AF449136

ACTA CONVENTUS
NEO-LATINI ABULENSIS

Medieval and Renaissance
Texts and Studies

Volume 207

ACTA CONVENTUS
NEO-LATINI ABULENSIS

*Proceedings of the Tenth International Congress
of Neo-Latin Studies*

Avila 4–9 August 1997

GENERAL EDITOR

RHODA SCHNUR

EDITED BY

JENARO COSTAS RODRIGUEZ, ROGER GREEN,
ANTONIO IURILLI, ELIZABETH McCUTCHEON,
ANTONIO MORENO HERNÁNDEZ, MONIQUE MUND-DOPCHIE,
and HERMANN WIEGAND

Arizona Center for Medieval and Renaissance Studies
Tempe, Arizona
2000

A generous grant from Pegasus Limited for the Promotion
of Neo-Latin Studies has helped meet publication costs of this book.

Library of Congress Cataloging-in-Publication Data
International Congress of Neo-Latin Studies (10th : 1997 : Avila, Spain)
Acta Conventus Neo-Latini Abulensis : proceedings of the tenth International
Congress of Neo-Latin Studies, Ávila, 4–9 August 1997 / general editor, Rhoda
Schnur ; edited by Roger Green . . . [et al.].
    p. cm. — (Medieval & Renaissance texts & studies ; v. 207)
Includes bibliographical references and index.
ISBN 0–86698–249–3 (acid-free paper)
    1. Latin literature, Medieval and modern—History and criticism—Congresses. 2.
Latin philology, Medieval and modern—Congresses. I. Schnur, Rhoda. II. Green,
Roger (Roger P. H.). III. Title. IV. Medieval & Renaissance Texts & Studies (Series)
; v. 207.
PA8002.I57 1997
470—dc21   99–055553

This book is made to last.
It is set in Bembo, smythe-sewn
and printed on acid-free paper
to library specifications.

Printed in the United States of America

In Gratam Memoriam Prof. J. IJsewijn (1932–1998)

The *International Association for Neo-Latin Studies* mourns the death of Professor Dr. Jozef IJsewijn, its founding father, its first president, and subsequently its distinguished member honoris causa.

Professor IJsewijn died on the evening of 27 November 1998 at the age of sixty-five. At the First International Congress for Neo-Latin Studies, held at Leuven in August 1971, he sowed the good seed, the 'granum sinapis', of the *International Association for Neo-Latin Studies* that grew out of it. Two years later, the Association had its official beginning and Prof. IJsewijn was elected its first President. He wrote the official version of its statutes in elegant Latin but, just as he stated many years later for his own *Companion to Neo-Latin Studies* (Leuven, 1990, p. IX), "Attamen ancilla haec Anglice quod loquitur, saeculum poposcit"; thus these were first discussed and drafted in English.

From the very beginning, Prof. IJsewijn was a prominent figure at every Congress of the Association. He not only served as the conscience and living memory of the Association, but was always most unselfishly prepared to share his rich experience and his vast knowledge of (Neo-)Latin with other colleagues. He welcomed young scholars with great enthusiasm, gave them confidence, inspired and stimulated them, and put them on the right track.

In this way, he was not only the living example and *exemplar* of a fine scholar but, for many of us, was in himself the *IANLS*.

Our wish had been to surprise him with a *Festschrift* during the Tenth Conference of our Association at Ávila. However, only a few weeks before that, he was struck by the first symptoms of the disease to which he had ultimately to yield. Being unable to attend that gathering, he was deeply touched by the good wishes of all participants in the Ávila Conference that accompanied the presentation of the volume at his home.

A few months later, he felt well enough to start the new academic year and personally taught every single course that was entrusted to him. Moreover, in a last heroic effort, he finished not only the second volume of his *Companion* but also the critical edition of his long cherished project of 'poetry in a Roman garden', the *Coryciana*.

> Ista reliquisti nobis monumenta per aevum
> Ingenii. Lugent Musae te grexque Latinus.

G. Tournoy

International Association for Neo-Latin Studies

Tenth International Congress

Avila, 4 – 9 August 1997

PROGRAMME

Sponsors

UNIVERSIDAD NACIONAL DE EDUCACIÓN A DISTANCIA (UNED):
Departamento de Filología Clásica
Vicerrectorado de Educación Permanente

EXCELENTÍSIMA DIPUTACIÓN DE ÁVILA
Fundación Cultural Santa Teresa de Ávila

MINISTERIO DE EDUCACIÓN Y CULTURA
Dirección General de Enseñanza Superior
Subdirección General de Formación y Promoción del Conocimiento

Excelentísimo Ayuntamiento de Ávila

Excelentísimo Ayuntamiento de Madrid

Universidad de Salamanca

Caja de Ávila

Advisory Board
for the Tenth International IANLS Congress

Professor J. Ijsewijn †
Katholieke Universiteit Leuven

Professor J. Starnawski
Uniwersytet Lodz

Professor J. Rice Henderson
University of Saskatchewan

Professor O. Merisalo
University of Helsinki

Professor C. Nativel
Paris

Professor F. Palladini
CNR Roma–Berlin

Monday, 4 August
Fundación Cultural Santa Teresa de Ávila

9.30 Registration

10.00 Opening Meeting

11.00 Coffee Break and Press Interview

11.30 Plenary Paper
J. F. ALCINA ROVIRA, Poesía neolatina y Literatura española
en los siglos XVI y XVII

16.00–18.00 Papers I

Linguistics   Chair: J. Glomski
L. CARRASCO REIJA, El sustrato castellano en el latín humanista de Diego López de
  Zúñiga
M. CONDE SALAZAR, La toponimia en los *Paralipomena* de Joan Margarit
C. MORANO RODRÍGUEZ, La actividad filológica de Isaac Newton y su conocimiento
  de las lenguas latina, griega y hebrea. A propósito de su obra: *El Templo de Salomón*

Linguistics   Chair: Th. Finan
T. O. TUNBERG, Longolius: Ciceronian Latinity?
P. STEENBAKKERS, True contents, false arguments: etymology and the emancipation of
  the vernacular
J. S. ROSE, Third declension i-stems and other non-classical morphology in Swedenborg's
  Neo-Latin

Linguistics   Chair: C. Chaparro Gómez
R. HOVEN, Les *Institutiones Grammaticae Latinae* de Nicolas Clénard
N. W. BRUUN, Zum Briefwechsel Thomas Bartholins
S. VALERIO, L'epistula *De amore* di Guiniforte Barzizza

Epistolography   Chair: M. S. Jensen
W. LUDWIG, Eine unbekannte humanistische Korrespondenz. Die Briefe zwischen
  Wolfgangus Rychardus und seinem Sohn Zeno (1520–1541)
J. STARNAWSKI, Les Lettres de Joan Dantiscus au Roi Sigismond I et à la Reine Bona
  Sforza
J. DE LANDTSHEER, From Ultima Thule to Finisterra: Surfing on the Wide Web of
  Justus Lipsius' Correspondence
O. VAN MARION, The Influence of Barlaeus' *Epistola Ameliae ad Henricum Fredericum* on
  the Dutch heroical epistles

Literary Genres   Chair: M. J. Chomarat
J. A. SÁNCHEZ MARÍN and M.ᴬ N. MUÑOZ MARTÍN, El tratamiento de los géneros
  literarios en J. C. Escalígero

a) Elegy
J.-L. CHARLET, Le mythe de l'âge d'or dans une élégie de G. Campano
B. MESDJIAN, La représentation des animaux dans l'*Eroticon* de Tito Vespasiano Strozzi

b) Panegyric
R. G. CZAPLA, Paul Schede Melissus als Dichter am Hof Elisabeths I von England
J. M. MAESTRE MAESTRE, La Presencia de Hércules en el *Panegyricum carmen de gestis
  heroicis divi Ferdinandi* de Juan Sobrarias Segundo
TH. CH. SCHMIDT, *Carmina laudatoria*. Humanistische Panegyriken als Textvorlagen für
  Staatsmotetten der Renaissance

18.30 Return to Ávila: guided visit to Ávila

21.00 Reception offered by Ávila Town Hall

22.30 Concert in the Palacio de los Velada

Tuesday, 5 August
Universidad Nacional de Educación a Distancia (UNED), Madrid

9.30 Departure

12.30 Plenary Paper
C. H. MILLER, Seventeenth-Century Latin Translations of Two English Masterpieces:
Hooker's *Polity* and Browne's *Religio medici*

13.30 Reception and lunch offered by Vicerrectorado
de Alumnos y Relaciones Institucionales de la UNED

16.00 Guided bus tour of Madrid

20.00 Reception offered by Madrid Town Hall

Wednesday, 6 August
Fundación Cultural Santa Teresa de Ávila

9.00–10.00 Papers II

New World   Chair: A. Moss
D. DEFILIPPIS, L' "invenzione" del Nuovo Mondo. Antica *auctoritas* e moderna *expe-*
rientia a confronto nella trattistica scientifica di Antonio Ferrariis Galateo
I. NUOVO, Il "mito" del Nuovo Mondo. Tradizione classica e *renovatio* cristiana nella
etica di Antonio De Ferrariis Galateo

New World   Chair: K. A. Neuhausen
PH. FORD, Anti-Colonialism in the Poetry of George Buchanan
R. FRANK, Black Passion in Ultima Thule

New World   Chair: E. McCutcheon
A. FRITSEN, Testing *Auctoritas:* The Travels of Paolo Marsi, 1468–69
G. EATOUGH, Peter Martyr's account of the first contacts with Mexico

New World   Chair: J. Mª Maestre Maestre
J. LENS-TUERO, Tradición e innovación en el *Omnium Gentium mores, leges et ritus ex*
multis clarissimis rerum scriptoribus de Juan Bohemio
S. RAMOS MALDONADO, El Nuevo Mundo en los *Commentariorum de sale libri V* del
humanista alcañizano Bernardino Gómez Miedes

New World   Chair: M. de la Garanderie
J. PAPY, *Hodie omnibus orior quasi tu!* Lipsius' Prophecy on the New World and Develop-
ment of an American Identity at the University of Lima
J. GONZÁLEZ VÁZQUEZ y M. LÓPEZ MUÑOZ, Granada, puerta de América. El
Reino de Granada y el Nuevo Mundo en algunas fuentes neolatinas

10.15 Plenary Paper

W. KÜHLMANN, Pagane Frömmigkeit und lyrische Erlebnisfiktion.
Präsenz und Funktion des antiken Mythos in der Dichtung
des Petrus Lotichius Secundus

12.00–13.30 Papers III

Poetry   Chair: J. Mª Núñez González

J. PASCUAL BAREA, Las poesías latinas del italiano Jacobo Alora en la Sevilla del Descubrimiento

D. CASTRO DE CASTRO, La poesía latina de Vicente Mariner

L. MUNDT, Die Eklogen Johannes Bocers (1524–1565)

Poetry   Chair: R. Green

E. S. GINSBERG, Joachim Du Bellay and Pierre Ronsard: a Revisitation

C. L. HEESAKKERS, The Ambassador of the Republic of Letters at the Wedding of Prince Philip of Spain and Queen Mary of England: Hadrianus Junius and his *Philippeis*

M. S. JENSEN, The Biblical paraphrases of Peter Griffenfeld

Poetry   Chair: H. Nellen

F. R. F. BLOM, *Barbarus ille mihi sermo est, ego barbarus illi.* The Latin poetry of Constantijn Huygens

D. SACRÉ, Latin Poetry in a Dutch Periodical: The *Algemeene Konsten Letterbode* (18th–19th Cent.)

F. J. NICHOLS, Why Sannazaro Took the Pastoral Muse to the Sea

Poetry   Chair: G. García-Alegre Sánchez

M.ᵃ M. PÉREZ MORILLO, El Tema del exilio en la poesía latina de Michele Marullo

J. SALVADÓ RECASENS, Poesía lulista y humanismo. El *De lege christiana* y las *Mysticae Lamentationes* de Jaume d'Olesa

S. T. DE PINHO, *De senectute* del humanista Lopo Serrão (1541–ca. 1581)

Poetry   Chair: M.ᵃ L. Arribas Hernáez

C. P. E. SPRINGER, Martin Luther's *De fonte oreadum Witerbergensium*

F. PALLADINI, Pettegolezzi intorno alla *Storia del Grande Elettore* (1695) di Samuel Pufendorf

16.30–18.30 Papers IV

Literary Theory   Chair: J. Lens-Tuero

R. FALCO, The *Prisci poetae* in Transition: Landino to Minturno

E. GALLEGO MOYA, Aportaciones de F. Arévalo a la teoría de la composición de Himnos Cristianos

J. R. HENDERSON, Temple's *Analysis* of Sidney's *Defence of Poesy:* Ramist Poetics and the Control of Imagination

J. M.ᵃ NÚÑEZ GONZÁLEZ, El *Ciceronianus* de Pierre de la Ramée

Historiography   Chair: J. González Vázquez

G. HINOJO ANDRÉS, La teoría historiográfica en la Retórica de Jorge de Trebisonda

G. GARCÍA-ALEGRE SÁNCHEZ, La falsa crónica de San Pedro de Taberna: un supuesto origen del Reino de Aragón

M.ᵃ J. LÓPEZ DE AYALA Y GENOVÉS, La guerra de África, un hecho clave en el *De rebus gestis* de Alvar Gómez de Castro

M.ᵃ V. FERNÁNDEZ-SAVATER MARTÍN, Ecos de Tácito en los *Indices rerum ab Aragoniae Regibus gestarum* de Zurita

Historiography   Chair: B. Hosington

M. PADE, Rome and Romulus in the work of Lapo da Castiglionchio and Giovanni
   Tortelli

E. HAYWOOD, *Quoniam nihil dignum in Hybernia gestum accepimus, ad res hispanicas festi-
   namus,* or why Italian humanists did not like Ireland

M. LAUREYS, The Roman Capitol scrutinized by Northern eyes: Justus Rycquius' *De
   Capitolio Romano*

P. J. OSMOND, Catiline and Catilinarianism in Renaissance Italy

Historiography   Chair: H. B. Norland

J. H. GAISSER, Pierio Valeriano and *De infelicitate litteratorum*

D. CHENEY, Making the List: Ravisius Textor and the Catalog of Learned Women

PH. DUST, Thomas More's Attitudes Toward Women in *The Epigrams*

M.ᴬ L. ARRIBAS HERNÁEZ, Reminiscencias Plinianas en las *Decades de Orbe Novo* de
   Pedro Mártir de Anglería

Humanistic Works   Chair: L. Valcke

D. MARSH, Mamma Roma, City of Women: Leonardo Bruni's *Address to the Prostitutes*

M. E. MILHAM, The neglected works of Bartolomeo Platina

F. RÁDLE, Andrea Guarna's *Simia*

M.ᴬ J. CEA GALÁN, El *Lexicon nauticum et aquatile* de Juan Lorenzo Palmireno

Humanistic Works   Chair: G. Tournoy

A. RASPA, John Donne and Neo-Latinist Humanist Works

A. V. VAN STEKELENBURG, A Latinist among the Hottentots. *The Descriptio Epistolaris
   Gentis Africanae circa Promontorium Capitis Bonae Spei* of Johannes Gulielmus de
   Grevenbroek. A.D. 1695

A. DÁVILA PÉREZ, Noticias bio-bibliograficas sobre Benito Arias Montano en su correspondencia latina con el impresor Juan Moreto (1591–1598)

Thursday, 7 August
Fundacion Cultural Santa Teresa de Ávila

9.00–10.30 Papers V

Classical Tradition   Chair: M. Trascasas Casares

B. ANTÓN MARTÍNEZ, El Brocense y la *receptio* de Tácito en España

B. CZAPLA, Von Terenz zu Karl Marx. Zeitgenössische Prologe und Epilog zu Terenz
   und Plautuskomödien in Westminster zur Jahrhundertwende

Poetry

J. L. NAVARRO LÓPEZ, *Anthologia Latina* 914 Riese: Galo falsificado

Classical Tradition   Chair: S. P. Revard

J. GLOMSKI, The imitation of non-classical models in the Renaissance: Italian Neo-Latin
   writing and the early Crakow humanists (1510–1525)

H. B. NORLAND, Seneca Redux: Alabaster's *Roxana*

M. SILVERTHORNE, *Leviathan, civitas* and *polis* in Thomas Hobbes' translation of Thucydides

Classical Tradition   Chair: M.ª J. López de Ayala y Genovés

D. CANFORA, Amore e matrimonio nel primo Quattrocento latino: per uno studio delle
   fonti

A. IURILLI, Episodi della fortuna europea de Properzio

Humanism   J. F. Alcina Rovira

A. MOSS, New Words, New Worlds, New Souls: Neo-Latin as an Instrument of Religious Change in the Early Part of the Sixteenth Century

S. MURPHY, Budé and the Heritage of Italian Humanism

L. PIEPHO, Andreas Vaurentinus' Commentary on the Eclogues of Baptista Mantuanus: Quattrocento humanism in the schools of France and England

Humanism   Chair: F. Tateo

J. MALINOWSKA, Pedro Ruiz de Moroz (1506–1571), a Spanish humanist at the Polish university and court

E. RUMMEL, Professional friendships among humanists: collaborators or collaborateurs?

A. WESSELING, In praise of Holland, Brabant, and Charles V

11.00 Business Meeting

16.30–18.00 Papers VI

Technical Prose   Chair: J. Costas Rodríguez

J. LL. BARONA y X. GÓMEZ FONT, Carolus Clusius, los naturalistas hispanos y la naturaleza americana

J. I. BLANCO PÉREZ, Antiguos y modernos en la obra del médico vallisoletano Lázaro de Soto

Y. HASKELL, Myth, Science and wonder in Neo-Latin astronomical didactic

Technical Prose   Chair: A. Carrera de la Red

A. I. MARTÍN FERREIRA y M.ᴬ J. PÉREZ IBÁÑEZ, El Nuevo Mundo en los textos latinos del Humanismo médico español

C. NATIVEL, Le *De pictura, plastice, statuaria libri duo* du Père Jules César Boulenger

Technical Prose   Chair: L. Carrasco Reija

R. F. GLEI, Novus Orbis: Melchior de Polignac über das Mikroskop

L. POELCHAU, Kosmographie und Geographie in Schriften von Humanisten aus Siebenbürgen (Transylvanien)

J. RAMMINGER, Ist der Dioscorides-Kommentar des Ermolao Barbaro vollendet?

Critics   Chair: P. Ford

P. M. CLOGAN, The Recovery of Statius in the Renaissance

A. COROLEU, Sixteenth-century commentaries on Poliziano: Pedagogical applications

J. V. MEHL, Characterizing the "viri obscuri" during the Reuchlin Affair

Critics   Chair: D. Marsh

M. DEL AMO LOZANO, Las anotaciones de L. J. Scoppa a la obra de Persio

M. MADRID CASTRO, Murrho and Badius' commentaries on Baptista Mantuanus' *contra poetas impudice loquentes*

E. SÁNCHEZ SALOR, Los "Nebrijas" reformados. El nombre de Nebrija contra la Gramática de Nebrija

Special Session
Wives and Monsters: The Construction of
Feminine Identity in Castilian Humanism

C. PERAITA, *Erudire inferiora*: Ludovico Vives' Defense of the Education of Women

S. MIGUEL-PRENDES, A Specific Case of the *Docta Foemina*. Luisa Sigea and her *Duarum virginum Colloquium de vita aulica et privata*

Friday, 8 August
Fundación Cultural Santa Teresa de Ávila

9.00–10.00 Papers VII

Philosophy Chair: C. Nativel
E. McCUTCHEON, Joseph Hall's *Mundus Alter et Idem:* Utopian Dream Turned Comic
  Nightmare
I. P. BEJCZY, L'Utopie et les limites de l'interprétation

Philosophy Chair: A. Mazzocco
G. PIRRELLI, L'elogio dell'amore profano in Giovanni Pontano da Bergamo
C. M. MURPHY, *Quia fecisti nos ad te:* Thomas More's Open Works

Neo-Latin Epic Chair: J. Ramminger
M. SCHEER, Die *Cortesiades* in der Nachfolge von Vergils *Aeneis*
B. MILEWSKA-WAZBINSKA, Lo spettacolo permanente. Il teatro e l'epica neolatina alla
  periferia di *Orbis latinus*

Politics Chair: C. L. Heesakkers
R. GINSBERG, The Founding of the Democratic State in Spinoza's *Tractatus Theologico-
  Politicus* (1670) and *Tractatus Politicus* (1677)
M. A. MASTRONARDI, L'immagine di Ferrara nella trattatistica estense

History of the Book Chair: J. M. Rodríguez Peregrina
A. J. E. HARMSEN, La bibliothèque néo-latine d'un jeune juriste Néerlandais
C. KALLENDORF, Proverbs, censors, and schools: Neo-Latin studies and book history

10.15 Plenary Paper
G. FERRAU, Umanisti e *Nuovi Mondi:* il codice ideologico e cultura
dell'Umanismo italiano nel confronto con le nuove etnologia e geografia

12.00–13.30 Papers VIII

Biblical Tradition Chair: E. Ginsberg
F. GONZÁLEZ-LUIS, La influencia de los himnos litúrgicos en los poemas latinos del
  padre José de Anchieta
M. GRÜNBERG-DRÖGE, *Latinitas Hebraeorum* or How the Jews of Rome said "Hallo"
  to the New Pope
F. ROUGET, Modèles séculaires et tradition biblique: les *Septem Psalmi* (1538) de Salmon
  Macrin

Neolatin of the XVIIth and XVIIIth Centuries Chair: E. Rodríguez Peregrina
L. BRAUN, Lateinische Epik im Frankreich des 17. Jahrhunderts
R. W. CARRUBBA, A Latin Epitaph for Dr. Engelbert Kaempfer's Three Children
H. WIEGAND, Hernán Cortés als epischer Held: J. B. Marienis *Cortesius* (1729)

Neolatin of the XVIIth and XVIIIth Centuries Chair: A. Moreno Hernández
P. KONING, Julius Caesar Scaliger, source d'inspiration poétique-philosophique à un prosateur du 17ème siècle de la Zélande
K. A. NEUHAUSEN, De Francisci Xaverii Trips Poetae Laureati Latinis, quae quidem
  permulta perpolitaque manserint, sed oblitterata nunc iacere videantur, operibus ad praesentes saeculo XVII status singulos omnium fere Europae spectantibus regionum
S. P. REVARD, Translation and Imitation of Johannes Secundus' *Basia* in England During
  the Civil War Era

Neolatin of the XVIIth and XVIIIth Centuries   Chair: R. Ginsberg

R. SARASTI-WILENIUS, *De peregrinatione*. Finnish scholars abroad

P. VAN BEEK, Minor Works: The *Opuscula Hebraea Graeca Latina et Gallica, prosaica et metrica* of Anna Maria van Schurman (1607–1678)

G. MARC'HADOUR, Latin in the Writings of Santa Teresa

Neolatin of the XVIIth and XVIIIth Centuries   Chair: F. Calero Calero

B. GARCÍA HERNÁNDEZ, La visión teatral del mundo y de la vida en Séneca y en Descartes

J. HIGUERAS MALDONADO, El humanista gienense y virrey del Perú, D. Diego de Benavides y de la Cueva (1607–1666)

Neolatin in America   Chair: E. Sánchez Salor

A. B. CARBÓN SIERRA, El neolatín en Cuba

A. CARRERA DE LA RED, El latín en la América del S. XVI: Análisis de las cartas de Pablo Nazareno

16.00–18.00 Papers IX

Erasmo-Vives   Chair: A. Kerson

R. P. H. GREEN, Erasmus and Prudentius

E. V. GEORGE, Rhetorical Strategies in Vives' Peace Writings: The *De pacificatione* and the Letter to the Grand Inquisitor

J. M. RODRÍGUEZ PEREGRINA, Una lectura renacentista de Virgilio: la *Praefatio in Georgica Vergilii* de Luis Vives

Vives   Chair: M. Conde Salazar

J. M.ª ESTELLÉS GONZÁLEZ, Unos *Proemia* poco conocidos de J. L. Vives

F. CALERO CALERO, Los *Diálogos* de Luis Vives en América

Sepúlveda   Chair: B. García Hernández

A. MORENO HERNÁNDEZ, El manuscrito *BNM* 5785 y la *Apologia* de Juan Ginés de Sepúlveda: crítica textual y variantes de autor

B. POZUELO CALERO, Modalidades historiográficas dominantes y finalidad de Juan Ginés de Sepúlveda en la Crónica de Carlos V, libros VI–X

J. J. SÁNCHEZ GÁZQUEZ, Juan Ginés de Sepúlveda. Un hispano a la altura del siglo XVI: Lutero y Erasmo

Sepúlveda   Chair: M.ª Victoria Fernández-Savater Martín

J. SOLANA PUJALTE, Los *Errata Petri Alcyonii in interpretatione libri Aristotelis de incessu animalium* de Juan Ginés de Sepúlveda: ¿obra perdida o inexistente?

J. J. VALVERDE ABRIL, El *Gonsalus sive de appetenda gloria dialogus*, primera obra filosófica original de Juan Ginés de Sepúlveda

20.30 Banquet

Saturday, 9 August
Universidad de Salamanca

11.00 Plenary Paper

M. MUND-DOPCHIE, Les Confins occidentaux du monde gréco-romain: les diverses fortunes d'une représentation antique à la Renaissance et au XVIIe siècle

13.00 Reception offered by Salamanca University

Sunday, 10 August

9.00 Excursion to El Escorial

12.30 Return to Madrid Airport

§§§

Executive Committee
President: Prof. Brenda Hosington, Université de Montréal
Past President: Prof. Francesco Tateo, Università di Bari
First Vice President: Prof. Gilbert Tournoy, Katholieke Universiteit Leuven
Second Vice President: Prof. Jenaro Costas Rodríguez, UNED, Madrid
Treasurer: Prof. Chris Heesakkers, University of Leiden
Secretary: Dr. Karl August Neuhausen, Universität Bonn
Chair of Publications: Mrs. Rhoda Schnur, St. Gallen

Organizing Committee
Chair: Prof. Jenaro Costas Rodríguez, UNED, Madrid
Prof. Leticia Carrasco Reija, UNED, Madrid
Prof. Matilde Conde Salazar, CSIC, Madrid
Prof. M.ª Victoria Fernández-Savater Martín, UNED, Madrid
Prof. Genoveva García-Alegre Sánchez, UNED, Madrid
Prof. M.ª José López de Ayala y Genovés, UNED, Madrid
Prof. Antonio Moreno Hernández, UNED, Madrid
Prof. Mercedes Trascasas Casares, UNED, Madrid

Scientific Committee
Prof. Juan Francisco Alcina Rovira, Universidad de Tarragona
Prof. Avelina Carrera de la Red, Universidad de Valladolid
Prof. César Chaparro Gómez, Universidad de Extremadura
Prof. Benjamín García Hernández, Universidad Autónoma de Madrid
Prof. Tomás González Rolán, Universidad Complutense de Madrid
Prof. José M.ª Maestre Maestre, Universidad de Cádiz
Prof. Elena Rodríguez Peregrina, Universidad de Granada

ACTA CONVENTUS NEO-LATINI ABULENSIS

BRENDA HOSINGTON, Presidential Address   1

PLENARY PAPERS

J. F. ALCINA, Poesia Neolatina y Literatura Española en los Siglos XVI y XVII   9

GIACOMO FERRAÚ, La prima ricezione del 'mondo nuovo' nella cultura dell'Umanesimo   29

WILHELM KÜHLMANN, Pagane Frömmigkeit und lyrische Erlebnisfiktion: Präsenz und Funktion des antiken Mythos in Petrus Lotichius Secundus' Elegie "Ad Lunam"   41

CLARENCE H. MILLER, Seventeenth-Century Latin Translations of Two English Masterpieces: Hooker's *Polity* and Browne's *Religio Medici*   55

MONIQUE MUND-DOPCHIE, Les confins occidentaux du monde gréco-romain: Les diverses fortunes d'une représentation antique à la Renaissance et au XVIIe siècle   73

COMMUNICATIONS

BEATRIZ ANTÓN MARTÍNEZ, El Brocense y la *Receptio* de Tácito en España   95

JOSEP LLUÍS BARONA y XAVIER GÓMEZ FONT, Carolus Clusius, los naturalistas hispanos y la naturaleza americana   105

ISTVÁN BEJCZY, L'*Utopie* et les limites de l'interprétation   113

FRANS R. E. BLOM, Barbarus ille mihi sermo est, ergo barbarus illi: The Latin Poetry of the Dutch Poet Constantijn Huygens (1596–1687)   119

NIELS W. BRUUN, Zum Briefwechsel Thomas Bartholins   129

FRANCISCO CALERO CALERO, Los Diálogos de Luis Vives en América   139

DAVIDE CANFORA, Amore e matrimonio nel primo Quattrocento latino: Le epistole di Guiniforte Barzizza e Giovanni Pontano   147

AMAURY B. CARBÓN SIERRA, El Neolatín en Cuba   155

ROBERT W. CARRUBBA, A Latin Epitaph for Dr. Engelbert Kaempfer's Three Children   163

MARÍA JOSÉ CEA GALÁN, El *Lexicon nauticum et aquatile* de Juan Lorenzo Palmireno: un proyecto de manualito para la composición en latín   169

DONALD CHENEY, Making the List: The Evolution of Ravisius Textor's Catalogue of Learned Women — 177

MATILDE CONDE SALAZAR, La toponimia en los *Paralipomena* de Joan Margarit — 183

ANTONIO DÁVILA PÉREZ, Noticias bio-bibliográficas sobre Benito Arias Montano en su correspondencia latina con el impresor Iohannes Moretus (1589–1598) — 193

PHILIP DUST, Thomas More's Attitudes toward Women in *The Epigrams* — 205

JOSÉ M. ESTELLÉS GONZÁLEZ, Unos *Prooemia* poco conocidos de J. L. Vives — 211

RAPHAEL FALCO, The *Prisci Poetae* in Transition: Landino to Minturno — 217

Mª VICTORIA FERNÁNDEZ-SAVATER MARTÍN, Ecos de Tácito en los *Indices rerum ab Aragoniae Regibus gestarum* de Zurita — 227

PHILIP FORD, Anti-Colonialism in the Poetry of George Buchanan — 237

GENOVEVA GARCÍA-ALEGRE SÁNCHEZ, La falsa *Crónica de San Pedro de Taberna*: un supuesto origen del Reino de Aragón — 247

EDWARD V. GEORGE, *"Suadendo, admonendo, hortando, precando"*: Rhetoric and Peacemaking in Juan Luis Vives' *De pacificatione* — 253

ELLEN S. GINSBERG, Du Bellay's Six Latin Poems in Praise of Ronsard — 265

ROBERT GINSBERG, The Founding of the Democratic State in Spinoza's *Tractatus Theologico-Politicus* (1670) — 275

REINHOLD F. GLEI, *Novus orbis*: Melchior de Polignac über das Mikroskop — 283

JACQUELINE GLOMSKI, The Imitation of Non-Classical Models in the Renaissance: Italian Neo-Latin Writing and the Early Cracow Humanists (1510–1525) — 293

JOSÉ GONZÁLEZ VÁZQUEZ y MANUEL LÓPEZ MUÑOZ, Granada, puerta de América: El Reino de Granada y el Nuevo Mundo en algunas fuentes neolatinas — 301

ROGER GREEN, Erasmus and Prudentius — 309

A. J. E. HARMSEN, Le *Wetsteen der vernuften* de Jan de Brune et la littérature Néo-Latine — 319

CHRIS L. HEESAKKERS, The Ambassador of the Republic of Letters at the Wedding of Prince Philip of Spain and Queen Mary of England: Hadrianus Junius and his *Philippeis* — 325

JUAN HIGUERAS MALDONADO, El humanista giennense y virrey del Perú D. Diego de Benavides y de la Cueva (1607–1666) — 333

GREGORIO HINOJO ANDRÉS, La teoría historiográfica en la retórica de Jorge de Trebisonda — 345

RENÉ HOVEN, Les *Institutiones Grammaticae Latinae* de Nicolas Clénard — 353

ANTONIO IURILLI, Episodi della fortuna editoriale dell'opera di Properzio — 361

CRAIG KALLENDORF, Proverbs, Censors, and Schools: Neo-Latin Studies and Book History — 371

PAULA KONING, Les "Desserts" de Julius Caesar Scaliger, nourriture spirituelle pour les "Emblemata" néerlandais de Johan de Brune — 381

Mª JOSÉ LÓPEZ DE AYALA Y GENOVÉS, La guerra de Africa, un hecho clave en el *De rebus gestis a Francisco Ximenio Cisnerio libri octo* de Alvar Gómez de Castro (1515–1580) — 389

MARIANO MADRID CASTRO, Badius' and Murrho's Commentaries on Baptista   397
Mantuanus' *Contra Poetas Impudice Loquentes*

JOLANTA MALINOWSKA, Pedro Ruiz de Moroz (1506–1571), a Spanish   403
Humanist at the Polish University and Court

GERMAIN MARC'HADOUR, Latin in the Writings of Santa Teresa   409

DAVID MARSH, Mamma Roma, City of Women: Leonardo Bruni's *Oration*   413
to the Prostitutes

MARIA AURELIA MASTRONARDI, L'immagine di Ferrara nella letteratura   423
estense

ELIZABETH McCUTCHEON, Joseph Hall's *Mundus Alter et Idem:* Utopian Dream   431
Turned Comic Nightmare

JAMES V. MEHL, Characterizing the *Viri Obscuri* during the Reuchlin Affair   439

SOL MIGUEL-PRENDES, A Specific Case of the *Docta Foemina:* Luisa Sigea   449
and her *Duarum virginum colloquium de vita aulica et privata*

MARY ELLA MILHAM, The Neglected Works of Platina   459

ANTONIO MORENO HERNÁNDEZ, El manuscrito 5785 BNM y la *Apologia* de   465
J. G. de Sepúlveda: Crítica textual y variantes de autor

COLETTE NATIVEL, Le *De pictura, plastice et statuaria* du Père Jules César   473
Boulenger, S.J.

CAROLUS AUGUSTUS NEUHAUSEN, De Francisci Xaverii Trips Poetae Laureati   481
Latinis, quae quidem permulta perpolitaque manserint, sed oblitterata
nunc iacere videantur, operibus ad praesentes saeculo XVII° status singulos
omnium fere Europae spectantibus regionum

JUAN Mª NÚÑEZ GONZÁLEZ, El *Ciceronianus* de Pierre de la Ramée   489

CARMEN PERAITA, *Sapientia* and Knowledge in the Construction of the   499
Renaissance *docta foemina:* Vives' *De institutione foeminae christianae*

MARIA DEL MAR PÉREZ MORILLO, El exilio en la *Poesía Latina* de Michele   507
Marullo

GIOVANNI PIRRELLI, Un'epistola "de amore" di Giovanni Pontano   519

FIDEL RÄDLE, Andrea Guarna: *Simia*   527

SANDRA RAMOS MALDONADO, El nuevo mundo en los *Commentariorum de*   533
sale libri V del humanista alcañizano Bernardino Gómez Miedes

ANTHONY RASPA, John Donne and Neo-Latin Humanist Works   543

STELLA P. REVARD, Translation and Imitation of Joannes Secundus' *Basia*   553
during the Era of the Civil War and Protectorate in England: 1640–60

FRANÇOIS ROUGET, Modèles séculaires et tradition biblique: les *Septem*   563
psalmi (1538) de Salmon Macrin

JOAQUÍN J. SÁNCHEZ GÁZQUEZ, Juan Ginés de Sepúlveda, Un hispano a la   575
altura del siglo XVI: Lutero y Erasmo

THOMAS SCHMIDT-BESTE, *Carmina laudatoria:* Humanistische Panegyriken als   585
Textvorlagen für Staatsmotetten der Renaissance

JULIÁN SOLANA PUJALTE, Los *Errata Petri Alcyonii in interpretatione libri*   597
Aristotelis de incessu animalium de Juan Ginés de Sepúlveda: ¿obra quemada,
no impresa o no publicada?

AGOSTINO SOTTILI, Università e Umanesimo   603

CARL P. E. SPRINGER, Martin Luther, the Oreads of Wittenberg, and *Sola Gratia* — 611

JERZY STARNAWSKI, Les lettres de Joannes Dantiscus au Roi Sigismond I et la Reine Bona Sforza — 619

SEBASTIANO VALERIO, L'epistola "de amore" di Guiniforte Barzizza — 623

JUAN JESÚS VALVERDE ABRIL, El *Gonsalus seu de appetenda gloria dialogus*, primera obra filosófica de Juan Ginés de Sepúlveda — 631

OLGA VAN MARION, Ovid's *Heriodes* in the Netherlands: A Dutch Princess in a Heroic Epistle of Caspar Barlaeus (1629) — 639

MARIÀNGELA VILALLONGA VIVES, Jeroni Pau en el umbral de un mundo nuevo: Quinto centenario de su muerte — 647

HERMANN WIEGAND, Die spanische Eroberung Mexikos im späten neulateinischen Epos: Giambattista Marienis *Cortesius nondum absolutus* von 1729 — 659

INDEX — 667

ACTA CONVENTUS
NEO-LATINI ABULENSIS

Presidential Address at the
Opening Ceremony of the Tenth
International Congress for Neo-Latin Studies

BRENDA HOSINGTON

L adies and Gentlemen, Señores and Señoras, dear colleagues and friends:
It is my great pleasure to welcome you all here for the Tenth International
Congress for Neo-Latin Studies. That we are all here this morning, on the first day
of what I know will be an extremely successful Congress, is thanks to the Rector of
the Universidad Nacional de Educación a Distancia, Professor Jenaro Costas Rodríguez, Second Vice-President of the International Association for Neo-Latin Studies.
He has worked very hard over the past three years to organize this congress, and has
been helped in this by his local Committee. We must also thank the Fundación Cultural Santa Teresa for taking care of the more material, yet essential aspects of any
congress: the lecture rooms, lodging, and local transport. Thanks are also due to the
Spanish Ministry of Education, the Ministerio de Educación y Cultura, which generously granted the sum of 1.000.000 pesetas to help in organizing the Congress, and
to the Diputación provincial, the Ayuntamiento de Avila, the Ayuntamiento de Madrid, the Universidad de Salamanca, and the Caja de Avila for their financial help.

As many of you know, the First International Congress for Neo-Latin Studies was
held in Leuven in 1971 and hosted by Professor IJsewijn. Two years later, at the Amsterdam Second International Congress for Neo-Latin Studies, the IANLS was created. The founding fathers, so to speak, came from several different countries and disciplines. This diversity has come to characterize the membership and nature of the
Association and is, indeed, to my way of thinking, one of its riches. The seven congresses that followed the Amsterdam meeting have been held in Tours, Bologna, St.
Andrews, Wolfenbüttel, Toronto, Copenhagen, and Bari. All have provided an international and interdisciplinary forum, as well as a friendly meeting-place, for the exchange of ideas. I have every reason to believe that at this our first meeting in the
Iberian peninsula, we shall encounter the same intellectual stimulus and cordial col-
legiality. At the same time, we shall learn of new Neo-Latin publications and research

projects and return at the end of the week to our home countries encouraged by what we have heard.

Indeed, there are plenty of new developments. In fact, contrary to what some of our colleagues in more trendy disciplines believe, Neo-Latin studies are alive and well. Interest in Neo-Latin has surged over the past twenty years. From the first important publications in the 1970s, IJsewijn's *Companion to Neo-Latin Studies*, Pierre Laurens and Claudie Belavoine's *Musae Reduces*, Alessandro Perosa and John Sparrow's *Renaissance Latin: An Anthology*, and Fred Nichols' *An Anthology of Neo-Latin Poetry*, books and articles on Neo-Latin writings have proliferated. There are anthologies, editions, translations, encyclopedic accounts of individual countries, and studies of individual authors. Nor are such works of scholarship confined to literary subjects, let alone poetry, as the earlier anthologies were. The plethora of publications in the fields of history, art history, translation, and philosophy, to name but a few, that have appeared in the 1980s and 90s bear witness to the truly interdisciplinary nature of Neo-Latin studies. One of the most fruitful areas of Neo-Latin research has been the reception of the classics in later periods; a fairly recent association and a journal devoted to the continuation of the classical tradition particularly welcome Neo-Latinists. Another area that has turned to Neo-Latin sources has been hermeneutics; yet another, philology, while for a time eclipsed (certainly in North America) by new schools of literary criticism, informs several recent studies of Neo-Latin authors.

No longer simply the fruits of a few classicists interested in Neo-Latin authors, or the equally few medievalists whose interest in Latin tempted them beyond the temporal confines of their field into the fifteenth and early sixteenth centuries, publications are being produced by colleagues in varied fields of Renaissance studies, but, most excitingly, by scholars working exclusively in Neo-Latin studies. Neo-Latin has come of age and can be considered a discipline in its own right, although it still appeals to those who have inter-disciplinary backgrounds.

This increased interest in Neo-Latin over the past twenty years or so can be seen in some other ways. Several journals are now devoted exclusively or almost exclusively to Neo-Latin: *Humanistica Lovaniensia*, founded by Joseph IJsewijn; *Medievalia et Humanistica*, refounded in 1970 by Paul Clogan, a faithful member of the IANLS, is the first journal in North America to promote the study of Neo-Latin authors; two journals privileging Neo-Latin, founded in Valencia and Cádiz; and the latest, founded one month ago by our own Secretary, Karl August Neuhausen, and his colleagues in Bonn, entitled *Neulateinisches Jahrbuch/Journal of Neo-Latin Language and Literature*.

Another manifestation of the fact that Neo-Latin is alive and well is the creation of research projects in various countries. Time will not permit me to enumerate all such endeavors. But I am thinking of the two Leuven-based projects on the correspondence of Justus Lipsius and of Juan Luis Vives, and a third on Dutch Humanism in the Low Countries; of the four Dutch publishing projects concerning Erasmus, Huygens, Grotius, and Vossius, as well as a new Leiden interdisciplinary research group under the umbrella of the "Leids Institute for the Renaissance"; and of two Eastern European centers of activity, the new Warsaw research group under the leadership of Jerzy Axer, which is editing humanist correspondence, and another at the

University of Pecs, in Hungary, whose subject is Neo-Latin poetry in that country from 1400 to 1600. Such cooperative projects have also gotten underway in other countries, but I should like to pass quickly to Spain, which has seen perhaps the greatest upsurge of interest in Neo-Latin of any country in the past ten years: thirty-one research groups are working on Humanism in Spain, of which a dozen concern Neo-Latin directly and another five or six touch on it. This is truly a remarkable feat and makes Spain a worthy and most suitable country to host our congress.

Although not able to compete with progress in research, teaching has nevertheless seen some innovations, and this should also warm the hearts of IANLS members, for one of the purposes of our Association, stipulated in our Statutes, is to promote the teaching of Neo-Latin at all appropriate levels. While we have looked on sadly over the past twenty years at the general decline in the popularity of Latin, both in the universities and the secondary schools—even in those countries with the strongest classical tradition—we have also witnessed the birth of some courses and seminars in Neo-Latin studies. In Leuven, two courses, "Neo-Latin Literature" and "The History of Renaissance Humanism," are taught to students in Classical Philology but also Romance Philology. In Germany, where the University of Hamburg has been teaching Neo-Latin in the Medieval and Neo-Latin Section of the Institute for Greek and Latin continuously since 1976, other universities are following suit, with traditional seminars in Classical Philology, Latin, Medieval Philology, and Medieval Latin now including classical *and* Renaissance or medieval *and* Renaissance Latin. Such is the case for the Universities of Erlangen, Göttingen, Heidelberg, Kiel, Marburg, and, within the past six months, Bonn, where the first appointment in medieval and Renaissance Latin has just been made. In France, some of the most innovative Neo-Latin teaching is now being done by classicists turned art historians, and a new post has just been opened up at the Ecole Pratique des Hautes Etudes in Renaissance Latin. At the Universities of Paris IV, Tours, Le Mans, Nanterre, Lyon, and Aix-en Provence, courses in sixteenth-century studies include seminars devoted exclusively to Neo-Latin. Perhaps one of the most encouraging pieces of news is that young Neo-Latinists have been appointed Maîtres de conférence in Grenoble, Le Mans, Reims, Rouen, Strasbourg, and Tours, while another thirty or so are preparing theses in Neo-Latin. In England, the University of Cambridge has a very successful post-graduate seminar entitled "Renaissance Literature and Society" that includes an optional course in Neo-Latin literature. In the United States, although Neo-Latin *per se* is taught in virtually no institutions, the Folger and Newberry Libraries have of late offered seminars on Neo-Latin philology and paleography, in part because of the Newberry's growing number of Humanist Latin manuscripts.

I have concentrated on these new manifestations of interest in Neo-Latin in this address because I personally find comfort in the fact that researchers and students are being inspired to work in an area that still holds out new challenges, that still presents "fresh fields and pastures new." This does not mean that we should not also take heart from the fact that older projects are still going strong. In Canada, the *Collected Works of Erasmus* continue to come off the press, as do Erasmus' *Opera Omnia* in Amsterdam. In the United States, the *Catalogus Translationum et Commentariorum: Medieval* and *Renaissance Latin Translations and Commentaries, Annotated Lists and Guides*, started by Paul Oskar Kristeller, continues into its seventh and eighth volumes. In Poland, the *Elementa ad Fontium Editiones* is still presenting a series of texts and documents that serve as source texts for studying Polish Neo-Latin. In the Czech Republic, the series on Humanism in Bohemia and Moravia continues, as does work on the Neo-Latin playwright, Balbino, both projects emanating from the Academy of Sciences and reuniting classical, Renaissance, and baroque scholars.

At the same time, some publishing houses are as interested as ever in producing new editions and translations of Neo-Latin works. In North America alone, Arizona State University has agreed to continue the Medieval & Renaissance Texts & Studies series as well as our own *Acta*, both of which it has taken over from the State University of New York, Binghamton; the University of California, Los Angeles, has a text and monograph series; the University of Toronto Press, in conjunction with the Pontifical Institute, publishes rare or unusual texts and translations; and the University of Ottawa Press publishes Renaissance Latin plays. And of course throughout Europe, presses still welcome editions and translations as well as monographs on Neo-Latin subjects. In Germany, for example, there are several, amongst which perhaps the most important are Teubner in Leipzig and Stuttgart; Fink Verlag in Munich, which publishes a series entitled the Humanistiche Bibliothek; and Peter Lang Verlag, which has a similar series entitled the Bibliotheca NeoLatina.

One of the most attractive aspects of the field is, as I said a while ago, the fact that there are still so many new areas in which to conduct research. There are so many works to discover or re-assess, so many texts to edit, or re-edit, to translate and interpret, that the title of our congress can in fact be applied to the whole realm of Neo-Latin studies—we are indeed "on the threshold of new worlds."

Perhaps I am being unduly hopeful for the field of scholarly endeavor that has brought us here today. Perhaps my enthusiasm for things Neo-Latin has blinded me to some less attractive realities. However, as I look at the program, I see promising signs of a continuing interest in this discipline, which is inherently interdisciplinary and brings together specialists who span a six hundred year period. This congress drew the largest number of abstracts that any member of the Executive Committee could remember. There were over two hundred. Although we could take only 141, we still have undoubtedly the largest program that the IANLS has ever had. A few of the papers you will hear will be read by doctoral students and post-graduate research assistants, and this I find particularly encouraging. To these younger Neo-Latinists we extend a warm welcome. Other papers are by teachers starting out on their careers, and they too deserve our gratitude and support. Lastly, we are delighted to see new faces, especially from our host country, and from countries like Cuba, which is represented for the first time here in Avila.

New projects, then, new publications, new teaching opportunities, and new members at a larger-than-ever congress. And we can add to this an occasional translation or composition in Neo-Latin—Beatrix Potter's beloved English "Peter Rabbit" transmogrified into "Petrus Cuniculus," for example, or the news broadcast, "Nuntii Latini," transmitted from Helsinki on weekends throughout the world on short-wave radio and available on the Internet Audio web site. It is therefore not surprising for us to feel, with the American novelist Mark Twain, that the report of our death has been greatly exaggerated.

On this positive and optimistic note, then, I declare the Tenth International Congress for Neo-Latin Studies open and I wish you all a very fruitful and thoroughly enjoyable time here in Avila.

Université de Montréal

Plenary Papers

Poesía Neolatina y Literatura Española en los Siglos XVI y XVII

J. F. ALCINA

El neolatín es parte de la historia y de los antecedentes de la literatura española. La imitación en castellano o intertextualidad de los autores de la Antigüedad siempre se hace a través de la hermenéutica creada por el humanismo y a través de los mecanismos de recreación que antes ha fijado la poesía neolatina. De hecho, por mencionar algo evidente, multitud de géneros poéticos neolatinos aparecen aclimatados en la literatura castellana: el emblema, los jeroglíficos y enigmas, la colección de *Tumuli*, las églogas piscatorias y venatorias, los epigramas preliminares en elogio del autor de un libro, etc.; además de los matices de contenido y forma con que el humanismo marcó otros géneros clásicos como la elegía, la epístola moral en verso o la épica cristiana renacentista[1].

Por su parte, la poesía neolatina que se escribe en España también influyó en la castellana o se tradujo al castellano. Podemos dar de ello un par de ejemplos: un famoso soneto de Hernando de Acuña que se ha fechado siempre mal hasta ahora: "Ya se acerca, señor, o es ya llegada / la edad gloriosa en que promete el cielo"[2] resulta que es traducción o paráfrasis de un poema coetáneo en latín del granadino Juan La-

---

[1] Véase Juan F. Alcina, "Entre latín y romance: modelos neolatinos en la creación poética castellana de los Siglos de Oro", en J. M. Maestre y J. Pascual, eds., *Humanismo y Pervivencia del Mundo Clásico*, I.1 (Cádiz, 1993), 3–27; "La elegía neolatina", en B. López Bueno, ed., *La elegía* (Sevilla, 1996), 15–40; Juan F. Alcina y Francisco Rico, "Prólogo" a Andrés Fernández de Andrada, *Epístola moral a Fabio* (Barcelona, 1993).

[2] Véase Chr. Maurer, " 'Un monarca, un imperio y una espada': Juan Latino y el soneto de Hernando de Acuña sobre Lepanto", *Hispanic Review* 61 (1993): 35–51. Es un soneto que había hecho verter mucha tinta malinterpretándolo con una datación temprana en torno a la batalla de Mühlberg como dedicado a Carlos V. Las raras lecturas de Maurer lo llevaron a la poesía neolatina de Granada y a la lectura de la *Austriada* del negro Juan Latino y la colección de epigramas que incluye. Entre ellos aparece uno dedicado a Felipe II por la batalla de Lepanto que es el que Hernado de Acuña traduce "epitomizándolo" como diría un poeta de la época.

tino y esto nos permite entenderlo y fecharlo con exactitud en 1572. Otro ejemplo puede ser la fortuna del poema épico *Diuae Magdalenae Libri IV* de Juan Petreyo. Nadie creería hoy que ese texto tuviera ninguna difusión, a pesar de sus dos ediciones (Toledo, 1552 y Córdoba, 1568). Sin embargo en el barroco se hace una traducción, a lo que yo sé anónima, que se conserva en la Biblioteca Nacional de Madrid[3].

Bucear en estas relaciones es una tarea demasiado amplia para una conferencia e incluso irrealizable para una sola persona. Yo en este trabajo sólo pretendo dar algunas notas dispersas en un recorrido por las literaturas hispanas de los siglos XVI y XVII empezando por la recepción de ciertos poetas y acabando con algunas calas en la poesía barroca, especialmente en la de Lope de Vega. Dejaré de lado los autores y temas más conocidos, como Garcilaso o las versiones de Sannazaro, por ejemplo, para centrarme en materiales menos transitados aunque no menos representativos.

La recepción de la poesía neolatina de Italia

A lo largo del siglo XVI hispano se editaron media docena de textos en verso de humanistas italianos y especialmente Poliziano, Sannazaro y Baptista Mantuano influyeron en la literatura española[4]. Pero evidentemente la pobre producción editorial de

---

[3] Ms. 3954, que contiene versos de Baltasar Elisio de Medinilla: fols. 98–183, *Los quatro libros de la vida de santa Maria Magdalena que compuso el Maestro Ioan Perez poeta ingeniosissimo en verso heroyco latino traduzido en octava rima en verso español*. Es probablemente la misma traducción que cita Nicolás Antonio, *Bibliotheca Hispana Nova*, s.v. "*Ioannes Petreius*": "*Magdalenam . . . poema, quod tamen, a nescio quo versum Hispane octoadibus, MS. extat in bibliotheca comitis de Villaumbrosa*".

[4] Dejando aparte a los italianos afincados en España como Lucio Flaminio Sículo, Antonio Geraldini, Lucio Marineo Sículo, Pedro Martir de Anglería etc. tenemos el *De divinis laudibus* de Pontano (Barcelona, 1498), los dísticos de Michele Verino (la edición más antigua conocida es de Tarragona, 1499) y en la edición de Zaragoza, 1535 lleva como apéndice los *Disticha* de Fausto Andrelini (todavía a mediados del s. XVII Pedro Soto de Rojas citará uno de los *Disticha* de Andrelini en el "Discurso contra el ocio", véase *Paraíso cerrado para muchos* . . . ed. A. Egido [Madrid, 1993], 144, las *Silvae* de Poliziano en ediciones de Alcalá, 1515 [por Nebrija] y Salamanca, 1556 [por Sánchez de las Brozas]). En Alcalá se editó también un Sannazaro en 1534. Junto con Verino, el neolatino italiano más veces impreso en España es Baptista Mantuano: sus *Parthenice septem* se publicaron por primera vez en Sevilla en 1515 al cuidado del profesor de gramática Pedro Núñez Delgado. Después se edita en los círculos erasmistas de Alcalá, primero en 1523, en una edición prologada por el bachiller Fernando de Briviesca que alaba al Mantuano por ser más amplio que otros poetas cristianos de la Antigüedad y por sus relaciones con España, empezando con el linaje del *Noster Mantuanus* "*noster inquam quia ab hispania oriundus*" [fol. a1v]. Esta edición, variando la dedicatoria, se reeditará en Alcalá en 1536. Por otra parte tenemos dos ediciones de Barcelona de parte de este texto: una de 1520, *Parthenice secunda que et Catharinaria inscribitur*, ed. A. Vaurentinus et J. Ascensius (Barcelona, 1520?), otra de 1525 con el título de *Parthenice Mariana* (Barcelona, 1525), ampliamente presentes en bibliotecas barcelonesas del siglo XVI: véase M. Peña, *El laberinto de los libros* (Madrid, 1997), 193–194. Además se editó en Alcalá el *Liber fastorum* del carmelita en dos ediciones, una de 1520 por Brocar y otra de 1527 por Eguía. Baptista Mantuano, preferido de Erasmo y Lutero, está presente en la literatura española desde Alonso Núñez de Reinoso a San Juan de la Cruz: véase E. Asensio, "Alonso Núñez de Reinoso, gitano peregrino, y su égloga *Baltea*", en *Studia Hispanica in honorem R. Lapesa*, I (Madrid, 1972), 131–132; y la edición de Reinoso de M. A. Teijeiro, *Obra Poética* (Cáceres, 1997), 163; Nicolas Antonio, *Bibliotheca*

la imprenta española no refleja ni de lejos lo que se leía y se vendía realmente en la Península. Sobre todo en cuanto a autores latinos clásicos y humanísticos la mayor parte de los libros eran de importación[5]. Por eso son muy importantes los catálogos de bibliotecas privadas y los catálogos de fondos editoriales que están apareciendo últimamente.

Lo que se encuentra en los catálogos de libros de la época se corresponde en general con el uso, citas y traducciones que aparecen en poetas concretos. Las obras de Poliziano aparecen en varias bibliotecas y en la práctica poética sin duda Poliziano es uno de los autores neolatinos más imitados[6]. Lo mismo podríamos decir de Sannazaro[7]. Pero también hay otros poetas menos conocidos actualmente que tuvieron una interesante vida y presencia en la poesía del XVI. Las valoraciones actuales no se corresponden con las del Renacimiento y los "Cánones Occidentales" son francamente dañinos si de verdad pretendemos hacer historia literaria. Hay dos casos curiosos que querría subrayar: una es la sorprendente fama de Girolamo Angeriano y la otra es la curiosa difusión de Petrus Bargaeus.

Girolamo Angeriano (1470–1535) es un interesante poeta petrarquista de formación napolitana influido por el preciosismo de Tebaldeo. Curiosamente su obra aparece en la biblioteca del Marqués don Pedro Fajardo, bibliófilo y diplomático, dueño de la hermosa fortaleza renacentista de Vélez Blanco en Almería. En el catálogo de 1581 de la parte de su biblioteca que fue a parar al Escorial encontramos unos "Hieronymi Angeriani poemata amatoria manuscripta"[8]. Y en consonancia resulta que Angeriano es un poeta bastante leído e imitado entre poetas castellanos: Francisco

---

Hispana Nova sive Hispanorum Scriptorum qui ab anno MD ad MDCLXXXIV floruere notitia, I (Madrid, 1783), 690, cita una traducción de alguna o todas las *Parthenice*, no lo sé, por Juan Fernández de Ledesma, *Historia virginal del insigne Poeta Baptista Mantuano* traducida de verso heroyco latino (ignoro si se conserva). Sobre las *Parthenice* en S. Juan de la Cruz, véase Marcel Bataillon, *Varia lección de clásicos españoles* (Madrid, 1964), 163.

[5] Véanse las conclusiones de Philippe Berger, "La evolución de la producción editorial española entre 1501 y 1520", en *El libro antiguo español*, I (Salamanca, 1993), 63–72, donde analiza los esfuerzos de los editores hispanos para enfrentarse al libro de importación en latín.

[6] Véase Juan F. Alcina, "Poliziano y los elogios de las letras en España (1500–1540)", *Humanistica Lovaniensia* 25 (1976): 198–222, especialmente 221–222; Francisco Rico, *Nebrija contra los bárbaros* (Salamanca, 1978), especialmente 54 y ss.; A. Romajo, "Notas sobre la recepción del Poliziano latino en España: una *monodia* del catedrático salmantino Blas López", *Criticón* 55 (1992): 41–52; Luis Merino, "Las *Silvae* de Poliziano comentadas por el Brocense", *Humanistica Lovaniensia* 45 (1996): 406–429; así como el artículo de Alejandro Coroleu en este congreso, y del mismo, "Poliziano at Alcalá, or a Witness to Antonio de Nebrija's Lectures on the *Silvae*", *Euphrosyne* 26 (1998): 253–260.

[7] Véase E. Clocchiatti, *El "Sannazaro español" de Herrera Maldonado* (Madrid, 1963); R. Reyes Cano, *La Arcadia de Sannazaro en España* (Sevilla, 1973); V. Bocchetta, *Sannazaro en Garcilaso* (Madrid, 1976); véase también el prólogo de Francesco Tateo a J. Sannazaro, *Arcadia* (Madrid, 1993).

[8] Véase Gregorio de Andrés, *Documentos para la Historia del Monasterio de San Lorenzo el Real de El Escorial*, VII (Madrid, 1964), 342; actualmente es el ms. d-IV-23 de la Biblioteca Escurialense.

de Figueroa imita el "De Venere et Cupidine" ("In fulua dum pulchra Venus spaciatur arena"), Pedro de Padilla traduce el "Sunt duri scopuli, sunt dura marmora, durum" y el "Caelia fatur, amor fatur, sua lumina pandit", Baltasar del Alcázar y Esteban Manuel de Villegas imitan el epigrama "Quum dormiret Amor, rapuit clam pulchra pharetram" sobre la amada que roba las armas a Cupido y ya en el Barroco, Sebastian de Covarrubias parafrasea el "Tempore tecta ruunt praetoria, tempore uires"[9]. Todavía Lope de Vega como veremos después elogia a Angeriano, junto con Marullo y Janus Secundus, en una pequeña lista de poetas neolatinos de la *Filomena*. Quizá la mención de los tres juntos obedezca a las antologías que los reunían como los *Poetae tres elegantissimi, emendati et aucti, Michael Marullus, Hieronymus Angerianus, Ioannes Secundus.*[10]

Los *Carmina* de Petrus Angelius Bargaeus (1517–1596), con seis ejemplares, aparecen en el catálogo de libros que tenía para la venta el librero Benito Boyer de Medina del Campo en 1592[11]. Estaba también en la biblioteca del duque de Osuna porque un ejemplar de Bargaeus con el fierro de su biblioteca se encuentra en la Biblioteca Universitaria de Barcelona[12]. Y en la biblioteca del poeta Luis Barahona de Soto (c. 1547–1595), amigo del duque de Osuna, don Pedro Téllez Girón, encontramos otra copia de Petrus Angelius[13]. No es de extrañar por tanto si Bargaeus es utilizado y citado frecuentemente por Herrera, en sus *Anotaciones a Garcilaso*[14], en las que colaboró Barahona, donde traduce un fragmento de su *Cynegeticon* y también en sus *Eglogas*[15].

Una cuestión particularmente interesante es la difusión de Antologías en España: en un catálogo de 1589 de la biblioteca del abogado barcelonés Francesc Serra aparece la entrada *Carmina Petri Bembi. Andreu Naugeri* que alude probablemente a alguna

---

[9] Da las referencias Joseph G. Fucilla, *Estudios sobre el petrarquismo en España* (Madrid, 1960 [Revista de Filología Española. Anejo LXXII]), 112 (Francisco de Figueroa), 164 (Baltasar del Alcázar), 174–75 (Pedro de Padilla), 215 (Covarrubias). La imitación poética de Villegas, que no señala Fucilla, es la "Cantilena XX. De Amor y Lidia", ed. N. Alonso Cortés, 216–217: "Sobre el margen de un río, / de árboles tanto umbrío"; véase Girolamo Angeriano, ed. A. M. Wilson, n° XLII.

[10] Parisiis, 1582 (Biblioteca Universitana de Valencia, *Catálogo*, n° 2323, II, 32).

[11] V. Bécares y A. L. Iglesias, *La librería de Benito Boyer. Medina del Campo 1592* (Salamanca, 1992), n° 378, p. 107.

[12] P. A. Bargaeus, *Poemata Omnia* (Florentiae, 1568), Biblioteca Universitaria de Barcelona, sign. 123/8/9 (el *Cynegeticon* lleva notas marginales en castellano con letra quizá del s. XVII con observaciones sobre zoología y las características del Uro, el tigre, el león, etc.); hay dos ejemplares de esta misma edición en la Biblioteca de la Universidad de Valencia, *Catálogo*, n° 171, I, p. 57, sign, Z-1/182 y Z-9/50.

[13] Véase F. Rodríguez Marín, *Luis Barahona de Soto* (Madrid, 1903), 345. Sobre el mundo de Barahona en Osuna, J. Lara Garrido, *La poesía de Luis Barahona de Soto (Lírica y épica del manierismo)* (Málaga, 1994), 49 y ss.

[14] Ed. Gallego Morell, 356.

[15] M. T. Ruestes Sisó, *Las églogas de Fernando de Herrera. Fuentes y Temas* (Barcelona, 1989), 340–341.

antología[16] como los *Carmina Quinque Illustrium Poetarum* y veremos después que Diego Hurtado de Mendoza también la utiliza.

En catálogos de bibliotecas actuales existen bastantes ejemplares de estas antologías. Teniendo en cuenta lo pobres que son las bibliotecas hispanas y los pocos libros antiguos que se han comprado, hay que suponer que una parte de estas antologías se adquirieron en la época. De los *Carmina Quinque* podemos localizar en España cuatro ejemplares por lo menos en diversas bibliotecas, ademas de otras antologías menos famosas[17]. Tampoco faltan las *Delitiae* barrocas preparadas por Gruter[18]. La presencia de las *Delitiae* en España es difícil de seguir. Quizá Esteban Manuel de Villegas las conociese porque utiliza el título *Delitiae* o "Delicias" para una de sus colecciones poéticas de 1617[19], aunque el término se había impuesto como sinónimo de antología

---

[16] Peña, *El laberinto de los libros*, 194. Se podría tratar de los *Carmina Quinque Illustrium Poetarum* con múltiples ediciones desde la de Venecia, Valgrisi, 1548 (véase J. Sparrow, "Renaissance Latin Poetry: Some Sixteenth-Century Italian Anthologies", en *Cultural Aspects of the Italian Renaissance* [Manchester, 1976], 389–392, que justamente empieza con "*Petri Bembi Carmina*" siguiendo con "*Andreae Naugerii . . . Lusus*", etc.). También podría tratarse del primer tomo de otra famosa antología, *Carmina Illustrium Poetarum Italorum. Io. Mathaeus Toscanus conquisiuit . . . Tomus Primus* (Paris, 1576), donde aparecen destacados los poemas de Bembo y Navagero entre otros.

[17] De los *Carmina Quinque Illustrium* hay tres ejemplares en la Biblioteca Nacional de Madrid en ediciones de Florencia (1449, 1552) y Venecia (1558), también hay un ejemplar de esta edición veneciana en la Biblioteca Pública de Toledo. Véase Mª Luisa Cerrón Puga, "Antología de poesía italiana (1532–1537)", *Edad de Oro* 12 (1993): 59–60, que describe los ejs. de la Biblioteca Nacional de Madrid; para la ed. de Venecia, 1558 que se conserva en Toledo, véase J. Méndez Aparicio, *Catálogo de los impresos del siglo XVI de la Biblioteca Pública del Estado, Toledo* (Madrid, 1993), n° 1405, 220. De los *Carmina quinque hetruscorum poetarum* (Florentiae, 1562), con poemas de F. Berni, B. Varchi, etc. hay un ejemplar en la BU de Barcelona, encuadernado con el Bargaeus antes citado sign. 123/8/9; De *Antoni Termini . . . Iunii Albini Terminii Senioris, Molsae, Bernardini Rotae . . . et aliorum illustrium poetarum carmina* (Venetiis, 1554) hay ej. en la BN Madrid R/21824 así como *Carmina praestantium poetarum Io. Antonii Taygeti* (Brixiae, 1565), sign. 3/4405, véase Cerrón, "Antología," 60; en la Biblioteca Serrano Morales de Valencia tenemos *Io. Baptistae Pignae Carminum . . . His adiunximus Caelii Calcagnini carm. Lib. III. Ludovici Areosti carm. Lib. II* (Venetiis, 1553) (*Catálogo*, n° 289, p. 148); en la BU de Valencia, *Poetae tres elegantissimi, emendati et aucti, Michael Marullus, Hieronymus Angerianus, Ioannes Secundus* (Parisiis, 1582) (*Catálogo*, n° 2323, II, 32) y *Fracastorii Opera Omnia . . . Accesserunt Andreae Naugerii . . . orationes duae carminaque nonnulla* (Venetii, 1555) (n° 1525, I, p. 500).

[18] En la Biblioteca Nacional de Madrid tenemos tres ejemplares de las *Delitiae C. poetarum gallorum* (Francofurti, 1609), sign. R-22943-5, 22938-40, y 5-5282; *Delitiae poetarum germanorum* (Francofurti, 1612), sign. R-21.357-62 y 5-4882, ambos ejemplares expurgados por la Inquisición; *Delitiae C poetarum belgicorum* (Francofurti, 1614), sign. 6-i/ 4331, con nota manuscrita en la portada de expurgo inquisitorial fechada "Matriti . . . 1754". En la Biblioteca de Catalunya de Barcelona encontramos unas *Delitiae poetarum scotorum* (Amsterdam, 1637), aunque este ejemplar probablemente no estuvo en España en el Barroco porque en la portada se indica a pluma "Collegii Lugdunensis".

[19] El título exactamente es "Síguense las Delicias que es el libro tercero de la primera parte de las Eróticas de don Esteban Manuel de Villegas", y "Segundas Delicias", ed. N. Alonso Cortés, *Eróticas o Amatorias* (Madrid, 1913), 188 y ss., 220 y ss. Ianus Gruter es un autor muy conocido y admirado en el Barroco español y el propio Villegas cita algunas obras suyas en las *Disertaciones*

lírica en otras lenguas. Por ejemplo aparece en *Les Delices de la poésie françoise ou Recueil des plus beaux vers de ce temps* editado por Du Bray en 1615 y el mismo Villegas utiliza el término *Deliciae* como genérico para referirse a las poesías de Ausonio[20]. Villegas era un erudito, autor de unos *Adversaria o Disertaciones críticas* en las que los capítulos con enmiendas a Propercio o Tibulo se alternan con otros capítulos dedicados a los ya consagrados poemas de "Ludovicus Gongora" o "Garcilassus". Naturalmente Villegas escribía poesía en latín y participó con un par de dísticos latinos en una justa poética[21]. Evidentemente además de admirar a los clásicos gustaba también de la poesía neolatina y así, en las *Eróticas*, entre sus epigramas con imitaciones de Marcial y Ausonio nos encontramos con una paráfrasis resumida—"epitomando" dice el poeta—de un epigrama a Hyella de Andrea Navagero, "Florentes dum forte vagans mea Hyella per hortos". Es el último de sus epigramas y reproduce primero el texto latino[22]. Para Villegas, Navagero está al mismo nivel que Marcial y Ausonio.

La poesía neolatina en tiempos de Garcilaso

La poesía neolatina bordea y acompaña la poesía italianizante desde sus inicios. Es conocida la producción poética en latín de Garcilaso. De él sólo se han salvado tres poemas aunque sabemos que tenía una producción mucho más amplia que envió a Pietro Bembo. Como decía McFarlane, los precursores de la *Pléiade* son los poetas neolatinos y la continuidad natural de estos últimos hay que buscarla en la poesía vernácula. En la poesía humanística de Garcilaso esta afirmación también es válida.

El caso de Diego Hurtado de Mendoza es paralelo al de Garcilaso, aunque no tengamos ningún poema latino suyo. Buen latinista y helenista interesado por el texto de Aristóteles estuvo profundamente inmerso en el mundo humanístico italiano y español. El mundo italiano en el que se movía don Diego Hurtado tenía muy presente la poesía latina humanística. Su propio sobrino, Juan de Mendoza, sucesor suyo en la embajada de Venecia (1545) era poeta en latín alabado por Sadoleto en carta de 1541 y por el portugués Britonio[23].

Mendoza estaba en contacto con una larga serie de humanistas y poetas neolatinos (aunque también podían escribir en italiano) como Pietro Bembo, Benedetto Accolti o Lazzaro Buonamici (Lazarus Bonamicus), uno de los interlocutores del *Dialogo delle Lingue* de Sperone Speroni al que se le aconseja escribir sólo en latín por que lo hace

---

críticas, véase la antología publicada por J. Bravo Vega que cito en la nota siguiente, 139 y 143.

[20] Aparece en una de las *Dissertationes* en la que intenta aclarar un epigrama de Ausonio a la cautiva Bissula y precisa: "Capta manu, sed missa manu, dominatur in eius / Deliciis, cuius bellica praeda fuit"; véase Julián Bravo Vega, *Esteban Manuel de Villegas. La obra literaria: manuscritos e impresos* (Logroño, 1989), 172.

[21] Véase Bravo Vega, *Esteban Manuel de Villegas*, 125. Algunos fragmentos de las *Disertaciones críticas* que quedaron inéditas se reproducen en este trabajo de Bravo Vega, 163 y ss.

[22] Fols. 83 vº–84 de la segunda parte de las *Eróticas* (Nájera, 1617). No se incluye en la ed. de N. Alonso Cortés (Madrid, 1913) y he tenido que utilizar el ejemplar de esta primera edición de la BNM.

[23] A. González Palencia y E. Mele, *Vida y obras de don Diego Hurtado de Mendoza*, I (Madrid, 1941), 180.

mucho mejor que en italiano. La afición de Hurtado de Mendoza por este tipo de poesía se refleja incluso en sus relaciones con Antonio Agustín al que protege de diversas formas. No es casualidad que Agustín, para congraciarse con Mendoza le envíe en una de sus cartas un poema, el "Carmen nuptiale" escrito para las bodas de la hermana Isabel Agustín que nos ha editado recientemente Joan Carbonell[24]. Es un poema fuertemente catuliano y lo subraya el propio Agustín en la epístola adjetivándolo "ad Catulli tui imitationem"[25]. Aparte de algunas reminiscencias aisladas el catulianismo de Mendoza habría que buscarlo en el lenguaje familiar y crudo de algunas de sus coplas castellanas paralelas al catulianismo de Castillejo.

Importante también para nuestro propósito es la relación de Mendoza con Juan de Verzosa. Verzosa formó parte de la guardia española en Siena que estaba al mando de Diego Hurtado. A él le dedicó Verzosa dos cartas. ¿Qué relación hay entre las epístolas latinas de Verzosa y las de Mendoza? La epístola horaciana en verso en castellano fue cultivada ya antes de 1543 por Mendoza en su famosa epístola a Boscán y es un género que cultivó ampliamente durante toda su vida. ¿Influyó Mendoza en las epístolas latinas de Verzosa? Verzosa sólo escribió en latín, quizá porque como Joachim Du Bellay, para hacerse entender en un mundo extranjero, entre Flandes e Italia, el latín era la lengua en la que mejor se podía refugiar[26].

Su poesía incluye algunos géneros nuevos no desarrollados por la poesía humanística de Garcilaso. Uno de ellos es el epigrama en octavas y en concreto algunos de ellos son traducciones de epigramas neolatinos de Marullo[27]. También parafrasea y adapta el lamento "Alcon" de Baltasar de Castiglione, pero sustituyendo los nombres "Alcon" y "Iolas" por "Damón" (el nombre pastoril del propio poeta en su poesía amorosa) y "Glauco". En el título mismo se indica "Ex libro quinque poetarum" que naturalmente es la famosa antología *Carmina quinque illustrium poetarum* antes citada[28]. En esos casos la influencia humanística es evidente, pero hay otros en que no se da una imitación concreta y, sin embargo, lo que se escribe en latín y lo que se hace en castellano resultan cosas semejantes. Un caso bastante curioso es el "Epitafio de doña

---

[24] "El *Carmen Nuptiale* d'Antonio Agustín", *Faventia* 16, 1 (1995): 87–98.

[25] González Palencia y E. Mele, *Vida y obras de don Diego Hurtado de Mendoza*, I, 270.

[26] Es la excusa que da Du Bellay para su producción en latín después de sus defensas del francés: "Ce n'est le fleuve Thusque au superbe rivage, . . . Qui ores (mon Ronsard) me fait parler Latin, / Changeant à l'estranger mon naturel langage, / C'est l'ennuy de me voir trois ans & davantage / Ainsi qu'un Promethé, cloué sur l'Aventin." (*Regrets*, son. 10): véase Y. Hoggan, "Aspects du bilingüisme littéraire chez Du Bellay: le traitement poétique des thèmes de l'exil dans les *Poemata* et *Les Regrets*", *BHR* 44 (1982): 76.

[27] J. P. W. Crawford, "Don Diego Hurtado de Mendoza y Michele Marullo", *Hispanic Review* 6 (1938): 346–348.

[28] Diego Hurtado de Mendoza, *Poesía completa*, ed. J. I. Díez Fernández (Barcelona, 1989), 335. El editor no identifica la fuente, pero se trata de los *Carmina quinque illustrium poetarum* (Florentiae, 1552), 57–62, o una edición similar. La fama del "Alcon" de Castiglione llega hasta el "Epitaphium Damonis" de John Milton; véase J. Montero, "Sobre las relaciones entre la elegía y la égloga", en López Bueno, ed., *La elegía*, 222.

María Pacheco", su hermana exiliada en Portugal, equivalente a un soneto-epitafio pero en la forma de una octava mixta[29]:

Epitafio de Doña María Pacheco

Si preguntas mi nombre, fue María,
Si mi tierra, Granada; mi apellido
de Pacheco y Mendoza, conocido
el uno y otro más que el claro día.
Si mi vida, seguir a mi marido;
mi muerte, en la opinión que él sostenía.
España te dirá mi calidad,
que nunca niega España la verdad.

Aunque no tiene relaciones textuales es el equivalente en romance de un epigrama neolatino en ocho versos, como octava, que quizá conocería don Diego:

Ad Illustrissimae D. Mariae Pacciechae Tumulum

Principibus genita et Padillae coniugis ultrix
    Maria sexus honos clauditur hoc tumulo.
Haec quia non potuit (uitam cum clauserit exul)
    coniugis ad bustum gressibus ire, uolens,
Sousa et Fico Rhous rara pietate ministri
    curarunt dominam condere sarcophago.
Viscera sed postquam dederit putrefacta cadauer,
    contumulanda ferent ossibus ossa uiri. Finis

Este epigrama se encuentra junto con otro en griego en el manuscrito escurialense V–II–3, fol. 12. El macabro y piadoso epitafio en latín parece destinado claramente al túmulo real de la esposa del líder comunero. El epitafio castellano parece más literario aunque quizá también tuviese una funcionalidad real[30]. Doña María Pacheco era una Mendoza "muy docta en latín y en griego" como su hermano y los epitafios en las dos lenguas están en consonancia con la cultura de la dama[31]. De cualquier manera lo que interesa reasaltar es la equivalencia de géneros y el trasvase de formas humanísticas al romance.

Las musas bilingües en España se podrían seguir en poetas como Alvar Gómez de Ciudad Real, Cristóbal de Cabrera o Alvar Gómez de Castro que escriben la mayor parte de su obra en verso latino, pero que también tienen una notable producción

---

[29] Ed. Díez Fernández, n° XXXIX. Sobre los tópicos de tradición clásica del epitafio en forma de soneto, coincidentes con la octava, véase E. L. Rivers, *El soneto español en el Siglo de Oro* (Madrid, 1993), 15–16.

[30] El diálogo con el caminante se coloca plausiblemente en la tumba portuguesa; desde el exilio tiene más sentido preguntar a "España" como se hace en los vv. 7–8.

[31] Véase A. Morel Fatio, "Doña María Pacheco", *Bulletin Hispanique* 5 (1903): 301–304, y Agustin Redondo, "Emergence et effacement de la femme politique: Isabelle la Catholique et María Pacheco", en *Images de la femme en Espagne aux XVIe et XVIIe siècles* (Paris, 1994), 302–304.

poética en verso castellano: en coplas castellanas en el caso de Gómez de Ciudad Real en su *Theológica descripción de los misterios sagrados* (1541) y en versos italianizantes en el caso de Cabrera y Alvar Gómez de Castro. Entrada la segunda mitad del siglo podríamos citar a Ramírez Pagán o Vicente Espinel[32] que producen la mayor parte de su obra en castellano, pero que nos han dejado también algunas muestras de poesía funeral en latín entre otras cosas plausiblemente perdidas.

El "Hermaphroditus" atribuido a Poliziano y Sebastián de Horozco

El latín es la lengua oculta, la lengua de lo sagrado y también la lengua de lo que se lee a escondidas. No es de extrañar que la poesía humanística crease una rica veta de poesía pornográfica al amparo de Marcial, Catulo y sobre todo la poesía Priapea. A esta veta poética dedicaron su ingenio Antonio Beccadelli, el Panormita, en su *Hermaphroditus*[33], Giovanni Pontano, Janus Panonius[34] o el mismísimo cardenal Pietro Bembo[35].

A este gusto por lo oculto y erótico obedece la inclusión de varias "Respuestas" a un epigrama medieval sobre Hermafrodito atribuido erroneamente al joven Poliziano en el *Cancionero* de Sebastián de Horozco (+ c.1578)[36], tan lleno por lo demás de coplas castellanas "no para damas" de regusto cancionero y groseramente obscenas.

Sebastián de Horozco incluye el texto latino que aparece en el "Liber graecorum epigrammatum" de Poliziano. Horozco se lo atribuye al mismo Poliziano, pero en el texto y en la carta a Urceo Codro el autor de los *Miscellanea* dice claramente que —aunque circulaba atribuida al espléndidamente salaz Panormita— es un epigrama antiguo del poeta Pulex[37]. El poema reza:

---

[32] Lope de Vega en el prólogo al *Laurel de Apolo* celebra a Vicente Espinel como "único poeta latino y castellano de aquellos tiempos"; véase L. Astrana Marín, *Vida azarosa de Lope de Vega* (Barcelona, 1935), 303.

[33] D. Coppini, *Antonii Panhormitae Hermaphroditus* (Roma, 1990).

[34] Janus Pannonius, *Epigrammi Lascivi* (Roma, 1993).

[35] Véase el "Priapus" que quizá fue el poema que acompañaba a la epístola latina que escribió el cardenal a Garcilaso; véase L. López Grigera, "Notas sobre las amistades italianas de Garcilaso: un nuevo manuscrito de Pietro Bembo", en *Homenaje a Eugenio Asensio* (Madrid, 1988), 291–310.

[36] Sobre Sebastián de Horozco véase Oleh Mazur, *El teatro de Sebastián de Horozco* (Madrid, 1977); la ed. de J. L. Alonso Hernández de S. de Horozco, *Teatro universal de proverbios* (Salamanca, 1976); M. Vitse, "Sobre las *Representaciones* de Sebastián de Horozco", *Criticón* 10 (1980): 75–92; y la edición de J. Weiner, *Relaciones históricas toledanas* (Toledo, 1981).

[37] Este poema se atribuye con más probabilidad a Hildebert de Lavardin o M. de Vendôme: véase la nota 56 a la introducción de Donatella Coppini, *Antonii Panhormitae Hermaphroditus*, I, CX, y las referencias bibliográficas que ahí se dan; véase también H. Walther, *Alphabetisches Verzeichnis Versanfängen mittellateinischer Dichtungen* (Göttingen, 1969), nº 3662 y 4902. Sobre la influencia de este poema latino en la literatura medieval castellana, véase F. Lecoy, *Recherches sur le Libro de buen amor* (Westmead, 1974 [1938]), 160–163. Atribuido a Virgilio se encuentra en el manuscrito escurialense I.III.21, fol. 56, del siglo XV de origen hispano, copiado por Pedro Marcilla, que corresponde al 4902 de Walther. Para el texto latino que da Poliziano utilizo A. Poliziano, *Opera Omnia,* II (Lugduni, 1533), 371–372; en carta a Antonio Urceo Codro, al que envía

Siguese una pregunta del hermafrodito, qu'es el que tiene sexo de varón
y de hembra

> ¿Quién es aquella que siendo preñada
> su madre del mismo soñó que paría,
> y estando en el parto pareció que oía
> dezir a tres dioses aquesta su hada?
> Será, dixo Marte, doncella sagrada,
> será, dixo Phebo, varón, y no es otro,
> será, dijo Juno, ni uno ni otro,
> y después fue todo, verdad muy probada.

Para respuesta desta pregunta es de saber una epigrama de Angelo Poliziano, que dize asi:

> Cum mea me genitrix grauida gestaret in aluo
>   Quid pareret fertur consuluisse deos.
> Mas est Phoebus ait, Mars foemina Iunoque neutrum;
>   Cumque forem natus Hermaphroditus eram
> . . . . . .

Responde agora el auctor a la pregunta conforme a la epigrama y pregunta lo demás de la muerte que había de haber.

> La dura quisitión que m'es preguntada
> me hizo algun rato pensar qué sería,
> hasta que supe que ya la tenía
> el gran Poliziano muy bien declarada.
> Así que parió la madre preñada
> un hermafrodito común en lo otro,
> aqueste es lo uno, y aqueste es lo otro,
> y siéndolos todo ninguno es, y nada.

Las respuestas de Horozco en este caso van en doctos versos de arte mayor. La sección de "Preguntas" en verso del *Cancionero* de Horozco incluye toda una serie de temas de tipo médico de tono un poco picante, como un enigma sobre el "Pedo", por qué la mujer que no pare es más lujuriosa, por qué las mujeres no tienen barba, por qué las mujeres morenas son más ardientes, los opuestos efectos sexuales de la planta llamada "ruda" en hombres y mujeres, etc. En ese ámbito el enigma de Poliziano encaja perfectamente con los temas trobadorescos y formas cancioneriles. Es un

---

éste y otros epigramas griegos, Poliziano explica que este epigrama en realidad era del poeta antiguo Pulex y que circulaba atribuido al Panormita: *"Hoc autem quod sequitur, non cum graecis iam, sed cum latino commisimus. Vertimus enim uetustum Poetae Pulicis in Hermaphroditum, quod uulgus Antonio Panormitano falso adiudicat, in quo laboriosissimum fuit reddere totidem uersibus, ac pene uerbis, imo uel syllabis eandem gracilitatem"*; para los poemas a Hermafrodito de Horozco utilizo la siguiente edición: *Cancionero de Sebastián de Horozco, Poeta Toledano del Siglo XVI*, ed. J. M. Asensio (Sevilla, 1874), 110–111 (añado acentos y corrijo el texto latino).

tema de ciencia, que enlaza con el gusto por los monstruos y prodigios de la naturaleza de moda en el Renacimiento en autores como Gema Frisio, Ambroise Paré por
ejemplo. Al mismo tiempo enlaza y se reviste de la tradición poética medieval del
"Perqué".

Por lo demás el epigrama de Poliziano tuvo uno cierta fama en España y una paráfrasis de este poema vuelve a aparecer entre los versos de Cristóbal de Castillejo[38],
también en coplas castellanas que en otros manuscritos se atribuye a Diego Hurtado
de Mendoza[39]. Después lo imitó Jaime Juan Falcó en un famoso epigrama, "Alma Venus praegnans, cum iam prope partus adesset", traducido varias veces en el barroco[40].

Emblema neolatino y traducción vernácula

Un punto importante de cruce entre neolatín y romance se da naturalmente en la
traducción. De hecho, todavía a mediados del siglo XVI la traducción en verso, con
una voluntad estética, de formas poéticas breves —por ejemplo la oda horaciana— no
estaba afianzada en la literatura española (otra cosa es la épica)[41].

En los tanteos por inventar una nueva lengua para la traducción en la segunda
mitad del siglo XVI, la poesía neolatina tuvo una especial importancia al crear una
interesante tradición de versiones al vulgar de epigramas latinos complementarios del
emblema, la iconografía y la pintura. El gusto por el símbolo y el emblema, al di-
fundirse en medios cortesanos y nobles habitualmente ayunos en latines, trajo consigo
la versión en vulgar del epigrama neolatino que lo acompañaba. Fruto de esa moda
es el hecho de que la primera colección amplia de traducciones en endecasílabos de
poemas breves latinos sea la de los *Emblemata* de Alciato por Bernardino Daza (1549).
Después, el profesor de humanidades Juan de Mal Lara, ligado a la nobleza y los
grupos intelectuales de Sevilla, se convierte en un especialista en esta búsqueda de
complementariedad entre imagen, creación latina y versión romance: en 1565 prepara
una colección de epigramas para seis cuadros de tema mitológico de Tiziano de la
colección de Felipe II. Nos ha llegado el de Prometeo acompañado de su versión en
una octava[42]. A su vez, su amigo y secretario de lenguas de Felipe II, Diego Gracián
de Alderete, escribirá una serie de epigramas semejante para las pinturas de Alonso
Sánchez Coello (al servicio de Felipe II de 1555 a 1588) y naturalmente irán acom-

---

[38] Ed. Dominguez Bordona, II, 255.

[39] "Cuando mi madre cuitada", ed. J. I. Díez Fernández, nº CCIV, 377–378.

[40] Véase el texto y algunas de las traducciones en la edición de D. López Cañete: Jaime Juan
Falcó, *Obras*, I (León, 1996), 122–23, 279–280; y R. Herrera Montero, "Alma Venus Praegnans.
Un epigrama de Falcó y sus versiones castellanas", *Cuadernos de filología clásica, Estudios latinos* 10
(1996): 205–215.

[41] La traducción de la lírica la fijarán por los años sesenta y setenta Juan de Mal Lara, Fernando
de Herrera y Fray Luis de León. Véase un útil resumen sobre la historia de la traducción poética
en el s. XVI en Mª I. Osuna Rodríguez, *Las Traducciones Poéticas en la Filosofía Vulgar de Juan de
Mal Lara* (Córdoba, 1997).

[42] Véase Rocío Carande, *Mal-Lara y Lepanto: los epigramas latinos de la Galera Real de Juan de
Austria* (Sevilla, 1990), 288.

pañadas de traducción, esta vez en prosa[43]. En 1570 Mal Lara, experto ya en el género de la *joyeuse rentrée*, publica el *Recibimiento* a Felipe II, con una larga serie emblemas con epigramas latinos y una doble traducción en prosa y en verso[44]; lo mismo hace en 1572 con los epigramas de la *Descripción de la Galera Real*, un texto que describe el arte efímero de imágenes, emblemas e inscripciones con que se adornó la galera de Juan de Austria tras la victoria de Lepanto. Los epigramas neolatinos llevan ya siempre su traducción o "declaración" en verso castellano, generalmente octavas. A finales del siglo XVI, Fray José de Sigüenza en su *Historia de la Orden de S. Jerónimo*, en la parte dedicada a describir El Escorial, se esfuerza por reflejar en endecasílabos castellanos los dísticos latinos con que Arias Montano adornó las figuras de pórfido de la sala Capitular del Monasterio. Por ejemplo, bajo la figura de Cristo, con el dístico: "Hic lapis offensus ferietque feretque ruinam. / Hic et inoffensus petra salutis erit." Traduce en verso nuestro jerónimo:

> Ofendida es piedra o despreciada
> mortal ruina e irremediable herida
> hará en el ofensor; mas si es temida,
> será refugio de salud cumplida.

Sigüenza considera estas figuras como emblemas y remite como equivalentes a los emblemas de los *Humanae Salutis Monumenta*: "quien quisiere ver mucho y muy excelente de este género lea el libro … *Humanae Salutis Monumenta*"[45]. Imagen, epigrama latino y traducción, generalmente poética, forman ya una unidad bastante fijada en España y seguirá así en el Barroco. El simbolismo de la imagen se explica y matiza en el epigrama en la lengua del Lacio. El latín a su vez se enriquece con sus equivalentes poéticos en romance. Además, evidentemente, la traducción cumple la natural función divulgadora para un público romancista.

Lope de Vega y la poesía neolatina

En el mundo de Quevedo y Góngora también circularon algunos versos neolatinos[46]. Pero entre los escritores del Barroco, sin duda Lope de Vega es el que

---

[43] Se conservan inéditos en la Biblioteca Nacional de Madrid, ms. 5572, fols. 43–50; por lo demás Gracián de Alderete es colaborador también con epigramas para emblemas en el *Real Apparato … con que Madrid … recibió a la Serma. Reina D. Ana* (Madrid, 1572), de J. López de Hoyos; véase Juan F. Alcina, *Repertorio de la poesía latina del Renacimiento* (Salamanca, 1995), nº 199.

[44] *Recibimiento que hizo la muy noble y muy leal ciudad de Seuilla a la C.R. del Rey D. Felipe n.s. …* (Sevilla, 1570). Sobre esta doble traducción véase Francisco Talavera, "La práctica de la traducción emuladora de Mallara y su contexto literario", *Analecta Malacitana* 17 (1994): 119–127.

[45] Fray José de Sigüenza, *La Fundación del Monasterio de El Escorial* (Madrid, 1988), 249–250 [=tercera y cuarta parte de la *Historia de la Orden de San Jerónimo*, ed. J. Catalina, NBAE, 12 (Madrid, 1909), 555]. En el dístico corrijo "*serietque*" por "*ferietque*", "*inoffensus*" por "*inofensus*".

[46] Véanse por ejemplo dos poemas de Quevedo dentro de esa tradición: uno es la silva al reloj de arena (ed. Blecua, nº 139) de compleja tradición y otro es un soneto de Quevedo (ed. Blecua, nº 520) y una redondilla de Góngora (ed. Millé, nº 192). El soneto de Quevedo: "Túmulo de la mujer de un avaro que vivió libremente, donde hizo

muestra una mayor admiración por la poesía humanística. El mismo es autor de una pequeña pero curiosa serie de epigramas latinos[47]. El elitista Góngora y el culteranismo desprecian a Lope, aunque de tanto en tanto el cordobés "se vuelve más humano"[48] en su trato con el comediógrafo. Lope debe justificar su lengua, la plenitud

---

esculpir un perro de mármol: Yacen en esta rica sepultura / Lidio con su mujer Helvidia Pada . . ." y la redondilla gongorina "A los ladrones ladré . . ." derivan de un dístico de Joachim Du Bellay de sus *Tumuli* (ed. G. Demerson, n° 9), señalada ya por Mª R. Lida de Malkiel, "Para las fuentes de Quevedo", *Revista de Filología Hispánica* 1 (1939): 371. El poema de Quevedo surge de estos dos dísticos: "Latratu fures excepi, mutus amantes: / Sic placui domino, sic placui dominae". Góngora ofrece también el texto en latín que presenta el primer verso ligeramente diferente: "Latraui ad fures: tacui cum uenit amator". La traducción de Góngora naturalmente se corresponde con esta lectura y también la de Quevedo que traduce: "Ladró al ladrón, pero calló al amante". Parece que la fuente no debió ser la de la edición de los *Poemata* de 1558. Evidentemente circuló por otros conductos. Podría tratarse del pareado italiano del bernesco Antonfrancesco Grazzini, el Lasca, la supuesta fuente de Du Bellay (véase Hoggan, "Aspects du bilingüismo littéraire chez Du Bellay", 65): "Latrai a'ladri, ed agli amanti tacqui; / Si che messere ed madonna placqui". Sin embargo, el texto de Góngora incluye el epigrama en latín y no parece probable que Quevedo tuviera un texto distinto titulándolo "Túmulo" y con el andamiaje de nombres latinos "Helvidia Pada" y "Lidio" con que desarrolla el tema.

El tema del reloj de arena con las cenizas del amante en la poesía del Siglo de Oro fue estudiada hace tiempo por Miguel Herrero García y otros autores en unos curiosos libros sobre el reloj en la cultura hispana de la "Biblioteca Literaria del Relojero" con poemas de Quevedo, Francisco López Zárate y Francisco de la Torre y Sebil (+1680), etc. Véase M. Herrero García, *El reloj en la vida española*, Biblioteca Literaria del Relojero, III (Madrid, 1955), 71 y ss., y R. Santo Torroella, *Los números del tiempo. Antología del reloj y las horas*, I (Madrid, 1953); véase. también R. M. Price, "The Lamp and the Clock: Quevedo's Reaction to a Commonplace", *Modern Language Notes* 82 (1967): 198–209, que analiza como emblemas los poemas citados por Herrero García. Más recientemente Eugenio Asensio, "Reloj de arena y amor en una poesía de Quevedo", *Dicenda. Cuadernos de Filología Hispánica (Homenaje a López Estrada)* II, 7 (1987): 17–32, señaló el origen de esta tradición en un poema de Hieronimus Amaltheus y en otro italiano de Tommaso Stigliani estudiando sus relaciones con Quevedo. El texto de Amaltheus puede verse en M. Toscanus, *Carmina Illustrium Poetarum Italorum*, I (Lutetiae, 1576), fol. 17v, citado por D. López Cañete, 133, que señala también la relación. El texto de Amaltheus, antes que Quevedo lo conocía ya Jaime Juan Falcó (1522–1594) al que dedica un par de epigramas (ed. D. López Cañete, I, 77 y I, 89). Véase también el trabajo de R. Herrera Montero, "Epigramas neolatinos en torno al reloj de arena y sus versiones castellanas", *Cuadernos de Filología Clásica, Estudios latinos* 8 (1995): 187–195, independiente al parecer del trabajo de E. Asensio, que señala la existencia de un ms. de la BNM (ms. 4141, fols. 297–298) con una sección dedicada al tema del reloj donde están reunidos los epigramas de Falcó, Amaltheo y traducciones de Salcedo Coronel y Luis de Ulloa Pereira. A principios del siglo XVII, Quevedo inicia la andadura de este tema en castellano con unas quintillas que traducen claramente a Amaltheus: "Este polvo sin sosiego" (ed. Blecua, n° 420) y después en la "Silva al reloj de arena" mucho más elaborado.

[47] Véase J. Millé y Giménez, "Una 'octava real' latina de Lope y el falso Avellaneda", en *Estudios de Literatura Española* (La Plata, 1928), 247–283; sobre el discutido tema de la latinidad de Lope véase la bibliografía reunida en E. Canonica-de Rochemonteix, *El poliglotismo en el teatro de Lope de Vega* (Kassel, 1991), 33, n. 2.

[48] "Otra vez me he visto con el de Góngora, que acaso le hallé por la tarde con el Almirante.

del castellano frente al latín, un castellano que no necesita latinizar, y al mismo tiempo busca su adscripción a una cultura humanística. Las críticas a su ignorancia en lengua latina que le hizo Torres Rámila en la *Spongia* de 1617 sin duda atizan sus alardes en las citas de vates neolatinos[49]. En ese marco del Lope bohemio, necesitado de dinero y de aprobación, los poetas neolatinos le sirven de defensa, de muestra de sus lecturas curiosas, de su equivalencia con Ronsard y su conocimiento del humanismo francés, tan envidiablemente protegido por los reyes. En este campo podemos seguir a Simón Anselmo Vosters que señala la relación de Lope con el humanista francés Simón Chauvel, poeta que participó con dos epigramas latinos y un jeroglífico en la Justa de San Isidro organizada por Lope en 1620 y que colaboró en la *Expostulatio Spongiae*[50]. Vosters nos ha demostrado también que Lope conocía la *Franciada* de Ronsard a través de la traducción latina de Jean Dorat, que cita un epigrama de este Poète Royal, como también conocería los *Poemata*, en la edición de Poitiers, 1596, de Scaeuola Sammarthanus[51].

En la segunda parte de *La Filomena*, un poema en clave bajo la forma de un debate entre diversos pájaros, el parlamento del "tordo" opuesto al del "ruiseñor-Lope" representa la crítica excesiva de ciertos gramáticos y presenta despreciativamente una pequeña lista de poetas neolatinos[52]:

> Perdono entre modernos a Pontano,
> Tarcañota, Segundo, Angerïano,
> Petrarca, los Estrozas y Vulteyo,
> Filelfo y Sanazaro, y tanta copia
> del estilo plebeyo,
> gente cansada, bárbara y impropia.

Como es sabido, las afirmaciones del "tordo" tienen siempre su ironía y son todas una crítica velada a la rigidez aristotélica del gramático de la Universidad de Alcalá Torres Rámila que había escrito la *Spongia* contra Lope. En *La Filomena*, Lope, al presentar a los poetas neolatinos como "de estilo plebeyo" y "gente bárbara y impropia," intenta caracterizar en negativo al pájaro y a Torres Rámila. Naturalmente Lope piensa todo lo contrario, pero le sirve para darnos una muestra de los autores que conoce: el "Tarcañota" es M. Marullo, "Segundo" es naturalmente Johannes Secundus, va seguido de Angeriano y aparecen los tres juntos como circulaban en la antología antes citada; "los Estrozas" remite evidentemente a la edición *Strozzii Poetae*

Está más humano conmigo, que le debo de haber parecido más hombre de bien de lo que él me imaginaba", fragmento de carta que reproduce José M. Blecua en la Introducción a Lope de Vega, *Rimas* (Barcelona, 1969), XLIII.

[49] Lope sabía suficiente latín como para incluir estrofas en un latín más o menos correcto en varias partes de la *Filomena*, como la "Descripción de la Tapada" (ed. Blecua, 719) y en la carta a "Elisio de Medinilla" (770–771).

[50] Véase S. A. Vosters, *Lope de Vega y la tradición occidental*, I (Madrid, 1977), 122.

[51] Vosters, *Lope de Vega y la tradición occidental*, II, 156–158.

[52] Ed. Blecua, 637 (Segunda parte, vv. 613–618).

Pater et filius[53] que muy probablemente poseía o había manejado y "Vulteyo" es el poeta Jean Visagier[54].

Espigando entre los sonetos finales de la miscelánea de epístolas de la *Circe con otras Rimas y Prosas* (1624) de Lope de Vega aparecen, con el texto latino al frente, traducciones más o menos fieles de uno de los poemas a "Hyella" de Marco Antonio Flaminio[55], de dos textos de Faustus Sabeaeus[56]; de uno de los *Epigrammata* de Johannes Secundus[57] y de otro de Sannazaro[58]. De estos poetas es lógico pensar que Lope tenía o edición o alguna antología de la que sacar los textos.

En la carta prólogo "A don Juan de Arguijo" de las *Rimas* de 1602 se incluye una defensa de los lugares comunes "pues ya son como adagios y términos comunes" y a la defensa de la literatura como reescritura. Para justificarlo, Lope se dedica a una desenfrenada erudición sacada como tantas otras veces de la *Officina* de Ravisius Textor[59]. Defiende el tópico de la comparación de lo innumerable con las estrellas

---

[53] Lope cita un verso de Hercole Strozzi de la colección de odas religiosas que encabeza el *Strozzi Poetae Pater et filius* (Parisiis, 1530) (Biblioteca de Catalunya E 3-IX-11) en *La Jerusalén Conquistada*, ed. cit. al verso "y abrió camino el mar" al margen remite: "Stroza filius, lib. I, ode 7: Qui iussit aequor fluctuosum diuidi", además de otras citas en la misma obra y en la *Arcadia:* véase J. de Entrambasaguas, *Estudios sobre Lope de Vega*, I (Madrid, 1967), 317–319. J. Secundus también cita juntos al padre y al hijo en la nómina de poetas neolatinos ilustres de *Elegiae*, 3, 7, 31–34.

[54] Visagier es citado anteriormente por Diego Salvador de Murga (aunque negativamente), en un poema "Ad librum suum" que cierra el "Epigrammatum liber" (*Poetica* [Salamanca, 1558], fol. XCIIIr). Diego Salvador tiene un excepcional conocimiento de lo que se escribe en esos momentos en Francia. Conoce por ejemplo la obra de Pierre de La Ramée y la nómina de poetas franceses a los que el *liber* debe agradar está particularmente cuidada, resaltando la protección que reciben de los Valois:

> Quod si a uatibus inde Gallicanis
> Ornatus legeris, placere cura
> *Macrino*, et inueni bono *Mureto*,
> Et salsis bene *Dampetro* phaleucis,
> Quos Valesius et creat, Poetis.
> *Vulteium* excipe cum suis phaleucis;
> Contemno iuuenem horridum, infacetum,
> Insulsum, illepidum, rudem, impudicum.

[55] Ed. Blecua, 1288. Son los versos 5 y ss. de "Hanc fistulam hospes, quam uides pinu sacra" del libro IV de Flaminio, *Carmina Quinque Illustrium Poetarum* (Florentiae, 1552), 251, con alguna pequeña diferencia como *obstupebant* por *obstrepebant*.

[56] Ed. Blecua, 1290, 1300, proceden de sus *Epigrammata* (Roma, 1556). No he podido comprobar las citas.

[57] Ed. Blecua, 1298. Vuelve a citar otra vez los *epigrammata* de Secundus, reproduciendo el verso latino correspondiente en el primer libro de *La Jerusalén conquistada*, ed. cit. fol. 3; también lo cita en el prólogo al *Triumfo de la Fe en los Reynos del Japón*, ed. J. S. Cummins (Londres, 1965).

[58] Ed. Blecua, 1305. Se trata del poema "De Aenea et Didone" del libro primero de los *Epigrammata, Iacobi Sannazarii Opera Omnia* (Romae, 1590), 153.

[59] *Officina Ioannis Ravisii Textoris Nivernensis, nunc demum post tot editiones diligenter emendata, aucta, & in longè commodiorem ordinem redacta. Cui hac editione accesserunt eiusdem Rauisii Cornucopiae*

y cita a Marulo:

> Marulo dijo:
> *Non tot signa micant tacente nocte*:
> y más abajo, por las arenas:
> *Non tantus numerus Libyssae arenae*;
> y Catulo lo mismo:
> *Quam magnus numerus Libyssae arenae*;
> y Silio Itálico por las estrellas:
> *Quam multa affixus coelo sub nocte serena.*

Naturalmente Lope no había buscado este ejemplo en Marullo, aunque quizá tuviera un texto de este poeta pues hizo una traducción de uno de sus epigramas a "Neaera"[60]. Ravisius Textor tiene una sección sobre "Descriptio magni et frequentis numeri, per similitudines & comparationes" donde están reunidos en una página los cuatro ejemplos[61]. De todas formas, no todas las citas las saca de la *Officina*. Hacia el final de la misma epístola habla de la imagen *Os roseum* traduciéndola literalmente como "boca de rosa" y cita ejemplos de Baptista Mantuano, Girolamo Vida[62], Poliziano y curiosamente dos versos de Arias Montano [63]:

---

libellus . . . (Venetiis, 1598); sobre Lope y Textor, véase Vosters, *Lope de Vega,* I, 193 y V. Infantes, "De *Officinas* y *Polyantheas*: los diccionarios secretos del Siglo de Oro", en *Homenaje a Eugenio Asensio*, 249, n. 24; y también A. Egido, "Lope de Vega, Ravisio Textor y la creación del mundo como obra de arte", en *Homenaje a Eugenio Asensio*, 171–184, recogido también en sus *Fronteras de la poesía en el Barroco* (Barcelona, 1990), 198–215.

[60] En el soneto 170 (ed. Blecua, 124) traduce el epigrama I, 49 (ed. Perosa, 22). Marulo por lo demás es un autor bastante difundido en España y además de las traducciones de Diego Hurtado de Mendoza y Juan de Mal Lara, *Filosofía Vulgar*, ed. A. Vilanova, III (Barcelona, 1958), 44 (es el epigr. III, 22), lo parafrasea en latín Hernán Ruiz de Villegas. Véase "Petrarquismo latino en España, II: Hernán Ruiz de Villegas y la imitación de Marulo", *Nova Tellus* 4 (1986): 43–62.

[61] *Officina*, fol. 185:

> Syllius lib. 7
> Quam multa affixus caelo sub nocte serena,
>
> . . . . . .
>
>   Marullus
> Non tot Attica mella, littus . . .
> Non tot signa micant tacente nocte, . . .
> Non tantus numerus Libyssae arenae . . .
>   Catullus
> Quam magnus numerus Libyssae arenae.

Dos páginas después da ejemplos latinos de la puesta de sol y otra vez echa mano de la misma sección de Textor de las múltiples citas clásicas de "Descriptio noctis seu aduentu eius": Textor, *Officina*, fols. 77v–78.

[62] Quizá conociese directamente su poética en verso porque lo cita en otros lugares como autoridad: véase *Rimas*, ed. Blecua, 848, habla de "versos debidos al albano Vida, / los que por Medinilla resplandecen" (¿hizo Elisio Medinilla una traducción de Vida?) y con otros autores de teoría literaria, 877.

[63] Ed. Blecua, 283. Vosters, *Lope de Vega*, II, 375–381, estudia ampliamente la influencia de

. . . y nuestro divino Arias Montano, en aquellos tetrastrofos, la llamó de
oro y de rosa:

> *Ut uultus rosae Virginis aureos*
> *Uxor Leuitici Pontificis uidet, etc.*

Proceden de los *Humanae Salutis Monumenta* (1571), de la "Ode tricolos tetra-
strophos XXXVI", vv. 1–2. Los *Monumenta* fueron uno de los libros de emblemas de
más éxito de la imprenta de Plantino, con cinco reediciones por lo menos. Sabemos
que Lope (que gustaba de los libros de emblemas) tuvo un ejemplar y es plausible
pensar que la cita ésta con la alusión exacta al título "tetrástrofos" no proceda de la
Officina o un libro similar, sino que realmente buscó el pasaje. En la "Respuesta a un
papel que escribió un señor de estos reinos en razón de la nueva poesía" Lope cita
como libros de su biblioteca junto con las obras de Justo Lipsio a "esse librito que
llamó Arias Montano *Humanae salutis monumenta,* cuyos versos no deben nada a
cuantos están escritos, la antigüedad perdone"[64]. No es de extrañar, por tanto, si en
las notas marginales de la *Jerusalén conquistada* (1609) en las que Lope daba pomposa-
mente las fuentes de algunos de sus versos nos encontramos con varias citas precisas
de los *Monumenta.* Arias Montano, como Virgilio o Horacio, le sirve a Lope para la
creación de imágenes atrevidas y misteriosas como por ejemplo en el fol. 3 vto. de la
Jerusalén[65] en el que al verso "la puerta de christal que abrió la vara" remite a "Arias
Mont[ano] od. Saph. 17: Fluminis portam uitream tumentis pandit"[66].

Digamos que la cultura de Lope es en parte de segunda mano, pero también tenía
sus lecturas directas. En un testamento de 1627, Lope dice que dejaba 1500 libros[67].
Algo más que *Officinae* y *Poliantheae* habría entre ellos.

En 1626 Lope inicia lo que Rozas ha llamado el ciclo *de senectute*[68]. Ya no puede,
ni físicamente, seguir escribiendo comedias para los hambrientos corrales y busca
patéticamente un mecenazgo que le dé una pensión para la vejez. Tiene entonces que
cambiar su imagen de hombre mujeriego y liviano por otra de hombre docto y serio
que le permita ser aceptado por la nobleza y la corte, aunque al final no lo consiga.
Para perfilar esa nueva imagen Lope dedica al Papa Urbano VIII, Maffei Barberini,

---

Montano en Lope y recoge otras citas que no trataré aquí como las que aparecen en el *Isidro* o el
epitafio de Montano de las *Rimas* de 1604 (ed. Blecua, 250) que implican el conocimiento de los
dísticos de *Virorum doctorum . . . effigies* (Amberes, 1572).

[64] Lope de Vega, *Obras Sueltas,* IV, 479, citado por M. Gascón, "Fuentes jesuíticas en el teatro
de Lope de Vega", *Boletín de la Biblioteca Menéndez y Pelayo* 17 (1935): 388, n. 1.

[65] Utilizo el ejemplar de la Biblioteca de Catalunya (Madrid, 1609).

[66] En fol. 52r al verso "Perficionó su humilde ser humano" referido a la Virgen, remite al
margen a "Arias Mont. Ode 38: Vt aucta amplius ipsa tuo numine perficiar"; y en fol. 15 al verso
"con que Israel sin pelear vencía" remite a "Arias Mont. ode 18: non gladio aut numero non ui".

[67] Véase Cayetano Alberto de La Barrera, *Nueva Biografía,* Obras de Lope de Vega publicadas
por la Real Academia Española, I (Madrid, 1890), 972, donde se reproduce el "Inventario" de los
bienes de Lope para un testamento que hizo en 1627.

[68] J. M. Rozas, *Lope de Vega y Felipe IV en el "ciclo de senectute". Discurso en la solemne apertura
de curso . . .* (Badajoz-Cáceres, 1982), recogido también en sus *Estudios sobre Lope de Vega* (Madrid,
1990), 73–132.

humanista y autor de una colección de poesía latina, la *Corona Trágica* sobre María Estuardo y le promete traducir sus odas latinas. El Papa le envía una carta y un epigrama latino que Lope inserta en los preliminares de la edición de 1627[69] añadiendo traducción castellana. El Papa, a través de su sobrino, el Cardenal Barberini que redacta la epístola, le dice:

> Eo cariores S[ancto].D[omino].N[ostro]. tuae fuerunt litterae ... quanti odas tu illas faceres, quas ipse uelut in seccesu a seueris curis, cum mansuetioribus olim Musis lusitare non est dedignatus. Id uero apertius quoque fit, dum tua in Epistola eximias laudes, quasi plena manu in easdem odas congeris, *quas etiam Hispanico exprimere carmine moliris*, iamque te manum admouisse scribis. Quod cum nisi felici conatu abs te fiat, dubitandum non est quin iis poematiis non exigua inde laus sit accesura ... ''[70].

Nada sabemos de estas traducciones de Lope. Sabemos que el poeta vallisoletano Gabriel del Corral, poeta latino y autor de la traducción de la *Argenis* de Barclay, tradujo estos poemas del Papa y Lope le dedicó un soneto a esta traducción en las *Rimas de Tomé Burguillos*[71]. De cualquier manera sus contactos con Roma sirvieron a Lope para conseguir el título de Doctor en Teología por la Sapienza, concedido junto con la carta, y para presentarse como fino degustador de versos neolatinos ante sus enemigos.

Por lo demás Lope es amigo de diversos humanistas que siguen cultivando la poesía en latín en el siglo XVII: Tamayo de Vargas que concurre con dísticos latinos en *Los Pastores de Belén*[72], el presbítero toledano Francisco Gutiérrez, que escribe un epigrama para la *Jerusalén conquistada*[73], Miguel Cejudo[74] o Luis Tribaldos de Toledo autor de una abundante producción en latín[75]. En los diversos certámenes o justas poéticas que organiza Lope para las celebraciones de Madrid y por los que recibe algún dinero, siempre se incluye alguna sección con sus premios para poesía latina.

---

[69] Véase La Barrera, *Nueva Biografía*, 401–402.

[70] La Barrera, *Nueva Biografía*, 409, donde se reproduce toda la epístola.

[71] *Rimas*, ed. Blecua, 1369–1370; La Barrera, *Nueva Biografía*, 403; y John V. Falconieri, *Obras de Gabriel del Corral* (Valladolid, 1982), 231 y ss. edita el centón latino en verso de Corral dedicado a Barberini y estudia la traducción de los poemas del Papa, que quedó inédita en un manuscrito de la Vaticana. También dedicó un soneto a "la traducción que ha hecho de los versos latinos de Su Santidad" el poeta Gabriel Bocángel, *La lira de las musas*, ed. Trevor J. Dadson (Madrid, 1985), 165. Junto con traducción de Manuel Salinas, lo cita también Gracián, *Agudeza y Arte de Ingenio* (Buenos Aires–México, 1944), 95 [Discurso XIV]. Conocía también la poesía latina de Urbano VIII el curioso poeta Francisco de la Torre y Sebil porque lo cita en los añadidos suyos a la traducción *Simbolos selectos y parábolas históricas del P. Nicolás Causino de la Compañía de Jesús* ... (Madrid, 1677), 132, 314, etc. Francisco de la Torre incluye en esta obra también algunos poemas latinos propios.

[72] Véase Vosters, *Lope de Vega*, 132–133.

[73] Véase *Rimas*, ed. Blecua, 646.

[74] Sobre los diversos poemas perliminares a obras de Lope de Cejudo véase de Etrambasaguas, *Estudios sobre Lope de Vega*, I, 319–320; Alcina, *Repertorio de la poesía latina del Renacimiento*, nº 115.

[75] Véase Alcina, *Repertorio*, nº 435, 200–201 y Vosters, *Lope de Vega*, 133.

En las comedias Lope utiliza también la mezcla de lenguas en la vieja tradición del *Poenulus* de Plauto, y naturalmente incluye el latín y su parodia en boca de estudiantes capigorrones, sacristanes y médicos[76]. Es un latín a veces incorrecto, palabras sueltas de español latinizado que no tienen la continuidad ni siguen una norma como el latín macarrónico. Veamos un ejemplo de la comedia *El poder en el discreto* (1623). En esa obra Celio se excusa de no poderse casar con Flora por estar enfermo—en realidad quiere casarse con otra—y su criado Alejo lo justifica en lenguaje médico:

> Dice Galeno, señora,
> que el hombre que *desmayatus*
> pretendiere ser *casatus*
> *morietur* de cantimplora.
> Donde *frigiditas* mora
> *nemo*, prosigue, *casetur*,
> porque no se *desmayetur*,
> que *caballerus galantis*
> aun *mulieribus estantis*
> es bien que *fortis mostretur*.

Otras veces el latín es correcto pero la hilaridad surge por la disparatada traducción, como en el examen del criado Crispín por Gregorio en *La niñez del Padre Rojas* (1625):

> Gregorio: Y ¿qué dirá, según eso / *satis est breuis oratio?*
> Crispin: Que son sastres los que hicieron / las bragas a Horacio[77].

Este uso cómico del latín está bastante extendido en comedias y entremeses del Siglo de Oro. Y, por ejemplo, Calderón todavía hace algunas referencias a la escritura en latín con cierto aire irónico. En el sainete o baile entremesado "El juicio de los poetas" con que se cierra la comedia *El gran duque de Gandía* (1671) se presenta un certamen o justa poética burlesca arbitrada por "Momo". Ante él corren con papeles de versos un ciego, un villano, un hombre vestido de mujer, un sacristán cojo y un médico corcovado, presentando todos ante el dios bufonesco sus obras poéticas. Y no faltan los latines que están en manos del pedante sacristán cojo[78]:

---

[76] En parte coincidentes con el "Pedante" de la comedia del quinientos italiana caracterizado por un "mistilinguismo" semejante, véase A. Stäuble, *"Parlar per lettera". Il Pedante nella commedia del cinquecento e altri saggi sul teatro rinascimentale* (Roma, 1991), 71 y ss. Evidentemente también detrás del lenguaje de los capigorrones, sacristanes o médicos de comedia se parodia la realidad de una lengua pedante (véase para Italia, Stäuble, "Possibili modelli viventi", *"Parlar per lettera"*, 107–111).

[77] Estos dos ejemplos aparecen recogidos en Canonica-de Rochemonteix, *El poliglotismo en el teatro de Lope de Vega*, 100 y 83.

[78] *El Gran Duque de Gandía. Comedia de don Pedro Calderón de la Barca publiée d'après le manuscrit de Mladá Vozice avec une introduction, des notes et un glossaire par Václav Cerny* (Praga, 1963), 175.

Momo: Llegue el seó beneficiado / ¿Qué papel?
Sacristán: Doce dísticos
Momo: *Distichos dicere debes*
Sacristán: Esto es de Calepinillo, / que yo llevo otra opinión.
Momo: Será del greco latino
Sacristán: Por no oler a romancista / ni una consonante admito.
Momo: ¿Por qué?
Sacristán: Por bocales todas / y por líquidas las mido.
Mujer (cant.) Pues medir sabe tanto / como blasona, / mida los pies
      con que anda, / porque no constan.

El sacristán es tan cojo como sus dísticos y los "pies" de sus versos, inusitados y desconocidos, se hacen cruelmente simétricos a su cojera. El sacristán supera el latín del diccionario de Calepino con un nuevo tipo de métrica que por apartarse de la rima consonante de la poesía romance sólo admite en sus versos vocales y líquidas. Probablemente hace burla aquí de los lipogramas o textos escritos sin una letra determinada que estaban de moda en el siglo XVII, como la novela de Francisco de Navarrete, *Los tres hermanos* (1640), escrita sin la vocal *a*[79].

Quiero acabar aquí, con el poliglotismo del teatro, este muestreo y recorrido entre latín y romance. El estado español fue siempre tacaño con las letras. La envidia de Lope de Vega al mecenazgo y protección de la poesía que había visto florecer en Francia está plenamente justificada. Fruto de esa falta de protección fue un humanismo aislado y endeble, aunque existió a pesar de todo. En cambio, el vernáculo floreció sin necesidad de ayudas ni políticas ni culturales. El puro mercado del libro le dio fuerza suficiente para consolidarse. Pero su floreciemiento estuvo siempre bordeado por el latín humanístico. El neolatín fue inevitablemente un elemento de fondo presente siempre como algo constitutivo en Garcilaso o de prestigio en Lope de Vega, por ejemplo. Y en ese sentido, el neolatín sigue vivo en la literatura española de los Siglos de Oro y llega hasta nosotros como una vieja savia escondida.

Universitat Rovira i Virgili
(Tarragona)

---

[79] *Novelistas Posteriores a Cervantes*, Biblioteca de Autores Españoles, XXXIII, 369–383; otros ejemplos en R. de Cózar, *Poesía e Imagen. Formas difíciles de Ingenio Literario* (Sevilla, 1991), 333.

La prima ricezione del 'mondo nuovo' nella cultura dell'Umanesimo[1]

GIACOMO FERRAÚ

In una lettera che accompagnava l'edizione delle prime tre deche, indirizzata a Carlo, re Cattolico, giovane sovrano dal grande destino, Pietro Martire d'Angera chiariva in termini esemplari la sua carriera di intellettuale italiano di formazione umanistica, la cui alta competenza culturale non aveva trovato adeguato campo di applicazione in una Italia oggetto di una vicenda ormai decisa altrove: era stato quindi

---

[1] A causa della ristrettezza dei tempi e dello spazio concesso, si pubblica la relazione così come è stata letta, con essenziali riferimenti alle fonti delle citazioni. Si rinvia innanzitutto alla raccolta delle *Fonti italiane per la storia della scoperta del Nuovo Mondo*, a c. di G. Berchet, II (Roma, 1892) (citato come Berchet), una silloge comoda anche se non sempre filologicamente sicura. La storia del Martire è citata da *De orbe novo* Petri Martyris Anglerii, Parisiis, apud Guillelmum Auvray, MDLXXXVII (citato come Martire). La citazione relativa alla *legatio babylonica* è tratta invece dall'edizione Petri Martyris *De orbe novo decades tres* [. . .] eiusdem praeterea *Legationis Babylonicae libri tres* (Basileae MDXXXIII). La *Historia Aphricae* di Scillacio è conservata in un manoscrtto della Biblioteca dell'Università di Valencia, ms. M782; il *De situ terrarum* del Galateo è compreso in Antonio de Ferraris Galateo, *Epistole*, ed. Altamura (Lecce, 1959), 23–31. Si offre in questa sede anche un rapidissimo ragguaglio bibliografico di quanto è sottinteso dal mio discorso, e innanzitutto dal classico e discusso libro di T. Todorov, *La conquista dell'America. Il problema dell'altro* (Torino, 1992), ricchissimo di suggestioni, al contributo di G. R. Cardona, *Moduli antichi e mondi nuovi: la storiografia delle scoperte*, in *La storiografia umanistica*, (Messina, 1992), I:93–111. Ancora notevoli osservazioni in R. Romeo, *La scoperta americana nella coscienza italiana del '500* (Milano-Napoli, 1954). Per la prospettiva 'edenica' colombiana, si veda G. Costa, *La leggenda dei secoli d'oro nella letteratura italiana* (Bari, 1972), 71–76. Per lo sfondo storico-culturale della vicenda, utile J. Bestard Contreras, *Barbaros, paganos, salvajes y primitivos. Una introducción a la Antropología* (Barcelona, 1987) e i più recenti B. Vincent, *1492, l'année admirable* (Parigi, 1991) e T. Gomez, *L'invention de l'Amérique. Mythes et réalités de la conquête* (Parigi, 1992). Su Pietro Martire: *Pietro Martire nella storia della cultura. Atti del secondo convegno internazionale di studi americanistici*, Genova-Arona, 16–19 ottobre 1978 (Genova, 1980); ulteriori spunti, anche di bibliografia: *Andando más más se sabe. Atti del Convegno internazionale 'La scoperta dell'America e la cultura italiana'*, Genova, 6–8 aprile 1992, a c. di L. Crovetto (Roma, 1994).

attratto dalla Spagna, dove veramente si compiva la storia di un'età nuova, "quia nullibi terrarum hoc tempore aeque praeclaras res fieri videbam" (*De orbe*, 1).

Così il vecchio umanesimo si apriva alla considerazione di una realtà diversa e decisiva per il futuro, ponendo al servizio della forza vitale di una nazione giovane le capacità raffinate ed estenuate di una civilizzazione giunta all'apice del suo destino e già in certa misura consapevole di un vicino tramonto che l'avrebbe posta ai margini della storia europea. Occorre subito dire che Pietro Martire si distingue nell'ambito del quotidiano umanistico, quasi sempre estraneo alle problematiche del 'nuovo mondo' e comunque portato a filtrare le novità attraverso un codice classicizzante troppo spesso inadeguato e mistificante.

D'altro canto, competenza umanistica e slancio vitale spagnolo sono le due forze la cui risultante è l'impresa stessa di Colombo: il quale poi, come è noto, non solo 'scopre' l'America, ma altresì la inventa, instaurando con le sue relazioni di viaggio una visione del nuovo mondo destinata a costituirsi in archetipo. Un archetipo, poi, a vario titolo presente in tutta la tradizione successiva, con risultati non sempre positivi per la comprensione della vicenda nei suoi termini reali.

In effetti, la fervida capacità visionaria del grande navigatore proponeva una descrizione delle terre da lui scoperte tanto mistificata quanto suggestiva, proprio perché in sintonia con aspirazioni, sogni, speranze di un mondo in crisi di profonda trasformazione, cui Colombo prospettava una visione edenica, di bontà naturale, in una società in cui non v'era il tuo e il mio e la religiosità naturalmente trovava la strada corretta di un culto ad una divinità creatrice senza tramiti idolatri. E ancora emergeva dalla prospettiva colombiana l'entusiasmo per una natura incantata e selvaggia, il cui impatto era spesso più diffuso e partecipe della stessa dimensione umana; e poi, ancora, il motivo dell'oro sublimato come potente mezzo per spingere le anime al paradiso. Tutte problematiche dietro cui, per altro, non è difficile ricostruire il classico modello dell'età dell'oro, una tipologia strutturante con cui dovranno fare i conti perfino le più avvertite considerazioni della grande etnologia spagnola del secolo seguente.

Ovviamente, d'altro canto, la prospettiva di Colombo non era poi oggettivamente neutra, dato che poteva essere utilizzata ai fini di una 'conquista' veicolata dai valori di incivilimento e di cristianizzazione, spesso destinati a nascondere diverse e meno nobili pulsioni: e valgano le considerazioni di un osservatore marginalmente interessato al problema, ma certamente formato alla scuola della politica più sottile, il Guicciardini, quando osservava che il pur nobile stato edenico dei nuovi popoli li rendeva facili prede della conquista (Berchet, 370). E tuttavia, la prospettiva impostata da Colombo era destinata a divenire il necessario punto di partenza di ogni discorso sul 'nuovo mondo', per cui, significativamente, i primi in Italia a riprendere motivi colombiani, non sono i rappresentanti della cultura 'alta', umanistica, ma piuttosto letterati appartenenti a tipologie popolareggianti, in cui aveva forte valenza la suggestione del meraviglioso, umano e naturale: il precocissimo recepimento di un Tebaldo de Rossi, di un Malipiero, di un Allegretti (Berchet, 1–3), ne percorreva in tale direzione gli elementi più fruibili, in una prospettiva che culmina nell'accattivante versificazione di Giuliano Dati, una puntuale ripresa delle tematiche più suggestive, dal valore tecnico dell'impresa, "che i nostri antichi non seppon trovare"; la smisurata e incombente natura, la prospettiva edenica di un mondo in cui "non si trova acciaro

o ferro", ma "credule e semplici brigate", dove "non ho veduto far né tuo né mio |
ma la vita è comun che vuole Dio". E ancora, la disposizione a farsi convertire, la
religiosità naturale, "non è fra loro idolatria nisuna", e il mito dell'età dell'oro, "o che
ricchezza | arei potuto in queste parti fare". Infine i *mirabilia*, uomini con le code,
cannibali, amazzoni (Berchet, 8–20). L'antropologia che ne emerge è ben in linea con
la prospettiva del 'buon selvaggio', destinata, una volta che se ne precisassero e
affinassero i termini ideologici, ad illustre fortuna nella cultura occidentale, ma che,
tuttavia, di per sé costituisce un ostacolo non lieve per una comprensione storica del-
l'evento, per cui, la prima vera storiografia umanistica della scoperta, nell'opera di un
Pietro Martire, dovrà necessariamente ricondurre la vicenda dal naturale al politico.
Ma, a sottolineare il significato della prima considerazione della scoperta, valga la
segnalazione della scarsa fortuna di più realistici resoconti, come quello di Michele da
Cuneo che, *et in Arcadia ego*, riporta in luce la filigrana dell'Eden colombiano, la violenza e la dura prospettiva economicistica sottesa alla storia della conquista (Berchet,
95–107).

Accanto al filone della ricezione popolare, immediata ed entusiasta, la linea più
propriamente umanistica tarda a comparire ed, è in ogni caso, soprattutto opera di
umanisti professionali che, privi del coraggio intellettuale di affrontare nuovi mondi,
dalla torre d'avorio della loro altissima civilizzazione guardano in modo distratto ed
episodico all'avvenimento epocale, non ne capiscono i termini reali e, se recepiscono
elementi del racconto colombiano, tentano tuttavia di riportarli nell'alveo caro e rassicurante del codice classico, come conferma a valori e significati consolidati: si veda
ad esempio il racconto del Sabellico che riscrive i *mirabilia* in chiave diodorea, quando
non si esibisce in giudizi di valore sul versante comparatistico, come la 'riducula per-
mutatio' di vasi di vetro con oro, un giudizio che esclude ogni possibilità di affrontare
la materia coi parametri di un necessario relativismo culturale (Berchet, 116). È una
prospettiva che approda persino al rifiuto di quella concezionee della pienezza del
tempo di rinascita (un'età che ha visto cose che gli antichi non conobbero), che pure
è mito ben umanistico: e si veda Lucio Marineo che, nella sua opera storica, rapidamente rende conto dell'avvenimento epocale, rilevando però che sulla nuova terra era
stata comunque rinvenuta una moneta romana,

> quae res nimirum nostri temporis navigantibus, qui se prius quam alios illuc
> navigasse iactabant, gloriam eripuit; quantum quidem numismatis huius argu-
> mento iam constat ad Indos olim pervenisse Romanos. (Berchet, 389)

È' un esempio forte della sordità ideologica della cultura umanistica, della pulsione
di ricondurre a codice gli elementi di novità, resecando le punte più incisive ed
inquietanti che potessero mettere a rischio valori consolidati. Ed è pure un indizio
evidente del fatto che ormai la cultura umanistica italiana aveva finito di essere
l'avanguardia europea, si era sclerotizzata nei termini, pur prestigiosi, di un classicismo
avviato a farsi sempre più scolastico ed incapace di recepire il nuovo. Ciò è valido
sostanzialmente anche per l'ambiente romano, dove una più puntuale ripresa della
problematica 'americana' era suggerita dal problema dell'evangelizzazione dei nuovi
venuti nell'ecumene civile: in tal senso la stessa religiosità naturale era un ottimo punto di partenza per un'operazione di recupero alla fede dei territori ad Occidente che

avrebbero compensato le perdite in Oriente causate dall'espansione turca. Una prospettiva non solo presente in territori culturali ecclesiastici: un Carvajal, corrispondente, per altro, di Pietro Martire, o un Fedra Inghirami; ma altresì a livello di umanesimo curiale, in un Cortesi ad esempio (Berchet, 142), o in un Maffei, che accoglie le scoperte nella sua enciclopedia, mantenendo la 'voce' sul doppio registro del confronto pliniano e dei *mirabilia* colombiani: "monstra [. . .] de quibus tam multa scriptoribus, licet, nusquam visa". Ma che tuttavia può accogliere un senso del nuovo insolito, registrando che "ad hos ‹populos› igitur Macedonum seu Romanorum neque arma neque nomen penetravere" (Berchet, 197).

Di certo, la generazione immediatamente a ridosso delle scoperte stenta a trovare linee di accostamento adeguate nei confronti della nuova realtà: tuttavia cominciano a prospettarsi tensioni che troveranno pieno sviluppo nella grande storiografia spagnola del secolo seguente, e tra queste emerge una linea di approccio critico che mette in primo piano le sofferenze dei popoli conquistati. Si veda ad esempio l'inferno a rovescio prospettato da un Galateo, in cui i valori edenici colombiani vengono riportati in negativo ai disvalori di cui si fa portatrice la Spagna nei paesi conquistati: tirannia, stragi, oppressioni, avidità, sete di sangue.

È' pur vero che la polemica del Galateo ha piuttosto di mira, col pretesto del 'nuovo mondo', le condizioni del Reame meridionale: tuttavia la pagina dell'umanista si configura come una delle più precoci manifestazioni di una 'leggenda nera' che, a ridosso della scoperta, trova echi in Giustiniani e soprattutto nella pagina di Alessandro Geraldini. Vale la pena di soffermarsi sulla relazione di questo ecclesiastico di famiglia dalle salde tradizioni umanistiche, proprio perché si tratta di documento di notevole spessore. Se infatti non è privo di spunti relativi al meraviglioso (i mostri marini che ne funestano il viaggio), come non mancano spunti in prospettiva edenica (gli indigeni "pii et bona in vera naturae lege [. . .] recti et integri, cum mira ubique aequitate": Berchet, 296) ed è presente il correlativo classicizzante, per cui l'America si identifica con l'Atlantide platonica e i cannibali inverano le leggende di Tieste e dei ciclopi (Berchet, 298 e 300), tuttavia è rilevabile un tentativo di descrivere incontri di culture, quando nei confronti del Geraldini che rimprovera il cannibale per il suo nefando costume, quest'ultimo si giustifica rispondendo che non si ciberebbe mai di uomini valorosi: "pietas in magno contemptu habenda est, si viribus magnis fulta non sit". O ancora interessante è la precoce testimonianza della crescita di una città coloniale, costruita 'ritu Italiae' e popolata da uomini di valore, giureconsulti, marinai, soldati, che, "res procul dubio admiranda", hanno scelto di compiere opera di civilizzazione, "patria sub axe Europae relicta" (Berchet, 299).

Ma certamente il significato della testimonianza del Geraldini risiede nel suo impegno di pastore che allarga la visione del nuovo mondo verso una considerazione più realistica della sorte degli indigeni: in tale direzione il punto di partenza può utilmente essere l'impostazione colombiana di tipo edenico, per cui gli indigeni del Geraldini

nullam alicui vim inferebant, matrimonia observabant, summum ius aequi et boni menti innocue affixum: [. . .] habebant regulos pii populi [. . .] quos miro cultu prosequebantur, nec ulla bella, nisi pro tutando regum limite, eis erant; omnia habebant communia praeter domos et privata opificia; minimi cibi erant, potus aqua, panem e radicibus faciebant. (Berchet, 304)

Su questi innocenti e sulla loro vita secondo natura si è abbattuta l'avidità dei colonizzatori: ciò che nelle pagine precedenti era rappresentato come slancio civilizzatore e fondatore di città, rivela un vero volto demoniaco

et tamen, cum miti adeo gente eo modo sevitum est, quod partim eorum, cum coniugibus liberis et tota familia coacti antiqua ab alveo flumina mutare, ut aurum inde eruerent, cum nullo plane alimento nisi paucorum piscium nutrirentur, in ipso labore periere; partim in longo opere fessi, et ob eam rem vulnere confecti sunt; foeminae foetae, cum quibus aliqua utendum indulgentia erat, cum opera longe maiora subirent, quam vires earum tolerarent, abortu emisso, statim cecidere. (Berchet, 305)

E questo è solo uno *specimen* di una lunga denuncia che anticipa temi e motivi familiari alla posteriore storiografia della conquista e che semmai, nel Geraldini, trova un limite nell'essere poi ricondotto sostanzialmente ad un alveo pietistico, con richiesta di instaurazione di strutture ecclesiastiche e relative reliquie.

Con tutti questi limiti tuttavia l'interesse per il nuovo mondo che caratterizza gli ambienti ecclesiastici e curiali non trova riscontro in altri momenti della cultura italiana del tempo: e, semmai, può essere appena segnalata una linea 'genovese' che mette in evidenza sostanzialmente le capacità tecniche del grande navigatore, una linea, per altro, di cui è facile misurare il provincialismo e l'ottusità di fondo (Battista Fregoso in Berchet, 75; Gallo in Berchet, 188–91).

Tuttavia almeno due casi di umanisti di formazione italiana evadono da queste coordinate: e si tratta di due personaggi le cui esperienze ispaniche fanno marcare un impegno più incisivo nei confronti della problematica delle scoperte, approdando a risultati di diverso valore e significato e tuttavia entrambi di buon interesse. Dei due, l'uno, Nicolò Scillacio, come siciliano, nasce suddito della corona di Aragona, partecipa di tipologie culturali umanistico-scientifiche, da medico, e può inoltre segnare al suo attivo una esperienza autoptica iberica; l'altro, Pietro Martire, dopo una formazione nella nativa Lombardia, aveva verificato la sua competenza umanistica nel prestigioso ambiente romano in cui operava l'esemplarità di Pomponio Leto (non a caso un umanista particolarmente interessato al 'diverso', come dimostrano le sue esperienze di viaggio 'scitiche'); il Martire si era quindi trasferito in Ispagna, per le fondate ragioni ricordate dalla lettera a Carlo V, approdando ad una prestigiosa carriera al 'Senato delle Indie', che avrebbe saputo sostanziare di motivazioni culturali di estremo interesse.

Per intrambi i personaggi, poi, occorre forse sottolineare come il loro interesse per il diverso etnico non si limita al versante del nuovo mondo e che, anzi, entrambi sono autori di ragguagli relativi al versante mediterraneo della diversità, un impegno certo non alieno alla Spagna del tempo.

In effetti, lo Scillacio è autore di una storia della vicenda magrebina del secolo XV, ancora inedita e certo più interessante dell'opera 'americana', una storia in servizio delle prospettive tradizionali siciliane ereditate dallo stato aragonese, verso le vicine Gerbe: in proposito basti rapidamente osservare come la ricezione del diverso a livello di storiografia non poteva strutturarsi secondo le consuete linee del modello dominante liviano-sallustiano, ma doveva trovare nuove forme capaci di accoglie il necessario referente etnico-geografico. Pertanto l'opera dello Scillacio non è esclusivamente narrativa, ma dedica larga parte ad una mappa dell'Africa del Nord impegnata sul versante dei costumi, dei prodotti agricoli, del teatro geografico della vicenda.

Pietro Martire, a sua volta, inviato dai Re Cattolici come ambasciatore al Cairo, fornisce un interessante e colorito ragguaglio dell'Egitto dei Mamelucchi, ancora un complesso tentativo di accorpare resoconto di viaggio, storia politica e sociale, costumi, storia naturale, per concludere nella prospettiva di un mondo alla rovescia, "regiones, in quibus servi dominantur, liberi serviunt; graves opprimuntur, stulti extolluntur, ubi nulla fides, nullum ius, nulla pietas, misericordia rara, avaritia immensa" (Martire, 84v). E si potrebbe riconoscere in questo *topos* la nobile ascendenza erodotea, laddove ancora lo stesso paese era un mondo alla rovescia rispetto alla grecità.

Comunque sia, una volta registrato in entrambi gli umanisti l'interesse per il diverso, occorre osservare che, per quel che concerne il versante mediterraneo, si tratta di un diverso in certo modo familiare, quello dei cari nemici con cui l'Occidente era da secoli abituato a confrontarsi, coloro che potevano essere sussunti nella categoria di barbari: e si sa che i barbari sono l'altra faccia della medaglia di ogni civiltà, la necessaria e contigua pietra di paragone, l'opposto, è possibile, ma non il totalmente diverso. La considerazione del nuovo mondo poneva invece la problematica di un diverso più sottilmente e radicalmente diverso: la trappola ideologica che Colombo aveva costruito mediante l'attribuzione di una dimensione edenica ai nativi aveva posto in essere una nuova categorizzazione, per cui non più barbari, dotati di una propria storia, ma selvaggi, popoli senza storia accoglieva il nuovo continente, popoli senza una tradizione di apprezzabile dimensione diacronica. E' questo che rende il mondo nuovo veramente nuovo, diverso dai quadri mentali della civiltà europea, in grado di interagire con tali quadri in direzione di una nuova dimensione ideologica capace di straordinaria incidenza nel tempo a venire, ma intanto problema fondamentale per coloro che per primi dovevano ricondurre la vicenda a storia.

È' un tentativo operato da entrambi gli umanisti, anche se deve essere innanzi tutto rilevato il diverso impegno dei due primi storici del nuovo mondo: vi è infatti una forte distanza tra lo scarno resoconto di Scillacio e il complesso, elaborato e motivato approdo di Pietro Martire, tra un'opera occasionale di non nascosta pulsione di intrattenimento e il risultato dell'operosità di una vita.

Di certo il lavoro dello Scillacio è ben povera cosa, troppo dipendente ancora dalla prospettiva colombiana e, per contro, fortemente strutturato dall'ipoteca umanistica: e innanzi tutto proprio perché, se si tratta di "insulae nuper inventae", non si tratta ancora di un 'nuovo mondo', ché anzi Colombo segue la rotta classica del cartaginese Annone: "meridiani maris ambitum enavigatum, Ethiopiae inferioris terminos exploratos, ... Arabiae beatas insulas deprehensas quae in mari Indico sparsae cernuntur". Inoltre il codice umanistico è presente a livello di immaginativa, con il mare popolato di Galatee e Nereidi, il *topos* della tempesta marina, con un orizzonte di riferimento per cui tutta la prima parte del viaggio di Colombo è letta in filigrana con la geografia di Plinio, identificando le isole scoperte con quelle arabiche, "cum Caii Plinii, tum aliorum testimonio certissimo" (Berchet, 83 e 88), mentre i singoli avvenimenti sono riconducibili a categorie storiografiche familiari, la magnanimità dei nativi, la gelosia per le donne individuata come sentimento universale. Non manca però qualche tensione verso aperture coloniali che segnano una 'reductio ad civilitatem', nel momento in cui, pur nella meraviglia di un mondo che spontaneamente produce i suoi frutti, si prevede l'intervento fabbrile del "colonus Hispanus" capace di rendere la natura "mitiorem [...] disciplina seminandi, adhibitis colonis, villicis adductis qui terram agitent, qui sarculis findant, aratione, runcatione domestica excitent". O ancora si veda la fondazione di città con l'auspicio che gli stessi re di Spagna, liberi ormai da cure domestiche, "e Gadibus profecti in tam beata regna penetrent [...] suas insulas visuri" (Berchet, 91).

È' un'apertura certo giustapposta alla linea maestra dell'opera schiettamente 'colombiana', sia nel descrivere la natura degli indigeni, mantenuta nelle ormai canoniche cordinate edeniche (non senza qualche concessione, nella dimensione che si è rilevata come cortigiana, al pittoresco esotico), sia nella tematica dell'oro e in quella della possibilità che "populi recogniti, gregatim sparsi sine lege [...] ad Christi religionem brevi traducentur" (Berchet, 93).

In realtà, lo Scillacio non riesce a trovare una linea unitaria di interpretazione: la sua narrazione rimane in buona misura distante da una vera e propria operazione storiografica, sospesa tra i due poli di un resoconto della prima conquista e una accettazione della dimensione metastorica e meramente 'naturale'. E se nella considerazione del più prossimo 'diverso' mediterraneo vi sono numerose aperture di rilevante interesse, alla base del recepimento della vicenda del nuovo mondo non vi sono categorie adeguate ad una comprensione degli elementi specifici di una ben diversa vicenda.

Poiché occorreva certo ridefinire le opzioni culturali necessarie all'approccio storiografico della nuova, complessa problematica: si poteva, ad esempio accogliere la dimensione metastorica di cui erano accreditati gli abitanti del nuovo mondo e fare storia solo della presenza europea; si poteva costruire una storia di tipo etnologico di quelle popolazioni; si poteva approdare ad una narrazione di viaggio che puntasse su una storia 'naturale' di *mirabilia* a livello zoologico, botanico, geografico; si poteva infine tentare una tessitura storiografica più complessa, che tenesse conto di tutti questi elementi e cercasse di strutturarli in un modello unitario: è la strada che, appunto, tenta di percorrere il Martire.

Occorre subito dire che il suo contributo è cosa ben diversa dall'occasionale intervento dello Scillacio: esso è piuttosto opera di una vita, che accompagna la vicenda americana, dal primo viaggio di Colombo sino a quando la morte dell'autore non interrompe l'opera. Proprio per questa sua caratteristica è una struttura costruita *in progress*, attraverso una prima forma epistolare che viene poi aggregata in una narrazione di cui sempre meglio si precisano le caratteristiche di opera storiografica, con raffinamento di tematiche e problemi sempre più evidente, sino a culminare con la quinta decade, la storia della conquista del Messico, opera veramente comparabile con i migliori approdi del genere in area umanistica.

La divisione in decadi, per altro, è da ritenersi un omaggio del tutto esteriore alla più illustre delle tradizioni classiche: nelle poche esplicitazioni relative a modelli storiografici, il Martire dichiaratamente rifiuta ogni prospettiva liviana, dal momento che si tratta, nel suo caso, di un'opera più complessa di quanto non sia il racconto di vicende meramente politico-militari, un'opera che potrebbe trovare riferimenti piuttosto nella composita struttura di un Plinio e di un Luciano, dal momento che punta piuttosto alla varietà della materia "de virorum casibus, de quadrupedibus, avibus, insectibus, arboribus, erbis, gentium ritibus et moribus et arte magica praesentiquae novae Hispaniae statu". Dunque una storiografia cospicua soprattutto sull'asse della totalità, non su quello della selezione, una storiografia che rifiuta di scegliere tra le varie opzioni, e in questa proposta radica i suoi pregi e i suoi stessi difetti; una storiografia che non trova fruibili, se non in alcuni momenti forti, i consueti modelli, ma che deve inventarsi nuovi e funzionali punti di riferimento. In questa direzione il Martire reinventa una struttura storiografica di tipo erodoteo, un modello certamente non utile ai consueti approdi di storiografia 'civile', dedicata alla vicenda di territori abbondantemente cartografati, come avveniva per la grandissima parte della storiografia umanistica italiana ed europea, ma certamente assai funzionale all'apprezzamento del 'diverso', nella prospettiva di una storia dalle molteplici e non sempre coerenti pulsioni. E certo è il primo grande merito di Pietro Martire quello di aver saputo costruire un modello innovativo rispetto ai fenomeni storiografici del tempo, tale da risultare sostanzialmente adeguato all'oggetto. È' da dire che il nome di Erodoto non figura esplicitamente nell'opera, ma a garantire la conoscenza di quell'antico esemplare, se fosse necessario all'altezza cronologica del lavoro del Martire, conforta la presenza nella sua opera del richiamo al già rilevato *topos* dell'Egitto come mondo alla rovescia o al paragone degli indigeni con il *mos Sciticus* o al ricordo dei rapporti tra Traci e Amazzoni.

Ma una storia integrale del problema 'americano' comportava innanzi tutto il superamento della prospettiva edenica colombiana, particolarmente nei libri più antichi, dato che, dall'ingresso degli Spagnoli nello Yucatan, il rapporto avviene chiaramente ormai con popoli che hanno case in pietra, moneta, leggi e vivono politicamente.

Ora, sin dal primo momento, quello più vicino tendenzialmente a prospettive colombiane, Pietro Martire rileva certamente che i nativi, "nudi, sine ponderibus, sine mensura, sine mortifera denique pecunia aurea aetate viventes [...] vitam agunt", ma tuttavia in essi è comunque presente una dimensione 'politica', nel momento in cui "ambitione et isti tamen imperii causa torquentur et se mutuis bellis conficiunt", poiché, anche nell'età dell'oro dell'Arcadia americana, "ea peste auream aetatem haudquaquam vixisse immunem credimus, quin et eo tempore 'cede', 'non cedam' inter mortales pererraverit" (Martire, 18).

Nella prospettiva educata al pragmatismo della storiografia umanistica la dimensione storico-politica è quindi consustanziale alla condizione umana, capace di generare conflitti anche nell'età dell'oro, sottraendo così ogni vicenda a prospettive metastoriche. In tale direzione il codice umanistico, lungi dall'essere nell'opera di Pietro Martire un filtro che distorce la visione dei problemi, risulta invece un potente ausilio alla comprensione, instaurando una prospettiva comparatistica che consente di superare le categorie di 'selvaggio' o di 'barbaro' in direzione di un primitivismo che lega storia e mito antichi, 'arcaici', a quelli dei nativi americani: in questa direzione il confronto è continuo e consente di riconoscere nella vicenda dei nuovi popoli una prospettiva schiettamente culturale di cui si può fare, non soltanto descrizione etnologica, ma altresì storia, correggendo la prospettiva colombiana, laddove, ad esempio, alla semplice religiosità naturale postulata dal primo contatto, si sostituisce una visione più consapevole ed articolata, non senza esplicite palinodie, in grado di ricostrure complesse tradizioni, a volte non senza un filo di 'illuministica' ironia, ma il cui significato è garantito da un agguerrito comparativismo con miti e riti della tradizione classica: anche nel nuovo mondo uomini generati da formiche, come la "Graecia verax" aveva tramandato "tot voluminibus [...] e formicis utpote Myrmidones procreatos", mentre la presenza di forze demoniache nella natura, gli *zemes*, ha un referente nel fatto che l'*antiquitas* "Dryades, Amadryades, Satyros et Panes aut Nereides, fontium, silvarum et pelagi curam habere putabat" (Martire, 90 e 93).

In questa prospettiva di primitivismo già il primo approccio colombiano nasce, non sotto l'insegna di una età edenica, ma sotto quello di una storia primitiva, e non per questo meno umana: nel nuovo mondo i navigatori

> varios ibi esse reges, hosque illis atque illos his potentiores inveniunt, uti fabulosum legimus Aeneam in varios divisum reperisse Latium, Latinum puta, Mezentiumque [...] qui angustis limitibus discriminabantur. (Martire, 18)

È' un paradigma che si configura come il filo rosso di una interpretazione della storia indigena capace di consentire la comprensione di fatti culturali diversi dal quotidiano europeo, come, ad esempio, la tradizione orale e gentilizia dei canti storici degli *areiti*. In tale prospettiva è concepibile il recepimento di figure di nativi politiche e 'magnanime' (senza arrivare alla quinta decade, la più propriamente e 'umanisticamente' storica, con la dialettica tra il 'magnanimo' Montezuma e il 'cesareo' Cortes). E basti qui riportare il discorso di un cacico che tenta di mettere assieme una coalizione antispagnola, la cui dimensione classicizzante non occorre neppure sottolineare, ma di cui occorre forse, invece, sottolineare la chiara connotazione politica e previsionale:

> Quae gens haec? Proh miseros, quae nos tranquilla pace fruentes exagitat? Quousque tandem patiemur horum saevitiam? Nonne satius est emori quam ea ferre quae [...] nostri ordinis principes ab his passi sunt? Uxores filiosque etiam ditionarios captivos duci et fortunas omnes in praedam trahi ante oculos? Me nondum attigerunt, sed exemplo aliorum non longe abesse meam perniciem aequum est credere. [...] Irruamus: iis trucidatis forte reliqui nos adoriri ultra verebuntur. [...] Quicquid evenerit aequanimius tolerandum erit. (Martire, 139)

È' una posizione culturale che consente, non soltanto di recuperare la lontana vicenda a dimensioni storiche concrete e umane, ma altresì di offrire una descrizione etnologica tendenzialmente accurata, ben consapevole di un relativismo di fondo che riesce a convalidare la cultura indigena, appunto come cultura, anche nelle sue manifestazioni più estranee e forse ripugnanti, come l'uso di forare le labbra con lamine d'oro,

> foedius nihil unquam me vidisse recordor. Putant tamen illi elegantius nihil

> esse sub orbe lunae, quo exemplo [. . .] quam fallamur omnes edocemur. Exis-
> timat Aethiops nigrum colorem esse candido pulchriorem [. . .] regiturque suo
> sensu quaeque provincia. (Martire, 312)

È' una prospettiva che conduce il discorso del Martire a riconoscere le ragioni
degli indigeni, a rilevare spesso le coordinate di oppressione con cui il vecchio mondo si riversava sul nuovo. E tuttavia, ciò senza dimenticare una prospettiva occidentale, per cui gli Spagnoli erano portatori di valori assolutamente condivisi, primo fra
tutti quello della religione cristiana: e del resto non sfuggiva al Martire la grandezza
della storia che la gente spagnola stava vivendo, sicché la sua narrazione spesso si
distende in una *laus gentis Hispaniae*: "vilescit quicquid manu Saturni, Herculis et
aliorum huiuscemodi heroum patefecit antiquitas, si quid indefessus labor Hispanorum detegat animadvertemus" (Martire, 221). Anche se non mancano momenti in cui
si sottolinea la crudeltà e l'*auri sitis*, si è in grado di valutare la funzione fondamental-
mente civilizzatrice e il coraggio dei conquistatori, con approdi epici e di alto valore
suggestivo. E si veda la narrazione della carriera di conquistatore del *gladiator* Balboa
che culmina nell'estatica, religiosa, catartica visione dell'Oceano Pacifico.

Non è possibile rende conto, nell'ambito limitato di una relazione, di tutta la ric-
chezza di interessi che emergono dall'opera complessa del Martire: sia comunque con-
sentita un'ultima osservazione relativa ad una delle tensioni più corpose della *Storia del
mondo nuovo*, quella della storia naturale.

In effetti, l'uomo occidentale, prima ancora che a una civiltà nuova, si era trovato
di fronte ad una natura lussureggiante ed incombente, ben diversa da quella europea,
ormai completamente ridotta a misura umana: proprio per questo assume un posto di
rilievo in ognuna delle relazioni, a partire dall'archetipo colombiano, la problematica
naturalistico-geografica, in modi e forme spesso prevalenti sulla stessa vicenda umana.

E' un fenomeno rilevabile anche a livello del Martire: la dimensione naturale della
sua *Historia* è altrettanto vivace e interessata di quella storica, sia nel recepire il pittoresco (la vicenda, ad esempio, del lamantino addomesticato Mato), sia nel raccogliere
mirabilia, ma anche problematiche scientifiche: le stelle del nuovo mondo, il problema
dei fiumi troppo grandi per l'esiguo retroterra, le correnti marine: tutte questioni di
cui occorrerebbe, in sede diversa, rendere puntualmente conto.

In questa sede forse basti sottolineare il codice interpretativo sotteso alle descrizioni
naturali: sostanzialmente questo si basa su due elementi, da un lato quello della esperienza originaria, per cui, ad esempio la descrizione di un tapiro viene offerta al pubblico occidentale per elementi di approssimazioni successive, tratte dall'' enciclopedia'
d'uso comune:

> est corpore bovem aequans; proboscide armatum est elephantina, non elephas;
> bovino colore, non bos; equinis ungulis, non equus; auriculis etiam elephan-
> tinis, sed minus patentibus et demissis. (Martire, 166: ma tutta la decade II per
> questioni naturali, ad es. i coccodrilli)

L'altra dimensione è quella della tradizione classica: e in effetti, il confronto con
tale tradizione è continuo e serrato, qualche volta per confermare, qualche volta per
correggere i dati. E si veda ad esempio la polemica contro la teoria che solo l'acqua

del Nilo nutrisce i coccodrilli, dove sono fatti valere i dati dell'esperienza. Ma che il codice delle *auctoritates* fosse un dato di partenza irrinunciabile, lo prova, ad esempio, il modo di identificare una tigre attraverso tutto l'apparato topico, "a maculis, a feritate, a dexteritate, a signisque aliis ab auctoribus datis" (Martire, 193). Ovviamente sbagliando l'identificazione in entrambi i casi, per difetto di una enciclopedia che non possiede elementi sufficienti alla categorizzazione dei ricordi di fenomeni naturali.

Col Martire la reazione 'umanistica' al nuovo mondo tocca il punto più alto e consapevole: certo, sono ancora numerosi i momenti in cui il codice umanistico si dimostra incapace di comprendere in tutto il suo significato rivoluzionario la nuova situazione dell'ecumene; certo è di là da venire la grande e impegnata etnologia di un Sahagún e di un Landa. E tuttavia, pur con i suoi condizionamenti culturali, ma forse anche per essi, l'opera storiografica di Pietro Martire si situa certamente tra gli approdi più significativi di una tradizione che aveva saputo in buona misura rinnovare le prospettive dello scriver di storia.

Università di Messina

Pagane Frömmigkeit und lyrische Erlebnisfiktion: Präsenz und Funktion des antiken Mythos in Petrus Lotichius Secundus' Elegie "Ad Lunam"

WILHELM KÜHLMANN

I

Die Aneignung der antiken Schrifttradition und des in ihr geborgenen Wissens vollzog sich, wie bekannt, in einem hochkomplizierten, zeitlich gestaffelten Prozeß der Selektion, Adaption und Transformation, in dem das Erbe Roms und Griechenlands einer sich nun christlich verstehenden Gesellschaft verfügbar gemacht wurde.[1] Dabei gehörte der antike Mythos, also die literarische, erst nach und nach als "Mythologie" systematisierte Welt der antiken Götter, zu den intellektuell äußerst sperrigen Überlieferungsbeständen. Jenseits aller—hier auszublendenden—epochalen und diskursiven Differenzierung[2] blieb die christliche Mythenrezeption seit den Kirchen-

---

[1] Dazu im weiteren Zusammenhang W. Kühlmann, "Poeten und Puritaner. Christliche und pagane Poesie im deutschen Humanismus. Mit einem Exkurs zur Prudentius-Rezeption in Deutschland," in *Humanismus und Theologie in der frühen Neuzeit*, hrsg. Hanns Kerner, Pirckheimer-Jahrbuch, Bd. 8 (Nürnberg, 1993), 149–190.

[2] Einen knappen Überblick über Methoden und Geschichte der Mythendeutung bietet Wolfgang Schmidbauer, *Mythos und Psychologie. Methodische Probleme, aufgezeigt an der Ödipus-Sage* (München/Basel, 1970), bes. 19–42; ferner Kurt Hübner, *Die Wahrheit des Mythos* (München, 1985), bes. 48–94; für Einzelheiten selbstverständlich immer heranzuziehen die bekannten Werke von D. C. Allen, *Mysteriously Meant. The Rediscovery of Pagan Symbolism and Allegorical Interpretation in the Renaissance* (Baltimore/London, 1970); Jean Seznec, *The Survival of the Pagan Gods. The Mythological Tradition and its Place in Renaissance Humanism and Art* (New York, 1961); Edgar Wind, *Heidnische Mysterien in der Renaissance.* Mit einem Nachwort von Bernhard Buschendorf, übersetzt von Christa Münstermann unter Mitarbeit von Bernhard Buschendorf und Gisela Heinrichs (Frankfurt/M., 1981); für unseren Zusammenhang (christliche Allegorese von Sol und Luna) wichtig im Kontrast Hugo Rahner, *Griechische Mythen in christlicher Deutung* (Darmstadt, 1957; Zürich, 1966), 124–228; ferner mit Entwicklungslinien bis ins 18. Jahrhundert Walter Sparn, "Hercules Christianus. Mythographie und Theologie in der frühen Neuzeit. Ihre Anwendung in den Künsten," hrsg. Walther Killy, Wolfenbütteler Forschungen, Bd. 27 (Wiesbaden, 1984), 73–108.

vätern[3] grundsätzlich angewiesen auf Deutungsverfahren, die jede numinose Macht der alten Götter, damit auch ihre kultische Rolle und spirituelle Verbindlichkeit zu entkräften suchten. Anknüpfend an die Mythen—und Dichterkritik der antiken Philosophie, auch aber an die Verteidigung Homers[4] wurde die weiterhin virulente Frage nach dem aktualisierbaren Sinnpotential der heidnischen Mythologeme nur noch unter der Voraussetzung ihres nicht mehr theologisch anstößigen Wahrheitsgehaltes gestellt. Diesen christlich integrierbaren Wahrheitsgehalt herauszuarbeiten war die Aufgabe einer allegorisierenden Hermeneutik, die in je zu unterscheidender Zweckrichtung und Akzentuierung den historischen, naturphilosophischen oder moralischen, wenn nicht sogar den heilsgeschichtlichen Aussage—und Referenzwert der mythischen "Fabeln" aus ihren überlieferten "Hüllen" zu befreien trachtete. Programm und Technik derart allegorisierender Mytheninterpretation lassen sich vornehmlich im Strom der mythographischen Handbücher[5], der Kommentare zu Ovids "Metamorphosen",[6] in den davon profitierenden Poetiken und in der weitläufigen

---

[3] Im Rückblick instruktiv Joachim Dyck, *Athen und Jerusalem. Die Tradition der argumentativen Verknüpfung von Bibel und Poesie im 17. und 18. Jahrhundert* (München, 1977), bes. 131–178 ("Der Sieg Davids über Apoll").

[4] Hinweise auf die moralische und physikalische Homerallegorese, zumeist apologetisch gefärbt, bieten Georg Finsler, *Homer in der Neuzeit von Dante bis Goethe* (Leipzig/Berlin, 1912; Hildesheim/New York, 1973), passim; Seznec, *Survival of the Pagan Gods*, bes. 84 ff.; Thomas Bleicher, *Homer in der deutschen Literatur (1450–1740). Zur Rezeption der Antike und zur Poetologie der Neuzeit* (Stuttgart, 1972), bes. 34 ff.; ergiebig Rahner, *Griechische Mythen*, Dritter Teil, 355–486; weiteres in der exemplarischen Untersuchung von Glenn W. Most, "Ansichten über einen Hund. Zu einigen Strukturen der Homerrezeption zwischen Antike und Neuzeit," *Antike und Abendland* 37 (1991): 144–168. Thematisch zentrierte Untersuchungen liegen vor von Sibylle Tochtermann, *Der allegorisch gedeutete Kirke-Mythos. Studien zur Entwicklungs- und Rezeptionsgeschichte*, Studien zur klassischen Philologie, Bd. 74 (Frankfurt/M.-Bern, 1992), und Sabine Wedner, *Tradition und Wandel im allegorischen Verständnis des Sirenenmythos. Ein Beitrag zur Rezeptionsgeschichte Homers*, Studien zur klassischen Philologie, Bd. 86 (Frankfurt/M.-Bern, 1994).

[5] Zu Boccaccios "Genealogia deorum gentilium" im weiteren Umkreis vgl. bes. Bodo Guthmüller, "Der Mythos zwischen Theologie und Poetik," in *Die Antike-Rezeption in den Wissenschaften während der Renaissance*, hrsg. August Buck und Klaus Heitmann, Mitteilung 10 der Kommission für Humanismusforschung (Weinheim, 1983), 129–148.

[6] Dazu Bodo Guthmüller, *Studien zur antiken Mythologie in der italienischen Renaissance* (Weinheim, 1986), bes. 37 ff. Die Fülle der Literatur zur Ovid-Rezeption, in der die Mythen-Rezeption berührt wird, muß hier ganz außer Betracht bleiben. Für den deutschen Kulturkreis wichtig und von Guthmüller erwähnt, doch sonst bisher kaum beachtet der Ovid-Kommentar des Melanchthon-Schülers Georg(ius) Sabinus (1508–1560), *Metamorphosis seu Fabula Poeticae, Earumque Interpretatio Ethica, Physica et Historica* (Wittenberg, 1555 u.ö. Nachdr. der Ausgabe Frankfurt/M., 1589: New York und London, 1976). Das Werk ist großenteils wohl Melanchthon zuzuschreiben. Eine knappe Charakterisierung bietet Max Töppen, *Die Gründung der Universität zu Königsberg und das Leben ihres ersten Rektors Georg Sabinus* (Königsberg, 1844), spez. 262–267. Zum Autor zuletzt Heinz Scheible, "Georg Sabinus (1508–1560). Ein Poet als Gründungsrektor," in *Die Albertus-Universität zu Königsberg und ihre Professoren* [. . .], hrsg. Dietrich Rauschning und Donata von Nerée, Jahrbuch der Albertus-Universität zu Königsberg 29 (1994) (Berlin, 1995), 17–31. Zum weiteren Umkreis s. Hermann Walter und Hans-Jürgen Horn (hrsg.), *Die Rezeption der "Metamorphosen" des Ovid in der Neuzeit: Der antike Mythos in Text und Bild* (Berlin, 1995).

Verarbeitung jener "Argumentationssysteme" verfolgen, die seit Augustinus, Laktanz, Tertullian und anderen Autoritäten die christliche Aufnahme der heidnischen Mythologeme zu begründen, zu begrenzen und zu steuern hatten.

Mythenkritik war dabei immer auch Dichterkritik. Spätestens bei Boccaccio setzte sich allerdings—wegweisend für das 18. Jahrhundert—gegen die plane rationalistisch-moralische Instrumentalisierung der christlichen Mythenexegese die Gewißheit durch, daß mit der Frage nach der "voluntas" der antiken Autoren auch die spezifisch poetische Funktion der Mythen, also ihre ästhetische, nicht mehr eindeutig allegorisierbare Attraktivität zu bedenken war.[7] Diese Erkenntnis umfaßte konsequenterweise auch die Beobachtung, daß gerade die mythenschaffende Phantasie der Dichter für jene Pluralisierung theologisch-kultureller Symbolsysteme verantwortlich zeichnete, die sich in der Kluft zwischen paganer und christlicher Frömmigkeit unzweideutig auch der Neuzeit als historisch anzuerkennendes und antiquarisch zu erschließendes Faktum darstellte.

Nicht präzise ließ sich in der weitgespannten Mythos-Diskussion und begleitenden mythographischen Literatur die Frage nach dem Spielraum beantworten, der modernen Autoren in der Fiktionalisierung, d. h. literarischen Restauration von Mythologemen zugestanden werden konnte oder sollte. Die Spannweite der christlichen Mythen—und Literaturkritik reichte bekanntlich von der zelotischen Verbannung jeder mythologischen Referenz aus der Dichtung[8] bis hin zu Kompromiß—und Harmonisierungsbemühungen, die mythische Namen nur dem ornamentalen Schmuck der poetischen Rede zuordneten oder zumindest jede theologische Valenz des poetisierten Mythos nach Maßgabe der bewährten allegorischen Interpretationsmuster verneinten. Anstößig blieb die mythographisch tingierte Poesie der Humanisten vor allem dann, wenn die in Frage kommenden Texte oder Kontexte keinen Anhaltspunkt für solche allegorische Depotenzierung, d. h. eindeutige Zweideutigkeit der mythischen Referenzen und Reminiszenzen anboten. Diese Anstößigkeit mußte sich zwangsläufig verstärken, wenn die antiken Götter sogar in die pragmatisch verstandenen Textsorten frommer Lebenspraxis eindrangen, also religiös definierte Genera der gebetshaften oder hymnischen Lyrik[9] ihren Adressaten oder ihr Objekt am antiken Götterhimmel suchten. Mag man auch, um das prominenteste Beispiel anzuführen, mit Walther Ludwig die *Hymni naturales* eines Michele Marullo, gedruckt 1497, auf dem Wege neuplatonisch-orphischer Kosmologie und im Zeichen

---

[7] Ich stütze mich hier auf die Darlegungen Guthmüllers, "Der Mythos," bes. 136 ff.

[8] Sprechende Belege für das 17. Jahrhundert bei Kühlmann, "Poeten und Puritaner," 176 ff.

[9] Conrad Celtis z.B. schrieb im Wettbewerb mit Horazens Götterhymnen drei Oden an christliche Heilige, acht an antike Gottheiten, wobei die antiken Götter nicht ins Christliche übersetzt, sondern zumeist als rhetorische Allegorien bzw. als Astralmythen expliziert wurden. "Der achristliche Charakter dieser Dichtung" wurde zum Teil als Provokation empfunden. "So veranlaßte die Theologische Fakultät in Wien eine Untersuchung gegen die Geldgeber und Herausgeber der 'Libri Odarum'," da diese für "rechtschaffene Ohren Anstößiges, Skandalöses, Gottloses, Irriges und nach Ketzerei Schmeckendes" enthielten. So mit weiteren Hinweisen Eckart Schäfer, *Deutscher Horaz. Conrad Celtis—Georg Fabricius—Paul Melissus—Jacob Balde* (Wiesbaden, 1976), 23.

der *theologia prisca* mit dem christlichen Monotheismus zur Deckung bringen können[10], so bleibt doch die Feststellung unbenommen, daß die hier manifeste Poetisierung antiker Mythologeme von vielen Zeitgenossen als Signatur eines modernen Heidentums verstanden wurde. Die Stimmen der scharfen Kritiker von Erasmus von Rotterdam[11] über Gianfrancesco Pico della Mirandola bis hin zu Julius Cäsar Scaliger[12] wurden freilich begleitet von mancherlei Apologien und Vermittlungsanstrengungen. Darunter verdient die von Ludwig zitierte Äußerung des niederländischen Juristen Guilelmus Cripius (Wilhelmus Criep, 1535–nach 1609) besondere Beachtung. Cripius besteht darauf, daß der Dichtung eine "ganz andere Freiheit" einzuräumen sei, als sonst gewöhnlich gewährt werde, und er verknüpft die fiktionale Suspendierung des Wahrheitsanspruchs literarischer Rede mit dem Zweck der Dichtung, "Vergnügen" zu bereiten.[13] Freiheitsspielraum und das Versprechen des Vergnügens sind dabei offenbar nicht als isolierte und isolierbare, sondern als interdependente Merkmale von Dichtung zu verstehen. Das aber bedeutet: Das Vergnügen an Dichtung hängt potentiell mit der Möglichkeit zusammen, im schützenden Schein der Fiktion Alternativen zu kulturellen Konventionen, in diesem Fall zum kirchlich-christlichen Auslegungsmonopol der mythischen Überlieferung, zu erproben und zu genießen.

Die sich mit dieser These anbietende Frage nach der Funktion paganer Mythen in modernen Texten und in ihrem dadurch bedingten Angebot an rezeptiven Freiräumen möchte ich im folgenden an einem deutschen Beispiel, der Elegie eines Dichters nachgehen, der bereits von den Zeitgenossen als "princeps poetarum" seines Jahrhunderts gefeiert wurde. Petrus Lotichius Secundus (1528–1560) aus dem hessischen Schlüchtern, zuletzt Medizinprofessor in Heidelberg,[14] veröffentlichte die Elegie

---

[10] Walther Ludwig, *Antike Götter und christlicher Glaube: Die Hymni naturales von Marullo* Berichte aus den Sitzungen der Joachim Jungius-Gesellschaft der Wissenschaften 10, Heft 2 (1992) (Hamburg, 1992). Zu den "griechischen Hymnois" s. Walter Burkert, in *Hymnen der alten Welt im Kulturvergleich*, hrsg. Walter Burkert und Fritz Stolz, Orbis Biblicus et Orientalis 131 (Freiburg/Schweiz und Göttingen, 1994), 9–17.

[11] "Marullus mihi videtur nihil aliud sonare quam Paganismum. Et ob hoc ipsum fortassis gratior est Marullus quam Mantuanus. Oderunt Christi nomen, quod nostra barbaries utinam perinde sinceriter ac vehementer amplecteretur": nach P. S. Allen, ed., *Opus Epistolarum Des. Erasmi Roterodami* (Oxford, 1906–1958), 2: 187 f.—ein Brief aus dem Jahre 1524; dazu und zu den im folgenden genannten Kritikern s. Ludwig, *Antike Götter*, 5 ff.

[12] Vgl. Ilse Reineke, *Julius Caesar Scaligers Kritik der neulateinischen Dichter* (München, 1988), 274–334, zu den Hymnen spez. 292 ff.

[13] S. Ludwig, *Antike Götter*, 12 f.: "[. . .] nec enim animadvertunt illi religiosuli longe aliam in poesi quam ceteris rebus libertatem permitti aliasque eius leges esse, quas qui tollunt, totam poesim eadem opera tollant oportet. Non veritas a poeta, sed oblectatio exigitur, quam qui consequitur, probe suo munere perfunctus est."

[14] Die Forschung zu Lotichius ist zusammengefaßt in dem Artikel (sub voce) von Bernhard Coppel, in *Literatur-Lexikon*, hrsg. Walther Killy (Gütersloh/München, 1990), 7: 352–354; weiteres nun in *Humanistische Lyrik des 16. Jahrhunderts*, hrsg. W. Kühlmann, Robert Seidel und Hermann Wiegand, Bibliothek der Frühen Neuzeit 5 (Frankfurt, 1997). Ich beziehe mich auf den hier abgedruckten Text samt Übersetzung (S. 416–423) und den Kommentar, S. 1194–1199; benutzt

"Ad Lunam. Cum noctu iter faceret" typographisch abgesetzt zuerst am Ende seines 1551 in Paris erschienen ersten Elegienbuchs. In den postum von Freunden herausgegebenen Sammelausgaben (ab 1563) wurde das Gedicht als Nr. V in die Mitte des elf Texte umfassenden Zyklus versetzt[15]. Dies ist insofern bedeutsam, als damit der autobiographische Aussagekontext des gesamten Buches auch für diese Elegie in Anspruch genommen wurde. Lotichius setzte sich nämlich hier mit Erfahrungen auseinander, die er als Soldat im Schmalkaldischen Krieg (1546/47) hatte sammeln müssen.[16] Es geht also nicht wie bei Marullo um einen Gedichtzyklus, der in seiner Makrostruktur auf ein antikes Vorbild, die Orphischen Hymnen, anspielte und in seinen semantischen Details religionsphilosophischen Systemcharakter erkennen ließ.[17] Indem Lotichius seine Hymne an Luna in autobiographischer Erlebnisfiktion motivierte, ging er auch wie seine Editoren das Wagnis ein, daß der Text nicht nur als ästhetisches Spiel, sondern auch als Produkt und Ausdruck praktischer Frömmigkeit verstanden werden konnte. Der Wagnischarakter dieser Elegie wird zu beachten sein, zugleich andeutungsweise die Position des Gedichts im weiteren Kreis vergleichbarer Poeme bestimmt werden müssen, die—früher oder später—unter dem so wirkmächtigen Titel „An den Mond" verfaßt wurden.[18] Letztlich dürften sich

---

wurden die Kommentare von Burmann (1754) sowie von Katherine Anne O'Rourke Fraiman, "Petrus Lotichius Secundus. *Elegiarum Liber Primus*. Edited with an Introduction, Translation, and Commentary" (Diss. Columbia Univ., 1973). Zum Biographischen nützlich Stephen Zon, *Petrus Lotichius Secundus. Neo-Latin Poet*, American University Studies, Series 1, Vol. 13 (New York, 1983), sowie Bernhard Coppel, "Petrus Lotichius Secundus," in *Deutsche Dichter der frühen Neuzeit (1450–1600). Ihr Leben und Werk*, hrsg. Stephan Füssel (Berlin, 1993), 529–544.

[15] Vgl. O'Rourke Fraiman, "Petrus Lotichius Secundus", 42, sowie dort den Abdruck der Erstfassung, 164–168. Daß die Luna-Elegie als isolierte Elegie am Ende der Pariser Publikation nach den "carmina" erscheint (Bl. 31v–40v), deutet auf die Sonderstellung des Gedichts, vielleicht auch auf seine Entstehung während der Frankreichreise hin. Für briefliche Hinweise zum Erstdruck danke ich freundlichst Prof. Dr. Walther Ludwig (Hamburg). Die kleineren Abweichungen vom Erstdruck sind für unsere Interpretation nicht von Belang, zumal wir beim Textus receptus (1563) mit späteren Autorenkorrekturen zu rechnen haben. Zum Verhältnis der Ausgaben grundlegend Bernhard Coppel, "Bericht über Vorarbeiten zu einer Lotichius-Edition", *Daphnis* 7 (1978): 56–106.

[16] Dazu im einzelnen Hermann Wiegand, "Krieg und Frieden im Werk des Petrus Lotichius Secundus", *Unsere Heimat. Mitteilungen des Heimat- und Geschichtsvereins Schlüchtern* 9 (1993): 131–153.

[17] Es gibt keine Indizien dafür, daß sich Lotichius durch die Homerischen Hymnen (darunter "Eis Selénen") oder durch die ihm wohl kaum bekannten Orphischen Hymnen hat inspirieren lassen; vgl. zu den Ausgaben des 15. Jahrhunderts und zur frühen Rezeption (u.a. Edition durch Ficino 1462) Ludwig, *Antike Götter*, 25–29.

[18] Vgl. die—Zeugnisse des deutschen Kulturraums freilich kaum berücksichtigende—Zusammenstellung der Mond-Motivik in Dichtung und bildender Kunst, in *The Oxford Guide to Classical Mythology in the Arts 1300–1990s*, bearb. von Jane Davidson Reid with the assistance of Chris Rohmann, 2 Bde. (New York/Oxford, 1993), 2: 984–987 (sub voce "Selene"); ferner George C. Schoolfield, "The Changes of the Moon: Lyric Poetry—Tradition and Transformation", in *German Baroque Literature. The European Perspective*, ed. Gerhart Hoffmeister (New York, 1983), 316–338; perspektivisch Kaspar Heinrich Spinner, *Der Mond in der deutschen Dichtung von der*

Beobachtungen zusammenfassen lassen, die das Gedicht als poetischen Widerruf der christlichen Mythenallegorese ausweisen. Denn deren Verfahren wird geradezu umgekehrt. Die Poesie erobert sich als Fiktion zurück, was die Theologie zu entkräften suchte oder zelotisch verwarf.

II

Der Text konstituiert sich als präsentische Rede eines Ichs in einer lokal-, temporal—und personaldeiktisch gekennzeichneten Sprechersituation. Damit wird eine inventionelle Strategie der "subjektiven Liebeselegie" der römischen Antike fruchtbar gemacht.[19] Motivationsgrund und äußere Bedingungen des sprachlichen Handelns sind in einem knappen Rahmen (V. 1–4; 115–20) exponiert bzw. am Ende des Textes als abgeschlossene, vergangene Wirklichkeit vorgestellt. Die Zeitdimension der Rede kongruiert suggestiv den inneren und äußeren Erfahrungsmomenten und Empfindungen des Sprechers zwischen Mitternacht und dem Morgengrauen, das vom Aufgang des Morgensterns verkündet wird. Der Untertitel des Gedichts verweist auf eine Reise, deren Ziel und Anlaß nur vage angegeben ist (*caussa gravis*, V. 7). Es geht nicht um die Beschreibung dieser Reise, sondern um die Gedanken und die Gefühlsreaktion eines Menschen, der um Mitternacht bei strenger Winterkälte durch ein von tiefem Schnee bedecktes (V. 21 f.), wegloses, offenbar unbekanntes und menschenleeres Gelände wandert (so V. 1–4 und ergänzend V. 21–24). Die Orientierungslosigkeit des Ichs erweckt Furcht (*timor*, V. 7, 113), ja Angst um das Leben (V. 20).[20] Überwindung der Bedrängnis und Bewältigung der Situation werden von einer Voraussetzung abhängig gemacht: Der von "pechschwarzen" Wolken bedeckte Mond (V. 10, 24) soll leuchten und nicht mehr daran gehindert werden, seinen hilfreichen Schein zu spenden. Aus der meteorologischen Deskription entwickelt sich ein Redevorgang, der die Natur in ein personales, ein mythisches Gegenüber verwandelt und den Dichter in die Rolle des Magiers versetzt, der seine inneren und äußeren Gefährungen im Medium und in der Wirkung seines "Gesangs" überwindet.

Lyrische Rede dient also nicht dazu, im Widerschein numinoser Mächte die eigene Geschichte zur Geltung zu bringen. Es wird gezeigt, wie sich die Situation des

---

Aufklärung bis zur Spätromantik, Abhandlungen zur Kunst-, Musik- und Literaturwissenschaft 67 (Bonn, 1969).

[19] Hilfreich im ganzen und im Detail Niklas Holzberg, *Die römische Liebeselegie. Eine Einführung* (Darmstadt, 1990).

[20] In der Motivkonstellation von Reise/Gefahr/Errettung läßt sich Lotichius' Elegie an bekannte Vorbilder der Antike anschließen; dort jedoch dominiert die "necessitas leti", die den Seefahrer bedroht: so etwa Horaz, *carm.* 1,22,5; 3,4,28 ff. (hier auch das in unserem Gedicht, V. 53 f., anklingende Vertrauen auf den besonderen Schutz, der den Dichtern zuteil wird); Ovid, *trist.* 1,2; 1,11 (hier wie bei Lotichius das Motiv des Votums in der Not). Neben den bekannten Kommentaren dazu immer wieder mit Gewinn zu lesen die großartigen Studien von Ernst Zinn, "Erlebnis und Dichtung bei Horaz", in *Wege zu Horaz*, hrsg. Hans Oppermann, Wege der Forschung, IC (Darmstadt, 1972), 369–388, sowie ders., "Aporos Soteria. Horaz im Rettungsboot (*carm.* III,29,62)", ibid, 225–257.

einsamen, potentiell sprachlosen Ichs, das sich einer bedrohlichen Naturgewalt ausgeliefert fühlen muß, dadurch verwandelt, daß sich das amorphe Gefüge rätselhafter Verhältnisse in der Sprache objektiviert, ja argumentativer Reflexion zugänglich erscheint. Mit V. 5, eingeleitet durch eine in religiöser Tradition nobilitierte Junktur ("adhibe vultus [. . .] tuos")[21] geht der Text in ein Bittgebet, ein Gelübde (V. 61), schließlich in einen kunstvollen Hymnus auf Luna (V. 67) über, den Mond also, der nun als weibliche Figur des mythischen Pantheons über Wohl und Wehe des Sprechers entscheidet. Erst die mythische Personifikation ermöglicht es dem isolierten Ich, Faktoren und Bedingungen, ja den "Absolutismus" (H. Blumenberg) der Wirklichkeit poetischer Sprache zu unterwerfen und diese Wirklichkeit dadurch als Produkt des schöpferischen Bewußtseins vorzuführen. Es ist, wie der Text in seiner fiktiven Genese bezeugen soll, der Dichter, dem diese Aufgabe zukommt und der sich in seiner mythischen Phantasie aus den Nöten und der Zwangsläufigkeit der Realität befreit.[22] Es ist, als ob Lotichius in der christlichen Moderne den archaischen Impuls und Vorgang der poetischen Mythenbildung rekonstruieren wollte. Dabei kombiniert das Gedicht Formen frommer Devotion und religiöser Redekultur, wie sie typologisch sowohl dem Heiden—wie dem Christentum zu Gebote standen. Jedoch werden alle Anklänge an christliche Redeinhalte, erst recht an die naheliegenden Gedanken göttlicher Providenz und Fürsorge ausgeklammert, ja offenbar ex silentio sogar verweigert. Lotichius' Hymnus an Luna präsentiert sich in aufreizender Manier mitten im literarischen Kampf des beginnenden Konfessionalismus geradezu als antikisierende Kontrafaktur[23] nicht eines Einzeltextes, sehr wohl aber einer spezifischen "Textklasse" der christlichen Frömmigkeit und des erbaulichen Schrifttums.

Es gehört zu den texttypologischen wie gattungshistorischen Merkmalen der Gebetslyrik, daß sie im sprachliche Akt des bittenden Anrufs, also durchaus "performativ", ihre Funktion erfüllt und ihren pragmatischen Zweck verwirklicht. So gliedert auch Lotichius den ersten Hauptteil der Elegie durch die variierte Wiederaufnahme des feierlichen "adhibe vultus [. . .] tuos" (V. 6), lockerte jedoch die appellative Reihe dieser Distichen (V. 19 f., 29 f., 39 f., 49 f., 55 f.)[24] durch zwei Einschübe auf. Der erste (V. 21–24) führt mit deutlicher Emphase die situative Exposition des Gedichtanfangs weiter aus, der zweite (V. 41–54) vergegenwärtigt in astralmythologischer, also gelehrter Umschreibung das Erscheinen der *astra minora* (V. 42) am Nachthimmel. Dadurch wird die "Evidenz" der Naturszenerie beglaubigt, ein Argument für das fromme Plädoyer nach dem topischen Schema "e contrario" bzw. "a minore ad

---

[21] Hier wohl in direkter Imitation der Gebetsformel bei Ovid, *am.* 2,13,16; ähnlich aber auch in erotischem Kontext wie Ovid, ibid. 2,1,37.

[22] Anregend wie immer in diesem Zusammenhang Hans Blumenberg, *Arbeit am Mythos*, 2nd ed. (Frankfurt/M., 1979), hier etwa S. 22 zur im Mythos gewonnenen "Appellationsfähigkeit" oder S. 32 zur Überführung der "numinosen Unbestimmtheit in nominale Bestimmtheit".

[23] Zu Theorie und Verständnis der "Kontrafaktur" vgl. die Klarstellungen von Theodor Verweyen und Gunther Witting, *Die Parodie in der neueren deutschen Literatur. Eine systematische Einführung* (Darmstadt, 1979), hier bes. 191 f.

[24] Nach wie vor gültig Eduard Norden, *Agnostos Theos. Untersuchungen zur Formengeschichte religiöser Rede*, 4 ed. (Darmstadt, 1956), 143–163 (zum "Du-Stil" der Prädikation).

maius" gewonnen. Wie kann Luna mit ihrem Schein noch auf sich warten lassen, wo doch ihre minderen Himmelsgefährten schon zu sehen sind? Deskriptive und appellative Partien bilden den Binnenrahmen für kleinere Textsequenzen, die in wechselnder Blickrichtung des Lesers, d. h. mit divergenter referentieller Zuordnung auf den Sprecher oder sein mythisches Gegenüber, reflektierende und erzählende Darstellungsmöglichkeiten verknüpfen. Dabei läßt sich eine chiastische Komposition der jeweils zusammengehörigen Versgruppen beobachten. Die Verse 7–12 und 25–28 berichten von den Wünschen und der Vergangenheit des sprechenden Ichs, während die Verse 13–18 sowie 31–38 Eigenschaften, Taten und Leiden der Mondgöttin berufen. Indem Lotichius wechselnde Prädikationen verwendet—zu Beginn *Cynthia* (V. 5), dann *stirps Latonia* (V. 29)—ist hier schon dafür gesorgt, daß eine plane allegorische Beziehung zwischen Naturphänomenen und ihrem mythischen Äquivalent vermieden wird. Denn im Anruf an Luna, griech. Selene, ist zugleich Diana/Artemis gemeint, später (V. 57 f.) sogar Hecate, die Zaubergöttin. Geschichte und Gestalt der Figur verschmelzen im Synkretismus mythologischen Wissens und werden in einen weiten Assoziationskreis numinoser Weiblichkeit überführt, der dann im folgenden Hymnus "der Reihe nach" (*ordine*, V. 66) abgeschritten werden kann.

In einem verkürzten Syllogismus, also einem Enthymem, dessen "präpositio" ausgeschlossen ist, beteuert der Wanderer, er sei nicht als "Verräter" oder zu Kriegslisten unterwegs (V. 11 f.). Mit solch unausgesprochener, sogleich entkräfteten Annahme, die Nöte des Ichs seien einer Schuld oder einem moralischen Makel zuzuschreiben, schlägt Lotichius für einen Moment auch den Bogen zum biographischen Konnex des ersten Elegienbuches, zu des Dichters Leben und Leiden im Schmalkaldischen Krieg. Mit V. 25 wird im Rückblick (*memini*) eine scheinbar autobiographische Anekdote ergänzt: Als der Sprecher einst die Tür seiner Geliebten nächtens bekränzte—hier ein wörtlicher Anklang an Tibull (1, 2, 14)—sah sich der *exclusus amator* in helles Mondlicht getaucht und so plötzlich verraten, ja allerlei böser Nachrede ausgesetzt. Luna soll also leuchten, weil sie es offenbar nach Belieben vermag, und sie soll nun zum rechten Zeitpunkt erscheinen. Lotichius unterlegt dem Gedicht bewährte Strukturen des rhetorischen Plädoyers, d. h. hier die Statusfrage nach dem *possibile* (vgl. Quintilian 3, 8, 25). Mögliche Hinderungsgründe Lunas werden vermutungsweise angeführt, zuerst (V. 15–18) in raffinierter Verschränkung mit einer Huldigung an ihre göttliche Schönheit—Reflex übrigens der antiken Liebeselegie wie schon die Gestalt des unglücklichen Liebhabers. Lotichius geht aus von den Mondflecken und dem wechselnden Aussehen des Himmelsgestirns[25], um diese Phänomene sogleich zu psychologisieren: Vielleicht schämt sich Luna ihrer mangelnden Anziehungskraft (V. 13). Diese Annahme wird dementiert im Vergleich mit Aurora, der Göttin der Morgenröte (V. 15 f.), und jener Trias holder Weiblichkeit, der sich eins Paris gegenübersah (V. 17 f.). Einzelheiten einer in der Naturszene motivierten Beobachtung (Mondflecken) werden so arrangiert, daß sich Übergänge zu mythologischen Aussagen anbieten. Mit

---

[25] Ob sich Lotichius bei astronomischen Einzelheiten nur auf die vorliegende Physica-Literatur stützte oder auch schon die ausführliche "Mond-Theorie" im Lehrgedicht des Giovanni Pontano (*Urania, sive de stellis*, in *Opera* [Venedig, 1505]) kannte, sei dahingestellt.

der Schönheit der Göttin, die nach ikonographischem Muster wie ihr Bruder, der Sonnengott (V. 39), auf einem Pferdegespann vorgestellt wird (V. 19, 39 f.), kommt auch das bekannteste Exempel ihres Liebeslebens ins Spiel, die Geschichte von Selene und Endymion (V. 35–38).[26]

Hier spätestens konnte der gelehrte Leser auf einen der leitenden Praetexte des Gedichtes aufmerksam werden: Ovid läßt in seinen *Heroides*, in der Versepistels Heros an Leander (Nr. 18), den Liebenden ein Gebet an den Mond sprechen, worauf vielleicht schon der nicht gerade geläufige Ausdruck "officiosa" (V. 6; bei Ovid V. 60) hinwies. Hero huldigt der Schönheit Lunas im Kreis der Göttinnen wie der einsame Wanderer des Lotichius, wobei allerdings die mythologische und sprachliche Reminiszenz hier anderes kontextualisiert erscheint. Lunas Liebe zum *pastor Latmius* fungiert bei Ovid als Argument für die Hilfe und das sympathetische Verständnis, das Hero von der Göttin erbittet. Bei Lotichius wird die erotische Komponente im Blick auf den Sprecher ausgespart. Stattdessen schiebt sich ein anderes Motiv in den Vordergrund. Möglicherweise wird Luna als Hecate durch magische Gesänge und Zauberkräuter (V. 31 f.; 57 f.) abgehalten, ja vom Himmel auf die Erde herabgezogen. Lotichius benutzt diese bei augusteischen Dichtern geläufige Vorstellung[27] dazu, sich—in unerwarteter Verschiebung der Ich-Du-Konstellation—als Helfer der Göttin zu imaginieren (V. 33 f.), gemäß dem alten Aberglauben an archaische Beschwörungspraktiken wider eine drohende Mondfinsternis.[28] Luna ist ersehnte Helferin und zugleich bedrohte Frauengestalt. In seiner poetischen Rolle befreit sich der Sprecher allmählich von dem, was ihn ausweglos und gefahrvoll umfängt. Zugleich wird ein zweiter Praetext vorausgesetzt, nämlich Medeas nächtliches Gebet an die Nacht und an den Mond, der an der betreffenden Stelle der Ovidschen Metamorphosen von der berühmten Zauberin "hernieder gezogen" wird (met. 7, 192–219, hier 207 f.).

Dem Gesang der Medea, den *magicae murmura linguae* (V. 57), ist nun genau in der Mitte des Textes (V. 61), am Wendepunkt der thematischen Gedankenführung, das Tun des Dichters entgegenstellt. Gesänge der schwarzen Magie sollen der Göttin nicht schaden, denn sie hat es mit einem *vates* zu tun, der sich wie seinesgleichen auch sonst besonderer numinoser Gunst zu erfreuen hat (so der Gehalt von V. 53 f.: das Exempel der Arion-Geschichte).[29]

---

[26] Vielleicht in kontrastiver Reminiszenz an Ovid, *am.* 1,13, bes. S. 43 f.: Dort geht es darum, das Aufkommen der Morgenröte mit Berufung auf das Endymion-Selene-Exempel zu verhindern.

[27] Vgl. etwa Horaz, *epod.* 5,46; Vergil, *ecl.* 8,69 ff; Tibull 1,8,21 f.; Properz 1,1,19; Ovid, *her.* 6,85; *met.* 7,207; 12,263 f. In der Magie-Literatur, namentlich bei Agrippa von Nettesheim, wurden derartige poetische Belege (mit Hinweisen auch auf Lukan und Apuleius) zum Beweis der "incantamentorum mirabilis potentia" zitiert; s. Cornelius Agrippa, *De occulta philosophia libri tres*, ed. V. Perrone Compagni, Studies in the History of Christian Thought 48 (Leiden, 1992), 237–239 (Buch I, Kap. 72).

[28] Vgl. Ovid, *met.* 4,332 f.; Livius 26,5,9.

[29] Lotichius hat den bekannten Stoff sehr eigenwillig in einer eigenen Elegie aufgegriffen; dazu erhellend Peter Leberecht Schmidt, " '. . . unde utriusque poetae elegans artificium admirari licebit'. Zur Ovid-Rezeption (*am.* 2,6) des Petrus Lotichius Secundus (*el.* 2,7)", in *Der altsprachliche Unterricht* 23.6 (1980): 54–71.

Das Bittgebet wandelt sich mit V. 61 in ein Gelübde. Der Dichter will die "tausend" Machtvollkommenheiten, die "tausend" Namen[30] seiner Göttin besingen. Nicht mehr der in der nächtlichen Winterlandschaft angefochtene Wanderer ergreift das Wort, sondern ein *vates*, dessen poetische Leistung und fromme Sprachgebärde magische Wirkungen zeitigen. Denn kaum ist das Versprechen verkündet, wandelt sich die Situation, und die Naturszene wird zum Ort mythischer Epiphanie (V. 63 f.): "Jetzt trittst Du silbern aus den weichenden Wolken hervor, die angestrahlte Erde erglänzt im Widerschein des Lichtes." Zur poetischen Rede gehört zwar auch hier mythologische Gelehrsamkeit, doch nicht oder hier jedenfalls nicht nur im antiquarischen Zitat, sondern in einer situativ gebundenen Kreativität, die psychisch begründet wird und die Macht des magischen "vates" mit einer antikisierenden Aura umgibt. Die Elegie erweist sich als Demonstration der ihr innewohnenden Poetik, als Manifest, das in der Assimilation heidnischer Frömmigkeit der Figur des Dichters huldigt, Anspruch und Wirkung seines Ruhms in der Bewältigung emotionaler Konflikte zugleich entdeckt und als fiktive Praxis demonstriert. In ihrer situativen Absicherung und polyhistorischen Einfärbung gehört die Elegie wie so viele andere zu den Exempeln der Humanistendichtung, zu Texten, die sich selbst thematisieren, indem sie den Poeten feiern und gegenüber möglicher Kritik in Schutz nehmen.

So darf der zweite Hauptteil der Elegie, der weit ausgreifende Lobgesang auf die das Dunkel erleuchtende weibliche Gottheit, als historische Antithese zu der nachmals so epochenmachenden Klage betrachtet werden, die der klassische Schiller unter dem Titel "Die Götter Griechenlands" anstimmte. Schiller trauerte um die entgötterte, die nur noch mechanischen Gesetzen gehorchende Natur und damit um den Verlust der Identität von Dichtung, Wirklichkeitsbild und mythischer Phantasie.[31] Lotichius verwandelt die Gegebenheiten des Natürlichen in einen Kosmos von Gestalten und wirkenden personalen Mächten, die nun in hymnischer Epiklese und dabei allerdings so vergegenwärtigt werden, daß christliche Assoziationen allenfalls noch in jener Anrufung der "Himmelskönigin" (V. 67) aufscheinen, die eigentlich zur Mariendichtung gehörte und dem Protestanten Lotichius vielleicht allenfalls in paganer Rückerinnerung möglich erschien.[32]

Im Zentrum des Hymnus stehen Ruhm (*gloria*, V. 78) und Macht (*vis*, V. 89) der Göttin. Sie erscheint zunächst als Mondgöttin in ihrer natürlichen himmlischen Umgebung: als Führerin der Sterne und Schwester des Sonnengotts. Astrologisch-naturkundliches Wissen wird integriert: im Hinweis auf die Erdnähe des Mondes oder die

---

[30] Man denke bei diesen genuin hymnischen Stilmomenten beispielsweise an das schon in den Homerischen Hymnen berufene Attribut "polyonymos".

[31] Dazu üppige Literatur, aus der erwähnt sei Heinz Gockel, *Mythos und Poesie. Zum Mythosbegriff in Aufklärung und Frühromantik*, Das Abendland, N. F. 12 (Frankfurt/M., 1981), 185–216.

[32] Zur humanistisch geprägten, antike Modelle und Junkturen ausnützenden, Mariendichtung s. Hermann Wiegand, "Humanismus", *Marienlexikon*, hrsg. Remigius Bäumer und Leo Scheffczyk, 3 (1991): 261–267; am Beispiel Jacob Baldes SJ, spez. den Odae Parthenicae, bes. ergiebig Urs Herzog, *Divina Poesis. Studien zu Jacob Baldes geistlicher Odendichtung*, Hermaea 36 (Tübingen, 1976), 105–146, zu "Regina coeli" und zur Mond- und Sonnenbildlichkeit spez. 118–126.

Tatsache, daß der Mond den Zodiakus, also den Tierkreis, schneller durchläuft als zum Beispiel die Sonne. Mit dem Hinweis auf das alte Mondjahr (V. 79 f.), damit auf eine Frühzeit der menschlichen Kultur, wird nicht nur ein wohl Ovids Fasten zu verdankendes antiquarisches Detail herausgehoben, sondern wohl sehr bewußt auch auf einen klassischen Praetext der hymnischen Gattung angespielt, der dem gelehrten Leser schon vorher in den Sinn kommen mußte: auf den Diana-Hymnus Catulls (34, V. 17 ff.). Der Mond steht nicht nur für den Wandel seiner äußeren Erscheinung und für seine Beweglichkeit im Wechsel der Himmelsgegenden, sondern garantiert auch als Geburtsgestirn künftigen Ruhm des neugeborenen Kindes. An dieser Stelle flicht Lotichius Persönliches ein. Luna als Phoebe (V. 87, also als Diana) weiß, warum er, der Dichter, so weite Wege zu gehen gezwungen ist. Was hier noch unklar bleibt, wird bald präzisiert. Lotichius widmete sich als Medizinstudent den Künsten Phoebus Apollos (V. 97). Luna gibt günstige Vorzeichen für den künftigen Arzt wie auch für die Tätigkeiten des Bauern oder Seemanns. Nur hier spielt Lotichius im ersten Elegienbuch auf seine Profession[33] an und untermauert naturkundliche Aspirationen[34] mit Tönen der klassischen Lehrgedichte: Vergils *Georgica* und Lukrez' *De rerum natura*. Lunas, des Mondes, Wirkung auf das erstaunliche Phänomen der Gezeiten bildet den ersten Beleg für den diesen Hymnus gliedernden Preis der göttlichen Macht über alle vier Elemente des Kosmos (V. 89 f.). Sichtlich aktualisiert der Text Lukrezens Prooemium des ersten Buches, den Hymnus auf Venus als Göttin der schaffenden und zeugenden Natur.

In Joachim Vadians zusammenfassender und zugleich wegweisender Poetik (1518) war die Leistung der Hymnographen in Berufung auf Orpheus, auf Catulls Dianahymnus, aber auch auf Marullus' Naturhymnen illustriert,[35] im späteren Kontext auch Lukrez' Venushymnus gerühmt worden. "Mir ist ganz eindeutig, daß die Alten unter dem Namen der Venus die der Erde innewohnende Kraft verstanden", heißt es hier.[36] Lotichius rühmt in der Tat die "vis" der Luna als *alma Venus*, überwindet und verschweigt allerdings im poetischen Moment die kulturelle und historische Distanz, die in Vadians Formulierung ("die Alten") anklingt. Auch Vadians Marullus-Verehrung darf gewiß in die Überlegungen zum Motiv- und Inventionsfundus dieser Elegie eingezogen werden. Die *Hymni naturales* waren in Deutschland recht früh bekannt.[37] Marullus' Gedicht unter dem lapidaren Titel "Luna" zeigt den Dichter im Zwiegespräch mit seinem Gefährten Hyllus.[38] Wie bei Lotichius ist die

---

[33] Dazu Joachim Telle und W. Kühlmann, "Humanismus und Medizin in Heidelberg," in *Semper Apertus. 600 Jahre Universität Heidelberg* (Festschrift), 6 Bde., 1: 255–290, zu Lotichius 259–265.

[34] Anspielung auf die Wetterzeichen *georg.* 1, 424 ff., dann auch (V. 99) auf *georg.* 2, 69–82.

[35] Vgl. Joachim Vadianus, *De Poetica*, Bd. 1: Kritische Ausgabe; Bd. II: Deutsche Übersetzung; Bd. 3: Kommentar, hrsg. Peter Schäffer (München, 1976), I: 76 f.

[36] Vadianus, ed Schäffer, Kap. XIX über "die Götter der Heide", 1: 157.

[37] Vor allem durch die Ausgabe der *Epigramma et Hymni* durch Beatus Rhenanus (Straßburg, 1508).

[38] *Michaelis Marulli Carmina*, ed. Alessandro Perosa (Zürich, 1951); Hymnorum Liber Tertius, 2: 145–147: "Lunae"; der Text greifbar auch in Alessandro Perosa und John Sparrow, hrsg.,

autobiographische Situation exponiert: eine Nachtszene und der Anbruch einer Reise, die Figur des Wanderers; als Gemeinsamkeit darf auch die Thematisierung des lyrischen Genus, also des Hymnus (V. 19 f.), und der Kontrast zwischen den Schrecken der Dunkelheit und dem wohltuenden Licht des Mondes angesprochen wurden. Sowohl Lotichius wie Marullus kommt es darauf an, die verschiedenen personalen Erscheinungsformen der Gottheiten möglichst weitläufig zu benennen. Dem dient bei Lotichius in etymologischer Explikation auch die Anrufung der Diana Lucina, der Schutzgöttin der Gebärenden (V. 105 f.)—vielleicht in Allusion wieder an Catull 34 (V. 13 f.),[39] die recht kryptische Identifikation von Luna mit Persephone/Proserpina (V. 107)[40] und mit der Göttin, die das Leiden der Lunatici verursacht (V. 109 f.),[41] oder die abschließende feierliche Invokation der Diana /Artemis als Jagdgöttin (V. 110 f. im Anschluß z. B. an Catull 34, 9–12 oder Horaz, carm. 1,3,1) in entlegener Assoziation mit Begleitern hier nicht des Dionysos, sondern der kleinasiatischen Kybele, den armenischen Tigern (V. 112).

Der Hymnus endet mit der Wiederaufnahme des Gebetsgestus, der auf den Begriff bringt, worum es in diesem Gedicht zunächst geht: um das im poetischen Akt verwirklichte religiöse Vertrauen, das "Furcht" verschwinden läßt und der Sache der Menschen dient. Der Dichter preist eine Göttin, die nicht furchterregend wirkt (*non metuenda,* V. 112 f.), nicht den strengen Vatergott, sondern Imaginationen des Weiblichen repräsentiert. Dazu paßt es, daß Lotichius am Schluß auf die Erlebnisfiktion des ersten Verses zurückgreift und die Elegie mit dem Abschiedsgruß an die Gottheit beschließt.

Renaissance Latin Verse (London, 1979), 120–122, sowie mit Übersetzung auch in Fred J. Nichols, hrsg., *An Anthology of Neo-Latin Poetry* (New Haven and London, 1979), 248–253. Neben der Studie von Ludwig (*Antike Götter,* mit weiteren Hinweisen) ist dazu heranzuziehen die übergreifende Würdigung von Marullos Werk von Georg Luck ("Marullus und sein dichterisches Werk", *Arcadia* 1 [1966]: 31–49: bes. wichtig der Hinweis auf M.s Lukrez-Studien!), die Monographie von Carol Kidwell (*Marullus. Soldier Poet of the Renaissance* [London, 1979]) sowie Christine Harrauer, *Kosmos und Mythos: Die Weltgotthymnen und die mythologischen Hymnen des Michael Marullus (Text, Übersetzung und Kommentar)* Wiener Studien, Beiheft 21, Arbeiten zur Religionsgeschichte 4 (Wien, 1994), hier auch umfassende Bibliographie.

[39] Paul Schede Melissus entfaltet die Topik in einer Glückwunschode zur Geburt von Erasmus Posthius, Sohn seines Dichterfreundes Johannes Posthius. S. Paul Schede Melissus, *Schediasmata Poetica* (Paris, 1586), 1: 431 f.: *Ad Lunam. Cum Joanni Posthio nasceretur Erasmus F[ilius];* Abdruck nun mit Einleitung und Kommentar in Kühlmann et al., *Humanistische Lyrik des 16. Jahrhunderts.*

[40] Antike Anregungen dürften weniger in Frage kommen als die Kenntnis der einschlägigen Ausführungen Agrippas: s. hier das Zitat Anm. 43; ähnliche Lizenzen finden sich in der französischen Renaissancedichtung: wenn etwa Baïf Hecate (nach Theokrit) als "Proserpine, ô royne aux trois visages" anredet oder die Dreiheit der weiblichen Gottheiten auf wechselnde Erscheinungsformen eines Numens zurückgeführt wird: "Hécate est Proserpine aux enfers, Diane en la terre, & la Lune au Ciel" (Jean Martin); nach Guy Demerson, *La Mythologie classique dans l'œuvre lyrique de la "Pléiade",* Travaux d'Humanisme et Renaissance, 119 (Genf, 1972), 560.

[41] Lotichius denkt an die Fallsucht oder Epilepsie; die von ihr Befallenen hießen *lunatici* (dem Mondwechsel unterworfen).

III

Freilich ist zu fragen: Geht es Lotichius nur um eine virtuose Kontrafaktur mythologischer Poesie und um die Erfüllung formaler Gattungsgesetze im Wetteifer mit renommierten poetischen Vorbilder? Darf man soweit gehen, in diesem Gedicht, das den christlichen Mythos so eklatant vermeidet, Spuren jener naturmagischen Theoreme neuplatonischer Provenienz zu entdecken, wie sie in Agrippa von Nettesheim berühmt-berüchtigten Werk *De occulta philosophia* (1533) kodifiziert waren? Hier erscheinen die antiken Dichter und Philosophen im Zeichen einer "hermetischen Verehrung" der in den Gestirnen wirkenden "Weltseele" als Protagonisten magischen Vermögens, denn "humanae imprecationes naturaliter imprimunt suas vires in res exteriores".[42] Ist die Identifikation des Dichters und des Magus in Lotichius' Elegie dann doch mehr als ein lediglich fiktional inszeniertes Bekenntnis zu der das Bewußtsein der Wirklichkeit verwandelnden Macht der Dichtung? In dieser Optik ließe dann unser Gedicht bei einem deutschen Medizinstudenten Spuren jener potentiell häretischen Naturfrömmigkeit wahrnehmen, die im Fall Marulls so manchen Zeitgenossen zum Widerspruch reizte. Jedenfalls erinnert Agrippa im Blick auf Gestirne und Planeten den der magischen Kunst Beflissenen expressis verbis an die orphischen Hymnen, nicht ohne zuvor eine Tabulatur jener *gloria* und *vis* der Mondgöttin kompiliert zu haben, die auch Lotichius rühmt.[43] In der potentiellen Anregung durch Marullus und in der Umsetzung der Praecepte Agrippas müssen wir wohl den aus dem Melanchthonschen Reformationshumanismus hinausweisenden geistigen und literarischen Impuls der vorliegenden Elegie fassen.

In ihrem thematischen Zuschnitt und in ihrer komplexen Formkombination unterscheidet sich die von Lotichius sichtlich angestrebte Rehabilitation des paganen Hymnus jedenfalls von lyrischen Varianten, die gerade in Deutschland im Gefolge der

---

[42] Agrippa, *De occulta philosophia*, 393 (Überschrift des Kap. 60 im zweiten Buch); hinzuzuziehen sind gleichsam als fundamentaler Kommentar zu Lotichius' Gedicht Agrippas Kap. 69–72 im ersten Buch über die magische Kraft der Sprache, darunter auch der poetisch-harmonischen "incantamenta".

[43] Agrippa, *De occulta philosophia*, 392 f. (Liber Secundus, Kap. 69): "Luna vocatur Phoebe, Diana, ‹Lucina,› Proserpina, ‹Hecate, menstrua, semiformis, noctiluca, errans, silens, bicornis, sospitatrix, noctivaga, cornigera,› regina coeli, summa numinum, prima coelitum deorum dearumque, regina manium, elementorum omnium domina, cui respondent sydera, redeunt tempora, serviunt elementa, cuius nutu spirant fulmina, germinant semina, crescunt germina, frugum parens initialis, Phoebi soror, lucens et fulgens, deferens lucem de uno planetarum ad alium, cuncta numina sua luce collustrans, stellarum varios meatus cohibens, solis ambagibus incerta lumina dispensans, domina magnae pulchritudinis, domina pluviorum et aquarum, datrix divitiarum, nutrix hominum, gubernatrix omnius statuum, pia et misericors, terra marique homines protegens, fortunae tempestates mitigans, cum fato dispensans, omnia terrae nascentia enutriens, lucos diversos inerrans, larvales impetus comprimens, terrae claustra cohibens, coeli luminosa culmina, maris salubria flumina, inferum deplorata silentia nutibus suis dispensans, regens mundum, calcans tartarum, cuius maiestatem perhorrescunt aves coelo meantes, ferae montibus errantes, serpentes solo latentes, beluae ponto natantes. Caeterum de his et similibus stellarum planetarumque nominibus, epithetis, cognomentis et invocamentis qui plura scire velit et curiosius illa scrutari is ad orphicos hymnos se conferat, ‹quos re vera qui intellexerit magnam naturalis magiae intelligentiam consecutus erit.›

sog. Empfindsamkeit unter dem Titel "An den Mond"—etwa bei Hölty oder Goethe —typenbildend wurden.[44] Biographisch-fiktionale Exposition dieses Textes, sein poetologischer Aussagegehalt sowie die intendierte Mimesis psychischer Bewegungen und magischer Frömmigkeit sind, soweit ich sehe, in der einschlägigen humanistisch-lateinischen Lyrik diesseits der Alpen ohne Beispiel. Ob Lotichius auf seiner Reise durch Frankreich Anregungen französischer Dichtung übernommen hat, muß ich hier ganz offen lassen. Jedenfalls beteiligte er sich in dieser Elegie nicht an der für die Zukunft wegweisenden Kontamination von Mond-Epiklese und implizierter Biographie des erotischen Begehrens. In solcher Kontamination (der Mond als Freund, Partner usw. des Liebenden) entwickelte sich bekanntlich eine reich variierte Topik, die Elemente des Hymnus durchaus integrieren konnte—in Deutschland etwa ablesbar an einem Sonett Paul Flemings.[45] Solange die Kunstgesetze des europäischen Klassizismus ihre Verbindlichkeit bewahrten, blieb daneben—gewiß seltener—das Modell der mythologisch-astralen Hymnik, damit auch der sakrale, nicht sentimentalisch übermalte Ursprung des archaischen Sprachrituals abrufbar.[46]

Universität Heidelberg

---

[44] Vgl. dazu und zum folgenden die in Anm. 18 genannte Literatur.

[45] Paul Fleming, "An den Mohn". "Du/ die du standhafft bist in deinem Unbestande// Steig"/ Hekate/ herab ich singe dir ein Lied/ [. . .]". Erstdruck in *Teutsche Poemata* (Lübeck, 1642; Ndr. Hildesheim, 1969), 632; vgl. Schoolfield, "Changes of the Moon," 323 f.

[46] Vgl. etwa George Chapman, "Hymnus in Cynthiam", in ders., *The Poems*, ed. Phyllis Brooks Bartlett (New York/London, 1941), 31–42; André Chénier, "Diane" (im Zyklus "Bucoliques"), in ders., *Œuvres complètes*, Bibliothèque de la Pléiade (Paris, 1958), 4 f.

Seventeenth-Century Latin Translations of Two English Masterpieces: Hooker's Polity and Browne's Religio Medici

CLARENCE H. MILLER

I was very pleased and honored when our president, Brenda Hosington, asked me to give a lecture at one of our plenary sessions at this congress, though I was somewhat concerned that the honor may have come so late in my life that I have nothing left to say. But for someone who has survived (and sometimes thrived) in academia for over forty years, merely having nothing to say is no serious obstacle to holding forth for three-quarters of an hour. It would not be surprising if the weather reports for this week noted a gaseous cloud hovering over Ávila and this part of Madrid.

In fact, it did not take long to think of a subject. I had been aware for a long time of Merryweather's translation of Sir Thomas Browne's English masterpiece, *Religio Medici*, and I wondered whether it had ever been fully or carefully compared with the English. Scholars had long been aware that another prose masterpiece of the English Renaissance, Richard Hooker's *Of the Laws of Ecclesiastical Polity*, had been translated into Latin by John Earle, but the translation was thought to have been lost until 1971, when the Folger Shakespeare Library acquired a copy of it. The Folger edition of Hooker's complete works made no use of it (perhaps because it arrived somewhat late in their enterprise), and, so far as I am aware, no one has examined it or compared it with the original. These two translations are part of a fairly extensive body of Latin translations of vernacular works, including (to speak only of English works) several partial and two complete translations of Milton's *Paradise Lost*[1] and a translation of Chaucer's *Troilus and Criseyde*. J. W. Binns has noted that in Elizabethan and Jacobean England alone over one hundred translations into Latin from English and

---

[1] The Latin translations of *Paradise Lost* have been discussed by John K. Hale, "The Significance of the Early Translations of *Paradise Lost*," *Philological Quarterly* 63 (1984): 31–38.

other vernaculars were printed.[2] It is safe to say that most of these translations have been neglected by scholars and critics of vernacular works, and in many cases perhaps rightly so. But by examining a very large sample of the Latin translations of Hooker and Browne, I have discovered that they throw some light on their English originals, in understanding both the literal meaning of the English texts and their places in the evolution of English prose.

But before we turn to the evidence to substantiate that claim, let me provide some information about the English works, their translators, and the sources and states of the translations.

Having been appointed Master of the Temple in 1585, Richard Hooker lectured in the mornings in defense of the Anglican ecclesiastical establishment. His opponents were Puritans who demanded that the English church abandon the prelatical structure set up by the Elizabethan Establishment of 1560–61 and adopt the ecclesiastical polity laid down by Calvin in his *Institutes* and actually established at Geneva. His antagonist Walter Travers lectured on the Puritan side in the afternoons, so that (as Thomas Fuller remarked) audiences were served pure Canterbury in the morning and pure Geneva in the afternoons. The great issue on which everything turned was the Puritans' insistence that the only source of ecclesiastical law is Scripture and Scripture alone, and that Scripture contains the church polity which they demanded. Hooker maintained that this simplistic position is untenable and that there are many different sources and kinds of law, not all of them scriptural, which must be taken into account in the moral and social guidance of individuals and the establishment of societies, civil as well as ecclesiastical. After he retired to rural parishes Hooker codified his arguments in five long books first published in 1593 and 1597. (The last three of the planned eight were not published till 1648 and 1662, long after Hooker's death, and their authenticity has often been questioned.)

The Latin translation of the preface and first five books of Hooker's *Polity*, the English of which fills 843 pages in the Folger Library edition, was made by John Earle (1600/01–1665), a distinguished churchman and writer best known for his extremely popular English masterpiece, a book of Theophrastan characters entitled *Microcosmography* (1628). As the chaplain of Charles II he went into exile at Cologne during the Cromwellian interregnum, when the Puritans opposed by Hooker finally had their way; after the Restoration he became bishop first of Worcester and then of Salisbury. On the continent he translated Hooker's defense of the English pre-Cromwellian church, partly, no doubt, because he had a good deal of time on his hands, but also because a Latin translation would make that defense available to a large continental audience, including many Roman Catholics, who in matters of church government were much closer to the Anglican establishment than to the Genevan model. Indeed, Hooker devotes Book 4 to refuting the Puritan position that wherever the English church agrees with Rome, it is for that very reason erroneous. Even apart

---

[2] J. W. Binns, *Intellectual Culture in Elizabethan and Jacobean England: The Latin Writings of the Age*, Arca: Classical and Medieval Texts, Papers and Monographs 24 (Leeds, 1990), 241, 253–57, 269.

from the main sticking point of papal authority, Hooker rejects some important papist doctrines, but in fact Earle's translation sometimes softens or even omits Hooker's infrequent remarks against the papists.[3] The translation, which was made between 1654 and probably 1664, was for centuries thought to have been lost. It was the usual story of servants using the loose manuscript leaves to light fires and wrap pies.[4] But in 1971 a manuscript of it (a somewhat careless copy, not the autograph)[5] turned up and was purchased by the Folger Shakespeare Library.[6] The manuscript is

---

[3] Folger MS, fols. 20 and 23v; vol. 1, p. 45, ll.20–21 [pref.8.7] and p. 54, ll. 20–22 [pref.9.4] in *The Folger Library Edition of the Works of Richard Hooker*, ed. W. Speed Hill et al., vols. 1–5, (London and Cambridge, MA, 1977–82); vol. 6, parts 1 and 2 (Binghamton, NY, 1993); hereafter cited as "Folger." I will cite the manuscript folia in the format "MS fol. 00"; the Folger edition by volume, page, and line number in the format "Folger 0.00.00"; and Hooker's book, section, and subsection in the format "[0.0.0]." The eighth book, which was not printed until 1648 and in a corrupt form, would have been the least acceptable part of Hooker's work to Catholics; we do not know whether Earle translated the last three books.

[4] In a letter of 13 September 1705 Thomas Smith noted that the manuscript was "utterly destroyed by prodigious heedlesnes and carelesnes; for it being written in Loose papers, onely pinned together, and put into a trunke unlocked after his death, and being looked upon as refuse and wast paper, the servants lighted their fire with them, or else put them under their bread and their pyes." See Peter Beal, *Index of English Literary Manuscripts*, vol. 2, part 1 (London and New York, 1987; repr. 1989), 431–32.

[5] A comparison with a Latin autograph manuscript by Earle (Public Record Office SP 16/215/31) shows that the writing is not Earle's, even though the autograph at the Public Record Office (11 April 1632) is some twenty-five years earlier than the translation. In the Hooker translation there are many cancellations and interlineations, but none are such as could only be made by the author. The copyist was none too careful. Apart from the omission of many brief phrases in the English (some but not all of which might be due to Earle himself) the copyist omitted a passage of 195 words at the end of the second section of the preface; he wrote it on a separate leaf at the beginning of the manuscript, with directions about where to insert it. At the beginning of Book 1 about six pages of the Folger edition of the English are missing from the Latin; the missing pages are Folger 1.55.1 to 1.60.25. Since at this point one manuscript page equals about two Folger pages, some three leaves of the translation are missing. Moreover the translation breaks off in the middle of section 78, subsection 5 of Book 5 (Folger 2.442.5). We do not know whether Earle or only the copyist did not reach the end of Book 5. Izaak Walton thought Earle had finished the translation, but a note in a copy of Walton's *Lives* at Yale states that it was "unperfect and deficient" at the time of Earle's death; see David Novarr, *The Making of Walton's Lives* (Ithaca, NY, 1958), 207, n. 72. The foliation in the Folger manuscript runs through, ignoring gaps; hence it was added later, probably when the manuscript was bound. Laetitia Yeandle has kindly provided the following entry (which occurs a few pages after October 1666) in John Ward's notebook (Folger Library V. a. 294, f. 50ʳ): "The works of Mʳ Hookʳ calld his Ecclesiastical policie translated into latine by Bishop Erles, and now in ye hands of Bishop Morly: Bishop Earles had first committed ye Revising of it to his Chaplaine who had alterd some thi[n]gs for ye worse, B. Morly committed it to Mʳ Littleton."

[6] Folger Library V. b. 34. It was purchased from Mr. Benjamin Weinreb, who wrote me on 21 August 1997, that he has no information about its provenance. The existence of the manuscript was announced to the scholarly world by W. Speed Hill in *The Times Literary Supplement* (31 January 1975), p. 112. I am grateful to the Folger Library for a microfilm and for the opportunity to compare my transcription with the original.

not easy to read; I have transcribed the preface and Book 1 (142 pages in the Folger edition) and have based my investigation on this fairly generous sample.

The publication of the English text of Browne's *Religio Medici* is complicated, though we do have a complete and fairly reliable text published by Browne himself. Suffice it to say that Browne wrote this series of essays on his personal religious beliefs and attitudes, replete with coruscations and scintillating paradoxes, about 1635 when he was some thirty years old, probably in response to a request from his friend John Power of Halifax. It circulated in manuscript and a corrupt version was printed and reprinted in 1642. In the following year Browne himself published an authorized edition, which was reprinted twice in 1645 and eight more times in the seventeenth century.[7] In 1644 a Latin translation by John Merryweather of Magdalen College, Cambridge, was printed twice in Leiden, with a brief prefatory letter by Merryweather and a translation of Browne's own preface. In the same year a piratical edition of the Latin was printed in Paris, of which Merryweather wrote to Browne: "When I came at Paris . . . I found it printed again, in which edition both the epistles were left out, and a preface by some papist put in their place in which making use of, and wresting some passages in your book, he endeavoured to show that nothing but custom and education kept you from their church." The Latin translation was reprinted in 1650, 1652, 1665, 1677, and 1692. The last four of these editions have a copious Latin commentary by Levin Nicolas von Moltke of Mecklinburg–Schwerin as well as the Paris preface.[8]

These Latin translations and the Latin commentary can contribute a good deal to our understanding of the original texts. To begin with the Hooker translation, which has never been examined by any of his editors, in several places the Latin specifies or clarifies the meaning of English words which often do not appear in the glossary of the Folger edition. A few examples:

Goodnesse in actions is like unto straightnes; wherfore that which is done well we term right. . . . (Folger 1.82.15–16 [8.1])

The Latin here is:

Bonitas in actionibus rectitudinis similis est, quare quod bene fit, rectum nuncupamus. (MS fol. 30)

---

[7] Geoffrey Keynes, *A Bibliography of Sir Thomas Browne*, 2nd ed. (Oxford, 1968), 3–8, 11–20.

[8] For Merryweather, see Keynes, *Bibliography*, 39. The annotator is identified only by his initials: L[evinus] N[icolas] M[oltkenius] E[ques] M[isniensis]. See Keynes, *Bibliography*, 38–41. I do not know the source for spelling out the name, which goes back at least as far as Samuel Johnson's life of Browne. *Religio Medici* was also translated into Dutch (1665, 1683, and 1688) and French (1668); see Keynes, *Bibliography*, 43–46. The Paris preface claims that Browne comes close to the Catholic doctrines of purgatory, praying to the saints, and guardian angels and that he ought not to be thought of as a heretic but as ripe for conversion to Catholicism. Some Catholic authorities disagreed, since the book was placed on the Index Librorum Prohibitorum. As a graduate student in 1951, when the pre-Vatican II church still prevailed, I obtained permission to read it from the archbishop of Boston.

Hence it is clear that Hooker uses right in the sense of "proper" and also the obsolete meaning "straight" (OED right *a*. I 1 a). Another example concerns the meaning of "deed":

> Wherefore as any mans deed past is good as long as himselfe continueth: so the act of a publique societie of men done five hundreth yeares sithence standeth as theirs, who presently are of the same societies, because corporations are immortall. (Folger 1.103.21–24 [10.8])

The Latin translates "deed" as "syngraphae" (MS fol. 37v), that is, not an action but a legal document. In another place we find that the translator understood "coast" in a sense now obsolete.

> For which cause the Lacedemonians forbidding all accesse of strangers into their coastes are in that respect both by Josephus and Theodoret deservedly blamed. . . . (Folger 1.108.31–33 [10.13])

The Latin translates "coastes" as "fines" (MS fol. 39v), that is, not shores but boundaries, an obsolete meaning of "coasts" (OED coast *sb*. 5).

It would be possible to give many similar examples from the translation of *Religio Medici*. Let one suffice:

> . . . even in doctrines heretical, there will be super-heresies; and Arians not only divided from their Church, but also among themselves. (1.8; 12–13)[9]

The Latin is as follows

> Ipsae Haereticorum doctrinae suas habent haereses, & non tantum ab ecclesia nostra[10] divisi sunt, sed etiam inter seipsos: . . . (sig. C6v)[11]

This translation lets us know that "super-heresies" does not mean principal or main heresies, but minor heresies superadded to the major one. Moreover, W. A. Greenhill, one of Browne's most copious and learned nineteenth-century editors, remarks several times that the Latin is plainer and makes the meaning of the English clearer,[12] as, for example, when Browne remarks concerning the literal or allegorical interpretation of Genesis:

---

[9] The first two numbers are the part and section of the work; they are followed by the page numbers of *Religio Medici* in volume one of *The Works of Sir Thomas Browne*, ed. Geoffrey Keynes, 6 vols. (London and New York, 1928–1931).

[10] A wrong translation of the English "their."

[11] I cite and quote the Latin of the translation and annotations from a microfilm of *Religio medici cum annotationibus* (Strassburg, 1652; Keynes, *Bibliography*, 63) in the Beinecke Library at Yale University. The volume is so tightly bound that on many pages a few letters on each side of the gutter cannot be read and have been supplied within square brackets. I give the locations by signatures within parentheses in the text.

[12] *Religio Medici, Letter to a Friend &c., and Christian Morals* ed. W. A. Greenhill (London and New York, 1881; reprint 1960), 263–64, 266.

. . . though Divines have to the power of humane reason endeavoured to make all go in a literal meaning, yet those allegorical interpretations are also probable, and perhaps the mystical method of Moses, bred up in the Hieroglyphical Schools of the Egyptians. (1.34; 43–44)

The Latin is certainly clearer:

Probabiles tamen sunt allegoricae illae interpretationes, & haud scio an forte mysticae Mosis methodo magis congruae, ut cui in Hieroglyphicis Aegyptiorum Scholis institui contigerat. (sigs. N6–N6v)

But the asymmetry of "probable" and "method," an adjective paired with a noun, is a deliberate and expressive feature of Browne's style that is not as much at home in the Latin, which simply matches adjective with adjective, "probabiles" with "congruae."

The Latin commentary on *Religio Medici*, for all its copia and prolixity, has been a valuable source of information for later editors. The first English annotator, Thomas Keck, whose learned and elaborate English commentary first appeared in print in 1656,[13] claims that his notes were gathered in 1644 and hence do not depend on von Moltke, whose learning he recognizes but whose prolixity and deficiencies he disparages;[14] but Keck himself several times takes note of von Moltke's opinions, even if only to disagree with them.[15] Certainly it is true that von Moltke goes off into learned digressions, as when he inserts a long essay on the limits of religious toleration (sigs. B4–B7), or disgorges his learning ad nauseam, as when he heaps up two and a half pages of misogynist quotations (sigs. Aa4–Aa5) to explain Browne's remark "I never cast true affection on a woman" (2.5; 82). But his learning and experience, however he sometimes mis- or overapplies them, are remarkably large and diverse. In the diplomatic service of the Duke of Holstein (C5v), he has resided in Italy, France, and England (P2), where he saw in the Tower of London the gold rose sent by Clement VII to Henry VIII when he was named Defender of the Faith (L8v). He has spoken with the Jesuit polymath Athanasius Kircher in Rome (S2v) and with the Abbess of the nun-witches of Ladun (M7). He is well versed in classical, patristic, and contemporary learning, secular and sacred. He can cite the glossa ordinaria (T5v) or Nicolas de Lyra (K2). He has read the Koran in French (I8v), Hobbes in English (K2v, K3v, M5v, M6v, M7), Petrarch and Machiavelli in Italian (E3, H1, H8). The two most learned of Browne's nineteenth-century editors complain about the prolixity not only of von Moltke but also of Keck. Of von Moltke Wilkins remarks that Browne's "text is absolutely buried beneath a mass of Latin notes."[16] Greenhill says of Keck that his notes are "learned and useful but unnecessarily prolix and tedious" and applies the same judgment to von Moltke, except

---

[13] Keynes, *Bibliography*, no. 6. It was reprinted in five later editions in the seventeenth century (Keynes, nos. 8–13). I have relied on a reprint of it in *The Works of Sir Thomas Browne*, ed. Charles Sayle, vol. 1 (Edinburgh, 1927), xi–lv.

[14] Sayle, Browne, xii–xiii.

[15] Sayle, Browne, xxxv, xlii, l, liii.

[16] Simon Wilkin, ed., *The Works of Sir Thomas Browne*, 3 vols. (London, 1852), 2:299.

that "unnecessarily" becomes "intolerably."[17] Both editors, however, make ample use of both commentators. But perhaps the true value of von Moltke's commentary is not merely the apposite information it provides but the sense it gives of the ordinary and accepted discussion and opinion which Browne ignores or presumes in order to play with the paradoxical edges and oddities of standard subjects such as angelology, creation, or the infusion of the human soul.[18]

In a larger sense, the two translations are a measure of what was happening to English prose during the sixteenth and seventeenth centuries. It is not necessary to remind an audience such as this of the dominance exercised by Latin over intellectual culture at the beginning of the sixteenth century. But it is sometimes hard to keep in mind how impotent and deficient English was in treating intellectual subjects—not, of course, that it was not capable of high literary merit in other types of writing. The deficiencies were partly lexical, partly syntactic or structural. Writing in 1531, Sir Thomas Elyot tries to outline the education of a Christian ruler, who ought to read

> ... the warke of Aristotell called *Ethicae*, wherin is contained the definitions and propre significations of every virtue; and that to be lerned in greke: for the translations that we yet have, be but a rude and grosse shadowe of the eloquence and wisedom of Aristotell.
>
> Forthe with wolde folowe the warke of Cicero called in Latin *De officiis*: whereunto yet is no propre englisshe worde to be gyven: but to provide for it some maner of exposition, it may be sayde in this fourme: of the dueties and maners appertaynynge to men.[19]

From the forties and throughout the century the so-called inkhorn controversy raged about whether to adopt Latin words into English.[20] In his *Art of Rhetorique* (1553), Thomas Wilson gives a parodic letter in which a Lincolnshire man Latinizes in his request for a benefice:

> Pondering, expending, and reuoluting with my selfe, your ingent affabilitie, and ingenious capacity for mundaine affairs: I cannot but celebrate, and extol your magnifical dexteritie aboue all other. For how could you haue adepted such illustrate prerogative, and dominical superioritie if the fecunditie of your ingenie had not been so fertile and wonderful pregnant? Now therefore being accersited to such splendente renoume, and dignitie splendidious: I doubt not but you will adiuuate such poore adnichilate orphanes, as whilome ware condisciples with you, and of antique familiaritie in Lincolneshire ... [21]

---

[17] W. A. Greenhill, ed., *Sir Thomas Browne's Religio medici, Letter to a Friend &c*, xxxvii, xlv.

[18] Von Moltke, Sigs. N4–N5v, N8–N8v, O2–O4. See note 45, below.

[19] Sir Thomas Elyot, *The Boke Named the Governour*, ed. Donald W. Rude (New York and London, 1992), 53.

[20] The controversy has been discussed at length by Richard Foster Jones in *The Triumph of the English Language* (Stanford, CA, 1953), 68–141.

[21] Thomas Wilson, *The Arte of Rhetorique*, ed. G. H. Mair (Oxford, 1909), 163.

As late as 1602 in *The Poetaster* Ben Jonson ridicules bombastic Latinate fustian. Horace and Virgil give Crispinus, a bad poet, an emetic to make him vomit up his inkhorn terms. Caesar, Maecenas, Gallus, and Tibullus are also present when the pill takes effect.

> Hora: A bason, a bason, quickly; our physick works. Faint not, man.
> Cris: O—*retrograde—reciprocal—incubus* . . .
> Gall: Thanks be to Jupiter.
> Cris: O—*glibbery—lubrical—defunct—ô* . . .
> Caes: What's that?
> Cris: —*Puffie—inflate—turgidious—ventositous* . . .
> Tibu: O terrible windie words!
> Gall. A signe of a windie braine.
> Cris; O—*oblatrant—furibund—fatuate—strenuous—* . . .
> Hora: Force yourself then, a little with your finger.
> Cris: O—*ô—prorumped.* . . .
> Hor: How now, Crispinus?
> Cris: O—*obstupefact.*
> Tibu: Nay: that are all we, I assure you.[22]

The fact that the words "retrograde," "reciprocal," "defunct," and "strenuous" are ordinary and accepted in modern English suggests that the purists mostly lost the battle. At least five thousand new words were added to English, most of them from Latin and most of them abstract terms like "anachronism," "allusion," "denunciation," "dexterity," "disrespect," "excrescence," "consolidate," "disregard," and "eradicate."[23]

An even more serious deficiency in the English of the early sixteenth century was structural. Consider the difficulty under which Sir Thomas Elyot labors when he attempts to explain that rulers, who produce nothing for themselves through their intellectual labors, should be supported by artisans whose products benefit both themselves and rulers and that artisans who do not work should not share in those products:

> But they that be governours (as I before sayde) nothinge do acquire, for theyr owne necessities, but do employe all the powers of theyr wittes and theyr diligence, to the only preservation of other theyr inferiours: Amonge whiche inferiours also behoveth to be a disposition and ordre accordynge to reason: that is to saye, that the slouthfull or idell persone, do nat participate with hym that is industrious, and taketh payne: wherby the frutes of his labours shuld be di-

---

[22] *Ben Jonson*, ed. C. H. Herford and Percy Simpson, 11 vols. (Oxford, 1925–63), 4:312–13.

[23] See Albert C. Baugh, *A History of the English Language*, 2d ed. (New York, 1957), 268. On the whole controversy see pp. 257–73.

minisshed, wherin shulde be non equalite, but therof shulde procede discourage, and finally dissolution for lacke of provision.[24]

This deficiency was remedied largely through translation and imitation of Latin[25] and through the intensive study of classical rhetoric.[26] The larger elements of rhetoric such as invention and disposition were crucial: the plan of Sidney's *Defense of Poesy* is modelled closely on the structure of a classical oration[27] and Hooker too, in a much larger fashion, arranges the *Polity* on the scheme of thesis, narration, disposition, confirmation, and refutation. But it was the branch of rhetoric called "elocutio," especially the verbal patterns and schemes, which was obsessively and narrowly pursued in Euphuism but which in the end contributed flexibility and articulation to the English sentence.

Hooker was the heir of this movement and his *Polity* was its culmination. The Ciceronian periodicity of Hooker's sentences is a commonplace of literary criticism,[28] but it is not always recognized that the long suspended sentence is not the primary feature of such periods, but rather the marshalling of interrelated, subordinated, often parallel or contrastive clauses into a focused and harmonious pattern.[29] Hooker's sentences match his outlook, for he sees all law, indeed all truth and all reality, as an intricate, interrelated, hierarchical system which cannot be reduced to *sola scriptura*. He himself describes his basic mindset:

> I have endevoured throughout the bodie of this whole discourse, that every former part might give strength unto all that followe, and every later bring some light unto all before. So that if the judgements of men doe but holde themselves in suspence as touching these first more generall meditations, till in order they have perused the rest that ensue; what may seeme darke at the first will afterwardes be founde more plaine, even as the later particular decisions will appeare, I doubt not more strong, when the other have beene read before. (Folger 1.57.25–33 [1.1.2])[30]

Because English intellectual discourse by Hooker's time had matured under the gui-

---

[24] Elyot, *Governour*, ed. Rude, 18–19.

[25] On translation see F. O. Matthiessen, *Translation, an Elizabethan Art* (Cambridge, MA, 1931).

[26] Of the many studies of classical rhetoric in sixteenth-century England, see, for instance, William G. Crane, *Wit and Rhetoric in the Renaissance: The Formal Basis of Elizabethan Prose Style* (Gloucester, MA, 1937; reprint 1964) and James J. Murphy ed., *Renaissance Eloquence: Studies in the Theory and Practice of Renaissance Rhetoric* (Berkeley, 1983).

[27] Kenneth Myrick, *Sir Philip Sidney as a Literary Craftsman* (Cambridge, MA, 1935; 2nd ed., Lincoln, NE, 1965), 46–83.

[28] Stephanie Stueber, C. S. J., "The Balanced Diction of Hooker's *Polity*," *Publications of the Modern Language Association* 71 (1956): 819–20 (n. 18).

[29] The finest discussion of Hooker's style is by Georges Edelen, "Hooker's Style," in *Studies in Richard Hooker: Essays Preliminary to an Edition of His Works*, ed. W. Speed Hill (Cleveland and London, 1972), 241–77.

[30] This sentence is missing in the translation.

dance of Latin, especially Ciceronian Latin, Hooker goes quite easily and comfortably into Latin. Earle's translation, at least in the form we have it, is sometimes inaccurate or erroneous, though not often. There are sometimes careless omissions, though these may be due to the copyist. Sometimes Hooker's wry irony or piquant vividness may be lost in the Latin. For example, when Hooker translates a sentence from St. Augustine, he seasons it with extra irony:

> *These good folke* (saith he, *that I may not trouble their wits with rehearsall of too many things) have not looked so far into the world as to perceive, that* Doe as thou wouldest be done unto, *is a sentence which all nations under heaven are agreed upon.* (Folger 1.91.14–17 [1.8.10])[31]

In Earle's translation the irony does not disappear but it is muted:

> Hi boni viri (inquit ille) vt non in plurimis illis molestiam inferam non animum adverterunt, quod facere, sicut sibi fieri velint apud omnes vbique nationes sibi consentaneum esse. (MS fol. 33)

The "rehersall of too many things" becomes simply "plurimis"; "trouble their wits" becomes "illis molestiam inferam"; "looked so far into the world as to perceive" becomes "animum adverterunt"; "under heaven" becomes "ubique." Similarly force and vividness are lost when "[rebels] *dayly run themselves, without feeling their owne hazard, upon the dint of the Apostles sentence*" (Folger 1.14.21–22 [pref.3.3]) becomes "quotidie incauti in illud Apostolicae censurae periculum incurrant" (MS fol. 7).

But usually the fit between the Latin and English is close and comfortable. Consider the most famous (but not most representative) sentence from the *Polity*:

> Now if nature should intermit her course, and leave altogether, though it were but for a while, the observation of her own lawes: if those principall and mother elements of the world, wherof all things in the lower world are made, should loose the qualities which they now have, if the frame of that heavenly arch erected over our heads should loosen and dissolve itself: if celestiall spheres should forget their wonted motions and by irregular volubilitie, turne themselves any way as it might happen: if the prince of the lightes of heaven which now as a Giant doth runne his unwearied course, should as it were through a languishing faintnes begin to stand and to rest himself: if the Moone should wander from her beaten way, the times and seasons of the yeare blend themselves by disordered and confused mixture, the winds breath out their last gaspe, the cloudes yeeld no rayne, the earth be defeated of heavenly influence, the fruites of the earth pine away as children at the withered breasts of their mother no longer able to yeeld them reliefe, what would become of man himselfe, whom these things now do all serve? See we not plainly that obe-

---

[31] Augustine's Latin is as follows: "Non intellexerunt, ne multa commemorem, Quod tibi fieri non vis, alii ne feceris, nullo modo posse ulla eorum gentili diversitate variari" (Folger edition 6/1 501, n. 1:9.7–10.g.).

dience of creatures unto the lawe of nature is the stay of the whole world? (Folger 1.65.20–6.6 [1.3.2])[32]

Earle's translation is as follows:

> Si iam natura cursum suum intermittat, et omnino vel parvo momento a legum suarum norma cesset, si illa prima et materna mundi elementa a quibus omnia in hoc mundo inferiore formantur qualitates suas quibus nunc imbutae sint, omittant: Si illius caelestis testudinis fabrica capitibus nostris superstructa laxetur et dissolvatur; si sphaerae caelestes motuum sibi solitorum obliviscantur et irregulari volubilitate, quo sors ferat, se vertant: si luminum caelestium princeps, qui nunc vt Gigas indefatigatum iter tenet quasi languescenti defectu consistere et quiescere incipiat: si luna a via sibi trita aberret, si anni tempestates confuse et inordinate se intermisceant, venti vltimum spiritum expirent, nubes pluuiam non effundant, influxu caelesti terra destituatur, terrae fructus exarescant vt pueri ad marcida matrum vbera languescentes non vltra nutrimenta largiri sustinentia, quid de homine ipso actum sit cui omnia haec nunc inserviant? Nonne luculenter videmus creaturarum ad legem naturae obedientiam totius mundi esse sustentaculum. (MS fol. 25)

No doubt, "vltimum spiritum" translates but does not express "last gaspe," and the triplicity of the three phrases "obedience of creatures," "the lawe of nature," and "the stay of the world" disappears in the Latin.[33] But otherwise very little is lost in the Latin. Even the contrast between the polysyllabic "irregular volubilitie" and the monosyllabic "any way as it might happen" is retained in "irregulari volubilitate, quo sors ferat."

In a more typical sentence Hooker presents not dissolution but the orderly gradations and interrelations of the scale of creatures, with parallel clauses within the large structure of "as this, so that":

> For as stones, though in dignitie of nature inferiour unto plants, yet exceede them in firmenesse of strength or durabilitie of being; and plantes though beneath the excellencie of creatures indued with sense, yet exceede them in the faculty of vegetation and of fertilitie: so beasts though otherwise behind men, may notwithstanding in actions of sense and phancy goe beyond them; because the endevors of nature, when it hath an higher perfection to seeke, are in lower the more remisse, not esteeming thereof so much as those thinges doe, which have no better proposed unto them. (Folger 1.75.7–6 [1.6.2])

Earle translates thus:

---

[32] It has long been recognized that Hooker bases his sentence on a passage in Arnobius of Sicca's *Adversus Gentes* (1.2); see Folger 6/1, p. 485, note on 1.65-20–66.6. Hooker shapes the separate and discrete elements of Arnobius into one large pattern of parallel, suspended clauses.

[33] Hooker is very fond of triplets; they seem to express for him stability, integrity, and harmony, as in his discussion of the "trinal tiplicities" (as Spenser called them) of the angels; see Folger 1.70.22–71.16 [1.4.1]. The Latin usually retains them.

> Nam vt lapides quamvis naturae dignitate plantis sint inferiores, in roboris tamen firmitate et essentiae duratione superant, et plantae quamvis sensu praeditis inferiores sint, in vegetationis tamen et fertilitatis facultate superant: sic bestiae quamvis alias sint inferiores, in sensuum et phantasiae actionibus facile superant: quoniam naturae conatus dum altiorem perfectionis gradum quaerunt, in inferioribus sunt magis remissi, non ea tanti aestimantes quanti illa quibus non est vlterior finis aestimant. (MS fol. 27v)

Latin and English are both congruent and equally expressive.

Let me give one more example of how easily Hooker's English goes into Latin before pointing out two characteristic features of Hooker's style which derive from Latin but work well in English. At one point Hooker gives the reason for the rewards and punishments specified by human laws:

> And because the greatest parte of men are such as prefer their owne privat good before all things, even that good which is sensuall before whatsoever is most divine, and for that the labor of doing good together with the pleasure arising from the contrarie doth make men for the most parte slower to the one and proner to the other, then that dutie prescribed them by lawe can prevaile sufficientlie with them: therfore unto laws that men do make for the benefit of men it hath seemed alwaies needful to ad rewards which may more allure unto good then any hardness deterreth from it, and punishments which maye more deterre from evill then any sweetnes therto allureth. (Folger 1.101.11–21 [1.10.6])

The Latin is as follows:

> Et quoniam maxima hominum pars privatis suis commodis omnia postponunt, sensuali etiam bono quicquid maxime est divinum: et quoniam bene agendi labor vna cum voluptate quae ex contrario oritur homines plerunque ad alterum taediores, ad alterum procliviores reddit quam vt officium lege constitutum satis apud illos valere possit: ad leges igitur quas homines hominum beneficio constituunt necessarium semper visum est mercedes addere, quae ad bonum magis alliciat, quam difficultas vlla ab eo terreat, et supplicia quae a malo magis terreant, quam vlla dulcedo ad illud alliciat. (MS fol. 36v)

Not only do the Latin and English run easily pari passu, but the sentence also illustrates one of the two characteristic features I mentioned: inversion of the normal English word-order. The usual order would be "it hath seemed alwaies needful to ad rewards unto the laws that men do make, etc." instead of "unto laws that men do make . . . it hath seemed alwaies needful to ad." Such inversion, which is very frequent in Hooker, often allows him to add and link up clauses, as here, where it enables him to attach a relative clause to "rewards." Or it may simply be emphatic, as in this sentence: "Deceived greatly they are therfore, who think that all they whose names are cited amongst the favourers of this cause, are on any such verdict agreed" (Folger 1.25.25–27 [pref.4.6]).[34] The Latin often manages to keeps such inversions

---

[34] The Latin is: "Graviter ergo hallucinantur, qui omnes illos quorum nomina inter huius causae fautores citantur in illud suffragium conspirasse existiment" (MS fol. 12).

quite easily, and in fact, they are sometimes more natural in the Latin than in the English. Consider, for example, the sentence:

> Of what accompt the Maister of sentences was in the Church of Rome, the same and more amongest the preachers of reformed Churches Calvin had purchased. . . . (Folger 1.11.5–7 [pref.2.8])

Because of its inflections the Latin runs more easily:

> Qua authoritate Magister Sententiarum erat in ecclesia Romana, eandem et ampliorem inter reformatarum ecclesiarum concionatores Calvinus acquisiverat. (MS fol. 5v)

In any case the translation highlights the fact that Hooker imported into his English a stylistic feature more natural in Latin, and he usually did so with great success.

The other Latinate feature which Hooker adapted to his English might be called an interruption or suspension. We tend to overidealize our heroes, according to Hooker, and:

> This with Germans hath caused Luther, and with many other Churches, Calvin to prevaile in all things. (Folger 1.26.33–27.1 [pref.4.8])

In Latin:

> Hoc apud Germanos Lutherum, apud multas alias ecclesias Calvinum in omnibus plurimum valere fecit. (MS fol. 12v)

Sometimes the Latin is even more suspended than the English:

> God has given us his law as a light which otherwise would have bene buried in darknes, not without the hazard, or rather not with the hazard, but with the certaine losse of infinite thousandes of soules most undoubtedly now saved. (Folger 1.121.26–29 [1.12.2])

Many things have been revealed, according to the Latin:

> quae aliter in tenebris sepulta iacuissent non sine periculo, aut potius non cum periculo sed certo infinitarum animarum quae nunc proculdubio servantur interitu. (MS fol. 43v)

The Latin frequently retains Hooker's suspensions,[35] and the translation confirms that this feature of Hooker's style is also borrowed from Latin.

These examples are sufficent, perhaps more than sufficient, to demonstrate the close affinity Hooker's style has to the Latin models cultivated so assiduously during the sixteenth century. When we come to Browne some forty years later, English

---

[35] Some suspensions, of course, either are not or cannot be retained in Latin, in particular those which depend on English auxiliar verbs which do not exist in Latin. For example: "this law, I say, comprehendeth all those thinges which men by the light of their naturall understanding evidently know, or at leastwise may know, to be beseeming or unbeseeming, vertuous or vitious, good or evill for them to doe." (Folger 1.90.23–25 [1.8.9])

prose has undergone a sea-change, and a Latin translator cannot hope to keep pace with his original, as Merryweather himself admitted in his preface: "... *sermonis elegantiam latinis auribus me reddere posse desperavi* ..." (sig. 6).[36]

The anti-ciceronian or baroque character of early seventeenth-century prose was first analyzed and discussed by Morris Croll in the years between 1914 and 1929,[37] and though Croll's work has been qualified and extended by George Williamson,[38] Jonas Barish,[39] and others, Croll's descriptions and distinctions are sufficient to examine how the Latin translation of *Religio Medici* reveals by its contrasts and deficiencies the special character of the new anti-ciceronian prose. According to Croll, baroque English prose falls into two categories: the curt style of the essayists and letter-writers, modelled primarily on Seneca and Tacitus, is characterized by brief members, lack of ligature, asymmetry, and a sort of repetitive, hovering progression which suggests the mind thinking rather than the thought thought. Here is an example which Croll himself gives from *Religio Medici*:

> The world that I regard is my self; it is the Microcosm of my own frame that
> I cast mine eye on; for the other, I use it but like my Globe, and turn it round
> sometimes for my recreation. (2.11; 91)

In the Latin the first two discrete and asymmetrical clauses are rounded into one, and in the final clause the mere additive force of "and turn it" is changed to a subordinate relative clause:

> Non alium mundum, quam me[ip]sum, quam meipsius fabricam, & mi[cro]cosmum curo, & contemplor. Altero [eg? ver?]o haud aliter ac globo meo utor, quem [int]erdum huc illuc animi causa versare so[leo]. (sig. Cc8r)

Far more characteristic of Browne, however, is Croll's second kind of baroque sentence, the loose style made up of long sentences in which the round period seems to have been exploded into a series of clauses which are loosely linked together by coordinating conjunctions or connectives like "whereas." Absolute-participle constructions are also a feature of this style. One might imagine that such loose sentences are a regression to the straggling sentences of Elyot, but they are actually deliberate and sophisticated structures which have not fallen back from the orderly Ciceronian sentence but have deliberately surged beyond it.[40]

---

[36] The Latin and early Dutch translations are discussed in C. W. Schoneveld, "Holland and the Seventeenth-Century Translations of Sir Thomas Browne's *Religio Medici*," in *Ten Studies in Anglo-Dutch Relations*, ed. Jan van Dorsten (Leiden and London, 1974), 128–71. The gathering is signed with the symbols)(.

[37] Croll's five essays on this subject are conveniently gathered and reprinted in *Style, Rhetoric, and Rhythm: Essays by Morris W. Croll*, ed. J. Max Patrick et al. (Princeton, NJ, 1966), 3–233. The last of the five essays, "The Baroque Style in Prose," pp. 207–33, places special emphasis on Browne.

[38] *The Senecan Amble: A Study in Prose Form from Bacon to Collier* (Chicago, 1951).

[39] *Ben Jonson and the Language of Prose Comedy* (Cambridge, MA, 1960).

[40] Other deliberate distortions of the Ciceronian period, somewhat different from Croll's loose

Let me quote one of Croll's examples. Browne, who had lived for long periods in France and Italy, as well as the Low Lands, saw no reason why a Protestant may not worship in a Catholic church:

> I could never perceive any rational Consequence from those many Texts which prohibit the Children of Israel to pollute themselves with the Temples of the Heathens; we being all Christians, and not divided by such detested impieties as might prophane our Prayers, or the place wherein we make them; or that a resolved Conscience may not adore her Creator any where, especially in places devoted to His Service; where, if their Devotions offend Him, mine may please Him; if theirs prophane it, mine may hallow it. (1.3; 6–7)

The Latin provides ligatures which eliminate the absolute construction and incorporate the detached clause "or that a resolved Conscience may not adore" into the structure of the sentence:

> Ex innumeris istis sacrae paginae locis, quibus Populo Israelitico edicitur, ne se Idolorum templis polluat, nullam adhuc satis validam consequentiam deductam vidi: Christiani enim omnes sumus, nec ejusmodi aliqua execranda impietate disjuncti, quae aut preces nostras, aut locum in quo factae sunt contaminare valeat, aut quae efficere possit, ut animus sibi constans reique tenax creatorem suum vel ubivis gentium adorare nequeat, nedum in locis istis qui cultui eius dedicati sunt; in quibus si cultus quem hi praestiterint, Divinum animum offensiorem reddat, meus forte placaturus est: si ille locum prophanet, fieri potest, ut meus expiet. (sig. A4r)

"We being all Christians" becomes a main clause linked by "enim": "Christiani enim omnes sumus." The non-matching phrases "as might" and "or that" fall into the parallel structure "quae . . . contaminare valeat aut quae efficere possit."

But apart from sentence structure, where the Latin sometimes could and sometimes does match the English fairly well, another feature of Browne's style is all but unattainable in Latin: his technique of playing off polysyllabic Latinate diction, the fruits of the Inkhorn importation, against simple English words. Other writers had done this. Consider the contrast between the first and second lines of Hamlet's parting plea to Horatio:

> Absent thee from felicity a while
> And in this harsh world draw thy breath in pain
> To tell my story. (V.ii.347–49)

And the contrast is common in *Paradise Lost*. But perhaps no English writer exploited it as fully and frequently as Browne.[41] It is especially important in a later work by

---

style, can be found in Milton or Donne. See Joan Webber, *Contrary Music: The Prose Style of John Donne* (Madison, WI, 1963). Unlike the curt style, which derived mainly from Seneca and Tacitus, the large, loose, baroque style has no close models in Latin.

[41] Browne's Latinisms are discussed and analyzed by Dietrich Bischoff, *Sir Thomas Browne*

Browne, *Hydriotaphia* or *Urn Burial*, where it occurs even in the title. In this work it usually highlights the melancholy contrast between man's aspirations to glory and perpetuity and the humility of his decaying flesh. At one point he contrasts the humble uncovered urns found in a field near Norwich with the urn of Patroclus in Homer:

> But in the *Homerical* Urne of *Patroclus*, whatever was the solid Tegument, we finde the immediate covering to be a purple peece of silk: And such as had no covers might have the earth closely pressed into them, after which disposure were probably some of these, wherein we found the bones and ashes half mortered unto the sand and sides of the Urne; and some long roots of Quich, or Dogs-grass wreathed about the bones. (chap. 3, para. 2)[42]

The lofty longings of "solid Tegument," "immediate," and "purple" are undercut by the lowly "earth," "bones," "ashes," "sand," "sides," "long roots of Quich, or Dogs-grass." In another place in the same work he speaks of the soul's longing for immortality:

> But the superiour ingredient and obscured part of our selves, whereunto all present felicities afford no resting contentment, will be able at last to tell us we are more then our present selves; and evacuate such hopes in the fruition of their own accomplishments. (chap. 4, last para.)[43]

Our earthly limitations are monosyllabic: "will be able at last to tell us we are more then our present selves." Our heavenly immortality is Latinate and polysyllabic: "evacuate such hopes in the fruition of their own accomplishments."

Sometimes he seems to be writing in both Latin and English at once. In *The Garden of Cyrus*, the companion work to *Urn Burial*, Browne pursues the multifarious appearances of the x-form of the quincunx in nature and the works of man. At one point he must be pulling our legs when he describes such instruments as nutcrackers, pliers, and scissors:

> ... who can but magnifie the power of decussation, inservient to contrary ends, solution and consolidation, union, and division, illustrable from Aristotle in the old *Nucifragium* or nutcrackers, and the Instruments of Evulsion, compression, or incision; which consisting of two *Vectes* or armes, converted towards each other, the innitency and stresse being made upon the *hypomochlion* or fulciment in the decussation, the greater compression is made by the union of two impulsors. (chap. 2, para. 11)[44]

This technique is less pervasive in *Religio Medici* but it is important and not

---

(1605–1682) als Stilkünstler: Ein Beitrag zur Deutung der englischen Barockliteratur, Anglistische Forschungen 88 (Heidelberg, 1943), 40–58.

[42] *The Works of Sir Thomas Browne*, ed. Keynes, 4:24.

[43] *Works*, ed. Keynes, 4:42.

[44] *Works*, ed. Keynes, 4:80–81.

uncommon. Making the point that unlike the religious writings of other men, those of Moses will last till the the end of the world, Browne writes:

> Mens Works have an age like themselves; and though they out-live their Authors, yet have they a stint and period to their duration: this only is a work too hard for the teeth of time, and cannot perish but in the general Flames, when all things shall confess their ashes. (1.23; 32)

The Latin is as follows:

> Sua scilicet est sicut scribentibus, sic scriptis aetas; quae licet authoribus suis supersint: certam tamen habent & definitam vitae periodum. Hoc solum opus temporis edacis dentibus insuperabile restat, [n]on ante periturum, quam universalis ista [fl]amma res omnes cineres suos fateri cog[e]t. (sigs. I7v–I8)

The English "stint" is set over against "duration"; "too hard for the teeth of time" contrasts with "the general Flames"; and the lofty "confess" ends with "ashes." Naturally, it is simply impossible to translate such dissonances or asymmetries into Latin, but the attempt to turn them into Latin highlights the artistry of the English.

One final example. Section 35 of Part 1 is an essay on creation, leading up to a concluding "O Altitudo" in the form of a paradoxical analogy between generation as Aristotle imagined it and divine creation. Generation is by contraries, as when the heat of the sun generates creatures in the humid mud of the Nile. So too creation:

> And herein is Divinity conformant unto Philosophy, and generation not onely founded on contrarieties, but also creation; God, being all things, is contrary unto nothing, out of which were made all things, and so nothing became something, and Omneity informed Nullity into an Essence. (1.35; 45)

The Latin is:

> Sic itaque & generationem & creationem in contrarietate fundatam videmus, adeoque Theologiae Philosophiam consonam. Deus omnia cum sit, *Nihilo* contrarius est, ex quo omnia producta sunt: Sic *Nihil aliquid* factum est,[45] & *Nullitas* ab *Omneitate* informata essentiam induit. (sigs. N7v–N8)

The English formulation "something became nothing" is paradoxical but not very striking because we are accustomed to the definition of creation as "to make something ex nihilo or out of nothing." But the sentence "Omneity informed Nullity into

---

[45] Von Moltke adds the interesting note: "Putant enim multi aliquid esse nihil, quod S. Augustinus refellit" (sig. O1). In fact, Augustine discusses the question at least three times: see *In Iohannis evangelium tractatus* 1.13.1-11, *Corpus Christianorum. Series Latina* (Turnholti, 1954–), 36:7; *De natura boni liber* 25, *Corpus scriptorum ecclesiasticorum latinorum* (Vindoboniae, 1866–), 25/2:866–67; and *Contra secundam Iuliani responsionem imperfectum opus*, 5.31–42, *Patrologiae Cursus Completus: Series Latina*, ed. J.-P. Migne, 221 vols. (Paris, 1884–1903), 45:1469–79. The question seems like a quibble, but some important issues derive from it, especially in the third passage from Augustine. This is a good example of how von Moltke's commentary can provide the traditional theological context which Browne often presumes in his search for paradoxes and coruscations.

an essence" uses Latinate diction derived from scholastic philosophy to boggle the mind.[46] To Latin ears "Nullitas" and "omneitas" are also odd but they are not so striking and initially puzzling as the English.

Let me conclude with an enlightening anecdote from Isaac Walton's life of Hooker. When Cardinal Allen and Thomas Stapleton praised Hooker's *Polity* to Pope Clement VIII, the pope desired

> that Doctor *Stapleton* should bring the said four Books, and looking on the English read a part of them to him in Latin; which Doctor *Stapleton* did, to the end of the first Book; at the conclusion of which, the Pope Spake to this purpose; *There is no Learning that this man hath not searcht into. . . . his Books will get reverence by Age, for there is in them such seeds of Eternity, that if the rest be like this, they shall last till the last fire shall consume all Learning.*[47]

Such an extemporaneous translation, even in an age when Latin was a spoken language, was an extraordinary feat, but it was rendered easier by the affinity of Hooker's English with its Latin forebears. But to imagine doing the same for the baroque style of Sir Thomas Browne does indeed boggle the mind, and the two Latin translations that were actually written tend to show us why this is so.

Saint Louis University

---

[46] "Informed" is also a technical term here, derived from Aristotelian form and matter. The combination of form and matter produces an individual essence.

[47] Isaac Walton, *The Lives of John Donne, Sir Henry Wotton, Richard Hooker, George Herbert, and Robert Sanderson*, intro. by George Saintsbury (London, New York, Toronto, 1927; repr. 1962), 212.

Les confins occidentaux du monde gréco-romain: Les diverses fortunes d'une représentation antique à la Renaissance et au XVIIe siècle

MONIQUE MUND-DOPCHIE

Introduction

> L'Asie, où la hauteur des rois s'épanouit,
> A ce contentement que l'univers est sombre;
> Ici la Cimmérie, au delà la Northumbre,
> Au delà l'âpre hiver, l'horreur, les glaciers nus,
> Et les monts ignorés sous les cieux inconnus;
> Après l'inhabitable on voit l'infranchissable;
> La neige fait au Nord ce qu'au Sud fait le sable;
> Le Caucase est hideux, les Dofrines font peur;
> Au loin râle, en des mers d'où l'hirondelle émigre,
> Thulé sous son volcan comme un daim sous un tigre;
> Au pôle, où du corbeau l'orfraie entend l'appel,
> Les cent têtes d'Orcus font un blême archipel,
> Et, pareils au chaos, les océans funèbres
> Roulent cette nuit, l'eau, sous ces flots, les ténèbres[1].

J'ai voyagé pendant des siècles d'un bout à l'autre du monde habité par les hommes jusqu'à l'Orient lointain et je suis revenu par le Septentrion. J'ai visité l'Hyperborée, et le blanc royaume de Thulé avant que les glaces ne l'engloutissent . . . J'ai connu l'Atlantide et les mages de Saturne qui ont su orienter les champs de pierres levées de Stonehenge et de Carnac en Petite-Bretagne . . .[2].

---

[1] V. Hugo, "Les Trois cents. I. L'Asie", *La légende des siècles* (1e éd. 1859), texte établi et annoté par J. Truchet (Paris, 1967), 70.

[2] P. Cothias–M. Rouge, *Les héros cavaliers. T.1. Perd-Cheval* (Grenoble, 1987), 36, case n°7.

Si j'ai choisi d'ouvrir mon exposé par ces deux textes à l'écriture contrastée, un poème tiré de La légende des siècles de Victor Hugo (1859), un phylactère d'une bande dessinée parue en 1987, c'est parce qu'ils me paraissent attester de façon exemplaire la pertinence culturelle et la richesse de toponymes renvoyant à ce qui était, pour les Anciens, les confins occidentaux du monde[3]. La Cimmérie, l'Hyperborée, la blanche Thulé, l'Atlantide sont incontestablement des noms qui "flattent l'oreille et l'imagination par le simple jeu de leurs sonorités"[4], mais ils ne sont pas uniquement cela, comme je m'efforcerai de le démontrer. Je me propose, en effet, de cerner les mécanismes conscients et inconscients qui ont assuré, à travers le recours à de tels vocables, la perpétuation de représentations antiques de l'espace, alors même que le savoir géographique a évolué. Ne pouvant dans le laps de temps qui m'est imparti retracer les différents épisodes de la survie de l'Extrême-Occident gréco-romain, je me contenterai d'envisager celle-ci dans les écrits de la Renaissance, qui a connu à la fois un retour en force de la Grèce et de Rome et la découverte de nouveaux mondes; et j'étendrai mes investigations au XVIIe siècle, qui en a assuré le prolongement[5]. Mais avant d'instaurer ce dialogue entre la vision antique du monde et celle de l'ère des Découvreurs, il importe de préciser comment les Anciens percevaient les marges de leur oecoumène. C'est ce que j'entreprendrai en premier lieu.

1. Les confins occidentaux du monde gréco-romain

(1)1. *Le mythe*

La première vision du monde qui s'imposa aux Hellènes a été forgée par le mythe. Celui-ci a posé d'emblée un ensemble de terres et de mers intérieures circonscrit par un vaste fleuve Océan, dont les eaux, dotées d'un mouvement perpétuel, reviennent à leur point de départ au terme d'un parcours circulaire. Les descriptions du bouclier d'Achille dans l'*Iliade* et de celui d'Héraclès dans le *Bouclier* pseudo-hésiodique ne laissent planer aucun doute à cet égard:

> Il y met la force puissante du fleuve-Océan, à l'extrême bord du bouclier solide.

> Enfin, le long du rebord circulaire roulait l'Océan—on eût dit un fleuve coulant à pleins bords—et il entourait tout entier l'écu aux mille ciselures[6].

Précisons tout de suite que le choix de l'Océan comme limite du monde est loin d'être neutre du point de vue symbolique. En premier lieu, celui-ci possède éminemment toutes les qualités attribuées à l'eau par la pensée mythique, à savoir un pouvoir

---

[3] Cf. Ch. Jacob, "Littérature et géographie en Grèce ancienne", in *Descriptions et créations d'espaces dans la littérature*, éd. E. Leonardy et H. Roland (Louvain-la-Neuve, 1995), 11–29 (p. 22).

[4] R. Baudry, "De l'exotisme au merveilleux", in *Exotisme et création. Actes du Colloque international (Lyon, 1993)* (Lyon, 1995), 331–344 (p. 335).

[5] Si cette synthèse m'est personnelle, elle a été alimentée par la lecture de nombreux livres et articles qui recoupent mes propres recherches. Étant donné les limites qui m'ont été imparties, je me contenterai de mentionner ici ceux qui ont appuyé directement cet exposé.

[6] *Il.* 18. 606–607; Hésiode *Sc.* 314–315 (trad. P. Mazon).

fécondant et cathartique[7]. Est-il besoin de rappeler que le soleil, par exemple, y plonge chaque soir, avec son char et son attelage, pour en ressortir reposé et purifié[8]? Mais l'infinitude de l'Océan le rend en même temps redoutable et difficilement accessible. Les Anciens et bon nombre d'humains après eux ont dès lors proclamé leur aversion pour l'étendue de la mer, investie par la peur: "Quelle folie de se confier à la mer", dit un personnage du Colloque érasmien *Naufragium*[9]. En second lieu, par sa masse d'eau confuse et désordonnée, l'Océan "constitue la relique de cette substance primordiale indifférenciée, qui avait besoin, pour devenir nature créée, de se voir imposer une forme"[10]; il évoque ce que les Grecs appelaient *Chaos* et *Apeiron*. Il incarne dès lors sans surprise le règne de l'inachevé et symbolise le désordre antérieur à la civilisation[11]. Or cette période est, selon la pensée grecque, caractérisée par l'ambivalence: elle a connu, en effet, et la prolifération de monstres, produits par une nature à l'exubérance anarchique, et l'état le plus heureux de l'humanité, celui de la race d'or—improprement désignée par la suite sous le vocable "âge d'or"—laquelle jouissait d'un bonheur parfait dans un cadre idyllique et ne se distinguait des dieux que par sa condition mortelle.

Par ailleurs, le cours occidental du fleuve Océan bénéficie d'un surcroît de richesse symbolique par rapport au reste de sa trajectoire. Car l'espace où le soleil se couche a été de tout temps perçu comme un espace de mort et d'au-delà; dans cette perspective, la navigation se transforme tout naturellement en un passage dangereux et initiatique. Les Grecs et les Celtes ont été particulièrement sensibles à cette dimension du Ponant[12]. Ils ont également opposé le Sud-Est, pays de la vie et de la lumière forte, et le Nord-Ouest, pays de la brume et de la lumière tamisée; ils se ménagent ainsi la possibilité d'avoir dans le second des séjours des morts fort différenciés, selon qu'ils privilégient la douce lumière du printemps ou la pénombre de l'automne[13].

Comme on pouvait s'y attendre, ce riche réseau de symboles a immanquablement influencé la perception hellène des contrées riveraines du fleuve Océan situées sur la terre connue, des îles océanes et même de la mystérieuse seconde rive, sur lequel le mythe n'apporte guère d'information et qui interférera par la suite avec la question des antipodes. Il n'est donc pas surprenant que les Grecs aient installé dans une périphérie marquée par la ressemblance des extrêmes—je me limiterai ici à son aire occidentale—des dieux et des monstres primordiaux: les Hespérides et leur dragon[14],

---

[7] Comme d'ailleurs à n'importe quelle eau, cf. J. Rudhardt, *Le thème de l'eau primordiale dans la mythologie grecque* (Berne, 1971), 83–89, 116–123.

[8] *Il.* 5. 5–6; *H. Soleil* 16; Eschyle frag. 192 N.

[9] Cf. J. Delumeau, *La peur en Occident (XIVe–XVIIIe siècle)* (Paris, 1978), 49.

[10] A. Corbin, *Le territoire du vide. L'Occident et le désir du rivage (1750–1840)* (Paris, 1988), 12.

[11] Corbin, *Le territoire du vide*, 12.

[12] Cf. S. Lewuillon, "Polémique et méthodes à propos d'une question historique: pour des 'îles Cassitérides'", *Dialogues d'Histoire Ancienne* 6 (1980): 235–266 (pp. 256–257, n.79).

[13] Sur cette vision des pays du Couchant, voir notamment A. Ballabriga, *Le Soleil et le Tartare. L'image mythique du monde en Grèce archaïque* (Paris, 1986); P. Fabre, "Les Grecs et la connaissance de l'Occident". Thèse présentée devant l'Université de Paris I le 20 juin 1977 (Lille, 1981).

[14] Cf. Hésiode *Th.* 215–216; Phérécyde frag. 33 (FHG,I); Euripide *Hipp.* 742.

les Gorgones[15], Atlas[16], Géryon aux trois têtes[17]. On y rencontre également, au-delà de Borée, un peuple heureux, oublié de l'histoire, les Hyperboréens, qui échappent aux misères de la vie normale—maladies et vieillesse—et consacrent leur vie à des activités ludiques[18]. On y découvre enfin des pays de l'au-delà: les Champs Élysées[19], les îles des Bienheureux[20], l'Enfer des Ombres avec son avant-poste tenu par les Cimmériens[21]. À l'ambivalence des habitants—aimables ou maléfiques—de l'Extrême-Occident correspond l'ambivalence des lieux. Le séjour des dieux, celui des Hyperboréens, les Champs Élysées et les îles des Bienheureux sont, en effet, organisés par une mère nature généreuse, qui maintient pour leurs occupants les délices de l'âge d'or:

> La plus douce vie est offerte aux humains, [...] sans neige, sans grand hiver, toujours sans pluie, on ne sent que zéphyrs, dont les risées sifflantes montent de l'Océan pour rafraîchir les hommes'[22].
>
> Le sol fécond porte trois fois l'an une florissante et douce récolte[23].
>
> Là, l'île des Bienheureux est rafraîchie par les brises océanes: là resplendissent des fleurs d'or, les unes sur la terre, aux rameaux d'arbres magnifiques, d'autres, nourries par les eaux[24].
>
> Des prairies fleuries de roses pourpres sont le faubourg de leur cité: l'arbre à encens l'ombrage, et des fruits d'or y font plier les rameaux [...]. Dans ce lieu aimable se répand sans cesse l'odeur des parfums de toute espèce[25].

En revanche, celui des Ombres et des Cimmériens apparaît lugubre et désolé:

> Nous atteignons la frontière et les courants profonds de l'Océan, où les Kimmériens ont leurs pays et ville. Ce peuple vit couvert de nuées et de brumes que jamais n'ont percées les rayons du Soleil, ni durant sa montée vers les astres du ciel, ni quand, du firmament, il revient à la terre; sur ces infortunés, pèse une nuit de mort[26].

La périphérie occidentale a donc bien exploité les virtualités de sa position géographique, puisqu'elle est à certains endroits—les plus nombreux—le pays de l'éternel printemps et à d'autres, celui de l'automne frileux et mélancolique.

---

[15] *Hésiode Th.* 274–279.
[16] Hésiode *Th.* 517–519.
[17] *Hésiode Th.* 287–294.
[18] Pindare *Py.* 10. 46–68; *Ol.* 3. 55–56.
[19] *Od.* 4. 565–568 (trad. V. Bérard).
[20] Hésiode *Op.* 166–173; Pindare, *Ol.* 2. 123–144.
[21] *Od.* 10. 508–512 et 11. 13–22.
[22] *Od.* 4. 565–568 (trad. V. Bérard).
[23] Hésiode *Op.* 173 (trad. P. Mazon).
[24] Pindare *Ol.* 2. 103–144 (trad. A. Puech).
[25] Pindare *Thrènes*, frag. 1 (trad. A. Puech).
[26] *Od.* 11. 13–19 (trad. V. Bérard).

(1)2. Mythe, géographie et fiction

Cet ensemble de représentations mythiques a profondément marqué, d'une part, les géographes—faute de documentation, nous ne pouvons, hélas, retrouver la fraîcheur des premières visions des explorateurs antiques—d'autre part, les poètes, les magiciens de la prose et les auteurs de fictions.

(1)2.1. Les géographes

Convaincus que les mythes comportent un noyau de vérité historique, dissimulé sous une gangue de merveilleux[27], les premiers ont tenté de concilier l'image du monde transmise par ceux-ci et l'expérience, ou plutôt le compte rendu de l'expérience des confins réels. Dès le VIe siècle a.C., ils transforment, d'après les informations véhiculées par des voyageurs phéniciens, carthaginois et grecs, le fleuve Océan en une continuité de mers reliées les unes aux autres, dont les eaux délimitent les trois continents, toujours conçus comme une grande île. L'insularité de l'ensemble constitué par l'Europe, l'Asie et l'Afrique devient un postulat de la géographie descriptive, dont la validité sera rarement contestée.

De même, ils s'efforcent régulièrement de situer les marges mythiques sur une carte, voire de les identifier à des lieux connus sous une autre dénomination. Dès le Ve siècle se manifeste ainsi le désir de donner aux errances d'Ulysse un cadre géographique dans le contexte méditerranéen ou sur l'Océan; ce type de quête se poursuit d'ailleurs de nos jours. En ce qui concerne les confins occidentaux de l'oecoumène, nous voyons notamment Pline l'Ancien appeler "Gorgades", c'est-à-dire "pays des Gorgones" et "îles Hespérides" des archipels situés au large de la côte occidentale de l'Afrique, dont l'existence lui a été révélée par le roi Juba Ier de Maurétanie:

> Face au promontoire de la Corne du Couchant se trouve, dit-on, les îles Gorgades, où séjournèrent autrefois les Gorgones, distantes du continent de deux jours de navigation, comme le rapporte Xénophon de Lampsaque. Hannon, le chef des Carthaginois, s'y rendit et raconta que les corps des femmes étaient velus et que les homme s'étaient échappés grâce à leur agilité; il plaça les peaux de deux Gorgones, comme preuve de l'historicité du fait et de son caractère merveilleux, dans le temple de Junon où on put les voir jusqu'à la prise de Carthage. Au delà des Gorgades se trouvent encore deux îles Hespérides. Tout ce qui a trait à ces régions est à ce point incertain que Stace Sebosus a rapporté qu'il fallait 40 jours de navigation pour se rendre des îles Gorgades jusqu'aux îles Hespérides après avoir doublé l'Atlas[28].

Strabon, de son côté, installe les Champs Élysées dans le Sud de l'Espagne, dont le climat idyllique correspond aux évocations d'Homère, et les îles des Bienheureux au large du Maroc, conformément au témoignage de Juba Ier:

---

[27] Cf. à ce sujet P. Veyne, *Les Grecs ont-ils crus à leurs mythes? Essai sur l'imagination constituante* (Paris, 1983), 27 et 143 (n.25).

[28] Pline *H.N.* 6. xxxvi. 198–201.

Homère, donc, ayant eu connaissance de toutes les expéditions guerrières qui avaient atteint les dernières terres de l'Ibérie, apprit aussi les richesses de celles-ci et leurs autres vertus—les Phéniciens en apportaient la révélation—et conçut l'idée d'y placer par fiction le séjour des âmes pieuses et ces Champs Élysées où Protée prédit qu'un jour s'établira Ménélas: [. . .]. La pureté de l'air et la douceur des souffles du zéphyr sont, en effet, les traits caractéristiques de cette contrée, puisqu'elle se trouve à l'occident et que le climat y est tiède. Et il est exact aussi qu'elle est située aux confins de la terre, où nous disons que la mythologie a placé l'Hadès [. . .] Quant aux poètes postérieurs, ils multiplient à l'envi les récits analogues, décrivant les expéditions faites pour conquérir les troupeaux de Géryon et les pommes du jardin des Hespérides, les fameuses "pommes d'or", et nommant Îles des Bienheureux certaines îles dont nous savons qu'elles se voient aujourd'hui encore non loin de l'extrémité de la Maurusie qui fait face à Gadéira[29].

Enfin, les géographes contribuent, dans leur grande majorité, à "mythifier" les confins découverts par les explorateurs et parcourus par les marchands, à métamorphoser ceux-ci en horizons oniriques, tels qu'ils sont imaginés par un public nourri de mythes dès la plus tendre enfance. Ils utilisent à cette fin divers mécanismes et techniques d'écriture, que Strabon a remarquablement mis en évidence et critiqués[30]. Ne pouvant, une fois encore, analyser ici leur démarche dans le détail, je me contenterai d'énumérer les procédés récurrents qui sont mis en oeuvre: recours aux mythes et aux prodiges autochtones, surtout s'ils recoupent des mythes et des prodiges gréco-romains; transfert de certains traits légendaires d'une marge à une autre, en vertu de leur situation commune aux abords de l'Océan; utilisation de métaphores pour évoquer aux riverains de la Méditerranée ce qui n'existe pas chez eux et pour quoi aucun mot n'existe[31]; amplification, grâce à différentes techniques d'écriture, des richesses et des périls bien réels rencontrés à la périphérie de la terre. D'une masse de documents sur l'Extrême-Occident, je retiendrai deux textes de Strabon particulièrement éclairants pour mon propos. Le premier concerne l'environnement de Thulé décrit par Pythéas de Marseille, son découvreur:

> Pythéas [. . .] a induit en erreur tant de monde [. . .] en débitant tant de fables sur Thulé et ces régions où l'on ne trouve plus ni terre proprement dite ni mer ni air, mais une matière composée de ces divers éléments, qui ressemble fort à la méduse (πλεύμονι θαλαττίωι) et dans laquelle, à ce qu'il dit, la terre, la mer et tous les éléments restent en suspension: c'est une espèce de gangue qui tient toutes choses ensemble et sur quoi l'on ne peut ni cheminer ni naviguer.

---

[29] Strabon 3. 2. 13.

[30] Strabon 1. 2. 35; 15. 1. 28.

[31] Cf. J.-N. Robert, *De Rome à la Chine. Sur les Routes de la Soie au temps des Césars* (Paris, 1993), 39.

En fait, cette matière semblable à la méduse, il l'aurait vue de ses yeux; le reste, il n'en parlerait que par ouï-dire. C'est là ce que raconte Pythéas[32].

Quelle que soit la réalité sous-jacente, *fog*, aurore boréale, banquise, plat pays où le sable des rivages se confond avec le gris de la mer et la brume du ciel, les Anciens devaient immanquablement songer à l'indifférencié originel d'Hésiode et d'Anaximandre; c'est pourquoi ils ont transformé Thulé en une terre primordiale, puisqu'elle était cise dans l'Océan primordial, dont elle reproduisait les caractéristiques.

Le second texte, fondé sur le témoignage de Posidonius d'Apamée, décrit, quant à lui, les grandes richesses vivrières et minérales du Sud de l'Espagne à travers différentes facettes de l'hyperbole: utilisation du comparatif de supériorité et du superlatif; vocabulaire de la bonne qualité, de la diversité et de l'abondance; énumération continue; affirmation d'une impossibilité de décrire etc. Il transforme de la sorte cette région en une caverne d'Ali Baba:

L'Ibérie n'est pas tout entière aussi fertile ni aussi favorisée que la Turdétanie, surtout là où les mines sont nombreuses. Il est rare, en effet, qu'un pays tire sa prospérité simultanément de ces deux sortes de ressources. Il est rare aussi qu'un même pays dispose en abondance sur un territoire restreint de mines renfermant différentes espèces de métaux. Or qui voudrait vanter sur ce point la supériorité de la Turdétanie et des contrées avoisinantes ne saurait trouver un langage qui y suffise. En aucun lieu de la terre on n'a pu voir jusqu'à présent ni l'or, ni l'argent, ni le cuivre, ni le fer être produits en quantités si grandes et avec une telle qualité[33].

(1)2.2. Les poètes et les prosateurs poétiques

Se tenant à l'écart de la démarche géographique, les poètes et les promoteurs d'une prose poétique ont, de leur côté, fabriqué à profusion des métaphores à partir des noms que leur fournissaient les mythes de l'Extrême-Occident et des toponymes désignant des pays lointains, mal connus et par conséquent auréolés de mystère. Ils instaurent de cette façon un code subtil, qui embellit le langage et fournit aux lettrés le plaisir d'une culture partagée. Peu leur importe, dans cette optique, la vérité ou l'évanescence de la réalité dénommée; il suffit que les noms charrient dans leur sillage des réminiscences de récits, de descriptions, de connotations symboliques. Tel est le sens de l'expression forgée par Virgile et appelée à une fortune considérable:

Ou bien César, deviendras-tu dieu de la mer immense? est-ce que les marins révéreront ta seule divinité? est-ce que Thulé, la plus lointaine des terres, te sera soumise (*tibi serviat ultima Thule*)?[34]

L'île du bout du monde, dernière terre du monde connu, visitée par le seul Pythéas,

---

[32] Strabon 2. 4. 1 (trad. G. Aujac).
[33] Strabon 3. 2. 8 (trad. F. Lasserre).
[34] Virgile *Géorg.* 1. 29–30 (trad. E. de Saint-Denis).

marque le point ultime jusqu'où s'étend la renommée de César, parce qu'il est impossible d'aller plus loin.

(1)2.3. *Les auteurs de fictions*

Enfin, des auteurs de fictions—penseurs utopistes et romanciers—ont installé sur les rives de l'Océan ou en son milieu des lieux qui brouillent les catégories du mythe et de la réalité. Contrairement à la première, ceux-ci ne véhiculent pas une tradition anonyme et multiséculaire, contrairement à la seconde, ils servent des buts qui n'ont rien de géographique. Mais ils empruntent suffisamment d'éléments aux confins mythiques et réels pour pouvoir être insérés à leur tour parmi les terres baignées par un océan que définit un double éloignement propice à ces nouveaux genres littéraires: l'éloignement dans l'espace, puisqu'il constitue la borne de la terre, l'éloignement dans le temps, puisqu'il conserve les caractéristiques de l'ère primordiale.

Ces contrées nouvelles ou réinterprétées de façon nouvelle abritent ainsi les sociétés que des penseurs épris de réformes décrivent à leurs contemporains comme des modèles ou des repoussoirs. Tel est le sens du récit platonicien de l'Atlantide, qui oppose une Atlantide industrieuse et maritime, trop ouverte sur l'extérieur pour ne pas être contaminée par ces contacts—telle est l'Athènes du IVe siècle—face à une Athènes ancestrale, terrienne, autarcique, austère, qui a manifestement les faveurs du philosophe[35]. D'autres terres abritent des sociétés idéales ou caricaturales: je songe en particulier à la Méropie de Théopompe de Chios[36], localisée dans l'antipode, ou encore à l'archipel d'Ogygie, habité par Cronos et une cour de sages, à cinq jours de navigation de l'Ouest de la Grande-Bretagne selon les estimations proposées par Plutarque dans son traité De la face visible de la lune[37].

La périphérie sert également d'espace pour des récits de voyages extraordinaires, qui prolifèrent à partir de la période alexandrine; merveilles et rencontres cauchemardesques s'y déploient à une cadence accélérée. De cette énorme littérature paradoxographique ne nous sont malheureusement parvenus que des jugements critiques sur ses invraisemblances, dont le roman pastiche de Lucien, *L'Histoire vraie*, des catalogues de prodiges et un résumé, dû au patriarche Photios (IXe siècle), du roman *Les merveilles au-delà de Thulé*, composé avant le IIIe siècle de notre ère par Antoine Diogène. Un couple d'amoureux y affronte, nous dit-on, lors de séjours dans des pays riverains de l'Océan, une série d'aventures rocambolesques, parmi lesquelles figure la découverte des étrangetés du Nord-Ouest:

> C'est dans cette course que Dinias vit les merveilles incroyables qui se passent au-delà de Thulé et qu'il est censé raconter maintenant à Cymbas. Il dit avoir vu ce que les astronomes enseignent, par exemple qu'il est possible que quelques habitants vivent sous le pôle arctique, qu'il y règne une nuit d'un mois avec de plus courtes et de plus longues, une nuit de six mois et, ce qui est plus extraordinaire, une nuit d'un an; que ce n'est pas seulement la nuit qui atteint

---

[35] Platon *Timée* 23d–25d et *Critias*.
[36] Élien *Histoires diverses* 3. 18.
[37] Plutarque "De la face visible de la lune" *Moralia* 941.

une pareille durée, mais que le jour connaît un phénomène analogue. Il prétend avoir vu d'autres étrangetés du même genre et il fait un récit extraordinaire sur des hommes et sur certaines merveilles d'autre sorte qu'il aurait vues et que personne, dit-il, n'aurait pu voir ni entendre raconter ni même imaginer[38].

Signalons en passant que la prolifération de lieux utopiques et romanesques à côté des confins mythiques et des confins réels a fini par poser aux anciens un véritable problème épistémologique. Puisque tous ces pays sont présentés comme véridiques par le mythe, par les voyageurs et les géographes, par les auteurs de fictions, puisque, d'autre part, l'Océan lui-même demeure hors d'atteinte et conserve jalousement ses secrets, il est impossible de vérifier l'exactitude des informations circulant à leur propos. Les seules réponses qui ont été trouvées pour résoudre cette aporie ont consisté dès lors à établir l'honnêteté et la fiabilité du témoin, ainsi que s'y est employé Strabon à propos d'Homère, ou à rejeter, à l'instar d'Ératosthène, comme pure affabulation, tout ce qui a trait aux confins, l'épithète "océanique" devenant en l'occurrence synonyme de "mensonger".

2. Fortunes de la représentation de l'Extrême-Occident à la Renaissance et au XVIIe siècle

L'héritage antique tel qu'il est parvenu jusqu'à nous comporte donc, en ce qui concerne l'Extrême-Occident, des mythes et des textes qui attestent diverses utilisations de ceux-ci: interprétations rationalisantes, adaptation du rêve à la réalité et vice versa, élaboration d'un langage fleuri, *mimésis* mise en oeuvre dans des fictions littéraires. Il ne fut cependant pas immédiatement accessible dans sa totalité. Les érudits du Moyen Âge ne disposèrent, en effet, que d'une partie des données relatives au Ponant. Il est vrai qu'ils pallièrent à cette lacune en intégrant dans leur horizon culturel des nouvelles légendes, telles que le voyage de saint Brandan et le peuplement de l'île des Sept Cités. En revanche, les humanistes et l'ensemble des lettrés de la Renaissance redécouvrirent et assimilèrent rapidement la quasi intégralité des écrits rescapés du naufrage de la civilisation gréco-romaine, sans renier pour autant l'apport médiéval. Or le monde atlantique qui leur était révélé par leurs lectures savantes était aussi celui que parcouraient leurs Découvreurs. Dans quelle mesure parvinrent-ils à concilier leurs références classiques et la nouveauté des espaces explorés? Telle est la question à laquelle je m'efforcerai de répondre dans la seconde partie de mon exposé.

(2)1. Usages littéraires de la représentation gréco-romaine

La littérature fut par excellence le domaine où se manifesta la permanence des schémas antiques, qu'il s'agisse du recours aux métaphores, de créations romanesques ou d'utopies.

On observe, en effet, sans surprise que prosateurs et poètes continuent à employer les toponymes des confins mythiques et géographiques du monde gréco-romain, comme si ce dernier était immuable et n'offrait aucune prise à l'actualité. On peut

---

[38] Antoine Diogène ap. Phot. cod. 166. 110b–111a (trad. R. Henry).

être tenté d'expliquer cette inertie par la progression extrêmement lente de la connaissance des explorations dans les milieux qui n'étaient pas directement concernés par elles, mais l'argument est loin d'être convaincant. Il convient plutôt de mettre en avant le souci de revenir au latin classique, largement répandu à la Renaissance, et celui d'enrichir les langues vernaculaires par des emprunts aux langues anciennes. Les métaphores qui sont ainsi réutilisées n'ont certes plus l'aura de sacralité issue du mythe ou le pouvoir évocateur d'un toponyme renvoyant à une terre mystérieuse, parce que inexplorée; en revanche, elles bénéficient du prestige attaché à un modèle incontournable et créent une complicité entre ceux qu'une érudition partagée réunit. Telle est la perspective dans laquelle s'inscrivent les mentions de Thulé dans une lettre de Gaspard Schalbe adressée à Érasme le 28 mai 1519 et dans le Tombeau de Joachim du Bellay composé par Jacques de la Taille en 1573:

> Nos sentiments étaient si forts, qu'en cours de route, toujours incertains de l'endroit où, toi, la perle unique du monde chrétien, tu pouvais bien te cacher, nous nous sommes solennellement juré d'aller te quérir fût-ce au fond des Indes, voire dans l'île la plus reculée: Thulé (ultima Thule). À plus forte raison donc en Brabant ou en France[39].

> Aussi delà la mer dont la terre est enclose,
> Voire de l'isle Thule, on viendra pour certain
> Voir quelque jour la tombe où Du Bellay repose[40].

Si elles conservent la belle sonorité du nom, ces références à l'île-borne, qui symbolisent le bout du monde, sont devenues obsolètes à une époque où l'on sait que la terre est ronde et que l'Amérique fait obstacle à ceux qui prétendent rejoindre l'Asie par l'Ouest.

Les romanciers, de leur côté, ne sont pas insensibles au charme suranné de l'Extrême-Occident antique. Le Tasse recommandait aux auteurs de récits d'aventures et aux créateurs de personnages exemplaires de situer l'action dans des contrées inconnues, dont les caractéristiques seraient de ce fait difficilement vérifiables. Cervantès, comme d'autres écrivains d'ailleurs, s'en est souvenu lorsqu'il a construit son roman *Persiles y Sigismunda* sur le modèle fourni par les *Éthiopiques* d'Héliodore. Tandis que les héros du roman grec effectuaient un voyage initiatique qui les menait du Nord au Sud depuis Delphes jusqu'en Éthiopie, Persilès et Sigismunda poursuivent une quête identique dans la même direction; mais ils partent cette fois en pèlerinage à Rome depuis l'Extrême-Nord. Car Persilès est originaire de Thulé et Sigismunda, de Frisland, une île septentrionale, que personne n'a vue, mais dont tous ont entendu parler depuis qu'Antonio Zeno en a publié une description en 1558. Thulé se voit dès lors brièvement évoquée en des termes que Pythéas aurait sans aucun doute jugé étranges, lui qui avait jugé bien frugale la vie des insulaires:

---

[39] *La Correspondance d'Érasme. Traduite en annotée d'après le texte latin de l'Opus epistolarum de P. S. Allen, H. M. Allen, et H. W. Garrod. Volume III: 1517–1519.* Par A. Gerlo, avec la collab. de C. Backvis, M. Delcourt, G. Schwers et H. Vannerom (Bruxelles, 1975), 621–622 (lettre 977).

[40] J. de la Taille, *Alexandre* (1573), éd. C. N. Smith (Exeter, 1975), 46.

Ie t'ay dit aussi qu'en la derniere partie de Norvegue, quasi au dessous du Pole Artique, est l'isle qu'on tient pour estre la derniere du monde de ce costé-là, dont le nom est Tile; Virgile l'appelle Tule en ces vers:

'. . . ac tua nautae

Numina sola colant, tibi seruiat ultima Thule'.

Cest Isle est aussi grande, ou peu moins que l'Angleterre, riche et abondante de toutes les choses necessaires pour la vie humaine[41].

Quant aux promoteurs d'utopies, ils furent nombreux au XVIe et au XVIIe siècle à décrire des pays sortis de leur imagination. Mais certains d'entre eux préférèrent ressusciter des terres vantées par les Anciens. Fénelon, par exemple, s'est souvenu des éloges adressés au Sud de l'Espagne. Sa Bétique, dont Strabon vantait autrefois les richesses vivrières et minérales ainsi que la population dotée d'une remarquable longévité, devient sous sa plume une enclave de l'âge d'or, où un peuple heureux et pur mène la vie idyllique des Hyperboréens mâtinée d'emprunts à l'*Utopie* de Thomas More. Qu'on en juge par les extraits que voici:

Le fleuve Bétis coule dans un pays fertile, et sous un ciel doux, qui est toujours serein. Le pays a pris le nom du fleuve [. . .]. Ce pays semble avoir conservé les délices de l'âge d'or. Les hivers y sont tièdes, et les rigoureux aquilons n'y soufflent jamais. L'ardeur de l'été y est toujours tempérée par des zéphyrs rafraîchissants, qui viennent adoucir l'air vers le milieu du jour. Ainsi, toute l'année n'est qu'un heureux hymen du Printemps et de l'Automne, qui semblent se donner la main. La terre, dans les vallons et dans les campagnes unies, y porte chaque année une double moisson. Les chemins y sont bordés de lauriers, de grenadiers, de jasmins, et d'autres arbres toujours verts et toujours fleuris. Les montagnes sont couvertes de troupeaux qui fournissent des laines fines, recherchées de toutes les nations connues. Il y a plusieurs mines d'or et d'argent dans ce beau-pays; mais les habitants, simples et heureux dans leur simplicité, ne daignent pas seulement compter l'or et l'argent parmi leurs richesses; ils n'estiment que ce qui sert véritablement aux besoins de l'homme [. . .].

Jamais peuple ne fut si honnête, ni si jaloux de la pureté. Les femmes y sont belles et agréables, mais simples, modestes, et laborieuses. Les mariages y sont paisibles, féconds, sans tache. Le mari et la femme semblent n'être plus qu'une seule personne en deux corps différents. Le mari et la femme partagent ensemble tous les soins domestiques: le mari règle toutes les affaires du dehors, la femme se renferme dans son ménage: elle soulage son mari; elle paraît n'être faite que pour lui plaire; elle gagne sa confiance, et le charme moins par sa beauté que par sa vertu. Ce vrai charme de leur société dure autant que leur vie. La sobriété, la modération et les moeurs pures de ce peuple lui donnent

---

[41] [M. de Cervantes], *Les amours de Persiles et de Sigismonde. [. . .] Histoire septentrionale. Traduite par le sieur Daudiguier* (Paris, 1628), 597.

une vie longue et exempte de maladies. On y voit des vieillards de cent et de six-vingts ans, qui ont encore de la gaieté et de la vigueur[42].

Notons pour terminer ces investigations dans le domaine de la littérature, que l'usage métaphorique des toponymes des confins et le recours à des espaces ultimes comme cadre de récits fictifs survécurent largement à la Renaissance et au XVIIe siècle. Les textes par lesquels j'ai introduit cet exposé relèvent de la première démarche. De même, notre époque connaît une pléthore de romans atlantidéens et thuléens. Tant est forte l'efficacité symbolique de ces anciennes représentations.

(2)2. *Usages géographiques de la représentation gréco-romaine*

Confrontés aux contraintes de la réalité—offrir des cartes soigneusement tenues à jour aux pouvoirs politiques et économiques, faire le point sur l'état des connaissances—les auteurs d'atlas et les cosmographes de la Renaissance et du XVIIe siècle ne purent, à l'instar des simples lettrés, se contenter de faire revivre la géographie gréco-romaine. Certes, celle-ci constituait un préalable, qui ne se laissait pas facilement éliminer: est-il besoin de rappeler que la découverte de la *Géographie* de Ptolémée fut un événement déterminant sur le plan scientifique et que les premiers atlas mis en circulation furent les recueils des cartes ptoléméennes dessinées par Agathodémon[43]? Mais la science antique se révéla très vite obsolète, quand il fallut rendre compte des résultats des explorations portugaises et espagnoles. Parce qu'ils n'osaient ou n'imaginaient pas faire l'impasse sur l'apport des Anciens—il fallut attendre Mercator et Ortelius pour que les cartes ptoléméennes soient définitivement distinguées des cartes modernes—les géographes furent forcés, dans une certaine mesure et d'aucuns plus que d'autres, de trouver des accommodements entre l'héritage gréco-romain et l'actualité. La représentation traditionnelle de l'Extrême-Occident fut particulièrement touchée par ce problème, car elle englobait à la fois la côte Ouest de l'Afrique et les îles océanes de l'Atlantique abordées par les Découvreurs. Il en résulta plusieurs tentatives de conciliation.

(2)2.1. *Création d'un passé vénérable*

La géographie antique permit, en premier lieu, de forger un passé à des régions qui en semblaient dépourvues aux yeux des Européens. Le cas de l'Afrique est exemplaire à cet égard. On ne connaît de ce continent, qu'il s'agisse de la partie occupée par les populations blanches ou de la partie peuplée de Noirs, que son état présent, révélé par les explorateurs, par les marchands et, partiellement, par Jean Léon l'Africain, dont *La description de l'Afrique* a été publiée une première fois en 1550. C'est pourquoi le cosmographe français François de Belleforest—et il n'est pas le seul à le faire—consacre deux rubriques à l'Afrique: l'une qui retrace son passé à coup de références classiques, l'autre consacrée à son état présent, fondée sur des récits de voyages récents et sur le traité de Léon l'Africain.

---

[42] Fénelon, *Les aventures de Télémaque*, édition Garnier (Paris, s.d.), livre 8, 102–144.

[43] Sur cette influence majeure des cartes ptoléméennes, voir notamment les réflexions de Ch. Jacob, *L'empire des cartes. Approche théorique de la cartographie à travers l'histoire* (Paris, 1992), 90–92.

Même quand le passé était connu, il apparut intéressant de privilégier la période antique, soit pour intégrer une contrée dans la culture occidentale et en réduire l'altérité, si celle-ci est éloignée du centre, soit pour en établir l'ancienneté et la pourvoir en quelque sorte de glorieux ancêtres. Tel est manifestement le but poursuivi par Ortelius lorsqu'il retrace l'état ancien de Cadix, connue des Grecs et des Latins sous le nom de Tartessos:

> Strabon, Pline et quelques autres semblent comprendre sous les Gades deux isles. Mela, Solin, Denis, Ptolemée, n'en comprennent qu'une seulement, laquelle ils nomment Gadira, avec une ville de mesme nom. Ceux qui en font deux, appellent l'une la Grande, l'autre la Petite. Ceste ci fut iadis appellée Erythia, et Afrodisie, comme escrit Pline, apres Philistides, Timaeus et Silenus, et Strabon après Pherecydes, lesquels l'ont aussi nommée l'isle de Iuno. La grande a esté aussi appellée particulierement des habitans Erythia, et Cotinusa. Les Carthaginois l'appellerent Gadir, et les Romains Tartesson, comme dit Pline. Il n'y a auiourd'huy qu'une Isle (qui est fort amoindrie par les inondations de la mer Oceane) laquelle les Espaignols nomment Cadiz, et vicieusement Caliz, ceux de nostre pays l'appellent, ie ne sçay pourquoy, Calis malis. En la moindre des deux isles y a eu iadis une ville, en la grande Iulia Gaditana Augusta, laquelle au paravant s'appelloit Naples, comme il semble, par Strabon, elle retient auiourdhuy le nom de l'isle, à savoir Cadiz. C'est à present ville Episcopale[44].

(2)2.2. *Réutilisation des toponymes antiques*

En deuxième lieu, l'Extrême-Occident antique fournit aux cartographes et aux cosmographes de la Renaissance une série de toponymes et quelques éléments descriptifs qui furent intégrés dans les savoirs nouveaux et apprivoisèrent par ce moyen l'étrangeté du jamais vu et de l'inconnu subitement révélé. Plusieurs lieux reçurent ainsi une double dénomination: le nom indigène ou récent et le nom mythique ou mystérieux transmis par les Anciens. On voit, par exemple, Ortelius signaler que les Canaries s'appelaient autrefois îles Fortunées et les îles du Cap Vert, îles Gorgades ou Hespérides, ou encore identifier l'Islande à Thulé. De même, certaines singularités du monde atlantique, voire du monde Pacifique, furent authentifiées par des témoignages d'auteurs grecs et latins. Le commentaire de la carte de l'océan Pacifique dessinée par Ortelius est révélateur à cet égard. Car le géographe anversois y affirme que les témoignages de Francisco Ulloa et d'Antonio Pigafetta donnent raison à Aristote et à Pline, lorsque ces derniers signalaient l'existence de forêts flottantes dans l'Océan:

> Ceux qui ont escrit du nouveau monde, disent, que ceste mer [sc. Mer de Zur] est fort profonde vers les isles Malheureuses, et de la part du Peru abondante en pierreries [. . .]. François Ulloa et Antoine Pigafetta rapportent qu'au fond de ceste mer croist une herbe de quatorze ou quinze toises, laquelle sorte hors de l'eauë la hauteur de quatre ou cincq; ainsi qu'aucunefois il semble plustost estre

---

44 A. Ortelius, *Théâtre de l'univers* (Anvers, 1598), fol. 20.

en quelques belles champaignes et verdes praieries, que sur la mer. Ie pense que c'est ceste mer laquelle Pline [H.N., VI, 87] et Antigonus [§.147] ont laissé par escrit, a sçavoir, que la mer Orientale, ou Indiane, est remplie de forestz; et aussi Aristote *de Admirandis* [§.136], n'accorde point mal avec cecy, où il dit, que les Cartaginois qui demeuroient en l'isle de Calez Malez, apres avoir passé les columnes de Hercule, sont arrivez en quelques regions pleines de feuillu et mousse marines, lesquelles herbes estoient arrousees par les exhalations et enflemens de la mer[45].

Ce type de démarche sous-tend, du reste, d'autres motivations en rapport avec les curiosités de l'époque, le regard porté sur l'élargissement des connaissances et les débats suscités par l'émergence de mondes nouveaux.

Forts de l'accroissement de leurs connaissances des pays lointains, certains géographes s'estiment, en effet, habilités à trancher le problème épistémologique qui s'était posé aux Anciens. Car ils s'efforcent désormais de fonder la vérité des explorations antiques, non plus sur la fiabilité des témoins grecs et latins, mais sur l'expérience liée à de nouvelles explorations. C'est dans cette perspective—qui n'est d'ailleurs pas la seule, comme nous le verrons plus loin—qu'il convient de situer les nombreuses discussions sur l'emplacement de l'*ultima Thule*, identifiée à l'Islande, aux Feroë, à la Norvège, aux Shetland, pour ne parler que des thèses les plus régulièrement avancées. Ce n'est pas un hasard non plus si le débat sur l'existence de l'Atlantide s'engage à la Renaissance après des siècles de silence et si l'île évoquée par Platon est présentée comme une île engloutie dans un océan Atlantique ouvert à la navigation hauturière ou comme une partie importante de l'Amérique. Le questionnement antique se trouve de la sorte réanimé et chaque lettré caresse le rêve d'être, dans son domaine, un décrypteur de mystères, qui emporte la conviction[46].

Les références à l'Extrême-Occident gréco-romain doivent également être replacées dans la réflexion qui s'élabore sur les rapports que la Renaissance entretient avec l'Antiquité. Comme l'a très finement noté James Romm[47], certains intellectuels inscrivent leur histoire dans un schéma cyclique et conçoivent leur époque comme une "renaissance" de l'Antiquité; ils sont dès lors naturellement portés à établir des passerelles entre les Découvertes des Anciens et les leurs. D'autres, au contraire, revendiquent pour eux une époque radicalement nouvelle sur les plans historique, scientifique et religieux; ils se veulent indépendants de la tradition, même s'ils ne parviennent pas pour autant à s'en abstraire complètement, et affirment la radicale hétérogénéité des nouveaux mondes.

Enfin, les informations véhiculées sur la périphérie occidentale par les Anciens ont

---

[45] Ortelius, *Théâtre de l'univers*, fol. 6.

[46] Sur la réactualisation du questionnement antique, voir notamment P. Mason, "Classical Ethnography and Its Influence on the European Perception of the Peoples of the New World", in *The Classical Tradition and the Americas. Volume 1. Part 1*, éd. W. Haase et M. Reinhold (Berlin–New York, 1994), 156.

[47] J. Romm, "New World and "*novos orbes*": Seneca in the Renaissance Debate over Ancient Knowledge of the Americas", in *The Classical Tradition and the Americas*, 80.

fourni des arguments aux lettrés engagés dans les controverses que suscitent la colonisation des Amériques et le statut des Amérindiens.

Sans entrer dans le détail de ces polémiques qui ont déjà fait couler beaucoup d'encre, rappelons que le *titulus occupationis* en ce qui concerne l'Amérique fut âprement disputé, d'une part, entre les conquistadores et la Couronne espagnole, d'autre part, entre l'Espagne et divers États européens (France, Angleterre, Provinces-Unies, Suède etc.). Les mythes et les mystères de l'Extrême-Occident contribuèrent à fournir aux antagonistes des précédents qu'ils invoquèrent en leur propre faveur et qu'ils contestèrent à leurs adversaires. Pour ne citer qu'un seul exemple—sans approfondir, du reste, toutes ses implications—Oviedo, le chroniqueur officiel de Charles Quint, utilise, dans une ingénieuse combinaison aussitôt répandue par de nombreux lettrés, le témoignage de Pline l'Ancien et de Solin sur les Hespérides, pour établir, contre les conquistadores, les droits de la Couronne sur les Indes occidentales. Prenant appui sur la généalogie des rois espagnols fixée par le faussaire Annius de Viterbe, il met en relation le roi Hesperos, descendant de Japhet, fils de Noé, et les Hespérides, qui doivent être identifiées, selon lui, aux Antilles, situées effectivement à 40 jours de navigation des Gorgades et de l'Atlas. Pour contrer cette thèse, il ne reste plus qu'à produire des ancêtres encore plus vénérables qu'Hesperos, comme le fait Guillaume Postel au profit du roi de France, ou proposer d'autres localisations, plus orientales, pour les Hespérides, comme s'y emploient notamment Fernando Colomb et Gómara pour défendre, l'un, les intérêts de sa famille, l'autre, la cause de Cortez[48].

De même, la question du peuplement des Amériques interpelle de nombreux érudits. D'aucuns revendiquent pour les Indiens l'autochtonie, qui leur confère une radicale hétérogénéité. Il n'existe dès lors aucun précédent qui justifie leur assujetissement ou leur conversion. D'autres leur trouvent des ancêtres européens ou asiatiques, d'une provenance unique ou d'origines multiples. Par ce biais, ils permettent à des colonisateurs d'établir leur droit sur les Amérindiens ou à l'Église de les christianiser et de les traiter comme son troupeau exclusif. Encore faut-il prouver que des migrations ont effectivement eu lieu dans le passé entre l'Ancien Monde et le Nouveau. Certains lettrés envisagent un passage par voie de terre, à travers l'Extrême-Nord. Les Scythes et autres barbares du Septentrion auraient ainsi fait souche en Amérique, ce qui peut expliquer la sauvagerie et le cannibalisme de ses habitants. D'autres privilégient les traversées océaniques en avançant différentes hypothèses: ils vantent les navigations hauturières des Anciens en invoquant les prouesses d'Hannon, de Pythéas de Marseille et des marins phéniciens et carthaginois; ils attribuent à l'Atlantide, engloutie par la suite, le statut d'île-passerelle; ou encore ils parsèment l'océan Atlantique d'un chapelet d'îles réelles ou supposées, qui ont offert aux Anciens la possibilité d'un cabotage sans péril. C'est la fonction que le pasteur hollandais Abraham Vander Milius assigne à Thulé, au Groenland, aux îles révélées par Antonio Zeno, à l'Ogygie de Plutarque, pour expliquer, à une époque où les Provinces-Unies

---

[48] Cf. G. Gliozzi, *Adamo e il nuovo mondo. La nascita dell'antropologia come ideologia coloniale: dalle genealogie bibliche alle teorie razziali (1500–1700)* (Florence, 1976), 16–18.

affichent leurs prétentions colonisatrices à l'égard du Nouveau Monde[49], le peuplement de celui-ci par les Cimbres, ancêtres des Hollandais et des Flamands:

> Enfin, il est évident que depuis une époque reculée, nos hommes ont habité ces parties de notre monde qui sont les plus proches du monde occidental, soit par l'Ouest, soit par l'Est. Ce sont, en effet, les voies les plus commodes pour se rendre en Amérique. Du côté occidental de notre monde connu, ce sont les îles Islande, l'antique Thulé, et Frisland [...]. Et que par là existe un chemin qui va de chez nous chez les Indiens et inversement, cela, me semble-t-il, Plutarque l'a pressenti. Dans son traité De la face visible de la lune, il signale quelque chose qui, à ce que je crois, n'est pas sans s'y rapporter[50].

(2)2.3. *Grille de lecture fournie par la périphérie ambivalente*

Il ne me reste plus, pour terminer cette seconde partie de mon exposé, qu'à évoquer l'influence exercée sur l'approche ethnologique des hommes de la Renaissance par l'*imago mundi* des Anciens avec ses marges ambivalentes. Certes, l'opposition centre-périphérie, qu'elle soit radicale—moi et les autres—ou qu'elle progresse en cercles concentriques depuis le centre jusqu'au cercle ultime, au-delà duquel il n'y a plus d'humains, est largement, sinon universellement, répandue. On l'observe, en effet, aussi bien chez les Perses, selon Hérodote[51], que chez les Chinois[52]. Mais elle a revêtu à la Renaissance l'habillage antique. Comme l'a remarquablement observé Peter Mason[53], les voyageurs et les intellectuels en chambre de l'époque ont régulièrement adopté les critères de sauvagerie élaborés par les Anciens, qui consistent en un ensemble de négations: pratiques alimentaires aberrantes, absence d'un langage articulé, absence de villes et de villages, absence d'industrialisation, ignorance des pratiques de la vie urbaine (lois, rapports sociaux, culte, art, philosophie). De même, ils sont partis à la recherche des merveilles attestées dans la périphérie et ils les ont bien entendu trouvées en Amérique: Amazones repérées par Christophe Colomb, Hernan Cortes, Thevet, Walter Raleigh, Francesco de Orellana, cyclopes et cynocéphales révélés à Colomb par des interlocuteurs indiens, géants de Patagonie et d'ailleurs, acéphales évoqués par Walter Raleigh, etc.

Cet imaginaire des marges a servi assurément de refuge pour les premiers découvreurs, confrontés à une réalité difficile à appréhender, "qui essayaient, logiquement, de recourir à des motifs connus". "Il rassura et permit de donner les explications indispensables à des phénomènes déroutants, à des observations surprenantes"[54].

---

[49] Cf. Gliozzi, *Adamo e il nuovo mondo*, 16.

[50] A. Vander Milius, *Lingua Belgica* (Leyde, 1612), 106.

[51] Hérodote 1. 134.

[52] Cf. A. Peyrefitte, *L'empire immobile* (Paris, 1989), 30.

[53] Mason, "Classical Ethnography and Its Influence", 135–172.

[54] J.-P. Sanchez, "L'Europe du Ponant et la découverte du Nouveau Monde: le rôle de l'imaginaire", in *Dans le sillage de Colomb. L'Europe du Ponant et la découverte du Nouveau Monde (1450–1650). Actes du Colloque International Université Rennes 2, 5, 6 et 7 mai 1992*, sous la dir. de J.-P. Sanchez (Rennes, 1995), 259.

Mais il fut plus que cela. Il intervint également dans le vieux débat sur la frontière qui sépare l'homme de l'animal et sur l'éventuel déficit en caractères humains dévolu aux Indiens, en particulier aux anthropophages, qui incarnaient au XVIe siècle "l'Autre vraiment autre, celui qui se place à l'extrémité de l'altérité, au pied de ce qui est fuite au–delà de l'horizon, de ce qui a cessé d'être un autre, pour se dissoudre dans le néant"[55].

3. Conclusion

Au terme de ce parcours, il apparaît que plusieurs mécanismes entrecroisés expliquent la perpétuation à la Renaissance de l'*imago mundi* élaborée par les Anciens et que l'attitude des lettrés du XVIe siècle face à cette dernière présente d'intéressantes analogies avec celle que les Grecs et les Latins ont adoptée à l'égard de leurs mythes.

Mentionnons en premier lieu l'importance "des images collectives brassées par les vicissitudes de l'histoire", qui sont léguées par les traditions et "circulent dans le monde diachronique des classes et des sociétés humaines"[56]. Pour reprendre une formule heureuse de François de Medeiros, ces "images mentales subissent une longue gestation et sont douées d'une grande force d'inertie"[57]. Tel est effectivement le cas de l'opposition centre-périphérie attestée dans de nombreuses civilisations, mais que la pensée antique a particularisée en insistant sur l'ambivalence primordiale des confins océaniques, enclaves de l'âge d'or épargnées par la marche du temps et antres de monstres et de sauvages en tout genre. Comme nous avons pu le vérifier, cette opposition, avec son habillage gréco-romain, a orienté de façon consciente et inconsciente le regard porté par de nombreux explorateurs sur les réalités de l'Extrême-Occident et influencé les jugements et classements proposés par diverses autorités centripètes à partir des informations qui leur étaient rapportées par les voyageurs.

Signalons comme deuxième mécanisme l'horreur du vide, qui pousse régulièrement les cartographes de la Renaissance et du XVIIe siècle à couvrir de toponymes, empruntés notamment à la géographie antique, des contrées lointaines, à peine effleurées par des explorations et demeurées de ce fait des terres abstraites, encore à découvrir. Dans le domaine qui nous a occupé, c'est plutôt la vacuité de l'espace temporel qui a été résorbée par ceux qui fabriquaient à coup de témoignages antiques un passé à des régions dont ils ignoraient l'histoire.

La passion du déchiffreur d'énigmes explique également certaines entreprises recontrées au cours de ce travail. On peut, en effet, attribuer au désir de résoudre les apories léguées par les Anciens et d'en tirer gloire l'acharnement avec lequel d'aucuns s'efforcent de situer de façon définitive sur une carte des pays mystérieux tels que Thulé, l'Atlantide, les îles des Bienheureux, Ogygie etc. Comme les sources qui en

---

[55] Préface de Pierre Chaunu à F. Lestringant, *Le cannibale. Grandeur et décadence* (Paris, 1994), 18.

[56] Cf. J. Le Goff, *L'imaginaire médiéval*, préface, VI.

[57] F. de Medeiros, *L'Occident et l'Afrique (XIIIe–XVe siècle). Images et représentations* (Paris, 1985), 268.

parlent sont lacunaires, voire contradictoires, cette démarche, qui se poursuit aujourd'hui encore, est immanquablement vouée à l'échec.

On peut en quatrième lieu mettre en avant le souci d'accorder à un pays déterminé—le sien ou celui d'autrui—des racines aussi profondes que possible. L'Extrême-Occident des Anciens se présente à cet égard comme un réservoir prestigieux auquel on recourt volontiers comme on le fit pour Cadix, identifiée par Ortelius à l'antique Tartessos. Ce type de procédé sert à l'évidence la glorification d'une contrée. Mais il peut constituer également une appropriation par la pensée, sinon dans les faits, d'un territoire étranger. Ainsi, les Hellènes balisaient leur empire commercial sur le pourtour de la Méditerranée en y localisant les étapes du retour des héros de la guerre de Troie. De même, les puissances coloniales n'hésitèrent pas, à l'ère des Découvertes, à se réclamer d'ancêtres grecs et romains pour établir leur droit de premier occupant et leur autorité sur les indigènes.

Plus généralement et ici aussi à l'instar des Anciens, on observe à la Renaissance une tentative de désamorcer l'étrangeté du jamais vu par la reconnaissance du déjà lu. Comment, en effet, rendre compte, faute de vocabulaire et de concepts adéquats, d'une altérité indicible, qui déconcerte et inquiète parce qu'elle remet en cause l'universalisme de la pensée judéo-chrétienne et les certitudes qui en découlent? Il suffit, répondent certains, de recourir aux comparaisons, qui évoquent l'indescriptible en décrivant ce qui est déjà connu[58], de fracturer la différence avec des noyaux de ressemblance. Déjà Hérodote, tout φιλοβάρβαρος qu'il fût, n'avait pu échapper au piège de l'ethnocentrisme, lui qui situait les nomades scythes à l'opposite des Athéniens autochtones. Pour notre part, nous avons rencontré ce mécanisme de l'identité retrouvée dans le commentaire de la carte de l'océan Pacifique rédigé par Ortelius et ce n'est là qu'un exemple parmi d'autres.

En sixième lieu, on ne manquera pas d'évoquer la croyance solidement établie en la vérité du mythe chez les Anciens, d'une part, en la vérité du témoignage des autorités antiques en Occident, d'autre part. Venues du fond des âges ou à tout le moins d'une époque reculée, véhiculées par une tradition, amplifiée plutôt que critiquée au fil des siècles, les informations sur l'Extrême-Occident ne pouvaient pas ne pas contenir, selon de nombreux Anciens et lettrés de la Renaissance, un fond de vérité historique; car la pensée humaine était incapable, à leurs yeux, de fonctionner dans le vide, sans repères fournis par la réalité. Plutôt que de rejeter le poids encombrant des Anciens—ce que certains n'hésitèrent pas à faire, à des degrés divers, dès le XVIe siècle—on préféra trouver des accomodements entre l'héritage antique et les révélations des voyageurs. De là ces tentatives d'intégrer dans la géographie moderne les éléments de vérité du mythe et de la tradition, une fois dégagés de leur gangue de merveilleux. C'est pourquoi les Gorgades et les îles des Bienheureux existent: ce sont les îles du Cap Vert et l'archipel des Canaries; Platon a fait correctement allusion au grand continent d'en face et Thulé est bien une île du Septentrion, même si on peut lui trouver divers emplacements.

---

[58] Cf. S. Greenblatt, *Ces merveilleuses possessions. Découverte et appropriation du Nouveau Monde au XVIe siècle*, trad. par F. Regnot (Paris, 1996), 206.

Il ne me reste plus qu'à évoquer la démarche des poètes et des auteurs de fictions, identique elle aussi durant l'Antiquité et à la Renaissance. Peu importe à ceux-ci l'éventuelle part de vérité historique que contiennent les mythes ou la tradition. Les utilisations scientifiques ou idéologiques des savoirs ainsi véhiculés ne les concernent pas davantage. En revanche, ils se révèlent sensibles à la musicalité des noms et perçoivent intuitivement, mieux que les géographes et sans que cela soit clairement formulé, la richesse symbolique charriée par des toponymes, dont le passé ne leur est pas nécessairement connu dans son intégralité. Le lien que Victor Hugo établit dans les vers cités au début de cet exposé entre l'océan et le chaos est révélateur à cet égard. Parce qu'ils traînent dans leur sillage des mythes et des voyages entourés de mystère, grâce aussi à leurs sonorités harmonieuses, les vocables de l'Extrême-Occident ont survécu à la civilisation qui les avait forgés et continuent à offrir à la création littéraire des possibilités, sans cesse renouvelées, de transfigurer la réalité. C'est ce qu'avait très bien compris Millotet, lorsqu'il célébrait la traduction de la Périégèse de Denys composée par Bénigne Saumaize en 1557:

> Tout ce que de ses rais le Soleil sans repos
> redore d'Orient au rivage de Thyle
> Tu le chantes, Denys, en si doux-grave style
> Que la terre et la mer sont moins beaux que tes mots[59].

Département d'Études grecques, latines et orientales
Université catholique de Louvain (UCL)

---

[59] Cité par Ch. Jacob, "L'oeil et la mémoire: sur la Périégèse de la terre habitée de Denys", dans *Arts et légendes d'espaces. Figures du voyage et rhétoriques du monde*, éd. Ch. Jacob et F. Lestringant (Paris, 1981), 80.

Communications

El *Brocense* y la Receptio
de *Tácito en España*

BEATRIZ ANTÓN MARTÍNEZ

Al estudiar el Tacitismo en España nos hemos encontrado en varias ocasiones con F. Sánchez de las Brozas, *Sanctius*, y pese a que no contribuyó de forma directa a la recepción de dicha corriente, hay datos suficientes para demostrar que, en el panorama tacitista español de fines del siglo XVI, un filólogo de la talla del Brocense trabajaba en los textos de Tácito y estaba al corriente de sus ediciones y comentarios. Sin embargo—como dejamos patente en el título—, quien atraía su atención era el Tácito clásico más que el movimiento de marcado signo político a que había dado origen: el Tacitismo.

Por otro lado, cuanto digamos del Brocense y de sus discípulos y amigos, probará una vez más que, en contra de lo afirmado, los españoles conocían a Tácito mucho antes de que se publicase la primera versión castellana (E. Sueyro, Antverpiae, 1613), y que analizaban sus textos, aunque los resultados de sus investigaciones no quedasen plasmados en ediciones críticas o en comentarios[1].

El propósito del presente trabajo es demostrar que en los estudios sobre la pervivencia de Tácito en España no puede pasar desapercibida la figura del maestro salmantino, cuya relación con el historiador romano—y con el Tacitismo—se estableció a través de cinco vías fundamentales que pasamos seguidamente a exponer:

1. El jurista milanés A. Alciato, que coadyuvó poderosamente a la introducción del Tacitismo en España, dejó escritas unas notas a la edición de Tácito de Beato Rhenano; también fue maestro de Derecho de A. Agustín, uno de los integrantes de la "vía hispánica" de la *receptio* del Tacitismo[2]. Pero sobre todo Alciato se hizo célebre por su *Emblematum libellus* (Mediolani, 1531), entre cuyas fuentes figura Tácito.

---

[1] Cf. Beatriz Antón, "La *receptio* del Tacitismo en España. La 'vía hispánica'", *Bibl H&R* 53, 2 (1991): 329–345, aquí 331 n. 4.

[2] Cf. Antón, "La *receptio* . . .", 334 ss; recogido en Beatriz Antón, *El Tacitismo en el siglo XVII en España. El proceso de "receptio"* (Valladolid, 1992), 91–106, aquí 95.

El libro fue traducido al castellano en 1549 por B. Daza, dando principio a la vulgarización del género[3].

También Sánchez de las Brozas contribuyó a la divulgación de Alciato con sus *Commentaria in Andr. Alciati Emblemata* (Lugduni, 1573). Pero estos comentarios en España quedaron lamentablemente limitados a una élite, pues los emblemistas españoles no mencionan al insigne extremeño "a pesar de ser, sin lugar a dudas, el mejor"[4]. Sus valores fueron, no obstante, ampliamente reconocidos allende los Pirineos: tras las primeras ediciones de Alciato, los impresores acostumbraban incluir la obra del primer comentarista de emblemas, y los comentarios del Brocense acompañaron varias de estas ediciones.

Otro dato a destacar es que, en marzo de 1599, el Brocense inició en la Cátedra de Latín la lectura y comentario de los *Emblemata* de Alciato con el rotulado "*Etiam ferocissimos domari*" (embl. 29), y en mayo todavía continuaba. Ello significa que Sanctius supo aprovechar para la enseñanza universitaria el valor pedagógico del *Libellus*, valor que tampoco pasó desapercibido a su yerno Baltasar de Céspedes[5].

El maestro salmantino comenta con fines científicos, indagando las fuentes de cada emblema, sin sujetarse a la orientación didáctica y moralizadora característica de la emblemática española. A juicio de Maravall, Alciato "fue comentado sabiamente en latín" por Sánchez de las Brozas, y la suya es "una de las primeras explanaciones amplias y eruditas de los *Emblemata*", en la que "aparece ya, entre las fuentes, repetidamente, el nombre de Tácito"[6]. En realidad el historiador latino sólo aparece en el comentario al embl. 2. *Mediolanum*, donde, a propósito de *Heduis,* enumera los autores clásicos que citan este pueblo y las diversas formas en que aparece la palabra; y también en el comentario al embl. 39. *Concordia*, donde cita las anotaciones que hizo Alciato a Tácito (*in scholiis, quae in Tacitum edidit*)[7]. A continuación informa que fue su amigo Alfonso Sánchez de la Ballesta[8] quien le indicó la procedencia tacitiana de este emblema[9].

La iniciativa del Brocense fue secundada medio siglo después por el eminente jurista Juan de Solórzano, uno de sus discípulos y el último autor de emblemas de importancia en España. Solórzano publicó en Madrid, en 1653, los *Emblemata centum regio-politica* para instruir a los príncipes. Pero esta obra, por estar escrita en latín, no

---

[3] Cf. Aquilino Sánchez, *La literatura emblemática española, Siglos XVI y XVII* (Madrid, 1977), 62; Alciato, *Emblemas,* ed. Santiago Sebastián (Madrid, 1985), 22–24.

[4] Cf. Sánchez, *La literatura emblemática,* 67.

[5] Cf. Gregorio de Andrés, *El Maestro Baltasar de Céspedes y su "Discurso de las letras humanas"* (El Escorial, 1965), 245.

[6] Cf. José A. Maravall, "La corriente doctrinal del tacitismo político en España", en *Estudios de Historia del Pensamiento español. El Siglo del Barroco,* 2ª ed. (Madrid, 1984), 75–98, aquí 82.

[7] Cf. *F. Sancti Brocensis Opera Omnia,* auctore Gregorio Maiansio (Genevae, 1766), III, 14, 112.

[8] Para Sánchez de la Ballesta, cf. Nicolás Antonio, *Bibliotheca Hispana Nova* (Matriti, 1783), I, fol. 47.

[9] Cf. *F. Sancti Brocensis Opera Omnia,* III, 112: *Posse hoc emblema elucidari ex Cornelio Tacito auctor mihi fuit amicus summus meus Alphonsus Sanctius Ballesta Talabricensis.*

fue tan conocida como la restante literatura emblemática en lengua vulgar.

Solórzano—según se lee en la cubierta de la citada edición—no sólo dirige su libro a los príncipes, *quibus, quicquid ad regum institutionem, et rectam Reip. Administrationem conducere, & pertinere videtur, summo studio disseritur*, también cree que puede ser de utilidad para los profesores universitarios: *Opus vel ipsa varietate, et utilitate Rerum, & Materiarum, quas continet, expetendum, & omnium Facultatum Professoribus summopere necessarium*. No pretende escribir un tratado meramente divulgativo, sino de rango universitario, y por ello lo redacta en latín. Ello lleva a decir a Sánchez que "Solórzano ha dado el primer paso para elevar el rango de la emblemática introduciéndola en los ámbitos universitarios", y añade: "este intento habría sido una verdadera novedad"[10]. Pero, después de lo apuntado sobre Sanctius, la novedad no es tanta, y es legítimo suponer que la idea de introducir la emblemática en la Universidad la concibiese tras escuchar a su maestro comentar a Alciato[11].

2. Entre los círculos españoles que mantuvieron intercambio epistolar con Justo Lipsio[12] sobresale el de Salamanca, constituido por el burgalés Manuel Sarmiento de Mendoza, profesor de Teología y amigo del Brocense.

Sarmiento remitió, en enero de 1600, una carta a Lipsio, que a juicio de Mayáns fue redactada por Sanctius, alegando como prueba el excesivo elogio que, en su respuesta, dedica Lipsio al autor de la misma; además, hay un párrafo del testamento del Brocense, documento considerado apócrifo, en que se alude a las epístolas que éste intercambió con Lipsio[13]. Aunque no es descartable que el humanista extremeño tuviera redactadas cartas a Lipsio, el "excesivo elogio" del erudito belga no nos parece razón suficiente para atribuirle la paternidad de ésta al Brocense.

Merece la pena detenerse en la epístola de Sarmiento[14], otro de los muchos españoles que, según confiesa, aprecia y venera a Lipsio, tanto que pasar el día entero hablando del humanista flamenco y de sus obras parecía breve a él y a sus amigos: *ad amicos, quibus cum mutuis de te & de tuis scriptis confabulationibus dies integros consumere nimis breue uidebatur*. Le envía algunas observaciones a su edición de Tácito, y le pide disculpas por haber visto en ella algo censurable, aunque "has examinado [a Tácito] con ojos muy perspicaces y lo has corregido con mil cuidados", *perspicacissimis oculis*

---

[10] Cf. Sánchez, *La literatura emblemática*, 151.

[11] Sobre esta faceta de Solórzano, cf. Beatriz Antón, "La mitología en la literatura emblemática del Siglo de Oro: Los *Emblemata Centum Regio-Politica* de Juan de Solórzano", en *Estudios de Religión y Mito en Grecia y Roma* (León, 1995), 221–236.

[12] Cf. Antón, *El Tacitismo*, 132–145.

[13] *Vita* del Brocense, en *Opera Omnia*, cc. CXCIV–CXCX, 83 s.: *Cur vero existimem Sarmenti epistolam scriptam fuisse a Sanctio, & non ab alio, dicam breviter* [. . .]. Sobre el testamento, cf. Marqués de Morante, *Biografía del Maestro F. Sánchez de las Brozas, El Brocense. Con algunas poesías suyas inéditas* (Madrid, 1859), 122; Pedro U. González de la Calle, *Ensayo biográfico. Vida profesional y académica de Francisco Sánchez de las Brozas* (Madrid, 1922), 436 ss.

[14] Cf. Alejandro Ramírez, *Epistolario de Justo Lipsio y los españoles (1577–1606)* (Madrid, 1966), epíst. 70 (11-I-1600) 280 ss. Publicadas por Pieter Burman, *Sylloges epistolarum a viris illustribus scriptarum* (Leidae, 1727), II, n° 767, 57–60.

lustraueris, et non una cura corrixeris. Elogia, a renglón seguido, la labor que ha realizado con el clásico: *Tacitum ab innumeris, quibus scatebat mendis, asseruisti, illustratum nobis exibuisti, lucem illi, atque salutem attulisti. Tuus totus ipse.*

Le informa que, en el año 1596, se dedicó en serio a leer a Tácito—antes sólo lo había probado a trozos— guiado por sus comentarios y sus obras. El juicio que le merece el clásico latino es altamente positivo: *stupui ad scriptorem magnitudinem, sententiarum pondus, sermonis puritatem, incorruptam historiae ueritatis, lepidam, simplicemque in dicendo breuitatem, continuam eloquentiam.*

Cuando se suspendieron las clases en el verano, determinó releer a Tácito bajo el estímulo de su amigo Sánchez de las Brozas, quien en sus conversaciones *inculcabat saepe scribentium ignorantia & grammaticorum imperitia in optimum quemque scriptorem plura inepta, barbara in Tacitum maxime irrepisse: et adhuc nonulla permanere.* Sarmiento, de acuerdo con las indicaciones de un experto filólogo como el Brocense y de su *Minerua,* decide enviarle unas cuantas notas sobre varios términos y expresiones que encuentra en Tácito y no cree que sean suyas: *Nonulla principio subodoratus aliena a grauitate Cornelii, et ab eius breuitate degenerantia.* Nadie, dice, creerá que puedan ser latinas frases como *cuncta ad senatum referendo, regendi cuncta, arma uitandi,* pues Sanctius y su *Minerua* (III, 8) le enseñaron que *referendo, regendi, uitandi* son pasivos (o gerundivos, como los llaman), y que no se les puede añadir un acusativo por su carácter de pasivos[15]. Envía un ejemplar de la *Minerva* a Lipsio y a él le remite. ¿Qué hacer, entonces?: *Delenda ne omnia iis similia? censeo. Leuius id peccatum (si tamen peccatum) quam frigide, et barbare loquutum existimare Tacitum.* Es más, *si alias eisdem uocibus, ut decebat latinum, eleganter utitur, cur non putem aliena, cum putide?.* Ya que la realidad muestra que a menudo se han añadido palabras, y la frase incorrecta resulta clara cuando se le quitan los vocablos intrusos (*uerba intrusa tollas*). Cita, para confirmar su sospecha, un ejemplo de *hist.* 2, 48, cuyas últimas cinco palabras (*laudando pietatem eius, castigando formidinem*) saben a otra mano, y por lo tanto deben suprimirse (*Delenda igitur, delenda*).

Parece que estemos escuchando a un ciceroniano, cuando Sarmiento declara que "esas expresiones ineptas y bárbaras" se habían deslizado en Tácito, o que este autor "no pudo expresarse de manera tan fría y tan bárbara". Llega, incluso, a proponerle que suprima todas las expresiones semejantes a éstas, por suponerlas errores de los glosadores.

Nos preguntamos si no será que tanto Sanctius como Sarmiento leen a Tácito y hacen sus observaciones sobre su lengua y estilo tomando como punto de referencia la *latinitas* de Cicerón. Después de todo, el Brocense "busca y encuentra el arquetipo de *latinitas* en Cicerón—o los de su tiempo—, arquetipo que puede estar proyectado en autores de otra época, pero que ha de ser médido siempre según el criterio del primero". En esto comparte la opinión de los ciceronianos, "quienes no decían que no hubiera que considerar otro autor que Cicerón, sino que el estilo (entendido como *latinitas,* esto es *estilo de lengua*) había que forjarlo sobre Cicerón, autor no sólo exento

---

[15] La doctrina de Sanctius es que "las formas en *-dus, -di, -do, -dum* tienen siempre significado pasivo, si no llevan un acusativo" (cf. *Minerua o De causis Linguae Latinae,* eds. Eustaquio Sánchez Salor y César Chaparro Gómez [Cáceres, 1995], 375).

de la sospecha de barbarie, sino considerado como la elocuencia personificada"[16].
Así pues, en el caso particular de Tácito, una cosa es que lo admirase como historiador, al igual que su amigo Sarmiento, y otra que en la *Minerua* se sirva reiteradamente
del clásico[17] para ofrecer testimonios de las *causae* o *rationes*, que no siempre coin-
ciden con lo propuesto como *Latine loquitur*, ya que para el Brocense "no todos los
autores, aunque se citen ejemplos de ellos, gozan de la misma fiabilidad"[18].

Respondió pronto Lipsio a Sarmiento[19], manifiestándole su sorpresa—como notó
Mayáns—de que semejante carta pudiese venir de esas riberas y de un teólogo: *Tales
ne epistolas ex iis oris, & a Theologo?*. Le hace saber que está ocupado en Séneca y va
a ilustrarlo con un breve comentario. Ya ha publicado a Tácito, *prudentiae (tuo quoque
iudicio) patrem*, y quiere publicar a Séneca, *sapientiae fontem*. Agradece sus elogios de
Tácito, sobre todo porque hay algunos que intentan rebajarlo y despreciarlo. Por lo
que respecta a las notas que le envió, señala que aprueba en ellas la sutileza, aunque
no siempre el juicio, y le reprocha el excesivo uso que hace del escalpelo y del cuchillo: *Nam scalpro aut cultro nimis interdum indulgere mihi visus, nec ausim sic residere
veteres omnes membranas*. Tras rechazar finamente sus sugerencias, manda saludos y
abrazos al Brocense: *Probitas & eruditio viri merentur, & te rogo non salutare tantum, sed
collum ille invadere, & pro me amplecti*.

3. El Neoestoicismo—para definirlo brevemente—fue "una corriente espiritual de
fines del siglo XVI y principios del XVII en Europa que, adaptándose en general a la
doctrina cristiana, aspiraba más o menos a un sistemático restablecimiento de la antigua Estoa y, sobre todo, de su ética tal como se hallaba en los escritos de Séneca y de
Epicteto"[20]. En efecto, en la herencia de la cultura greco-latina hay una doctrina particularmente hecha para ser recuperada por el Humanismo cristiano: la de los estoicos.
Más aún, dentro del pensamiento católico, Estoicismo y Cristianismo son como "des
couleurs qui, fondues les unes dans les autres, donnent de multiples nuances"[21].

Su origen se sitúa en los Países Bajos y tiene en Lipsio a su principal protagonista.
El *sospitator Taciti*, como se le llamó, se encargó también de reconstruir el Estoicismo
romano con *De constantia* (1593), los *Politicorum libri* (1589), la *Manuductio ad stoicam*

---

[16] Cf. Juan Mª Núñez, *El Ciceronianismo en España* (Valladolid, 1993), 118.

[17] Cf. *Minerua*, referencias a Tácito (no recogido en el índice final de nombres): Lib. I, 84
(*bis*), 92. Lib. II, 132, 140 (*bis*), 160. Lib. III, 230, 244 (*ter*), 246 (*pluries*), 250 (*pluries*), 270, 272
(*bis*), 278, 280, 290, 298 (*bis*), 300, 304 (*bis*), 306, 312, 324, 332, 346, 384 (*bis*), 394, 410 (*bis*).
Lib. IV, 468 (*pluries*), 486, 496, 514 (*bis*), 554 (*bis*), 572 (*bis*), 592, 602 (*ter*), 664 (*ter*).

[18] Cf. Núñez, *El Ciceronianismo*, 118 y 115.

[19] Cf. Ramírez, *Epistolario de Justo Lipsio*, epíst. 72 (Lovaina, 14-III-1600), 294 s. Recogida en
los *Opera omnia* de Lipsio (Antuerpiae, 1637), II, *Centuria ad Italos et Hispanos* nº 89, 315 s. También Abraham Ortelio, corresponsal de Lipsio, se interesó por el Brocense (cf. Antón, *El Tacitismo*,
141 n. 169).

[20] Cf. Karl A. Blüher, *Séneca en España. Investigaciones sobre la recepción de Séneca en España desde
el siglo XIII hasta el siglo XVII* (Madrid, 1982), 369. Véase, además, Léontine Zanta, *La renaissance
du Stoïcisme au XVIᵉ siècle* (Paris, 1914).

[21] Cf. Henry Gouhier, *L'anti-humanisme au XVIᵉ siècle* (Paris, 1987), 113–114, 119.

philosophiam (1604), y su edición crítica de Séneca (1605). No sólo quería proporcionar una doctrina moral para el individuo, sino que sus ideas fueron primariamente de carácter político. Lo cual explica la conexión entre la *Constantia* y las *Políticas*[22]. Después de todo, el Neoestoicismo fue "an important and constructive element in the political thought at the turn of the sixteenth century", cuyo objetivo era incrementar el poder y la eficiencia del Estado; exigía autodisciplina y una vida de trabajo, frugalidad, acatamiento y obediencia[23]. Por consiguiente, la filosofía neoestoica fue el fundamento del neoestoicismo político de Lipsio, quien se hizo merecidamente acreedor del título de "inventor del neoestoicismo del Renacimiento"[24], por compaginar Estoicismo y Cristianismo.

El Neoestoicismo entró en España tardíamente, cuando ya se había divulgado ampliamente en el resto de Europa. Y si bien es cierto que Lipsio fue quien en mayor medida contribuyó a difundir la nueva corriente filosófica—simultáneamente con el Tacitismo—, destaca la figura de Sánchez de las Brozas, que en edad avanzada estudió a Epicteto y tradujo su *Encheirídion*. El comentario a esta traducción se publicó en 1600, poco antes de su muerte, y llevaba por título *Doctrina del estoico filósofo Epicteto*. Mientras que Lipsio toma como principal modelo a Séneca, Sanctius centra su atención en Epicteto, cuyo comentario constituye "el primer documento de importancia del Neoestoicismo en España"[25]. Aun cuando el neoestoicismo español no comienza con Séneca, sino con Epicteto, es gratificante y revelador que sea un humanista como Sánchez de las Brozas quien siente las bases para el arranque de este movimiento en España. Por otro lado, el Brocense se hallaba empapado del espíritu de Erasmo, lo que facilitó su acercamiento a Lipsio[26]. El Neoestocismo -en opinión de Bataillon- marca un renacimiento del humanismo filosófico. Y es que el afán de conciliar su fe moral con el Cristianismo hizo de éste un nuevo género de *philosophia Christi*, y fue Lipsio el maestro de este género desde que, convertido al catolicismo, pasó a enseñar a Lovaina. Entonces, "todos los ojos se volvieron al nuevo gigante de las letras como se habían vuelto hacia Erasmo tres cuartos de siglo antes"[27].

De este modo Sanctius, casi al final de sus días, se encontraba frente a este movimiento en situación muy parecida a la de Nebrija frente al Erasmismo: "el uno, discípulo de Valla, allanaba el camino a Erasmo; el otro, discípulo de Erasmo, allanaba el camino a Justo Lipsio"[28].

Hay que subrayar el esfuerzo del Brocense por presentar del modo más aceptable la doctrina estoica mediante una interpretación y armonización cristianas. Su neoestoicismo "ajustado, de la forma más aproximada posible y que muchas veces vela las diferencias, a la doctrina cristiana, conserva ciertamente la posición fundamental de la

---

[22] Cf. Blüher, *Séneca en España,* 490.

[23] Cf. Gerhard Oestreich, *Neostoicism and the Early Modern State* (Cambridge, 1982), 8.

[24] Cf. Jacqueline Lagrée, *Juste Lipse. La restauration du Stoïcisme* (Paris, 1994), 12.

[25] Cf. Blüher, *Séneca en España,* 370.

[26] Cf. Blüher, *Séneca en España,* 370.

[27] Cf. Marcel Bataillon, *Erasmo y España* (México, 1995), 772.

[28] Cf. Bataillon, *Erasmo y España,* 773.

ética estoica"[29]. Resulta evidente que "el Neoestoicismo español emerge del humanismo cristiano del siglo XVI, que se halla en la misma línea de Erasmo y de Vives"[30]. El Brocense, es cierto, allanó el camino a Lipsio, pero lo que realmente le franqueó el camino en España fue su conversión al catolicismo en 1593.

4. Lorenzo Ramírez de Prado publicó un libro misceláneo intitulado *PENTH-KONTARXOS, siue qinquaginta militum ductor* (Antuerpiae, 1612). Se cree que la obra fue escrita por el Brocense, siéndole usurpada por su discípulo Ramírez de Prado. No vamos a tratar aquí de la paternidad del *Pentecontarchos*, pero convenimos con la mayoría de los estudiosos que atribuye su autoría al Brocense[31].

El título es alegórico: el capitán de los cincuenta no es sino el autor de los 50 capítulos que componen la obra. Cada uno de ellos trata de cuestiones diferentes. Nuestro interés se centra concretamente en el apartado, del c. XXII, "*Tacitus interpunctione sanatus*", dedicado a aclarar un pasaje del texto tacitiano[32]. Este apartado, brevísimo, constituye el único comentario filológico a Tácito impreso del siglo XVII del que tenemos noticia. De ahí su importancia. En el se hace referencia al pasaje de Tácito (*ann.* 3, 49–51) donde se menciona la acusación de que fue objeto el caballero Clutorio Prisco y de su condena a muerte, a la que se opuso Marco Lépido en un famoso discurso, del que se recoge el siguiente párrafo: *Vita Lutorii in integro est, qui neque seruatus in perniciem, neque damnatus in exemplum ibit* ("Se mantiene intacta la vida de Clutorio, cuya salvación no representará un peligro para el Estado, y cuya muerte no servirá de ejemplo"). Mientras que Lipsio aconseja leer "*in integro esto*" ("manténgase intacta"), para el autor de la miscelánea la solución está en la puntuación, pues si se pone coma detrás de *integro* y se explica la ausencia del imperativo *esto* por elípsis (figura frecuente en Tácito), queda resuelto el problema: "*Vita Lutorii in integro, est qui neque, etc.*"[33]

5. Por último, nos ocuparemos de Gaspar de Guzmán, el célebre Conde-Duque de Olivares, valido de Felipe IV. Este personaje, al igual que su rival Richelieu, desempeñó un papel decisivo en la política europea del siglo XVII y, al igual que aquél, ha quedado como paradigma de político tacitista[34].

Nace en 1587 en Roma, donde su padre es embajador; reside en diversas ciudades de Italia hasta que regresa a España. Hacia 1600 encontramos al joven Gaspar—contaba tan sólo trece años—en las aulas salmanticenses, destinado, como segundón que era, a la carrera eclesiástica. Pese a su lujoso tren de vida, su estancia en Salamanca lo

---

[29] Cf. Blüher, *Séneca en España,* 386 s.

[30] Cf. Blüher, *Séneca en España,* 388.

[31] Cf. Antón, *El Tacitismo,* 86 n. 110.

[32] Cf. fols. 184 s.

[33] Las ediciones modernas tienen *uita Clutorii in integro est, qui* etc. Los traductores de Tácito al castellano Sueyro (1613) y Alamos (1614) siguen la lectura *esto,* propuesta por Lipsio. Cf. Antón, *El Tacitismo,* 87.

[34] Cf. John H. Elliott, *Richelieu y Olivares* (Barcelona, 1984), 37–49.

marcó profundamente, dejándole una evidente erudición en materia de leyes[35]. Si el Brocense ejercía de Catedrático todavía a comienzos del curso 1600/1601, hay que apuntar la posibilidad—sin duda, remota—de que Olivares, quizá ya instalado en la capital castellana en 1600[36], alcanzase todavía a ser alumno de Sanctius. En cualquier caso, sí debió asistir a las lecciones de su yerno Céspedes, su sucesor en la Cátedra, quien demuestra en el *Discurso de las Letras Humanas*[37] ser un buen conocedor de varios trabajos lipsianos: los comentarios a Tácito, las *Saturnales,* el *De pronuntiatione veteri,* las *Inscriptiones* y las *Políticas.* Esta última es considerada por Céspedes una obra "admirable", donde Lipsio "va cosiendo diferentes lugares griegos y latinos, de tal manera que parece que los mismos authores los hicieron mas para el propósito de Lipsio que para el suyo propio"[38]. En otra parte[39] cita como ejemplo de comentario el de Lipsio a Tácito, aunque con la siguiente puntualización: "quiso servir su Commentario mas para ostentación de su erudición con los hombres muy doctos que para la interpretación de la letras de aquel author, que es obscurissima". Opinión poco favorable que recuerda aquella carta, con algunas correcciones a la edición de Tácito, que remitió Sarmiento a Lipsio, y que nos lleva a sospechar que detras del teólogo burgalés no sólo estuviese el Brocense, sino también su yerno Céspedes.

En suma, un gran lector de Tácito como Olivares, que parece haber inspirado toda su carrera política en doctrinas tacitistas[40], debió conocer desde muy temprano al historiador romano y a su editor flamenco, siendo decisiva su estancia en Salamanca, donde uno y otro contaban con seguidores de renombre.

§

A modo de corolario insertamos aquí el entusiasta elogio que Lipsio, por medio de Sarmiento de Mendoza, hizo llegar al Brocense en la primavera de 1600: *Ille Mercurius, ille Apollo est, Hispaniae vestrae, atque utinam multos excitet trahatque ad splendidas verasque artes; neque armis tantum, ut semper, sed ingeniis etiam, ut olim floreat ille* tractus![41]

Ojalá los deseos de Lipsio sobre el Brocense, *ille Mercurius, ille Apollo,* se hubiesen cumplido. Hoy nos conformamos con saber que, en una España entregada casi por

---

[35] Solórzano dedicó al Conde-Duque, su compañero de estudios, el segundo tomo del *De Indiarum Iure* (1639).

[36] Cf. Richard L. Kagan, *Universidad y sociedad en la España moderna* (Madrid, 1981); Juan Pérez de Guzmán, "La labor político-literaria del Conde-Duque de Olivares", *Revista de Archivos, Bibliotecas y Museos* 8–9 (1904): 81–111. En cambio, Gregorio Marañón (*El Conde-Duque de Olivares. La pasión de mandar* [Madrid, 1998[26]]) y John H. Elliott (*El Conde-Duque de Olivares* [Barcelona, 1990[2]]) retrasan la fecha hasta 1601.

[37] El *Discurso* fue escrito en 1600, pero no se publicó hasta 1784. Cf. Nicolás Antonio, *Bibliotheca Hispana Nova,* I, fol. 181.

[38] Cf. *Discurso,* 246.

[39] Cf. *Discurso,* 230.

[40] Cf. Beatriz Antón, "Tácito, ¿inspirador de la carrera política del Conde-Duque de Olivares?", *Minerva* 6 (1992): 285–312.

[41] Cf. Ramírez, *Epistolario,* 29 (epíst. 72).

completo a escribir comentarios histórico-políticos a Tácito y a destilar su pensamiento en forma de aforismos, el maestro salmantino, insensible a la moda, urgaba en los textos del "padre de la prudencia política" y de ellos extraía numerosos ejemplos para ilustrar su *Minerua*. Al fin y al cabo, la relación de Sánchez de las Brozas con Tácito—como con la emblemática—, a diferencia de la mayoría de los españoles de los siglos XVI y XVII, era la propia de un filólogo, de un científico, no la de un moralista o un político.

Universidad de Valladolid

Carolus Clusius, los naturalistas hispanos y la naturaleza americana[1]

JOSEP LLUÍS BARONA y XAVIER GÓMEZ FONT

En el curso del viaje realizado entre 1564 y 1565 por la Península Ibérica, el naturalista Carolus Clusius (Utrecht 1526–Leiden 1609)[2] descubrió la importancia de la naturaleza americana a través de la tradición naturalista hispana. Buena prueba de ello son sus traducciones. Clusius conoció la obra del naturalista portugués García de Orta titulada *Coloquios dos simples*, obra que tradujo al latín, con el título *Aromatum et simplicium aliquot medicamentorum apud indos nascentium historia* (Antwerpen, 1567); asimismo, años más tarde traduciría al latín la obra de Monardes *Primera y Segunda y Tercera Partes de la Historia Medicinal de las Cosas que se traen de nuestras Indias Occidentales que sirven en Medicina . . .* (Sevilla, 1574) bajo el título *De simplicibus medicamentis ex occidentali India delatis quorum in medicina usus est* (Antwerpen, 1574); en 1582 traduce al latín el *Tractado de las drogas y medicinas de las Indias orientales* de Cristóbal de Acosta, con el título *Aromatum et medicamentorum in orientali India nascentium liber* (Antwerpen, 1582), e imprime unas *Aliquot notae in Garciae aromatum historiam* (Antwerpen, 1582), que completaban las observaciones de Garcia de Orta a partir de las anotaciones sobre las costas occidentales americanas que le había brindado Francis Drake a su regreso de la expedición al Pacífico.

Durante este viaje quedó impresionado por las características de su territorio y no sólo tuvo ocasión de herborizar determinadas zonas de Castilla, Andalucía y el País Valenciano, sino que a partir de entonces inició una relación epistolar y científica estable con naturalistas y médicos españoles.

Una vez alcanzada Lisboa, tras una breve estancia en la ciudad portuguesa, Clusius

---

[1] La presente comunicación forma parte de un estudio monográfico más amplio: *La correspondencia entre Carolus Clusius y los naturalistas españoles* (València: Seminari d'Estudis sobre la Ciència/ Universitat de València), que se publicará en breve por la Universitat de València. Este trabajo forma parte del proyecto de investigación PB92–1048 de la DGICYT, titulado *La comunicación con Europa de la medicina española (siglos XVI–XVIII)*.

[2] Sobre la figura de Clusius, cf. la monografía antes citada.

se separó de su compañero de viaje Jacobo Fugger para recorrer una parte importante del territorio español. Se dirigió inicialmente a Sevilla, donde comenzó una larga relación con médicos y botánicos, en unos momentos en que la ciudad andaluza era el centro de las relaciones comerciales con las colonias del Nuevo Mundo. Allí no solamente vivía Nicolás Monardes, sino también el núcleo principal de los que después serían sus corresponsales. Asimismo se desplazó por el sur hacia las costas del Mediterráneo y en su itinerario visitó Cádiz, Gibraltar, Málaga, Granada, para llegar a Valencia a finales de 1564[3]. De sus datos autobiográficos parece desprenderse que Clusius permaneció unos tres meses allí, donde probablemente estableció una relación de amistad con Juan Plaza, que ha sido reiteradamente comentada por la historiografía, aunque no hay datos fehacientes y en el epistolario de Clusius no ha quedado testimonio de ella[4].

A mediados de abril de 1565 regresó a Madrid, iniciando el viaje de regreso hacia Antwerpen, donde llegó durante los primeros días de junio. Sin duda la estancia en España había transformado sustancialmente su pensamiento científico y sus intereses. Baste recordar su labor como traductor y divulgador de las obras ya mencionadas; pero además aprovechó la estancia en tierras ibéricas para aprender español y portugués, para recolectar una colección importante de plantas nuevas, de las que en torno a doscientas jamás habían sido descritas anteriormente. Fruto de estos trabajos fueron *Rariorum aliquot stirpium per Hispanias observatarum historia* (Antwerpen, 1576), *Rariorum plantarum historia* (Antwerpen, 1601), que reúne la descripción de más de un centenar de especies desconocidas hasta entonces, y *Exoticorum libri decem* (Leiden, 1605)[5].

Por último, inició una serie de relaciones con científicos españoles que se tradujeron, en muchos casos, en una correspondencia principalmente científica, que ahora presentamos. De ella se desprende un vivo interés por las plantas americanas y por el intercambio de especies y semillas.

Tres fueron los nexos de unión de Clusius con España: por una parte el núcleo de científicos de la corte del monarca Felipe II, especialmente a través de su amistad con Benito Arias Montano[6], con quien ya mantuvo una relación de amistad desde la estancia de éste en los Países Bajos; por otra parte el núcleo sevillano representado por Rodrigo Zamorano, Juan de Castañeda y Simón de Tovar; y finalmente el valenciano Juan Plaza, responsable del Jardín Botánico de la Universitat de València. Entre 1568 y 1573, durante los años en que estuvo viviendo en Malinas en casa de su amigo Jean

---

[3] Son datos que proceden de su autobiografía, y que son recogidos por Ch. de Backer y L. J. Vandewiele, "Le botaniste flamand Carolus Clusius (1526–1609) et ses relations avec l'Espagne", en *Medicamento, historia y sociedad. Estudios en memoria del profesor D. Rafael Folch Andreu* (Madrid, 1982).

[4] de Backer y Vandewiele, "Clusius".

[5] Una edición póstuma de sus trabajos fue publicada en 1611 por Plantin bajo el título de *Curae posteriores*.

[6] Sobre la figura del famoso humanista, cf. T. González Carvajal, *Elogio histórico del Dr. Benito Arias Montano*, t. VII (Madrid, 1832), así como B. Rekers, *Arias Montano* (Madrid, 1973). Por lo que se refiere a su correspondencia con diferentes personalidades, es de obligada referencia B. Rekers, "Epistolario de Benito Arias Montano (1527–1598)", *Hispanófila* 9 (1960): 25–37.

de Brancion, Clusius dedicaba su tiempo a completar su *flora hispanica*, al tiempo que trabajaba en el diseño de una carta geográfica de la Península Ibérica[7]. Son aspectos de su trabajo que se han convertido en testimonios históricos de difícil acceso, puesto que su impresor Plantin no pudo imprimir la, sin duda, novedosa *Flora Hispanica* una vez concluida por Clusius debido a dificultades financieras, y de su mapa apenas se localizan dos ejemplares en todo el mundo[8].

Benito Arias Montano (1527–1598), cabeza del humanismo en la época de Felipe II, responsable de la célebre *Biblia Políglota Complutense* y coordinador general durante un tiempo de la Biblioteca de El Escorial, había vivido en Antwerpen entre 1568 y 1575 y durante ese período se integró en el círculo de intelectuales y científicos agrupados en torno a la figura del gran impresor Christophe Plantin. Desde ese momento sirvió de nexo de comunicación entre los grandes intelectuales y científicos de los Países Bajos (Ortelius, Mercator, Gemma Frisius, Dodoens, Clusius ...) y la cultura científica española. Diversos testimonios indican que envió a España libros e instrumentos y dio a conocer las obras científicas españolas a los científicos flamencos, pero también abrió las puertas de las grandes imprentas europeas a diversos médicos y naturalistas españoles (Francisco Arceo, Simón de Tovar ...). La amplitud de sus conocimientos le hizo concebir al final de su vida una obra frustrada, que trataba de ilustrar la historia natural que aparece en la Biblia, y de la que sólo llegó a publicarse un primer volumen tres años después de su muerte en Antwerpen bajo el título de *Historia Naturae*[9]. Cabe resaltar que intentó poner al frente de esta empresa a Clusius, con quien—deseaba nuestro humanista—colaborarían los naturalistas hispanos[10].

A través de su mediación, interesado por la flora del Nuevo Mundo, Clusius entró en contacto con el grupo de naturalistas sevillanos, en unos momentos en que Sevilla era—no hay que olvidarlo—el centro del intercambio comercial con América. Sin embargo, no hemos encontrado testimonios de una relación directa con Nicolás Monardes, que entonces trabajaba allí de médico y había creado una amplia colección de productos tropicales. Ni las cartas ni los datos autobiográficos de Clusius apuntan nada al respecto.

Simón de Tovar (m. 1596)[11] era un médico sevillano que desarrolló toda su labor científica en su ciudad natal, donde contribuyó a la fundación de un importante jardín botánico, que serviría de base a los intercambios científicos con Bernardo Paludano y Carolus Clusius, a los que remitió importantes listados de plantas y semillas que más tarde Clusius incluyó en sus obras ya citadas[12]. Su principal actividad cien-

---

[7] de Backer y Vandewiele, "Clusius", hacen referencia a la absoluta dedicación de Clusius al estudio de la naturaleza hispana.

[8] de Backer y Vandewiele, "Clusius".

[9] Benito Arias Montano, *Naturae Historia, prima in magni operis corpore pars* (Antverpiae, 1601).

[10] Carta de Benito Arias Montano a Clusius de fecha 19-II-1596 (= Rekers, "Epistolario", nº 376).

[11] Cf. Nicolás Antonio, *Bibliotheca Hispana nova sive Hispanorum scriptorum ...*, II (Roma, 1672), 232.

[12] La labor científica del médico y naturalista sevillano bien merecería ser objeto de un estudio histórico del que actualmente carece. Las dos cartas a Clusius que incluimos en el epistolario, y

tífica se centró en las plantas curativas y en el análisis de la composición de los medicamentos[13] y sólo ocasionalmente nos ha legado testimonio de su interés por otros aspectos de la ciencia, como es el uso de la ballestilla para la navegación[14].

Rodrigo Zamorano (m. 1620) era principalmente cosmógrafo y matemático, y trabajó desde 1575 en la sevillana Casa de Contratación, donde estaba encargado de la enseñanza del arte de navegar y de la fabricación de instrumentos científicos y de navegación. Su actividad científica fue muy extensa y no sólo se limitó a la navegación hacia las Indias, sino que abarcó también la cartografía y la observación astronómica, lo que le reportó gran prestigio y el nombramiento de piloto mayor de la Casa de Contratación, lo que le convertía en el máximo responsable de la actividad científica en la institución sevillana [15]. Por ese tiempo, Zamorano creó una colección de rarezas procedentes de los lugares más remotos y un jardín botánico, que denota su interés por el mundo vegetal.

Menos información poseemos de Juan de Castañeda, apenas mencionado por la erudición bio–bibliográfica española y al que la *Enciclopedia Universal Ilustrada Europeo–Americana* (Barcelona, vol. 12, 211) describe no sin errores como un "ilustre botánico español del siglo XVII, nacido en Sevilla. Escribió al célebre Clusio muchas cartas científicas, catorce de las cuales han sido impresas. Le envió también semillas y otros elementos de estudio y compuso un discurso y *Quaedam carmina*, destinados a una obra de aquel famoso naturalista." Por algunas de las referencias que aparecen en sus cartas, Castañeda debió pertenecer al círculo científico de Rodrigo Zamorano y seguramente a través de él inició su larga relación epistolar con Clusius.

La correspondencia entre Carolus Clusius y los médicos y naturalistas españoles fue recopilada en gran parte y presentada por Ignacio Jordán de Asso a finales del siglo XVIII en una obrita latina titulada *Cl. Hispaniensium atque exterorum epistolae cum prefatione et notis* . . . publicada en Zaragoza en 1793, de difícil acceso para el estudioso actual. A mediados de los años 1770, Asso ocupaba el consulado español en Amsterdam, lo que le permitió entrar en contacto con el mundo académico y científico holandés. En una estancia en Leiden descubrió casualmente, entre la amplísima correspondencia que había legado Carolus Clusius, una serie de cartas manuscritas de españoles, que son las que después incluiría en esta obra cuya *Praefatio* viene a ser como una síntesis de los momentos estelares de la tradición científica española, principalmente entre los siglos XVI y XVIII. Algunas de las cartas que hemos estudiado y traducido pasaron desapercibidas al jurista aragonés[16]. Hemos podido corroborar

---

otras en las que se le menciona directamente, son un testimonio fehaciente de la importante relación que mantuvo con ambos.

[13] Este aspecto se hace explícito a lo largo de la correspondencia que mantuvo con Clusius y es la consecuencia de su actividad práctica en Sevilla donde mantenía un avanzado jardín botánico.

[14] Se hace eco de ese interés J. M. López Piñero, "Tovar, Simón de," en *Diccionario Histórico de la Ciencia Moderna en España* (Barcelona, 1983), vol. 2: 371–372.

[15] Cf. U. Lamb, "Zamorano, Rodrigo de", en *Diccionario Histórico de la Ciencia Moderna en España*, vol. 2: 443–444.

[16] Tal es el caso de la carta de 22-IV-1569. En este caso podría pensarse que esta epístola todavía no figuraba en los archivos. Hay que resaltar asimismo que Rekers no reseña en su citado

además la existencia de un manuscrito en 4° de Asso, que data de 1788, titulado *De Claris Hispaniis Historiae Naturalis Cultoribus*, el cual al parecer estaba listo para la imprenta, pero no llegó a publicarse[17]. Comprende una especie de historia cronológica de los naturalistas españoles semejante a la que forma el prefacio de la obra posterior y hace referencia ya a las cartas a Clusius que había encontrado en Leiden. Tal vez por su interés por la tradición naturalista española y por el mundo de la botánica, Asso decidió por esas fechas iniciar una incipiente labor de naturalista aficionado, y existen testimonios de su labor herborizadora por tierras aragonesas y de su interés por la geología y la paleontología[18].

La recopilación y edición latina de las cartas a Clusius de Asso, aunque incompleta y carente de cualquier tipo de análisis de contenido (no podemos decir que destaque por su meticulosidad), resulta de utilidad, porque nos ha permitido constatar varias cuestiones metodológicamente importantes para analizar las relaciones científicas de Clusius con España. En primer lugar, el hecho de que en la época de Asso no existiera en Leiden mayor número de cartas manuscritas de científicos españoles que en la actualidad, es decir, que no ha habido pérdidas ni deterioros considerables, aunque parte del material que ahora presentamos se encontraba en condiciones de lectura y transcripción francamente difíciles. Pero además hemos podido ampliar el número de cartas con otras que Asso no descubrió y con las que hemos encontrado en el archivo del Museo Boerhaave de Leiden. Globalmente, el *corpus epistolare* está compuesto por seis cartas de Benito Arias Montano, escritas entre 1568 y 1596; catorce cartas de Juan de Castañeda, escritas entre 1600 y 1604; una carta temprana de Pedro Martín (1569) y otra de Hipólito Martín (1570); dos de Simón de Tovar, de 1596, y una de Rodrigo Zamorano, datada en 1603, lo que hace un total de veinticinco cartas, frente a las diecinueve transmitidas por Asso. Es interesante considerar que, a pesar de que la estancia de Clusius por tierras españolas tuvo lugar entre 1564 y 1565, los intercambios epistolares con el núcleo científico sevillano no se verificaron hasta los últimos años del siglo XVI y primeros del XVII. Únicamente la relación personal con Arias Montano abarca todo el período, y las cartas de Pedro e Hipólito Martín hacen referencia a cuestiones personales relacionadas con la milicia, lo que nos hace pensar que tal vez se haya perdido una posible correspondencia anterior a las primeras cartas de Simón de Tovar, las cuales son inmediatamente posteriores a la publicación por Clusius en 1593 de las tres obras de Monardes, Acosta y García de Orta, lo que tal

---

artículo dos cartas de Arias Montano a Clusius, una de fecha 7-VIII-1568 y otra de 13-II-1573, que tampoco son transcritas por Asso, por lo que son inéditas. Lo mismo cabe decir sobre la misiva de Pedro Martín, de Valencia, de fecha 7-X-1570, y la de su hermano Hipólito Martín, desde Huenter, en 9-X-1570, de similar contenido.

[17] Ignacio J. de Asso, *Historia de la Economía Política de Aragón. Zaragoza, 1798; prólogo e índices de José Manuel Casas Torres* (Zaragoza, 1947), XXVI–XXVII.

[18] Sobre la personalidad de Ignacio J. de Asso, véase el *Diccionario Histórico de la Ciencia Moderna en España*, vol. 1, así como el prólogo de José Manuel Casas Torres a la edición facsímil de Ignacio J. de Asso (*Historia de la Economía Política de Aragón*). Su labor naturalista se refleja en varios de los trabajos incluidos en la obra colectiva *Linneo en España* (Zaragoza, 1907).

vez avivó el interés de los médicos y botánicos españoles por mantener informado al ya anciano naturalista holandés.

La correspondencia entre Arias Montano y Clusius se inició durante la estancia de aquel en los Países Bajos. Las primeras cartas de Arias están escritas desde Antwerpen y van dirigidas a Malinas, donde residía Clusius amparado por su común amigo Branción. Ya en esas fechas (1569) el intercambio de semillas y las listas de especies botánicas constituían un asunto de interés común para ambos, además de otras cuestiones intelectuales, sociales y personales. A través de las cartas se evidencia el papel de Chr. Plantin como nexo de unión entre ellos y otros muchos eruditos, intelectuales y científicos, en el envío de libros, paquetes y otros objetos, que incluso llegaron a causar algún problema entre ellos debido al impago de los costes. Ocasionalmente aparecen referencias a ciertos naturalistas españoles como Bernardino de Burgos o Durano, que servían a Arias de corresponsales sobre la flora española, y de los que apenas hay testimonio histórico. En la última de sus cartas, Benito Arias Montano hace una referencia explícita al intercambio de semillas y a la participación de Simón de Tovar en esos intercambios. Surge en esa última misiva un problema que no debía ser ajeno a los intercambios de la época: la pérdida de las etiquetas identificativas de las semillas, al haber sido abierta la correspondencia durante el itinerario.

La carta de Pedro Martín data del 15 de diciembre de 1569 en Valencia y hace referencia a una recomendación transmitida a través del médico Juan Plaza. A pesar del talante personal de la misma, Martín da cuenta de los desplazamientos que Plaza hacía a los Pirineos para herborizar, y de la recepción de la versión latina del libro de García de Orta que Clusius le había remitido. También se refiere a la habitual correspondencia entre el flamenco y el catedrático valenciano.

Las cartas de Simón de Tovar tratan cuestiones estrictamente botánicas. Responde a cartas de Clusius y hace referencia al intercambio de semillas y al delicado estado de salud de ambos. Se lamenta de las dificultades añadidas a los intercambios, debido a los hurtos de las plantas y simientes, y añade listados importantes de plantas que eran requeridas de una o otra parte. En otras ocasiones es la tardanza en zarpar las naves o la prolongada travesía la que echaba a perder las semillas. Clusius solía enviar a Tovar listas de plantas que deseaba aclimatar y éste hacía todo lo posible por remitirle las semillas, aunque expresaba las dificultades inherentes a la aclimatación. Son frecuentes las referencias a los nombres latinos y vulgares de numerosas especies nuevas, y la discusión en torno a las dificultades que plantea el cultivo. También se hace explícita una relación semejante entre Simón de Tovar y Bernardo Paludano. Tovar afirma que está preparando un catálogo, describe ciertos ejemplares americanos con todo lujo de detalles—como en el caso del *narciso jacobeo*, llamado en las Indias *Azcal Xochitl*—y aporta una amplia y valiosa terminología botánica. Pero la relación de intercambio científico es recíproca, como se advierte cuando Tovar enumera los bulbos y semillas que ha recibido de Clusius, o le solicita el envío de ciertas especies concretas, que originan largas compilaciones. Ocasionalmente aparece su interés por el desarrollo de la cartografía y las recientes cartas de marear.

La desaparición de Simón de Tovar hizo pasar a primer plano en los intercambios con Clusius a Juan de Castañeda y eventualmente a Rodrigo Zamorano. De la carta de éste último se desprende este hecho y la importancia que el intercambio de especies y semillas nuevas había adquirido a comienzos de siglo XVII, hasta el punto de establecerse un verdadero entramado internacional, que daba lugar, en algunos casos como el narrado por Zamorano, al hurto y pirateo de nuevas semillas.

Las catorce cartas de Juan de Castañeda abarcan un período de cuatro años al iniciarse el siglo XVII, están escritas en castellano, lo que expresa el mencionado conocimiento de dicha lengua por parte de Clusius y la condición extraacadémica, ajena al uso del latín, de algunos de los cultivadores de la botánica hispana. A menudo responden a peticiones concretas de Clusius acerca de semillas de especies que deseaba incorporar y a las que no tenía acceso, además de otras *yerbas de Indias*. Son frecuentes las lamentaciones por haber llegado las plantas o semillas en mal estado. Por otra parte, la relación de amistad y colaboración científica entre Castañeda y Zamorano hace que en algunas ocasiones las cartas del primero incluyan referencias a materiales enviados por el segundo, o inclusive especies animales desconocidas que Castañeda sugiere a Clusius que sería de gran interés reproducir en la imprenta.

El interés de Zamorano por establecer una relación continuada con Clusius se hace evidente a través de algunas de las cartas de Castañeda. Siendo como era *Piloto Mayor de las Yndias* y aficionado a la botánica y la zoología, Zamorano intentaba atraer el interés de Clusius por su trabajo y reitera con insistencia la obtención de aceite de romero para uso terapéutico, a lo que Clusius no parecía dedicar demasiada atención[19].

En la carta remitida a Clusius el 29 de abril de 1601, Castañeda responde a un requerimiento del holandés diciendo "... procuraré saber de aquél libro que se encomendó a Leonardo Recco Neapolitano y avisaré a Vm. de lo que ubiere a quién Dios guarde ..."[20]. La frase da a entender el interés de Clusius por tener acceso a los excelentes materiales que Hernández había traído del continente americano, los cuales, como se recordará, acabaron en manos de Recchio para su impresión resumida. Se trata de un testimonio más del interés de Clusius por la obra de los naturalistas españoles, y de su buena información al respecto.

Otro aspecto importante de la colaboración era la descripción y dibujo de las nuevas especies. Probablemente algunos de los dibujos que Plantin compró a Clusius podrían haber procedido de los botánicos españoles. Por último, se hace evidente en algunas de las cartas el interés por la farmacopea y las aplicaciones terapéuticas de las plantas, hasta el punto que Juan de Castañeda contaba con la colaboración de un especialista flamenco para la preparación de medicamentos, que, según su propio testimonio, siendo gran conocedor de su oficio acumulaba en Sevilla grandes riquezas por el desempeño de su trabajo. El conjunto de los materiales intercambiados por Clusius y sus corresponsales españoles, así como la identificación de las plantas y sus usos, los problemas terminológicos y las vías de adaptación y difusión de semillas procedentes del Nuevo Mundo son algunas de las cuestiones principales que estamos analizando, cuyos resultados ofreceremos en un futuro inmediato.

Universitat de València

---

[19] Rodrigo Zamorano a Clusius, carta de 3 de junio de 1603.
[20] Juan de Castañeda a Clusius, carta de 29 de abril de 1601.

L'*Utopie* *et les limites de l'interprétation*

ISTVÁN BEJCZY

On dit parfois qu'un soir suffit pour lire l'*Utopie* de Thomas More, tandis que pour comprendre l'*Utopie*, il faut toute une vie humaine. Cette dernière estimation semble même plutôt optimiste. Cinq siècles d'interprétation n'ont pas permis d'établir définitivement le sens de l'*Utopie*; au contraire, chaque génération de lecteurs a ouvert de nouvelles perspectives sur l'ouvrage de Thomas More, et les seules interprétations que l'on puisse juger mauvaises semblent celles qui imposent des restrictions au sens. Depuis quelques décennies on reconnaît que la pluri-interprétabilité de l'*Utopie* fait partie du caractère de l'ouvrage: c'est le *libellus* de Thomas More qui, par sa structure ouverte, invite ses lecteurs à s'engager dans un processus d'interprétation sans fin.[1] Comprendre l'*Utopie*, c'est donc avant tout respecter son ouverture permanente à de nouvelles significations.

J'aimerais développer ici l'idée que l'*Utopie*, à mon avis, ne s'oppose pas seulement au concept d'une interprétation limitée par sa structure, mais aussi, d'une façon plus directe, par son contenu. Ce que les commentateurs de l'ouvrage, pour autant que je sache, ont négligé jusqu'ici, c'est que le problème de l'interprétation est admis, de façon explicite, par les habitants de l'île d'Utopie.[2] Dans son récit sur l'île d'Utopie, le personnage narrateur, Raphaël Hythlodée, nous donne, en effet, quelques exemples des habitudes de l'interprétation pratiquées par les citoyens utopiens. Ces exemples montrent que donner un sens au texte ne va pas de soi pour les Utopiens. L'interpré-

---

La préparation de cet article ainsi que ma participation au congrès d'Avila ont été financées par l'Organisation Néerlandaise de Recherche Scientifique (N.W.O.). Les citations de l'*Utopie* seront accompagnées par les références P et Y. P se rapporte à la traduction d'André Prévost, *L'Utopie de Thomas More* (Paris, 1978); Y au texte latin de l'édition yaloise, *Utopia*, éd. Edward Surtz et J. H. Hexter, *The Yale Edition of the Complete Works of Thomas More* 4 (New Haven, 1965).

[1] Je pense avant tout au travail d'Elizabeth McCutcheon, notamment *My Dear Peter. The Ars Poetica and Hermeneutics for More's Utopia* (Angers, 1983). Voir aussi Dominic Baker-Smith, *More's Utopia* (Londres, 1991).

[2] J'ai traité cet aspect de l'ouvrage dans *Pape Jansland en Utopia. De verbeelding van de beschaving van middeleeuwen en renaissance* (Nimègue, 1994), 242–245.

tation, pour eux, est un problème qui requiert une solution.

Le problème de l'interprétation en Utopie se pose surtout face aux lois et aux procès judiciaires. Je vous invite à comparer le passage suivant (le texte français est repris de la traduction d'André Prévost):

> Les lois sont très peu nombreuses: elles suffisent à des gens qui ont de telles institutions. Ils reprochent avant tout aux autres peuples d'utiliser une quantité infinie de volumes de lois et de commentaires et, malgré cela, de n'en avoir jamais assez. C'est, disent-ils, une très grave iniquité que d'obliger des hommes à respecter des lois trop nombreuses pour qu'on puisse les lire ou trop obscures pour qu'elles puissent être comprises par le premier venu.
>
> Au surplus, les avocats, ces hommes qui font appel à la ruse pour plaider un procès et usent de fourberie pour discuter les lois, sont absolument exclus de chez eux. Ils estiment, en effet, que normalement la cause doit être défendue par les plaignants eux-mêmes: c'est à eux à expliquer au juge ce qu'ils auraient raconté à un avocat. On évite ainsi bien des complications et la vérité est plus facilement mise en lumière, puisque celui qui la rapporte n'a pas appris de son avocat l'art de feindre. Le juge apprécie dès lors, avec compétence, les détails de l'affaire et donne raison aux gens simples en dépit des roueries des chicaniers. Dans les autres nations, de telles pratiques sont difficiles à observer, en raison de l'accumulation invraisemblable des lois et de leur caractère extrêmement compliqué. Mais, chez eux, tout le monde est expert en droit. Car, comme je viens de le dire, d'une part les lois sont très peu nombreuses et, d'autre part, plus l'interprétation proposée en est simple, plus ils la considèrent comme conforme à la justice. Ils estiment, en effet, que la seule raison pour laquelle toutes les lois sont promulguées est de permettre à chacun d'être par elles averti de son devoir. Or, si l'interprétation du droit exige trop de subtilité, très peu de gens—les rares personnes capables d'en saisir le sens—seront avertis de leur devoir; au contraire, si c'est le sens le plus simple et le plus courant qui s'impose, la loi est claire pour tout le monde (P 125–126; Y 194/6–27).

On peut déduire de ce passage que les Utopiens veulent éviter que la vérité ne soit ensevelie sous un verbiage consistant en lois et en discours interprétatifs. Il s'agit de deux sortes de vérité: premièrement de la vérité sur le droit (c'est-à-dire sur les règles qui gouvernent la vie sociale); deuxièmement de la vérité sur les faits (c'est-à-dire sur l'état des choses à la base des litiges). Ce que les Utopiens désirent avant tout, c'est l'exclusion de chaque forme d'ambiguïté. La cause de l'ambiguïté, dans leur opinion, est triple: d'abord la présence d'un grand nombre de lois; ensuite la difficulté des lois; et finalement la capacité de l'homme d'expliquer les lois ainsi que les faits toujours à son avantage. C'est pourquoi les Utopiens, pour combattre l'ambiguïté, restreignent le nombre et la difficulté des lois ainsi que leur interprétation: il y a peu de lois; les lois sont simples; et seule l'interprétation la plus évidente (*crassus*, *simplex*, *obvius*) est valable. Dans la situation idéale, les discours devant les tribunaux sont transparents, afin que la vérité sur le droit et sur les faits soit visible à travers les mots.

Le moyen principal dont se servent les Utopiens pour obtenir la transparence du discours, c'est l'usage d'un langage simple et sobre. La simplicité de la parole est en effet favorisée par la langue utopienne. Cette langue ne possède pas seulement un vocabulaire riche et une sonorité agréable, comme Raphaël Hythlodée nous le dit, mais aussi "aucune autre [langue] n'interprète plus fidèlement la pensée" (P 101, Y 158/13–14). Il existe apparemment un rapport étroit entre les mots et les choses: la langue représente la réalité aussi directement et carrément que possible, ce que semblent souligner les formes raides et carrées des lettres de l'alphabet utopique. Outre la parole, la langue aussi évite l'ambiguïté et tend à la transparence. La transparence de la langue fait d'ailleurs pendant à celle de la musique utopienne, louée par Raphaël Hythlodée pour son aptitude "à reproduire et à exprimer fidèlement les sentiments naturels de l'âme; elle harmonise si bien les sonorités avec ce qu'elles signifient (*sonus accomodatur ad rem*) . . . , elle accorde si parfaitement le dessin de la mélodie au sens profond (*rei sensum melodiae forma repraesentat*), que l'âme des auditeurs en est saisie, pénétrée et enflammée d'une admirable manière" (P 155, Y 236/5–9).

Le problème de l'interprétation est donc reconnu par les Utopiens. Ils abhorrent l'idée d'une interprétation sans fin et s'efforcent par conséquent de limiter l'interprétation autant que possible. Leur solution consiste à prôner une naïveté, voire une primitivité: l'interprétation la plus apparente, qui est évidente pour le premier venu, est valable chez eux. Moins l'interprétation est compliquée, plus elle laisse entrevoir la vérité.

Qu'est-ce que cela veut dire? On pourrait croire que l'auteur de l'*Utopie* a dessiné dans les passages cités son propre idéal de l'interprétation. Après tout, beaucoup d'humanistes à l'époque de Thomas More s'opposaient à la quantité et la difficulté du droit canonique et de ses commentaires, ainsi qu'à l'élaboration compliquée de la morale chrétienne dans la théologie scolastique. La simplification des préceptes légaux et moraux était certainement un objectif important de l'humanisme chrétien. On a cependant du mal à croire que Thomas More ait été capable d'approuver sérieusement le primitivisme interprétatif des Utopiens, et cela pas uniquement parce que son *Utopie* nous frappe comme une *opera aperta* par excellence, pour emprunter ce terme d'Umberto Eco.[3] Rappelons que More, dans la même année 1515 où il composait son récit sur l'île des Utopiens, écrivait sa fameuse lettre à Maarten van Dorp, théologien de Louvain impliqué dans une polémique avec Erasme. Dans une lettre à ce dernier, Dorp avait remarqué, entre autres, qu'un théologien était obligé de traiter des questions bien plus difficiles que l'interprétation de la Bible *ad litteram* ou même au sens spirituel. Comprendre la Bible, selon Dorp, ne représentait qu'une étape propédeutique vers l'étude approfondie de la dogmatique.[4] Dans sa réaction, Thomas More niait fortement l'idée selon laquelle la compréhension de la Bible était une chose facile et se demandait si le processus de l'interprétation pouvait jamais prendre fin. Le sens littéral de la Bible me semble contenir déjà tant de difficultés, avouait More

---

[3] Umberto Eco, *Opera aperta* (Milan, 1962); traduction française: *L'Oeuvre ouverte* (Paris, 1965).

[4] *Opus epistolarum Desiderii Erasmi Roterodami*, éd. P. S. Allen e.a. (Oxford, 1906–1958), Ep. 347, l. 323–336.

à Dorp, que je ne sais pas s'il y a une seule personne capable de le comprendre.[5] Supposer qu'un homme qui s'exprimait ainsi puisse embrasser comme idéal le primitivisme interprétatif des Utopiens, c'est presque un blasphème, même si en Utopie il ne s'agit pas de textes sacrés.

Comment alors interpréter l'interprétation utopienne? Je crois que Thomas More nous a fourni la clé de la réponse dans son texte. Quand on étudie plus attentivement les habitudes interprétatives des Utopiens, on voit que l'idéal de la transparence du discours ne se réalise pas dans leur île.

D'abord, la langue des Utopiens, qui devrait stimuler la limpidité de la parole, n'existe pas dans sa pureté. Elle n'est pas vraiment identique dans toutes les régions, comme Raphaël Hythlodée le dit au début de son récit (P 71–72, Y 112/17–18). Plus tard il précise que la langue "reste à peu près la même" partout dans l'île, mais qu'à chaque endroit elle est sujette à des déformations différentes (P 101, Y 158/14–15).[6] Dans la réalité on ne parle donc que des dialectes en Utopie, qui dans leur imperfection manifeste (*corruptior* est le mot employé dans le texte latin) obscurcissent sans doute la parole.

De surcroît, le passage sur les lois et les procès judiciaires que nous avons lu est paradoxal, sinon contradictoire. Les Utopiens se contentent *consciemment* de l'interprétation la plus évidente de la loi. Ils sont donc capables d'imaginer des interprétations plus compliquées. Or imaginer une interprétation équivaut à interpréter tout court. Les interprétations que les Utopiens prétendent exclure sont par conséquent présentes dans leur île. L'interprétation de la loi n'est dès lors pas vraiment limitée en Utopie; elle est seulement barricadée d'une façon artificielle et irréelle. De plus, on pourrait se demander pourquoi les Utopiens éprouvent le besoin d'interpréter la loi. Si la loi était évidente (*self-evident*), il ne faudrait pas l'effort conscient d'une interprétation. Apparemment la loi n'est pas si évidente que cela: elle fait naître de nombreuses interprétations, parmi lesquelles les Utopiens font valider celle qui est considérée comme la plus simple. Mais comment décider laquelle des interprétations est la plus simple? Pour cela, il faut un discours interprétatif sur les interprétations. Et quelles sont les règles qui gouvernent ce discours interprétatif? Pour cela, il faut un méta-discours interprétatif. *Et cetera et ad infinitum.* Dès qu'on reconnaît le problème de l'interprétation, on ne peut échapper à la sémiosis illimitée, c'est-à-dire au processus où chaque interprétation devient l'objet d'une nouvelle interprétation. Même parmi les Utopiens, la transparence du discours doit rester une chimère.

Les Utopiens ne sont donc pas mieux protégés contre l'idée d'une interprétation sans fin que les habitants du vieux monde. Ils ont beau louer leur primitivisme interprétatif; ceci montre seulement que, comme le faisait Maarten van Dorp, les Utopiens

---

[5] *Letter to Dorp*, The Yale Edition of the Complete Works of Thomas More 15 (New Haven, 1986) 60/2–4 = *The Correspondence of Sir Thomas More*, éd. Elizabeth F. Rogers (Princeton, 1947), Ep. 15, l. 762–764.

[6] La traduction de Prévost: "Elle reste à peu près la même, sauf quelques corruptions locales, dans les vastes régions de cette partie du globe" ne correspond pas tout à fait au sens du latin: "eadem fere (nisi quod ubique corruptior, alibi aliter) magnam eius orbis plagam peruagatur".

méconnaissent la nature de l'interprétation. Le récit de Raphaël Hythlodée montre d'ailleurs que les Utopiens ne reculent pas toujours devant les ruses interprétatives. Hythlodée raconte que les Utopiens ne signent pas de traités, vu qu'ils sont toujours violés par les étrangers, qui utilisent délibérément des expressions ambiguës dans les traités au moment de leur rédaction pour pouvoir échapper à leurs obligations en cas de besoin:

> Il n'est pas difficile de chicaner sur les expressions employées car, de propos délibéré, au moment de la rédaction [des traités], elles [les expressions] ont été dictées avec tant d'habileté que ... il est toujours possible d'échapper à certains [liens] d'entre eux, et d'éluder du même coup les obligations du traité et la parole donnée (P 128, Y 198/1–4).

Encore une fois les Utopiens reconnaissent que l'interprétation est une chose problématique et que le sens du texte reste souvent obscur. C'est pourquoi ils préfèrent ne pas conclure de traités: incapables d'éviter la prolifération de leurs sens, les Utopiens n'ont pas les moyens de maîtriser les affaires étrangères. Toutefois ce ne sont pas seulement les étrangers qui exploitent la pluri-interprétabilité du droit international. En cas de guerre, les Utopiens n'hésitent pas à exciter d'autres pays contre leurs ennemis après avoir cherché une vieille formule juridique pour justifier le conflit (P 133, Y 204/28–31). Dépourvus de moyens pour limiter l'interprétation de la loi, les Utopiens sont parfaitement capables de profiter de son caractère flou, tout comme les parties et leurs avocats devant les tribunaux en Europe.

Je crois qu'on peut conclure que les passages de l'*Utopie* sur la pratique utopienne d'interprétation ont un caractère ironique. Si le lecteur se limite au sens apparent de ces passages, on peut croire que l'interprétation en Utopie est limitée au sens apparent. Cependant si le lecteur va au-delà des apparences, il constate que l'interprétation en Utopie va, elle aussi, au-delà des apparences. Cette dernière est illimitée pour ceux qui sont prêts à reconnaître que le sens profond du texte reste toujours hors de portée. Je crois que par l'impossibilité de restreindre l'interprétation en Utopie, Thomas More nous propose une leçon pour l'interprétation de son ouvrage: loin de se limiter au sens apparent, le lecteur est invité à s'engager dans un processus d'interprétation sans fin. L'histoire de l'interprétation de l'*Utopie* prouve que cette leçon reste toujours opportune.

Pour terminer j'aimerais attirer l'attention sur un passage de l'*Utopie* où la difficulté de l'interprétation n'est pas seulement reconnue, mais aussi mise en valeur. A la fin de son récit sur l'île d'Utopie, Raphaël Hythlodée parle des services religieux dans les temples utopiens. Il raconte que les prêtres des Utopiens portent des vêtements composés de plumes d'oiseaux. Dans ces plumes et dans leur disposition "sont contenus, disent-ils, de mystérieux arcanes (*arcana mysteria*). L'interprétation de ces symboles—soigneusement transmise par les ministres du sacrifice—rappelle les bienfaits divins envers eux et la piété qu'ils doivent à Dieu en retour, les obligations aussi qu'ils ont les uns envers les autres" (P 154, Y 234/22–26).

On voit que, quand il s'agit de textes plus ou moins sacrés, les Utopiens abandonnent leur primitivisme interprétatif: ni eux ni Raphaël Hythlodée d'ailleurs ne se contentent de l'interprétation la plus évidente des manteaux de plumes. Le sens du texte ne se dévoile pas facilement au premier venu; il ne se dévoile même pas du tout, car, de plus d'une façon, le sens se trouve dans le voile lui-même. Inutile de lever le manteau du mystère. Devant le sens profond des choses, il n'y a de place que pour l'étonnement éternel.

Katholieke Universiteit Nijmegen, Pays Bas

Barbarus ille mihi sermo est, ego barbarus illi:

The Latin Poetry of the Dutch Poet

Constantijn Huygens (1596–1687)

FRANS R. E. BLOM

Introduction

Possession and desire are two different things. In Latin the two different things are referred to by two different verbs: *habere* and *avere*. What, however, remains of the difference in the mouth of Spanish people with their own elegant way of pronouncing the letter -*v*- ? If we go back in history, and read the poet Constantijn Huygens, we may believe that the great war between Spain and the Netherlands had its origin in this matter. From his witty epigram about the letter B, in Spanish written as V, it becomes clear that the possessions of the one country were the desires of the other, just as the desires of the one country were the possessions of the other:

B. HISPANIS V
De Beta totum Batavis certamen Ibero est:
 Quidquid habent, hic havet: quidquid havent, hic habet.[1]

This is Constantijn Huygens, one of the most prominent figures of the Dutch Golden Age, in daily life working as a secretary to the Princes of Orange, and, as a poet, gifted with a sharp intellect and an insatiable passion for puns.

Attitude towards the Classics

Huygens was brought up with a broad humanist education. The classics played a predominant role in his curriculum. From the early age of nine years on he read, reread and memorized ancient poets, orators and historiographers in Latin and Greek. Soon he started to write his first poems in shaky Latin, as he put it.[2] During an early

---

[1] *Momenta Desultoria* 1655, 346 (ed. J. A. Worp, *De gedichten*, vol. 4, 39D).
[2] *De vita propria* 1. 97–9 (ed. J. A. Worp, *De gedichten*, vol. 8, 182):

period of seven years his muse had a Latin voice only. But then, probably under the influence of the rapidly growing status of the vernacular, his poetry took up the Dutch language alongside Latin. French poems, as well, flowed from his pen. As he was against the traditional worshipping of Latin and Greek, he disagreed entirely with people who considered any modern language inferior to classical languages. "Complete madness, I call it, to have these rich resources from our own land, and still leave them unused, just to make the learning process harder than it could be, if we used the vernacular!"[3] Thus, Huygens took his position in the *question of languages*, that had started in Italy long before it finally reached the Netherlands. "No, I will not submit my pen only to Rome. Enough and more than enough has it been, that one Rome ever existed, that thirsty Rome alone filled itself with triumphs and the world with Caesars. Those were the days when that city was no smaller than the whole world, and the whole world no bigger than the *Collis Quirinalis*. That was the time when languages were strange if they didn't know the strange language of Latium. That was the time when vernacular languages were strange if they dared to call themselves not strange in their own country".[4]

The picture that I have just drawn does not justify Huygens' attitude towards the classics, and needs correction. In the first place, let it be clear that these biting remarks on the classics are made in Latin. Moreover, they are made in a specific context. In fact, rejection of the classics can be found only in passages where defence of the vernacular is at work. Thus, his statements against antiquity must always be interpreted according to their function of advocating the status and use of modern languages. Huygens does not hate Vergil, he hates blind admiration of antiquity.

  Quippe rudis tiro et nondum tria sana Latine
  Iungere verba potens, coepi insanire pedesque
  Metiri digitis et ineptum cudere carmen.

[3] Taken from the Latin prose autobiography of his youth, edited by J. A. Worp, "Fragment eener autobiographie van Constantijn Huygens," *Bijdragen en Mededeelingen van het Historisch Genootschap* 18 (1897), 45: "Nam quae haec insania est, cum abunde domi suppetat, quo in artium difficultate partim subleveris, negligere opes patrias vel contemnere, ut operosius erudiare?"

[4] Vss. 1–8 of the Latin poem addressed to the *pur sang* Latinist Caspar Barlaeus, edited by J. A. Worp, in *De gedichten*, vol. 2, 121:

  At mihi non uni calamum submittere Romae,
  Quo Latio legar ore, libet: satis una superque
  Quod fuit, una fuit, satis una oppleta Triumphis,
  Non satiata, sui vidit nil Caesaris expers,
  Quando nec Urbs olim Orbe minor, nec Colle Quirini
  Amplior hic, Mundi una domus fuit, una Quiritum,
  Barbara quae linguae nesciret lingua Latinae
  Barbariem, et patriae auderet non barbara dici.

The Latin *oeuvre* of Constantijn Huygens

The overall view of his writings in poetry supports this attitude.[5] The multilingual poetic works of Huygens add up to a total of approximately eighty thousand lines.[6] More than half of these have been written in the vernacular. Second best is the Latin language, scoring almost twenty thousand lines. So the Latin poetry adds up to a quarter of his complete *oeuvre*.

However, it would be naive to stick to these numbers, because they do not show the actual nature of his Latin poetry. Therefore, let us first compare his Dutch and Latin poems and place the Latin works in the broader spectrum of his complete works. Is Huygens the same poet in the Latin language as he is in the vernacular? Are we to believe him when he proclaims: *omne solum vati patria est*, the poet's home is everywhere?[7]

At a cursory glance it seems that Huygens composed his Latin verses just as easily as he wrote his poems in Dutch. This, also, is the image that the author himself puts forward in his autobiography. Reconstructing his life, he suggests that his ever present Muse was bilingual. Both Latin and Dutch poems are proof of his *insania*.[8]

But, with all these superficial similarities, there is, of course, a significant difference. The Latin language, for Huygens, was the proper medium for shorter poems: occasional poetry and epigrams.[9] Hardly any Latin poem can be found exceeding the number of twenty-five lines, whereas most of them consist of fewer than ten verses. In Dutch, these two types of short poetry can be found as well. The difference, however, becomes clear if we look at his more extensive poems. For these larger compositions are all exclusively written in Dutch. The native language, therefore, is the vehicle *par excellence* for longer and more ambitious works, but Latin is restricted to short poetry. Huygens, indeed, shows himself at home in the Netherlands as well as in Latium, although he is slightly more comfortable in the language of his home country than in Latin.

Latin Poetry in Print

Huygens published his edition of exclusively Latin poetry for the first time in 1644, at the age of nearly fifty.[10] For years these poems had circulated among

---

[5] Because of limitations in time his prose writings (e.g., correspondence) have not been studied in this respect.

[6] Following J. A. Worp's edition of Huygens' poetry the total sum of lines is 75,555, of which 48,590 are in Dutch (64.3 percent), 19,962 in Latin (26.4 percent), 6579 in French (8.7 percent), 146 in Italian, 31 in Greek, 24 in German, 24 in Spanish.

[7] Ed. J. A. Worp, *De gedichten*, vol. 2, 121C vs.42f. The full passage reads:

> Omne solum vati patria est, ille incola mundi
> Ille domi in patriâ, ille foris, ille omnibus idem.

[8] *De vita propria* 2. 307–311 (ed. J. A. Worp, *De gedichten*, vol. 8, 212).

[9] The fourteen books of his *Momenta Desultoria* (1655) consist of one book called *Farrago*, one book of *Iuvenilia*, and twelve books of epigrammatic poetry.

[10] The *Momenta Desultoria* appeared for the first time in 1644. A second, larger, edition followed in 1655. His *Otia* (1625) includes Latin verse as well, but since that is not an edition entirely in Latin we will not be dealing with this work here.

friends and fellow poets only in manuscript, but at that moment they were brought together for a wider public. It needs to be said here that the initiative for the edition was not taken by the poet himself. Actually he didn't want to publish at all. It was only at the instigation of one of his friends that he decided to show them to the world.[11] However, this step from manuscript to the printed edition is quite important, because here we find indications of the author's view on the quality of his own Latin poetry.

During his preparations Huygens was anything but confident about the impact of his Latin poems. Among friends, of course, his poetry had been praised loudly, but this was no guarantee at all of a favourable reception by a wider public. The poet was fully aware of the Catos, the censors, who were waiting to get their sharp teeth into his Latin poetry. And he did not fail to realize that this enterprise could end in a serious disgrace, so that his Latin muse on her first journey could be shipwrecked.[12]

So to prevent the critics from defaming his Latin edition, Huygens decided to call in a recognized authority in Latin. He needed, in his own words, a judge, an Horatian *doctus Trebatius*, who, with a thorough knowledge of Latin, could give an expert judgement of his use of the language.[13] This, in a way, reveals a degree of uncertainty. Faced with the question whether his poems were in tolerable Latin, Huygens had to rely on the judgement of a professional.

View of his Latin Poetry: Quantities and Style

Thus the poet piled up his impressive amount of epigrams and sent them to his judge in Amsterdam, the famous professor of Latin, Caspar Barlaeus. The eminent scholar was instructed to read the poems not as a friend, but as if he were a general reader, just to find out whether Huygens as a Latin poet would be received favourably by his public or be laughed off.[14]

Then the instruction goes into details, and this is where we get a close and interesting view of the poet's attitude towards his Latin writings. There were two things in particular that had to be focused on: a technical and a stylistic point. Technically, the poems needed attention in respect of quantities, the correct use of long and short syllables in the metrical schemes. Huygens, indeed, shows that he is aware of possible lapses, when he says: "You may find me violating the quantities of syllables, because I lost attention or by a slip of my memory. Please check this point, for you are im-

---

[11] In the preface to the *Momenta Desultoria* 1655 (fol. 83r): "Quae enim ille [sc. Huygens] edi operae precium non putabat, seculo doctissimo et acutissimo, adeoque inter amicos perire volebat."

[12] Letter to C. Barlaeus, 21 Aug. 1643 (ed. J. A. Worp, *De briefwisseling*, vol. 3 no. 3377): "Quantulacumque enim sint, nolim ludibria ventis volare, aut naufragio absorberi."

[13] Letter to C. Barlaeus, 21 Aug. 1643 (ed. J. A. Worp, *De briefwisseling*, vol. 3 no. 3377). Huygens, quoting Hor. *Sat.* 1. 1 vs. 78, describes his judge as *docte Trebati* and credits him with the quality of authority in the field of Latin language by quoting *Ars Poetica* 72: "te penes arbitrium est et norma legendi."

[14] Letter to C. Barlaeus, 21 Aug. 1643 (ed. J. A. Worp, *De briefwisseling*, vol. 3 no. 3377): "Sumendus est habitus, quo publice tolerari statuamus vel explodi, pro captu lectoris, aequi aut iniqui."

peccable".[15] Now, quantities are problematic for the type of Latin poet whose knowledge of the language is not as thorough as his mastering of the vernacular. Therefore this remark may be taken as another piece of evidence that Huygens was not too sure about the quality of his Latin verse.

In the case of quantities censorship would be relatively easy, for the Latin was either right or wrong. The stylistic point, however, was more complicated. Huygens had a great love of unusual expression. His verse is dense, strained, and ingeniously contrived. His poetry is a labour of sharp intellect. And one of his most beloved instruments is word-play. No wonder, therefore, that his favourite genre was the epigram. A stupendous example is a poem on the famous Hugo Grotius. When this scholar had published his study on law in the Netherlands (*The Introduction to Dutch Law*) he had succeeded in giving a very structured overview of the formerly incomprehensible mass of Dutch private law. Now Huygens praised the work in enigmatic diction, playing on almost every possible word in the poem, especially on the double meaning of *putare*, "to cut back" and "to consider":[16]

> IN H. GROTIJ INSTITUTIONES IURIS BATAVICI
> Quae patriam observat Grotius servare, reservat,
>   Quae putat in patriâ non patria esse, putat.
> Quid scriptore putas, Lector, tam sana putante,
>   Quid melius tam non sana putante putas?
> Non puto, quae putat hic lectu bene digna, putanda,
>   Quae putat hic lectu non bene digna, puto.

Ignoring every pun, the interpretation should be something like:

> ON GROTIUS' INSTITUTIONS OF DUTCH LAW
> Grotius retains the things he considers fruitful for the country
> And he cuts back the things in the country he considers as
>   not belonging to the country.
> Now, reader, what do you consider better than a writer with
>   such wise considerations,
> who cuts back the things that are not wise?
> I don't consider the things he considers worth reading as
>   things that should be cut back,

---

[15] Letter to C. Barlaeus, 21 Aug. 1643 (ed. J. A. Worp, *De briefwisseling*, vol. 3 no. 3377): "Potero in syllabarum quantitates impegisse aliud agendo, aut memoriae lapsu." An example of wrong quantity is given in line two of the epigram *Nauta in procinctu* (ed. J. A. Worp, *De gedichten*, vol. 3, 201). The manuscript reads: "Iam lacessitus tot quaesitoribus, Eurus" with the short syllable *lac-*, whereas a long syllable is required. The printed version, instead, reads: "Saepe lacessitus" (*Momenta Desultoria*, ed. 1655, 173).

[16] Ed. J. A. Worp, *De gedichten*, vol. 2, 224; *Momenta Desultoria* 1655, 73. In a letter to Daniel Heinsius (ed. J. A. Worp, *De briefwisseling*, vol. 1 no. 581), Huygens was very amused about his "putidum epigramma, quod in ore est omni populo et totam curiam pro aenigmate exercet".

> And I do consider the things he considers not worth reading
> as things that should be cut back.

Of course, this epigram is a rather extreme example of Huygens' love of word-play. However, as much as this was his strength, it was a target of criticism as well. Although among friends and fellow poets this style had been received with joy, more than once he had been called difficult, affected and obscure. So now, when he was aiming at a wider public, this was the second point of concern. Would his unusual Latin style be acceptable? Again, he asked the Amsterdam professor to look at his poems not as a friend but as a severe judge. For Huygens knew that his Latin poetry now was to meet a wider circle of readers. And, unlike his friends, these people had not before experienced his peculiar Latin style, his unusual obscurity and, as some would have it, his affectedness. So the professor was ordered to pick out everything that needed either correction, illustration, or even complete deletion.[17]

From these remarks, made in private correspondence, we may conclude that Constantijn Huygens must not have felt too comfortable in publishing his Latin poems. He feared serious criticism both for his style and for lapses in quantity. Latin, indeed, was a strange language to him, just as he, in his poems, had a strange command of Latin.

Barlaeus *ad lectorem*

This, also, was the representation of the poet in the preliminary pages of the edition of his Latin poetry. The editor, the same Amsterdam professor who had read the poems in preparation, did not even take the trouble of hiding these possible points of criticism. Echoing the poet's attitude toward his mastery of the Latin language, the editor wrote: "This book is a banquet for well-educated, cheerful readers of good taste. Please stay away, captious critics, who would scowl on a wrong syllable or accent, and raise a storm in a teacup."[18] So here again we find the evidence that Huygens' use of Latin, at some points, is not impeccable.

As for the second point, his style, the editor anticipated critics as well. Of course, some readers would blame the poet's *obscuritas*. But, in fact, these critics had better blame themselves for not understanding: the poems had not been written for tasteless Boeotian peasants. Instead, they were meant for intelligent people who liked close reading and taking small bites, and enjoyed the taste of refined food.[19] Snobbish as it may sound, this is, of course, a way of defending the poet's unusual style.

---

[17] Letter to C. Barlaeus, 21 Aug. 1643 (ed. J. A. Worp, *De briefwisseling*, vol. 3 no. 3377): "Rogo itaque, ne, dum parcere mihi studes, male consultum velis. Intelligo nimirum, quid intersit, amico poenas dem, an imperitiae vulgi in obscuro fere autore prave et cum praejudicio affecti. (. . .) Excerpas hinc inde quae vel corrigenda vel illustranda censeas, vel penitus eliminanda."

[18] *Momenta Desultoria* 1655, fol. *6v: "Abesse jubeo vitilitigatores, et minutiarum anxios sectatores, qui ob voculae situm aut accentum, frontem corrugant, et fluctus in simpulo excitant."

[19] *Momenta Desultoria* 1655, fol. *7r: "Aquarum potoribus et in Boeotia natis haec non scribuntur, verum Lectori attento et cui repetita lectio secreta aperit. quae diluti et fatui saporis sunt, gustamus cum fastidio et contemptu, quae vero erecti, attentâ pitissatione, et frictione crebrisque morsicationibus."

Function of his Latin Poetry

So from his own words, as well as from the preliminary remarks in the edition, it is clear that Huygens was not a Latin poet in the classical tradition. Too much a man of his own day and age, he rejected servile imitation and the uncritical worship of ancient models. Instead, he used the dead language for a show of wit and intellect.

But above all, Huygens did not *claim* to be a professional in the field of Latin poetry. His public should know that he, first and foremost, was *occupatus* in the service of his country. Among his duties as a secretary to the Princes of Orange, his poems were merely *nugae*, a profit of leisure hours and odd moments. "I spent my free time on poetry", he wrote in his autobiography, "and I hope, posterity, that you will not disapprove of a poet who worked for his country and only when possible for you."[20] Now this is the wider context in which his Latin poetry must be seen. The *negotium* in the service of the country did not leave the poet much *otium* for thorough study and writing. For this reason the edition was given the appropriate title of *Momenta Desultoria*, since the poems were actually written in scattered moments and had scattered subjects.

So the social background of the poet played a predominant role in the nature of his poetry. In fact, the brevity of the poems and the diversity of their subjects were determined by the poet's circumstances. Even his peculiar style, tending towards obscurity, fitted his social position. For, taking part in European high society, Huygens in his Latin poetry presented himself as a *cortigiano* in the way Baldassare Castiglione had prescribed. With his word-play, puns, and contrived style Huygens deliberately aimed at *acutezza*, so that his readers, by cracking the hard nuts in his poetry, would enjoy the ingenuity and sagacity of the writer.[21]

Especially in confrontation with major authorities in the field of classical literature, we find Huygens using this motif. Among the great scholars and professional Latin poets of his day he was a poet of a different kind. When, for example, he presented his Latin poetry to the Leiden University professor Petrus Scriverius, he instructed the scholar about the type of poet he actually was: "You will find a cackling courtier here, rather than a poet, as a poet should be."[22]

---

[20] *De vita propria* 2. 314–317 (ed. J. A. Worp, *De gedichten*, vol. 8, 212):

> Tu quoque, Posteritas, nisi vani pascimur umbrâ
> Nominis, Hugenijs aliquot bene perdere nugis
> Et momenta voles, et non odisse Poetam
> Res Patriae alternisque tuas, ubi posset, agentem.

[21] B. Castiglione, *Il Cortegiano*, 1 cap. 30: "Se le parole che usa il scrittore, portan seco un poco non dirò di difficultà, ma d'acutezza recondita, e non cosi nota, come quelle che si dicono parlando ordinariamente, danno una certa maggior autorità alla scrittura, e fanno ch'il lettore va più ritenuto e sopra di se, e meglio considera e si diletta dell' ingegno e dottrina di chi scrive." Huygens used these words in defense of his style, in the Dutch poem *Daghwerck* (ed. J. A. Worp, *De gedichten*, vol. 3, 49).

[22] *Momenta Desultoria* 1655 fol. ★★7v (ed. J. A. Worp, *De gedichten*, vol. 3, 312 vs. 4–5): "Si poëtae non poëtae, si dicacis aulici Non gravaris esse lector."

In conclusion, a clash between Huygens and Hugo Grotius may be instructive. Although he had always held him in high esteem, one day Huygens wrote a very sharp epigram against Grotius. The poem was a fierce attack on Grotius' plea for the unity of all churches. Hurtful as it was, it was published in a pamphlet anonymously to prevent any criticism. However, within a few days, it was found out, probably because of the style, that the epigram had been written by Huygens. Of course, Grotius felt very much offended and took his revenge. In his counter-attack the scholar denounced the quality of the Latin verse, and called the author of the epigram a bad poet. In fact, he called him Santra Salebrosus, the inferior poet known from the epigrams of Martial. Although this was a painful point for Huygens, he knew that in confrontation with such a great scholar and expert in Latin any refutation would be useless. Therefore, he decided to take it as a compliment and as a confirmation of his poetic practice. In reply he said: "La qualité de mauvais poète m'a tousjours semblé des plus compatibles aveq celle d'honest' homme."[23]

Conclusion

Constantijn Huygens in his Latin poetry was quite a peculiar phenomenon. For, as far as models are concerned, he refused to be a servile imitator of the classical writers. Furthermore, the practice of his poetry would not let him be a thorough follower of the classical tradition. When scholars blamed him for writing *parum Latine,* or when they missed the typical *color Romanus* in his verse, the poet agreed.[24] On the contrary, Huygens had his own ideas of writing Latin poetry. For him, it was a game of word-play and wit, an entertaining show of intellect. His merits were not to be found in the authentic use of Latin, but in the original mastery of a language that for him was dead. To put it in his own pregnant style: *Barbarus ille mihi sermo est, ego barbarus illi.*[25]

Leiden University

---

[23] For a full discussion on the clash between Huygens and Grotius see H. J. M. Nellen, 'Een Haags dichter over "de Delftse Cicero": Hugo Grotius in de brieven en gedichten van Constantijn Huygens,' *De zeventiende eeuw* 3–2, 1987, 125–137.

[24] In a letter from Willem Grotius to Hugo Grotius, 21 April 1642, (ed. P. C. Molhuysen et al., *Briefwisseling van Hugo Grotius,* 15 vols. ['s-Gravenhage, 1928–1996] vol. 13, no. 5689), the style of Huygens' epigram is characterized as "stilum non satis Latinum". Another negative judgement by Hugo Grotius on a poem by Huygens in a letter to Willem de Groot, 17 July 1631 (*Briefwisseling,* vol. 4 no. 1660): "carmen inelegans nec latinum". Cf. also P. Hofman Peerlkamp, *De vita doctrina et facultate Nederlandorum qui carmina Latina composuerunt,* 2nd ed. (Haarlem, 1838) 438: "Mihi ita videtur. Hugenio, quominus excellens poeta fieret, natura non obstitit. Sed natura sine arte et exercitatione parum valet. Arti autem et exercitationi non multum tribuere, nec luxuriem ingenii usu depascere potuit; quo factum est, ut lusus verborum captare, et negligentiam in scribendo adhibere coeperit, a venustate et nitore Romano alienam."

[25] *De vita propria* 1. 5 (ed. J. A. Worp, *De gedichten,* vol. 8, 180).

References

Constantijn Huygens, *Momenta Desultoria*, ed. C. Barlaeus, Hagae-Comitis 1644

———, *Momenta Desultoria*, Ed. altera, multo priore auctior, ed. L. Huygens, Hagae-Comitis 1655

———, *De gedichten*, ed. J. A. Worp, 9 vols. (Groningen, 1892–1899)

———, *De briefwisseling,* ed. J. A. Worp, 6 vols. (The Hague, 1911–1917)

http://iias.leidenuniv.nl/huygens/home.html

Zum Briefwechsel Thomas Bartholins[1]

NIELS W. BRUUN

Als der dänische Polyhistor und Grundleger des ersten dänischen Naturalienkabinetts, Ole Worm 1654 starb, hinterliess er eine umfangreiche Briefsammlung, nämlich den Briefwechsel, den er von Jugend an mit Gelehrten in Dänemark und im übrigen Europa geführt hatte. Die Briefe, deren wissenschafts- und geistesgeschichtliche Bedeutung kaum zu überschätzen ist, befanden sich viele Jahre lang im Besitz der Familie, bis Frederik Rostgaard, dessen Name heute vor allem mit der verdienstvollen Ausgabe dänischer neulateinischer Dichtung verbunden ist, der *Deliciæ Poetarum Danorum* von 1693, das Material mit Hinblick auf eine Veröffentlichung übernahm. Die Briefe sind jedoch nicht von Rostgaard herausgegeben worden, sondern von seinem guten Freund, dem klassischen Philologen Hans Gram, dessen kritische Durchsicht der Brieftexte 1728 abgeschlossen war.

Der Philologe Hans Gram arbeitete mit äusserster Sorgfalt und in dem Manuskript, das er während der Editionsarbeit an den Briefen benutzte, hat er mehrfach seine Überlegungen die Briefe betreffend schriftlich festgehalten, die in zwei mehr oder weniger voneinander abweichenden Fassungen vorlagen—vermutlich zum späteren Gebrauch in dem Vorwort, das er aus verschiedenen Gründen jedoch nie schrieb.

Die Schwierigkeiten begannen, als Hans Gram zu dem Briefwechsel zwischen Ole Worm und dessen Neffen, dem Sohn seiner Schwester, Thomas Bartholin kam. Letzterer hatte in den Jahren 1663 bis 1667 unter dem Titel *Epistulæ Medicinales* eine aus 400 Briefen bestehende Auswahl seiner Korrespondenz mit Gelehrten in In- und Ausland veröffentlicht, unter anderem auch einige Briefe von seinem Onkel Ole

---

[1] Mein Vortrag liegt hier in der gleichen Form vor, in der er auf dem IANLS-Kongress 1997 in Avila gehalten wurde. Aus platzmässigen Gründen ist es mir nicht möglich gewesen, den Text mit erklärenden Anmerkungen zu versehen oder meine Standpunkte näher zu erläutern und zu begründen. Stattdessen weise ich auf meinen Aufsatz "Über die redaktionellen Prinzipien des Thomas Bartholin bei der Herausgabe seines Briefwechsels" hin, in dem ich eine umfassende Dokumentation vorlege und meine Auffassung eingehend begründe und diskutiere. Der Artikel ist in Vorbereitung und wird in absehbarer Zeit in der dänischen Zeitschrift *Danske Studier* erscheinen.

Worm. Hans Gram stellte ganz richtig fest, dass Ole Worms eigenhändigen Briefe, die in seinen noch bewahrten Konzeptbüchern überliefert sind, in Thomas Bartholins Ausgabe der Briefe eine andere Form erhalten hatten. Einen dieser Briefe hat Hans Gram mit folgender Anmerkung versehen:

> *Hæc epistula, sed multò auctior, præsertim ab initio & circa finem, legitur in Thomæ Bartholini Epistulis Medicinalibus . . . ut appareat, eam postea quàm in adversariis scripserat Wormium auxisse.*

Grams Erklärung, Ole Worm habe während der Reinschrift der Briefe Korrektionen vorgenommen und Zusätze gemacht, erscheint unmittelbar ganz plausibel und an anderer Stelle in seinem Manuskript vertieft er diese Auffassung noch mit folgender Erklärung:

> *Hinc NB disco (id quod in Præfatione monendum) non profiteri nos Epistolas Wormii aliter repræsentari in nostra hac editione quàm quales in Autographis beati Viri adversariis . . . inventæ sunt, primis adeo lineis ductæ conceptæque, cum inter rescribendum multa postea immutasse Wormium & addidisse vel his epistolarum, quæ ex datis ad se Bartholinus edidit, exemplis satis edoceamur.*

Gram ist also der Auffassung, dass Ole Worms Briefe in der Form, in der sie in seinen Konzeptbüchern vorliegen, lediglich als flüchtig entworfene Skizzen zu betrachten sind, die erst während der Reinschrift ihre endgültige Form erhielten. Nach Gram ist es eben gerade diese Originalfassung, die Bartholin in seiner Briefausgabe *Epistulæ Medicinales* wiedergegeben hat.

In neuerer Zeit haben die Neulatinisten H. D. Schepelern und Niels W. Bruun einige Originalbriefe von Ole Worms Hand untersucht und mit der in Ole Worms Konzeptbüchern vorliegenden Fassung verglichen. Aus diesen Untersuchungen, die keineswegs Anspruch auf Vollständigkeit erheben, geht klar hervor, dass Ole Worm sich, abgesehen von ganz geringfügigen Korrekuren, bei der Reinschrift an seine Vorlage gehalten hat. Wenn von Ole Worms Briefen die Rede ist, begeht man deshalb wohl kaum einen Fehler, wenn man zwischen Konzeptfassung und Originalbrief ein Gleichheitszeichen setzt. Jedenfalls ist Grams Auffassung von der Konzeptfassung als eines flüchtigen Entwurfs, dem Worm erst während der Reinschrift seine endgültige Form gegeben hat, als nicht haltbar zurückzuweisen. Gleichzeitig sei zu Grams Entschuldigung jedoch gerechterweise der Umstand hervorgehoben, dass Gram ja nicht die ungleich bequemeren Bedingungen des modernen Herausgebers hatte, dem bei seiner Materialsuche ausländische Bibliotheken und Archive zur Verfügung stehen, und dass es ihm deshalb praktisch unmöglich war, genauere Untersuchungen über das Verhältnis zwischen Kladde und Originalbrief anzustellen.

Es war nicht leicht für Hans Gram, sich Klarheit über den Briefwechsel zwischen Ole Worm und Thomas Bartholin zu verschaffen und diese Schwierigkeiten nahmen noch zu, als er im Laufe seiner Herausgebertätigkeit auf einen an Ole Worm gerichteten Originalbrief von Thomas Bartholins Hand stiess. Der betreffende Brief war schon in Thomas Bartholins Briefsammlung *Epistulæ Medicinales* herausgegeben worden, jedoch in einer Fassung, die in vielen, nicht unwesentlichen Punkten von dem Originalbrief abwich, den Gram in der Hand hielt. Diesen Umstand meint Hans Gram folgendermassen erklären zu können:

*Crediderim Thomam Bartholinum, cum raptim & ex tempore scriberet multas episto-
larum, quas ad Wormium aliosque mittebat, ut indicia cum alia tum ipsi in autographis
characteres literarum & ductus velocissima manu ... ostendunt, argumenta tantum
earum in adversariis ac antigraphis suis consignata retinuisse, ex quibus postea, cùm sta-
tuisset Wormii responsorias ... Epistolis à se vulgandis ... inserere, novam Epistolam
... conflaverit.*

Daraus geht hervor, dass sich auch in Thomas Bartholins Konzeptbuch skizzen-
hafte Briefkladden fanden, und dass Bartholin, der laut Gram Ole Worms Briefe an
Bartholin selbst nach der reingeschriebenen Fassung, wie er sie empfangen hatte, ab-
druckte, jetzt einen gewissermassen neugeschriebenen Brief an Ole Worm veröffentlicht, dem eine unvollständige Kladde zugrundeliegt.

Wenn Hans Grams Erklärungsversuch nicht zu überzeugen vermag, ist der Grund
dafür in dem Umstand zu suchen, dass Thomas Bartholin in dem Zeitraum, in dem
er mit Ole Worm korrespondierte, nach eigener Aussage meist gar kein Konzeptbuch
gebrauchte, sondern seine Briefe ex tempore verfasste. Dazu kommt, dass Thomas
Bartholin, als er zwischen 1660 und 1663 die Herausgabe seiner Briefe vorbereitete,
Zugang zu Ole Worms hinterlassener Briefsammlung hatte und damit auch zu dem
betreffenden Originalbrief, den er infolgedessen in der Form hätte reproduzieren
können, in der er vorlag—wenn er das wirklich gewollt hätte.

Wenn Thomas Bartholin seine Antwortbriefe nicht in ihrer ursprünglichen Fassung herausgegeben hat, sondern ihnen manchmal sowohl sprachlich als auch inhaltlich eine andere Form gegeben hat, ist die Erklärung hierfür in Umständen und Er-
wägungen zu finden, die er im Vorwort zur dritten Zenturie oder Sammlung seiner
1667 erschienenen *Epistulæ Medicinales* darlegt:

*Non ægrè ferent amicæ mentes ... si responsionibus meis non pauca hic, forsan etiam
diversa viderint esse addita. Hanc enim mihi licentiam condonari velim, qvod interdum
novas substituerim, si qvando vel amanuensium exemplaria deessent vel dignæ lectoribus
aliis epistolæ. Hinc plerisqve meis velut condimenta in Medica exercitatione obvias
Historias vel ab amicis Naturæ Consiliariis communicatas inserui, ut gratior familiaris
esset pagina.*

Bartholin bittet also seine Brieffreunde um Verständnis dafür, dass die veröffentlichten Antwortbriefe entweder kleine Zusätze enthalten oder auch einen fast neuen
Inhalt bekommen haben, so dass sie nicht mehr viel Ähnlichkeit mit dem ursprünglichen Antwortbrief haben. Als einen der Gründe für diese wohl auch zu jener Zeit
recht überraschende Disposition gibt er offen und ehrlich zu, in gewissen Fällen gezwungen gewesen zu sein, einen ganz neuen Antwortbrief zu verfassen, da er seiner-
zeit keine Kladde angefertigt habe und sich jetzt nicht mehr daran erinnere, was er
damals eigentlich geschrieben habe. Als den anderen Beweggrund für diese redaktionellen Änderungen führt er Rücksicht auf den Leser an. Bartholin ist sich vollkommen darüber im klaren, dass die Voraussetzungen für einen privaten Brief, der veröffentlicht und damit öffentlich wird, grundlegend verändert sind und es sei, wie er
erkennt, notwendig, den Text unter anderem mit unterhaltsamen Geschichten und

Berichten zu würzen, wenn man sichergehen wolle, dass die Briefe bei einer breiteren Leserschar Anklang fänden.

Vergleicht man heute Thomas Bartholins Antwortbriefe mit den gedruckten und von ihm selbst revidierten Fassungen, kann man feststellen, dass nur einige wenige originale Antwortbriefe so radikal verändert worden sind, dass man von einem vollständig neuen Brief sprechen kann. Als Beispiel hierfür verweise ich auf Nr. 1a und 1b, die jeweils den Anfang eines Briefes darstellen, den Bartholin im Jahre 1662 an seinen alten Jugendfreund, den Polyhistor Aprosio Vintimiglia in Italien schrieb. Wie Sie sehen, wird in dem Originalbrief (1a) viel Wert darauf gelegt, der aufrichtigen Freude darüber Ausdruck zu verleihen, dass die Verbindung mit einem alten Freund wieder aufgenommen wurde, und dass es diesem Freund gutgegangen ist im Leben, während die revidierte Fassung diesen Punkt nur ganz kurz berührt und stattdessen in weitläufigen Wendungen auf Bartholins Bruder, den Orientalisten Jacob Bartholin zu sprechen kommt. Dieser Bruder wird im Originalbrief überhaupt nicht erwähnt, wird aber für die revidierte Fassung—den öffentlichen Brief—herangezogen, teils, weil man davon ausgehen kann, dass das gelehrte europäische Publikum daran interessiert ist, etwas über Leben und Arbeit des verstorbenen Verwandten zu erfahren, teils aber auch, weil Thomas Bartholin selbst den Wunsch hatte, seinem übrigens schon damals recht unbekannten Bruder ein Denkmal zu setzen.

Bevor wir den Brief an Aprosio verlassen, möchte ich gerne darauf aufmerksam machen, dass dieser Brief von allen heute existierenden Bartholin-Briefen der einzige ist, in dem Thomas Bartholin sich selbst gestattet, einem anderen Menschen gegenüber aufrichtige und warme Gefühle zum Ausdruck zu bringen. Dass die echte Herzenswärme des privaten Briefes in der gedruckten Fassung des Briefes nicht zum Ausdruck kommt, ist, was mich überrascht hat, auf einen redaktionellen Beschluss Bartholins zurückzuführen, auf den er im Vorwort der zwei ersten Briefsammlungen wie folgt selber hinweist:

Id qvamqvam proprium epistolis sit & germanum, veris affectibus plenum, publica tamen luce indignum censeo.

Er vertritt also den Standpunkt, dass persönliche Gedanken und Gefühle, die ja ganz normal sind in einem privaten Brief, beim Redigieren gestrichen werden müssen, wenn der betreffende Brief veröffentlicht werden soll. Er begründet seinen Standpunkt nicht näher, ich vermute jedoch, dass er von der damaligen Brieftheorie übernommen wurde und nicht als Ausdruck der traditionellen Unlust des nordischen Mannes zu verstehen ist, persönliche Gefühle oder—mit Bartholins eigenen Worten—*veri affectus* zu zeigen. Daraus erklärt sich, warum ein Teil der Briefe Bartholins in der gedruckten Briefsammlung von einer merkwürdigen Steifheit geprägt sind.

In den Auszügen 2a und 2b zeige ich, dass Bartholin während der redaktionellen Arbeit an seinen eigenen Briefen diese auch verkürzte und im vorliegenden Fall derart drastisch und umfassend, dass der Leser der revidierten Fassung kaum versteht, worum es eigentlich geht. Erst bei der Lektüre des Originalbriefes begreift man, dass Ole Worm in der Abhandlung mit dem Titel *De aureo Domini Christiani Qvinti ... cornu* den Fund eines etwa aus dem vierten Jahrhundert n.Chr. stammenden Goldhorns beschreibt, und dass der Werktitel aufgrund einer Änderung in der Wortstellung zu *De Aureo Principis Cornu* in Frankreich Anlass zu Heiterkeit gegeben hat. Im Scherz meinte man nämlich zu wissen, das Buch handle von dem Erbprinzen Christian von Dänemark, den man zum Hahnrei gemacht habe!

In Nr. 3a und 3b lege ich den Abschluss eines Briefes vor, den Bartholin 1643 an den neapolitanischen Arzt Marcus Aurelius Severinus geschrieben hat. Die revidierte Fassung selbst schliesst sich, abgesehen von einigen kleinen Änderungen—*tantæ* ist ausgetauscht gegen *magnæ* und anstatt des umfassenden *virtutum* heisst es einschränkend *eruditionis*—eng an den Originalbrief an, am Schluss des Briefes findet man jedoch eine Hinzufügung, mit der Bartholin hofft, die Unterlassungssünde wieder gutzumachen, die er als junger Mann 1643 beging, als er vergass, dem alten Freund seines Vaters, Mario Schipano, einen Gruss zu überbringen. Jetzt kommt der Gruss—mit zwanzigjähriger Verspätung. Dass sowohl der Adressat des Briefes als auch der Freund des Vaters längst das Zeitliche gesegnet haben, spielt dabei keine Rolle, denn mit dieser Hinzufügung liegt der Brief endlich in der Form vor, in der der junge Thomas Bartholin ihn hätte schreiben sollen. Ich mache darauf aufmerksam, dass derartige Zusätze auch in anderen von Bartholins gedruckten Briefen zu finden sind.

Ausschnitt 4a ist einem Brief an den bekannten Johan Schefferus in Uppsala entnommen, in dem Bartholin um dessen Meinung über die Beschreibung der Pygmäen bei dem römisch-griechischen Schriftsteller Aelianus bittet. Im Originalbrief war der Name Aelianus im stillschweigenden Einverständnis der Eingeweihten ausgelassen worden, in der revidierten Fassung jedoch wurde er zur Orientierung des Lesers vernünftigerweise wieder eingesetzt. Wir sehen auch, dass das etwas seltenere *accensenda* des Originals gegen das gebräuchlichere *annumeranda* ausgetauscht wird. Dieser Art von Änderungen, bei denen ein selten vorkommendes Wort gegen ein gängigeres ausgetauscht wird, begegnen wir häufig in den Briefen. Am Schluss von 4a bemerken Sie, dass der Gedanke, den Bartholin mit *certè fabulosi Dij fabulæ huic ibi immiscentur* auszudrücken versucht, erst mit der Formulierung *certè fabuloso ævo contigit, quia Dii Deæqve fabulæ huic immiscentur* der revidierten Fassung klar und deutlich zum Ausdruck kommt.

Im selben Brief—ich verweise auf 5a—erwähnt Thomas Bartholin einige seiner literarischen Arbeiten, die sich zu dem Zeitpunkt, als der Brief geschrieben wurde gerade im Druck befanden. Die Schrift über die Lungen versieht er mit der zusätzlichen Information, sie sei vor ein paar Tagen fertig geworden und zwar *celerrimo calamo*, denn, wie er seinem Freund Scheffer anvertraut, 'so pflege ich ja zu arbeiten'. Für den, der einige von Bartholins Büchern gelesen hat, ist dieses Eingeständnis keine grosse Überraschung, sondern bestärkt einen in der Vermutung, dass Thomas Bartholin sich sicher nicht immer die notwendige Zeit für die Ausarbeitung seiner Schriften genommen hat. Bartholin selbst schreibt an einer Stelle, allerdings in Bezug auf seine eigenhändigen Briefe *bis non scribo, vix bis lego*. Ich glaube jedoch, dass diese Äusserung Bartholins Arbeitsmethode im allgemeinen beschreibt, und dass dies bis zu einem gewissen Grad auch zu erklären vermag, wie es möglich war, dass ein Mann allein eine so ungeheuer umfangreiche und allseitige, an die 100 Arbeiten umfassende literarische Produktion hat hinterlassen können.

Aus 5 b geht hervor, dass Thomas Bartholin beim Wiederlesen dessen, was er seinem Freund Scheffer in einem privaten Brief anvertraut hatte, angesichts der ursprünglichen und offenherzigen Formulierung *celerrimo calamo* Bedenken gekommen sind, und dass er es für besser hielt, diese Formulierung abzuschwächen und gegen das harmlosere *calamo extemporaneo* auszutauschen, denn niemand in der gelehrten Welt sollte hören, wie er öffentlich zugab, seine Schriften eilig zusammengeschrieben zu haben.

Mit 6a sind wir zum Schluss des Briefes gekommen und hier teilt Bartholin auf eine wie mir scheint rührende Weise mit, den Brief an Scheffer an seinem Geburtstag, also dem 20. Oktober, geschrieben zu haben. Diese private und ein wenig sentimentale Notiz erscheint nicht in der revidierten Fassung, da Gefühlsäusserungen oder *veri affectus*, wie wir schon gesehen haben, allein dem privaten Brief vorbehalten waren.

Nachdem wir uns nun davon haben überzeugen können, dass Thomas Bartholin mit Hinblick auf eine Veröffentlichung an seinen eigenen Briefen redaktionelle Änderungen vornahm, liegt die Überlegung nahe, ob er nicht auch die von ihm selbst empfangenen Briefe einer kritischen Überprüfung unterzog, bevor er sie in den Druck gab. Es ist merkwürdig, dass Thomas Bartholin weder in den Vorwörtern zu seinen gedruckten Briefen noch anderenorts über diese wichtige Frage Auskunft gibt. Im Anhang finden Sie jedoch die Antwort auf diese Frage.

Im ersten Beispiel (7a) hat Bartholin das ein wenig warmherzige *svavissime* gestrichen—eine Anredeform, die man in den gelehrten Kreisen nördlich der Alpen durchaus nicht schätzte—und es gegen das akademische und völlig ungefährliche *sapientissime* ausgetauscht. Etwas Ähnliches sehen Sie in 8a, wo das emotionale *in dies viridiorem* gestrichen und an seine Stelle ein Gruss an zwei Personen gesetzt wurde, denen gegenüber der Briefschreiber Thomas Bartholins Auffassung nach seine Hochachtung hätte zum Ausdruck bringen müssen. Die nachfolgende Textprobe, in der das stark betonte *cuiquam* gegen das gebräuchlichere *alicui* ausgetauscht wird, enthält ebenfalls eine Ergänzung zum Text, die dem Leser als Aussenstehendem erklären soll, warum Severinus Thomas Bartholin bittet, als Zwischenhändler aufzutreten.

Die Auszüge 10 und 11 enthalten ein paar kleinere sprachliche Änderungen, auf die ich hier nicht weiter eingehen will, da sie wohl für sich selber sprechen. Stattdessen möchte ich kurz auf Nr. 12 zu sprechen kommen. Sie finden hier das ungebräuchliche Substantiv *monumen*, das Bartholins Brieffreund Marcus Aurelius Severinus bei dem Grammatiker Priscianus gefunden haben muss, wenn er es nicht gar selbst gebildet hat. Da die singuläre Form möglicherweise Unsicherheit darüber hätte aufkommen lassen können, was der gelehrte Briefschreiber ausdrücken wollte—er weist ja auf William Harveys epochemachende Abhandlung über den Blutkreislauf hin—hat Bartholin in dem öffentlichen Brief die Normalform *monumentum* eingesetzt. Nr. 13, der letzte Textauszug den ich hier vorlege, ist ein Beispiel für die am häufigsten auftretende Korrektur in Thomas Bartholins Briefen: die Änderung der Wortstellung.

Wir haben uns nun an Hand der Beispiele selbst Gewissheit darüber verschaffen können, dass Thomas Bartholin redaktionelle Änderungen mit Hinblick auf eine Veröffentlichung nicht nur an den Briefen vornahm, die er selbst geschrieben hatte, sondern auch an denen, die er empfangen hatte. Die redaktionellen Eingriffe an den empfangenen Briefen könnte man in etwa folgender Weise zusammenfassen:

1) Es werden sprachliche Änderungen vorgenommen, die entweder Deutlichkeit, Verständlichkeit und Genauigkeit anstreben oder lediglich den Charakter der Normalisierung haben. Das Vorbild ist natürlich klassisches Latein.

2) Die Wortstellung wird geändert.

3) Hat der Briefschreiber dem Adressaten gegenüber warmherzige persönliche Gefühle zum Ausdruck gebracht, sind diese Äusserungen in dem öffentlichen Brief meist, jedoch nicht konsequent, weggelassen worden.

4) Der Text wird durch kurze Zusätze ergänzt, die erklärenden oder vertiefenden Charakter haben oder es werden Personen eingeführt, die der Briefschreiber nach Bartholins Auffassung hätte erwähnen müssen.

Es sei hier betont, dass die Ergänzungen normalerweise mit Umsicht und mit mit vollem Respekt vor dem Absender vorgenommen worden sind. Ich möchte gleichzeitig darauf aufmerksam machen, dass es keine Beispiele dafür gibt, dass Bartholin durch Weglassen längerer Passagen in dem empfangenen Brief Meinungen oder Gesichtspunkte, die ihm irgendwie nicht passten, im Sinne einer Zensur unterdrückt hätte. Er verhält sich mit anderen Worten loyal gegenüber seiner Vorlage.

Das soeben Gesagte gilt jedoch in keiner Weise für die Briefe, die Bartholin von seinem Onkel Ole Worm empfangen hat. Es ist ein auffälliges Paradox, dass Bartholin die Briefe des Mannes, dem er sonst so viel Hochachtung entgegenbrachte, bei der Veröffentlichung fast respektlos behandelte. Ich kann auf diesen Sachverhalt hier nicht näher eingehen, sondern beschränke mich darauf kurz darzulegen, wie dies meiner Meinung nach zu erklären ist: Als Thomas Bartholin zwischen 1660 und 1663 die Herausgabe seiner Briefe vorbereitete, besass er die Briefe, die er im Laufe der Jahre von Ole Worm erhalten hatte, nicht mehr, fandt sie jedoch alle in Ole Worms hinterlassenen Konzeptbüchern wieder. Gerade der Umstand, dass die Briefe dieses Absenders nur in Kladde vorlagen, hat bewirkt, dass Bartholin sich nicht wie sonst der Vorlage gegenüber verpflichtet gefühlt hat, sondern meinte, sie mit grosser Freizügigkeit behandeln zu können.

Doch nun zurück zu Thomas Bartholins eigenhändigen Briefen! Für die redaktionelle Arbeit an diesen Briefen hat Thomas Bartholin die gleichen Richtlinien befolgt, die er für die empfangenen Briefe aufgestellt hatte, darüber hinaus stellen wir jedoch fest, dass er seine Darstellung entweder ausbaut oder verkürzt, so dass die Botschaft klarer und deutlicher zum Ausdruck kommt. Der entscheidende Unterschied zwischen der Redaktion fremder und der eigener Briefe besteht jedoch darin, dass er sich seinem ursprünglichen Brief gegenüber gelegentlich sehr freizügig verhält, indem er ihn derart umarbeitet, dass eigentlich eine vollkommen neue Fassung vorliegt.

In der Einleitung zu meinem Vortrag habe ich den dänischen Philologen Hans Gram und dessen Auffassung über den Entstehungsprozess einiger der Bartholinischen Briefe erwähnt. Ich habe gezeigt, dass er mit viel Energie versucht hat, das zu bemänteln und wegzuargumentieren, was er meiner Vermutung nach bereits gesehen und erkannt hatte, nämlich, dass Bartholin seine Briefe revidierte, bevor er sie veröffentlichte. Der Hintergrund für Grams vergeblichen Versuche war wahrscheinlich eine tiefe Enttäuschung darüber, dass eine europäische Berühmtheit wie Thomas Bartholin seine Briefe nicht in der Form veröffentlichte, in der sie ursprünglich vorlagen. Als

Trost für Hans Gram und alle diejenigen, die in Verbindung hiermit von einer 'nicht so strengen Herausgebermoral jener Zeit' sprachen, sei daran erinnert, dass Thomas Bartholin sich in guter Gesellschaft befindet. Schon Plinius der Jüngere tat es, Sidonius Apollinaris tat es ebenfalls und alle die Vielen, die ihnen seitdem gefolgt sind und selbst die Herausgabe ihrer eigenen Korrespondenz besorgten, taten dasselbe: Sie redigierten ihre Briefe sorgfältig bevor sie sie herausgeben liessen. Zu erwarten, dass Thomas Bartholin sich selbst von dieser uralten und ehrwürdigen epistolographischen Tradition, die sich meines Wissens bis heute lebendig erhalten hat, hätte ausschliessen sollen, ist meiner Auffassung nach nicht zu verlangen und übrigens auch nicht wahrscheinlich.

Anhang:
Textproben aus Briefen, die von Thomas Bartholinus geschrieben sind

(1a)   *An Aprosio Vintimiglia in Venezia. 24.2. 1662.*
Vir Religiose & Reverendissime,
Summam mihi lætitiam attulerunt literæ desideratissimæ scriptæ X. Nov. 1661, ex quibus commodè mihi allatis vivere Te & valere magna cum voluptate intellexi, nec minus altero nuncio affectus sum, quod nostri adhuc servaveris memoriam. Albo calculo hunc diem notavi. Quamquam enim multi iam effluxerint anni, ex quo nihil literarum vel dederim vel acceperim ob remotorum locorum difficultatem, tamen Vintimigliæ mei candidus animus, humanitas incredibilis & amicitia haud fucata animo meo semper insedit & ante oculos versata est. Tibi interea, Rev. Pater, quod cuncta ex animi sententia fluxerint & amplissimi Romæ honores obtigerint, gratulor publicoque nomine jam gaudeo, quod patriæ tuæ redditus in edendis varij argumenti libris occuperis, quibus nomen tuum ad posteritatem diffundas.

(1b)   Angelico Aprosio Vintimiglia, Genoam.
Lectis Tuis humanissimis literis rediit mihi animus & revixit ingenti rigidæ hyemis frigore penè extinctus. Gaudeo qvod adhuc vivas valeasqve, utinam diutissimè, in literarum vestrarum, qvibus assiduè magna fama vacas, solatium. Nos valemus & cum fratribus tui memoriam semper recolimus. Salutant illi Te perofficiosè, qvi inter vivos sunt. Sextus enim frater *Jacobus Bartholinus,* designatus olim in Academiâ Regia & Eqvestri Sorana Professor Historiarum, ante plusculos annos in Germania qvum reditum in patriam meditaretur, doloribus colicis confectus obiit. Ante obitum tamen Ebræorum nonnullos Magistros publica luce donavit in lingvis orientalibus perfectissimus, qvos Tibi in fasciculo mitto, ut videas nec illum Bartholinum ignotum vixisse, & si fata vitam illi prorogassent, qvamplurima in schedis relicta promisisse.

(2a)   *An Ole Worm in Kopenhagen. 31.3. 1642*
Id hactenus silentio involvi non semel in Gallia Tituli et Inscriptionis Ordinem turbasse multos et extemporanei joci de Aureo Principis Cornu festivioribus ingeniis materiam ministrasse, ut sunt ad captiunculas prompti leviorum animi.

(2b)   Faceta alia ingenia nescio quid de cornu aureo jocantur.

(3a)   An Marcus Aurelius Severinus in Napoli. 17.9. 1643.
        Apud Columellam igitur pro *vipera* legendum *uiuerra* censuit Vir Summus Pe-
        trus Victorius, quod an recte ab alio nolim exquirere quam à Severino nostro,
        Naturæ arbitro & intimiori mysteriorum eius scrutatore, cui perennaturam *tantæ*
        famæ vitam ex meritis uoueo, *virtutum eius sincerus amatoset Cultor indefessus*
        Thomas Bartholinus, Casp. f.
        Pat. 17. Sept. 1643.

(3b)   Apud Columellam igitur pro *vipera* legendum *uiuerra* censuit Vir Summus Pe-
        trus Victorius, quod an rectè ab alio nolim exquirere quam à Severino nostro,
        Naturæ arbitro & intimiori mysteriorum eius scrutatore, cui perennaturam
        magnæ famæ vitam ex meritis uoueo, *eruditionis illius* indefessus *cultor. Officio-*
        sissimam salutem nomine meo nunciabis Cl. Viro Mario Schipano, Parentis amico
        veteri, quem lætus humanis adhuc interesse accepi, utinam diu. Scripsi Pat. XVII.
        Sept. 1643.
        T.T.
        Thomas Bartholinus.

(4a)   *An Johan Scheffer in Uppsala. 20.10. 1662.*
        Quid sentias de Pygmæorum Historia lib. XV. cap. 29. consignata, nisi grave
        sit, indicabis. Fabulisne *accensenda? Certè fabulosi Dij fabulæ huic ibi immiscentur.*

(4b)   Quid sentias de Pygmæorum Historia lib. XV. cap. 29. Æliani consignata, nisi
        grave sit, indicabis. Fabulisne *annumeranda? Certè fabuloso ævo contigit, quia Dii*
        Deæqve fabulæ huic immiscentur.

(5a)   Operæ nostræ Typographicæ in epistolis meis desudant et in Diatribe de Pul-
        monum Substantia & Motu, *celerrimo calamo*, qui meus est mos, nudius tertius
        conscripta.

(5b)   Operæ nostræ Typographicæ in epistolis meis desudant et in Diatribe de Pul-
        monum Substantia & Motu, calamo extemporaneo, qui meus est mos, nudius
        tertius conscripta.

(6a)   Hafniæ XX Octobr. MDC LXII, *qui mihi ante annos XLVII natalis fuit.*
        T.T.
        Thomas Bartholinus

(6b)   Hafniæ XX Octobr. MDC LXII.
        T.T.
        Thomas Bartholinus

Textproben aus Briefen, die an Thomas Bartholinus geschrieben sind

Von Marcus Aurelius Severinus. 30.5. 1643
(7a)   Hactenus de his carptim & compendiosè, qvæ tu, *svavissime* Bartholine . . .
        commode valebis exercere ac dilatare.

(7b)   Hactenus de his carptim & compendiosè, qvæ tu, *sapientissime* Bartholine . . . commode valebis exercere ac dilatare.

(8a)   Amorem mei fove *in dies viridiorem.*

(8b)   Amorem mei fove *foveqve Clarissimorum Virorum Veslingi & Rhodi gratiam.* Von demselben. 20.2. 1645

(9a)   Rogabaris, ut *cuiquam* Amico Lugdunensi Docto Viro commendares editionis meæ castigationem.

(9b)   Rogabaris, ut *alicui* Amico Lugdunensi Docto Viro commendares editionis meæ castigationem. *Tuo isthoc officio plurimum opus est.*

Von demselben. 15.10. 1643

(10a)   Si condonent id liberi perturbationibus.

(10b)   Si condonent id liberi *a* perturbationibus.

Von demselben. 1.7. 1643.

(11a)   Nisi meus me animus meque dissertatio *fallant.*

(11b)   Nisi meus me animus meque dissertatio *fallunt.*

Von demselben. 13.4. 1643

(12a)   Judicium meum quoddam quod de Harvei *monumine feceram.*

(12b)   Judicium meum quoddam quod de Harvei *monumento feceram.*

Von Thomas Reinesius. 22.4. 1657.

(13a)   Sin autem propter verecundiam suam *minus se Tibi* obtulit.

(13b)   Sin autem propter verecundiam suam *Tibi se minus* obtulit.

Bagsvaerd, Denmark

Los Diálogos de Luis Vives en América

FRANCISCO CALERO CALERO

Importancia de los dialogos dentro del _corpus vivista_

A diferencia de la Edad Media, durante el Renacimiento el latín se enseñó preferentemente sobre diálogos escritos en latín, que solían tener por argumento aspectos de la vida escolar. Muchos de aquellos libritos alcanzaron gran éxito editorial, como los de Petrus Mosellanus[1] y los de Mathurinus Corderius[2]. Sin embargo, los de mayor repercusión fueron los famosísimos de Erasmo[3], de los que se contabilizan más de cuatrocientas ediciones. También Vives, después de la muerte de Erasmo, redactó unos diálogos[4], que fueron muy utilizados durante los siglos XVI, XVII y XVIII, llegando a contabilizarse sobre las trescientas treinta ediciones.

La finalidad de la obra es expresada claramente por Vives en la dedicatoria al príncipe Felipe[5] (futuro Felipe II):

> Quam ob causam non gravabor, inter maiorum studiorum occupationes, hac quoque parte pueritiae rudimenta adiuvare. Conscripsi in usum latinae linguae primam loquendi exercitationem, quam pueris, ut spero, conducibilem, tibi Principi puero visum est dicare.

Además de esa finalidad evidente, la enseñanza del latín, podemos descubrir otras motivaciones que le influirían en tomar aquella decisión en su edad madura: 1ª El extraordinario éxito de tales obritas, sobre todo, la de su amigo Erasmo. 2ª La posibilidad de solucionar sus dificultades económicas. 3ª La muerte de Erasmo, con quien tal vez no quiso competir en vida. 4ª Ayudar a su alumna y protectora Mencía de Mendoza en el aprendizaje del latín.

A pesar de que estas obritas eran consideradas como de poca importancia, como expresó el propio Vives "inter maiorum studiorum ocupationes", examinándolas con

---

[1] Petrus Mosellanus, _Paedologia_, s.l.s.a.

[2] Mathurinus Corderius, _Colloquiorum scholasticorum libri III_ (Genf, 1564).

[3] Desiderius Erasmus, _Familiarium colloquiorum formulae_ (Basilea, 1518).

[4] Luis Vives, _Linguae latinae exercitatio_ (Basilea, 1539).

[5] Luis Vives, _Linguae latinae exercitatio_, dedicatoria.

la perspectiva de los muchos años transcurridos, adquieren dimensiones de mucho mayor relieve. Esto es evidente en el caso de Erasmo, quien en sus *Familiarium Colloquiorum formulae* fue dejando las ideas por las que tanto luchó, hasta el punto de que en sus sucesivas ediciones podemos percibir la evolución de su espíritu. En los de Vives las esencias están más escondidas, pero es indudable que en la actualidad la *Linguae latinae exercitatio* ha de ser considerada como una obra importante, tanto por los datos autobiográficos que encierra como por las ideas educativas, sin olvidar sus numerosas indicaciones sobre juegos, deportes, comidas, bebidas, vestido, calzado, etc. También se pueden percibir entre líneas algunos rasgos de su personalidad, como el amor al estudio, el amor a la naturaleza, su frustración poética, la terrible enfermedad, su sentido práctico y su carácter moralista. De todo esto he tratado con amplitud en otro lugar, por lo que se remite allí[6] al lector interesado.

Un aspecto que aquí nos interesa especialmente es el de los comentarios a la *Linguae latinae exercitatio*. En su deseo de que los alumnos adquirieran un vocabulario lo más amplio posible, y dado su extraordinario dominio del léxico latino de todas las épocas, Vives se sirvió en su obra de palabras poco utilizadas. Él mismo se dio cuenta, ya que puso notas marginales en las que explicaba el significado de los términos más raros. Pero quien propiamente llevó a cabo el primer comentario sobre los Diálogos de Vives fue Pedro Mota, un complutense alumno de Nebrija. La edición más antigua con los comentarios de Mota es la de Lyon de 1544, hecha por Guillermo de Millis[7]. Decía que nos interesaban especialmente los comentarios, porque quien llevó los Diálogos de Vives a América escribió otros, precisamente para completar los de Mota. En efecto, la obra de Vives no sólo enseñó el latín a buena parte de Europa, sino que también lo hizo en América gracias a su amigo Francisco Cervantes de Salazar, de quien me he ocupado en otra ocasión.[8]

Francisco Cervantes de Salazar

No se conoce el año exacto del nacimiento de Cervantes Salazar, pero debió ser en la segunda década del siglo XVI. Nació en la ínclita Toledo, donde tuvo como maestro al insigne Alejo de Venegas, autor, entre otras obras, de *Primera parte de las diferencias de libros que hay en el universo*. Estudió cánones en Salamanca, obteniendo sólo el grado de bachiller. Por esos años acompañó al licenciado Girón en su viaje a Flandes, donde tuvo ocasión de tratar con personas eruditas de aquellas tierras, entre las que sobresale Luis Vives.

A su vuelta a España ocupó el cargo de secretario latino del cardenal García de Loaysa, arzobispo de Sevilla, gran inquisidor y presidente del Consejo de Indias; parece que dejó de estar a su servicio con anterioridad al 22 de abril de 1546. Fue

---

[6] Francisco Calero, *Los Diálogos de Luis Vives* (Valencia, 1994).

[7] *Ioannis Lodovici Vivis valentini linguae Latinae Exercitatio. Accessit etiam Graecarum priscarumque dictionum, et locorum subobscurorum interpretatio, per P. Mottam, una cum rerum et verborum memorabilium diligentissimo indice* (Lugduni, 1544).

[8] Francisco Calero, "Francisco Cervantes de Salazar autor de la primera biografía de Luis Vives", *Epos* 121 (1996): 53–64.

catedrático de retórica en la Universidad de Osuna, si bien no aparece su nombre en la relación de profesores de dicho centro. Gracias a la documentación utilizada por Millares Carlo[9] conocemos la razón de su paso a México el año 1550 ó 1551; se decidió a tal viaje por la invitación de su primo Alonso de Villaseca, dueño de una gran fortuna en Nueva España; también sabemos que posteriormente tuvo grandes desavenencias con este pariente.

Al principio de su estancia en México fue profesor de latín en una escuela particular, pero poco después, al fundarse la universidad, se le concedió la cátedra de retórica, con el encargo honorífico de pronunciar el discurso inaugural en latín; su permanencia en la universidad duró desde 1553 a 1557. Al mismo tiempo que enseñaba la retórica, se graduó de licenciado y maestro en la facultad de artes el mismo año de 1553; al año siguiente se presentó al examen de bachiller en cánones; también en este año recibió las sagradas órdenes, si bien los grados de bachiller, licenciado y doctor en teología los obtuvo años después.

No se sabe con exactitud cuándo fue nombrado cronista de la ciudad de México, pero el 15 de enero de 1560 solicitaba Cervantes permiso para ausentarse de la ciudad a fin de cumplir mejor su encargo de cronista. En 1563 presentaba ante el cabildo de México una real provisión que le otorgaba una canonjía. No pararon ahí los deseos de Cervantes, ya que se tienen noticia de las gestiones realizadas para obtener el cargo de chantre y el de maestreescuela, sin ningún resultado positivo. La causa de este fracaso debió ser el mal concepto que de él tenía el arzobispo Moya de Contreras, quien en su informe al rey de España afirmaba (se cita por Millares Carlo)[10]:

> El canónigo Francisco Cervantes de Salazar, natural de tierra de Toledo, de hedad de más de sesenta años, a veynte y cinco que está en esta tierra, a la cual vino lego, en opinión de gran latino, aunque con la hedad a perdido algo desto: leyó muchos años la cáthedra de rethórica de esta Universidad. Graduóse de todos tres grados en artes por suficiencia: ordenóse avrá veynte años de todas las órdenes, y oyó theología quatro años al fin de los cuales se graduó de bachiller, y después de licenciado y doctor, auiéndose graduado a los principios de bachiller en cánones por remisión de cursos. Es amigo de que le oygan y alaben, y agrádale la lisonja: es liuiano y mudable, y no está bien acreditado de honesto y casto, y es ambicioso de honra, y persuádese a que a de ser obispo, sobre lo cual le an hecho algunas burlas. A doze ques canónigo; no es nada eclesiástico, ni hombre para encomendarle negocios.

Tanto García Icazbalceta[11] como Millares Carlo consideran injustos estos juicios del arzobispo, que contradicen los de otras importantes personas así como las buenas relaciones de Cervantes con el Consejo de la inquisición, que le nombró consultor en

---

[9] Agustín Millares Carlo, *Apuntes para un estudio bibliográfico del humanista Francisco Cervantes de Salazar* (México, 1958).

[10] Millares Carlo, *Francisco Cervantes de Salazar*, 53.

[11] J. García Icazbalceta, *México en 1554. Tres Diálogos latinos que Francisco Cervantes Salazar escribió e imprimió en México en dicho año* (México, 1875).

1571. Además el propio arzobispo le había nombrado dos meses antes de su informe examinador de los aspirantes a oficios y beneficios eclesiásticos. También entran en contradicción con el informe del arzobispo los cargos desempeñados por Cervantes en la universidad, ya que en 1567 había sido nombrado diputado de hacienda de la misma, y el 10 de noviembre del mismo fue elegido rector, repitiéndose esta elección para 1572.

Por la declaración de los testigos de la apertura de su segundo testamento conocemos la fecha de su muerte, ocurrida el 14 de noviembre de 1575.

La Edición Mexicana de los *Diálogos*

Gracias a la iniciativa de Francisco Cervantes de Salazar salieron de las prensas mexicanas los *Diálogos* de Vives. Desgraciadamente no conocemos el título exacto por carecer de portada el único ejemplar conocido[12].

La historia de este rarísimo libro es contada por García Icazbalceta,[13] de la que entresacamos los datos más interesantes; en 1849 D. José María Andrade descubrió el ejemplar, falto de portada y de los dos últimos folios, y se lo regaló a García Icazbalceta, quien durante muchos años albergó la esperanza de encontrar otro y poder completarlo; en 1866 se descubrió otro ejemplar en muy mal estado, que permitió no obstante conocer el último folio; perdida ya la esperanza, García Icazbalceta se decidió a publicar parte de la obra en el año 1875.

El contenido del volumen es el siguiente: en el folio 3r empieza la *Compendiosa Ludovici vita*; el texto de los *Diálogos* de Vives empieza en el folio 4r y termina en el 227r; el comentario a los *Diálogos* se intercala con el texto; en el folio 228r hay una portada propia de los *Diálogos* añadidos por Cervantes Salazar a los de Vives: *Francisci Cervantis Salazari Toletani ad Ludovici Vivis Valentini exercitationem, aliquot Dialogi. 1554*; a continuación viene una dedicatoria al arzobispo Montúfar y los cuatro *Diálogos* compuestos por Cervantes en España, que terminan en el folio 247v; en este mismo folio empiezan los tres *Diálogos* mejicanos y terminan en el 290v; el volumen concluye con 4 hojas sin numerar que contienen una epístola de Alfonso Gómez, la fe de erratas del comentario a Vives, otra de los *Diálogos* de Cervantes, una epístola del impresor Juan Pablos y el colofón, que reza así:

> Impositus est finis huic operi, anno ab asserto in libertatem genere humano, millesimo quinqentessimo [sic] quinquagessimo [sic] quarto. Die vero sexta: mensis Novembris. Ex commisione Prorregis & Archiepiscopi Mexicani, probatum est opus, Doctori Matheo Sedeño Areualo, Decretorum interpreti, & Magistro Alfonso a uera Cruce Theologiae primario moderatori, Mexici anno me[n]-se & die ut supra.

---

[12] Actualmente en la biblioteca de la universidad de Texas, Austin. En el lugar de la portada aparece un título escrito a mano: *Commentaria in Ludovici Vives Exercitationes linguae latinae* (México, apud Ioannem).

[13] J. García Icazbalceta, *México en 1554*, XVIII.

En 1875 Joaquín García Icazbalceta en la obra citada en la nota 11 reimprimió los tres *Diálogos* de Cervantes de Salazar con notas. De los mismos *Diálogos* se publicó también una traducción inglesa[14] en 1953.

Los Comentarios de Cervantes a los *Diálogos*

Por el testimonio del propio Cervantes de Salazar sabemos que, estando todavía en España, hizo unos comentarios a los *Diálogos* de Vives[15]:

Elucidationes, quas olim in Vivem, quum agerem in Hispania composueram, recognitas, una cum aliquot Dialogis, Vivis instituto faventibus, evulgare constitui.

También explica la finalidad de los comentarios, que no era otra que aclarar la obrita de Vives, considerada por Cervantes como la más útil para aprender el latín. Por otra parte, para que los profesores de latín tuviesen a mano unos comentarios completos añadió los de P. Mota[16]:

Partim ut hic liber preceptoribus, quorum nonnullis negotium facessebat, dilucidior accederet. Partim vero ut una cum adiectione colloquiorum, utilior et proinde commendatior sermonis latini studiosis velut renasceretur. Adieci item quo labor meus magis commendaretur, permixtas lucubrationibus meis, interpretationes quas ante me iam pridem Motta Complutensis, vir certe doctissimus, in autoris cognitionem publicaverat, ne quid esset quod sedulus institutor et cupidus auditor desiderare potuissent. Eo namque oportebat linguae latinae Exercitationem (hic enim est libro titulus dignissimus) explicatiorem et magistris et discipulis tradi, quo ad comparandum latinum idioma ex multis libris utilior est.

Los comentarios de Cervantes se detienen en la explicación de los términos difíciles, dando la traducción en castellano, si bien las aclaraciones están redactadas en latín. En general podemos decir que la elección de las palabras comentadas es atinada, y también su interpretación castellana, como podemos comprobar con algunos ejemplos tomados del *Diálogo* primero:

— *recentem subuculam*: camisa limpia.
— *thoracem*: el jubón; simplum an diploidem? el sencillo o el esfofado nam diplos, u, interpretatur duplex, unde diplois, dis, por cosa doblada o aforrada.
— *minus graver*: esté más suelto o más ligero.
— *schola ipsa vocatur ludus*: schola interpretatur vacatio et eadem vocatur ludus, sed

---

[14] Life in the Imperial and Loyal City of Mexico in New Spain and the Royal and Pontifical University of Mexico as Described in the Dialogues for the Study of the Latin Language prepared by Francisco Cervantes de Salazar for use in the Classes and Printed in 1554 by Juan Pablos. Now Published in Facsimile with a Translation by Minnie Lee Barrett Shepard and an Introduction and Notes by Carlos Eduardo Castañeda (Austin, 1953).

[15] Commentaria in Ludovici Vivis . . . Dedicatoria.

[16] Commentaria in Ludovici Vivis . . . Dedicatoria.

litterarius, quod in eo cum singulari animi voluptate, quasi ludentes, litteris indulgeamus.

— *per rimulam ostii observabam*: observare, hic propie significat quod hispane dicimus asechar, in quam sententiam ita Plautus: observabo quam rem agat.

Una de las ideas recurrentes de Cervantes es que quien no hubiese estado en Flandes no podía entender bien la ambientación de los diálogos de Vives, y por ello son numerosas las alusiones relativas a dicha región. En este congreso, de carácter internacional, parece adecuado detenerse especialmente en algunas de dichas explicaciones por constituir una unidad temática.

En el diálogo primero, comentando las palabras "aperiam fenestras hasce ambas ligneam et vitream", dice Cervantes[17]:

Ne qui Flandrie morem ignoraverit ambas fenestras duas esse putet, sciat propter frigus, quod maximum est in ea regione, vitreis et ligneis ianuis eamdem fenestram claudi solere, ut die apertis ligneis vitreae, quae clausae manent, frigus propellant a cubiculo lucemque admittant. Sonat hispane abriré los dos pares de encajes: el de madera y el de vidrio. Id genus sunt alii multi loci, quos exponendos censui, intelligens nimirum nisi ab eo qui apud Flandros versatus fuerit percipi non posse.

En el mismo *Diálogo* al comentar "Utros, longo obstragulo an brevi?", dice Cervantes[18]:

¿cuáles? ¿los zapatos enteros o los medios? Hieme namque tectis, hoc est, longo obstragulo, propter lutum, apertis vero qui sunt brevi obstragulo aestate Flandrenses homines uti solent

En el *Diálogo* quinto en la expresión "*cape tabellam*" comenta[19]:

Toma la cartilla, *tabellam dixit quod prima illa elementa, quae ante lectionem pueri solent ediscere, papyro exarata ne propter tenuitatem chartae dilacerentur, de more est apud Flandros ut tabellae affingantur, qua propter tabellam dixit abecedariam, id est, in qua alphabeticum inscriptum sit.*

En el *Diálogo* sexto, al comentar *"prope est ut sublatis carnibus"* dice[20]:

Ya casi acabamos de comer, *solet enim prandium apud Flandros praesertim, sublatis carnibus, pomis et caseo claudi.*

En el *Diálogo* séptimo al comentar *"Prodigium, Flander sine cutello"* dice[21]:

Milagro es, flamenco sin cuchillo, *ideo dictum quod omnis fere aetatis et viris et*

---

[17] Commentaria in Ludovici Vivis . . . Fol. 5v.

[18] Commentaria in Ludovici Vivis . . . Fol. 7v.

[19] Commentaria in Ludovici Vivis . . . Fol. 19r.

[20] Commentaria in Ludovici Vivis . . . Fol. 22v.

[21] Commentaria in Ludovici Vivis . . . Fol. 30v.

foeminis Flanderensibus mos est cultellum secum gestare, nullius ponderis, in tot usus necessarium, deferri oportere merito quidem asserentibus.

En el mismo *Diálogo* comenta así *"praebibo tibi"*[22]:

Bébote, *quod est*, convídote bebiendo para que bebas, *quem morem, veluti magnum mutuae benevolentiae signum, ita religiose servant Germani et Flandri ut, nisi paria cum ipsis feceris, te inimicum arbitrentur.*

En el *Diálogo* octavo en *"via salaria ad leonem galeatum peperit ter geminos"* hace el siguiente comentario[23]:

En la calle salaria a la seña del León con capacete seis días a parió de un vientre seis hijos. Admonui iam apud Flandros et Gallos viis civitatum non solum indicta esse nomina, ut inquirenti melius occurrant, sed ex domibus pendere tabellas, in quibus effigies depictae domum inquirentem quae sit commonefaciant.

En el *Diálogo* noveno comenta "Immo equis trahetur" así[24]:

Cymbam ab equis posse trahi qui id non viderit mirabitur forsam, praesertim Flandriae et Galliae fluvios si nostris qui praecipites plerique et inter perruptissima saxa feruntur similes putet; sunt enim illi omnes lenes admodum et utrimque littora habentes latissima, et qui propterea navigabiles sunt, unde fit ut si adverso flumine navigentur equi quos Helciarios vocant, cymbam funibus collo ligati, littore incedentes facile contra cursum amnis trahant, contra la corriente del río.

También en el noveno insiste en la dificultad de entender los *Diálogos* de Vives si no se ha estado en Flandes; al comentar "rotam sufflamina imprudens" dice[25]

Hic locus torquet illos praessertim qui in ea regione non fuere; apud nos, nempe, rotis tantum duabus currus fertur, tametsi raro quatuor, Flandrenses vero omnes redhae quatuor aguntur rotis atque ea de causa, nostris sunt illae multo longiores angustioresque, ac ne in proclivi descensu seu procursu praecipites ferantur decurrantque plus iusto sufflammine, hoc est, retinaculo quodam rota una retinetur et comprimitur. A quo machinae genera sufflamminare dictum est; sufflamminare, est, rotam comprimere et retinere ne per declive decurrens rheda, ut saepe fit, frangatur. Quod, ut in descensu iuvat, ita plano itinere et salebroso, si sufflamminetur, procedere non potest, nec minus periclitatur quam si non sufflamminata per declive descendat. Hispane sufflamminare calzar o agarrotar la rueda. Sufflamminabant et Romani vehicula, quod intelligi ex illo loco potest Seneca 4 declamationes: tanta illi erat velocitas orationis ut

---

[22] Commentaria in Ludovici Vivis . . . Fol. 31v.
[23] Commentaria in Ludovici Vivis . . . Fol. 40v.
[24] Commentaria in Ludovici Vivis . . . Fol. 53r.
[25] Commentaria in Ludovici Vivis . . . Fol. 56v.

vitium fieret, itaque D. Augustus optime dixit alterius noster sufflamminandus est, había calzado la rueda sin mirar lo que hacía o descuidadamente.

Como puede comprobarse por las muestras elegidas, los comentarios de Cervantes de Salazar tienen gran interés, ya que no se limita a dar la equivalencia en castellano sino que además explica las costumbres y usos que hacen las expresiones completamente inteligibles. En este sentido, podemos decir que puede ser una fuente importante para el estudio de la vida cotidiana en Flandes en la primera mitad del siglo XVI.

Aunque nuestro interés en esta comunicación se centra en el singular hecho de haber servido los *Diálogos* de Vives para la enseñanza del latín en América, sin embargo no queremos dejar de resaltar la importancia de los *Diálogos* compuestos por Cervantes de Salazar, sobre todo, los tres referentes a Méjico: *Academia Mexicana, Civitas Mexicus interior* y *Mexicus exterior,* ya que constituyen un documento de gran valor para la historia de la universidad de Méjico y para la de la ciudad.

Universidad Nacional de Educación a Distancia, Madrid

Amore e matrimonio nel primo Quattrocento latino:
Le epistole di Guiniforte Barzizza
e Giovanni Pontano

DAVIDE CANFORA

La discussione *de amore* suscitata dalla lettera di Guiniforte Barzizza al cavaliere spagnolo Francesco Centellies (marzo 1439) e proseguita con la replica di Giovanni Pontano a Guiniforte medesimo si fonda su un ricco apparato di fonti. Si intende qui prospettare una interpretazione "ideologica" delle scelte operate da Barzizza e da Pontano nell'ambito degli *auctores*. Tali scelte vedremo che non paiono dipendere da un gusto superficialmente accumulativo per l'aneddotica varia. Sembra anzi ragionevole affermare che la scelta degli *auctores* è sempre mirata e attenta ai contenuti. La lettera di Barzizza prospetta una visione "spirituale" dell'uomo e contiene dunque un elogio dell'amore inteso come esercizio di virtù; la lettera di Pontano, invece, contrappone al tradizionalismo di Barzizza una visione negativa e misogina dell'amore coniugale[1].

L'epistola di Pontano si fonda su due tipologie fondamentali di *auctoritates*: la

---

[1] Nella produzione letteraria umanistica numerosi sono gli scritti aventi come tema l'amore. Quanto agli elogi del matrimonio in genere e alle orazioni nuziali, le edizioni moderne non sono numerose. Ricordo qui M. De Nichilo, *Oratio Nuptialis* (Bari, 1994), dove, oltre all'edizione critica dell'orazione per le nozze di Uguccione Contrari e Camilla Pio, si offre un quadro d'insieme del genere. È noto poi che Giovanni Pontano da Cerreto scrisse la raccolta poetica *De amore coniugali*, dedicata alla moglie (se il Pontano autore della lettera in risposta a Guiniforte Barzizza sia Giovanni Pontano da Cerreto o il meno noto Giovanni Pontano da Bergamo è questione qui discussa da Giovanni Pirrelli: cf. "Un'epistola 'de amore' di Giovanni Pontano". Una visione dell'amore come scelta di fedeltà verso una donna virtuosa—visione non priva di analogie con l'esposizione di Barzizza—si ha nella lettera di Niccolò della Valle a Francesco Colonna (M. De Nichilo, "Una miscellanea umanistica e una lettera di Niccolò della Valle a Francesco Colonna", *Roma nel Rinascimento* [1992], 343–386). Quanto alle manifestazioni di aperta ostilità verso il matrimonio, è da ricordare almeno la celebre lettera di Ermolao Barbaro ad Arnoldo di Bost (13 febbraio 1486) e il trattato *De coelibatu* dello stesso autore.

Bibbia vulgata e i classici latini. Sono ricordati diversi luoghi dell'Antico e del Nuovo Testamento. In apertura della lettera si rievoca "Israeliticus ille Ioseph, qui Egiptie concubitum fugiens palium in manu mulieris dereliquit" (fol. 42r)[2]. L'episodio—risalente a *Genesi*, 39, 11–12—si accompagna alla veloce menzione di due figure della mitologia greca: Ippolito e Bellerofonte. Altri riferimenti ai personaggi celebri del mito antico sono numerosi nella lettera di Pontano: può certo trattarsi di reminiscenze derivanti dalla lettura dei classici—reminiscenze che l'autore via via raccoglie nel corso dell'esposizione—ma non è escluso che, ancora per un umanista, il tramite più semplice per la conoscenza dei miti fossero le *Genealogie* del Boccaccio.

Altri esempi sono: Davide che, "visa de solario Bersabee, statim exarsit" (fol. 42v)—è un riferimento a *Samuele*, II, 11, 2–4—e il noto "vidit Deus quod esset bonum" (fol. 44v), ricavato da *Genesi*, 1, 8; si ricordino inoltre gli "Evangelii verba" citati a proposito dei "frutti"—cioè dei comportamenti adottati nella "mutua consuetudo"—da cui è possibile riconoscere il vero amore degli sposi (fol. 45r)[3]. Naturalmente la conoscenza e l'utilizzazione—da parte di Pontano—del Testamento, Vecchio e Nuovo, non suscita sorpresa. Anche gli umanisti più laici e attenti alla riscoperta degli antichi, come Poggio Bracciolini, non si lasciavano sfuggire—dove esso era possibile—il ricorso alla somma *auctoritas* biblica. Penso al *De infelicitate principum* (1440), in cui Poggio, a fianco di un'ampia serie di citazioni di autori greci e latini sul tema della connessione tra infelicità e potere, afferma: "[. . .] divina veritas, que mentiri nequit, [. . .]: 'homo' inquit 'cum in honore esset non intellexit, comparatus est iumentis insipientibus et similis factus est illis' "[4]. L'allusione, in Poggio, è ai *Salmi* (48, 13); significativo il giudizio: "divina veritas, que mentiri nequit".

Si noti, comunque, che il ricorso ai testi sacri, in uno scritto vivace e sostanzialmente antitradizionalista come l'epistola di Pontano, potrebbe anche avere una finalità provocatoria, come vedremo.

Quanto ai "gentiles", Pontano dimostra di avere una larga conoscenza della letteratura romana: Terenzio, Cicerone, Virgilio, Orazio, Ovidio, Valerio Massimo, Giustino, Giovenale, Gellio etc. Una gustosa combinazione tra Valerio Massimo (VI, 7, 1) e Gellio (VII, 8) è costituita dall'aneddoto—uno dei primi che figurano nell'epistola pontaniana—riguardante Scipione Africano "qui, cum in Hispania se a formosa et nobili virgine temperasset, demum etate provectior humilis pediseque et patinas culinamque redolentis sequutus amorem dicitur" (fol. 42r–v)[5].

---

[2] Le citazioni dell'epistola di Pontano sono fatte dal *ms. 44* (fols. 42r–48v) della Biblioteca Civica Guarneriana di San Daniele del Friuli, che risulta essere testimone unico del testo pontaniano. Esso è stato edito in forma mendosa, sulla base del Guarneriano, da P. Pirri ("Le notizie e gli scritti di Tommaso Pontano e di Giovanni Gioviano Pontano giovane", *Bollettino della Regia Deputazione di Storia Patria per l'Umbria* 18 [1913], app. II: 107–126). Si osservi che, nel Guarneriano, l'epistola di Pontano si interrompe bruscamente a metà del fol. 48v con le parole "idem amor". Il resto della pagina è bianco, il che fa supporre che mutilo fosse già il modello.

[3] Il riferimento, alquanto generico, agli "Evangelii verba" sembra trovare riscontro in *Matteo*, 12, 33: "dal frutto si riconosce l'albero".

[4] Poggio Bracciolini, *Opera omnia*, tomus I (Basileae, 1538), 403; cfr. anche: Poggio Bracciolini, *De infelicitate principum*, a cura di D. Canfora, Roma, 1998, 29 (23–27).

[5] Da Valerio Massimo Pontano ha ricavato l'episodio dell'amore senile di Scipione, da Gellio

Terenzio—autore caro agli umanisti—affiora invece quando Pontano si rivolge con ironia a Guiniforte, rievocando gli *Adelphoe*: "Terentiani illius Mitionis quam Demee similis esse, ymo vero ut ille Demea *ex duro liberalis* fieri voluisti" (fol. 42v). È evidente la ripresa dai vv. 662–4 di Terenzio: "factum a vobis *duriter* [. . .] atque etiam, si est, pater, dicendum magis aperte, *inliberaliter*". Ovidio è citato da Pontano ripetutamente, ora in modo esplicito, ora in modo implicito. Il primo rinvio ad Ovidio, espressamente citato, è nella frase "quod et Ovidio placet, eligi que ametur potest" (fol. 42v), rifatta sul pentametro "elige cui dicas: 'tu mihi sola places'" di *Ars amatoria*, I, 41 (v. anche i vv. seguenti). Il nome di Ovidio viene ricordato da Pontano altre due volte, e alle sue opere l'autore dell'epistola sembra attingere in modo sistematico.

Interessante il caso di una citazione da Giovenale (IV, 2–4). Scrive Pontano: "inter reliqua vitia obicit Crispano Iuvenalis quod, cum in modicis ceterarum amoribus ardeat, delitias vidue tamen aspernatur adulte" (fol. 47r). Il passo—così come è tràdito dal *ms. 44* della Guarneriana—è corrotto. Il v. 4 di Giovenale recita infatti così nella forma corretta tramandata dai codici più antichi: "deliciae, viduas tantum aspernatus adulter". Anche il nome di Crispino è in Pontano alterato in Crispano. Non è questo, del resto, il solo caso in cui il nostro manoscritto presenta corruttele di nomi propri[6].

Crispino è definito da Giovenale :

> monstrum nulla virtute redemptum
> a vitiis, aegrae solaque libidine fortes
> deliciae, viduas tantum aspernatus adulter

Questo il testo che si legge nelle edizioni moderne, fondato sulle lezioni dei mss. Montepessulanus Bibl. Med. 125 ("deliciae, viduas") e Vindobonensis 107 ("aspernatus"). Il testo di Pontano, invece, coincide con quello della famiglia Φ dei codici di Giovenale, rappresentata da un gruppo di almeno sette codici vergati dal IX al XII secolo: "eorum adfinitates—osserva Clausen—[. . .] tam variae sunt ac mutabiles, ut nullo stemmate, sit licet vel implicatissimum, designari possint"[7]. È certo quindi che Pontano si servì di uno di questi testimoni, ovvero di un loro discendente recenziore, e ne ha ereditato gli errori.

Un altro caso di citazione da Giovenale: Messalina—scrive Pontano—"imperatoria videlicet coniunx nocte lupanar ingrediebatur et lassata viris, nunquam satiata recessit" (fol. 47v). Pontano riprende l'episodio dalla satira VI, 116-ssg, dove si descrive la "meretrix Augusta" che "intravit calidum lupanar" (v. 121). Le parole "et lassata viris, nunquam satiata recessit", in particolare, ripetono il v. 130 di Giovenale.

Il frequente ricorso da parte di Pontano alla *auctoritas* virgiliana appare quasi scon-

---

il riferimento alla sua condotta in Spagna nei confronti della nobile ragazza.

[6] Altri casi di nomi propri corrotti nel Guarneriano sono: "Penolopes" in luogo di "Penelopes" (fol. 42v); "Cateline" in luogo di "Catiline" (fol. 43v); "Catone Censorino" in luogo di "Catone Censore" (fol. 43v); "Graccium" in luogo di "Grecinum" (fol. 43v); "Athomas" in luogo di "Athamas" (fol. 44r); "Arogonum" in luogo di "Aragonum" (fol. 46v).

[7] Persi et Juvenalis *Saturae*, edidit W. V. Clausen (Oxonii, 1959), 12; cf. anche R. J. Tarrant, "Juvenal," in: *Text and Transmission* (Oxford, 1983), 201–202.

tato: Virgilio fu autore citatissimo nel Medioevo e nell'Umanesimo[8]. Per la vicenda di Gige e Candaule (fol. 45r) è più verosimile pensare come fonte a Giustino (I, 7, 14–19) piuttosto che ad Erodoto (I, 8, 13): si tratta infatti di un episodio ben noto e non pare il caso di pensare che Pontano abbia utilizzato fonti greche, almeno per quanto riguarda la parte di lettera che ci è dato leggere nel manoscritto[9].

Ciceroniano è l'aneddoto su Ulisse, "qui, cum amore coniugis cuperet se a Troyana expeditione immunem reddere, furorem simulavit ac nihilominus deprensus et ignominia non caruit et profectionem ipsam vitare non potuit" (fol. 48v). La fonte di Pontano è qui la parte finale del *De officiis* (III, 97–98):

> utile videbatur Ulixi, ut quidem poetae tragici prodiderunt (nam apud Homerum, optimum auctorem, talis de Ulixe nulla suspicio est), sed insimulant eum tragoediae simulatione insaniae militiam subterfugere voluisse. Non honestum consilium, at utile, ut aliquis fortasse dixerit, regnare et Ithacae vivere otiose cum parentibus, cum uxore, cum filio[10].

Anche nel caso di Cicerone la scelta della fonte non sorprende: Pontano, piuttosto, si distingue per l'acuta capacità di cogliere il riferimento alle donne e all'amore anche in testi che non sono specificamente di contenuto erotico[11]. Cicerone infatti si occupa, nel finale del *De officiis*, della possibilità di separare l'"utile" dall'"honestum", e in questo contesto fa rientrare anche l'aneddoto su Ulisse.

Un intreccio di fonti diverse si registra nella presentazione di una coppia di aneddoti:

> neque tamen utetur vir fortis vanitate mendatii neque delectabitur aut Punica fraude [. . .] aut Tracio‹rum› vaframento, qui, pactis dierum indutiis, nocte Beoticorum agros populabantur, asserentes dierum, non noctium, indutias esse pactas. (fols. 46v–47r)

C'è qui la ripresa di Valerio Massimo, capitoli terzo e quarto del VII libro, capitoli intitolati rispettivamente *Vafre dicta aut facta o Strategemata*. È da Valerio Massimo che Pontano ha ricavato il riferimento alla "Punica fraus" (cfr. in particolare la "Punica calliditas" di VII, 4, 4) e il raro vocabolo "vaframentum" (presente in: VII, 3, ext. 2,

---

[8] Le citazioni provengono da tutte e tre le opere. Non mi diffondo su questo punto e segnalo solo le più evidenti: "sed danda vela ventis" (fol. 43r; cf. *Georg.*, II, 41); "Ibo armis contra magnum vel prestet Achillem" (fol. 44r; cf. *Aen.*, XI, 438); "vix ossibus herentem" (fol. 44v; cf. *Ecl.*, III, 102).

[9] Cf. n. 2.

[10] L'episodio di Ulisse fintosi pazzo per evitare la guerra di Troia è nella tradizione sovente collegato a quello di Palamede e a quello di Achille, e si legge in varie fonti. Si vedano, a titolo di esempio: *Cypria*, 118–121; Apollodoro, *Epitoma*, 3, 12; Hyg., *fab.*, XCV (*Ulixes*); Myth. Vat., I, 35 (*Historia Palamedis*). Solo in Cicerone, tuttavia, l'episodio è descritto privo di alcuni particolari assenti anche in Pontano, come quello di Ulisse che si dedica all'agricoltura; solo Cicerone e Pontano si soffermano sul concetto del "vivere cum uxore".

[11] L'epistola di Pontano, in questo senso, rappresenta un ricco catalogo umanistico di situazioni connesse con la presenza di figure femminili.

4 e 7 [12]; si osservi che in quest'ultimo passo si parla proprio di Annibale). "Vaframentum", comunque, è vocabolo usato da Pontano con riferimento non già ai Cartaginesi, bensì ai Traci, i quali—racconta Pontano—saccheggiavano di notte le campagne dei Beoti, perchè la tregua era stata pattuita per il giorno e non per la notte. Ora, l'aneddoto sullo stratagemma della tregua risale probabilmente a Cicerone, *De officiis*, I, 33, come confermano le forti analogie verbali riscontrabili tra il testo pontaniano e quello ciceroniano, che qui di seguito si riporta:

> ut ille qui, cum triginta dierum essent cum hoste indutiae factae, noctu popula
> batur agros, quod dierum essent pactae, non noctium indutiae.

Cicerone non fa il nome dell'autore di questo stratagemma: la stessa astuzia è attribuita da Plutarco a Cleomene, re di Sparta, nella guerra contro gli Argivi (*Apophtegmata Laconica*, 223 B[13]). Nè in Cicerone nè in Plutarco si nominano i Beoti o i Traci: Pontano potrebbe avere ricavato l'attribuzione dell'aneddoto ciceroniano ai Beoti e ai Traci di seconda mano, per esempio da una glossa erronea collocata a margine del testo da lui posseduto del *De officiis*; ovvero potrebbe avere in proprio stabilito quella attribuzione, sulla base della proverbiale stupidità, unanimemente riconosciuta dalle fonti antiche, dei Beoti. Ad essi, però, solitamente vengono contrapposti gli Ateniesi; cf. Cicerone, *De fato*, 7: "Athenis tenue caelum, ex quo etiam acutiores putantur Attici; crassum Thebis, itaque pingues Thebani et valentes". I Traci costituiscono una novità: nel codice si legge "Tracio vaframento"; la correzione nel genitivo plurale "Traciorum" è parsa necessaria allo scopo di non lasciare pendente il nominativo plurale "qui" immediatamente successivo. Ma "Tracio" potrebbe celare una più grave corruttela: il codice Guarneriano non manca di nomi propri corrotti, anche vistosamente[14].

Si è notato che Pontano non sembra servirsi di fonti greche. Anche quando una *auctoritas* greca viene nominata, essa si direbbe citata attraverso un referente latino. È il caso di Platone, di cui Pontano afferma che, "in constituenda re publica", propose uno stile di vita, ispirato alla comunione dei beni, risalente alla "aurea etas" (fol. 48r). Non è escluso che Pontano abbia consultato la traduzione latina della *Repubblica* platonica, approntata dal Decembrio nel 1439–41[15] (l'epistola di Pontano è ovviamente successiva alla composizione—avvenuta nel marzo 1439—della lettera di Guiniforte Barzizza). Tuttavia è anche possibile che, dietro al riferimento alquanto generico a

---

[12] "Vaframentum" è attestato solo in questi passi di Valerio Massimo; cf. *Oxford Latin Dictionary*, s.v., e *Thesaurus linguae Latinae* CD-ROM (PHI).

[13] L'aneddoto è raccontato da Plutarco in questi termini: "Cleomene, avendo pattuito con gli Argivi una tregua di sette giorni, dopo avere appurato che quelli, confidando nella tregua, nella terza notte stavano dormendo, li attaccò e in parte li uccise, in parte li fece prigionieri. Quando gli fu rinfacciato di avere violato il giuramento, egli negò che in esso fossero comprese, con i giorni, anche le notti".

[14] Cf. n. 6.

[15] La prima traduzione umanistica della *Repubblica*, quella di Umberto Decembrio, è di inizio '400. Al 1439–41 risale la versione di Pier Candido. Cf. E. Garin, *Ricerche sulle traduzioni di Platone* in *Medioevo e Rinascimento. Studi in onore di Bruno Nardi* (Firenze, 1955), 341–357.

Platone da parte di Pontano, si nasconda un brano di Lattanzio (*inst.* 3, 21, 3)—riprodotto dagli editori moderni ad integrazione della fine perduta del IV libro del *De republica* di Cicerone (IV, 5, 5)—in cui si stigmatizza Platone appunto perchè "omnia omnibus voluit esse communia". Le *Divinae Institutiones* di Lattanzio furono pubblicate per la prima volta nel 1465, ma ovviamente circolavano già prima[16]. Interessante il fatto che l'esuberante Pontano dell'epistola *de amore*, a differenza del moralista Lattanzio, tessa le lodi di Platone e della "communio bonorum".

Latine, sacre e profane, sono dunque le fonti utilizzate da Pontano. Il risultato è, come si diceva, un catalogo umanistico di aneddoti legati a figure femminili, di tono misogino e ironico nei confronti della posizione tradizionalista di Guiniforte Barzizza, anch'egli incline alla misoginia e tuttavia fiducioso che la virtù maschile possa riscattare la debolezza congenita delle donne. In questo quadro, gli episodi tratti dalla Bibbia, ripetuti in forma rispettosa del modello originario e tuttavia miranti a scardinare le argomentazioni di Guiniforte, debbono forse intendersi come la più vivace ed esasperata delle provocazioni dell'antitradizionalista Pontano. Egli in sostanza dimostra a Guiniforte di poter attingere a testimonianze di adulterii e ad argomenti ostili all'amore non soltanto—come era in fondo prevedibile—dalla letteratura latina pagana, erotica e non, ma anche da quegli stessi testi sacri di cui Barzizza aveva fatto uso allo scopo di elogiare il "perennis, singularis atque immaculatus amor".

Nel complesso, le *auctoritates* utilizzate da Guiniforte Barzizza sono diverse—o diversamente utilizzate—rispetto a quelle pontaniane. Si tratta di fonti antiche—greche e latine, sacre e profane (Aristotele, Ovidio, Bibbia)—e di fonti medievali e preumanistiche (Cappellano, Petrarca, Boccaccio): si veda qui "*L'epistola 'de amore' di Guiniforte Barzizza*" di Sebastiano Valerio. È possibile, quindi, a partire da questi dati, fare un confronto tra il testo dell'epistola di Barzizza e quello dell'epistola di Pontano.

Pontano ha dunque in comune con Barzizza alcune fonti. A parte la Bibbia, che—si è visto—Barzizza e Pontano usano con finalità opposte, Barzizza cita ad esempio Ovidio. "Iuvenilis animus plerumque solet in vetitum niti et novitatibus delectari" (pp. 127–128)[17] scrive Barzizza citando gli *Amores* (III, 4, 17): "nitimur in vetitum semper cupimusque negata". Tuttavia Ovidio serve a Barzizza per fare una concessione, in fondo moralistica, alla passionalità dell'animo giovanile, a cui Barzizza contrappone la solidità della ragione adulta. E su di una serie di sane "rationes"—non certo sulla sola bellezza, che attrae l'irruenza dei giovani: "prohibeo quidem, ne te

---

[16] Cf. L. Caeli Firmiani Lactanti *Opera omnia*, ed. S. Brandt–G. Laubmann, pars I (Pragae-Vindobonae-Lipsiae), X–XII (*Prolegomena*). Si osservi che—poco prima della stigmatizzazione della "communio bonorum" platonica—Lattanzio aveva scritto: "non dissimile Platonis illut est, quod aiebat se gratias agere naturae: primum quod homo natus esset potius quam mutum animal, deinde quod mas potius quam femina, quod Graecus quam barbarus, postremo quod Atheniensis et quod temporibus Socratis [. . .] quasi vero si aut barbarus aut mulier aut asinus denique natus esset, idem ipse Plato esset ac non illud ipsum quod natus fuisset" (3, 19, 17–18). Il tono misogino di questa affermazione attribuita da Lattanzio a Platone e il riferimento all'"asinus" potrebbero trovare una eco nell'epistola di Pontano, come si vedrà in conclusione.

[17] Cito da: Gasparini Barzizii Bergomatis et Guiniforti filii *Opera*, pars I (Romae, 1723).

sola pulchritudine incendi patiaris", scrive Barzizza (p. 128)—si fonda tutta la lettera a Francesco Centellies, tesa sostanzialmente a rendere nobile e a "normalizzare" una "animi perturbatio—la passione amorosa—[. . .] iunioribus applicabilior" (p. 122).

Tradizionale e, per così dire, "rassicurante" si può definire la *auctoritas* di Aristotele (*Etica Nicomachea*, IV, 8, 30, 1124b), che Barzizza chiama in causa per la definizione della categoria del "magnanimus" (p. 125). Analogamente al caso della ripresa dei testi biblici, è lecito pensare che Pontano, nel citare la "communio bonorum" platonica, abbia voluto replicare ad una *auctoritas* di Barzizza—appunto Aristotele—con il nome di una *auctoritas* altrettanto autorevole, Platone. Dunque non a caso Pontano potrebbe avere rievocato una delle teorie platoniche più "scomode" e imbarazzanti, quella della comunione di ogni cosa all'interno della Πόλις, a partire dalle donne[18].

Purtroppo non conosciamo la parte finale dell'epistola di Pontano: non possiamo quindi dire se la conclusione della lettera di Barzizza a Francesco Centellies, che termina con tre citazioni tratte dal Petrarca volgare, abbia prodotto riprese o imitazioni. Nel testo superstite di Pontano non c'è mai mescolanza di latino e volgare. Lasciando dunque da parte questa possibile, diversa scelta di fonti, sono l'ispirazione e il tono moralistico e tradizionale che distinguono piuttosto Barzizza da Pontano: nelle ultime righe Guiniforte sottolinea con forza—come per prevenire l'accusa di assumere una posizione eccessivamente censoria—di avere affidato il compito di stigmatizzare l'amore-passione alle parole non dello stoico Seneca, bensì dell' "amans Petrarcha" (p. 131), di cui cita ben 58 versi del *Triumphus Cupidinis*. La chiave di lettura del testo di Barzizza sembra dunque la seguente: è certo ammissibile qualche paternalistica e del tutto umana concessione alla "violentia iuvenilis amoris" (p. 131), ma un animo "generosus" (p. 125) deve puntare ad un amore più profondo, fedele e rasserenante. Petrarca, allo scopo di sorreggere questo teorema, si presenta come la *auctoritas* più

---

[18] Nell'epistola a Guiniforte, Pontano—come detto—attribuisce la comunione delle donne nella Πόλις al tempo dell'"aurea etas", quando gli esseri umani erano ancora ignari dei vizi. Egli soggiunge quindi—non senza ambiguità—che, su questo punto, ci sarebbe altro ancora da dire, ma lo spazio a disposizione non lo consente. Giovanni Pontano da Cerreto, nell'esordio del III libro del trattato *De obedientia*, affronta il medesimo problema della comunione delle donne, anzitutto indicando nella "medietas" aristotelica il mezzo per trasformare l'"appetitus" umano in "virtus" e poi contestando apertamente il modello platonico: "Et appetitus proprium est appetere, inde enim nomen ipsum ductum est, sic rationis est illum corrigere et coercere. Hoc enim pacto solum est quae honesta videantur, expetemus, et quae natura insunt nobis, ea certo ac recto modo tempe- rabimus, medium illud retinens, quo remoto frustra omnis noster ad virtutem conatus est [. . .] Quo magis damnanda est illorum opinio, qui optimum esse arbitrati sunt ac civitatibus maximum conducere, si mulieres communes essent, qui mihi nihil aliud videntur suasisse, quam ut promiscue ac sine ullo discrimine et in propatulo coeamus omnes, sublata de rebus humanis pudicitia, labe- fectemusque arctissimum retinaculum societatis humanae, coniugalem fidem" (G. Pontano, *Opera omnia* [Venezia], 1518, 20). Appare evidente la differenza di tono tra l'epistola a Guiniforte e il *De obedientia*: la cosa—si è visto—potrebbe spiegarsi con la diversa identità degli autori delle due opere, ovvero con quella "varietà" che non è rara negli umanisti e che è stata individuata come la caratteristica dell'ispirazione di Pontano da Cerreto anche nella strutturazione dei dialoghi: "la mancanza di uno schema prestabilito, di un modello particolarmente caro all'autore" (F. Tateo, *Tradizione e realtà nell'Umanesimo italiano* [Bari, 1967], 319).

adatta, in ragione del suo apparente e artefatto oscillare continuo tra il ricordo della bellezza di Laura e il pentimento, tra l'amore terreno e l'amore celeste: di essi Petrarca sembra sempre sul punto di abbandonarsi al primo, per poi immancabilmente rifugiarsi nel secondo.

Pontano oppone alla teoria nobile ma astratta di Barzizza la prassi di una umanità inevitabilmente soggetta alle passioni e di un sesso femminile, a giudizio di Pontano, incompatibile con la predisposizione alla virtù che Barzizza ad esso aveva potenzialmente attribuito. "Meo iudicio sunt et asine mulieres", afferma pesantemente Pontano (fol. 42r), replicando alle parole di Barzizza: "amorem dico in mulieres, nec de asinino intelligo" (p. 123)[19]. È dunque evidente che anche la scelta delle *auctoritates* da parte di Pontano sarà sulla linea della rottura rispetto a Barzizza. Rottura talora esplicita, con la prevalente presenza delle fonti pagane; e con particolari scelte nell'ambito delle stesse, per esempio Platone opposto ad Aristotele o l'Ovidio del piacere ("placet") opposto all'Ovidio del divieto ("vetitum"). Ovvero rottura operata attraverso l'arma dell'ironia e la manipolazione dei testi, per esempio attraverso il ribaltamento—a cui già si è fatto cenno—delle sacre scritture in funzione misogina e apertamente anticoniugale.

Università degli Studi di Bari

---

[19] Sia Barzizza sia Pontano si rifanno, in modo diverso, ad una consolidata e proverbiale tradizione dell'asino come simbolo di stoltezza ("inepta et prorsus asinina cogitatio" si legge in Apul., *met.* 6, 2, 5).

El Neolatín en Cuba

AMAURY B. CARBÓN SIERRA

El latín llegó a Cuba con los colonizadores españoles en 1510. Fue aquí, como en otras partes del mundo, la lengua de la ciencia, la cultura y la liturgia católica, y, por lo tanto, el núcleo de la segunda enseñanza, ya que sin su dominio no se podía acceder a los estudios universitarios ni a la bibliografía científica y profesional básica. Estas circunstancias explican el hecho de que fueran muchos los que en nuestro país—y fuera de él—poseyeran la lengua de los antiguos romanos y la emplearan de forma oral, escrita, o combinadamente en sus ejercicios académicos, o los que en el desempeño de su profesión y con diferentes fines y motivaciones, sobre todo docentes, se expresaran en ella.

Nuestra investigación se limita exclusivamente a los textos o escritos que vieron la luz pública, con lo que se prescinde de centenares de cuodlibetos en latín o ejercicios de grado no publicados ni citados, que están en los archivos pendientes de un profundo estudio paleográfico. Con esta decisión quedan fuera personalidades de la cultura cubana que por sus actividades docentes, estudios realizados o testimonios de sus contemporáneos se sabe que fueron latinistas, como Justo Vélez, Ángel Cowley, Francisco Ruiz, y muchos más, de quienes no se conservan impresos ni manuscritos significativos.

De acuerdo con la revisión bibliográfica y de archivo realizada, todo parece indicar que los primeros textos en latín que se hicieron públicos en Cuba fueron las inscripciones funerarias, en las que—como es costumbre—no se identifica el autor. Así, de 1524, menciona Juan Miguel Dihigo en su folleto *La epigrafía en Cuba* la colocada en la sepultura del Adelantado Diego Velázquez de Cuéllar, descubierta a principios del siglo pasado en las excavaciones de los cimientos de la nueva catedral de Santiago de Cuba. Unidos los pedazos de la lapida y suplida alguna letra por el contexto, pudo reconstruirse la inscripción[1].

Miguel Rodríguez-Ferrer, sin embargo, considera que esta inscripción, algo ruda en su latín, es posterior al epitafio en versos latinos que ha conservado Juan de Caste-

---

[1] Juan M. Dihigo y Mestre, *La epigrafía en Cuba* (La Habana, 1928), 21.

llanos en sus *Elegías de varones ilustres de Indias*, publicadas por primera vez en 1589[2]. Ambos textos epigráficos demuestran la presencia en nuestra antigua capital de personas cultas, capaces de apreciar y preocuparse por estos detalles a unos pocos años de fundada la villa[3] y constituyen testimonios visibles y perdurables de la extensión y el arraigo que, desde los días de la conquista, ha tenido el uso del latín[4]. Por ello, aunque este trabajo no se ocupa de la epigrafía por las especificidades de las inscripciones que son a veces citas o adaptaciones de otros textos, no se puede prescindir de algunos ejemplos relevantes e ilustrativos como los señalados, y otros más, sobre todo porque la imprenta no llega a América hasta alrededor de 1535 cuando se establece en México. En Cuba probablemente la hubo a fines del siglo XVIII[5], aunque el folleto más antiguo que se conoce, *Arancel o tarifa general de precios de medicina*, es de 1723[6].

Dihigo cita también, de 1557, la inscripción que se halla en el monumento más antiguo de nuestro país, empotrado en una de las paredes del Palacio de los Capitanes Generales, hoy Museo de la Ciudad: una pequeña lápida funeraria, erigida en memoria de doña María de Cepero y Nieto, dama principal de la villa de La Habana, en el mismo lugar donde se dice que cayó mortalmente herida ese año por un disparo casual de arcabuz, mientras rezaba en la Parroquial Mayor, que allí existía[7]. Por la fecha de estas inscripciones es de suponer que ninguna fuera redactada por un natural del país, o es poco probable que así hubiera ocurrido, aunque ya en 1544 el primer maestro de origen cubano, Miguel Velázquez, daba clases de gramática (latina) en Santiago de Cuba, después de haber estudiado en España.

El mismo autor registra en su folleto la inscripción de 1754 de El Templete, monumento conmemorativo del lugar donde se efectuó la primera misa y el primer cabildo en la villa de San Cristóbal de La Habana. El texto fue corregido en 1903 por el eminente lingüista, a petición del ayuntamiento de la ciudad.

El primer libro escrito en latín o al menos editado en esa lengua por un cubano parece haber sido *Arechaga Commentaria juris civilis* (Salamanca, 1662), del jurista y poeta Juan de Aréchaga y Casas, nacido en La Habana en 1637 y fallecido probablemente en México en 1688. Realizó estudios en la Universidad de Salamanca, donde se graduó de doctor en Leyes en 1662 y ejerció como profesor. Fue después gobernador de Yucatán en 1679 y Oidor de la Audiencia de México en 1672. En La Habana fundó con sus bienes y los de cinco hermanas el monasterio de religiosas dominicas Santa Catalina de Siena (1688)[8]. Aréchaga dio también a la imprenta *Extemporaneae*

---

[2] Miguel Rodríguez-Ferrer, *Naturaleza y civilización de la grandiosa isla de Cuba* (Madrid, 1887), 445 s.

[3] César García del Pino y Alejandro de la Fuente, "Introducción a la cultura de Cuba en los siglos XVI y XVII. Elementos para un nuevo enfoque", *Revista de la Biblioteca Nacional José Martí* (1989): 10.

[4] J. M. Rivas Sacconi, *El latín de Colombia* (Santafé de Bogotá, 1993), 455.

[5] Guillermo Furlong, *Orígenes del arte tipográfico en América* (Buenos Aires, 1947), 24.

[6] Editado en La Habana por el flamenco Carlos Habré.

[7] Dihigo, *Epigrafía en Cuba*, 24.

[8] La Real Cédula que declaró el permiso se dictó en 2 de agosto de 1684. Con esta acción piadosa tal vez quiso también Aréchaga lavar las faltas de su padre como funcionario público.

commentationes. Ad textus sorte oblatos pro petitionibus Cathedrarum Academiae Salmanticensis, Edit. Salmanticae apud Josephum Gomez de los Cubos, 1666, el único que se conserva, y que tal vez sea—o incluya—el que los bibliógrafos cubanos Félix de Arrate y Francisco Calcagno citan como de 1662. Escribió igualmente un *Epigramma in obitum Philippi IV, Magni Hispaniarum & Indiarum Regis* publicado por Francisco Roys o Roix en *Pyra real* que erigió la Universidad de Salamanca ... (Salamanca, 1666). Consta de siete dísticos elegíacos.

Otro jurista habanero que alcanzó significación intelectual fuera de la Isla fue Tomás Recino y Hormachea nacido en 1642 y graduado en ambos derechos en la Universidad de Salamanca, donde desempeñó varias cátedras de su especialidad. Publicó, quizás en España, su tratado *A quibus adquiri et constituti servitutes* (1666). Se dice que terminó su carrera de magistrado como Oidor de la Audiencia de Manila. Lamentablemente la obra de Recino no se ha hallado en Cuba ni en la Biblioteca Nacional de Madrid, como tampoco se han podido obtener muchas más informaciones sobre su vida que las relativas a sus estudios en la Universidad de Salamanca, labor en la que ha sido decisiva la colaboración del director del Archivo Histórico de esa Institución, Don Severiano Hernández y de la jefa de sala Dña. Concha Álamo. Abundan, sin embargo, en nuestro país los datos de Dionisio Recino, su hermano, quien fuera obispo de 1704 hasta su muerte en 1711 a los sesenta y seis años. Hay que recordar que hasta 1728, fecha de la fundación de la Real y Pontificia Universidad de San Gerónimo de la Habana, los jóvenes con recursos debían trasladarse a España, Santo Domingo o México a cursar sus estudios superiores.

Escribió en latín su *Cursus Complutensis Carmelitanus in clariorem methodum pro commodiori magistrorum ac discipulorum usu redactus* (*circa* 1730) el docto y grave fraile cubano Manuel de San Juan Bautista, cuyo nombre verdadero se ignora. Fue rector del colegio San Ángel, prior de México y dos veces provincial de dicha jurisdicción donde murió seguramente. Según Beristáin de Souza en su *Biblioteca hispanoamericana septentrional*, su texto se conservaba en la librería del Santo Desierto de México[9].

Otra obra neolatina importante fueron los *Commentaria in selecta Petri Lombardi Distinctiones* del habanero Antonio Pimentel y Sotomayor (1711–1753), colegial de oposición en el Colegio de San Ildefonso de México, doctor en teología y catedrático de la Universidad, visitador del obispado de Michoacán y canónigo lectoral de la catedral de Valladolid, según Beristáin. Este mismo bibliógrafo menciona como publicado en La Habana en 1725 el tratado *Endimiones Habanensis* del médico y matemático Marcos Antonio Gamboa Riaño y Vargas (La Habana, 1672–México, 1729), profesor de la Universidad de México y revisor de libros de la Santa Inquisición. No obstante la intensa búsqueda realizada, no se han hallado estos textos en ninguna de nuestras bibliotecas y archivos.

Tampoco se han localizado las obras que publicó en latín José Julián Parreño Espinosa (La Habana, 1728–Roma, 1785), uno de los restauradores de la oratoria sagrada en México, donde integró la Compañía de Jesús y enseñó retórica, filosofía

---

9 José Mariano Beristáin de Souza, *Biblioteca hispanoamericana septentrional*, 3 vols. (México, 1816–1821), 2: 141.

y teología. En 1767 se fue con sus hermanos a Roma, donde continuó estudios y publicó sus *Eloquentiae Praecepta* (1778) y otros libros en latín que consigna su bibliografía activa. Falleció en el convento de Val-humbrosa. Un año antes había escrito su propio epitafio en el que recuerda la tierra natal[10].

Orador de renombre en México llegó a ser, igualmente, Francisco Javier Conde y Oquendo (La Habana, 1733–Puebla, México, 1799). Después de graduarse de abogado y de ejercer el cargo de Fiscal de la Curia Eclesiástica de La Habana, entre otras funciones, se trasladó a España y más tarde a México donde profesó en la Iglesia de Puebla. En 1796 ocupó el cargo de canónigo de la Catedral. Además de traductor de latín, parece haber escrito en esa lengua su *Oratio in funere Caroli III Hispaniarum atque Indiarum Regis Catholici et Potentissimi, habita in Templo Maximo Angepolitano.* . . . (Madrid, 1779).

De las pocas obras escritas en latín en el siglo XVIII que se conservan en nuestras bibliotecas, una es la *Parentalis oratio in funere, quod pro gratia, et pia memoria beneficentissimae D.D. Mariae Teresiae Chacon Torres & Castellon; commissae de casa Bayona, et Dynastae civitatis Sanctae Mariae del Rosario &&&.* Su autor, Tomás Pascual y Villegas, la pronunció el 2 de julio de 1788 en el convento de San Juan de Letrán, y fue publicada en La Habana en la Imprenta de la Curia Episcopal. Pascual fue rector de la Real y Pontificia Universidad en 1790 y 1793, además de ocupar otras responsabilidades. Falleció en 1827. María Teresa Chacón y Torres hizo por testamento grandes aportes financieros al convento de San Juan de Letrán y a la Universidad.

Con motivo del traslado a Cuba de los supuestos restos de Cristóbal Colón procedentes de la isla Dominicana, el obispo Felipe Tres Palacios compuso en 1796 su extenso epitafio para cubrir la pared donde se enterrarían las cenizas del Descubridor. Según Eugenio Sánchez de Fuentes el texto fue el mismo que figuró en las exequias celebradas en honor del Navegante[11]. Como se ha dilucidado, los restos de Colón reposan en Sevilla. Los traídos a Cuba fueron quizás los de su hijo Diego.

Al año siguiente se dio a conocer el tratado *Philosophia electiva ad usus academicos accommodata* del presbítero José Agustín Caballero y Rodríguez de la Barrera (La Habana, 1762–1835), iniciador de la reforma filosófica antiescolástica en Cuba. Su texto, escrito para los alumnos del Colegio Seminario de San Carlos y San Ambrosio, fue el primero entre nosotros, aunque la publicación tuvo lugar en 1944, casi siglo y medio después de redactado y de haber circulado en copias manuscritas. Caballero también escribió un epitafio en latín a la muerte del obispo Juan José Díaz de Espada y Landa (1832) y tradujo textos de Juan Ginés de Sepúlveda *(Historia del Nuevo Mundo en especial de México, y Cartas de Sepúlveda a Melchor Cano),* y el libro I de los *Fastos* de Ovidio, a partir del cual compuso su "Canto al día de la consagración del Ilmo. Sr. Dr. Don Luis Peñalber y Cárdenas, Dignísimo obispo de la Luysiana".

Discípulo de Caballero fue el presbítero Felix Varela y Morales (La Habana, 1787–San Agustín de la Florida, E.U., 1853), quien con sus *Institutiones Philosophiae eclecticae*

---

[10] Enrique Saínz, *La literatura cubana de 1700 a 1790* (La Habana, 1983), 168.

[11] Eugenio Sánchez de Fuentes, *Cuba monumentaria, estatuaria y epigráfica* (La Habana, 1916), 482.

ad usum studiosae juventutis editae (1812) introdujo en el país desde la cátedra del Seminario de San Carlos un cambio más radical de los estudios filosóficos en relación con las reformas de su maestro y amigo. De su obra en tres tomos se conservan sólo el primero, de Lógica, y el tercero, escrito en español porque pensaba que se le declararía lengua oficial. El segundo, de metafísica, descrito por Bachiller y Morales, debe darse por perdido. De Varela se ha dicho que fue el primero que nos enseñó a pensar.

Un documento que permite conocer el nivel de la filosofía que se daba aún en la Universidad dos décadas después del cambio de orientación dado a estos estudios por Varela, lo constituyen las notas de clase del estudiante de derecho Agustín Saavedra Palacios tomadas entre 1828 y 1831, y adquiridas recientemente por la Biblioteca Nacional José Martí. Las lecciones, de lógica y física escolástica, fueron dictadas por fray Pedro Infante, lector de la asignatura y rector de la Real y Pontifica Universidad en 1837. Parecen apoyarse en el manual de Antonio Goudin recomendado por el Plan Salamanca de 1771 como más completo y panorámico y porque es conciso y tiene un buen latín[12].

Tres composiciones en verso con motivo de la muerte del obispo Espada se dieron a conocer entre 1832 y 1834. Fueron sus autores José Agustín Caballero, ya mencionado; el presbítero Santiago Comas, y el médico español radicado en Puerto Rico, José Espaillat, quien obtuvo premio en el concurso convocado por la Sociedad Patriótica para honrar al prelado, lo que le valió ser corresponsal de esta institución. Constituyen estas elegías, junto con la de Aréchaga y la lápida de Velázquez, los únicos textos en verso de carácter funerario que se conservan pues sólo se tienen noticias de los dedicados a Juana Rosa Téllez y Clara Morales. De esta época es también la oración pronunciada por Comas en el Seminario de San Carlos al colocarse allí el retrato del obispo (1834).

En 1840 el profesor Manuel González del Valle y Cañizo (1802–1884) tuvo a su cargo en la Real y Pontificia Universidad la lección inaugural de la cátedra de Filosofía Moral, publicada ese año por la imprenta de Bolonia en edición bilingüe latín-español. Se halla en la Biblioteca Nacional José Martí. El latín era la lengua oficial de ésta y otras cátedras, excepto en las prácticas de Medicina.

En 1842, con la secularización de la Universidad convertida en Real y Literaria, el latín dejó de ser lengua oficial académica para convertirse en una asignatura de formación cultural básica como hasta hoy. Disminuye por ello el número de obras neolatinas a partir de entonces, si bien sigue usándose como lengua de la Iglesia Católica y de algunas ramas científicas como la Biología.

Precisamente, se publican en latín en Cuba y en el extranjero a finales del siglo pasado los *Icones plantarum in Flora Cubana descriptarum ex Historia Phisica, Politica et Naturalis a Ramon de la Sagra* . . . (París, 1863); la *Flora Cubana* . . . de Francisco Adolfo Sauvalle (Havanae, 1873), y la *Enumeratio piscium Cubensium* de Felipe Poey y Aloy (Madrid, 1876). A estas debe agregarse la disertación sobre algunas plantas cubanas publicadas en folletos el siglo anterior por Baltasar Manuel Boldó (1798), quien for-

---

[12] Mariano y J. Luis Peset, *La Universidad Española* (Madrid, Taurus), 224.

maba parte de la comisión de exploración dirigida por Tomás de Villanova, profesor de Botánica de Valencia. Boldó era natural de Zaragoza. Este folleto se localiza en la Biblioteca Central Rubén Martínez Villena de la Universidad de La Habana.

Hasta aquí algunos de los textos neolatinos más representativos. Si a ellos se agregan los que por razones de espacio no es posible siquiera mencionar, podemos decir que hasta 1842, fin de lo que pudiera llamarse en una periodización particular la primera etapa del uso del latín por su empleo como lengua viva, vieron la luz pública al menos 48 tesis de medicina, 12 de jurisprudencia y 14 de filosofía, para un total de 74 títulos. A las publicaciones anteriores habría que agregar las dos proposiciones defendidas en época posterior a 1842, y las 19 obras en formas de libro y folleto y de naturaleza varia (tratados de derecho, retórica, fisiología, religión, etc.) dados a la imprenta en estos cinco siglos de tradición europea, junto con seis inscripciones fundamentales, ocho epitafios, cuatro certificaciones o títulos, cinco oraciones o discursos, una décima jocosa, un poema de tono satírico y tres traducciones de sánscrito al latín, que representan 49 obras más, y un total general de 123 textos neolatinos de un número aproximado de autores equivalente. Los años de los que se conservan más textos impresos son: 1841 con ocho, 1837 con seis, y 1827 y 1832 con cinco cada uno.

Las funciones básicas que cumplen estos documentos son cuatro:

— búsqueda de la solemnidad y tono elevado: no se considera la lengua vernácula apropiada para la exaltación de las grandes figuras o los hechos luctuosos, de modo que se emplea el latín en inscripciones funerarias, fundacionales o religiosas, títulos, etc.
— búsqueda de precisión jurídica o científica: es así que aparecen en latín tratados científicos y filosóficos.
— en ocasiones se trata sólo de una voluntad de erudición, y así encontramos discursos y poemas. Esta tendencia se vio favorecida por los concursos sobre temas relacionados con la muerte de alguna personalidad, como los convocados al fallecer Felipe IV y el obispo Espada.
— ejercicios docentes a que estaban obligados los educandos: tesis o cuodlibetos. En esta función escasean o faltan trabajos durante el segundo período constitucional de España y sus colonias (1820–1823), dado que se deja a opción del estudiante, por reglamento, presentar la tesis en español o en latín.

Agréguese a esto que el latín continuó siendo la lengua oficial de la Iglesia Católica, por lo que era empleado en toda su documentación: constituciones sinodales, almanaques, etc.

Resultaría muy difícil evaluar la calidad de la autoría de los textos en latín por varias razones: por ejemplo, no se conservan los de algunos latinistas notables como Tranquilino Sandalio de Noda, Ángel Cowley y otros; la muestra de un autor es a veces demasiado pequeña, o bien los escritos no tienen todos las mismas características, y por lo tanto no son comparables. Por otra parte, habría que hacer estudios de cada uno de los textos, incluida su traducción, para valorarlos *per se*, y en relación con otros. Añádase a lo dicho que no existen, como constata el profesor Joseph Ijsewijn, gramáticas ni diccionarios de latín humanístico o neolatín, diferente del de

Roma, sino algunos artículos y monografías sobre los más encumbrados autores como Petrarca y Erasmo, y unos pocos índices y glosarios[13].

Con todo, y sin desconocer la importancia de otros empeños, se destacan entre los escritores cubanos en latín el padre José Agustín Caballero y el presbítero Félix Varela, autores respectivos de los textos *Philosophia electiva* (1797) y *Philosophia ecclectica* . . . (1812), que marcan la reforma filosófica en Cuba y la modernización de estos estudios.

Universidad de La Habana

---

[13] Joseph Ijsewijn, *Lenguaje y estilo*, traducción de José Quiñones (México, 1989).

$$A\ Latin\ Epitaph\ for$$
$$Dr.\ Engelbert\ Kaempfer's\ Three\ Children$$

ROBERT W. CARRUBBA

The tragedies of the private life of the celebrated German physician, traveler, and author Engelbert Kaempfer stand in sharp contrast to the achievements of his professional life. Born in Lemgo in 1651 as the son of the Lutheran pastor of the Nikolaikirche,[1] Kaempfer studied at a number of institutions in Central Europe as well as across the Baltic Sea in Stockholm, Sweden.[2] In 1683 he undertook what was to be a decade of cultural and scientific exploration through Russia, Persia, India, Java, Siam, and, most importantly, Japan.[3] During these travels, whether as the secretary of the Swedish mission to the Persian Court at Isfahan or as a physician in the Dutch East India Company (VOC), Kaempfer made superb use of his extensive education in languages, history, and the sciences to record observations and discoveries. We may note three works: his thesis, for which he was awarded the degree M. D. in 1694, *Disputatio Medica Inauguralis;*[4] the multifaceted *Amoenitates Exoticae* (1712);[5] and his most famous work, *The History of Japan* (1727).[6] In these publications, Kaempfer presents original observations, discoveries, and analyses concerning such widely varying items as the bitterness and mythological whirlpools of the Caspian Sea, the remains of the ancient monuments at Persepolis, the state of the Persian

---

[1] Kaempfer's father, Johannes (1610–1682), became pastor primarius of the Nikolaikirche in 1644. Kaempfer's mother, Christine Drepper, died about 1654, when Engelbert was still quite young.

[2] This large number includes institutions at Lemgo, Hameln, Lüneburg, Lübeck, Danzig, Krakow, Königsberg, and Uppsala.

[3] Kaempfer left Stockholm in March 1683 and returned to Amsterdam in October 1693.

[4] See John Z. Bowers and Robert W. Carrubba, "The Doctoral Thesis of Engelbert Kaempfer on Tropical Diseases, Oriental Medicine, and Exotic Natural Phenomena," *Journal of the History of Medicine and Allied Sciences* 25 (1970): 270–310.

[5] Engelbert Kaempfer, *Amoenitatum exoticarum politico-physico-medicarum fasciculi V, quibus continentur variae relationes, observationes & descriptiones rerum Persicarum & Ulterioris Asiae* (Lemgo, 1712).

[6] *The History of Japan*, trans. J. G. Scheuchzer, 2 vols. (London, 1727).

empire, the electric torpedo fish of the Persian Gulf, diseases endemic to India and its so-called snake dances, sexual magic in Malabar, the date palm, Japanese tea, the oriental surgical techniques of moxibustion and acupuncture, and the culture and history of Siam and Japan. These fruits of his "considerable labor, expense and danger,"as Kaempfer himself termed them,[7] earned him during his lifetime, and especially thereafter, an international reputation among scholars, scientists, and the educated lay public.

Yet, such splendid achievements came at a high personal price: he was seriously ill for a period in Persia,[8] his explorations by land and sea were physically trying as well as dangerous,[9] his personal liberty was restricted in the manner of his two-year imprisonment at Nagasaki,[10] and his style of life demanded that he postpone marriage and a family until his return home to Germany. When nearly fifty, he married Maria Sophia Wilstach[11] in December of 1700. The doctor looked forward to the joys of conjugal life, to the improved lifestyle that his wife's dowry would provide, and to children. As things turned out, Kaempfer was to experience deep disappointment and sorrow in all three areas. From his correspondence with his Dutch friend Daniel Parvé[12] and from his will,[13] we learn that Kaempfer did not receive the financial benefits he had expected from his father-in-law and on which he counted to be free from the "slavery of his work," and that the doctor literally came to hate his wife, whom he specifically disinherited. Of his marriage, Kaempfer says in a letter to Parvé, that in the evening of his life he did something insane.[14] Whether written in partial jest or not, these sentiments reveal an aspect of Kaempfer which is scarcely flattering. As for children, Maria Sophia bore two daughters and a son, but unhappily all three died early and from the same cause, smallpox:

Amalia Florentine	Born 1702	Died 1705
Amalia	Born after 1705	Died 1714
Friedrich Adolph	Born 1710	Died 1715

Tragically, all of Kaempfer's children had passed away before the doctor's own death. During the last years of his life, Kaempfer's health greatly deteriorated from

---

[7] See Kaempfer, *Amoenitates Exoticae*, Preface, 1.

[8] While serving as a physician in the service of the Dutch East India Company at its factory in Bandar Abbas on the Persian Gulf (December 1685–June 1688).

[9] We need only cite Kaempfer's perilous crossing of the Caspian Sea in November 1683.

[10] Kaempfer, *The History of Japan* (Glasgow, 1906), 2: 191: "Thus we live all the year round little better than prisoners, confin'd within the compass of a small Island, under the perpetual and narrow inspection of our Keepers."

[11] Maria Sophia Wilstach (1684–1761) was quite young when she married Kaempfer, shortly after whose death she remarried.

[12] Karl Meier-Lemgo, *Die Briefe Engelbert Kaempfers. Akademie der Wissenschaften und der Literatur. Abhandlungen der mathematisch-naturwissenschaftlichen Klasse 6* (Mainz, 1965).

[13] Heinrich Schwanold, "Engelbert Kaempfers Testament," *Mitteilungen aus der lippischen Geschichte und Landeskunde* 5 (Detmold, 1907): 41–61.

[14] See Kaempfer, *Briefe*, 41f.

colic. He managed to recover from serious attacks and to continue his duties as physician to the Count of Lippe, but in September 1716 he was again stricken with fever, fainting, and vomiting of blood. Toward the end of October, his condition worsened with fever, nausea, loss of appetite, and increased vomiting of blood. Mercifully, his suffering ended shortly thereafter with his death on 2 November 1716.

Funeral services for Kaempfer were held at Nikolaikirche in Lemgo. Johann Berthold Haccius, the church pastor, delivered the funeral oration in German. Haccius published this oration along with additional materials in both German and Latin on the life and achievements of Kaempfer, including Pastor Hermann Gerard Weland's interesting and creative Latin *Elegy for Engelbert Kaempfer*.[15] Toward the end of Haccius' book we find the Latin invitation extended by Christoff Meier, Rector of the Lemgo Gymnasium, which Kaempfer had attended as a boy, to all persons of letters and all citizens to attend the last rites for Kaempfer. A second announcement, this time in a mixture of German and Latin, ends with the following lines:[16]

Introduced with a Distraught Pen

by

Christoff Meier

Rector of the Lemgo Gymnasium

There follow several pages of German verse reflecting in a religious manner on Kaempfer's life and death, after which appears on an unnumbered page the Latin epitaph for Kaempfer's three children, presumably composed by Meier himself. This piece, which to my knowledge has not been published or translated elsewhere, provides us with a tender but powerful insight into that dichotomy of professional achievement and private tragedy which is a hallmark of Kaempfer's life. In addition, this epitaph reminds us that the Latin language in 1716 was still a living vehicle for communicating learned and religious thoughts. Finally, the epitaph, if a bit contrived in its botanical metaphor,[17] nonetheless conveys genuine compassion in a simple but sophisticated form.

---

[15] Johann Berthold Haccius, *Die beste Reise Eines Christlichen Kämpffers nach dem himmlischen Orient* (Lemgo, 1716). See also Robert W. Carrubba, "Pastor H. G. Weland's Latin Elegy for Engelbert Kaempfer," *Gesnerus: Swiss Journal of the History of Medicine and Sciences* 51 (1994): 34–44.

[16] The original text is: Mit beſtürtzter Feder vorgeſtellet
von
Chriſtoff Meiern/
des Lemgoiſchen Gymnaſii Rectore.

[17] The metaphor, which compares a loved one who has died to a flower which has been cut down or which loses its bloom after only a short time, is traditional. The reference may also be intended to reflect Kaempfer's extensive contributions to botany, e.g., reports on the date palm and Japanese plants.

EPITAPHIUM

In tres B. DOCTORIS liberos, aliquot annis ante
obitum eius defunctos.

STA. VIATOR.

ET.

SI. PEREGRINUS. ES. LEGE.
SI. CIVIS. ETIAM. LUGE.
VTERQUE. AUTEM. INTELLIGE.
FLORUM. AMOENIORUM. TRIGAM.
VARIIS. COLORIBUS. DISTINCTAM.

SED.

VARIOLIS. PROH DOLOR! EXTINCTAM.
VEL. VT. RECTIUS. DICAM,
IPSO. AETATIS. VERE.
IN MELIOREM PARADISUM. TRANSLATAM.

ESSE.

NAM.

QUOD. FLORET. FELICITER.
DEFLORESCIT. VELOCITER.

ET

AESTATES. VIVUNT. ROSAE.
NON. AETATES.

SCILICET.

MAGNI. PARENTIS.

DOMINI.

ENGELBERTI. KAEMPFERI.

MED. DOCTORIS. ET. ILLUSTRISSIMAE. AULAE.
LIPPIACAE.
ARCHIATRI CELEBERRIMI.
FILIOLAE. DUAE.
CUM.

CUM. VNO. FILIOLO.

AMALIA. FLORENTINA.

AMALIA. POSTERIOR.

FRIDERICUS. ADOLPHUS.

HIC. IUXTA. OSSA. B. PARENTIS.
RESURRECTIONEM. EXPECTANT.

EPITAPH

For the BLESSED DOCTOR'S three children, deceased some years
prior to his death.

STAND TRAVELER

AND

IF YOU ARE A FOREIGNER, READ;

IF YOU ARE A CITIZEN, ALSO GRIEVE.

BOTH OF YOU, HOWEVER, UNDERSTAND THAT

THE TRIAD OF MORE PLEASANT FLOWERS,

WITH VARIOUS COLORS WAS DISTINCT,

BUT

BY SMALLPOX - ALAS THE SORROW! - BECAME EXTINCT,

OR THAT I MIGHT SPEAK MORE CORRECTLY,

IN THE VERY SPRING OF LIFE

TO A BETTER PARADISE WAS TRANSPORTED.

FOR

THAT WHICH FLOWERS HAPPILY

LOSES ITS FLOWER QUICKLY

AND

ROSES LIVE FOR SUMMERS

NOT FOR YEARS.

TO BE SURE,

OF A GREAT PARENT,

MASTER

ENGELBERT KAEMPFER,

DOCTOR OF MEDICINE AND OF THE MOST ILLUSTRIOUS COURT

OF LIPPE

MOST RENOWNED CHIEF PHYSICIAN,

TWO LITTLE DAUGHTERS

WITH

ONE LITTLE SON,

AMALIA FLORENTINE,

AMALIA THE LATER,

FRIEDRICH ADOLPH,

HERE BESIDE THE BONES OF THEIR BLESSED PARENT

AWAIT THE RESURRECTION.

After the Latin epitaph, the last page of Haccius' compilation presents six lines (two triptychs) in German, in which the deceased Kaempfer children speak. Their words encourage friends to be of good cheer and to consider that the souls of the three children have quite agreeably risen to heaven, where there is pure joy. The children also reason that their curtailed period of life receives its compensation by an eternity in heaven with Jesus, in accordance with their struggles. And by extension, of course, all human beings are to be heartened by the reflection that human suffering will find joy in the next life. A final illustration with two human figures and a skull expresses the shortness of life and the inevitability of death.

Fordham University

El Lexicon nauticum et aquatile *de Juan Lorenzo Palmireno: un proyecto de manualito para la composición en latín*[1]

MARÍA JOSÉ CEA GALÁN

Preliminares

Por evidentes razones de espacio el objetivo de la presente comunicación no será el estudio en profundidad del *Lexicon nauticum et aquatile* de Juan Lorenzo Palmireno. Futuras investigaciones nuestras vendrán a completar en lo sucesivo los contenidos de este trabajo.

La obra en el contexto filológico de la época

El *Lexicon nauticum et aquatile* del humanista aragonés Juan Lorenzo Palmireno[2] se inserta en la línea de los *apuntes* o *vocabularios* tan en boga en el Renacimiento y cuyo interés habían señalado mucho antes que él humanistas de la talla de Erasmo o Vives. En efecto, Erasmo había advertido en su *De ratione studii* la importancia de los apuntes para obtener la *copia uerborum*. Vives, por su parte, entre las ideas acerca del modo de enseñar a los niños apuntaba la necesidad de que éstos se hicieran con un vocabulario de los objetos inmediatos que les rodeaban en la vida para poder nombrarlos en latín; en la *Exercitatio* Vives adapta palabras antiguas a significaciones nuevas con el fin de que el alumno componga en latín a partir de textos escritos previamente en la lengua materna, discerniendo los sinónimos y antónimos e insertando los adagios y frases hechas que ha recopilado y, en su caso, memorizado[3].

---

[1] Este trabajo ha sido realizado en el marco del proyecto de investigación PS93–0130 subvencionado por la DGICYT.

[2] Para el estudio bio-bibliográfico de este humanista cf., principalmente, A. Gallego Barnés, *Juan Lorenzo Palmireno (1524–1579): un humanista aragonés en el Studi General de Valencia* (Zaragoza, 1982), *passim*; C. L. de la Vega y Luque, "Vida y obra de Juan Lorenzo Palmireno", *Teruel* 49–50 (1973): 112–186; L. Esteban Mateo, "Juan Lorenzo Palmireno, humanista y pedagogo", *Perficit* 95 (1976): 73–106; J. Mª Maestre Maestre, *El humanismo alcañizano del siglo XVI. Textos y estudios de latín renacentista* (Cádiz, 1990), 127–195.

[3] Cf. A. Fontán, "El latín de Luis Vives", *VI Congreso de Estudios Clásicos. Homenaje a Luis Vives* (Madrid), 52–53.

A través de la lectura de estos humanistas Palmireno asimila el método vivista y él mismo declara haberlo adoptado como otros tantos estudiosos que había conocido[4]. Es este método el que inspiró sus numerosos glosarios, de los que es quizá especialmente famoso el *Vocabulario del humanista compuesto por Lorenço Palmireno, donde se trata de aues, peces, quadrúpedos, con sus vocablos de caçar y pescar, yeruas, metales, monedas, piedras preciosas, gomas, drogas, olores, y otras cosas que el estudioso de letras humanas ha menester. Dirigido Al Illustríssimo y Reuerendíssimo señor don Ioan de Ribera Patriarcha de Antiochia y Arçobispo de Valencia, &c. Hay también un uocabulario de antiguallas para entender a Cicerón, César y Virgilio*, obra ésta publicada en Valencia por Pedro de Huete en 1569 y en cuya reedición de 1575 se añadieron otros apartados, como *Selecta animalia, Stromata, &c*[5]. En la misma línea se insertan sus colecciones de adagios, de emblemas y jeroglíficos, los listados de árboles, colores, panes, medallas y símbolos, los refraneros, los manuales para la improvisación en latín y las explicaciones de frases oscuras de autores clásicos.

Contenido de la obra

Según las investigaciones actuales, la obra que nos ocupa no fue dada a la imprenta en su totalidad: sólo conocemos un fragmento de la misma que aparece publicado en la primera edición de la *Rhetorica* de nuestro humanista a modo de apéndice del libro tercero junto con unos adagios, declamaciones y extractos de comedias[6].

Aclara en ese lugar Palmireno que años atrás, cuando explicaba en clase los *Comentarios* de César y describía en el libro tercero las anclas, los bancos de remeros y las naves de los galos, había prometido a sus alumnos un *Lexicon nauticum et aquatile* en latín, mas, aunque tenía confeccionada una buena parte de él, "sucede a veces que los malvados ojeadores[7] de las buenas obras destruyen la cosecha todavía en la hierba. No está en mi mano hablar con más claridad, sólo añado lo siguiente: que contra mi voluntad aplazo el asunto para otra ocasión. Entretanto, para que no sigan molestos mis discípulos, que me la reclaman a diario, ofrecemos los principales capítulos de la obra futura, pidiendo solamente del benigno lector que, si en ellos ve algo mal explicado, calle hasta que podamos hacer visible lamiendo el informe parto de la osa"[8].

En efecto, los capítulos de los que se componía la obra proyectada son relacionados a continuación por el humanista: vocablos de lugares acuáticos; partes y aparejos de las naves, sus tipos y formas; términos, expresiones y frases propios de la navegación; metáforas náuticas selectas, adagios, sentencias, apólogos, símiles y apotegmas náuticos; jeroglíficos, monedas y emblemas; peligros y tormentas, los vientos; problemas relacionados con la navegación; presagios; el combate naval; vocablos de pesca, su

---

[4] Gallego Barnés, *Juan Lorenzo Palmireno*, 97.

[5] Gallego Barnés, *Juan Lorenzo Palmireno*, 98.

[6] Cf. J. L. Palmireno, *Tertia & ultima pars rhetoricae Laurentii Palmyreni in qua de memoria & actione disputatur* (Valentiae, 1566), 84–101.

[7] Término éste del vocabulario cinegético—en latín *alatores*—que designa a aquellos que acosan con gritos a la caza por los flancos del camino que ha sido fijado previamente.

[8] Palmireno, *Tertia & ultima pars rhetoricae*, 84.

método, los peces diversos; y, por último, algunos secretos y arcanos de la navegación[9].

De estos capítulos desarrolla entonces Palmireno sólo algunos, dejando el resto para la redacción definitiva. Así, encontramos en primer lugar los vocablos de lugares acuáticos, una copiosa relación de términos latinos que, de una forma u otra, guardan relación con el líquido elemento; hallamos, en efecto, los nombres de las masas o corrientes de agua (*fluuius, mare, lacus, palus, fons*, etc.), de accidentes geográficos u obras de ingeniería relacionados con aquellos (*isthmus, sinus, portus, aquae ductus*, etc.), y algunas expresiones que tienen que ver con el agua (*aquaria prouincia*, "intendencia de las aguas", *aqua et igni interdicere*, "privar a alguno del agua y del fuego", es decir, "desterrarlo", *frigidam suffundere*, "echar un jarro de agua fría", etc.). Comenta Palmireno que estos términos y otros muchos se explican en español en su *Lexicon* y que añade otros por el estilo incluyendo además los nombres de algunos mares, o de la grava, la arena, la marea, etc[10].

Se dan luego los nombres de algunos vientos con su equivalencia en español (*Eurus-Syroco, uulturnus-sudoeste*, etc.)[11] y seguidamente los nombres de las naves y sus diferencias; es ésta una extensísima lista en que se detalla la equivalencia latín-español tanto de los nombres de navíos (*nauis praetoria, la capitana; nauicula, una góndola*, etc.) como de sus partes y aparejos (*corbis, la gabia; cornua, los cabos de las antenas*, etc.), de los tripulantes de una nave (*nauta, el marinero; proreta, el que va sentado en la proa para gouernar; piratae et praedones, cossarios*, etc.) y de otros términos marinos tan peculiares a veces como el *nauticus panis, vizcocho* o la *nausea, el vómito que padescen los que se marean*[12].

Siguen a esto los milagros náuticos, capítulo no anunciado pero que quizá se corresponde con aquellos presagios anteriormente citados. Entre ellos se mencionan, por ejemplo, las estrellas de Cástor y Pólux como equivalentes de las *lumbres de S. Elmo*, o a Tritón, que lo es de *la serena del mar*. Palmireno comenta aquí de nuevo que en su *Lexicon* se desarrollan ampliamente estas historias y otros milagros de las aguas y lo que la gente piensa erróneamente[13].

A continuación encontramos los peligros del mar, una relación de términos breve aunque diversa: *turbo, fluctus, procella, Scylla, Charybdis, Syrtes, breuia, scopuli, beluae et marina monstra, tempestates, latrocinia, praedones, piratae* y *naufragium*[14]. Siguen los problemas náuticos, con tres ejemplos como es: *cur remus in aqua inflexus uidetur?*[15]

El último capítulo desarrollado es el de los símiles náuticos. Recoge Palmireno cuarenta y dos símiles, como el siguiente: *ut aqua marina ad potum inutilis melius sustinet nauem quam fluuialis dulcis et potui aptior, ita suum unaquaeque res usum habet, si quis utatur ad id quod oportet*[16].

---

[9] Palmireno, *Tertia & ultima pars rhetoricae*, 84–85.

[10] Palmireno, *Tertia & ultima pars rhetoricae*, 85.

[11] Palmireno, *Tertia & ultima pars rhetoricae*, 86.

[12] Palmireno, *Tertia & ultima pars rhetoricae*, 86–94.

[13] Palmireno, *Tertia & ultima pars rhetoricae*, 94.

[14] Palmireno, *Tertia & ultima pars rhetoricae*, 94–95.

[15] Palmireno, *Tertia & ultima pars rhetoricae*, 95.

[16] Palmireno, *Tertia & ultima pars rhetoricae*, 95–101.

El *Lexicon nauticum et aquatile*: ¿Una obra no publicada en su totalidad?

Como dijimos más arriba, al parecer la obra completa nunca fue dada a la imprenta. Ya nos aclaraba Palmireno al presentarla en la *Rhetorica* que la falta de medios económicos le había impedido publicarla. Añádase a ello la falta de tiempo de nuestro humanista, pues con las clases diarias en la Universidad, las que daba de forma particular en su casa, las incomodidades que le ocasionaba su numerosa prole y las frecuentes visitas que recibía apenas le quedaba ocasión para la actividad editorial, cuando las más de las veces llevaba al impresor los propios apuntes de clase que tomaban sus discípulos[17].

Queda por averiguar—aunque sea prácticamente imposible—si lo que era un proyecto de 1566 no se vio repartido luego en otras obras. Recordemos a este respecto que el *Vocabulario del humanista* incluye un catálogo de peces y vocablos de pesca y que también hemos mencionado listados de medallas, emblemas, adagios, etc. elaborados por nuestro humanista, entre los que hubiera podido incluir también los propiamente *náuticos*. Pero la inexistencia del apunte proyectado e incluso la pérdida de varias de sus publicaciones nos hace imposible hoy por hoy la tarea. Lo que sí es presumible es que el proyecto alcanzó una notable madurez y, probablemente, tomó forma de apuntes, según nos hace pensar la impronta de estos conocimientos teóricos en los ejercicios "escolares" del autor. En efecto, si la principal utilidad de estas recopilaciones era su aplicación posterior en las composiciones en latín, entonces sus escritos latinos podrán darnos una idea aproximada de lo que había concebido a nivel teórico. De manera que extraeremos a continuación de una parte de su obra—concretamente los discursos latinos[18]—aquellos pasajes que tengan que ver con la navegación para someterlos a análisis.

De la teoría a la praxis

Encontramos en los discursos latinos de Palmireno dieciocho pasajes relacionados con la navegación de extensión y sentido ciertamente variables:

A. Con frecuencia el propio discurso es una nave con la que se navega al hablar y cuyas velas, una vez concluido, se recogen para retornar a puerto:

1. *Profecto si orationis uela pandere et quasi aperto inuectus mari per Salayae laudes decurrere instituam*[19]

---

[17] Gallego Barnés, *Juan Lorenzo Palmireno*, 49, 78–79.

[18] Actualmente nos encontramos realizando en la Universidad de Cádiz nuestra Tesis Doctoral sobre los discursos latinos de Palmireno bajo la dirección de los Dres D. Juan Gil Fernández y D. José Mª Maestre Maestre.

[19] Cf. J. L. Palmireno, *Laurentii Palmyreni oratio qua suam Hispanicam quam in Aragonia habuerat defendit in Academia Valentina anno 1574 mense Ianuario*, en *Campi eloquentiae in quibus Laurentii Palmyreni ratio declamandi, Orationes, Praefationes, Epistolae & Epigrammata continentur* (Valentiae, 1574), 5. El estudio, edición crítica y traducción anotada de esta obra constituyó nuestra Tesis de Licenciatura inédita realizada bajo la dirección del Dr. D. José Mª Maestre Maestre con el título "Discurso de Juan Lorenzo Palmireno sobre la defensa del castellano frente al latín" (Universidad de Cádiz, 1993).

2. *Nam quo longius in altum inuehor eo mihi amplior et patentior orationis quasi cursus ostenditur*[20]

3. *Sed, quorsum pelagus hoc ingredior?*[21]

4. *Sed longum pelagus ingredior*[22]

5. *Ego ne uobis molestus sim, ad silentii portum me recipio*[23]

6. *Temporis me ratio ut uela contraham portumque tandem aliquando respiciam monet*[24]

B. Otras veces la Universidad es la nave: sufre tempestades y goza de la bonanza:

7. *Non enim studiosorum nauis, ut solebat, placido mari secundis conspirantium uentorum flatibus impulsa fertur: horribiles eam procellae et turbinum uis, uel exercitatissimis metuenda rectoribus, agitant ut, quanquam a naufragio quidem nullum periculum est, non mediocris tamen animos teneat metus ne tam saeua tempestas multos hisce dictatorum dialecticae fluctibus inuolutos in ea breuia praecipites abripiat, unde postea nec enatare ipsi nec euadere atque emergere alieno auxilio possint*[25]

8. *[Academia Valentina] eam pacem, id otium amplectebatur ut tranquillis fluctibus addita malacia crederetur et omnes passim in foro esse alcedonia dictitarent*[26]

9. *Nam, quae tempestas, Deum immortalem, . . . academiae fuisset?*[27]

C. En la nave de la Universidad el Rector es el timonel:

10. *Audieram enim Blasium Nauarrum, insignem theologum, in academia Valentina ad clauum sedere*[28]

---

[20] Cf. J. L. Palmireno, *Laurentii Palmyreni orationes duae aduersariae quarum prior dictata quae uocant miris laudibus extollit; altera uero acerbo conuicio reprehendit. In Academia Valentina 1572 recitata prior a Petro Peralta, posterior a Francisco Tarrega*, en *El latino de repente de Lorenço Palmyreno, añadido e emendado* (Valentiae), 284.

[21] Cf. J. L. Palmireno, *Oratio Laurentii Palmyreni in laudem classium habita in academia Valentina 14 Calendas Nouembris 1561*, en *Rhetoricae Laurentii Palmyreni pars secunda in duos libros distributa, quorum prior elocutionis praecepta, alter exercitationem & exempla complectitur* (Valentiae, 1565), fol. 64r y *Campi eloquentiae* . . . , 185–186.

[22] Cf. Palmireno, *Oratio in laudem iurisperitiae recitata in Academia Valentina a Ioanne Ynsa Caspensi*, en *Campi eloquentiae*, 143.

[23] Cf. Palmireno, *Oratio Laurentii Palmyreni in laudem classium*, en *Rhetoricae Laurentii Palmyreni pars secunda*, fol. 64r y *Campi eloquentiae*, 186.

[24] Cf. Palmireno, *Laurentii Palmyreni orationes duae aduersariae*, en *El latino de repente*, 284.

[25] Cf. Palmireno, *Laurentii Palmyreni oratio qua suam Hispanicam*, en *Campi eloquentiae*, 7.

[26] Cf. Palmireno, *Laurentii Palmyreni orationes duae aduersariae*, en *El latino de repente*, 270.

[27] Cf. Palmireno, *Laurentii Palmyreni oratio Valentiae habita mense Decembri 1563*, en *Tertia & ultima pars Rhetoricae*, 141, y en *Campi eloquentiae*, 192.

[28] Cf. J. L. Palmireno, *Laurentii Palmyreni oratio post reditum in Academiam Valentinam mense Augusto 1572*, en *Phrases Ciceronis obscuriores in Hispanicam linguam conuersae a Laurentio Palmyreno. Item eiusdem hypotyposes clarissimorum uirorum ad extemporalem dicendi facultatem utilissimae. Eiusdem Oratio post reditum in Academia Valentina mense Augusto 1572* (Valentiae, 1572). Es éste el primer discurso latino de Palmireno que ha contado con una edición moderna, acompañada de traducción anotada y estudio introductorio, realizada por Maestre Maestre, *El humanismo alcañizano del siglo XVI*, 196–227. Para el pasaje que se cita Maestre Maestre, *El humanismo alcañizano del siglo XVI*, orat. 12, 1–2.

D.　O, por extensión, quien se halla al frente de una comunidad o institución:

11.　*Qui tam feliciter sedes in puppi clauumque tenes*[29]

E.　En otra ocasión la vida es una travesía y la muerte prematura, un naufragio:

12.　*Nimirum ut ante in ipso cursu obruamur quam possimus exoptatum portum con-spicere*[30]

F.　Asimismo, hallamos la imagen del náufrago:

13.　*Naufragium facit natationis ignarus, arripit tabulam et amplexu tenens ad littus inco-lumis a fluctibus appellitur, num idcirco natandi peritiam negabimus esse utilem, quod sine ea qui fuit e periculo tempestatis euaserit?*[31]

G.　Y del áncora de salvación:

14.　*Ad dictata ceu ad sacram anchoram confugiunt*[32]

15.　*Sibi enim persuadebant sacram anchoram in illis esse*[33]

H.　La imagen de la tempestad y la tormenta se aplica también a veces a algo distinto de la Universidad:

16.　*Sedata est tempestas illa non secus ac mare sublatis procellosis uentis tranquillum fit et iucundam malaciam ostendit*[34]

I.　El ánimo es como un escollo que soporta impasible las sacudidas de las olas:

17.　*Stat enim ut in medio mari edita et altissimis defixa radicibus rupes cuius summa fluc-tus ne attingunt quidem, infima sic uerberant non ut eam commoueant, sed ut ipsi frangantur*[35]

J.　Por último, el estudioso que se toma un descanso es como la nave que se retira a puerto:

18.　*Tanquam in portu, complicatis uelis caeterisque armamentis omnibus compositis, quie-scentem senatus Valentini autoritas expergisci denuo et subductam iam nauim, mutato consilio, deducere et uela uentis pandere coegit. Nam ex quo tempore horum iucundae exoptataeque litterae redditae sunt, tanta cupiditate fui ad reditum incensus, ut mihi nulli neque remi neque uenti satisfacerent*[36]

En estos pasajes hallamos términos incluidos en el listado de vocablos de lugares acuáticos del *Lexicon*, como *aperto mari* (pasaje número 1), *portus* (pasajes 5, 6, 12 y

---

[29] Cf. Palmireno, *Oratio Laurenti Palmyreni recitata a quodam theologo in collegium Calatrauae cooptato*, en *Campi eloquentiae*, 208.

[30] Cf. J. L. Palmireno, *Oratio funebris in qua immaturam mortem Pontificis seu Archiepiscopi Valentini deflebamus. Obiit autem Asisclus Moya de Contreras mense Maio 1564*, en *Laurentii Palmyreni de copia rerum et artificio oratorio libellus in quo Topica Oratoria & Dialectica uariis exemplis eloquentiae illustrata cernuntur* (Valentiae, 1564), fol. 38v.

[31] Cf. Palmireno, *Laurentii Palmyreni orationes duae aduersariae*, en *El latino de repente*, 273.

[32] Cf. Palmireno, *Laurentii Palmyreni orationes duae aduersariae*, en *El latino de repente*, 275.

[33] Cf. Palmireno, *Laurentii Palmyreni orationes duae aduersariae*, en *El latino de repente*, 278.

[34] Cf. J. L. Palmireno, *Oratio prima aduersus iurisperitos recitata a Ioanne Çapater Fresnedensi in Academia Valentina die diui Lucae 1573*, en *Campi eloquentiae*, 136.

[35] Cf. Palmireno, *Laurentii Palmyreni oratio qua suam Hispanicam*, en *Campi eloquentiae*, 17.

[36] Cf. Palmireno, *Laurentii Palmyreni oratio post reditum* (cf. Maestre Maestre, *El humanismo alcañizano del siglo XVI*, orat. 11, 3–8).

18), *littus* (13) y *mare* (16 y 17); otros términos aparecen entre las partes y aparejos de las naves aclarados en español, como *velum* (pasajes 1 y 6): *velum, la vela; clavum* (10 y 11): *clauus, el timón del gouernalle de la naue; puppi* (10 y 11): *puppis, la popa postrera parte de la naue; remi* (18): *remi, los remos;* o *sacra anchora* (13 y 14): *sacra anchora, es la que los marineros tienen guardada, y no la sacan sin grande necesidad.*

Especialmente significativo es el pasaje número 7, donde se acumulan términos incluidos en la relación de los peligros del mar: *horribiles eam **procellae** et **turbinum** uis, uel exercitatissimis metuenda rectoribus, agitant ut, quanquam a **naufragio** quidem nullum periculum est, non mediocris tamen animos teneat metus ne tam saeua **tempestas** multos hisce dictatorum dialecticae **fluctibus** inuolutos in ea **breuia** praecipites abripiat, unde postea nec enatare ipsi nec euadere atque emergere alieno auxilio possint.* Ejemplos como éste se entienden mejor a la luz de lo que ya apuntara el Profesor Fontán sobre el latín de Vives, cuya influencia en Palmireno ha sido ampliamente demostrada: "la aparición de un tema, arrastrado por un símbolo o metáfora, por ejemplo, la comparación con una nave, es generalmente utilizada para acumular seguidamente varios términos del vocabulario técnico correspondiente"[37]. De ahí, pues, la gran importancia que tenían los listados y apuntes como el *Lexicon.*

Pero echamos de menos determinados capítulos de aquel proyecto donde encuadrar, por ejemplo, términos, expresiones y frases propias de la navegación: falta la aclaración de no pocos vocablos como *malacia* o *alcedonia* o *procellosus* o bien los usos poéticos de *pelagus* y *altum,* falta la recopilación de numerosas expresiones y frases, como *uela pandere, uela complicare* o *contrahere, in puppi sedere* o *clauum tenere,* o *e periculo tempestatis euadere.* Tampoco contamos con lo que sería un utilísimo listado de metáforas, como la tan frecuente en el Renacimiento de la nave del Estado o la del timonel, o de imágines, como la del náufrago. Sin embargo, creemos muy probable que todo ello se encontrara en los apuntes de Palmireno y, por tanto, en su proyecto de edición, como lo avalan tanto el hecho de que los utilice con cierta frecuencia en sus composiciones latinas como el que gran número de esas expresiones, símiles o metáforas sean deudores precisamente de Cicerón[38], cuyo léxico había estudiado en profundidad nuestro humanista, según demuestra el análisis de sus obras[39].

En definitiva, en el estado actual de las investigaciones resulta imposible saber si el proyecto concebido por Palmireno tomó cuerpo de imprenta o no. No descartamos que futuros hallazgos bibliográficos puedan sacarnos de esta duda, pero, en tanto la realidad sea la que tenemos, lo que sí es cierto es que los textos de Palmireno—tanto teóricos como prácticos—que hoy conocemos ofrecen un vastísimo campo para los estudios del latín renacentista.

Universidad de Cádiz

---

[37] Cf. Fontán, "El latín de Luis Vives", 57.

[38] Por citar sólo las más significativas, *uela pandere* (*Tusc.* 1, 119), *orationis cursus* (*Brut.* 325), *contraxi uela* (*Att.* 1, 16, 2), *horribiles procellas* (*div.* 1, 14), *sedebamus in puppi et clauum tenebamus* (*epist.* 9, 15, 3), *tabulam . . . adripuerit* (*off.* 3, 89) o *neque remi neque uenti* (*epist.* 12, 25, 3).

[39] Para la influencia de Cicerón en Palmireno, véase, fundamentalmente, Maestre Maestre, *El humanismo alcañizano del siglo XVI,* 127–195, y M. J. Cea Galán, "Defensa del castellano frente al latín", XV–XLVII.

Making the List: The Evolution of
Ravisius Textor's Catalogue of Learned Women

DONALD CHENEY

At the time of her death in Prague in 1612, the Neo-Latin poet Elizabeth Jane Weston appears to have enjoyed the greatest international fame of any English writer who was not—like Sidney or More—of predominantly extra-literary interest to Europeans. Widely celebrated as the "Virgo Angla," Westonia exchanged correspondence and verse tributes with the major humanists of her time; one indication of her eminence is that Thomas Farnaby's 1634 *Index Poeticus*, a list of eminent ancient and modern writers, includes her as one of seven English writers and the only woman of any place or time.

The ways we might account today for her fame are likely to be influenced by our understanding of the position of such learned women in early modern culture. She was a genuinely talented Latinist, widely praised for her mastery of the elegiac form as another Ovid or Tibullus. At the same time, her personal circumstances doubtless worked to her advantage, creating a sense of pathos that could only enhance the emotions triggered by the Neo-Latin enterprise. As the stepdaughter of Edward Kelley, the Emperor Rudolf's alchemist, with whom she lived in Prague from early childhood, she enjoyed the advantages of an affluent and cosmopolitan upbringing. Although none of her vernacular writings survive, we are told she was fluent in numerous languages, and this seems likely from her family's connections with Bohemian and German aristocrats in the Rudolfine circle. When Kelley was imprisoned in 1597 and died in disgrace and penury, she further enjoyed (I suspect) the privilege accorded a talented and attractive orphan in need of benevolent patronage. Her brother was sickly and away at the University of Ingolstadt, where he would die presently; her poems and letters spoke eloquently of her destitute condition, and that of her mother, and she was able to write and publish without anyone's wondering why any kinsman could have permitted such a thing. Accordingly, she did not want for devoted patrons throughout the international republic of letters. The most notable among them was the Silesian aristocrat Georg Martin von Baldhoven, who undertook to edit and (sometimes rather ineptly) correct her poems. He published a two-book edition of *Poëmata* in 1602 and an expanded three-book collection of poems and letters that appeared probably in 1608,[1] under the slightly imprecise title of *Parthenica*, maidenly writings, since Westonia had married in 1603 and her role as English Virgin had ended in the same month that the other English Virgin, Elizabeth I, had died.

The subject of this essay is less the status or stature of Westonia than the question of canonicity that is reflected or embodied in a catalogue of learned women which Baldhoven appended to the *Parthenica* (III, fols. F3r–7v). Baldhoven copied verbatim a 1552 catalogue with some fifty-seven entries and added a few names of his own at the end, culminating in Westonia's. As we shall see, he is following in a tradition of borrowing and extending such compilations. I would suggest that this catalogue both consciously seeks to glorify Westonia by placing her in the context of other learned women, and at the same time inadvertently (from our historical perspective) illustrates a moment when the position of a learned virago like Weston was possible and less contentious than it would become a century later.

Baldhoven's immediate source is a late edition of Ravisius Textor's *Officina*,[2] one of the more notable instances of those collections of miscellaneous information made possible by the state of book production in the early sixteenth century. In a 1974 essay,[3] Walter J. Ong provides the fullest—and indeed almost the only—description of the work of Jean Tixier, Seigneur de Ravisi (c. 1475–1524), although T. W. Baldwin's *William Shakspere's Small Latine & Less Greeke*[4] had already shown the importance of that writer's *Epitheta* for the Elizabethan schoolboy in search of epithets for every occasion. Ong surveys the wide-ranging and frequently zany lists that Textor collects in his "workshop" or *Officina*—lists of suicides and parricides, fat men and skinny men, places with snakes and places with no snakes. The list of learned women, "Mulieres doctae," immediately follows a list of lovers of literature and a list of those who were unlearned and hated literature ["Indocti, et qui literas oderunt"], and it is followed by a list of those who wrote a great deal ["multa"] and a list of those who wrote works about slight matters ["de modicis rebus opera"].

Furthermore, and not very surprisingly, entries in one list turn up in others. A list of bellicose women includes Deborah and Zenobia, items 1 and 14 on Baldhoven's list of the learned; a list of prophets early on in the volume includes the learned Cassandra, Manto, Phaemonoe, Sosipatra, and Amalthea (items 34, 15, 11, 12, and 19). A list of women who wore men's clothes naturally features Pope Joan (item 49).

---

[1] *Poëmata* (Frankfurt am Oder, 1602); *Parthenicon . . . Libri III* (Prague, n.d.). Although the traditional date given the *Parthenica* in most library catalogues is c.1606, the catalogue of learned women cites Helena Maria Wackeriana von Wackenfels as having died in Prague. Since her death occurred on 30 May 1607, the book must have gone to press sometime after that date. A copy in the National Library of Prague (signature II.Ff.12) bearing the bookplate of Prince von Lobkovitz has a contemporary vellum binding with the date 1608 stamped on it.

[2] (Basel, 1552), cols. 751–759; first edition (Paris, 1520).

[3] "Commonplace Rhapsody: Ravisius Textor, Zwinger and Shakespeare," in *Classical Influences on European Culture, A.D. 1500-1700. Proceedings of an International Conference held at King's College, Cambridge, April 1974,* ed. R. R. Bolgar (Cambridge, 1974), 91–126.

[4] (Urbana, 1944).

Frequently, too, Textor repeats the items verbatim, sometimes with sources given and sometimes not.

Ong observes that Textor's work is located on the threshold of what he describes as "the new visual world of the inscribed word, which . . . in Textor's day was . . . maturing through the newly developing alphabetic print of the West" (108). The rapid evolution in the sixteenth century of capacious and consistently alphabetized indexes further facilitated information retrieval and encouraged the proliferation of lists and categories that one was scarcely aware of wanting, or recognizing previously. Today we have a term for such works that was not available to Ong in 1974; that is, these are early modern search engines. Anyone who has surfed the web will recognize the elusive, evanescent joys of such activity as well as the impressionistic terminology that grows up to describe it. It is hard to identify the precise kind of work that goes on in such a workshop or *Officina* as Textor's (or that of his contemporary cybernetic counterparts); *copia*, mere copiousness, is what one asks of a copy-book or *cornucopia*, not argumentation or hierarchy or, typically, value judgments.

Textor does not try to give us the extended analyses of individuals or the patterned juxtapositions of individuals that we find in more polished literary collections like Ovid's *Heroides* or Boccaccio's *De claris mulieribus* or Chaucer's *Legend of Good Women*. Nor does he intend, evidently, the comic, openly parodic listing of "authorities" that Chaucer's Franklin provides in Dorigen's complaint, a day or two long, ever purposing that she would die; yet the miscellaneity of his catalogue of learned females does carry a hint of unconscious absurdity.

Still, by the simple, mechanical process of scanning earlier histories, encyclopaedias, "rhapsodies," or commentaries, and of pulling down all the names of women who (in the case of the present catalogue) may be considered learned by one standard or another, Textor does manage to weave together (as his name suggests) the strands of the various traits that constitute the identity to which Westonia either aspires in her own writing or to which her admirers and editor would consign her. The appearance of Deborah and Minerva at the head of Textor's list suggests Biblical and classical sources for vatic prophecy and the "liberal arts," *bonae artes*, in strong and independent female figures. Corinna (item 3) is a name that links Weston to her principal model, Ovid, but it is also, we are told, the name of a poet who vanquished Pindar. Learning and poetic mastery (and, not incidentally, feminine charms) are intertwined from the outset.

The conditions of an encyclopaedic omnium gatherum of names support, however incidentally, a gloss on parallels to Westonia's glory which her correspondents have predictably cited in their letters included in the *Parthenica*. Innumerable admirers compare her to Sappho, a poet without peer; to the degree that this catalogue serves as an index of, or witness to, such citations, it is useful to be told of the variant accounts of Sappho's life: the husband by whom she has a daughter in one account, the tragic love for Phaon in another. If Westonia is a new Theano to her admirers— in her resemblance to the Theano who "excelled in lyric" (item 13)—it is additionally valuable to know of another Theano who wrote both poems and Pythagorean apophthegms. Westonia may not greatly resemble Zenobia (item 14) in her principal role as a tyrannical conqueror, a female Tamburlaine, but she does share with her a knowledge of languages and a concern to educate her children in letters.

Indeed, the happenstance that Diogenes Laertius should have provided Textor and his predecessors with a cluster of philosophically inclined women, especially in the circle of Pythagoras, may have seemed especially apt to readers of the *Parthenica*, or to its editor Baldhoven, in view of the fact (known to contemporaries but virtually unmentioned in the work itself) that Westonia was (by virtue of her connection to Kelley) at the center of the alchemical, "Spagyric" philosophy and its practitioners and allies throughout Europe. Although it is unclear just how much her popularity depended on such connections, and indeed just how much of an alchemical fraternity with larger social or political goals actually existed at this time, the association of Westonia with this multifarious catalogue encourages the casual reader to speculate on such possibilities, almost infinite in their range.

At times, of course, Textor either misinterprets his sources or passes on the misinterpretations of other glossators. Mycale (item 22) is a Thessalian witch mentioned by Ovid in *Metamorphoses* 12.263; since the dying centaur Nessus alludes to her in Seneca's *Hercules Oetaeus*, Textor mistakenly assumes she is a female centaur who (in the tradition of centaurs) taught Thessalian women the art of love. In the context of this catalogue she may seem to be akin to the Ovidian poet Westonia, but a better informed reader will balk at the comparison. "Istrina" (item 18) is an Istrian wife of the Scythian king Ariapithes. That she should have taught their son Scyles Greek culture is for Textor proof of her learning, but the point made by Herodotus is that she is the reason that Scyles will later be beheaded by his countrymen for having been corrupted by being exposed to Greek practices. She is thus a questionable model for the English matron who is raising her children by a German husband in the multicultural milieu of Rudolfine Prague.

As Textor's catalogue moves (somewhat erratically, by fits and starts) into Christian and modern times, the parallels at first seem rather less perilous. Westonia's piety seems comfortably akin to that of the matrons praised by St. Jerome, just as her sharing of poetic skills with brother and husband makes comparisons with Cornificia and Statius' Claudia or Lucan's Polla appropriate (items 42 to 44). A concern for transmitting eloquence within the humanistic household of the Holy Roman Empire is also properly compared to that of Cornelia, mother of the Gracchi (item 38); and Proba Valeria in particular (item 46) is a worthy source for Westonia's adaptations of classical formulae to Christian mysteries.

Here, however, a new peril lurks, one that apparently had seemed harmless enough to Textor in the earlier part of the sixteenth century. Item 49, the story of an "English Joan" whose love of learning brought her to Athens and Rome in male disguise to facilitate her studies (and, no doubt, her travelling arrangements), is at first a touching story (like Singer's *Yentl*) of a girl's scholarly diligence which receives the supreme prize of her election to the papacy. Yet as Valerie Hotchkiss has shown,[5]

---

[5] "The Legend of the Female Pope in the Reformation," in *Acta Conventus Neo-Latini Hafniensis: Proceedings of the Eighth International Congress of Neo-Latin Studies, Copenhagen 12 August to 17 August 1991*, ed. Ann Moss et al. (Binghamton, 1994), 495–505.

this thirteenth-century legend was to become an increasingly contested site for Protestant critics of the papacy. On the one hand, the election itself would have created a gap in the apostolic succession from Peter and cast doubt on the authority of the College of Cardinals; on the other hand, the titillating story of her giving birth during her ceremonial passage through the streets of Rome reinforces the rumors of sexual scandal at the highest levels of the Catholic hierarchy. Thus, although Textor's entry is itself a model of discretion, it alludes to a scandalous tale that would have resonated in seventeenth-century Prague, with its history of Protestant and Catholic coexistence under Rudolf, even before one considers its implied applicability to a learned English maiden named Elisabetha *Joanna* Westonia (the names Jane and Joan are of course indistinguishable in Latin, and hardly distinguished in English usage at the time). Not surprisingly, in at least two copies of the *Parthenica* the entry on Pope Joan is heavily scored with the remark in Latin, "Sabellicus, and those who cite him, are liars."

For the most part, however, it seems that Textor's catalogue probably coexisted comfortably with the poems and letters of the *Parthenica*, as Westonia's editor doubtless expected it to do. Specific analogies to Westonia, of the sort I have been suggesting, were probably neither inevitable nor indeed as important as the general sense of a pervasive presence, throughout history, of learned women who embodied in varying combinations the traits being praised in this present-day bard. To a degree, in fact, the catalogue serves as an explanatory index of the names which recur in the text as terms of praise for Westonia.

Moreover, compiling such a catalogue is evidently an endless task. Textor took his names and descriptions from numerous sources, frequently verbatim and often with explicit citation, not only from the classic and early Christian writers such as Diogenes Laertius or St. Jerome but also from Renaissance compilers like himself, most frequently Raffaele Maffei of Volterra, known as Volaterranus (1455–1522). Baldhoven derives his version of the catalogue from a posthumous 1552 version of the *Officina*, edited by Conrad Lycosthenes (or Wolffhardt, 1518–1561), an Alsatian collector of such materials in the following generation. Textor's list of learned women ends with item 54; the next three items are attributed to Baptista Fulgosus, apparently the Baptista Fregoso whose *De dictis factisque memorabilibus collectanea* (Milan, 1509) is listed in the British Library catalogue. Lycosthenes has simply taken the Milanese compiler's list of these three Italian women and silently appended them to Textor's list, much as Baldhoven, a generation later, will add his own list of northern women, concluding with his own Westonia.

Of these three Italian additions, item 55 speaks of a Battista who was the daughter of Galeazzo Malatesta and the wife of the count of Urbino, whereas in fact Battista was Galeazzo's wife and the count's daughter. Once imbedded in the list, errors reproduce themselves much as they do in latter-day search engines. Similarly, Baldhoven's Catherine Albert (item 64) seems to have been named Elizabeth, to judge from another manuscript correction in a copy of *Parthenica*.

Finally, although it seems that Textor's catalogue was generally well suited to the purpose to which Baldhoven adapted it, namely the demonstration of a genealogy for his exemplary poet, it has to be noted that Westonia was not entirely grateful for his efforts. Two copies of the *Parthenica*, one in Prague and another in the British Library,[6] contain manuscript poems signed by "Elizabeth Jane ... wife of Johannes Leo" and dated 16 August 1610, in which the writer complains that although the reader can find her authentic writings here, they are assembled in such disorder, and with such misprints, that she regrets her works should have appeared in this form. Besides, she notes, some of the writings that are here listed as "maidenly," parthenic, were written after she had married. She is not too happy either, she says, with some of the names with whom she is linked in that catalogue of learned women. She concludes by hoping that the time will come for a more accurate and complete edition of her works. Unfortunately, she was to die two years later, having given birth to seven children in her nine years of marriage. The fortunes of the catalogue of learned women were not entirely happy, either. As Woods and Fürstenwald have shown in their study of German catalogues of "Das gelehrte Frauenzimmer" from Baldhoven's time to the present,[7] such lists of learned women were destined to be subordinated to the emerging, often extremely bitter debate in the later seventeenth century over the suitability of education for women. In retrospect, Westonia and her eminent successor in mid-century, Anna Maria von Schurman, were to seem bizarre exceptions to the general rule of separate realms for the two sexes—admirable exceptions, to be sure, but not to be considered branches of a flourishing tree of *Mulieres doctae*.

University of Massachusetts, Amherst

---

[6] Prague, National Museum Library, 49 E. 38; British Library, C.61.d.2.

[7] *"Das Gelehrte Frauenzimmer," Kataloge der Schriftstellerinnen, Künstlerinnen und gelehrten Frauen von 1606 bis zur Gegenwart* (Stuttgart, 1984).

La toponimia en los *Paralipomena*
de Joan Margarit

MATILDE CONDE SALAZAR

Introducción

Joan Margarit nace en o cerca de Gerona en 1421 y muere en Roma en 1484[1]. Su producción literaria, en consonancia con su calidad de humanista, está escrita en latín[2]. Estudió en la Universidad de Bolonia; sirvió en las cortes de Alfonso V y Nicolás V, quienes prestaron gran aliento a los estudios históricos; estuvo en Roma cuando se estaban produciendo las principales traducciones de los historiadores y geógrafos griegos (1447–1453) que tuvo ocasión de manejar[3].

Sus *Paralipomenon Hispaniae libri X*[4], dedicados a la historia de España Antigua, aunque aún permanecen inéditos[5], son anteriores en concepción y datación a las *Décadas* de Nebrija. El propósito que persigue con esta obra es el de proporcionar a

---

[1] Robert B. Tate, *Joan Margarit i Pau, cardenal i bisbe de Girona*, trad. Teresa Loret (Barcelona, 1976); "Margarit i el tema dels Gots", en Justino Bruguera y Josep Massot i Muntaner, eds. *Actes del Vè Col·loqui de Llengua i Literatura catalanes* (Montserrat, 1980), 151–168.

[2] A excepción de algunas cartas y del discurso de bienvenida a Juan de Navarra pronunciado en las Cortes de Barcelona (1454); cf. Robert B. Tate, "El *Paralipomenon* de Joan Margarit, cardenal obispo de Gerona", en *Ensayos sobre la historiografía peninsular del siglo XV* (Madrid, 1970), 121.

[3] Hace referencia, por ejemplo, a una traducción de Dionisio Alejandrino hecha por Antonio Basseo; una visión más completa sobre las traducciones empleadas por Margarit en Lluis Lucero Comas, "La tradición manuscrita y el uso de las fuentes en el Libro II de *Paralipomenon Hispaniae*", en *IV Congreso de Postgraduados en Estudios Hispánicos. 4th Hispanic Studies Postgraduate Conference, University of Nottingham, 4–5 Enero 1996* (Londres), 101–111, esp. 103–105.

[4] Su faceta historiográfica ha sido minuciosamente estudiada por Tate en diferentes trabajos. A los ya citados podemos añadir: "La geografía humanística y los historiadores españoles del siglo XV", en Eugenio Bustos, ed., *Actas del Cuarto Congreso de la Asociación Internacional de Hispanistas II* (Salamanca, 1982), 691–698.

[5] La edición la lleva a cabo Lluis Lucero bajo la dirección de Mariàngela Vilallonga y creemos que verá la luz en breve.

España un renombre paralelo al que los historiadores humanistas italianos habían exigido para Italia mediante la resurrección de la historia clásica. Pero Margarit comprende la necesidad de concebir una historia antigua propia para España, aislada del entorno universal en que la presentaba Trogo[6], en la línea del ideal humanista de "patria" introducido por Bruni[7].

Parte de un profundo conocimiento de las fuentes clásicas que une con otras posteriores dignas de crédito y reconstruye un pasado de la Península.

Las principales fuentes clásicas que utiliza son: Estrabón, Ptolomeo, Polibio, Diodoro Sículo, Plutarco, epítome que hace Justino de Trogo, Plinio, Mela, Livio, César y sus epitomadores, Floro, Eutropio, *Itinerario* de Antonino etc. También cita autores como los Analistas, Salustio, Aulo Gelio, Solino, Prisciano, Flavio Josefo, Heródoto, Valerio Antias, Dionisio de Alejandría. Fuentes clásicas no específicamente históricas: Varrón, Cicerón, Virgilio, Ovidio, Marcial, Macrobio y Lucano. Fuentes eclesiásticas: Sagradas Escrituras, San Agustín, Orosio, San Jerónimo, Lactancio e Isidoro. No menciona a ninguno de los historiadores locales posteriores a Rodrigo Jiménez de Rada[8], síntoma incipiente de la actitud crítica de los humanistas ante el inmediato pasado medieval. Los contemporáneos mencionados son todos humanistas italianos: Petrarca, Boccaccio, Bruni y Sozómeno de Pistoia a los que habría que añadir los traductores que emplea y no menciona. A veces, a lo largo de su narración, hace alusión, de forma general, a *veteres* o *antiqui scriptores* y a *moderni scriptores*; asimismo emite su propia crítica cuando habla de *veridici, approbati* o *grati scriptores*. Cuando los testimonios de dos autoridades discrepan, Margarit expone su opinión personal y, a veces, se inclina por testimonios contemporáneos[9]. También explicita si hay algo que no ha encontrado mencionado en las fuentes consultadas[10].

Toponimia de los *Paralipomena*

Los fragmentos de cinco versiones distintas que se conservan en el manuscrito 5554 de la Biblioteca Nacional[11] hacen suponer que la obra sufrió varias refundiciones, posible fruto de una redacción en diversas etapas de la vida de Margarit[12]. La

---

[6] *superiores tres (sc. Trogus Pompeius, Orosius, Isidorus) singuli sua historia delectati, nobilissima maximaque Hispaniae gesta praetermiserunt (Paralipomenon L. I, De historiographis Hispaniae, fol. Iv; en adelante se cita solamente libro, capítulo y folio).*

[7] A quien denomina *nostrae aetatis historiographorum princeps (L. I, De primis Hispaniae incolis, fol. VIIr).*

[8] *caeteri vero ignorantium caterva plurima, qui divinationes et somnia contexuerunt (L. I, De historiographis . . . , fol. Ir).*

[9] *Casytecides ad Austrum in pelagus, quamquam Strabo dixerit ad Aquilonem, quod satis charta nauigationis ostendit (ibid.).*

[10] *Promontorium ab antiquis praetermissum (ibid., fol. IVv).*

[11] Tate indica que la versión del Codex G-1, de la colección de Salazar en la Real Academia de la Historia, abarcando una serie de historias peninsulares medievales, está todavía por estudiar. Lluis Lucero la tiene en cuenta para su edición.

[12] Hace referencia a ella en *Templum Domini*; cf. Fidel Fita i Colomer, *El Gerundense y la España primitiva* (Madrid, 1879), 179: *libro quem de oblita antiquitate Hispaniae futurae posteritate conscripsi.*

muerte le pudo impedir elaborar la redacción final.

Consta de diez libros dedicados a: etnografía y topografía (L. I); una historia de España de época precartaginense (L. II–III); las guerras púnicas en España (L. IV–VII); dominación romana hasta César Augusto (L. VIII–X). Margarit desarrolla una especie de geografía histórica con la identificación entre los nombres antiguos y modernos a fin de lograr conectar la historia pasada con la presente, propósito fundamental de los *Paralipomena*. La equiparación entre onomástica antigua y moderna es constante a lo largo de toda la obra, pero muy especialmente en la parte más original constituida por los libros I y II. Relaciona las colonias más antiguas con los sucesivos invasores y luego con su localización moderna.

> In his quoque tribus provinciis, populis ac regionibus plurimi sunt, qui sua nomina mutaverunt taliter, quod difficillimam reddant lectionem rerum antiquarum, quum propter obliterationem antiquorum nominum ignorationem faciant legentibus tum circa provincias, tum etiam montes, et flumina, urbesque deletas, quae quum non extent, neque quibus in locis fuerint, neque res apud eas gestae facile deprehendi possunt. Igitur primum de populis, provinciis, et regionibus. Secundo de urbibus. Tertio de fluminibus. Quarto de montibus. Quinto et ultimo de deletis urbibus agendum est. (*L. I, De provinciis Hispaniae, quae nomina mutaverunt*)

La variedad de recursos utilizados por Margarit para, a través de la onomástica, unir pasado y presente, denota una preocupación filológica: explicaciones etimológicas verdaderas o simbólicas; alternancia de nexos para establecer la relación entre nombres antiguos y modernos; atribución, a menudo, de un origen popular al nombre actual; amplia utilización y enumeración de fuentes en que continuamente basa su exposición y, sobre todo, frecuente discrepancia de las mismas.

Por limitación de espacio sólo nos ocuparemos aquí de los dos primeros apartados:

1. Explicaciones etimológicas:

1.1. El nombre del reino de Portugal se explica a partir del de la ciudad de Oporto: *Portus civitas, a qua urbe Portugalliae regnum nomen habet* (*L.I, De urbibus Hispaniae, quae propria nomina mutaverunt*, fol. XVIv); *portus Galleciae etiam ipsa urbs appelletur, a quo nomine recipit Portugalliae Rex* (*L. I, Hispaniae descriptio et terminatio per maritima littora et Pyrenaeum*).

1.2. Dos términos pueden ser, según los autores consultados por Margarit, los que están en el origen del nombre de *Hispalis* (Sevilla): *pālus, -ūdis* "laguna" y *pālus, -i* "estaca", y lo repite varias veces. Entre ellas: *Hispalis, quae Metropolis Baeticae a palude, quae urbi circunfertur sic dicta, sive ut aliqui voluerunt, quia urbs eo in loco constructa sit in fixis palis, in quibus urbs fundata est propter aquarum redundanciam* (*L. I, De provinciis Hispaniae quae . . .*, fol. XVv).

Para el nombre "vulgar" de Sevilla, propone una evolución a partir de *Civitas Iulia: Hispali dicta est a prioribus antiquis. Postea vero a Iulio Caesare Iulia Romulea appellata, ut Straboni placuit, a cuius nomine vulgata locutio originem traxit, ut Sivilla appelletur tanquam a Iulio Caesare instaurata, et dicatur Civitas Iulia . . . Potuit tamen Iulius Caesar illam instaurasse labentem, auxisse, ac dilatasse, obtinuit tamen moderna literarum locutio, ut pristino nomine ab eis nuncupetur* (ibid.).

Para Nebrija, sin embargo, el nombre de Sevilla es una evolución de *Hispilia*[13].

1.3.   Otros nombres tienen un origen griego:

1.3.1. Siguiendo a Diodoro y Apiano, hace derivar el nombre de los Montes Pirineos de πῦρ (aunque ya de antemano nos avisa de que *de istorum . . . montium nomine diversi diversa sentiunt L. I, De montibus Hispaniae, qui . . . , fol. XIIIr): ab ardenti Pyra, quae est lignorum congeries ardens, Pyrenaei montes appellati sunt. Haec Diodorus. Idem etiam censuit Appianus. Aliqui a crebris fulminum ictibus illic cadentium Pyrenaeos dixere, a Pyr, quod est ignis* (ibid., fol. XIIIv)[14]; *ferunt priscis temporibus igne a pastoribus iniecto montanas omnes regiones fuisse combustas. Qua ex re montes, aiunt, cognominatos Pyrenaeos, ardente continuis diebus igne, pluresque ex montium incendiis argenti puri rivuli effluxerunt* (*L. I, De Pyrenaeis montibus ac metallis eorum*, fol. Xr).

1.3.2. El nombre de las islas Baleares proviene de la destreza en el uso de la honda ("balera"[15]) que tenían sus habitantes[16].

1.3.3. También inventa una etimología para el nombre de Barcelona (*Barchino*), provendría de un término griego con que se denominaban las chozas hechas de palos[17]: *nomen veraci historia Graecum est, et significat domunculas ex virgultis contextas, quae ad maris littora ad piscandum sunt, in quibus se piscatores recipiunt, quarum quum ibi magnus esset numerus, loci, ac aeris salubritate prospecta Barchinon urbem eodem in loco constituit, sicque eam ab eisdem domunculis appellavit* (*L. II, De urbibus quae quondam florentissimae in Hispania sunt deletae*, fol. XXIIv).

1.4.   Determinadas características del lugar habrían propiciado algunas denominaciones:

1.4.1. El Moncayo debe su nombre a las nieves perpetuas de sus cimas: *mons altissimus in vertice Pyrenaeia canicie Canus appellatus, quoniam aestate et hyeme semper*

---

[13] *Romuleamque quondam Hispalim vocitatam praeterlabitur. Haec a poenis deinde Ispilia, et a barbaris postea inversis literis prioribus, et p in b mutata Sibilia dicta, nunc* "Sevilla" *nominant* (Antonio de Nebrija, *Hispanarum rerum . . . gestarum Decades duae, Excusatoria praefatio, De maximis fluminibus Hispaniae*).

[14] También Nebrija alude a esta etimología, junto con la de Silio Itálico que rechaza Plinio y a la que Margarit se refiere de forma general: *dixerunt quidam Pyrrhenaeos a Pyrrho Hispani successore vocitari* (*L. I, De montibus Hispaniae, qui nomina mutaverunt*, fol. XIIIr): *Nam quod de Pyrene nympha ab Hercule compressa Silius Italicus prodit, tanquam fabulam Plinius excludit. Illa vero quae de Caco sive Caio monte, et de Hispano, Liberia Pyrroque dicuntur, a nugivendo quodam fabulatore conficta sunt* (Nebrija, *Decades duae, Ad benevolum candidumque lectorem*; cf. ibid., *De montibus Hispaniae*).

[15] Palabra inexistente en griego donde encontramos, o bien el verbo βάλλω o βέλος "proyectil"; cf. Lluis Lucero, "Juan Margarit i Mallorca: presència de les Illes Balears en el *Paralipomenon Hispaniae Libri Decem*", en *Homenatge a Miquel Dolç. Actes del XII Simposi de la Secció Catalana i I de la Secció Balear de la SEEC (Palma, 1 al 4 de febrer de 1996)* (Palma de Mallorca, 1997), 495–498.

[16] En otro lugar dice *graeca lingua Baleae appellantur* y prefiere seguir a Ptolomeo que a Diodoro: *in quo potius Ptolemaeo credendum esse puto* (*L. II, De adventu Herculis . . .* , fol. XXr).

[17] El origen es latino.

inibi nives inhabitent (*L. I, De terra Ruscilionis an sit in Hispania*, fol. Vv)[18].

1.4.2. Córdoba a su enclave respecto al Guadalquivir: *Corduba insuper civitas, quae in medio pene fluminis cursu est, ab eodem flumine denominationem habet, ut tanquam cor Baetis dicta sit Corduba* (*L. I, De fluminibus quae nomina mutaverunt*, fol. XIVr).

1.4.3. Huesca provendría de la unión de *os* y *Caci*: *urbs Osca, tanquam os Caci* (*L. II, De reditu Herculis ab Hispania in Graeciam*, fol. XXIIIv).

1.4.4. Compostela, de la unión de *compos* y *stella*: *quumque ad eam partem Hesperum stellam oriri vidissent, ipsamque tanquam regionibus illis salubrem, Compotem stellam nominarunt. Unde et Compostellam urbs vicina denominationem trahit* (*L. I, De urbibus Hispaniae quae . . .*, fol. XVIv).

1.4.5. Encuentra una explicación bastante fantástica para el nombre de Ibiza: *Dicta Ebusa a candore salis, quod ebori simillimum est* (*L. I, De urbibus Hispaniae quae . . .*, fol. XVIIr)[19].

1.5. Siguiendo a Jerónimo, sostiene Margarit que las regiones adoptan, a menudo, el nombre de los árboles o frutos que en ellas se cultivan: *Consuevere arborum fructus appellari a regionibus, ubi iidem fructus ab initio sunt reperti, ut ait Hieronymus in Epistola ad Eustochium . . .* (*L. I, De urbibus Hispaniae quae . . .*, fol. XVr). Así se explica el nombre del reino y la ciudad de Granada: *Granata mala punica dicta sunt, quia ii fructus apud Poenos primum reperti sunt. Quum vero Hispania diutius sub Poenorum fuerit potestate, perfacile fuit, ut illius generis arbores de Aphrica translati sint in Hispaniam, et ea urbs, a qua forte per Hispaniam translati sunt, ab eorum fructu conversionem nominis fecerit, ut Granata dicatur, Hispano siquidem nomine mala punica Granata appellantur* (*L. I, De urbibus Hispaniae quae . . .*, fol. XVr).

1.6. De un intercambio entre sinónimos hace derivar el nombre de la ciudad portuguesa de Silves: *Ab ipso itaque Saltu Sylva urbs Portugalliae hodierno idiomate nuncupatur, quoniam Latino sermone Saltus, et Sylva idem sunt* (*L. I, De urbibus Hispaniae quae . . .*, fol. XVv).

1.7. Muchas ciudades, montes, ríos y regiones recibieron, tradicionalmente, el nombre de sus fundadores (mitológicos o históricos): *Certum est enim quod urbes sive ab autoribus, sive a fluminibus inundantibus nomina receperunt. Unde . . . a Belo Babylonia . . . a Nino Ninive . . . a Romulo Roma . . . a Constantino Constantinopolis . . . Osca civitas, cuius initium a Caco Hispano est* (*L. I, De urbibus Hispaniae ante Herculis adventum*, fol. VIIIr).

Otros ejemplos:

1.7.1. Mérida: *urbem aliam illi vicinam instituit ex dispersis populis, et veteranis Hispaniae militibus, qui cum Caesaribus Iulio, seu Augusto militaverant, quoniam emeritos ap-*

---

[18] Nebrija (*Ad benevolum . . .*): *Illa vero quae de Caco sive Caio monte, et de Hispano, Liberia Pyrroque dicuntur, a nugivendo quodam fabulatore conficta sunt.*

[19] Nebrija (ibid.): *Pityusam, id est, Ebusum et Ophiusam.*

pellabat, ideo Emeritam urbem vocavit (*L. I, De urbibus quae quondam* ..., fol. XVIIIr).

1.7.2. Mahón: *Maho est, a Magone filio Amilcaris Hannibalis fratre conditum* (*L. I, De urbibus Hispaniae quae* ..., fol. XVIIr).

1.7.3. Gibraltar: *Nunc vero mons iste mutationem nominis fecit ab adventu Arabum, qui eandem inhabitant regionem, et Gibeltarich appellatur. Gibel itaque Arabica lingua montem significat tanquam mons Tarich. Hic itaque Tarich primus Dux Arabum fuit, qui classe instructa Arabibus de Africa traicit in Hispaniam* (*L. I, De montibus Hispaniae quae* ..., fol. XIIIv).

1.7.4. Incluso se permite inventar algunos como el de la isla de Ibiza: *Nunc autem eadem insula Alviza dicta est ab Avicena Arabe medico, quem ibi regnasse ferunt Arabum tempore* (*L. I, De urbibus Hispaniae quae* ..., fol. XVIIr).

1.8. Otras ciudades reciben el nombre del río cercano: *prout ab antiquis fieri solitum est, ut maximae enim a fluminibus nominentur provinciae, sic Indi ab Indo flumine, Alamanni ad Alamanno amne, Iberi ab Ibero, a Baeti Baetici, ab Ana Lusitania* (*L. I, De terra Ruscilionis* ..., fol. Vv):

1.8.1. Lusitania: *Lusitania vero dicitur ab Ana flumine, quod hodie Gaudiana appellatur* (*L. I, De provinciis Hispaniae quae* ..., fol. Xv).

1.8.2. Bética: *vocitaturque Baetica ab ipso amne Baeti, provincia intersecante* (*L. I, Divisio Hispaniae*, fol. IIIr).

1.8.3. Limia: *ab amne Limino illius agri incolae Limicae dicti sunt* (*L. I, De urbibus quae quondam* ..., fol. XVIIIr).

1.8.4. Gerona: *dicitur Gerunda a Geryone, et unda flumine, quod per urbis medium fluit* (*L. I, De urbibus Hispaniae ante Herculis adventum*, fol. VIIIr).

1.9. En otros casos busca una etimología gramatical:

1.9.1. Río Tech: *flumen Illiris dictum* ... *quod a Romanis Tetrum est appellatum, quia per diversas metallorum venas maximeque ferri scaturiens, nigrum colorem gestat, et propterea ad irrigandum maxime nocet. Quod vulgus vocabulum corrumpens ethymologiae ignarus Techum appellat* (*L. I, De terra Ruscilionis* ..., fol. Vv).

1.9.4. Sagunto: *Saguntum* ... *quae hodie Murivetus appellatur* ... *devastata, ac diruta, sola antiqua arcis menia exstant. Unde a sucessoribus muri veteres dicti sunt, et a modernis Murivetus oppidum dictum est* (*L. I, De urbibus Hispaniae quae* ..., fol. XVIIv).

1.10. Una evolución fonética ha originado los nombres de los ríos Llobregat y Fluviá:

1.10.1. Llobregat: *ab antiquis Rubricatus dictus est, a nostris vero, R litera est mutata in L, et dicitur Lubricatus* (*L. I, De fluminibus quae* ..., fol. XIVv).

1.10.2. Fluviá: *Cluvianus, qui non longe ab Emporio quondam maxima urbe Gerundensis agri per Occasum influit in Mediterraneum, solam unam mutavit literam c in f, et Fluvianus dicitur, quanquam Plinius de Naturali historia libro tertio illum Flumialbum appellat* (*L. I, De fluminibus quae* ..., fol. XIVv).

2. Utilización de recursos lingüísticos que ponen de manifiesto un importante esfuerzo del autor por aliviar la inevitable enumeración, de por sí repetitiva y monótona, al mismo tiempo que reflejan una preocupación de Margarit por la be-

lleza formal y estilística a la hora de redactar en lengua latina. La unión entre nombre antiguo y moderno se hace:

2.1.   Unas veces anteponiendo el nombre antiguo y, en ese caso, el moderno va introducido por:

2.1.1. Adjetivos como:

moderni/hodiernus (die, idioma): *montem Canum, qui hodie Canigo mons a modernis nuncupatur* (*L. I, Hispaniae terminatio*, fol. IIr); *Illiridi, qui Achei sunt, et apud nos hodierno idiomatae Sclavones dicuntur* (*L. I*, cap. *De urbibus ab Herculi in Hispania conditis*, fol. XXIIr).

2.1.2. Sustantivos como:

modernitas/nostrum tempus: *Iulium Oppidum erat, a Iulio Caesare conditum, quod nunc modernitas Lyncam appellat* (*L. I, De citeriori Hispania*, fol. XIIr); *oppidum, quod nostris temporibus Civitatella dicitur* (*L. II, De adventu Herculis in Hispaniam*, fol. XXr).

2.1.3. Adverbios como *nunc/hodie*, acompañados de verbos de lengua (*dicere, appellare, vocare, nuncupare, nominare*): *Bibali ab oppido Bibalo, nunc Birbao* (*L. I, De provinciis Hispaniae quae . . .*, fol. XIv); *Promontorium Sacrum, quod nos hodie Caput Sancti Vincentii appellamus* (*L. I, Hispaniae terminatio*, fol. IIIr).

2.2.   En alguna ocasión no logra una identificación actual para el topónimo, como *Secabur: quondam Secabur dicebatur ab antiquis, nunc vero -----* (*L. I, De fluminibus quae . . .*, fol. XIVv).

2.3.   Otras veces el nombre moderno va en primer lugar y, a continuación, el antiguo y, en ese caso, los términos empleados son:

2.3.1. Adjetivos sustantivados como:

antiquus/veteres: *ab antiquis omnis Hispania citerior Celtiberia dicta est* (*L. I, Descriptio Hispaniae per Mediterranea*, fol. IVr); *Hanc sequitur Ulisbona urbs ad oram fluminis Tagi, haec autem apud veteres Scalabus dicebatur* (*L. I, De urbibus Hispaniae quae . . .*, fol. XVIv).

2.3.2. Adverbios como:

antiquitus/quondam/per antea: *Colimbria urbs est sita, quam antiquitus Mundam aliqui dixerunt* (*L. I, Hispaniae descriptio*, fol. IVr); *Ecclesia de finibus terrae sita, quae quondam Solis Ara dicebatur* (*L. I, Hispaniae descriptio*, fol. IVr); *Erat enim per antea ibi urbs Calpe dicta a monte ipso* (*L. I, De montibus Hispaniae quae . . .*, fol. XIIIv).

2.4.   En otras ocasiones el paralelismo conlleva una doble formulación para nombre moderno y antiguo: *Perpiniani etiam oppidum a recentissimis etiam temporibus dicitur, Stabulum enim antiquitus vocabant* (*L. I, De terra Ruscilionis . . .*, fol. VIr).

Margarit y Nebrija

Nebrija hacía preceder su obra histórica *Rerum a Ferdinando et Elisabe decades duae* de unos capítulos introductorios en los que se puede comprobar que persigue un objetivo semejante al de Margarit, a saber, trazar un panorama geográfico de la Península Ibérica.

Dos son, sin embargo, las diferencias fundamentales entre ambos autores: en primer lugar, la distinta metodología a la hora de exponer por escrito unas ideas. Las

Décadas de Nebrija son una traducción, más o menos elaborada, de la obra de Hernando del Pulgar siendo precisamente esos capítulos introductorios la parte más original del autor y en la que, como Margarit, se presenta Nebrija preocupado por trazar unas líneas generales y claras de la Península. Para ello elabora, también Nebrija, una especie de geografía histórica nacional. Pero Nebrija es, ante todo, filólogo y gramático y su preocupación se centra en que la obra refleje una buena dicción latina de aquellos nombres que en su relato deberá inevitablemente de latinizar (*Excusatoria praefatio: nihil tamen est, quod me magis a scribendo deterreat, quam locorum atque hominum, propria nomina, quae maiori ex parte usque adeo sunt aspera et dura, ut nullo cultu moliri, nulla diligentia possint mansuescere*). Para subsanar errores, dedica un capítulo a los montes: *De montibus Hispaniae* y otro a los ríos: *De maximis fluminibus Hispaniae*, en la misma línea que hemos visto en Margarit, si bien de forma mucho más reducida y sin ese interés fundamental que tiene la obra de Margarit por estrechar continuamente la unión entre pasado y presente ni por una descripción geográfica tan detallada y exhaustiva, aunque también sea pormenorizado el recorrido de Nebrija. Al final de la descripción de los ríos anuncia que va a hablar de regiones, pueblos y ciudades, pero este capítulo se ha perdido.

La segunda diferencia importante, por la repercusión que pueda tener en la obra, es el distinto lugar de nacimiento de ambos autores que hace que, inevitablemente, conozca mucho mejor cada uno aquella zona en la que ha crecido e instintivamente se detengan, con más minuciosidad, en la descripción de los nombres de los lugares que les son familiares. Como muestra baste observar la detallada descripción por parte de Margarit de la zona de Cataluña, especialmente de Gerona y sus alrededores, mientras Nebrija lo hace, al hilo de la narración de las batallas contra los moros, en los diferentes pueblos de Andalucía próximos a su Nebrija natal.

Pero son, nos parece, muchas más las semejanzas entre uno y otro ya que, para trazar este panorama, con estilos propios como vemos, se sirven, en general de las fuentes comunes. Los mismos autores básicos: Ptolomeo, Estrabón, Mela, Plinio . . . que, mientras en Margarit aparecen citados de forma reiterada, en Nebrija a veces son utilizados pero ni siquiera citados.

Conclusión

Tanto Nebrija como Margarit son profundos conocedores de los clásicos y en la obra de ambos encontramos citas de historiadores, geógrafos, enciclopedistas y autores técnicos en general, pero también de poetas.

La obra del gerundense se podría considerar más técnica que la de Nebrija en lo que respecta a la historiografía y, concretamente, a la geografía. Nebrija busca más una belleza de la composición y una perfección en el empleo de la lengua latina, por lo en su obra son mucho más abundantes las citas de poetas, como Virgilio, Ovidio, Lucano, que las de tratados técnicos. Margarit, sin embargo, recurre continuamente, sobre todo a lo largo del libro primero y, aunque en menos medida, del segundo, a obras técnicas como la de Estrabón, Ptolomeo, Diodoro o Plinio.

Margarit persigue un objetivo claro que consiste en trazar, a través de la geografía, una línea directa de unión entre pasado y presente peninsular. Para evocar el pasado tiene que recurrir a los autores que han dejado constancia del mismo.

Sin embargo, la unión con el presente la hace nuestro autor a través de recursos literarios y lingüísticos de los que hemos analizado aquí algunos que nos muestran a Margarit como un profundo conocedor de la lengua latina y de sus estructuras. Aunque la temática que aborda hace inevitable que el relato resulte a menudo árido y reiterativo, se percibe el esfuerzo del autor por huir de esta monotonía recurriendo a los diversos recursos que le brinda el lenguaje para conseguirlo.

Consejo Superior de Investigaciones Científicas, Madrid

Noticias bio-bibliográficas sobre
Benito Arias Montano en su correspondencia latina
con el impresor Iohannes Moretus (1589–1598)[1]

ANTONIO DÁVILA PÉREZ

La correspondencia privada de cualquier personaje histórico es una de las fuentes de datos más apreciadas por los investigadores; así sucede con los hombres del Renacimiento, como demuestran los epistolarios de Erasmus, Laeuinus Torrentius o Iustus Lipsius[2]. El caso de Benito Arias Montano, una de las cumbres del humanismo español de la segunda mitad del XVI, sigue clamando al cielo: existen cartas suyas esparcidas por bibliotecas y archivos de medio mundo, muchas de las cuales aún permanecen inéditas[3]. Además, no hay que emplear mucho tiempo en rastrear catálogos de manuscritos; una visita al Museo Plantin-Moretus, casa de los ilustres impresores de Amberes con los que Arias Montano mantuvo estrechísima relación, regala documen-

---

[1] Este trabajo forma parte del Proyecto de Investigación PS 93-0130 de la DGICYT.

[2] Por citar sólo algunos. Cf. P. S. Allen, *Opus epistolarum Des. Erasmi Roterodami*, 12 vols. (Oxford, 1906–1958); M. Delcourt y J. Hoyoux, *Laeuinus Torrentius: correspondance*, 3 vols. (París, 1950–1954); y, por último, las *Iusti Lipsi Epistolae*, 7 vols. (Bruselas, 1978–1997), en los que han trabajado A. Gerlo, M. A. Nauwelaerts, H. D. L. Vervliet, S. Sué, H. Peeters, J. Kluykens y, actualmente, J. De Landtsheer.

[3] La correspondencia de Benito Arias Montano se ha conservado en tres bloques principales: las cartas del Archivo General de Simancas, publicadas en su mayoría en la Colección de Documentos Inéditos de la Historia de España (tomo XLI) y en la gran monografía de T. González Carvajal, *Elogio Histórico del Doctor Benito Arias Montano* (en *Memorias de la Real Academia de la Historia*, t. VII [Madrid, 1832], 1–199); el segundo bloque está en el manuscrito A 902 de la Kungliga Biblioteke de Estocolmo (trabajado por B. Macías Rosendo en su tesis doctoral inédita "La Políglota de Amberes en la correspondencia de Benito Arias Montano (ms. Estoc. A 902)" Sevilla, 1994; el tercero—del que actualmente preparo la edición y traducción anotada—se encuentra precisamente en los archivos del Museo Plantin-Moretus de Amberes (a partir de ahora citados MPM Arch.), publicados parcialmente por M. Rooses y J. Denucé en los ochos volúmenes de la *Correspondance de Christophe Plantin* (Amberes, 1883–1920), a partir de aquí citada *CP*.

tos inéditos y sin catalogar que aportan no poca luz a lo que se conoce hoy de la vida y obra de Montano. En este trabajo me propongo presentar una parte de la correspondencia entre el humanista español y Iohannes Moretus, aprendiz, yerno y heredero del célebre Cristóbal Plantino. Para ello me planteo un triple objetivo: primero, catalogar las cartas entre Moretus y Montano posteriores a la muerte de Plantino; en segundo lugar, ordenar los datos que éstas encierran sobre el tramo final de la vida de Arias Montano y sus relaciones con la imprenta del *Compás de Oro*[4]; por último, seleccionar y presentar las principales noticias que contiene este grupo de cartas—muy homogéneo y casi desconocido—en torno a las obras de vejez de nuestro humanista.

Inventario detallado

Ya el investigador holandés Bernard Rekers confeccionó en los sesenta un primer catálogo de cartas de Montano conservadas en el Museo Plantin-Moretus dentro de su acercamiento a la correspondencia del sabio frexnense[5]; sin embargo, se ha avanzado poco desde este punto y, aún hoy, se ignora la existencia de muchas de estas epístolas fechadas entre 1589 y 1598. En mi inventario voy a omitir tres cartas de 1589 y una de 1590 publicadas en la *Correspondance de Christophe Plantin*; sí cuento, sin embargo, las misivas inéditas de Arias Montano a su hombre de confianza, el banquero Luis Pérez, dirigidas en último término a la imprenta—según se ve por su contenido y por el hecho de que actualmente se conserven en los archivos plantinianos[6]:

1. **[1589 07 08]**: Iohannes Moretus [Amberes] a Arias Montano [Sevilla]
   Incipit.: *Animi tui, Clar^{me} D^{ne} ac patrone colende, tenerum affectum* . . .
   b: MPM Arch. 10, fol. 246v.

2. **1589 10 04**: Iohannes Moretus [Amberes] a Arias Montano [Peña de Aracena]
   Inc.: *Quam gratae acceptaeque semper mihi sint fuerintque* . . .
   b: MPM Arch. 10, f. 256v.

3. **1590 02 08**: Iohannes Moretus (Amberes) a Arias Montano [Sevilla]
   Inc.: *Elapso mense dedi ad D. T. satis ampliores.*
   b: MPM Arch. 10, fol. 269v.

---

[4] Una perspectiva general de las actividades e importancia de la tipografía plantiniana puede extraerse de la obra de L. Voet, *The Golden Compasses: A History and Evaluation of the Printing and Publishing Activities of the Officina Plantiniana at Antwerp* (Amsterdam, 1969–1972).

[5] Cf. B. Rekers, "Epistolario de Benito Arias Montano (1527–1598)", *Hispanófila* 9 (1960): 25–37; véase también su monografía *Arias Montano* (Madrid, 1973). En ambos catálogos se omiten 13 de las 28 cartas incluidas en el nuestro (números 1, 2, 3, 4, 5, 6, 7, 8, 9, 14, 18, 19 y 22).

[6] Comentamos brevemente el significado de los signos y abreviaturas usados en el elenco que sigue: 1) La fecha de las cartas se indica con el número de ocho cifras a la derecha del guión; las cuatro primeras cifras corresponden al año, las dos siguientes al mes y las dos últimas al día. 2) Se emplean paréntesis para los datos confirmados; corchetes, para datos sólo conjeturados. 3) En cuanto a las abreviaturas: MPM Arch. / MPM Ms. (Museo Plantin-Moretus, Archivos / Manuscritos), **b**: borrador; **c**: copia; **e**: edición; **o**: original.

4. 1590 03 19: Iohannes Moretus [Amberes] a Arias Montano [Sevilla]
Inc.: *Meas 29 Octobris ad D. T. scritas tradittas esse intellexi.*
b: MPM Arch. 10, fols. 272r–272v.

5. 1590 06 27: Iohannes Moretus [Amberes] a Arias Montano [Sevilla]
Inc.: *Nunquam (Vir Clar^me) aliquas accipio a te quin . . .*
b: MPM Arch. 10, fols. 276r–276v.

6. 1590 09 03: Iohannes Moretus [Amberes] a Arias Montano [Sevilla]
Inc.: *Febris quae me per dies aliquot decumbentem detinuit . . .*
b: MPM Arch. 10, fol. 281r.

7. 1590 10 18: Iohannes Moretus [Amberes] a Arias Montano [Sevilla]
Inc.: *Quas nouissime misi tertia elapsi mensis scripsi . . .*
b: MPM Arch. 10, fols. 285r–285v.

8. 1590 10 28: Iohannes Moretus (Amberes) a Arias Montano [Sevilla]
Inc.: *Scripsi 18 huius de iis quae tunc indicanda existimaui . . .*
b: MPM Arch. 10, fols. 288v–289r.

9. 1591 08 24: Iohannes Moretus [Amberes] a Arias Montano [Sevilla]
Inc.: *Accepi quas XV Iunii ad me dedisti . . .*
b: MPM Arch. 11, fol. 8r.

10. 1592 05 04: Arias Montano (Madrid) a Iohannes Moretus (Amberes)
Inc.: *Nuper ad te litterarum fasciculum dedi Ludouico nostro Perezio inscriptum . . .*
o: MPM Arch. 76, pág. 113–114.

11. 1592 05 13: Iohannes Moretus [Amberes] a Arias Montano [Madrid]
Inc.: *Iam tertias scribo quas R. T. misi . . .*
b: MPM Arch. 11, fol. 28r.

12. 1592 06 18: Iohannes Moretus (Amberes) a Arias Montano [Madrid]
Inc.: *D. Ludouicus Perezius, patronus meus semper mihi colendus, . . .*
b: MPM Arch. 11, fol. 31v.

13. 1592 07 01 Fechada erróneamente el 22 de julio por Rekers, quien lee 22 en
vez de *p^a* (*prima*, primero de mes)
Iohannes Moretus (Amberes) a Arias Montano [Madrid]
Inc.: *Postremas meas dedi 18 elapsi mensis.*
b: MPM Arch. 11, fol. 34v.

14. 1592 07 21: Iohannes Moretus [Amberes] a Arias Montano [Madrid]
Inc.: *Paucis respondebo, Clar^me D^ne, l^ris ad me XIX junii scriptis . . .*
b: MPM Arch. 11, fols. 38v–39r.

15. [1592 11 12]: Iohannes Moretus (Amberes) a Arias Montano [Peña de Aracena]
Inc.: *L^ris D^ni Ludouici Perezii patroni mei hon^di . . .*
b: MPM Arch. 11, 42r.

16. 1592 12 10: Iohannes Moretus [Amberes] a Arias Montano [Peña de Aracena]
Inc.: *Ex li^{ris} D^{ni} Lud^{ci} Peresii, patroni mei,* . . .
b: MPM Arch. 11, fol. 44r.

17. 1593 03 15: Iohannes Moretus [Amberes] a Arias Montano [Sevilla]
Inc.: *Indies experior quantum accrescat tuus in me Plantinianamque familiam affectus* . . .
b: MPM Arch. 11, fol. 49v.

18. 1593 05 16: Arias Montano [Madrid] a Luis Pérez [Amberes]
Inc.: *Los s^{es} dottores Tovar y Fran. Sánchez piden y ruegan* . . .
o: MPM Arch. 76, págs. 117–118.

19. 1593 06 14: Arias Montano (Sevilla) a Luis Pérez (Amberes)
Inc.: *Praefatio: animae magni operis praefigenda* . . .
o: MPM Arch. 76, págs. 115–116.

20. 1594 02 28 Registrada en el índice de Rekers con fecha del 25 de enero de 1593; en efecto es éste el día que anota Montano al concluir su carta, pero en el *post scriptum* se hace constar que la misiva salió el 28 de febrero por problemas de correos.
Arias Montano (Sevilla) a Iohannes Moretus (Amberes)
Inc.: *Tibi, mi dilectissime Iohannes, primam ex corpore magni operis partem mittimus* . . .
o: MPM Arch. 76, págs. 119–121.

21. 1594 07 06: Iohannes Moretus (Amberes) a Arias Montano [Sevilla]
Inc.: *Hodie D. Lud^{us} Perezius expectatas et gratissimas l^{ras}* . . .
b: MPM Arch. 11, fol. 75v.

22. 1595 01 31: Arias Montano (Sevilla) a Iohannes Moretus [Amberes]
Inc.: *Mitto tibi, Morete optime, promissam pridem linguarum omnium artem* . . .
o: Bibliothèque Royale, Bruselas III 1483, n° 7.

23. 1596 01 16: Arias Montano (Sevilla) a Luis Pérez (Amberes)
Inc.: *Olvidéme en la que ha tres días encaminé a v. m.* . . .
o: MPM Arch. 76, pág. 123.

24. [1596 07 30–1596 10 10]: Iohannes Moretus [Amberes] a Arias Montano [Sevilla]
Inc.: *D^{nus} Lud^{us} Perezius (quem uere tecum patronum optimum habeo)* . . .
b: MPM Arch. 11, fol. 91r.

25. 1596 11 01: Arias Montano (Sevilla) a Iohannes Moretus (Amberes)
Inc.: *Breueis equidem tuas literas nuper accepi sed gratissimas illas* . . .
o: MPM Arch. 76, págs. 124–125.

26. 1597 05 08: Iohannes Moretus [Amberes] a Arias Montano [Sevilla]
Inc.: *Plurimi nunc elapsi sunt menses e quo nulla a R. D. T. acceperim* . . .
b: MPM Arch. 11, fol. 96r.

27. 1597 08 03 Registrada en el índice de Rekers con fecha del 5 de agosto, por un error en la traducción de la fecha latina (el tercer día antes de las *Nonas* de agosto, es decir, el tres y no el cinco de agosto).

Arias Montano (Peña de Aracena) a Iohannes Moretus (Amberes)

Inc.: *Literas tuas IX maii datas ad idus Iulias accepi* . . .

o: MPM Arch. 76, pags. 129–130; **c**: BNM ms. 8.588, fols. 346v–347v; **e**: J. López de Toro, "Arias Montano escribe a Justo Lipsio y a Juan Moreto", *Revista de Archivos, Bibliotecas y Museos* 60, 2 (1954): 542–543.

28. 1598 06 22: Iohannes Moretus [Amberes] a Arias Montano [Sevilla]

Inc.: *Iam menses aliquot elapsi sunt quod nullas R. D. T. scripserim* . . .

MPM Arch. 13, fol. 8r.

Noticias biográficas:

El 8 de julio de 1589, Iohannes Moretus comunica a Arias Montano la muerte de Cristóbal Plantino. Las numerosas tachaduras y correcciones de este borrador indican el dolor que sufría el impresor y su preocupación por no afligir demasiado a uno de los más íntimos amigos de su suegro; sin embargo, Moretus no puede reprimir su pluma al reclamar, en medio del dolor, una subvención oficial del Rey de España para hacer frente a los acreedores ([1589 07 08]). En posteriores contactos, el tipógrafo llega a rogar a Montano, temiendo por su salud, que acepte con resignación la pérdida de Plantino (1589 10 04); desde ese momento Iohannes Moretus hereda a un tiempo el oficio de su suegro y la correspondencia que mantenía la imprenta con numerosos personajes de los Países Bajos y del extranjero.

La estrecha relación personal que habían mantenido Arias Montano y Cristóbal Plantino durante treinta años se tradujo en cartas plenas de sugerencias, expresiones afectivas e, incluso, mutuo apoyo espiritual. Esta riqueza de vínculos y guiños se atenúa bastante en la correspondencia entre Arias Montano y Iohannes Moretus. Tras la muerte del gran tipógrafo, las cartas que llegan y salen de la imprenta son eminentemente prácticas; su principal objetivo es resolver los problemas que van surgiendo durante la publicación de las obras. Como consecuencia, el tono se hace mucho más frío y el estilo extremadamente conciso[7]. En casi todas aparece el nombre de Luis Pérez, banquero de Amberes, como mediador entre Arias Montano y la imprenta. Luis Pérez, y no Moretus, es quien comunica a Montano el fallecimiento de la viuda de Plantino (1596 11 01), el que le informa del estado de salud de toda la familia plantiniana ([1589 07 08], 1590 03 19, [1592 11 12], 1592 12 10, etc.) e, incluso, el que recibe los encargos de libros y las copias manuscritas de la obras montanianas junto con las instrucciones de estampado (1593 03 15, 1593 05 16, 1593 06 14, 1596 01 16). Por desgracia, nos ha llegado muy poco de lo que, con seguridad, fue un buen número de cartas entre Montano y Luis Pérez.

Desde la década de los setenta Iohannes Moretus se venía encargando del envío de libros y otras mercancías. Arias Montano siempre ocupó un lugar especial entre los

---

[7] Tan sólo en dos cartas del bloque que estudiamos se detiene Iohannes Moretus para hablar de su situación familiar: 1590 10 18 y 1598 06 22.

clientes del *Compás de Oro* como protector y amigo personal de la casa plantiniana; en nuestra correspondencia se registra el envío de un retrato de Plantino, dos epigramas funerarios en su honor (1590 09 03, 1590 10 18 y 1591 08 24) y algunas semillas (1590 06 27 y 1590 09 03). Desde España, Arias Montano solicitaba a la imprenta listados de libros para sus amigos y conocidos, entre los que figuraban Alfonso Ramírez, tío de Pedro de Valencia, el capitán Francisco Márquez, el canónigo Francisco Pacheco, los médicos Simón de Tovar y Francisco Sánchez de Oropesa y el poeta Fernando de Herrera, por citar sólo a algunos (p. ej. 1593 03 15 y 1593 05 16). El gran valor de estos *"memoriales"* que encomienda personalmente Arias Montano es que llevan marcados al margen los libros que debían enviarse también para el extremeño; gracias a estos listados, podemos saber con exactitud qué obras manejaba el sabio español desde 1585 hasta 1596[8]. Entre sus propias creaciones, la que reclama Montano con más insistencia es el *Dictatum Christianum*, libro de texto incluido en el plan de estudios de la cátedra fundada por el extremeño en la Peña de Aracena y también solicitado por muchos libreros y monasterios porque "hay algunas iglesias en las que para ser admitidos en las órdenes sagradas se obliga a los aspirantes a superar un examen de conocimientos de la lengua latina y de la doctrina de la piedad a partir de este mismo librito" (1596 11 01).

Tras la muerte de Plantino, Iohannes Moretus se esfuerza por demostrar que el trato recibido por Montano y sus obras no va a cambiar en absoluto. De hecho, desde 1589 a 1592 el contacto epistolar fue frecuente y el ritmo de impresión, notable: durante este período Moretus escribió dieciocho cartas (frente a sólo cinco desde 1593 a 1598) y salieron de la casa plantiniana de Amberes tres obras de Montano (frente a ninguna en los seis años siguientes). Hay que marcar, pues, un antes y un después en el año 1593. Arias Montano, por su parte, disfrutaba en su vejez de más tiempo de ocio que nunca, entregándose a sus estudios a un ritmo frenético. Ocupaba sus horas de trabajo en el macro-proyecto denominado *Opus Magnum*; por esta razón, no andaba muy satisfecho con los crecientes retrasos que sufría la publicación de sus escritos. A pesar de su característica templanza, se puede entrever en las palabras del extremeño cierto tono de queja (1596 11 01):

> [. . .] De nostrorum uero scriptorum impressione ut nihil est quod potius optem quam ut illa munere nomineque tuo in lucem prodeant ita *nihil etiam quod moneam superest praeter breuitatem ac temporis compendium* [. . .]

De hecho, Arias sospecha que en Amberes se difiere la impresión de sus libros por temor a que se vendieran a corto plazo peor que otras obras; anticipándose a esta objeción, el teólogo español no deja nunca de sostener económicamente sus propias impresiones. Una vez más detectamos cierto tono de reproche, que se hace evidente

---

[8] Actualmente trabajo en la edición de estos memoriales para incluirlos como apéndice en mi tesis doctoral que llevará por título "La correspondencia del humanista Benito Arias Montano conservada en el Museo Plantin-Moretus". En total manejo diecinueve listados, repartidos en distintos volúmenes de los archivos, cuyas fechas van desde el 28 de marzo de 1585 hasta 1596.

cuando Montano pone ante los ojos de Moretus el ejemplo desinteresado y eficiente de su suegro (1597 08 03): uero

> Qua de scriptis nostris per te edendis commemoras, [. . .] cupio *quam maturrime expediri* [. . .] Volo autem commodo tuo, quantum a me fieri possit, per D. Perezium ista curantem consuli: atque utinam multo plus posse daretur; praestarem profecto ut nulla prorsus nummaria difficultate haereres. Verum *optimi parentis ac soceri sancti memineris, mi Iohannes, cuius magnis inceptis et conatibus Deus feliciter semper prouidebat.*

Lo cierto es que Arias Montano no pudo ver publicadas las dos obras que desde 1593 se venían imprimiendo en Amberes: los *Commentaria in Isaiae Prophetae Sermones* y la *Naturae Historia*. Pedro de Valencia, discípulo predilecto de Montano, asume la tarea de editar las últimas creaciones del maestro; las palabras que dirige el humanista zafrense al director de la imprenta resultan mucho menos templadas y diplomáticas que las de Montano:

> [. . .] Haec ego quam primum exscripta (qui mihi in uiri huius scriptis antiquus et gratus labor) ad uos transmittam excudenda. Hoc officii mei arbitror, *uestri autem et haec et quae pridem apud uos Commentarium in Isaiam, Naturae historiam, Rhetoricam, Dialecticam et Grammaticam quamprimum etiam excudenda curare.* Hoc honoris et officii ARIAE MONTANO uestro *maiore cum cura mortuo quam uiuenti praestare debetis.* Homini optimo et sapientissimo atque in omnem ingenii partem excellentissimo et omnino magno, amicorumque omnium et uestrae praecipue familiae amantissimo *tam cito amicos deesse, turpissimum fuerit* atque in aliis hoc, ut hominum mores sunt, *fortasse timendum in Plantini familia monstro simile foret* [. . .][9].

Noticias bibliográficas

La mayor riqueza de estas cartas entre Iohannes Moretus y Arias Montano radica en los datos que contienen sobre el proceso de impresión de las cinco obras que se trabajaron entre 1590 y 1598:

1. *De Varia Republica*[10]

Los comentarios de Montano sobre el libro de los *Jueces* es la única obra de las cinco estudiadas aquí que abarca la última etapa de la vida de Cristóbal Plantino y la primera de Iohannes Moretus como sucesor de su suegro. Plantino, enfermizo y acosado por sus acreedores, tuvo noticias en sus últimos años de vida de que Arias

---

[9] Pedro de Valencia a Iohannes Moretus, 18 de octubre de 1598, en MPM Arch. 94, págs. 139–142. El Museo Plantin-Moretus conserva otras tres cartas de Moretus a Pedro de Valencia: 1599 02 25, MPM Arch. 12, fols. 63r–63v; 1599 08 21, MPM Arch. 12, fol. 83r; 1604 06 03, MPM Arch. 12, fols. 258v–259r.

[10] *De Varia Republica, siue Commentaria in Librum Iudicum, Benedicto Aria Montano Hispalensi descriptore. Antuerpiae, ex officina Plantiniana* [. . .] *M. D. CXII.* Registrado con datos sobre formato, papel empleado, precio y tirada en MPM Ms. 296, fol. 11v y MPM Ms. 39, fol. 12r.

trabajaba en estos comentarios; y, ávido por publicarlos, incluso apremia a su protector a que acelere el trabajo. Moretus se muestra casi impaciente por recibir la copia de la obra (1590 03 19, 1590 06 27, 1590 09 03 y 1590 10 18).

Montano la concluye a finales de 1589 y aguarda la ocasión de entregársela a alguien de confianza para enviarla a la imprenta (1590 01 03, nº 1515 en *CP*). En cuanto a las condiciones de impresión, el teólogo español no sólo no gana dinero con su obra, sino que subvenciona económicamente su estampado, reservándose tan sólo algunos ejemplares para regalar a sus amigos. El manuscrito llega a Amberes en la segunda mitad de 1590. Revisado por Laeuinus Torrentius, pasa después a manos de Henricus Ciberti de Donghen, *alias* Dungheus, a la sazón canónigo de la catedral de Amberes; pero quedaban detalles por aclarar: faltaba la dedicatoria y había algunos cabos sueltos en torno a las veinte ilustraciones que iban a insertarse en los comentarios (1590 10 28). Un año después, el impresor parece preocupado por demostrar su diligencia y se cree en el deber de disculpar los que, por ahora, no son excesivos retrasos: "nos ha retenido algo—alega Moretus—el segundo tomo de los *Anales* de Caesar Baronius, que gracias a Dios ya se ha terminado" (1591 08 24). Los *Comentarios sobre el libro de los Jueces* se acabaron de imprimir antes del 13 de mayo de 1592, fecha de la carta en que Iohannes Moretus notifica a Montano el envío de un ejemplar de su obra. Este libro salió en 4º, empleándose 91 folios y medio por ejemplar; según los registros del Museo se tiraron 1.250 ejemplares, vendidos a 35 placas cada uno.

2. *Hymni et Secula*[11]

En 1587 recabamos la primera noticia de esta obra: Pedro de Valencia anuncia en el prólogo a la anterior colección poética de Montano la futura aparición de nuevos poemas sagrados de su maestro. Desde entonces no se sabe más de este proyecto hasta 1592, año en que Arias envía a su impresor desde Madrid la copia manuscrita corregida de su obra (1592 05 04)[12].

Los *Hymni et Secula* llegan a la imprenta a mediados de junio. A partir de este momento comenzaba a funcionar la máquina burocrática: el primer paso era la censura eclesiástica, a cargo de Dungheus; más tarde se había de enviar la obra a Bruselas para ser provista de la preceptiva licencia por el Consejo Privado del Rey (1592 06 18). Este documento llegó a la imprenta a principios de julio (1591 07 01). La semana siguiente comenzaron a trabajar las prensas en los *Hymni et Secula*, extendiéndose la impresión hasta principios de noviembre de 1592 ([1592 11 12]). Sin embargo, la obra no ve la luz definitivamente hasta 1593, tras la corrección de las erratas detectadas por el propio Montano (1593 06 14). El resultado fue una típica edición de bolsillo: formato de 16º, para el que se necesitaron sólo 10 folios y cuarto de papel por

---

[11] *Benedicti Ar. Montani Hymni et Secula. Antuerpiae, ex officina plantiniana* [. . .] *M. D. XCIII.* Registrado en MPM Ms. 296, fol. 11v y MPM Ms. 39, fol. 12v.

[12] El 19 marzo de 1592 Luis Pérez había escrito a Montano: "A[ni]ma magni operis está en manos de censor, a quien no aprovecha dar priesa porque se excusa con ser letra menuda, y que será Pentecoste antes que pueda acabar de leerlo; ¿qué hará con *himni et secula* de letra minutísima? Buscarle hemos buenos antojos que hagan parescer la letra gruesa" (Archivo General de Simancas, E 169/176).

ejemplar; en consecuencia, nuestra colección de poemas—de la que se tiraron 1.250 ejemplares—se vendió al módico precio de cinco placas.

3. *Liber Generationis et Regenerationis Adam*[13]

El proyecto más ambicioso de todos los que había acometido Arias Montano llevaba por nombre *Opus Magnum*, y quedaba dividido en dos partes, *Anima* y *Corpus*: la intención era crear una enciclopedia filosófico-teológica que, como el propio autor proclama en la dedicatoria del *Anima* a la Iglesia, recapitula "el principal argumento de todos mis escritos" (1593 06 14). Como en todos sus escritos anteriores, la Sagrada Escritura es la única cantera de la historia del alma humana expuesta en *Anima*, y de los variopintos tratados de historia natural, lingüística, retórica, arquitectura, etc. que habría de contener el inconcluso *Corpus*.

Los trabajos de impresión del *Anima*, al igual que los de las dos obras precedentes, fueron relativamente rápidos en comparación con las obras de años posteriores. A mediados de 1591, el ejemplar manuscrito ya se encontraba en Lille a punto de ser transportado a Amberes (1591 08 24). En mayo del año siguiente andaba el *Anima* en manos del censor Dungheus, quien se quejaba una vez más de la pequeñez de la letra (1592 05 13); el mes siguiente, pasa por el trámite del privilegio real esta obra, que entra en prensa inmediatamente después de la finalización de *Hymni et Secula* ([1592 11 12]). Prueba de la meticulosidad de los trabajos de la imprenta plantiniana es la consulta que hace Iohannes Moretus a Montano sobre el título de la obra: le plantea dos opciones, cuya diferencia principal radica en escribir "*Opus Magnum. Pars Prima*" o conectar ambos sintagmas con el genitivo "*Operis Magni pars prima*"; como se deduce de los ejemplares conservados, Montano eligió la segunda de ellas (1592 07 01).

En diciembre de 1592 las prensas continúan trabajando. Arias Montano había propuesto que se elaborara en la imprenta el índice de la obra, aunque Moretus le previene de la dificultad de tal tarea encontrándose tan lejos el autor y habiéndose de emplear suma pulcritud especialmente en materia teológica (1592 12 10). El *terminus ante quem non* para la impresión de la obra es el 14 de junio de 1593, fecha en que Montano envía el prefacio. Poco después sale el *Anima* en un volumen en cuarto; se emplearon 78 folios para la impresión de cada ejemplar, que fue vendido a 30 placas. La tirada constó de 1.000 ejemplares.

4. *Commentaria in Isaiae Prophetae Sermones*[14]

Después de las tres obras montanianas que vieron la luz en 1593, el ritmo de los trabajos de la imprenta se decelera en exceso. Por este motivo, durante el lapso de cinco años que transcurre desde la aparición del *Anima* hasta 1598 Montano no disimula su malestar y eleva claramente el tono de sus quejas. Tenemos testimonios de

---

[13] *Liber Generationis et Regenerationis Adam, siue De Historia Generis Humani. Operis Magni pars prima, id est Anima. Bened. Aria Montano Hispalen. descriptore. Antuerpiae, ex officina plantiniana,* [. . .] *M. D. XCIII.* Registrado en MPM Ms. 296, fol. 11v y MPM Ms. 39, fol. 12v.

[14] *Benedicti Ariae Montani Hispalensis Commentaria in Isaiae Prophetae Sermones. Antuerpiae, ex officina plantiniana* [. . .], *M. D. XCIX.* Registrado en MPM Ms. 39, fol. 12v.

que el *Isaías* estuviera en prensa en 1596 ([1596 07 30–1596 10 10]); un año después, Montano escribe a Moretus que son muchos los que ya esperaban con impaciencia sus *Comentarios*. La impresión de esta obra se simultaneaba con la del *Cuerpo* del *Opus Magnum*; y Arias Montano, deseoso de ver las dos estampadas, exige a Moretus que se organicen los trabajos y se distribuyan los subsidios económicos que envía al efecto (1596 11 01).

En dos ocasiones Moretus justifica los retrasos del *Isaías*: primero alega la falta de papel, debido a las dificultades de transporte por la guerra (1597 05 08); más tarde se queja de nuevo de la pequeñez de la letra del amanuense, lo que les obligaba a perder tiempo consultando los lugares más confusos a algunos eclesiásticos competentes (1598 06 22). Con todo, Moretus anuncia el término del trabajo para octubre de ese mismo año de 1598. Para esta obra en 4° se consumieron 184 folios y medio por ejemplar, vendido a 4 florines con 10 placas; el número de ejemplares tirados ascendió a 950.

5. *Naturae Historia*[15]

Como continuación del *Alma*, que vio la luz en 1593, la primera parte del *Cuerpo* sale en 1601 (en 4°; se emplearon 67 folios por ejemplar, que fue vendido a 35 placas, y se tiraron 1.000 ejemplares). Después de haber trazado la historia del género humano desde su creación a su redención, Arias Montano produjo en esta parte de su *Opus Magnum* un exhaustivo tratado de historia natural, siempre con el referente directo de la Biblia.

Sin embargo, desde julio de 1594 andaba el ejemplar manuscrito de la primera parte del *Corpus* en la imprenta antuerpiense a punto de ser enviado al censor, que, al igual que los compositores, temía la diminuta e ilegible letra del amanuense (1594 07 06). Arias Montano lo había remitido a principios de año (1594 02 28), dictando a su impresor instrucciones precisas sobre el formato de la edición, que había de coincidir con la del *Alma*: volúmenes en cuarto, letras diferenciadas para las citas bíblicas, citas al margen de autores usados para la argumentación. . . . El objetivo era que todos los volúmenes editados y por editar coincidieran a modo de enciclopedia. Para enjugar las dificultades de impresión, el sabio español colabora de nuevo con una aportación económica de 200 florines, cien de regalo y los otros cien a cambio de los ejemplares que se le enviaran una vez impresa la obra.

Hasta 1596 no pasa la *Naturae historia* a manos de los compositores; mientras tanto, Montano envía nuevo material, como la relación de ilustres botanistas cuyos nombres debían aparecer en el capítulo *De cognitione herbarum* (1596 01 16). Sin embargo los correctores se topan con serios problemas para leer algunos lugares, anotados por Iohannes Moretus en un folio y enviados a Montano ([1596 07 30–1596 10 10]).

Desde 1594 Arias Montano concentraba todos sus esfuerzos en la siguiente parte del *Cuerpo*. Pero ésta nunca llegó a publicarse, y no fue a causa de la indolencia del teólogo español, quien seguía enviando nuevo material a marchas forzadas. Las misi-

---

[15] *Naturae Historia, Prima in Magni Operis Corpore pars, Benedicto Aria Montano descriptore. Antuerpiae, Ex officina plantiniana* [. . .], *M. D. CI.* Registrado en MPM Ms. 39, fol. 16v.

vas que van desde 1594 a 1598 encierran datos preciosos para reconstruir el plan e intenciones del resto del *Corpus*, que nunca vio la luz.

En la misma carta que remite Montano a Moretus el 28 de febrero de 1594, junto con la que viajaba la primera parte de su *Corpus*, explica al impresor casi en secreto en qué consiste su proyecto: en ningún momento desvela Arias Montano de cuántas partes constará el *Cuerpo*[16]. Lo que sí se deja claro es que el material debe agruparse en partes conforme vayan saliendo de su pluma, cosa que no suponía ningún problema debido a la uniformidad de criterios de formato que se venía empleando para todos los volúmenes del *Opus Magnum*. De hecho, el autor pretende crear, a partir de las Sagradas Escrituras, tratados de todas las disciplinas, recogiendo la universalidad de saberes diseminados a lo largo de toda su producción exegética. Desgraciadamente, Montano sólo pudo trabajar en tres de estos tratados: una Dialéctica, una Retórica y una Lingüística comparada. Reunamos aquí los datos que poseemos en torno a éstos: ya en su carta del 28 de febrero de 1594 habla Montano de su Gramática Comparativa, obra que, aunque podía venderse por separado, debía imprimirse con el mismo formato y diseño que las demás partes del *Cuerpo*. Al final de este tratado, y como ayuda para el estudiante, debía añadirse un apéndice con las conjugaciones y declinaciones del mayor número de lenguas posible. Arias Montano sugiere que se utilicen, para el griego, los tratados de Palmireno o de Pedro de Valencia, para el hebreo, los de Clenardus, para el Sirio, las del tomo correspondiente de la *Biblia Regia*, de las arábigas se podría encargar el ilustre Franciscus Raphelengius y, así sucesivamente con el latín, el francés, el flamenco, el español, el italiano, etc.

El tratado de lingüística comparada habría de añadirse a los de Dialéctica y Retórica que Montano tenía en proyecto. A primeros de 1595 se envía la gramática comparativa a la imprenta (1595 01 31); Iohannes Moretus ha recibido ya las tres obras dos años más tarde (1597 05 08). En su carta de esta fecha, el heredero de Plantino expone a Arias Montano dos dificultades que parecen presentar los manuscritos recibidos, una en relación al final de la *Dialectica* y otra en torno al comienzo de la *Rhetorica*. Gracias a esta misiva y a la respuesta de Arias escrita meses después podemos conocer algo de éstos que debieron de ser interesantísimos tratados.

La *Dialéctica* parecía terminar con una argumentación inconclusa; constaba de quince capítulos, el último de los cuales se intitulaba *De habitu*. La *Retórica* terminaba con un poema dedicado al Espíritu Santo; sin embargo, había sido remitida a la imprenta sin título ni prefacio, hecho que extrañó a Luis Pérez y al propio Moretus, quienes llegaron a sospechar la posibilidad de que Montano quisiera englobar Dialéctica y Retórica bajo un mismo nombre. En su misiva de agosto de 1597, el sabio extremeño se sorprende de aquel extravío y copia de memoria el título de su segunda retórica que jamás llegó a publicarse:

---

[16] Pedro de Valencia comunica posteriormente a la imprenta que el *Corpus* constará de tres partes: "[. . .] *Hispalim contendi, omnesque quas inuenire potui illius chartas et chirographa collegi, inter quae et alia non mediocris eruditionis et doctrinae, sed quae ipse elaborauerat et editioni destinauerat, Secunda et Tertia corporis in magno opere partes,* [. . .]": Pedro de Valencia a Iohannes Moretus, 17 de noviembre de 1598 (MPM Arch. 94, pág. 139).

A B I G A I L

siue

De ratione dicendi ex sacrorum eloquiorum obseruatione
Benedicti ARIA MONTANO descriptore
Ad communem studiosorum
omnium utilitatem

Conclusión

Las cartas aquí presentadas aportan valiosos datos que nos sumergen en el desconocido e interesante terreno de las relaciones entre humanista e impresor. Iohannes Moretus hereda la correspondencia de su suegro con Arias Montano; y, como es normal, hubo un cambio sensible con respecto a la situación anterior: por un lado, a pesar de los primeros esfuerzos de Moretus, Montano acaba echando de menos las emblemáticas diligencia y constancia que caracterizaban a Plantino; por otro lado, Moretus limita sus contactos epistolares al ámbito profesional, acotando sensiblemente la intimidad y complicidad que unía al sabio español y al célebre Cristóbal Plantino. Sin embargo, este carácter práctico determina que nuestra correspondencia revele al detalle el proceso de impresión de algunas obras de vejez de Arias Montano, e incluso ayude a concebir los proyectos que nuestro ilustre humanista tenía en cartera cuando le alcanzó la muerte.

Universidad de Cádiz

Thomas More's Attitudes toward Women
in The Epigrams

PHILIP DUST★

To ignore the treatment of women in the *corpus* of Thomas More's epigrams is to overlook sixty-three (including three of the Progymnasmata) of the two hundred and eighty-one as they were arranged by Erasmus for publication in the *Utopia-Epigrammata* volume, which finally came from Johann Froben's press at Basel in March 1518.[1] This is a considerable number and merits special consideration. Was More, as Richard Marius suggests, so sexually inhibited as to downgrade women?[2] Or, as Lee Cullen Khanna argues, did More create a balanced perspective on women, seeing them "not simply [as] stereotypes, but . . . either good or bad—both good and bad." So she concludes: "He at least wished them good."[3] So, too, Revilo P. Oliver has contended that More was an upright example of fatherhood and a model as a husband.[4] I would agree with the two latter. I see More as a man of strong moral convictions regarding the sacrament of marriage. It is not so much that he considers women as sex-objects, or as ideally good in themselves, as that he considers them, as he considered himself, as morally obligated partners in God's plan for the procreation and proper education of children, and as helpmates for their mutual salvation.

★ Philip Dust died following a brief illness on 3 May 1998. The IANLS mourns the passing of a longtime and faithful member, whose scholarly interests were Renaissance Humanism, especially Erasmus and Thomas More, and the writings of John Milton.

[1] St. Thomas More, *Latin Poems, Complete Works of Thomas More*, vol. 3, pt. 2, ed. Clarence H. Miller, Leicester Bradner, Charles A. Lynch, and Revilo P. Oliver (New Haven, 1984), 57–58. All citations of Latin poems (identified by number) and English translations are from this edition.

[2] Richard Marius, *Thomas More* (New York, 1982). This is one of the major contentions of the book.

[3] "No Less Real Than Ideal: Images of Women in More's Work," *Moreana* 14, nos. 55–56 (1977): 50. This study deals with the *Dialogue of Comfort against Tribulation*, the *Utopia*, and *Richard III*, not the epigrams.

[4] *Latin Poems*, 57–58.

In some part, the women who are in More's epigrams are found in the *Planudean Anthology*, and are not More's original creations. But he did choose them for inclusion in his work and, therefore, bears responsibility for the selection. Must we conclude, however, with Marius, that he was so sexually repressed as to be anti-feminist in the epigrams? I think not. There is no question that the poems in the *Planudean Anthology*, gathered over so many centuries of ancient and medieval life, are anti-feminist. But More is merely selecting them in keeping with a literary framework, the epigrammatic satire, a genre inherited from Martial and Juvenal.

More important is the moral position More is working from as a Christian satirist. In his own personal life, as well as that of the women in his family, this was the ethical imperative of chastity—that is, of a monogamous marriage primarily directed toward the procreation and education of children. This family-unit's main purpose in life was to live for the honor and glory of God. As a satirical literary artist, then, More assumed the artistic responsibility for setting out in sometimes stark relief the terrible evils in family relationships that followed from conduct not in keeping with More's moral ideals. So, while he follows the medieval anti-feminist literary tradition, it is not out of sexually repressed bitterness, but out of positive principles, expressed in negative moralities. If we see in the epigrams much negative morality, we can best set them off against the lengthy and very noble ideas that More also presents of virtuous women. In the discussion that follows, I have classified the relevant poems into four categories: 1) Morally objectionable women, 2) Morally questionable women, 3) Ideal women, and 4) More's female children.

Morally objectionable women

There are several poems on the astrologer's adulterous wife, an occasion for satire on both feminine adultery and astrology. "Aliud in Astrologvm Vxoris Impvdicae Maritvm" (61), "In Evndem Iambicvm" (62), "Alivd in Evndem" (63), "Alivd in Astrologvm Evndem" (64), "Alivd in Astrologvum" (65), and "De Astrologo de Qvo Svpra" (67) all show the futility of both. In 65, he concludes, "Hinc factum astrologe est, tua quum capit uxor amantes, / Sydera significent ut nihil inde tibi" (11.8–9) ["That is why, astrologer, when your wife takes lovers, the stars give you no hint of the matter"] (p. 137). What is important here is the satire on the moral evil of adultery and the epistemological evil of astrology. Neither fits the standards of morality for a Christian. Also, *both* women *and* men are being satirized.

Unfaithful wives, engaged in adultery, are again under attack in "In Amicam Foedifragam Iocosvm, Versvm e Cantione Anglica" (82), "In Virginem Moribvs Havd Virgineis" (84), "In Vxorem Impvdicam" (165), "Ad Sabinvm, Cvi Vxor Absenti Concepit" (196), and "Ad Sabinvm" (205). Epigram 82 speaks of a young man's depression when he learns, after an exalted moment of infatuation, of his mistress' unfaithfulness: "Heus tua iam pactam fregit amica fidem" (1.8) [" 'Just look, your mistress has broken the promise she made' "] (p. 147). Epigram 84 plays on the term "uirgo" as "Blanda, salax, petulans, audax, uaga, garrula" (1.1) ["seductive, wanton, saucy, footloose, talkative"] (p. 147). Number 165 mockingly commiserates with Aratus, whose children are not his own. Number 196 to Sabinus does the same.

Mythological and biblical women who were reprehensible, mostly taken from poems in the *Planudean Anthology*, also form a category of satirical poems: Phaedra (123), Clytemnestra (136), Herodias and Salome (224, 226, 227). Phaedra reappears (241) as a prototype of evil women, much in the tradition of anti-feminism; she is also an example of a truly evil woman who violated all moral values.

Again to Sabinus is 205, where More conjectures about the thoughts of the mother at conception. The one child Sabinus claims as his own is his because its mother was thinking about her husband. Or was she? As More concludes: "Dum pertimescit anxia / Ne tu Sabine incommodus / Velutque Lupus in fabulam / Superuenires interim" (11.43–46) ["She was worried for fear you, Sabinus, might inconveniently arrive on the scene, as we say 'speak of the devil'"] (p. 237). Epigram 220 attributes Sabinus' misfortune of having had three unfaithful wives to his fate. At least that is what the third unfaithful wife says (11.12–13).

"In Pictvram Herodianae Mensae" (226) compares the deaths of John the Baptist with the execution of a murderer, both deaths requested by women of ill repute. And the next epigram, "In Eandem Pictvram" (227), compares the saint's death to the death of Itys, Tereus' son, effected by the two sisters Procne and Philomela.

"De Fabvlla Et Attalo" (245) is a satire on a whore, Fabulla. "In Pvellam Divaricatis Tibiis Eqvitantem" (235) satirizes a girl who can ride a man as well as a horse. "In Privignvm Collapsa Novercae Statva Oppressvm e Graeco" (239) and "In Novercas e Graeco" (241) make fun of bad stepmothers, so unlike More's second wife Alice. "In Vxorem Impvdicam" (165) is about a woman who bore children three times without the help of her husband. "De Pvella Qvae Raptvm Finxit" (167) describes an attempted rape on a girl who pretends to resist but who, threatened with not being assaulted, is only too glad to give sexual assent. "De Herode Et Herodiade" (224) is another poem on the vile Herodias.

Morally questionable women

Nagging wives, the subject of *The Second Shepherd's Play*, are also a subject of satire, much in the vein of the Middle Ages. "In Vxores" (85), "In Easdem" (86), "In Digamos e Graeco" (138), "Ad Qvendam Cvi Vxor Mala Domi" (174), and "De Philomeno Et Agna Conivgatis Mala Fide" (253) all fit this category. The male counterpart of the Wife of Bath complains about marriage; still, as the epigram says at the end of 85: "Quin sex sepultis, septimam ducit tamen" (1.6) ["Yes, when his sixth wife dies, he marries a seventh"] (p. 147). Such is the nature of life. Number 86 speaks of a wife's bequest as her best part, 138 bemoans a second marriage as shipwreck, 174 castigates a typically shrewish wife, and 253 sings the happy marriage of two ill-fated partners, where the husband becomes a cuckoo and the wife a she-wolf: "Mox Philomenus auem quauis aestate canentem, / In cuculum, inque auidam uertitur Agna lupam" (11.13–14) ["Soon Philomenus was changed to the bird which sings each summer, the cuckoo; and Agna became an insatiable she-wolf"] (p. 267). The lamb has become a wolf.

There remains a group of More's poems which satirize false beauty in women: Number 54, about an Athenian courtesan who has grown old; Number 58, where dye is used in vain to make a Helen of Hecuba. Numbers 154, 155, and 156 satirize ugly women, while numbers 216 and 217 satirize Gellia, a black woman. While the last two are certainly censurable by an enlightenment which condemns racism, Elizabethan England was far from such an understanding. More was no more to blame than his age. "De Forma Dilemma Iambis Trimetris Scazontibvs" (66) makes fun of the superficiality of feminine beauty in matters of true love.

Ideal Women

Even as early as "In Ancillam Mortvam" (46), More was writing about positive feminine virtues. It reads: "Ante fuit solo Sosime corpore serua, / Nunc fato pars est haec quoque missa manu" (11.1–2) ["Before Sosima was a slave only in body. Now even that part of her has been freed by death"] (p. 127). With her inward freedom of soul, the woman Sosima was only bound as a slave; death freed her from even this. True being of both men and women alike for More consists in the soul, not the body.

Epigram 143, containing the proper criteria for choosing a wife, is addressed to Candidus. Money and beauty are not among them (11.35–61). True love is inspired by a woman who is "Virtutis inclytae" (11.62–67) ["glorious in virtue"] (p. 183). Sexual conduct is categorically excluded (11.91–101). Her education is of paramount importance both for her and for her children and grandchildren (11.102–124). Her education will be reflected in her "Summa eloquentia / Iam cum omnium graui / Rerum scientia" (11.154–156) ["perfect power of expression and her thoughtful understanding of all kinds of affairs"] (pp. 189–191). Learned women from antiquity are cited as models (11.157–177).

"Excvsat Qvod Dvm Loqveretvr Cvm Eximio Qvodam Patre, Nobilem Qvandam Matronam Ingressam Thalamvm, Atqve Aliqvandiv Colloqventibvs Illis Adstantem Non Animadverterat" (265) is an elaborate apology on More's part for not noticing the entrance of a beautiful French woman into the room where he was absorbed in conversation with a prelate. This poem reveals another side to More, one of the utmost courtesy, which he felt on this occasion he had not lived up to. As he says hyperbolically: "At uel hiulca prius mihi terra dehisceret optem / Quam sit in hoc animo tam fera barbaries, / Vt si quando, leues ueluti mihi missa per auras / In thalamum penetret candida nympha meum, / Non saltem aspiciam (si plura licere negetur) / Quaque licet memet candidus insinuem." (11. 38–43). ["But I would that the earth split open and swallow me rather than that there be found in my heart a rudeness so brutal that when a fair nymph, wafted so to speak by some breath of air, enters my room, I fail to look at her at least (if the occasion allows no more) and, if it is permitted, fairly win her favor"] (p. 285). He concludes even more courteously by suggesting that the prelate's speech in which he had been so absorbed might "Dedecus hoc lepidae debent purgare fabellae / Meque meae dominae conciliare tuae" (11. 54–55) ["wipe away this disgrace and restore me to my lady's good graces"] (p. 285). If all of this seems excessive, it was one of the better features of an age of courtesy, as Sir Thomas Hoby's translation of Castiglione's *Il Cortegiano* testifies, and one which reflects well on More.

More's high ideal of womanhood is nowhere better expressed than in his epigram, which is an epitaph, to his two wives: Jane, who has passed away, and Alice, who remains with him. A More who could not sanction divorce found epigrammatic point in the belief that he would be reunited with them in death, and live in heaven with both wives. In "Epitaphivm in Sepvlchro Iohannae Olim Vxoris Mori, Destinantis Idem Sepvlchrvm Et Sibi Et Aliciae Posteriori Vxori" (258), he sings the praises of Jane, who "Me uocet ut puer et trina puella patrem" (1.8) ["(Jane who) has made me father of a son and three daughters"] (p. 271), and of Alice, who is "Altera priuignis (quae gloria rara nouercae est) / Tam pia, quam gnatis uix fuit ulla suis" (ll.9–10) ["the other has been as devoted to her stepchildren (a rare and splendid attainment in a stepmother) as very few mothers are to their own children"] (p. 271). More here is not only speaking about his love for both women, but he is speaking very selflessly of their roles as mothers to his children. But both a "fatum" which makes death inevitable and a "relligio" which does not permit bigamy will be overcome in the permanence of immortality as More says, "societ nos obsecro coelum" (1.15) ["I pray that heaven will unite us too"] (p. 273).

That More could write "Gratvlatvr Qvod Eam Reppperit Incolvmem Qvam Olim Ferme Pver Amaverat" (263) in his advanced years indicates a romantic, sentimental side to him which his busy life as a public servant suppressed. It was not, as Marius suggests, sexual suppression that concealed this side of his nature, but the drowning out of emotional life in the day-to-day carrying-out of legal and political duties into which More had been channeled by his father.[5] Young romance had bloomed in More at sixteen years with all the natural enticements puberty offers. More remembers his early attraction: "Cum uelut attactu stupefactus fulminis haesi" (1.28) ["I was helpless, as though stunned by a lightning-stroke"] (p. 277). The epigrammatic point comes with his memory that she too had been attracted to him in those early years of his manhood: "Namque tui consors arcani conscia pectus / Garrula prodiderat concaluisse tuum" (11.38–39). ["For a gossipy companion of yours who was in on the secret revealed that your heart, too, was moved"] (p. 277). More's encounter years later with his first love and his remembrance of things past reveal a human attraction to a member of the opposite sex which all who are human have experienced and most have not forgotten.[6]

More's Female Children

As More's love and devotion to his two wives was the subject of Number 258 because of their care of his children, so his love and care for his children, Margaret, Elizabeth, Cecilia, and John is the subject of "T. Morvs Margaretae Elisabethae Ceciliae Ac Ioanni Dvlcissimis Liberis S. P." (264), giving further evidence of his role, not as a possessive husband, but as a father giving all of himself to his offspring, three of whom are daughters. That More reveals himself as a parent who is near to doting on his son and daughters, even as they have grown older, is a decisive refutation of the view that he was emotionally repressed. He speaks of having taken his children

---

⁵ J. A. Guy, *The Public Career of Sir Thomas More* (Brighton, 1980), 3–4.

⁶ In the *Latin Poems*, Oliver says the poem has "unmistakable and simple veracity" and is "honest and rational," 58.

into his arms, a very motherly act, indeed, "Vos tam saepe meo sueta fouere sinu" (1.25) ["to take you so often into my arms"] (p. 287) and of having done that "saepe," often. He says he gave them cake, ripe apples, and fancy pears, again a very motherly act: "Inde est uos ego quod soleo pauisse placenta, / Mitia cum pulchris et dare mala piris" (11.26–27) ["That is why I regularly fed you cake and gave you ripe apples and fancy pears"] (p. 281) and that as a regular practice ["soleo"]. Like a mother, he dressed his children: "Inde quod et Serum textis ornare solebam" (1.28) ["That is why I used to dress you in silken garments"] (p. 281). And that again regularly ["solebam"]. He could not endure their tears: "Quod nunquam potui uos ego flere pati (1.29) ["and why I never could endure to hear you cry"] (p. 281). As for corporal punishment, his whip was a peacock's tail: "Flagrum pauonis non nisi cauda fuit" (1.31). It is a very sentimental More who writes here, expressing deep feelings that in bygone years would have been considered "weak" and "feminine." In short, it is a modern More who fulfilled the roles of both father and mother.

If the first part of the epigram reveals More's intimate feelings about his children when they were young, the latter part reveals his role as father-teacher to them, and not just to his male offspring preparing for the universities, but to his daughters who would never enter the doors of a university. Hardly chauvinistic was a father who would instruct his daughters in humanistic learning for their own sakes rather than for any degree they might have gotten from such instruction. As his children have gotten older, the instruction has taken effect: "Hoc faciunt mores puerili aetate seniles, / Artibus hoc faciunt pectora culta bonis. / Hoc facit eloquio formatae gratia linguae / Pensaque tam certo singula uerba modo" (11.42–45). ["This is because you combine the wise behavior of old age with the years of childhood, because your hearts have been informed with genuine learning, because you have learned to speak with grace and eloquence, weighing each word carefully"] (p. 281).[7] This is said not only of Margaret, who is so often cited as an example of More's humanistic efforts, but also of his daughters Elizabeth and Cecilia. His children's accomplishments mean much more than mere biological procreation for More. As he says: "Vt iam quod genui, quae patribus unica multis / Causa est adfectus, sit prope nulla mei" (11.48–49) ["(Their accomplishments) bind me to my children so closely, that what, for many fathers, is the only reason for their affection—I mean the fact that they begot their children—has almost nothing to do with my love for you"] (p. 281). If his instruction has made More think that he had been a doting father when they were young, then what more can come? In epigrammatic point he urges them to continue their learning so that he will love them that much more.

Northern Illinois University

---

[7] Elizabeth McCutcheon has made a strong case for More's enlightenment about the education of women in the Christian context of modesty and virtue, and about his daugherts as examples or prototypes of the educated woman. See McCutcheon's study, "The Education of Thomas More's Daughters: Concepts and Praxis," in *East Meets West: Homage to Edgar C. Knowlton, Jr.*, ed. Roger L. Hadlich and J. D. Ellsworth (Honolulu, 1988), 193–207, and the review by James A. McGoldrick in *Moreana* 27, no. 103 (1990): 89–92.

Unos Prooemia *poco*
conocidos de J. L. Vives

JOSÉ M. ESTELLÉS GONZÁLEZ

Los primeros contactos que tuve con los Comentarios de J. L. Vives al *De ciuitate Dei* de S. Agustín con el fin de editarlos de nuevo[1], me revelaron que además del seguimiento cuidadoso del texto agustiniano que lleva a cabo el humanista valenciano, éste introdujo unos preámbulos, *praefationes* o *prooemia*, situados estratégicamente a lo largo de dichos Comentarios. Con ellos Vives intenta situar al lector, hacerle reflexionar sobre lo que se ha tratado anteriormente y al propio tiempo introducirle en los capítulos siguientes de la obra. La densidad del trabajo de S. Agustín, que Vives ha experimentado en sus propias carnes, obliga a que se haga un descanso, que sirva tanto de recopilación de ideas anteriores, como de soporte para cobrar nuevas fuerzas y así poder afrontar dignamente la tarea que se avecina. El obispo de Hipona tabién emplea el mismo método, cosa que no nos debe extrañar en una obra tan amplia. Así nos encontramos con pequeños *prooemia*—dejando de lado el del libro primero—que tiene un carácter recapitulatorio la mayoría, como, por ejemplo, los que se insertan en II 2, IV 1, y en los inicios de los libros V, VI y VII.

Refiriéndonos a Vives tres son los *prooemia* que el humanista incluye en sus *Commentarii*: al inicio del libro IV, al del VIII y al del XVIII. También son tres los

---

[1] *Ioannis Lodovici Vivis Opera Omnia* I: I: Volumen Introductorio coordinado por A. Mestre. II: *Philologica, 1: Commentarii ad Diui Aurelii Augustini De Ciuitate Dei. Libri I–V* (València, 1992). III: *Philologica III: Commentarii ad Diui Aurelii Augustini De Ciuitate Dei. Libri VI–XIII* (València, 1993). *Philologica IV: Commentarii ad Diui Aurelii Augustini De Ciuitate Dei. Libri XIV–XXII* (en prensa). Curauerunt F. Georgius Pérez Durà et Iosephus M. Estellés González. Igualmente puede leerse un detallado estudio sobre las diferentes ediciones de los comentario de Vives en C. Coppens, "Une collaboration inconnue entre Caroline Guilard et Huges de la Porte en 1544: le *De ciuitate Dei* d'Augustin, edité par Jean Louis Vives," *Gutenberg–Jahrbuch* (1988): 126–140. También cf. E. González y González, *Joan Lluís Vives. Del Escolasticismo al humanismo* (València, 1987); "La lectura de Vives, del siglo XIX a nuestros dias," en *Ioannis Lodovici Vivis Opera Omnia* I, 1–76, y "Vives. De la edición príncipe hacia el texto crítico," en E. González, S. Albiñana y V. Gutiérrez, eds., *Vives. Edicions Princeps* (València, 1992), 13–57, con excelente bibliografía en todos ellos.

problemas que plantea con suma nitidez y que nos demuestran la finura y rigurosidad intelectual en que se mueve el humanista valenciano. En el *prooemium* al libro cuarto (A) se abunda en aspectos relacionados con la *religiosidad* del pueblo de Roma fundamentalmente. En el que introduce el libro octavo (B) es la *filosofía*—el platonismo y su herencia—el tema que mueve a Vives. Por último, en el que antecede al libro diez y ocho (C) contempla *aspectos historiográficos*. Llama poderosamente la atención el sentido crítico que Vives evidencia y que le lleva a analizar con detalle ideas y opiniones, criticándolas con dureza si llega el caso, sin que quede al margen el propio S. Agustín. Pero conviene entrar en detalles.

Libro IV

IOANNIS LODOVICI VIVIS VALENTINI, IN QVARTVM LIBRVM DE CIVITATE DEI DIVI AVRELII AVGVSTINI COMMENTARII

S. Agustín, tras desencadenar un fuerte ataque al mundo pagano que acusa al cristianismo de ser el causante de la caida de Roma y de señalar que los bienes y males de este mundo deben aplicarse a buenos y malos (libro I), comenta que Roma se vió inmersa en un cúmulo de vicios e inmoralidades estando vigentes y colaborando a ello aquellos dioses paganos (libro II) los cuales tampoco liberaron a Roma de los males físicos y externos que la afectaron desde su fundación (libro III).

Vives, al inicio de su comentario al libro IV expone con mucha claridad su propósito: *Nunc ex rebus gestis Populi Romani ad religionem eius sacra ceremoniasque transeundum.*

Tras los aspectos históricos tratados en los tres libros anteriores deben tratarse aspectos relacionados con la religión y sus ritos. Vives constata que en sus comentarios a los libros anteriores no se le han planteado problemas que tuvieran difícil solución, pues la historia romana, en lo que a aspectos religiosos se entiende, ha podido reunirse, si no al menos en su totalidad, al menos en parte. Desgraciadamente Tito Livio nos ha llegado fragmentado, por lo que Vives solicita de antemano el perdón por si *uel diligentiam nostram lector desiderarit uel ingenium.*

Pero no solo Livio es el que ha sufrido la agresividad del tiempo. Pérdida más importante la constituye una obra de Varrón, *uir totius ueteris aeui consultissimus*, sus *Antiquitates, quas unas si haberemus satisfacere potuissemus Augustino.* No obstante Vives ha debido actuar—exactamente dice: *emendicanda nobis a uariis fuerunt*—, y lo ha hecho a plena conciencia, plenamente seguro de sus propias fuerzas, *ne nudi omnino et inopes, omnique non modo cultu ac ornatu, sed instrumento quoque domestico egeni uideremur.*

Tras recordar alguna modalidad cultual romana, se sorprende de que se pueda perder el tiempo en aspectos en los que casi no importa insistir: *Quid enim confert eruditioni flagitia Iouis aut Veneris nosse? quibus diis quae sacra fiant? quae ostenta, quibus hostiis sacrisque procuranda? quae auguria prodigiaque a quibus mittantur? quomodo experientur?* Non obstante Vives es consciente de que los aspectos mitológicos de la religión, los misterios augurales, la propia experiencia religiosa importan a mucha gente, aunque él les conceda menor importancia; por lo tanto no tendrá inconveniente en comentar en relación a cualquier dios o diosa su naturaleza (*genus*), sus templos y altares (*templa, aras*), sus fiestas y celebraciones (*festa, cerimonias*), sus ritos (*sacra*). De todo ello va a hacer un seguimiento, *ne lector harum rerum studiosus uacuus earum a lectione nostrorum commentariorum discedat.*

Libro VIII

IOANNIS LODOVICI VIVIS VALENTINI IN OCTAVVM LIBRVM
DE CIVITATE DEI DIVI AVRELII AVGVSTINI COMMENTARII.
VIVIS PROOEMIVM IN TRES SEQVENTES LIBROS

Vives expresa claramente el ámbito al que se dirije este pequeño prólogo: a los tres libros siguientes. Son los libros del *De ciuitate Dei* octavo, noveno y décimo. Hagamos primero un pequeño resumen de lo que dichos libros ofrecen. En el octavo Agustín se refiere a la teología natural y a los dioses que con ella se relacionan. Al tratar el tema del más allá, preguntándose si el culto que a aquellos dioses se ofrece es provechoso para conseguir la vida eterna, habla de los platónicos, a los que considera muy cercanos a la fe cristiana. Pone a continuación grandes objeciones a Apuleyo y a todos aquellos que defienden el culto a los demonios.

En el noveno, siguiendo la estela del anterior, el obispo de Hipona polemiza con aquellos filósofos que creen en la existencia de demonios buenos y demonios malos. Y en el décimo se refiere a los ángeles buenos, afirmando rotundamente que el culto de latría únicamente debe ofrecerse a Dios. Cierra el libro discutiendo con Porfirio acerca de temas relacionados con el alma.

Como he indicado más arriba el platonismo es, desde el punto de vista filosófico, una de las preocupaciones fundamentales del humanista. Por ello proclama al comienzo que los *Commentarii* a los tres libros siguientes que acabamos de mencionar se centran en discutir *cum uiris acutissimis summaque praeditis eloquentia, qui ex Platonis schola caeteris bonis artibus instructi religione sola caruerunt.* Desgraciadamente no todos sus colegas participan de su entusiasmo, pues *sententiae* [. . .] *sectae principis Platonis* [. . .] que Vives se ha esforzado en explicar concienzudamente *a nostris hominibus qui in philosophorum scholis theologorumque uersantur prorsus sunt ignotae.*[2] La alusión al mundo de la enseñanza escolástica—aquellos "Pseudodialécticos"—es clara y no se lo perdonarán jamás, a pesar de que Vives no hace más que estar plenamente de acuerdo con lo dicho por Agustín en el libro VIII. El capítulo XI del citado libro octavo lleva un título significativo y que ahorra cualquier comentario con vistas a explicitar cuál es la mentalidad de S. Agustín al respecto. Dice: *Vnde Plato eam intelligentiam potuerit adquirere, qua Christianae scientiae propinquauit.* No es de extrañar pues que Vives afirme lo siguiente: *Cum sint tamen cognosci dignissimae [Platonis sententiae], tum propter subtilitatem rerum magno ingenio curaque extusarum, tum uel maxime quod uicinae sunt nostrae pietati.*

Acto seguido Vives pasará revista a los filósofos que Agustín cita, atreviéndose, y no es la primera vez, ni será la última, a corregir y emendar las opiniones de S. Agustín.

Para terminar el humanista da paso a una amplia disquisición en la que pide disculpas al lector, pues la enjundia de los temas que debe comentar le ha llevado, aún

---

[2] Esta útima frase de Vives fue suprimida por la censura en muchos ejemplares de las distintas ediciones. En la revista del Departamento de Filología Clásica de la Universitat de València, *Studia Philologica Valentina* se publicará en el próximo número el primero de una serie de artículos del firmante de esta comunicación sobre Vives y la censura inquisitorial a los Comentarios.

sin quererlo, a excederse en amplitud, superando con creces la brevedad exigible a unos simples comentarios.

Libro XVIII

IOANNIS LODOVICI VIVIS VALENTINI PROOEMIVM IN DECIMVM OCTAVVM LIBRVM

Todo el que haya manejado los *Commentarii* de Vives se habrá dado cuenta de que los correspondientes al libro XVIII superan con creces a todos los restantes. Nos encontramos ante un conjunto que suma casi cuatrocientas notas, muchas de gran amplitud, las cuales podrían ocupar sin duda un amplio volumen independiente. Y es que Agustín ha dado pie al humanista, pues en el libro anterior se ha dedicado de lleno a hablar de la ciudad celestial, mietras que en éste se refiere a la ciudad terrena, en la que halla ciertos paralelismos con la anterior, tratando de sus orígenes hasta el final de los tiempos.

Claramente nos damos cuenta de que la materia a tratar por Vives es inmensa y le desborda. Con la mayor humildad a sí lo proclama al comienzo: *Volumine operis huius duodevicesio multa nobis inter tenebras spatia fuerunt conficienda*; y la razón de la afirmación anterior tabién nos la ofrece: *non iam in una ciuitate unoque populo manendum, ut prius in Romano, sed per totum terrarum orbem inter procul dissita peregrinandum regna. . . .* Agustín ha planteado un gran reto y Vives se encuentra con grandes dificultades, pues debe viajar para conocer pueblos tiempo ha alejados, investigar en linajes reales perdidos en el tiempo. Por ejemplo, tiene que comentar aspectos relacionados con Asiria, con Sición, con los pueblos argivos, con el Ática, etc.

No obstante el sentido crítico del humanista en estado puro emerge. A pesar de que depende de otros no por ello puede aceptar lo que S. Agustín admite sin pestañear. Efectivamente, según dice Vives, *Augustinus etiam fabulas ceu durissima nuces, iuglandes aut amygdalas, aut etiam pineas spargit, in quibus frangendis non parum sit negotii, quo nucleum gestae rei altissimo cortice contectum eruamus.* Las imágenes que emplea Vives, las cuales descienden a niveles coloquiales y conversacionales, y que destilan causticidad a manos llenas, se comentan por sí solas e invitan a compartir sonrisas con el valenciano.

El que igualmente se traten temas más cercanos en el espacio no quiere decir que se presenten limpios de toda clase de corruptelas. El historiador riguroso, aconseja Vives, debe saber distinguir. Así, por ejemplo, en asuntos relacionados con la península itálica en la antigüedad, *accedunt commentis et dissidiis scribentium incertissima facta.* Igual puede ocurrir con Roma o con los territorios en los que se asienta el pueblo hebreo.

Ante tal cúmulo de dificultades Vives debe dar explicaciones, valiosísimas para nosotros, pues nos informa de sus fuentes, tanto principales como secundarias, y de su manejo. Nos dice: *Quod si ita est, quanto aequius erit mihi ueniam dari, si quando forsan aut casu quippiam aut ignorantia in auium aliquod concessi. . . .*

Y Vives a continuación va citando autores y obras que hubiese podido consultar con gran provecho, como las ya citadas *Antiquitates* de Varrón, *quae unae si adfuissent Mercuriorum nobis fuissent uicariae.* Del mismo modo cuando, por ejemplo, ha tenido que referirse a Asiria, su única fuente ha sido Eusebio, con algunos detalles tomados de Diodoro Sículo.

También Vives alude a dos autores, cuya citación le presenta en bandeja la ocasión para arremeter con saña contra autores que, al ser editados, pasan por ser excelentes, cuando en realidad son deleznables. Se trata de Beroso y de Juan Annio[3]. El ataque contra estos escritores no puede ser más furibundo: *ab illis prorsum abstinui, ne de fece, quod aiunt, uiderer haurire, hoc est e libellis frivolis et incertorum autorum, quod ad stupefaciendos imperitos lectores Graecia lusit otiosa.* El sentido crítico de Vives es más que evidente, llegando incluso a expresiones de carácter escatológico. Somos testigos del afloramiento de la actitud combativa de los humanistas frente a las manipulaciones, contradicciones y falsedades que adornaban los libros de historia.

Eusebio y Pausanias también conducen a Vives a través de Sición o del Peloponeso, a pesar de que la información que se transmite no deja de ser elemental, pues *contenti nuda regum nomina percensuisse.* Poca cosa para las exigencias de un historiador riguroso.

Al referirse a Judea advierte Vives que tiene muy claras cuáles son sus fuentes, que no son otras que los *certisssimi illi et fidissii prophetae.* Hijo de su tiempo y de la corriente erasmiana a la que pertenece el humanista valenciano—no olvidemos que es Erasmo el que le encarga comentar a S. Agustín—también se siente capaz de interpretar y aclarar aquellos pasajes de las Sagradas Escrituras, sobre todo cuando escritores no eclesiásticos opinaban sobre aspectos relacionados con la historia de los hebreos. No obstante Vives nos dice que opta por no nombrar a aquellos que se muestran de acuerdo con lo que nos dicen los textos sagrados: ... *explicuimus interdum, quid prophani scriptores de illis ipsis rebus indicarent, si modo alia ostendebant* ... *nam ubi inter se congruebant satis fuit sanctorum sententias declarasse,* como, por ejemplo, Alejandro Polyhistor, que escribe basándose en la traducción bíblica de los Setenta.

Por último alude a lo que geográficamente toca más de cerca, como Grecia y Roma y sus antecedentes argivos y latinos, cuyas noticias ha tomado *ex uariis.* Consciente de la enorme ambigüedad de la expresión Vives concluye reenviando al lector a sus *Comentarii,* donde encontrará cumplida respuesta. La frase de Vives pueden muy bien servir de conclusión a estas líneas: *caetera lector ex ipsis commentariis cognoscet.*

Y para concluir he aquí tres aspectos que me han llamado la atención, además de otros muchos que el humanista hace florecer ante nosotros, abriendo múltiples caminos de investigación:

---

[3] Beroso, historiador y astrónomo babilonio (330 a. de C.–?). Se dice que en la isla de Cos daba clases de astrología. Inventó un cuadrante solar y escribió a comienzo del siglo III una historia de Babilonia, cuyos escasos fragmentos recogen Flavio Josefo, Clemente de Alejandría y Eusebio. Por otro lado Giovanni o Nanni Annio (1432–1502), dominico italiano y experto en lenguas orientales, fue también historiador y arqueólogo. Dedica a los Reyes Católicos sus "Comentarios de las antigüedades" (1498), obra en la que se recoge la historia fabulosa de la Hispania primitiva a partir de la llegada del legendario Túbal. Sus opiniones se basan casi por entero en textos falsificados, atribuidos a Beroso o al egipcio Manetón. No obstante gozó de gran predicamento y fue muy apreciado, incluso por Nebrija. No es extraño que Vives los una.

1. La continua alusión al lector, que está siempre presente en el momento de investigar y de redactar los comentarios.
2. Las dificultades enormes que la densísima obra agustiniana le plantea desde todos los puntos de vista, tanto textuales como ideológicos, de los cuales tenemos cumplida constancia, y que quedan claramente en evidencia en las líneas anteriores.
3. En relación con la idea anterior he podido constatar que Vives en la medida en que avanza en sus comentarios se va afirmando y manifestando más seguridad en sus propias opiniones. Los *prooemia* comentados son vivo ejemplo de lo dicho.

Universitat de València

The Prisci Poetae *in Transition:*
Landino to Minturno

RAPHAEL FALCO

I

This paper examines changes in the origin myths of poetry in *artes poeticae* of the late fifteenth and early sixteenth centuries. The implications of my discussion should have resonance, I think, in the analysis of all cultures "en el umbral de nuevos mondos" (to quote the title of the international congress). The manipulation of the poetic origin myths resembles the highly rationalized transplanting of cultural symbols that we find in justifications of colonial or imperial ambition, and the humanists' rediscovery of Latin and Greek literature and culture provides an interesting analogy for the discovery and conquest of far-off lands. Both humanist scholars and *conquistadores* often justified their activities as triumphs over barbarism. And both often took possession of their chosen realms by invoking a more ancient, divine connection to the origins of civilized society. Indeed, establishing a genealogy of the charismatic ideals of culture, whether they are poetic or religious or martial ideals, seems to be an inevitable first step in the discovery (*inventio*) of New Worlds—from San Salvador to the *res publica litterarum*.

The artes poeticae contain much evidence of this genealogical impulse. Virtually all poetic treatises of the period contain discussions of Orpheus, Linus, Amphion, and Musaeus, and most Renaissance theorists acknowledge the significance of the origins of poetry in the development of civilized culture. Yet, despite ubiquitous references to the *prisci poetae*, the treatise-writers often have considerably different explanations of the meaning of the poetic origin myths. I have found, for example, that the familiar category of the *poeta theologus* does not dominate characterizations of Orpheus and Amphion after the fifteenth century, nor is that category consistently defined. Even in the work of Cristoforo Landino we find an attempt to accord a more tangibly civic role to the poet than one would expect from a Neoplatonist. Similarly, the notion of the *furor poeticus* is far less stable than modern critics have indicated, ranging from an utterly ventriloquized ecstatic utterance, as in Marsilio Ficino's theories, to something more like the twentieth-century idea of inspiration as a controllable element in artistic production. This range of differences is interesting in itself. But there are also important ramifications of these different interpretations for our understanding of the development of Renaissance poetics in a cultural context. In the *artes poeticae*, the origin myths provide the genealogical link between the charismatic figures of antiquity and contemporary poetic practice, and the differing versions that we find in various treatises offer a key to the motives, ambitions, and shifting ideals of Renaissance authors.

Yet it is difficult to know where to begin because the origins of the origin myths are fragmentary, scattered throughout the literature of antiquity. From Aristotle to Pausanias, from Apollodorus to Diodorus Siculus, philosophers, poets, historians, and chroniclers all provide versions of the life and times of Orpheus and his fellow originals. But perhaps the most reasonable starting-place is Horace's familiar and influential passage on the *prisci poetae* in the *Ars poetica*, which contains a description of what might be called the primal scene of poetry.[1] Horace refers to Orpheus as *sacer interpres*, priest or sacred interpreter of the gods, and both he and Amphion are called *vates*. But Horace does not associate their divinity with worship or prophecy per se. They seem to be civic rather than religious heroes, manifesting a consummately utilitarian presence as lawgivers and builders.

These socializing virtues provided a model of poetic heroism which would keenly interest the sixteenth-century authors. In fact, Bernard Weinberg long ago called the civilizing function of poetry a commonplace in Renaissance criticism.[2] But this commonplace has many variations to which I think it worthwhile to pay closer attention. If myths have meaning, then, as Ernst Cassirer suggested, they probably describe "a world of becoming." To my mind, the small revisions in the poetic origin myths reflect just such a world: an intellectual milieu self-consciously aware of itself in a chrysalis. We homogenize the variations in the myths at the risk of losing that incipient world and of ignoring the evolving relation of the humanist movement to its own mythography.

That mythography can be as densely layered as the branches of a family tree, and comparably difficult to disentangle. For example, the civilizing function of the *prisci poetae* does not spring full grown from Horace's forehead into the poetic treatises of the Renaissance. Rather, it emerges gradually from the more prevalent myth of the *vates* as a theologian first and a citizen second. In fact, as Craig Kallendorf has argued, "the theory of the poet as theologian became the cornerstone of humanist poetics."[3] The concept of the *poeta theologus* thrived throughout the early modern period, hardily enduring such ideological paradigm-shifts as Neoplatonism, Neo-Aristotelian poetics, and Reformation Protestantism. Moreover, it should be noted that the genealogy of the *poeta theologus* is not the same as that of Horace's *vates*, although as we

---

[1] Horace, *Ars Poetica*, Loeb Classical Library (Cambridge, MA and London, 1926; rpt. 1978), ll. 391–401.

[2] Bernard Weinberg, "The Poetic Theories of Minturno," in *Studies in Honor of Frederick W. Shipley By His Colleagues* (St. Louis, 1942), 103; cf. 110–111.

[3] Craig Kallendorf, "From Virgil to Vida: The *Poeta Theologus* in Italian Renaissance Commentary," *Journal of the History of Ideas* 56 (1995): 45.

will see the two branches eventually come together. The notion of the *poeta theologus* originates in Aristotle's *Metaphysics* where he refers to "the disciples of Hesiod and all the theologians."[4] Aristotle uses the word *theologisantes* to mean "one who speculates about the gods," distinguishing the Hesiodic *theologisantes* from philosophers and genuine poets. But the Aristotelian distinction was not preserved by later commentators, who, if they knew Aristotle at all, tended to collapse the separate categories.

Among Christian apologists for poetry the poet-as-priest became an important means of joining Hellenistic origin myths to Hebrew prophecy—in myriad commentators from Isidore to Boccaccio, Moses is cited as a *priscus poeta*, with David and Solomon following close behind. This Hebrew version of the poet-priest had little to do with Aristotle's *theologisantes*, but the grafting of the supposedly true religion onto the pagan verse forms provided a new origin myth from which later Christian poets could safely claim descent. In Isidore of Seville's *Etymologiae*, for example, Moses is credited as the Ur-poet who not only invented Hebrew letters and wrote Exodus long before Homer's time, but who also wrote in hexameters, dactyls, and spondees. Moreover, Isidore was the first commentator to define the term *vates* clearly; as Concetta Greenfield has noted, "[h]is notions reappear in every humanist treatise on poetics" until the late fifteenth century.[5] Isidore maintains that "according to Varro's authority, [the poet] was called *vates* because of the power of his [or presumably her] mind" ["Vates a vi mentis appellatos Varro auctor est"].[6] He mentions their "near madness" ["quasi vesania" (8.7.3)] and concludes with the statement that "at one time the poets were said to be Theologians because they composed songs about the gods" ["Quidam autem poetae Theologici dicti sunt, quoniam de diis carmina faciebant" (8.7.9)].

Isidore's characterization of the vates finds its way to fourteenth-century Italy virtually unchanged. Both Albertino Mussato and Petrarch subscribe to the myth of the *poeta theologus*, although their remarks are somewhat perfunctory. Soon after their efforts, however, Boccaccio produced the *De genealogia gentilium deorum*, books 14 and 15 of which contain a remarkable interweaving of origin myths liberally seasoned with the author's skepticism regarding the ancient sources and the actual date of poetry's inception. For example, Boccaccio refuses to choose among the Hebrews, the Babylonians, or the Greeks, although he agrees with the theory that praise of the Deity is the most likely origin for poetry. He suggests that it was necessary to invent a form of address suitable for the "unum esse," and that this task fell to the priests: "Some of these [priests]," he argues, "though few—and among them it was believed were Musaeus, Linus, and Orpheus—divinely moved by the prompting of the mind fashioned and devised strange songs in regulated time and measure in praise of God" ["Ex quibus aliqui, pauci tamen, quos interfuisse creduntur Museus, Lynus, et Or-

---

    ⁴ Aristotle, *Metaphysics*, trans. Richard Hope (Ann Arbor, 1960), 53 (1000b).

    ⁵ Concetta Carestia Greenfield, *Humanist and Scholastic Poetics, 1250–1500* (Lewisburg, PA, and London, 1981), 35–36.

    ⁶ Isidore of Seville, *Etymologiarium sive originum, libri xx*, 2 vols., ed. W. M. Lindsay (Oxford, 1911), 8.7.3 (no page numbers in text). Translations are mine unless otherwise noted.

pheus, quadam divine mentis instigatione conmoti, carmina peregrina mensuris et temporibus regulata finxere, et in dei laudem invenere"].[7] But, while Boccaccio repeatedly asserts that poetry springs from God's bosom, he never settles on a definitive theory of its earthly origins. Even the Greeks in the end do not satisfy him because he cannot believe that such a great art would have been bestowed on Musaeus, Linus, or Orpheus, unless—and this is a curious compromise—"as some judge, Moses and Musaeus were one and the same" ["nisi, ut arbitrantur aliqui, Musaeus et Moyses unus et idem sint" (2:704–705)]. Finally Boccaccio too subscribes to the myth of Moses as an epic poet, the Ur-figure of Isidore's *Etymologiae*.

II

I would like to turn now to Cristoforo Landino, who wrote his prefaces and commentaries nearly a century after Boccaccio's *De genealogia*. For Landino the most important development of the fifteenth century in regard to the *prisci poetae* had been Marsilio Ficino's translations of the *Hermetica* and his singing of the Orphic Hymns, along with the virtual canonization of Orpheus by the Neoplatonists. But Ficino paid little heed to the origin myths of poetry, preferring to isolate Orpheus as a semidivine figure analogous to Hermes Trismegistus. Moreover, Ficino repeatedly asserted that poets were mere instruments, who, when seized by the divine frenzy, were sounded through by the deity "as through trumpets."[8] This extreme version of the *furor poeticus* left little consciousness to the human poet, plausibly weakening the value of poetry as a useful civic virtue.

Landino seems to have taken it upon himself, as a literary critic, to temper Ficino's Orpheus and, judiciously, to socialize the divine frenzy. In myriad texts he returns to the primal scenes of poetry, integrating the origin myths into the Christianized Neoplatonic landscape, while at the same time awarding the *prisci poetae*—and by extension all their contemporary descendants—with something akin to pragmatic consciousness. He merges the Neoplatonic origin myths with the *poeta theologus* handed down from revisionary Christian tradition:

> Neque enim alius est magnus verusque poeta quam theologus, quod non solum Aristotelis tanti philosophi auctoritas testimoniumque ostendit, sed ipsorum quoque scripta apertissime docent. Duplex enim theologia est: altera quam priscam vocant, cuius divinus ille vir Mercurius cognomine Trismegistus primus fontem aperuit, altera nostra est, quae non modo verior comprobatur, sed ita verissima, ut neque addi quicquam nec imminui inde possit.[9]

---

[7] Boccaccio, *Genealogia deorum gentilium libri xv*, 2 vols, ed. V. Romano (Bari, 1951), 2: 703–704).

[8] Marsilio Ficino, *Opera Omnia*, 2 vols. (Turin, 1962; facsimile of Basel edition, 1571), 1: 614 (letter to Antonio Pelotti): "quod multa furentes canunt, et illa quidem mirabilia, quae paulō post deferuescente furore ipsimet non satis intelligunt, quasi non ipsi pronunciauerint, se Deus per eos ceu tubas clamauerit."

[9] Cristoforo Landino, *Scritti Critici e Teorici*, ed. Roberto Cardini, 2 vols. (Rome, 1974), 1: 230.

[No other poet is as great and ancient as the theologian, not only as the authority of the testimony of that great philosopher Aristotle shows, but as (the poets') writings themselves also openly teach. Theology, however, is twofold: one kind is known as the ancient theology, of which that first divine man Mercury (called Trismegistus) uncovered the source; the other kind is our theology, which not only was established more true (than the first kind), but is thus the truest, so that nothing whatever can be added or diminished thence.]

Landino deftly separates the *prisca theologia* from what he terms *nostra theologia* without losing the force of the earlier poetry. He modifies the *poeta theologus* by linking the concept to Hermes Trismegistus, thus combining the Neoplatonic program with the traditional theological authority accorded the first poets. This passage comes from Landino's introduction to the *Aeneid*. In another passage from his "Proemio al commento dantesco" he manages to bring Hermes and Moses together:

ne' più antichi secoli fu Moisé, uomo e per disciplina militare e per dottrina maraviglioso, el quale dagl'Etiopi liberó gl'Egizi e dagl'Egizi gl'Ebrei; e secondo Eupolemo greco scrittore, perché fu inventore delle letere fu dagl'Egizi chiamato Mercurio Trimegisto. (1:146)

[In more ancient times there was Moses, a man wonderful for military discipline and for doctrine, who from the Ethiopians freed the Egyptians and from the Egyptians the Hebrews; and according to the Greek writer Eupolemos, because he was the inventor of letters he was called by the Egyptians Mercurius Trismegistus.]

In terms of origin myths one could not ask for more than that last assertion, that Moses and Hermes were the same person. Not only does Landino go beyond Boccaccio's suggestion that Moses and Musaeus were identical, but his myth also confirms an archaic connection between Hebrew and pagan culture. Still, doctrine and military discipline notwithstanding, Landino quickly associates Moses with ancient *literary* culture, noting that "as is clear from his writing, [Moses] was not an ignoble poet" ["come appare ne' suoi scritti, fu poeta non ignobile" (1:146)]. He then concludes the passage by reminding us that Moses led the people from Israel when Cecrops ruled in Athens and "all the excellent things done in Greece are after the time of Cecrops" ["uomo tanto antico che quando trasse el popolo d'Israel d'Egitto, Cecrope regnava in Atene; e tutte le cose eccellenti fatte in Grecia sono dopo e' tempi di Cecrope" (1:146)]. Thus Moses, also known as Hermes Trismegistus, was the first poet of antiquity from whom all the Greek poets descended—a brilliant bit of genealogical *inventio*.

Landino returns innumerable times to the original succession of poets because, as Roberto Cardini has remarked, in showing that the poets were present at the foundation of civilization he can demonstrate the preëminence of poetry in all the liberal disciplines.[10] Consequently he associates the pagan *prisci poetae*—Orpheus, Linus,

---

[10] Roberto Cardini, *La Critica del Landino* (Florence, 1973), 85; cf. Landino, *Scritti*, 2: 49.

Musaeus, and Amphion—with the *prisca theologia*. Again in his introduction to the *Aeneid*, following the passage quoted above, Landino asks:

> In prisca igitur nonne Orpheus ita versatur, ut multa de Deo, multa de angelis, multa de incorporeis mentibus, multa de humanis animis describat? Is enim ostendit Deum unum esse, eundemque ubique nullis locis aut temporibus circunscriptum esse, omnia agere, omnia servare, in omnibus operari. (1:230)

> [Is not Orpheus therefore versed in ancient theology, insofar as he describes many things about God, angels, bodiless intellects, and human souls? He thereby reveals the one God to be everywhere the same and bounded by no place or time, to set all things in motion, to serve all things, and to be at work in everything.]

So Orpheus can join Moses as a purveyor of the poetic truth, since in singing about the many gods he in fact paradoxically proves that everything is linked by "Deum unum . . . ubique" [one God everywhere]. Landino suggests that the same might be said of the other *prisci poetae* and, for that matter, even of Homer. Invariably his impulse is to allegorize the pagan texts as a means of refitting the ancient myths to modern rationalizations. But in doing so he rescues the *prisci poetae* from denunciation and integrates them into a genealogy that now embraces not only Hebrew origins but also the newly translated Hermetic manuscripts.

This amalgamated genealogy is not all that Landino offers, however. As I suggested earlier, he also grafts the Horatian idealization of the *vates* onto the *prisca theologia*, thus adducing a civic function to the poet's ancient divinity. Here is his version of Horace's primal scene:

> veggiamo in Orfeo, el quale per nessuna altra cagione dicono avere con la citara potuto fermare e' fiumi, muovere e' sassi, mitigare le fiere, se non perché con la suavitá de' suoi versi poté reprimere l'empito e el furore di molti, e' quali nelle forze del corpo fidandosi tutti gl'altri abbattevono e conculcavono, e altri e' quali erono d'efferato ingegno o stupido o quasi insensati condusse a vita razionale e civile. . . . Similmente interpreterremo che Anfione con sua citera [*sic*] movessi le pietre a congiugnersi e fare le tebane mura; perché con la suavitá de' versi gl'uomini e' quali sanza leggi, sanza costumi vagando pe' propinqui monti vivevono in solitudine, ridusse insieme e mollificando la lor dureza gli compose in vita civile. (1:145)

> [We see (the genius and diligence mentioned above) in Orpheus, who they say with his cithara made rivers stop, stones move, fires cease, for no other reason than that with the sweetness of his verses he was able to hold back the violence and the fury of many, who, placing faith in the power of the body, attacked and violated each other; others as well who were of savage mind or were foolish or almost without sense he brought to civil and rational life. . . . Similarly we understand that Amphion with his cithara moved the stones to join themselves together and make the Theban walls; for with the sweetness of his verses the men who lived without laws, without customs wandering the nearby

mountains in solitude, he brought together and, mollifying their harshness, organized them in civil life.]

In echoing Horace so closely this passage might be seen as a challenge to the Neo-platonic Orpheus. For instance, Orpheus and Amphion are remarkably similar, just as they are in the *Ars poetica* but as they never could be for Ficino. Orpheus moves stones as well as stopping rivers and extinguishing fires, rare miracles only occasionally associated with his legend, yet his poetic magic is unencumbered by doctrine. Equally significant is Landino's observation that both poets "reduced" humanity from savagery to "civil and rational life." In this remark we see that the theological role of these first civilizers dovetails with their social responsibilities. These poets are not Ficinian trumpets, infused with a rhapsodic divine frenzy. Landino resists the extreme notion of the ventriloquized poet. He combines the divine auspices of Moses and Hermes with the pragmatic civic function of Horace's *prisci poetae*, deliberately noting that Orpheus and Amphion brought rationality to the barbarism of prehistoric times. For Landino, more definitively than for his predecessors, metrical language, worship of the gods, divine frenzy, theological doctrine, moral law, and civil society all share the same origin myth. His signal contribution to the origin myths, therefore, is the balancing of the supra-rational with the rational, the integration of the *poeta theologus* with a poetic prototype of the civic humanist as administrator, governor, and educator.

III

Although it is difficult to generalize about the many sixteenth-century treatises, we should nevertheless recognize that after Landino the categories and classifications of the *prisci poetae* began to change. I am not sure how far we can credit Landino himself with influencing the changes, beyond noting the popularity of his commentaries on Virgil and Dante. More important may be the increasing interest in Horace and the proliferation of commentaries on the *Odes* and *Epistles*. Many treatise-writers, such as Bernardino Daniello in 1536, simply re-write Horace's primal scene of poetry, taking more or less for granted that the poet is chiefly a civilizer who also knows "the things of God and Nature" ["quelle anchora di Dio et di Natura"].[11] But Horace is not the whole story. As is well known, the evolution of interest in Horace coincided with the rediscovery of Aristotle's *Poetics* and the development of Aristotelian classifications. While a number of militant Aristotelians eventually emerged, the most influential treatises seem to offer a more moderate, if quirky, mixture of Horace, Plato, Aristotle, and a bit of homegrown theory. Where the *prisci poetae* are concerned, this tendency to mix theories results in a pronounced secularization, as is evident, for example, in Antonio Minturno's *De poeta* of 1559.

Minturno treats the origins of poetry historically, without skepticism but also without awe. He calls poetry the first form of writing:

---

[11] Bernardino Daniello, *La Poetica*, reprint ed. Bernhard Fabian (Munich, 1968), 11.

Quam ob rem cùm prisca illa secula erudita, et elegantia fuisse sit conceden-
dum, nec aliud scribendi genus, atque Poëticum, iam vigeret, affirmandum est,
quacunque de re esset aliquid explicandum, id versibus commendari opor-
tuisse.[12]

[Hence it is understood that during the first erudite and elegant age, there was
no other kind of writing than Poetry, which, as is affirmed, was much esteemed: it was customary to write in verses whatever subject might have been
enlarged upon.]

Acknowledging Apollo as the source of poetry, Minturno goes on to discuss the
function of the *prisci poetae* among the ancients:

Deorum . . . filii de rebus divinis, Linus, quem debuit Pater Phoebus erudire,
et Orpheus, qui potuit à matre Calliope didicisse, ut Deos laudare, ut precari
deberemus, ornatissima carmina condiderunt. (14)

[The sons of the gods composed highly embellished songs about divine things,
in order to praise the gods in the manner that (in those times) we were obliged
to make entreaties—Linus, whom Father Phoebus was bound to instruct, and
Orpheus, who was enabled by his mother Calliope to disseminate (his songs).]

This passage somewhat echoes Boccaccio's idea that the first poets were chosen to
address the gods because vulgar language was inappropriate to divine praise.

Minturno describes a descent of poetry that begins with pre-Socratic philosophy,
issuing in the divine Poemata and praising what he terms "other gods and other
origins." This material would be found in Thales, Anaximander, Xenophon, Empe-
docles, and Pythagoras—would be found there, that is, if we had their works. He
explains that poetry acts to preserve the ancient ideas, providing an invaluable service
to culture. With his eye on their service, Minturno recalls that Amphion built the
Theban walls and that Orpheus "reduced" ["deduxisset"] the wild animals, the for-
ests, and the mountains, civilizing society by taming the wilderness and erecting walls
to defend against enemies:

Civibus autem ita in unum locum congregatis iura et instituta Poëticis condita
numeris fuisse facile concesserit, qui memoria repetierit in Hispania quondam
Turdetanos, qui sapientiam coluisse plurimum gloriabantur, solitos esse mirifi-
cae vetustatis monimenta, legesque versibus descriptas ostendere. (15)

[Thus he (or she) will easily grant (my point), who will remember that the
erstwhile Turdantanians in Spain, who boasted exceedingly of having cultivated
wisdom, were accustomed to show that the rights and ordinances of society
were preserved in poetry to exhibit in verse descriptions customs, monuments,
and laws of extraordinary antiquity.]

---

[12] Antonio Minturno, *De poeta*, reprint ed. Bernhard Fabian (Munich, 1970), 14.

The juxtaposition of the *prisci poetae* and the lost works of the ancient philosophers is provocative. It allows us to conjecture that, for Minturno, the importance of poetry is coterminous with the survival of culture: the poets not only establish the first civic institutions, but through their verse they also preserve the most meaningful cultural artifacts of antiquity.

In the *De poeta* the *prisci poetae* have vast, somewhat undefined powers. Yet Minturno stops just short of calling these first poets theologians, even though he refers to them in his marginal note as *vates*. The marginal note is interesting:

> Poetae omnes Qui vates, aut sacerdotes erant, quique Remp. gubernabanti.
> (15, margin)

There may be an allusion to Cicero's *Pro Roscio Amerino* in the use of "Remp." with a variation of "gubernare." But in any case the important connection is that of the vates with the civic responsibility of directing the republic. In the body of the text Minturno offers this summary:

> Quapropter qui apud priscos illos veteres essent interpretes Deorum, et sacer-
> dotes, qui sapientes, qui eloquentes haberuntur, qui rectè, ac prudenter in pu-
> blicis rebus versarentur, omnes Poëtae dicebantur. (15)

> [Wherefore, among those first ancient ones, who were the interpreters of the
> gods who had both wisdom and eloquence, (and) who were justly and pru-
> dently engaged in public matters—all were called poets.]

The burden of Minturno's message is the poet's comprehensive public function. His *prisci poetae* may be privy to divine wisdom, but they display that wisdom in social contexts—as tamers, builders, and lawgivers. This universal centrality of the poet, and particularly the civic or public emphasis, while echoing Horace, extends the primal scenes of poetry to something more accessible to sixteenth-century sensibility: specifically, the governance of an idealized republic. A few years later in his vernacular treatise, *L'Arte poetica della poesia toscana*, Minturno calls poetry "queen of all the sciences" ["di tutte le scienze reina"] and names the Muses "governatrici di tutte le cose."[13] As much as any other critic, Minturno underscores the analogy between the *res publica* and the so-called *res publica litterarum*.

Without oversimplifying his treatment of the *prisci poetae*, it is plausible, I think, to note in Minturno's treatise a secularization of the origins of poetry. Minturno was a bishop, and he could hardly exclude the *poeta theologus* from his conception. But he never mentions such a figure by name in the *De poeta*, and he shies away from the association of Orpheus, Linus, or Amphion with patently theological truths. In the *Arte poetica* he lists the "theologi" with Moses, the Prophets, Orpheus, Linus, Mercury, Homer, and Pythagoras, adding the Evangelists for good measure. But the point of the genealogical catalogue is to associate a particular set of techniques with highly regarded philosophical and religious truths, rather than to establish the primacy of

---

[13] Antonio Minturno, *L'Arte poetica* (Naples, 1725), Preface (unnumbered first page).

theological doctrine. This association provides an imprimatur for poetic production. Yet Minturno seems just as intent on distinguishing poetry as a consistently practiced skill from among the welter of ideological, spiritual, and nationalistic discourses with which it has become confused. He mixes Hebrews, Greeks, and Christians in the passage in the *Arte poetica* only to extract from the mixture a stable notion of poetic feigning.

Minturno's revisions of emphasis have counterparts throughout the second half of the sixteenth century. Indeed, with a little creative interpretation of the primal scenes, commentators were able to expand the contributions of the *prisci poetae*. For instance, the English critic George Puttenham, supplementing the categories of lawgiver, governor, and philosopher, adds that poets were also the first astronomers, historiographers, musicians, and politicians.[14]

Of course, it is difficult to draw exact correspondences between changes in the origin myths of poetry and new social or literary concerns among humanist writers. Yet I think it would be useful to recognize the transition that I have sketched briefly in this paper. The impulse among Renaissance literary critics to alter the myths of the *prisci poetae* reflects a comparable impulse among intellectuals in different disciplines to revise, re-invent, and reinscribe other cultural myths in pursuit of rationalizations for new religions, new conquests, and new modes of moral conduct.

University of Maryland, Baltimore County

---

[14] George Puttenham, *The Arte of English Poesie* (facsimile), with an introduction by Baxter Hathaway (Kent, OH, 1988), 24–25.

Ecos de Tácito en los
Indices rerum ab Aragoniae Regibus gestarum
de Zurita

Mª VICTORIA FERNÁNDEZ–SAVATER MARTÍN

Jerónimo de Zurita y Castro (1512–1580), nacido en Zaragoza, de ilustre familia (del linaje de los Zuritas de la Villa de Mosqueruela, según Latassa[1]), llevó a cabo sus estudios en Alcalá de Henares, y llegó a dominar el latín y el griego. Así mismo aprendió francés, italiano, portugués, catalán y valenciano. Ejerció desde su adolescencia cargos de relevancia; Carlos V lo nombró Merino de Barbastro y Almudévar, y Continuo de la casa Real. Ya en su madurez, en 1566, fue escogido por Felipe II como secretario de su Consejo y Cámara. Sin embargo, una de sus principales actividades, junto con la de secretario del Santo Oficio, y que es precisamente la que me trae hoy aquí, fue la que desarrolló a partir de 1548 cuando es nombrado primer Cronista del reino de Aragón.

Los diputados de aquellas Cortes acordaron que, como cronista, al llevar a cabo su obra, hiciera "dicha Coronica una en romance y otra en latín", para que "fuese más universal la noticia de nuestras acciones"[2].

Como cronista de Aragón, Zurita llevó a cabo, en castellano, su más grande e importante obra, a la que dedicó 30 años de su vida: *Anales de la Corona de Aragón*, extensa crónica dividida en diez libros. Pero, a la vez, y siguiendo el deseo de los diputados del reino de Aragón, como él mismo señala en el Prólogo a su obra latina, "… dum ea, quae … decem superioribus libris annalium accommodare nitimur, in ueritatis lucem patrio sermone proferuntur …," se dedica a llevar a término en latín, "ex multiplici et perpetuo annalium contextu summas quasdam …"; estos resúmenes

---

[1] *Bibliotecas antigua y nueva de escritores aragoneses* de Latassa, aumentadas y refundidas en forma de diccionario biográfico-bibliográfico por M. Gómez Uriel (Zaragoza, 1885).

[2] Latassa, *Escritores aragoneses,* ed. Gómez, 429.

son los *Indices Rerum ab Aragoniae Regibus gestarum*[3]. Se trata de un epítome de los dos tomos de la primera parte de los *Anales*, concebidos como preparación y ayuda para su gran obra histórica en castellano, y que comprenden desde los orígenes del reino hasta 1410.

Zurita, que debía de ser un hombre verdaderamente culto, según dice Angel Canellas en su edición de los *Anales*, "ha bebido con singular delectación los textos de prosistas historiadores, y entre estos ha hallado un alma gemela a sus gustos, en la obra ingente de Publio Cornelio Tácito". Reconozco que fue precisamente la admiración por Tácito[4] que siente Zurita, y que comparto sin reservas, la que me animó a comenzar un estudio que rastrease las huellas del clásico en el humanista. Trabajo del que hoy tan sólo puedo ofrecerles los primeros y vacilantes pasos. En este estudio que acabo de emprender, trato de determinar mediante un examen detenido, es decir lectura atenta y repetida, en qué aspectos y hasta qué extremos llega la influencia de los *Annales* de Tácito en la obra latina de Zurita[5]. Digo en la obra latina por que, desde luego esta influencia se extiende también a la obra castellana, no sólo en el método histórico que se sigue en ella, sino también en la forma de narrar, en el estilo; lo que acarrea como consecuencia que una de las características más destacadas de los *Anales* sea la obscuridad, y la dificultad de su lectura.

Pero volvamos a la obra latina y comencemos por examinar esta influencia en su manifestación más global: Zurita ya trasluce su relación con Tácito en la forma de exponer la historia; sigue estrictamente el método analístico, adoptando el viejo principio de la exposición año por año pues le parece la más útil; así lo dice en su Prólogo a los *Indices*, entre ". . . tam uaria ac paene infinita rerum commemoratione . . ." señalará "origines ipsas . . . conexa temporum serie," lo que según él, "magno mihi usu fuisse saepe". Y así lo hace indicando en el margen de su obra explícitamente los años en los que van sucediendo los acontecimientos y, en ocasiones, también los días.

En lo que a la intención del autor se refiere, recordemos que Tácito, en un momento de sus *Annales*[6], precisa que no señalará entre las propuestas hechas al Senado "nisi insignis per honestum aut notabili dedecore", y lo hace así, "quod praecipuum munus annalium reor, ne uirtutes sileantur utque prauis dictis factisque ex posteritate et infamia metus sit."(III, 65) Zurita recuerda y hace suya la mitad de esta opinión de Tácito acerca de la labor del analista, cuando, de nuevo en el Prólogo de su obra, asegura que intenta sacar a la luz ". . . tot inuoluta signa uirtutis et probitatis". Nada dice de los ejemplos nefastos, quizás para resaltar la parte positiva de la historia,

---

[3] La obra, en tres libros, fue publicada por Domingo de Portonariis de Ursinis en Zaragoza en 1578 y reeditada por Andres Schott en Francfurt, 1606, en su *Hispania Illustrata,* tomo III.

[4] Encontrar un escritor renacentista que abandone el modelo ciceroniano para seguir a Tácito es realmente sorprendente; parece avanzado para su tiempo.

[5] Me animan a seguir mi investigación las palabras de un estudioso de la talla de J. Mª Maestre Maestre, cuando afirma que "Faltan investigaciones que hayan intentado comprobar el lógico impacto de la *receptio* en la prosa latina de los humanistas . . ." :"En torno a la prosa latina de los humanistas: el tacitismo de Juan de Verzosa", en *La recepción de las Artes Clásicas en el siglo XVI* (Cáceres, 1996), 231.

[6] Cito la edición de Heinz Heubner (Stuttgart, 1983).

aunque veremos más adelante que, si bien no se muestra, desde luego, tan durísimo como Tácito, si comparte con él la visión turbulenta de muchos de los acontecimientos que narra.

De sobra conocidas son las palabras que Tácito incluye al inicio de sus *Annales* y que se interpretan como una declaración de principios del autor a la hora de narrar la historia: "sine ira et studio" ("sin encono ni parcialidad"). Se trata sin duda este de un intento de imparcialidad del que no es momento para discutir si alcanzó o no el éxito pretendido. Lo que nos interesa es la búsqueda por parte del historiador de la objetividad, cualidad que necesita para materializarse que no haya "ni encono, ni parcialidad", esto significa verdad en el relato y, sin duda, libertad, externa o interna, a la hora de narrar. Pues bien, ahora es Zurita quien, no al comienzo de la obra sino durante su desarrollo como Tácito en otras ocasiones, hace su declaración de principios también en términos de "verdad" y "libertad", cuando asegura que "vere et libere ut institutum nostrum postulat, hoc dici potest . . ." (Año 1387. Lib. III, 365).

También investigador serio como Tácito, cita Zurita entre sus fuentes documentos oficiales, algunos de cuyos textos, esto no lo hace Tácito, inserta en su relato. Sin embargo, también como Tácito, la mayor parte de las veces recurre a testimonios anónimos que se repiten con mucha frecuencia; si en Tácito encontramos "ferebatur, dicerentur, quidam sunt qui existiment . . .", e incluso en alusión más evidente a consulta de fuentes: "diuersa non modo apud auctores sed in ipsius orationibus reperiuntur . . .", cita Zurita, así mismo, testimonios anónimos del tipo "satis constat . . .", pero también de consulta de fuentes: "maior scriptorum pars . . . , extant uetusti annales . . .", e incluso: "cum aequalibus illis temporibus scriptor nullus extet in summa obscuritate rerum gestarum uersamur . . ."

Es momento de pasar al texto mismo de la historia, para señalar algunos momentos de ella en la que se aprecian rasgos taciteos. Iremos de aspectos más generales y repetidos, los que más destacaron cuando iniciamos el acercamiento, hasta algún detalle particular, calco del autor clásico.

Desde la primera lectura de los tres libros de los *Indices* de Zurita, la obra de este autor "suena" a Tácito, y empleo "suena" literalmente porque hay en la sintáxis de Zurita un empleo de los usos de Tácito, y esto se ve y se oye. Me estoy refiriendo concretamente y en primer lugar, a la ausencia total de discurso en estilo directo; es cierto que domina totalmente en el epítome la narración, se trata de un resumen, pero en las ocasiones en que un personaje podría haber tomado la palabra, Zurita la reproduce empleando, normalmente, la subordinación, con gran profusión de oraciones de infinitivo; esto ocurre incluso en los escasos discursos que aparecen, porque en los *Indices*, contra lo que sucede en los *Annales*, no hay nunca reproducción de discursos[7].

La presencia constante del "discurso trasladado"[8] en Zurita, hizo que yo aplazara la idea de recoger los testimonios de éste en la totalidad de los *Indices* y, lo que sería

---

[7] Los únicos textos en estilo directo son los documentos reales que el autor incluye de vez en cuando en su crónica.

[8] Cf. Gerard Genette, *Nouveau discours du récit* (París, 1983).

aun más ambicioso, pero interesante, compararlos con su empleo en Tácito. En este primer estadio de mi trabajo, les pido que confien en mi lectura de Zurita. Por ahora, simplemente les ofrezco un ejemplo:

Discurso de Martín I

In eo consessu, una in orbe terrarum Aragonensium rationem regium imperio fidelissima haberi praedicat: atque in omni fortuna perutilem semper Regibus eius gentis operam, atque fidelitatem fuisse: eosque veros esse Celtiberos: qui superesse proelio nefas ducerent, cum is occidisset, pro cuius salute spiritum deuouerant. Demum pollicetur accitu suo, se Siciliam Regem filium arcessiturum: ut prouideat, praesensque animum intendat, qua ratione leges, institutaque maiorum sarta tecta ab omni vi, impressioneque conseruentur. Nam adepto, aditoque regno, graue id nimis regnandi impotentia, principibus visum iri: quod cetera regna, non ratione legibus parendi, sed repentina, maiore ex parte, voluntatum inclinatione, gubernentur. (Año 1404; Lib. III, p. 391)

En segundo lugar hace Zurita un constante y variado uso de las construcciones participiales que trae a la memoria, sin duda, la forma en la que Syme[9], en su imprescindible estudio sobre el historiador latino, se refiere el empleo que éste hace del participio; Syme, muy descriptivamente, dice que en Tacito "the participle becomes omnicompetent"[10]. Intentar presentarles aquí una relación de las construcciones participiales, tanto en Zurita como en Tácito, hubiera sido aún menos factible que lo anterior: el material sería inabarcable. Así pues, de nuevo, y de momento, se tendrán que conformar sólo con mi palabra; también como botón de muestra, les propongo el siguiente ejemplo:

Pactos de Enrique de Trastamara

Henricus Trastamarensis ingentes copias ex Gallia, in expeditionem aduersus fratrem educens, . . . , Montionem ingreditur. Eius aduentu, facta commutatione rerum, admirabili, et prope incredibili confidentia regnum appetens, Rege fratre praepotenti, et rebus feliciter gestis victore, et rerum potiente, et Ferdinando iusto, ac legitimo regni herede, in aetatis flore proceres paene omnes Castellae in suas partes omni cautione, et foedere deuincente, Regis fidem in eam diem, et stipendia secutus, . . . cum rege transigit: suadetque, ut se regali solio deturbantem fratrem, regnumque occupantem, atque inuadentem iuuet, tueatur, atque conseruet. (Año 1363; Lib. III, 324)

En tercer lugar, encontramos en los *Indices* un recurso sintáctico-estilístico, de extensión más limitada, que Zurita toma sin ningún género de dudas de Tácito. Concretamente me estoy refiriendo a esas dos posibles causas de un hecho que Tácito presenta en forma de disyuntiva, como para que el lector escoja la que le parezca más verosímil, es decir: "causa offensione Vistilo fuit seu composuerat quaedam in C. Caesar ut impudicum, siue ficto habita fides". (VI,9)

---

[9] Ronald Syme, *Tacitus*, 2 vols. (Oxford, 1989).
[10] Syme, *Tacitus*, I: 347.

Las alternativas sólo en alguna ocasión son atribuidas a la opinión popular: "morte fortuita an per uenenum extinctus esset, ut quisque credidit, uulgauere" (XII,52). En el resto de los casos son razones esgrimidas por el propio autor.

Se trata éste de un rasgo muy taciteo que a mi siempre me ha parecido definitorio del autor, porque, aunque estilísticamente llegue a parecer algo casi formular (y en Tácito la repetición, tampoco carece de sentido), al mismo tiempo, cada vez que se presenta, es la manifestación de una reflexión única y personal del autor en la búsqueda de las posibles causas de un acontecimiento o de un actuar concreto.

A Tácito le interesan las causas; su búsqueda es constante: "causa eius mutationis quaerere libet"; y no duda en señalarla cuando cree conocerla: "haec causa necis . . . , scelerum causae . . . , causas odiorum . . . , causae irarum . . . , belli causa . . . , cladis causa . . . , causa tam prauae morae, . . .". Pues bien, también Zurita, quien ha aprendido de Tácito que es importante buscar las causas y comparte con él esta inquietud, cuando reconoce en el Prólogo su estilo repetitivo precisa: "sed . . . fastidiose hoc arido et austero modo, . . . tum a primo repetitionibus temporum, tum in extremum non modo casuum, et euentorum, sed rationum et causarum . . . recidentibus repetitionibus explicarim".

He recogido, si no todos, la mayoría de los textos de los *Annales* de Tácito en los que se plantea la disyuntiva, y todos los que aparecen en la edición de Zurita que manejo.

TACITO:

1.   . . . sincera adhuc inter matrem filiumque concordia **siue** occultis odiis. (III,64)

2.   . . . Tiberioque etiam in rebus quas non occuleret, **seu** natura **siue** adsuetudine, suspensa semper et oscura uerba. (I,11,2)

3.   . . . is fatali quodam motu . . . **seu** praua sollertia . . . (V,4)

4.   . . . neque enim segnem ei fuisse indolem ferunt, **siue** uerum, **seu** periculis commendatus retinuit famam . . . (XII,26)

5.   . . . **siue** explenda simulatione, **seu** periturae matris supremus adspectus quamuis ferum animum retinebat. (XIV,4)

6.   . . . caesis Hirtio et Pansa, **siue** hostis illos, **seu** Pansam uenenum uulneri adfusum, sui milites Hirtium . . . (I,10)

7.   . . . interrogantibus quid adspiceret, respondisse tempestatem ab Ostia atrocem, **siue** coeperat ea species, **seu** forte lapsa vox in praesagium uertit. (XI,31)

8.   . . . legiones, metu **an** contumacia, locum deseruere . . . (I,65)

9.   . . . eaque perfecta, contemptu ambitionis **an** per senectutem, haud dedicauit. (VI,45)

10.   . . . morte fortuita **an** per uenenum extinctus est. (XII,52)

11.   . . . nec uim medicaminis statim intellectam, socordiane **an** Claudii uinolentia. (XII, 67)

12.   . . . incertum metu **an** per inuidiam. (I,11)

13.   . . . Tiberius . . . nullo metu **an** ut firmitudinem animi ostentaret. (IV,8)

14.   . . . quando uxore ab Octauia, . . . fato quodam, **an** quia praeualent inlicita, abhorrebat. (XIII,12)

15.   ... ut solitum egit, altitudine animi, **an** compererat modica esse et uulgatis leuiora. (III,44)

16.   ... inferius maiestate sua rati, ..., **an** ne omnium oculis uultum eorum scrutantis falsi intelleguntur. (III,3)

17.   ... Vologaeses, quo bellum ex commodo pararet, **an** ut aemulationes suspectos ... amoueret. (XIII,9)

18.   ... uelata parte oris, ne satiaret adspectum, **uel** quia sic decebat. (XIII,45)

ZURITA:

1.   ... **siue** eorum culpa, **siue** infelicitate Imperatoris, ignominiosa clades accepta. (Lib. II, 238)

2.   ... Leonora Regina intimo in privignum odio **siue** metu concitata ... (Lib. III, 256)

3.   ... satis ex vetustis monumentis constat, a Raimundo fratre, **seu** dira regnandi cupidine, **siue** caeca, ac temeraria ulciscendi insania, fuisse interemptum ... (Lib. I, 32)

4.   ... quod Rex uxori ... probrum intulerat, **siue** Caiae filiae illuserat. (Lib. I, 2)

5.   **Siue** fieri diuortium et affinitatis dissidium Rex doleret, **seu** quod nouas res moliretur; (Lib. I, 46)

6.   ... **siue** quod vetustas credidit, eius ferae vixus noxius sit ... **seu** quod credibile est, immodica exercitatione, et graui immoderatoque cibo obstupefactamente contexerit animum ... (Lib. III, 375)

7.   Nam **siue** ludibrio et despectui se omnibus esse videns, illustre exemplum edi voluit, **siue** maior procerum pars ab eo defecisset. (Lib. I, 62)

8.   Initia regni Alfonsi Regis ... pacata fuisse comperio: **siue** occisis Alcobacensi proelio hostium rebus ... **siue** ad Castellanas res conuersus, propagandi imperii cupidine concitatus ... (Lib. I, 44)

9.   Post finitima vi, **vel** metu subacta castrorum et castellorum munimentis oppleta Aragonia est ... (Lib. I, 33)

Como verán, frente a Tácito, quien, fiel a su estilo, hace gala de una mayor *uariatio*[11] para expresar la disyunción y la causalidad, Zurita se limita al uso de las conjunciones *siue* y *seu* fundamentalmente; claro que a Zurita no le podemos reprochar la monotonía, pues como hemos visto ya se ha acusado de ella en su Prólogo.

En lo que a las causas mismas esgrimidas por los historiadores, vemos que Tácito, excepto en los ejemplos 6, 7, 10 y 11, interpreta los condicionamientos internos que llevan a las diferentes actitudes, incluso hay un esbozo de frase sentenciosa de alcance general, a las que es tan aficionado: *quia preualent inlicita*. Zurita, por su parte, hace intentos psicologistas en el ejemplo 3 y 5, e insinúa algo también en el 1 y 7.

Dejo el ejemplo 2, que podría muy bien haber pertenecido al propio Tácito, para el final porque me ayudará a enlazar con el siguiente aspecto que quiero comentarles; hay duras palabras en este texto, palabras como *odium* que no son, ni mucho menos, infrecuentes en Zurita.

---

[11] Este aspecto merecería un comentario profundo que no es hoy la finalidad de mi trabajo, aunque espero llevarlo a cabo pronto.

Dice también Syme en el estudio antes aludido[12] y refiriéndose explícitamente a los *Annales* de Tácito que: "his theme was savage and sinister, with no place for hope or ease or happiness", y sigue diciendo que hay que señalar que "among other words of his predilection are *acer* and *atrox* . . ." a estas a mi me gustaría añadir *odium*, incluso *ira*.

El tema de Zurita también se muestra en muchos momentos salvaje y siniestro; Zurita está tratando en un mundo de poderosos, al fin y al cabo, como Tácito, de la lucha por el poder, y sobre todo la forma de mantenerse en él. Los enfrentamientos, las emboscadas, los resentimientos, el odio, en una palabra, dominan gran parte de las relaciones que en la historia de Zurita tienen lugar. O, al menos, así lo ve e interpreta Zurita con un enfoque similar al que Tácito dió a los acontecimientos de su historia.

Es innecesario recordar a todos aquellos que hayan leído a Tácito, la multitud de veces que se hace mención expresa del odio: el odio del pueblo al emperador, de éste hacia su madre, odio de ésta hacia todo aquel que se interponga en el camino de su hijo o que pueda aminorar su influencia sobre él: esposa, amante, confidente; el odio del pueblo hacia personajes siniestros como Sejano y Tigelino, los odios de ambos hacia todos los demás . . .

Sentimientos turbulentos como el odio y la ira se repiten también en la obra de Zurita. Así, entre otros muchos:

Odio al rey: ". . . caede Caprerae patrata Regi tali facinore incredibile odium . . . procerum omnium contrahitur". (Año 1364, Lib. III, 332)
Odio al papa: "Inde magnum Philippi Regis adversus Pontificen odium . . .". (Año 1302, Lib. II)
Odio entre padre e hijo: "Dionysius Portugalliae Rex et Alphonsus eius filius, qui patrem regno evertere summe concupivit, capitali odio inter se dissident". (Año 1320, Lib. II)

Igualmente, por supuesto, es posible encontrar en el texto del humanista los duros y favoritos términos de Tácito: *acerbum odium*[13] (en 3 ocasiones), *acre bellum* (en 3 ocasiones), *atrox bellum* (en 3 ocasiones).

Zurita, que como Tácito[14] no hace retratos de sus personajes, sí los describe indirectamente por sus acciones y sentimientos, por su carácter. He encontrado un ejemplo de personaje masculino en la obra de Zurita, de gran carácter y dominado por la ira cuya actitud final el aragonés parece identificar con la de un personaje de los *Annales*, mediante un sintagma que tan sólo aparece una vez en esta obra: "Petrus Castellae . . . ira exardescens et pro rei indignitate concitatus . . . mentis insania ac furore et ira efferato . . ." ¿Le recuerda al cronista este rey a Agripina, la esposa de Germánico, mujer *ingens animi*, que tenía como rasgo importante de carácter, según su marido, la *ferociam*? Tácito describe su forma de sentir, después de las agresiones su-

---

[12] Syme, *Tacitus*, I: 348.

[13] Las expresiones *summo odio* y *magno odio* aparecen tanto en los *Annales* como en los *Indices* sólo en una ocasión.

[14] Tan sólo el magistral e irrepetible de Tiberio.

fridas, cuando enferma recibe a Tiberio, como *peruicax irae*[15], "obstinada en su ira" (IV, 53,1). Pues bien, Pedro de Castilla, también *praeferocis animi* . . . , sintiéndose injuriado, "irae pervicax et scelerum ferox spes omnem pacem perpetuo eripit".

En este mundo de poderosos, del que trata Zurita, en el que los pactos, las alianzas y los matrimonios convenidos están a la orden del día, a un rey no se le permite permanecer "solo" jamás. Los reyes enviudan o repudian a sus esposas y tiene lugar el nuevo matrimonio; así, los hijos de una madre y otra se suceden y están allí para disputar la herencia del padre. Aparece entonces una figura que Zurita resalta identificándola totalmente con la que su modelo Tácito había tratado magistralmente en sus *Annales*, convirtiéndola en inmortal: la *noverca*, la madrastra. Supongo que a Zurita al caracterizar los sentimientos de sus madrastras, le era imposible o no quería olvidar, los términos en los que Tácito se refiere a los de Livia.

Hay en los *Indices* de Zurita 2 historias de madrastras. La primera es la de un infante Pedro que se siente desbancado parcialmente por el infante Fernando, hijo de la nueva esposa de su padre, la reina Leonor. Y es que el rey padre estaba *uxorio arbitrio deuinctus*, así que el hijastro heredero ha de huir *metu nouercae*. Y tenía motivos para ello, pues, según nos dice después Zurita la madrastra Leonor sentía *acerbum in priuignum odium*. (Año 1333, Lib. III, 254). Cuando llega el momento de que el *priuignus* acepte los legados que se han hecho a su hermanastro, no lo hace, pues está **nouercalibus odiis** *imbutus* . . . (Año 1334, Lib. III, 256). Como **nouercalibus odiis** seguramente mató Livia a su nieto Agripa Póstumo (I, 6,11); y precisamente para evitar estos sentimientos, Narciso recomienda a Claudio que se case con Antonia, familiar directo, que no mirará a sus hijos **nouercalibus odiis** (XII, 2,3).

Depués es el infante Juan, hijo del anterior una vez convertido en el rey Pedro IV de Aragón, quien se ve despojado de su condición de heredero. Y recurre al Justicia de Aragón, "exploratis in se patris **nouercae odiis**" (Año 1386, Lib.III, 359). En este caso parece que Zurita está recordando la historia que Tácito cuenta acerca de Radamisto (XII, 44), hijo de Faresmanes rey de los Iberos. Aquel deseaba el reino de su padre y por ello, *simulata aduersus patrem discordia tamquam* **nouercae odiis** *impar pargit ad patruum*. Creo que es la presencia del padre junto a la madrastra, la que fuerza el *nouercae odiis* de Zurita, que aparece sólo en este contexto en Tácito.

Zurita cuenta como el odio de la madrastra se dirigirá ahora también contra la esposa del heredero, doña Violante, pues, contra el deseo de su padre y madrastra, "Iohanes . . . Iolantem filiam Berensis Ducis . . . ducit". Como consecuencia se produce el cisma familiar, que Zurita nos cuenta en estos términos: "Eo feminarum aemulatio eruperat ut in partes domum regiam distraxerit" (Año 1384, Lib. III, 357). Al hacerlo, sin duda, tiene en mente un episodio de los *Annales* en el que también peligra la unidad de la casa Imperial y están implicadas dos mujeres: Sejano trata de convencer a Tiberio de que le permita casarse con Livia, hermana de Germánico; Tibero, dudoso, le plantea los problemas que existen para ello: ". . . simplicius acturum, de inimicitiis primum Agrippinae, quas longe acrius arsuras, si matrimonium Liviae

---

[15] Aparece únicamente esta vez en los *Annales*.

velut in partes domum Caesarum distraxisset. sic quoque *erumpere aemulationem feminarum . . ."* (IV, 40).

Pero es el momento en el que Zurita trata de describir la relación nefasta de madrastra y nuera, cuando sin ambajes, ni cambio alguno, recurre a Tácito palabra por palabra: haciendo del comportamiento de doña Leonor hacia Violante una réplica exacta del de Livia hacia Agripina.

Zurita:

> *Accedebant muliebres offensiones nouercalibus* Reginae *in* Iolantem *stimulis.* (Año 1387, Lib. III, 361)

Tácito:

> *Accedebant muliebres offensiones nouercalibus* Liuiae *in* Agrippinam *stimulis . . .* (I, 33,3)

Y ya que estamos en ello, sería interesante comentar el tratamiento que de las mujeres hacen ambos autores, pero como hemos de terminar ya, sólo les haré una breve anotación relacionada con este adjetivo usado por Zurita y tan querido para Tácito: *muliebris*. En ambos siempre es despectivo, aquí también Zurita aprende de Tácito; tanto, que vean la forma que tienen los dos de calificar el consejo de las mujeres: habla Zurita en su historia de una decisión tomada por el Rey a instancias de su mujer, **consilio muliebri** *ut aiunt* **deteriori** (Lib. III, 362). Tácito cuenta del traidor liberto Mílico *uxoris quoque* **consilium** *adsumpserat,* **muliebre ac deterius**.

Espero que este recorrido panorámico, general y variado, nos deja por lo menos creo yo, una primera impresión en la que destacan la intención de Zurita de asemejarse en la forma de contar la historia a su modelo, y el profundo y detallado conocimiento que de éste tiene el autor zaragozano.

Que Zurita no es Tácito está a la vista, no tiene ni su calidad ni su profundidad, y desde luego esta obra no le hará alcanzar la gloria que el clásico consiguió; pero como nos dice el mismo en el Prólogo a los *Indices*, tampoco era esa su intención: "Non enim in minima, tenuisimaque opera futilem aucupari gratiam et inanis rumoris popularem auram confectari mei consilii fuit".

Universidad Nacional de Educación a Distancia, Madrid

Anti-Colonialism in the Poetry of George Buchanan

PHILIP FORD

The Scottish humanist and poet George Buchanan (1506–1582) passed a good part of his life, following his self-imposed exile from Scotland in 1539, teaching on the continent, with extended periods spent in Bordeaux, Paris, and Coimbra.[1] Many influences contributed to forming his outlook on life: the cosmopolitan world in which he moved (in addition to French scholars, he came into regular contact, in the various colleges in which he taught, with teachers from Portugal, Spain, Italy, and elsewhere); the growing tide of feeling against the established Church in France; and his deep-seated knowledge of classical literature. In the course of this paper, I intend to explore, through a consideration of the literary and historical background of a small group of poems, Buchanan's approach to the subject of colonialism, one of the central moral issues in the sixteenth century, and one of which he would have been made particularly aware by the period he spent in Portugal.

Buchanan's decision to leave France for Portugal was intimately bound up with his friendship for a group of teachers at the Collège de Guyenne in Bordeaux whom he had known for much of his life. These included André de Gouveia, the principal of the Bordeaux college, who as early as 1542 had entered into negotiations with the king of Portugal, Dom João III, with a view to founding a new humanist college in Coimbra to teach Latin, Greek, Hebrew, mathematics, and philosophy. Gouveia went to Coimbra towards the end of 1546 to organize the new Colégio das artes, and a large part of the teaching staff of the Collège de Guyenne followed him there in March 1547, including Buchanan, who was appointed regent of the primus ordo, or rhetoric class. Although Buchanan appears to have settled down quickly in Coimbra, his academic peace was shattered on 10 August 1550 when he was arrested by the Inquisition along with two Portuguese colleagues, Diogo de Teive et João da Costa. After prolonged interrogation in Lisbon, he was sentenced in July 1551 and imprisoned in the monastery of San Bento in Xabregas, to devote himself to pious pursuits. He was provisionally released in December 1551, and unconditionally freed on 29

---

[1] For details of the life of Buchanan, see I. D. McFarlane, *Buchanan* (London, 1981).

February 1552, leaving Portugal later that year on a Cretan ship bound for England.

It is no doubt after his experiences in Portugal that he wrote a number of poems condemning colonialism, in particular as practised by the Portuguese,[2] and these sentiments also found their way into the unfinished didactic poem *De sphaera*, a work in five books which was begun while the author was private tutor (from around 1554 to 1560) to Timoléon, the son of the successful French marshal, Charles de Cossé. Buchanan's accusations are both general and specific, but in essence he views colonial expansion as being inspired only by greed, and the colonists as sexually depraved and warmongering, bringing Christianity, and by implication Catholicism, into disrepute by their behaviour.

One of the most general charges is made in *Miscellaneorum liber* 5, a hendecasyllabic epigram entitled "In Polyonymum."[3] The title refers to the king of Portugal as being endowed with many names, a reference to the enormous colonial expansion of Portugal since the fifteenth century.[4] These possessions take in parts of India (including Calcutta, Cochin, Goa), Arabia and Persia, Portuguese Guinea, and vast sections of Africa, although surprisingly Brazil is left off the list in this poem. The reason given for this expansion is purely mercantile greed:

> Nec portus, neque merx, neque insula ulla est,
> Lucelli unde levis refulget aura,
> Quæ te non titulo augeat. . . . (ll. 9–11)

[There is no port, trade, or island from which a slight gleam of profit shines which does not enhance you with a title.]

However, Buchanan warns, it would take only a war or bad weather at sea to bring an end to the spice trade upon which this empire is based:

> Si belli furor, aut mare æstuosum
> Occludat piperariam tabernam, . . .
> Versuram faciet vel esuribit. (ll. 15–16, 18)

[. . . if the fury of war or the raging sea shuts down the pepper stall, . . . he will borrow money, or go hungry.]

---

[2] It was not until 1530 that Spain began to expand its empire in real terms. This, in addition to Buchanan's direct experience of the Lisbon authorities, no doubt explains his concentration on the Portuguese, whose empire would have been far more established in the 1550s than that of the Spanish.

[3] All quotations are based on the *Opera omnia* of Buchanan, ed. Peter Burman, 2 vols. (Lugduni Batavorum, 1725), abbreviated as *OO*. On this poem, see Philip J. Ford, *George Buchanan, Prince of Poets; with an Edition (Text, Translation and Commentary) of the "Miscellaneorum Liber,"* Philip J. Ford and W. S. Watt (Aberdeen, 1982), 145–146 and 186–187.

[4] On colonial expansion in general, see Pierre Chaunu, *L'Expansion européenne du XIIIe au XVe siècle* (Paris, 1969), and Chaunu, *Conquête et exploitation des nouveaux mondes: XVIe siècle* (Paris, 1969). Portuguese colonial expansion really began around 1474, when the king gained direct control of all overseas ventures. Buchanan is therefore justified in identifying colonialism directly with the king.

Thus the precarious nature of the Portuguese empire is emphasized here. Although Buchanan mentions only pepper, which was by far the most commonly traded of the spices, trade would also have included the other common spice, ginger, along with the luxury spices, cinnamon, cloves, and mace.[5]

When Buchanan does consider the Portuguese presence in Brazil, however, his criticism is of the colonists themselves and is presented largely in terms of their sexual morals.[6] This is apparent in the six-line epigram *Fratres fraterrimi* 29 ("Brasilia," *OO* II. 293):

> Africa deseritur, miles mendicat egenus,
>   . Vi sine tuta fugax oppida Maurus habet.
> Accipit obscœnos Brasilia fusca colonos,
>   Quique prius p‹ueros›[7] foderat, arva fodit.
> Qui sua militibus tollit, dat rura cynædis,
>   Jure sub adverso nil bene Marte gerit.

[Africa is deserted, the needy soldiery is begging, without fighting the fleeing Moors have safe cities. Dusky Brazil receives the disgusting colonists, and he who previously had ploughed boys is ploughing fields. He who removes his estates from the soldiers is handing them over to perverts. Truly he has no success when Mars is against him.]

Although the Portuguese had various trading posts in Africa, their hold there was far more tenuous than in their other territories, partly on account of the size and geography of the continent, partly on account of its many diseases, partly too as a result of native resistance. As Chaunu writes:

> Au XVIe, le Continent noir ne s'ouvre pas aux Portugais comme le Brésil. ... Résistance des hommes, configuration du relief et de l'hydrographie, la barre qui gêne l'accès des côtes, l'implacable concurrence de l'Amérique et de l'Asie sont autant d'obstacles.[8]

Buchanan must have this in mind, then, when he notes the shift of forces to Brazil, where the principal charge laid against the colonizing soldiers is not mercantile greed but sodomy, a theme which is developed more fully in the following poem in the

---

[5] On the Portuguese and the spice trade, see Chaunu, *Conquête et exploitation des nouveaux mondes,* 315–323. Chaunu writes (p. 315): "Le poivre et les épices ont joué, à l'est, le rôle des trésors à l'ouest. Ce sont des forceurs de blocus, des réducteurs de distance, des fédérateurs d'univers." Buchanan mentions other spices and luxury items in *De sphaera* I. 207–210: "... nunc decolor Indus / Zinziber & piper accumulat, nunc cinnama dives / Cogit Arabs: nunc fœcundo de vulnere matris / Thus & Myrrha fluunt ..." (*OO* II. 433).

[6] The Portuguese presence in Brazil dates from 1500, when Pedro Álvares Cabral first discovered the mainland of that country, but it is only after 1530 that the Portuguese were there in any numbers (see Chaunu, *Conquête et exploitation,* 221).

[7] The Burman edition here has "p . . . . ." rather than "pueros," but earlier editions have the word in full. On the use of the verb *fodio* as a metaphor for sexual penetration, see J. N. Adams, *The Latin Sexual Vocabulary* (London, 1982), 151–152, who cites Juvenal 9. 45–46: "seruus erit minus ille miser qui foderit agrum / quam dominum."

[8] *Conquête et exploitation,* 370.

collection, entitled "In Colonias Brasilienses, vel Sodomitas a Lusitanis missos in Bra-
siliam" (*OO* II. 293–294).

This forty-four-line poem, written in the solemn Alcaic metre, assumes right from
the beginning a hieratic tone, reminiscent of Buchanan's Psalm paraphrases[9] in the
way in which it combines Horatian diction, intertexts, and metre with biblical, and
particularly Old Testament, allusions. This is exemplified in the first stanza with its
Horatian opening (see *Odes* III. 4) combined with the picture of the avenging angel,
coming to punish the inhabitants of Sodom and Gomorrha.

> Descende cœlo turbine flammeo
> Armatus iras, Angele, vindices,
>   Libidinum jam notus ultor
>   Exitio Sodomæ impudicæ. (ll. 1 4)

[Descend from heaven, Angel, with your avenging wrath armed with a fiery whirl-
wind, renowned as a punisher of lust through the destruction of shameless Sodom.]

Although Horace's ode, in the same metre, begins with a call for divine inspiration,
it also incorporates towards the end an allusion to the Gigantomachia and Jupiter's
punishment of the Giants, a well-established allegory of human hubris,[10] and no
doubt in Buchanan's mind when he was writing his own ode:

> . . . scimus ut impios
> Titanas inmanemque turbam
>   fulmine sustulerit caduco
>
> qui terram inertem, qui mare temperat
> uentosum et urbes regnaque tristia
>   diuosque mortalisque turmas
>   imperio regit unus aequo. (Horace, Odes III. 4. 42–48)

Only God can truly control all the regions and seas of the world, not man.

Buchanan implies that Brazil, with its hot climate, particularly encourages sexual
depravity, a notion perhaps also linked to the well-known nakedness of the inhabitants. The Protestant traveller, Jean de Léry, refers to this idea in order to dispel it in
his *Histoire d'un voyage faict en la terre du Brésil*, but it is clear from this that there was a
widespread European prejudice in this matter, to which Buchanan himself subscribes:

> Toutesfois avant que clorre ce chapitre, ce lieu-ci requiert que je responde,
> tant à ceux qui ont escrit, qu'à ceux qui pensent que la frequentation entre ces
> sauvages tous nuds, et principalement parmi les femmes, incite à lubricité et
> paillardise.[11]

---

[9] During his incarceration in the monastery of San Bento, the pious pursuit to which Buchanan devoted himself was the paraphrase of the Psalms. Thus this style of writing would have been
quite fresh in his mind.

[10] Cf. Du Bellay's use of the myth in *Les Antiquitez de Rome,* 4 and 12.

[11] See *Histoire d'un voyage faict en la terre du Bresil* (1578), edited by Frank Lestringant (Paris,
1994), 234.

Elsewhere, he writes of the natives:

> Je diray davantage, veu la region chaude où ils habitent, et nonobstant ce qu'on
> dit des Orientaux, que les jeunes gens à marier, tant fils que filles de ceste
> terra-la, ne sont pas tant adonnez à paillardise qu'on pourroit bien estimer ...
> toutesfois, à fin de ne les faire pas aussi plus gens de bien qu'ils ne sont, parce
> que quelques fois en se despitans l'un contre l'autre, ils s'appellent *Tyvire*, c'est
> à dire bougre, on peut de la conjecturer (car je n'en afferme rien) que cest
> abominable pesché se commet entr'eux.[12]

Buchanan too refers to

> Pars ista mundi, quam sibi propriam
> Sedem dicavit mollis amœnitas
>   Luxusque ... (ll. 9–11)

[That region of the earth, which effeminate delight and debauchery have
appropriated as their own abode ...]

Mollis frequently has the pejorative sense of "effeminate" in Latin, while *luxus* means
"excess, debauchery" in this context. The result of this on the already corruptible
Portuguese is to cause them to lose all restraint:

> Abominandis arsit amoribus
> Strigosus æstu, pauperie & fame,
>   Glandis vorator, virulentum
>   E rhaphanis redolens odorem. (ll. 12–16)

[Thin from the heat, poverty, and hunger, he has burnt with abominable desires, a glutton for acorns, stinking of the powerful smell of horseradish.]

The insinuations here are clear, through a mixture of punning innuendos and intertextual allusions. The literal meaning of "glandis vorator," a glutton for acorns, in the
context of the smell of horseradish clearly has a sexual sense, alluding to the *glans
penis* and thus the idea of the Portuguese as given over to fellation.[13] The horserad-
ishes refer to Catullus 15 ("Commendo tibi me ac meos amores"), where the inser-
tion of a horseradish into the anus is presented as a punishment for sexual abuse. In
fact, the entire Catullus poem is a very fitting subtext to Buchanan's ode, as the Roman poet warns his friend Aurelius to keep his hands—and other parts of his anatomy—off his beloved (assumed by commentators to be the young man Juventius):

---

[12] *Histoire d'un voyage*, 429–430. In his note on this passage, Lestringant remarks: "La plupart
des récits sur les Indiens les accusaient de sodomie," which no doubt helped to create the idea of
the Portuguese settlers taking advantage of this tendency. Léry also reports that it was common for
fathers to prostitute their daughters before they married "au premier venu," including Europeans,
although adultery was not tolerated (429).

[13] See Adams, *The Latin Sexual Vocabulary*, 72–73, on the sexual use of *glans,* which he believes is used for the entire organ at Martial XII. 75. 3, and pp. 138–139 for the verb *uoro* used of
the sexual activity usually known as *fellatio.*

> verum a te metuo tuoque pene
> infesto pueris bonis malisque.
>
> . . . . .
>
> quod si te mala mens furorque uecors
> in tantam impulerit, sceleste, culpam,
> ut nostrum insidiis caput lacessas,
> a! tum te miserum malique fati,
> quem attractis pedibus patente porta
> percurrent raphanique mugilesque.
>
> (Catullus 15. 9–10, 14–19)

Even the lean appearance of the Portuguese in Buchanan's poem, "Strigosus æstu, pauperie & fame" (l. 14), suggests a moral as well as a physical wasting.[14]

Later in the ode, the religious dimension of what Buchanan has to say becomes clear, coupled with the more classical notion of the transgressive nature of taking to the sea in ships, especially in the pursuit of trade.

> O Christiani infamia nominis!
> O fœda labes & nota temporum!
>   O turpium turpisque caussa, &
>   Exitus, & pretium laborum!
> Ignota rostris verrimus æquora,
> Gentes quietas sollicitavimus
>   Terrore belli, orbisque pacem
>   Miscuimus misero tumultu.
>
> (ll. 21–28)

[Oh disgrace to the name of Christian! Oh loathsome and notorious discredit to our times! Oh shameful cause, result, and reward of our shameful labours! We have swept across unknown seas with our prows, roused up unwarlike nations with the horror of war, and disturbed the peace of the world with wretched uproar.]

The classical intertexts here are all about transgression and the corruption and decline of mankind. For example, compare Catullus 64. 4–7 on the Argonauts:

> cum lecti iuuenes, Argivae robora pubis,
> auratam optantes Colchis auertere pellem
> ausi sunt uada sala cita decurrere puppi,
> caerula uerrentes abiegnis aequora palmis

where the theme of the search for the Golden Fleece can readily be allegorized as a search for gold in the New World, or Ovid's equally famous description of the Age of Iron in *Metamorphoses* I:

---

[14] Virgil describes the Harpies, for example, as having "pallida semper / ora fame" (*Aeneid* III. 217–218), as quoted below.

vela dabat uentis neque adhuc bene nouerat illos
nauita quaeque diu steterant in montibus altis
fluctibus ignotis insultauere carinae
communemque prius, ceu lumina solis et auras,
cautus humum longo signauit limite mensor.
nec tantum segetes alimentaque debita diues
poscebatur humus; sed itum est in uiscera terrae
quasque recondiderat Stygiisque admouerat umbris
effodiuntur opes, inritamenta malorum.
iamque nocens ferrum ferroque nocentius aurum
prodierat; prodit bellum, quod pugnat utroque
sanguineaque manu crepitantia concutit arma.
(*Metamorphoses* I. 132–143)

In his ode, Buchanan develops the theme of the corrupting power of European civilization, bringing turmoil to "gentes quietas" and disturbing the peace of the world, simply for motives of greed and to provide sexual gratification for the Portuguese settlers: "Ne deesset impuris cinædis / Prostibulum Veneris nefandæ" ("So that the unclean perverts would not lack partners in wicked love") (ll. 31–32). In another common topos on the subject of European barbarity, Buchanan notes that the cannibalistic savagery of the natives of Brazil has been outdone by that of the colonists:

Gens illa nullos mitis in hospites,
Et ora victu assueta nefario,
    Portenta conspexit Cyclopum
        Sanguinea dape fœdiora. (ll. 33–36)

[That nation which is gentle to no strangers and whose lips are accustomed to impious nourishment has gazed upon horrors more shameful than the bloody feast of the Cyclopes.]

The Homeric allusion to the Cyclopes, and particularly to Polyphemus' devouring of Odysseus' crewmen in book 9 of the *Odyssey*, makes the nature of the "victu … nefario" of line 34 clear, and Buchanan continues in Homeric mood in the next stanza, where he calls upon Scylla and Charybdis to destroy the Portuguese ships (ll. 37–40), or, in the final stanza, for the earth or sky to swallow them up. Again, the final lines link the Portuguese to the notion of anti-Christian behaviour, referring to them as "Christianæ / Dedecus opprobriumque terræ," the dishonour and shame of Christendom.

These accusations against the Portuguese have to be seen in terms of the anti-Catholic rhetoric which surrounds the whole issue of colonialism in the sixteenth century, and in that context it is clearly important to consider the collection in which these two poems are found, the largely anti-Catholic *Fratres fraterrimi*. If we consider the main accusations against the Portuguese, they fit in more generally with the accusations made against leading members of the Catholic hierarchy by Buchanan. For example, the principal charge made here of sodomy is very much associated by Buchanan with Rome. *Fratres fraterrimi* 13, "In pontifices" (*OO* II. 287), begins by making this accusation against Pope Paul IV, who had been active in trying to eradicate Protestantism in France,[15] "Pædicat Paulus, contemnit fœdera Clemens" ("Paul commits sodomy, Clement despises agreements") while the much longer poem 17 (*OO* II. 289), in which the statue of Pasquillus in Rome is speaking, looking over all the different identities which he can assume,[16] ends with the following barb aimed at the cardinals (the "purpureos . . . cinædos"):

> Denique transiero cuncta in miracula rerum,
> Sed puero Romæ non licet esse mihi.
> Hoc quoque ero per purpureos aliquando cinædos,
> Si liceat laxas non habuisse nates.
> (*Fratres fraterrimi* 17. 13–16)

[In short, I shall change into all manner of marvellous things, but in Rome I am not at liberty to be a boy. This too I will become one day with the permission of the purple-clad perverts, if I am allowed not to have well-buggered buttocks.]

The abuse of the Brazilian Indians by the Portuguese can thus be seen as an extension of the general Catholic tendency to exploit and corrupt everything which is other. Moreover, the physical rape of the Brazilian population is also a parallel to the more general rape of the land for the purposes of profit, and this theme of greed and exploitation is another one with which Buchanan taxes the religious orders. Once again, Pope Paul IV is the butt of satire for his sacrilegious greed (*OO* II. 287):

> Paulus ab Hebræo scis quantum distet Iuda?
> Hic cœli Dominum vendidit, ille domum.
> (*Fratres fraterrimi* 12)

[Do you know the difference separating Paul from Judas? The latter sold the Lord of heaven, the former his abode.]

Elsewhere in Buchanan's poetry it is the Franciscans who are presented as exploiting and robbing the poor.

This theme of greed is the one that Buchanan develops in book I of the *De sphaera,* in a parenthetical passage ostensibly aimed at demonstrating that the earth is spherical (*OO* II. 432–435). He concentrates here on the notion of *avaritia,* which has led men to visit the most inhospitable regions of the world, to go to "Omnia . . . vasti . . . / Claustra orbis" (ll. 186–187), and to witness "rerum longis incognita seclis / . . . secreta" (ll. 187–8). Again, Ovid's description of the Age of Iron comes to mind here, with its idea of delving into the hidden entrails of the earth to extract hidden

---

[15] Cf. McFarlane, *Buchanan,* 15: "In France, the first synod of Paris met in 1559; but two years earlier—and this shows the speed with which the new religion was spreading—Pope Paul IV had appointed a commission to extirpate Calvinist tendencies in France."

[16] On the subject of the statue of Pasquino and the pasquinade, see G. Dickinson, *Du Bellay in Rome* (Leiden, 1960), 155–207. Buchanan in this epigram has in mind Propertius IV. 2, a poem on a statue of the god Vertumnus which, like Pasquillus, could be dressed up to take on different identities; cf. l. 21: "opportuna meast cunctis natura figuris." (I am grateful to Philip Hardie of New Hall, Cambridge, for this suggestion.)

wealth. In typically epic manner, Buchanan includes a hypotyposis of Avaritia in order to fix in the reader's mind the dreadful nature of this vice (lines 188–195):

> . . . namque insatiabile monstrum
> Orcus Avaritiam Stygiis emisit ab antris
> Germanam Harpyis: facies inculta, situque
> Tristis, hiant rictus, tetricis frons aspera rugis,
> Ora fame pallent, corpus miserabile curæ
> Attenuant, virus promptam ad perjuria linguam
> Inficit, & trepidam exercent insomnia mentem,
> In vigiles ne blanda quies irrepat ocellos.

[. . . for Hell sent forth from its Stygian caverns the insatiable monster Avarice, sister to the Harpies: her appearance is rude and gloomy from neglect, her mouth gapes open, her brow is rough with stern wrinkles, her face is pale from hunger, cares enfeeble her wretched body, poison stains her tongue which is quick to perjure itself, and dreams disturb her restless mind, lest pleasant repose steal into her wakeful eyes.]

The Scottish poet here has in mind Virgil's description of the Harpies in book III of the *Aeneid:*

> tristius haud illis monstrum, nec saeuior ulla
> pestis et ira deum Stygiis sese extulit undis.
> virginei uolucrum uoltus, foedissima uentris
> proluuies uncaeque manus et pallida semper
> ora fame.
>   (*Aeneid* III. 214–218)

Once again, the allegory is clear. The settlers, like the Harpies,[17] not only pillage everything they can lay their hands on, they also befoul and corrupt what they leave behind. In addition, their lust for wealth causes them to abandon everything they should hold dear in their native land. Buchanan paints a vivid picture of the sadness and devastation they inflict on their own families:

> His animum illusi formis, duraque premente
> Pauperie, & magnum magni spondente laboris
> Spe pretium, linquunt patriamque thorumque laremque,
> Grandævosque patres, flentesque in limine natos,
> Præcipitantque animas in aperta pericula viles
> Auspice avaritia. . . .
>   . . . . .
>   . . . at postquam cum lucro audacia crevit,
> Alta petunt, caraque procul tellure relicta

---

17 In allegorical terms, the Harpies are generally linked with the idea of avarice, being etymologically derived from the Greek verb meaning "to snatch," ἁρπάζω.

Velivolas verrunt rostris spumantibus undas.
(*De sphaera* I. 212–217, 220–222)

[With their minds destroyed by these images and at the urging of harsh hunger, and with the hope of great toil promising a great reward, they abandon their country, their marriage-beds, and their homes, their aged parents and their children weeping at the doorway, and urge on their base minds to open dangers under the inspiration of Avarice. . . . But after their audacity has grown with the love of profit, they seek the depths, and leaving the dear land far behind sweep the ship-bearing waves with foaming prows.]

He goes on to describe how their "auri scelerata cupido" ("wicked passion for gold") (l. 249) drives them from Africa, further and further afield, to places "qua nec Romana aut Barbara traxit / Arma odium, bellive furor" ("where hatred or rage for war have not brought Roman or barbarian arms") (ll. 245–246).

Thus Buchanan's view of colonialism is very much mediated by classical attitudes to the notion of sea-travel and Protestant mistrust with regard to the Catholic presence in the New World. Perhaps unsurprisingly for someone with no first-hand experience of Brazil, the specific nature of the indigenous inhabitants is absent from Buchanan's poetry: they are simply presented as the victims of physical and sexual aggression. Rather, it is the corruption of the settlers themselves that forms the basis of these poems. The theme of greed, however, is mentioned even by those who went to Brazil, although they sometimes give the Indians their own voice. The Protestant Jean de Léry, again, reports a conversation with a Topinambou Indian, who cannot understand why the French and Portuguese travel so far afield to obtain brazilwood, when they have wood in their own countries:

Vrayement, dit lors mon vieillard (lequel comme vous jugerez n'estoit nullement lourdaut) à ceste heure cognois-je, que vous autres *Mairs,* c'est à dire François, estes de grands fols: car vous faut-il tant travailler à passer la mer, sur laquelle (comme vous nous dites estans arrivez par-deçà) vous endurez tant de maux, pour amasser des richesses ou à vos enfans ou à ceux qui survivent apres vous? la terre qui vous a nourris n'est-elle pas suffisante pour les nourrir?[18]

Buchanan may not himself give the Brazilian Indians a voice, but his clear moral stand on colonialism and the corrupting nature of colonization on the settlers themselves was expressed in clear and committed terms. The natives may not be presented as noble savages, but they are shown as victims of an economic, religious, and social system which is as corrupting for those charged with applying it as it is devastating for those regions of the world which are directly affected. With Buchanan we may be some way from the cultural relativism and anthropological interest of his pupil Montaigne, but his calling into question of European claims to dominate and exploit the world is in tune with an enlightened if conservative attitude to nationhood and the right of the individual not to be tyrannized by a foreign power.

Clare College, Cambridge

---

[18] See *Histoire d'un voyage*, 311.

La falsa Crónica de San Pedro de Taberna:
un supuesto origen del Reino de Aragón

GENOVEVA GARCÍA-ALEGRE SÁNCHEZ

Jerónimo de Blancas, Cronista de Aragón entre 1581 y 1590, en su *Aragonensium rerum commentarii* (Zaragoza, 1588)[1], incluye, componiéndola él mismo, una supuesta *Crónica de San Pedro de Taberna*, que explica el origen del Reino de Sobrarbe, núcleo primitivo del futuro Reino de Aragón. Con esta fabulación trata de que Aragón tenga una antigüedad propia, independiente de los reinos vecinos (Castilla y Navarra), siguiendo la tradición que en el siglo XV ya iniciaran Pedro Tomic Cauller en su obra *Histories e conquestes dels Reys de Aragó e Comptes de Barcelona* (Barcelona, 1495)[2], o Gauberto Fabricio de Vagad—Cronista Mayor del rey Fernando el Católico—en su *Crónica de los reyes de Aragón* (Zaragoza, 1499), quienes inician la ficción de los reyes y los fueros de Sobrarbe.

Pertenece Blancas a la oligarquía zaragozana de la segunda mitad del siglo XVI. Sus estudios están enmarcados dentro de la formación humanística de la época, estudiando las letras latinas en Valencia con Pedro Juan Núñez, de quien aprenderá su característico estilo ciceroniano. Al morir Jerónimo Zurita, quedó vacante el cargo de Cronista de Aragón, y fue designado Blancas para el mismo por los Diputados del Reino. Ya había desempeñado con anterioridad alguna actividad emparentada con esta función, pues había preparado, por encargo de los Diputados, la censura o supervisión de la Segunda Parte de los *Anales* de Zurita.

---

[1] Existe una traducción del texto de Manuel Hernández, *Comentarios de las cosas de Aragón* (Zaragoza, 1878), y una edición facsímil de esta edición (Zaragoza, 1995), con una introducción de Guillermo Redondo Veintemillas y Esteban Sarasa Sánchez. También las Cortes de Aragón han publicado (Zaragoza, 1996) una edición facsímil de las *Inscripciones latinas a los retratos de los Reyes de Sobrarbe* (Zaragoza, 1680), con una introducción de Guillermo Redondo Veintemillas y Carmen Morte García; en esta edición traducen y amplían Martín Carrillo y Diego José Dormer la obra de Blancas *Ad regum Aragonum veterumque Comitum in Regia Deputationis Caesaraugustanensi aula depictas imagines inscriptiones.*

[2] La redacción es de mediados del s. XV.

Se debe integrar, pues, a Jerónimo de Blancas en esa rica tradición de cronistas de Aragón que van configurando su historia y que trabajaron a expensas de la Diputación del Reino desde finales del siglo XV y a lo largo del siglo XVI. Sigue los pasos de Vagad y de Zurita, quienes a su vez, tuvieron como precedente la *Crónica de San Juan de la Peña*, escrita, al parecer, por iniciativa de Pedro el Ceremonioso en las tres versiones–latina, catalana y aragonesa–durante los últimos años de su reinado. Esta crónica recogió asimismo otros textos anteriores de carácter narrativo y que fueron sus fuentes originarias.

Pero el cronista Blancas no llevó a cabo una obra de la envergadura de los *Anales de la Corona de Aragón* de Zurita. El propio título de los *Commentarii Aragonensium Rerum* indica explícitamente que se trata de unos dispersos *Comentarios de las cosas de Aragón* que nuestro cronista ordena temáticamente. La narración de algunos episodios históricos y la descripción de algunas instituciones aragonesas tienen un verdadero interés, que incluso hoy se conserva. Sin embargo, no pone reparos en mezclar indiscriminadamente la realidad de esos hechos históricos y la descripción de estas instituciones propias de Aragón con el carácter legendario de los orígenes del reino, invención que ya había despreciado Zurita huyendo de la fabulación y encaminándose hacia una concepción historiográfica más moderna.

Parece probado que los *Commentarii Aragonensium Rerum*, estaban ya redactados mucho antes (1584), pero no verían la luz hasta 1588. Es muy posible que el excesivo énfasis con que resalta Blancas los caracteres peculiares y propios del Reino de Aragón, tanto por la figura del Justicia de Aragón como por los orígenes propios del Reino de Sobrarbe, pudiera ser interpretado como un ataque a la política de su monarca, Felipe II.

En efecto, el Consejo Supremo de Aragón fue partidario de denegar la licencia para su impresión por "ir este libro encaminado a levantar el Magistrado del Justicia de Aragón", si bien el Soberano consideró que podía publicarse con la condición de que "se viera si se podía quitar o enmendar lo que trata del Justicia".

Sin embargo, el hecho de que la lengua utilizada en la edición, latín y, además, culto, permitiera únicamente su acceso a un grupo reducido de eruditos, quizá posibilitara que pudiera finalmente publicarse en 1588.

Y es que, precisamente, todo el esfuerzo de Blancas va encaminado a sintetizar y destacar todo cuanto hacía de Aragón y de sus instituciones un Reino independiente, con una historia diferente, antigua y rica, que no quería perder su identidad, basándose en un pasado ejemplar y en unas instituciones propias y justas.

Por todo ello, no se trata de una historia simplemente inventada o recreada al gusto de la época, sino más bien inventada en el sentido medieval de la "invención" y para crear un arma contundente frente a la nebulosa en la que estaba sumida la historia más remota de Aragón.

Se trata, sobre todo, de un intento, más o menos logrado, de fijar y sostener un pasado discutible con unos orígenes fabulados que deberían engrandecer el protagonismo de Aragón en la política española de su tiempo. No olvidemos que Blancas murió en el año 1590, y un año después, en 1591, se desató la rebelión aragonesa que tanta literatura iba a producir en torno al ajusticiamiento de Juan de Lanuza, la intervención de la política castellana en Aragón y la política de la monarquía absoluta.

Así, Jerónimo de Blancas, con una motivación política, se instala en una técnica historiográfica ya superada en su época por muchos historiadores, y, desde luego, por su antecesor como Cronista del Reino de Aragón, Jerónimo Zurita.

Además, va totalmente en contra de lo que el espíritu del humanismo había supuesto de avance contra el anacronismo y de intento de recuperación del sentido histórico de todo documento o vestigio del pasado. Baste recordar los comentarios bíblicos de Nebrija, en sus *Tertia Quinquagena*, o cómo Lorenzo Valla, en la *Donación de Constantino*, va a desentrañar por medio de una concienzuda investigación histórica y filológica el engaño de un falso texto que autentificaba y justificaba un hecho histórico. Es un paso adelante en la concepción historiográfica moderna que Blancas sin duda retrocede[3].

Al comienzo de sus *Comentarii*, nuestro historiador nos cuenta cómo en la época del obispo Bencio de Zaragoza, pocos años después de la caída de la monarquía Visigoda ante el ataque y la ocupación árabe, un grupo de cristianos huyen a los Pirineos y, en torno a un primitivo núcleo surgido junto al monasterio de San Pedro de Taberna, crean el Reino de Sobrarbe, futuro Reino de Aragón. Queda así establecido el paralelo con el origen del Reino de Castilla, siguiendo el modelo de los seguidores de Pelayo que huyeron a las montañas de Asturias, formando el núcleo de lo que más tarde conformaría el Reino de León, origen, a su vez, del Reino de Castilla. Y queda, además, dignificada la monarquía Aragonesa al quedar entroncada con la nobleza cristiano-visigoda.

Para corroborar estos hechos, interpola Blancas esta supuestamente antigua *Crónica de San Pedro de Taberna*, que dice haber encontrado en un viejo códice junto a la *Crónica de San Juan de la Peña*. Veamos el texto:

Venerandus pater Dauidius suo tempore praeerat in monasterio Tabernae. Et beatus Belascutus sub ipso erat primus in ipsius congregationis collegio et merito. Qui beatus Belascutus quadam die ad scribendi studium fecessit. In quo studio eum infirmitas corporis percussit. Qua infirmitate diu grauiterque aegrotauit. Infirmitate ergo tanti uiri cum omni congregatione contristatus est ualde Dauidius pater praedicti monasterii. Solito more, cum omni reuerentia et religione, ut tanto uiro erat dignum, uenerunt eum uisitare, et secundum consuetudinem Sanctae Ecclesiae ex Apostolica iussione Domino commendare, beato Iacobo dicente: "Infirmatur aliquis in uobis, inducat presbyteros Ecclesiae, et orent super eum, ungentes eum oleo In nomine Domini, et oratio Fidei saluabit infirmum". Qua itaque reuerentia uisitato et . . . . . omni cura, Ecclesiastico ordine, coeperunt reuocare memoria condicionem monasterii Tabernae. Sed quia ceteris erat difficillimum, et antiqua uetustate contradictum, omni solicitudine a beato Belascuto condicionem Ecclesiae Tabernae uoluerunt inquirere; ut qui, ut diximus, sicut erat maior merito, ita et aetate. Hic itaque beatus uir

---

[3] La invención de documentos para justificar históricamente un entramado político o ideológico, así como la reacción crítica que trata de desenmascarar estas interesadas ficciones, ha sido una práctica nada rara en la historia de nuestra cultura, como lo atestigua el interesantísimo estudio de Anthony Grafton, *Faussaires et critiques*, traducción francesa de Marielle Carlier (París, 1993).

acquiescens precibus Abbatis et congregationis fideliter ueraciterque reuocauit memoriae pro posse condicionem monasterii Tabernae. Et sic incipit narrare: "Nullus enim posset hoc dicere, postquam ipse esset egressus e corpore".

Hic plura continentur, quae ad propositum sermonem nihil attinent. Quae uero omnino pertinere uisa sunt, ea sunt huiusmodi.

Decimoquinto anno Ordinationis suae (loquitur autem de Bentio, quem saepius beatissimum Caesaraugustanum Episcopum appellauerat) furor perse-quutionis inualuit. Quo tempore Rudericus Rex praeerat Hispaniae, et Sarra-ceni Hispanias sunt ingressi. Quorum furore persequutionis nullus Christia-norum ante eorum oculos uiuus remanere potuit. Hac persequutione comperta, sanctus Episcopus Bentius omnes discipulos suos in unum congregauit, et cum lacrymis ait: "Videte Fratres, quanta sunt peccata Christianorum, ut diuina uin-dicta super nos mittat impiissimam gentem Sarracenorum. Nunc ergo filii ac-quiescite consiliis patris uestri et cum codicibus uestris et cum brachio Sancti Petri Apostoli et cum aliis Sanctorum Reliquiis aut Romam pergamus, aut ad montes, ubi nos Sarraceni inuenire non possint, fugiamus". Cui unus discipulus proteruamente respondit: "Nuntius uenit ad nos de impiissima gente Sarrace-norum, per quem promittunt et iurant ut quicunque Christianorum cum eis habitare uoluerit, se eis nullum malum facturos". Isto malo consilio turbati ce-teri non acquieuerunt consilio patris. Cum ergo audisset sanctus Episcopus, quod discipuli sui non acquiescerent consilio salubri, nocte superueniente, bra-chium Sancti Petri Apostoli et Reliquias multorum aliorum Sanctorum accepit, et cum paucis de suis occulte de ciuitate fugit. Eodem tempore in terra ista Armentarius Comes erat. Ad quem beatus Episcopus fugiendo peruenit. Et ipse clementissimus Princeps ut eum uidit, quod conquereret, quid uellet, interro-gauit. Cui beatus Episcopus ait: "Caesaraugustanus Episcopus fui, a facie Sarra-cenorum nunc fugi; et rogo te multum ut, si habes in terra tua Ecclesiam in loco tutissimo positam, dona eam mihi, ut habitans in ea brachium Sancti Petri Apostoli et Reliquias beatorum Martyrum seu Confessorum, quas mecum ha-beo, recondam ibi". Cui benedictae memoriae Armentarius respondit: "Habeo Ecclesiam terminis locis positam, in honorem Sancti Petri Apostoli aedificatam; placet accipere eam et has pretiosissimas Reliquias recondere in ea". Beatus igitur Episcopus Bentius audiens, magno gaudio repletus, ad monasterium nos-trum uenit. Et, ut decebat, Abbas noster Domnus Donatus cum congregatione tota eum honorifice suscepit. Venit enim cum magno thesauro. Et tempore suae uitae transiens felici fine, requiescit in eodem loco.

Eodem tempore strenuissimus Rex Carolus super gentem Francorum regna-bat. Ad quem misit me Domnus Donatus: et indicaui omnia, quae erant gesta. Igitur ipse, ut audiuit talia, promisit se uenturum cum maximo exercitu et cum nimio alimoniarum apparatu Hispanias; ut Sarracenos inde eiiceret, et liberta-tem patriae recideret. Et propter amorem Sancti Petri Apostoli dedit mihi auc-toritatem libertatis monasterii nostri; et insuper multa munera mihi concessit, et cum omni prosperitate ad nostrum monasterium me remisit. Ergo post re-gressum meum a Francia, sanctus Episcopus Bentius adhuc uiuebat; et ordinauit diem, ut dedicaret noua Altaria, in quibus sanctissimas reconderet praedictorum

Sanctorum Reliquias. Consecrauit igitur Altare in honore Sancti Petri Apostoli, in quo reposuit brachium eiusdem Apostoli; et Reliquias de uestimento Beatae Virginis; et Reliquias de corpore Sancti Pauli Apostoli; et Sancti Andreae; et Sancti Iacobi, fratris Sancti Ioannis Evangelistae; et pretiosissimas Reliquias de Sancto Laurentio Leuita et Martyre; et alias multas Sanctorum Reliquias, quas modo non ualeo nominare mea humilitate. Consecrauit Altare in honore Sancti Ioannis Baptistae. In quo reposuit Reliquias: Vasculum argenteum, plenum ex beatorum Apostolorum pretioso sanguine, et hoc dictum est certissime; et cineres de corpore Sancti Ioannis Baptistae; et de uestimento et capillis Sancti Ioannes Euangelistae; et Reliquias aliorum plurimorum Sanctorum, quas propter numerositatem non potui reddere memoriae. Consecrauit etiam Altare in honore Sancti Stephani Protomartyris. In quo reposuit duos digitos de corpore eiusdem Martyris; et Reliquias de corpore Sancti Bartholomaei Apostoli, Sancti Barnabae Apostoli et Sancti Cipriani Martyris; et caput Sanctae Nulionis; et spatulam Sanctae Alodiae; et Crucis particulam de lignum Domini. His ergo rebus uenerabiliter completis, conuocatis Episcopis totius prouinciae, ordinauit diem Dedicationis Ecclesiae. Et fuit dedicata cum magna honorificentia. Huic dedicationi interfuerunt septem Episcopi et praedictus Comes Armentarius et uir nobilissimus, nomine Redemptus, et ego peccator Belascutus. Et iuro uobis fratribus meis dilectissimis per diem tremendi iudicii quod hoc, quod uobis exposui, in ueritate dixi, quia oculis meis uidi, et aliqua, quae non uidi, de ore fidelium audiui . . . . . Haec Beatus Belascutus dixit, et infirmitate pressus siluit, et bonis operibus . . . . . Kal. Aprilis ad caelorum regna transiuit, et iusta Altare Sancti Petri Apostoli sepultus . . . . . Imperante Domino nostro Iesu Christo, qui uiuit et regnat per omnia saecula . . . . . Sunt Reliquiae multae quorum delectatu sunt notamina. Et ibi est caput . . . . . In minori uero est Vasculum argenteum, in quo habentur multae Reliquiae Sanctorum . . . . . Iusti et Pastoris et Sanctarum Iustae et Rufinae. Et est ibi scriptum, sicut superius praenota . . . Belascuti. Ita uidimus esse in Altaribus.

Este falso texto de la *Crónica de San Pedro de Taberna*, que—como ya mencionamos—asegura Blancas haber hallado con caracteres antiguos en el Códice de la *Crónica de San Juan de la Peña* (de mediados del siglo XIV), sin embargo, no difiere —si exceptuamos la también simulada fragmentación— del resto del texto de sus *Commentarii*, que tiene una marcada pretensión ciceroniana. Es más que probable que nadie creyera esta fabulación, aunque muchos se sintieran identificados con su ideología, y el propio Blancas tiene que reconocer finalmente, quizá para tratar de dejar a salvo su dignidad de historiador:

Haec itaque in ea Sancti Petri Coronica memorantur. Quibus quae fides adhibenda sit, affirmare non ausim. Affirmabo autem nimis uere, me ita ea omnia exarata inuenisse in dicto peruetusto Codice Pinnatensi, antiquis literis, atque adeo ueteri pergameno descripta, ut magnam speciem prae se ferant, mei quidem iudicio, ueritatis.

Sólo el aspecto más superficial (los supuestos caracteres y el pergamino) proporcionarían una base para confirmar su antigüedad, aunque difícilmente se puede disimular en papel antiguo un estado de lengua que no corresponde a la época deseada. De todas formas, la política hace milagros de interpretación de la realidad, presente o pasada, y no es aventurado pensar que el ambiente exigía un documento como el inventado por Blancas.

Universidad Nacional de Educación a Distancia, Madrid

"Suadendo, admonendo, hortando, precando": *Rhetoric and Peacemaking in Juan Luis Vives'* De pacificatione

EDWARD V. GEORGE

In the 1520s, Juan Luis Vives, the transplanted Spanish humanist who spent most of his career in the Low Countries, produced a series of politically oriented writings, ending with an ensemble in 1529 which included the treatise *De pacificatione*.[1] This treatise has been studied by Philip Dust as a pacifist writing, and by George McCully as part of his work on Vives and the problem of evil.[2] In this paper I wish to take a different approach, as part of my own series of essays on the uses of rhetoric in Vives' writing.[3] In brief my argument will be as follows. First: the *De pacificatione* is *inter alia* a treatise about the communal role of persuasive discourse, and hence of rhetoric. Second: in this treatise, persuasive discourse is ultimately incumbent upon

---

[1] Citations of Vives' works are from *Ioannis Ludovici Vivis Opera Omnia*, ed. G. Majansius (Valencia, 1782–1790; repr. London, 1964), abbreviated *VOO*, by volume and page number, or by page number alone. The *De pacificatione* occurs at *VOO* 5.404–446. Other political writings by Vives from the 1520s include the *De Europae dissidiis et bello Turcico*; epistles to Henry VIII, Pope Adrian, and John Longland, bishop of Lincoln; translations of two of Isocrates' political orations: the *De concordia et discordia*, and the *De conditione vitae Christianorum sub Turca*.

[2] Philip C. Dust, *Three Renaissance Pacifists: Essays in the Theories of Erasmus, More, and Vives* (New York, 1987), 191–214; George E. McCully, Jr., *Juan Luis Vives (1493–1540) and the Problem of Evil in His Time* (Ph.D. diss., Columbia Univ., 1967), 391–428.

[3] Edward V. George, "The *Sullan Declamations*: Vives' Intentions," in *Acta Conventus Neo-Latini Guelpherbytani*, ed. Stella P. Revard et al. (Binghamton, 1988), 55–61; "The *Declamationes Sullanae* of Juan Luis Vives; Sources and Departures," *Humanistica Lovaniensia* 38 (1989): 124–151; "Rhetoric in Vives," in Juan Luis Vives, *Ioannis Lodovici Vivis Opera Omnia*, ed. Antonio Mestre (València, 1992–1993), 1: 113–177; and "Rhetorical Strategies in Vives' Peace Writings: The Letter to Charles V and the *De concordia*," in *Ut Granum Sinapis: Essays on Neo-Latin Literature in Honor of Jozef IJsewijn*, ed. Gilbert Tournoy and Dirk Sacré (Leuven, 1997), 249–263.

virtually every adult in the community. Third: among all classes, including (and especially) those with the greatest power and influence, Vives encourages what I shall describe as a "rhetoric of submission" on behalf of the peace of the community, a notion at odds with what Wayne Rebhorn, in a recent book, finds to be generally true of Renaissance culture.[4] And fourth: at the conclusion of the *De pacificatione* Vives departs to a mystical plane, on which conformity to the life of Christ renders all his previous advice unnecessary.

The *De pacificatione* falls into three main parts with gradual transitions from division to division:

De pacificatione: Summary

I. (406–411)
   A. Similitude (= harmony) preferable to difference (=conflict).
   B. One who appears just but doesn't possess the virtue of justice is fraudulent. Test of genuineness: whether one responds when *others* are treated unjustly.
   C. Cato the Elder, ready to give up his life for the community (parallel: Jesus), is thereby a paragon of justice in the community.

II. (411–441) Contains, in loose and repetitive order:

Categories of People Who Can Be Peacemakers	Resources for Creating Conflict/ Harmony
superiores	*claritas generis*
pater familiae/ mater/ mariti	*honor*
institutor/ magister	*opes*
amici	*nobilitas*
viri fortes	*leges*
milites	*pecuniae*
docti/ eruditus/ doctrinis ac prudentia excellentes	*possessiones*
boni	*familiae*
sacerdotes	*clientelae*
rex/princeps	
consiliarii	
(illi) in vicinia/ civitate	
interpretes sanctorum voluminum	
pontifices	
liberi (children)	
subditi (with reference to the prince)	

III. Conclusion (441–446)
   A. Upright life and submission to the Holy Spirit are most pleasing and beneficial to people.

---

[4] Wayne A. Rebhorn, *The Emperor of Men's Minds* (Ithaca, 1995).

B. *Peroratio*: rhetorical activity left behind. Fidelity to the model of the self-humbling, submissive life of Christ (see Phil. 2:8–9) is the foundation of community peacemaking.

Part I, the Introduction, affirms the natural preferability of similitude over difference, that is, of harmony over conflict. For instance, injustice offends the just man even when the injustice is committed against someone else rather than himself. If a man who claims to be just stands by idle while injury is done to another party, his claim is thereby found to be fraudulent. On the contrary, there are those who actually do not shrink from immersing themselves in the troubles of their community in order to promote peace. Vives' star ancient exemplum is Cato the Younger, as remembered in Lucan's *Pharsalia*:

> O utinam caelique deis Erebique liceret
> hoc caput in cunctas damnatum exponere poenas!
> Devotum hostiles Decium pressere catervae;
> me geminae figant acies, me barbara telis
> Rheni turba petat; cunctis ego pervius hastis
> excipiam medius totius vulnera belli;
> hic redimat sanguis populos, hac caede luatur
> quidquid Romani meruerunt pendere mores.
> (*VOO* 5. 407–408; Lucan *Phars.* 2.306–313)

Cato, like Jesus Christ, surpasses his human limitations by utter submission of himself to the good of the community; his pronouncement itself succeeds in having a persuasive effect on his hearer Brutus, in whom (rather ironically, considering the context for which Vives cites the passage) it arouses "excessive passion for civil war" (*Phars.* 2.325). Cato's subsequent career in actual history, climaxing in his suicide, attests to his ability to put his life on the line in defense of principle. Vives merges persuasion, submission to the community, and peacemaking in this striking cry from the hero of the dying Roman republic.

After this introduction, Vives observes that the soul is the source of both concord and discord, and proceeds to list influences on the soul's emotions: *opes, pecuniae, possessiones, familiae, clientelae,* and then *claritas generis* and *honor* (411, 412). The stage is thus set for Part II, the bulk of the treatise, which provides a catalog of various classes of people in the community, pointing out how they are to promote peacemaking and citing the harmful effects that ensue when they fail. Interspersed are comments on qualities or resources that can be used for or against communal harmony: the elements just mentioned, along with *nobilitas* and *leges*.

Concentrated in Part II are numerous indications of the critical importance of persuasion, a role which Rebhorn recognizes as present at all levels of social discourse, but which he finds to be universally associated with ruler-subject conceptions of relationship.[5] Thus the *De pacificatione* echoes an idea found in Vives' rhetorical

---

[5] "I contend that rhetoric is political in the Renaissance not because of the uses to which it is put or the styles it engenders but because, in the imagination of the period, the relationship

advisory, the *De consultatione* of 1523 (not published until 1533, as far as we know), that the art of persuasion is applicable and important at various levels of public and private life.[6] In the *De pacificatione* the persuasive powers of the *rex* and the *consiliarius* are in many ways not on a plane apart, but on a continuum with the persuasive duties laid upon large numbers of lesser members of the community.

Meanwhile, the great are under the same onus as was Cato, the embodiment of the spirit of community service: they prove themselves by giving up their resources. The wealthy could put their goods to no better use than to support laws, contribute to equity, stand up for righteousness and justice ["faveant legibus, adiuvent aequitatem, adsint iuri ac iustitiae" (414)], all activities which imply use of persuasive abilities. *Nobilitas* is sought by conferring benefits on the citizenry. In the following excerpt, true nobility is associated with self-sacrifice:

> Nobilitas quaesita est per beneficia publica civium, nempe quod magni aliqui et excelsis animis viri, conservandis civibus, legibus, patria, non solum magnam et strenuam operam, sed *se ipsos quoque, cum opus esset, impenderunt: haec est vera et propria origo nobilitatis.* (*VOO* 5.414: my emphasis)

Again, implicit in this statement is the union of persuasive activity and self-abnegation.

Unfortunately, people of honor in the community often pass up opportunities to do good:

> Possent, veneratione ac maiestate sola, iura et leges fulcire ac sustentare, *componere controversias, inimicitias tollere, odia comprimere ac sedare, quietem, pacem, caritatem in civitate fundare ac constituere, denique ea perficere auctoritate, quae vix ullis vel armis perficerentur vel viribus.* . . . Timent quidam ne detrimentum auctoritatis suae accipiant, si tam multos curent, et tam multa. (*VOO* 5.416; my emphases)

The link among power, risk, and persuasive activity emerges. The word *auctoritas*, which occurs at least a dozen times in the *De pacificatione*, refers to a quality whose employment for communal benefit the reader will readily associate with persuasion.

Vives then broadens his scope and takes the *vulgus* at large to task for not calling to account the people who have a reputation for wisdom or goodness but who do nothing useful for the community: "Stulte vulgus, cur tu sapientem aut bonum eum vocas, et ut talem revereris, cuius bonitatem sapientiamque gravem tibi saepe experiris, utilem numquam?" (417). The duty of a king, Vives continues, is to cultivate peace among the citizenry [*pacem inter cives suos curet et colat* (418)], unlike the *tyrannus*, whose role is to inflame hearts and sow the seeds of discord [*irritet animos, et spargat semina discordiarum* (418)]. Again, the language chosen evokes the weapons in the orator's arsenal.

---

between rhetor and audience is conceived fairly consistently in political terms as one between ruler and subject, and that that conception of rhetoric remains central to the discourse throughout the entire period" (Rebhorn, *Emperor*, 9).

[6] *VOO* 2.239–240; George, "Rhetoric in Vives," 140.

The cleric—and here the population under discussion widens in another direction beyond those at the very top of the political pyramid—possessed of *vis quaedam et auctoritas divina*, has a full complement of persuasive duties:

> Sacerdos, si modo officio ac munere suo probe defungitur, a vitiis *dehortatur* ac *deterret, incitat* atque *impellit* ad pietatem, *consolatur* maestos, iacentes tamquam porrecta manu *erigit, domat* contumaces, *lenit* asperos, denique quidquid est in pietate vel fractum *consolidat*, vel pravum *corrigit*: hi omnes *velut vox quaedam* sunt *divina*, quorum auctoritatem his verbis sanxit ipse idem Deus et Dominus omnium: *Qui vos audit, me audit*. (*VOO* 5.413; emphases mine)

As with the *sacerdos*, the persuasive role of the *consiliarius* is self-evident: he is the *mens regni*, alongside the *rex* who is the *voluntas regni*; his importance is affirmed with the dictum that having a good king with bad counselors is a worse situation than the reverse (420). The duties of a *consiliarius,* not surprisingly, include "regere ac cohibere voluntatem, docere meliora, deterrere a pravis, monere, incitare, exstimulare ad pulchra et praestantia" (420–421). For the purposes of this essay, suffice it to say that the *consiliarius* is the very raison d'etre for Vives' rhetorical treatise *De consultatione*.

Teachers likewise use their gifts of persuasion to promote communal harmony: "Quid poterit congruentius cum munere ac professione sua facere, quam adhortari, impellere quantum consilio, iussu, auctoritate, verbis et re valeat?" (421).

The obligation of husbands and wives to nurture love and not hate is an imperative affecting subordinates and superiors throughout society (425). The wife should avoid insulting her husband, while the husband should avoid the behavior of a man beating a horse and refrain from inflicting misery on his wife (427). The *pater familiae* must keep his house in order or else he will compromise his larger civic *auctoritas*. Philip of Macedonia and Gorgias of Leontini are cited as examples of people who lost public credibility because of their private failures:

> Nam rex domi dissidentes habebat filium et uxorem, orator vero uxorem et ancillam: non adducebantur Graeci ut crederent suas querelas, rixas, discordias ab iis hominibus sapienter posse componi, qui ipsi privatas domi, vel auctoritate vel prudentia, non sedassent. (*VOO* 5.426)

In other words, public persuasive leverage fades when the persuader's abilities are seen to fail in private life.

Subditi, subordinates of the prince, receive attention as a class. Their first duty listed here, where the topic is peacemaking, is not to obey but almost always to avoid getting embroiled in the quarrels of the prince. Sovereigns who neglect their domestic duties to prosecute wars against other sovereigns are bringing the worst kind of misery on their own people:

> Quantum *auctoritate*, quantum *suadendo, admonendo, hortando, precando*, denique quibuscumque rebus subditum erga superiorem, tamquam filium adversus patrem valere ac posse fas iusque est, salva maiestate omni ac reverentia magistratus et principis, tantum laborare ac contendere [subditi] deberent, ut principem suum et conventus rectorem a turbis illis odii ac tempestatibus ad quie-

tissimam pacis tranquillitatem traducerent, ut ex illa suavitate capitis multum in cetera omnia membra derivaretur. (*VOO* 5.427)

Vives thus observes a balance: criticism is the responsibility of the *subditi*, but only within bounds that preserve the prince's paternal status and prestige, and hence the stability of the community.

After considering other classes of people, such as friends—who are not true friends if they get pleasure out of seeing their companions in discord—strong men, and soldiers, Vives takes to task those who cause ruptured relationships among fellow Christians and fellow citizens. They are like one who hurls a barbed and poisoned lance into a crowd, creating hostile confrontations (434). From this consideration Vives proceeds to a traditional litany of the evils of war.

Interpreters of scripture are next (436). They will be called to account for how clearly they have explicated the sacred word—and here we have a foreshadowing of the rhetorical and ethical significance Vives will give to commentaries and other learned works in the third book of the *De ratione dicendi* of four years later, Vives' main treatise on rhetoric.

We now return to priests (*sacerdotes*, 436). They must be effective preachers, as was Jesus Christ, the greatest preacher of all, and as were the apostles. Vives' low opinion of contemporary preaching, later expressed elsewhere,[7] gets exposure here. The priests' obligations include:

Ad pacem *suadeant, hortentur, impellant; efficacissimas* de pace *afferant rationes*, quae non leviter summis animis haerentes, levissima quaque aura deleantur, sed quae alte penetrent, quae aculeum in auditorum praecordiis infixum relinquant, *quemadmodum Periclem* fecisse, *magnum Athenis oratorem*, scriptores veteris comoediae significant. . . . Sic mundus conversus est ad rectam pietatem, cum homines viderent eosdem habere operis auctores quos consilii, *nec ab oratione vitam discrepare*. (*VOO* 5.437, 438: my emphases)[8]

Discrepancy between a priest's life and discourse leads to loss of credibility and damage to society. Contrariwise, when preachers show no such discrepancy, that is, when *iustitia* and *sermo* are in harmony, peacemaking can occur.

In the presence of such people of integrity, connoisseurs of wisdom are awestruck: who are these people, they wonder, who talk as they live? By contrast, what sort of people is it that will equip others with impious subtleties, tools for dissension?

Cuiusmodi sunt illi qui ansas odiis ac simultatibus praebent impia subtilitate? "Odisse non potes, odii signa potes ostendere; non potes non amare, amoris

---

[7] Cf. Vives, *De causis corruptarum artium* 4.3 (*VOO* 6.163–167; and George, "Rhetoric in Vives," 149), where modern preachers are said to surpass their forebears only in the quality of their subject matter.

[8] The allusion to Pericles comes from Cicero's *De oratore* 3.34.138 and *Brutus* 9.38. Jacques Chomarat, *Grammaire et rhétorique chez Erasme* (Paris, 1981), 2: 1105, cites its use in Erasmus' *Paraclesis* at *Desiderius Erasmus Roterodamus: Ausgewählte Werke*, ed. Hajo Holborn (Munich, 1933), 139, 22–25. I am indebted to Professor Chomarat for these references.

indicia potes subtrahere." Non disputo nunc de eiusmodi invento: illud dico, nolim quemquam tam periculose esse ingeniosum. Potes tu rivum prohibere, cum fontem vel aperueris, vel reliqueris? Potes tu ita ignem includere, ut se non proferat? Ego vero vix fieri posse credo ut non se amare indicet, prodat, testetur, quisquis amat:

> "Quis enim bene celaverit ignem,
>> lumine qui semper proditur ipse suo?"
>> (*VOO* 5.438: Ovid *Her.* 1.16.7–8)

Purveyors of dangerous subtleties, such as the pseudodialecticians Vives obviously alludes to here, teach others how to stir up conflict. Articulate and honest people are peacemakers, and frauds will inevitably be found out.

For priests, Vives continues, stirring up support for war is inadmissible:

Quoties res postulabit, exerendus est zelus ille zelo Christi simillimus, et proferenda est libertas, *non tacendum, non dissimulandum, non connivendum:* "propter Sion, clamat ille, *non tacebo,* et propter Hierusalem *non quiescam.*" Et alio loco: *"Exalta vocem tuam* qui evangelizas Sion." . . . Hoc est praedicatoris munus, sicut Isaias inquit: *annuntiare* pacem, *praedicare* salutem, quae in sola sita est pace; hoc repetant, hoc infigant, inculcent; tot bella iam continenter gerunt duo capita orbis Christiani [Charles and Francis]. (*VOO* 5.439; my emphases)

Again, persuasive power is implicitly demanded.

And thus at the end of Part II of the *De pacificatione*, the eternal quarrel between Charles V and Francis I of France is brought to the surface, followed immediately by a cry of exasperation that people remain silent: "Quid hic tacemus? Quid mussamus?" (439). The exemplum now produced is, like Cato, another character remembered for sacrificing his very life to the good of the community: Telemachus, the monk of late antiquity, who jumped into the arena to halt the brutal gladiatorial games, exclaiming, "Quid facitis, fratres? Quae causa est tantae discordiae?" Vives experiences Telemachus' distress, and adds a first person castigation of himself and his fellow citizens:

Nos omnes Christianum orbem tamquam in arenam digladiantem, et sese conficientem *taciti* spectamus! Quin *clamamus,* quin ostendimus, nec hunc vocari posse Catholicum, nec sacrum, neque illum Christianissimum, nec alium fidei defensorem, nisi ea exequantur quae sunt Christiani, nempe bene velle, amare, non nocere, prodesse qua possit? (*VOO* 5.439: emphases mine)

The references in this passage, to Charles, Francis, and Henry VIII (*hunc, illum, alium*) are clear. Persuasive speech of the most urgent kind is associated with subordinates, and at the same time with ultimate submission to the common welfare, even at the risk of one's life. Vives reinforces the point by recommending to prelates the model of Saint Paul, whose choice to serve Christ rather than to please humans provides the path to justice and harmony.

We now break into Part III of the *De pacificatione*, with Vives' language signaling a major transition:

Iam vero converto orationem meam, et dico eos magis placituros hominibus, et *in maiore futuros pretio, modo sermoni moderato ac prudenter pio vita respondeat*, et intelligant homines non illos vel respectu suorum commodorum latrare, vel servitute pravi alicuius affectus, sed Dei se exhibere ministros, ut *tamquam fistulae quaedam sint, quae sacro illo divino Spiritu animatae, sonum illum emittant* ad eorum salutem quibus aliquid significant. Id facile vita declarabit, *sine qua fucata et simulata existimatur omnis adhortatio.* Tum etiam *oderunt omnes consultorem*, qui non ad utilitates eorum quibus consulit refert quae dicat, sed ad suos vel suorum. (*VOO* 5.441: my emphases)

The moderate and prudent discourse of priests should echo their lives and should resound as if they are but reeds, musical instruments of the Holy Spirit. Ambrose, using the status of his episcopate, defeated Theodosius. Leo the Great, turning away Attila the Hun at the gates of Rome, relied on "sacred oratory, but sacred oratory which came from a faithful heart!" [*pia oratione, sed quae pio ex pectore nasceretur* (441)]. The Christian martyrs are extolled next. Underpinning these people's feats is *veneratione et cultu piae libertatis.* Princes and magnates valued heroes like Ambrose, Leo, and the early martyrs as the *tubae* of the Holy Spirit, a metaphor comparable to the *fistulae* envisioned earlier (441: see citation above). Socrates, under indictment and in the darkness of uncertainty, declares that he will obey God before the Athenians; will the Christian, facing another Christian in a situation of safety and even prestige, fail to be as firm as the condemned Greek philosopher who knew not what lay before him (443)?

The treatise then takes a turn which, in light of all the importance hitherto given to persuasive discourse, exhibits a mystical quality:

Sed quid nos rationes ad id suadendum conquirimus, et non potius ipsius unius Christi vita et actiones omnes pro omnibus argumentis sufficiunt, pro omnibus exemplis sunt exemplum unum, quod aemulemur, ad quod nos fingamus et componamus? (*VOO* 5. 443–444)

I choose the term mystical to describe this moment in the *De pacificatione* because Vives, after pages of exhortation to constant, moderate, and carefully chosen speech, envisions a level at which, if the citizen can live the life of Christ, all those precepts cease to matter. The secular gesture of submission by Cato at the beginning of the *De pacificatione* reappears spiritually in Jesus' own voluntary emptying of himself, taking the humble role of a slave and persisting even to death, as portrayed in Philippians 2:5–11. Rhetorical obligations are left behind. Implicitly, the life we must lead for the sake of communal justice and harmony is the submissive life of Jesus, meaning for the good citizen the life of subordination of his interests to those of the community. This is the life to which the overlay of *sermo*, persuasive discourse, must faithfully correspond.

I have tried to show that for Vives persuasive discourse is incumbent on people throughout society, at all levels upwards through superiors and the supremely powerful. This phenomenon gathers added interest when observed in the light of Rebhorn's study mentioned earlier, which surveys how Renaissance writers "thought about or, rather, wrote about it [i.e., rhetoric] and how they imagined its powers and its limits, its value to the individual and to society, its characteristic uses, its relationship to other disciplines and activities." In Rebhorn's view,

> The particular political vision of Renaissance rhetoric distinguishes it from that of both classical antiquity and the Middle Ages: the rhetor is imagined as a ruler, his audience becomes his subjects, and power and control are the central issues.[9]

Expanding on his case, Rebhorn refers to such evidence as the aetiological myth of the civilizing orator who by his persuasive power gathers and acculturates scattered, wild, mankind into civilized life; or, for another example, to the visual illustrations of Hercules who overpowers and subjects humanity by the skill of his eloquence. Rebhorn is discussing evidence for Renaissance thinking *about* rhetoric, and if we can accept the *De pacificatione* as an example of thinking or writing *about* rhetoric and its social role—and I hope I have proven that we can—the presence of persuasive discourse in this treatise is at odds with the pattern Rebhorn finds in his broad analysis, on one crucial count. In the *De pacificatione* rhetoric is associated not with hunger for power, but with employment in an attitude of submission to the community, as manifested in many ways, but crystallized with especial force in the figures of Cato the Elder, Telemachus the ancient monk, and Jesus Christ as he empties himself. This attitude is recommended to those who are at or near the pinnacle of political power and to all great players on the communal stage, just as it is to virtually everyone else, whether superior or subordinate. Vives departs from Rebhorn's model, offering a synthesis of ideas about rhetoric in the Christian community, which we might call, paradoxically, a rhetoric of communal submission. It is this rhetoric through which *iustitia* and *sermo*, the bonds of the community in Vives' thought, are united; it is also through this rhetoric that Vives' status as a rhetorical preceptor is reconciled with his non-combative character, echoed in his personal motto *sine querela*.

Finally, the dedicatory epistle of the *De pacificatione*, addressed to Alfonso Manrique, the archbishop of Seville, gives us a valuable opportunity to observe whether and how Vives follows his own precepts; for here we can glimpse his rhetorical demeanor toward an important player in the political environment of his time. Manrique was at the moment the Grand Inquisitor, and the period was a hard one for Vives' converso Jewish family in Valencia. His father had been executed in 1524, and his mother's remains were disinterred and burned in 1529, the year the *De pacificatione* was published. On the other hand, a harsh prison sentence meted out to Vives' uncle was commuted by Manrique himself in 1534.[10] And Manrique was a defender of the Spanish Erasmists; his support was critical to their success in the cele-

---

[9] Rebhorn, *Emperor*, 13–14.
[10] Angelina Garcia, *Els Vives: Una familia de Jueus Valencians* (València, 1987), 280.

brated theological conference at Valladolid in 1527.[11] Finally, Manrique was a councillor in the circle of Charles V. In fact, deVocht surmises that it may have been as a result of their presence in Charles' court in 1517 that Manrique and Vives first crossed paths.[12]

Vives' dedication is a cautious compliment, so artfully phrased as to mislead at least one modern scholar into seeing there a generous encomium.[13] Here is the list of reasons Vives gives why people should feel entitled to regard Manrique as a *pacificator* (*VOO* 5.404-405): 1) He has noble ancestry. 2) He is of an age at which eagerness for war should have cooled. 3) He is a counselor to the king, and counselors *should* restrain their sovereigns (*qui et principum cupiditates refrenent, et concitatos motus inhibeant, et illos, ulterius quam expedit, se rapientes revocent sistantque*: note the use of the characteristic subjunctive). 4) He is an archbishop, and prelates should watch their flocks like good shepherds. In this capacity he has the added responsibility of Inquisitor, about which more in a moment. And 5) he has shown a humane spirit toward scholars (*in studiosos omnes humanitas*), of whom he names four Spaniards who are both acquaintances of Vives and known to have been in Manrique's entourage.

A careful reading of the litany shows that the only item on the list which confers acclaim for something Manrique has actually done is the fifth. Vives' circumspection also comes out in his allusion to Manrique's Inquisitorial position, a grave and perilous duty in which one can sin gravely if he is not aware of how he touches the lives and safety of many people:

> Accedit his omnibus maximis, ut vides, pignoribus, pacificationis munus inquisitionis haereticorum, quod cum tantum sit tamque periculosum, nisi sciat quis quo pertineat, eo peccat gravius quo de plurium salute, fortunis, fama, et vita agitur: mira dictu res, tantum esse permissum vel iudici, qui non caret humanis affectionibus, vel accusatori, quem nonnumquam ad calumniam, odium, vel spes, vel prava aliqua impellit animi cupiditas. In tanto discrimine tempestatis non unica spectanda est sacra illa, ut Graeci dicunt, ancora, sed bonus et sapiens rector clavi. (*VOO* 5.405)

And despite this citation of risks and pitfalls, Vives affirms that the Inquisition is a *munus necessarium* (405)! We have no evidence of direct involvement by Manrique in the condemnation of Vives' dead mother, which made it necessary for him to prepare the journey of his destitute sister to the Low Countries in 1531.[14] But in any event we may suppose that in the dire straits in which his relatives found themselves, Vives had hopes that some unforeseen good might come of his choice of Manrique as the dedicatee. In addition to the aforementioned release of his incarcerated uncle,

---

[11] See Marcel Bataillon, *Érasme et l'Espagne*, ed. Daniel Devoto (Geneva, 1991), 1: 253. On Manrique's position see also McCully, *Problem of Evil*, 391–393.

[12] Henry deVocht, ed., *Monumenta Humanistica Lovaniensia: Texts and Studies about Louvain Humanists in the First Half of the XVIth Century* (Louvain, 1934), 429.

[13] McCully, *Problem of Evil*, 394.

[14] *VOO* 7.139; Vives' letter to Honorato Juan, March 1531. Ep. no. 180 in Gilbert Tournoy, *Pour une nouvelle edition de la correspondance de J. L. Vives* (Kortrijk, 1992), 31.

Vives even secured employment later as tutor to Manrique's son Rodrigo.[15] Mc-Cully suspects that some of Vives' remarks on community harmony might have been intended as advice to the Inquisitor.[16] Manrique, while complimented only in guarded terms, is at the same time immune to pointed accusations. These are reserved for the *De pacificatione* proper, and for Charles, Francis, and Henry. Here, in other words, Vives is employing a rhetoric of submission toward Manrique in the interest of harmony and peace.[17] If so, it must be a bitter peace, and a grievous harmony, to which Vives is resigning himself personally. Perhaps he chooses to suffer private anguish as the price for staying in a role where he has a chance to be heard through the medium of a royal counselor on other matters affecting the peace of Europe as a whole. His explicit and condemnatory attention to the devastating conflict between Charles and Francis would support this assumption.

Texas Tech University

---

[15] DeVocht, *Monumenta*, 430.

[16] McCully, *Problem of Evil*, 395.

[17] I have argued for similar indirection and circumspection in Vives' *De concordia* (see George on the Letter to Charles V in "Rhetorical Strategies"). My view is at odds with McCully's generally valuable analysis when he sees a degree of presumptuousness on Vives' part (*Problem of Evil*, 393–394).

Du Bellay's Six Latin Poems
in Praise of Ronsard

ELLEN S. GINSBERG

A goal of the group of poets known as the Pléiade is the search for self-identity. This is seen in Joachim Du Bellay's *Deffence et Illustration de la langue française* (1549), where he attempted to create an identity for the upcoming group of young poets by opposing them to earlier poets and by formulating a new poetics opposed to that of earlier writers of the sixteenth century. In addition, Du Bellay created his own identity by opposing himself to Pierre de Ronsard, friend, companion, fellow-scholar, and acknowledged leader of the Pléiade. This "rivalry" between colleagues can best be seen in the poems which Du Bellay wrote during the four years he spent in Rome (1553–1557). These poems, which included both French and Latin poetry, were later divided into four volumes (three in French and one in Latin) and published after Du Bellay's return to France at the end of 1557. The introductory sonnets of the *Regrets*, in which Du Bellay consciously opposes his style and manner to those of Ronsard, have been principally examined by scholars from this point of view.[1]

At the same time that Du Bellay was writing poems in French, he wrote a series of Neo-Latin poems (the *Poemata*) which formed one of the volumes published after his return to France. The *Poemata* are divided into four sections: the "Elegiae," the "Epigrammata," the "Amores," and the "Tumuli." Since the publication of the excellent edition of Du Bellay's Latin poetry by Geneviève Demerson,[2] scholars have shown much interest in this poetry. It has been commented on extensively and compared to the French poetry that Du Bellay was writing at the time. Scholars have concluded that the themes exemplified in Du Bellay's French poetry, especially in the *Regrets* (1558), generally acknowledged to be his masterpiece, also appear in his Latin poetry.

---

[1] See Gilbert Gadoffre, *Du Bellay et le sacré* (Paris, 1978); Floyd Gray, *La Poétique de Du Bellay* (Paris, 1978); Richard A. Katz, *The Ordered Text: The Sonnet Sequences of Du Bellay* (New York, 1985); Josiane Rieu, *Esthétique de Du Bellay* (Paris, 1994).

[2] Joachim Du Bellay, *Oeuvres poétiques*, vols. 7–8 (Paris, 1985).

This volume of Latin verse contains some ten poems addressed to Ronsard which detail the relationship between the two poets in those difficult years for Du Bellay when he was "exiled" in Rome, while Ronsard remained in France, producing much poetry and becoming increasingly successful.

Within the first section of "Elegiae," is Elegy 6, "Ad P. Ronsardum," which Du Bellay translated into French as "A Pierre de Ronsard." The Latin version of the poem is addressed to Ronsard as "lyrae Gallicae principem," while the French version is addressed simply to Pierre de Ronsard. Demerson, who has compared the two versions, concludes that Du Bellay is more direct in his description of his relationship to Ronsard in his Latin poetry and also praises Ronsard more highly in Latin.[3]

The second section, the "Epigrammata," contains a larger number of poems to or about Ronsard.[4] Epigram 11, although ostensibly on the *Amours de Francine* of J.-A. de Baïf, contains praise of Ronsard as leader of the Aonian band. It exhorts Ronsard to abandon love poetry and to oppose his Francus to Baïf's Francine, that is, to get started on his epic.[5] Epigram 14 continues this theme, as its title indicates: "Ad P. Ronsardum, ut relictis Amoribus Heroica scribat." The title has been translated by Demerson as, "A Ronsard, pour qu'il abandonne les Amours et écrive des vers héroïques."[6]

Epigram 31 appears to be the only poem in which Du Bellay states outright that Ronsard has made hardly any response to the many poems which Du Bellay sent him from Rome. Du Bellay laments Ronsard's forgetfulness and threatens to send henceforth only verses crueler than those of Archilochus.[7]

Epigrams 43–48 constitute a series dealing with the silver statue of Minerva which Ronsard was awarded by the Jeux Floraux de Toulouse (1555) and which he then dedicated to King Henry II of France.[8] Although many of Du Bellay's Latin poems are "translated" or transposed into the French poems he was writing concurrently, this is not true of the six Minerva poems. They form a set of variations on the same theme: "des exercices de style." Although the subject is ostensibly quite different from those of the other Latin poems written to Ronsard, when looked at in detail the six epigrams contain many themes found in the *Regrets* and other poems written during Du Bellay's Roman sojourn, including other *Poemata*.

Why did Du Bellay devote six Latin epigrams to the subject of Ronsard's award? It may be simply a poetic game, showing the author's ability to treat a subject in six different ways. But I suggest that the answer is linked to many of Du Bellay's concerns during his Roman years and throughout his creative life. It reveals his personal "obsessions" as well as his aesthetic and poetic theories. I wish to focus on this set of poems.

---

[3] Geneviève Demerson, "Du Bellay traducteur de lui-même," in *Neo-Latin and the Vernacular in Renaissance France*, ed. G. Castor and T. Cave (Oxford, 1984), 113–128.

[4] I am indebted to Oliver Millet, whose fine article, "Les *Epigrammata* de 1558: Sens et fonction du recueil," in *Du Bellay: Actes du Colloque d'Angers (1989)*, 2 vols., ed. Georges Cesbron (Angers, 1991), 569–586, supports some of my own findings.

[5] Du Bellay, *Oeuvres poétiques*, 7: 59–62.

[6] Du Bellay, *Oeuvres poétiques*, 7: 110.

[7] Du Bellay, *Oeuvres poétiques*, 7: 101.

[8] Du Bellay, *Oeuvres poétiques*, 7: 111–115.

Though Du Bellay dedicated six Latin poems to the award given Ronsard, he did not talk about this event in his French poetry. In the *Deffence et Illustration*, Du Bellay had treated the Academy of the Jeux Floraux at Toulouse with considerable scorn.[9] It was a provincial academy with a medieval origin. Yet Du Bellay looks upon the awarding of the Minerva as a triumph for Ronsard. Several reasons for Du Bellay's praise of this event are plausible.

A clear relationship exists between Minerva (Pallas Athena), goddess of wisdom and of war, whose talisman is the olive branch, and *l'Olive*, Du Bellay's first major poetic work, a sonnet sequence dedicated to a mysterious lady identified only as Olive.[10] As the first poem of *l'Olive* shows,[11] Du Bellay places his love and his poetry under the protection of "la sage Déesse," who has chosen the olive branch to honor her sacred altar, an olive branch with which he hopes to be crowned. Du Bellay thus indicates the symbolic value of Olive, the name of his lady, and announces his poetic program, based on the desire to create an elevated and erudite poetry, worthy of Pallas Athena. Throughout his life, Du Bellay dedicates many of his poems, including *l'Olive* and the *Poemata*, to "Madame Marguerite, seur unique du Roy," Marguerite de Valois, Henry II's sister, who protected the poets of the Pléiade. Both Ronsard and Du Bellay celebrated her as a new Minerva, protector of letters and of poets.[12] Marguerite/Minerva, accompanied by the Muses, is the symbol of the elevated view of poetry exemplified by the Pléiade. Du Bellay's desire to commemorate the awarding of the Minerva to Ronsard may draw upon his personal interest in Minerva as a symbol of his lady, Olive, and of his patron, Marguerite de Valois.

I will briefly describe the six poems. They are epigrams 43–48 in the *Epigrammata*, the second section of Latin poems within the *Poemata*. They differ in length, in theme, and in meter, but have many similarities. As far as I can see, these poems do not exhibit the technique which D. Sacré has so well analyzed in his article on epigrams 22–26 (a series of cancrine lines), but they are interesting in other ways.[13]

Epigrams 43, 45, and 47 are composed of Phalaecian hendecasyllables, while 44, 46, and 48 are in elegiac couplets.[14] Thus, a regular alternation occurs in the meter of these Latin epigrams. This is similar to what Du Bellay did in French in the *Antiquitez*, for example, where we find a regular alternation between ten-syllable and twelve-syllable verse as we move from sonnet to sonnet.[15] The length of the poems

---

9 Du Bellay, *Deffence et Illustration*, ed. H. Chamard, (Paris, 1948), vol. 2: iv, 108.

10 Du Bellay, *L'Olive, L'Anterotique, XIII Sonnetz de l'Honneste Amour*, vol. 1 of *Oeuvres poétiques* de Du Bellay, ed. H. Chamard (Paris, 1909).

11 Du Bellay, *L'Olive*, 27.

12 Dorothy Coleman, "Minerve et *l'Olive*," in *Du Bellay: Actes du Colloque International d'Angers (1989)*, ed. Georges Cesbron (Angers, 1990), 161–169.

13 Dirk Sacré, "Sur quelques épigrammes latines de Joachim du Bellay," *Les Etudes classiques* 52 (1989): 1, 56–59.

14 Du Bellay, *Oeuvres poétiques*, 7: 277.

15 Marie-Madeleine Fontaine, "Le Système des *Antiquités* de Du Bellay: l'alternance entre décasyllabes et alexandrins dans un recueil de sonnets," in *Le Sonnet à la Renaissance: Des origines au XVIIe siècle*, ed. Y. Bellenger (Paris, 1988), 67–81.

also differs, the longest having 22 verses (no. 47) and the shortest having 4 (no. 48), while the first four poems have 14, 6, 6, and 8 lines, respectively. An effect of variety related to meter and length is thus created within this group of poems dealing with the same theme.

Epigram 43, being the first, is quite circumstantial in its detail, as it introduces the event which is the subject of the entire six-poem sequence.

In Mineruam argenteam
a S.P.Q. Tholosano
Petro Ronsardo ludis Floralibus decretam
et postea ab ipso Ronsardo
Herrico Regi Christianiss. dicatam

> Absenti neque tale quid petenti,
> Sed toto Aonidum probante coetu,
> Doctus Palladiae chorus Tholosae
> Perpulchram tibi detulit Mineruae,
> Ronsarde, effigiem, et quidem merenti:
> Nam si pro merito aestimare quenque
> Fas est, cui potius Minerua detur
> Quam cui in pectore tota sit Minerua?
> Tu uero ingenuo pudore tantum
> Decerni tibi non ferens honorem,
> Sed malens propria locare sede
> Sacrum Palladium, pius sacerdos,
> Regi Pallada rite dedicasti,
> Sub quo Palladii uigent honores. (p. 111)[16]

This describes how Ronsard was awarded a beautiful image of Minerva by the assembly of Toulouse, although he had in no way sought such an honor. Du Bellay explains that no one is more worthy of such a statue than Ronsard, whose heart is full of Minerva. Ronsard, however, was not willing to accept such an honor but dedicated the statue of Pallas to the king, under whom the cult of Pallas flourishes.

Epigram 44 is a short resumé of the previous poem:

Aliud

> Grata tuis studiis nuper studiosa Tholosa,
>> Sub qua Palladiae nunc uiget artis honos,
> Argento e nitido spirantia Palladis ora
>> Carminibus posuit, magne poeta, tuis.
> Tu uero haec Regis iussisti tecta subire,
>> Pallada qui solus nouit utramque simul. (p. 113)

---

[16] The six epigrams analyzed and quoted herein come from the critical edition of the Latin poems of Du Bellay, edited by Geneviève Demerson (see note 2 above).

Ronsard, a great poet, was awarded a living [*spirantia*] image of Pallas, made of silver, to reward him for his verses. Ronsard placed the statue in the palace of the king, who alone is able to unite the two vocations of Pallas: wisdom and war.

Epigram 45, also 6 lines, again resumes the essential elements of the incident:

Aliud

Tholosa ingenua, et Tholosa uere,
Tam bellam tibi quae dedit Mineruam.
Tu quoque ingenuus, tibi datam qui
Regi Pallada maximo dedisti.
Nunc suo posita est loco Minerva:
Quid Princeps tibi maximus rependet? (p. 113)

The emphasis is on nobility (*Tholosa ingenua/ingenuus* referring to Ronsard). The poem ends with the suggestion that the king, in order to prove himself noble, must reward Ronsard for the gift that Ronsard gave him.

Epigram 46 is addressed to Henry II to persuade him to give a generous gift to Ronsard:

Ad Herricum Reg. Christianiss.
in eandem sententiam

Vilius argentum est auro, uirtute minora
    Carmina, magnanimo Rege poeta minor.
Sed tu, quem fas est, Rex o ter maxime Regum,
    Vel paruis meritis praemia larga dare,
Quae tibi Ronsardus uates argentea misit,
    Aurea Ronsardo dona remitte tuo.
Aurea nanque decet solum dare munera Regem,
    Qui solus nobis aurea secla dedit. (p. 113)

Silver, poetry, and a poet are of less value than gold, virtue, and a magnanimous king. Henry, who is three times as great as any other king, and who is authorized to give great recompense, even for small merit, should make a golden gift to Ronsard, who has made Henry a silver gift. This king, who has given France a golden age, should only offer golden presents. The emphasis on Henry's virtue, magnanimity, and greatness is linked to the emphasis on gold (mentioned four times). This poem is the culmination of the theme of demanding recompense for Ronsard's gift to the king. I wonder if Du Bellay wants to receive a similar gift.

Epigram 47, the longest, is quite different in its structure from the others:

Ad P. Ronsardum

Cur Ronsarde, nouo atque inusitato
Decreto tibi nobilis Tholosa
Caelatam modo detulit Mineruam?
Vt, qui scilicet usitata Gallis
Sic vestigia linquit ut Pelasgum
Primus detegat abditos recessus,

Is novo quoque munere augeatur.
At cur iudicio gravi Senatus
Decreta est potius tibi Minerua
Quam Phoebus fidicen neposue Atlantis,
Aut una Aonidum e choro sororum?
Vt te non modo uersibus sonoris
Cantus edere (quod solent inepti),
Sed constet potius tuis inesse
Doctis uersibus et laboriosis
Rerum multiplicem eruditionem.
Cur uero tibi candido ex metallo
Haec facta est Dea? Nempe quod poeta
Purus, candidus, omnibus poetis
Praestes ingenuo tuo nitore,
Candore ut proprio nec aduocato
Argentum solet omnibus metallis. (pp. 113–115)

It is organized by three questions which Du Bellay asks of Ronsard: (1) Why did
Toulouse recently offer you (Ronsard) a sculptured Minerva? (2) Why did the Senate
of Toulouse award you a Minerva rather than a Phoebus Apollo, a Mercury, or a
Muse? (3) Why is this goddess made of a white and brilliant metal? The answers to
these questions are linked to praise of Ronsard: (1) Toulouse offered you a statue of
Minerva because you merited an extraordinary recompense for having abandoned the
traditional paths of the French to enter the hidden retreats of the Pelasgians (aboriginal non-Greek inhabitants of Greece), in other words, by having imitated early Greek
poetry, Pindar in particular. (2) Toulouse awarded you a *Minerva* to show that you
are not content to create songs that are sonorous but vapid, for we can find great
variety of erudition in your learned and artfully crafted verses. The contrast between
the *versibus sonoris* of the *inepti* and Ronsard's *(d)octis versibus et laboriosis /Rerum multiplicem eruditionem* suggests the difference between poetry of the new school and that
of its predecessors, as sketched in the *Deffence et Illustration*.[17] (3) Toulouse has
awarded you a *silver* Minerva, because you have a pure and candid soul like the silver
of the Minerva. You triumph over all other poets through your noble brilliance, just
as silver triumphs over all other metals through its native brilliance.

The last Epigram, only four lines long, offers the epigrammatic conclusion to the
entire series:

Ad eundem
Strinxerat in saevos quod fortiter arma Tyrannos

---

[17] Du Bellay, *Deffence et Illustration*, vol. 2: iv, 107–108, where Du Bellay recommends
constant reading of Greek and Roman authors: "Ly donques & rely premierement (ò Poëte futur),
fueillete de main nocturne et journelle les exemplaires Grecz & Latins: puis me laisse toutes ces
vieilles poësies Francoyses aux Jeuz Floraux de Thoulouze & au Puy de Rouan: comme rondeaux,
ballades, virelaiz, chantz royaulx, chansons, et autres telles episseries. . . ."

> Alcaeus uates, aurea plectra tulit.
> At quod Barbaries nostris, te uindice, tectis
> Exulet, hoc posita est docta Minerua tibi. (p. 115)

It is composed of a comparison/contrast between Alcaeus, the ancient Greek poet who received a gold plectrum as a reward for writing satirical and revolutionary songs against tyranny, and Ronsard, who, having chased barbarism from France, was presented with a wise Minerva. This contrast could be viewed as indicating that Ronsard received the reward he deserved [*docta Minerva*], but the *gold* plectrum awarded Alcaeus suggests that Ronsard deserves a *golden* reward for his success in outlawing barbarism from France and thus participating in, if not instigating, the return of the golden age.

These poems are encomiastic in nature, devoted to themes of praise: (1) Praise of Toulouse which awarded Ronsard the statue ["Doctus Palladiae chorus Tholosae . . . studiosa Tholosa . . . Tholosa ingenua, et Tholosa uere . . . nobilis Tholosa"]; (2) Praise of the statue itself and what it symbolizes ["Perpulchram . . . Minervae; spirantia Palladis ora; Tam bellam . . . Minervam; docta Minerva"]; (3) Praise of Ronsard, who merited the statue for his poetic achievements, his revival of Greek poetry, and his erudition; (4) Praise of Ronsard's "noble reserve" which made him dedicate the statue to the king, and of Ronsard's pure and candid soul; (5) Praise of the king who has supported the cult to Pallas and who is creating a new golden age. According to Millet, "ces six variations sur la Minerve d'argent . . . servent à définir autour d'une célébration de la poésie et du Roi les relations de Ronsard, de Henri II et de Du Bellay sur un ton unanime sans aucune des plaintes ou des réticences que l'on peut entendre dans la première partie des *Regrets*, mais aussi dès les premières épigrammes."[18] It seems at first glance that Du Bellay is praising Ronsard and his poetry without any of the complaints or recriminations that are found in the *Regrets* and in the other *Epigrammata*.

What is the purpose of all this praise? To encourage the king to offer a substantial gift to Ronsard in return for the gift which Ronsard has made him. This message is explicitly presented in poems 45 and 46, and indirectly in poem 48 through the comparison between Alcaeus' reward for his satiric and political poetry and Ronsard's reward for eliminating barbarism from France.

The praise of Toulouse, Ronsard, and King Henry is extravagant, as can be seen in the vocabulary, in the repetition of expressions from poem to poem, and in the repetition of the theme. We may ask to what extent Du Bellay is seriously praising Ronsard and demanding that the king reward him generously. Is Du Bellay ironic? Is he, in effect, talking about himself, suggesting that the same treatment be accorded to him? Do we have here an implicit or explicit self-contrast with Ronsard? The expression *paruis meritis* of poem 46 could apply to Du Bellay.

To look into this matter more closely, we should determine the dates of composition of these poems and compare them with similar poems written in Latin or in

---

[18] Millet, "Les *Epigrammata* de 1558," 577.

French by Du Bellay at the same time. This is difficult to do. The date of the event which is the subject of the poems is clear. On 3 May 1554, Ronsard was awarded an eglantine by the Jeux Floraux of Toulouse. He did not receive the flower, but in the following year (1555), he was awarded the solid silver statue of Minerva which was sent to him in Paris.[19] Ronsard did not keep the statue, but sent it to Henry II, who declared himself well pleased with the gift: "l'estimant beaucoup davantage qu'elle ne valait, pour avoir servi de marque à la valeur infinie d'un tel personnage."[20] The six epigrams, therefore, could not have been written before 1555, perhaps not before 1556, since they all speak of the awarding of the Minerva to Ronsard and of his giving it to the king. We cannot be more precise than this. No reference to this event occurs in any of Du Bellay's other poems, either those written in Rome and published upon his return, or those written between 1558 and 1560, the year of his death.

Several of Du Bellay's poems and letters deal with his poverty, his search for a noble patron, and his hope for a stable and secure existence. This is the story of his life, as it is of many other poets of the time. As a younger son, he had no claim upon the estate of his father. He needed to make his way in the world. After having abandoned law for letters, he took minor orders and hoped to obtain benefices and rewards from patrons for his skill in poetry. His departure for Rome in 1553 with his cousin, Cardinal Jean Du Bellay, was an attempt to assure his future as well as to satisfy the humanist dream of visiting Rome.

Physical and spiritual insecurity was a major theme of Du Bellay's life. His reiterated insistance on the award to Ronsard, on Ronsard's noble act in giving it to the king, and on Henry's obligation to give Ronsard a golden award, reflect Du Bellay's inferiority complex *vis-à-vis* Ronsard, and his chronic lack of financial security. Yet the award touched a chord in Du Bellay's psyche. Du Bellay is at once praising Ronsard, rejoicing in his success, while regretting his own lack of recognition.

While these serious themes may underlie the meaning and the motivation for this series of poems, another reason surely exists for them, which may explain why Du Bellay never used any of this material in his French poetry. The six epigrams are without doubt a series of "exercices de style." The description of the award, Ronsard's reaction, and the suggestion as to how Henry should react, are repeated in various fashions, longer or shorter, with an internal development that leads to the epigrammatic closure in poem 48. Du Bellay creates as much variety as possible without deviating from the subject he has chosen to illustrate. Thus, poems 44 and 45 are shorter versions of 43, in which Du Bellay had presented all his themes. Poem 45, however, is not identical to 44; it turns on a threefold notion of nobility, that of Toulouse, that of Ronsard, and that of the king. The king should reciprocate Ronsard's gift to demonstrate his own nobility. Poem 45 provides a development of the original theme. Poem 46 is a direct plea to the king to reward Ronsard with a golden present. The theme of gold is found throughout the poem. Poem 47, the longest, by

---

[19] See Pierre de Nolhac, *Ronsard et l'humanisme* (Paris, 1921), 297–298.
[20] Pierre Champion, *Ronsard et son temps* (Paris, 1925), 107–108.

the use of the question and answer format, allows Du Bellay, answering his own questions, to paint a glowing picture of Ronsard, his poetry, and his character, without mentioning Henry or the gift. Although this poem is the culminating point of the earlier theme of praise of Ronsard, it is meant to make Henry realize that he must reward Ronsard for his outstanding talents and qualities. Poem 48 brings the series to a close with the comparison/contrast between Alcaeus and Ronsard, and the rewards each has received.

The series of six poems can be treated as a single discourse or speech, with a variety of stylistic techniques used to embellish the themes. Du Bellay rings the changes. While this set of poems was surely intended for Du Bellay's Roman humanist colleagues or for his French humanist readers, we may ask, was it intended for Ronsard? The repetition of the elements of the incident sound more ironic or even parodic than heartfelt. They intimate that Ronsard is the court poet [*le poète courtisan*] *par excellence*. The same ambivalent attitude toward the "poète courtisan" is found in Du Bellay's *Regrets* and elsewhere. Du Bellay's praise of Ronsard and Henry may turn out to be a mock encomium after all.

The Catholic University of America

The Founding of the Democractic State
in Spinoza's
Tractatus Theologico-Politicus *(1670)*

ROBERT GINSBERG

The social contract theory, prominent in European thought in the seventeenth and eighteenth centuries, proposed an account of government, in its various forms, in terms of an originating act of contract. Contract theory has been dismissed as fanciful pseudo-history, or pseudo pre-history. David Hume, for instance, in his essay, "Of the Original Contract" (1748), offered the stunning objection to the social contract that such an enactment had never occurred.

But the contract envisioned by its great theorists was not proposed as historical; it was intended as conceptual. Its virtue lies in its justificatory power, not in its historical accuracy. While we may read the contract theorists as writing primarily to justify government in general and then to express a preference for one form of government over others, we might also see their primary effort as making the case for the best form of government. The best is then identified with the form that is the closest to the spirit of the originating contract. "Origin" in this sense is not temporal but purposive. In Aristotelian terms, it is the final cause, the goal intended. So a social contract theory may turn out to be a case made for one form of government by means of a theoretical account of the purpose of government in general.

What is intellectually exciting about the great contract theorists is how they rearrange the theory to support a preferred form of government. Hobbes, the most celebrated of such theorists, argues in Latin in *De Cive* (1642), and in English in *Leviathan* (1651), that monarchy is the best form of government, since it places in one person's hands the protection of all parties, for whose very protection civil society is instituted. The worst form of government, according to Hobbes, is democracy, in which people rule themselves. This is too close to the state of nature where each person is judge to their own cause; thus, democracy is scarcely government. It approaches the greatest evil: civil war.

Locke, in his *Two Treatises of Government* (1690), counters the Hobbesian position by making the case for majority rule, since it is closest to a contractual act by a multitude of parties. For Locke, the worst form of government is that which consigns the exercise of power over the multitude to one person; thus, absolute monarchy is scarcely government at all. It approaches the greatest evil: tyranny. We can see that political programs are implicit in the political theories of Hobbes and Locke.

I wish to introduce Spinoza into this discussion. Writing anonymously in Latin in his *Tractatus Theologico-Politicus* (1670), Spinoza gives a remarkably clear and forceful version of contract theory, in chapter 16, on the Foundation of the State (*De Reipublicæ Fundamentis*).[1] Spinoza is all for democracy. "Of all forms of government," he declares, it is "the most natural, and the most consonant with individual liberty" (E, p. 207); "de quo præ omnibus agere malui, quia maxime naturale videbatur, & maxime ad libertatem, quam natura unicuique concedit, accedere" (L, p. 195). By "natural," the most powerful term in Spinoza's vocabulary, he means "the sovereign law and right of nature that each individual should endeavor to preserve itself as it is, without regard to anything but itself" (E, p. 200); "Et quia lex summa naturæ est, ut unaquæque res in suo statu, quantum in se est, conetur perseverare, idque nulla alterius, sed tantum sui habita ratione" (L, p. 189). Democracy favors the preservation of all contracting parties because its conduct will most likely be guided by reason. "It is almost impossible," says Spinoza confidently, "that the majority of a people . . . should agree in an irrational design" (E, p. 206); "Nam fere impossibile est, ut major unius cœtus pars . . . in uno absurdo conveniat" (L, p. 194). Locke was to share this confidence in the majority. While one person or a few people may be mistaken in their exercise of reason, the chance that reason will be soundly used is compounded if we rely on the majority of people, according to both Locke and Spinoza. Safety lies in numbers, when we are talking about the safety of all and when the activity is open to reason. This is an almost self-evident axiom.

In Spinoza's view reason is crucial to democracy. He tells us, "the basis and aim of a democracy is to avoid the desires as irrational, and to bring men as far as possible under the control of reason, so that they may live in peace and harmony" (E, p. 206); "deinde propter ejus fundamentum & finem, qui, ut etiam ostendimus, nullus alius est quam absurda appetitus vitare, & hominis sub rationes limites, quoad ejus fieri potest, continere, ut concorditer & pacifice vivant" (L, p. 194). This ideal of democracy is more than a form of government; it is an instrument of humanization. Democracy, in this vision, democratizes. Peace and harmony are to be achieved in accordance with the supreme natural law of self-protection, and such achievements require the transformation of our lives. To overcome our passions and live under the guidance of reason serves the interests of everyone. But this is the task of ethics, as

---

[1] Spinoza, *Tractatus Theologico-Politicus*, in *Opera*, ed. Carl Gebhardt, vol. 3 (Heidelberg, 1972 [originally published in 1925]). Page references to the Latin edition will be signalled in the text by L. Cf. R. H. M. Elwes, trans., *The Chief Works of Benedict de Spinoza*, 2 vols. bound as one (New York, 1951 [originally published in 1883]). Page references to this English translation will be signalled in the text by E.

conceived by Spinoza in his posthumous masterpiece, *The Ethics, Demonstrated in Geometrical Order* (1677).

Rousseau in his classic, *Du Contrat social* (1762), was to share with Spinoza the insight, or the insistence, that the institution of civil society transforms persons such that the moral life becomes feasible. Rousseau was concerned with the internalization of the social self, so that every individual bore within himself (or herself) due regard for others, whereas Spinoza is concerned with the assistance that democracy provides for each individual in order to lead a truly moral life through reason's mastery over passion. The state is concerned with the moral well-being of its subjects, because, in Spinoza's terms, this is conducive to peaceful relations between its subjects. In other words, if individuals are fulfilled (instead of being driven by their desires) then they are not likely to cause trouble to one another.

Part four of the *Ethics*, subtitled, "Of the Power of the Passions," has as its main title, "Of Human Bondage" (appropriated by W. Somerset Maugham for his autobiographical novel [1915]). The problem Spinoza raises in part four is answered in part five, entitled "Of the Power of the Intellect; or of Human Freedom." The project of the *Ethics* is to assist people to overcome their slavery to passion through the liberating power of reason. Such freedom is bliss. I speak of the *Ethics* as a project because it can be used as a manual for self-improvement, although due to its propositional form it is usually taken as a demonstrative treatise. The axioms and propositions are ladders that allow readers to get into the act through the exercise of reason, regardless of the stage at which they find themselves. This is cognitive therapy, since our understanding of irrational causes will lead to our release from their sway. Psychoanalysis, invented in the late nineteenth century by Freud, is in this tradition. Therefore, for Spinoza and Freud, self-awareness frees us. Our suffering is self-inflicted insofar as our unconscious desires disrupt the course of our lives.

Thus, for Spinoza, ethics is an epistemology. Self-awareness, in turn, is connected to metaphysics, for we must grasp reality under its different aspects. Everything comes down to *Deus sive Natura*. Spinoza works within the Cartesian spirit to link all the branches of philosophical inquiry.

Democracy, as Spinoza conceives it, is a political project that facilitates the life of reason within individuals and within the society. Social harmony and personal fulfillment go hand-in-hand. This vision of a mutually supportive relationship between the society and the individual stands in contrast to modern views, which call for the appropriate formal treatment of persons by the state while keeping private life out of the purview of government. Be as irrational as you want, as long as you stay within the law! is the password of liberal democracies nowadays. But irrationality, argues Spinoza, is in no one's interest, since it is self-destructive. To follow one's passion is not to be free.

Liberation is the overarching project for Spinoza. Thus, the state is created as a rational act in the need to free ourselves from the inadequate and dangerous conditions found in the state of nature. For "without mutual help, or the aid of reason," says Spinoza, we "must needs live most miserably" (E, p. 202); "hominis absque mutuo auxilio miserrime, & absque rationis cultu necessario vivere" (L, p. 191). Hobbes had spoken of such life as "solitary, poore, nasty, brutish, and short." The key to the contract is in replacing the uncontrolled exercise of desire with a conduct guided by reason, thanks to our mutual transfer of power to the body politic (E, p. 205; L, p. 193). All contract theories turn upon giving something up for the sake of something desirable or necessary. While we each give up liberty, power, and right, which are three facets of the same thing in Spinoza's eyes, in return we receive the protection of liberty, power, and right. Reason would have to consent to this, since nothing of value is really lost and everything of value is made secure. The democratic state places everyone's interests in the forefront. So what we have surrendered is only the caprice of living by passion. We are now free to live in reason. That is why Spinoza sees democracy, in the passage quoted earlier, as "most consonant with individual liberty" (E, p. 207; L, p. 195).

The Spinozaic concept of liberty is inseparable from the exercise of reason. Thus, Spinoza says, "he alone is free who lives with free consent under the entire guidance of reason" (E, p. 206); "solus ille liber, qui integro animo ex solo ductu rationis vivit" (L, p. 194). This type of liberty has nothing to with the Hobbesian notion of being unimpeded in one's actions. For Spinoza, true liberty is a willing conformity, not to arbitrary law, but to the dictates of reason, which demands adherence to the laws that regulate the body politic for everyone's protection. Rousseau was to further develop the apparent paradox of freely choosing to be bound.

Spinoza sees that the exchange of natural right in the creation of democracy in effect preserves each individual's exercise of the right insofar as each individual is constitutive of the majority which rules the society (E, p. 207; L, p. 195). Your liberty and my liberty are thereby enhanced rather than lost. Locke was to develop further this virtue in majority rule.

Spinoza adds that under democracy "all men remain, as they were in the state of nature, equals" (E, p. 207); "Atque hac ratione omnes manent, ut antea in statu naturali, æquales" (L, p. 195). Equality is the natural condition from which all contract theories start. A contract, covenant, compact, pact, mutual promise, or whatever you wish to call it, presupposes equal willingness to agree. Our equality in the supposed natural state may be described in a variety of ways by the contract theorists. Thus, according to Hobbes, we are each equally capable of killing one another. But the theorists are in general agreement that we all equally desire self-protection. We may all be equally threatened by the lawless condition of the natural state. This is the reason for all of us to enter into a contract that changes this condition. We are equal in reason in being able to understand that the contract is in our mutual interest. Remember that we are not speaking historically but hypothetically; we are making a case for what people at any time or place would do. This hypothetical projection is clearest in the great twentieth-century revival of contract theory by John Rawls, *A Theory of Justice* (1971).

Equality is essential to social contract theory. Without equality as the justificatory origin of polity, we would be beset with a grounding in social coercion. If force has formed our forms of governments, then force may be used to disobey or to alter them. And if only might makes right, then we invite the collapse of civil society into civil war, in which we are no better off than in the state of nature. Voluntary agreement is the antidote to lawless aggression.

The problem for all contract theorists is how to justify the inequalities that appear in civil society, given the origination of that society in universal equality. The magistrate and the pickpocket are obviously not equal, as I was reminded recently while sitting in the Plaza Mayor in Madrid, although we might recognize their equality under due process of law. Hobbes, as I have earlier reported, totally rejects equality once the contract is equally entered.[2] Spinoza, then Locke, then Kant, insists that our original equality remains with us under the right form of government. For Spinoza, each person has the right in a democracy to self-protection and self-fulfillment; each should have the opportunity, thanks to the state, to achieve happiness in the peaceful ordering of individual life in accordance with reason. The American Declaration of Independence (1776) declared as unalienable the rights to "Life, Liberty, and the Pursuit of Happiness." Government was instituted to protect such rights for "all Men," since they "are created equal."

The Declaration penned by Thomas Jefferson was a justification of the American Revolution, as Locke's *Two Treatises* were a justification of the Glorious Revolution. Rousseau's case for revolution in *Of the Social Contract* is the broadest, and was used to justify the French Revolution.

Hobbes made the strongest case against revolution as civil war by stating that it is better to live under a bad government than in a state of war, which is the state of nature. All government, according to Hobbes, might be thought of as tyranny, since we are bound absolutely to obey. This is the price we pay for peace and safety. Yet Hobbes allows that since the individual's natural right to self-preservation always persists, we would save our necks by fleeing from so-called tyrants—and even from legitimate executioners. In such grave instances, we would be getting out of the contract.

Spinoza takes into account the tyrannical abuse of power by the sovereign. In such a case, the contracting parties have the natural right to replace the sovereign.[3] We must keep in mind that in the great contract theories, the contract is between the individual citizens, allowing them to designate a sovereign. It is not a contract between the people and the sovereign. So for Spinoza what we call "revolution" could be justified as a revision of the contract. The American Declaration speaks of the people's right "to alter or to abolish" forms of government destructive of the other rights of the people.

Spinoza has another answer—a foolproof one—to the question of revolution, which is that democracy will prevent tyranny. For the people to oppress themselves is a contradiction. Yet John Stuart Mill, in his *On Liberty* (1859), was to persuasively warn us against the tyranny of the majority. The individual needs protection against

---

[2] Robert Ginsberg, "Equality in Hobbes's *De Cive*," in *Acta Conventus Neo-Latini Hafniensis: Proceedings of the Eighth International Congress of Neo-Latin Studies*, ed. Ann Moss et al. (Binghamton, 1994), 339–444.

[3] See Spinoza, *Tractatus Politicus*, in *Opera*, ed. Gebhardt, vol. 3, chap. 7, sect. 30, 322. Cf. Elwes, trans., *Chief Works of Spinoza*, 343.

the people. Spinoza's response might be that democratic government increasingly becomes more rational in its conduct, and its subjects themselves become more rational. Oppression of individuals or groups is avoided when the universality of our rights is recognized. Spinoza's optimism likely received a serious blow in 1672, two years after the publication of his *Tractatus Theologico-Politicus*, when the great statesman Jan de Witt, along with his brother Cornelius de Witt, were hacked to death and strung out on several lampposts by a mob. Spinoza himself was in danger of mob action.

In his writings on politics and ethics, Spinoza contributes to the recognition of human dignity. Kant, in *Zum ewigen Frieden* (1795), was to build one of the best cases during the Enlightenment for a social contract grounded in human dignity. The Universal Declaration of Human Rights (1948), which is among the greatest achievements of the twentieth century, insists on the universality of the dignity and the equality of all humankind. This Declaration, like the Spinozaic ethics and democracy, is couched as a project: all persons, and all governments, have the obligation to advance the recognition of human rights. Recognition entails realization. Thus, my duty, even as scholar, is to make the world more suitable for humanity. Spinoza helps in this effort. His great achievement in the *Tractatus Theologico-Politicus* is the rejection of theocratic intervention within the state. This stands alongside the similar efforts of Hobbes and Locke, and earned Spinoza a place on the Index. Great ideas need not remain caught in the nets of the past. Like doves, they may take wing and soar with the joy of freedom.

I cannot leave Spinoza's contribution to the liberation of humanity without pointing to some shortcomings. Spinoza's last word on democracy demands our attention. It comes in the closing section of the last chapter, "Of Democracy," of the posthumous *Tractatus Politicus* (1677): "one may assert with perfect propriety, that women have not by nature equal right with men," so women should be ruled by men; "affirmare omninò licet, fœminas ex naturâ non æquale cum viris habere jus, sed eas viris necessariò cedere."[4] To this we may suitably apply the technical term, ¡Merda!

Spinoza has mistaken the historical and empirical situation which prevented women from ruling over men as evidence of their own natural weakness. This mistake, which devalues half of humanity, shows us how deceptive reason can be in understanding humanity. If I have learned anything in my unsuccessful career as a philosopher, it is to distrust the passion for reason. I would also make room in ethics and politics for the understanding that comes with illuminating passion. The value of passion for insight and fulfillment was movingly demonstrated by Teresa of Avila. A passion for human decency and a compassion for one another would balance Spinoza's beautifully naive faith in blind reason.

What is chiefly lacking in Spinoza's case for democracy is the specification of the formal structure of government that would accomplish the aims of democracy. To echo the motto of the people of the state of Missouri, "Show me!" How is it to work? What checks must be created to prevent the people from becoming a mob,

---

[4] Spinoza, *Tractatus Politicus*, in *Opera*, ed. Gebhardt, vol. 3, chap. 11, sect. 4, 360. Elwes, trans., *Chief Works of Spinoza*, 387.

ruled not by reason but by inflamed passion? What balances must be instituted within government to prevent it from becoming a tyranny if officeholders are corrupted by power? In trying to answer these questions, we move toward a republic as a form of government in which the people rule by representatives rather than directly, and in which ruling powers are divided into legislative, judicial, and executive branches. This is the tradition of Locke, Montesquieu, the Federalist Papers, and Kant.

In the *Tractatus Politicus* (chapter 11, sections 1, 3), Spinoza insists that democracy means the right of the people to vote and to stand for office. Is that all there is to democracy? All the rest, Spinoza might argue, will follow from the use of reason by the multitude or by the officers they elect. The right persons will be elected because all citizens are eligible for office, and presumably those who are the most rational will be recognized by the people. Voting is reason confirming itself.

This is not enough protection for me. Spinoza's democracy lacks institutional structure; therefore, we have to fill this in for him. The *Tractatus Politicus* breaks off at the point where democracy cries out for modes of implementation and protection.

But if instead of speaking of democracy as a form, we were to treat it as a spirit or ethos of government, then Spinoza belongs at the heart of the modern liberal tradition of political thought. "Democratic" government is almost universally applauded these days, even if democracy is not quite the form manifested. Thus, great oppressive regimes have called themselves "People's Democratic Republics." Constitutional monarchies, federated states, and presidential regimes also pronounce themselves democratic. Several of these current forms might legitimately be called democracies in the spirit of Spinoza, insofar as they are organized to advance, under peaceful conditions, the human dignity of all their subjects.

Spinoza's parents fled the Iberian peninsula, accused of the high crime of being Jews. We are indebted to their son for a clear and distinct political theory, which may be corrected and expanded to include respect for all human beings, women and men. Such liberating ideas are the true *Patrimonio de la Humanidad*. That democratic government can flourish with happy results is amply evident today in the Iberian peninsula.

The Pennsylvania State University

Novus orbis: *Melchior de Polignac*
über das Mikroskop

REINHOLD F. GLEI

Vor 250 Jahren erschien in Paris die *editio princeps* des monumentalen, enzyklopädischen Lehrgedichts *Anti-Lucretius sive de Deo et Natura libri novem*[1] des illustren Kardinals Melchior de Polignac (1661–1741).[2] Das "doppelt verwaiste Werk", wie es der Herausgeber Charles LeBeau, Professor der Beredsamkeit an der Pariser Universität, in seiner Vorrede nennt[3], hatte der 80 jährige Kardinal 1741 auf dem Totenbett seinem langjährigen Freund und Hausgenossen, dem Abbé Charles d'Orléans de Rothelin, unvollendet hinterlassen, der sich der Aufgabe unterzog, die *disiecti membra poetae* zu sammeln, zu ordnen und in eine sinnvolle Reihenfolge zu bringen. Rothelin selbst starb 1744, ohne seine Aufgabe vollendet zu haben, so daß sich schließlich LeBeau des Gedichts annahm und es 1747 herausbrachte.

Im Keim entstanden ist der *AL* aber bereits 50 Jahre früher, 1697, und damit vor nunmehr 300 Jahren. Damals befand sich Polignac—ein junger Diplomat in den Diensten Ludwigs XIV.—auf der Rückreise von Warschau, wo er die Nachfolge des polnischen Königs Johann III. Sobieski im Sinne Frankreichs hatte regeln sollen; als ihm dies nicht gelang und der sächsische Kurfürst August der Starke König von Polen wurde, berief Ludwig XIV. Polignac ab. Dieser reiste über Holland zurück und hielt sich einige Zeit in Rotterdam auf, wo er u.a. mit Pierre Bayle (1647–1706) zusammentraf, der seine aufklärerischen Ansichten gern mit Lukrezversen zu untermauern

---

[1] Anti-Lucretius, sive de Deo et Natura, libri novem. Eminentissimi S.R.E. Cardinalis Melchioris de Polignac opus posthumum; Illustrissimi Abbatis Caroli d'Orleans de Rothelin curâ & studio editioni mandatum. Parisiis, Apud H.-L. & J. Guerin, M.DCC.XLVII. (Exemplar der Bayerischen Staatsbibliothek München). Am weitesten verbreitet ist der (leider mit zahlreichen Fehlern behaftete) Pariser Nachdruck von 1754.—Verf. bereitet eine kommentierte Textausgabe des *Anti-Lucretius* (im folgenden: *AL*) mit deutscher Übersetzung vor.

[2] Zur Biographie cf. Pierre Paul, *Le Cardinal Melchior de Polignac (1661–1741)* (Paris, 1922).

[3] Praef. p. xxiij: "Nos aliquot difficultatibus diutiùs, quàm vellemus, retardati, opus bis posthumum, & parente & tutore orbatum, adoptandum nunc tradimus Religioni & Litteraturae."

pflegte. Da faßte Polignac den Plan, Lukrez, "den Oberpriester der Atheisten"[4], in Gattung, Sprache und Stil mit dessen eigenen Waffen zu schlagen und dem honigsüßen Gift des römischen Dichters die bittere Medizin der wahren Lehre entgegenzusetzen. Er sollte dazu bald Gelegenheit haben, denn Ludwig XIV. verbannte den glücklosen Diplomaten für fünf Jahre in die einsame Abtei Bonport in der Normandie. Die verwickelte Geschichte des Werkes, die sich, wie gesagt, über 50 Jahre hinzieht, kann hier nicht weiter verfolgt werden; Ziel der folgenden Ausführungen ist es, die Argumentationsweise und Methode Polignacs exemplarisch aufzuzeigen und deutlich zu machen, daß er nicht nur Lukrez bzw. Epikur bekämpft, sondern sich auch kenntnisreich und engagiert in zeitgenössische Debatten einmischt.

Bevor dies an einem konkreten Beispiel demonstriert werden kann, muß ein grober Überblick über den Aufbau des ca. 18.000 Hexameter umfassenden Werkes gegeben werden. Das erste Buch *De Voluptate* erörtert zunächst die negativen Folgen der epikureischen Lustlehre, die in ihrer Konsequenz zum Verlust der Moral und damit zu individuellem wie kollektivem Unglück führe. Im Zentrum des Buches steht die Kritik an den neuzeitlichen Apologeten Epikurs, insbesondere an Pierre Gassendi (1592–1655) und den Gassendisten, ferner an den Pyrrhonisten und schließlich an Thomas Hobbes (1588–1679). Den dritten Teil bildet eine umfassende Synkrisis der Religion und des Epikureismus im Hinblick auf soziale Verantwortung und individuelles Glück. Nach dieser programmatischen Exposition, die man als Pendant zum umfangreichen Proömium von *De rerum natura* (im folgenden: *DRN*) verstehen kann, erfolgt die Widerlegung der lukrezischen Lehre im einzelnen. Weil Lukrez mit der Atomphysik begonnen hatte und weil—nach einem treffenden Diktum von Rainer Specht—"Polignac ... davon überzeugt [war], daß Vacuumtheorie wie Atomistik direkt zu Atheismus, Atheismus direkt zu Unmoral und Unmoral direkt zu Unglückseligkeit führt"[5], mußte Polignac vordringlich die epikureisch-lukrezisch-gassendische Atomphysik[6] widerlegen; dies geschieht in den Büchern 2 *De Inani* (Darlegung der Nichtexistenz eines physikalischen Vakuums), 3 *De Atomis* (Teilbarkeit der Materie *in infinitum*) und 4 *De Motu* (Bewegung im Äther, Unmöglichkeit akausaler Bahnabweichung). Mit Buch 5 *De Mente* geht Polignac dann vom Bereich des Mikrokosmos in den des Mesokosmos über und behandelt die Natur der menschlichen Seele, die er im Anschluß an René Descartes (1596–1650) als immaterielle *res cogitans* versteht. Buch 6 *De Belluis* und Buch 7 *De Seminibus* behandeln anschließend höchst aktuelle Probleme der Biologie, nämlich in Buch 6 die Frage nach der Existenz einer Tierseele (Diskussion der Automatenhypothese), in Buch 7 das Problem der Entstehung des Lebens sowie der Mechanismen der Fortpflanzung und Verer-

---

[4] Praef. p. xj: "Lucretium Atheorum antistitem atque oraculum".

[5] Rainer Specht, "Über Polignacs 'Antilucretius'", in *Epirrhosis. Festgabe für Carl Schmitt* (Berlin, 1968), 697–707; Zitat: 703.

[6] Cf. Howard Jones, "An Eighteenth-Century Refutation of Epicurean Physics: The *Anti-Lucretius* of Melchior de Polignac (1747)", in *Acta Conventus Neo-Latini Torontonensis* (Binghamton, 1991), 393–401.

bung.[7] Mit Buch 8 *De Mundo* begibt sich Polignac schließlich in den Bereich des Makrokosmos und beschreibt das heliozentrische Weltbild im Anschluß an Johannes Kepler (1571–1630); Buch 9 *De Terra et Mari* sollte geophysikalischen Problemen gewidmet sein, ist aber bis auf das Proömium verloren.[8] Polignac folgt damit im wesentlichen dem Aufbau von Lukrez' *DRN*, setzt aber, wo es nötig erscheint, andere Akzente.[9]

Zu einem konkreten Beispiel: Zu Beginn des siebten Buches[10] wird die von Lukrez in *DRN* 5,805ff. dargestellte Theorie der Urzeugung behandelt; als Hauptargument gegen sie führt Polignac an, daß Urzeugung nicht beobachtet werden könne und daß der von Lukrez behauptete Verlust der Fruchtbarkeit von Mutter Erde unerklärlich sei; außerdem widerspreche er der im Venushymnus gepriesenen Fertilität der Natur. Natürlich bekämpft Polignac damit nicht nur Lukrez oder Epikur, sondern auch die modernen Verfechter der Urzeugung wie z.B. den gelehrten Jesuiten Athanasius Kircher (1601–1680), der den sog. Panspermismus vertrat, wonach die *semina rerum* das All durchdringen und spontan Leben erzeugen.[11]

Weiterhin lehnt Polignac auch die aristotelische Theorie vom Samen als wirkendem Formprinzip (*forma artifex*)—wie im übrigen den gesamten Hylemorphismus— ausdrücklich ab; auch hier bezieht sich Polignac ausdrücklich auf Versuche, die alte *doctrina Lycei* wiederzubeleben, namentlich die Lehre von der *natura plastica*, die von Ralph Cudworth (1617–1688) und Nicolas Hartsoeker (1656–1725) vertreten wurde.[12]

Polignacs eigene Theorie von der Entstehung des Lebens, die in vielen Punkten mit der Lehre von Jan Swammerdam (1637–1680) übereinstimmt[13], läßt sich etwa

---

[7] Buch 7 wurde bereits unmittelbar nach Erscheinen des *AL* besonders gelobt: cf. e.g. *Nova Acta Eruditorum* (Lipsiae, 1. Januar 1748), 17: "[liber VII], qui Physiologiae compendium dici potest". Cf. auch Paul, *Melchior de Polignac*, 354: "Son étude des semences est peut-être bien la plus originale de ce long poème."

[8] Das unauffindbare neunte Buch wurde von Rothelin durch eine "Conclusio totius operis", eine schwache Retractatio des ersten Buches, ersetzt.

[9] *AL* 2–4 entsprechen also *DRN* 1–2, *AL* 5 entspricht *DRN* 3–4, *AL* 6–9 entsprechen *DRN* 5–6. Die geplante Ausgabe wird die Anti-Textur des AL auf der Makro- und Mikroebene zu untersuchen haben; zur Theorie und Methodik cf. einstweilen R. F. Glei, "Der interepische poetologische Diskurs: zum Verhältnis von *Metamorphosen* und *Aeneis*", in H. L. C. Tristram, ed., *Neue Methoden der Epenforschung* (Tübingen, 1998) [im Druck].

[10] Überblick über Buch 7: *Journal de Trévoux* 48 (1748), Article LI: 1081–91; Edouard Patry, "L'Anti-Lucrèce du Cardinal de Polignac" (Thèse, Faculté des Lettres de Nancy, Auch 1872), 149–168; Casimir-Alexandre Fusil, *L'Anti-Lucrèce du Cardinal de Polignac* (Paris, 1917), 89–102.

[11] Athanasius Kircher, *Mundus subterraneus* (Amsterdam, 1665).

[12] *AL* 7, 169–171: "Haec fuit antiqui celebris doctrina Lycei; / Quam renovare velint, quibus haec natura vocatur / Plastica". Cf. Ralph Cudworth, *The True Intellectual Systeme of the Universe* (London, 1678; repr. Hildesheim, 1977); lateinische Übersetzung von Johannes Laurentius Moshemius: *Systema intellectuale huius universi* (Jena, 1733; secunda editio Leiden, 1773); Nicolas Hartsoeker, *Principes de physique* (Paris, 1696); ders., *Conjectures physiques* (Amsterdam, 1706).

[13] Swammerdams berühmtes Hauptwerk, die *Biblia Naturae* (Leiden, 1737), erschien zwar erst kurz vor Polignacs Tod, das Wesentliche ist jedoch bereits in der *Historia insectorum generalis* (Leiden, 1685; secunda editio Utrecht, 1693) enthalten.

so umschreiben: Gott schuf im Anfang ein für allemal den Prototyp jeder Art von Lebewesen, die sich seitdem unverändert mithilfe der Samen fortpflanzen.[14] Spontanentstehung/Urzeugung von Lebewesen ist also keinesfalls möglich: Lebewesen können nur aus den entsprechenden Samen entstehen- bis auf jenes erste Lebewesen jeder Art, das von Gott geschaffen wurde (cf. *AL* 7,1673–76). Ein Problem, das sich in diesem Zusammenhang ergab, war die Frage, ob die Vererbung patri- oder matrilinear vonstatten geht; denn eine Synthese männlicher und weiblicher Teilsamen nach Art einer 'Legierung' hielt Polignac mit anderen angesichts der Komplexität der Lebewesen und zumal des Menschen nicht für möglich. In diesem Streit der 'Ovulisten' und 'Spermatisten'[15] ergriff Polignac eindeutig für die letzteren Partei: Danach liegt der Samen ausschließlich im männlichen Wesen, das weibliche dient nur der Ernährung und Aufzucht des Samens.

Polignac folgt in diesem Punkt also nicht dem Ovulisten Swammerdam, sondern einem anderen großen holländischen Naturforscher: Antoni van Leeuwenhoek (1632–1723)[16] aus Delft, dem 'Delphi Batavorum'. Mithilfe selbstgebauter einfacher Mikroskope von z.T. erheblichem Vergrößerungsfaktor machte der Autodidakt zahlreiche Entdeckungen, die er der Londoner Royal Society in Briefen, die eigens dafür ins Lateinische übersetzt werden mußten, mitteilte.

Damit kommen wir zu Polignacs Äußerungen über das Mikroskop. In der dem unten abgedruckten Text vorangehenden Passage hatte Polignac, wie es im *Argumentum* des siebten Buches heißt, "aus der dauerhaften Ähnlichkeit der Generationen und deren äußerst kunstfertiger Anlage gefolgert, daß die Samen nur von einer planenden, allgemeinen, mächtigen und ewigen Ursache geformt werden konnten"[17]; so sei das gesamte Menschengeschlecht bereits im ersten Menschen angelegt gewesen. Daß die entscheidenden Lebenskeime sich in den männlichen Wesen befänden, davon könne man sich jetzt mit eigenen Augen überzeugen:

Nempe Microscopium, Batavis quod nuper in oris
Divinâ sapiens reperit Levenockius arte,
Perspicuamque facem in tenebris dedit esse profundis,
Arripe & observa. Nihil est nisi vitrea lenti   1025
Lacryma convexæ similis, quam lamina duplex
Continet infixam, tenuique foramine circùm

---

[14] Daß dies eine prinzipiell unendliche Teilbarkeit der Samenkörper voraussetzt (cf. *AL* 7,1396: "segetem aeternam, & sine fine feracem"), war für Polignac unproblematisch, hatte er doch in Buch 3 die Atomhypothese gründlich widerlegt und eine Teilbarkeit der Materie *in infinitum* nachgewiesen.

[15] Bis zur Entdeckung der Spermatozoiden im Jahre 1677 beherrschten natürlich die Ovulisten das Feld: cf. F. S. Bodenheimer, *The History of Biology: An Introduction* (London, 1958), 54–63; Paolo Rossi, *Die Geburt der modernen Wissenschaft in Europa* (München, 1997), 246–251, mit weiteren Literaturangaben.

[16] Biographische Daten bei A. Schierbeek, *Introduction to* Antoni van Leeuwenhoek, *On the Circulation of the Blood* (Nieuwkoop, 1962), 25–29.

[17] Argum. libri septimi, p. 287: "Ex constanti generationum similitudine earumque arte eximiâ probat, semina nisi à causâ providâ, communi, validâ & aeternâ formari non potuisse."

Includit. Minimum quodcunque objeceris, ingens
Apparet visu confestim, atque intima pandit.
Nec præsens adeò nostris obtutibus unquam   1030
Auxilium venit: novus illo sistitur orbis;
Et nova Naturæ facies reseratur, apertis
Visceribus mixtorum, & tegmine nuda remoto.
Est oculorum oculus, sine quo cæci esse videmur,
Saltem hebetes tardique: quibus vix antè licebat   1035
Nosse superficiem, atque hærere in cortice summo,
Nunc aditus liber patet in præcordia rerum.
Nec jam vestibulum ante ipsum atque in limine portæ
Stamus, at in medias juvat ire profundiùs ædes;
Atque ibi thesauros fluxi & reparabilis ævi   1040
Hactenus occultos, quodque est ante omnia mirum,
Æternæ contemplari vestigia Mentis
Indita Materiæ, ut speculis mandatur imago. (*AL* 7,1022–43)

[Denn nimm das Mikroskop, das der kluge Leeuwenhoek kürzlich in Holland mit göttlicher Kunstfertigkeit erfand und das er ‹uns› in tiefer Dunkelheit als helle Fackel gab: Nimm es zur Hand und beobachte! Es ist nichts als eine gläserne Träne, einer gewölbten Linse ähnlich, die eine doppelte Platte im Innern festhält und mit einer kleinen Öffnung rings umschließt. Was immer an ganz Kleinem man betrachtet, erscheint dem Blick gleich riesengroß und öffnet ‹ihm› sein Innerstes. Niemals kam unserer Beobachtung etwas so deutlich zu Hilfe: Eine neue Welt wird dadurch präsentiert, ein neues Antlitz der Natur eröffnet sich, man blickt ins Innere ihrer Verbindungen, die Blöße der Natur ist nicht mehr bedeckt. Es ist das Auge der Augen, ohne das wir blind erscheinen, zumindest stumpf und schwerfällig: Uns, denen es vorher kaum möglich war, die Oberfläche zu erkennen und an der äußersten Schale zu haften, steht jetzt der Zugang offen zum Herzen der Dinge. Nicht mehr stehen wir bloß auf der Schwelle des Tores, selbst noch vor der Eingangshalle, sondern freudig gehen wir tiefer hinein ins Zentrum des Hauses und betrachten dort die bisher verborgenen Schätze des flüchtigen, aber sich fortpflanzenden Lebens und, was vor allem bewundernswert ist, die Spuren des ewigen Geistes, die der Materie innewohnen wie das Bild dem Spiegel.]

Dieser hymnische Preis des Mikroskops[18] ist in zweifacher Hinsicht besonders bemerkenswert: in technischer und in philosophischer. Was die technische Seite angeht, so liegt in den zitierten Anfangsversen eine exakte Beschreibung desjenigen

---

[18] Polignacs Verse beeindruckten bereits die Rezensenten: cf. *Nova Acta Eruditorum* (Anm. 7), 21; *Journal de Trévoux* (Anm. 10), 1089. Auch J. G. Kerkherdere pries in seinem *Carmen Panegyricum* auf Leeuwenhoek ("Leogonus") ausführlich das Mikroskop: abgedruckt in Antonii à Leeuwenhoek *Opera Omnia*, tom. 1 (Lugduni Batavorum, 1722; repr. Hildesheim, 1971), 3–8.

Typs von Mikroskop vor, den Leeuwenhoek konstruiert hatte[19]: Zwischen zwei
dünnen Metallplättchen aus Messing, Silber oder auch Gold war eine kleine, stark
geschliffene Linse angebracht; auf der einen Seite des Instruments befand sich ein
verstellbarer Dorn, auf dem das Objekt befestigt wurde, von der anderen Seite blickte
man mit einem Auge gegen das Licht hindurch (s. die Abbildungen). Das Ganze war
eine recht primitive Konstruktion, führte aber durch Leeuwenhoeks Fähigkeit, stark
brechende Linsen mit bis zu 270-facher Vergrößerung zu schleifen, zu hervorra-
genden Ergebnissen. Polignacs äußerst präzise Beschreibung in V. 1025ff. sowie die
einleitende Wendung "Arripe et observa" legen die Vermutung nahe, daß er ein
Leeuwenhoek'sches Mikroskop gesehen und ausprobiert hat: Leeuwenhoek wollte die
Konstruktion seiner Mikroskope aus verständlichen Gründen nicht allzu offen preis-
geben und veröffentlichte keine Abbildungen oder Beschreibungen. Polignac muß
ihn daher in Delft aufgesucht und den Meister um einen Blick auf und durch dessen
Mikroskope gebeten haben. Dazu hatte er z.B. 1697 Gelegenheit, als er sich, wie
erwähnt, längere Zeit im nahe gelegenen Rotterdam aufhielt. Zu dieser Zeit war
Leeuwenhoek bereits eine Berühmtheit; seine Briefe an die Royal Society waren
erstmals 1695 unter dem Titel *Arcana naturae detecta* in Delft erschienen. Polignac hat
seine eindrückliche Begegnung mit Leeuwenhoek dann später in den *AL* an passen-
der Stelle eingearbeitet.[20]

Bezüglich des philosophischen Aspekts sei hier nur en passant erwähnt, daß Polignac die durch das Mikroskop ermöglichten Einblicke in die Natur (wie umgekehrt
auch die Ausblicke durch das Teleskop) im Sinne des physiko-theologischen
Gottesbeweises interpretiert: Die Wunder der Natur, die sich so dem Auge erschließ-
en, zeigen die Spuren des göttlichen Geistes, offenbaren den faszinierenden Plan der
Schöpfung und widerlegen gleichzeitig die epikureische Lehre vom Zufall. Damit
(und nicht zuletzt mit sprachlichen Anklängen) stellt Polignac der Hybris des atheis-
tischen Naturforschers, wie sie sich in Lukrez' Epikurelogien (besonders in *DRN*
1,62–79) manifestiert, die Ehrfurcht und Demut des christlichen Wissenschaftlers
gegenüber.

Doch bleiben wir noch ein wenig bei Leeuwenhoek und seinen Entdeckungen.
Polignac bringt ein Beispiel, das seine Argumentation im Rahmen der Fortpflanz-
ungstheorie stützt:

> Ergò lenticulæ opponas, dum pura dies est,   1055
> Aut canis, aut galli stillantem è semine guttam;
> Protinus ecce tibi ante oculos (mirabile visu)

---

[19] Cf. W. Scheffer, *Das Mikroskop, seine Optik, Geschichte und Anwendung gemeinverständlich
dargestellt* (Leipzig, 1902), 21–24; Reginald S. Clay and Thomas H. Court, *The History of the
Microscope* (London, 1932), 33–36; Maria Rooseboom, *Microscopium* (Leiden, 1956), 31–33.39–43.

[20] Damit dürfte sich auch die These von Wolfgang Bernhard Fleischmann, "Zum Anti-
Lucretius des Kardinals de Polignac", *Romanische Forschungen* 77 (1965): 42–63, die Bücher 6–9 des
AL stammten nicht von Polignac selbst, sondern vom Abbé de Rothelin, erledigen. Im übrigen
erwähnt Polignac das Mikroskop (zusammen mit dem Teleskop) auch bereits *AL* 2,530ff. mit
Verweis auf den speziellen Glasschliff.

Vermiculorum ingens populus, quasi in æquore magno
Mobilis, atque natans, celer, irrequietus, & omne
Per spatium ludens certatim ac præpete cursu.   1060
Quàm multæ spectantur apes æstate serenâ
Surgere confertim, totisque erumpere cellis;
Cùm priscis laribus pulsæ novitatis amore,
Fragrantes cunas & cæca palatia linquunt:
Agglomerant se se in nubem, rapidasque choreas   1065
Ad Solem exercent: pennis micat effera pubes,
Et magno circumvolitat per Inane susurro.
Sic genitale suâ fremit agmen & ardet in undâ,
Quàm durat calor ille diu quem è fonte paterno
Attulerant: sensim nam defervente liquore   1070
Languescunt, tenuesque animas jam frigida ponunt. (*AL* 7,1055–71)

[Bring also, wenn es heller Tag ist, einen Tropfen vom Samen eines Hundes
oder eines Hahnes vor die Linse: Sogleich erscheint vor deinen Augen (ein
Wunder zu sehen) eine riesige Schar von Würmchen; wie in einem großen
Meer schwimmen sie beweglich herum, schnell, rastlos und über die ganze
Strecke in spielerischem Wettkampf dahineilend. Wie man an einem heiteren
Sommertag viele Bienen beobachten kann, wie sie sich dichtgedrängt erheben
und überall aus ihren Waben ausbrechen, wenn sie die Neugier aus ihren alten
Wohnungen vertreibt und sie ihre duftende Wiege, den dunklen Palast, verlassen, sich zu einer Wolke ballen und ihre geschwinden Sonnentänze aufführ-
en; in jugendlicher Ausgelassenheit lassen sie ihre Flügel blitzen und schwirren
mit lautem Gesumme durch den Raum: So wimmelt das Heer der Spermien
in seiner Flüssigkeit, solange die Hitze andauert, die sie aus der väterlichen
Quelle bezogen haben; wenn die Flüssigkeit sich abkühlt, erschlaffen sie allmählich und legen bald schon, kalt geworden, ihr zartes Leben ab.]

Diese wiederum äußerst präzise und realistische Beschreibung[21] läßt sich—neben
anzunehmender Autopsie—detailliert aus Leeuwenhoeks Werken belegen.[22] Entdeckt hatte die Spermatozoiden zwar bereits 1677 ein gewisser Hammius, *medicinae
studiosus*[23], genauer untersucht und dargestellt aber wurden sie erst von Leeuwenhoek. Die Entdeckung dieser "animalcula" gab natürlich den Spermatisten Auftrieb,
die nun im Spermium den Homunculus zu sehen glaubten, der sich in die weibliche
Eizelle zwecks Wachstum einnistete. Der Präformationslehre, die Ende des 17. Jahr-

---

[21] Cf. V. 1058–60, besonders den die Lebhaftigkeit der Spermien malenden daktylischen Vers
1059.

[22] Cf. insbesondere den ausführlichen Brief "De diuturna vita Animalculorum in Semine
Masculo Canis etc." an die Royal Society aus dem Jahre 1685 (in *Opera Omnia*, 1: 149–177).

[23] Cf. J. Halbertsma, "Johannes Ham von Arnhem, Entdecker der Spermatozoiden", *Archiv für
holländische Beiträge zur Natur- und Heilkunde* 3 (1864): 322–326.—Cf. auch Leeuwenhoeks Brief
an Hermann van Zoelen (Epist. 113 in *Opera Omnia*, 3: 57–69).

hunderts von den meisten Biologen vertreten wurde (während Leeuwenhoek selbst eine epigenetische Theorie bevorzugte), folgt auch Polignac: Er beobachtet am Spermium nicht nur Kopf und Schwanz, sondern auch ein "molle rudimentum membrorum" (*AL* 7,1072f.); zwar gibt er zu, daß die von der Theorie geforderte Existenz männlicher und weiblicher Spermien wegen der feinen Unterschiede nicht beobachtbar sei, hält aber dennoch daran fest, daß das Spermium den ganzen Menschen enthalten müsse, der im Mutterleib dann nur noch heranwachse (*AL* 7,1080ff.).

Ziehen wir ein Fazit unserer Beobachtungen! Polignac hat die wissenschaftliche Diskussion, wie sie in der Biologie im späten 17. Jahrhundert geführt wurde, genauestens verfolgt und sich eine eigene Meinung gebildet. Dabei ging er—im positiven, ciceronischen Sinne—eklektisch vor und hat sich gemäß dem *probabile* bald der einen, bald der anderen Richtung angeschlossen, ohne sein Beweisziel, den Nachweis eines einmaligen göttlichen Schöpfungsaktes, dabei aus den Augen zu verlieren.

Der Eindruck, der durch die Betrachtung eines gleichsam mikroskopischen Ausschnitts des *AL* gewonnen wurde, bestätigt sich bei der Lektüre des Gesamtwerkes: Polignacs Lehrgedicht ist eine wahre Fundgrube, ja Enzyklopädie der Naturforschung seiner Zeit: Welches Thema man auch anschneidet, Polignac zeigt sich stets auf der Höhe der Diskussion. Freilich erwiesen sich im Laufe der Zeit manche seiner Ansichten als veraltet, und als der *AL* 1747 endlich erschien, hatte der Fortschritt der Wissenschaft natürlich bereits vieles überholt.[24]

Worin liegt also—über die wissenschaftsgeschichtliche Bedeutung hinaus—der bleibende Wert des *AL*? Zweifellos in dem wissenschaftstheoretischen Axiom, in der unbeirrbaren Überzeugung Polignacs, praktische Philosophie und Theologie dürften den Erkenntnissen der Naturwissenschaft nicht nur nicht widersprechen, sondern müßten sich gleichsam aus ihnen ableiten. Die disparaten, hochspezialisierten modernen Wissenschaften zusammenzusehen und die zwischen Natur- und Geisteswissenschaften herrschende Sprachlosigkeit zu überwinden—das ist die Aufgabe, vor die uns Polignacs Lehrgedicht stellt.[25]

Ruhr-Universität Bochum, Germany

---

[24] In besonderem Maße gilt dies z.B. von Polignacs Ablehnung der Newtonschen Gravitationstheorie, der er die obsolete Cartesische Wirbelhypothese vorzog: zur Auseinandersetzung zwischen Cartesianern und Newtonianern cf. Ferdinand Rosenberger, *Isaac Newton und seine Physikalischen Principien* (Leipzig, 1895; repr. Darmstadt, 1987). Es ist eine Ironie des Schicksals, daß im Jahre 1741, dem Todesjahr Polignacs, die Pariser Académie des Sciences (der Polignac seit 1717 angehörte) ihren Widerstand gegen den Newtonismus endgültig aufgab (Rosenberger, *Newton*, 525).

[25] Cf. die publizistischen Versuche des Verfassers, diese Aufgabe einer gelehrten Öffentlichkeit nahezubringen: R. F. Glei, "Über Gott und die Welt. Kardinal Melchior de Polignacs lateinisches Lehrgedicht 'Anti-Lucretius'", *Forschung an der Universität Bielefeld* 12 (1995): 36–40; ders., "Poesie und Strategie—Schach im lateinischen Gedicht", *RUBIN: Forschungsmagazin der Ruhr-Universität Bochum* 7/2 (1997): 6–12.

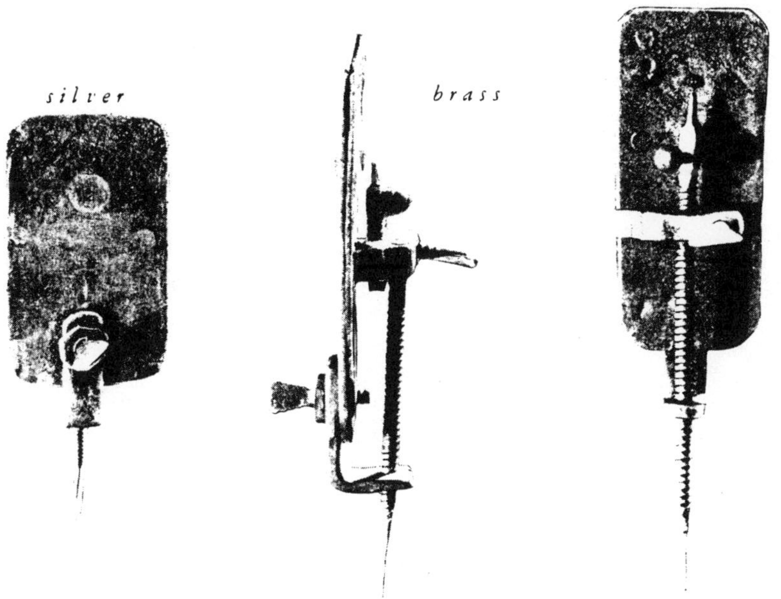

50. *Three microscopes, made and used by Antoni van Leeuwenhoek between 1673 and 1723: slightly enlarged.*

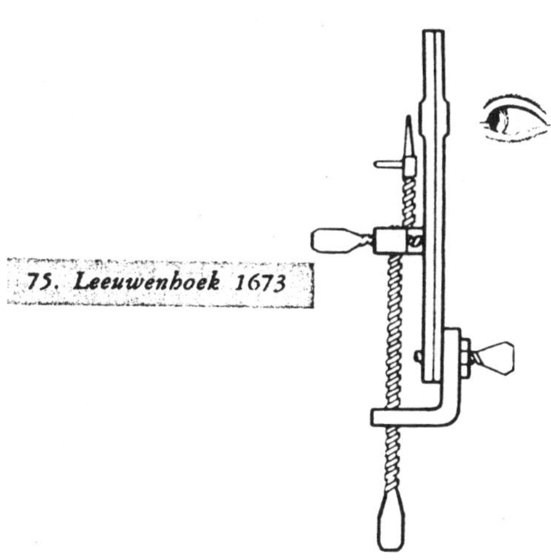

Maria Rooseboom, *Microscopium* (Leiden, 1956).

The Imitation of Non-Classical Models in the Renaissance: Italian Neo-Latin Writing and the Early Cracow Humanists (1510–1525)[1]

JACQUELINE GLOMSKI

By the time the humanist movement crossed the Alps at the end of the fifteenth century, the imitation of classical literary models had been practised by Italian writers for over a hundred years. The early humanists had succeeded both in establishing a canon of classical texts and, through their doctrine of *imitatio*, in producing a body of Latin literature which, though derivative in nature, came quickly to be admired for its purity of language and elegance of expression. Italian Neo-Latin literature itself became a model and increased the repertoire of approved texts available for humanist teaching. The humanists of central Europe were among those who valued the achievements of the previous generations of Italian scholars. As part of their goal to perfect the knowledge of Latin among their students and to create a national literature written in Latin, German humanists set up the work of the Italians as a standard which they claimed their own writers could surpass. Aside from their expressions of rivalry, though, the central European humanists acknowledged the benefits of employing Italian models along with the classics in the teaching of a correct Latin style.

Humanists connected with the University of Cracow were no exception to this trend, as they too integrated non-classical models into their educational and literary projects. The activities of three young teachers, Rudolf Agricola Junior, Valentin Eck, and Leonard Cox, demonstrate that Italian Neo-Latin writing was a factor in the attempt not only to introduce humanist studies into the University, but also to im-

---

[1] I would like to thank Professors Juliusz Domański (University of Warsaw) and Nicholas Mann (Warburg Institute, University of London) for their suggestions during the course of my research. I am also grateful to the rare book librarians at the Ossoliński Institute, the University of Cracow (Jagiellonian Library), and the Czartoryski Library, as well as to Janet Zmroczek of the British Library. Any errors or omissions remain my own.

prove the standards of Latin composition generally at Cracow. Agricola Junior, Eck, and Cox, during their residence at Cracow in the first quarter of the sixteenth century, exhibited their enthusiasm for the Italian humanists by republishing Italian Neo-Latin texts for use by students and by emulating Italian Neo-Latin authors in their own writing. In fact, Agricola, Eck, and Cox adopted a complex version of *imitatio*, conditioned by their own eclecticism and by the indirect route through which they received the writings of the Italians.

In spite of their admiration for Italian Neo-Latin literature, neither Agricola nor Eck nor Cox ever set foot south of the Alps. Agricola, whose German name was Baumann, was a native of Wasserburg on Lake Constance.[2] He came to Cracow in the summer of 1510, after studying for two years at Leipzig and passing through Breslau (Wrocław). Valentin Eck, from Lindau, also on Lake Constance, followed Agricola to Cracow from Leipzig, arriving in the Polish city in 1511.[3] Leonard Cox traveled to Cracow from England through Paris and Tübingen, and matriculated at the University of Cracow in the autumn of 1518.[4] These three young scholars were exposed to Italian humanism in their early places of study, and then developed their familiarity with Italian Neo-Latin writing at Cracow.

When Agricola, the first of the group to reach Cracow, arrived in the city in 1510, he found the academic community already well aware of Italian humanist currents. As we know from the work of Professor Juliusz Domański, scholars at the University of Cracow were interested in the writings of the Italians as early as the 1430s. In the 1450s the Bishop of Cracow and Chancellor of the University, Zbigniew Oleśnicki, wrote a letter to Aeneas Silvius in which he reflected on the problems confronting the Poles in creating a good Latin style and held up the Italians as models for imitation.[5]

From 1470, the Poles had an example of Italian Neo-Latin writing living among them, Filippo Buonaccorsi Callimachus, who had come to Poland in 1470, fleeing

---

[2] On Agricola Junior, see Gustav Bauch, *Deutsche Scholaren in Krakau in der Zeit der Renaissance 1460–1520* (Breslau, 1901), 68–69; Bauch, "Rudolphus Agricola Junior. Ein Beitrag zur Geschichte des Humanismus im deutsch-polnisch-ungarischen Osten," *Wissenschaftliche Abhandlung zum Jahresbericht der Evang. höh. Bürgerschule II in Breslau, Ostern 1892* (Breslau, 1892); C. Morawski, *Histoire de l'Université de Cracovie. Moyen Age et Renaissance* (Paris, 1900), 3: 107–110; Henryk Barycz, *Historja Uniwersytetu Jagiellońskiego w epoce humanizmu* (Cracow, 1935), 31–37; *Polski Słownik Biograficzny*, s.v. "Agricola, Rudolf młodszy."

[3] On Eck, see G. Bauch, "Valentin Eck und Georg Werner. Zwei Lebensbilder aus der Zeit der Besitzergreifung Ungarns durch die Habsburger," *Ungarische Revue* 14 (1894): 40–57; *Polski Słownik Biograficzny*, s.v. "Eck, Walenty."

[4] Neither Cox's birthplace nor date of birth are known. Some sources give his place of birth as Monmouth in Wales. See A. Breeze, "Leonard Cox, A Welsh Humanist in Poland and Hungary," *The National Library of Wales Journal* 25 (1988): 399–410. More recently, S. Ryle, "An English Humanist in Eastern Europe: Leonard Cox (c. 1495–c. 1550)," *Studi Umanistici Piceni* 12 (1992): 223–231, notes that Cox gave his birthplace as Thame in Oxfordshire on the matriculation records of both Tübingen and Cracow.

[5] J. Domański, "Filippo Buonaccorsi e la cultura filosofica del '400 in Polonia," in *Callimaco Esperiente Poeta e Politico del '400*, ed. Gian Carlo Garfagnini (Florence, 1987), 33–34.

Rome because of involvement in a conspiracy to assassinate the Pope. Buonaccorsi became an advisor to the Polish kings Kazimierz Jagiellończyk and Jan Olbracht, and remained in Cracow until he died in 1496. He wrote erotic poetry, historical biography, and political treatises.[6]

Buonaccorsi was supported in his efforts to cultivate humanism in Poland by Conrad Celtis, who was resident in Cracow from 1489–91, arriving there after his journey to Italy. Together they created the literary society, *Sodalitas litteraria vistulana*. Moreover, two other Italian humanists, Johannes Silvius Amatus and Constantius Clariti, taught at the University of Cracow in the first decade of the sixteenth century and helped to organize the study of Greek there.[7] Rudolf Agricola Junior was instructed by both of them.

In addition, Agricola, Eck, and Cox came into a city where the works of the Italian humanists were already being printed.[8] For example, Franciscus Niger's *Compendiosa ars de epistolis* was published in 1503, 1506, and 1508. Baptista Mantuan's *Contra poetas impudica scribentes* was printed in 1504, while Francesco Filelfo's *Epistolae* were published in 1505 and his *Epistolae breviores* in 1509. Meanwhile, Augustino Dati's *Elegantiolae* came out in 1505. Finally, Pomponio Laeto's *De Romanorum magistratibus* appeared in 1507, and Leonardo Bruni's *Comoedia poliscenae* in 1509.

These publications were most likely connected with interests developing at the University as most of these texts were also being lectured on at the time in the Collegium Maius.[9] Niger's *Epistolae sive de conscribendis epistolis* was extremely popular, appearing on the list of official lectures at the Collegium Maius in the 1490s and continuing to appear almost without a break from 1500 to 1530. Filelfo's *Epistolae* were lectured on in 1501, 1502, and 1506, while classes on Pomponio Laeto's *De Romanorum magistratibus* were given in 1509. Augustino Dati's *Elegantiolae* were taught in 1492, 1496, and 1508. Although Bruni's *Comoedia poliscenae* did not appear on the lecture list until the winter of 1518, his *Introductorium philosophiae moralis* was being studied in 1509 and 1510. This work would be printed in 1511 with a commentary by the Cracow master, Johannes de Stobnica.

From these titles it is clear that in the first decade of the sixteenth century scholars at Cracow were interested in the educational writings of the Italian Neo-Latin authors for the purpose of teaching prose composition, and especially the art of epistolography. Like their predecessors, Agricola, Eck, and Cox would take a pedagogical approach to the Neo-Latin texts of the Italians. Agricola published Beroaldo's *Modus epistolandi* in 1512, and Antonio Mancinelli's *Opusculum de componendis versibus* and *Opusculum de poetica virtute* in 1513.[10] Eck incorporated the work of the Italian

---

[6] On Callimachus, see Harold B. Segel, *Renaissance Culture in Poland* (Ithaca, 1989), 36–82.

[7] Henryk Barycz, *W błaskach epoki Odrodzenia* (Warsaw, 1968), 161–209.

[8] See Alodia Kawecka-Gryczowa et al., eds., *Polonia typographica saeculi sedecimi* (Wrocław, 1959–), fasc. 1, *Kasper Hochfeder*; fasc. 3, *Florian Ungler*; fasc. 4, *Jan Haller*.

[9] See W. Wisłocki, ed., *Liber diligentiarum Facultatis Artisticae Universitatis Cracoviensis. Pars I (1487–1563)*, Archiwum do Dziejów Literatury i Oświaty w Polsce, vol. 4 (Cracow, 1886).

[10] Besides Mancinelli's works, according to the Polish bibliographical tradition, Agricola Junior also edited Antonius Filippo Beroaldo's *An orator sit philosopho et medico anteponendus* (1514), but

grammarians Tortelli, Politian, Perotti, Mancinelli, Niger, and Ferretus into his handbook on the composition of poetry, *De versificandi arte opusculum*, in 1515.[11] Cox referred to the Italian educational theorists Pier Paolo Vergerio, Battista Guarino, Aeneas Silvius, and Maffeo Vegio in his treatise on schooling, *Libellus de erudienda iuventute*, in 1526.[12]

Nevertheless, the work of Agricola, Eck, and Cox reveals an evolution in the imitation of Italian Neo-Latin writing at Cracow, which embraces both the form and content of the models. Agricola, Eck, and Cox wished their students to be able to capture the purity of the Latin style of the Italians, while at the same time they stressed the moral values imparted by their works. We can observe a bias toward content earlier on, but from 1515 imitation of form seems to gain more importance.

Agricola's prefaces to the Italian texts which he edited reveal choices based on moral content. In his introduction of 1511 to Octavius Cleophilus' *Coetus poetarum*,[13] a lengthy elegy in praise of classical poetry, Agricola expresses his belief in the permanence of Cleophilus' work. Agricola wishes his edition of the poem to be a monument to his friendship with the dedicatee, the young Swiss student Sebastian Grubel from Sankt Gallen, and to be an incentive for Sebastian to the study of letters. In his dedication of his edition of Maffeo Vegio's *Philalethes*, a dialogue on the nature of truth, to his teacher at the University of Cracow, Michael of Breslau (Michał z Wrocławia),[14] in 1512, Agricola states that he has edited the book for the young students at Cracow. Although Agricola praises Vegio as a famous poet and orator, and terms his book "venustissimus," he highlights the moral side of *Philalethes*. Agricola notes that the dialogue is full of cultured aphorisms and that Vegio condemns the perverse habits of evil men.

In 1520, Leonard Cox's statements in his introduction to Pontano's *De laudibus divinis opusculum*[15] indicate a choice of text influenced by both the content and the

---

Kawecka-Gryczowa et al., eds., *Polonia typographica* (see note 7, above) lists all three titles as "egzemplarz niedostępny," indicating no known location.

[11] See Cyprian Mielczarski, "Podręcznik 'De arte versificandi' Walentego Ecka na tle humanistycznej teorii wersyfikacji," unpublished Master's Thesis, University of Warsaw, Department of Classical Philology, n.d.

[12] See A. Breeze and J. Glomski, "An Early British Treatise upon Education: Leonard Cox's *De erudienda iuventute* (1526)," *Humanistica Lovaniensia* 40 (1991): 112–167, for the text with an introduction, translation, and notes.

[13] Cleophilus (1447–1490) was born at Fano, studied at Rome, where he was a disciple of Pomponio Laeto, and taught at Viterbo. See *Biographie Universelle Ancienne et Moderne* (Paris, 1854), 8: 430. The earliest edition of *Coetus poetarum* listed in the British Library Online Catalogue is Rome, Eucharius Silber, 1485 [?].

[14] On Michael of Wrocław (Michał Falkener z Wrocławia), see *Polski Słownik Biograficzny*, s.v. "Falkener, Michał." In his dedicatory letter, Agricola Junior addresses him as a teacher at the Collegium Maius. Later that year (1512), Michael would move to the Faculty of Theology. Agricola had completed his baccalaureate the preceding year. *Philalethes* was first printed at Cologne, c. 1470. For a description of the work, see Luigi Raffaele, *Maffeo Vegio. Elenco delle opere. Scritti inediti* (Bologna, 1909), 113–115.

[15] *De laudibus divinis* was composed in Pontano's youth, about 1456–1458, and then revised

form of the work. In this dedicatory preface to Pontano's collection of short poems in honour of Christ and the saints, which Cox wrote during Lent, he tells the young Cracow patricians Andrew (Andrzej) and Nicholas (Mikołaj) Salomon that he has decided to edit Pontano's poetry not only because it makes inspirational reading, but also because from it one can learn good morals and eloquence at the same time. Cox not only attaches a short summary of the contents to each of the fourteen hymns, but also concludes his edition of the cycle with a hymn of his own, written, obviously, in imitation of Pontano.

On the other hand, clear testimony for the imitation of Italian Neo-Latin style can be found in Valentin Eck's handbook on the composition of Latin poetry, *De versificandi arte opusculum*, the first edition of which was published at Cracow in 1515.[16] In the treatise Eck ranks Baptista Mantuan alongside the ancients, employing ninety-six citations from Mantuan's poetry as examples of versification, and citing only Ovid and Virgil more frequently.[17] Eck draws on Mantuan's *Eclogues*, *Fasti* ("De sacris diebus"), *Parthenice*, *Brixianum*, *Lucianum*, and *Alphonsus*.[18] Moreover, Eck quotes from Mantuan's *Apologeticon* for his definition of metre,[19] and he refers to Mantuan as "Vergilius neotericus."[20] Eck also uses the poems of the Italian poets Ludovico Bigi, Faustus Andrelinus, and Filippo Beroaldo as *exempla*.[21]

Furthermore, the Cracow humanists could approximate to the style of the Italians in their own compositions, as Leonard Cox's attempt at a slavish imitation of Pontano demonstrates. In his "Ad Diuum Ioannem Baptistam," with which he closes his aforementioned edition of Pontano's *De laudibus divinis*, Cox uses the same meter as Pontano, the elegiac distich, and follows the outline of Pontano's hymns, beginning with an invocation to the saint and proceeding to a narrative, in this case the birth of the Baptist, his preparation of the way for Christ, and the baptism of Jesus in the River Jordan. Cox ends in the manner of Pontano, with praises of the saint and a prayer, here, for his patron, Jan Konarski, Bishop of Cracow. Cox follows Pontano's mixing of pagan and Christian images, as in the phrase, "Angelus excelso Zacharie missus olympo," describing the announcement by the Angel Gabriel of John the Baptist's conception to his father Zachariah.[22] Perhaps the only feature to distinguish Cox's poem from those of Pontano is Cox's less frequent use of anaphora.

In spite of their ability to emulate one author closely, the Cracow humanists tended to espouse an eclectic method of *imitatio*. In his dedicatory preface to his 1524

---

years later. The revision was first printed in Naples in 1505. Erasmo Percopo, *Vita di Giovanni Pontano*, ed. Michele Manfredi (Naples, 1938), 148–151, and Liliana Monti Sabia, "Per l'edizione critica del *De laudibus divinis* di Giovanni Pontano," *Invigilata Lucernis* 9 (1989): 361–409.

[16] A second, enlarged edition was published at Cracow in 1521 and 1536.

[17] Mielczarski, "Podręcznik 'De arte versificandi'," 53.

[18] Mielczarski, "Podręcznik 'De arte versificandi'," 53.

[19] Mielczarski, "Podręcznik 'De arte versificandi'," 45.

[20] In the first edition of *De versificandi arte opusculum*, B4r. Mielczarski, "Podręcznik 'De arte versificandi'," 53, 71.

[21] Mielczarski, "Podręcznik 'De arte versificandi'," 52.

[22] Luke 1:5–25.

edition of Adriano Castellesi's *Venatio*, a 427-line poem on hunting and banqueting,[23] Cox informs his patron, Jodocus Ludovicus Decius, secretary to the Polish king, that he intends the book for students and he argues for its beautiful and pure latinity. Cox claims he has put his best effort into the scholia, and he expects that his work on *Venatio* will open the way for students who are just beginning to a felicitous imitation of the princes of Latin eloquence. Cox echoes the old comparison of the poet to the bee, asserting that here the learner has the honey produced from many flowers gathered from the fields of Latium.[24]

This eclecticism becomes more complex when we consider that the student is not only to imitate the Italians imitating the ancients, but also the Italians themselves, as Cox makes clear in his commentary to *Venatio*. In his notes, which explain grammatical constructions, vocabulary, phrases, and proverbs, Cox refers both to classical writers as well as to the "recentiores": Valla, Erasmus, Melanchthon, Beroaldo, Aldus Manutius, Wimpheling, Politian, Perotti, and Ermolao Barbaro. Cox considers contemporary writers to be as reliable authorities as the ancients and declares that their style can be as refined.[25]

Finally, the twisted path which the texts of the Italians traveled in order to reach Agricola, Eck, and Cox affected their reception. An attempt to trace the roots of Valentin Eck's *An prudenti viro sit ducenda uxor*, composed at the very beginning of 1518,[26] illustrates this complication. Here, Eck takes a theme popular in humanist prose treatises and turns it into verse, in an effort to instruct his pupils.[27] In the first section of the poem Eck argues against taking a wife, citing examples of insidious wives from the Old Testament, the classics, and the Church Fathers. The traditional malicious habits of women are described: they gossip, they are shrews, they are unfaithful. In the second section, he refutes these allegations and presents the virtues of married life, explaining that a man and a woman should be together in order to produce children and that a woman can be a helpmate to a man. Eck gives examples of the good, faithful, and wise wife drawn, again, from the classics and the Old Testament.

Because the theme of whether or not to take a wife had been so favored by the Italian humanists from Petrarch onwards,[28] there were a number of sources which

---

[23] *Venatio* was first published in 1505. For further information, see S. F. Ryle, "Hunting, Feasting and Church Reform: The Background to Adriano Castellesi's *Venatio*," in *Memores Tui. Studi di Letteratura classica ed umanistica in onore di Marcello Vitaletti*, ed. Sesto Prete (Sassoferrato, 1990), 165–170.

[24] On the bee metaphor, see J. von Stackelberg, "Das Bienengleichnis: Ein Beitrag zur Geschichte der literarischen *Imitatio*," *Romanische Forschungen* 68 (1956): 271–293.

[25] E3v–E4r.

[26] *An prudenti viro sit ducenda uxor* was printed twice at Cracow, in 1518 and 1524.

[27] The poem was dedicated to Alexis Thurzo, royal secretary to Louis II of Hungary. Eck was teaching at Bardejov (now in Slovakia) at the time. On Thurzo, see P. G. Bietenholz and T. B. Deutscher, eds., *Contemporaries of Erasmus* (Toronto, 1985–87), 3: 322–323.

[28] For a discussion of the literary tradition of this topic, see Max Herrmann, *Albrecht von Eyb und die Frühzeit des deutschen Humanismus* (Berlin, 1893), 315–327; William Melczer, "Albrecht von

Eck could have had at his disposal. It is possible that Eck knew Poggio's *An seni sit uxor ducenda*, which was circulating in manuscript,[29] and Francesco Barbaro's *De re uxoria*, first printed in 1513 in Paris,[30] five years before Eck wrote his poem. On the other hand, Eck's familiarity with this Italian topic may have come via the work of German humanists. It is likely that Eck knew the work of Albrecht von Eyb, the Franconian humanist,[31] whose writings on women and marriage were influenced by Petrarch, Poggio, and Barbaro. Eck could also have been inspired by Heinrich Rybisch's *Disceptatio an uxor sit ducenda*, a disputation relying on Urceo Codro's *An uxor sit ducenda* (*Sermo IV*), which Rybisch delivered at Leipzig in the autumn of 1509 while Eck was a student there.[32]

We see, then, in the editorial work and in the writings of Rudolf Agricola Junior, Valentin Eck, and Leonard Cox an esteem for and a desire to imitate Italian Neo-Latin. Agricola, Eck, and Cox were proud of their familiarity with the Italian humanists. This generation progressed from the mere use of Italian handbooks on Latin composition to the promotion of the Latin literature written by the Italian humanists, especially poetry. Although they continued to value this literature for its moral content, these early Cracow humanists increasingly emphasized style and the aim of writing a pure and elegant Latin. Agricola, Eck, and Cox developed a sophisticated form of imitation in their employment of Italian Neo-Latin models, and thus paved the way for the next generation of Cracow humanists to create a golden age of Polish Neo-Latin writing.

The Warburg Institute

Eyb (1420–1475) et les racines italiennes du premier humanisme allemand," in *L'Humanisme Allemand (1480–1540). XVIIIe Colloque Internationale de Tours* (Munich; Paris, 1979), 36–37.

[29] Poggio's treatise was composed in 1437, but was not printed until the early nineteenth century. Riccardo Fubini, ed., *Poggius Bracciolini Opera omnia. Tomus Secundus. Opera miscellanea edita et inedita* (Torino, 1966), 677. Wacława Szelińska, *Biblioteki Profesorów Uniwersytetu Krakowskiego w XV i Początki XVI Wieku* (Wrocław, 1966) mentions that manuscripts of Poggio's works were owned by scholars at Cracow in the late fifteenth and early sixteenth century. She notes that Poggio was present at the Council of Constance, to which the Poles sent a delegation (p. 288).

[30] Barbaro's treatise had been composed in the early fifteenth century. Attilio Gnesotto, ed., *Francisci Barbari De re uxoria liber in partes duas* (Padua, 1915), 14–15, 18–20; Percy Gothein, *Francesco Barbaro. Früh-Humanismus und Staatskunst in Venedig* (Berlin, 1932), 88–99.

[31] Von Eyb's Latin writings, *Clarissimarum feminarum laudatio* (1459), *Inuecta in lenam* (1459), and *An uxor uiro sapienti sit ducenda* (1460), remained in manuscript, while his vernacular *Ehebuch* appeared in print, first in 1471. For more information, see Herrmann, *Albrecht von Eyb*, above, note 27; Joseph Anthony Hiller, *Albrecht von Eyb, Medieval Moralist* (Washington, D.C., 1939); Albrecht von Eyb, *Ob einem manne sey zunemen ein eelichs weyb oder nicht*, ed. Hulmut Weinacht (Darmstadt, 1982).

[32] On Rybisch's activities at Leipzig, see Richard Foerster, "Heinrich und Seyfried Ribisch," *Zeitschrift des Vereins für Geschichte Schlesiens* 41 (1907): 183–187.

Granada, puerta de América:
El Reino de Granada y el Nuevo Mundo
en algunas fuentes neolatinas

JOSÉ GONZÁLEZ VÁZQUEZ y
MANUEL LÓPEZ MUÑOZ

Se podría pensar, en un primer momento, que hemos dado un título un tanto pretencioso a nuestra comunicación por aquello de "Granada, puerta de América". Creemos, sin embargo, que se pueden esgrimir una serie de razones y de hechos, nucleados en torno a algunas fuentes neolatinas, que demuestran que ello no es así.

En primer lugar, hay que tener en cuenta el hegemónico protagonismo de la ciudad de la Alhambra en la génesis de la aventura del Descubrimiento. Recuérdese, de una parte, que "en Santa Fe y en la propia Granada los Reyes firmaron las Capitulaciones y los documentos complementarios que satisfacían las desmesuradas exigencias de Cristóbal Colón"[1]. De otra, resulta evidente que "la empresa americana estaba supeditada a la terminación de la costosa guerra de Granada por razones económicas"[2]. La mejor prueba de ello la tenemos en el hecho de que el 2 de enero se producía la entrada oficial de los Reyes Católicos en Granada y el 17 de abril otorgaban a Cristóbal Colón las Capitulaciones de Santa Fe, que daban luz verde a la aventura americana.

Otra relación que se podría establecer entre la conquista de Granada y el descubrimiento de América es la misma motivación religiosa latente en ambos hechos. "La estrecha coincidencia entre la caída de Granada y la autorización de la expedición colombina puede hacer pensar que esta última fuese a la vez una acción de gracias y un acto de renovada dedicación de Castilla a la tarea, aún incompleta, de la guerra contra los infieles"[3]. Y es que el impulso de cruzada o exaltación mística producidos

---

[1] A. Domínguez Ortíz, "Granada, América. Razones de un protagonismo", en *El Reino de Granada y el Nuevo Mundo* (Granada, 1994), I, 23.

[2] Domínguez Ortíz, "Granada, América", 24.

[3] J. H. Elliott, *La España imperial (1469–1716)* (Barcelona, 1982), 58.

por la reconquista de Granada había suscitado el deseo de los Reyes Católicos de ganar más almas para la cristiandad. De ahí que, por ejemplo, Julio César Stella, en el mismo comienzo de su *Columbeida,* nos diga lo siguiente:

> inventum pugnata cano pia bella per orbem
> magnanimum Ducem, terris qui primus Iberis
> axis ad oppositi populos, ignota Quiqueiae
> littora fecit iter secretaque regna retexit.
> Ille graves rerum constanti pectore casus
> pertulit et magnos pelago terraque labores,
> inceptis dum monstrum Erebi felicibus obstat
> multaque bellando expertus, dum tecta locaret
> tuta suis ritusque pios moremque sacrorum
> conderet, unde novas passim venerata per aras
> in summos nunc relligio successit honores[4].

Como podemos comprobar, Stella deja claro desde el comienzo mismo de su poema que la intención principal de Colón era la de cristianizar a los pueblos amerindios, idea que se repetirá a lo largo de los dos libros.

Si el objetivo de Colón es extender la cristiandad, la del diablo es impedírselo: de ahí los diversos ataques que las fuerzas infernales, asociadas a la noche y la oscuridad, llevan a cabo contra los proyectos de Colón[5]. Pero, al final, las fuerzas del bien, asociadas a la luz, triunfarán y arrancarán a los indios de las garras del diablo[6].

De ahí que la Bula de la Santa Cruzada, que había actuado como acicate espiritual de la Reconquista de Granada, se continuara aplicando después en las Indias: "Fernando el Católico conseguirá la renovación de la Cruzada y su extensión al Nuevo Mundo por la bula '*Dum Turcharum Sarracenorumque*' (6-XII-1514) y el breve '*Nuper felicis recordationes*' (27-II-1515)"[7].

Pues bien, la misma cercanía en el tiempo y vinculación de estos dos acontecimientos favoreció, a juicio de Domínguez Ortíz, el hecho de que se pusieran pronto de manifiesto las semejanzas y paralelismos entre ambos: así, si la reconquista de Granada suponía completar el mapa de España, el descubrimiento y conquista de América completaba el mapa del mundo. En este sentido, ha sido bastante frecuente entre los historiadores el considerar la toma de Granada, como final de la reconquista y de la unidad española, antecedente obligado del descubrimiento y colonización de América: "De hecho, la estimación de la empresa americana como una prolongación de la reconquista, constituye un lugar común historiográfico"[8].

---

[4] J. C. Stella, *Columbeida,* I, 1–11.

[5] Stella, *Columbeida,* I, 53 y sigs., esp. 104–261.

[6] Stella, *Columbeida,* I, 311 y sigs.

[7] J. A. Benito Rodríguez, "La Bula de Cruzada: de la reconquista de Granada a su implantación en las Indias", en *El Reino de Granada y el Nuevo Mundo,* I, 537.

[8] M. A. León Coloma, "Imágenes plásticas de la realeza en Granada: Fernando el Católico, el rey conquistador", en *El Reino de Granada y el Nuevo Mundo,* II, 388. Cf., en este mismo sentido, C. Sánchez de Albornoz, *España, un enigma histórico* (Buenos Aires, 1962), II, 501–509.

Y habría posiblemente todavía una razón más para incluir una alusión a la Guerra de Granada en estos poemas colombinos: nos referimos a lo que ya apuntara Mª D. Rincón de que "la Toma de Granada tuvo mayor resonancia que los anuncios colombinos porque suponía también una victoria definitiva, mientras que el otro acontecimiento no obtuvo al principio la consideración que le correspondía"[9] De ahí que, como la propia Mª D. Rincón comenta, en casi todas las primeras celebraciones de la gesta del descubrimiento se aluda asimismo a la definitiva victoria de los Reyes Católicos sobre las tropas de Boabdil.

Pero con ser todas estas razones más que suficientes para titular así nuestra comunicación, lo hemos hecho en atención, sobre todo, al tratamiento que algunos autores neolatinos hacen de textos referentes a la guerra para la reconquista de Granada. Nos referimos, en concreto, a la curiosa inserción de sendos pasajes relativos a la Guerra de Granada que hacen en sus respectivas *Columbeidas* Julio César Stella y Ubertino Carrara: Stella, humanista del siglo XVI, en el libro II, versos 270–351, de su *Columbeis*, y Carrara, jesuíta de finales del XVII y principios del XVIII, le dedica prácticamente todo el libro V de su *Columbus*. No se trata, evidentemente, de textos con ninguna pretensión histórica, sino de relatos poéticos exclusivamente tales. Sin embargo, en ambos casos los pasajes relativos a la Guerra de Granada prefiguran bastante bien los poemas referidos a la empresa de Colón en tierras americanas. Veamos.

Stella nos presenta el episodio como motivo de la decoración del yelmo con que Colón obsequia al rey nativo Narilo y aprovecha su descripción para hacernos un verdadero alarde de composición poética de neto cuño virgiliano.

Tras presentarnos a los reyes Fernando e Isabel con una demostración de síntesis sorprendente y magistral, hace lo propio con los enemigos, los moros, a los que comienza caracterizando como gente poco fiable que rompe los pactos y que ataca por sorpresa:

> tortis ibi crinibus Afros
> non expectato rumpentes foedera bello
> cernere erat[10].

Para asociarlos inmediatamente después a la noche que encubre y protege sus insidias:

> nox favet, insidiasque umbris defendit amicis[11].

Aliados suyos son los azotes infernales y las fuerzas del mal con todos los efectos perniciosos a que éstos conducen:

> simul ilicet adsunt
> pallentes Erebi pestes, quas Orcus aperto
> expuerat gremio, captaeque immiserat urbi
> exitium, flammas illae ferrumque ministrant,

---

[9] Mª D. Rincón, "La divulgación de la Toma de Granada y el descubrimiento. Una edición de Basilea de 1494", en *El Reino de Granada y el Nuevo Mundo*, II, 29–30.

[10] Stella, *Columbeida*, II, 274–276.

[11] II, 277.

> inspirantque viris caedes, fluit undique sanguis,
> undique mors nigra, luctusque in veste vagantur[12].

Donde destacamos los dos últimos versos:

> fluit undique sanguis,
> undique mors, nigra, luctusque in veste vagantur,

que recuerdan tanto aquellos otros de Virgilio:

> crudelibus ubique
> luctus, ubique pavor et plurima mortis imago[13],

en los que la repetición de *undique* y la acumulación de términos como *sanguis, mors, nigra* y *luctus* hacen que el texto rezume la idea de una ciudad repleta de heridos y muertos y ennegrecida del luto por ellos.

Así nos presenta Stella en este episodio a los moros, enemigos de los cristianos, de la misma manera que la noche aparece también como aliada de las asechanzas planeadas contra el almirante y asociada con las religiones autóctonas que los cristianos acaudillados por Colón encuentran en América:

> cum nox tenebras optata reduxit,
> [. . .]
> iamque potens voti secum graviora volutat
> monstrum informe Erebi Stygiaque ab sede Pavore
> excitat, ut classem caecis terroribus omnem
> impleat inceptisque metu desistere cogat.
> Protinus ille humeris alas pallentibus aptat
> seque tremens agit ad naves, cui frigidus Horror
> it comes et lento repens Ignavia gressu[14].

En contrapartida, la luz aparece asociada tanto a los cristianos, en la Guerra de Granada,

> quo praevius anteit
> armatas acies manifesta in luce Iacobus
> candidus aurato clara inter nubila ferro,
> pergere iter, Loscaeque agros atque oppida vastat[15],

como a las fuerzas del bien que protegen al almirante y sus hombres durante su gesta americana:

> ille volat. Nitido perfusum lumine caelum
> risit et obstantes penitus cessere tenebrae

---

12 II, 280–285.
13 *Aen.* II, 368–369.
14 Stella, *Columbeida*, I, 230–240; cf. también II, 725 y sigs.
15 II, 292–295.

> pictaque non solita tremuerunt aequora luce.
> forte Duci serus labentia lumina somnus . . .[16]

No es, pues, de extrañar que a lo largo de todo el poema el triunfo cristiano vaya siempre acompañado por una explosión de luz que lo inunda todo, luz que queda aún más de manifiesto por su oposición a la oscuridad y tenebrosidad que envuelve a los enemigos.

Y podríamos referirnos, asimismo, al hecho de que el fragmento relativo a la Guerra de Granada contiene en síntesis los procedimientos narrativos fundamentales que vamos a encontrar en el resto del poema referido a la gesta americana: caracterización de los héroes[17], desfile de guerreros[18], etc.

Por su parte, el poema *Columbus* de Carrara nos parece claramente inspirado en el de Stella, al menos por lo que se refiere a este particular de la inserción de la Guerra de Granada en la epopeya colombina, si bien difiere de él en algunos aspectos, como es su mayor extensión y, sobre todo, por la diferente función literaria que desempeña en el texto: mientras que en Stella, el episodio granadino aparece como motivo de la decoración del yelmo con que Colón obsequia a Narilo, en Carrara es el propio almirante el que narra a sus tripulantes su participación en dicha guerra, convirtiéndose, de este modo, en una auténtica *aristía* que utiliza Colón para enardecer a sus hombres de cara a los combates que se avecinan con los amerindios.

En el texto de Carrara nos encontramos, además, claramente enunciado que la empresa descubridora de Colón está condicionada por la reina a que el almirante actúe dirigiendo parte de la escuadra española contra los moros en el puerto de Málaga,

> classem quam poscis habebis.
> ante sed obscuris maribus quam proelia portes,
> dux nostro prolude mari, qualisque futurus
> a Lybicis Indos iam nunc ordire triumphos[19],

campaña ésta decisiva para la definitiva toma de Granada. Por ello, una vez finalizada la batalla malagueña con resultado exitoso, la reina cumple su palabra y ofrece a Colón las naves con las que éste abordará su proyecto americano:

> hunc habuit tandem laurus Neptunia finem.
> Belli tempestas in quas iactaverit oras
> Aethiopis fluitantis opes, implevit ut omnes
> utriusque maris portus, ut clade marina
> eminus audita Granata recluserit urbis
> ostia Fernando, cumque illa Hispania tota
> libera tunc primum libaverit oscula regi,
> dicere longa mora est . . .

---

[16] I, 339–342.
[17] Vv. 273 y 337 y sigs.
[18] V. 336.
[19] V, 110 y sigs.

[. . .]
promissi regina dati non immemor, oris
reddimur ut Malacae incolumes, multosque subinde
ut tenuere dies festa solemnia pugnae,
me vocat, et numero ratium, quas cernitis, ornat[20].

Hay, pues, una explícita relación causal entre el final de la guerra de Granada y la partida de Colón hacia el Nuevo Mundo en los relatos neolatinos, relación a no dudarlo inspirada por el manejo de las fuentes historiográficas y presente en la producción poética que, de modo más o menos tangencial, trata este tema. Así sólo hace un par de días tuvimos ocasión de oir al profesor Maestre comentar que en el panegírico de Fernando de Aragón, redactado por Juan Sobrarias II, se elogia al Rey Católico, entre otras cosas, aludiendo a una secuencia de hazañas entre las que aparecen, y en ese orden cronológico normal, la guerra de Granada, la expedición colombina y las campañas norteafricanas.

Así pues, lo realmente interesante de esta tirada de versos que aquí presentamos no radica tanto en la secuenciación Granada-América cuanto en la propia funcionalidad estructural de los elementos narrativos del pasaje. Veamos unos pocos rasgos.

Podemos comenzar señalando que el relato de la toma de Granada aparece como un extenso "flashback" inserto en el relato de la peripecia colombina. El Almirante quiere elevar la moral de sus compañeros de viaje—y por las crónicas sabemos lo feble que ésta era—, a un tiempo legitimando la expedición, y a su propio comandante, todo sea dicho.

En efecto, relata Colón cómo fue la propia reina de Castilla la que vinculó el éxito de la guerra de Granada a la autorización para aprestar las naos y zarpar. Pero hay una pequeña variante: primero tendrá él que capitanear un buque en la batalla que se librará frente a las costas de Málaga; así, hará méritos ante su protectora, que aprovechará las habilidades marineras de aquel aventurero. Es como debemos entender que primero le endulce la existencia con un argumento de peso—"a pesar de tu elocuencia, nadie te ha hecho caso, pero yo sí estoy dispuesta"—para luego dejarle clara la contrapartida con un razonamiento que contiene un evidente *quid pro quo*, típico de quien negocia en una posición de ventaja: "antes, tendrás que hacer algo por mí".

En el mismo momento de aceptar, Colón se encuentra convertido en parte combatiente, cosa que nos lo sigue separando del universo de la Historia para situarlo en la esfera de la acción poética. Desde luego, el autor no puede tampoco alterar demasiado los hechos conocidos, y utiliza la mirada del navegante para enfocar toda una secuencia típicamente épica, con aristías y anagnórisis incluidas. Simplemente, la trama dramática lleva al poeta a hacer de la guerra de Granada un relato que se utiliza para que el Cristóbal Colón poético esté en condiciones de justificar el viaje, pero también de hacerles ver a sus compañeros que están acaudillados por un hombre al que ningún azar del mar le es ajeno: ni la navegación, ni la batalla.

Se puede, pues, concluir que el relato de la campaña granadina, superando la mera

---

[20] V, 833 y sigs.

secuenciación cronológica del relato historiográfico, tiene una clara funcionalidad narratológica, al aumentar poéticamente la vinculación de la guerra contra el moro y la expedición por la procelosa Mar Océana.

Podemos, pues, concluir diciendo que la inserción del episodio de la Guerra de Granada en los poemas colombinos de Stella y Carrara, lejos de ser puramente casual o secundaria, obedece a profundas motivaciones que van desde el terreno meramente histórico por el que tenemos pleno conocimiento de la estrecha vinculación de las dos gestas, pasando por el de las similares o idénticas razones de carácter religioso que subyacen a los dos acontecimientos, para acabar en el campo estrictamente poético, en el que podemos interpretar dicha inserción, de una parte, como un adelanto o prefiguración de la gesta colombina y, de otra, en el caso concreto del texto de Carrara, como un recurso literario que desempeña una clara función psicológica tendente a inflamar la moral de los guerreros.

En razón de todo ello, no creemos aventurado ni pretencioso decir, como hacemos en el título de nuestra comunicación, que Granada aparece en las epopeyas colombinas de Stella y Carrara como "puerta de América".

Universidad de Granada / Universidad de Almería

Erasmus and Prudentius

ROGER GREEN

It is well known that Erasmus had a high opinion of Prudentius, the Spanish Latin poet of the fourth and fifth centuries, whom he valued for doctrinal, moral, and poetic reasons, and above all as an inspiring example of what Erasmus called Christian eloquence. In this paper I will conduct a careful study of two poems in which Erasmus makes very intense allusion to some of Prudentius' poems, numbers 114 and 110 in the CWE (*Collected Works of Erasmus*) edition[1]. Nowhere else, with the possible exception of poem 105 in CWE, entitled *Elegia de patientia*, which is closely based on the *Psychomachia* of Prudentius, does Erasmus make such detailed use of Prudentius. Nowhere else, indeed, does he make such continuous use of a poem or passage of any poetic predecessor: Vergil and Horace he certainly quotes much more often, but he does not rework particular passages in the same thoroughgoing way, because, unlike Prudentius, they are not Christian writers expounding Christian truth. The present study will be an opportunity to see what Erasmus made of Prudentius in poems where he is clearly using him as an inspiration and a model. It will show that he knew Prudentius extremely well, and that he borrowed boldly and altered confidently as he thought fit. It also raises the question of how and when he acquired this thorough knowledge of Prudentius and how he retained it throughout his life, as he appears to have done.

Poem 114 in CWE, entitled *aliud epitaphium, metro anapaestico*, is the second of two epitaphs for Berta de Heyen of Gouda, which, as Vredeveld has shown in the introduction to his notes, must have been written in October 1490, along with the first epitaph and the *Oratio Funebris* in prose. Although only the last twelve of the

---

[1] See H. Vredeveld (ed.), *Collected Works of Erasmus* (hereafter CWE): *Poems*, vols. 85 and 86 (Toronto, 1993), 276–299 and 330–332 (texts) and 646–663 and 688–689 (notes). There is also an edition and commentary in H. Vredeveld (ed.), *Erasmi Omnia Opera* 1. 7 (Amsterdam, 1995) at pages 355–377 and 406–407. The poems are nos. 13 and 19 respectively in C. Reedijk (ed.), *The Poems of Desiderius Erasmus, with introduction and notes* (Leiden, 1956). Poem 114 is in fact translated and annotated twice in CWE: see also B. Inwood (ed.), *Collected Works of Erasmus*, vol. 29 (Toronto, 1989), 29–30 and 429–430.

thirty-two lines of this poem are relevant now, the whole poem is quickly summarised, for notwithstanding the anapaestic metre it has the same conciseness and discipline, as well as the same length, as the Ambrosian stanza often used for hymns.

Erasmus begins with an address to the *viator*, the passer-by, who was addressed in so many classical epitaphs, in six lines. This is followed by six lines on the eternity of Berta's fame, followed by four lines each on her virtues in general—none had greater *pietas* or *aequitas*—her virtues as a mother (or matron) to all people, and her virtues as a nurse, which she exercised in the hospital of St. Elizabeth at Gouda as well as in her own home. The final eight lines describe the resurrection and the subsequent unity of soul and body. The poem of Prudentius which is used by Erasmus, which is in the same metre, is number 10 of his *Cathemerinon*, the series of lengthy hymns which he composed for various feast days or solemn occasions. As its *title hymnus circa exsequias defuncti* ("hymn concerning the funeral of a deceased person") suggests, this was not written for the funeral of a particular person, but is a hymn that might be used at any funeral[2].

To simplify comparison of these texts, the relevant parts are now quoted, with highlighting of verbal similarities. First, Erasmus, lines 21–32:

Nutrix fuit omnibus illa
Quos dira premebat egestas,
Spes una dolentibus, una
Aegris *reparatio vitae*.
Humili licet *aggere terrae*   25
Lateant modo lucis egena
Et nescia sanguinis ossa,
Ea saecula sed tamen olim
Venient, quis *prisca revisens*
Vivax habitacula sensus   30
Putribus rediviva sepulchris
Secum super aethera tollat.

Then Prudentius, *Cathemerinon* 10.29–43:

At, si generis memor ignis
contagia pigra recuset,   30
vehit hospita viscera *secum*
pariterque reportat ad astra.

Nam quod requiescere corpus
vacuum sine mente videmus,
spatium breve restat ut alti   35
repetat collegia *sensus*.

Venient cito *saecula* cum iam

---

2 Or none: since the hymns of Prudentius have further literary and theological aims which cannot be explored here.

socius calor *ossa revisat*
animataque *sanguine vivo*
habitacula pristina gestet.   40

Quae pigra cadavera pridem
tumulis *putrefacta* iacebant
volucres rapientur in auras
animas comitata priores.

Hinc maxima cura sepulchris   45
impenditur . . .

The first verbal allusion of note is in line 24, where Berta is described by Erasmus as *aegris reparatio vitae:* for the sick, she is the renewal of life. As nurse, her work was to renew or rather prolong earthly life for the sick. Interestingly, the phrase *reparatio vitae*, which surely derives from Prudentius *Cathemerinon* 10.120 (rather than the earlier Juvencus), does not refer, as it does in Prudentius, to the new life, the heavenly life, which the deceased will obtain. Erasmus used the phrase in a more literal sense, although he was no less convinced than Prudentius of the life to come: perhaps he meant to say that Berta will receive a new life just as she created new life for her patients, but if so then it is surprising that he is not more explicit in this very simple and straightforward poem.

The following eight lines draw on material from about four stanzas, or sixteen lines, of Prudentius' hymn. In Erasmus we have a single sentence at this point, in which a clause introduced by *licet* ("although") occupies three lines and contrasts strongly with the remainder, which describes what takes place at the resurrection. In lines 25–7 there is only one possible allusion to Prudentius, in the phrase *aggere terrae:* that phrase can be found elsewhere in this hymn (*Cath.* 10.62), but also in Vergil, *Aeneid* 11.212; it is perhaps pointless to ask which was the source of it. The phrases *lucis egena* and *nescia sanguinis ossa* have no close counterparts in Prudentius. But the central section of our passage is much closer to Prudentius: compare Erasmus, who has *Ea saecula sed tamen olim venient* ("but those ages will come one day"), with Prudentius' line 37, *venient cito saecula cum iam:* they are strikingly similar except in word-order (but even here both poets begin a line with *venient*). The replacement of *cito* by *olim* is theologically significant: Prudentius has already emphasised the point *with spatium breve restat ut* ("there remains a short interval before . . ."). Erasmus chooses not to make the point that the resurrection will happen soon. A second difference is purely grammatical: Prudentius has *cum*, Erasmus *quis* ("in which")[3].

Erasmus then very economically describes the resurrection of the body in twelve words, a simple sentence involving one participial clause. The subject is *vivax sensus*, with *sensus* taken from line 36 in Prudentius and *vivax* suggested by his phrase in 39, *sanguine vivo*. This "enlivening sense" is then described as *prisca revisens habitacula*, "revisiting its former dwelling," that is, the particular body with which it was formerly

---

[3] *Quis* is actually an emendation of the manuscript's *quibus*, but there would be no justification to consider *cum* as the true reading in Erasmus.

united. The same notion of *habitacula* was used in Prudentius, but in his poem *socius calor* "unifying heat" was said to put on, like a garment, its *habitacula pristina*. Erasmus has no need of Prudentius' *animataque sanguine vivo*, since he has already used *nescia sanguinis ossa* in line 27. He goes on in line 31 to speak of "enlivening sense" bearing with it (*secum*) above the sky these *habitacula* which newly arise from their rotting sepulchres (*putribus*). For the last word compare Prudentius' *putrefacta* in 42, but it is noteworthy that in Erasmus this is just about the only word that could be described as appealing to the senses, which Prudentius does copiously. Lastly, a note on Erasmus' *super aethera*, which is chosen carefully: it might be seen as a correction, since the phrase *volucres in auras* in Prudentius[4], which it replaces, could convey the misleading notion that the resurrected bodies were liable to be dispersed by the winds.

Erasmus, in general, is briefer because he is not being didactic like Prudentius. Prudentius wished to make as emphatically as possible his point about the reunion of body and soul, and to explain why such care is lavished on Christian tombs in preparation for the second coming. For example, *pariter* in 32 immediately after *secum* in 31, *hospita viscera* ("hospitable flesh") in the same line, and *then alti . . . collegia sensus* ("partnership with deep sense"), and *animas comitata priores* ("accompanying their previous souls"), in quick succession. But Erasmus has no need of Prudentius' *copia*. He also drops all reference to "fire" or "heat," which for Prudentius is the catalyst of the process, and indeed a leading motif of his whole poem, which began *deus ignee fons animarum*. It is also prominent in the first line of the passage quoted above. For Prudentius, at least here[5], God is fire; Erasmus sticks to the plainer notion of divine light.

§

The second poem, 110 in CWE, is entitled *Paean divae Mariae, atque de incarnatione verbi* ("Paean to the Virgin Mary and on the incarnation of the Word"). It is some 400 lines long, and in the Sapphic metre. According to the Scriverius ms. it was written by Erasmus when *fere puero*, and so has been dated to his time at Steyn, c. 1490; but Vredeveld (646–647) put forward a different dating, based on the notion that this poem was used by Erasmus in his *acerrimum certamen* with Gilles van Delft referred to in a letter of May 1499. I will return to this point later.

In this poem Erasmus alludes clearly to at least six of the twelve poems in Prudentius' *Cathemerinon*, namely 2, 3, 5, 6, 9, 11, as can be seen from the valuable notes in Vredeveld's edition. In what follows most attention will be given to reminiscences of three of these, nos. 3, 5, and 11, since reference to the other three are on a small scale, and indeed in the case of *Cath.* 2 might be thought non-existent. A single word, *speculator*, is involved, and Erasmus uses it quite differently from Prudentius (*Cath.* 2.105), to refer to St. John the Divine rather than God. From *Cath.* 6 Erasmus takes the phrase *mendax . . . imago*, using it of the Old Testament foreshadowings of

---

[4] Almost a classical tag: Vergil, *Aeneid* 5.503, 11.795, Ovid, *Metamorphoses* 13.307.

[5] The notion, on the classical side, is a Stoic one.

the Virgin Mary where Prudentius (*Cath.* 6.46) had applied it to the dreams of the
wicked. In spite of a difference in context, the identical combination of adjective and
noun leaves little doubt about the allusion. That Erasmus makes striking use of a
passage of *Cath.* 9 (lines 25–27) will be seen from the quotation below. Poem 5 of
Prudentius gives him rather more: a passage of twelve lines (113–124) on Paradise
provides various details for Erasmus' description of the Garden of Eden. The same
flowers are named, in slightly different verbal form, but in the same order, by both:
roses, violets, cinnamon and nard. Most remarkably, Erasmus ends his description
with *balsama surclo* in line 132, echoing Prudentius' *balsama surculo* in 117, with a
minimal change to suit the metre.

From Prudentius' third hymn Erasmus takes the programmatic *Sperne, Camena,
leves hederas* . . . (26–27) and reworks it into a sentiment worthy of the Virgin. The
ivy should be replaced by lilies:

> Pone serpentes hederas, odoram   5
> Liliis nectens niveis coronam:
> Quaeritat frondes fugiens prophanas
>   Lilia virgo.

Later in his poem he follows Prudentius' account of the creation and the Fall in *Cath.*
3.96–155, but is noticeably selective. To say simply that Erasmus imitates these passages, as a commentator may do in the interests of brevity, is potentially misleading,
for Erasmus subtly varies the intensity of his allusion. The most obvious allusions
occur in lines 113–120 of Erasmus (which actually precede the passage already discussed in connection with Prudentius' fifth hymn). Here Erasmus borrows the verbs
iubere (in 118, from 101), *habitare* (line 118, from 102), and the phrase *quadrifidus* . . .
amnis (119/120), which Prudentius had used in 105 (*quadrifido . . . amne*). Thereafter,
although he follows the general order of Prudentius, echoes are not intrusive: compare *socium . . . coniugem* (157–158) and *socium . . . virum* in *Cath.* 3.113; *vitiata* (165)
with Prudentius' *vitiosa* (131), *morte luunt* (167) with *morte luit* (135). Much later in his
poem Erasmus uses Prudentius' *numine . . . rutilante* (141–142) in 267–268, merely
reversing the order of the words—a notable tribute to a remarkable phrase. We shall
also see evidence of *Cath.* 3. 136–140 in the passage about to be analysed.

Erasmus' use of *Cath.* 11 is best illustrated with the help of quotation, again with
emphasis of the significant similarities. First, Erasmus:

> *Scisne* quid clausa teneas in alvo?   290
> *Scisne*, ter felix, tua quid recondant
>   Viscera, virgo?
>
> . . . Sed puer lenis, puer a *vetustis*
> Imminens *saeclis*, face qui secunda
> Saecla iamdudum miseris daturus   315
>   Aurea terris,
>
> *Emica* caecis uteri latebris
> Pusio dulcis, trepido tumultu

Cerne nutantem fabricam, sacratam
    Exere frontem.   320

O dies omni venerandus aevo,
Quo patris Iesu soboles superni
Carne vestitus *lutea* silenti
    Proderis orbi.

O, tui quantum iubili tulere,   325
Nate, *vagitus*: redeuntis illi
Nuntii vitae, reducis fuere
    Signa salutis.

En tibi vultu iubilant sereno
Cuncta nascenti, prope iam recisam   330
Excitat lucem meliore currens
    Tramite Phoebus.

Nubibus coeli chorus e supernis
En modos gaudens ciet insolentes;
Orbis extremi duce te requirunt   335
    Sydere Chaldi.

Te *pecus* prono *veneratur* ore
Bruta, te cantu modulans agresti
Laudat, exultat pietas relictis
    Rustica bubus.   340

Quin et umbrosas subito renatis
Frondibus sylvas videas, et omne
Floribus densis viruisse pratum et
    Gramine laeto.

Iam fluunt amnes celeres Lyaei   345
Dulcibus rivis, sapit unda vitem,
Rore iam *stillant* hilares benigno
    Balsama coeli.

Iam ferunt duri nova *mella scopli*,
Ismarae cautes redolente nardo   350
Iam calent, Syrum spatiosa *sudat*
    Quercus amomum.

Inter haec *quanto* saliisse rere
Gaudio castae tenerum puellae
Pectus immensi impedientis orbis   355
    Gaudia pannis?

Prudentius, *Cathemerinon* 11. 53–84:

> *Sentisne*, virgo nobilis,
> matura per fastidia
> pudoris intactum decus   55
> honore partus crescere?
>
> O *quanta* rerum *gaudia*
> alvus pudica continet.
> ex qua novellum *saeculum*
> procedit et lux *aurea*!   60
>
> *Vagitus* ille exordium
> vernantis orbis prodidit;
> nam tunc renatus sordidum
> mundus veternum depulit.
>
> Sparsisse tellurem reor   65
> rus omne *densis floribus*
> ipsasque harenas Syrtium
> flagrasse nardo et nectare.
>
> Te *cuncta nascentem*, puer,
> sensere dura et barbara   70
> victusque saxorum rigor
> obduxit herbam cotibus.
>
> Iam *mella de scopulis* fluunt,
> iam *stillat ilex* arido
> *sudans amomum* stipite   75
> iam sunt myricis *balsama*.
>
> O sancta praesepis tui,
> aeterne rex, cunabula
> populisque per saeclum sacra,
> mutis et ipsis credita!   80
>
> *Adorat* haec *brutum pecus*,
> indocta turba scilicet,
> adorat excors natio,
> vis cuius in pastu sita est.

The quotation from Erasmus began with lines 290–292 in order to show a clear imitation of Prudentius, *Cath.* 11.54 (*sentisne* . . . ?). The next stanza in the above quotation of Erasmus introduces the theme of the Golden Age, with the help of a passage from Prudentius' ninth hymn (lines 25–27, already mentioned) which is conspicuous in *vetustis . . . saeculis* and *emica* (317). There is also, incidentally, a reference to the Fourth Eclogue of Vergil in 319 (*nutantem fabricam*). Then the stanza *O dies omni venerandus aevo* (321) makes a clear allusion to Prudentius *Cath.* 3.136–140, marked by the use of *luteus* (literally "muddy"—used of mortal flesh) and the distinctive use of *prodo* ("reveal"). From this point only the eleventh hymn of Prudentius is relevant, and reference will be made to that poem alone.

Erasmus now takes up the Prudentian motif of *vagitus* (the crying of the infant Christ). It is particularly interesting that although both writers go on to describe the Golden Age, they do so by different routes, as it were, and with different objectives. Erasmus contrasts the *vagitus* of the holy infant with the *iubili* of the whole created order, and there follows a description of the general jubilation. Notice the closely similar phrases *cuncta nascenti* (Erasmus, line 330) and *cuncta nascentem* (Prudentius, line 70), each summing up the reaction of all nature and the universal significance of the event, but with the difference that Erasmus is referring to the whole created order, Prudentius to all inanimate things. In what follows Erasmus mentions Phoebus (the sun); the chorus of heaven, i.e., the angels; the Chaldaean wise men; the beasts—here he is thinking first of the beasts that witnessed Christ's birth, but also of the whole animal world. This leads on to a picture of the joy of inanimate nature, which quickly modulates into a picture of the Golden Age. From there he returns to the theme of Mary's joy as she ties "the joy of the whole wide world" in its baby clothes (a remarkable piece of writing this, in a stanza that is in some ways intricate, even convoluted, but gives a clear articulation of her joy that is to be echoed by that of all creation). The description of the Golden Age—with honey flowing from rocks and all the rest—is in many ways conventional, but also close to Prudentius: his *densis floribus* is simply reversed, his *mella de scopulis* becomes the rather bold *mella scopli*, the *ilex* becomes the similar *quercus*. Before that his *pecus . . . bruta* (337/8) showed little change from Prudentius' *brutum pecus* (81).

But although the presence of Prudentius is so strongly felt in this passage, the order in which Erasmus deploys this material is significantly divergent. For Prudentius the *vagitus* was the announcement of a new world, a world greeted and symbolised by flowers in the countryside, nard and nectar even in the quicksands of the Syrtes, and grass growing on rocks. Even inanimate vegetation, and brute animals, could recognise the new world—but the Jews could not. Prudentius is polemical and allegorical, and to make this clear lines 82 and 83 are given over to explaining that the animals signify untaught paganism. Again Erasmus' objectives are quite different and, it seems, more simple.

§

The variety and depth with which we have seen Erasmus treat Prudentius can stem only from a very close reading, and I would argue that he could do this only immediately after studying Prudentius or with the text open on his desk at the time. This is perhaps what he did in 1523, when he presented Margaret Roper with a Christmas present consisting of a line-by-line commentary on two of Prudentius' hymns (numbers eleven and twelve)—unless of course these were earlier compositions that he simply took out of a drawer and blew the dust off. This is a possibility which should be taken seriously, although my present concern is with the verse that he composed in the last ten years or so of the fifteenth century.

I return to the dating of poem 110. Vredeveld's introduction, as stated earlier, discussed the evidence for two datings of poem 110, and preferred the later; but perhaps these dates are not in fact incompatible. The date of c. 1490 implied by the ms. could indeed be wrong, but one could retain it by arguing that the poem was written then but also used nine years later in his competition with Gilles van Delft, whether with a little revision or none. (It could also have been used at this time for Erasmus' prose hymn to the Virgin Mary, which is securely dated to 1499 by a reference in *Ep.* 93). The earlier date actually fits in rather better than Vredeveld allowed with the other chronological evidence of Erasmus' close acquaintance with the *Cathemerinon*. From his index of patristic, medieval and Renaissance references (pp. 775–776), after excluding references which point out only a general similarity of theme, or where the similarity could easily be derived from a source other than Prudentius, one can quickly arrive at a rather small number of poems containing reference to Prudentius' *Cathemerinon*, of which only a few have been given a date other than c. 1490. The justification for positing a use of Prudentius at other times is not in fact particularly strong. The similarity of *Cath.* 3.23, *liquor . . . ambrosius* and Erasmus 2.133, *ambrosio . . . liquore* (the poem is dated tentatively to 1506) could be explained by the fact that both independently use Statius, *Thebaid* 9.731, or another source unknown to us. In Poem 9.15 the link with Prudentius (*Cath.* 10.143) is in fact the single word *cinisculus*, which could have been remembered from an earlier reading, or noted down because exceptional. In poem 49—the verses written for the new St. Paul's School sometime after 1510—there is an apparent echo in *animas sortita priores* (lines 28–29) of Prudentius *Cath.* 10.414; this phrase is actually a part of the passage carefully reworked to celebrate Bertha von Heyen, and might therefore have stuck in his memory.

There remain two poems in which the allusion to Prudentius is less easily dismissed, and for which Vredeveld has claimed a date of c. 1499: poems 111 and 112. Given their position in the manuscript, they ought to be in the same case as 110. Vredeveld argues that the later dating is corroborated by thematic or verbal similarities with poems of exactly that date: in the case of 111, parallels with the *Carmina* of Tifernate (Venice, 1498), and in the case of 112 parallels with the poem of M. Mutius, *De triumpho Christi* (1499), which, Vredeveld claims, must have been Erasmus' inspiration. These arguments are less sure than they appear. First, the parallels to Tifernate cited in Vredeveld's notes show a similarity of theme, but no obvious similarities in expression; and as for the parallelism of Mutius and Erasmus in their descriptions of the harrowing of hell—essentially a matter of the order of their narratives— could this not be due to the use of a common source? Secondly, if indeed there were borrowings from one writer to the other, must we assume that Erasmus was the borrower, and not the source? And in such situations must one poem have been written immediately after the other? There is certainly a case for placing poems 111 and 112 earlier, along with 110[6].

---

[6] Vredeveld also argues that poem 36 disproves the dating implied by the Scriverius ms., but his argument that its "Christocentrism" (only a single line in fact refers to Christ) separates it from such poems as 1 and 110 and links it in time with the *Enchiridion* seems weak.

I tentatively suggest that the efflorescence of Prudentius' hymns in the poems of Erasmus was the result of close reading at one particular short period of his life: the years leading to 1490. One can agree with Reedijk that Prudentius may have been introduced to him at school in Deventer; but he evidently paid him particular attention at Steyn and, if I am right, very little after that. The references to Prudentius in Erasmus' prose works are admittedly many, but (with the possible exception of the commentary) contain nothing that must come from a recent study of Prudentius; some derive from the liturgy, others no doubt come from annotations made much earlier, and some are clearly generalities. To argue, as I have just done, that there was perhaps only one time in his life when he gave close attention to Prudentius is not to doubt his sincere and lifelong admiration of the Spanish poet, but simply to take into consideration what a remarkably busy scholar Erasmus was.

University of Glasgow

Le Wetsteen der vernuften *de*
Jan de Brune et la littérature Néo-Latine[1]

A. J. E. HARMSEN

Caractéristiques du *Wetsteen*

A Amsterdam fut publié en 1644 le *Wetsteen der vernuften* (L'affiloir des esprits) par Jan de Brune, jeune écrivain néerlandais.[2] Le livre contient quarante essais, dans lesquels sont traités des sujets de caractère divers et ayant trait à la conversation entre jeunes gens. Il semble que ce livre eut beaucoup de succès si l'on considère les fréquentes rééditions et le fait qu'en 1659 une seconde partie, posthume et incomplète, fut à son tour publiée.[3] En témoigne, du reste, Jan de Brune lui-même. Dans la même année 1644, il publiait une collection d'anecdotes, intitulée *Jok en ernst* (Jeux et gravités), à la fin de laquelle il se montre enchanté de l'accueil favorable et du prestige obtenus par le *Wetsteen*.[4] Ceci explique pourquoi il a travaillé assidûment à une deuxième partie de l'ouvrage, qu'il n'a cependant pas pu achever.

Le *Wetsteen* constitue un enchevêtrement impressionnant de citations. Les trois cent cinquante pages de l'édition originale ne comprennent pas moins de 800 allusions et citations, dont à peu près un quart fut emprunté à la Bible. Le phénomène s'observe commence dès la page de titre, avec une citation tirée des sonnets de Marino: "Il men si scopre, il più vien che s'asconda"—le détail apparaît, mais l'ensemble reste dissimulé. De Brune enchaîne ces citations de deux façons différentes: parfois il propose une idée qu'il étaye à l'aide d'une série de citations; le plus souvent il lie une citation à la suivante. Il laisse divaguer ses pensées, parfois même en oubliant son idée de départ. À cet égard la construction de ses essais est donc très différente de celle de Bacon ou de celle de Montaigne, lesquels maintiennent une structure

---

[1] Traduction de Caroline Gauthier

[2] J. de Brune: *Wetsteen der vernuften, oft beqvaam middel, om, van alle voorvallende zaken, aardighlik te leeren spreken.* Het eerste deel (Amsterdam, 1644; réimpr. Rotterdam, 1994).

[3] J. de Brune: *Wetsteen der vernuften, oft beqvaam middel, om, van alle voorvallende zaken, aardighlik te leeren spreken.* Het tweede deel (Amsterdam, 1659).

[4] J. de Brune: *Jok en ernst* (Amsterdam, 1644), 411.

beaucoup plus rigide; Bacon traite seulement un thème par essai et Montaigne ne laisse aucune liberté à sa fantaisie, comme le fait Jan de Brune.

Le premier chapitre du *Wetsteen* commence par une citation du *De ira* de Sénèque, évoquant un médecin qui cachait son scalpel dans un chiffon pour le dissimuler à une princesse paniquée qu'il s'apprêtait à opérer. Une telle façon d'agir n'est pas concevable selon De Brune; mais elle sert de base à maints aphorismes célèbres de la littérature. Six réponses avisées sont passées successivement en revue. La première est l'histoire d'un officier trapu, appelé Samson, dont on dit, ironiquement, qu'il pourrait battre une armée entière. "Oui," répondit ce Samson à son railleur, "mais alors il me faudrait une de vos mâchoires." L'allusion au livre des Juges 15:15 est évidente—où le Samson de la Bible combat mille Philistènes avec une mâchoire d'âne. Mais ce passage comprend également une référence historique: l'histoire d'un certain officier italien Samson Pignatelli. Les autres anecdotes dans ce chapitre sont de la même façon empruntées à des sources espagnoles, italiennes et juives.

Par ailleurs, De Brune bannit la théorie selon laquelle un chrétien ne doit pas rire parce que Jésus n'a jamais ri. Pourtant le rire est traité dans les Psaumes, dans le livre des Proverbes et dans l'Évangile de saint Luc. Le rire est le propre de l'homme, créé par Dieu; par conséquent il doit être une bonne chose. De Brune ajoute à cela une observation très personnelle: lui-même aime rire et rit beaucoup. Ce qui lui rappelle l'anecdote d'une jeune femme avec laquelle il se divertit récemment. Elle faisait éclater des pétales de roses sur son front. Ce bruit, selon De Brune, est causé par la pression de l'air. L'érudit apporte ce fait comme une découverte physique de grande importance, ce qui montre que sa connaissance de la physique est très restreinte. Il fait bien souvent des digressions sur des phénomènes élémentaires. Par la suite, il emprunte deux longues citations à la *Gerusalemme liberata*: tout comme lui couché auprès d'une jeune femme, Reinout (Rinaldo) était couché auprès d'Armida. Cette indiscrétion le mène à un éloge de Maria Tesselschade Roemers, une des poétesses néerlandaises les plus connues de la première moitié du dix-septième siècle. Il l'admire parce qu'elle s'occupait d'une traduction du Tasse, traduction qui par ailleurs ne fut pas achevée et dont il ne reste pratiquement rien.[5] Néanmoins De Brune lui consacrera deux pages entières. Ensuite, il revient sur le thème des pétales de roses, qu'il compare à des lèvres de femme. D'une part, c'est une raison pour émettre des considérations sur la douceur des pétales de roses—le sybarite Smyndirides dormait dessus— d'autre part pour évoquer la douceur des lèvres, particulièrement les lèvres inférieures: qui n'a point de lèvre inférieure, ne pourra jamais bien embrasser; ainsi De Brune transforme le proverbe italien qui annonce: qui n'a point de lèvre inférieure ne pourra jamais bien siffler. Il renforce ces théories sur la rose avec les citations de Martial, Ronsard, Amalthée, Arioste, Elien, Achille Tatius, Lactance, Homère et avec des expressions néerlandaises et grecques. Le thème de la rose est du reste inépuisable; il y revient également dans d'autres chapitres.

---

[5] Voir A. A. Sneller et O. van Marion (eds.): *De gedichten van Tesselschade Roemers* (Hilversum, 1994), 100–103.

Education de Jan de Brune

Jan de Brune a été élevé au milieu de livres. S'il existait des Néerlandais beaucoup plus érudits que lui à son époque, le cercle familial de l'auteur le prédestinait à une large érudition. Du côté maternel, il était le neveu de trois érudits renommés: Gérard Vossius (1577–1647),[6] professeur à l'université de Leyde et à l'Athénée d'Amsterdam, Franciscus Junius (1590–1677),[7] historien d'art et fils du célèbre théologien, enfin François Gomarus (1563–1641).[8] Ce dernier s'était engagé à Leyde dans les querelles théologiques qui se développaient en Hollande dans le premier quart du dix-septième siècle. Après cela, il se retira à Middelbourg en Zélande, où Jan de Brune naquit et passa sa jeunesse. Il étudia ensuite le droit à Leyde et à Amsterdam, puis il passa quelques années en Angleterre chez son oncle Franciscus Junius, auteur du précis de la peinture antique, *De pictura veterum*. Jan de Brune a ajouté une dédicace et une introduction détaillées à la traduction néerlandaise de ce livre.[9] Les membres de la famille s'entraidaient: les oeuvres posthumes de G. J. Vossius furent ainsi éditées par Franciscus Junius.

Jan de Brune le Jeune avait un oncle du même nom, que nous appelons Jan de Brune l'Ancien. Ce magistrat de Zélande et auteur de poésie, puis de prose en forme d'essais, avait une prédilection pour la création de collections littéraires; il écrivit de courts morceaux de prose à partir de collections de proverbes.[10] Il différait beaucoup de son jeune neveu, car il était moralisateur, grave et calviniste. Par contre, les essais de Jan de Brune le Jeune dégagent une atmosphère ludique, un modernisme éclairé. Toutefois, Jan de Brune l'Ancien aura sans aucun doute marqué son jeune neveu par sa passion de collectionneur.

En septembre 1638, Marie de Médicis séjourna à Amsterdam, et c'est à cette occasion que Jan de Brune composa un éloge en français, intitulé *À Sa Maiesté*. L'année suivante il publia une collection de poésies d'amour intitulée *Veirzjes*.[11] Dans ce petit livre, nous trouvons trois odes. La première est de François Vossius (fils du professeur Gerardus Vossius), la deuxième de Pieter de Groot (fils de Hugo Grotius) et la dernière de Isaac Gruterus (fils de Petrus Gruterus). Nous pouvons en déduire que Jan de Brune était membre d'un cercle de jeunes étudiants, érudits de science et de littérature. Au fil des ans, il a répondu à tous ces poèmes, par exemple par la dédicace à Pieter de Groot dans sa traduction de l'anglais des paraphrases de Baker sur le Notre Père. Ce texte est également agrémenté d'une élégie de Isaac Gruterus. De Brune

---

[6] C. S. M. Rademaker: *Life and Work of Gerardus Joannes Vossius (1577–1649)* (Assen, 1981).

[7] Voir F. Junius: *De pictura veterum libri tres* (Roterodami 1694). Ed. du livre I par C. Nativel (Genève, 1996).

[8] En effet, Gomarus était l'oncle de la mère de Jan de Brune. Ses parents étaient Isaac de Brune et Johanna Junius, une demi-soeur de l'épouse de G. J. Vossius et une nièce de F. Gomarus.

[9] F. Junius: *De schilderkonst der oude, begrepen in drie boecken* (Middelbourg, 1641).

[10] Voir P. J. Verkruijsse c.s.: *Johan de Brune de Oude, een Zeeuws literator en staatsman uit de zeventiende eeuw* (Middelbourg, 1990).

[11] J. de Brune: *Veirzjes* (Amsterdam, 1639).

honora un autre fils de Vossius, Matthaeus, avec un épithalame construit sous forme de dialogues.[12]

Même si la poésie dans les *Veirzjes* ne témoigne pas d'un grand niveau littéraire, ce recueil comprend des imitations néerlandaises des *Basia* de Janus Secundus, ainsi qu'une poésie érotique et religieuse d'un style très personnel. Cependant Jan de Brune se fait remarquer surtout comme un prosateur: l'introduction légère entrecoupée de proverbes et de citations est un chef d'oeuvre.

Quelques années plus tard, en 1644, parut son oeuvre principale, le *Wetsteen der vernuften*. Dans ce livre, Jan de Brune montre son intérêt pour des lectures variées: la littérature antique, grecque et romaine, puis la littérature moderne. Il cite des textes latins et grecs, italiens, espagnols, français, anglais et néerlandais. Le livre est précédé de deux poèmes dédicacés, l'un de Daniel Mostart, qui compare le *Wetsteen* aux essais de Bacon et de Montaigne, et l'autre de Joost van den Vondel, le plus grand poète néerlandais du dix-septième siècle, déjà célèbre de son vivant et appelé par la suite le prince des poètes. Il importe de savoir que Vondel avait beaucoup d'admirateurs, mais qu'il ne faisait pas parti du monde littéraire de son époque et que par conséquent il avait très peu de contacts littéraires. Les poèmes dédicacés de sa main sont rares et il ne cite que dans quelques cas d'autres poètes. Notre Jan de Brune constitue vraiment une exception à la règle. Dans son éloge Vondel s'adresse à Franciscus Junius le Jeune, et il écrit: "Si vous passez en revue votre famille vous voyez la noblesse, pas l'épée mais la plume; maintenant votre neveu vous suit au galop." Phrase curieuse, mais il faut savoir que Junius a écrit un livre dont un chapitre est consacré à l'art du dressage.[13] Vondel poursuit: "La façon d'assembler différents matériaux à une chaîne est unique. Cette diversité enrichit superbement le texte." Dans le travail préliminaire de la première édition de la poésie complète de Vondel (également sortie en 1644),[14] la lettre que Jan de Brune a insérée dans le trente-septième chapitre du *Wetsteen der vernuften* est citée sans en mentionner le destinataire—et qui semble donc être écrite pour Vondel. De Brune nomme également Hooft avec sympathie, lorsqu'il imite plusieurs fois la poésie de Huygens. Il s'avère qu'il a un goût général pour la poésie néerlandaise, et pourtant il ne semble pas posséder un grand talent lorsqu'il écrit lui-même ses poèmes; mais il essaie de faire de son mieux pour s'exprimer de la même manière que les grands poètes.

Le but du *Wetsteen*

Cependant De Brune est remarquable en tant qu'homme de lettres. Ses essais ont été construits à partir de notes prises pendant ses nombreuses lectures érudites et sont beaucoup plus que de simples extraits de littérature. De Brune a réussi à rassembler ses citations de façon divertissante. Le lecteur se sent souvent visé personnellement.

---

[12] Voir L. Strengholt: "Donne als model. Donne, Hooft en Huygens in Jan de Brunes Minnepraet," *Voortgang* 7 (1985): 213–239.

[13] Voir L. C. Michels: "Franciscus Junius en Jan de Brune de Jonge" in: *Filologische opstellen* III (Zwolle Thieme, 1961), 211–227.

[14] J. van den Vondel, *Verscheide gedichten* (Amsterdam, 1644).

De Brune a écrit de merveilleux discours à l'aide de quelques formules "type" et d'une association de thèmes. Des intermezzi philosophiques y ont été ajoutés, dans lesquels il donne sa vision de la condition humaine; il situe toujours sa lecture dans un cadre bien défini. La longue liste d'auteurs qu'il cite montre la richesse de l'érudition de De Brune. En ce qui concerne la littérature néolatine, par exemple, il cite des auteurs connus et obscurs: Marsilio Ficin, Coelius Rhodiginus, Artémidore, Pancirolle, Cardan, Ribera, Lessius, Maffaeus, Melanchthon, Meursius, Vossius, Muret, J. J. Scaliger, Amalthée, Aeneas Sylvius, les médecins Almenar, Torella, Monardis, Faloppius, Fracastorius et le juriste frison Ausonius Popma. Cette liste n'est pas complète, parce qu'il a souvent omis les références. Pour le lecteur moderne les citations ne sont pas faciles à identifier. Derrière les formules telles que "quelqu'un dit", "un juif érudit soutient", ou "j'ai ouï dire", il cache des auteurs moins réputés ou des auteurs dont les noms lui échappent. Il arrive parfois que ses citations soient des paraphrases ou qu'elles proviennent de commentaires; elles sont parfois si mal répertoriées que le lecteur peut les chercher longuement sans le moindre résultat. Il attribue par exemple le vers "Oscula si dederis fiam manifestus amator" à Cicéron, vers qui, en l'occurrence, n'existe pas dans la littérature classique latine.

Le principe rhétorique qui se cache derrière cet enchevêtrement est celui de la recherche de bonnes *"inflexiones"* et de bons exemples. Il ne faut pas toujours philosopher d'une manière sévère et syllogique dans la probation rhétorique. En ce qui concerne le discours juridique, les préceptes sont plus sévères: Vossius cite l'empereur Justinien: *"Non exemplis, sed legibus, judicandum."* Cela est encore différent dans le discours apodéictique dans lequel une induction peut être utilisée.

Les idées de Jan de Brune

Dans l'ensemble nous observons que Jan de Brune comprend mal la physique, comme nous l'avons déjà remarqué. Par contre ses opinions éthiques et sociales éclairées ont été présentées d'une façon agréable. Il cite avec sympathie quelques anecdotes à propos des juifs, dans lesquelles il prend la défense de ce groupe de la population. Ainsi il raconte que les juifs en Italie doivent porter un chapeau jaune afin d'être reconnus et qu'un valet embarrasse un juif en échangeant son chapeau avec lui. Le chevalier du valet ordonne à celui-ci de rendre le chapeau jaune au juif, "parce que," dit-il "il préfère être un véritable juif qu'un chrétien déshonoré." Le juif est de cette manière sorti de l'embarras, ceci rejoint l'opinion du milieu intellectuel de Vossius qui en tant que calviniste convaincu fait des recherches sur les autres religions du monde et laisse à chacun sa propre valeur.[15]

Un thème qui revient souvent est le combat contre les superstitions. Nombre de ses anecdotes montre la bêtise de la superstition parfois avec une foule d'arguments, et d'autres fois avec une ironie supérieure et hautaine.

Nous retrouvons beaucoup d'éléments de De Brune dans l'oeuvre de Gérard Vossius. L'oeuvre de ce dernier a un style beaucoup plus scientifique et par conséquent moins distrayant, du fait que les associations libres de De Brune en sont absentes.

---

[15] Rademaker, *Vossius,* 307.

Néanmoins Vossius se laisse facilement guider pour des citations bien choisies de la littérature classique, la Bible et la Patrologie. Nous rencontrons souvent pour introduire des digressions savantes dans son travail, des phrases telles que *"etsi vero ad rem non multum hic refert . . ."*

Le fait que De Brune utilise de longues citations du latin sans s'excuser, comme il le fait amplement lorsqu'il s'agit d'un sonnet en anglais ou en italien, semble indiquer qu'il attend de son public une connaissance certaine du latin. Cette érudition ne se limite pas au canon renommé; il utilise également les petits opuscules et les auteurs inconnus. Il paraît avoir rassemblé des fiches dans certaines catégories lors de sa lecture—il dit qu'il ne traite pas de certains sujets parce qu'il y réserve spécialement un chapitre entier.

Bien que De Brune ait certaines aspirations littéraires, comme le prouvent ses citations nombreuses d'oeuvres littéraires et maints exemples de sa propre poésie insérés dans son livre, il ne se limite vraiment pas à la littérature en ce qui concerne ses sources. Il attache aussi beaucoup d'importance aux oeuvres juridiques (comme les *Institutions* de Justinien), théologiques (comme l'oeuvre de Lessius), et des traités de physique (comme celles de Libertos Fromondus).

Jan de Brune connaît donc parfaitement la littérature de son époque: non seulement la littérature néerlandaise, mais aussi la littérature européenne et classique lui sont familières. Toutefois, il est peu vraisemblable qu'il exerça une influence déterminante sur ses contemporains. En ce qui concerne son érudition, il est digne des grands érudits, en ce qui concerne sa mentalité il appartient aux groupes de jeunes gens de son époque qui s'entretenaient de tous sujets lors de conversations galantes. Son éducation exceptionnelle auprès de grands érudits qui possédaient d'extraordinaires bibliothèques privées a fait de lui une personnalité unique de la littérature néerlandaise. C'est avec raison que le poète Jan Vos compare cette "pierre à affiler" avec un diamant.[16]

Université de Leyde

---

[16] Poème de J. Vos dans J. de Brune: *Alle de volgeestige werken* (Harlingen, 1665), fol. **v.

The Ambassador of the Republic of Letters
at the Wedding of
Prince Philip of Spain and Queen Mary of England:
Hadrianus Junius and his Philippeis[1]

CHRIS L. HEESAKKERS

Hadrianus Junius (1511–1575) is considered to have been the most important Dutch humanist, philologist and historian in the period between Erasmus' death and the foundation of the first Dutch university in 1575. He published editions or Latin translations of four Greek texts, edited four Latin texts, composed two dictionaries, and wrote two historical works, one collection of philological emendations and explanations, and one volume of *adagia*.[2]

Among his contemporaries, and particularly his young admirers, Junius also enjoyed great prestige as a Latin poet. He published a collection of *Emblemata* and two larger poems, one being the *Philippeis*, an epithalamium on the wedding of Prince Philip of Spain and Queen Mary of England in the summer of 1554.[3] He contributed many verses to engravings and other works of artistic friends in his home town of Haarlem. In April 1575, three months before his death, he wrote to a friend announcing his decision to publish his more than twenty books of poetry, "Poema-

---

[1] For the correction of my English, I am indebted to Mrs. Atmo Carlisle (Amsterdam) and Mrs. S. G. van Romburgh (Leiden).

[2] For an overview of Junius' life and works, see C. L. Heesakkers, "Junius (Hadrianus) (1511–1575)", in *Centuriae Latinae—offertes à Jacques Chomarat*, ed. C. Nativel (Genève 1997), 449–455.

[3] PHILIPPEIS, SEV, IN NVPTIAS DIVI PHILIPPI, AVG. PII, MAX & HEROINAE MARIAE AVG. FELICIS, INVICTAE, Regum Angliae, Franciae, Neapolis—Carmen Heroicum. HADRIANO IVNIO Hornano *Medico Auctore*. LONDINI. 1554.

tiorum supra viginti libri".[4] A collection of poems on political and military events around Leiden, entitled *Carminum Lugdunensium Sylva*, was published in April or May 1575. This collection was part of what I tend to call the frontispiece or the prospectus of the newly opened Leiden University, the very first tangible and lasting proof of its existence within the *Respublica Literarum*. I am referring to the *Nova poemata* of the prolific young poet Janus Dousa, with its remarkable imprint "In nova academia nostra Lugdunensi excusum".[5] Dousa had been the most important member of the committee that prepared the foundation of the university. This committee was transformed into three so-called *Curatores* who, together with the four burgermasters of the town, formed the board of the university after the opening ceremony on 8 February. Being a friend of Dousa for ten years, Junius' name was soon mentioned as a future professor of medicine.[6]

In an extensive and programmatic poem adressed to his fellow *Curatores*, Dousa, eagerly expecting Junius' arrival, heralded his friend as

> . . . pater omnium leporum,
> Noster Iunius, ille Erasmus alter
> Huius temporis alter et Secundus.[7]

Now, even if we are prepared to interpret this as a eulogistic exaggeration, which is so typical among humanists and Neo-Latin poets, the equation of Junius to Erasmus sounds rather surprising to our ears. Junius was certainly a good scholar with a wide range of interests, but his own modesty would have prevented him from comparing himself with the giant that Erasmus had become to posterity. Junius himself suggested in one of his last books that Erasmus' fame had almost totally eclipsed his fellow scholars: "Ille fulgure suae claritatis caeteris propemodum tenebras obduxit".[8] To compete with Janus Secundus, "ingenium felicissimum et ab ipsis Musis effictum", "that most fertile genius, shaped by the hands of the Muses", was also a risk that a person with average self-knowledge would wisely avoid.[9] A reincarnation, however, of the two extremes, Erasmus and Janus Secundus, in one human being would seem to result in an unparalleled hybrid. The fusion, to quote Junius again, of the bearer of the laurel wreath of all kinds of learning, but particularly biblical learning, on the one

---

[4] H. Junius, *Epistolae*, D(ordrecht MDLII [=1652]), 492 (to Nic. Vorstius, 8-4-1575): Quod si pax coeat, id quod speramus, Bataviam cum Poematiorum supra viginti libris in lucem dare decretum est.

[5] *Iani Duzae Nordovicis Nova Poemata. Quorum Catalogum altera ab hac pagina indicabit. Item Hadriani Iuni Carminum Lugdunensium Sylva. In nova academia nostra Lugdunensi excusum. Anno 1575. Impensis Ioannis Hauteni.*

[6] P. C. Molhuysen, *Bronnen tot de geschiedenis der Leidsche universiteit* I (s-Gravenhage 1913), 24* (ca. 1-5-1575): "voorts dat men voir teerste soude moegen volstaen met een professor in re medica als Mr. Gerard Bont ende ter gelegender tijt Doctorem Adrianum Iunium soude solliceteren".

[7] Dousa, *Nova Poemata* [above n. 5], fol. Q iij recto.

[8] H. Junius, *Batavia* (Leiden, 1588), 234.

[9] Junius, *Batavia,* 236.

hand, with the poet, whose most graceful *Basia* will live as long as mouths of lovers are open to give and receive each other's kisses, on the other, would be a monstrosity.[10]

Tradition has it that Justus Lipsius had described Junius as the most learned Dutchman after Erasmus. This description has survived in almost all the histories and dictionaries of scholarship or of national or general biography. Junius' fame as a poet, however, soon faded away, notwithstanding the posthumous publication of an extensive collection of his religious poetry. Georg Ellinger, the excellent critic of the Neo-Latin poetry from the Low Countries, allowed Junius only a place in the wake of Dousa, in the chapter entitled "Freunde Dousas". He devoted a sympathetic page to Junius, to conclude (I translate): "The impulse to express his feelings in poetry is there, but the ability to give poetic expression to these feelings does not keep pace with it".[11] This seems like a kind way to say that Junius had the ambition to be a poet, but lacked any poetic gifts.

A much more explicitly negative view can be found in a still unsurpassed pioneer work, the monograph devoted to Latin poets from the Netherlands by the philologist Petrus Hofman Peerlkamp. The book was first published in 1822. A revised and enlarged edition followed in 1839. To illustrate his opinion of Junius' poetic talents, Peerlkamp quoted a line from Homer's *Iliad*, where Patroclos leads the Greeks to the battlefield instead of his wrathful friend Achilles. Staying behind, Achilles prayed to Zeus to give his friend Patroclos great courage and eternal glory, as well as a safe and sound return from the fight. Then the *Iliad* continues, in Peerlkamp's slightly adapted version: "Zeus granted Achilles some of the favours he had prayed for, but refused the last one". According to Peerlkamp, the same applies to the appreciation of great geniuses. While granting them great talents, Zeus sometimes withholds less important ones. In the case of Junius, what Zeus withheld was certainly of less importance than what he granted him. To paraphrase Peerlkamp's Latin, Junius was a brilliant scholar in Greek and Latin, and excelled in philosophy, medicine, and all aspects of historiography. He should not be blamed for trying his hand at poetry too. He is to be blamed, however, for publicising the fruits of these efforts, since they do not match his fame in the other disciplines. Peerlkamp then quotes ten lines from Junius' *Philippeis*, which contain a description of the dance of the Muses, just before Philip and Mary prepare themselves for their wedding night, and concludes: "Quae sane et in verbis et in rebus Junio indigna sunt", i.e., these lines befit Junius neither in phrasing nor in contents. To forestall any objection to this merciless condemnation, Peerlkamp immediately gave the poet Junius the coup de grâce by adding that Junius did not merit inclusion in the ranks of the poets as far as the *Emblemata* was concerned

---

[10] Junius, *Batavia,* 234: "Certe vniuersi prope orbis testimonio doctrinae omnigenae ac praesertim sacrae lauream meruit [sc. Erasmus]"; p. 236: "cuius [sc. Secundi] in poematijs omnes Veneres et elegantiae Catullianae renident, qui, si par contigisset a fatis aetas, Vmbrum vatem in Elegijs longo post interuallo reliquisset: cuius Basia viuent, dum basijs amantium ora patebunt".

[11] Georg Ellinger, *Geschichte der neulateinischen Lyrik in den Niederlanden vom Ausgang des fünfzehnten bis zum Beginn des siebzehnten Jahrhunderts* (Berlin-Leipzig, 1933; repr. Berlin, 1969), 136: "der Drang, das ihn Bewegende poetisch nahezubringen, ist vorhanden, aber mit ihm hält die Fähigkeit, den Ausdruck zu meistern, nicht gleichen Schritt".

either: "Nec Emblemata obstant, quominus eum ex choro poetarum ejiciamus". Concluding his paragraph, the severe philologist proved to be aware of the favourable opinion on Junius as a poet of no less famous a critic than Pierre Bayle. However, he brushed this aside with the remark: "Hoc nempe dictu quam probatu facilius est" ("this is easier to say than to prove").[12] I cannot imagine that Hofman Peerlkamp shed many tears over the loss of the more than twenty books of Junius' poetry, as mentioned above.

The devastating criticism of the authoritative critic Peerlkamp is not a great encouragement to the readers of Junius' epithalamium. Nevertheless, I consider it worth while to dwell a few more minutes on it. As is the case with much Neo-Latin poetry, it is not the poetic and aesthetic qualities of the *Philippeis* that draw our attention in the first place, but rather its function within the historical and cultural context. Such a situational approach was probably inconceivable for a pure classicist like Peerlkamp, in a period in which the discipline of Neo-Latin Studies had still to be invented. Moreover, I wonder whether Peerlkamp read the *Philippeis* in the original edition or in the re-edition within the *Delitiae C poetarum Belgicorum* by Janus Gruterus.[13]

Gruterus included most of the additional texts of the first edition, but he dropped the long title-page and the dedicatory letter. Now a most interesting detail of this letter is the way the author tried to get access to the royal couple. The wedding of the Emperor's son Philip and the English monarch Mary had brought many noblemen, diplomats and other people to England, more precisely to Winchester and London. One of them was the well-known humanist and compatriot of Junius, Gislenus Busbequius, who left us a short account of the events.[14] Junius too travelled to England and witnessed the impressive cortège of ambassadors and representatives of the kings and nations who had gathered from almost the whole continent.[15] It is possible that he hoped to present the original copy of his poem in person, but it is not clear whether he succeeded in doing so. To be sure, he had lived in England for some four years and had dedicated a publication to Mary's predecessor, King Edward. He was acquainted with Stephen Gardiner, the bishop who performed the wedding ceremony in Winchester, and with the bishop of London, Edmund Bonner. As for the bridegroom, Junius was soon to become his subject, for Philip succeeded his father Charles V in the Netherlands the following year. Nevertheless, he had scarcely any right to present himself at the wedding, or even have his poem presented to the bridal couple by others. As a real humanist, however, Junius assigned himself, or

---

[12] Petrus Hofmannus Peerlkamp, *Liber de vita doctrina et facultate Nederlandorum qui carmina Latina composuerunt* (Haarlem, 1838), 112–113; the Greek quotation is from Homer, *Iliad* 16.250, slightly adapted.

[13] Gherus, Rhanutius [=Janus Gruterus], *Delitiae C poetarum Belgicorum, huius superiorisque aevi illustrium* (Frankfurt, 1614), III, 7–28. ["Hadriani Iunii Hornani] In nuptias Philippi & Mariae, Hispaniae, Angliae, &c." Peerlkamp gives the title "Philippeidem, carmen heroicum, in nuptias Philippi II regis Hispani et Mariae Angliae".

[14] Cf. Z. R. W. M. von Martels, "Augerius Gislenius Busbequius. Leven en werk van de keizerlijke gezant aan het hof van Süleyman de Grote", thesis, Groningen, n.d., col. 546.

[15] *Philippeis*, [Ai verso]: "nos quoque oculata fide attestari possumus".

rather his poem, a surprising role, which allowed him to join the congratulations of the international embassies. He invested his *Philippeis* with the dignity of ambassador of the supranational Republic of Letters or Republic of Poetry: "Vos itaque felicissimi Principes", he wrote to Philip and Mary, "poemation istud, cui Philippeidi nomen indidimus, velut Reipublicae literariae Poeticesue nomine ad vos venientem ac gratulabundam legationem, benigna fronte suscipite" ("You, most fortunate princes, will accept with a benevolent smile this small poem, which we entitled *Philippeis*, as if it were the embassy, coming to you to congratulate you on behalf of the Republic of Letters, or the Republic of Poetry").[16]

It may be useful to give a very concise summary of the contents of the poem, which consists of 729 hexameters, so as to convey an impression of its subject matter and structure.

After the introductory verses, Junius describes the wars which seriously menace all European countries. The situation forces the assembly of the Olympian gods to interfere. Although Queen Mary seems to be successful in pacifying England, the dynasty should be safeguarded to ensure a lasting peace. The best husband for the Queen is Philip of Spain. At Jupiter's proposal, Mercury is sent to Philip. In the shape of the councillor Lamoraal Count of Egmont, the godly messenger suggests that he marry Mary. Wicked little Cupid secretly follows Mercury, and after the latter has left, successfully wounds Philip with his arrow of love, and causes him to have sleepless nights and happy dreams. Then Cupid hurries back to his mother Venus to accompany her on her trip to the English Queen and to help her to persuade Mary to wed. A huge fleet brings Philip to England and the marriage is celebrated amid enormous public applause. During the ceremony the four nymphs Britannia, Hispania, Hibernia and Belgica, representing the countries of the monarchs, solemnly congratulate the couple, all four predicting the birth of a royal offspring before Phoebe, Delia or Luna will have ten times completed her orbit. After the ceremony, feasts, meals and dances follow until Venus prepares the bride to enter the wedding suite. Meanwhile, London has prepared itself for a warm reception of the couple. The bishop, Edmund Bonner, delivers his welcoming speech; cannons pound; congratulations and a prayer from a spectator are heard; and the company moves in procession to Whitehall. At this point the tired Muse stops inspiring Junius, so that Apolline poets can take over.

So far the contents of the poem. Grammatically and prosodically there is little or nothing blameworthy in it. All possible poetic and rhetorical devices, such as anaphora, apostrophe, alliteration and comparisons are used, albeit not always in a very subtle manner. The vocabulary seems somewhat overwhelmed with rare and unpoetical words. A description like "Antistes, dignum cui vox dat Graeca coronae / Nomen" ("a bishop to whom the Greek word for crown has been given as a worthy name"), to indicate Bishop Gardiner is rather far-fetched.[17] Gardiner's Christian name was Stephen, *stephanos* being the Greek word for crown. There is an almost fastidious abundance of reminiscences and more or less modified quotations from classical

---

[16] *Philippeis*, [Ai verso].
[17] *Philippeis*, ll. 379–380.

authors. As a *poeta doctus*, with his "multiplex lectio et recondita eruditio", as his correspondent Daniel Rogers remarked in this connection[18], Junius certainly made some impression on his contemporaries, as he may still do on his modern readers.

The title *Philippeis* suggests an epic poem, although the opening lines immediately alert the reader that the material is different from that of the great ancient epics. It is therefore not surprising that the phraseology of the poem reveals Junius' familiarity with Latin epic idiom everywhere. The borrowings from Virgil's *Aeneid* are most frequent by far, but his *Georgics* are also present. The way in which Jupiter sends Mercury to Philip and Mercury's disguise as the Count of Egmont (ll. 120 ff.) show affinity with *Aeneid* 4.220–278. Mercury's interest in sightseeing in the regions he sees below during his flight through the air reminds us, however, of Ovid's *Metamorphoses* 4.662 ff.. The "Concilium deorum" in Book I of Ovid's *chef-d'oeuvre* inspired Junius for his description of the gathering of the gods (ll. 36 ff.). Most elements of the description of Philip's voyage by ship from La Coruña to England draw freely from similar scenes in the *Aeneid*, and the many gods and nymphs of the sea who admire the enormous fleet are directly borrowed from Neptune's train in *Aeneid* 4.816 ff. Other epic favourites of Junius are Statius and, to a lesser extent, Valerius Flaccus. Lucan has almost exclusively been used in the beginning of the poem. The presence of Claudian's *Epithalamium in nuptiis Honorii* could be expected, but other poems of Claudian have also provided Junius with some formulae. We should pass over other names, including those of some prose writers, like Cicero and Tacitus, which we could mention here.

When Hofman Peerlkamp considered even the poetic phraseology, the "verba", of the *Philippeis* unworthy of the scholar Junius, he obviously judged him from the limited, aesthetic point of view of the traditional nineteenth-century classicist. And he certainly had no regard for the character of the poem as *poesis docta* which was highly esteemed in Junius' time.

Another characteristic of the *poeta doctus* is the use of ancient mythology. Here too Junius seems to surpass the norm of Neo-Latin poetry. In this case, however, the mythology seems to serve a very particular goal. Not without reason, the poem opens with a description of the miserable political and social situation in Europe. War dominates everywhere and peace seems so far away that it cannot be attained without supernatural intervention. The mythical beings represent the cosmic, divine forces, the only source from which help may still be expected. Therefore the mythical personalities are stripped of their pagan characteristics. For instance, on his trip to Philip Mercury is secretly followed by *Amor*, but this is "Ortus Amor coelo," the celestial *Amor*, or *Amor Uranius*, as a marginal note needlessly explains (l. 171). Later on, Junius adds that this *Amor* is not the son of Dione, whom the Greeks thought to be blind (ll. 197 ff.). Similarly, the "Coelica Venus" sent to Mary has nothing to do with "Cypris desultoria", the playful Venus of the ancients (ll. 203–204). With this in mind, it is not difficult to equate a Christian God, the Father pitying the miserable

---

[18] Junius, *Epistolae*, 629; Rogers asks for the source of Junius' line 476, stating that Hibernia, Ireland, had been well-known to the ancient Argonauts.

world, with Jupiter presiding over the godly council. Olympus is simply identical with Heaven, and with Christian Providence caring for humankind. It is Heaven's, God's decision to come and rescue the human race through the marriage of two very powerful monarchs, who will be able to restore and maintain peace within Christian Europe by joining forces. The marriage receives a cosmic and a providential dimension. Philip and Mary are in the first place instruments in God's hands.

Although much of the mythological lore in the poem may be understood within the framework of Junius' text, it does not necessarily fit in well from a poetic point of view. In my opinion, however, it fits better here than, for instance, in Sannazaro's *De partu virginis*.

Though it may fit an epithalamium, Junius' emphasis on the advisability of ensuing the speedy birth of a male offspring is undeniably a lack of subtlety and good taste towards the princely couple from a modern point of view. Of course, it was "now or never" for the thirty-eight and a half year-old bride, if she wanted an heir apparent. Obviously, Junius considered his worry about the succession quite normal and he was probably never criticized for it, at least not apparently by the Queen herself, for he dedicated to her his next publication, *De Anno*, one and a half years later. Had she criticized the poem, Junius would hardly have dared approach her again and he certainly would not have reminded Mary of the *Philippeis*, as he explicitly did in that dedication.

A final question demands our attention. We have seen that Junius was an eye-witness of at least the procession into the capital, London. One therefore wonders whether the poem contains any historical information or views on historical facts of the event which could be of interest to us. Actually the historical facts in the poem are rather scanty. True, the Count of Egmont, who was to be the first and most famous Dutch victim of the Duke of Alva's government on behalf of Philip fourteen years later, played a part in the preparation of the engagement. It was he who was sent to England to perform the marriage "per procurationem", as Philip's proxy, early in 1554. This was a delicate duty which implied, among other activities, that he had to lie down at Mary's side for a short time, in a suit of armour, but with one bare leg. Another passage of the poem refers to Mary's struggle with the faction of Jane Grey and its leader John Dudley, Duke of Northumberland, but it contains no details apart from a mention of the coronation day just one year before. The two bishops, Gardiner of Winchester and Bonner of London, both correspondents of Junius', are mentioned without specific information and without a word about their recent release from prison, thanks to the Queen. The dignity with which the noblemen Pembroke and Derby bear the double-edged sword, and Philip's reception of the Order of the Garter, are skipped by a handy *praeteritio* (ll. 531–550), because, as the poet remarks, no less a poet than a Homer or Virgil was needed to describe it.

Thanks to Junius' correspondence we know something about the fortune of the poem. In two undated letters, Junius seems to suggest that the whole affair cost him about six months, a period which he obviously spent in England.[19] While still

---

[19] H. Junius, *Epistolae selectae*, ed. P. Scheltema (Amsterdam-Leipzig, 1839), 7 (to Perezius):

working on the text, Junius consulted one of his correspondents, Nicolaus Guldensterrius, in an undated letter. First, he asked whether he had to send a manuscript or
a printed copy of the poem, and secondly, whether his personal presence was needed
or whether he could limit himself to sending it to Guldensterrius.[20] A letter from 9
September tells us that he finished the text and decided to have it printed in London,
where he was impatiently waiting for the typographer's return to the city.[21] On 24
September, Junius could send two printed copies from London to Malinaeus, the
secretary of Philip's father, the Emperor Charles V, asking him to offer one copy, as
well as a warm recommendation of it, to the Emperor.[22]

As might be expected, the correspondence also informs us that Junius' poetic
praise of the marriage was at least partly inspired by rather down-to-earth motives.
When the poem was rewarded with only thirty-six golden crowns, Junius was bitterly
disappointed. In an undated letter, he wrote to Gonsalvo Perez to say that his voyage
and his stay in London, for which he had had to borrow money, had cost him much
more than double the amount: "certe duplum amplius multoque amplius".[23] Now
he regretted his long stay in England and his expenditure on the special, nicely bound
copies.[24] History would soon reveal that Philip was not at all inclined to be generous towards the inhabitants of the Low Countries. I wonder whether that was the
reason why Junius tried his luck by dedicating his next publication, a second edition
of his *De Anno et Mensibus commentarius*, exclusively to Philip's wife, Queen Mary. I
cannot tell whether he had more financial success this time.

University of Amsterdam / State University of Leiden

"pro eo qui quinque imo sex plus minus sumptus non parvos fecerit"; 11 (to NN.): "tot mensibus,
sex plus minus".

[20] Junius, *Epistolae selectae*, 74 (to Guldensterrius): "optime laboribus meis consulet Tua Excel-
lentia, si me tribus dignetur verbis certiorem facere. manuve descriptum exemplar an typis pro-
cusum mittendum videatur; adde huc an etiam praesentia sit opus nostra, an vero tibi in manum
submitti praestet".

[21] Junius, *Epistolae selectae*, 2 (to Perezius, 7-9-1554): "Carmen Heroicum—Philippeidos nomine a me donatum, jam absolutum, praelo tradere constitui, Regique et Reginae offerre. Jamque
a praeli labore respirasset, nisi jam totos octo et amplius dies ingrata remora illud tardasset, dum
Regius Typographus mihi expectatur peregre profectus".

[22] Junius, *Epistolae*, 214–215 (to Malinaeus): "Nunc orandus mihi es, ut Philippeidem typis
Anglicis efformatam, memoris animi testimonium benigne excipias, alterumque exemplar Carolo
Imp. cui quod sis longe omnium gratissimus tua meretur virtus, exhibeas, ornesque verbis nostram
operam, si videbitur, ita ut Caesar tuis verbis intelligat, ipsum filii laudibus cumulatius laudari, earumque fructum uberrimum hoc quoque modo in ipsum redundare".

[23] Junius, *Epistolae selectae*, 7 (to Perezius).

[24] Junius, *Epistolae selectae*, 11 (to NN.).

El humanista giennense y virrey del Perú
D. Diego de Benavides y de la Cueva (1607–1666)

JUAN HIGUERAS MALDONADO

Don Diego de Benavides y de la Cueva había nacido en la villa de Santisteban del Puerto (Jaén), en donde fue bautizado un 25 de febrero del 1607. Era hijo primogénito del VII Conde de Santisteban, D. Francisco de Benavides y de la Cueva, y de su primera esposa y prima hermana Doña Brianda de Bazán y Benavides, hija de D. Álvaro de Bazán, I Marqués de Santa. Cruz, Comendador Mayor de León en la Orden de Santiago y del Consejo de Felipe II.[1]

Heredó, pues, el título de VIII Conde de Santisteban; Felipe IV le otorgó además el de Marqués de Solera, en premio a sus servicios prestados a la corona (según luego veremos). Por su matrimonio con Dª Antonia Ruiz de Corella Dávila, Condesa de Concentaina y Marquesa de las Navas y del Risco, acumuló también dichos títulos nobiliarios.[2]

Humanísticamente se había formado con los jesuitas en el Colegio Imperial de Madrid (del que posteriormente fue su óptimo patrono), junto con otros varones ilustres en las armas y en las letras, tales como el príncipe D. Fernando de Austria (gran admirador de su erudición), y sus propios hermanos D. Antonio, D. Enrique y D. Álvaro de Benavides, e igualmente D. Antonio Zapata (Conde de Barajas y profesor del Palacio Real), D. Antonio de Luna (Conde de Salvatierra), D. Alfonso de Velasco

---

[1] Joaquín Mercado Egea, *La muy ilustre villa de Santisteban del Puerto* (Madrid, 1973), 121 ss.; Manuel Caballero Venzalá, *Diccionario bio-bibliográfico del Santo Reino de Jaén* (Jaén, 1979), I, 232–233, nº 1988; Joaquín Mercado Egea, *D. Diego de Benavides y de la Cueva, XVIII Virrey del Perú* (Jaén, 1990), 15 ss., 28 ss.; Miguel Molina Martínez, *Jaén y el mundo hispanoamericano* (Jaén, 1987), 113 ss.

[2] Mercado, *D. Diego de Benavides,* 33 ss.; Caballero, *Diccionario bio-bibliográfico,* nº 1988; Bartolomé Ximénez Patón, *Historia de la antigua y continuada nobleza de la ciudad de Jaén* (Jaén, 1983) (edición facsímil sobre la de 1628), fols. 155–159; Gonzalo Argote de Molina, *Nobleza de Andalucía* (Jaén, 1957) (sobre la edición de Jaén, 1866), 577. "Condado de Santisteban" en la revista *D. Lope de Sosa* (edición facsímil de Riquelme y Vargas-Machuca, Jaén, 1982) (1918): 213, 326, 363; (1919): 362 ss.; Julio de Atienza, *Nobiliario español,* 2ª edición (Madrid, 1959), 970.

Córdoba (Marqués de Celada), etc. Así nos lo testifica el jesuita Andrés Salo (profesor de teología en el colegio de la Compañía de Jesús en Pamplona), en la censura oficial que formuló, el 30 de enero de 1660, sobre su obra antológica (en prosa y versos latinos)[3].

Nuestro conde de Santisteban ejerció la carrera militar, conforme se usaba durante esa época entre las personas de su rango social noble. Destacó en la campaña de Milán (1637), primero como soldado particular, y después como capitán de infantería en el Tercio de Saboya. También sobresale militarmente durante las campañas de Aragón (1642) y Portugal (1643); aquí fue nombrado Gobernador de las Armas para defender la frontera de Extremadura contra los lusitanos, al igual que por el norte estaba defendida por el Duque de Alba. No menos logra distinguirse como buen político en sus funciones de gobernador y capitán general en Navarra (1653), y finalmente de Virrey, Gobernador y capitán general en las provincias del Perú (1660). De este último cargo tomó posesión el 30 de julio de 1661.[4]

Las instrucciones reales para el gobierno del Perú (expedidas el 16 de agosto del 1660) fueron aplicadas por D. Diego de Benavides con toda prudencia y rectitud. Supo afrontar y paliar, de modo equitativo, los graves problemas de aquel virreinato, cuales eran la actitud abusiva de los propios españoles o de los criollos enriquecidos, las relaciones con la Iglesia y con la Hacienda Real, y particularmente la situación social de los indios. A este respecto, sólo unos días después de su toma de posesión como virrey, despachó una provisión (el 10 de agosto de 1661) para reducir el número de mitayos. Con posterioridad redactaba unas ordenanzas a favor de los indios, en las cuales fijó la jornada máxima de trabajo, el salario mínimo, las excepciones por razón del sexo, edad y resistencia. Eran unas normas plenas de sentido humano y cristiano, y de profundo y sincero respeto hacia los indios. También como militar tuvo que intervenir allí (ante las incursiones piratas) para defender las costas y fortificar Panamá, Arica, Guayaquil y Valparaíso.[5]

Tras el fallecimiento de su primera esposa contrajo segundas nupcias con su cuñada Dª Juana Dávila y Corella, mediante capitulaciones matrimoniales otorgadas en Madrid, a 12 de abril del 1651. Enviudado por segunda vez, vuelve a contraer matri-

---

[3] Fue recopilada y publicada por sus hijos D. Manuel y D. Francisco Dávila y Corella, bajo el título *Horae Succissiuae* (Lugduni, 1660), 30 fol., 361 pp. 8°.- Madrid, Biblioteca Nacional 2/66586. La Diputación Provincial de Jaén acaba de adquirir otro ejemplar (para la biblioteca del Instituto de Estudios Giennenses), impreso en Lugduni, sumptibus Ioannis de Argaray, 1664 (signatura n° 3.851); Antonio Palau y Dulcet, *Manual del librero hispanoamericano*, t. 2° (Barcelona, 1949), 158, n° 27.185. Caballero, *Diccionario bio-bibliográfico*, n° 1992; Mercado, *D. Diego de Benavides*, 128–129.

[4] *Memorial en que representa al Rey N. S. la antigüedad, calidad y servicios de sus Casas, D. Diego de Benavides y de la Cueva . . . Conde de Santisteban, Marqués de Solera . . . En Madrid. Año de M. DC. LX.* Madrid, Biblioteca Nacional 3/73177. Cf. también el *Memorial* presentado ante el Rey por el IX Conde de Santisteban D. Francisco de Benavides Dávila. Instituto de Estudios Giennenses, 3.853: *Historia General de España y América* (Madrid, 1987), IX,2, 364.

[5] Mercado, *D. Diego de Benavides*, 103 ss.; Caballero, *Diccionario bio-bibliográfico*, n° 1988; Molina, *Jaén y el mundo hispanoamericano*, 114 ss.

monio con Dª Ana del Silva Manrique de la Cerda, probablemente a comienzos del 1654. Falleció en Lima el 19 de marzo del 1666.[6]

§

Tanta actividad militar y política, dentro y fuera de España, supo compaginarla perfectamente con su amor por la cultura clásica. Así aparece reflejado en una serie de escritos en prosa y poesías latinas, que según anticipamos (cf. supra nota 3) fueron recopilados y publicados por sus hijos.

De la categoría poética de sus composiciones pueden darnos idea los elogios de sus contemporáneos. Así, por ejemplo, uno de los censores oficiales de su libro, D. José Moreto, jesuita y cronista del reino de Navarra, asegura que

nihil his versibus dulcius, utilius nihil praeceptionibus his ... Hic purum, ac suaue halat et diuersis flosculis consertus e medio Parnasso, et lectissimis areolis decerptis.

Parecidamente se expresa el otro ya referido censor D. Andrés Salo, a través de estas palabras dirigidas a los editores e hijos del Conde:

Rem feceritis vobis gloriosam, nobis iucundam, omnibus salutarem. Opus enim hoc est lucem orbi late affusurum, adeoque luce ac aeternitate dignum.

No menos expresivo resulta el elogio del librero D. Juan Coronneau:

Nam cum multos habeat, qui res magnas gerant, pauciores qui scribant; quanta dignitas nancisci in Te vno, qui praeclara faciat et praeclara scribat ... Tibi debet Hispania vt in te legat quae per te patrauit, et transmittat per te ad posteros, quae fortiter et prudenter per te confecit.

Como colofón a todas estas alabanzas, y a modo de epifonema, puede valernos el retrato que de él nos legó Nicolás Antonio:

Vir non equestri modo virtute, sed felicissimo ingenio, florenti eruditione, prudentia et pietate singulari, flos et ornamentum Hispanae nobilitatis. (*Bibliotheca Hispana Nova I,* 270)

La ya aludida antología, bajo el título de *Horae Successivae,* comprende 361 páginas, más 30 folios de preliminares, sin numerar, en 8º. Su contenido es el siguiente: Se inician los folios preliminares con la típica y tradicional epístola dedicatoria al papa reinante Alejandro VII (1655–1666) por parte de los hermanos D. Francisco y D. Manuel de Benavides, en su calidad de compiladores-editores e hijos de D. Diego; asimismo, otra al lector. Seguidamente las habituales y elogiosas censuras de los respectivos censores, D. José Moreto, jesuita cronista en el reino de Navarra, y D. Andrés Salo, también jesuita y profesor de teología en el colegio de la Compañía de Jesús en Pamplona, con fechas 6 de febrero y 30 de enero del 1660, respectivamente.

---

[6] Mercado, *D. Diego de Benavides,* 33 ss.; Caballero, *Diccionario bio-bibliográfico,* nº 1988, 233.

Tras la aprobación oficial a cargo de D. Francisco Ruiz de Palacios, doctor en derecho y vicario general en el obispado de Pamplona, se adjunta una extensa (17 ff.) y elogiosa carta de este curial, dirigida a los sobredichos hermanos. En estos mismos términos laudatorios se expresan (como acabamos de anticipar) los elogios, en prosa y verso, del impresor de la "editio princeps" D. Juan Coronneau. (Por contraste en la posterior edición, Lugduni, 1664, no existe elogio alguno del impresor pamplonica D. Juan de Argaray). Como colofón a estos amplios preliminares se insertan un breve epigrama de tres dísticos, compuesto por los hermanos Benavides, y dedicado al ya referido papa Alejandro VII; otro epigrama de cinco dísticos por D. Guillermo Subrigerio, y el índice general analítico de todo el libro.

Éste se presenta estructurado en tres partes o secciones: *Carmina* (tres libros, entre las pp. 1 a 193), *Elogia Varia* (pp. 203–284) y *Oracvla Divina* (pp. 285–361). El libro I de los *Carmina* incluye poemas latinos en honor de ilustres personajes y amigos: Alejandro VII con motivo de su elección para romano pontífice, al cardenal infante D. Fernando, hermano del rey D. Felipe IV, a D. Juan Isasio, conde de Piedeconcha y preceptor del príncipe, a D. José Moreto, cronista del reino de Navarra y censor de su libro, a D. Diego de Guzmán, marqués de Leganés, gobernador en el estado de Milán, a los jesuitas D. Gerardo Montano y D. Diego Oquete, al excmo. D. Luis de Haro, ministro de D. Felipe IV, al propio rey con motivo de la reconquista de la ciudad de Lérida, y por último en alabanza a la Compañía de Jesús (pp. 6–74).

El libro II de los *Carmina* se inicia con un epigrama, en paráfrasis a otro en español (pp. 75–76). Continúan luego diversos epigramas al nombre de Jesús e institución de la Compañía, a la muerte de Dª Margarita de Mora, hija del marqués de Castelrodrigo, a diferentes santos jesuitas (S. Luis Gonzaga, S. Francisco de Borja ...) y del santoral católico (S. Francisco de Asís, S. Bartolomé, patrono de Pontevedra, Sto. Tomás de Aquino, S. Isidro Agrícola, S. Fermín, patrono de Pamplona ...) y a diversas advocaciones marianas: Inmaculada Concepción, Nª Sª de las Nieves, Asunción ... (pp. 77–107). También dedica epigramas a personajes literarios e históricos: Tarquinio "El Soberbio"; M. Anneo Lucano, Lucio Anneo Floro, Julio César, Dª Urraca, al Cid Campeador, a D. Fernando III "El Santo", D. Felipe IV, la batalla de las Navas de Tolosa contra los moros ... (107–126). Vienen seguidamente otros poemas a las cuatro virtudes cardinales y a las tres teologales, una oda para festejar el nacimiento del príncipe D. Felipe, epigramas a D. Gonzalo Fernández de Córdoba, al rey D. Pelayo, a sus propios hijos D. Francisco y D. Manuel de Benavides, y en homenaje a la paz de Fuenterrabía. Finaliza este libro con un epigrama al obispo de Pamplona D. Diego de Tejada y la Guardia (pp. 127–150).

Comienza el libro III de los *Carmina* con un extenso poema histórico a los reyes de España (entre los cuales incluye también a los emperadores romanos) hasta el coetáneo Felipe IV (pp. 151–172). Sigue una larga epístola monitoria a su hijo D. Francisco por haber heredado el marquesado de las Navas y el condado de Concentaina, tras la muerte de su hermano D. Pedro; asimismo, una poética descripción de la modesta casa de madera, en donde se firmó la paz de Fuenterrabía entre españoles y franceses, el año 1659 (pp. 173–184). Por haber fallecido entonces, en ese mismo lugar y circunstancias, su hijo D. Pedro, le dedica una sentida elegía (pp. 185–191). Finaliza este tercer libro de sus Carmina con unas *Notas*—en prosa latina—a un poema suyo sobre el asedio a la ciudad italiana de Vercelli (pp. 193–201).

La segunda parte de esta antología incluye una serie de *Elogia Varia* en honor de la Virgen María, que forma un verdadero tratado poético sobre mariología: concepción inmaculada, natividad, presentación, nupcias con S. José, encarnación, visita a Sta. Isabel, parto, purificación, huida a Egipto, junto a la cruz, muerte y asunción (pp. 203–30). De igual modo, en honor de España por su geografía, por sus habitantes y distintas denominaciones; canta además a una *Hispania Gothica, Nautica, Literata* y *Religiosa* (pp. 231–248). Tras unos preámbulos—en cuidada prosa latina—aparecen sendos Elogia a D. Luis de Hara y Guzmán (condeduque de Olivares y plenipotenciario para la paz firmada entre Felipe IV y Luis XIV de Francia) y al cardenal D. Julio Mazarino (también plenipotenciario francés para firmar dicha paz). De esta misma guisa—pero sin preámbulos en prosa—figuran *Elogia* a D. Francisco Ramos del Manzano, al marqués de Sta. Cruz D. Álvaro Bastano, a sus censores los jesuitas D. Andrés Salo Hiberno y D. José Moreto, y al vicario general de Pamplona D. Francisco Ruia de Palacios (pp. 249–284).

La tercera y última parte de este florilegio (con prólogo al lector por parte de sus hijos D. Francisco y D. Manuel, y un proloquio del autor de toda la obra) recopila un amplio ensayo filosófico-teológico, en prosa, bajo el título de *Oracvla Divina* (pp. 285–361). A base de unas paráfrasis sobre los tres primeros capítulos del Génesis va desarrollando una serie de reflexiones aplicadas a la política y a los políticos. Son continuas las citas textuales y las referencias conceptuales no sólo de autores eclesiásticos (S. Agustín, S. Ambrosio, S. Jerónimo, Sto. Tomás de Aquino ...), sino muy señaladamente de escritores grecolatinos: Homero, Platón, Aristóteles, Demóstenes, Jenofonte, Tucídides, Plutarco, Polibio, Filón ... ; y entre los latinos: Ennio, Cicerón, Catulo, Ovidio, Horacio, Séneca, Salustio, Plinio, Tácito, Lucano, Suetonio, Aulo Gelio, Veleyo Patérculo, Lucio Floro, Boecio, Casiodoro, Justiniano, Amiano Marcelino, Claudiano, Ennodio, Petrarca y Arias Montano.

El latín que utiliza es un neolatín cuidado y formalista, de escuela jesuítica, con un gran dominio de la métrica grecolatina y los recursos estilístico-literarios clásicos. En cualquiera de sus poemas (ya sean de tema religioso, literario o histórico) pueden apreciarse todas estas cualidades, que acabamos de apuntar. Aunque prevalecen los esquemas métricos del dístico epigramático, también utiliza las estrofas, en particular la sáfica. En relación a la prosa, debemos añadir el profundo y extenso conocimiento que poseía tanto de la cultura cristiana, como de la clásica. Prueba de ello queda patente en el elenco de autores, más arriba enumerados, entre los cuales figuran no únicamente los "auctores probati", sino bastantes más, tanto de época posterior, como incluso de la humanística. A pesar de ello, su prosa neolatina adolece de excesivo énfasis y demasiado retoricismo, que en ocasiones puede resultarnos un tanto empalagoso.

§

Para que también nosotros podamos directamente sopesar su inspiración y formación humanística, hemos seleccionado—con la correspondiente traducción y comentario estilístico-literario—dos composiciones: el Epigramma LXVIII del Liber II, y el Elogivm V (*Hispania Navtica*) de los *Elogia Varia*.

LIBER II
EPIGRAMMA LXVIII[7]
De Classi ab India Occidentali Hispaniam
repetenti, An. 1659.

Expectata diu uictrix super aequoris undas
Cardine ab occiduo classis onusta redis.

Diuitias Orbis quas congerit ultimus, atque
Argenti, atque auri pondera prome sinu.

Americae impositus curae Ludouicus ab Aula
Hispana incolumen per sua iussa uehit.

Defuit haud quaquam precibus placare Tonantem,
Regis ut obsequijs promptus honore prior.

Gratulor, et faustum pacis tibi uendicat omen,
Munia qui rerum summa Philippus obit.

Nequicquam obsistet ferrum auro, saecula condes
Aurea; nam cunctas hic feret annus opes.

LIBRO II
EPIGRAMA LXVIII
*Sobre una flota que regresa a España desde
las Indias Occidentales. A. 1659.*

¡Esperada tiempo ha y victoriosa sobre las
olas del mar, desde las regiones occidentales, oh flota, cargada regresas!

Las riquezas, que acumulan los confines
últimos de la tierra, además de tanta cantidad en plata y oro, sácalas de tu seno.

El gobernador de América, Luis, nombrado
por la corte real hispana, la conduce incó-
lume merced a sus mandatos.

En modo alguno descuidó aplacar con sus
preces a Júpiter Tonante, para poder expresar con obsequios su primacía en el honor
del rey.

Te doy mis parabienes, y el fausto augurio
de la paz te otorga Felipe[8], quien asume
las supremas funciones del Estado.

En vano se enfrentará la espada con el oro:
vas a crear unos siglos de oro, pues toda
clase de riquezas logrará esta época.

---

[7] *Horae Successivae*, 115.
[8] Felipe IV (1605–1665).

Comentario

Inicia el ciclo de los epigramas que podemos denominar como de tema histórico. Éste, en concreto, más bien se asemeja a un cántico triunfal en honor de una flota española, que, cargada de riquezas, felizmente arriba hasta la nación, desde las Indias Occidentales, en el año 1659. Justo dos años antes de que D. Diego de Benavides y de la Cueva navegase hacia allá, tras haber sido nombrado en 1660 como virrey, gobernador y capitán general de las provincias del Perú.

El actual epigrama triunfal incluye tres claros protagonistas: la flota, su almirante el gobernador de América D. Luis[9] y el rey D. Felipe IV (1605–1665).

Comienza el poema con un patético y entusiasta apóstrofe hacia la flota, en dos dísticos. En el primero de los cuales, se describe a la misma mediante tres expresivos calificativos: *Expectata, uictrix, onusta*, completados los dos primeros con su respectiva epexegesis: *diu, super aequoris undas*, embellecido éste a su vez por la poética metonimia de *aequoris* y la circunlocución *cardine ab occiduo* v. 2. El último calificativo queda desarrollado ampliamente por todo el segundo dístico, en el cual la anticipación de *diuitias* v. 3. se especifica en cuanto a su procedencia (por conducto de la perífrasis *Orbis ultimus*), y en cuanto a su contenido (*Argenti / auri* v. 4), unidos ambos gracias al polisíndeton *atque*, para enfatizar esa frase y obligar a los lectores / -ras a fijarse con detenimiento en los dos materiales preciosos.

El tercer protagonista indicábamos que era el rey D. Felipe IV. Éste, en su calidad de jefe supremo del estado español (amplia circunlocución de un pentámetro para definirlo, v. 10) es quien le otorga a D. Luis el *faustum pacis omen* v. 9. (Notemos el *uendicat* menos etimológico que "uindicat" v. 9). Pero también el poeta quiere unirse a tales momentos de triunfo y felicidad. Y para ello lanza sus entusiastas parabienes con ese *Gratulor* v. 9, anticipado y alegre mediante un pie dáctilo, que contrasta con los dos pies espondáicos siguientes del hexámetro.

Concluye este poema de cántico triunfal con los clásicos augurios de paz y bienestar. Nos recuerdan al pacifismo triunfalista de un Virgilio en su misteriosa égloga IV 8–9 (*quo ferrea primum / desinet ac toto surget gens aurea mundo*) o el de Ovidio en su *Metamorphosis* XV 832 ss.

Por desgracia tales deseos de un nuevo siglo de oro para España, pletórico de paz y riquezas, no responde—ni mucho menos—a la realidad histórica de nuestra patria, durante esas fechas. Tal vez se deba a la imaginación, buena voluntad o incluso adulación hacia su rey, por parte del Conde de Santisteban, muy en consonancia con el pensamiento barroco sobre la realeza en esa época, particularmente entre los nobles españoles. Recordemos, por el contrario, que precisamente ese mismo año 1659, el 7 de noviembre, se firmaba el tratado de los Pirineos, que supuso el final de la hege-

---

[9] Nuestro poeta probablemente se refiera a su antecesor en el virreinato del Perú, D. Luis Henríquez de Guzmán, Conde de Alba de Liste y Grande de España. Este personaje fue primeramente virrey en Nueva España (México), desde 1650 hasta 1653. Más tarde, el 24 de febrero de 1655, recibía el mando del virreinato del Perú, que le transmitió su sobrino, el Conde de Salvatierra. En dicho cargo se mantuvo hasta 1661, en el cual fue sustituido por nuestro D. Diego de Benavides (1661–66): *Historia General de España y América* IX,2, 363; Lewis Hannke, *Virreyes del Perú durante los Austrias* (Madrid, 1976).

monía europea de España y su transferencia a Francia. En contraste con el reinado de Felipe III "el buen rey", que elevó la grandeza española hasta su cenit, el reinado de Felipe IV—en honor a la verdad—constituyó la caída y ruina de nuestra nación, en el interior y en el exterior. No sabemos si el humanista giennense, al escribir "toda clase de riquezas" en el final del epigrama, se refiera al auge logrado en la explotación de las minas de oro de la Concepción y Santiago de Turlurú, en Panamá. Esto, sin duda, fue lo más sobresaliente para la economía española en América por esas fechas.[10]

Una solemnidad majestuosa, pero pacífica, se manifiesta métricamente en el hexámetro 11 (que es holoespondáico), y no menos en el contraste sereno de las sinécdoques *ferrum / auro*, justificado con la derivación etimológica *aurea*, en una clara hipérbole encabalgada *saecula / aurea*, cuya explicación cierra ya todo el poema: *cunctas hic feret annus opes* v. 12. Aunque también cuenten las razones métricas y las literarias a causa del siguiente *aurea* v. 12, parece que el poeta ha buscado en *auro* v. 11, además de la sinécdoque poco ha señalada, una "variatio" en sustitución de los sinónimos anterior y posterior: *diuitias* v. 3 y *opes* v. 12.

En este contexto final, el hipérbaton de anticipación en la forma pronominal *cunctas* v. 12, le ha conferido a esta palabra secundaria un valor enfático muy significativo.

<table>
<tr><td>

HISPANIA NAUTICA
ELOGIVM V.(*[11])

</td><td>

TRADUCCIÓN

</td></tr>
<tr><td>

I   Vel in Oceano expiscatur laudes
      Hispania!
   Nec toto pelago circunscriptos
   Quam laxos sortitur praeconiorum
[5]   Cancellos.

</td><td>

¡Que hasta en el Océano obtenga elogios
     Hispania!
Ni circunscritas ni laxas, por todo el piélago pueden surgir barreras a sus elogios.

</td></tr>
<tr><td>

II   Num quodlibet par Orationis curriculum,
     per immensum currenti?

   Extollitur vndis, sed ad Coelum.
     Sola in tantos salo;
[10]   Et tunc non sola,
   Cum alter iam sit Typhis, et altera
     Quae vehat Argo
   Cum classis extra classem:
   Sonant illius acclamationes fluctus.

</td><td>

¿Acaso existe cualquier otra liza semejante en palabras de encomio hacia quien recorre la inmensidad del mundo?
Se ve ensalzada por las olas hasta el Cielo.
Sola entre tantos por alta mar;
Pero ahora no se halla sola,
Porque ya tiene un Tifón, y otra
Argos que conduzca
su flota más allá de cualquier otra flota.
Las olas hacen sonar las aclamaciones suyas.

</td></tr>
</table>

---

[10] Ramón Menéndez Pidal, *Historia de España* (Madrid, 1986), XXVI, 589 ss.; *Historia General de España y América,* IX,1, 24; IX,2, 294; J. Alcalá-Zamora y Quiepo de Llano, *Razón y crisis de la política exterior de España en el reinado de Felipe IV* (Madrid, 1977); A. Domínguez Ortiz, *Política y hacienda de Felipe IV* (Madrid, 1960).

[11] *Horae Succissiuae,* 192–193 (en la edición del 1660, 138–139). Las indicaciones con números romanos y arábigos las añadimos para facilitar la lectura del texto en su traducción y en el comentario, pero no figuran en el original.

[15]   Cessit Herculi feroci in terris
          Morem, in pelago haud auscultat
          Plus vltra, à meta illi praescripto

               Euecta est:
          Et primum Atlantico superato
[20]   Exantlandas inaugurauit
               Nauigationes.
          Vela dantium Virtus honori velificatur
          Non ab re extra orbitam
[25]   Cursus, cùm extra orbem.

III   Pietati incrementum; Imperium
          Sibi; Mundo Partem Hispania
               Nautica addidit.

IV   At cum Americam subiectis nomen
[30]   Indidit Prouinciis, cur ab Aduena
          Nauclero deducitur
               Apellatio?
          In hoc opificem imitata summum,
               Qui condita sua
[35]   Alijs dedit; hoc est, Adamo
          Negotium nuncupandi.

V   Porrò
          Nulla Hispanis Gens in maritimis
               Illustrior;

[40]   Cum totum vno nauigio suo orbem
               Lustrauit.
          Et quae hoc magnum facinus testatur
          Carina, Victoriae nomen.
               Ecce tibi
[45]   Quidquid fragile, vel apud eam
               Laureatum.

Ella amainó al Hércules feroz su deseo por
nuevas tierras; en el piélago ya no escucha
Plus vltra (Más allá); la meta, que a él se le
había prescrito,
          Quedó franqueada:
Y, tras haber rebasado por primera vez el
Atlántico, inauguró el que se pudieran achi-
car las Navegaciones.
La Virtus de quienes se dan a la vela navega
en su honor, a través de una ruta efectiva
no fuera de órbita, sino más bien fuera del
orbe.

Para la Piedad le ha añadido la Hispania
Naútica un incremento; un Imperio, para
sí misma; para el Mundo, unos nuevos
          Lugares.

Sin embargo, cuando el nombre de América se dio a las sometidas Provincias, ¿por
qué se le quitó el nombre de su Navegante
          Extranjero?
En esto ha imitado ella al sumo creador,
El Cual sus propias creaciones
A Otros les confió el denominarlas; a saber,
a Adán le encomendó la tarea de imponerles un nombre.

          En definitiva:
No existe entre los pueblos marítimos una
estirpe más Ilustre que la de los Hispanos;
          ella, en efecto, Ha recorrido

todo el orbe con su único navegar.

Más aún: esta gran proeza la atestigua una
Nave bajo el nombre de Victoria.
          Ahora bien,
Cualquier cosa que para ti pueda resultarte
efímera, para ella significa incluso
          El Laurel de su victoria.

Comentario

El texto literario aparece enmarcado por 46 líneas irregulares con 13 / 12 / 11 sílabas, que alternan de forma asistemática con otras de 5 / 4 / 3 y una sola con 2 (lín. 37).

Su contenido temático se puede sintetizar bajo el siguiente esquema:

I: Introducción (lín. 1–5). II: (lín. 6–25). La Hispania Nautica, favorecida por la protección mitológica del Tifón, de Argos y de Hércules, franqueó la meta del Non Plus Vltra. Los protagonistas fueron los navegantes hispanos, protegidos por su Virtus. III: (lín. 26–28). El resultado de tal gesta fue el siguiente: incremento de la religión, un gran Imperio para Hispania, y un Nuevo Mundo. IV: (lín. 29–36). ¿Por qué se le impuso el nombre de América?. V: Conclusión (lín. 37–46). Esta proeza corona a la Hispania Naútica con el laurel de la victoria, como a la raza más ilustre de entre los pueblos marineros.

I.   Comienza la composición con un fuerte exabrupto optativo y además temático e hiperbólico. ¡No existen límites ni fronteras por todo el mar para elogiar a Hispania!. Se resalta dicha optación con un *Vel* inicial; con el objeto elogiado colocándolo en línea independiente (*Hispania*, lín. 2), y mediante las simili-cadencias antitéticas *circumscriptos . . . laxos . . . Cancellos* (lín. 3–5).

II. Como mero adorno enfático, el autor formula una interrogación no retórica, en la cual justifica objetivamente (pero de nuevo en forma hiperbólica) su encomio: con sus conquistas marinas cubre la inmensidad del mundo, y consigue encumbrarse hasta los cielos (lín. 6–8). En tal empresa no se hallará sola, pues le va a proteger el gigante Tifón, hijo de Tártaro y de Gea, y padre de la Quimera, de la Esfinge, el Gerión, la Hidra y la Gorgona, etc. Este monstruo de la mitología griega, con sus cien cabezas e incontables brazos, era la personificación de los vientos tempestuosos y de las erupciones volcánicas. Aquí nuestro humanista Benavides alude sin embargo a su protección benigna y protectora. Lo mismo hace respecto a la famosa nave Argos, en la que los héroes legendarios griegos, los famosos Argonautas (capitaneados por Jasón) embarcaron rumbo a la Cól-quida, en busca del vellocino de oro.

Como estilemas convergentes con estas alusiones a la mitología clásica, desta-camos la figura etimológica *curriculum . . . currenti* (lín. 6–7), así como también los parónimos geminados en poliptóton y con epanadiplosis: *sola . . . salo . . . sola . . . alter . . . altera classis . . . classem* (lín. 9–13). Asimismo es destacable la personificación del oleaje marino haciendo resonar esas alabanzas (lín. 14), según habíamos observado igualmente en el *extollitur* de la lín. 8.

De nuevo surge otra alusión a la mitología greco-romana: Hércules / Hera-cles, hijo de Zeus y de Alcmena, ilustre por su fuerza y por su valor sobrehuma-nos. Le cuadra, pues, perfectamente el epíteto *feroci*, con el que se le califica en la lín. 15. Entre los famosos doce trabajos, que, por designio de la diosa Hera, el rey de Micenas, Euristeo, impuso a Heracles, figuraba el robo de los bueyes al gigante Gerión. Para lograrlo tuvo que separar las denominadas Columnas de Hércules, esto es, los montes Abila / Ceuta (en el norte de Marruecos) y Calpe / Gibraltar (en el sur de España), y así consiguió abrir el estrecho de Gibraltar.

Al concluir esta hazaña, sostiene la leyenda que Hércules colocó allí la conocida frase *non plvs vltra* para indicar y advertir que no existía tierra "más allá", y por tanto ahí finalizaba el mundo clásico por occidente. Sin embargo, fueron los navegantes hispanos quienes obtuvieron el franquear esa meta (prescrita hasta al mismo Hércules), rebasando los primeros el mar océano Atlántico.

Merecen resaltarse la antítesis complementaria *in terris* . . . . *in pelago* (lín. 15–16) y la posición destacada, al principio de la lín. 17, de la frase *Plus vltra*, junto con las expresivas y fuertes aliteraciones dentales y nasales en *Atlantico superato Exantlandas . . . Navigationes* (lín. 19–21).

Los auténticos protagonistas de esta verdadera proeza transoceánica, "fuera del orbe" (lín. 25) occidental entonces vigente, son los navegantes hispanos protegidos y honrados por su propia *Virtus*, es decir, su varonía, su hombría valerosa. Es muy elocuente el paralelismo antitético que juega con la etimología de los vocablos *extra orbitam . . . extra orbem* (lín. 24–25).

III. El resultado muy positivo de dicha gesta es triple: La Religión se verá incrementada con nuevos fieles; la Nación Hispana consigue un gran Imperio, y el Mundo amplía su geografía, merced a la conquista de estos nuevos lugares (lín. 26–28). Esta enumeración la realiza nuestro autor a través de una gradación en cierto modo ascendente: primero la Religión, luego nuestra Nación Hispana, y por último el Mundo entero.

IV. A modo de digresión (lín. 29–36) se pregunta D. Diego de Benavides el por qué al Nuevo Mundo le impusieron el nombre de América, en lugar del de su descubridor, Cristóbal Colón, a quien define como *Aduena Nauclero*, "Navegante Extranjero" (lín. 30–1). Y él mismo responde por medio de una moralizante comparación bíblica: Hispania ha emulado al Dios creador supremo del universo, quien—en vez de imponerles personalmente el nombre a cada una de sus criaturas—con suma liberalidad encomendó a Adán esta honrosa tarea, conforme refiere el libro sagrado del Génesis (2: 19–20).

V. La conclusión (lín. 37–46) de todo el razonamiento anterior viene resumida en una pintoresca y descriptiva hipérbole: ¡No existe entre los pueblos del mar ninguna otra estirpe más noble que la española, pues sólo ella ha recorrido todo el orbe con sus navíos!. Esta proeza se simboliza a través de una metonimia, que sustituye el nombre de las tres famosas carabelas (Sta. María, la Pinta y la Niña) por el de la nave Victoria. Tal vez quiso nuestro humanista tipificar este laurel victorioso de Hispania, aludiendo simbólicamente a la antigua diosa romana (la Niké helénica), la cual solía representarse como una mujer alada, en actitud de ceñir una corona de laurel a los vencedores triunfales.

Universidad de Jaén

La teoría historiográfica en la retórica
de Jorge de Trebisonda

GREGORIO HINOJO ANDRÉS

P uede parecer sorprendente y paradójico, pero el Renacimiento Italiano tan preocupado por la elocuencia, por el cuidado de la forma y por la expresión "elegante y bella", es decir, por la retórica, tardó un tanto en dar a la luz un manual completo de esta disciplina y tuvo que ser un griego-bizantino, prófugo y exiliado, el que escribiera el primer tratado completo. Nos referimos a Jorge de Trebisonda con sus *Rhetoricorum libri quinque,* obra publicada por primera vez en Venecia en 1433–1434. En España fue editada en Alcalá, dedicada al Cardenal Cisneros[1], en 1511, precisamente por las fechas en que Elio Antonio de Nebrija acababa de ser nombrado cronista regio y se establecía en la Universidad Complutense al amparo del mismo Cardenal.

La influencia y repercusión de la obra fueron inmensas y se prolongaron durante todo el siglo XVI, como ha señalado J. Monfasani[2], y puede ser considerada como un "best-seller" de la época, en expresión feliz y acertada de Robert B. Tate[3]. Un testimonio y una prueba evidente de su aceptación general son las palabras de Fernando de Herrera, maestro de retórica en Alcalá y, posteriormente, en el Estudio salmantino, en su dedicatoria a Cisneros, que no nos resistimos a reproducir:

Nam Quintiliani institutiones tum prolixissime sunt, tum opinionum superuacuarum referctissime quas non est necesse nouiciis huius artis ingerere. Adde quod mendis adhuc ob iniuriam temporum scatent, ideo ad lectionem priuatam sunt potius reseruande. Sed nec Marci Ciceronis ullum opus inuenias quod hanc pueris de se utilitatem prebeat ut in manus instituende iuuentutis ueniat.

---

[1] *Opus absolutissimum rhetoricorum Georgii Trapezuntii cum additionibus Herrariensis* (Compluti, 1511).

[2] J. Monfasani, *George of Trebizond. A Biography and a Study of his Rhetoric and Logic* (Leiden, 1976), 261–299, 318–337.

[3] R. B. Tate, "Alfonso de Palencia y los preceptos de la historiografia", en *Nebrija. III Academia Literaria Salmantina* (Salamanca, 1983), 43.

Nam liber ad herennium tam breuis est ut nihil fere contineat quod uotis adolescentulorum satisfaciat. Opera uero de oratore et perfecto oratore non nisi post magnos in hac facultate profectus sunt legenda. Noster autem Trapezuntius inter Quintiliani fastidiendam prolixitatem et Ciceronis concisam breuitatem medius incedit. Et ex utriusque extremis temperatur.

En este tratado de Retórica se dedica un apartado especial y destacado, aunque muy breve, a la escritura de la historia: *De historico dicendi genere*. Para los humanistas la historia es un *modus dicendi* más, y, por tanto, debe tratarse como un género retórico. Se convierte así la *Retórica* de Trebisonda en el primer manual o método de escribir historia, del que, de alguna forma, van a depender todos los tratados renacentistas.

Es la primera vez que en un manual de Retórica se presta una atención específica y exclusiva a la escritura de la historia, en un capítulo completo y monográfico. En Cicerón, por el contrario, la teoría de la historia aparece dispersa a lo largo de toda su amplia obra retórica, no está sistematizada ni claramente definida, y presenta algunas contradicciones o divergencias que, con frecuencia, se pretenden explicar o conciliar con lecturas e interpretaciones no siempre convincentes. Es innegable que el gran orador ha dedicado numerosas consideraciones teóricas a la redacción, al estilo y al contenido de la historia, pero no encontramos en sus escritos una doctrina coherente y estructurada sobre la historiografía.

La ausencia de esta teoría sistemática y coherente en el tratadista más importante de retórica en Roma sólo puede explicarse porque la redacción de la historia no era objeto directo y obligado de dicha disciplina, y porque se pensaba que no era imprescindible ni necesario saber redactar la historia, ni conocer o dominar las leyes del género para la formación del orador, aunque sí era muy útil la lectura y conocimiento de las obras históricas. Incluso probablemente el que Cicerón le haya dedicado una especial atención y un tratamiento amplio, muy superior al de otros autores, —como Quintiliano—, podría explicarse por sus gustos y circunstancias personales, o por su interés en instaurar la historiografía literaria en Roma y llenar, o procurar que se llenara, este vacío de las Letras Latinas, como le reclamaban sus coetáneos[4].

Nos encontramos ya ante una diferencia esencial entre la concepción y consideración de la historia de Cicerón y sus coetáneos y la de Jorge de Trebisonda y los renacentistas. Para éstos últimos la historia es claramente, como hemos indicado, un género retórico; pertenece al dominio de la *eloquentia* y tiene, por ello, un espacio y un lugar en los tratados teóricos. De hecho, para los autores de la época, especialmente desde Petrarca, la elocuencia es el objetivo y la meta de todas las artes y las ciencias, y, por ende también, el de la historia.

Entre los múltiples testimonios que pueden citarse para probar este aserto,

---

[4] Cic., *Leg.* 1, 5: "Postulatur a te iam diu uel flagitatur potius historia. Sic enim putant, te illam tractante effici posse, ut in hoc genere Graeciae nihil cedamus . . . Abest enim historia litteris nostris, ut et ipse intellego et ex te persaepe audio. Potes autem tu profecto satisfacere in ea, quippe cum sit opus, ut tibi quidem uideri solet, unum hoc oratorium maxime". Son muy numerosos los pasajes en los que Cicerón afirma que la historiografía latina no ha logrado un nivel literario digno y que no puede competir con la griega: *epist.* V12,5; *de orat.* 2,52; *rep.* 2,33; *Brut.* 228.

elegimos la siguiente definición de la *eloquentia* del brillante humanista Coluccio Salutati:

> Hec est illa facultas, que cunctas alias scientias, sive speculative sive practice sint, et omnes vite nostre partes exornat, colit celebratque et ad cuius perfectionem omnium etiam maximarum rerum scientia, sive divine sive humane sint, neccesaria est, de cuius laudibus post Ciceronem dicere temerarium est[5].

Ideas y expresiones similares encontramos en Lorenzo Valla y el propio Jorge de Trebisonda[6]. La historia es una disciplina y un *modus dicendi* como cualquier otro y, por ello, es un género retórico orientado y dirigido por las normas de la *eloquentia*. Este carácter retórico de la escritura de la historia, recogido y defendido por numerosos humanistas, se encuentra formulado de forma explícita, entre otros, en Petrarca, el Veronese y Lorenzo Valla[7].

Por ello no nos puede sorprender que en este manual aparezca un estudio sistemático y especializado de la escritura de la historia, que puede considerarse, como con acierto ha señalado Girolamo Cotroneo, el primer método: "Il testo del Trapezunzio si presenta como el primo tentativo di offrire una sistematica regolamentatione delle tecniche attraverso le quali condurre il raconto storico: e per tale motivo può essere considerato come il primo trattato di *ars historica*"[8].

Además, en nuestra opinión, el incluir el estudio y la reglamentación de la escritura de la historia dentro de los manuales supone claramente un cambio en la consideración y en la teoría retórica con respecto a la época clásica, ya que en la Antigüedad nunca la escritura de la historia tuvo un apartado específico y monográfico en los manuales, ni en los griegos ni en los latinos; esto es un giro decisivo y un indicio del cambio introducido por la teoría humanista. Incluso se puede afirmar que en la teoría de Trebisonda hay una mayor aproximación, casi una identificación, entre el *genus oratorium* y el *historicum*. Por ello no duda el autor de que Cicerón hubiera sido el mejor historiador, muy superior incluso al propio Livio, si hubiera escrito historia, y que el mérito principal de éste último es ser un gran orador:

> Quod T. Liuius adeo mirifice consecutus est, ut idem pene sit *de perfecta historie forma dicere et de ipsius oratione disceptare;* neque hoc dico quod putem summum illud eloquentie Ciceronis flumen, si in historia deriuatum fuisset, non multo prestantius, elegantius, iocundiusque fuisse . . . Quare illos insanire credendum

---

[5] C. Salutati, *Epistolario,* ed. F. Novati (Roma, 1891–1911), v. III: 411.

[6] L. Valla llama a la elocuencia *regina rerum . . . et perfecta sapientia* en *Elegantiae, Praefatio* IV: *Opera omnia* (Torino, 1962), vol. 1: 120; G. Trapezuntii, *Rhetoricorum*, M_{iiii}, escribe: "sic, qui mundi se ambitum, caelestium naturam, unde quaelibet fiant, quo ruant, scire profitetur, nisi orationis quoque copia tanto quam auro, aut gemma exornet, et illustret doctrinam, omni scientia inops videri debet".

[7] Petrarca, *Rerum memorabilium libri,* ed. G. Billanovich (Florencia, 1937), 18: "Opus . . . ut ab arce eloquentiae non multum abesse videatur"; G. Veronese, *"De historiae conscribendae libellus", Epist.* II, 458–465; L. Valla, *Praefatio*, 6: "etsi plerique conditores oratoriae artis, quae historiae mater est".

[8] G. Cotroneo, *I trattatisti dell' "Ars historica"* (Napoli, 1971), 40.

est, qui magna uoce audent praedicare Ciceronem si historiam conscribere uoluisset, T. Liuium exaequare non potuisse[9].

Las breves páginas dedicadas por Trebisonda a la redacción de la historia, pese a su formación bizantina y griega, parecen estar calcadas y con citas literales de la obra de Cicerón; como muestra ofrecemos unos fragmentos de los dos autores:

Cic., *de orat.* II, 63: . . . rerum ratio *ordinem temporum* desiderat, regionum descriptionem; uolt etiam, quoniam *in rebus magnis memoriaque dignis consilia primum, deinde acta, postea euentus* exspectantur, et *de consiliis* significari *quid* scriptor *probet* et *in rebus gestis* declarari *non solum quid actum aut dictum sit, sed etiam quo modo* et cum de euentu dicatur, *ut causae explicentur omnes uel casus uel sapientiae uel temeritatis hominumque ipsorum non* solum *res gestae, sed etiam qui fama ac nomine excellant, de cuiusque uita atque natura.*

G. *Trapezuntii rhetoricorum libri*[10]: Qui historiam scribit, primum dabit operam, ut rerum *et temporum ordinem seruet.* Quod erit, si *in rebus magnis memoratu dignis consilia primum, deinde acta, post euentus* exequatur, hisque omnibus addet quod cuique proprium est: *de consiliis quid probet,* quid improbet, *significabit.* In *rebus gestis nos solum quid actum aut dictum sit, sed etiam quomodo* et cur demonstrabit. Euentus ita declarabit, ut *causae explicentur omnes, uel casus uel sapientie uel temeritatis* . . . ; *hominum quoque ipsorum non tantum res geste, sed etiam qua fama ac nomine excellant, qua uita atque natura sint breuiter* ostendet.

La coincidencia es tal que podría afirmarse que se trata de una simple copia de una edición distinta o de unos cambios motivados por las exigencias contextuales. Con todo, los textos anteriores muestran que Trebisonda no sólo se ocupa de los aspectos estilísticos y literarios de la redacción de la historia, sino que también se interesa por el contenido, por los temas que debe tratar, por el análisis de los acontecimientos, por las causas de los mismos y por el juicio moral. Es evidente que en su corto tratado se dedica mucha mayor atención y espacio a las cuestiones estilísticas, pero no puede afirmarse que sólo le preocupan los aspectos literarios.

Es innegable que en su estudio no encontramos analizados los problemas filosóficos que se plantean a los tratadistas posteriores de la escritura de la historia ni tampoco las relaciones, coincidencias y diferencias, entre poesía, filosofía e historia que van a discutir y examinar con detalle y polémica los historiadores renacentistas de los siglos XV y XVI. Pero, como hemos visto en los textos citados, se ocupa del contenido, de la selección del material, de las causas del devenir histórico, y de los valores morales de las acciones. Y dedica numerosas consideraciones a la integración de los episodios secundarios en el hilo de la narración, a la ordenación de los acontecimientos, a su combinación y a la variedad y diversidad para evitar la monotonía y el tedio del lector; en una palabra, a la *dispositio*, entendida en sentido preciso y técnico:

---

[9] Trapezuntii, *Rhetoricorum,* Q$_{iiii}$.
[10] Trapezuntii, *Rhetoricorum,* Q$_{iiii}$.

Nec a totius historie serie separavit, aut quamquam rem alienam a ceteris dividet, sed rebus gestis inseret ... Preterea si multa diuersaque in eodem facta tempore sunt, nil artificiosus quam ita dicere ut altera res alteri inserta, et aliud alii negotio implicitum sit ... Nam preterquam quod supinum et omnino deiectum sit nusquam egredi, nihil interponere, nec dignitatem orationi addit, nec auditori, quem in longo historie ambitu varietate mulcendum puto, eventumque rerum semper retinendum ullam afferre potest delectationem, expositioni quoque rerum que ordine peragenda est nimirum adversatur. Nam quum longum temporis spatium pleraque negotia conterant, si nisi quod inceperis, absolueris, aliis manum iniciendam non putes, revolvi sepe atque universa confundere tibi necesse est; sed modus est adhibendus ne maiores fiant circuli quam opus sit, neve tota historia sic implicetur, ut aut rarius quies habeatur quam fesso lectori congruat, aut rerum oppresso multitudine nisi que legerit sepius repetat confusio iungatur. Ad hec paucis verbis eventum, ut cupiditatem legendi exsuscitet, nonnumquam preocupare oportet historicum[11].

Hemos citado un párrafo tan amplio porque en este fragmento se exponen, en nuestra opinión, algunos de los aspectos fundamentales de la historiografía renacentista y los rasgos que la diferencian de las crónicas y narraciones medievales. En éstas se acumulan gran cantidad de datos y de acontecimientos, insertados y yuxtapuestos sin mucho orden y sin un plan determinado; no hay un interés explícito por lograr la atención del lector ni por obtener la *delectatio* ni por destruir el tedio y el cansancio con la diversidad temática o estilística. Los renacentistas, en cambio, organizan y estructuran los materiales con una técnica adecuada para lograr la claridad narrativa y suscitar el interés de los lectores. Nos parecen muy acertadas las palabras de N. S. Struever cuando afirma que la función primordial de la historia renacentista es dar forma a los brutos materiales de la narración histórica[12]. La ordenación y estructuración de los materiales y de los acontecimientos simultáneos es una de las diferencias esenciales entre las obras históricas de Nebrija —del que luego nos ocuparemos— y las fuentes escritas en vulgar en las que se inspira.

El autor se ocupa también de la selección de los acontecimientos—tema muy discutido en la historiografía renacentista — y de la mayor o menor extensión con que debe tratarse cada uno de ellos:

Preter hec omnia non parvam historico curam adhibendam iudicamus, ut quid perstringendum breuius, quid sibi latius exponendum sit percipiat. Qua de re quid precipi possit difficile dictu est[13].

Como se deduce de la lectura del texto, el autor no tiene un criterio preciso sobre esta materia a la que han dedicado mucha atención numerosos historiadores humanistas. Esto puede explicarse por el carácter excesivamente teórico de su tratado y por

---

[11] Trapezuntii, *Rhetoricorum,* Q_{iiii}.

[12] N. S. Struever, *History in the Renaissance. Rhetoric and Historical Consciousness in Florentine Humanism* (Princeton, 1970), 62.

[13] Trapezuntii, *Rhetoricorum,* Q_{iiii}.

no haber cultivado nunca, como su modelo y paradigma, Cicerón, la escritura de la historia. En numerosos escritos y ensayos se insiste en que la selección se fundamente en criterios morales o ejemplarizantes, en la utilidad práctica o en el interés nacional y patriótico.

Por este carácter teórico ya señalado, Jorge de Trebisonda no dedica atención en su tratado a la importancia y utilidad de la escritura de la historia, ni a su carácter práctico y pedagógico, tópicos que se comentan en todos los tratados, introducciones teóricas y prólogos programáticos de los historiadores renacentistas. Piensa nuestro autor que estos valores le vienen dados a la historia por pertenecer al dominio de la *eloquentia,* de cuya utilidad e importancia para la vida social y pública y para el progreso de los pueblos y de la cultura, ya ha hablado ampliamente en los primeros capítulos de su *Retórica.* Tampoco presta especial atención a la verdad y objetividad de la historia, y sólo de pasada dice que *uerisimile flagitat fide.*

En cuestiones de estilo, en las que se extiende de forma especial, sigue —así lo confiesa expresamente— la teoría ciceroniana del *De oratore* con bastante fidelidad. Parte de la proximidad del *genus historicum* y el *oratorium,* y las diferencias entre ambos *modi dicendi* son de escasa relevancia y difíciles de determinar:

> Non licet historico ut causas agenti, elegantia sepius circumductionis duritiam evitare . . . Non enim ut in causis pro pondere rerum mutanda, sed eadem fere ubique oratio affectanda est. Quare non mirum si quum rebus orator orationem accommodet, orationi res historicus coaptare conetur[14].

Como ha señalado G. Cotroneo[15], son dos *modi* diferentes y deben ser redactados de forma diversa, pero resulta difícil precisar en qué consisten estas diferencias y cómo puede armonizar y adaptar el historiador el estilo a los diversos acontecimientos. Tampoco es muy claro el valor, alcance y significado de la *elegantia circunductionis:* este último término, *circunductio,* aparece varias veces y es interpretado de forma diversa por los comentaristas[16]. No podemos detenernos en este momento a discutir sus posibles valores ni a precisar las diferencias entre ambos estilos, no muy claras para el propio tratadista, ya que alargaría esta breve disquisición, pero sí queremos señalar que todavía no se ha realizado un estudio exhaustivo y riguroso de este tratado y de que se manejan lecturas erróneas con frecuencia.

Como conclusión de este apartado se puede señalar la valoración y estima que muestra nuestro autor por la obra de Salustio, especialmente como modelo de la historia monográfica, *carptim,* término utilizado por el propio Trebisonda. Parece lógico que, dada su formación y sus presupuestos ciceronianos, el historiador más valorado, el que se presenta como paradigma y modelo sea Tito Livio, pero nos parece destacable el juicio tan positivo que ofrece sobre Salustio, que tuvo, en nuestra opinión, más importancia e influencia de la que generalmente se le otorga en la historiografía

---

[14] Trapezuntii, *Rhetoricorum,* Q$_{iiii}$.

[15] Cotroneo, *Ars historica,* 45.

[16] R. Sabbadini, *Il metodo degli humanisti* (Firenze, 1920), 80.

renacentista y del que no podemos olvidar la alta consideración que mereció a dos insignes humanistas, Erasmo y Luis Vives[17].

Jorge de Trebisonda y Nebrija

Como ya hemos indicado, Nebrija profesa en Alcalá por las mismas fechas en que se publica el tratado de Trebisonda y debe, además, redactar unas obras históricas, ya que en 1509 fue nombrado cronista regio.

Antes de analizar las posibles relaciones entre el tratado de Trebisonda y las obras históricas de Nebrija, *Decades* y *Bellum Navariense,* nos parece conveniente detenernos brevemente en un hecho sintomático, sorprendente y digno de análisis. En 1515 Nebrija publica en Alcalá un tratado de Retórica con un título muy ambicioso: *Artis Rhetoricae compendiosa coaptatio ex Aristotele, Cicerone et Quintiliano. Antonio Nebrissense concinnatore, Absolutum opus VI Kal. Martii anno a Natali Christi M.D. XV*[18].

Llama poderosamente la atención, como acertadamente ha señalado Luisa López Grigera[19], que, con un corto intervalo, se impriman, para uso de los estudiantes de la universidad de Alcalá de Henares, dos manuales de retórica. Probablemente haya que interpretar la obra de Nebrija, como indica la investigadora citada, como un intento de desautorizar y desprestigiar la obra del autor extranjero y con influencias bizantinas; de ahí un título tan pomposo que quiere indicar que su retórica es una síntesis de las tres autoridades del mundo antiguo, frente a la de Trebisonda que se inspira sólo en la tradición ciceroniana más el aporte de Hermógenes.

El temperamento de Nebrija y la elevada autoestima —puesta de manifiesto en otras obras suyas y en el continuo desprecio hacia sus colegas de Claustro— pueden confirmar esta hipótesis; por otra parte encuadra con la tendencia de numerosos humanistas que pretendieron revalorizar a Quintiliano y luchar contra el excesivo ciceronianismo de la época: Nebrija pertenecía, sin ninguna duda, a este grupo. Llama también la atención que se nombre a Aristóteles en el título, aunque, según ha mostrado James J. Murphy, no hay citas explícitas ni referencias a las ideas del tratadista griego[20]; este hecho puede explicarse por el afán de elevarse sobre la obra de Trapezuncio, maestro y amigo de un rival y adversario suyo, Alfonso de Palencia[21].

En su tratado de retórica no se ocupa el Nebrisense de la teoría de la historia, ni dedica un apartado a la misma, pero en sus obras históricas, redactadas en los últimos años de su vida y editadas después de su muerte, las *Decades* y el *Bellum Nauariense,*

---

[17] Des. Erasmus, *De ratione studii, Opera omnia, Lugduni* MDCCIII, t. I: 521; L. Vives, *Obras completas* (Madrid, 1948), t. II: 331.

[18] Un estudio de esta obra, de sus fuentes y de sus características puede verse en J. J. Murphy, "Antonio Nebrija in the European Rhetorical Tradition", en C. Codoñer, y J. A. González, eds., *Antonio de Nebrija. Edad Media y Renacimiento* (Salamanca, 1994), 447–457.

[19] L. López Grigera, "Introducción al estudio de la retórica en el siglo XVI en España", *Re,* 105.

[20] "There are no citations directly traceable to Aristotle's *Rhetoric*": Murphy, "Nebrija", 453.

[21] Lopez Grijera, "Introduccion", 106. Sobre las relaciones y admiración de Palencia hacia Trebisonda, cf., entre otros, R. B. Tate, "Alfonso de Palencia," 42 ss.

sigue con bastante fidelidad muchos de los postulados de Trebisonda, como vamos a intentar mostrar.

Son muy numerosos los pasajes en los que Nebrija, a diferencia de las fuentes vulgares en las que se inspira, expone las distintas causas de los hechos históricos, enumera los planes y proyectos de los protagonistas, discute sus ventajas e inconvenientes, y enjuicia la oportunidad o las ventajas de los hechos[22]. También cuida con mucho detalle la selección de los acontecimientos y la supresión de los poco importantes o intranscendentes, así como evita repetir episodios. La *Crónica* de Pulgar, por ejemplo, nos ofrece los nombres de los que participan en la batalla y luego los repite al describir los ejércitos o al ensalzar la victoria.

Más importante nos parece todavía la labor de nuestro historiador en la ordenación y distribución del material. En su relato no se cortan los episodios, se concentran los sucesos a la acción principal, se marcan con procedimientos formales las digresiones y *excursus,* se insertan adecuadamente los datos necesarios para la comprensión del devenir histórico y no se advierten desfases en el hilo narrativo. Puede afirmarse que la teoría de Jorge de Trebisonda sobre la claridad, comprensión, variedad e inserción de los hechos —a la que hemos aludido anteriormente— es realizada con éxito por el debelador de la barbarie hispana, como quiso calificarse Nebrija.

Es muy probable que, pese a las rivalidades, Nebrija leyera la obra de Trapezuncio; pero ello no es necesario en absoluto, ya que la teoría de éste es la inspirada en la tradición antigua y, en consecuencia, la oficial en todo el humanismo. Si Trebisonda aportó innovaciones y postulados bizantinos en otros dominios de la teoría retórica, es evidente que su doctrina sobre la historia es de raigambre claramente ciceroniana; por tanto, para redactar sus obras históricas no tuvo el Nebrisense que leer el tratado de su rival, ya que no aportaba ideas originales ni desconocidas para un humanista bien formado; incluso en el prólogo de sus escritos históricos Nebrija muestra conocer, como en otro lugar hemos mostrado, las teorías historiográficas de los humanistas más destacados, Lorenzo Valla y Flavio Biondo[23].

También fue él, Nebrija, insigne y preclaro humanista, y por ello mereció el siguiente elogio de Erasmo de Rotterdam: *precipuum ornamentum Academie Complutensis, egregius ille senex, planeque dignus qui multos uincat Nestoras, Antonius Nebrissensis*[24].

Universidad de Salamanca

---

[22] Remitimos a los interesados a nuestro trabajo: *Obras históricas de Nebrija. Estudio filológico* (Salamanca, 1992), 37–51.

[23] G. Hinojo, "Nebrija y la traducción de términos históricos e institucionales", en *Estudios filológicos en homenaje a E. de Bustos Tovar* (Salamanca, 1993), 470 ss.; "La norma lingüista en el latín renacentista", en *Actas del VIII Congreso Español de Estudios Clásicos* (Madrid, 1994), 344–345.

[24] Erasmus, *Epistulae, Opera omnia,* t. III, nº DCXI, 689.

Les Institutiones Grammaticae Latinae
de Nicolas Clénard

RENÉ HOVEN

L'année 1531 représente dans la vie de Clénard une date-charnière. À l'exception d'un récent séjour de quelques mois à Paris, Nicolas Clénard (Clenardus, Cleynaerts), à ce moment âgé de 37 ou 38 ans, a jusqu'alors vécu uniquement en Brabant: à Diest, sa petite ville natale, et à Louvain, la ville universitaire où il a fait ses études et où il enseigne le grec et l'hébreu, comme il vient d'ailleurs de le faire à Paris. En outre, il a déjà publié, à Louvain également et presque coup sur coup, les trois manuels qui lui vaudront une bonne part de sa notoriété: dès 1529, une *Tabula in grammaticen Hebraeam*; en 1530, une grammaire grecque intitulée *Institutiones in linguam Graecam*; en juillet 1531, un ouvrage destiné spécialement aux autodidactes, les *Meditationes Graecanicae in artem grammaticam*.

Rien ne semblait devoir modifier profondément le cours de cette vie et de cette carrière de prêtre-professeur quand, en octobre 1531, Clénard reçoit à Louvain la visite de Fernand Colomb, le fils de l'explorateur, et signe bientôt avec lui un contrat de trois ans pour l'organisation à Séville de la "Biblioteca Colombina"; son élève et ami, le Brugeois Jean Vasaeus[1], à peine âgé de vingt ans, s'engage également. À vrai dire, si l'on en croit ses déclarations ultérieures[2], Clénard rêvait de l'Espagne depuis quelque temps déjà: désireux de se perfectionner en arabe, qu'il avait commencé à apprendre seul, il espérait y trouver des conditions favorables et surtout un professeur capable. Il quitte donc Louvain—qu'il ne devait plus revoir—et se met en route vers la péninsule ibérique; mais, contrairement à Vasaeus, il ne va pas jusqu'à Séville: il résilie son contrat et on le trouve bientôt à Salamanque où, tout en étudiant l'arabe,

---

[1] Sur ce personnage (Bruges, 1511 ou 1512–Salamanque, 1561), cf. A. Roersch, *L'Humanisme belge à l'époque de la Renaissance. Études et portraits, Deuxième série* (Louvain, 1933), 79–96; Idem, "Vasaeus" in *Biographie Nationale . . . de Belgique*, t. 26 (Bruxelles, 1936–1938), col. 504–508.

[2] Lettre de Clénard "aux Chrétiens", *ca.* 1540–1541: cf. A. Roersch, *Correspondance de Nicolas Clénard* (Bruxelles, 1940), t. I, lettre 63, lignes 345–367.

il enseigne le grec et le latin—notons que l'enseignement du latin est pour lui une nouveauté; vers la fin de 1533, il passe au Portugal, à Evora; plus tard, il séjourne à Braga, où il jette les bases d'un nouveau Collège qui doit être dirigé par son ami Vasaeus et où il publie en 1538 le manuel que je me propose d'examiner avec vous: ses *Institutiones Grammaticae Latinae.*

Pour les chercheurs, le problème préalable et non résolu pendant des décennies a été de découvrir un exemplaire de cette édition princeps. Déjà, V. Chauvin et A. Roersch, dans une étude publiée en 1900, ne connaissent cette édition que par un témoignage indirect, qui leur permet cependant de donner le libellé exact de la page de titre[3]; de même, en 1926, A. J. Anselmo dans sa bibliographie des œuvres imprimées au Portugal au xvie siècle[4]. Plus récemment, vers 1960, quand L. Bakelants a entrepris pour la *Bibliotheca Belgica* une bibliographie des œuvres de notre auteur, il n'a pas été plus heureux sur ce point; moi non plus d'ailleurs quand, après le décès de L. Bakelants, j'ai repris ce travail, qui a connu bien des vicissitudes avant d'être finalement publié en 1981[5].

Et pourtant, un exemplaire "dormait", depuis longtemps sans doute, dans une Bibliothèque peu connue de Lisbonne, la "Biblioteca Duarte de Sousa", située cependant en plein centre-ville, au Palacio Foz.

C'est F. Leite de Faria qui, le premier, dans une étude bibliographique consacrée à Damien de Goes et à son époque, et publiée à Lisbonne en 1977, a brièvement signalé le fait[6]. Encore fallait-il qu'un chercheur s'intéressant à Clénard aille y dénicher cette mention; ce mérite revient à Monsieur Gilbert Tournoy, qui a fureté partout en vue de préparer l'exposition qui a marqué à Diest en 1993 le cinquième centenaire de la naissance de Clénard; il s'est procuré pour cette exposition une reproduction complète du précieux exemplaire, reproduction aujourd'hui déposée à la Bibliothèque de la "Katholieke Universiteit te Leuven" (K.U.L.)[7]. Avec une grande obligeance, M. Tournoy a mis aussi une photocopie à ma disposition; je tiens ici à l'en remercier vivement et publiquement. Il est donc possible désormais de connaître cette grammaire latine non plus seulement à travers ses rééditions posthumes, mais en édition princeps, la seule publiée sous la responsabilité de Clénard.

L'ouvrage, imprimé en caractères gothiques, compte 208 pages in-8°; aucune pré-

---

[3] V. Chauvin et A. Roersch, *Étude sur la vie et les travaux de Nicolas Clénard* (Bruxelles, 1900), 202.

[4] A. J. Anselmo, *Bibliografia das obras impresas em Portugal no século xvi* (Lisbonne, 1926), 313, n° 1074.

[5] L. Bakelants (†) et R. Hoven, *Bibliographie des œuvres de Nicolas Clénard 1529–1700*, 2 vols. (Verviers, 1981) (Coll. "Livre-Idées-Société", n° 1). Pour l'édition en question, n° 535, t. I, 173.

[6] F. Leite de Faria, *Estudos bibliograficos sobre Damião de Gois e a sua época* (Lisbonne, 1977), 214, n° 171.

[7] G. Tournoy a mentionné pour la première fois l'existence de cet exemplaire dans l'ouvrage collectif *Évora. Schone slaapster van Portugal* (Louvain, 1991), éd. A. Provoost, 5, appendice n° 4; cf. surtout sa contribution à *Nicolaes Cleynaerts (1493–1993) van Diest tot Marokko*, in *Brabantse Folklore en Geschiedenis*, n° 278–279 (juillet–octobre 1993), 263–265, notice n° 68, avec reproduction de la page de titre.

face, introduction ou lettre-dédicace n'est là pour nous éclairer sur les circonstances de la publication.

On y retrouve les trois grandes parties habituelles: morphologie[8], syntaxe, prosodie et métrique. Mais si l'on veut pousser plus loin l'analyse, on reste quelque peu perplexe, essentiellement à cause de la présence et de l'emplacement des rubriques annoncées par le titre-courant *"Adnotationes"* (p. 131) et où l'on trouve notamment *"adnotationes in nomina "*, *". . . in pronomina"*, *". . . in verba"*, *" . . . in syntaxin"*—ajoutons, tout à la fin du volume, *"adnotationes in rationem metricam"*—rubriques qui, à ma connaissance, n'ont aucun équivalent dans les autres grammaires latines antérieures ou contemporaines. Seule, la comparaison avec la grammaire grecque que notre auteur avait publiée huit ans plus tôt pourra nous éclairer[9]. Si l'on veut bien tenir compte du fait que, dans ces *Institutiones in linguam Graecam* de 1530, la syntaxe est limitée à quatre pages—destinées à mettre en relief les différences entre la syntaxe latine supposée connue et la syntaxe grecque—et que prosodie et métrique en sont complètement absentes, on constate pour le reste un très grand parallélisme dans l'intitulé et l'ordre des matières des deux manuels; c'est ainsi que l'on rencontre déjà dans la grammaire grecque les rubriques *"Annotationes in nomina"* et *"Annotationes in uerba"*. Mais ce qui me paraît plus significatif encore, c'est l'analogie frappante et quasi textuelle entre les remarques qui introduisent d'un côté comme de l'autre ces annotations. À la page 131 de sa grammaire latine, Clénard écrit: *Hactenus de partibus orationis et ratione syntaxeos ea conscripsimus quae ferme catholica sunt. Iam quae praeterea restant, carptim adnotabimus.* En 1530, à la page 71 de sa grammaire grecque, il avait écrit, un peu plus longuement mais tout à fait dans le même sens: *Hactenus de partibus orationis ea conscripsimus quae Graecas literas auspicantibus omnino putamus necessaria et citra quorum cognitionem frustra legendis autoribus operam impendant. Nunc quae praeterea dicenda sunt de nomine et uerbo, carptim et breuiter annotabimus.* Dans un cas comme dans l'autre, l'auteur a donc divisé son manuel en deux sections: la première présente les règles qu'il considère comme générales et nécessaires (*catholica, necessaria*), la deuxième section contient les remarques qu'il estime accessoires et qui peuvent être apprises plus tard. Il y a là de toute évidence une volonté délibérée, une prise de position que l'on peut qualifier de pédagogique, mais qui ne fut peut-être pas du goût de tous: ainsi en 1533, une réédition parisienne de la grammaire grecque insère les *Annotationes* au fur et à mesure dans le texte principal et annonce fièrement à la page de titre: *Omnia in ordinem studiosis commodiorem restituta*[10]; cette initiative non respectueuse de la volonté de Clénard a été imitée dans une vingtaine de rééditions ultérieures[11]. Pour

---

[8] On sait que le terme "morphologie" date seulement du xixe siècle; les grammairiens de la Renaissance parlent tantôt simplement de *"Prima pars grammaticae"*, tantôt de *"Octo partes orationis"*, parfois aussi d'*"Etymologia"*, donnant ainsi à ce mot un sens différent de l'usage courant. Clénard lui-même n'attribue aucun titre d'ensemble à cette partie de sa grammaire; toutefois, p. 131, il la synthétise en parlant de *"de partibus orationis"*.

[9] Voir le tableau ci-joint.

[10] *Institutiones in linguam Graecam* (Paris, 1553); cf. L. Bakelants et R. Hoven, *Clénard*, t. I, 53–54, n° 127; reproduction de la page de titre t. II, 78, n° 127.

[11] Liste dans L. Bakelants et R. Hoven, *Clénard*, t. I, 54.

en revenir à la grammaire latine, il faut bien constater que Clénard n'y a pas poussé jusqu'au bout la logique du système, qui aurait dû le conduire à présenter les notions générales de prosodie et de métrique avant les *"adnotationes"* des diverses parties; aurait-il décidé tardivement d'inclure dans son manuel prosodie et métrique et aurait-il alors renoncé à modifier l'ordre de ce qui était déjà écrit, voire imprimé? Nous ne le saurons sans doute jamais.

Si Clénard a rédigé plusieurs grammaires, il est très conscient que la grammaire n'est pas tout pour l'apprentissage d'une langue: trois fois déjà dans sa grammaire grecque, une douzaine de fois dans ses *Institutiones Grammaticae Latinae*, il renonce à donner plus de détails et préfère renvoyer l'apprenti helléniste ou latiniste à l'usage et aux auteurs; il écrit par exemple: *Nemo unquam recte linguam didicit, qui nimium tribuit praeceptis grammaticis. Ex authoribus discenda est et eorum familiari consuetudine qui pure ac terse loquuntur* (p. 172). À propos de certains points de métrique, il renvoie (p. 199) à Horace pour les vers lyriques, à Ovide pour les élégiaques, à Virgile et à Lucain pour les vers "héroïques". Sa grammaire compte de nombreux exemples; les auteurs de ces exemples sont assez fréquemment mentionnés, particulièrement dans les *"Adnotationes in syntaxin"* et dans le chapitre relatif à la métrique; il s'agit de Cicéron, Salluste, Tite-Live, Quintilien, Pline le Jeune, des poètes qui viennent d'être cités, ainsi que de Térence, Plaute, Catulle, Martial. Si l'on ne connaissait déjà par la page de titre et par des renseignements externes l'endroit où le manuel a été rédigé et publié, très peu de passages le laisseraient deviner: *"Discedo Bracara, facturus iter Conimbrica"* (p. 130); *"Postridie quam uenissem Bracaram"* (p. 170). Deux autres passages donnent une note plus personnelle: le premier révèle une certaine nostalgie, qui pourrait faire penser à celle d'Érasme au soir de sa vie: *"E Brabantia migrasse dolet. Per Galliam redeundum est"* (p. 130). Le deuxième est une assez longue allusion à la langue arabe: Clénard y déclare qu'il a composé des *Institutiones Arabicae*, mais qu'il ne les a pas encore éditées, faute de disposer des caractères adéquats; il y insiste aussi sur l'utilité de cette langue pour les médecins[12]; on sait que cette grammaire arabe n'a jamais été publiée et que le manuscrit encore signalé en Espagne au début du xviie siècle semble avoir disparu[13].

En novembre 1538, Clénard quitte le Portugal pour l'Espagne, où il séjourne à Grenade. De là, en 1540, il se rend au Maroc, où, en tant que prêtre catholique, il veut préparer une "croisade pacifique", c'est-à-dire la conversion des Musulmans au christianisme, non par la guerre mais par la persuasion; une condition préalable et essentielle est évidemment la connaissance de l'arabe. Ce séjour au Maroc se termine mal pour Clénard, on le sait: blessé et malade, il retourne à Grenade, où il meurt en novembre 1542.

Alors qu'une dizaine d'années plus tôt, Clénard avait pu se réjouir du succès de ses manuels d'hébreu et surtout de grec, un seul écho, très négatif, nous est rapporté par

---

[12] *". . . et nos aliquando, Deo propitio, de hoc loquemur in Institutionibus Arabicis, quas hactenus non edidimus, typorum auxilio destituti. Eos ubi primum tolerabiles nacti fuerimus, Arabicas literas nostris hominibus commonstrabimus, rem medicis in primis utilem"* (p. 107).

[13] Cf. Chauvin et Roersch, *Clénard*, 124; Roersch, *Correspondance . . .*, t. II, 108.

l'auteur lui-même à propos de sa grammaire latine: le 21 août 1541, il écrit de Fez à Jean Petit, qu'il avait connu archidiacre d'Evora et qui était devenu évêque de Saint-Jacques du Cap Vert: *Valde, ut intelligo, uapulat ea Grammatica quam edidi Braccarae, nec placet Lusitaniae*[14]. Nous ignorons qui étaient les auteurs de ces vives critiques et sur quoi elles portaient: s'agissait-il de l'emploi de caractères gothiques? de l'ordre des matières, que nous avons évoqué? de l'absence de vers mnémoniques, traditionnels depuis le Moyen Âge et encore utilisés dans maintes grammaires, comme celle de Nebrija et de Despautère? À propos de Nebrija, il convient de rappeler que le grammairien le plus fameux de la péninsule ibérique avait, dans la première édition de ses *Introductiones Latinae*, publiée à Salamanque en 1481, présenté un texte rédigé uniquement en prose, mais que, quelques années plus tard, pour faire taire les critiques, il s'était résolu à y introduire des vers mnémoniques[15]; cet état d'esprit subsistait-il encore après un demi-siècle?

Quoi qu'il en soit, les *Institutiones Grammaticae Latinae* de Clénard ont connu seulement, sauf ignorance de ma part, quatre rééditions, toutes les quatre posthumes et présentant de notables différences avec l'édition princeps. Je n'insisterai pas sur la réédition de Louvain, 1550, ni sur celle de Lyon, 1551, dont les responsables sont inconnus et qui ne comportent aucune préface; voyons plutôt les deux rééditions dues à Jean Vasaeus et publiées dans la péninsule ibérique: celle de Coïmbre en 1546, celle de Salamanque vers 1551[16].

La lettre-préface de l'édition de Coïmbre est datée d'Evora, où Vasaeus enseignait alors et elle est adressée "au Sénat et au peuple de Diest"[17]; Vasaeus explique aux anciens concitoyens de Clénard que celui-ci lui avait souvent demandé de revoir sa grammaire latine et d'y supprimer ou d'y ajouter ce qui lui semblait opportun. Ce qu'il n'a pas voulu faire du vivant de Clénard, il estime maintenant le devoir "aux mânes du défunt"; il a donc relu très attentivement le texte et y a ajouté très peu de chose[18]. Une comparaison entre l'édition princeps et cette réédition de 1546 permet de constater que Vasaeus a corrigé quelques lapsus, qu'il a entièrement respecté la structure du manuel, qu'il n'a rien supprimé, mais qu'il a fait à travers tout l'ouvrage

---

[14] Roersch, *Correspondance . . .*, t. I, lettre 58, lignes 228–229.

[15] On constate le fait pour la première fois dans la réédition de Venise, 1491; mais celle-ci ne serait que la reprise d'une édition qui aurait été publiée en Espagne entre 1481 et 1491 et qui serait aujourd'hui perdue. Cf. A. Palau y Dulcet, *Manual del Librero Hispanoamericano*, t. X (Barcelone, 1957), 459–460; J.-Cl. Margolin, "Des '*Introductiones Latinae*' (Salamanque, 1481) d'Antoine de Nebrija au '*De constructione octo partium orationis*' (Bâle, 1515) d'Érasme de Rotterdam: étude comparative" in *Antonio de Nebrija: Edad Media y Renacimiento*, éd. Carmen Coroner (Acta Salmanticensia. Estudios Filologicos, 257) (Salamanque, 1994), 259–276, notamment 261 et 265–266.

[16] Sur ces rééditions, cf. Bakelants et Hoven, *Clénard*, t. I, 171–174; t. II, 318–320.

[17] "*Senatui Populoque Diestensi*" ; texte reproduit par Roersch, *Correspondance . . .*, annexe V, t. I, 257–258.

[18] Ibid., lignes 34–39: "*quum . . . Clenardus adhuc superstes me rogasset frequenter ut eas recognoscerem et si quid opus uideretur uel delerem uel adderem, tamen quod uiuo saepe denegaueram, defuncti manibus praestandum constitui. Relegi igitur quam diligentissime et paucula admodum apposui*".

un grand nombre d'ajouts, le plus souvent très brefs il est vrai. Ainsi se confirme la mention de la page de titre, qui met en relief les additions dues à Vasaeus: *Institutiones Grammaticae Latinae Nicolai Clenardi. Per Ioannem Vasaeum Brugensem auctae et recognitae*[19]. Parmi ces ajouts, relevons tout d'abord un renseignement d'ordre bibliographique: après les quelques lignes consacrées par Clénard à l'accentuation latine, Vasaeus mentionne un opuscule que Franciscus Menesius a "récemment" publié à Salamanque sur le sujet[20]. Effectivement, le Franciscain espagnol Francisco Meneses venait d'éditer à Salamanque, en cette même année 1546, *Breuis ac dilucida accentuum collectio, quae Summula prosodiaca uocatur*[21]; il avait d'ailleurs déjà publié, une vingtaine d'années plus tôt, *Difficilium accentuum compendium*, dont curieusement la seule édition connue est celle de Paris, Robert Estienne, 1527[22]. Parmi les autres additions de Vasaeus, il faut signaler aussi un certain nombre de renvois aux auteurs anciens, généralement ceux que nous avons déjà mentionnés. Mais d'une manière générale, la masse d'ajouts très brefs nous amène à nous demander si Vasaeus n'éprouvait pas avant tout la crainte d'omettre tel ou tel détail et s'il ne s'est pas mis ainsi en contradiction avec le principe proclamé et répété par Clénard; l'élève aurait-il en quelque sorte, consciemment ou non, "trahi" son maître?

En 1550, Vasaeus quitte Evora pour Salamanque, où il avait déjà séjourné et enseigné. Vers 1551, il y publie une nouvelle réédition de la grammaire de Clénard; je dis "vers 1551" parce que la page de titre ne porte pas de date et qu'il n'y a pas de colophon, mais que le privilège et la lettre-préface sont tous deux de 1551. Dans cette lettre-préface, adressée cette fois à ses étudiants de Salamanque, Vasaeus ne fait aucune allusion à la réédition de Coïmbre, alors qu'il reprend en partie le texte du message aux habitants de Diest; il s'exprime comme si c'était uniquement pour ses étudiants de Salamanque qu'il avait entrepris une révision et une réédition de cette grammaire! Par rapport à l'édition de 1546, le nombre des additions a encore augmenté, sans que les caractéristiques générales du manuel soient modifiées.

Vasaeus fait suivre ces deux rééditions de la grammaire latine d'un texte d'une quarantaine de pages qu'il intitule *Nicolai Clenardi praeceptiones aliquot de ratione docendae atque exercendae linguae Latinae*; il s'agit en fait de fragments de lettres que Clénard lui avait adressées en 1535–1536[23]. Du même coup, Vasaeus fait ainsi le premier pas dans la publication posthume de la Correspondance de son ami, publication

---

[19] Reproduction de cette page de titre dans Bakelants et Hoven, *Clénard*, t. II, 318.

[20] "*Qui plura de accentuum ratione uolet, consulat libellum F. Francisci Menesii, uiri docti et religiosi, quem de hac re Salmanticae nuper aedidit non minus utilem quam compendiosum*".

[21] Cf. Palau y Dolcet, *Manual del Librero*, t. IX, 1956, 68, n° 164.446.

[22] Cf. A. Renouard, *Annales de l'imprimerie des Estienne* (Paris, 1843), 26; *Inventaire chronologique des éditions parisiennes du xvi*e *siècle, d'après les manuscrits de Philippe Renouard*, t. III, 1521–1530 (Abbeville, 1985), 358, n° 1271.

[23] Cf. lettre-préface de la réédition de Coïmbre dans Roersch, *Correspondance* . . . , t. I, 258, lignes 47–49: " . . . *diuersarum ipsius (= Clenardi) epistolarum fragmenta quae ille de iis rebus subinde scripsit ad me, dum in Salmanticensi Academia literas graecas et latinas publice docerem*"; texte des *Praeceptiones*: éd. de Coïmbre, 238–280; éd. de Salamanque, fol. 147 r°–169 v°; reproduction partielle dans Roersch, *Correspondance* . . . , t. I, n° 64, 239–249 (notes t. II: 157–159).

qui fera connaître le nom de Clénard à un public partiellement différent et sans doute plus large encore que celui de ses manuels[24]. Enfin, Vasaeus, désireux de prouver à ses étudiants sa sollicitude personnelle, clôture la réédition de Salamanque par la publication (fol. 170 r°–179 r°) d'un petit traité de sa composition: *De orthographia praeceptiunculae aliquot.*

Pour revenir à la grammaire latine de Clénard, je dirai simplement en conclusion que, même si ce dernier manuel composé et publié par l'auteur n'a pas été son plus grand titre de gloire, il m'a paru intéressant de tenter à son propos de dissiper le flou qui l'entourait immanquablement tant qu'on ne disposait pas de l'édition princeps; je suis heureux que le présent Congrès m'ait donné l'occasion de le faire dans cette péninsule ibérique où précisément l'édition princeps et les deux rééditions revues par Vasaeus ont été composées et publiées.

Marche-en-Famenne, Belgique

---

[24] Cf. entre autres Roersch, *Correspondance . . .*; Bakelants et Hoven, *Clénard*, t. I, 175–185; t. II, 321–329.

<table>
<tr><td>

Institutiones Grammaticae Latinae, 1538

p. 3 Literae
p. 3 Partes orationis octo
p. 4 Declinationes nominum
p. 42 Pronomina
p. 44 (Prima) coniugatio

p. 100 Aduerbia

p. 103 Coniunctio
p. 103 Interiectio
p. 104 Syntaxis
p. 131 Hactenus de partibus . . . Iam . . . Adnotationes
p. 132 Genera nominum
p. 139 Numeralia
p. 140 Adnotationes in nomina
p. 146 Adnotationes in pronomina
p. 147 Adnotationes in verba
p. 152 Adnotationes in syntaxin
p. 177 Accentus

p. 178 Quantitas syllabarum
p. 188 Ratio metrica
p. 200 Adnotationes in rationem metricam

</td><td>

Institutiones in linguam Graecam, 1530

p. 3 Graecorum literae
p. 4 Partes orationis octo
p. 5 Declinationes nominum

p. 16 Coniugationes
p. 68 Pronomina
p. 70 Articuli
p. 71 Aduerbium, coniunctio et prae-
      positio

p. 71 Hactenus de partibus . . . Nunc
      . . .

p. 72 Annotationes in nomina

p. 81 Annotationes in uerba

p. 105 Accentus
p. 108 Ratio syntaxeos
p. 112 Abbreviationes

</td></tr>
</table>

Episodi della fortuna editoriale
dell'opera di Properzio

ANTONIO IURILLI

Il breve catalogo di un modesto tipografo italiano, Federico de' Conti, registra al 1471–72, accanto ad una delle più antiche edizioni della *Commedia* di Dante Alighieri, l'*editio princeps* delle *Elegie* di Properzio, stampata in un agile *in-quarto* di meno di cento pagine.[1]

Non voglio sottolineare la sensibilità letteraria che induceva il de' Conti a stampare per la prima volta, insieme a un testo capitale della letteratura volgare italiana, l'opera di un elegiaco latino separandolo dalla trilogia canonica (Catullo-Tibullo-Properzio) propria della tradizione manoscritta dei *flores* medievali.[2] Si trattava, senza dubbio, di una scelta 'aristocratica', non pensata per il mercato scolastico, e anzi destinata a cedere proprio alla ripresa *sub specie typographica* della trilogia medievale, più spendibile su quel mercato. Gli incunabuli properziani che si succedono immediatamente alla *princeps* riproducono infatti quest'ultimo modello.

---

[1] E' ormai certa la identificazione della *princeps* del *corpus* properziano con l'edizione pubblicata a Venezia da Federico de' Conti nel febbraio del 1472 (*Sexti Aurelii Propertii nautae umbri incipit liber Elegiarum vel monobiblos*, [s.l.], [s.t.], II, 1472: BMC VII 1135, CR 4888, Flodr 260, IGI 8086, ISTC P 1014). Di qualche mese successiva (ma dello stesso anno 1472) è infatti l'edizione di Tibullo, Properzio, Catullo, Stazio pubblicata sempre a Venezia da Vindelin de Spira. Su Federico de' Conti, oltre a Giuseppe Fumagalli, *Lexicon typographicum Italiae . . .* (Firenze, 1905), 177–179, e a Victor Scholderer, "Federico de' Conti and the First Books Printed at Jesi", *Gutenberg-Jahrbuch* 7 (1932): 110–113, cf. *Cinque secoli di arte tipografica jesina. Mostra della stampa a Jesi dal 1472 al 1972*, aprile–maggio 1973, Giovanni Annibaldi e Edoardo Pierpaoli, eds. (Jesi, 1973), che propone un catalogo di sette edizioni del tipografo.

[2] Sulla fortuna medievale di Properzio cf. soprattutto Janus L. Butrica, *The Manuscript Tradition of Propertius* (Toronto-Buffalo-London, 1984). Sulla presenza dei tre elegiaci in Petrarca cf. B.L. Ullman, "Petrarch's Acquaintance with Catullus, Tibullus and Propertius", in *Studies in the Italian Renaissance* (Roma, 1973²), 177–196. Cf., comunque, per una informazione complessiva sugli studi properziani, P. Fedeli–P. Pinotti, "Bibliografia properziana (1946–1983)", *Atti dell'Accademia Properziana del Subasio*, serie VI, n. 9 (1985), (Assisi, 1985).

Al contrario, il modello dell'autore singolo proposto dalla *princeps* sopravvisse nel Properzio che il tipografo dalmata Bonino de Boninis stampò a Brescia nel 1486, e in quello che Benedetto Faelli stampò un anno dopo a Bologna. La scelta non appare casuale. Entrambe le edizioni sono infatti corredate dai due più importanti commenti umanistici a Properzio: quello di Domizio Calderini per il rarissimo incunabulo bresciano; quello di Filippo Beroaldo per l'incunabulo bolognese. L'incunabulo bresciano tenta anzi di valorizzare proprio il commento abbozzando una primitiva disposizione sinottica su due colonne del testo properziano e delle *Elucubrationes in quaedam Propertii loca* del Calderini, con risultati tipografici pessimi: fastidiosi spazi bianchi svuotano frequentemente la pagina là dove la discontinuità del commento non consente alle due scritture di procedere parallele.[3]

Anche il primo Properzio romano si presenta in forma monografica. Ma la sua storia editoriale merita maggiore attenzione. Eucario Silber, tipografo noto nella Roma sistina per il suo catalogo "anticonformista", stampa nel 1482 il testo di Properzio curato da Antonio Volsco, maestro nello *Studium Urbis*, e, contemporaneamente, un'antologia ciceroniana curata da Martino Filetico, collega del Volsco, che contiene un attacco a un *corruptor latinitatis*, cioè ad Antonio Volsco: sicuro, il Silber, di scatenare un lucroso *affaire* letterario proprio nel turbolento *milieu* filologico dello *Studium*.[4]

Dal Volsco, che si vantava di esercitare l'arte del commentare "ut in arena gladiator", non era infatti difficile attendersi risentite repliche, che puntuali giunsero quattro anni dopo, in una edizione non più romana, ma veneziana del suo commento a Properzio, nella quale il bersaglio non fu tanto il Filetico, quanto il filologo Pietro

---

[3] Sull'edizione del Boninis cf. H 4761, BMC VII 970, ISTC P 1016. Sull'edizione del Faelli cf. BMC VI 822, HCR 13406, ISTC P 1017. Sull'officina tipografica del Faelli cf. Fernanda Ascarelli, Marco Menato, *La tipografia del '500 in Italia* (Firenze, 1989), 51; D. E. Rhodes, "Benedictus Hectoris of Bologna and his Complaint against Typographical Pirates" in idem, *Studies in Early Italian Printing* (London, 1982), 229–231; Albano Sorbelli, *Storia della stampa in Bologna . . .* (Bologna, 1929). Sui primordiali tentativi, attribuibili presumibilmente ai tipografi o agli editori, di assemblare testo e commento cf. Francesco Lo Monaco, "Alcune osservazioni sui commenti umanistici ai classici nel secondo Quattrocento", in *Il commento ai testi. Atti del seminario di Ascona*, ottobre 1989, Ottavio Besomi e Carlo Caruso, eds. (Basel-Boston-Berlin, 1992), 103–139. Sulla qualità del commento del Calderini cf. Donatella Coppini, "Il Properzio di Domizio Calderini", in *Commentatori e traduttori di Properzio dall'Umanesimo a Lachmann*, Atti del convegno internazionale, Assisi, ottobre 1994 (Assisi, 1996), 27–79.

[4] *Sexti Aurelii Propertii Elegiae. Recognovit Antonius Volscus*, [Roma, non prima del 13.I.1482]: BMC IV 104, HC ★13402, IERS 754, IGI 8087, ISTC P 1015; cf. Butrica, *Manuscript Tradition*, 167. L'edizione del Filetico è descritta in Giovanni Battista Audiffredi, *Catalogus historico-criticus Romanarum editionum saeculi XV* (Romae, 1783), 401; cf. anche BMC IV 120; GW 6874. Sulla protostampa romana cf. "Materiali e ipotesi per la stampa a Roma", in *Scrittura, biblioteche e stampa a Roma nel Quattrocento. Aspetti e problemi. Atti del I e II seminario*, C. Bianca et al., eds., 2 vols. (Città del Vaticano, 1980 e 1983), I: 213–244. Sul Silber cf. Alberto Tinto, *Gli annali tipografici di Eucario e Marcello Silber (1501–1527)* (Firenze, 1968). Sui rapporti fra *Studium* e prototipografia romana cf. Maria Grazia Blasio, "Lo 'Studium Urbis' e la produzione romana a stampa: i corsi di retorica, latino e greco", in *Un pontificato ed una città: Sisto IV (1471–1484). Atti del Convegno* (dicembre 1984) (Città del Vaticano, 1986), 481–501.

Marso, anch'egli maestro nello *Studium Urbis*. La polemica coinvolse anche due esponenti di spicco dell'inquieto mondo accademico romano: Domizio Calderini, peraltro scomparso già da alcuni anni, e l'ormai attempato Pomponio Leto, non estraneo alle fortune accademiche dello stesso Volsco. Come era prevedibile, il Marso replicò al non disprezzabile commento properziano del Volsco definendolo *Tenebrae Propertianae*.[5]

Ma l'officina romana del Silber si distinse per un'altra importante iniziativa editoriale che, alla fine del secolo, richiamò per la prima volta l'attenzione sulla parte eziologica della poesia properziana, sull'onda del culto per l'antiquaria e per le religioni prelatine vivo nel *milieu* culturale del papato sistino e alessandrino. Il Silber inserì infatti la sola elegia seconda del quarto libro, la celebre "vertumniana" (che, come è noto, ricostruisce le origini, il nome e le metamorfosi del dio Vertumno), nell' edizione di un *best seller* della nascente filologia antiquaria, le *Antiquitates* di Annio da Viterbo, il quale aveva appunto commentato l'elegia properziana. Sempre attraverso la mediazione di Annio, il testo eziologico di Properzio si era anche inserito nel recupero editoriale di un altro classico della letteratura antiquaria, i frammenti delle *Antiquitates* del mitico sacerdote babilonese Beroso.[6]

Diverso è invece l'esordio editoriale di Properzio al di là delle Alpi: l'edizione lipsiense di 82 fogli, prodotta da Martin Landsberg nel 1495, che inaugura la fortuna di Properzio a stampa in terra germanica, propone, infatti, nel frontespizio un singolare *hapax* semantico ("*calores*" al posto di "*elegiae*"), probabilmente influenzato dai due luoghi properziani in cui il termine figura (*Eleg.* I,12, v. 17 e III, 8, v. 9): un *hapax* fortemente indicativo di una lettura dell'elegia properziana in chiave eroticosentimentale, forse voluta per assecondare il gusto classicistico della media borghesia germanica.[7]

Al contrario, quasi a voler marcare un netto contrasto con questa tendenza all'accentuazione dei contenuti erotici della scrittura elegiaca properziana, la produzione postincunabulistica dei Paesi Bassi documenta un impiego didattico-pedagogico dell'opera di Properzio. L'importante *officina literatoria* dei fratelli Pafraet, attiva in uno dei centri più avanzati dell'editoria olandese, Deventer, confeziona, infatti, nel 1503, un'antologia che, in appena ventiquattro carte, accoglie i "selecti versus" di Tibullo, Properzio e Ovidio, promettendoli "magis memorabiles atque puerorum institutioni aptiores". La prevalente fruibilità scolastica dell'edizione era peraltro garantita dal grande prestigio cui la scuola di Deventer era assurta alla fine del Quattrocento sotto

---

[5] *Sexti Aurelii Propertii Elegiae* [comm. di Antonio Volsco] (Venezia, 1488): BMC V 354, H ⋆4762, IGI 9664, ISTC P 1018). Sull'esercizio filologico del Volsco cf. Carlo Dionisotti, " 'Lavinia venit litora'. Polemica virgiliana di M. Filetico", *Italia Medievale e Umanistica* 1 (1958): 283–315, esp. 295–300. La replica del Marso si legge nella seconda edizione del suo commento al *De officiis* di Cicerone (Venezia, 15.III.1491: GW 6960).

[6] Cf. Anna Maranini, "Le traduzioni properziane di Benivieni e Cartari", in *Commentatori e traduttori di Properzio . . .*, 81–133.

[7] *Propercii Umbri Elegiographi calorum libri quatuor* (ex officina Martini Lantzpergersis Herbipolensis . . . prima Martis (sic: forse "mensis") Februarii anno salutis nostre nonagesimoquinto supra millesimum et quadringentesimum: H 13403, BMC III 638).

la direzione di un umanista del calibro di Alexander Hegius, quando aveva avuto fra i suoi allievi Erasmo da Rotterdam; mentre la qualità della selezione era garantita dalla competenza pedagogica del curatore, il limburghese Johann Murmell, professore a Münster, che aveva curato edizioni scolastiche di autori latini, classici e cristiani con una netta inclinazione pedagogica.[8]

Intanto, riproponendo la sua esemplare innovazione tipografica, Aldo Manuzio immetteva sul mercato la trilogia degli elegiaci latini. Apparsa nel 1502 in ben tremila esemplari nella serie degli enchiridi aldini, i quali avevano segnato una svolta nella storia del libro e della lettura dei classici, ma con un vistoso refuso nel frontespizio che colpiva proprio il nome *Propertius*, ridotto a *Propetius* in alcune copie e poi emendato in corso di tiratura, la trilogia degli elegiaci latini era stata dedicata da Aldo ad un colto borghese veneziano, Marino Sanudo, emblematico esponente di un nuovo pubblico che si affacciava al mercato del libro, assicurandogli un'amena lettura.[9]

Ma quella silloge, che usciva solo pochi mesi dopo i celebri Virgilio e Orazio "da mano", voleva in realtà andare ben oltre il pur auspicato successo editoriale legato all'innovazione tipografica e sottolineato dalla eccezionale tiratura. La sua specifica competenza metrico-filologica, confortata dalla collaborazione di un attento studioso del testo catulliano quale Girolamo Avanzo, professore di Filosofia a Padova, induceva, infatti, Aldo a produrre un'edizione degli elegiaci latini non imbrigliata dai commenti, eppure testualmente corretta, accettabile anche da quegli umanisti che ancora guardavano alla stampa come ad una pericolosa corruttrice di testi.

L'esemplare edizione aldina degli elegiaci sembra tuttavia concludere il dinamismo filologico dell'Umanesimo italiano nei confronti del testo properziano. Sintomatico di una ormai perduta egemonia esegetica italiana appare proprio l'intervento che Paolo Manuzio, figlio di Aldo, sollecita presso il francese Marc-Antoine Muret per il restauro dell'ormai vetusta trilogia di elegiaci del padre: un restauro del quale il Muret andò orgoglioso, al punto da sollecitare l'editore a rinunciare parzialmente al glorioso ottavo paterno e a produrre una tiratura speciale di grande formato, atta a valorizzare, come l'antico libro da banco tanto ostico ad Aldo, soprattutto il commento.[10]

Che invece l'agile enchiridio di Aldo fosse destinato a dettare legge ancora a lungo sul mercato editoriale degli elegiaci latini, lo dimostra la scelta addirittura del sedicesimo fatta sessant'anni dopo da un tipografo del calibro di Cristophe Plantin per la

---

⁸ *Ex elegiacis trium illustrium poetarum Tibulli, Propertii ac Ovidij carminibus selecti versus magis memorabiles atque puerorum institutioni aptiores* ([Deventer], 1503: Nijhoff-Kronenberg 3949).

⁹ *Catullus, Tibullus, Propertius* (Venetiis, in aedibus Aldi, 1502: Renouard Man. 39). Sulla tiratura di questa edizione, il cui numero dichiarato dallo stesso Manuzio nella dedica al Sanudo va forse riferito al solo Catullo ("Idem et Tibullo et Propertio fecimus, quos ad tria millia voluminum, et plus eo, hac minima forma excusos in manos tuas et caeterorum commode assidueque una cum Catullo et ire et redire speramus": *Aldo Manuzio editore. Dediche, prefazioni, note ai testi*, introd. di Carlo Dionisotti. Testo latino con traduzione e note di G. Orlandi, 2 vols. (Milano, 1975), 2: 56, cf. Harry George Flechter III, *New Aldine Studies. Documentary Essays on the Life and Works of Aldus Manutius* (San Francisco, 1988), 100–106, esp. 100–102.

¹⁰ *Catullus, et in eum Commentarius M. Antonii Mureti ab eodem correcti et scholiis illustrati Tibullus et Propertius* (Venetiis, 1558: Renouard Man. 174).

sua prima edizione di Catullo, Tibullo e Properzio, apparsa nel 1560. Si tratta di
un'edizione che, contando proprio sulla *brevitas* degli elegiaci, Plantin aveva investito
del rischioso compito di lanciare sul mercato editoriale la serie delle *pocket-editions* dei
classici che egli avrebbe successivamente prodotto per favorire la divulgazione.
Trent'anni dopo, all'apice delle sue fortune editoriali, Plantin ripubblicava in piccolo
ventiquattresimo la trilogia degli elegiaci, annunciando orgogliosamente al dedicata-
rio, Cornelius Prunius, di volerla destinare alla lettura degli studenti poveri e dei
viaggiatori. Contrariamente a quanto aveva fatto per un altro classico come Orazio,
il tipografo fiammingo evita particolari impegni esegetici per gli elegiaci, puntando
solo sulle agili e prudenti chiose di Theodor Poelman e Victor Giselin per Catullo e
Tibullo, e di William Canter per Properzio.[11]

La ripresa dell'attività esegetica sui testi degli elegiaci è segnata, alla fine del secolo,
dall'apparizione a Parigi nella celebre officina degli Estienne delle audaci congetture
di Giuseppe Scaligero sul testo dei tre elegiaci. L'uscita delle *Castigationes*, destinate
a sollevare polemiche, come gran parte dell'esercizio filologico dello Scaligero, coincideva con una più movimentata domanda della scuola, che aveva riscoperto la poesia
elegiaca nel clima della disputa classicistica sulla poetica e della imitazione metrico-sti-
listica degli alessandrini.[12] In quel clima maturarono anche le note filologiche agli elegiaci degli olandesi Dousa (padre e figlio), e l'impegno critico del portoghese Achille
Stazio, mirato al restauro filologico del Catullo di Paolo Manuzio e del Muret.[13]

Erano, dunque, maturi, alla fine del secolo XVI, i tempi per un impegno editoriale
capace di presentare la storia dei testi degli elegiaci e degli interventi critico-filologici
frattanto stratificatisi sulla loro opera: si delineava, cioè, l'*editio variorum* a commento
plurimo. A produrla per prima nel 1592 fu l'officina plantiniana di Leida, frattanto
passata nelle mani del Raphelingen: il ponderoso *in folio* di 272 pagine, pur fondan-
dosi sul commento critico-filologico di Janus Dousa, era concepito in realtà come una
rassegna storicamente documentata e criticamente esposta delle *coniectaneae* sul testo
degli elegiaci, e in particolare su quello di Properzio: una svolta, senza dubbio, nella
storia della fortuna editoriale degli elegiaci, che avrebbe indotto gli editori parigini
Marc Orry e Claude Morell a produrre qualche anno dopo una vera e propria *editio*

---

[11] *Catullus, Tibullus, Propertius, Cornelii Galli Fragmenta. Omnia ex vetustissimo exemplari multo
quam antea emendatiora, additis annotationibus* (Antuerpiae, 1560: Voet 933).

[12] Cf. Schreiber 248. Le 250 pagine delle *Castigationes* dello Scaligero sono contenute nel secondo tomo. Sullo Scaligero e sul suo ruolo nella scuola umanistica cf. A. Grafton, "Joseph Scaliger's Edition of Catullus (1577) and the Traditions of Textual Criticism in the Renaissance", *Journal of the Warburg and Courtauld Institutes* 38 (1975): 155–181; A. Grafton, *Joseph Scaliger: A Study
in the History of Classical Scholarship* (Oxford, 1983). Si veda A. Grafton–H.J. De Jonge, *Joseph Scaliger: A Bibliography (1852–1982)* (The Hague, 1982).

[13] *Caii Valerii Catulli, Albii Tibulli, Sexti Aurelii Propertii quae extant. Accesserunt uberiores anima-
dversiones in quibus praeter doctorum virorum coniecturas et castigationes accurate expensas nunc demum
infinita post Beroaldum, Muretum, Achillem Statium, Gulielmum Canterum, Josephum Scaligerum, Dousas,
Passeratium indicio mss. codicum illustris Bibliothecae Palatinae eruuntur eorundemque loca vitiosa corriguntur,
dubia constituuntur, suspecta deciduntur aut vindicantur, denique obscura illustrantur conspersis perquam utili-
bus in alios scriptores observationes. Opera et studio Jani Gebhardi* (Hanoviae, 1618).

variorum dei tre elegiaci, corredata per la prima volta, oltre che di ben diciotto apparati esegetici, anche del primo *index rerum et verborum* degli elegiaci latini.

Il commento agli elegiaci di Jean Passerat, professore al Collège de France, uscito a Parigi nel 1608 e fondato sulla *recensio* di un bellissimo codice fiorentino della metà del Quattrocento, il *Memmianus*, costituisce un momento—credo— particolarmente significativo della fortuna di Properzio nella cultura francese.[14] Esso insiste, infatti, sugli aspetti formali della scrittura elegiaca properziana, riflettendo una sensibilità particolarmente attenta a cogliere dall'impegno filologico le premesse di una ricerca stilistica che frattanto era entrata negli interessi classicistici dei poeti della Pléiade, dei quali il Passerat fu a lungo amico. Si tratta di un episodio che prelude al costituirsi in Francia di un filone traduttorio degli elegiaci ispirato da alcune tendenze proprie del classicismo manieristico francese. In quel clima culturale viene messa a stampa, a metà Seicento, la prima traduzione completa delle elegie di Properzio, curata da un ecclesiastico, Michel de Marolles, non nuovo a *performances* traduttorie, e incline alla versione in prosa come antidoto contro le degenerazioni sia delle parafrasi infedeli, sia delle piatte imitazioni.[15]

Il Marolles era letterato in vista nei salotti della Parigi di primo Seicento, che, sul modello dell'Hotel de Rambouillet, professavano—come si disse—"l'affinement du gout". La sua versione di Properzio, in prosa, recava espliciti riferimenti alla "delicatesse du sujet" e alla "difficulté d'y réussir, estant d'un Autheur très élégant et très poli". E rivendicando altrove il diritto ad una calcolata infedeltà là dove l'originale risulta ostico alla sensibilità moderna, polemizzava contro chi costruiva traduzioni con passiva fedeltà.

Ma neanche l'impegno filologico tace in quegli anni. Mentre Jean Bogard tenta di integrare la lettura degli elegiaci nel sistema scolastico della Riforma cattolica riproponendoli nel 1621 "omni obscaenitate sublata", l'editoria dei Paesi Bassi diffonde le migliori prove filologiche sui testi degli elegiaci, maturate durante tutto il XVII secolo in alcune università olandesi. A Utrecht esce una nuova *editio variorum*, curata da un modesto filologo frisone, Simon Gabbema: in apparenza un *reprint*, ma accanto alle ormai classiche chiose del Muret, dello Scaligero, dell'Estace e dei due Dousa, quella edizione presenta la nuova (e forse apocrifa) *recensio* allestita da Giovan Giorgio

---

[14] *Joannis Passerati, professoris et interpretis regii, commentarii in Caium Valerium Catullum, Albium Tibullum et Sextum Aurelium Propertium cum tribus accuratissimis rerum, verborum, autorum et emendationum indicibus* (Parisiis, 1608). Sui commenti del Passerat (Troyes 1534–Parigi 1602) agli elegiaci cf. *Catalogus transl.* 7 (1992): 275–278.

[15] *Catulle, Tibulle, Properce, de la traduction de M. de Marolles* (Paris, 1653–1654). Michel de Marolles (Marolles 1600–Parigi 1681), abate di Villeloin, noto a Parigi nei salotti letterari di Isaac Habert, Guillaume Duval, Coëffeteau, fu anche il primo traduttore di Lucano (1623); tradusse anche Lucrezio (1650), Orazio (1652), Persio e Giovenale (1653), Marziale (1655), Stazio (1658), Plauto (1658), Terenzio (1659), Ovidio (1660), Seneca (1660). Accanto a questa intensa attività letteraria, svolse anche ricerche di indole storico-erudita, geografica, biografica: cf. Jean-Pierre Arnaud, "De Joachim du Bellay à Pierre Daru: les traductions et adaptations françaises de l'ode 'Exegi monumentum' (III,30) anterieures au XIX siècle", in *Présence d'Horace*, ed. R. Chevalier (Tours, 1989), 1–23, esp. 8.

Graevius, notissimo filologo tedesco che da ormai non pochi anni era titolare della cattedra di eloquenza all'Università di Utrecht.[16]

Appariva solo all'inizio del Settecento, preceduta da una proposta di sottoscrizione cui aderirono, fra gli altri, Robert Walpole e John Locke, la prima edizione in terra inglese dei tre elegiaci. Il volume uscì dall'officina di Jacob Tonson, tipografo dell'Università di Cambridge.[17] Il tardivo interesse dell'editoria inglese per gli elegiaci coincide dunque, all'inizio del Settecento, con la ripresa di una cultura classica rinnovata secondo un gusto sensistico-razionalistico, ma anche con una moda letteraria che rilancia nella cultura mondana europea la lirica ellenistica e le sue filiazioni latine nei termini di una lirica, come si disse, "da cantare alla spinetta con la dama".

Da questa tendenza nascono, nello stesso anno, il 1743, ben due traduzioni italiane di Properzio, le prime riservate all'elegiaco dal pur affollatissimo Parnaso di volgarizzatori italiani dei classici. A propiziarle sono Guido Riviera, pastore arcade, abate, tipico traduttore settecentesco dei classici; Giulio Cesare Becelli, scrittore di teatro, ex-gesuita, approdato, dopo un transito in alcune accademie, a posizioni decisamente anticlassicistiche e vagamente preromantiche.[18]

Se nell'esercizio traduttorio del Riviera riconosciamo il corredo tecnico di un classicista ansioso di riprodurre le forme poetiche classiche con una decorosa fedeltà che spesso è la ragione stessa della versione, nella traduzione del Becelli riaffiorano con più forza i motivi, della "libertà" del traduttore, una libertà decisamente antifilologica.

In quegli stessi anni, credo non a caso, il Μονοβίβλος properziano usciva tradotto, insieme al Catullo erotico, dal laboratorio poetico di John Nott, esponente di spicco del filone esotico-odeporico della letteratura inglese, autore anche delle belle versioni del poeta persiano Háfiz Shirazi.[19]

Anche le prime traduzioni tedesche degli elegiaci maturano in un clima letterario schiettamente protoromantico: quella di Franz Xavier Mayr, del 1786; quella di Karl Hoffmann, del 1798; quella infine di Karl Ludwig von Knebel che, amico e corri-

---

[16] *Catullus, Tibullus et Propertius et quae sub Galli nomine circumferuntur. Cum selectis variorum commentariis. Accurante Simon Abbas Gabbema* (Trajecti ad Rhenum, 1659). Simon Abbas Gabbema (Leeuwarde, 1620–1700) fu conservatore degli archivi frisoni e storico della sua regione. Fu editore di Petronio (dalla sua edizione fu costruita l'*editio variorum*) e di Ausonio.

[17] *Catulli, Tibulli et Propertii opera ad optimorum exemplarium fidem recensita. Accesserunt variae lectiones quae in libris mss. et eruditorum commentariis notatu digniores occurrunt* (Cantabrigiae, 1702: cf. McKitterick 64).

[18] *Corpus omnium veterum poetarum latinorum cum eorundem italica versione . . . Raccolta di tutti gli antichi poeti latini colla loro versione nell'Italiana favella. Tomo XXIII. Contiene i versi di Sesto Aurelio Properzio tradotti dal signor dottor Guido Riviera Piacentino, fra gli Arcadi di Trebbia Ugildo* (Milano, 1743: Paitoni 186). *I quattro libri dell'Elegie di Sesto Aurelio Properzio tradotte in terza rima con alcune brevi e chiarissime note* [da Giulio Cesare Becelli] (Verona, 1743: Paitoni 185).

[19] *Propertii Μονοβίβλος, or that book of the Elegies of Propertius entitled Cynthia translated into English verse with classical notes* (London, 1782). John Nott (Worcester 1751–Clifton 1826), dopo aver studiato chirurgia, si imbarcò su un vascello della Compagnia delle Indie alla volta della Cina, da dove iniziò una lunga sequenza di peregrinazioni nell'Oriente. Tradusse anche Catullo, Lucrezio, Orazio.

spondente di Goëthe, privilegia, tra gli elegiaci, Properzio, affiancandogli Lucrezio.[20]

Singolare è infine il caso di un modesto letterato bretone, Pierre de Longchamps, del quale mi sarebbe difficile fornire altre notizie, autore di una versione properziana che conobbe una eccezionale fortuna editoriale spiegabile solo nel clima di sensibilità romantica alla musa elegiaca di Properzio. Consegnata a un ponderoso *in-quarto* di ben 610 pagine, che uscì contemporaneamente ad Amsterdam e a Parigi nel 1772, la traduzione ebbe una riedizione parigina nel 1795, nella collana dei "Poètes erotiques" dell'editore Volland, e, quel che ancor più sorprende, un'altra riedizione parigina uscita nel 1802 in una veste tipografica inconsueta per la sua magnificenza anche per una traduzione prestigiosa.[21]

Nei ben quattro tomi di cui essa si compone non solo si leggono le elegie properziane "dans toute leur intégrité" (quindi, senza limiti censori, come recita il frontespizio), ma si godono soprattutto splendide incisioni (un *primum* assoluto nella storia editoriale del *corpus* properziano), opera di Nicolas Ponce, il più celebre incisore dell'Illuminismo francese, illustratore di Voltaire e Rousseau, e di Clément Marillier, disegnatore espertissimo, conteso da tipografi e editori, collaboratore del Ponce in quella altissima iniziativa iconografica dei cinquantasei *Illustres Français*.

La nascente sensibilità romantica cercava, evidentemente, con sempre maggiore convinzione, fra i "triumviri rei amatoriae" (come si amò definire gli elegiaci), il più "difficile" e "introverso" Properzio: al punto da volerlo godere anche attraverso una lettura visiva dei suoi versi, secondo l'antico concetto dell'*ut pictura poesis* che, non a caso, ha accompagnato, nelle letterature dell'Occidente, altri momenti di intensa riflessione sull'esercizio lirico.

Università di Bari

Opere citate nelle note per acronimo:

Arbour: Roméo Arbour, *L'ère baroque en France. Répertoire chronologique des éditions de textes littéraires* . . . 6 vols. (Genève, 1977–1985).

Argelati: Filippo Argelati, *Biblioteca dei volgarizzatori o sia notizie dell'opere volgarizzate d'autori, che scrissero in lingue morte del sec. XV, coll'addizioni e correzioni di Angelo Teodoro Villa*, 5 vols. (Milano, 1767).

Baudrier: Henry, Louis and Julien Baudrier, *Bibliographie lyonnaise. Recherches sur les imprimeurs, libraires, relieurs et fondeurs de lettres de Lyon au XVI siècle . . . publiées et continuées par Julien Baudrier*, 12 vols. (Lyon, [poi: Brossier, poi: Paris, Picard], 1895–1925, reprint Georges Tricou ed., con l'aggiunta del 13° vol. di tavole,

---

[20] Cf. rispettivamente: *Catull, Tibull, Properz, aus dem Lateinischen, von F. X. Mayr* (Leipzig, 1786), 2 vols., *Vier Bücher Elegien übersetzt u. mit erklärender Anmerkung begleitet* (Erfurt, 1786). *Elegieen von Properz* . . . (Leipzig, 1798).

[21] *Elegies de Properce traduites par M. de Longchamps* (Paris et Amsterdam, 1772). *Elegies de Properce traduites dans toute leur intégrité. Avec des notes interprétatives du texte et de la mythologie de l'auteur; et des figures gravées sous de direction de Ponce d'après les dessins de Marillier. Nouvelle édition revue, corrigée et considérablement augmentée par M. de Longchamps* (Paris, 1802).

Paris, 1964–1966 [con *Supplément provisoire à la Bibliographie lyonnaise du Président Baudrier*, Y. De la Perrière ed., Paris, 1967, I]).

BB: *Bibliotheca Belgica. Bibliographie générale des Pays-Bas par le bibliothécaire en chef et les conservateurs de la Bibliothèque de l'Université de Gand* (Gand, 1880–).

BLC: *British Museum. General Catalogue of Printed Books to 1955*, 263 vols. (London, 1964 [con i relativi supplementi periodici]).

BMC: *Catalogue of Books Printed in the XVth Century now in the British Museum* (London, 1908–85).

BNP: Bibliothèque Nationale, Paris, *Catalogue général des livres imprimés de la Bibliothèque National. Auteurs* (Paris [vols. 1–21], Imprimerie nationale [vols. 22–231], 1897–1981).

Brunet: Jean Charles Brunet, *Manuel du libraire et de l'amateur de livres . . .* 6 vols. (Paris, 1860–65, 5° ed., [supplem. di P. Dechamps e G. Brunet, Paris, 2 vols., 1878–80], rist. anast. Milano, 1990).

Catalogus transl.: *Catalogus translationum et commentariorum: Mediaeval and Renaissance Latin Translations and Commentaries*, Virginia Brown ed., vol. VII (Washington, 1992).

CR: Consensus *Copinger-Reichling.*

DBI: *Dizionario Biografico degli Italiani* (Roma, 1960–).

Flodr: Miroslav Flodr, *Incunabula Classicorum. Wiegendrücke der griechischen und römischen Literatur* (Amsterdam, 1973).

Giorgetti-Vichi: Anna Maria Giorgetti-Vichi, *Gli Arcadi dal 1690 al 1800. Onomasticon* (Roma, 1977).

H: Ludwig Hain, *Repertorium bibliographicum, in quo libri omnes ab arte typographica inventa usque ad annum MD, typis expressi ordine alphabetico vel simpliciter enumerantur vel adcuratius recensentur*, 4 vols. (Stuttgartiae & Lutetiae Parisiorum, 1826–1838 [ristampe nel 1920, 1925, 1948, 1964]).

HC: Consensus *Hain Copinger.*

IGI: *Indice generale degli incunabuli delle biblioteche d'Italia*, T. Guarnaschelli, E. Valenziani, E. Cerulli, P. Veneziani, eds., 6 vols. (Roma, 1943–1981).

ISTC: *Incunable Short-Title Catalogue* (base-dati in allestimento dal 1979 a cura della British Library di Londra, attualmente interrogabile in linea; ne è prevista la pubblicazione su cd-rom).

McKitterick: David McKitterick, *Four Hundred Years of University Printing and Publishing in Cambridge 1584–1984. Catalogue of the Exhibition in the University Library, Cambridge* (Cambridge, 1984).

Nijhoff–Kronenberg: Wouter Nijhoff–Maria E. Kronenberg, *Nederlandsche Bibliographie van 1500 tot 1540*, 8 vols. (s'Gravenhage, 1923–1966).

Paitoni: G. M. Paitoni, *Biblioteca degli autori antichi greci e latini volgarizzati*, 5 vols. (Venezia, 1766–67).

Renouard: Philippe Renouard, *Bibliographie des éditions de Simon de Colines (1520–1546)* (Nieuwkoop, 1990, seconda rist. anast. dell'ed. Paris, 1894).

Renouard Man.: Antoine Augustin Renouard, *Annales de l'imprimerie des Aldes ou histoire des trois Manuce et de leurs éditions* (Paris, 1834), [poi:] *Annali delle edizioni Aldine. Con notizie sulla famiglia dei Giunti e repertorio delle loro edizioni fino al 1550 . . .* (Bologna, 1953).

Schreiber: Fred Schreiber, *The Estiennes. An Annotated Catalogue of 300 Highlights of their Various Press* (New York, 1982).

VD 16: *Verzeichnis der im deutschen Sprachbereich erschienenen Drücke des XVI Jahrhunderts. Herausgegeben von der Bayerischen Staatsbibliothek in München in Verbindung mit der Herzog-August-Bibliothek in Wolfenbüttel* (Stuttgart, 1983–1992).

Voet: Leon Voet, Jenny Voet Grisolle, *The Plantin Press (1555–1589). A Bibliography of the works printed and published by Christopher Plantin at Antwerp and Leiden*, 6 vols. (Amsterdam, 1980–1982).

Proverbs, Censors, and Schools:
Neo-Latin Studies and Book History

CRAIG KALLENDORF

"Texts, books, and discourses really began to have authors (other than mythical, 'sacralized' and 'sacralizing' figures) to the extent that authors became subject to punishment, that is, to the extent that discourses could be transgressive. In our culture (and doubtless in many others), discourse was not originally a product, a thing, a kind of goods; it was essentially an act—an act placed in the bipolar field of the sacred and the profane, the licit and the illicit, the religious and the blasphemous. Historically, it was a gesture fraught with risks before becoming goods caught up in a circuit of ownership."[1]

The subject of this paper is a sixteenth-century book which presents several questions to the modern scholar. The book is titled *Sententiae et proverbia ex poetis Latinis* ..., and it is actually in two parts. The first is a collection of extracts from classical Latin authors commonly read in the Renaissance, arranged by author. Another collection of extracts, this time arranged by key words in the quotations, has been added, as the title page notes: *His adiecimus Leosthenis Coluandri sententias prophanas, ex diuersis scriptoribus, in communem puerorum usum, collectae.* The title page names the author of the second part but not the first, and the book lacks any sort of prefatory matter to enlighten us further.[2] Who, then, is the author of the first part?

This is not, however, the only question posed by this book. The only other words on the title page are *Venetijs. M D XLVII.* The problem, of course, is that the name of the printer is not given, as we would expect it to be. Initially, William Ward solved this problem by tracing the printer's mark, which is on the title page, through the appropriate reference books to two men named Francesco Bindoni and Maffeo Pasini, who worked cooperatively from 1524 to 1551 and printed over two hundred

---

[1] Michael Foucault, "What Is an Author?" in David Lodge, ed., *Modern Criticism and Theory* (London, 1988), 202.

[2] The book, an octavo of 114 folios, is described in Hesketh and Ward, Catalogue 17, 49, no. 90.

books ranging from translations of Lucian and the Bible to vernacular literature by Ariosto and Boccaccio.[3] Ultimately, however, a mystery remains. I have looked at about forty other books published by this cooperative, and I have found only one that appears to have been published anonymously.[4] Why did Bindoni and Pasini feel constrained to abandon their usual practice and leave their names off their *Sententiae et proverbia* . . . ?

The third question this title page raises focuses around the declaration that Coluandrus' *sententiae* had been *in communem puerorum usum collecta[e]*. Who were the boys envisioned as an audience for this book, and how were they expected to use it?

The questions raised by this book are slightly different from the ones that Neo-Latinists generally consider. To be sure, we sometimes attempt to reduce the corpus of that most prolific of all early authors, *Anonymous*, but we generally know who wrote the works we study. And it is even less often that our work takes us into questions about who printed a book or who a reader or group of readers mentioned in an early edition might be. Yet I want to suggest that Neo-Latinists should consider these questions more often, because some works can only be understood fully by answering them. What is more, I would like to suggest that a developing field generally referred to as "history of the book" offers a useful way for us to do this. History of the book encourages us not to look *through* a book as a semiotically insignificant carrier of text, but rather to look *at* it as a physical object which conveys meaning along with the text it carries.[5] In the language of the book historian, my artifact raises questions about production (who wrote it?), distribution (how was it printed and circulated?), and consumption (who read it, and for what purpose?)

First, who wrote the *Sententiae et proverbia ex poetis Latinis* . . . ? Some bibliographical detective work has generated a stemma which is not free of ambiguity but which clearly ends in other editions whose authorship is certain. Another edition with exactly the same titles for both parts was published in Venice by Ioannes Patavinus, but this edition lacks a date, so it is impossible to say whether it precedes or

---

[3] Hesketh and Ward, Catalogue 17, 49, no. 90. The printer's device, found on the title page and the last page of the book, is illustrated in Emerenziana Vaccaro, *Le marche dei tipografi ed editori italiani del secolo XVI nella Biblioteca Angelica di Roma* (Florence, 1983), fig. 287. Information on Bindoni and Pasini may be found in Fernanda Ascarelli and Marco Menato, *La tipografia del '500 in Italia* (Florence, 1989), 349–350, 360–361.

[4] I have examined the books printed by Bindoni and Pasini in the collections at the University of Texas and the University of Pennsylvania, and added information on ten other titles from the catalogues of the Giuseppe Martini sale, *Bibliothèque Joseph Martini*, Première vente aux enchères 27–29 août 1934 Lucerne (Milan, 1934), and Deuxième partie vente aux enchères 21–23 mai 1935 Zurich (Milan, 1935). Only two of the Martini lots, one of which is a four-page, ephemeral tract, lack the printers' names.

[5] The seminal event in the development of this approach is generally taken to be the publication of Lucien Le Febvre and Jean Martin, *L'apparition du livre* (Paris, 1958), translated into English as *The Coming of the Book: The Impact of Printing, 1450–1800,* trans. David Gerard (London, 1976).

follows the 1547 edition being investigated.[6] The same works had also been published six years earlier by Sebastianus Gryphius, an important and prolific Lyons printer.[7] Books moved easily between Lyons and Venice and copyright laws were difficult to enforce—remember the infamous Lyons counterfeits which so angered Aldus Manutius[8]—so either Bindoni and Pasini reprinted the Lyons edition directly, or indirectly via the Ioannes Patavinus edition as intermediary. Our problem remains, however, because the *Sententiae et proverbia ex poetis Latinis . . .* is anonymous in both these editions.

All three of these editions, however, have extracts from almost exactly the same poets, in exactly the same order, as a book printed in Paris in 1534, 1536, and 1540, and titled *Sententiae et proverbia ex Plauto, Terentio, Virgilio, Ovidio, Horatio, Iuvenale, Persio, Lucano, Seneca, Lucretio, Martiale, Silio Italico, Statio, Valerio Flacco, Catullo, Propertio, Tibullo, Claudiano*. These editions were published by Robert Estienne (Robertus Stephanus), of the well-known family of French scholar-printers, but they, too, lack an author's name on the title page.[9] Further investigation, however, indicates that Estienne himself selected and edited the extracts.[10]

The stemma, however, does not end here. The 1547 Venice edition is striking for the amount of space it devotes to extracts from Plautus and Terence—over fifty pages, or a full third of the text, as opposed to the two pages devoted to Virgil, whose works were far more popular in sixteenth-century Europe. Some further investigation reveals that pages 3–57 of the 1547 Venetian edition contain the same extracts from Plautus and Terence as pages 465–574 of a book printed by Robert Estienne's son Henri (Henricus Stephanus). This book was printed in 1569,[11] but the

---

[6] The *British Library General Catalogue of Printed Books to 1975* (London, 1983), 185:135 dates the book, with considerable hesitation, to 1552. The *National Union Catalogue, Pre-1956 Imprints* (London, 1977), 538: 453 indicates that the catalogue of the Bibliothèque Nationale dates the book to 1547, but my examination of that catalogue leaves me uncertain about precisely which edition of the *Sententiae et proverbia . . .* the Bibliothèque Nationale holds.

[7] Copies of this book may be found in Trinity College Library, Cambridge (H. M. Adams, *Catalogue of Books Printed on the Continent of Europe 1501-1600 in Cambridge Libraries* [Cambridge, 1967], 2: 204 [942]); and in the Biblioteca Apostolica Vaticana, shelf mark Legatura De Marinis 86.

[8] Aldus printed a warning to counterfeiters at the end of his 1501 Martial, but the warning itself was reprinted in a Lyons counterfeit published shortly afterward; see H. George Fletcher, *In Praise of Aldus Manutius: A Quincentenary Exhibition* (New York and Los Angeles, 1995), 56.

[9] The three editions are recorded in A. A. Renouard, *Annales de l'imprimerie des Estienne, ou, Histoire de la famille des Estienne et de ses éditions*, 2nd ed. (Paris, 1843), 40 (1534.13), 43 (1536.14), and 50 (1540.9), respectively. A copy of the 1540 edition may be found at the Cambridge University Library (Adams, *Catalogue*, 2: 92 [1517]).

[10] The National Union Catalogue, 162: 612, assigns authorship of the 1536 edition to Robert Estienne, and Fred Schreiber confirms that this attribution is correct (private correspondence, 19 November 1996).

[11] *Comicorvm / Graecorum sen- / tentiae, id est* γνῶμαι, */ Latinis versibus ab Henr. / Stephano redditae, & an- / notationibus illustratae . . . anno M. D. LXIX / Excudebat Henr. Step.* (f. ¶1r), with an internal title at p. 465 introducing the relevant section: *Comicorvm Latinorvm / sententiae, & ea*

material from Plautus and Terence had originally been printed in 1530 by Robert[12] and again by Antoine Bonnemere in Paris in 1536.[13] In other words, Robert had begun by making a collection of extracts from Plautus and Terence, and then he added the extracts from other Latin authors to make the collection which ultimately found its way into Bindoni and Pasini's book.

To summarize: the collection of extracts printed by Bindoni and Pasini had begun as a group of citations from Plautus and Terence gathered by Robert Estienne and was later expanded by the editor to include other classical Latin authors. The expanded collection was printed in Lyons, from which it appears to have travelled to Venice, where Bindoni and Pasini either reprinted it directly, or indirectly from the book published by Ioannes Patavinus.

We are now in a position to address the second question posed by the 1547 edition: why did the men who printed this book abandon their usual practice and leave their names off the title page? The answer, I would suggest, derives from the fact that at the time this book was printed, its author was already in deep trouble with the religious authorities.

As a scholar-printer, Robert Estienne had obtained an appointment from the king of France to print in Greek, which led to nine *editiones principes* of early Greek authors. Estienne also printed Bibles, and here lay the source of his troubles. His first Bible was a Vulgate, printed in 1527–1528, which ran afoul of the Faculty of Theology at the University of Paris, and each new edition brought further conflict. Francis I, who had offered powerful protection to Estienne, died in 1547, and in October of that year the Faculty of Theology condemned all of Estienne's biblical writings in Latin, claiming that the explanatory matter was filled with heresy and the received text of the Vulgate had been modified. Henry II authorized this condemnation in November of 1548, where it passed first into the *Catalogue of Prohibited Books* of 1551, then into the Papal *Index* of Paul IV in 1559, which also allowed the complete prohibition of all books by any author or printer who had disseminated heresy. By 1551 Robert had converted to Calvinism, moved to Geneva, and opened a new press.[14]

At this point Paris and Venice were the two most important publishing centers in

---

qui- / bus usi sunt pro- / verbia. . . . This book is described in Fred Schreiber, *The Estiennes: An Annotated Catalogue of 300 Highlights of Their Various Presses*, with an introduction by Nicolas Barker (New York, 1982), 153–154 (no. 175). I have examined the copy at the University of Texas; another copy is at the University of North Carolina at Chapel Hill, to which the collection described by Dr. Schreiber was sold.

[12] *Sententiae et proverbia ex omnibus Plauti et Terentii Comoediis* (Paris, 1530); see Renouard, *Annales*, 34, (1530.12); and Adams, *Catalogue*, 2: 92 (1515).

[13] *Sententiae et proverbia ex omnibus Plauti et Terentii Comoediis* (Paris, 1536); see Adams, *Catalogue*, 2: 92 (1516).

[14] The most thorough study of the life and work of this printer remains Elizabeth Armstrong's *Robert Estienne, Royal Printer: An Historical Study of the Elder Stephanus*, rev. ed. (Abingdon, England, 1986), from which most of the information in this paragraph is taken (165–227). See also Schreiber, *The Estiennes*, *passim*, esp. 45–46.

Europe, and there is little chance that the woes of the dominant printer in one city would remain unknown for long in the other. There was no way of knowing in 1547, of course, that Robert would abandon Catholicism in 1551, but the peculiar reprinting of the *Sententiae et proverbia ex poetis Latinis* . . . does make sense when we balance what we know about the situation in Venice at precisely this point against the problems we have noted on the title page. On the one hand, Paul Grendler has characterized the 1540s as a decade that was unusually open to the printing of new books and ideas, including those connected to Protestantism.[15] Venetian printers still came under suspicion for a willingness to sacrifice piety to commercial opportunities, yet at times the state intervened on their behalf with the religious authorities because the book trade played an important part in the general prosperity of the Venetian republic.[16] On the other hand, however, there were risks involved. It is hard to imagine how heresy could creep into a collection of aphorisms from classical authors, but it is important to remember that in a city renowned for its piety, not everyone defended classical literature enthusiastically. Once a book was condemned, the printer faced the possibility of having his entire stock confiscated and losing whatever he had invested in having it printed. And once the Inquisition became upset over Bibles, it was an easy matter to condemn whatever else was associated with the man who had edited and printed them. Ultimately, Bindoni and Pasini devised an elegant way to balance risk against opportunity: they printed the book, but without their names or the name of the author. If the book was traced back to them, perhaps through its printer's mark, they could at least claim that they did not know who wrote it and escape the worst of the Inquisition's ire.

The fate of another of Robert's books, his *Dictionarium, seu . . . Latinae linguae thesaurus* . . . , parallels that of the *Sententiae et proverbia ex poetis Latinis* . . . and provides confirmation for this interpretation. Estienne's dictionary was also reprinted in Venice in 1550–1551, just a few years after the book of extracts. And just like the *Sententiae et proverbia ex poetis Latinis* . . . , the Venetian edition of the dictionary lacks the names of both author and printer. The heirs of Pietro Ravani, who reprinted the dictionary, seem to have balanced opportunity and risk in the same way.[17]

Now that we know why Bindoni and Pasini were reluctant to identify themselves openly as the printers of this book, it is time to look more closely at why they were willing to take the risks associated with the project. To answer this question, we need to return to the *pueri* for whom the title page says the book was prepared.

---

[15] Paul Grendler, *The Roman Inquisition and the Venetian Press, 1540–1605* (Princeton, 1977), 225–233.

[16] In addition to Grendler's study mentioned above, the relations between the Venetian press and religious authorities may be traced in Horatio F. Brown, *The Venetian Printing Press, 1469–1800: An Historical Study Based upon Documents for the Most Part Hitherto Unpublished* (London, 1891; reprint, Amsterdam, 1969); and Conor Fahy, "The Index Librorum Prohibitorum and the Venetian Printing Industry in the Sixteenth Century," *Italian Studies* 35 (1980): 52–61.

[17] The dictionary, which was published in two volumes in 1543 and 1544, is described in Renouard, *Annales*, 55–57; and Schreiber, *The Estiennes*, 70 (no. 68); see also Armstrong, *Robert Estienne*, 87–94.

The statement that the *sententiae* were *in communem puerorum usum collecta[e]* suggests that the book was intended for an academic market. Humanistic schools with curricula based on classical texts represented a huge potential market in Renaissance Europe, which explains in good part why Bindoni and Pasini were willing to take some risks to print this book.

To understand fully the appeal of books like this, however, we shall have to look briefly at how classical authors were studied in these schools. Contrary, perhaps, to our expectations, few teachers read a work straight through from beginning to end; instead, they tended to dip in at certain key episodes, which were explicated slowly and fully.[18] There were several reasons for this. One was tied to the physical way in which the text was presented. Early printed books mimicked the appearance of medieval manuscripts, which often presented the text accompanied by one or more commentaries; this encouraged the reader to proceed slowly as the eye went back and forth between text and commentary.[19] What is more, as Roger Chartier has shown, passing freely and casually through a large number of texts is a comparatively modern way of reading. The older alternative privileged slow, attentive study of language and meaning as a way of inculcating a common set of references and quotations. Both physical layout and mode of reading tended to fragment the text—to reduce it to a series of formulas, proverbs, maxims, and ready-made expressions.[20]

These expressions, as Battista Guarino explained, were to be collected by the student and entered into notebooks, one of which was to be based on rhetorical forms and idioms (*Methodice*), the other on content, especially moral content (*Historice*).[21] From these notebooks, the results of the students' reading could be applied to their own compositions and, presumably, to their lives as well. Sometimes these common-place books themselves were published, as was the case with the *Osservationi . . . sopra l'opere di Virgilio* of a Venetian schoolmaster named Orazio Toscanella.[22]

Books like Toscanella's—and Estienne's—were aimed at this market, at students (and teachers) whose educational environment valued the collected proverbial wisdom of the ancients. In terms of its content, the only remarkable thing about the *Sententiae et proverbia ex poetis Latinis . . .* is its heavy reliance on Plautus and Terence, which can be explained once the book has been situated into the corpus of its editor, for Estienne was drafting a text of Plautus, preparing editions of both Plautus and Terence, and working on a dictionary based largely on these two authors at the same

---

[18] There are occasional exceptions to this generalization, one of which is Venice, Biblioteca Nazionale Marciana, Aldine 628, a copy of Virgil which was marked throughout by a teacher for classroom use.

[19] Ruth Morris, *Truth and Convention in the Middle Ages: Rhetoric, Representation, and Reality* (Cambridge, 1991), 24–26.

[20] Roger Chartier, *The Cultural Uses of Print in Early Modern France*, trans. Lydia G. Cochrane (Princeton, 1987), 221–225.

[21] R. R. Bolgar, *The Classical Heritage and Its Beneficiaries* (Cambridge, 1954), 270.

[22] Toscanella's importance emerges clearly from Paul Grendler, *Schooling in Renaissance Italy: Literacy and Learning, 1300–1600* (Baltimore, 1989), 222–224 and 240.

time as he was editing his little book of extracts.[23] Other than this, Estienne's book resembles many others of its kind which Ann Moss has recently studied.[24] From *Aeneid* 4, for example, Estienne draws three bits of wisdom: *Nusquam tuta fides* (line 12), *Improbe amor, quid non mortalia pectora cogit?* (line 412), and *Varium et mutabile semper / Foemina* (lines 569–570).[25] Such wisdom was the common intellectual stock of its day, and it retains its value for us by providing a window into which of the many possible interpretations of a given author were developed in Renaissance schoolrooms.

Further evidence of how books like these were intended to be used can be derived from examining some of the surviving copies. A copy in my possession obviously belonged to a schoolboy, for the rear flyleaves contain a drawing of a well dated "1629" and a page of additional *sententiae* entered by hand.[26] Similarly, the copy now at the Biblioteca Nazionale Marciana in Venice contains manuscript notes and various citations in sixteenth- and seventeenth-century hands,[27] indicating that once again, early owners simply added additional proverbs from whatever texts they were studying at school. The copy now at the University of Illinois is particularly interesting, for a stamp on the title page tells us where it came from: *Domus S. Anton. de Padua*. Since the Basilica of St. Anthony of Padua has a renowned collection of music manuscripts, it should not surprise us to discover that this copy is bound in a vellum page taken from one of these choirbooks (see plate 1), and the book was undoubtedly used in one of the schools attached to the basilica, which is still an active educational center.[28]

As we would expect, most of the surviving copies reflect their humble origins: the Marciana copy, like the one now in Illinois, is bound in discarded parchment, the humblest option in the culture of its day. The methodology of the history of the book, however, quickly teaches us to expect the unexpected, which comes to pass here with a copy of the 1541 Lyons edition now in the Vatican Library. This book once belonged to Apollonio Filareto, secretary to Pier Luigi Farnese (the natural son of Pope Paul III, he was assassinated in 1547, two years after receiving the Duchy of Parma and Piacenza). The book is covered in leather, with one side containing the

---

[23] Schreiber, *The Estiennes*, 51–53 (no. 39) and 54 (no. 43).

[24] Ann Moss, *Printed Commonplace-Books and the Structuring of Renaissance Thought* (Oxford, 1996), who lists the 1534 and 1536 editions of the *Sententiae et proverbia ex poetis Latinis . . .* (anonymously, of course) in the list of primary sources she consulted.

[25] P. 58 of the Bindoni and Pasini edition.

[26] The student owner signed his name on the verso of the original flyleaf, but the signature was cancelled by a later owner and only the first part, *Sebastianus de . . .* , is legible.

[27] I am grateful to Stefania Rossi Minutelli and Marino Zorzi of the Biblioteca Nazionale Marciana for supplying me with information on the copy in Venice (personal correspondence, 25 November 1996).

[28] I know of two other copies of this book in the United States, at the University of Texas and Yale University, and one other copy in Italy, at the Biblioteca Provinciale Cappuccini in Reggio Emilia (see *Le cinquecentine della Biblioteca Provinciale Cappuccini in Reggio Emilia* [Parma, 1972], 245 [no. 616]).

owner's name and the other side containing a medallion depicting an eagle soaring over a rocky sea with the Virgilian motto *procul este* (*Aen.* 6.258) (see plate 2).[29] Medallion bindings were the most sumptuous option available during the Italian Renaissance, and Filareto was one of only four men to have owned groups of them.[30] The other volumes in his collection are mostly standard Latin curriculum authors,[31] and I would suggest that when Filareto prepared his library of the humanistic literature so valued by the courtiers of his day, he included the 1541 Lyons proverb collection because he remembered how valuable its interpretive approach had been to him in his student days.

As we have seen, then, the 1547 *Sententiae et proverbia ex poetis Latinis* . . . only yields its full range of information when we learn to look *at* it as a physical object at the same time as we look *through* it into the text it carries. As a text, it joins other printed commonplace books in telling us a good deal about the educational practice of its day. Only as a book, however—a printed object with its own production, distribution, and consumption—does it stand apart and take on a life of its own. Early printed books, as Natalie Zemon Davis has reminded us, are "carriers of relationships,"[32] and that is certainly true here, for it is indeed a tangled web that runs through this seemingly innocent schoolboy tool to link one of Europe's greatest scholar-printers to a powerful servant of the church against which he ultimately took his stand. Yet at the same time as this book survives as a witness to the religious conflict that divided Renaissance Europe, it also attests to how difficult it really was to stop the free flow of ideas in a culture where educated people on both sides of the divide spoke the same language. The history of this book, in short, confirms that in the final analysis, there was only one *res publica litterarum* in Renaissance Europe.

Texas A & M University

---

[29] The book itself, now Legatura de Marinis 86, once belonged to the scholar/bookseller Tammaro de Marinis, who included it in *La legatura artistica in Italia nei secoli XV e XVI* (Florence, 1960), 1: 814–826.

[30] The best recent treatment of Filareto and the medallion bindings is A. R. A. Hobson, *Apollo and Pegasus: An Enquiry into the Formation and Dispersal of a Renaissance Library* (Amsterdam, 1975).

[31] The other volumes are listed in Hobson, *Apollo and Pegasus*, 91–95.

[32] Natalie Zemon Davis, "Printing and People," in *Society and Culture in Early Modern France* (Stanford, 1975), 192. I would like to thank Fred Schreiber, William Stoneman, and Steven Ferguson for their comments on an earlier draft of this essay.

1547 *Sententiae et proverbia ex poetis Latinis . . .*
Vellum binding from the Basilica of St. Anthony, Padua.
Courtesy of the Rare Book and Special Collections Library
at the University of Illinois at Urbana-Champaign.

1541 *Sententiae et proverbia ex poetis Latinis . . .*
Medallion binding of Apollonio Filareto.
Courtesy of the Biblioteca Apostolica Vaticana.

Les *"Desserts" de Julius Caesar Scaliger,*
nourriture spirituelle pour les "Emblemata" néerlandais
de Johan de Brune

PAULA KONING

Le dernier recueil de poésie de Julius Caesar Scaliger, édité après sa mort par son fils Joseph Juste en 1573, est intitulé *De Sapientia et Beatitudine libri octo, quos Epidorpides inscripsit.* Depuis 1574, année de la première édition des *Poemata,* l'oeuvre poétique complète, ce recueil *De Sapientia et Beatitudine* est intitulé *Epidorpides* (Desserts) tout simplement.[1] Joseph Juste s'est chargé de faire éditer la poésie de son père et il en a aussi propagé la lecture. Dans le cercle des humanistes académiques à Leyde, où Joseph Juste était devenu professeur, Dousa par exemple connaissait aussi bien les vers du père Scaliger que ceux de Sannazaro et de Pontano. Donc, Julius Caesar Scaliger était connu et lu comme poète aux Pays-Bas à la fin du XVIe et du XVIIe siècle. De plus un choix de 89 de ses poèmes d'amour furt diffusé dans les *Veneres Blydenburgicae* (Dordrecht 1600). Mais Nichols a constaté que dans la poésie néolatine des érudits néerlandais, on ne trouve pas de traces d'imitation directe de Julius Caesar Scaliger.[2] Mes études des rapports littéraires entre Scaliger et Johan de Brune, entamées grâce aux recherches récentes sur l'oeuvre de De Brune, permettent de corriger cette vision d'une non-existence de l'influence scaligerienne en Hollande.[3]

L'abondance, vice ou vertu?

Parmi les admirateurs des poèmes du père Scaliger se trouvait Juste Lipse, qui

---

[1] J. C. Scaliger: *Poemata in duas partes divisas* ([Genève: s.é], 1574). Toutes les citations sont de cette édition. Les *Epidorpides* se trouvent dans part II.

[2] F. J. Nichols, *The Literary Relationships of the "Poemata" of Julius Caesar Scaliger* (Ann Arbor, 1967), 209.

[3] Voir K. Porteman, "Johan de Brunes emblematische essays," in P. J. Verkruijsse (ed.): *Johan de Brune de Oude (1588–1658). Een Zeeuws literator en staatsman uit de zeventiende eeuw* (Middelbourg, 1990), 110.

critiquait toutefois l'édition du fils. Lipse est d'avis que la qualité irrégulière du matér-
iel poétique est un mauvais point et que Joseph Juste aurait dû faire une sélection.
L'intérêt pour l'oeuvre poétique se concentre d'ailleurs en général sur d'autres recueils
tels que les *Heroes, Heroinae, Urbes, Nova Epigrammata, Anacreontica* et non pas du tout
sur les *Epidorpides*. Pourquoi ne parle-t-on pas des *Epidorpides*? Je crois que la critique
de Lipse en ce qui concerne l'abondance est juste et applicable à ces poèmes.

Le recueil *Epidorpides* comprend une longue dissertation de 226 pages due à un
vieil humaniste chrétien qui emploie tout son talent d'écrivain et son érudition pour
nous convaincre de la meilleure manière d'accomplir notre vie. Il prête beaucoup
d'attention aux péchés que l'homme a commis depuis la chute d'Adam; maintenant
l'homme doit sans cesse combattre les attaques et les tentations du diable. Les livres
I–IV ont été composés de poèmes courts—le plus souvent de deux à cinq vers—sur
les vices et les vertus. Dans le livre I (p. 99), on explique comment la béatitude
absolue se cache derrière ces trois règles fondamentales:

> Numen cole summum. Tibi prima, ultima, meta haec.
> Ne prodige te: nec tua prode negligendo.
> Ne cui facias, quae tibi facta non placerent.
> Istis tribus omnis capitur beatitudo.
> Quam qui nihil fecerit, exibit inanis. (p. 99)

> Vénère le plus grand Dieu. C'est ta première et dernière
>   mission.
> Ne te dissipe pas et ne néglige pas tes talents.
> Ne fais pas à autrui ce que tu ne voudrais pas qu'on te fasse.
> La béatitude se cache dans ces trois règles.
> Celui qui ne trouve pas cela important est indigne.

La béatitude n'est donc pas une situation sainte où l'on est inactif; nous devons agir
et nous améliorer afin de trouver le juste milieu entre l'exagération et l'insuffisance de
nos talents reçus et nous devons également chercher l'harmonie avec autrui. Tout cela
est précédé par le commandement principal qui est celui d'honorer Dieu.

Après cette introduction religieuse vient l'*Initium praeceptorum* (p. 100), "le début
des préceptes", où Scaliger annonce le passage aux *Sapientium dicta vetusta*, "les beaux
proverbes des sages", sous la forme de centaines de vers intitulés *Nosce te; A te pende
& virtute; Sustine & abstine; Taciturnitas; Voluptas noxia; Virtus; Lites fuge* etcetera. Les
Epidorpides sont donc la reproduction personnelle d'un mélange de sagesse de la Bible
et des philosophes anciens, formulée en vers. A partir du livre IV, la longueur moy-
enne des poèmes augmente et, à partir du livre VI, l'oeuvre a comporté à l'evidence
un caractère passionnément religieux. Je cite une des nombreuses exclamations
religieuses:

Jesu mea spes, lux mea, deus meus, meus Rex (l. VII, p. 298)

Le ton vif des oraisons et des poèmes, ton qui valait à Scaliger en tant qu'humaniste
érudit de solides ennemis (Erasmus, Rabelais, Cardan), se retrouve dans les poèmes
exaltés qui s'adressent à Jésus et à Dieu. Les thèmes des trois derniers *Libri octo* sont

quasiment empruntés aux textes bibliques, la plupart au Nouveau Testament.

Ces qualités, l'émotion et la force d'une dévotion poétique, ont inspiré Johan de Brune de Oude (l'Ancien) qui vivait à peu près un siècle plus tard (1588–1658) que Scaliger (1484–1558). Johan de Brune a étudié le droit à Leyde où il fit la connaissance du professeur Joseph Juste Scaliger (décédé en 1609). Il a passé le plus clair de son temps, avant et après ses études, à Middelbourg, la capitale de la province de Zélande, où il commença une carrière d'avocat en 1617, et ensuite débuta comme magistrat communal. De plus il s'occupa pendant plusieurs années des fonctions dans l'Eglise Réformée. Sa carrière politique culmine lorsqu'il obtient la fonction la plus importante du gouvernement provincial, celle de grand pensionnaire. En même temps que son travail de fonctionnaire, il écrit des poèmes et de la prose. Nous retrouvons les deux genres dans les *Emblemata of Sinne-werck* de 1624.[4]

Les *Emblemata* ont été illustrés par 51 merveilleuses gravures d'après des dessins d'Adriaan van der Venne, dans lesquelles nous ne trouvons aucune trace de la mythologie conventionnelle, mais un grand nombre d'intérieurs et d'extérieurs très réalistes comme il en existait en Zélande et en Hollande. Les images innocentes, parfois attendrissantes prennent leur signification la plus profonde dans la composition fixe d'une devise, une subscription de huit vers et une explication en prose fréquemment agrémentée de citations et de poèmes. L'explication peut nous surprendre par rapport à ce que l'on observe à première vue.

Ceci s'observe par exemple dans l'Emblème 10, illustré avec l'image d'un couple avec un enfant pleurant pendant la nuit. La mère le nourrit et le père le console. La devise est: "Crie dans le besoin pour le pain du ciel" et l'épigramme explique que Dieu nous console avec une chanson joyeuse de la mort. Le thème général de l'emblème est le dégoût de la vie terrestre avec une perspective réconfortante de l'au-delà, auquel De Brune consacre huit pages d'explication. L'objectif général des *Emblemata*, selon le sous-titre, est de montrer et de pallier les erreurs de notre siècle à l'aide d'images, de poèmes et d'explications. La calomnie, le désir charnel, l'ingratitude, l'hypocrisie, les litiges, la simulation, l'impudeur, l'indiscrétion, l'oisiveté, l'amour-propre, la cécité, voilà quelques erreurs humaines dont De Brune traite dans ses 51 chapitres. Si les vertus existent, elles sont presque absentes et doivent être réanimées. C'est avec des raisonnements de ce genre, qui foisonnent dans toute son oeuvre, que De Brune rejoint la compagnie de Scaliger et de tant d'autres écrivains moralistes.

Grâce à la présence dans les *Emblemata* d'auteurs de la Pléiade comme Ronsard, contemporain de Scaliger, nous pouvons parler d'un ouvrage assez moderne. Le style des explications est également moderne, dans le sens où il fait penser au style des *Essais* de Montaigne par la façon de donner au lecteur un jugement personnel sur toutes sortes de sujets en lui parlant à la première personne. Montaigne était bien connu dans le monde de la littérature néerlandaise mais le Zélandais introduit quelque chose de nouveau en pratiquant ce style aux Pays-Bas.

---

[4] J. de Brune, *Emblemata of Sinne-werck: voorghestelt in beelden, ghedichten, en breeder uijtlegginghen, tot uyt-druckinghe, en verbeteringhe van verscheijden feijlen onser eeuwe* (Amsterdam, 1624).

Il y a dix-neuf poèmes latins de Scaliger dans quatorze des 51 *Emblemata*.[5] Les poèmes latins sont intégralement repris (sauf deux) et accompagnés de la traduction néerlandaise réalisée par De Brune. La qualité de cette traduction est très bonne et pleine de trouvailles poétiques. Il y a de petites fautes d'impression dans les textes latins qui en général ne figurent pas dans les poèmes traduits. Je crois que l'opinion de Lipse en ce qui concerne la technique d'édition de Joseph Juste Scaliger n'est pas partagée par De Brune, même si celui-ci l'a connue. Il a pu lui-même faire une sélection parmi le nombre excessif de ces poèmes qui rejoignaient les thèmes de ses emblèmes.

Une autre religion, les mêmes pensées

De quelle façon De Brune présente-t-il Scaliger dans ses emblèmes? Prenons l'Emblème 5 avec la devise: "Tout est trop petit, si c'est ordinaire". L'image représente un enfant attrapé par deux femmes. Si l'enfant était lâché, il ferait ce que ferait tout enfant, symbole de la bêtise enclin au péché. L'homme ne veut pas prendre le chemin qui se présente devant lui, mais bien au contraire prendre celui qui lui est interdit. L'homme refuse ainsi le chemin éclairé de Dieu et recherche plutôt les secrets cachés et obscurs. L'explication développe le thème que l'homme ne doit pas chercher à expliquer le monde entier par la raison. Ce plaidoyer en faveur de la foi est argumenté de citations d'autorités telles que Euclide, Socrate, l'Apôtre, Lipse, Augustin, Platon, Plutarque et bien d'autres. Vers la fin du cento il y a un poème latin, sans indication d'auteur ou de référence. Nous remarquons la même construction dans les Emblèmes 6, 7 et 10, commentés également par des poèmes latins anonymes, qui se révèlent être tous empruntés à Scaliger. La solution apparaît dans l'Emblème 15 où De Brune révèle sa source: "(Epidorpid. lib.)", et qualifie l'auteur comme "ce grand Jules". Enfin dans l'Emblème 21 le nom complet de "Jules Scaliger" est révélé. De Brune exprime encore son admiration pour Scaliger par exemple en le qualifiant de "génie immortel" (Emb. 22) ou en l'appelant "cet aigle supérieur dans ses desserts" (Emb. 24). Le nom complet de Jules Scaliger n'apparaît donc qu'une seule fois, mais cette seule fois supprime la supposition que De Brune a craint de nommer sa référence peut-être parce que lui-même un véritable protestant, ne pouvait citer un fervent catholique. Cette citation unique, placée au beau milieu des citations de Scaliger, était suffisante pour honorer Scaliger comme il se doit. J'interprète toutes les autres allusions avant et après comme un élément du jeu littéraire pour le lecteur.

Le protestant De Brune se montre d'ailleurs dans son oeuvre un homme du piétisme, tendance chrétienne qui dépasse les Nations et les Eglises, en surmontant les différences réligieuses et dogmatiques.[6] Nous verrons (ci-dessous) que De Brune a une grande prédilection pour les poèmes de Scaliger qui sont basés sur des textes bibliques.

---

[5] Les vers signalés de Scaliger se trouvent dans les emblèmes 5, 6, 7, 10, 15, 19, 20, 21, 22, 24, 26, 28 et 29.

[6] Voir W. J. op 't Hof, "De godsdienstige ligging van De Brune," in P. J. Verkruijsse (ed.): *Johan de Brune de Oude (1588–1658). Een Zeeuws literator en staatsman uit de zeventiende eeuw.* (Middelbourg, 1990), 26, 27.

Discordia Christiana

Son choix a été facilité par les titres que Scaliger a donné a ses poèmes (les titres manquent dans les emblèmes de De Brune à une seule exception). *Sobria sapientia* (l. IV, p. 208) est le premier poème qu'utilise De Brune dans sa thèse que l'homme doit tout d'abord se fier à la foi et non à la raison (Emb. 5). On y note avec intérêt que, si les Etats ont bien leurs secrets sans lesquels ils ne pourraient bien gouverner, pourquoi ne serait-il pas permis à Dieu d'avoir ses secrets? Cet écho observé dans le travail de De Brune en tant que fonctionnaire politique, reparaît plusieurs fois dans les emblèmes.

Un exemple très évident du rôle politique joué par De Brune est visible dans l'Emblème 6, "L'union fait la force". Le poème de Scaliger *Discordia Christiana* (l. VI, p. 251) est la conclusion parfaite du discours de De Brune sur les conséquences terribles d'un manque d'union dans la patrie. Il s'écrie:

> Qui ne voit pas les cicatrices honteuses (et Dieu permet que la croûte de la plaie soit tombée aujourd'hui) du corps de l'état dont nous nous réjouissons d'être des membres vivants? N'avons-nous pas frôlé un immense bain de sang général, un massacre mutuel? Et pourquoi donc? Pour une partialité amère et pour quelques têtes lunatiques qui auraient préféré voir la révolution de notre état au lieu de se défaire des excréments de l'estomac infecté? (p. 49)

De Brune veillait prudemment à ce que cette condamnation sévère soit appuyée par maints exemples de la Bible et de l'Antiquité, parce qu'il s'agit d'un événement actuel: la jeune république néerlandaise, par un conflit interne entre les remontrants et les contre-remontrants sur l'interprétation de la doctrine de la prédestination, avait frôlé une guerre civile. Le prince Maurits, qui avait choisi le côté du part contre-remontrant, avait mis fin au conflit en 1618 par l'emprisonnement de quelques-uns de ses adversaires les plus importants, entre autres Hugo Grotius et le vieux politicien Johan van Oldenbarnevelt. Grotius, condamné à la prison à vie, put échapper, mais Oldenbarnevelt fut exécuté en 1619 sur l'ordre du prince. De Brune, sympathisant du prince, me semble faire allusion à la mort d'Oldenbarnevelt en parlant de "cicatrices honteuses" et de "la plaie" encore très sensible, et en utilisant les mots "où nous nous réjouissons d'être des membres *vivants*", suivis immédiatement de l'antithèse du bain de sang. Je crois que le poème *Discordia Christiana*, du reste, ne permettait pas uniquement de commenter l'emblème, mais servait de point de départ pour arriver à cette conclusion.

Scaliger décrivait une telle expérience douloureuse, lorsqu'il écrivait l'élégie *Discordia Christiana*. Le calme de la petite ville d'Agen, située entre Bordeaux et Toulouse, où il habitait, avait été troublé par le schisme de l'Eglise en 1538, lorsque l'inquisiteur dominicain Louis de Rochette y arriva pour enquêter sur les doctrines fausses et réprouvées. Ce dernier constitua 71 dépositions dont quatre accusaient Scaliger.[7]

---

[7] A. C. Fiorato, "Jules-César Scaliger bien ou mal sentant," in *Acta Scaligeriana. Actes du Colloque International organisé pour le cinquième centenaire de la naissance de Jules-César Scaliger.* Recueil des travaux de la Société Académique d'Agen, 1986, 14, 15. Et: V. Hall, "Life of Julius Caesar Scaliger," in *Transactions of the American Philosophical Society* 40 (1950): 119, 120.

Bien que le jugement du tribunal fut favorable à Scaliger, l'événement le choqua profondément.

Dans les emblèmes cités jusqu'ici, j'ai supposé que De Brune avait pris Scaliger comme source de ses thèmes. Or, à l'Emblème 15 la supposition devient une certitude. L'utilisation de Scaliger y est maximale: quatre poèmes (et quelques citations d'autres auteurs) pour illustrer le thème que l'amour du prochain s'est éloigné à cause de la discorde des hommes. La devise de l'emblème est "Comment êtes-vous donc, Christ, ainsi divisé?" L'image montre l'histoire biblique de Samson (Juges 15:4–5), qui par vengeance jette dans un champ de blé des renards dont les queues sont attachées les unes aux autres par des torches enflammées, pour détruire la récolte. "Les queues sont attachées mais les têtes sont divisées", explique l'épigramme. De Brune parle ici sans détour avec grande fermeté:

> Nul besoin de construire ni de remplir le cerveau avec toutes les sagesses et les sciences profondes, visant même à scruter les secrets du ciel. Si vous n'avez pas l'amour, vous serez vaincu par le diable, dont vous n'atteindrez pas la raison. Les gens qui semblent m'arracher les dents, ont la bouche pleine de la parole de Dieu et le coeur plein d'aigreurs, empêtrés dans la haine et dans toutes les injustices. (p. 117)

Johan de Brune a de façon cohérente introduit les quatre vers, répartis dans les livres VI et VIII des *Epidorpides*, pour composer le texte développent le thème de l'emblème. Au point de départ *Caritas refrixit* (l. VI, p. 253) est le centre de la thèse amère qui veut démontrer que l'amour a disparu. Ensuite la situation que chacun n'en fait qu'à sa scandaleuse volonté est éclairée par *Sibi quisque Deum fecit* (l. VI, p. 258). Suit l'incitation de retourner à l'amour à travers le poème *Caritatis commendatio* (l. VIII, p. 317). Le texte termine en demandant d'arrêter la fureur et la vengeance avec *Non nocere nocentis* (l. VIII, p. 318). De Brune a bien observé que Scaliger a puisé essentiellement son inspiration dans l'Evangile de Saint Luc, comme celui se vérifie en beaucoup d'autres poèmes dans ces livres. *Caritas refrixit* est basé sur Luc 11:30–33, l'histoire du voyageur dévalisé et molesté qui n'est secouru ni par un prêtre ni par un Lévite, mais bien par le Samaritain méprisé de tous. Par *Caritatis commendatio*, une parabole remarquable d'un bûcheron qui se lève pendant le gel matinal pour couper le bois lui procurant un peu de chaleur, nous sommes exhortés à chasser le froid infernal qui nous menace par le feu de l'amour. Ceci représente à mon avis une paraphrase poétique de Luc 3:9, nous incitant à couper à la hache les racines de l'arbre qui ne porte pas de bons fruits et à jeter au feu le bois de cet arbre. *Non nocere nocentis* est un développement de Luc 9:54–56 où les disciples Jacques et Jean sont à ce point irrités, quand Jésus est mal accueilli en Samarie, qu'ils veulent que les Samaritains soient frappés par la foudre. A la fin de cet emblème, De Brune nous conseille d'être aussi bien Marie que Marthe, qui incarnent la foi et le travail. C'est une interprétation pragmatique de la Bible (Luc 11:38–42) laquelle nous dit plutôt qu'il vaut mieux être comme Marie, c'est à dire faire prévaloir le spirituel. En ceci De Brune rejoint également Scaliger, non pas dans l'écriture mais dans l'esprit à travers les vers intitulés *Et credere & facere* (l. VII, p. 292).

Après le sommet quantitatif de l'Emblème 15, le nombre de poésies de Scaliger diminue de la même manière qu'il avait augmenté auparavant. Après l'Emblème 29 il n'y en a plus.

"Sobria sapientia": la valeur de la raison

Les textes et les raisonnements que De Brune a empruntés à Scaliger nous montrent que le fondement religieux est l'aspect essentiel de leurs rapports littéraires. On le voit aussi dans leur usage fréquent du motif biblique de l'effrayante oisivité. Tous deux sont également convaincus que le bon chrétien doit rendre son *Otium negotiosum* (l. I, p. 130), une conviction dont leurs vastes oeuvres sont la preuve.

Face à l'abondance moraliste et chrétienne des *Epidorpides*, De Brune a été capable de nuancer ses opinions dans les *Emblemata* à travers les emblèmes divers avec la même cohérence que nous avons remarquée dans l'Emblème 15. Regardons par exemple le développement des idées en ce qui concerne le motif de la raison dans quelques emblèmes. Dans son plaidoyer en faveur de la foi qui échouerait à cause de la raison (Emb. 5), *Sobria sapientia* soutient son avis que la raison est sans valeur pour une vie chrétienne. Puis, dans l'Emblème 21 intitulé "L'homme est aveugle dans ce qu'il aime", De Brune regrette la perte de la raison parfaite et esquisse avec nostalgie la situation originale et idéale du "petit monde que nous appelons l'homme" (donc le microcosme), lors de sa création. Alors la raison était illuminée par une clarté céleste, notre seul éclaireur menant le chemin de la volonté. La volonté ne voulait rien qui ne soit pas d'abord autorisé par la raison. Et l'âme avait un pouvoir absolu sur les sens. Mais à l'heure actuelle: *Quantum mutatus ab illo* sommes-nous! Le motif de l'homme maintenant aveugle et corrompu est soutenu par *Caecitas in praesenti vita* (l. VIII, p. 316) et *Perversitas* (l. V, p. 241). Entre parenthèses, la combinaison de "petit monde" et de ce *quantum mutatus*, perfection et chute (p. 154), nous la trouvons aussi dans l'ouvrage de Robert Burton, *The anatomy of melancholy*, ce qui m'a suggéré que De Brune connaissait ou possédait très tôt une édition de ce livre publié en 1621. En tout cas il était bien informé des publications importantes de la République des Lettres malgré son isolement insulaire.

Cependant, cet état déplorable de l'homme devenu la proie du diable après la chute offre quelques espoirs. Nous voilà devant une tournure positive dans l'Emblème 26 intitulé "Celui qui multiplie la science, multiplie la peine (Solomon)", dans lequel De Brune explique que "les lettres constituent un secours valable pour acquérir la vertu et un joyau précieux pour orner celle-ci" (p. 186). Si l'homme fait ses études à l'école de la sagesse, il peut rendre son âme plus invincible et plus invulnérable, qu'un bouclier ne le fait pour le corps. *Literae sine iudicio* (l. IV, p. 219) de Scaliger vient à l'appui de ce motif, dans lequel la raison retrouve sa dignité.

La suite logique est le sujet de l'importance d'une bonne éducation, présenté dans l'Emblème 28 "La coutume rend calleux". L'image nous montre un rat qui, contrairement à sa nature, éclaire sans peur avec une bougie une compagnie de personnes. La coutume, raisonne De Brune, est notre seconde nature, non, elle est même plus forte que notre nature et l'on ne saurait commencer trop tôt à cultiver les coutumes désirées. Le *Naturam studiis augere* de Scaliger (l. V, p. 243) est dès lors à sa place dans le cadre de l'approche adéquate de la jeunesse. On découvre avec surprise dans cet emblème (p. 197) une trace de l'influence exercée sur De Brune par les *Exercitationes exotericae*, l'oeuvre de Scaliger fulminant contre les opinions scientifiques de Hieronymus Cardanus.[8] Cela montre que son intérêt pour Scaliger ne se limitait pas aux *Epidorpides* (il y en a d'autres marques dans les livres de De Brune).

En résumant, nous pouvons constater que Johan de Brune de Oude a trouvé un coreligionnaire dans Julius Caesar Scaliger. Le protestant De Brune a été influencé surtout par les *Epidorpides*, le dernier ouvrage poétique et d'inspiration chrétienne-moraliste du catholique Scaliger. De Brune a montré son admiration pour le poète spirituel néo-latiniste d'un siècle auparavant, par la sélection et la traduction d'une vingtaine des *Epidorpides* dans les explications de ses *Emblemata*, un essai également d'inspiration chrétienne-moraliste. Les poèmes de Julius Caesar Scaliger dans les *Emblemata* constituent ainsi une contribution importante au chapitre de l'influence littéraire de Scaliger sur les Pays-Bas du dix-septième siècle.

Rotterdam

---

[8] J. C. Scaliger, *Exotericarum Exercitationum liber XV, De Subtilitate, ad Hieronymum Cardanum* (Frankfurt, 1612), 705.

La guerra de Africa, un hecho clave en el De rebus gestis a Francisco Ximenio Cisnerio libri octo *de Alvar Gómez de Castro (1515–1580)*

Mª JOSÉ LÓPEZ DE AYALA Y GENOVÉS

El período que abarca este libro se desarrolla en la línea del asentamiento de unas bases nacionales sólidas que desde 1482, tres años después de que el matrimonio entre Isabel y Fernando uniera las coronas de Castilla y Aragón, se emprendieron a lo largo de diez años mediante una serie de campañas, que consiguieron expulsar a los musulmanes del Reino de Granada, donde gozaban de todos los derechos desde el siglo XIII[1]. Esta fórmula simplificada de las guerras como parte de un proceso de autodefinición territorial, dentro de unas fronteras más o menos tradicionales y de unas lenguas aproximadamente nacionales, se fue abriendo paso por toda Europa. El emperador era, por aquel entonces, la fuente en la que bebía un sistema de honores y patronazgo que obligaba a las ciudades y príncipes ambiciosos a buscar sus favores.

En el mapa político, prescindiendo de la conquista de Granada, las fronteras de Europa occidental permanecieron ostensiblemente estables entre 1450 y 1618, hecho sorprendente si lo comparamos con los masivos avances de los turcos en el sureste y el mediterráneo.

Los temas que la época heredó de la tradición medieval constituyen el núcleo de la teoría política del Renacimiento, que se basa, en gran medida, en un substrato donde afloran todas las teorías filosóficas resultando difícil sobreestimar la evolución del pensamiento político español, aunque la importancia tipológica de éste estriba en que expresa la primera fisura social y cultural, que se produce en el tránsito de la Edad Media a la Edad Moderna, concretamente en el tema social y político que nos ocupa, pues frente a algunos seguidores que hacen contribución al estudio del problema de la guerra, otros abogan por el retorno al pacifismo bíblico, por lo que las doctrinas antimilitaristas no quedan confinadas sino que se desarrollan por toda Europa.

---

[1] J. R. Hale, *Guerra y Sociedad en la Europa del Renacimiento (1450–1620)* (Madrid, 1990), 21.

En este marco debe establecerse una distinción entre las guerras civiles o internacionales por un lado y, por otro, las rebeliones armadas variables en su intensidad. La 'guerra' atañía a la sociedad y para los hombres de Estado la paz global era un mito. La vida intelectual española en esta época era rica, influenciada por las teorías agustiniana, tomista y erasmista. Al igual que Francia e Italia, España contribuyó a un desarrollo significativo del pensamiento político, como se ve al principio del siglo XVI, cuando Castilla era el Reino europeo, en el que se habían establecido más firmemente los cimientos de un estado nacional, aunque esta situación se vio alterada por una doble crisis institucional. Trás la muerte de la Reina Isabel (1504), Castilla se encontró con un emperador en su trono y dueña de un mosaico de territorios ultramarinos, que no encajaban en ningún sistema político conocido. Castilla, en un primer momento, se ve obligada a seguir una ambigua vía intermedia para, en años posteriores al 1520, ser el símbolo de España y convertirse en el centro del Imperio respondiendo al sistema renacentista de estados. En este marco territorial, político, religioso y social, nace, se educa y escribe el autor al que nos vamos a referir.

Alvar Gómez de Castro (1515–1580) nace en Santa Eulalia o Santa Olalla (Toledo), cursó estudios de Humanidades en la Universidad de Alcalá donde fue discípulo de Juan Ramírez de Toledo; en 1539 obtuvo la cátedra de Griego y ese mismo año se graduó como maestro en Artes; en 1550 marchó a Toledo donde desempeñó la cátedra de Retórica y Griego, que alternó con el cargo de capellán de la Universidad de Santa Catalina. Impulsó la edición de las obras de San Isidoro (1599) y en los últimos años se ocupó de la revisión de los códices de las *Origenes seu Etimologiae*. Murió el 16 de septiembre de 1580.

Este autor legó a la posteridad el *De rebus gestis a Francisco Ximenio Cisnerio libri octo*, obra escrita en buen latín y ejemplo de una biografía muy completa, que responde a la categoría que la genealogía adquirió en esta época y a la que se dedicaron los cronistas oficiales, historiadores de este tiempo, quienes elaboraron escritos genealógicos de interés histórico, escasos de crítica, y, por lo general, carentes de valor literario.

Con el Renacimiento parece señalarse un nuevo punto de vista, que acoge, como esencialmente históricas, manifestaciones de actividad social diferentes de la política, que también constituyen la materia histórica, a saber, los hechos del sujeto, individual o social, cuya vida se estudia y que pretenden ahondar en el estudio de esta misma. La variación en el modo de concebir el sujeto de la historia se venía perfilando desde hacía siglos, siendo una de las características el concentrar la vida de un Estado o de una sociedad particular en la persona de su representante legítimo u otra persona influyente. Se cumple, en cierto modo, una ley de herencia que la historia traía de su progenitora la epopeya viniendo a ser historia heroica, en vez de historia social, con lo que vuelve aflorar el pensamiento de Quintiliano quien se remite a la tradición de una historia heroica cuando escribe: *est enim (sc. historia) proxima poetis, et quodam modo carmen solutum est.*[2]

---

[2] Quintiliano, *Institutiones Oratoriae* 10,1,31: "la historia está muy cerca de la poesía y es una suerte de poema en prosa".

En primer lugar nos referiremos[3] al valor de la biografía como un subgénero literario en el que queda constancia evidente de la categoría de su creador, el autor y, por lo tanto, a la explicación literaria de la misma, que debe ser enfocada en función de la personalidad y vida del escritor.

Esta biografía juzgada a la luz que arroja sobre la obra poética puede considerarse satisfactoria. En este sentido cabe defenderla y justificarla como estudio del hombre genio, de su desenvolvimiento moral, intelectual y emocional, lo que la reviste de interés intrínseco propio, es decir, el arte del autor desplaza el foco de atención a la personalidad humana[4] de Jiménez de Cisneros de quien dice que: *ubi ita integre vitam instituit, ut ab omnibus bonis eius amicitia certatim ambiretur.* En esta obra se recoge una biografía[5] muy completa, que rastrea los antecedentes del cardenal y está considerada como la mejor e indispensable para conocer su persona y su época; de él se dice: *magnum virum Ximenium esse, et augurari se, ab illo coenobio ad praeclarissimam aliquam dignitatem abducendum*[6] y añade el biógrafo: *enim vero pugilem deus hactenus in umbra exercitum, in mediam ecclesiae arenam parabat immittere.*[7]

Con esta y otras obras de la época la genealogía adquirió ahora gran desarrollo. No sólo se aplicaron a ello muchos de los escritores que laboraban y publicaban bajo la protección de los nobles, sino especialmente los cronistas oficiales, a quienes los gajes de su cargo independizaban económicamente.

En segundo lugar nuestro trabajo ha intentado analizar el contenido del libro cuarto del *De rebus gestis* en el que se recogen dos hechos fundamentales: *Inter alia multa quae sunt per Ximenium praeclare suscepta et confecta, duo sunt in oculis omnium posita, Academia Complutensis de qua hactenus egimus, et bellum Africanum de quo nunc sumus dicturi.*[8]

---

[3] Remitimos para información bibliográfica sobre el autor al trabajo de Antón Alvar Ezquerra, *Acercamiento a la poesía latina de Alvar Gómez de Castro (Ensayo de una biografía y edición de su poesía latina)*, 2 vols. (Madrid, 1980); idem, "Alvar Gómez de Castro, humanista", *RFE* 72 (1982): 193–210; idem, "Alvar Gómez de Castro y la historiografía del siglo XVI. La vida de Cisneros", en Manuel Revuelta Sañudo y Ciriaco Morón Arroyo, eds., *El Erasmismo en España*, Ponencias del coloquio celebrado en la Biblioteca de Menéndez Pelayo del 10 al 14 de junio de 1985, Estudios de literatura y pensamiento hispánicos (Santander, 1985).

[4] Alvar Gómez de Castro, *De las hazañas de Francisco Jiménez de Cisneros*. Edición, traducción y notas por José Oroz Reta (Madrid, 1984), 34; para el texto latino *De rebus gestis* I 933, cf. *Hispania Illustrata* (Frankfurt, 1603) I, 927–1156: "llevó una vida tan recta que todas las personas honradas se disputaban a porfía su amistad . . . dio muestras evidentes de un espíritu amigo del cultivo de las letras".

[5] J. López de Toro, *Perfiles humanos de Cisneros, Trayectoria de una biografía* (Madrid, 1958), 12; A. de la Torre y del Cerro, en el prólogo a su edición del *Memorial* de Vallejo, publicado hace 70 años con el título: *Memorial de la vida de Fray Francisco Jiménez de Cisneros* (Madrid, 1913).

[6] Gómez de Castro, *De las hazañas*, 37, cf. *De rebus gestis* I 934: "Jiménez era un varón extraordinario y, según el Cardenal Mendoza, saldría de aquel convento para alguna elevada dignidad, y eso cedería en gran provecho para toda la República cristiana".

[7] Gómez de Castro, *De las hazañas*, 39; cf. *De rebus gestis* I 935: "en realidad Dios entrenaba a su atleta, hasta ahora soldado de retaguardia, para lanzarlo en medio del estadio de su Iglesia".

[8] Gómez de Castro, *De las hazañas*, 249; cf. *De rebus gestis* IV 1035: "pareció oportuno abarcar

La idea de la guerra, esto es, cómo se ha difundido, articulado y relacionado en determinadas épocas constituye un asunto de gran importancia histórica[9]. Se ha llegado a decir que la historia no debe detenerse en el relato de las guerras y de las batallas, sino ocuparse principalmente en las relaciones de la vida civil y política, pero en este caso dice Gómez de Castro: *Nescires ad quam rem ille propendior natura esset, disciplinis provehendis, et pacis muneribus obeundis, an potius bellicis studiis exercendis*[10]. El *De rebus gestis* al hacer un análisis de las causas y del perfil de su personaje, nos presenta un testimonio único en relación con la actitud y postura ante la conquista de Orán: *magis ad bellica exercitia a natura effictum esse iudico . . . Sed hoc nostro de eo iudicium ex Africano bello certum esse, luce clarius, ut existimo, apparebit . . . summis ducibus fuisset procul dubio annumerandus.*[11]

Planteado el tema, tendríamos que hacernos algunas preguntas ¿qué lugar ocupa Jiménez de Cisneros en el tema de la paz y de la guerra dentro del ámbito de los humanistas del Renacimiento? ¿cuáles son las huellas clásicas en la estrategia, ataque, composición de la armada etc.? ¿es Jiménez un adelantado en la expansión y conquista en las tierras africanas? ¿qué aporta la colonización del norte de África?

En el tema de la paz y de la guerra Jiménez se encuentra emparentado con Ginés de Sepúlveda, quien defendía la licitud de las guerras de conquista de todas las tierras de los indios como base y condición previa para su evangelización y para imponerles la conversión a la fe cristiana casi a la fuerza. En su obra *Democrates Secundus* se hace eco de todas las opiniones en que se basaba la vieja teoría imperialista y de dominación que justificaba la intervención de los cristianos y la fundamenta con argumentos tomados del Antiguo Testamento, de la teología y la filosofía, teniendo en cuenta que la mayoría de los juristas de la corte opinaban como él e incluso los colonizadores, apoyados en estos principios, defendían los privilegios adquiridos y los abusos de encomiendas. También Sepúlveda comprueba con agrado que un tanto por ciento de los jóvenes españoles se entregan por igual a las letras y a las armas, aunque a muchos se les plantee el grave problema de ser soldado y cumplir con su obligación y, a la vez, ser un buen cristiano; ante este dilema él confía en la autoridad de los príncipes.

En sus escritos se evidencia que la colonización es la dominación de la perfección sobre la imperfección, de la fuerza sobre la debilidad, de la más alta virtud sobre el vicio[12]. En su teoría sobre la guerra justa, que justifica a partir de la noción de

---

en un solo libro de nuestra historia estas dos materias tan amplias (la Universidad de Alcalá y la guerra de Africa) para que, por el cotejo de ambas entre sí, llegue a ponerse de manifiesto cuánto poder tenía, en la paz y en la guerra, este varón magnífico y sensato".

[9] Hale, *Guerra y Sociedad*, 17.

[10] Gómez de Castro, *De las hazañas*, 249–250; cf. *De rebus gestis* IV 1021: "no sabríamos a cuál de los dos asuntos estaba por naturaleza más inclinado, si en promover las disciplinas y en cumplir sus deberes de paz o en llevar a cabo sus afanes bélicos".

[11] Gómez de Castro, *De las hazañas*, 250; cf. *De rebus gestis* IV 1021: "creerán sin duda que era amigo de la paz y la cultura . . . sin embargo . . . estimo que estaba hecho por naturaleza más para las prácticas militares y belicosas . . . Y si los testimonios que él dejó relativos a la paz son más famosos, su plan de vida y la persona de su pontificado no obró nada que no se ajustara más a las heridas y a la muerte . . . y habría sido contado entre los grandes generales de su tiempo".

[12] Juan Ginés de Sepúlveda, *Democrates Secundus*, 16: *Maneat igitur constitutumque sit sapientissimis*

orden, exige comenzar por un análisis de la paz, que nos llevaría a reconocer que es necesario querer la paz y no hacer la guerra nada más que por necesidad[13]. En definitiva, intenta justificar los caracteres de una guerra justa, fundamentada en la autoridad del príncipe; en que la guerra justa venga las injurias y en que siempre prima la intención recta. El concepto de 'guerra' debía ceñirse a su verdadero significado: las guerras se entablan por anhelos de gloria, por la esperanza de obtener un buen botín, por miedo a que más tarde sobrevenga una catástrofe, por vengar un agravio y por defender a los amigos.

En el período que nos ocupa la Europa política era como el plano de una finca, y la guerra una forma social de adquisición de la propiedad. El escalón más amplio de personas, cuyo asentamiento era necesario para poner en marcha la máquina de guerra, incluía a los clérigos influyentes, los terratenientes y los ciudadanos ricos. Se trataba, en conjunto, de un sector instruido. La caraterística más notable es la consideración creciente de la guerra como un fenómeno seglar, distinto de los castigos divinos.

Con este enmarque podemos situarnos ante lo que nosotros hemos llamado 'un hecho clave': la Guerra de África en la vida política y social de Jiménez de Cisneros, pues como dice Gómez de Castro desarrolló una gran parte de su vida y pensamiento en planificar de qué modo y manera arbitraría todos los medios a su alcance: *ut oram illam maritimam nostram faceret*[14]. En esta decisión, aunque él gozó de la confianza de la reina Isabel, muerta ésta, se enfrentó a todas las dificultades y arbitró los medios necesarios para el diálogo, buscando conocer las intenciones con un solo objetivo: *ut Guletae praesidium occuparet*.[15] Una vez más quedan igualmente patentes las razones de Jiménez de Cisneros para comenzar la guerra, a lo que podemos añadir los deseos de toda la juventud cortesana, que estaba ansiosa de aquella guerra.

Todo lo anterior motiva la preparación de una armada bien equipada, con varones selectos y peritos en el arte de guerrear, poniendo al frente de la misma al Alcaide de los Donceles Diego Fernández de Córdoba. La reacción no tarda en llegar y los africanos intentan ahuyentarlos con "hondas, proyectiles y saetas", y no siendo suficiente, ayudados por los mauritanos y númidas de a caballo e infantería, utilizan "las hogueras".

Diego Fernández de Córdoba muere el 15 de julio en combate y entonces Jiménez quiere que se le nombre y encomiende tal empresa pues, a pesar de su formación y del decoro de la personalidad que ostentaba, anhelaba llevar la lanza y el escudo, en vez del báculo y el capelo. El rey accede a la petición alegando que había

---

viris auctoribus, prudentes, probos, et humanos dissimilibus imperare iustum esse, et naturale (*Democrates Segundo, Apología*, ed. Alejandro Coroleu [*Dem.*], Antonio Moreno [*Ap.*] [Pozoblanco, 1997]).

[13] Ginés de Sepúlveda, *Democrates Secundus*, 2: *Ad summam nunquam bellum est, nisi cunctanter, et gravate, et iustissimis, atque adeo necessariis ex causis suscipiendum.*

[14] Gómez de Castro, *De las hazañas*, 251; cf. *De rebus gestis* IV 1021: "lo que más admiré en el empeño de Jiménez fue que, nacido para labrar la salvación y felicidad de la sociedad, se preocupó durante toda su vida de esto sólo: hacer nuestras aquellas costas africanas".

[15] Alvar Gómez de Castro, *De las hazañas*, 251; cf. *De rebus gestis* IV 1021: "hizo que el rey Fernando conquistara Bugía y Trípoli, una vez conquistada Orán y logró que el emperador Carlos V ocupara la fortaleza de la Goleta".

que darle gracias, según se merecía, porque siendo un hombre tan entrado en años y casi agotado por sus constantes trabajos, se ofrecía con ardor juvenil a una guerra durísima.

A partir de este momento comienzan los preparativos de un nuevo ataque. Se organizan los trirremes del Reino, las naves de guerra y de espolón, los barriles para el agua, la pólvora, que pudieran comprar o el azufre o nitro, que pudieran tomar de las minas de los particulares. Se hacen levas de soldados y se forma un ejército de cuatro mil de a caballo y diez mil de a pie. Todo exige una situación económica favorable, que es respaldada en su totalidad por los eclesiásticos, en especial el cabildo de Toledo. Este gran montaje muestra el poder de un hombre para dilatar la religión y defender la nación. De nuevo las insidias atacaban a Jiménez de Cisneros considerando que era vano y temerario que se ocupara de una asunto de tanta importancia.

El día fijado la armada, compuesta de ochenta naves ligeras, diez trirremes, que ahora se llaman galeras; naves pequeñas; diez mil infantes, cuatro mil jinetes . . . tuvo un viento favorable y levadas las anclas zarpó del puerto de Cartagena. El desarrollo de todo el ataque lleva intercalado dos augurios "el de la cabeza cortada" y "el de las nubes" que indicaban la victoria de los españoles, por lo que Jiménez de Cisneros dice a su prefecto que mande a sus soldados a trabar combate, y la seguridad y firmeza de sus palabras hace que se interpreten como un oráculo divino más que un consejo de hombre. Está muy clara la descripción del botín: grande y rico, alrededor de quinientos mil ducados.

Termina la descripción con una serie de prodigios: la señal de una cruz y la exclamación del obispo "con esta cruz venceremos"; la aparición de un jabalí, ante el que todos gritaron que era Mahoma y fue atravesado con las flechas; una bandada de buitres que revoloteaba sobre el ejército y hacía predecir el dicho "los buitres siguen a los ejércitos"; finalmente la aparición de dos arcos iris suspendidos sobre Orán como señal de victoria.

Todos estos hechos concluyen con la toma de la ciudad y la comunicación a Jiménez, quien con la cruz delante y rodeado del ejército victorioso entró en la Alcazaba y se le entregaron las llaves. Ante tan sorprendente resultado, él alabó públicamente la labor de los jefes y tribunos militares y conforme a la categoría de cada uno les regaló collares, brazaletes, adornos númidas, etc. A su vez se recogieron más de sesenta armamentos de guerra hechos de bronce y bien pertrechados: *catapultarum, scorpionum, balistarum et iaculorum immensus numerus.*[16]

Escribe Gómez de Castro que se corría la anécdota de aplicar a Jiménez la frase que César, una vez vencido Farnaces, escribió al senado: *Veni, vidi, vici,*[17] que se presenta como un fuerte contraste ante una duda que queda sin aclarar ¿estuvo en Orán Jiménez de Cisneros?, la respuesta parece clara: *quare Ximenii virtus et fortuna, omnium literis et memoria hominum est celebranda, qui Oranum nondum visam, eo ipso quo appulerat die vicerit, subegerit et occupaverit.*[18] Y aquí se cumple lo que dice el pro-

---

¹⁶ Gómez de Castro, *De las hazañas*, 290; cf. *De rebus gestis* IV 1038: "gran número de catapultas, escorpiones, ballestas y armas arrojadizas".

¹⁷ Gómez de Castro, *De las hazañas*, 290; cf. *De rebus gestis* IV 1038: "Llegué, vi, vencí".

¹⁸ Gómez de Castro, *De las hazañas*, 291; cf. *De rebus gestis* IV 1038: "fue digno de ser

quanquam nunc verum esse, ..., suam quemque moribus et industria fortunam fingere, ostendemus.[19]

No nos detenemos en la amplia descripción de los numerosos sucesos que siguieron a la conquista de Orán, sus jefes, soldados, emboscadas etc. Jiménez de Cisneros se marchó definitivamente de la ciudad el 23 de mayo en dirección a Cartagena; pasados los años y diferentes hechos y situaciones: *hic ergo tunc erat rerum nostrarum in Africa status. Ximenius postquam Orani victoriam non ita recentem in hominum memoria esse credidit et se minus seris gratulationibus obtuendendum, Compluto Toletum ... venit ... Durant ad nostram aetatem sacri dies in monumentum Africanae victoriae instituti.*[20]

Concluimos nuestro trabajo con una referencia al tema de la guerra y de la paz desde la visión inevitable de la primera y la justificación del uso de la fuerza en algunas circunstancias por motivos de la responsabilidad de gobierno, aunque las guerras libradas con talante agresivo, nunca fueron aprobadas. Había, pues, una amplia gama de ideas orientadas hacia la búsqueda de la paz que podían irse filtrando hacia los niveles en los que solicitaba el apoyo de la guerra. Pero, por supuesto, ninguna idea tuvo más influencia que el cálculo de ventajas y desventajas en el entorno local inmediato.

La divulgación de las ideas sobre la guerra y la paz, en general, era canalizada a través de proclamas, panfletos, etc. La diferencia de religión, la ampliación de territorios o la ambición de un príncipe no justificaban una guerra. La conclusión es que si una guerra no era un mal *per se*, sin embargo, y dado que puede provocar muchas desgracias, era una de esas empresas que muchas veces se hace mal y, por tanto, exige muchas condiciones para que fuera justa.

Los humanistas cristianos se van a ver obligados a aceptar lo que la tradición clásica admitía desde un principio: la única esperanza de alcanzar la paz radica en el estado. Sus teorías políticas, como las del neoescolasticismo, guardan una estrecha relación y dependencia con sus ideas sobre la guerra. Se comparte la convicción de la época de que la guerra y la autoridad política caminan estrechamente de la mano y se encontrará en los principios de la guerra justa el nexo que le permita mantener unidos dos elementos antitéticos: una sociedad universal, cuya formulación era imprescindible para los intelectuales españoles tras el descubrimiento del Nuevo Mundo, y un concepto de estado basado en los principios dinásticos y territoriales.

La guerra de África una de las constantes de nuestra historia y uno de los yunques más eficaces en que se habrán de forjar los ejércitos españoles, fue, desde el principio, propicia a terribles desastres motivados por la naturaleza del suelo, por la astucia, la tenacidad y el fanatismo de los naturales y por las inagotables reservas de hombres del continente.

---

ensalzado el valor y la suerte de Jiménez quien sin haber visto siquiera la ciudad de Orán, la sometió y ocupó el mismo día en que arribó".

[19] Gómez de Castro, *De las hazañas*, 291; cf. *De rebus gestis* IV 1038: "cada uno se labra su suerte por medio de sus costumbres y actividad o habilidad".

[20] Gómez de Castro, *De las hazañas*, 316; cf. *De rebus gestis* IV 1049: "cuando se dio cuenta que la victoria de Orán ya no era tenida en consideración en el recuerdo de los hombres ... vino desde Alcalá a Toledo ... allí aún perduran los días festivos en recuerdo de la victoria de África".

Al amparo de esta guerra civil Jiménez de Cisneros, quien había nacido en Torrelaguna en 1436, de una familia hidalga, político sagaz, de indomable energía, ya Cardenal, pudo intentar la realización de su sueño de extender por el norte de África el nombre de Cristo. Las guerras de Italia y de África eran una gran escuela donde se formaban quienes habían de ser conquistadores de las Indias. Cisneros resulta un utópico[21], pero con capacidad suficiente para contagiar a reyes, a guerreros y a contemporáneos.

Universidad Nacional de Educación a Distancia, Madrid

---

[21] J. García Oro, *El Cardenal Cisneros. Vida y empresas* (Madrid, 1943), II, 567.

Badius' and Murrho's Commentaries

on Baptista Mantuanus'

Contra Poetas Impudice Loquentes

MARIANO MADRID CASTRO

Baptista Mantuanus' poem *Contra poetas impudice loquentes*, dated in Rome, 20 October 1487, was printed for the first time in Bologna on 1 April 1489[1]. In its one hundred and fifty-six verses the author criticized a literary genre which was validated by the prestige of the works of ancient authors, in particular Catullus[2]. Beccadelli, Pontano, and Marullo were some of the writers who cultivated this genre, which was an added danger to the use of pagan literature in schools. This piece was well-accepted as it illustrated each one of the disciplines which constituted the *studia humanitatis*: grammar, rhetoric, poetry, historiography, and moral philosophy. This poem is in elegiac distichs, with historical references[3], many mythological allusions, and with an unwavering morality which condemned obscenity and all reminders of Epicurean doctrine. In sum, it fought against that plague which Erasmus defined as *nihil aliud (. . .) quam paganismum*[4].

Shortly after the *Contra poetas* appeared in print, two commentaries were published. Both commentaries, however, had been composed almost at the same time, one by Jodocus Badius Ascensius and the other by Sebastianus Murrho. Badius, who also worked as a printer, was well known for his *commentarii familiares*. Among his earliest works is the commentary on the poem of Mantuanus. Murrho, on the other hand, did not become as famous as Badius because of his early death. His only com-

---

[1] Bolonia, Benedictus Hectoris Faelli, 4 April 1489. See M. Madrid Castro, "Baptistae Mantuani contra poetas impudice loquentes," *Humanistica Lovaniensia* 45 (1996): 93 ff.

[2] An author rediscovered in the fourteenth century. See W. Ludwig, "*Catullus renatus*— Anfänge und frühe Entwicklung des catullischen Stils in der neulateinischen Dichtung," in *Litterae Neolatinae* (München, 1989), 162–194.

[3] E.g., the reference to Cato the censor, v. 151.

[4] See Ludwig, "*Catullus renatus*," 187.

mentaries were on three works of Baptista Mantuanus: *Contra poetas* and *Parthenices primae et secundae libri*, and we cannot even be certain as to when they were composed. We do know, however, that they must have been written between 1489 and 1494. At this time, both men were living in relatively close cities, Lyons and Sélestat. Taking this into account, along with the fact that they both commented on the same work, we may ask ourselves if they might have known each other, but let us first review their lives briefly.

There is some doubt as to the birthplace of Badius (1462–1535): Asche (in Brabant) and Ghent (in Flanders) have both been proposed. He himself, however, states on two occasions that he is from the second[5]. He studied in Ghent, Louvain, Ferrara, and Mantua. His trip to Italy must have been before December 1488 or after the academic year 1489[6]. After travelling to Italy, he went to France and established himself in Valence and Lyons, where he taught Latin. His first *commentarii familiares* are based on the classes that he taught there. In Lyons he began working as a printer for Jean Trechsel, where he worked until the end of 1498 or the beginning of 1499. Later he moved to Paris and settled down there.

His stay in Italy seems closely connected with his commentary on *Contra poetas*. As the poem was printed in 1489, he could have had access to it while he was there. It does not seem likely, however, that Badius had contact with the Carmelite, who was in Rome from 1487 to 1489 and later went back and forth between Rome and Bologna.

Badius' commentary on *Contra poetas* was first printed in Lyons, on 14 November 1492. It was included in the *Sylvae morales*, an anthology of the following authors: Virgil, Horace, Persius, Juvenal, Ennius, Baptista Mantuanus, Sulpicio di Veroli, Pseudo-Cato (*dicta*), and Alain de Lille. In this work Badius begins publication of his *commentarii familiares*, which he worked on all his life[7]. The commentary of 1492 was revised in the following edition of 1499, also published in Lyons and by the same printing house.

Murrho's name must have been Sebastian Mor, Murr, or Mörer, in Latin Sebastianus Murrho (1452–1494)[8]. He was born in Colmar, in Alsace, and studied in Sélestat in the prestigious school of Ludwig Dringenberg[9]. He died at the early age of 42 on 19 October 1494[10].

---

[5] See Ph. Renouard, *Bibliographie des impressions et des oeuvres de Josse Badius Ascensius, imprimeur et humaniste. 1462–1535* (repr. New York, ca. 1965), 1: 5ff. It seems, however, that there is still no unanimous opinion with respect to this. Cf. M. J. Desmet-Goethals, "Die Verwendung der Kommentare von Badius, Mancinellus, Erasmus und Corderius in der *Disticha Catonis*-Ausgabe von Livinus Crucius", in *Der Kommentar in der Renaissance* (Boppard, 1975), 75.

[6] Renouard, *Bibliographie*, 1: 9.

[7] Until 1529.

[8] See H. G. Wackernagel, *Die Matrikel der Universität Basel* (Basel, 1951), 1: 54. Cf. Renouard, *Bibliographie*, 1: 147.

[9] C. G. Jöcher, *Allgemeines Gelehrten-Lexicon* (repr. Hildesheim, 1961), s.v. Murrho: "(Murrho) wuchs zu einer Zeit heran, wo Ludwig Dringenberg, aus Westphalen, eine Schule in Schlettstadt errichtet hatte, in der er seine Schüler nach einer eben so angenehmen als leichten Methode, zu einer richtigen Kenntniß der lateinischen Sprache anwies".

[10] On his birth and death, we follow P. Joachimsen, *Jakob Wimpfelings Epitome rerum Germa-*

The well-known Alsatian humanist Jakob Wimpfeling, who was a friend of the commentator, began the correction of Murrho's brief work in September of that same year[11]. It is likely that Wimpfeling began the task of revising the work before Murrho's death, as we can infer from his letter to Amerbach[12]. A series of difficulties arose at this time and delayed the final edition. Let us see what happened to the commentaries.

In September 1495, Wimpfeling was in Heidelberg and had Murrho's original copy. Sebastian Brant, author of the *Navis stultifera*, had a manuscript copy of it in Basel with him in order to supervise the printing of the work[13]. In December of that same year, Wimpfeling worked day and night in Speyer on the commentaries[14]. In February 1496, Wimpfeling wrote to Johannes Amerbach, who was from Basel[15]. In January 1499, Amerbach had—we suppose for a long time—the now-corrected copy of Murrho's commentaries, but he did not print it. Wimpfeling asked him to send the corrected copy to him in Heidelberg or to Craft Hofmann in Sélestat[16]. In March 1500, Amerbach still had the manuscript with him[17]. Wimpfeling had waited in vain for about five years and demanded Amerbach send the manuscript back so that it could be printed elsewhere. The commentary was finally edited that year, or the next[18].

The above-mentioned circumstances allow us to formulate an opinion about the composition of both commentaries.

1. When Badius wrote his commentary, he did not know about Murrho's for two reasons:

    a. It is very unlikely that Murrho had finished his commentary before 1492, because when he died in 1494 Wimpfeling still had to correct the original copies in order to send them to the printer's.

---

nicarum, Festgabe Hermann Grauert (Freiburg i. Br., 1910), 171–181. Jöcher, *Gelehrten-Lexicon*, maintains he died from a plague which broke out in 1495.

[11] The commentaries on *Contra poetas* and *Parthenices primae (Mariae Virginis) et secundae (Sanctae Catharinae) libri*, which were written at the insistence of Wimpfeling. He also completed and edited the *collectanea*, a collection of news and historical material related to his country's past. According to Jöcher, it contained the following titles: *Vita M. Catonis, Sextus Aurelius: de vitiis Caesarum, Beneventus: de eadem re, Phil. Beroaldi et Thomae Vvolphii Junioris disceptatio de nomine imperatorio, Epithoma rerum Germanicarum usque ad nostra tempora* (all published in Strasbourg 1505). Cf. O. Herding and D. Mertens, *Jakob Wimpfeling Briefwechsel* (München, 1990), 223 and 446.

[12] Dated Speyer, 28 February 1496. See Herding-Mertens, *Briefwechsel*, 247, *ep.* 60.

[13] As interpreted by Wimpfeling's letter of 26 September 1495. See Herding-Mertens, *Briefwechsel*, 237, *ep.* 52a,b.

[14] Letter of 31 December 1495. See Herding-Mertens, *Briefwechsel*, 243, *ep.* 57.

[15] Letter of 28 February 1496. See Herding-Mertens, *Briefwechsel*, 247, *ep.* 60.

[16] Letter of 27 January 1499. See Herding-Mertens, *Briefwechsel*, 297, *ep.* 89.

[17] Letter of 29 March 1500. See Herding-Mertens, *Briefwechsel*, 336, *ep.* 106.

[18] The *editio princeps* of the commentary was printed, according to Herding and Mertens, in Strasbourg by Johannes Schott in 1501. The copy I consulted, sent me by the Bayerische Staatsbibliothek, uncatalogued, without editor or place of publication, is dated c. 1500. There are small differences with respect to the edition of 1501.

b.   The possibility that he knew of the unpublished commentary seems very remote.

2.   Murrho could have known about Badius' commentary. However, it seems that he did not know about it when he wrote his own if we consider its practical purposes. It is unlikely that he would repeat a work already written by Badius.

By 1513—and probably much earlier, we suppose—Badius knew of Murrho's work. In the edition of the complete works of the Mantuan of that year, the commentary of the humanist from Colmar was included, as well as those of other authors (Brant and Dati). This was not the first time that he had edited other commentaries along with his own[19].

Let us now consider briefly the text of the two commentators. Moral philosophy is always present in both[20], perhaps because of the Mantuan's intentions and the particular content of his verses. They also deal with various aspects of grammar, with special attention to prosody[21] and metrics[22], the selection and use of words[23],

---

[19] The editions of 1523, 1527, and 1533 of the *Disticha Catonis* contain commentaries by Badius and Erasmus. See Desmet-Goethals, "Kommentare", 86.

[20] Cf. P. G. Schmidt, "Jodocus Badius Ascensius als Kommentator", in *Der Kommentar in der Renaissance,* 70: "Nicht als Philosoph, sondern ausschließlich als Grammatiker will Badius kommentieren". Perhaps in other works: *De disciplina scholarium* by Pseudo-Boethius, *Parabolae* by Alain de Lille, even in the *Eclogae* by Mantuan. In the *Contra poetas*, his interest in moral philosophy is the most important or, at least, as important as grammar, rhetoric, or history. The references to ethics are constant.

E.g., *Comm. Bad.*, ad *Sunt quibus eloquii datur aurea vena poetae*: "Dat ergo statim in principio egregiam doctrinam benignitate solius naturae neminem bonum esse neminemque laudatum. (. . .)".

Comm. Bad., ad *Sancta prophanari scelus est delebile multo* etc.: "Facit syllogismum, qui sit, ut docet Servius, ex propositione, assumptione et conclusione. Propositio, quam maiorem vocant, est 'Quaecumque sancta et sacra sunt, nephas est prophanari'. Assumitur sive subsumitur in minore sic *Spiritus vatum est sanctus et sacer*. Concluditur ergo 'spiritum vatum nephas est profanari'. Et iterum 'Quaecumque sancta et sacra sunt, nephas est prophanari'. Carmina sunt sancta et sacra, ergo ea nephas est prophanari. Maior nota est, quia illud sanctum est, quod pollui non licet. Minor patet, quia spiritus vatum divinus est".

Comm. Murrho, l. 43, ad *Verba movent animos*: "Notent id adolescencie praeceptores et a scandalo caveant neve innocentes seducant".

Comm. Bad., ad *Vita decet sacros et pagina casta poetas*: "Docet ergo non satis esse vitam poetarum esse castam, immo oportet, ut verba etiam casta sint. Unde videtur improbare illud Catullianum *Castum esse decet pium poetam ipsum, versiculos nihil necesse est (. . .).* Et quod Ovi. de se dicendo *Crede mihi, mores distant a carmine nostro. Vita verecunda est, musa iocosa mihi.* Et Martia. *Lasciva est nobis pagina, vita proba est*".

[21] *Comm. Murrho,* ad *Thracius*: "apud Graecos Θρᾷξ habet iota subscriptum (quae appellatur diphthongus impropia, quam si diviseris Θρᾶιξ, id est *Thraix*) dissyllabum dicetur, cuius foemininum erit *Thraissa* et adiective *Thraicius*".

[22] *Comm. Bad.*, ad *subtrahe colla iugo*: "notum est et commodatitium hemistichium: Propertius *Dum licet iniusto subtrahe colla iugo*".

[23] *Comm. Bad.*, ad *arma*: "Arma sunt cuiuslibet artificis instrumenta, ut agricolae arma sunt aratrum, sarcula, marrae, bidentes; sutoris formae et scalpra; (. . .)".

morphology[24] and syntax[25]; they pay attention to topics related to rhetoric[26], etymology[27], mythology[28], sacred history[29], geography[30], ethnography[31], natural
science[32], and many other different subjects[33]. The explanation is usually—but not
always—based on quotes from classical, mediaeval, and even contemporary authors.

Even though these commentaries no longer follow the practices of most mediaeval
commentaries, the philological rigour of other humanists of their time is not present.
There are many parallel texts (a typical feature from the Middle Ages) and, above all,
in Badius there is a lack of conciseness[34]. This characteristic is partly explained by
Badius' and Murrho's pedagogical intentions. We must consider here that their
commentaries had no other purpose than to help students of Latin[35]. Therefore at
times the criticism about them is unjustified[36].

There is a certain logic in placing Badius among both the mediaeval commentators
and the most representative humanists of his time[37]. We can extend this to Murrho.
They exhibit features belonging to humanism[38], such as a rupture of the limits of

---

[24] *Comm. Bad.*, ad *Iessei*: "Iessei autem a nominativi *Iesseus*, qui a *Iesse* formatur, ut a *Crete
Creteus*".

[25] *Comm. Bad.*, ad *Dona Dei carmen nitidum*: "(. . .) appositio est".

[26] E.g. *Comm. Bad.*, ad *aurea vena* et *lutum*: "Perstat autem docte in metaphora, nam, sicut
mundius purgatiusque nihil est quam aurea vena —ut qua aurum purgatum fornacibus effluit—,
ita obscoenius atque fetidius nihil est luto".

Et item ad *Laurus*: "per metonymian *Daphne* aliquando pro *lauro* ponitur".

[27] *Comm. Bad.*, ad *profanari*: "Prophanum autem dicitur, quod *procul* debet esse a *phano* et a
templo deorum". The example here is obviously wrong.

[28] *Comm. Bad.*, ad *Cupido*: "Cupido filius Veneris amoris deus in altera manu sagittam ignitam,
in altera flammam habet".

[29] *Comm. Bad.* ad *Hieremias*: "Est enim is Hieremias, cuius libri extant [*sic*] in biblia nostra, qui
carmine plura scripsit (. . .)".

[30] *Comm. Bad.*, ad *Stygia palus*: "Secundum Homerum Peneum flumen Thessaliae manat nec
ab eo (Stygia palus) recipitur (. . .)".

[31] *Comm. Bad.*, ad *Cyprus*: "Libido autem et lascivi mores eius gentis illam (Venerem) sibi
asciverunt. Nam virgines Cypriae non ante nubebant quam apud portum advenas excipientes
concubitibus dotes lucrarentur".

[32] *Comm. Bad.*, ad *Ambrosia*: "apud medicos herba est, de qua Dioscorides *Ambrosia, quam multi
brotim aut artimisiam vocant. Frutex est multas virgas habens longas palmis tribus et folio initio, simillima
rutae. Virgae sunt plenae semine, ut sint quasi acini odorem vini habentes. Nascitur in Cappadocia*".

[33] Above all, in the area of natural science: medicine, pharmacy, etc.

[34] Such as we find, for instance, in the edition of the *Disticha Catonis* by Erasmus. See Desmet-
Goethals, "Kommentare", 85.

[35] See Schmidt, "Jodocus Badius Ascensius", 68 ff.

[36] Testimonies to this effect are collected abundantly by Renouard, *Bibliographie*. E.g., 140;
142: in the commentary on Boethius, 1498, Badius writes: *In qua re potissimum sudavimus ut cum
bonis doctrinis atque institutis etiam bonas litteras imbecilior aetas addiscat*. The same affirmation is in
Schmidt, "Jodocus Badius Ascensius", 70. Neither was Murrho's intention different, since he knew
Dringenberg's methods of teaching in Sélestat and was encouraged by Wimpfeling to write a
commentary which would make pupils read the Mantuan more easily.

[37] See Schmidt, "Jodocus Badius Ascensius", 71.

[38] Schmidt considers Badius to be a humanist and he contrasts him with the mediaeval

tradition in order to explain the reasons behind facts and phenomena[39], frequent allusions to antiquity, and an interest in language (in contrast to the mediaeval commentaries). In this respect Badius was influenced by the *Elegantiae* of Valla, to which he refers in his explanations[40]. Their content and the way of presenting it make these commentators an example of what, until this century, constituted the teaching of Latin at school, which is basically reading texts and commenting on them.

On the other hand, each one presents peculiar characteristics and quotes certain authors' divergent testimonies[41]. In Badius there are many references to the pagans; however, the whole commentary revolves around the moral message of the poem, whereas Murrho is more concise in his ethical reflections. Badius gives us many details, at times somewhat disordered; however, it would be unfair to accuse him of being disorganized, as he repeats the central idea, making sure that the reader does not become confused. Indeed, this practice, that of explaining the verses in hyperbaton and other such procedures, makes his commentary more school-like in format and intent. Murrho, in general, is more ordered and precise; hence his commentary is much shorter and the tone more philological.

In spite of these differences, we must not forget that they interpret the same work and it is logical that they often approach the text on the same terms. They also exhibit, at times, the same quotations for the clarification of doubtful words, but from a close reading of the commentaries we are led to the conclusion that in neither can we detect indications—at least, not evident indications—of the influence of the other.

Granada

---

commentators. He writes in his article about a similar affirmation of Pierre Courcelle, who considers the commented edition of Boethius as the "first humanist commentary on the *Consolatio*". See P. Courcelle, *La Consolation de la Philosophie dans la tradition littéraire. Antécedents et postérite de Boèce* (Paris, 1967), 361 ff.: quoted by Schmidt, "Jodocus Badius Ascensius", 67.

[39] *Comm. Bad.*, ad *cadaver:* "*Multae autem sunt apud ignaros ridiculae etymologiae, quibus etiam docti illusi sunt (. . .)*".

Comm. Murrho, ad *Nectar:* "immortalitatem significat a νε, quod privacionem, et κτείνω, id est *occido*, neque a *necto nectis* deducitur, cum Catholico Ugucio somniavit".

[40] E.g.: "Elogium est (inquit Valla) testificatio de aliquo sive vituperationis sive honoris causa". In the opinion of Desmet-Goethals, the framework in which Badius moves is more extensive than Valla's. See "Kommentare", 78.

[41] In the explanation of Dyrce, but also in many other cases, e.g., ad *gremium . . . solvis:*

Comm. Bad.: "*Gremium* intra foemora, unde et omne genitalis seminis receptaculum gremium vocant, ut *gremium* terrae. *Solvis* ergo quia utrumque conclusum nullique pervium virgines habent".

Comm. Murrho: "*Gremium* (. . .) tractum est a ritu nuptiarum. Nam novae nuptae vir seu maritus cingulum *solvebat*. Nam pro pudiciciae custodia puellarum venter cingulo laneo cinctus servabatur, quod vir in lecto *solvebat*".

Pedro Ruiz de Moroz (1506–1571), a Spanish Humanist at the Polish University and Court

JOLANTA MALINOWSKA

The journeys abroad undertaken by the humanists with the aim of acquiring knowledge of the world and science were characteristic of Renaissance times. Although Spain was too far away to keep up frequent literary and diplomatic contacts with it, this does not mean that no Polish traveller reached this country. From the beginning of the fifteenth century Polish pilgrims visiting the grave of Saint James the apostle in Santiago de Compostela, or the knights attempting to find fame in fighting with Moors, are met there. The political importance of Spain and its position in Europe in the time of the Emperor Charles V resulted in an increasing interest in this country, which was accompanied by a new fashion in clothes and made Spanish a fashionable language. Poland under the rule of Sigismund I the Old and his son Sigismund Augustus carried on, as we know, fairly lively trade relations and maintained vigorous diplomatic relations with Spain. The list of Polish ambassadors undoubtedly begins with the royal secretary, Jan Dantyszek, a precursor of Erasmianism in Spain and the well-known groups known as *erasmitas*.

Spanish-Polish literary relations developed, first of all, through Italy where, as we know, a majority of young people travelled to improve and broaden the education acquired in their motherlands. A considerable influx of students to Bologna encouraged and facilitated the establishing of international relations. The relationships between Poles and—to say nothing of the Italians—the Spanish and Portuguese were lively, but the attempts to settle them in Poland were finally unsuccessful. The crowning success was the invitation of Pedro Ruiz de Moroz, in Latin called Royzius Maureus, with whom Poles made friends in Bologna between 1537 and 1541. He was invited to Poland most probably by Bishop Piotr Gamrat, although the official invitation for the post of professor at the Jagellonian University must have come from the chancellor of the university, the bishop of Cracow, Samuel Maciejowski. In Cracow the post of professor at the Department of Roman Law was offered to Royzius and because the proposition was attractive to him, as it seems, he arrived in Cracow most probably in the middle of 1541 or at the beginning of 1542. He lectured at the

Jagellonian University, as he says himself, for about nine years:

> Bina suum dixit nam me per lustra magistrum
> Audivitque artes tradentem iuris et aequi
> Solventem nexus et legum aenigmata caeca[1].

The information concerning Royzius' stay at the university is essentially based on his works, because the official records of the Law Department of that time were destroyed in a fire. Unfortunately those were not the best times for the Academy of Cracow, whose times of splendour were past and gone. The excessively conservative attitude of the majority of professors towards new humanistic trends and their fears of more radical changes were the cause of a massive exodus of young people to universities abroad. In order to hold back this process Sigismund I the Old banned travelling to universities abroad; but he withdrew his ban in 1543. This situation at the Jagellonian University was undoubtedly one of the reasons for which Royzius was invited to Cracow. After all he was an excellent humanist, well-acquainted with classical antiquity, an outstanding lawyer, an eager and eloquent disputant, and also an ardent Catholic.

There is no doubt that during the nine years of his activity in Cracow Royzius did not limit himself to lectures on Roman law, but at the same time, as he had used to do in Bologna, he tried to popularise general knowledge about ancient literature and culture, Greek and Roman, especially poetry, of which he was himself a connoisseur and keen imitator. We can only speculate about the subject matter of his lectures and how numerous his students were. A certain kind of evidence that he lectured according to the spirit of his master Andrea Alciati, intertwining and colouring strictly scientific considerations of Roman law with quotations and reminiscences from classical literature, is present in his treatise published in 1563 entitled "Decisiones Lithuanicae". We find a longer reference to the Jagellonian University in one of Royzius' first works written in Poland, the "Epithalamium Sigismundi Augusti et Elisabes." His opinion is rather favourable, but too general, because the poet's aim was praise of King Ladislaus Jagello, the reformer of the Academy.

From Royzius we learn very little about the professors from the university. It is known that he was disappointed with his low wages and with the fact that the post of professor did not have due respect in Poland. These remarks of a contemporary professor and poet find confirmation in the latest research. The wages and income of the professors of the Academy of Cracow, as a result of the loss of value of the currency, were insufficient, and badly subsidized departments did not attract distinguished scholars. The privilege given by king Sigismund I the Old in 1535, on the basis of which a professor of the Cracow University after twenty years of work there would receive nobility, did not change the situation.

Unfavourable relations at the university and his inborn social talent resulted in many contacts outside the university spheres, and surely there were few educated

---

[1] *Petri Royzii Maurei Alcagnicensis Carmina*, ed. B. Kruczkiewicz (Cracoviae, 1900), 1: 25, v. 29–31.

people in Cracow who did not know Royzius. Very early he became acquainted with Andrzej Frycz Modrzewski, if as early as 1545 in one of his works he called him "Fricius meus"[2]. It is possible that he had already met Stanisław Orzechowski and Marcin Kromer in Italy, and he must have met Mikołaj Rej and Andrzej Trzecieski, with whom they were friends for a long time. Acquaintance with members of the upper and influential classes, where he was admitted owing to his international refinement, and where his knowledge and especially his exceptional poetry could win him due appreciation and rewards, were of no less importance to him. At the court of the bishop of Cracow, Samuel Maciejowski, Royzius had the opportunity of being introduced to the leading literary and political celebrities in Poland of that time. We can be sure that he met there two of the most powerful magnates: Jan Tarnowski and Piotr Kmita. He tried to maintain and develop these relationships, realizing that they would bring him nearer to the royal court. He was aware that in order to achieve his goal making their acquaintance as such was insufficient, so he soon learned about Polish history and Polish customs, and even studied Polish.

At the same time, he was considering writing a longer poem of lasting value. Amidst the fight for respect for Roman law, and his indignation at the fact that in Poland a lawyer was respected less than a doctor, or even an astrologer, an idea of presenting the origins and development of law in a separate longer poem inevitably was born in his mind. Thus a plan of a poem entitled "De origine iuris" crystallized, from which four fragments of manuscripts have been preserved, amounting together to 235 verses. But there was another poetic purpose, in that Royzius desired to make himself distinguished and make his contribution to the society which he became a part of and now belonged to. He was thinking about writing an epic on the history of Poland similar to the *Annals* of Quintus Ennius. The poem was to be entitled "Sarmatis" or "Historia Polonica". The content of the poem is given in the following words:

> Sauromatum prima reges ab origine dicam
> Saecula ad haec, addam pugnatas ordine pugnas
> Et multis olim crescentia regna tropaeis[3].

Unfortunately he did not manage to realize this idea either. He wrote only the first volume, which has 133 verses in which he described the mythic history of Poland up to the foundation of Cracow. He was more successful with another poem in which patriotic and religious plots are interwoven. This is a composition presenting the martyr's death of the patron of Poland, Saint Stanislaus. Although in this attempt Royzius had a predecessor, Paweł of Krosno, he handled his task in a better way. The poem, one of his longest, imitating Virgil and dedicated to Bishop Samuel Maciejowski, appeared in print in 1542 under the title "Carmen de sancto pontifice caeso sive Stanislaus".

---

[2] He wrote this in an introductory epigram for the oration entitled "Ad senatum oratio secunda de poena homicidii" by Andrzej Frycz Modrzewski in 1545.

[3] Kruczkiewicz, ed., *Carmina*, 1: 17.

At this time, however, relationships at the court changed for the worse. After Bishop Gamrat's death in 1545 Royzius intended to return to Spain, but most probably Bishop Maciejowski's friendly attitude and persuasion stopped him from doing so. But even the bishop's support was not sufficient to improve the situation, since in the epigram to Stańczyk the poet complains that only a king's jester is allowed to point out the mistakes of the king and the clergy[4]. In another work he says: "You often ask me how I like the life at the court?", and he answers: "In the same way as a thief likes the halter"[5]. Meanwhile in 1548 King Sigismund I the Old died. The misunderstandings between the young king Sigismund Augustus and his mother, Queen Bona Sforza, are well known. Royzius could expect that with the change on the throne his prospects would also be more favourable. So he wrote an elegy, one of his most beautiful and most carefully written works, so precise and exact in details that it can be used as a historical source. Indeed, together with the death of Sigismund I the Old the relationships at the court changed favourably for Royzius, so he gave up the intention of going back to Spain and stopped complaining. The influence of Bona and her favourites was neutralized, and bishop Maciejowski won greater prestige from the king.

At this time Royzius was frequently called to the court in order to give advice on legal and judicial matters. Soon, as early as in 1549, King Sigismund Augustus appointed him his courtier and counsellor, and in the spring of next year he was guaranteed a salary of 200 florins. Let us quote a passage from the king's decree which is of interest to us:

> Cum in aulam nostram nobilem Petrum Roizium Maureum Hispanum iuris utriusque doctorem, quem ingenium ac generis nobilitas, quam non obscuris testimoniis cognovimus, nobis commendant, et virtus ac iuris civilis peritia, quam annis pluribus in civitate ipsa nostra publice profitendo declaravit,—propterea, ut illius opera et consiliis, cum postulaverit necessitas in quibuscunque causis tamquam eius, qui iuris utriusque peritiam habet, utamur, sicut in aliis litteris nostris continetur, accersi iussimus—visum est nobis necessarium esse, ut prospiceremus illi, unde habere posset sumptus, quos in aula nostra facere illum oportebit. Quam ob rem illi annuam pensionem ducentorum florenorum numeri et monetae regni nostri in salinis Vieliciis constituendam duximus ... [6].

As a court counsellor he took part, as he mentions himself, in chancellor's cases under the presidency of Bishop Maciejowski. Private clients were also not scarce and so his income improved considerably. This favourable period was interrupted by Bishop Maciejowski's death in autumn 1550. Jan Lange tried to help Royzius in this troublesome situation by obtaining an invitation from the Roman king Ferdinand to

---

[4] Kruczkiewicz, ed., *Carmina*, 2: 246.

[5] Kruczkiewicz, ed., *Carmina*, 2: 69.

[6] B. Kruczkiewicz, *Royziusz, jego żywot i pisma* [Royzius, his life and works] (Kraków, 1897), 76–77.

take the position of professor of law at Vienna University. Then Sigismund Augustus offered him the permanent post of judicial advisor at the royal court in order not to lose a lawyer who was talented and well-disposed towards the humanist monarch. Royzius accepted the king's proposal, and his situation changed only to such an extent that his accidental contacts with the court turned into permanent ones, and that he became a court counsellor in a non-nobleman's court with an official title of *consiliarius*, and was no longer a professor at the university. This new post carried a permanent salary of 500 florins.

It is very probable that Royzius counted on getting a lucrative post in the Church, but in principle it was unattainable. A king in Poland was constrained by the privileges of the nobility, and the nobility protected these privileges to such an extent that it was difficult for him to give Royzius, who did not have the title of nobleman, a suitable and advantageous position in the Church without exposing himself to the discontent of the nobility. On the other hand, the king still had the unrestricted rights of a hereditary prince in Lithuania before the union, and thus he could reward his court lawyer with such a post. Perhaps this was one of the important reasons for Royzius' leaving for Lithuania, especially because after the death of Barbara Radziwi-łłówna the king was more frequently present in Vilnius than in Cracow, wanting by suitable reforms to modernize to some extent the Lithuanian institutions and courts. After moving from Cracow to Lithuania in 1552, he lived in Vilnius, where he died in 1571.

To sum up, it should be stated that Royzius as a clear-headed and versatile humanist, an exceptionally competent lawyer, a man endowed with sincerity, openness, eloquence and wit, combined with social refinement, won the hearts of the Poles. His sincere attachment to cold Poland as his second motherland earned him the name of "gentis polonae amicus". Many flattering references about him can be found in practically all contemporary Polish writers, but surely none of them devoted so many and such hearty poems to Royzius as the greatest of poets of that time, Jan Kochanowski. Let us quote as an example one of his epigrams:

> Ultima te produxit Iberia, docte Royzii,
>> Erudiit Latium, Sarmatis ora fovet,
> Nec gens ulla adeo est a nobis dissita, quo non
>> Ingenii penetret fama secunda tui[7].

Although Royzius, while in Cracow, complained of many things about his life there, he should have admitted in retrospect that his teaching and writing were a significant contribution to the scholarly and cultural life of the Cracow republic of scholars and to the Polish renaissance as well.

Lublin

---

[7] J. Kochanowski, *Epigrammata* (Warszawa, 1896), 3: 201, epigr. 33.

Latin in the Writings of Santa Teresa

GERMAIN MARC'HADOUR

Although Teresa never studied Latin, she ought not to be absent from a Congress held in her native Ávila. Not only did she pray and chant every day in the language of St. Jerome, but all her writings, even familiar epistles, are studded with echoes of the Vulgate Bible or the Roman liturgy. She would be at home among us, because she was fond of the *letrados*—the word occurs a hundred times under her pen, always with affectionate reverence: "Siempre fui amiga de letras ... y buen letrado nunca me engañó".[1] For her spiritual guide, she chose the greatest scholar available in Ávila, "el mayor letrado que había en el lugar" (*Vida* 32/16), reckoning him even probably the most learned member of his order, that of the Dominicans. In selecting confessors for her convents, she placed learning above piety.

Allow me to connect Teresa, on the map of the Renaissance, with several eminent practitioners of Latin verse and prose. She saw the light of day in the very year 1515 when *Utopia* went into production. She left her father's house on 2 November 1535, a few months after the execution of John Fisher and Thomas More, and a few months before the death of Erasmus. The second of November was All Souls' Day, *el día de las ánimas.* The Latin form *ánimas,* retained on account of the liturgical context, is still current in modern Spanish to designate the departed souls. Teresa prefers it to *alma* when the epithet is *animosa,* not for "animosity," but for "animus" in the sense of "spirited."[2]

The vernacular romances which young Teresa, like her mother, read avidly were not a bad training school for the brilliant *raconteuse* her writings would reveal, but she began, at an early age, to read also books of spirituality. Her personal copy of Osuna's *Tercer Abecedario,* preserved as a relic in this city, bears her autograph response, glosses

---

[1] *Libro de la vida,* ch. 5 section 3. Henceforth references will be given in parenthesis after the quotation, using Teresa's *Obras Completas* in the edition of Efren de la Madre de Dios and Otger Steggink (Madrid, 1982).

[2] E.g., *el ánima animosa.* Various moods, in fact, admit the Latin form, for instance, *anda el ánima tan señora* or *me inquieta mucho el ánima.*

and underlinings.[3] These treatises would often quote Latin phrases or sentences from the Vulgate or the Christian classics. Teresa, brought up by Augustinian nuns, was *muy aficionada a san Agustín,* especially his *Confessions* (*Vida* 9/7, 13/3), and the *Soliloquia,* which she calls *Meditaciones* (*Camino,* 46/2). She also quotes from St. Jerome's epistles (*Vida,* 3/11, 11/11) and St. Gregory's *Moralia in Job* (*Vida* 5/8, 31/11).

She read those works in Castilian, but they familiarized her with an ascetic vocabulary which remained close to the Latin matrix. The title she gave to her *Vida* was *De las misericordias de Dios.*[4] As a native speaker of a Romance language, I can witness that a considerable amount of deciphering is available to keen readers of liturgical Latin. Compare Teresa's *Sol de Justicia* (*Vida* 20/19, 20/29) to its source, the *sol justitiae* of Malachi 4:2, and her *Ordenó en mí la caridad,* which occurs half a dozen times in her commentary on the Song of Songs (ch. 6), to the *ordinavit in me caritatem* of Solomon's canticle (2:4).

This familiarity, which was shared by her audience of nuns, clergy, and educated middle-class laity, accounts for the phonetic spelling she uses as she writes *currente calamo.* The spoken quality of her prose can best be sampled through her exposition of the *Pater noster:* "*santificetur nomen tun . . . adveniad rrenun tun . . . fiad voluntas tua sicud in zelo et yn terra . . . panen nostru cotidiano da nobis odie*" (*Camino,* chs. 52 to 60). She explains the *Our Father* because her nuns used to recite it "so often each day" (ch. 68/5), and she wants them all to understand what they are praying for (ch. 51/3). She meant to do a similar *explication de texte* for the *Ave Maria* (ch. 73/2), but did not get round to it. In Tudor England, "a paternoster while" was a current measure of duration; in Teresa's Castile, this method of reckoning was extended to the *Credo* and the *Ave Maria,* e.g., "*no sé si era avemaría*" (*Vida* 4/17), "*estar quedo* [to stay quiet] *un credo*" (*Vida* 30/16).

The English word *patter* testifies to repeated prayers ending up as parrot-like utterances. Teresa fought that danger: "When I say the creed", she writes, "it sems to me reasonable, and indeed an obligation, to know what I believe; when I say the 'Our Father', love prompts me to understand who that Father is" (*Camino* 40/1).

Another text which she and her communities knew by heart was that of the *psalms,* and she acknowledges that their meaning was at times beyond her grasp (*Vida* 15/8). A few verses will complete our sampling of the highly Hispanic orality of her Latin: "*Quemadmodun desiderad cervus a fontes aguarun*" (*Ps* 41:1); "*Letatun sun yn is que dita sun miqui* (*Ps* 121:1); "*Un verso que decimos a Prima . . . : Cun dilatasti cor meun*" (*Ps* 118:32).[5]

The nuns learnt their psalter from books, but some liturgical formulas came to

---

[3] She mentions it repeatedly, and as early as ch. 4 of her autobiography (p. 35).

[4] "Intitulé ese libro *De las misericordias de Dios,*" says her letter of 19 November 1581 (p. 1078). The verse *Misericordias Domini in aeternum cantabo* was used as a caption under the portrait of the Madre.

[5] (*Moradas* 1/5). The long Psalm 118 (Hebrew 119) was recited in full each day. Teresa quotes this hemistich again, in *Moradas* 2/5, with *dilataste.* Sounding *i* as *e* was also common in the England of her day: it is not wrong for the film producer of Shakespeare's *Henry V* to make the army chant "sed nomine tuo da gloriam" where Psalm 113:1 has nomini.

them by word of mouth, and Teresa's rendering of these can be the more distant from the correct Latin. Thus she writes *"Sid nomen Domine benedicto Eso nunque edusque in secula"* (*Constituciones* 10/12), which it may take us a few seconds to recognize as *"Sit nomen Domini benedictum ex hoc nunc et usque in saecula."* Daily Vespers included Mary's canticle (Luke 1:46f.), and Teresa singles out some words in it which she found enlightening: *las palabras de la Magnificat "Exultavid espiritus meus"* (*Obras*, p. 487, §2, and cf. p. 473, *cuenta* 47).

In a famous essay on Teresa's style, Ramón Menéndez Pelayo says she used popular pronounciation for words she had often read in their correct spelling, so as to sound *rusticana,* and distance herself from the professional *letrados:* hence her spellings of Latinate terms such as *pusilaminidad, supresticiosas, trobulaciones,* and, yet more consistently, *relision, ilesia, ispiriencia.*[6]

Shall we leave it for linguists to distinguish Teresa's idiosyncracies from her phonetic *hispanismos*? Among the traits that jump to the eye is the substitution of *−n* for *−m,* familiar to us through *corazón, Colón, Carmen* etc. The final *−d* may have retained the sound of *−t* as it does in other languages. The unstressed endings of Latin words had become blurred and were apt to be muted. The *c* before *t* has been dropped in all Romance languages, so Teresa's *fatus sun* for *factus sum* (*Vida* 20/10, quoting Psalm 101:8) should cause no surprise. What is the more surprising is that she retained the final -f in *Josef,* although *José* was already the current form.

Speaking of a saint, I wish to end with two of her quotations from the New Testament: *"Domine, da miqui aguan"* (John 4:5, *Vida* 30/19) and *"Miqui bivere cristus es"* (*Ephesians* 1:21, *Moradas* 2/6), perhaps adding the Hebrew *Amén* with which she so often punctuates her texts, whether in assertion or in prayer. No wonder that her literary heirs promoted her *patrona de los escritores españoles* on 18 September 1965, ten years before the papal brief *Lumen Hispaniae* of 27 September 1970 proclaimed her *Doctor Ecclesiae.*

Université Catholique de l'Ouest

---

[6] "El Estilo" etc. is reproduced by Luis Santullano in his edition of *Obras Completas* (Madrid, 1966), 37–50.

/ *Mamma Roma, City of Women:*
Leonardo Bruni's Oration to the Prostitutes

DAVID MARSH

lthough the humanist Leonardo Bruni (1370–1444) is generally portrayed as a
solemn statesman who dedicated his leisure hours to the higher disciplines of
history and philosophy, he too contributed to the revival of the Lucianic spirit of
irony, only a few years after he studied Greek with Chrysoloras and thus became familiar with Lucian. In 1407, while he was employed as a papal secretary to Gregory XII, Bruni composed a paradoxical oration which forms a singular contrast to his
generally high-minded works, the *Oration of Heliogabalus to the Prostitutes* (*Oratio Heliogabali ad meretrices*).[1]

This risqué composition apparently reflects a shift in Bruni's attitude as he moved
from Florence to Rome. In Florence, the chancellor Coluccio Salutati had died the
year before, but Bruni now found himself unable to write a serious eulogy of his former mentor.[2] Now under the influence of his ribald colleague Poggio Bracciolini,
Bruni evidently sought relief from the onus of serious eulogy in composing a paradoxical encomium.[3] (Like other declamations, ancient and humanist, the speech is
preceded by an *argumentum*, presumably supplied by Bruni himself.) From the idealized republic of Florence, Bruni had passed to decadent Rome, capital of the debauched emperors and perennial home of prostitutes.

In the *Scriptores Historiae Augustae*, a late Latin collection of forged imperial biogra-
phies, the life of Antoninus Heliogabalus (or Elagabalus) relates how the dissolute

---

[1] For the dating, see Leonardo Bruni, *Humanistisch-philosophische Schriften*, ed. Hans Baron
(Leipzig-Berlin, 1928), 162. Citations (as "*Oratio*") are to the text in *Historiae Augustae scriptores*
(Venice, 1519), fols. 291–295.

[2] On Bruni's difficulties with the Salutati eulogy, see James Hankins, "The Latin Poetry of
Leonardo Bruni," *Humanistica Lovaniensia* 39 (1990): 9–10.

[3] Hankins, "Latin Poetry," 14, notes that Poggio owned a codex of the *Historia Augusta*, now
Vat. Pal. lat. 899, which preserves marginal notes written by both Poggio and Bruni.

ruler assembled all the prostitutes of Rome and addressed them in a quasi-military oration:

> Omnes de circo, de theatro, de stadio et omnibus locis et balneis meretrices collegit in aedes publicas et apud eas contionem habuit quasi militarem, dicens eas commilitones, disputavitque de generibus schematum et voluptatum.[4]

Using this biographical hint as a starting point, Bruni set himself the task of writing this scandalous discourse, in which he shrewdly applied encomiastic rhetoric to this unlikely topic. As the author of the *Panegyric of the City of Florence*, Bruni was well acquainted with the rhetoric of praise. In his *Dialogues to Pier Paolo Vergerio*, moreover, he had explored ways of arguing both for and against the same topic—in this case the merits of Dante, Petrarch, and Boccaccio.[5] His *Oration of Heliogabalus* was clearly intended as an amusing form of irony. For the eloquent emperor of the *Oration* had already been condemned as a monster in Bruni's *Panegyric of the City of Florence*, in the same breath with Nero and Domitian.[6]

Indeed, Bruni was aware of the provocative nature of his fictional oration, as we may deduce from the postscript to the work, which reads as follows: "Leonardus Arretinus recreandi ingenii causa ludens ridensque dictitauit. Unde seueriores rogat ne legant, urbaniores ne efferant."[7] His request that witty readers should not promulgate the work—*urbaniores ne efferant*—echoes the conclusion of the *Dialogues to Pier Paolo Vergerio*, in which Niccolò Niccoli asks his friends not to reveal what he is about to say in criticism of Petrarch.[8]

As a military harangue, Bruni's oration offers both praise and prizes for martial valor. Like orators of any age, Heliogabalus contrasts the present state of decadence by citing *exempla* from an earlier age. To counteract the hypocritical devotion of today's Roman wives to chastity, Heliogabalus proposes a glorious new law which will encourage all to enter the service of Cupid. Decreeing that all women are shared in common, the emperor will banish frigidity and shame. Even in the decadent Rome of today, a veteran prostitute can show the way. I exhort you, he concludes, to serve your country and to claim the rewards I offer!

---

[4] *Scriptores Historiae Augustae* 17 (=Aelius Lampridius, *Antoninus Heliogabalus*), 26.3. The noun *schemata* must mean gestures (cf. *Heliogabalus* 19: "vasa schematibus libidinosissimis inquinata"). Bruni has included this detail in his physical instructions to the prostitutes, cited below.

[5] See the critical edition in Leonardo Bruni, *Dialogi ad Petrum Paulum Histrum*, ed. Stefano Ugo Baldassari (Florence, 1994). For a discussion of their rhetorical dimension, see David Marsh, *The Quattrocento Dialogue: Classical Tradition and Humanist Innovation* (Cambridge, MA, 1980), 24–36.

[6] See Bruni's *Laudatio Florentinae Urbis* in *Schriften*, ed. Baron 1928, 247: "At si hi [Tiberius and Caligula] teterrimi et pernitiosi, tamen qui postea secuti sunt, meliores fuere? Quinam isti? Nero scilicet et Vitellius et Domitianus et Heliogabalus?"

[7] The postscript is found in codexes like University of Chicago Library, MS. 32; and London, British Library, Harl. 2268.

[8] See Bruni, *Dialogi*, ed. Baldassari, 256: "Verum ego libere dicam quod sentio: vos autem rogo atque obsecro ne hanc meam orationem *efferatis*."

The oration may be divided into roughly three sections. (1) Heliogabalus begins his oration by citing Ovid's poetic tag—"militat omnis amans"—but complains that the rewards of Cupid go unclaimed in the Rome of his day. The emperor confirms his point by contrasting the folly of present-day Roman matrons to the sexual exploits of the great imperial mistresses of the past. (2) The heart of the speech is Heliogabalus' glorious law proclaiming that all women shall be shared in common. Under this new law, the emperor now exhorts the women assembled to do their duty as Cupid's warriors. Shunning frigidity and false modesty, they should imitate the example of a veteran whore who recently accosted a timid young man. (3) In his peroration, Heliogabalus cites the many civic prizes which can be won for service to Rome.

Although the immediate inspiration for Bruni's oration came from Roman history, it owes little or nothing to Roman historians, whether to Livy, who glorifies republican virtue, or to Tacitus, who scorns imperial corruption. Instead, Bruni draws on the tradition of Roman poetry. Thus, in praising the martial aspects of lovemaking, Heliogabalus paraphrases Ovid's *Amores* 1.9.1: "Militat omnis amans, et habet sua castra Cupido." More centrally, Bruni's imaginary polity of vices—the sensual body politic of prostitutes governed by a debauched tyrant—recalls the satirical tradition of Juvenal, whose famous sixth satire castigates the very promiscuity which Heliogabalus so ardently celebrates. (When Bruni defended his oration in a letter to his friend Niccolò Niccoli, he cited a line from Juvenal 2.3: "nec Curios simulant, nec Bacchanalia vivunt".)

To cite one example, after censuring the fatuous chastity of Roman matrons, Heliogabalus appeals to Roman tradition, the *mos maiorum*, by citing the example of women who have served the fatherland well:

> Pro dii boni, hocne Clodia et Paulina timent? hoc Caesonia et Seruilia, hoc Pompeia, uel Quinta, uel Octauia, uel aliae innumerabiles huius urbis foeminae nobiles, ignobiles, uiduae, maritae?[9]

Despite his appeal to all Roman women, patrician and plebeian, Heliogabalus' catalogue of women reflects his imperial status by citing highborn women linked with prominent men, including the Julio-Claudian emperors. Clodia is famous as the lover of Catullus and Caelius. Paulina was the wife of Caligula. Caesonia was the mistress of Caligula, and Servilia the mistress of Caesar. Pompeia, Caesar's third wife, was suspected of a liaison with Clodius. Octavia was the daughter of Claudius and the wife of Nero, who accused her of adultery.[10]

The highpoint of Heliogabalus' oration is a sexual emancipation proclamation for the women of Rome, a decree ironically inspired by the idealist Plato. When he wrote his *Oration*, Bruni had already embarked on his series of translations from Plato.

---

[9] *Oratio*, fol. 292v.

[10] On Paulina, see Suet. Calig. 25; Tac. A. 12.1; on Caesonia, Suet. Calig. 25; Juv. 6.616. On Servilia, see Cic. Att. 14.21.3; 15.11.1; 15.12.1. On (Claudia) Octavia, see Suet. Claud. 27; Ner. 7.

By 1407, his attention had turned from the dialogues which offer the most vivid portraits of Socrates—Plato's *Phaedo*, *Apology*, and *Crito*—to the discussion of rhetoric in the *Gorgias*.[11] Heliogabalus' oration forms an ironic celebration of Plato's most notorious doctrine, namely, the common possession of women which Socrates proposes in Book 5 of the *Republic* (461E). Distressed by the sham pudicity of Roman matrons, Bruni's Heliogabalus offers his imperial authority to a new social program by declaring all the women of Rome common property. Introducing this decree, the emperor makes oblique reference to Plato's imagined legislation, in a passage which is unfortunately garbled in the 1519 Aldine edition:

> Sed de mulieribus nostris ipse uidero, experiarque profecto an minus mihi Romae liceat, quam philosopho nescio cui in sua quadam ciuitate, quam ipse finxerit, licuerit ... Est, inquam, mihi cordi legem ferre, per quam mulieres omnes fiant communes.[12]

By satirizing *Republic* 5, the ironic humor of Bruni's oration exorcises Plato's troubling doctrine of communal marriage, which Quattrocento humanists were hard pressed to accept and defend.[13] Beyond that, there is also a clear literary precedent for such satire in the writings of Lucian. The second book of his *True Story*, for example, describes the Isle of the Blest, which is the permanent abode of countless heroes and great men. "Only Plato was absent," Lucian comments (2.17), "for it was said he was living in a city he had invented with its own constitution and laws." In *Philosophies for Sale* 17, Lucian likewise mocks the holding of women in common. In words that echo the *True Story* passage, the figure of Socrates says that he lives in an invented city with its own constitution and laws. When a potential buyer asks to hear one of his laws, Socrates replies that his greatest is that one that allows women to be held in common.

What is essential to the ironic tone of the work is that Bruni's Heliogabalus is a notoriously unreliable character: his oration is the discourse of a madman, if not of a liar. Thus, Bruni's work is an early example of the kind of ironic declamation which a Lucianist like Erasmus would later transform into his masterpiece *The Praise of Folly*. Characterized by its ironic use of military jargon, Heliogabalus' oration constitutes the first humanist example of paradoxical rhetoric of the Italian Renaissance. The peroration illustrates Bruni's ironic tone:

> Vos autem interea hortor ut exempla ueteranarum uobis ante oculos praeponatis, nec solum impudentiae, uerum etiam caeterarum rerum, quae ad me-

---

[11] On Bruni's early translations of Plato, see James Hankins, *Plato in the Early Italian Renaissance*, 2 vols. (Leiden, 1990), 1: 40–58.

[12] *Oratio*, fol. 293, corrected using University of Chicago Library, MS. 32.

[13] In the 1430s and 1440s, *Republic* 5 proved a stumbling-block to its translator, Pier Candido Decembrio, and to his Milanese circle. See Hankins, *Plato in the Early Italian Renaissance*, 1: 149–153, on Antonio da Rho's *Dialogi in Lactantium* (1443), which attempts to counter the anti-Platonic polemics of Aristotle, Lactantius, and contemporary humanists.

retriciam pertinet. Nullus ferme earum gestus, siquis diligenter respiciat, artificio caret. Non uox, non manus, non oculus, non supercilium, non labia, non lingua, non genu, non pes, non tibia iners unquam inuenitur. In quorum imitationem uos diligentissime tradere debetis, et enixissime conari, ut pares ac similes illis efficiamini. Nam si dura et laboriosa essent illa, ad quorum studium uos cohortor, tamen pro adipiscenda artis uestrae laude, esset a uobis omni conatu in illis elaborandum. Cum autem non modo facilia sunt, uerum etiam dulcia ac uoluntaria, quaenam uos excusatio tutari potest, quo minus ad summum gradum eiusdem artis assidua exercitatione contenderitis? Accedit quod amplexus et basia, caeteraque perfectae libidinis opera, quae duris legibus antea coercebantur, non solum permissorem nunc habent, uerum etiam fautorem atque suasorem, qualem uidetis. Ego nanque in hoc dignitatis gradu constitutus omnia uobis concedo, omnia permitto, omnia uobis licere uolo, excipiens nihil, nec locum, nec tempus, nec personam. Quare excitemini, precor, commilitones, et alacriter ac prompte operi uestro incumbite, nec expectate ut petamini. Sed uos ultro offerte, ac postposito omni fatuo atque degeneri pudore, per uicos, per plateas, per fora, per campos, per theatra, per ipsa denique immortalium deorum templa discurrite, capite, rapite, seducite omni tempore omne genus hominum, omnis quidem etatis, sed praecipue adolescentes. Quantum ad augustalem munificentiam attinet, ut in sanguinolenta Martis militia, coronae murales, uallares, nauales, ciuicae, rostrataeque fortibus uiris propositae sunt, sic ut quaeque uestrum egregia lasciuiae opera ediderit, in hac Cupidinis militia dona magnifica reportabit.[14]

As a paradoxical encomium, the *Oratio Heliogabali* exemplifies the oratorical freedom which early humanists were so often at pains to defend—especially historians who (like Bruni) composed speeches in the classical manner for the great protagonists of their narratives—and his praise of erotic pleasure anticipates by two decades the *succès de scandale* of Lorenzo Valla's *De voluptate*.[15] There was, moreover, classical precedent for such rhetorical liberties. In antiquity, the ability to argue both sides of a question constituted an ideal both of Academic skepticism and of Ciceronian eloquence—although when the Greek philosopher Carneades had dared to argue publicly on behalf of injustice in second-century Rome, he was banished from the city.[16] But like other humanists, Bruni was conscious of the dangers of provoking readers by excessive rhetorical freedom. In a letter dated Siena, 7 January 1408, he defended his *Oration of Heliogabalus* to his friend Niccolò Niccoli by various arguments:

---

[14] *Oratio*, fol. 295r–v.

[15] See, for example, the praise of prostitution in Lorenzo Valla, *De vero falsoque bono*, ed. Maristella Panizza Lorch (Bari, 1970), 38: "melius merentur scorta et prostibula de genere humano quam sanctimoniales virgines et continentes."

[16] In his dialogue *On Pleasure*, Lorenzo Valla was to cite Carneades as emblematic of provocative rhetorical freedom: see Marsh, *Quattrocento Dialogue*, 68–69.

Leonardus Nicolao S. Tu me philosophum esse censes, et nichilominus Elio-gabalum postulas. Vide ne non conhereant petitiones, et exhortationes tuae. Nisi forte hanc eandem Philosophiam interpretare; et si ita est, accipies opus sane philosophicum non ex Zenonis disciplina, sed ex intimo Epicuri sinu de-promptum. Ridebis, ut opinor, hanc incestissimam contionem: quamquam multis peperci, quorum michi copiam suscepta causa ultro largiebatur, et in ta-berna vinaria abstemius fui. Itaque ualde equidem uereor, ne utrique me subac-cusare non immerito possint: severis quia rem non satis gravem susceperim; urbani quia in causa pingui et copiosa jejunior fuerim. Ac in me fortassis illud jactabitur: aut undique religionem tolle, aut usquequaque conserva. Se de urba-nis quidem non multum laboro, si me continentiorem fuisse arbitrabuntur. Cum severis autem et tristibus plus michi, ut opinor, negocii supererit. Verum ut Lucilius non Romanis, quid erant peritiores, et in poematibus judicandis nimium curiosi, sed Tarentinis et Reginis se scripsisse affirmauit [Cic. *de fin.* 1.3.7]; sic ego tristibus et severioribus nego me scripsisse, nec ab illis legi volo. Est autem aliud quoddam genus hominum, qui in joco severi et in severitate jocosi sunt; qui neque Catonis rigiditatem, nec Sardanapali [ed. Scipii] disso-lutionem sectantur: Hoc est qui nec Curios simulant, nec Bacchanalia vivunt [Juv. 2.3]. Isti, ut spero, hanc mediocritatem meam et legent non inviti, et pro-babunt non simulate. Denique loquantur omnes ut libet. Ego si michi et tibi uni satisfecero, ceteros omnes cum suis judiciis floccipendo, eorumque opi-niones et oblocutiones vix unius assis existimo. Tu vale mi dulcissime et sua-vissime Nicolae. Laudationem Colucii Salutati viri clarissimi scribere incepi. Oratio erit luculenta et copiosa. Non possum nunc plura scribere ad te. Vale. Andreas noster tibi Heliogabalum portat. Senis, VII. Id. Ianuar.[17]

Bruni's letter is notable for three elements. First, he associates his composition with an ethical ideal that combines severity with jesting, although he claims (in loose philosophical terms) to prefer the Epicurean outlook to the Stoic. Next, Bruni de-fends his paradoxical speech as a form of *satire*. He adduces the Roman satirist Luci-lius—Horace's predecessor and principal model—as an example of literary modera-tion, *mediocritas*, and he cites a verse of Juvenal which describes men of exaggerated severity or hedonism.[18] Finally, he mentions that he is engaged in writing a eulogy, *laudatio*, for his mentor, Coluccio Salutati, who had died the year before. Bruni thus implies that his exercise in paradoxical encomium may constitute a leisurely pastime to the more serious business of commemorative eulogy. (The oration on Salutati, which does not survive, was probably never completed.)

Whether serious or paradoxical, epideictic rhetoric was not limited to single speeches or treatises. Here too Lucian proved a guide to rhetorical possibilities, since he employed encomium not only in the essay *The Fly*, but also in his dialogue *The*

---

[17] Epistle II.16 in Leonardo Bruni, *Epistolarum Libri VIII*, ed. Laurentius Mehus (Florence), 53–54, dated and supplemented according to Bruni, *Schriften*, ed. Baron, 199–200.

[18] Juvenal in fact impugns the hypocrisy of people who pretend to be righteous while living dissolutely, but in Bruni's context the verse describes two ethical extremes to be avoided.

Parasite. In reviving classical dialogue, Quattrocento humanists often employed three successive speakers to discuss a topic from different perspectives. In so doing, they ostensibly acknowledged the strictures of Augustine concerning Cicero's two-sided debates, and let a "Christian" speaker conclude the discussion. But such apparent orthodoxy could be used to offset the more radical remarks of the first two speakers, who were thus granted greater liberties in arguing their case. Two of the earliest examples of neo-Ciceronian dialogue explore the use of encomiastic rhetoric in this "protected" context by interpreting a controversial topic in a positive light. In his *On Avarice (De avaritia)* of 1428, Poggio Bracciolini proposes avarice as an essential trait in civic enterprises. Surplus wealth can only be amassed by someone with a passion for profit and the accumulation of capital.[19]

For obvious reasons, Bruni did not include the *Speech of Heliogabalus* in later anthologies of his more respectable work. Nevertheless, this paradoxical oration exercised some influence on other humanists, most notably Sicco Polenton and Lorenzo Valla.

The Latin "comedy" *Catinia* (1419), by the Venetan humanist Sicco Polenton (c. 1376–c. 1448), is dedicated to the Venetian nobleman Giacomo Badoer. *Catinia* is a comic debate in Latin most likely intended for reading rather than performance, although it has often been called a "humanist comedy."[20] Set in a tavern where five patrons dispute who should pay the bill, Polenton's dialogue shares with its Lucianic model a spirit of hedonism and paradox. The dialogue takes its name from the rustic Catinius, an itinerant seller of pots (from Latin *catinus*, "pot"), who eventually loses the debate and must pay the host. The other interlocutors are likewise of humble station: the friar Questius, the fisherman Cetius, the wool-carder Lanius, and the inn-keeper Bibius. They agree in denouncing other professions—philosophers, lawyers, physicians, soldiers, and scholars—and in praising their own devotion to the pleasure of the table.[21] In particular, Sicco echoes Lucian in ridiculing scholars as starving wretches, a theme that Leon Battista Alberti was to develop a decade later in his essay *On the Use of Literary Studies*.[22]

Polenton's crude dialogue occasioned a minor controversy which affords us a glimpse into the literary attitudes of early Quattrocento humanists. When some severe Venetian patricians took the *Catinia* amiss, Polenton wrote a letter defending

---

[19] Latin text in Poggio Bracciolini, *Opera omnia*, ed. Riccardo Fubini, 4 vols. (Turin, 1964–69), 1 (=1538 Basel edition): 1–31; English translation in Bracciolini 1978. Longhi 1983, 147–148, describes Poggio's use of paradoxical discourse as a heuristic rhetorical device.

[20] See Sicco Polenton, *Catinia*, ed. Giorgio Padoan, Memorie dell'Istituto Veneto di Scienze Morali, Lettere ed Arti 34 (Venice, 1969). For the influence of Guarino's version of Lucian's *Parasite* on Polenton's *Catinia* and Alberti's *Momus*, see Emilio Mattioli, *Luciano e l'Umanesimo* (Naples, 1980), 48–49.

[21] For Polenton's debt to Lucian, see Padoan's introduction in *Catinia*, 19–21. The work is discussed as a "humanist comedy" in Douglas Radcliff-Umstead, *The Birth of Modern Comedy in Renaissance Italy* (Chicago and London, 1964), 26–27, with a synopsis on 246.

[22] For Alberti's *De commodis*, see Leon Battista Alberti, *De commodis litterarum atque incommodis*, ed. Laura Goggi Carotti (Florence, 1976).

the work to Fantino Dandolo, the *podestà* of Padua.[23] In his apology, he cites the precedent of other illustrious authors who indulged in composing humorous and risqué works. Polenton begins with an example from ancient poetry, citing the precedent of Virgil who composed the lewd poems collectively known as *Priapeia*. As for Latin prose, Polenton names two contemporaries who, in no wise inferior to the ancients, have engaged in humorous paradox. The eloquent Leonardo Bruni recently composed an *Oration of Heliogabalus*, in which the dissolute emperor urges the prostitutes of Rome to do their duty, and now the learned Guarino has written a defense of the parasitic life.[24] Polenton appears to be expressing what was a widespread predilection for such literary recreations. Bruni's *Oratio Heliogabali*, for example, survives in Venetian codexes which also contain Guarino's translation of Lucian's *Parasite* (Marc. lat. VI 134) and Polenton's *Catinia* (Marc. lat. XI 61).[25]

Following Bruni's lead, Lorenzo Valla's dialogue *On Pleasure (De voluptate)*, of 1430, redefines pleasure as a primary ethical goal in human behavior. In his praise of pleasure and his provocative attacks against the Stoics and Epicureans, Valla seems to echo Lucian's *Parasite*. And although the concluding speaker in the dialogue identifies pleasure with celestial beatitude, the second speaker provocatively celebrates physical pleasure, including a passage which (in apparent tribute to Bruni's oration) celebrates prostitution. In a notorious passage (1.43), Valla asserts that prostitutes serve mankind better than nuns and virgins: "melius merentur scorta et prostibula de genere humano quam sanctimoniales virgines et continentes."[26] Valla echoes Bruni in pointing to the connection between *meretrix* "courtesan" and *bene mereri* "to serve well."[27] This humanistic use of etymology to examine Latin vocabulary without preconceptions is also found in Poggio Bracciolini, who analyzes the adjective *nobilis* in similar fashion. But by the 1440s, Poggio had become Valla's implacable enemy, and in his second invective against Valla, Poggio denounces this very passage.[28]

The second book of Valla's *De voluptate* concludes with an address delivered by a fictitious Vestal virgin before what Valla calls a "Platonic senate." The allusion to

---

[23] Text in *Catinia*, 23–24; Padoan's discussion, 30–31.

[24] *Catinia*, 23–24: "Maro nanque (ut non a rudibus et minimis, sed viris maximis et litteratissimis ordiar), qui poetarum omnium princeps carmine suo illustravit nomen latinum, Priapeiam scripsit, et ita scripsit quod nihil preter rem lupanarem pluris fecisse videatur. Leonardus Aretinus prope eadem, que ille metro, soluta et ornatissima oratione persuasit. . . . Guarinus item Veronensis, quem litteris et latinis doctissimum et grecis doctiorem illis ipsis quos Grecia genuisset fatentur omnes, de parasitica vita, que gulosa et scurrilis est, multa dixit cum iocunditate summa."

[25] See Padoan in *Catinia*, 29 n. 60, and 34–35.

[26] Valla, *De vero falsoque bono*, 38.

[27] Cf. Bruni, *Oratio*, fol. 293: "An fortasse meretricii nomen eas mouet, quod mercedis inest mentio, et mercenaria uidetur opera? Detractent hoc quantum libet; tamen utcunque faciant, et siue domi sese contineant, siue in publico uersentur, iam antea meretrices sunt. Nec equidem uideo quid sordis huic uerbo insit. Nam et milites quoque mereri dicimus, et emerita stipendia, et honorem et praemia mereri, et magna merita appellamus. Nec dubitandum est, quin omnes quae modo aliquid merentur, meretrices sint nuncupande; siquidem et illas, quae aliquid inueniunt, inuentrices, et quae uicerunt, uictrices recte appellamus."

[28] Bracciolini, *Opera omnia*, 1: 232.

Plato recalls Bruni's parody of Platonic communism, and the appearance of a Vestal virgin in Valla's prosopopoeia recalls Cicero's oration *Pro Caelio*, which had supplied Bruni with information about Clodia, the first of the Roman women praised by Heliogabalus.[29]

By the 1430s, the dignified chancellor of the Florentine commune may have been embarrassed by the success of this risqué composition of his earlier years. But the influence of the *Oration of Heliogabalus* makes clear that it reached the "urbane" readers he originally had in mind.

Rutgers University

---

[29] In Cicero's oration, the blind censor Appius Claudius appears in a celebrated example of proposopoeia, and invokes the Vestal virgin Claudia as a reproof to the immoral Clodia. See Cicero, *Pro Caelio* 14.34: "Nonne te, si nostrae imagines viriles non commovebant, ne progenies quidem mea, Q. illa Claudia ... non virgo illa Vestalis Claudia ... ?"

L'immagine di Ferrara nella letteratura estense

MARIA AURELIA MASTRONARDI

I

O Ferraria, quantum Borsio Estensi debes, qui, sua magnanimitate, inveteratam sordidam maculam tuam ab oculis Germanorum tanto cum splendore detersit, ut, cum te denigrare solebant aeris infectione et nascentium rerum tuarum intemperantia, in praesentiarum illam extollant, res omnesque tuas mirum in modum laudent et magnificent nomenque tuum gloriosum per orbem reportantes, inveteratam tuam infamiam sepelientes praedicantesque totius Italiae alteram te paradisum esse[1].

Culmina idealmente nell'immagine di Ferrara quale città perfetta ed ideale il *De felici progressu Borsii Estensis* di Michele Savonarola. Proprio nel momento centrale della ascesa al potere di Borso, quando cioè l'imperatore Federico III sta per conferire all'Estense l'ambito titolo di duca di Modena e Reggio, la narrazione dell'evento pare interrompersi per lasciare spazio ad una breve, ma non per questo meno incisiva, descrizione delle "meraviglie" ferraresi. In una scrittura che della ambiguità sembra aver fatto la sua cifra essenziale (nella prima parte dell'opera si giunge infatti, progressivamente, alla esaltazione di Borso, dopo aver discusso dei pregi di monarchia e repubblica, della superiorità dei regimi ereditari o di quelli elettivi, delle virtù dell'ottimo governante, riscontrate tutte, puntigliosamente, nella figura e nell'operato

---

[1] M. Savonarola, *De felici progressu Borsii Estensis ad marchionatum Ferrariae, Mutinae et Regii ducatum comitatumque Rodigii*, m.s. conservato presso la Biblioteca Estense di Modena, con la segnatura α.W. 2.15: c.30r. È presente anche una redazione in volgare dell'opera (ms. conservato presso la Biblioteca Classense di Ravenna, con la segnatura Cl. 302), di cui ho di recente curato l'edizione (M. Savonarola, *Del felice progresso di Borso d'Este*, a cura di M. A. Mastronardi [Bari, 1997]). Per un profilo del medico umanista, docente a Padova e presso lo Studio ferrarese, archiatra presso Niccolò III, Leonello e Borso, cf. in assenza di una moderna monografia, A. Segarizzi, *Della vita e delle opere di Michele Savonarola* (Padova, 1900); T. Pesenti Marangon, "Michele Savonarola a Padova: l'ambiente, le opere, la cultura medica", *Quaderni per la storia dell'Università di Padova*, 9–10 (1976–1977): 45–102.

dell'Estense, in una ripresa, in forma oratoria, aperta e problematica, di alcuni capitoli fondamentali del *De regimine principum* di Egidio Romano, filtrati umanisticamente attraverso la lezione di Isocrate, Cicerone, Plutarco e Seneca[2]), la *laus Ferrariae* viene enunciata dagli stupefatti Germani, che, al seguito di Federico ammirano non tanto la bellezza del luogo, quanto la magnificenza della vita ferrarese. Se la meraviglia dei visitatori stranieri è un *topos* dei panegirici umanistici di città (si pensi alla *Laudatio Florentinae urbis* di Leonardo Bruni e al *De laudibus Mediolanensium urbis panegyricus* di Pier Candido Decembrio[3]), nel passo savonaroliano alcuni particolari, apparentemente minuti, caricano il tema di una propria specificità. Ai *topoi* della amenità del luogo, della salubrità dell'aria o della bellezza in genere del paesaggio, motivi tutti che connotano in maniera essenziale Firenze o Milano, si contrappone infatti una Ferrara posta in un sito non certo felice dal punto di vista geografico, caratterizzata da un clima non certo salubre e dunque posta in una situazione di iniziale svantaggio. Proprio questa situazione sembra però totalmente sovvertita dal dominio di Borso. Emerge così quella totale identificazione tra Ferrara e la signoria estense che costituirà la nota dominante di vari elogi della città. Se infatti anche l'eccellenza di Firenze e di Milano coincideva, antiteticamente, con l'eccellenza delle rispettive forme di governo e con la *virtus* degli abitanti, la grandezza di Ferrara coincide con il governo perfetto dei suoi signori, in una identificazione totale città-dinastia. Quella città splendida, quel *paradisum mundi inferioris*, appare, in questa prospettiva, diretta emanazione delle virtù del "principe". E non certo a caso il "panegirico di Ferrara" è collocato nella seconda parte dell'opera, quella relativa alla investitura imperiale, risalente al 1452 e dunque cronologicamente successiva alla prima, ove si descriveva l'elezione avvenuta alla morte di Leonello nel 1450 e la assunzione del potere da parte di Borso. Il saggio governo dell'Estense, la saldezza delle istituzioni, la consolidata concordia interna, il mecenatismo del signore hanno reso quindi Ferrara un *alterum paradisum*, una città *imperio digna*, una *altera Roma*[4]. Ma non è solo la perfezione del regime signorile a colpire i Germani: è anche, e in misura non inferiore, lo splendore della corte e la raffinatezza della vita quotidiana[5].

---

[2] Per un'analisi della struttura, delle fonti e dei modelli dell'opera cf. l'*Introduzione* dell'edizione da me curata (M. Savonarola, *Del felice progresso*, 9–55).

[3] La *Laudatio Florentinae urbis* è edita in H. Baron, *From Petrarch to Leonardo Bruni. Studies in Humanistic and Political Literature* (Chicago and London, 1968), 232–263; il *De laudibus Mediolanensium urbis panegyricus* è edito da G. Petraglione in *Archivio Storico Lombardo* (1907): 27–45. Sulla valenza politico-ideologica delle due opere cf. H. Baron, *La crisi del primo Rinascimento italiano* (Firenze, 1970[2]), 209–229.

[4] "Et tanta eo pro tempore fuit hominum frequentia et nobilium virorum multitudo generosa, ut Ferraria veluti altera vetus Roma splenderet" (*De felici progressu*, c.28v).

[5] "Interea in plateis magnificum tribunal ligneum, sedilibus magnificis constructum, parabatur, tapetis ornatum magnificis, mirandisque figuris laneis fulgens, cuius splendore Germani omnes, veluti stupidi facti, mirabantur, opinati tot tamquam magnifica ornamenta apud unicum Italiae minime esse posse, eoque maxime cum Borsii ingens palatium similibus ornamentis undique splenderet. Nam in auribus loquentes, inquiebant:—Princeps is Federicum in ornatu tantarum rerum superat ceterosque omnes Germaniae principes—[. . .] Ceteri vero Germani, non tam hominum multitudinem quam vestimentorum aureorum et sericorum preciositatem stupebant, ut in vicem

Pare affiorare, allusivamente, la topica contrapposizione *civilitas* italica/*immanitas* germanica, secondo un meccanismo strutturale che sembra riprendere alcuni dei nuclei essenziali della *Descriptio urbis Viennensis* di Enea Silvio Piccolomini[6], opera in cui l'umanista italiano, in questo caso visitatore "straniero" della città, pur esaltando i pregi architettonici della capitale austriaca, criticava l'attardata cultura dello Studio e, soprattutto l'eccessivo attaccamento dei Viennesi ai piaceri della gola[7]. L'attonita *comparatio* dei Tedeschi (ben più ampia nella redazione volgare) sembra segnare quindi la sottile, forse ironica, acquisizione del tema: a colpire l'immaginario del seguito di Federico III non è tanto l'ottimo governo di Borso, lo splendore della sua corte, o la vivacità della cultura ferrarese, ma, soprattutto la raffinatezza del vitto e la prelibatezza di cibi e bevande. In quest'ottica, quindi, la differenza tra i due universi, appare, umanisticamente, irriducibile antinomia.

Sono presenti quindi nel *De felice progressu Borsii Estensis* le coordinate essenziali attorno alle quali verrà costruita l'immagine ideale di Ferrara all'interno di quel complesso "sistema" che è la letteratura estense.

II

Già alcuni spunti essenziali affioravano nella *Politia literaria* di Angelo Decembrio, in cui, pur nell'estrema stilizzazione degli elementi, l'immagine idealmente trasfigurata della corte (e dunque della città in essa rispecchiantesi) si imponeva con particolare pregnanza, fino a giungere, nel VI libro, dopo la significativa, topica, discussione tra gli ambasciatori di Firenze e quelli di Milano sui pregi di monarchia e repubblica[8], a identificare nel regime ferrarese (e in particolare nel dominio del "sapiente" Leonello) la più perfetta forma di governo e in particolare una restaurata "età dell'oro"[9].

L'immagine della città e dei suoi assetti politici, della sua connotazione urbanistica e della sua quotidianità, sembra sfumare a tutto vantaggio della dimensione precipuamente culturale: è la corte come luogo di incontro e di dibattito, animata dal reggente-filosofo Leonello e dal suo maestro e consigliere Guarino ad essere delineata, al bivio tra essere e dover essere, quale suprema e rarefatta incarnazione del mito platonico, in una rappresentazione che troverà una sorta di singolare *pendant* nella

---

loquentes, dicerent Germaniam ipsam totam non tot preciosis vestibus esse refertam [. . .] Nam et in memoria tenebant panis ferrariensis pulchritudinem et bonitatem, vini amoenitatem, quadrupedum carnium delectabilem gustum, volatilium preciositatem . . ." (*De felici progressu*, cc. 29r, 30r).

[6] E. S. Piccolomini, *Descriptio urbis Viennensis*, in *Opera omnia* (Basilea, 1571), 718–720.

[7] "Omnes fere cives vinarias tabernas colunt, stubas calefaciunt, coquinam instruunt, bibulos et meretrices accersiunt, hisque cibi aliquid cocti gratis praebent ut amplius bibant sed minorem mensuram dant. Plebs ventri dedita, vorax, quicquid hebdomada manu quaesivit, id festo die totum absumit lacerum et incompositum vulgus" (*Descriptio urbis Viennensis*, 718).

[8] A. Decembrio, *Politia literaria* (Basilea, 1562), 539–544.

[9] "Uti vos quoque, ferrariensis populus imo aurensis, si dici liceat, magis in aurea velut aetate degentes, sub optimo principe Leonello illustrique Estensium, felicissime gubernamur" (Decembrio, *Politia*, 542).

orazione in morte del Veronese di Ludovico Carbone (1460). Sarà infatti l'intera Ferrara, profondamente modificata dalla svolta impressa dall'umanista e permeata dalla nuova cultura a stringersi in maniera corale attorno alla salma del maestro[10].

La puntigliosa enumerazione dei personaggi, membri di spicco della corte e della Cancelleria o semplici funzionari, ma tutti egualmente partecipi della lezione guariniana[11], sembra segnare una sorta di ulteriore realizzazione del mito platonico. Ferrara è dunque una sorta di "città ideale" perché la lezione umanistica non è più soltanto patrimonio di pochi, della eletta schiera degli interlocutori di Leonello, ma è fondamento ideologico e culturale comune per tutti coloro che, a livelli diversi, provvedono alla amministrazione dello stato.

Ma, al di là del vagheggiamento del mito umanistico, che nella sua dirompente essenzialità rimarrà circoscritto alla sola età di Leonello, è l'identificazione contemporaneità-età dell'oro a costituire il tema più foriero di sviluppi e di implicazioni.

III

Ai primi anni Sessanta è riconducibile la composizione dei *De laudibus Estensium carmina* e dei *Pastoralia*[12] di Matteo Maria Boiardo. Tali opere appaiono addirittura permeate dalla concezione escatologica dei *Saturnia regna*, in quella speculare fusione dei due archetipi virgiliani (*Buc.*, IV; *Aen.*, VI, 791–793) che diverrà un vero e proprio *topos* in ambito ferrarese. I *De laudibus Estensium carmina* sono organizzati secondo una precisa linea narrativa: prendendo infatti le mosse dai progenitori troiani, si giunge ad esaltare Ercole d'Este e si ripercorrono i momenti salienti della sua vita. Viene introdotta così l'identificazione tra l'età di Borso, caratterizzata da pace e prosperità, e la rinnovata "età dell'oro", fino a giungere, nel componimento conclusivo, alla ripresa dello schema ciclico delle età del mondo, culminante nell'affermazione secondo la quale solo sotto la signoria estense potranno rinnovarsi gli *aurea saecla*[13]. Allo stesso modo, nell'egloga IV, in cui l'ovvia adesione al modello virgiliano diviene umanistica *aemulatio*, l'età di Borso (ma anche di Ercole e Sigismondo) raggiunge l'idealizzazione estrema. E se scompare totalmente, nell'eterna primavera dell'età di Saturno, qualsiasi riferimento concreto alla corte o alla città, la trasfigurazione degli elementi non fa che trasporre la contemporaneità e, nello specifico, un preciso disegno dinastico, nella dimensione assolutizzante del mito[14]. Se si considera infatti

---

[10] Cf. G. Bertoni, *Guarino da Verona fra letterati e cortigiani a Ferrara* (Ginevra, 1921) (l'orazione del Carbone è edita alle pagine 160–175).

[11] Bertoni, *Guarino*, 166.

[12] Cf. M. M. Boiardo, *Le poesie volgari e latine*, a c. di A. Solerti (Bologna, 1894), 407–470. Su queste opere e sul ruolo in esse ricoperto dal mito dell'"età dell'oro", cf. E. Bigi, "La poesia latina del Boiardo", *Giornale storico della letteratura italiana* 146 (1969): 321–338; G. Costa, *La leggenda dei secoli d'oro nella letteratura italiana* (Bari, 1972), 59–72.

[13] "... Namque iterum Estensis sub pectore tuta resedit / Herculis alma fides, / iustitiaeque decus simul isdem sedibus alba / relligio subiit, / aureaque Estensi rursus sub principe saecla / reddita sunt populis" (Boiardo, *De laudibus Estensium carmina*, 15, vv. 45–50).

[14] "Haec primum incipient, bis septem saecula postquam / transierint, decimumque eadem post saecula lustrum / quo Deus omnipotens hominis sub imagine terras / diluit et veterum noxas

che queste opere, dedicate a Ercole d'Este, furono composte subito dopo il suo ritorno dall'esilio napoletano e la nomina a governatore di Modena (1462) e che dunque esse risalgono al momento in cui è proprio il problema della successione ad essere al centro del dibattito politico ferrarese, nello scontro tra il partito della Vela, facente capo al giovane Niccolò di Leonello, e quello del Diamante, facente capo ad Ercole, traspare come lo stesso impiego di *topoi* e di modelli classici in genere vada ben al di là di un processo di riscrittura in senso piattamente e aproblematicamente encomiastico, ma come esso risponda ad un ben più complesso meccanismo di rifunzionalizzazione in senso schiettamente politico, in una sorta di dialogo, fondante ed ineludibile, con la contemporaneità.

IV

Tito Vespasiano Strozzi, nel IV libro della sua *Borsias*, ripropone l'immagine della rinnovata età di Saturno quale conseguenza diretta delle virtù di Borso, in una elencazione in cui lo schema canonico perde qualsiasi genericità per calarsi nella concreta realtà ferrarese ed offrire, ancora una volta, l'immagine dello stato perfetto, in cui giustizia, clemenza ed intestina concordia sono davvero principi di governo[15].

Lo stesso *topos* del superamento della logica delle armi a tutto favore della pace[16] si colora in questo contesto di una propria intrinseca specificità. Viene introdotto infatti il tema di Borso pacificatore, Borso arbitro delle controversie fra gli stati italiani, Borso fautore ed artefice della pace all'interno dello stato e nell'intera penisola, secondo un meccanismo di ufficiale autorappresentazione, oltremodo pregno di implicazioni. Tutte le opere prese in esame sono infatti ascrivibili al periodo successivo alla pace di Lodi (1454), agli anni in cui il signore estense, costretto ad abbandonare qualsiasi mira di espansione o consolidamento territoriale, attraverso una ostentata opera di mediazione, tenta di assumere un ruolo non secondario quale arbitro

---

tulit inde malorum. / Tunc iterum mores, terrenaque corpora menti / astrorum regis suberunt, tunc Borsia virtus / immortale decus caelo mittetur ab alto. [. . .] Ver dabit et flores, te praeside, frugibus aestas / dives erit multis, tunc poma Autumnus et uva / conferet ac pleni vix stabunt pondere rami, / brumaque iam tepido mitescet dura sereno; / tunc grandes pecudum foetus, tunc copia lactis. / Tunc nec sanguinei radiabit stella cometae, / nec vastum insanis consurget fluctibus aequor; / non catulum rabies, pecudem non tabida pestis / corripiet, flavas rubigo haud horrida messes / eruet, haud tristi procumbent gramine vites" (*Pastoralia*, 4: 18–24; 76–85).

[15] W. Ludwig, *Die "Borsias" des Tito Strozzi* (Monaco, 1977), 4: 13–67. I primi quattro libri dell'opera sono anch'essi ascrivibili agli anni Sessanta.

[16] "Horridaque armorum studiis exercitus inter / bella ferox quamvis iuveniles egerit annos / non animi praestantis egens, non inscius artis / militiae, quam poscit opus, tamen otia pacis / dat patriae strepitumque insani a finibus arcet / Martis et externas componit foedere gentes. / Tantane Maeonii sacro de pectore flucit / vena senis, tantum divinae Aeneidos autor / praestitit ingenio, si luce fruatur uterque / rursus, ut exilem res condere principis huius / materiam esse putet ac tot benefacta referre? / Tu, cui pandit iter virtus et gloria coelo, / cuius ab aethereis fatalem sedibus aevum / indulsere dei terris, Saturnia quo sub / saecula nunc redeunt, unde, olim fulgere mundo / vicinum Erigone non indignabitur astrum, / dexter ades, Borsi! Te nil praesente monere / magnum ego ausim; nec me fiducia linquit, / quod mea Permessi libarit parcius undam / te duce Sandalio sitis exaturata liquore" (Ludwig, *Die "Borsias"*, 4: 48–67).

inter pares nel concerto delle potenze italiane. In questo senso anche il *topos* squisitamente umanistico del superamento delle arti della guerra e della esaltazione della pace foriera di civiltà, al di là delle sue matrici ideali e culturali, acquista un concreto significato di ordine politico: i *Saturnia regna* restaurati corrispondono quindi, in quest'ottica, proprio a quella pace, a quella concordia, a quel rifiuto di qualsiasi conflitto da Borso tenacemente perseguito a livello ufficiale. Dopo gli aspri conflitti che avevano dilaniato, nel serrato gioco delle mutevoli alleanze, l'Italia della prima metà del XV secolo, la *renovatio* sembra finalmente aver avuto inizio proprio ad opera dell'Estense, in questo senso moderna trasposizione del *puer* virgiliano.

V

Il medesimo schema e le medesime tematiche sono presenti nel *De excellentium virorum principibus ab origine mundi per aetates* di Antonio Cornazzano. Tutte le età della terra e tutte le vicende dei grandi eroi della Bibbia e del mondo classico, da Adamo a Noè, da Mosè a David, da Omero a Romolo, da Annibale a Scipione, da Pompeo a Cicerone, da Cesare a Carlo Magno, ritenuto il capostipite degli Estensi, vengono rappresentati in un disegno strutturale in cui ordine cronologico e prospettiva ideologica sembrano coincidere e culminare nella conclusiva esaltazione della casa d'Este e di Borso in particolare. Egli appare così, ancora una volta, quale supremo pacificatore[17] e, in una ulteriore, sottile, identificazione con il modello augusteo, quale artefice del nuovo, splendido volto della città[18].

Lo stesso schema della ciclicità sembra in questa prospettiva infrangersi, o meglio coesistere con il senso di una evoluzione costante, per cui l'età presente, l'"aurea Ferrara", non appare soltanto l'incarnazione di una mitica età perduta, quanto il punto di arrivo di un lungo cammino, in cui sembrano davvero concretizzarsi le attese dell'età nuovo i *Saturnia regna* non sono più soltanto il sogno di una vagheggiata palingenesi, ma sono divenuti, nel presente, realtà. Lo stesso richiamo costante al signore d'Este, dalla dedica al continuo dialogo a distanza istituito tra lui e tutti i grandi della Bibbia e dell'antichità, non fa che suggerire un continuo confronto e, el contempo un precise un percorso di lettura: ogni evento, ogni personaggio, nella tutta ideologica fusione tra dimensione "storica" e dimensione propriamente narrativa, non è, in questa prospettiva, che un momento di preparazione all'"età dell'oro", che Ferrara, erede consapevole di tutto un patrimonio classico e cristiano e in questo senso quasi punto di arrivo della millenaria vicenda dell'umanità, sembra vivere sotto la casa d'Este.

---

[17] "Verus enim princeps discordibus acta tyrannis / sumptibus emendat consilioque praemit / et tot mutantes scelerum sub pondere terras / adiuvat ac casus firma columna tenet. / Tum sibi bellorum cessit scelerata libido / nec Iani ancipitis post patuere fores. / Orbi pulchra fuit pacis Ferraria templum / et circum haec tenuit Mars loca sancta nihil" (A. Cornazzano, *De excellentium virorum principibus ab origine mundi per aetates*, ms. conservato presso la Biblioteca Estense di Modena, con la segnatura α P. 6.4, c.56r).

[18] "Huic invenies aequam a palatio coelo / subque oculis mundum, nil nisi marmor erit. / Tum quasi divinam mutus miraberis urbem / et dices nostri motus honore ducis" (Cornazzano, *De excellentium*, c.56v).

VI

Ma sarà Ludovico Carbone nella sua opera sovrabbondante e multiforme a delineare l'immagine forse più ricca e completa della magnificenza di Ferrara.

Nell'epitalamio per Giovanni Romei e Polissena d'Este (figlia di Meliaduse, fratellestro di Borse) il legame tra le canoniche virtù del sovrano e la perfezione dello stato ferrarese, nello splendore della corte e dell'intera città, appare oltremodo cogente, in una ulteriore ambigua rifunzionalizzazione del *pattern* di ascendenza classica e medievale. Vengono esaltate, ancora una volta, concordia e prosperità interna e torna l'immagine di Borso quale infaticabile artefice della *pax Italiae*[19]. Ma culmine ideale dell'intero segmento relativo alle virtù dell'Estense e al suo ottimo governo può essere considerata quella singolare rappresentazione dello sfarzo del signore e della sua corte, attuata attraverso una rutilante *congeries*[20].

È, ancora una volta, l'immagine di una irripetibile "età dell'oro" quella che emerge da questa descrizione preziosa, ma di una "età dell'oro" dai connotati fortemente e ostentatamente cortesi, a conferma ulteriore di come, ancora a questa data, a Ferrara il modo di vedere, leggere, interpretare e riscrivere l'antico sia ancora pervicacemente cortese[21]. È, in sostanza, lo stesso programma che governa la fascia mediana del Salone dei Mesi del palazzo di Schifanoia, in cui il tema conduttore delle virtù del signore si stempera nella rappresentazione sfarzosa della vita di corte, dei suoi rituali e delle sue mitologie, con lo sfondo di una Ferrara reale, ma al tempo stesso fortemente idealizzata nella sua stilizzazione. Ancora una volta, a conferma di quei sottilissimi nessi che fanno della cultura estense un reticolo oltremodo ricco di collusioni e rimandi intertestuali, si assiste alla fusione dei *topoi* relativi alle virtù del principe e alla

---

[19] "Contra Fortuna parum valet umana diligentia sed maxime in re bellica Fortuna vult esse domina. Unde plurimum collaudandi summique laudibus efferendi estis, o Italiae principes, qui, tandem furore deposito, otio, tranquillitate, concordiae pacique Italiae consulere voluistis, tuque in primis, mitissime ac placidissime dux, qui tantos labores, tantasque impensas suscepisti ad componendam hanc italicam pacem" (L. Carbone, *Opera*, ms. conservato presso la Biblioteca Universitaria di Bologna, Misc. Tioli, 36, c.197r).

[20] "Eius animi magnitudinem declarat ornatissimus ac nitidissimus aulae apparatus, tantus famulatus, tanta purpuratorum iuvenum multitudo, tot auro intertexta vestimenta, tot vasa ex solido argento auroque perfecta, tot aulea tapeta, peristromata, segmenta, monilia, tantus numerus margaritarum et omnis generis gemmarum, carbunculi, adatae, hyacintia, corallia, syrtites, veientanae, poenitae, ponticae, smaragdi, cyaneai, crystalli, galleici, ceraunia, gagatae, nasamonitae, chrisoprasi, hematitae, sardonices, malachitae, andiodiamantes, magnites, lychnitae, berylli, ametisti et omnis generis lapilli qui preciosi habentur, in quibus natura vires suas occultavit; tot accipitres, tot falcones, tot canes, tot equi sonipedes, quot maximi Persarum reges non habuerunt, tot sumptuosissima aedificia, et urbana et rusticana et omnia fere distributa et donata" (Carbone, *Opera*, c.201r). Il medesimo segmento, secondo una prassi non infrequente nel Carbone, torna, immutato, nell'orazione pronunziata dinanzi a Federico III (1469) e nell'orazione in morte di Borso (1470) (Carbone, *Opera*, c.240r; c.220r).

[21] Su questo aspetto essenziale della cultura ferrarese cf. A. Tissoni Benvenuti, "L'antico a corte: da Guarino a Boiardo," in *Alla corte degli Estensi. Filosofia, arte e cultura a Ferrara nei secoli XV e XVI* (Modena, 1994), 390. Sul ruolo dell'oratoria cfr. M. A. Mastronardi, '*Officina eloquentiae*'. *Oratoria e politica nella ferrara estense* (Patenza, 1999).

rappresentazione, in un contesto generale che non può non far pensare alla rinnovata instaurazione dei *Saturnia regna*, della città e della corte ideale. La presenza di questa griglia di *topoi* all'interno di generi diversi, dalla trattatistica alla poesia encomiastica, dall' oratoria al dialogo, fino a giungere al complesso e totalizzante programma di Schifanoia, non può che costituire una prova ulteriore della straordinaria duttilità delle maglie del reticolo, della complessa organicità di un sistema che permea ed ingloba generi e forme diverse in una suprema ricerca di autorappresentazione, in cui parola, scrittura, arte figurativa e immaginario collettivo concorrono a costruire un modello, una identità cittadina altra e diversa rispetto a quella dei vari centri italiani. Lo stesso *topos* della *Ferraria felix*, nella sua collusione tra età dell'oro e città ideale, diviene in questa prospettiva una spia oltremodo pregna di significazioni della "diversità" ferrarese, del complesso meccanismo di ricezione/riuso di temi e motivi desunti dal mondo antico, dall'immaginario cavalleresco e dal coevo dibattito umanistico, ambiguamente fusi in quel variegato ed inquietante crogiolo che fu oppunto la Ferrara del XV secolo.

Univerità delle Basilicate, Potenza

Joseph Hall's Mundus Alter et Idem: *Utopian Dream Turned Comic Nightmare*

ELIZABETH McCUTCHEON

In 1605, almost ninety years after More's *Utopia* was first published, *Mundus Alter et Idem* appeared, purportedly written by Mercurius Britannicus. Like *Utopia*, the *Mundus* is well aware of contemporaneous explorations in the new world and their material, psychological, and philosophical impact there and in Europe.[1] Like *Utopia*, too, it is grounded in a putative traveler's report of the customs and institutions of hitherto unknown people and places.[2] But where the *Utopia* abjures any discussion of monsters, preferring to inquire about "well and wisely trained citizens,"[3] the *Mundus* is about peoples whom its audience would have considered monstrous,[4] yet who turn out to resemble us. This generates an almost metaphysical wit, one dependent upon finding similitudes in differences. The *Mundus* offers apparently inexhaustible instances of people who seem so very different and whom Mercurius describes with an ironically straight-faced hyperbole. But even as the *Mundus* exploits a fascination with the "Other"—hence its subsequent English translation as *The Discovery of a New World* (1609)[5]—it collapses these differences; both *Alter et Idem*, it insists that hope is illusory and transforms eutopian dream to dystopian nightmare. Intensifying the satiric element of the *Utopia*, the *Mundus* becomes an anti-utopia or dystopia; while ostensibly describing another world, it magnifies the folly and depravity of ours.

---

[1] See the discussion in David Fausett, *Writing the New World: Imaginary Voyages and Utopias of the Great Southern Land* (Syracuse, 1993), 42–51.

[2] John M. Wands, "Antipodal Imperfection: Hall's *Mundus Alter et Idem* and Its Debt to More's *Utopia*," *Moreana* 18 (March 1981): 85–100, has a fuller discussion of Hall's similarities to More.

[3] Thomas More, *Utopia: Latin Text and English Translation*, ed. George M. Logan, Robert M. Adams, and Clarence H. Miller (Cambridge, MA, 1995), 49.

[4] On the significance of the nomenclature and types of people considered "monstrous" in the middle ages and early Renaissance, see John B. Friedman, *The Monstrous Races in Medieval Art and Thought* (Cambridge, MA, 1981). Many of these types appear in Hall's work.

[5] This version of the *Mundus* was translated by John Healey. See the edition of Healey edited by Huntington Brown (Cambridge, MA, 1937); the notes are invaluable.

Its actual author, Joseph Hall (1574–1656), sometimes called the "English Seneca" because of his Christian Stoicism and English prose style,[6] had a long and generally successful career as cleric and writer. In 1597 and 1598, while still at Cambridge, he published six books of verse satires, staking out his claim to be the first English satirist.[7] Ordained in 1600, he became the rector of Hawstead, Suffolk, a year later, and it was here that he finished the *Mundus*, although he may well have begun it at Cambridge.[8] Certainly Hall's intended audience is young, male, and academic enough to enjoy the many allusions to and parodies of classical, medieval, and Renaissance texts;[9] the learned marginalia; the almost Joycean wordplay; and the linguistic prowess: Hall drew on at least seven languages in making up the names of places and persons, which he highlighted by way of an elaborate glossary.

The prefatory address, signed by Hall's friend, William Knight, claims that the work, which purports to have been printed in Frankfurt, was finished many years earlier and published against the express will of the author, who has given himself wholly to theology. But the *Mundus* was actually printed in London by Humphrey Lownes, who printed Hall's first devotional work, *Meditations and Vowes*, the same year.[10] Moreover, the *Mundus* is dedicated to Henry Hastings, the fifth Earl of Huntingdon. Hall dedicated two later works to him, calling him "the first patron of my poor studies."[11] It looks, then, as if the *Mundus* was, in part, an early and ambitious effort, by Hall himself, to promote his career at a time when he felt himself both underpaid and underappreciated.[12]

---

[6] Leonard D. Tourney, *Joseph Hall* (Boston, 1979), 17; George Williamson, *The Senecan Amble: A Study in Prose Form from Bacon to Collier* (London, 1951; repr. Chicago, 1966), 246–248.

[7] Joseph Hall, *The Collected Poems*, ed. A. Davenport (Liverpool, 1949), 11.

[8] John Millar Wands, trans. and ed., *Another World and Yet the Same: Bishop Joseph Hall's "Mundus Alter et Idem"* (New Haven, 1981), xviii.

[9] To the audience traditionally singled out, fellow students of the University of Cambridge, we need to add those who had attended the Inns of Court, like Hall's dedicatee. For a fine analysis of the way Tudor and Jacobean schoolboys were taught to read and for evidence of actual Tudor reading, see Eugene R. Kintgen, *Reading in Tudor England* (Pittsburgh, 1996), 18–98. Kintgen documents the radically intertextual nature of Tudor writing; studies of intertextuality in the *Mundus* include Sandford M. Salyer, "Renaissance Influences in Hall's *Mundus Alter et Idem*," *Philological Quarterly* 6 (1937): 321–334; and Giampaolo Zucchini, "Utopia e satira nel *Mundus alter et idem* di Joseph Hall," *Il Pensiero politico* 9 (1976): 248–275. The best discussion of the *Mundus*, in Richard A. McCabe, *Joseph Hall: A Study in Satire and Meditation* (Oxford, 1982), 73–109, includes some fascinating material on the ways in which Hall combined the diverse works he drew upon.

[10] See, in particular, John Millar Wands, "The Early Printing History of Joseph Hall's *Mundus Alter et Idem*," *The Papers of the Bibliographical Society of America* 74 (1980): 1–12.

[11] Wands, *Another World*, xvii.

[12] Biographical studies include Tourney, *Joseph Hall*, and Tom Fleming Kinloch, *The Life and Works of Joseph Hall* (London, 1951); see, in particular, Kinloch, *Life and Works*, 17–24. Hall himself comments on difficulties in his years at Hawstead; see *Observations of Some Specialties of Divine Providence in the Life of Joseph Hall* (1659), included in *Works of the Right Reverend Joseph Hall, D. D.*, ed. Philip Wynter, 10 vols. (Oxford, 1863; repr. New York, 1969), 1: xxvii and xxxiii–xxxv.

Like Hall, the narrator, Mercurius Britannicus, is an academic stay-at-home with an inexhaustible thirst for learning. Persuaded by his friend, Peter Beroaldus, he decides to emulate such explorers as Francis Drake, Thomas Cavendish, Sebastian del Cano, Christopher Columbus, Ferdinand Magellan, Francisco Pizarro, and Hugh Willoughby, and sets out with Beroaldus and another friend to discover yet another new world. Early on, then, Hall invokes the utopian dream and eschatological fervor that inspired a figure like Columbus, whose name he links with the dove (*columba*) that showed Noah signs of land.[13] But Mercurius soon finds himself continuing the journey alone, heroically or rather, pseudo-heroically preferring "innumerable and unknown perils" to the "derisive laughter" of his friends, should he abandon the voyage to the southern land of *terra australis* (17).[14] Naïve, but ever "alacer" (eager) (18), he sails beyond the Fortunate Isles and the Cape of Good Hope to land at the Black Cape of Crapulia. Thus the *Mundus* turns into a symbolic survey of human-kind's depravity. Playing moral and social issues out spatially—there are five hand-some maps (themselves parodies of Ortelius' and Mercator's)—it generates a brilliant, if wholly negative, allegorical geography, as Mercurius explores four huge regions in terra australis: Crapulia, Viraginia, Moronia, and Lavernia.[15]

Mercurius' first stop, Crapulia, the subject of Book I, is "a large and splendid region" (19), made up of two provinces, Pamphagonia, a land of gluttons, and Yvronia, a land of drinkers. This is, perhaps, the most amusing part of his journey, although the comedy is bizarre. Crapulia is an embodied monomania and a *reductio ad absur-dum*; everything is defined by way of food and/or drink. Pamphagonia, for instance, has ten commandments—all concerned with the consumption of food; the people have no use for money, buying and selling goods (all edible) by barter; they worship the God of Time, Saturn, who is the "*edax rerum*" (eater of things) and appears in the shape of RUC, a monstrous bird of prey (49); they wage war with the Hambrians or hungry ones and the Frugionans; and they have a knife and broad spoon attached to their right hand, while the inhabitants of Ucalegonium, a so-called free city, live by Sybarite law: "Coenant, dormiunt, surgunt, prandent, recumbunt" (44): "They dine, they sleep, they rise, they breakfast, they lie down" (32).

There is a lot of local satire: geographically, the two provinces are mirror oppo-sites of England and Germany, and some of the drinking customs parody those at Cambridge, for instance. But satire quickly becomes dystopian. Crapulia is a gro-tesque version of the land of Cockaigne, a popular quasi-utopia that envisions a land of plenty that satisfies all appetites and can be enjoyed without effort.[16] In its present

---

[13] Mercurius Britannicus [actually Joseph Hall], *Mundus Alter et Idem* (Frankfurt [actually London], n.d. [1605]), 11. Subsequent citations from the Latin text will be from this edition and included in the text.

[14] Normally, citations from the English text are to the translation by John Millar Wands and will be included in the text with page number; a few short translations without page numbers are my own.

[15] McCabe, *Joseph Hall*, includes Map One from Ortelius' *Epitome of the Theatre of the Worlde* (1603), facing 87, and discusses Hall, Ortelius, and Mercator, 85–88.

[16] On Cockaigne as a people's utopia and Hall's contempt for it, see A. L. Morton, *The English*

form, it represents a wholly sensate or corporal existence, one devoid of anything spiritual. For Crapulians, then, the "swine [is] the best and most useful of all animals" (30). And their "slaves" or bondsmen (actually the undersized) are given the well-fed bodies of wealthy aristocrats, who drank too much and died, to feast upon—a kind of cannibalism that appears to be a perverse parody of both the Christian eucharist and the revolutionary politics implicit in the idea of Cockaigne. In fact, cannibalism, one of Europe's greatest fears in its new world encounters, is a recurrent motif in the *Mundus*, where it comes to symbolize the way that people prey upon one another. Later, then, we hear about Orgilia, located in Moronia Aspera, where the citizens "feed on raw flesh, usually human" (84), and become drunk on the blood; the legs of men hang in the butcher shops; and the palace of the Duke, who dines on the head of any unwary traveler, rests on top of a mountain of human skulls—anticipating the killing fields of Cambodia and other examples from current newspaper headlines. Book I, though, has a half-comic explanation: the Crapulians hate to see good food go to waste.

Book II of the *Mundus* relies upon reversal and multi-focal word play as well as exaggeration. In Viraginia, also called New Gynia, the gender relationships of early modern England are turned upside down; now men are the subordinate sex and women are on top. Thus the region's names and practices simultaneously satirize the colonial enterprise in Northern America, such as that led by Sir Walter Raleigh, whose book on Guiana had been published in 1596. Raleigh's motives—which he himself characterized as "To seeke new worlds, for golde, for prayse, for glory"[17]— are repeatedly impugned in the *Mundus*, as is the imagined nature of women. Viraginia, it seems, is where geographers locate the Land of Parrots, and Viraginians are insatiably talkative and lustful as well as shrill and dangerous viragoes who wear the trousers and compel their husbands to do all the domestic chores that were normally woman's lot in England.

Some of this anti-woman satire is traditional. Hall exploits banal notions of women's loquacity and vanity, taps Erasmus' colloquy on the parliament of women, draws upon legends about the fabled Amazons,[18] and enters "Land of Shrewes," (almost the only English words in the *Mundus*, appearing in black letter in the margin [104]) while the narrator, who was arrested and carried away from Crapulia by the Viraginians, saves himself by capitalizing on the proverbial (albeit fallacious) notion that England is a paradise for women. Such satire was particularly topical by 1605; King James, who had succeeded to the throne in 1603, was a misogynist, and attacks on women who cross-dressed, wore make-up, and/or challenged the status quo in any way became increasingly virulent. Once again, though, satire triggers deeper, dystop-

---

Utopia (London, 1952), 11–26. J. C. Davis, *Utopia and the Ideal Society: A Study of English Utopian Writing: 1516–1700* (Cambridge, 1981), has a more theoretical discussion of Cockaigne, 20–22. Hall's opposition to the land of Cockaigne is one aspect of a more general conservatism that permeates the *Mundus*.

[17] *The Poems of Sir Walter Ralegh*, ed. Agnes M. C. Latham (London, 1951), 27.

[18] See, in particular, Celeste Turner Wright, "The Amazons in Elizabethan Literature," *Studies in Philology* 37 (1940): 433–456.

ian reverberations. Some are sexual and erotic: the text taps the masculine fear of sexual exhaustion even as it arouses male fantasies, to judge by the almost pornographic frontispiece in the 1643 Utrecht edition of utopian fictions by Hall, Campanella, and Bacon.[19] Even more telling are the power plays dramatized by the shift in relationships, all of them pictured as awry because women have won the traditional battle of the sexes. The government, for instance, is a "democracy," since every woman wants to govern. At the same time, males are victimized—by indirection saying something about the problems women faced in England, a situation the *Mundus* otherwise only hints about.[20]

Book III, Moronia, is the core of the *Mundus*, if we can speak of a "core" or "center" when the boundaries are permeable, the situation global. In this way the *Mundus* resembles an illustration (around 1590–1600) at the Bodleian Library, Oxford: a fool's cap encloses a world map based on one by Ortelius, and the motto above it reads, "*Stultorum infinitus est numerus*" [The number of fools is infinite].[21] Moronia's population is equally large, although Mercurius, for once, understates the case, remarking that, by contrast with Moronia, a country like China appears depopulated. Moronia is also "*incultissima*" (very squalid) (113), "*multiplex*" (changeable), and "*multiformis*" (diverse) (115), given its five sections: Moronia Variana, Aspera, Fatua, Felix, and Pia. Seemingly every imaginable sort of folly is satirized, then, and Moronia teems with instances of physical, intellectual, moral, and spiritual aberrations. One person is convinced he is made of glass. Some have turned themselves into chimneys by smoking tobacco. And huge numbers of "religious clergy," also called Morosophi, roam the region; like the people in Erasmus' *Moria*, "they light candles in the middle of the day" (71)—one of the mildest charges made in the *Mundus* against Roman Catholic practices.[22]

But Mercurius' narrative is most powerful, and most dystopian, when it creates highly charged moral-psychological landscapes that resemble comparable moments in Spenser's *Faerie Queene*. There is the Cave of Maninconicus, for example, where huge icicles, like gigantic teeth, hang from the roof, and "the disturbed souls of melancholic people are tortured by the most intense cold" (82).[23] Or the Paradise of Moronia

---

[19] This frontispiece is conveniently reproduced in Joseph Hall, *Un Mundo distinto pero igual*, trans. with introduction and notes, Emilio García Estébanez (Madrid, 1994), 30.

[20] See the beginning of Book II, chapter 4, which comments on the cruelty in England that led some women to escape to Viraginia; cf. Tourney, *Joseph Hall*, 39–40.

[21] Included in Stephen J. Greenblatt, *Marvellous Possessions: The Wonder of the New World* (Chicago, 1991), figure 10, labeled "Travel as folly." There is a fine discussion of this fool's cap map in Anne S. Chapple, "Robert Burton's Geography of Melancholy," *Studies in English Literature* 33 (1993): 100–130.

[22] Such satire is virtually omnipresent in the *Mundus*; see Claude Lascassagne, "La satire religieuse dans *Mundus alter et idem* de Joseph Hall," *Recherches anglaises et nord-américaines* 4 (1971): 141–156. For the analogy in Erasmus, see *The Praise of Folly*, trans. Clarence H. Miller (New Haven and London, 1979), 75.

[23] McCabe, *Joseph Hall*, 90, points out that the geography here is based upon Richard Eden's *Decades of the New World*.

Felix, which, set at the top of a glittering mountain built out of gold—or what appears to be gold—is given its own story-line. The Goddess Fortune (whom the text identifies with the Madonna) has her throne here, and innumerable pilgrims attempt to find her favor. But even the very few who apparently succeed are the victims of a dream turned nightmare; day-old kings, they mourn for a lost, but delusive, past. Scenes like these illuminate the psychology of Moronians—which is to say everyone, everywhere—as people try to be something they are not, dwelling in a world of illusion, and having either no knowledge or understanding of self or a misplaced faith in something or someone other than the true God. There is a crucial societal aspect too: we witness the breakdown of community. Everyone is isolated, incapable of constructing positive relationships. Hermits and tyrants live here, the latter guided by the rule of "Vince & Fruere" [Conquer and Enjoy] (145), while the original inhabitants walks on all fours, have no houses, can neither cook food nor make clothes, and, perhaps most frightening of all, do not know their parents, children, or spouse—some do not even know how to feed themselves (87).

Lavernia, the last major region Mercurius visits, is a logical outgrowth of the personal and communal breakdown pictured in Book III. A land of thieves and deceivers who are more like beasts than human beings, it is in a constant state of civil war: "*nunquam non intestina bella*" (197). Everyone lives for himself by "*dolus*" or "*vis*," deceit or force (193); everyone seeks to appropriate "*peculium*" [money or property] for himself. Even babes in arms are taught to steal, beginning with small pins and coins, and are beaten if they're not quick enough. Lavernia is, then, a complete dystopia that anticipates Thomas Hobbes' terrifying picture of the natural condition of humankind as "solitary, poore, nasty, brutish, and short."[24] The last province we hear about, indeed, is populated by monstrous men who resemble the aboriginal inhabitants of Moronia: they have hog's heads, walk on all fours, never look skyward, grunt rather than speak, and live in lairs rather than homes. But Halls casts his "remedy"—insofar as there is one—in fictional and psychological, rather than political, terms. Mercurius claims to have founded a school in Lavernia, where, "as the omniscient soothsayer," he "boldly wrote the truest prophecy of this age" (113). Playing, in good Lucianic and Morean fashion, on the paradox of lying and truth-telling in fiction, and satirizing Mercurius' role, Hall indirectly invites reflection on the whole of the *Mundus*.

Unlike More's *Utopia*, this work does not end in an expression of hope, however ambiguous. Rather, after gazing upon, being astonished by, and laughing at men, customs, and cities for thirty years, Mercurius returns home, exhausted by his travels (117).[25] He may be older (although he doesn't seem to be), but he is none the wiser. Instead, he has moved ever more deeply into the dystopian world, exhausting any hope of discovering a eutopia or a truly new world. In fact, if we plot his travels on the map of *terra australis*, he has gone in a complete circle, failing to discover

---

[24] Thomas Hobbes, *Leviathan*, ed. Richard Tuck (Cambridge, 1991), 89.

[25] Critics have suggested that the thirty year figure may be significant; Hall himself was thirty years old in 1605.

either Frugiona, on the eastern border of Viraginia, or the Holy Land, which is next to Moronia Pia and still *"ignota"* (unknown). For the narrator, then, there is no question of insight or self-knowledge.

But how do we as readers interpret Mercurius Britannicus' self-conscious performance? For one answer, we could step back and, mindful of the message implied by Frugiona and "terra sancta ignota etiam adhuc" [the holy land still as yet unknown], consider the value of moderation and sobriety while starting to search for the true holy land. We could also remember *"Nosce teipsum"* [know yourself][26]—words that are above the fool's cap on the illustration at the Bodleian Library and implicit throughout the *Mundus*. Or we could look to Hall's many meditative and devotional works, which he began to publish in 1605, seeing the *Mundus* as a transitional work as Hall, later an Anglican bishop, turned from satire to religion. Or, if we want a more specifically political answer that shows Hall as both staunchly Protestant and staunchly conservative, we could read the moral commonwealth Hall extrapolated from Proverbs and Ecclesiastes (1609), a dreary collection of texts on law and order that could be summarized as, "Feare God and keep his Commandments."[27]

But these answers are all too easy, and partial, at best. Hall himself early and continuously believed that "Mundus senescit, the World groweth old."[28] Certainly the *Mundus* evinces almost no sense that improvement is possible. If change occurs, then, it will be for the worse, by analogy with Mercurius' own travels to the antipodes; here as later, Hall satirizes the very idea of travel.[29] Characteristically, Hall identifies himself at only one point in the *Mundus* (and then obliquely); he includes his initials, inverted, in the middle of an epitaph directed to the traveler, who is encouraged to *"Mane, Lege, Ambula"* [Stop, Read, Walk on] (127)—the imperatives miming the reader's process through the text. The subject of the inscription is equally telling: one Andrew Vortunius, who "lived his life not in the city, not in the country, not at home, not abroad, not on the sea, not on land, not here, not anywhere, but everywhere" (75). But "Neque hic, nec alibi, sed vbique" (128) is itself an inversion of a Senecan sententia that Hall must have held dear: "Nusquam est, qui ubique est" [He is nowhere who is everywhere].[30]

Finally, though, I think we have to reckon not just with the pessimism of the work and its ability to puncture any small bubble of hope, but with its irrepressible energy. However negative, however obsessed with things nugatory and depraved, this energy also reveals a deep interest in and fascination about the very matters the young traveler abhors or mocks. This means that both the work and the author's stance are

---

[26] See Greenblatt, *Marvellous Possessions*, figure 10.

[27] Joseph Hall, *Salomons Diuine Arts* (London, 1609), sig. A3. Davis, *Utopia and the Ideal Community*, 30, discusses the political aspects of this work.

[28] Wands, "Antipodal Imperfection," 86; see too McCabe, *Joseph Hall*, for analysis of Hall's themes.

[29] In 1617 Hall published *Quo Vadis? A Just Censure of Travell as It Is Commonly Undertaken by the Gentlemen of Our Nation.*

[30] Seneca, *Ad Lucilium epistolae morales*, trans. Richard M. Gummere, 3 vols. (London, 1917; repr. London and Cambridge, MA, 1953), Epistle II, 2.

more complex and ambivalent, and hence more interesting, than Hall himself was willing or able to admit.[31]

Throughout the seventeenth century, *Mundus Alter et Idem* was a very popular text on the continent as well as in England. On the other hand, John Milton, a political opponent of Hall's, attacked it, calling Hall a "petty prevaricator of *America*, the zanie of *Columbus*," and an "anticreator."[32] Dismissing the comic and parodic dimension of the *Mundus*, for him a "universall foolery," "a meer tankard drollery," and "a venerous parjetory for a stewes [salacious decorations for a brothel],"[33] Milton either was or pretended to be oblivious to the ironies and moral concerns of what we today call a dystopia—Hall's *Mundus Alter et Idem* was the first one in early modern England. In either case, Milton correctly sensed how the visionary, eutopian elements of Columbus and More had been transformed into a dystopia by a sceptical and anxious consciousness that did not believe the world could become better and cast a large question mark over any and all human endeavors.

University of Hawaii

---

[31] Similarly, the liveliest part of *Salomon's Diuine Arts* is a satiric picture of the wanton woman, who, unlike "modest wiues," is babbling, perverse, and ever gadding about. From a different perspective McCabe, *Joseph Hall*, notes how "Satire and meditation reflect the two most prevalent modes of his [Hall's] moral and religious outlook," 2.

[32] *An Apology against a Pamphlet Call'd A Modest Confutation of the Animadversions upon the Remonstrant against Smectymnuus* (1642) in *Complete Works of John Milton*, ed. Don M. Wolfe (New Haven, 1953), 1: 880, 881.

[33] Milton, *Apology* in *Works*, 1: 880, 881.

Characterizing the Viri Obscuri
during the Reuchlin Affair

JAMES V. MEHL*

The Neo-Latin construction, *viri obscuri*, originated in the humanist literature of the most famous pre-Reformation controversy in Germany, the Reuchlin affair. The term was fashioned for the title of a collection of fictional letters, the *Epistolae obscurorum virorum*.[1] The humanist supporters of Johannes Reuchlin circulated the *Epistolae* as propaganda, as a means of satirizing the efforts of Jacob Hoogstraten and other scholastic theologians who opposed the preservation of Hebrew books for scholarly use. The satirical letters appeared successively in several early editions, printed between 1515 and 1517. Crotus Rubeanus, Ulrich von Hutten, Hermann Buschius, and possibly other writers participated in the planning and authorship of the scandalous letters, which, on the surface, had been written by the "obscure men" of Cologne. The actual humanist authors, inspired by ancient satirists such as Lucian, devised the fictional letters in the literary form of mimic satire.[2] This satirical form allowed the obscurantist correspondents—some real-life and others contrived—to condemn themselves through the humor of their macaronic Latin style and the burlesque of their ignorance and lascivious lifestyles. In my paper I shall discuss the origins and evolving use of both the term and the satirical meaning of the *viri obscuri* as reflected in several texts published during the Reuchlin affair.

---

* James V. Mehl died very suddenly on 16 November 1998. A Reformation historian and an author of articles on Neo-Latin prose, James will be sadly missed by members of the IANLS and the Neo-Latin community at large.

[1] See James V. Mehl, "Characterizations of the 'Obscure Men' of Cologne: A Study in Pre-Reformation Collective Authorship," in *The Rhetorics of Life-Writing in Early Modern Europe: Forms of Biography from Cassandra Fedele to Louis XIV*, ed. Thomas F. Mayer and D. R. Woolf (Ann Arbor, 1995), 163–185.

[2] On the relationship of the *Epistolae* to other genres of Neo-Latin satire, see Jozef IJsewijn, "Neo-Latin Satire: *sermo* and *satyra menippea*," in *Classical Influences on European Culture, A.D. 1500–1700*, ed. R. R. Bolgar (Cambridge, 1976), 41–55, esp. 41, n. 2.

By the nineteenth century the vernacular terms, "Dunkelmänner," "obscure men," "obscurantist," and other modern equivalents of *viri obscuri* had taken on specific secular and negative connotations.[3] However, the original meaning of the Latin term was related more exactly to the opponents of Reuchlin, whom the authors of the *Epistolae* formulated as a group of reactionary scholastic enemies of the enlightened humanists. Both the concept and the precise term, *viri obscuri*, emerged shortly after the publication, in 1514, of the *Epistolae clarorum virorum*, a collection of serious letters in Reuchlin's behalf. Their publication came at about the same time as the Speyer decision in March 1514, which favored Reuchlin's cause. These actions were important events in shifting the Reuchlin affair from primarily a legal procedure motivated by anti-Jewish bias to a conflict that included greater hostility between the humanist supporters of Reuchlin and those scholastic theologians who wished to ban Jewish books.[4] And these events also marked a significant progression in the humanist-scholastic debate during the early sixteenth century.[5]

The formulation of the *viri obscuri* is rooted in the polemical exchanges and name-calling that developed in the early controversial literature of the Reuchlin affair. Between 1507 and 1509 two converted Jews, Johannes Pfefferkorn and Victor von Karben, published a series of slanderous pamphlets in which they attacked the Jews for their stubbornness in refusing Christian baptism. These zealots also called for a banning of Jewish books, including the Talmud. In 1509 the Cologne arts professor and humanist, Ortwin Gratius, probably collaborated with Pfefferkorn and von Karben by translating some of their works into Latin and overseeing their publication at the Quentell press, where he also worked as a corrector. In that same year, the Emperor Maximilian authorized Pfefferkorn to collect Hebrew books in the presence of local officials. The archbishop of Mainz, who was the leading churchman in Germany, objected to this practice. The emperor turned the matter over to the archbishop, who solicited the opinions of the universities of Mainz, Cologne, Erfurt, and Heidelberg, as well as several experts (*periti*). Besides the judgments of Cologne, Mainz, and Erfurt, which supported Pfefferkorn's efforts, two important experts issued strong views on the threatened confiscation of Jewish books. One was Hoogstraten, a member of the Cologne theological faculty who, in 1510, was elected prior of the Dominican convent in Cologne. This office also made him papal inquisitor for the ecclesiastical province of the lower Rhineland. Hoogstraten supported the opinion of Cologne, which he had helped to draft. The other expert was Reuchlin, a humanist and jurist who was generally recognized as the leading Hebrew scholar in

---

[3] Erich Meuthen, "Die 'Epistolae obscurorum virorum,'" in *Ecclesia Militans: Studien zur Konzilien- und Reformationsgeschichte*, ed. Walter Brandmüller, Herbert Immenkötter, and Erwin Iserloh, 2 vols. (Paderborn, 1988), 2: 76.

[4] Hans Peterse, *Jacobus Hoogstraeten gegen Johannes Reuchlin: Ein Beitrag zur Geschichte des Antijudaismus im 16. Jahrhundert* (Mainz, 1995). See also James H. Overfield, *Humanism and Scholasticism in Late Medieval Germany* (Princeton, 1984), 247–297.

[5] Erika Rummel, *The Humanist-Scholastic Debate in the Renaissance and Reformation* (Cambridge, 1995), for the Reuchlin affair, 87–89.

Europe at the time. In his judgment supporting the retention of the Talmud and other serious Hebrew texts, Reuchlin also questioned Pfefferkorn's motives for converting to the Christian faith. Pfefferkorn responded to this personal attack by issuing his *Handt Spiegel* in 1511, where he accused Reuchlin of not being the true author of his own works and of accepting bribes from the Jews. The attacks *ad hominem* continued. In August 1511, Reuchlin published his famous *Augenspiegel* (*Speculum oculare*), assaulting Pfefferkorn and the faculty of theology at Cologne.

When Pfefferkorn and the Cologne theologians continued to press him by securing an imperial ban on the printing and sale of his *Augenspiegel*, Reuchlin expanded his personal assaults in the *Defensio contra calumniatores suos Colonienses* (1513). He especially attacked Arnold Tongern, who had recently issued his *Articuli* (1512), claiming that the leader of the Cologne theologians had twisted his arguments. Reuchlin mocked Pfefferkorn as a "semi-Jew" (*semijudaeus*) and even called into question the virtue of his wife.[6] Reuchlin further demeaned Gratius as an unlearned poet and teacher of humanistic subjects. Rather than a professor of liberal arts, Reuchlin branded him a "perversor bonarum artium" and an agent of the theological faculty.[7] The incensed Reuchlin no longer considered his detractors in the theology faculty at Cologne to be true theologians, but rather *theologistas*, as he explains the clear distinction between the two: "notissima inter theologos et theologistas differentia est, qualis inter virtutem et vitium, inter bonum et malum, inter fucatum et meram, inter falsum et verum."[8] By listing opposites in this way, Reuchlin was imputing specific characteristics for his scholastic enemies, as men of vice, evil, deceit, and falsehood. By implication, he and his humanist supporters were men of virtue, goodness, honesty, and truth. Thus the idea of two opposing sides or camps begins to emerge in the literature of the Reuchlin affair, with each having identifying characteristics. It is the theologistas, those false or counterfeit theologians, who will shortly take on the personification of *viri obscuri* and *magistri nostri* in the *Epistolae*.

Reuchlin's cause gained the support of many humanists as the attacks against him expanded in 1514. Prompted by the Cologne theologians, the faculties at Louvain, Mainz, and Erfurt joined in the condemnation of the *Augenspiegel*, and Hoogstraten summoned Reuchlin to the court of inquisition in Mainz. Again the archbishop of Mainz objected, declaring the legal proceedings improper. Reuchlin appealed his position to Rome, whereby the archbishop of Speyer was appointed to adjudicate the case. Following a lengthy investigation, the archbishop found in Reuchlin's favor in March 1514. The inquisitor quickly traveled to Rome where he continued to press his case for some years. Even the Emperor Maximilian came out in Reuchlin's favor. In France, however, King Louis XII, upon the urging of his Dominican confessor,

---

[6] *Defensio contra caluminatores suos Colonienses* (Tübingen, 1513), fol. E3r.

[7] *Defensio*, fol. E3r. Also cited, along with other derisive names for Gratius, in Eduard Böcking, ed., *Ulrichi Hutteni, equitis Germani, opera quae reperiri potuerunt omnia*, 5 vols., suppl. 2 vols. (Leipzig, 1859–70; repr. Aalen, 1963), suppl. 2: 572.

[8] *Defensio*, fol. B4r. See also Peterse, *Jacobus Hoogstraeten*, 32.

Guillaume Petit (Parvus), collaborated with the theological faculty at Paris in having the *Augenspiegel* banned and the Talmud burned.[9]

This action in Paris prompted a short satire, *Contra sentimentum Parrhisiense* (1514), that introduces a literary prototype of the *vir obscurus*.[10] The satire, probably written in Germany by Crotus Rubeanus, was a mock debate on the merits of the Paris condemnations. The disputation is between two fictitious Paris students: Cutius Gloricianus, a bachelor of laws who opposes the action of the theologians, and Hackinetus Petitus, a cursor in theology, who takes the affirmative side. Cutius presents twelve well-developed arguments against the actions of the Paris theologians, followed by twelve rather anemic responses by Hackinetus. Some of Cutius' arguments are stated in technical legal language, as in his second statement: "Secundo si dicere vellent se doctrinaliter consuluisse, hoc non deberet valere in iudicio neque ullum iudicem movere, nisi puncta dubia iudex ipse dederit, vel partes litigantes illa inter se composuerint prout de iure."[11] To this Hackinetus responds simply: ". . . quod quamvis possit esse de subtilitate iuris, tamen theologi non curant iura, quia non sint de facultate eorum."[12] This student representative of the theological side cannot be bothered with the subtleties of such juristic argument, because theologians are not members of that faculty and do not care for the law. Here the author of the satire was ridiculing both the ignorance and the arrogance of the scholastic theologians, who were the most powerful faculty at Paris.

In yet another example of the pretensions of the theologians, Hackinetus answers the tenth argument against the condemnations of the *Augenspiegel* and the Talmud. He restates and emphasizes the traditional authority of the theological faculties, as expressed in the writings of Tongern at Cologne: "Ad decimum quod credat Parrhisienses ita fuisse informatos a Coloniensibus, et maxime a Magistro nostro Arnoldo de Tungari collegii Laurentiani primario regente, qui plurimum laudatus est a Magistris nostris Parrhisiensibus super illo libro quem articulatim composuit contra speculum oculare Ioannis Reuchlin."[13] It is simply enough for the theologians to speak and all must listen and follow their directives. The derisive use of the title for the theologians, "magister noster," in this passage anticipates its appearance in the *Epistolae*. Thus, in his ignorance and ostentation, Hackenetus serves as a literary model for the characterization of the *viri obscuri*.

The characterizations for the "obscure men" were also developed in the *Triumphus Doctoris Reuchlini*, of which an initial draft was probably circulated by Buschius in 1514. A revised and expanded copy of the *Triumphus* was published in 1518, probably under the direction of Hutten.[14] This later edition included a large woodcut illus-

---

[9] *Acta Doctorum Parrhisiensium* (Paris, 1514).

[10] The text is in Böcking, suppl. 1: 318–322; see also Peterse, *Jacobus Hoogstraeten*, 54–55.

[11] Böcking, suppl. 1: 319.

[12] Böcking, suppl. 1: 321.

[13] Böcking, suppl. 1: 321.

[14] On the authorship of the *Triumphus*, see Thomas W. Best, *The Humanist Ulrich von Hutten: A Reappraisal of His Humor* (Chapel Hill, 1969), 48–53. The text of the *Triumphus* is in Böcking, 3: 413–447.

tration, the "Triumphus Capnionis," where the *viri obscuri* are depicted as a defeated band of Reuchlin's enemies.[15] The written text provides derisive descriptions of individual opponents, such as Hoogstraten, Gratius, and Tongern, along with a more general characterization of the enemies of the Hebrew scholar. Gratius, for instance, is identified as a scorpion who, in spite of having two eyes, can see only wickedness. He is an unlearned and spiteful man who is to be blindfolded "lest he cast a spell over all men [ne fascinet omnes]!"[16] In the woodcut, Gratius is portrayed with a blindfold. The blindfolding could be a playful allusion to his opposition to Reuchlin's *Augenspiegel*. How could a sightless Gratius condemn the very thing that would clarify vision? In the *Triumphus*, Reuchlin's opponents are also mocked as a group with specific physical characteristics; they may speak a thousand arguments, but they are a truly sad and depressed lot with their gaping mouths, crooked noses, protruding teeth, and down-turned eyes hidden beneath their cowls.[17] Moreover, these spiritually depraved men worship the false gods of superstition, barbarism, ignorance, and envy, which are carried before them as idols in the illustration.[18] Such a group of dispirited monks was also used to illustrate the title page of the first edition, part two, of the *Epistolae obscurorum virorum*.[19]

Probably the most important and direct inspiration for the characterization of the *viri obscuri* was a serious collection of letters, the *Epistolae clarorum virorum*, which had been written by Reuchlin's supporters and published in 1514. The decision to circulate another collection of letters, but this time fictional and satirical, followed quickly. This new collection would be a mimic satire of Reuchlin's opponents, cast as the "obscure men" of Cologne. If Reuchlin's supporters had been "viri clari," then his detractors must be their opposite, "viri obscuri." In August 1514, Erasmus met with Reuchlin, Hutten, and Buschius in Mainz, where the literary project may have been discussed. And Erasmus may have been given a manuscript copy of some of the first letters during a second meeting with Hutten and Buschius in Frankfurt am Main in April 1515. In any case, the first edition of the *Epistolae obscurorum virorum* was printed anonymously by Heinrich Gran, in the autumn of that same year, in Hagenau.[20]

Most scholars credit Crotus Rubeanus with the conception of the satire, along with the authorship of most of the forty-one letters in the first part of the *Epistolae*. In his literary construction, Crotus may have had in mind the inversion of Conrad Mutianus Rufus' humanist circle in Gotha, in which he was active, by creating a new

---

[15] The foldout woodcut illustration is reprinted in Ludwig Geiger, *Renaissance und Humanismus in Italien und Deutschland* (Berlin, 1882), opposite 522.

[16] Böcking, 3: 432–434.

[17] Böcking, 3: 427–428: "Mille argumenta hic, et mille feruntur elenchi,/ Et multis nocuum murmur, linguaeque prophanae,/ Sacrilegaeque manus, promptique invadere rictus,/ Exertique labris dentis, nasique recurvi,/ Luminaque obliquum deflexa, superciliisque/ Contractae frontes, oculique horrenda tuentes,/ Lividulaeque genae, et rabiosa silentia pressis/ Intercepta labris, plenique errore cuculli."

[18] Böcking, 3: 428–429.

[19] Böcking, suppl. 1: 183.

[20] Aloys Bömer, ed., *Epistolae obscurorum virorum*, 2 vols. (Heidelberg, 1924; repr. Aalen, 1978).

circle of obscurantist correspondents seeking the foolhardy advice of their leader in Cologne, Ortwin Gratius.[21] Hutten contributed the first letter for the initial install-ment, seven additional letters appended to the initial installment in the second edition of 1516, and most of the sixty-two letters published in 1517 as a sequel to the first volume. Buschius also wrote letters for both parts and, in my view, played a greater role in the literary project than has generally been recognized.[22] His personal feud with Gratius, in 1509, over the teaching of Donatus' *Grammar* at Cologne, along with Gratius' switch in positions during a controversy involving Peter of Ravenna and the increasingly active role he had played in the Reuchlin case, made the would-be hu-manist an obvious target.[23] In the opinion of Buschius and his fellow humanist con-spirators, Gratius was a turncoat humanist, an ally of the Cologne theologians, who deserved to be lampooned in the satire.

Two letters from the *Epistolae* must suffice to exemplify the fully developed char-acterization of the *viri obscuri*. The first is the rather well known opening letter to part one, which features a mock banquet and debate on the "Feast of Aristotle."[24] Attributed to Hutten, the salutation is exaggerated in the manner of the rest of the letters: "Thomas Langschneyderius, baccalaurius theologiae formatus quamvis indig-nus, salutem dicit superexcellenti necnon scientificissimo viro domino Ortvino Gratio Daventriensi, poetae, oratori, et philosopho, necnon theologo, et plus si vellet." The fictional correspondent, "Langschneyderius," is a good example of the macaronic style used in the letters, when a Latinate ending, "us," is added to a German name meaning "Tall Tailor."[25] The pretensions of the obscurantists are immediately indi-cated by the claims that Gratius is a famous and learned poet, orator, philosopher, and even theologian. Such academic boastings are reinforced in the subject of the mock debate: whether Doctors of Divinity should be addressed as *magister nostrandus* or *noster magistrandus*. The question, of course, is a ridiculous one, since the preference for placing the two Latin words was a satire aimed at the corrupted Latin (Küchen-latein) that had developed in the common discourse of late medieval universities. Certainly the distinction was not based on learned linguistic knowledge or study of ancient Roman texts, as the humanists would have argued.

The obscurantist correspondent, Langschneyderius, relates the two sides of the de-bate. A "Magister Warmsemmel," who is identified as a Scotist and a professor for eighteen years, argues that doctors should be called by one word, *nostermagistrandus*, because *magistrare* signifies "to make magister," like other academic titles: ". . . quia 'magistrare' significat 'magistrum facere,' et 'baccalauriare' 'baccalaurium facere,' et 'doctorare' 'doctorem facere'; et hinc veniunt isti termini 'magistrandus,' 'baccalau-

---

21 Mehl, "Characterizations," 170.

22 Mehl, "Characterizations," 171.

23 On the disagreement over Donatus, see James Mehl, "The 1509 Dispute over Donatus: Humanist Editor as Controversialist," *Publishing History* 16 (1984): 480–506.

24 Letter I.1 in Bömer, *Epistolae obscurorum virorum*, 2: 7–9.

25 I have discussed elsewhere the demeaning associations of class and occupation for the ficti-tious correspondents: James Mehl, "Language, Class, and Mimic Satire in the Characterization of Correspondents in the *Epistolae obscurorum virorum*," *Sixteenth Century Journal* 25 (1994): 289–305.

riandus,' et 'doctorandus.'" Again the corrupted Latin style of the scholastics is ridiculed by the turning of nouns into verbs. This convoluted argument, which betrays both the ignorance and arrogance of the university professorate, is followed by a false humility and perverted sense of their Christian faith: "Sed quia doctores in sacra theologia non dicuntur doctores, sed propter humilitatem et etiam sanctitatem, et propter differentiam nominantur seu appellantur magistri nostri, quia stant in fide catholica in loco domini nostri Iesu Christi, qui est fons vitae."[26] Since Christ was *nostrorum omnium magister*, the theologians should also be called *magistri nostri* because it is appropriate for them to instruct us in the way of truth, and God is the truth! Langschneyderius agrees that the scholastic theologians should be called *magistri nostri*, for it is the serious duty of all to accept their teachings and refrain from saying anything against them, since they are our masters.

The opposing side is given by a "Magister Andreas Delitzsch," described as a "poeta . . . artista, medicus et iurista," who lectures on Ovid's *Metamorphoses*, explaining all the fables both allegorically and literally.[27] So Delitzsch is, like Gratius, a would-be humanist. Again, a garbled argument is presented for *magister nostrandus*: "Quia sicut est differentia inter 'magister noster' et 'noster magister,' ita etiam est differentia inter 'magister nostrandus' et 'noster magistrandus'; quia 'magister noster' dicitur doctor in theologia, et est una dictio, sed 'noster magister' sunt duae dictiones, et sumitur pro unoquoque magistro, in quacunque scientia liberali, seu mechanica manuali, seu capitali."[28] In short, the title ought to be in two words because "magister" is used to signify a teacher for any of the liberal sciences. The study of mechanical subjects, of course, was excluded from the scholastic curriculum. The correspondent requests that "Magister Ortvinus" determine the truth of the matter and send the answer to him, because Gratius was profound and had been his teacher in the third class at Deventer!

My second example is the opening letter, also attributed to Hutten, for part two of the *Epistolae*.[29] The correspondent is "Joannes Labia," a "prothonotarius apostolicus" in Rome. Labia acknowledges his recent receipt of a printed copy of the *Epistolae* which Gratius has sent to him from Cologne. Labia reports that, only yesterday, he had taken the opportunity of a feast, attended by members of the Roman curia, to inquire as to the reasons for Gratius entitling the book "Epistolae obscurorum virorum" and calling his friends and cohorts obscuros viros. After dinner, several of those in attendance had offered different reasons for these usages. The first speaker was a learned priest and jurist from Münster, who responded that *obscuritas* had many possible meanings. It might be a family name, since it is written that the parents of the Roman Emperor Diocletian and other kings were "Obscuri." Next, a pompous Carmelite theologian from Brabant suggests that Gratius, who was a learned man who knew the scriptures, called his friends *obscuros viros* in a mystical sense, "quia semel

---

[26] Bömer, *Epistolae obscurorum virorum*, 2: 8.

[27] Bömer, *Epistolae obscurorum virorum*, 2: 8.

[28] Bömer, *Epistolae obscurorum virorum*, 2: 8–9.

[29] Letter II.1, Bömer, *Epistolae obscurorum virorum*, 2: 91–93.

legi unam auctoritatem, quod veritas latet in obscuris." Several mangled passages from the Hebrew Bible, along with one from Virgil—"Obscuris vera in obscuris," are cited to support his contention and conclusion: "Et datur intelligi, quod magister Ortvinus et sui amici sunt tales, quod inquirunt secreta scripturarum et veritatem, et iustitiam et sapientiam, quae non potest intelligi ab omnibus nisi ab his, qui sunt illuminati a domino."[30] Such playful and mocking inversions of enlightenment and obscurity must have struck the humanist readers as very humorous.

Finally, a younger man, "Bernhardus Gelff," identified as a master of theology at Paris, offers an explanation that includes several twists of irony. Ortwin has referred to his friends as *obscuros viros* out of a sense of humility. Having noticed that Reuchlin, three years ago, had printed a collection of letters from his friends, which was entitled "Epistolae clarorum virorum," Gratius organized his own collection, which he called "Epistolae obscurorum virorum," to show that he also had many learned and talented friends. Bernhardus believes that Gratius' collection is much superior to that of Reuchlin: "Non intelligendo, quod istud epistolare amicorum magistri Ortvini non est artificialiter compositum, quia amici Ioannis Reuchlin in vita sua numquam componerent melius, etiam se deberent perdere capita sua."[31] The use of the double negative in this passage reinforces the irony of its mimic satire. As in the previous example, this letter concludes with the correspondent Labia asking Gratius to resolve the issue by communicating his real motive for entitling the *Epistolae obscurorum virorum*.

What might be concluded, then, from this analysis? The Neo-Latin formulation, *viri obscuri*, was a product of the controversial literature during the Reuchlin affair. The negative and slanderous characterizations associated with the "obscure men" developed out of the dialogue of personal attacks that permeate the early pamphlets of the controversy. Reuchlin himself played an important role in initiating the character assassination of his opponents by questioning Pfefferkorn's sincerity in converting to the Christian faith. Pfefferkorn responded in kind, in his *Handt Spiegel* of 1511, by accusing Reuchlin of not being the real author of his works and of accepting Jewish bribes. The Hebrew scholar broadened his attacks in the *Augenspiegel*, taking on the entire theological faculty at Cologne. And in his *Defensio* of 1513 Reuchlin satirized his opponents individually, ridiculing Gratius and even Frau Pfefferkorn. The scholastic theologians at Cologne and other universities who had condemned his works were not true theologians, but rather their opposite, *theologistas*. These counterfeit theological opponents were men of vice, evil, deceit, and falsehood, and would soon take on the personification of the *magistri nostri* in the *Epistolae obscurorum virorum*. Another anticipation of the *viri obscuri* occurs in the little satire, *Contra sentimentum Parrhisiense*, where the fictional theology student, Hackinetus Petitus, betrays the ignorance and arrogance of the *magistri nostri* at Paris. Although more difficult to interpret, because it was printed in final form in 1518, the *Triumphus Doctoris Reuchlini* also includes many well developed characterizations of the "obscure men."

---

[30] Bömer, *Epistolae obscurorum virorum*, 2: 92.

[31] Bömer, *Epistolae obscurorum virorum*, 2: 93.

The real genius in the formulation of the *viri obscuri* occurs, however, in the literary response to the appearance of Reuchlin's *Epistolae clarorum virorum* in 1514. Crotus Rubeanus, Hutten, Buschius, and perhaps other humanist supporters of the embattled Reuchlin planned and executed, over the next several years, a literary counterpart in mimic satire, the *Epistolae obscurorum virorum*. If so many famous humanists could come out publicly in Reuchlin's favor, then the publication of a satirical collection of letters, from the pens of the *viri obscuri*, would further serve to undermine the authority of his scholastic enemies. The two letters discussed here indicate the effectiveness of the mimic satire written in a doggerel Latin style. The ridiculous debate, in the first example, over the proper title for Doctors of Divinity—whether *magister nostrandus* or *noster magistrandus*, and the inane discussion, in the second letter, on why Gratius named his book and called his friends *viri obscuri*, were intended to expose, in a very humorous and entertaining way, the ignorance, arrogance, and luxurious lifestyle of Reuchlin's clerical opponents. This intertextual play of satirical images and themes continued into the later stages of the Reuchlin affair, with the publication of a number of satires of the "obscure men" type. An especially good example of these later texts is the *Ex obscurorum virorum salibus cribratus dialogus*, printed anonymously around 1519.[32] Taken together, these projections of the *viri obscuri* in the controversial literature of the Reuchlin affair contributed significantly to the growing conflict between humanists and scholastics on the eve of the Reformation.

Missouri Western State College

---

[32] The text is in Böcking, suppl. 1: 301–316.

A Specific Case of the Docta Foemina: *Luisa Sigea and her* Duarum virginum colloquium de vita aulica et privata

SOL MIGUEL-PRENDES

Luisa Sigea embodied the sixteenth-century's ideal of the female humanist: a lady well-versed in the Classics. Contemporary humanists called her "Docta Sygaea" or "virgo admirabilis."[1] Joannes Vaseus described Pope Paul III's amazement after reading a letter from Luisa, who at twenty-two had written in Latin, Greek, Hebrew, Arabic, and Aramaic.[2] Yet, Joannes Vaseus attributed Luisa's astonishing accomplishments to her father, Diego Sigeo. Diego had studied at the University of Alcalá under such famous humanists as Antonio de Nebrija, Diego López de Zúñiga, and Alonso de Zamora; he became a language teacher and a preceptor of María Pacheco de Padilla, and later served the Duke of Braganza. A classical education was the only wealth he could bequeath his children, and he passed it on not only to his two sons, but to his two daughters as well.[3] Although it is unclear whether Luisa's sister,

---

[1] Manuel Serrano y Sanz, *Apuntes para una biblioteca de escritoras españolas* (Madrid, 1903), 270 part 2: 399–400.

[2] Admiratus tam multiplicem ingenii fructum et donum multiplicis linguarum scientiae in viris quoque rarum, nedum in feminis. [Amazed at such varied talent and knowledge of languages, so infrequent among men, even more among women.] Serrano y Sanz, *Apuntes*, 400. My translation unless otherwise indicated.

[3] Debetur haec laus optimo patri et viro doctissimo Didaco Sygaeo, qui non contentus filios optimis quibusque disciplinis instituisse, tantam in filia tot linguis imbuenda diligentiam adhibuit; nec in ea solum hanc operam posuit, sed alteram quoque filiam Angelam graece latineque pro aetate et sexu non mediocriter eruditam, tam exacta Musices scientia curavit perdocendam, ut cum praestantissimis illius artis professoribus contendere posse putem. [We must praise for her achievements Diego Sigeo, excellent father and very learned person who, having instructed his sons in all the best disciplines, dedicated such great effort to teach his daughter so many languages; and also his other daughter, Angela, rather learned in Latin and Greek for her age and sex. He instructed her so well in the science of music that I believe she was able to compete with the leading teachers of that art.] Serrano y Sanz, *Apuntes*, 400.

Angela, drew any practical benefit from her father's teachings—Vasaeus only mentions that she excelled in music—Louisa served as "dama latina" [Latin preceptor] at the court of Maria of Portugal for thirteen years. However, after marrying Francisco de Cuevas, a member of the lower nobility, she abandoned the Portuguese court for Burgos in 1555 and spent the last five years of her life petitioning in vain for a post at the court of Philip II for herself and her husband.[4]

The events of Luisa Sigea's life raise the question of what purpose was served by providing women with humanist schooling. Why, for example, did Diego Sigeo subject his daughters to relentless drilling in Latin grammar and to intense instruction in the finer points of usage, history, and geography required by such training, rather than preparing them to be good Christian wives? Could he have reasonably expected that his daughters would become professors of the *studia humanitatis,* like himself, or even personal secretaries in court? Certainly, as her contemporaries attest, Luisa was well-equipped with all the necessary skills. Alonso Fernández de Madrid, Archdeacon of Alcor, described her in his *Silva palentina* as "muy docta en Philosophia y Oratoria y Poesía, y principalmente en las lenguas latina, griega, hebrea y caldea, en las quales tan facilmente habla y escriue como la nuestra castellana" [well-versed in philosophy, oratory, and poetry, and especially in Latin, Greek, Hebrew, and Chaldean, languages she speaks and writes as easily as Castilian].[5] Even though the art of oratory was considered useless for women, who had no role outside the household or convent,[6] she could speak *ex tempore* on any subject either in classical Latin or Greek and was equally versed in rhetoric. Her extensive correspondence[7] reveals her ability to compose formal letters in the classical idioms, and the request of the Portuguese royal family that Luisa be sent as "moça de camara" [lady-in-waiting] for Queen Catherine and, later, as Princess Maria's preceptor speaks for her ability as a teacher. Luisa's *studia humanitatis* provided her with a strong foundation for a successful career, and, in that

---

[4] Serrano y Sanz, *Apuntes,* 394–401; Odette Sauvage, "Recherches sur Luisa Sigea," *Bulletin des études portugaises* 31 (1970): 36–60: Sauvage, ed., *Louise Sigée: Dialogue de deux jeunes filles sur la vie de cour et la vie de rétraite (1552)* (Paris, 1970), 17–22; Inés Rada, "Profil et trajectoire d'une femme humaniste: Luisa Sigea," *Images de la femme en Espagne aux XVIe et XVIIe siecles: des traditions aux renouvellements et à l'emergence d'images nouvelles: Colloque international, Sorbonne et College d'Espagne, 28–30 septembre 1992* (Paris, 1994), 339–349.

[5] Serrano y Sanz, *Apuntes,* 397; Sauvage, "Recherches," 134.

[6] Cf. Luis Vives: "De eloquentia nihil sum sollicitus. Non indiget ea mulier, probitate ac sapientia indiget. Nec turpe est feminam tacere; foedum et abominandum non bene sapere, male vivere." [I am not all concerned with eloquence. A woman has no need of that; she needs rectitude and wisdom. It is not shameful for a woman to be silent; it is disgraceful and abominable for her not to have wisdom and to live a bad life.] *De institutione feminae Christianae. Liber primus,* ed. C. Fantazzi and C. Matheeussen, trans. C. Fantazzi (Leiden, 1996), 38–41.

[7] Of the thirty-three Latin letters mentioned by Joannes Vaseus and Nicolás Antonio, only fifteen are extant. Serrano y Sanz, *Apuntes,* 409; Alfonso Bonilla y San Martín, "Clarorum Hispaniensium epistolae ineditae," *Révue hispanique* 8 (1901): 280–296; and L. Bourdon, "Recherches sur Luisa Sigea," *Bulletin des études portugaises* 31 (1970): 61–133.

sense, the polyglot letter she wrote to Pope Paul III[8] could very well have served as an elegant resumé, addressed by any young humanist to a prospective employer.

But the tangible rewards that a classical education might secure—that is, a comfortable post as a teacher or personal secretary—were generally restricted to men. It is more likely that Diego Sigeo educated his daughters not so much for careers at court as to negotiate better matches for them, since the *studia humanitatis* did provide other practical values more fitting to devoted wives. In this regard, he was a man of his time and may have been following the curriculum for the schooling of women as outlined by Luis Vives in his *De institutione foeminae christianae,* published in 1524.[9] Vives recommended that young girls be taught to read and proposed a Latin reading list that included selections from the Bible, Church Fathers, philosophers, and secular poets. Yet Margaret King notes that while Vives opened the door to the serious education of women, he sharply limited the scope and purpose of their learning. Vives conceived women's instruction along the same lines as Erasmus: as a "weapon against idleness" and as a means of impressing upon a girl's mind some basic precepts that would improve her moral behavior.[10] In King's words, "the education Vives prescribed for the young woman of the Renaissance was not one that would cultivate her mind, but one that would encourage her obedience to familiar duties and virtues" (165).

The teaching methods employed in humanist schooling encouraged obedience and docility. Grafton and Jardine, describing the methods of Guarino Guarini's school at Ferrara a century earlier, claim that as a consequence of the narrow cumbersomeness of classroom instruction, "students became accustomed to taking their orders and direction from an authority whose guiding principles were never revealed, much less questioned"; the resulting product was a crop of "fluent and docile young noblemen ... a commodity of which the oligarchs and tyrants of late fifteenth-century Italy could not fail to approve."[11] When applied to the education of women, this method of instruction—methodical grammar drills and memorization—was intended to promote an enlightened passivity by replacing the constant spinning of the distaff in the upbringing of upper-class women. Instead of mechanical spinning or the mindless repetition of rosary prayers, Vives advised that a girl be given "sententiola" [short excerpts] from the Sacred Book or from moral anthologies, "which should be copied out many times so that they will remain fixed in the memory."[12] Daily contact with

---

[8] In Bonilla y San Martín, "Clarorum," 122–123.

[9] Besides *De institutione,* Vives wrote other works dealing with the topic: the 1528 *De officio mariti* and two shorter texts aimed at the education of a specific woman, the first letter of *De ratione studii puerilis* (1523)—a plan of study for teaching Latin and Greek to seven-year-old Mary Tudor—and *Satellitium animi* (1524), a collection of apothegms intended to guide young Mary to govern wisely. See Carmen Peraita, "*Sapientia* and Knowledge in the Construction of the Renaissance *docta foemina:* Vives' *De institutione foeminae christianae,*" included in this volume.

[10] Margaret King, *Women of the Renaissance* (Chicago, 1991), 181.

[11] Anthony Grafton and Lisa Jardine, *From Humanism to the Humanities* (Cambridge, 1986), 24.

[12] Ex litteris Sacris aut philosophorum monumentis sententiola, quam saepius scriptam tenacius memoria affigat. *De institutione,* 40–41.

a carefully selected assortment of the *bonae artes* could prompt moral behavior. In Vives' opinion, the majority of female vices sprang primarily from ignorance, "because women did not read or hear tell of those splendid exhortations of the Fathers of the Church concerning chastity, solitude, silence, and feminine adornment and attire."[13]

It was precisely this kind of obedient behavior that humanist schooling was meant to foster, which Diego Sigeo hoped to instill in his daughters. And Luisa Sigea was undoubtedly a dedicated student. Her *Duarum virginum colloquium de vita aulica et privata,* addressed to Princess Maria of Portugal in 1552, is a monument of female cultivation, an accomplished outcome of the training for women described above. In the letter that precedes the *Colloquium,* Luisa Sigea thanks Princess Maria for providing her with the opportunity to cultivate herself in the royal library.[14] The product of her efforts is the *Colloquium,* which is based on the best works contained in that library and which she is submitting to the Princess.[15] Sigea mentions the little drop ("guttam") of that immense knowledge she has recollected and that she will never be capable of imitating.

> Vtriusque sententiam sapientissimorum uirorum dictis comprobare atque impugnare nitimur, paucis admodum ex Minerua nostra interpositis, tum quod imbecilles ad id uires nostras plane esse non ignorem, tum etiam ut, quorum doctrinam ab ipsis paene incunabulis uoluimus, in medium proferamus, ac uideat quicumque leget meam, quantulacumque est, eruditionem me eis autoribus debere faterique ingenue debitum. . . . Accedit quod si ex uberrima illorum copia quantum fructum debuissem decerpere non ualui, nouerim tamen me unquam soluendo non esse quod debeo: cum ingenue fatear ne minimam quidem exuberantissimae illorum scientiae guttam adbibisse, nedum illos plene imitari unquam posse praesumere. (69)

> [I try to justify and argue each character's points of view by quoting the words of the greatest philosophers, inserting just a few words of mine, in part because I am fully aware that I do not possess the strength required to attain such a goal and in part because I want to disseminate those authors on whose teachings I have meditated almost since I was in the cradle; in this way, anyone who reads me will see that I owe to these authors the little knowledge I have and I declare my debt to them openly. . . . If I did not have the expertise to collect from their abundant richness as much fruit as I should, I know, however, that

---

[13] Egregia illa sanctorum patrum monita de castitate, de solitudine, de silentio, de ornamentis et cultu muliebri neque legerunt neque audierunt. *De institutione,* 31.

[14] Inter tot ac tanta beneficia quibus me semper ornare curasti, Serenissima princeps, . . . litterarum otium et destinatum ad id locum mihi ultra concesseras. [Among all the abundant benefits you have always honored me, most serene Princess, . . . you provided me with the time and appropriate place to study.] Sauvage, *Louise Sigée,* 69.

[15] Cuius auctor pedissequa tua est, editionis locus tuum Musaeum atque operi edendo tui optimi libri adiutores (69). [Its author is your servant, the place where I have composed it your library, and for its composition your best books have come to help me.] Sauvage, *Louise Sigée,* 69.

I will never be able to pay the debt I owe to them; since I frankly confess that I limited myself to drinking a very small drop from their wisdom and that I will never dare to imitate them.]

Beyond the customary modesty required in her letter's *captatio benevolentiae,* the image of the drop indicates clearly the tradition she is following. It refers to the scholastic method of *inventio* that consists in collecting materials—traditionally designated as "drops" or "honey"—from the river of eloquence found in the works of the canonical authors.[16]

Luisa Sigea's work is based precisely on those authors that Vives advises young women be given when learning to write, so that, by their very repetition, they impress virtue. Since she is addressing the *Colloquium* to Princess Maria, she has selected subjects in classical and patristic literature that Vives suggested women study: a moral content, focusing specifically on chastity, seclusion, silence, and proper feminine attire. As Carmen Peraita indicates in her treatment of the *De institutione,* Vives thought that the authors he endorsed as instructionally sound—theologians and philosophers who dealt with intricate issues—*de facto* had written very few simple precepts that could be safely given to girls. Hence, he conceived his *De institutione* as a compilation of simple rules governing virtuous life for women. It seems plausible that Sigea's writing method was to summarize the most pressing educational issues treated by Vives, which she later supported with further quotations painfully retrieved from the royal library ("tanto sudore tamque indefessis uigiliis") and inserted in the text.

The *Colloquium* is presented, first, as an argument for the superiority of a retired life over one in the court. It appears to be modelled on the Christian standard outlined by fray Antonio de Guevara in his *Menosprecio de corte y alabanza de aldea,* written in 1539. Luisa Sigea associates courtly life with the world and, therefore, with its vices and evils. The other term of the contrast, a virtuous retreat from the social milieu, becomes associated with monastic life, specifically with a nunnery. The *Colloquium* takes place over a three-day period of which the first is devoted exclusively to a discussion of courtly life.

Flaminia, the younger of the two interlocutors, defends the court from the objections made by Blesilla, a woman whose authority stems from having experienced both types of life (159). Young Flaminia relishes the opportunity afforded by court life to engage in discourse with intellectuals, because it provides her with a sense of *dignitas* and *libertas* (77); but above all, she commends the joy of being ruled by ideal monarchs whose virtue is patterned on Plato's philosopher-king and who, therefore, can bring happiness to their subjects (77). Blesilla, however, demonstrates that Flaminia's *dignitas* and *libertas* are superficial, because they stem from the vanity of

---

[16] Curtius, referring to Dante's invocation of Virgil as "fonte," indicates that the term *fiume* is a stylistic latinism that corresponds to the Latin expression *flumen oratoris,* used to praise the eloquence of an author. Ernst Curtius, *Literatura europa y edad media latina,* trans. Margit Frenk Alatorre y Antonio Alatorre (México, 1955), 2: 511. The same image is used by Gregory the Great in his *Moralia in Job* to refer to the inexhaustible depth of the divine word. Beryl Smalley, *The Study of the Bible in the Middle Ages* (Oxford, 1983), 33.

courtly pleasures. She also shows that the portrait of the ideal ruler drawn by Flaminia is far removed from the reality of contemporary courts, where princes are whimsical and their judgment is generally blinded by sycophants. Accordingly, Blesilla counsels young Flaminia to flee this world: a world described as a labyrinth, implicitly associated with the realm of Fortune in its constant change and uncertainty.

None of these motives, belonging to a long tradition and already present in Guevara's work, is developed with any ingenuity. Both Blesilla and Flaminia, for example, present their arguments mechanically, and, although they are supposed to represent opposing views, the dialogue lacks any logical progression, as Flaminia, for no clear reason, abruptly agrees with Blesilla by the end of the first day. The conventionality and lack of originality also taint Luisa Sigea's choice of Latin names for the two characters ("Flaminia romana" and "Blesilla senensis"). The naming reveals a common humanist whim but has no relation to the content whatsoever. The same can be said of the three brief recesses, when the characters celebrate the beauty of nature, a prevailing literary topos in the dialogue genre that is not well blended into the work. Sigea is obediently following the humanist training accepted for women, repeating the received models.[17] Moreover, Sigea bases her dialogue on the very works that Vives recommends that girls read, and both characters argue their points by resorting to citations and examples drawn from those authors, a method that Odette Sauvage likens to film editing[18] or, more in the spirit of the time and the mechanical nature of the experiment, like patchwork. In other words, the *Colloquium* is an exercise in translation framed as a *controversia*, another classroom exercise.

On the other hand, the *Colloquium* brings to fruition the ideal of a woman's curriculum espoused by Vives. Accordingly, at the end of the first day, Blesilla encourages Flaminia to renounce the company of princes in order to avoid the flattery common to courtly life (121). This injunction is expanded on the second day when the two discuss the proper ornamentation and demeanor of a young woman. What was supposed to have been a debate on the "vita aulica et privata" is instead an exposition on specific issues related to the proper behavior of women in court. Since Luisa Sigea supports the characters' arguments with the authors recommended by Vives, Blesilla, accordingly, arrives at the same conclusions as Vives in his *De institutione:* a

---

[17] The Archdeacon of Alcor saw it very well: "Lo que tengo aquí en mucho es, que aunque esta señora en este libro no pusiera nada de su cassa, sino buscar para su propósito sentencias tan notables de Platon, Aristóteles, Genofon, Plutarco, y otros muchos autores griegos, y ponerlas á la letra enteras en su propia lengua y characteres griegos, y trasladarlas luego letra por letra en latin, y juntamente las authoridades de Profetas y Psalterio y Salomon, escriptas en lengua y characteres hebreos, y trasladadas en latín, digo que aunque más no hiciera havía hecho mucho." [What I have here is a lot, and although this lady has not included anything of hers, except looking for notable sentences by Plato, Aristotle, Xenophon, Plutarch, and many other Greek authors to suit her purpose, and writing them in their own language and Greek characters, and translating them, letter by letter, into Latin, and along with them testimonies from the Prophets, the Psalter and Solomon, written in Hebrew characters and translated into Latin, although she did not do but that, as I say, she had accomplished a lot.] Serrano y Sanz, *Apuntes,* 397.

[18] "Ce travail complexe de montage"; Sauvage, *Louise Sigée,* 51.

woman is the embellishment of sin and should strive to remain chaste, modest, and submissive, first to God and then to either her prince or her husband.

Blesilla's opinion prevails throughout this second part of the dialogue, in spite of the mild complaints of her young companion. She also replies now to one of the points in defense of "vita aulica" made by Flaminia the first day, namely, that the court is a place where women have the freedom to speak their minds. Blesilla points out the dangers of eloquent conversations with men. Accusing articulate women of both making fools of themselves and inciting men, Blesilla links feminine oratorical skills with make-up and high fashion; in other words, she equates a woman's public display of wit with her sexual appetite and with licentiousness. She advises that the proper way to find a suitable husband is for a woman to offer her tongue in sacrifice and to ornament herself with restraint and modesty. It becomes clear why Blesilla counseled Flaminia to stay away from the flatterers who always surround princes: they foster wit and embellishment, the very inclinations a woman should resist to maintain intact her *pudicitia*.[19]

As a remedy against idleness for upper-class women, Blesilla proposes that a proper woman should devote her time to philosophy, but those who are not inclined to do so (the majority of them, we must assume), should at least familiarize themselves with the lives of exemplary women. She mentions the need for routine repetition ("exercitatione et assiduitate") in reading those lives so that their beneficial lessons permeate women's characters and improve their conduct ("cum frequens imitatio saepe transeat in mores, et consuetudinis, teste Cicerone, magna sit uis" [161]). Sigea is referring to Vives' educational program of teaching morals through the repetition of specific passages and is presenting it to the princess as an agenda.

Finally, on the third day, Blesilla recommends a life of retreat as the only way to prevent danger and attain true inner happiness. But in spite of Blesilla's long disquisition, young Flaminia refuses to accept her friend's proposal and instead chooses to remain at court, enduring a life of struggle, realizing that, as Blesilla has pointed out, she will never be at peace.

Blesilla and Flaminia embody the only two alternatives for educated women: total retreat or constant struggle. There is no consensus at the end of the *Colloquium* on which one is more appropriate. The length of Blesilla's lecture could indicate that Luisa Sigea favors the "vita privata," but besides being a conventional humanist viewpoint, we find no statements in the dialogue that indicate clearly her personal preference. She seems to be merely stating the characteristics of both avenues.

We are left with the question of whether there is a distinctive woman's voice in Sigea's *Colloquium*. Inés Rada has identified a specific feminine discourse based on the dialogue: Blesilla, she argues, speaks like a man, while Flaminia's role consists in refuting her friend's arguments (33–34). From this we may conclude that Flaminia speaks like a woman. But the truth is that both women speak like men. Luisa Sigea,

---

[19] *Pudicitia* is a key term in Vives' vocabulary, as Peraita notes; it indicates not only chastity of the body, but more importantly, it is the virtue that ensures a woman's control of her passions and provides her "with a modest, sober spirit that engenders appropriate subordinate behavior."

as a woman and a woman in court, writes within linguistic and social structures that do not permit her to transcend her role. First of all, she confines herself to translation, one of the fields allowed to women writers, and she excels in it as an accomplished student, as the Archdeacon of Alcor indicates. But she stops short when it comes to imitating or recreating the models she so expertly translates, to speaking in her own voice.

She accepts the humanist curriculum, formulated to train a social élite to fulfill its predetermined social role. In the case of women, this program emphasized repetition over performance as a means of encouraging obedience and, therefore, silence. Acceptance of this subjected role was her only safe-conduct into speech, but precisely because she was so willing to embrace it, her personal life was caught in the conflict between the expected female characterization and her public position as a humanist. We may ask if her voice can be found anywhere in the *Colloquium,* when the dominant discourse refuses her words. Edward George has signaled a marked difference in the two characters' mode of argumentation. Both women make abundant use of quotations, but while Flaminia maintains intact her personality and relies more heavily on the line of reasoning, trying to adapt the excerpts to her own circumstances, Blesilla uses the authorities in greater number and actually adopts the personality of the authors being quoted.[20] In that sense, I believe Luisa Sigea can only be heard in Flaminia: not in Flaminia's words, borrowed from male language, but instead in her behavior and, specifically, in her silence and adamant resolution to stay at the court. Thus, the *Colloquium* cannot be interpreted as a dialogue on the "vita aulica et privata"; it is instead a dialogue between the humanist construct of the feminine and a learned woman. Flaminia's decision reveals a fierce independence at the expense of her potential happiness. Luisa Sigea may well have employed Vives' method of conveying proper feminine humanistic principles, but, in the final analysis, it is Luisa Sigea who wins the argument, because Flaminia rejects the advice given by Blesilla. By doing so, I would argue, Luisa Sigea represents the sixteenth-century "humanist woman," and her *Colloquium* plays out the dilemma she faced in her life: a peaceful existence as a silent and docile spouse—be it of Christ or of a man—versus active independence. The *Colloquium* is a work of protest, based on an argument concealed in a humanist vocabulary to articulate the place of the new woman.

Yet, to follow Flaminia, or Luisa, is to make great personal sacrifice. Very likely, Diego Sigeo considered Angela a success, for she married and settled down,[21] while Luisa was a failure. But Diego Sigeo had underestimated the power of the *bonae artes*, for education leads to enlightenment, not passivity, and, in that sense, Luisa was an accomplished product. But by making her an assertive woman, Luisa's education no doubt hampered her life.

As a *femina erudita,* she was caught between societal expectations for feminine passivity and her need to speak. Like other female humanists before her, she felt that her

---

[20] Edward George, "Luisa Sigea's Dialogue on Court versus Countryside: The Evidence of the Participants' Rhetoric" (paper delivered at the Conference on Spanish Golden Age Women Writers, Texas Tech University, 10 October 1996).

[21] Serrano y Sanz, *Apuntes,* 395 n. 1, and Sauvage, "Recherches," 53.

acceptance of male discourse and the power of her eloquence made her an exception to other foolish women. Her *Colloquium* accepts the dominant discourse on the weakness of feminine nature, as did those of over learned women, such as Isotta Nogarola[22] and Laura Ceretta,[23] a century before. Luisa castigates women who pay too close attention to their looks, and encourages silence, for, as Vives had said, a woman does not need to be concerned with rhetoric. As for herself, she undoubtedly thought that her extraordinary skills made her superior to her female contemporaries and, as her correspondence attests, she supported her claim to a post at the court of Philip II with her own exceptionality.[24]

But her very rarity (her "rara perfecçión" says Pedro Laínez) and the fact that she wrote well transformed her into an oddity, a monster; the Archdeacon of Alcor even described Luisa Sigea as a "cossa monstruossa" (a monstrous thing).[25] Providing women with the most current Christian education was a double-edged sword. Some of them became too independent, too indecorous, and had to be married off quickly to end all that nonsense. This was the case of Luisa Sigea, according to Jeremy Lawrance's reading of the historical evidence provided by Ismael Ramila.[26]

Active learning and writing, beyond the few precepts and rules on how to live endorsed by Vives, were considered unwomanly; they were tolerated only when women renounced what identified them as women, marriage and childbearing, and gave themselves to the asexual or celibate life of monastic retreat, the quiet life extolled by Blesilla. If Luisa Sigea was a rarity as a young woman, she became twice a monster after her marriage. The Archdeacon of Alcor, after describing all her unnatural accomplishments, ends his account by noting that, most surprisingly, the burdens of marriage did not prevent her from cultivating the *bonae artes*.[27] Contemporary humanists chose to ignore her marital status when praising her, and after her death, Luisa Sigea was extolled as the tenth muse by Fernando Ruiz de Villegas ("illa

---

[22] See her "Defense of Eve" in Margaret King and Albert Rabil Jr, eds., *Her Immaculate Hand: Selected Works by and about the Women Humanists of Quattrocento Italy* (Binghamton, 1983), 57–69.

[23] See her "Curse Against the Ornamentation of Women," in King, *Her Immaculate Hand*, 77–80.

[24] Ac si apud te bonarum artium peritiam idem viget, ac apud celsos olim Reges, vt spero, memineris, id a te muneris eam suppliciter efflagitare foeminam, quæ ceteras suae ætatis foeminas Musarum cultu (si fas est dicere) facile excelluit. [And if, as I expect, you are familiar with the liberal arts, like the excellent kings of antiquity, grant this little benefaction requested by a woman who, if I am allowed to say so, has surpassed all the other women of her time cultivating the Muses.] Bonilla y San Martín, "Clarorum," 280.

[25] For Laínez, see Serrano y Sanz, *Apuntes*, 395. Cf. the Archdeacon of Alcor: "Sobre todas paresçe cossa mostruossa, y que se deue contar por cossa de prodigio en este tiempo." From Serrano y Sanz, *Apuntes*, 397.

[26] Jeremy Lawrance, "The Universities in Spain at the End of the Middle Ages," *Atalaya* 6 (1995): 21–40; Ismael García Ramila, "Nuevas e interesantes noticias, basadas en fe documental, sobre la vida y descendencia familiar burgalesa de la famosa humanista, Luisa de Sigea, la 'Minerva' de los renacentistas," *Boletín de la Institución Fernán González* 145 (1958): 309–321; 146 (1959): 465–492; and 147 (1959): 567–593.

[27] Serrano y Sanz, *Apuntes*, 397.

novem Aoniis addita virginibus") or "tanta puella" by Juan de Merlo.[28] As a married, learned woman, she could not fit in any category. Her husband, as we may expect, remembered her as a woman—his epitaph is the only praise that addresses her as "foemina"—but the humanists exalted her as a virgin, a nonwoman, the model for complete chastity that was the only virtue open to a learned lady.

Luisa Sigea was fully aware of her contradictory situation, and she described it in a bitter letter to her brother-in-law shortly after her marriage.[29] As a *femina erudita*, she was a burden for her husband; as a married woman, she would never be able to secure a position at court doing what she knew best, much less become an active civic figure, like her male contemporaries. In spite of her proven skills, she could never develop a professional career. The dominant discourse categorized her as a woman endowed with *pudicitia*[30] and that same *pudicitia* condemned her to silence and restraint incompatible with public life.

Wake Forest University

---

[28] Serrano y Sanz, *Apuntes*, 397.

[29] Quum tot linguarum atque aliarum artium studiis a teneris annis desudarim, ac de inde in Regum aula adscita fuerim . . . ac post tredecim annorum spatium sedulae servitutis, fratri tuo, mihi conjugi dulcissimo, ipsorum permissu nuptarim, videamque studiorum atque aulicae illius onerosae servituis sat debita praemia negari et me iterum marito, dum ut feminam extra aliorum aleam positam decebat, commodo futura essem, esse incommodo. [Having devoted my efforts since my tenderest years to the study of so many languages and other arts, I have been admitted to the royal courts of the kings and placed at their service . . . and now, after thirteen years of diligent services, having married your brother, my dearest husband, with the princes' permission, I find that I am denied the reward due to my studies and to the wearisome service in court, and that I am a burden for my husband instead of helping him as it would be appropriate for a woman who is beyond the common destiny.] Sauvage, "Recherches," 101–102.

[30] Her husband's epitaph praises her as "Loisiae Sigaeae Foeminae incomparabili cuius pudicitia cum eruditione linguarum quae in ea ad miraculum fuit aequo certabat." [To Luisa Sigea, unequaled woman whose pudicitia rivalled her learning of the languages in which she was a miracle.] Serrano y Sanz, *Apuntes*, 399.

The Neglected Works of Platina

MARY ELLA MILHAM

Bartolomeo Sacchi, called Platina, has been known for more than five hundred years for his librarianship of the renewed Vatican Library (immortalized in a famous painting of Melozzo da Forlì); for his composition of *De honesta voluptate et valetudine*, that curious work on foodstuffs, medicine, and recipes; and for *The Lives of the Popes*, which even served the Protestant Reformation. My first complete biography, which accompanies my new critical edition of *De honesta voluptate*, has revealed his authorship of more than thirty items, nearly all cast in print but some much more widely known than others.[1] Of the most outstanding, several have been badly neglected since their last printings in the sixteenth century.

Perhaps the most important work of Platina's to have been neglected is his tract on moral philosophy, *De falso et vero bono*. It seems clearly to have been written while he was incarcerated in Castel Sant'Angelo for the second time by Pope Paul II (1468–69), on a charge of having been party to the so-called Conspiracy of 1468. It seems to represent the period of incarceration when Platina was being kept segregated from those fellow members of the Roman Academy who were jailed on similar charges and from nearly all visitors, except the Greek Teodoro Gaza and the doctor and associate in the academy, Tommaso Valeri da Viterbo. The opening book is based upon an exchange in prison between Platina and the warden, Roderigo Sanchez de Aravalo, on the classical *consolationes* akin to Boethius from Plato and Aristotle. It considers the capacity of the human mind to rise above pain and adverse fortune and to find comfort in contemplation, aid to mankind, self-sufficiency, and friendship. In Book II the interlocutor is Gaza, and in Book III attention turns to Valeri.

The volume on humanistic philosophy in Saitta's monumental work, *Il pensiero italiano nell' umanesimo e nel rinascimento*, places Platina among the eight chief humanist-philosophers of the Italian Renaissance. Much of his discussion centers on *De falso et*

---

[1] Mary Ella Milham, *Platina: On Right Pleasure and Good Health*, Medieval & Renaissance Texts & Studies, vol. 168 (The Renaissance Society of America, Renaissance Texts Series, vol. 17) (Tempe, AZ, 1998).

vero bono. Saitta did not agree with Gaida[2] and others who had seen this work simply as a Boethian exaltation of the ascetic and contemplative life; rather, he believed that it contained·a philosophic justification for true happiness, constructed out of the sufferings of prison, which was founded on a spiritual vision in some ways similar to the later and more profound views of Pico and Ficino. To Platina, the possibilities of man's mind are marvellous and infinite, desiring to know everything in heaven and earth, not only in science and the arts but in morality and politics.[3]

New lines of research which include *De falso et vero bono* have begun to appear in recent years, as are shown in Onofri's studies.[4] She has investigated themes in the work in light of various kinds of Aristotelianism, Platonism, and Neo-Platonism, and places certain ideas of Platina outside the mainstream of Roman Platonism. One wonders how this relates to Platina's intellectually formative years studying philosophy in Florence under Giovanni Argyropulo (1457–62) where he was a classmate of Lorenzo and an acquaintance of many Florentine humanists. It seems obvious that *De falso et vero bono* is in need of a modern study similar to Lorch's investigation of Valla's *De voluptate*.[5] In fact, *De falso et vero bono* invites comparison with *De voluptate*, for which Valla used several titles, that of the final version being *De vero et falso bono*. We know that about 1462, Platina had written *De flosculis quibusdam linguae latinae*, directly based upon a work of Valla's, but we do not know whether there is a relationship between the two tracts on moral philosophy. Kristeller long ago proved that Platina was not the tutor of Ficino, as had been believed, but this does not deny his knowledge of Florentine thought and thinkers.[6]

It is interesting that *De falso et vero bono*, with its title reminiscent of Valla, was first dedicated to Platina's nemesis, Paul II, about 1470–71, presumably in an attempt to regain his good will, although the pope was known to scorn Valla's treatise on pleasure. After Paul II's death in 1471 it was rededicated to Sixtus IV in the version widely disseminated in manuscripts. This important work was first printed with several other shorter tracts in an appendix to an edition of Platina's *Lives of the Popes* in 1504, which was reissued several times in the sixteenth century.[7] It deserves not only reprinting but editing from the manuscripts and translation into a major modern language, which would assure it of further investigation.

---

[2] Giacinto Gaida, *Liber de vita Christi et omnium pontificum*, in *Rerum Italicarum Scriptores*, new ed. 3,1 (Città di Castelli, 1913–33).

[3] Giuseppe Saitta, *Il pensiero italiano nell' umanesimo e nel rinascimento*, vol. 1, 2d ed. (Florence, 1961), 391.

[4] Laura Onofri, "Figure di potere a paradigmi culturali," in *Uno principato ed una città: Siste IV* (hereafter called *PCS*), ed. Massimo Miglio (Vatican City, 1986), 58–63.

[5] Maristella Lorch, ed., *De voluptate*, by Lorenzo Valla (Bari, 1980), 37–38.

[6] Paul O. Kristeller, "Per la biografia di Marsilio Ficino," *Civiltà Moderna* 10 (1936): 295.

[7] Platina, *Platynae hystoria de vitis pontificum*, 2 parts (Venice, 1504). The appendix to this publication contains: Dialogus . . . de falso et vero bono; Dialogus contra amores; Dialogus . . . de vera nobilitate; Diversorum academicorum panegyrici in parentalia B. Platynae. This edition and appendix were·reprinted a number of times until at least the late 1560s.

Another dialogue which has not, so far as I am aware, been given a modern edition, translation, or complete study is *De amore*, also found in the same 1504 edition, although it had first appeared in 1481 in a P. A. Filelfo edition of Platina's *De flosculis quibusdam linguae latinae*.[8] Benvenuti has given us its previously unknown first manuscript version, which would date its composition to about 1465 at Rome.[9] Now we know that it was issued in manuscript with three different dedications within about six years, and that only the last, to one Stella (fictitious, or a pseudonym for Ludovico Agnelli), sometimes called *In amores* and sometimes *Contra amores*, was cast in print. This is a misogynistic critique of women; its influence on later writers appears to have been significant.

De amore seems to be inspired by Plutarch's "Dialogue on Love" in the *Moralia*,[10] but at least twice after Platina's death it was probably the point of departure for the rather different works of others who knew him. In 1487 Paolo Pompilio produced a work entitled *De vero et probabili amore*, which is dedicated to Platina's dearest friend, Pomponio Leto. In the dedication Pompilio states that Pomponio will find much from his own writings, but he makes Platina the chief speaker in the dialogue, which is unlike Platina's original.[11] Platina carries on this imaginary dialogue with Alessio Stati in 1476 in the presence of two Spanish prelates.[12] In the sixteenth century a member of the second Roman Academy, Marcantonio Altieri, composed another and more famous dialogue, *Li Nuptiali*, in which he made Pomponio and Platina the speakers, discussing marriage with him. He claimed that he had often heard them discussing the question with each other, but we do not know whether he was reporting fact or setting the stage for his own work.[13]

In a study by Trevor Peach of the sixeenth-century *Dialogues* of the French Jacques Tahureau we have a truly modern, though limited, analysis of *De amore*. Peach discusses the popularity of Platina's dialogue in France and uses the attitudes toward love of Platina and Stella in discussing the dialogue between Democritic and Cosmophile. He sees the antifeminist views of Platina/Democritic as deriving from a fourteenth-century tradition, while the views of Stella/Cosmophile are in the tradition of the neo-Platonists and Castiglione's *Cortegiano*.[14] Since the date of composition of *De amore* is about 1465, the ideas of the Florentines on love were perhaps not fully formed, but it is possible that some of them were already being discussed when

---

[8] *De flosculis . . . Contra amores*, ed. P. A. Filelfo (Milan, 1481).

[9] Antonia Tissoni Benvenuti, "Due schede per il Platina," in *Bartolomeo Platina, detto Il Platina*, ed. Augusto Campana and Paola Medioli Masotti (Padua, 1986), 209–210.

[10] Plutarch, "The Dialogue of Love (Erotikos)," *Plutarch's Moralia* (Greek), trans. Edwin L. Minar, Jr., F. H. Sandbach, and W. E. Helmbold, Loeb Classical Library (London, 1961), 301–439.

[11] MS Vat. lat. 2222, fols. 45–47, dedication to Leto; fol. 47v, Dialogus de amore Pauli Pompilii, loquitur Alexis Eustathius ad Platynam. . . .

[12] Maria Chiabo, "Paolo Pompilio professore dello *Studium urbis*," in *PCS*, 508.

[13] Stephen Kolsky, "Altieri's Roman Weddings," *Renaissance Quarterly* 40, 1 (1987): 76–79.

[14] Trevor Peach, "Une source négligée de l'antiféminisme XVIe siècle: le 'Contra amores' de Platina et les 'Dialogues' de Jacques Tahureau," *Studi francesi* 19, 2 (1975): 201–213.

Platina was studying under Argyropulo in 1457–62. Saitta feels that Platina's misogyny in this dialogue is tempered by psychological insights into women quite advanced for the fifteenth century and that perhaps his antifeminism is merely a manifestation of the masculine ethic that he shared with Machiavelli.[15] All of this suggests that *De amore* needs not only editing and translating but a full modern assessment, including its relationship to Plutarch, its philosophic roots, its imitators, and its place in gender studies.

Both *De falso et vero bono* and *De amore* seem, then, to have been too often ignored, or only superficially assessed, but the political philosophy has fared somewhat better. In this half-century *De principe*, to the young Federigo Gonzaga, and its revision, *De optimo cive*, to Lorenzo de'Medici, have been given serious attention by several European scholars, as have his historical works, though chiefly by Italians. Another short work on political philosophy is *De vera nobilitate*, which has recently been fully addressed by Rabil as one of the nine essays on that topic to be produced in the Quattrocento.[16]

Most of Platina's known compositions were laudatory, biographical, or historical, or were simply clerical records (of the workings of the Vatican Library); they continue to be studied. But a few minor works have been so recently discovered that they are not yet in discussion. Although I found and identified MS Berlin: SBSPr lat. Quart. 488, I later found that Virginia Brown had previously discovered and transcribed Platina's brief works on Vergil which are contained in it; she will no doubt deal with them in her volume on Vergil for *Catalogus translationum et commentariorum*. Similarly, in his article on Pliny in the *Catalogus*,[17] Nauert reported MS London: BL Harl. 3475, which contains a fragment of Platina's *Epitome* to the *Historia Naturalis* of Pliny. Since, however, Nauert did not notice an error in his sources, his account of the dedication of this work is flawed, and analysis of the fragment (from the Geography) was outside his mandate. This work is well worth an extensive study which would deal with all its problems, including its probable use in *De honesta voluptate*.

Finally, I am convinced that a sizeable body of poetry by, to, and about Platina should be collected and studied. I have found that he already had a reputation as a poet as a mature student at Florence, which Sixtus IV later utilized in his commissions for the dedicatory inscriptions on the Ponte Sisto and elsewhere. But there must certainly be biographical material in the many poems written to and about Platina, both during his lifetime and after his death. Some poems about him are well known, but Kristeller's *Iter Italicum* alone lists many more recorded in manuscript (including one about an unknown illness) and held in Venice.[18] A volume of eulogistic poetry, called the "Parentalia" and published after his death, was also reissued in 1504 in the

---

[15] Saitta, *Il pensiero*, 395.

[16] Albert Rabil, Jr., "On True Nobility," in *Knowledge, Goodness, and Power: The Debate over Nobility among Quattrocento Humanists* (Binghamton, 1991), 269–298.

[17] Charles G. Nauert, Jr., "Caius Plinius Secundus," *Catalogus translationum et commentariorum*, vol. 4 (Washington, 1980), 335–337.

[18] Kristeller, *Iter Italicum*, 7 vols. (London, 1963–).

same appendix to *The Lives of the Popes* mentioned above, but it seems not to have been examined since.

We have seen many of Platina's compositions ignored until the post-World War II era, which has brought great advances in the study of all Renaissance figures. I hope that my introduction to the edition and translation of *De honesta voluptate*, with its account of the life and works of Platina, will help to spur interest in the important works which remain obscure.

University of New Brunswick

El manuscrito 5785 BNM y la Apologia de J. G. de Sepúlveda: Crítica textual y variantes de autor

ANTONIO MORENO HERNÁNDEZ

Dentro de la extensa producción de Juan Ginés de Sepúlveda se incluye una obra que bajo el título de *Summa quaestionis ad bellum Barbaricum sive Indicum pertinentis* ha sido considerada tradicionalmente como una pieza independiente del humanista pozoalbense dentro de sus trabajos relativos al derecho de gentes[1].

Este opúsculo, transmitido por un único manuscrito[2] (ms. 5785 de la Biblioteca Nacional de Madrid, ff. 309–317) y editado por A.M. Fabié en 1879[3], se inscribe dentro de la polémica que entre 1540 y 1550 surge en torno a la legitimidad de la conquista al calor de las cortapisas con que chocó la publicación del *Democrates secundus* (*Dem. sec.*).

El título completo de esta *Summa* alude claramente a su carácter de epítome del *Dem. sec.*[4], elaborado con el fin de responder a las objeciones planteadas por las Universidades de Salamanca y Alcalá en contra de la publicación del *Dem. sec.*[5]

---

[1] Así en Ángel Losada, *Juan Ginés de Sepúlveda a través de su 'Epistolario' y nuevos documentos* (Madrid, 1949, rpt. 1973), 331, 652–653.

[2] Para una descripción de este ms., cf. la introducción a la edición de la *Apologia* que aparece en *Juan Ginés de Sepúlveda. Obras Completas* III, ed. Antonio Moreno Hernández (Pozoblanco, 1997), CLXI–CLXI. Las referencias a la numeración y a las ediciones y mss. de la *Apol.* se hace sobre la base de esta edición.

[3] Antonio María Fabié, ed., "Objeciones y respuestas relativas al *Demócrates Alter*", en *Vida y escritos de Fray Bartolomé de las Casas, Obispo de Chiapa* (Madrid, 1879), Apéndice XXIII, 519–537. La transcripción de Fabié es, como hemos tenido ocasión de comprobar, extremadamente deficiente: cf. Juan Ginés de Sepúlveda, *Obras Completas* III, Introducción a la *Apologia*, CLXII, n. 102.

[4] El título íntegro es *Summa quaestionis ad bellum Barbaricum sive Indicum pertinentis, quam latius persequitur G. Sepulueda in libro, quem de* Iustis belli causis, *in qua omnes obiectiones Salmanticae et Compluti proponuntur et solvuntur.*

[5] Sobre los avatares de esta polémica, cf. la introducción a la *Apología* en *Juan Ginés de Sepúlveda. Obras Completas*, III, Introducción a la *Apologia*, CXXXVII–CXLIV.

Pues bien, el propósito de este artículo es intentar demostrar que la vinculación fundamental de esta obra no es con el *Dem. sec.* sino con la *Apologia* (*Apol.*) del mismo Sepúlveda, publicada en Roma en 1550, con la cual guarda una relación, como veremos, más profunda de lo que podría parecer. La confrontación entre la *Summa* y la *Apol.* permite extraer un primer dato relevante: el ms. 5785, que ha sido copiado por uno de los amanuenses habituales de Sepúlveda y revisado por él mismo[6], presenta un texto que coincide casi exactamente con la sección central de la *Apologia* (*Apol.* 3–27), aunque no es idéntico a ella. El análisis de la afinidad y la divergencia entre uno y otro texto permite determinar con más claridad la relación entre ambos y explicar, en última instancia, el procedimiento de composición de la *Apologia*.

Contraste entre la *Apologia* (*Apol.*) y el texto del ms. 5785 BNM (*M*)

La colación de ambos testimonios permite advertir que la afinidad entre uno y otro es, en efecto, muy alta, con un grado de coincidencia que ronda el 90% del volumen total de texto.

1. Conexión de M *con la tradición de la* Apol.

Desde el punto de vista de la filiación manuscrita, pueden advertirse en *M* variantes—tanto gráficas como de otra naturaleza—que revelan cómo el texto que porta este manuscrito entronca nítidamente con la tradición representada por el grupo de las ediciones de la *Apol.* (*rcm*) frente a los mss. *SJ* y *G*. Algunos ejemplos son éstos:

3,7	difficillimum *Mrcm* : difficilimum *S* : dificillimum *G*
4,3	et praestantioribus *Mrcm* : et prestantioribus *S* : praestantioribus *G*
5,3	aversatur *Mrcm* : abersatur *S* : adversantur *G*
5,3	quaerat *Mrcm* : querat *GS*
5,7	idololatria *Mrcm* : idolatria *GS*
7,7	mulctari *Mrcm* : multari *GS*
12,2	saepe *Mrcm* : sępe *G* : sepe *S*
20,1	poenis *Mrcm* : penis *GS*
21,1	haereticorum *Mrcm* : hęreticorum *G* : hereticorum *S*
24,2	causa iusta *1° Mrcm* : causa iuxta *S* : iusta causa *G*
24,3	praetermisso *Mrcm* : pretermisso *S* : praemisso *G*

Igualmente *M* presenta sus propias variantes gráficas y fonéticas frente a toda la tradición de *Apol.*:

5,7	scripsisset *GMrcm* : scripsiset *M*
5,8	idolorum *GMrcm* : ydolorum *M*
6,2	spiritualibus *GSrcm* : spiritalibus *M*
7,7	praeparentur *GSrcm* : preparentur *M*
15,1	admitterent *GSrcm* : admiterent *M*

---

[6] Cf. *Juan Ginés de Sepúlveda. Obras Completas*, III, Introducción a la *Apologia*, CLXII.

2. Variantes de redacción

Pero las diferencias entre *M* y *Apol.* no se limitan a variantes derivadas del proceso de copia, sino que revelan una voluntad deliberada de modificar la redacción del texto. Estas divergencias se producen a diversos niveles, como acreditan los ejemplos que siguen:

A) Alternativas de redacción de un mismo pasaje (*Apol.* 3,8):

M: *Non pertinet ad Papam de paganis quibus moribus aut legibus utantur inquirere, auctore Paulo, qui Ad Corinthios 5, "Quid", inquit, "ad me pertinet de iis, qui foris sunt, iudicare?"; non igitur eos propter idolorum cultum bello lacessere.*

Apol.:   *Non est iuris aut potestatis Ecclesiae siue Pontificis de infidelibus iudicare; Papa ergo nec per se nec per alium potest infideles ad cuiuspiam legis observationem compellere. Nom enim fuit talis potestas apostolis concessa, ut Paulus testatur 1 Ad Corinthios 5, dicens "Quid enim pertinet ad me de iis, qui foris sunt, iudicare?"; ergo nec Ecclesiae*

   . . .

En este pasaje recoge Sepúlveda una de las objeciones cruciales de sus oponentes: la ilegitimidad de la autoridad eclesiástica para obligar a los indios a abrazar la fe. Sin embargo hay dos diferencias muy significativas entre *M* y *Apol.*: por un lado, el mayor grado de elaboración argumental y jurídica de *Apol.*, y, por otro, la inclusión en el razonamiento, en esta segunda, no sólo del Papa, sino también de la Iglesia, que debe acatar la autoridad papal. Esta sutileza, lejos de responder a una modificación caprichosa, se explica a partir de la filosofía que inspira la *Apol.*: la necesidad de que los distintos estamentos eclesiásticos—y por tanto también las órdenes religiosas, como las franciscanos y los seguidores de Bartolomé de las Casas—cumplan con las ordenanzas papales que, a juicio de Sepúlveda, se desprenden de la Bula *Inter Caetera* de Alejandro VI (4 de mayo de 1493) sobre la conquista de América, y en la que se apoya reiteradamente nuestro autor a lo largo de la *Apol.* para avalar su posición[7].

B) Pasajes documentados en *M* y no en *Apol.*:

Al final de *Apol.* 5,9: *qui si aliter sentiret, non esset audiendus, atque eo magis quod in confirmatione suae sententiae bis ibidem lapsus est, quod stropha utitur haereticorum de Christi exemplo, qui neminem coegit, ab Augustino multis in locis confutata, et quod de causa delendi gentes peccatrices contraria tradit, ut docuimus, Scripturae Sacrae.*

---

[7] Sobre esta Bula, cf. Alfonso García Gallo, *Las Bulas de Alejandro VI y el ordenamiento jurídico de la expansión portuguesa y castellana en Africa e Indias* (Madrid, 1958); B. González Alonso, "Aspectos jurídicos de la conquista y colonización de América", en *Actas del Congreso Internacional sobre el nacimiento del Dr. Juan Ginés de Sepúlveda* (Córdoba, 1993), 199–210; Manuel Giménez Fernández, *Nuevas consideraciones sobre la historia, sentido y valor de las Bulas Alejandrinas de 1493 referentes a las Indias* (Sevilla, 1944); Emma Falqué, "Bulas alejandrinas de 1493. Texto y traducción", en Juan Gil y José M. Maestre, eds., *Humanismo latino y descubrimiento* (Sevilla-Cádiz, 1992), 11–35.

Al final de *Apol.* 14,5: *Nam licet potestas, quam Christus communicavit Vicario suo in rebus spiritalibus potissimum, et ad salutem animarum pertinentibus versetur, non tamen a temporalibus excluditur, quatenus haec ad spiritalia diriguntur, ut Thomas testatur De Reg. prin. Lib. 3, c. 3, iuncto c. 10 (ut supra diximus M^2).*

Se trata de dos pasajes que insisten en sendas argumentaciones y que en la redacción de *Apol.* se han desestimado, por considerarlos prescindibles o redundantes.

C) Pasajes presentes en *Apol.* pero no en *M*:

7,2 *ut autem infideles evangelicam praedicationem audire et legem naturae servare cogantur, necesse est ut Christianorum imperio subiiciantur, causaliter igitur, ut utar verbo pontificio, hoc quoque pertinet ad potestatem Papae, quod magnopere dirigitur ad spiritualia quae sunt eiusdem potestatis, cap. "per venerabilem", tit. "Qui filii sint legitimi"* . . .

11,2 *quae eadem est Constantii*

10,5 *primum a Constantino ut Eusebius in Historia Ecclesiastica et Hieronimus in Chronicis testantur latam, et post a Constantio filio et aliis imperatoribus confirmatam.*

17,4 *ex ordine ad finem sortiuntur; quare, quae finem impediunt, non habent rationem boni.*

El primero de estos pasajes (7,2) resulta ilustrativo de cómo la *Apol.* intenta matizar la formulación de *M*: en una exposición sobre la necesidad de que los infieles abracen la fe, Sepúlveda aduce que para ello es necesario que éstos se sometan al poder de los cristianos (*necesse est ut Christianorum imperio subiiciantur*), y que este poder está legitimado por la autoridad papal (*ad potestatem Papae*). Otra vez la Bula de Alejandro VI parece esgrimirse implícitamente como razón de fondo para la legitimación de la conquista por la fuerza.

D) En algunos contextos se han introducido alteraciones sistemáticas entre *M* y *Apol.*

Así *M* recurre con alguna frecuencia a fórmulas de cierto regusto escolástico para recoger la argumentación anterior, como es el uso de *antecedens*, que ha sido eliminado en la redacción de la *Apol.*

    3,2   illud *GSrcm* : antecedens *M*

    3,3   namque *GSrcm* : antecedens probatur *M*

    26,1   nego antecedens ad confirmationem iterum antecedens negatur nam *add.* M

    17,4   non enim *GSrcm* : probatur antecedens quia nec *M*.

E) Lecturas alternativas:

5,3 Sic enim scriptum est in *Deuteronomii* cap. 9, "Ne dicas, cum deleverit eos Dominus ‹tuus M› in conspectu tuo, . . ."

9,2 Iure igitur ‹isti M› Barbari salutis suae causa ad iustitiam compelluntur.

27,1 is per ignorantiam affectatam et malitiam [et malitiam *om.* M] seu per scandalum Pharisaeorum deliquisse facile convincetur.

5,4 omnia enim peccata, quae hic memorantur, theologorum consensu ad idolorum

cultum referuntur aut impiam superstitionem *GSrcm* : referuntur *post* superstitionem *transp. M*

19,2 (*Apol.*) Nam nec iniustum bellum inferre, nec iustum illatum, si rite fuerit indictum, propulsare licet, sine iniuria, non enim solum, contumeliam inferre, sed
ut cumque iniuste in quemquam facere iniuria est.

19,2 (*M*) Nam iniustum bellum *nec* inferre, nec *illatum,* si *recte* fuerit indictum, propulsare licet, sine iniuria, non enim solum, contumeliam inferre, sed ut cumque iniuste in *quemque* facere iniuria est.

3. Correcciones de M

Otro aspecto fundamental a estos efectos de *M* es que el manuscrito ha sido
revisado por el propio copista (*M¹*) y por la mano del propio Sepúlveda (*M²*). La
confrontación de estas correcciones con el texto de la *Apol.* permite comprobar cómo
las mayoría de éstas van en la línea de converger con el texto de la tradición
mayoritaria de la *Apol.*, de forma que ya sobre la propia redacción de *M* se conformó,
al menos en parte, el texto de la *Apol.*

A) Correcciones del propio copista (*M¹*):

  3,1   Christianorum *JGSM¹rcm* : iure Cristianorum *M*
  3,1   iure *JGSrcm M¹ i.l.* : *om. M*
  3,2   quaest. 2 *JGSrcm* : *M¹ i.l.*
  3,3   Sincera *JGM¹* : Syncera *M*
  4,2   ut *JGSM¹rcm* : ut testatur *M*
  5,5   *Exodi* 32 *JGSM¹rcm* : *Exodi* 232 *M*
  5,8   itaque *JGSrcm M¹ i.l.* : unde *M* s
  7,5   Aristoteles *JGSM¹cm* : Aristotiles *r* : Augustinus *M*
  9,5   prophetia *JGSMrcm* : quod tunc ecclesia *add. M* [*del. M¹*]

B) Correcciones y anotaciones del propio Sepúlveda (*M²*):

  3,3   lib. 2 adversus literas Petiliani *M² m.g.*
  5,3   iustitiam *JGSM²rcm* : iustificationem *M*
  5,9   Caietanus *JGrcm M² i.l.*: Gaietanus *S* : Gae. *M*
  9,5   qua de re – et habetur *Srcm* : qua de re Augustinus *M* : epistula ultima
         et habetur *M² i.l.* : *om. JG*
  11,7   est *JGSrcm M² i.l.* : *om. M*
  14,5   ut supra diximus *M²*
  18,1   esset *JGSM²rcm* : essent *M*
  18,1   quam *JGSrcm M² i.l.* : q. *M*
  18,2   nisi ad – impietatem redirent *JGSrcm M² i.l.* : *om. M*
  27,1   et quid *JGSm M² m.g.* : et *M* : et quod *rc*

Conclusiones

Pues bien, a la vista de estos datos textuales podemos extraer la siguiente conclusión: El texto del ms. 5785, un documento académico inédito, concebido para refutar a las Universidades de Alcalá y Salamanca, ha servido de base, con ciertos retoques en su redacción, para la sección central de la *Apologia* publicada inicialmente en Roma en 1550.

Pero esta reutilización de un texto privado anterior permite explicar además una peculiaridad significativa de la estructura argumental de la *Apologia*[8], la presencia de dos registros discursivos diferentes:

1) El comienzo y el final de la *Apologia* contiene la respuesta de Sepúlveda a Ramírez de Haro, al que se dedica la obra. Ocupa los caps. 1 y 2, y reaparece en los caps. 28–33, y sirve para vertebrar todo el escrito, con estas características formales:

    a) Alusión constante a su interlocutor, Ramírez de Haro, a la sazón obispo de Segovia, a través de la 2ª persona.
    b) Ausencia de referencias eruditas y una casi total ausencia de citas, con concomitancias en el tono y en la expresión con el género epistolar y con la oratoria forense.

2°) La sección central (caps. 3–27), que corresponde a la respuesta de Sepúlveda a las Universidades de Salamanca y Alcalá (= ms. 5785 BNM). Los rasgos que definen esta sección de la *Apologia* responden al modelo escolástico de 'suma':

    a) Ausencia de alusiones a Ramírez de Haro ni a sus objeciones concretas. Desaparición de la 2ª persona: se refiere siempre en plural a sus oponentes, sin citarlos por sus nombres.
    b) El discurso es estrictamente argumentativo, basado en un esquema de argumento/refutación, acompañado de un abundante aparato de citas.

El ms. 5785 permite entender, en efecto, el procedimiento seguido por Sepúlveda para componer la *Apologia*, ya que para responder a Ramírez de Haro recurre a un texto previo concebido originariamente con otra finalidad. Sepúlveda aprovechó este texto insertándolo con las modificaciones de distinta índole que hemos apuntado, desde la adición o supresión de palabras o frases enteras, hasta la alteración de la redacción, aprovechando para matizar aspectos de su argumentación que con sutileza intenta introducir en aras de una mejor formulación de sus intenciones. La revisión que como hemos visto sufrió un pasaje como el de *Apol.* 3,8, por ejemplo, deja entrever su deseo de vincular la posición de toda la iglesia con la autoridad papal, representada por la Bula de Alejandro VI, con la pretensión de restar peso a las instancias que desde la misma iglesia se oponían a su posición.

Esta forma de proceder permite, así mismo, entender mejor cómo la *Apologia* no es un texto lineal, sino que surge del ensamblaje entre el compendio de objeciones y refutaciones y la respuesta a Ramírez de Haro, dentro de la cual se inserta el primero.

---

[8] Para un estudio detenido de la estructura argumental de la *Apol.*, cf. *Juan Ginés de Sepúlveda. Obras Completas* III, Introducción a la *Apologia*, CXLIV–CXLVIII.

Un buen ejemplo, en fin, del afán de Sepúlveda por revisar escrupulosamente sus textos, como puede apreciarse en otras muchas facetas de su producción, pero que cobra en este caso una importancia muy significativa, por ser aquí donde intenta defender con sus mejores armas dialécticas y los argumentos de autoridad la esencia de su posición sobre la legitimidad de la conquista.

Universidad Nacional de Educación a Distancia, Madrid

Le De pictura, plastice et statuaria
du Père Jules César Boulenger, S.J.

COLETTE NATIVEL

Le traité *De pictura, plastice et statuaria* de Jules César Boulenger est depuis long-temps oublié des historiens d'art et de l'archéologie. Seul Ellenius, dans son *De arte pingendi* (Uppsala, 1960), en donne un bref survol qui s'appuie sur le vague résumé du *Systematik und Geschichte der Archäologie der Kunst* de Stark, paru il y a plus d'un siècle, en 1880, alors que Schlosser (*Die Kunstliteratur*, Wien, 1924) ne consacre qu'une ligne au "savant archéologue" qu'il mentionne. Plus récemment, *L'histoire de l'histoire de l'art* (Paris, 1996) de Germain Bazin ne le nomme même plus. La même indifférence règne chez les historiens de l'archéologie: Boulenger n'a droit à aucune notice dans les synthèses de Schiering (*Allgemeine Grundlagen der Archäologie*, 1969) ou de Schnapp (*La conquête du passé: aux origines de l'archéologie*, Paris, 1993).

Pourquoi donc exhumer ce texte qui n'a certes pas, dans l'histoire de la pensée artistique, l'importance du *De pictura* d'un Leon Battista Alberti, du *De pictura ueterum* d'un Franciscus Junius, du *Laocoon* d'un Gotthold Ephraim Lessing? Parce qu'il est nécessaire, à qui veut évaluer exactement l'apport de ces grands textes à la pensée de l'art, de dessiner précisément le paysage intellectuel dans lequel ils s'inscrivirent. Cela ne se peut faire qu'en tentant de comprendre de l'intérieur la démarche que les huma-nistes suivirent, en examinant les questions qu'ils se posaient et en utilisant les outils critiques qui étaient les leurs, donc en étudiant systématiquement toute la production contemporaine que nous avons conservée, même lorsqu'elle est de médiocre qualité à nos yeux.

Je dis bien à nos yeux car Boulenger (Bulengerus), l'auteur, lui-même peu connu, du *De pictura, plastice et statuaria* eut son heure de gloire et fut lu par ses grands con-temporains comme Vossius, Junius ou Dati. Plusieurs de ses traités furent assez fa-meux pour figurer encore dans les *Thesauri* d'antiquités grecques et romaines que réunirent à la fin du XVIIe siècle Johannes Georgius Graevius et Johannes Fredericus Gronovius—le *Thesaurus antiquitatum romanarum* (Utrecht, 1694–1699) et le *Thesaurus graecarum antiquitatum* (Leyde, 1697–1702). Ces *Thesauri*, qui réunissent dans un groupement thématique les textes majeurs d'histoire et d'archéologie antiques publiés depuis le XVIe siècle, constituent sans doute la première grande encyclopédie de l'antiquité. Le *De pictura, plastice et statuaria* parut dans le volume IX du *Thesaurus graecarum antiquitatum*, *"Festiua, mensurarum ac picturae, temporis et numeri ac pecuniae diuersa exsequens"*, dans la section *pictura* qui compte quatre autres traités (complets ou partiellement réédités): le *De sculptura* de Pomponio Gaurico (Naples, 1504); les deux livres sur la sculpture et la peinture du *Gallus Romae hospes* de Louis de Montjosieu (Rome, 1585); le *De caelatura* d'Alde Manuce extrait du *De quaesitis per epistolam libri duo* (Venise, 1576); et le *De pictura* (*sic*) de Philostrate (les premiéres lignes des *Images*). Une étude précise du choix et des regroupements de ces textes permettrait d'ailleurs de mieux appréhender la vision de l'Antiquité à la Renaissance et à l'âge classique car ils mettent en question les notions mêmes d'antiquité et d'histoire: il est clair que Gaurico, même s'il se réfère aux anciens, n'écrit à aucun moment une histoire de l'art antique. De plus, aucun des traités réunis dans ce volume dédié aux antiquités grecques, sauf celui de Philostrate, ne concerne spécifiquement la Gréce; on les attendrait dans le *Thesaurus antiquitatum romanarum* qui, de son côté, ne propose que la description par Lucas Holstein d'une peinture représentant un nymphée, trouvée à Rome dans les jardins Barberini et celle des peintures de la tombe des Nasons par Bellori: la peinture, grecque ou romaine, est abordée dans le cadre d'une réflexion plus large sur la peinture antique.

Les outils biographiques dont nous disposons donnent peu de renseignements sur Boulenger. Son père, Pierre, un grammairien, professeur de grec et de latin à Loudun, jouissait déjà d'une certaine notoriété puisque Cosme II de Médicis l'appela, pour enseigner la théologie, à Pise où il mourut en 1598. C'est à Loudun que naquit Jules César en 1558. Entré au noviciat en 1582, il sortit, en 1594, de la Compagnie de Jésus, avec l'autorisation de ses supérieurs, pour se consacrer à l'éducation de ses frères et neveux. Il enseigna à Paris, Toulouse et Pise. Il rentra en 1620 dans la Compagnie et prêcha avec succès. Il mourut à Cahors en 1628.

Il laissait une œuvre importante et variée: des ouvrages directement liés à son état religieux—des prêches, l'*Oraison funèbre sur la mort d'Henri III*, des textes polémiques contre Casaubon qui avait attaqué Baronio dans les *Exercitationes*, contre Du Plessis Mornay. Il fit aussi œuvre d'historien, donnant une *Historia sui temporis* qui couvre la période de 1560 à 1612 et confirme ses sentiments monarchistes exposés dans le *De officiis regni Galliae* (1617), le *De sancta et inuiolabili regum maiestate libri tres* (s.l.n.d.), et le *Tractatus de iure*. Il taquina la muse dans un poème sur Florence, *Florentia* (Pise, 1615), dédié à Charles de Médicis. Nous avons de lui encore un *Triomphe du roi*. Mais surtout il laissa une importante série de traités sur les antiquités romaines dans laquelle s'inscrit le *De pictura*:

En 1598, à Paris, le *De uenatione circi et amphitheatri liber* et le *De circo romano, ludisque circensibus* accompagné de l'*Oratio de circo* de Jean Chrysostome traduite en latin pour la première fois d'après un manuscrit inédit, nous dit-on.

En 1601, à Paris, le *De spoliis bellicis, trophaeis, arcubus triumphalibus et pompa triumphi*, accompagné du *De triumpho et ludis circensibus* d'Onuphrio Panvinio et dédié à Jacques-Auguste de Thou.

En 1603, à Troyes, le *De theatro, ludisque scenicis libri duo*.

En 1612, à Toulouse, le *De tributis ac uectigalibus populi romani liber*, dédié au poète

Jean de La Ceppède, alors président de la cour des comptes.

En 1615, à Paris, le *Romanus Imperator*, repris en 1618, à Lyon, dans une version augmentée (douze livres), intitulée *De imperatore et imperio romano*, dédiée à Cosme II de Médicis.

En 1621, à Lyon, un *Opusculorum systema* qui regroupait en deux tomes trois livres : *De instrumento templorum, in quorum primo agitur de ueste Pontificum, Episcoporum et sacerdotum; in secundo de Donariis; in tertio de forma templorum in quibus difficillima quaeque Anastasii bibliothecarii libro de uitis Pontificorum explicantur;* une série de traités sur la divination—*De tota ratione diuinationis, de oraculis, satibus, auguriis et auspiciis, etc.* Le second volume comprenait des rééditions du *De triumpho*, du *De circo romano, ludisque circensibus*, du *De theatro* et du *De uenatione circi*.

En 1627, enfin, à Lyon, les *De pictura, plastice et statuaria libri duo*, les *De conuiuiis libri quatuor* et le *De ludis priuatis, ac domesticis ueterum*.

Ces traités s'inscrivent dans la tradition philologique européenne. Boulenger a lu les philologues italiens. Le lien avec les travaux d'Onuphrio Panvinio, par exemple, est clairement marqué par l'édition du *De spoliis bellicis* conjointe à celle du *De triumpho et ludis circensibus* du même auteur. Il connaît les traités d'art italiens comme le *De sculptura* de Gaurico, la *Bibliotheca selecta* de Possevin.

Il a lu aussi les savants du Nord. Bien plus, ses études balaient le même champ de la vie publique et privée des Romains que celles, à peine antérieures, que Lipse écrivit—le cirque et ses jeux (Lipse publia des *Saturnalia* en 1582 et un *De amphitheatris* en 1584), l'armée (Lipse donna en 1596 un *De militia Romana* et un *Poliorceticon*)—Boulenger traite de surcroît des triomphes, le dernier volume sur le sujet, que Lipse n'avait pas eu le temps d'écrire; les institutions enfin (de Lipse parut en 1605 un *De magistratibus*). Boulenger connaît son prédécesseur flamand qu'il mentionne à l'occasion et dont il adopte la démarche résolument didactique: avant d'aborder l'étude des us et coutumes, il s'efforce de définir précisément le vocabulaire qui leur est pertinent et de décrire les lieux qui leur servent de cadres. Voici, par exemple, le plan du début du *De circo*: 1) *De origine circensium et nomine*; 2) *Circus unde dictus*; 3) *De forma circi*; 4) *De circo maximo*; 5) *De aliis circis romanis*; 6) *De circis aliarum gentium*. Puis commencent les chapitres qui décrivent l'organisation et le déroulement des jeux. Cette archéologie de philologue, plus que sur les vestiges, s'appuie, comme chez Lipse, sur un florilège de textes anciens, cités, commentés, éventuellement corrigés. À la différence de Lipse, d'ailleurs, Boulenger ne cherche pas à les expliciter par des illustrations: trois planches seulement, ce qui est peu. Ce qui le distingue davantage encore de son prédécesseur, c'est qu'il n'affiche pas le même souci éthique que lui. Son point de vue est celui d'un antiquaire soucieux de comprendre le monde antique, plus que d'un moraliste qui cherche dans les vestiges de la Rome antique une leçon à l'usage des modernes.

Une troisième source aux travaux de Boulenger est à chercher dans la tradition française. Le jésuite s'appuie à maintes reprises, nous y reviendrons, sur les travaux de Blaise de Vigenère—*doctorem meum*, comme il l'appelle, sans qu'on sache s'il suivit ses cours, ou s'il le nomme ainsi parce qu'il traduit souvent en latin de longs extraits de ses *Plattes Images*.

Le *De pictura, plastice et statuaria* présente les mêmes caractéristiques. C'est un ouvrage complexe. Plus proche de l'essai que du traité en forme, il ne s'ordonne pas (à la différence des autres ouvrages) dans un plan d'une grande clarté et l'exposé suit des méandres difficiles à suivre. En voici un rapide sommaire.

La première partie s'ouvre sur une présentation générale de la peinture et de la sculpture. Le 1ᵉʳ chapitre—*de pictura*—définit cet art comme une imitation, et, après avoir affirmé le primat du talent, suivant Alberti, montre sa dette aux autres arts: aux sciences, à la géométrie, pour la *symmetria* (Parrhasios), à l'arithmétique (Eupompe), à l'optique et à la perspective; mais aussi à la philosophie morale, la peinture représentant tous les sentiments; le second—*de plastice et pictura in genere*—envisage l'objet de cette imitation, qui est la nature. Il élargit cette définition à la plastique, la statuaire, la sculpture et la ciselure; après s'être attaché à distinguer ces arts par une étude du vocabulaire grec et latin qui en désigne les productions, il amorce une rapide histoire de la peinture, puis de la sculpture, conéue, selon la tradition plinienne, en termes de progrès vers un meilleur rendu de la vérité. Le chapitre suivant porte sur la seule peinture, cette fois définie en tant que technique (*Pingere nihil est aliud quam penicillo lineas ducere et colores addere, quibus homines, planta arbores aliaeque res exprimantur*), puis rapprochée de l'écriture par une série de preuves philologiques, les verbes *graphein* et *scribere* signifiant écrire aussi bien que peindre. On revient ensuite à l'histoire de la peinture, qui part cette fois de ses origines pour en montrer les progrès techniques—relevés d'ombres, monochromes, polychromes, emploi des ombres et des lumières, des contrastes, des dégradés, des mélanges de couleurs—ainsi que ceux de la sculpture. Suivent cinq chapitres consacrés à la technique picturale: le 4ᵉ et le 5ᵉ, sur les couleurs, adoptent le classement de Pline (*floridus/auster*) et en expliquent la fabrication, puis l'emploi; les 6ᵉ et 7ᵉ, sur la peinture à l'encaustique s'appuient sur Brisson, Perotti et Vigenère; le 8ᵉ est consacré à la mosaïque. Le chapitre 9 revient sur les peintres et les sculpteurs célèbres. Le 10ᵉ traite des peintures "honnêtes et honteuses", le 11ᵉ regroupe les anecdotes connues sur les trompe-l'œil, les chapitres 12 à 16 traitent encore d'aspects techniques: toiles peintes, outils du peintre—pinceaux et le burin, la *pergula* d'Apelle (traitée comme s'il s'agissait d'une pratique courante), pinacothèques et galeries, échafauds. Le chapitre 17, le dernier sur la peinture, regroupe, sans qu'on sache bien pourquoi, des définitions de Pollux et Théophraste. Les cinq chapitres suivants portent sur la seule sculpture: au chapitre 18, images et simulacres sont abordés d'un point de vue surtout religieux, qu'il soit chrétien ou païen, avant que soit traitée la question du matériau, le chapitre suivant énumère sans ordre des statues antiques mentionnées dans les textes et des sculpteurs célèbres, le 20ᵉ traite du culte et de l'ornement des simulacres des dieux, le 21ᵉ revient sur les statues élevées aux grands hommes, le 22ᵉ évoque assez rapidement les *tituli*, le 23ᵉ revient sur les simulacres des dieux.

Le second livre se consacre plus à la technique de la peinture telle que les contemporains la pratiquaient, bien qu'il s'ouvre par un nouveau chapitre sur les origines de la plastique et de la peinture. L'ordre est alors plus rigoureux: un chapitre *de pictura qua uulgo utimur*, un sur la peinture sur verre qui renvoie aux techniques antiques, deux sur l'émail, le second discutant l'assimilation de l'encaustique au smalte, un chapitre *de plastice, sculptura et statuaria* qui distingue les trois techniques. Après les matériaux—marbre, gemmes et pierres précieuses, pierres—sont envisagées les statues de bronze, l'enduit en smalte et en étain, la soudure des œuvres en métal et pour finir les outils des sculpteurs.

Outre le désordre de l'ensemble, à l'intérieur des chapitres règne une certaine confusion: les répétitions abondent (le sommaire l'a montré), tout est juxtaposé sans transition, sans classement, voire sans problématique. Les contemporains ont souligné l'incohérence de l'ouvrage: Carlo Dati l'appelait, dans le *Prœmion* de ses *Vite*, un *confuso e piccolo repertorio*; Junius, déçu, écrivait qu'il manquait à ce *tractaculus* un *nescio quid plus est*. Quel principe d'organisation trouver à cette compilation déséquilibrée ? On constate que si Boulenger ne répartit pas toujours méthodiquement, dans le première livre, ses remarques sur les divers arts dans des chapitres bien séparés et traite indistinctement de la peinture, la plastique et la sculpture, la seconde partie, malgré de nombreuses références aux textes anciens, traite plus souvent de la pratique moderne de la peinture. De plus, l'intérêt porté au vocabulaire technique, encore imprécis dans les langues vernaculaires aussi bien qu'en latin, est aussi remarquable: dans la première partie (pp. 4–5), Boulenger tente d'expliquer ce que sont *caelatura* et *sculptura*, il étudie le vocabulaire de la statue (*statua, imago, conflatile, effigies, figura, similitudo, sculptile, sigillum*) et il distingue *marmorarius, aerarius, sculptor* et *excusor, signum* et *simulacrum*. Dans le second livre, il donne, en outre, chaque fois que cela est possible, des équivalents français aux mots latins qu'il emploie. *Tunc opus dicitur inchoatum, ebauché Gallice, quod sinunt sensim exsiccari, ut deinde iterum nouos colores floridiores, uegetioresque inducant, quibus uestium natiua elegantia exprimatur, uulgo uocant draperies, ce linge est bien drapé, les plis bien estendus, ces draperies sont bien faictes* . . . (p. 107) Cet extrait montre assez le caractère de fiches que prennent parfois les chapitres. Mais surtout on y reconnaît la marque de Vigenère qui affirmait, dans l'épître à Barnabé Brisson, vouloir "accumuler force vocables et locutions", "pour exerciter", à l'exemple de Philostrate, "la jeunesse à sçavoir deviser et escrire à propos, non seulement des peintures, mais d'infinies autres belles choses dont il a curieusement recherché les mots convenables, et appropriez à toutes sortes de professions et mestiers." En cela, le *De pictura* s'apparente aussi aux *Merveilles de la nature*, presque contemporaines (1620), du père jésuite Étienne Binet, qui prétendait fournir au prédicateur un lexique moderne souvent emprunté aux métiers, voire des expressions toutes faites. Enfin, un souci stylistique comparable à celui qu'exprimait Vigenère dans la même épître à Brisson est sensible dans d'autres travaux de Boulenger. Ainsi il s'inquiète dans l'épître au lecteur du *De spoliis bellicis* de l'aspect disparate que revêt le collage de citations qui composent l'ouvrage:

> Hoc te monitum uelim . . . me, in hoc libello, ea quae sunt ab Ammiano Marcellino, Gellio, Plinio, Vopisco, aliisque auctoribus ita cum meis contexuisse, ut pene idem orationis contextus uideri possit, cum in eorum uerbis quaedam sint horridiuscula, et minus nitida, quae uelim ex suo quaeque auctore ut sunt recognoscas, et a meis internoscas, ne dictionis ac stili uarietas tibi nauseam pariat.

Le plan général du *De pictura* répondrait donc à un double but, la première partie étant un répertoire destiné à l'érudit, la seconde visant à former l'honnête homme et à lui fournir, comme les *Plattes Images* ou les *Merveilles de la nature*, des outils linguistiques capables d'orner à la conversation. Plus que construire une théorie de l'art, Boulenger espère apprendre à parler précisément des techniques.

§

Car l'intérêt de Boulenger pour les techniques est important. Dans la tradition de Vigenère, encore, il recense toute sorte d'informations non seulement sur les œuvres antiques mentionnées dans les textes, mais encore sur les techniques et les matériaux employés. Les pages consacrées aux couleurs (I, chap. 4 et 5), aux vitraux, aux textiles, aux techniques du vitrail, du "plomb calciné" dans la fabrication de la faïence, à la peinture à l'encaustique (II, chap. 3 à 6), ou à la mosaïque sont une mine tant sur l'art antique que sur l'art moderne.

C'est ainsi que Boulenger prétend former le goût du lecteur. Il écrit dans la dédicace: *Quo quisque peritior artis est, et judicii limatioris, eo magis admirabilem operis industriam et sollertiam opificis demiratur.* Il ne suffit pas de rester stupéfait devant les œuvres, il faut encore savoir apprécier l'habileté de l'artiste—son *industria* et sa *sollertia*. Cette démarche est celle d'un connaisseur plus que celle d'un esthète qui jugerait l'œuvre en fonction d'une certaine idée de la beauté, comme le voulait Cicéron.

La théorie de l'art se réduit donc à énumérer les lieux communs que la tradition avait dégagés et que Boulenger ne cherche ni à remettre en cause, ni même à illustrer. L'affirmation que la peinture et la sculpture, comme la poésie, imitent la nature lui sert de point de départ. Il emprunte au Socrate des *Mémorables* sa définition de la peinture: *Socrates dicere solitus erat . . . picturam esse imitationem et repraesentationem eorum quae uidentur . . .* (p. 4), pour l'élargir à la plastique et à la sculpture et critiquer les grotesques en suivant certes le classicisme d'Horace, Vitruve et Pline, mais au nom surtout de la valeur pédagogique des images réaffirmée par la tradition post-tridentine (p. 3). Le premier chapitre, soulignant la parenté entre les arts, s'ouvre sur le fameux parallèle *ut pictura pœsis* qu'il reprend d'ailleurs au chapitre 3. Adoptant la topique traditionnelle depuis Simonide—*Pœticam esse picturam loquentem, picturam uero pœsim mutam*—il trouve trois éléments de comparaison entre les deux arts: *utraque multa invenit, multa fingit, multa mentitur.* A quoi il ajoute la "preuve" philologique que Gauricus avait apportée dans son *De sculptura*: les anciens, comme Virgile, employaient la formule *perlegere oculis* pour désigner l'acte de regarder des sculptures (*Aen.* 6, 34).

Boulenger mêle à la démarche d'antiquaire, qui était celle de ses autres traités, celle d'un amateur d'art moderne. Dès le premier chapitre apparaît son souci de mettre en perspective l'art moderne et l'art antique. Il s'exprime de plusieurs façons. Parfois, il se fonde sur son expérience personnelle pour étayer ses affirmations. A propos du primat du talent sur l'art—*nascitur artifex, non fit*—il relate avoir "vu à Florence un peintre dont la main d'enfant enlevait la palme aux plus grands peintres." Il donne en exemple des différentes techniques qu'il expose des œuvres visibles: les mosaïques de Sainte Sophie à Constantinople (sans doute d'après des estampes), à Rome, celles de Saint Paul, de Sainte Agnès, Sainte Cécile, Sainte Marie Majeure, à Florence, celles de Saint Laurent (pp. 36–37). Il a vu une statue de Cybèle à Venise (p. 57). Il compare enfin les techniques anciennes et modernes quand il traite des couleurs à l'encaustique (p. 12), de l'émail (pp. 113–122), ou des couleurs en général (*Colores superioris aevi posuimus, his et nostri aevi colores adiiciamus*, p. 109), du marbre et des stucateurs (p. 135).

Mais toujours, les critères esthétiques des anciens servent à son évaluation des œuvres modernes. Ainsi, (p. 3), il propose une liste ("canonique", puisqu'on la trouvait déjà chez Possevin, et d'autres avant lui) de six artistes modernes qui ont respecté le précepte horatien de l'*Art poétique, serueteur decorum*: Michel-Ange, Raphaël, Le Corrège, Jules Romain, Sebastiano Veneto, Andrea del Sarto; mais, lorsqu'il évoque les modernes qui "ont ravi la palme à Apelle et Protogène", il n'en cite plus que trois: Michel-Ange, Raphaël et le Parmesan. Le premier l'emporte pour le dessin, le second pour la couleur, le troisième pour l'invention (p. 108): c'est une des traces de la démarche rhétorique qu'avaient adoptée, après Alberti et Vasari, les théoriciens italiens, mais que n'exploitera pas Boulenger. Michel-Ange est encore loué pour ses talents de peintre et les effets de relief du plafond de la Sixtine. Pour la statuaire (pp. 123–126), Boulenger cite des œuvres visibles à Rome, en suivant encore une de ces listes obligées depuis Doni: l'Adonis et le Méléagre, l'Apollon du Belvédère, le Laocoon (qu'il croit monolithique), l'Hercule Farnèse, l'Hercule du Capitole, la statue équestre de Marc Aurèle, les colonnes trajane et antonine, les collections du palais des Conservateurs, à Venise le quadrige de saint Marc et parmi les modernes, à nouveau Michel-Ange dont il souligne que ses talents conjugués de peintre et de sculpteur lui ont permis de corriger l'architecture de Saint-Pierre, mal conçue par Bramante et Sangallo. Il ne néglige pas les artistes français et leurs œuvres. Il mentionne, par exemple, Jacques d'Angoulême et Germain Pilon, la statue équestre d'Henri IV sur le pont Neuf, coulée, il est vrai, par un bronzier florentin (p. 149). Pour la gravure, qu'il semble préférer, avec le modelage et la sculpture, à la peinture, il évoque Dürer (p. 125). Ce ne sont pas de simples noms pour lui: il a vu les œuvres de plusieurs d'entre eux, bien qu'il en parle un peu sèchement, malgré l'admiration qu'il dit avoir pour elles.

Peut-on dire qu'il y a chez lui une conception de l'histoire de l'art? Sa démarche "historique" suit essentiellement la topique évolutionniste des livres XXXV et XXXVI de l'*Histoire naturelle* de Pline. La première forme de peinture est la *skiagraphia*: *Prima pictura fuit umbra hominis lineis circumducta, secunda singulis coloribus, monochromatos dicta, alii monogrammon uocant* (p. 8). Aux monochromes succédèrent les couleurs, puis s'ajoutèrent les ombres et les lumières, les progrès de l'art étant associés à des inventeurs. La même évolution est notée dans la sculpture. Pourtant le Jésuite discute sa source latine en la confrontant aux textes bibliques pour tenter de trouver les origines des arts. Il s'oppose ainsi à son affirmation que la peinture était inconnue à l'époque de la Guerre de Troie: *Negat Plinius bello Troiano pingendi artem extitisse, ostendo ante bellum Troianum in Iudaeis multis annis et sculpturam et caelaturam et picturam et plasticem ceterasque artes fuisse* (p. 70). Gaurico avait ouvert la voie, en affirmant que, selon Moïse, le modelage était l'art le plus ancien "non sans raison, car Dieu lui-même fut son premier inventeur. On ne peut qu'en effet reconnaître qu'il a dû être le meilleur modeleur lui qui a si admirablement formé ces mondes." C'est là évidemment le motto du *Deus artifex*, depuis longtemps répété à l'envi pour donner aux arts leurs lettres de noblesse. Boulenger reprend la démonstration; il l'amplifie et l'atteste par toute sorte de références empruntées à la Bible et à Eusèbe qui lui permettent d'établir une sorte de chronologie de la naissance des arts: d'abord parut le modelage, avec Séruch; le père d'Abraham, Tara, fut statuaire. L'*Exode* 31 prouve "… que la peinture, la plastique, la statuaire, la sculpture, la ciselure furent transmises aux hommes, dans leur plénitude, par Dieu, lorsque fut construite l'Arche d'alliance." (p. 51). Ainsi, les plus anciens artistes sont Beçaléel et Oholiab, contemporains de Moïse (p. 70). L'épisode du Veau d'or (*Exode* 32) montre que l'art de fondre l'or et le bronze est antérieur à la guerre de Troie (p. 71). Pour la peinture, il trouve une preuve supplémentaire de son existence à l'époque homérique dans les descriptions des armes d'Achille et d'Hercule chez Homère et Hésiode: *Si erat caelatura, erat et pictura, quae utraeque pedetemptim et per gradus, non uno tempore absolutionem consecutae sunt* (p. 9). Puis, il prend des exemples dans la Bible: avant Hercule, les Chaldéens pratiquaient la peinture, au temps de Moïse, et, avant lui, d'Abraham (p. 9).

Cette analyse qui reste bien sommaire ne vise sans doute pas à reconstituer une histoire de la peinture et de la statuaire. Elle n'emploie pas non plus le motif, récurrent dans les traités d'art renaissants, du *Deus artifex* pour prouver la grandeur de l'artiste. Elle a plutôt, me semble-t-il, un enjeu religieux: il s'agit, dans le contexte post-tridentin, de réhabiliter l'image et de prouver la grandeur des arts par leur origine divine et leur antiquité.

Cet ouvrage pédant qui accumule les sources, s'il ne comporte pas de réflexion philosophique, ni de théorie de la peinture, témoigne donc d'un certain nombre de questions que l'art posait aux humanistes. Son approche délibérément technique annonce ce que sera la *Realphilologie*, en même temps qu'elle propose un mode d'appréciation de l'œuvre qui en valorise l'exécution, tout en évacuant sa signification. Ce manuel, sans doute le dernier de ce genre avant le *De pictura ueterum* de Junius, et surtout les grands traités de Piles et de Félibien, pose le problème du passage du discours savant sur l'art des philologues au discours à la première personne du moderne amateur, mais aussi, et surtout, celui de la pédagogie de l'art dont Junius traitera abondamment dans son second livre.

Université de Paris I Panthéon-Sorbonne

De Francisci Xaverii Trips Poetae Laureati Latinis,

quae quidem permulta perpolitaque manserint, sed

oblitterata nunc iacere videantur, operibus ad praesentes

saeculo XVII° status singulos omnium fere

Europae spectantibus regionum

CAROLUS AUGUSTUS NEUHAUSEN

Acroasis huius exordium ac divisio

Franciscus ille Xaverius Trips Rhenana quadam stirpe ortus pastor Romano-Catholicae fidei semper addictus idemque suis temporibus Poeta Laureatus usque celebratus, cuinam esset saeculo tribuendus, quot opera Latina pedestri non secus ac poetico sermone reliquisset eleganter admodum singula contexta, quam denique fortunam irrita tamen eadem essent iniquam apud posteros passa, paucis equidem adumbravi iam tum, cum inter conventum Hafniensem, quem octavum instituit sexennio ante societas nostra, disserere fusius sum connisus, quomodo urbs Bonna Latinis litteris inde a decimo sexto ineunte saeculo descripta traderetur esse sive laudata.[1] Accessit interim ea commentatio, qua nuper Tripsianorum operum postremum illud quidem idque sublimitate vel maximum, sed antea prope prorsus ignotum in lucem mihi primo protrahere contigit[2]; istud enim opus grande, quo res praeclare cum in omni Europa tum in Germaniae finibus paenultimo exeunte decennio decimi septimi saeculi gestae subtiliter ornateque memorantur, inscriptum est optimo iure *Tractatus historico-poeticus.*

Quibus de causis, praesertim quoniam adhuc selectos tantummodo Tripsii scriptoris ac poetae Latini textus ab oblivione vindicandos divulgavi, consentaneum est eo

---

[1] Et hac igitur symbola (cuius inscriptio praecisa reperietur infra sub appendicis priore capitulo) et altera ilico (adn. 2) alleganda sequens oratio omnis innititur.

[2] Quocirca fieri non potuit, quin ista quoque relatio cardinalis in tripertitam bibliographiam praelectioni huic adiectam reciperetur.

magis me gaudere, quod Abulensem hanc opportunitatem nactus totum velut corpus Tripsianum nunc quamvis breviter primo praebere possum Neolatinitatis homini gnarissimo cuique, cuius id novisse atque adeo forsitan admirari vel plurimum interest. Itaque ut ante triennium, dum Bariensis noster agitur ille congressus, de non pluribus quam quattuor, quae feruntur, opusculis Latinis Dominici cuiusdam Cyllenii Graeci hucusque non editis rettuli[3], sic hodie in innumerabilia paene multoque praestantiora Tripsii illius (ut iunioris aliquatenus ita dotibus ingenii vique facundiae aliquanto superioris) Latine scripta, quorum exigua pars recentioribus typis exstat cusa, at longe maxima latet abscondita, mihimet est inquirendum, ut nec virium nec temporis permissi mensura tam ingenti tamque indigestae textuum moli responsura videatur.

Iam vero, ne nimis exili Latine dicendi ratione, quali huius quoque conventus participum equidem audeo solus uti, fatigaretur animus attentissime cuiusque auscultantis aut ab ipsius auctoris egregii verbis hic in medio ponendis avocaretur, eundem ipsum profecto quam saepissime tamquam ab inferis suscitatum inducere mallem loquentem. Sed angustiis spatii coercitus vereor, ut queam plus efficere quam Latina deinceps opera, quae Tripsii fuisse perhibeantur, certum in ordinem sistere redacta.

Tractatio

I. Perpauca de Tripsii tam vita quam operibus generaliter praemonenda

Etenim quominus in medias res incurramus, nihil iam est, quo nos oporteat impediri. Namque num Tripsius anno 1630° sit (ut opinio vult communis) Coloniae natus, utrum celeberrimo praeclarae huius urbis gymnasio, quod Tricoronatum nuncupabatur, bonis artibus imbutus an aliis instructus scholis maturitatis testimonium sibi pepererit, quatenus denique quamque diu adulescens sacerdos Iesuitis applicatus exstiterit[4], et parum liquet nec magni nostra scire nunc refert. Etsi enim satis est causae, cur miremur Tripsium ante quadragesimum fere aetatis annum nihil ne Latine quidem exaratum, quod memoriae proderetur, videri publicavisse, hoc tamen apparet saltem perfectum eundem esse necesse iam dudum evasisse poetam Latinum, cum anno 1670° parochi munus obiturus ad Honneffensis perveniret communitatis oppidum id, quod paulo superius urbe Bonna situm adiacet dexterae Rheni fluminis ripae perinde atque clarissimis montibus septem.

Atque in eadem hac sede Honneffensi deinde Tripsius idem auctor Latinus semet ipse *Septimontanum* appellare consuevit et Benedictorum quasi quadam loci stabilitate petita viginti sex per annos usque ad mortem suam (a. 1696°) ita moratus est, ut ibidem plurima, quae quidem innotuerint, opera Latina conscripsisse videatur[5]. Interiectum est enim temporis nihil nisi illud sexennium, quod post annum 1682[um] Tripsius honorifice aulicus ab ipso Maximiliano Henrico tum Archiepiscopo Coloniensi

---

[3] *Acta Conventus Neo-Latini Bariensis*, Medieval & Renaissance Texts & Studies, vol. 184 (Tempe, 1998).

[4] Hisce de quaestionibus singulis consulendus est is liber, quo Tripsianum iter omne stravit indagaturis E. Nellessen (v.i. passim).

[5] De paucis minoris certe momenti libellis, quos quidem Theodisco sermone conflatos sub subditivis nominibus Tripsium edidisse sit simillimum veri, cf. E. Nellessen p. 223.

sacellanus bibliothecariusque delectus degebat in illius augusta sede Bonnensi eademque etiam universitatis studiorum Bonnensis aede perenni futura. Ita factum est, ut
Tripsius vir eximie doctus, quia per aevi medii tempora Bonnam acceperat nomina-
tam esse Veronam, humanistarum proprio more naviter observato *Veronensem* quoque
scriptorem esse contendere se solitus est[6].

II. De Tripsii quattuor libris in urbibus Bonna Coloniaque (a. 1683°–1688°) impressis

Quae cum ita fuerint, haud mirum est, si Tripsius est numquam nisi tam felici
Bonnensis intervalli illius ambitu consecutus, ut quadriga quaedam eorum, quae Latine chartis suis mandavisset, prelo denique subiecta prodiret. Vix enimvero biblio-
thecarius idem insigni munere suo coeperat aulico fungi, cum Coloniae typis Arnoldi
Metternich a. 1683° emissum est id carmen excellens illi Archiepiscopo Coloniensi
dono datum dedicatumque, cuius poematis plus quinquaginta paginas continentis haec
est inscriptio duplex: *Lignum vitae rex arborum fagus, in salutifero et sacrosancto nomine
Iesu supra omnes arbores exaltata, sive Prodigiosa SS. NOMINIS IESU prope Rhenobacum
in Arbore Fago reperta effigies, Poeticis coloribus et septem Artium Liberalium suffragiis exor-
nata*[7]. Fictum id quidem, sed ex vera quadam re sollerter ingenioseque deductum
singulare certamen, ex quo fagus Rhenobacensis cum ceteris arboribus iisque emi-
nentibus comparata discedit victrix, tam splendidis et imaginum luminibus et sententiarum scatet, ut perpetuis explanationibus sit opus ad interpretandas series versuum
singulas.

Exceperunt mirificum hoc Tripsii poema quadriennio post (a. 1687°) foras ab
eodem auctore et apud eundem typographum datae laudes eorum, qui Rhenobaci
fines angustos vicinaeque etiam limites urbis Bonnae latissime transgressi inscribuntur
(adhibitis iterum sollemniter chronogrammatum quidem litteris, sed iisdem hic ne-
glectis) *Heroes Christiani in Ungaria & alibi adversus iuratos hostes Otomannos strenue pugnantes . . . seu Elogia eorum qui pro Deo enses strinxerunt contra barbaros. Elegiacis versibus
adumbrati atque pro xenio praesentis anni praesentati*[8]. Quam autem late pateat elegorum
haec corona quantumque momenti tribuendum sit eiusdem singulis partibus, vel inde
colligi potest, quod huic operi centum decem paginas complenti insunt insertae cum

---

[6] Quisquis istud ignorat, perquam inepto cuidam vix potest esse non obnoxius errori. Sunt
enim nonnulli, quos cum effugerit, qualem Bonnensis Tripsius cum Verona sibi prisca necessi-
tudinem intercedere simulavisset, eundem humanistam opinentur in Italiae septentrionalis urbe tam
pulchra genitum sua poemata pepigisse.

[7] Hunc titulum in eiusdem libelli frontispicio sequuntur haec verba: "Serenissimo ac Reveren-
dissimo S. R. Imperii Principi Electori MAXIMILIANO HENRICO . . . Sanctissimi NOMINIS
IESU Cultori Ter Eminentissimo, Ipso S. HENRICI Patroni sui Augustissimi Festo, Id est, Post
evolutum Trium ex ordine et continuata serie, in Sede Archiepiscopali sibi succedentium
Bavaricorum Ducum SECULUM Die quinta supra quinquagesimam *Affectu et corde summississimo*
OBLATA a FRANCISCO XAV. TRIPS . . . Anno ELeCtorIs BaVarI In seDe VbIa eX Voto
regnantIs trIgesIMo tertIo."

[8] Adiectae sunt eiusdem rursus artis chronogrammaticae gratia voces hae: Anno salutatoris
Domini Iesu Christi authore Fran. Xaverio Trips . . . Typis vero atque expensis Arnoldi Metter-
nichii prope Augustinianos Agrippinae.

aliorum prope totius Europae principum populorumque descriptiones luculentae tum Venetiarum, quibus in delineandis poeta quattuor hisce distichis exorditur:

> Aemula Romani Respublica Regia fastus:
>> quae maris in mediis nata, superbit aquis.
> Adriatici Regina freti mundique Theatrum:
>> Urbs, quam non homines, quam posuere Dii.
> Urbs, quam nec murus nec propugnacula firmant,
>> Solo naturae fortis ubique situ.
> Urbs a divitiis, a Maiestate, regendi
>> Forma, structura, Nobilitate, fide.

Clauserunt eorum agmen librorum, quos Tripsius Bonnae curavit edendos, duo opuscula variis referta carminibus, quae cum ad eundem hominem pertineant laudibus extollendum, quam artissime videntur inter se cohaerere. Utrumque enim ad maiorem illius Archiepiscopi Coloniensis gloriam ita compositum est, ut prius, quippe quod inscribatur *Musa Genethliaca sive bene ominata nativitas*[9], cum alia huiusmodi poemata natalicia tum duodecim omina complectatur, quibus idem princeps a. 1686° tredecim lustris felicissime iam peractis tamquam divinus efferatur ad caelum. Posterius autem opusculum biennio post (a. 1688°) prolatum, simulatque vatis ille defunctus est nobilis fautor, nihil aliud est nisi laudatio funebris uberrime condita poetico more; nam superior eius titulus exhibetur Idea infulatae virtutis, quae concisa notionum iunctura triplex quid significet ceteris inscriptionis partibus interpositis[10] hac denique appendice planius enucleatur: "VITAM, VIRTUTES, MORTEM, Symbolice repraesentans *in Solemnibus Exequiis* Ac communi totius Patriae tam Dilecto Principe viduatae Luctu Ad Tumbum Funeralem Anathematis Loco appensa".

III. De Tripsianis operibus post auctoris obitum saeculo XVIII° editis

At vero reliqua eaque longe copiosissima materies illorum, quae Latino sermone Tripsius elaboravit, dum versatur cum in urbe Bonna tum in eius finitimo scilicet oppido Honneffensi, nusquam eadem lucem aspexisse videtur auctore vivo. Quamquam enim constat Tripsium iam, cum aulicae praeesset bibliothecae Bonnensi, seditionem perniciosam in urbe Coloniensium id temporis exortam (qui tumultus prope sexennium devoravit) compluribus deinceps articulis totam ingressum esse Latinis versibus persequi, inchoatum hoc opus magnificum idque pedetemptim tribus quattuorve gradibus adauctum ac denique absolutum octo demum annis (a. 1704°), postquam eiusdem scriptor decesserat vita, Lipsiae illud quidem (ut praetendebatur) apud Petrum Marteau, sed re vera nimirum in ipsa urbe Colonia Agrippinensi tandem est editum[11] ita, ut elegiacum volumen omne ducentas septuaginta paginas complecte-

---

[9] Longiorem, qui limatissimus sequitur, complurium particularum catervum, quibus omnis conglutinatus est titulus, depromere supersedendum hic quoque esse queror deficientibus chartis.

[10] Istas aeque ac largam libelli ipsius silvam praedicationum, quibus a poeta gratissimo mortui Coloniensis Archiepiscopi persona concinitur, expedire nunc nequeo, nedum relecturis hoc loco plura suppeditentur excerpta.

[11] Huius quidem editionis paucissima supersunt exemplaria, quae quanti hodie pendantur, vel

retur hac inscriptione praemissa: *Quinquennalis seditio atque rebellis Ubiorum status etc. absque omni passione prout vere extitit poetice delineatus. Urbi Ubiae Agrippinae et orbi universo ad cautelam repraesentatus*[12].

Perpetuus igitur huius tituli tenor non tantum prae se putandus est ferre, quam peritum chronogrammata fingendi semet artificem vates noster ille coronatus hic pariter atque alias toties ubique praestiterit[13], verum etiam perspicue simul ostendit omnino triplicem fuisse auctoris et historiographi scopum et poetae: Primum enim se profitetur ut veritatis amantissimum sine ira et studio calamum fortiter movere consuesse, deinde asseverat tragicam illam Coloniensium rebellionem, quam inter quam plurimos unicus describere sit ausus, et huic *urbi* et *orbi* terrarum (id est non tam Agrippinatum animis quam cunctis gentibus mundi) speciminis instar offerre se velle, tum asserit genuinum se natum esse talem poetam, qualis existimandus sit, quicumque intendat nulli nisi vel summo Nasoni parem esse aut similem. Namque in ea praemonitione, qua benevole legentium mentes temptat allicere, de semet ipso Tripsius haec praedicare non dubitat:

Stylo usus sum non quem ars, sed quem natura indidit. Fluxum amo, quem nec elisio durior absorbeat nec distorta vitiorum aut pedum cacophonia retardet. Elegia ni tersa, ni facilis, ni fluida sit, ni Ovidianae quid prae se fert elegantiae, confestim desipit et sua ipsius lectione amarescit.

  Quod natura negat, nemo feliciter audet.

Poeta nasci, non formari debet, et quamquam ars naturam poliat, hac tamen non adminiculante ceu corpus spiritu destitutum exanimis iacebit.

Proinde, siquidem istud Coloniense poema magnum ex multis milibus versuum constat, exordii saltem Tripsiani prima nunc disticha tria citare sufficiat:

> *Corruga faciem, dentes preme, rade capillos,*
> *Deplora miserum moesta elegeia statum,*
> *Indue pullatam (sic mandant tempora) vestem*
> *Innatat heu lachrymis uda Camoena suis.*
> *Heu! redeat Graeco novus Heraclitus ab orbe,*
> *qui fleat ingentis (quod gemo) syrma mali . . .*

Quibus cognitis rebus nihil videtur esse causae, cur miremur, quod triginta tribus annis, postquam diem supremum Tripsius obierat, Pantaleon Eschenbrender in suo *Tyrocinio poetico*[14], cuius manuductionis editio princeps a. 1729° Coloniae promulgata futuris est vatibus destinata, neminem nisi Septimontanum nostrum sive Vero-

---

ex eo perspici potest, quod unum comperi nuperrime sub hasta sex milibus venisse marcarum.

[12] Non chronogrammata modo neglecta praeterii, sed de reliquis quoque tacui membris, quae libri huius sive fronti leguntur aspersa sive aliis affixa paginis haerent.

[13] Eadem haec ars Tripsiana, cum et mirum quantum ipsa per se praecipua sit et ad singulorum terminos textuum temporumque definiendos maxime semper idonea, videtur esse dignissima, de cuius exquisitae ponderibus quam proxime subtilius disseratur.

[14] Ne hoc quidem de compendio cum lecturis communicare nunc licet plura, quam nos fecit iam Ernestus Nellessen (v.i.) certiores.

nensem ipsum Tripsium, quippe qui praeter ceteros floruisset poetas, imitandum commendari graviter iudicavit debere. Etenim illi enchiridio, quod eodem saeculo duodevicesimo bis etiam (annis 1746° et 1763°)[15] prodiit reimpressum, annexum est tamquam singulare velut exemplar id florilegium, cui titulus est *Conatus poeticus posthumus* (sic) *ob claritatem, facilitatem, historiae amoenitatem tenebris et tineis subductus et excerptus e manuscriptis Francisci Xaverii Trips quondam sacellani aulici et pastoris in Honneff.*

Atqui praestantis huius anthologiae, qua replentur paginae centum (sc. 36-136), principem amplissimumque locum obtinet non ille *Tractatus historico-poeticus* aut *Quinquennalis seditio atque rebellis Ubiorum status* aut aliud opus Tripsianum a me modo laudatum, sed elegorum ea collectio, quae distributa viginti quattuor in articulos inscribitur *Europae status descriptio metrica sub Sanctissimo Pontifice Innocentio X. et Leopoldo I. imperatore augustissimo.* Hac itaque farragine distichorum similiter atque in illo poemate, quod inscribitur *Heroes Christiani* (etc.), idem auctor poeta laureatus effecit, ut contemporaneus omnium fere totius Europae principum tam ecclesiae quam civitatum singularum comprehensus quidam gyrus pateret expositus.

Sed universi huius orbis Europaei tabulam speculumve sequuntur cum duo Bonnensia carmina a me iam Hafniae commemorata (v.s.) tum alia perpolita eademque ut nostra quidem aetate e plerorumque doctorum etiam hominum memoria pridem elapsa ita tum temporis tironibus ante oculos ea mente proposita, ut ipsi talia videlicet exemplaria continuo humanistarum ritu scilicet aemularentur, quo commodius celeriusque eadem aliquando possent aequare vel vincere.

IV. De Tripsii tribus libellis nuper emissis deque ceteris eiusdem operibus cunctis venturo denique millennio prodituris

Adicienda vero Tripsianis poematibus illo *Tyrocinii poetici* volumine comprehensis permulta porro sunt alia Latina Tripsii manuscripta, quae scaenam imprimis Batavicam illustrantia cum adhuc exstent in bibliothecis compluribus asservata[16], tamen Eschenbrender ille in suum artis poeticae compendium asciscere noluit aut (id quod veri similius est) inscius omisit.

Verumenimvero haec omnia non minus quam illa Latina, quae quidem creberrima tamque diligenter Tripsius elucubravisset, inde a mediante fere saeculo XVIII° iam obsoleta tam subito desierunt in manibus esse legentium, ut ipsa suarum esse virtutum velut victimae reddita videantur; exceptis enim paucissimis frustulis corporis Tripsiani nihil deinceps plus quam duo per saecula factum est publici iuris. Atque etiam nescio an nomen quoque Tripsianum funditus fuerit ad inferos delapsurum, nisi post *Tyrocinii poetici* illius auctorem vir alter, qui de Tripsianis studiis optime mereretur, exstitisset ante haec decennia duo paene Ernestus Nellessen eruditissimus[17].

---

[15] Utramque hanc editionem accuratius expertus est idem Hermannus Wiegand, qui de talibus aliis quoque rebus se disputaturum esse promisit.

[16] Ne hanc quidem congeriem testimoniorum hic explicari posse eo vehementius est dolendum.

[17] Quapropter eidem soli, cum fundamentalis a me bibliographia Tripsiana (v.i.) constitueretur, impertitus est principatus.

Qui quidem theologus Bonnensis brevi, antequam praematura morte (a. 1982°) ipse decessit, non modo primus eos edidit tres Latinos Tripsii libellos prosa oratione conscriptos, quorum unus ad ecclesiae Honneffensis consuetudines pertinet, alter inservit instruendo optimo cuique pastori, tertius oppidi Honneffensis enarrat fatum prope radicitus eversi. Immo maiorem etiam eisdem Honneffensibus opusculis publicatis Nellessen ille simul adeptus est gloriam, quod prioribus elenchis multo locupletiorem eum operum Tripsianorum indicem concinnavit, qui quamvis non vacaret erroribus et certe supplendis aliquot indigeret, utique fundamentum quoddam aliquatenus iecit omnibus cuicumque textui Tripsiano posthac operam navare paraturis.

Conclusio

Perorantibus igitur iam nobis totumque orbem Tripsianum collustrantibus illum quidem oblivione diutius obrutum, sed nunc aperte satis patefactum duplex esse via ratioque reputandi videtur ineunda.

Nam primum quidem necesse est concludamus universas res aut gestas aut suscipiendas, quas quidem Tripsius variis suis operibus sumpserit enodandas, ad eiusdem ipsius aetatem usque accommodatas spectare vel passim singulas referri debere; est ergo Tripsius, etsi quam plurima semper et verba solebat et exempla nimirum ex aptissimis quibusque antiquitatis arcessere fontibus, non actorum eorumque iam pridem praeteritorum descriptor temporum sive laudator, sed potius, cum praesentium solarum utique rerum gravissimas quasque tractaverit, proprie contemporaneus et is auctor vere Neolatinus existimandus, qui spreta fere tam vernacula quam extera voce quavis recenti veterem linguam Latinam ceteris omnibus sermonibus superiorem putaverit tanti, ut eadem usus et suas ipsius curas atque cogitationes novissimas quaslibet exprimeret et sui temporis reliquos tam personarum quam rerum omnium publicarum status eventusque commentaretur.

Deinde dubitari nequit, quin talis auctor, qualis tot tantisque cuiusvis generis operibus Latinis excellens sui saeculi cum historicus viguit tum litterarius testis, dignus denique sit ducendus, qui tandem resurgat et ita quidem resuscitatus evadat, ut omnium suorum operum editione principe tam diu desiderata carere desistat; iam enim aliquamdiu, priusquam haec occasio est Abulensis arrepta, non doctis modo civibus concupiveram penitus esse persuasum, si disiecta dumtaxat pergeremus habere quaedam Tripsii membra, nocentes opimum amissuros fuisse nos et feracem litterarum thesaurum; sin autem quando textus Tripsianos Latinis litteris mandatos omnes in decem fere voluminum seriem[18] digestos coegissemus eosque critica quidem singulos editione recognitos, fore, ut novus quidam si non alter at dimidiatus certe tam Sallustius redux emergeret quam redivivus Ovidius—nedum pro auri fulgore velut orichalchi lamina vilis aut vesca substitutum iri videretur.

Ex Universitate Bonnensi

---

[18] Totum hoc corpus Tripsianum decem in capita divisum exhibetur appendicis altera parte, qua commentatio haec omnis concluditur absolute.

Appendix

A. Bibliographia brevis eademque novissima

1. Franz Xaver Trips. Honnef vor 1700—Aufzeichnungen zur Ortsgeschichte, herausgegeben und übersetzt von Ernst Nellessen, Bad Honnef 1978 (cf. *Humanistica Lovaniensia*, vol. 37, 1988, 321).
2. K. A. Neuhausen: "Urbs Bonna quomodo Latinis litteris inde a decimo sexto ineunte fere saeculo descripta sit et laudata," Acta Conventus Neo-Latini Hafniensis, Medieval & Renaissance Texts and Studies, Vol. 120 (Binghamton, 1994), 165–178.
3. Idem, "*Urbs Bonna exusta.* Eine unbekannte zeitgeschichtliche Darstellung der völligen Zerstörung Bonns 1689 - Zum noch nicht veröffentlichten *Tractatus historico-poeticus* des Poeta Laureatus F. X. Trips," in *Zeitgeschehen und seine Darstellung im Mittelalter / L'actualité et sa représentation au Moyen Age*, herausgegeben von Christoph Cormeau, Studium Universale, Schriftenreihe der Universität Bonn, 20 (Bonn, 1995), 237–259.

B. Conspectus operum Tripsianorum succinctus[19]

Francisci Xaverii Trips opera omnia Latina, quae quidem adhuc cuncta fere non tradita nisi manuscriptis aut ineptius edita supersint, his decem voluminibus denique sunt comprehendenda:

I.   *Tractatus historico-poeticus.*

II.   *Europae status descriptio metrica sub sanctissimo pontifice Innocentio X. et Leopoldo I. imperatore augustissimo.*

III.   *Heroes Christiani in Ungaria et alibi contra iuratos hostes Otomannos strenue pugnantes (etc.).*

IV.   *Quinquennalis seditio atque rebellis Ubiorum status* . . .

V.   Elegiae Bonnenses duae: *Bonna lamentans* et *Querela ac suspirium urbis Bonnae.*

VI.   Duo poemata Maximiliano Henrico tum Archiepiscopo Coloniensi deinceps oblata: *Musa Genethliaca* . . . et *Idea infulatae virtutis* . . .

VII.   *Lignum vitae rex arborum fagus* . . . (sc. Rhenobacensis)

VIII.   Honneffenses libelli tres prosa oratione conscripti.

IX.   Varia scaenae Batavicae carmina.

X.   Reliqui multiplices textus hucusque inediti.

Sed ne quis soli mihi tantum oneris impertire ne Herculeis quidem laboribus levioris umquam voluisse me suspicetur, velut foveam praetergressurus hoc utique commonefaciendum esse reor omne corpus fere Tripsianum robigine diutius iam obsitum, quo celerius manuscriptorum illuvie veternoque ablutum tandem protraheretur in lucem, compluribus aliis—iisque adulescentibus duce Marco Laureys collega Bonnensi naviter promovendis—ita iam pridem esse commissum, ut mihimet ipsi scilicet exigua pars perpurganda restare videatur. Tantum igitur abest, ut unus equidem idemque senectutis limen interim consecutus totum tamquam Tripsiadis munus susceperim transigendum, ut iuvenilis turba quaedam satis docta deinceps in eandem hanc materiem se potissimum inquisituram esse promiserit.

---

[19] Plura his de operibus suo singula loco supra sunt indicata.

El Ciceronianus *de Pierre de la Ramée*

JUAN Mª NÚÑEZ GONZÁLEZ

Pierre de la Ramée (Ramus) publicó su *Ciceronianus* en 1557 (el privilegio y la epístola dedicatoria al Cardenal Charles de Lorraine son de 1556), es decir, casi 30 años después de la aparición de la obra homónima de Erasmo de Rotterdam. Tal ensayo con el que pretende *ut tanti oratoris imitatio discipulis nostris facilior esset*[1], constituye una *subductio* de su ensayo anterior *Brutinae quaestiones*[2], donde trató de establecer cuál era la doctrina retórica que regía la composición ciceroniana, basándose en su propia praxis, dado que de la Ramée rechaza de plano la doctrina teórica de los antiguos Aristóteles, Cicerón y Quintiliano[3]. A diferencia de los otros dos rétores de esta tríada, Cicerón se le revela con sus discursos y producción literaria creativa como el modelo sobre el que levantar su 'libro del estilo' latino[4].

De la Ramée, tras indicarnos que en su época los eruditos que desean ser considerados ciceronianos desprecian al resto como si de huéspedes y extranjeros de la lengua latina se trataran[5], pretende delimitar quién debe ser considerado ciceroniano, valiéndose del testimonio y autoridad de Cicerón. Según de la Ramée hay dos bandos en su época, *aliorum sese Ciceronianos esse profitentium, aliorum liberiorem quandam uiam insistentium*[6]. De la Ramée no dice adscribirse a ninguno, pero tras manifestar que tratará de delimitar *quid Ciceronianum sit, et quid non Ciceronianum: quid hic sequendum nobis,*

---

[1] Citamos por la edición de Basilea de 1573. La frase citada corresponde a la epístola dedicatoria, fol. A2r.

[2] Primera edición (Paris, 1547). Publicadas posteriormente como una parte de sus *Scholae in liberales artes* (Basilea, 1569; facsímil por W. Ong, Hildesheim-New York, 1970).

[3] "In Rhetoricis uero et Dialecticis labor ingens ac prope desperatus uideatur, aduersus summos authores et tot saeculis ueluti consecratos Ciceronem, Quintilianum, Aristotelem dicere: . . . Ciceronisque et Aristotelis artes Ciceronis et Aristotelis usu corrigendas et emendandas esse moneo" (Scholae, Lectori S., fol. α2).

[4] Remitimos a nuestro "La recepción del *ars rhetorica* por P. de la Ramée", en E. Sánchez Salor et al., eds., *La recepción de las artes clásicas en el siglo XVI* (Cáceres, 1996), 345–351.

[5] Pierre de la Ramée, *Ciceronianus*, 1: "qui se Ciceronianos dici desiderant: caeteros autem uelut hospites in lingua Latina et peregrinos aspernantur".

[6] de la Ramée, *Ciceronianus*, 2.

quid etiam cauendum et fugiendum sit[7], el lector comienza a comprender que se le está proponiendo la imitación de Cicerón. Y, en efecto, un poco más adelante dirá que no sólo propone la imitación de la latinidad de Cicerón, sino también de todo lo que en él es virtuoso y elogiable[8]. De la Ramée propone, además, para todas las lenguas, el método de imitación ciceroniana, esto es, del uso aprobado: *sic nos Ciceronem omnibus populis et linguis proponimus*[9]. Y hace uso de los mismos planteamientos que Pietro Bembo: *Graecae, inquam, litterae Tullio externae fuerunt, familiares autem et domesticae, Latinae: Francis Graecae pariter ac Latinae peregrinae sunt, francicae uero populares et uernaculae*[10].

Más adelante, tras utilizar la metáfora de la abeja, que liba de distintas flores para elaborar un producto mejor, la miel, tópico senequiano una y otra vez retomado en las polémicas sobre la imitación ya desde Petrarca[11], se desmarca de los ciceronianos con las siguientes palabras: *Verumtamen a Ciceronianis nostris longissime aberro, qui Ciceronem et totum et solum pueris imitandum esse, neque preterea quicquam ex aliis assumendum censent: Haec enim est Ciceronianorum persuasio et religio (. . .) In ea certe haeresi minime connumerari uelim, ut Ciceronianum in sermone statuam et totum et solum, quod in Ciceronis libris hodie legimus*[12]. ¿En qué consiste entonces, para él, ser ciceroniano? En ser consecuente con la norma lingüística establecida por la costumbre recta y cuidada. Esta fue la regla que siguió Cicerón: *Vsum loquendi (aiebat ipse Tullius) populo concessi, scientiam mihi reseruaui.*[13] Ahora bien, no hay ya pueblo que tenga competencia en la lengua latina. El uso correcto hay que aprenderlo en los libros. La lengua latina tuvo, por otra parte, su infancia y su vejez. Ninguna de ellas recomienda de la Ramée, sino la edad intermedia. No se ha de acudir a las antiguallas obsoletas de Catón o de Plauto, ni a las formas recientes de Livio, Séneca, Plinio, Celso, Quintiliano o Tácito, si bien, ni en los primeros todo es viejo, ni en lo segundo todo moderno, sino que se ha de perseguir el aspecto (estilo de lengua) de Terencio, Varrón, Salustio, César y sobre todo Cicerón, *in qua omnes Latinae linguae uirtutes, perfectionem suam et maturitatem habuisse uideantur*[14]. En consecuencia, ¿a qué se le puede llamar ciceroniano? *Quod illius aetatis purae et incorruptae consuetudini conueniat, id Ciceronianum nobis esto.*

Por lo que respecta al léxico, *singula uerba in Cicerone propria, lecta, splendida sunt, ideoque Ciceroniano imprimis imitanda: uix contrarium quicquam reperies: nisi forte uerbum*

---

[7] de la Ramée, *Ciceronianus*, 3.

[8] de la Ramée, *Ciceronianus*, 4.

[9] de la Ramée, *Ciceronianus*, 11.

[10] de la Ramée, *Ciceronianus*, 13. Cf. P. Bembo, *Prose della volgar lingua* (1525) (Milán, 1880), I, 145: "Che si come i romani due lingue aveano, una propria e naturale, e questa era la latina, l'altra straniera, e quella era la greca, cosí noi due favelle possediamo altresí, l'una propria e naturale e domestica, che è la volgare, istrana e non naturale l'altra, che è la latina".

[11] Cf. H. Gmelin, "Das Prinzip der Imitatio in den romanischen Literaturen der Renaissance", *Romanische Forschungen* 46 (1932): 83–360. Sobre el tópico de la abeja, cf. 122 ss.

[12] de la Ramée, *Ciceronianus*, 18.

[13] de la Ramée, *Ciceronianus*, 19.

[14] de la Ramée, *Ciceronianus*, 19.

aliquod a Cicerone ipso reprehensum[15]. Pero también es posible acudir a otras fuentes y considerarlas ciceronianas: *multa certe, quae Ciceroniana sint, ex aliorum libris repetentur. Innumerabilia sunt artium uocabula propria, quibus Cicero usurus fuerat, si res et occasio fuisset: Ea cum reperiam in Plauto, Catone, Varrone, Columella, caeterisque probatis authoribus et scriptoribus, an non Ciceroniana ducam?*[16] No obstante, en algunos casos será necesario utilizar alguna prefación del tipo '*ut ita dicam*', '*si licet dicere*', '*quodanmodo permitte mihi sic*'. Por lo tanto, el imitador de Cicerón utilizará como si fueran ciceronianas palabras que Cicerón nunca usó, pero esto no lo hará nunca caprichosamente y sin aplicar ningún criterio *(sed tamen nihil temere, nihil sine iudicio*[17]). En las páginas siguientes seguirá insistiendo en la misma idea: no hay que limitarse a un solo autor, sino a todos; no obstante en el mejor y más sobresaliente hay que detenerse durante muchísimo tiempo: *Hoc certe Ciceronianum est, non ex uno authore aliquo, sed ex omnibus cuiuscunque generis, copiam uerborum et bonitatem parare: in optimo tamen et excellentissimo quoque diutissime permanere*[18].

Al igual que le sucediera a Cortesi y otros ciceronianos, para de la Ramée la composición rítmica de los periodos constituye una de las características más importantes que debe imitar el ciceroniano, pero en esto no ha de seguir la doctrina de los antiguos, sino la práctica del propio Cicerón: *Nulla parte mihi Cicero Ciceronianus minus est, quam in compositionis et numeri doctrina: tot scholasticis ineptiis eam refersit, ut in Brutinis quaestionibus exposuimus; Nulla parte Cicero magis Ciceronianus uidetur, quam in orationis compositione et structura: tam eleganter et uenuste orationem composuit*[19]. Método que, como puede apreciarse, responde al principio ciceroniano citado, en virtud del cual concedía al pueblo la *auctoritas* del uso, pero se reservaba su conocimiento científico.

La doctrina de Pierre de la Ramée es compleja y controvertida. Buena prueba de ello es la distinta valoración o catalogación de la misma que nos han dejado los distintos estudiosos, a lo que ha contribuido su producción escrita anterior, especialmente sus *Brutinae quaestiones*, donde hace una crítica negativa de la doctrina retórica de Cicerón y, con él, de Aristóteles e igualmente con el primer 'ciceroniano' de la historia en sus *Distinctiones in Quintilianum*. Esta actitud crítica impelía a valorar el *Ciceronianus* de Ramus en el mismo sentido que el de Erasmo. De hecho un contemporáneo suyo, Joachim Perion (*Ioachimus Perionius*), publicaría inmediatamente a la aparición de sus comentarios al *Orator* ya citados, su *Pro Ciceronis oratore contra Petrum Ramum oratio* (Paris: 1547).

En efecto, resulta controvertido, a primera vista, que proponga la imitación de Cicerón, incluso de sus cadencias rítmicas (lo que Erasmo satirizó en su diálogo homónimo), pero al mismo tiempo afirme que él se aparta de los ciceronianos actuales y proponga la imitación de todos, aunque principalmente de Cicerón, así como que acepte el léxico de otros autores, aunque haga determinadas restricciones y apela-

---

[15] de la Ramée, *Ciceronianus*, 20.
[16] de la Ramée, *Ciceronianus*, 21.
[17] de la Ramée, *Ciceronianus*, 27.
[18] de la Ramée, *Ciceronianus*, 35.
[19] de la Ramée, *Ciceronianus*, 94 s.

ciones al buen criterio. Claro está que la controversia surge porque se parte del principio indiscutido de que los ciceronianos no admitían término que no estuviera en las obras conservadas del Arpinate. Así, C. Lenient[20] parece adscribirlo entre los partidarios de Erasmo. R. Sabbadini[21] presta poca atención a Ramus, por considerarlo un epígono del holandés. I. Scott[22] no duda tampoco en adscribirlo como anticiceroniano e, igualmente, H. Gmelin, autor de un espléndio trabajo sobre la imitación en el renacimiento[23], considera que "der bedeutendste Vertreter dieser Richtung der freien Imitatio endlich ist Petrus Ramus (1515–1572) gewesen, er hat den Impuls des Erasmus am stärksten weitergegeben"[24] y tampoco manifiesta ninguna duda al hablar de su anticiceronianismo y de su ideal ecléctico en la formación del estilo[25]. No obstante, un poco antes había dejado constancia de lo controvertido de esta figura al decir: "er bekämpft zwar auch die Sekte der Ciceronianer, aber es ist selbst Ciceronianer in einem anderen Sinne, sein Ciceronianus ist keine Spottfigur wie bei Erasmus, sondern eine zu formende Idealfigur wie etwa der *Cortegiano* des Castiglione"[26]. El ideal ecléctico de Ramus queda patente, según Gmelin, en sus comentarios de las Instituciones de Quintiliano, cuando asegura: *Plures imitandos, non unum Quintilianus existimat; id etiam libenter accipio, ut potius multorum uirtutes quam uel unius etiam uitia consectemur*[27]. Pero Gmelin no parece haber reparado en que el texto de la *Institutio Oratoria* que Ramus está comentando en ese pasaje propone la imitación de Cicerón (*qui maxime imitandus*), si bien no única y exclusivamente, por la sencilla razón de que resulta insuficiente[28]. Tal es lo que dice aceptar de la Rameé, aunque añadirá una restricción (que tampoco parece que se haya tenido en cuenta) *modo tamen in optimis quibusquam confirmatus prius fueris*, y a eso mismo parece responder la doctrina de su *Ciceronianus*.

Más recientemente, los estudiosos han empezado a valorar de distinta forma este tratado ramista, subrayando especialmente lo que tiene en común con los ciceronianos. Así, M. Fumaroli[29] advierte que "en matière de style, moins pragmatique et

---

[20] C. Lenient, *De ciceroniano bello apud recentiores* (Paris, 1855), 50 ss.

[21] R. Sabbadini, *Storia del ciceronianismo* (Torino, 1885), 73.

[22] I. Scott, *The Imitation of Cicero* (New York, 1910), 99: "On the side of the anti-Ciceronians, a disciple of Erasmus, a prominent leader, and a valiant fighter stood out in the person of Peter Ramus". Cf., también, 101.

[23] Gmelin, "Das Prinzip der Imitatio".

[24] Gmelin, "Das Prinzip der Imitatio", 337.

[25] Gmelin, "Das Prinzip der Imitatio", 340: "Aus dem Werdegang und der Stiltheorie Ciceros selbst entwickelt Ramus seinen Anticiceronianismus, sein freies eklektisches Stilideal".

[26] Gmelin, "Das Prinzip der Imitatio", 339.

[27] Pierre de la Rameé, *Ciceronianus*, col. 390.

[28] Quintiliano, 10, 2, 24s.: "*Sed non qui maxime imitandus, et solus imitandus est. Quid ergo? Non est satis omnia sic dicere, quomodo M. Tullius dixit? Mihi quidem satis esset, si omnia consequi possem (. .) Ideoque cum totum exprimere quem elegeris paene sit homini inconcessum, plurium bona ponamus ante oculos, ut aliud ex alio haereat, et quod cuique loco conueniat aptemus*".

[29] M. Fumaroli, *L'âge de l'éloquence. Rhétorique et 'res literaria' de la Renaissance au seuil de l'époque classique* (Genève, 1980; 2ª ed., Paris, 1994).

éclectique qu'Erasme, il est proche des thèses du 'cicéronien' Scaliger"[30] pero "il refuse l'étroitesse du cicéronianisme italien, et s'il accorde un préjugé favorable au vocabulaire tiré de Cicéron, ce n'est pas sans liberté critique (...) D'ailleurs on peut enrichir le fonds cicéronien en y agrégeant le vocabulaire de Térence, et en accordant droit de cité à certains mots archaïques, ou nouveaux, employés dans un sens figuré"[31]. K. Meerhoff, tras considerar que de la Ramée ha actuado como el propio Erasmo al combatir a los falsos ciceronianos que dominaron la primera mitad del XVI, reconoce que "si, à côté de Dolet, il y a eu un Cicéronien en France, c'est bien Ramus. Mais, nous l'avons vu, son Cicéronianisme a été guidé, sinon bouleversé, par les travaux de la Pléiade ..."[32]. Y, finalmente, Christian Mouchel cataloga decididamente a Ramus entre los que él denomina 'cicéroniens souples', esto es, los que frente a los 'stricts', admitían la utilización de léxico que no apareciera en las obras de Cicerón, o bien léxico de Cicerón utilizado con otro sentido al que tiene en sus obras[33].

En el catálogo de Mouchel, entre los ciceronianos flexibles o moderados, se encuentra también Scaliger, quien—recuérdese—publicó como respuesta al satírico diálogo de Erasmo dos discursos contra el holandés y en defensa de Longueil. Este humanista ha sido siempre considerado ciceroniano y antierasmista, precisamente por estas publicaciones. En el primero de estos discursos, publicado en 1531, niega que sea verdad la acusación, realizada por Erasmo a los ciceronianos, de que no admitían todo aquello que no se encontrara en las obras del Arpinate[34]. El propio Cicerón— dirá Scaliger—al haber acuñado nuevos vocablos al escribir sobre filosofía, siguiendo en esto el ejemplo de Aristóteles, nos enseñó el camino por donde nos podremos aventurar sin peligro. Nuestro criterio no consiste en rechazar una palabra o expresión porque Cicerón no las haya usado, sino que consideraremos que porque deben ser rechazadas éste no las utilizó. No es, así pues, cierto eso que dice Erasmo, que los ciceronianos no usan otras palabras que las que se conservan en los libros de aquel. La falsedad de este aserto se aprecia observando la actitud del mismo Cicerón, que empleó términos, incluso ya obsoletos, tomados de los poetas antiguos. Los ciceronianos—continúa diciendo Scaliger—admiran a Tito Livio, juntamente con Cicerón, y a Salustio, aunque su estilo resulta raro y angosto, y a Terencio. Ahora bien, para los ciceronianos, determinados géneros de autores han de ser imitados intensamente y ciertas épocas "reproducidas" y otras totalmente rechazadas; en algunas se ha de aplicar cierta ponderación. Nadie que se tilde de ciceroniano rechazará a César, Bruto, Catón o Celio Luceyo[35].

---

[30] Fumaroli, *L'âge de l'eloquence*, 454.

[31] Fumaroli, *L'âge de l'eloquence*, 456.

[32] K. Meerhoff, *Rhétorique et poétique au XVIe siècle en France, Du Bellay, Ramus et les autres* (Leiden, 1986), 39.

[33] Ch. Mouchel, *Cicéron et Sénèque dans la rhétorique de la Renaissance* (Marbourg, 1990), 83 ss.

[34] Hemos manejado una edición de 1620: *I. Caes. Scaligeri Pro M. Tullio Cicerone, contra Desid. Erasmum Roterodamum, Oratio I* (Tolossae, 1620), 30: "Neque quod tu ais Ciceronianis unquam persuasum fecit, ut quod ille non scripsisset statim damnatum uellent sed quod ille expunxit, Romanus apud Romanos, apud doctos doctus, Romanae linguae censorem agens, ab eo tamquam a Barbarie scopulo cursum flectere nos debere commonent".

[35] Scaliger, *Pro Cicerone*: "Quoniam et ipse quae ad Philosophiam spectant, et quae ad forum

Pero no es por lo anterior, por lo que se le considera a Scaliger ciceroniano 'moderado', sino por su más conocida y leída obra, *Poetices*, donde censura a Bembo por haber utilizado *heros* en lugar de *Iesus,* advirtiendo que no convienen tales ficciones a nuestro Dios[36].

Lo que nos extraña es que Mouchel no haya visto que también Dolet, a quien él cataloga entre los 'estrictos' o radicales, ha negado que Longueil, y con él los ciceronianos, fuera tan escrupuloso como para no aceptar otro léxico que el ciceroniano:

> neque mehercule tam morosa fuit Longolii in uerbis cura, uocum ut nullam nisi ex elencho Ciceronianae dictionis erutam, in scripta sua coniiceret: neque ea in compositionis ornatu, stilique forma solicitudo, ut omnia ad Ciceronis lineamenta superstitionis exigeret. Ridiculam uerborum calumniam fugiebat, uocem nullam reformidabat, quae uernacula esse, et urbis Romanae propria, quaeue autore aliquo non pessimo defendi posset (. . .) Ducem Ciceronem in scribendo habuit, non in illius uerba sic iurauit, ut nihil non arbitratu tentaret.[37]

Es decir, Dolet era de la misma opinión que Scaliger y, por tanto, tan 'strict' o tan 'souple' como él.

Pero lo más curioso es lo siguiente: El diálogo *de imitatione ciceroniana adversus Desiderium Erasmum Roterodamum pro Christophoro Longolio* (Lyon, 1535) se desarrolla entre dos personajes: T. More (*T. Morus*), el portavoz de Erasmo, y el que fuera maestro de Dolet, Neufville o Villaneuve *(Villanouanus)*, ciceroniano y portavoz del autor. Como nos advierte el propio Dolet, todas las palabras que pronuncia More han sido tomadas literalmente del *dialogus Ciceronianus* de Erasmo y constituyen por tanto la opinión del holandés. Pero en este caso Dolet ha manipulado con técnica centonaria el texto erasmiano, pues Erasmo, o mejor los personajes de su satírico diálogo,

---

pertinent aliter, atque aliter pertractauit, multa noua nomina Aristotelico exemplo felicissime meditatus, 'proloquium' et 'qualitatem' atque eiusmodi [cf. *Acad.* 1,25], proposuit nobis rationem qua nos quoque felicius auderemus (. . .) Non igitur quoniam Cicero non posuit, damnabimus: sed quoniam damnanda essent, ipsum non posuisse iudicamus. Quod autem ait Ciceronianos nullis aliis uocibus quam quae in illius extant libris uti consueuisse, quantum id falsum sit uel ex ipso Cicerone uidemus, qui Terentii, atque Ennii, atque aliquot aliorum Poëtarum uel obsoletis uocabulis usus est. (. . .) Liuium cum Ciceronianis, atque cum Cicerone pariter admiramur, pariterque imitamur. Neque uero Sallustium politissimum autorem reiiciunt, sed anxium illud atque insititium dicendi genus, sed multa superstitiosa uerba non ipsi primum [31] notauerunt. At quem magis amplectuntur quam Terentium? (. . .) Sed ita Ciceroniani censent, certa genera autorum tota penitus imitanda, certasque aetates effingendas, alia tota reiicienda, in quibusdam iudicium adhibendum (. . .). Quis tibi Ciceronianus unquam Caesarem reiecit? Quis Brutum, quem tanti fecit Cicero? quis Catonem? Caelium? Luceium, a quo ipse Cicero incredibili cupiditate ardet sua gesta memorari?

[36] J. C. Scaliger, *Poetices libri septem* (Lyon, 1561; edic. facsímil con introd. de A. Buck, Stuttgart, 1964), 6, 309: "Idem etiam cum Dominum Iesum Heroa uocat, ualde me commouit sane vox impia et utraque indigna. Ne argutetur quispiam Heroem e semisse deum, ex altero semisse hominem. Non possunt monstrorum figmenta uero Deo nostro conuenire".

[37] Emile V. Telle, *L'Erasmianus sive Ciceronianus d'Etienne Dolet (1535)* (Genève, 1974), 56.

no dijeron nunca que Longueil estuviera afectado por una *superstitio* tal que no leyera otro autor que Cicerón. Es más, Buléforo, el portavoz de Erasmo, cuando habla de Longueil, asegurará:. *Quanquam ille non uni Tullio assidebat, sed per omne autorum genus sese uoluerat, disciplinas liberales omnes diligenter edidicerat, ultra iuris peritiam, nec erat contentus exprimere lineamenta Ciceronis, sed in inuentione rerum peracutus fuisse uidetur et copiosus, etc.*

Y añadía Buléforo (esto es, Erasmo): *Nihil est igitur quod isti Ciceronis simii nobis Longolium obiiciant, aliis dotibus ille magnus erat, etiamsi ciceronianus non fuisset.*[38]

Dolet ha puesto en boca de More: *Annos septem totos nihil attigit, praeter libros Ciceronianos Longolius, a caeteris non minore religione temperans, quam Carthusiani temperant a carnibus, nequid alicunde haereret alienae phraseos, ac ueluti labem apergeret nitori Ciceroniani sermonis,*[39] pero lo cierto es que en el diálogo erasmiano estas palabras son pronunciadas por Nosopono[40] y van referidas a él mismo, esto es, al personaje ficticio y no a Longueil. Dolet ha confeccionado en este caso un centón con las palabras referidas a Nosopono y las referidas al personaje real, si bien es verdad que todo el mundo entendió que Longueil estaba bajo la persona de Nosopono. Pero lo que aquí nos interesa destacar es que Dolet asegura que Longueil no era un ciceroniano tan estricto como pretendía hacer creer Erasmo de forma subliminar. Ahora bien, Erasmo lo que había dicho de Longueil era que no podía ser presentado como modelo por parte de los *Ciceronis simii,* porque el belga no era así de fanático. ¿Quiénes eran, entonces, los ciceronianos ridículos? Nuestra sospecha es que lo que creemos ser una característica de los ciceronianos radicales no sea sino una invención del holandés para desprestigiar a quienes se habían atrevido a censurar su latinidad, lo que nos obligaría a replantearnos la historia del ciceronianismo, desprendiéndonos de tales prejuicios[41]. Obsérvese que Erasmo dice en el texto anteriormente citado que "no nos echen en cara esos ciceronianos a Longueil, porque Longueil no era así de fanático".

Por lo que se refiere a Ramus, nos preguntamos, si éste no estaría en realidad planteando el mismo programa que todos los ciceronianos, haciendo ostentación solamente de las diferencias con los fantasmas que había creado el diálogo de Erasmo. Téngase en cuenta que Ramus dice haber leído todos los tratados que sobre la imitación de Cicerón y sobre la polémica suscitada en torno a ello se han publicado. Ello significa que ha leído a Scaliger y Dolet y, por tanto, una versión del ciceronianismo muy diferente a la que él mismo atribuye a éstos y muy cercana, en cambio, a la suya propia.

Esta hipótesis de trabajo—que hemos llamado sospecha—se confirma cuando leemos al valenciano Luis Vives:

---

[38] D. Erasmo de Rotterdam, *Il Ciceroniano o dello stile migliore,* Edición crítica y trad. de A. Gambaro (Brescia, 1965), ls. 3717 ss. La primera edición del *Ciceronianus* de Erasmo (Basilea, 1528).

[39] Telle, *L'Erasmianus,* 55.

[40] Erasmo, *Il Ciceroniano,* ls. 163 ss.

[41] A reforzar esta hipótesis de trabajo contribuye ahora el trabajo de T. O. Tunberg, "Longolius: Ciceronian Latinity?", presentado en este mismo Congreso, en tanto que nos revela un Longueil no tan radicalmente ciceroniano.

Nostra aetate quidam ridicule sese alligant imitationi tamen, nec in uerbis solum latini sermonis et graeci, quod necessarium est, propterea quod eae linguae amissae in uulgus monumentis ueterum authorum continentur ac conseruantur, sed in phrasi, quod minime est necessarium, quippe collectis e lectione uocabulis, et loquendi formulis, tamquam lignis et lapidibus, sic unusquisque extruere orationem potest[42].

Ahora bien, tras esta denuncia general, cuando tiene que dar nombres concretos de los que *ridicule sese alligant imitationi*, resulta que los nombres más significativos escapan de esa caracterización, que sólo aparece concretada (?) en un indefinido *quidam* o un despectivo *isti*, pero que no llega a materializarse nunca en nombres concretos; y, cuando éstos aparecen, es para decirnos que sus métodos de imitación son muy diferentes de los de los *ridiculi*:

Similior patri filius qui mores reddit, quam qui liniamenta oris. Cur tantum uirum non totum imitantur, et potissimum animum, quo praestat corpori, quod recte praecipit Pau. Cortesius, qui aliam multo uiam imitandi ostendit, quam isti sequuntur, eamque merito deplorat ab hominibus nostris aut neglectam esse, aut mutatam. neque enim uult nos Ciceronis similes, ut simias, sed ut filios parentum. simiae externa solum repraesentant, filii etiam interna. nec simiae aliud quam liniamenta et deformitates quasdam gestus, filii uultum, incessum, statum, motum, uocem (. . .) Eadem est sententia hominis omnium Ciceronianissimi Christophori Longolii[43].

En todos los humanistas españoles por nosotros estudiados[44], y que bien porque abiertamente lo declaren o bien porque determinados indicios los relacionan con el movimiento de los imitadores de Cicerón, se suele repetir este tópico del desmarcarse de los *ridiculi ciceroniani*.

Ahora bien, lo que resulta desconcertante, a primera vista, es una carta de Erasmo dirigida a Ursino Velio, datada en 1531 (sólo tres años después de publicado su *Ciceronianus*), en la que manifiesta su admiración por el estilo de Bembo, entre otros ciceronianos:

Vacat audire nouarum rerum aliquid? Accipe: Quanquam inter adynata numerari scio senis mutare linguam, tamen ego meditor mutare stylum. Ac primum applicui memet ad exemplar structurae Budaicae: legi plerasque illius epistolas feliciter elaboratas, annisus sum sedulo, sed conatus successu caruit. Nunc in effingendo Cicerone sum totus. Dices, quid accidit? Huc exstimularunt me trium hujus aetatis in dicendo felicissimorum epistolae, Jacobi Sadoleti, Petri Bembi, et Julii Pflug, quorum postremum nuper amicum habere coepi, ex re mala magnum nactus bonum. Phrasis horum ita consentit, ut dicas a teneris unguiculis eodem in ludo doctos et educatos. Deum immortalem! qui candor

---

[42] Luis Vives, *De disciplinis libri XX* (Antuerpiae, 1531), fol. 54r.

[43] Vives, *De disciplinis,* fol. 55r.

[44] J. Mª Núñez, *El Ciceronianismo en España* (Valladolid, 1993).

orationis, quam felix facilitas, quanta sensuum sanitas, quam omnia cohaerent, amnisque limpidissimi in morem inoffense labuntur, nulla salebra, nullo uortice lectorem remorante! Tales Ciceronianos toto pectore possum amare, utinam et assequi liceat. Sed arbitror consultius, ut sexagenarius ab his comitiis abstineam, ne per juuentutem tumultuantem fiam depontanus[45].

Si a todo esto se añade que no contamos (o, al menos, no hemos visto que se aduzca nunca) con ninguna carta o escrito de cualquier clase de Bembo o Longueil[46], donde se exponga un programa tan estricto como el caricaturizado por Erasmo, nuestra sospecha o hipótesis de trabajo puede llegar a convertirse en tesis. Y en ese caso, Pierre de la Ramée debe ser considerado un ciceroniano, sin más, como Bembo, Longueil, Scaliger o Dolet. Y no pugna tampoco contra esta interpretación el hecho de que en sus *Brutinae quaestiones* haya criticado o censurado a Cicerón, pues, en realidad, estas críticas van dirigidas a su doctrina retórica, pero no a su actividad creadora ni a su estilo, que constituyen para él la manifestación literaria más importante de la prosa latina: *eloquentiam Ciceronis in toto genere orationis in uerbis, in figuris, in nobilibus et eximiis exemplis argumentorum magnificentiam uel in caelo pono: magistrorum, qui te isto modo quaestiones propositas tractare docuerunt, requiro prudentiam.*[47]

No obstante, es verdad que ya en su época se le interpretó, precisamente por las críticas vertidas contra su doctrina, como enemigo de Cicerón y suscitó la respuesta de Ioachimus Perionius (*v. supra*) en 1547. Por ello, quizás, haya que pensar que su respuesta a esta falsa interpretación o acusación fuera su *Ciceronianus*, que lejos de ser una crítica de este movimiento, constituye una especie de manifiesto o de programa de imitación, no sólo de su latinidad—cosa que no pone en duda en ningún momento—, sino incluso de su trayectoria y formación como orador. No olvidemos que, según su propia declaración, el *Ciceronianus* constituye una puesta en práctica de sus comentarios críticos denominados *Brutinae quaestiones*.

Universidad de Oviedo

---

[45] Erasmo, *Opera omnia* (Lugduni Batavorum, 1703; reimp. Hildesheim, 1961–62) III,2, col. 1372, epist. 1570, de 15 de marzo de 1531.

[46] Mouchel considera que el radicalismo de Longueil es atestiguado por su biógrafo R. Pole, cuando nos dice que pasó cinco años leyendo exclusivamente a Cicerón. Tal testimonio constituye una evidente exageración, pues Longueil no vivió ni mucho menos ese tiempo desde que conoció a Bembo y, además, entra en contradicción con otros datos de esa misma Vita en la que se nos refieren sus variadas lecturas y ocupaciones literarias y filológicas. Por otra parte, no parece dársele mucho crédito, en la actualidad, a la autoría de tal biografía por parte de Pole; cf. G. B. Parks, "Did Pole write the 'Vita Longolii'?" *Renaissance Quarterly* 26 (1975): 274–285.

[47] Pierre de la Ramée, *Scholae*, col. 246.

Sapientia *and Knowledge in the Construction of the Renaissance* docta foemina: *Vives'* De institutione foeminae christianae

CARMEN PERAITA

Vives' *De institutione foeminae christianae* (1524) represents the most influential defense of feminine access to education in the sixteenth century. This paper offers an interpretation of the text, nuanced by, and contextualized in, the evolving notions of *sapientia* in the Renaissance.

The analysis reveals two insights into Vives' model for Christian instruction. On the one hand, Vives views education in *bonae litterae* as a seminal enterprise for both women and men, one that leads not only to virtue and self-knowledge, but also to greater obedience. On the other hand, Vives proposes education as a method for reinforcing in women the notions of their theological and natural inferiority. The present analysis suggests that his paradoxical view of education—only educated women can understand, and implicitly accept, their subservience—can be resolved by reference to the extant relation between Christian humanist perceptions of wisdom as a naturally acquired moral virtue and Vives' desire to reinforce the existing patriarchal social order.

The study also indicates that Vives' writing proffers a somewhat progressive notion. Contemporary received ideas had characterized female *eruditio* as morally dangerous, an activity which leads to lasciviousness and disorder in the body politic: wise women should be ignorant and virtue and illiteracy are linked. Vives, in contrast, avers that reading fosters in women *pudicitia*, in addition to the beneficial effects of simply occupying women's minds. Thus while his writing appears on one level to support the status quo (reading as a tool to reinforce patriarchial authority), it appears subversive on another (*pudicitia* is reinforced through reading, not through ignorance, and reading does not lead to lust but to virtue).

The study begins by exploring how notions of *sapientia* changed during the Renaissance and how these ideas shaped Christian humanistic discourse on the education of women. The discussion then turns to how the Spanish humanist educator applied the concept of wisdom to his defense of feminine learning. Some remarks on the tensions arising in Vives' defense of female education, on the grounds that it reinforces social control of women, conclude the paper.

During the Renaissance, the classical idea of wisdom suffered what Eugene Rice calls a "moralizing process" (149), whereby emphasis on knowledge is transferred to virtue.[1] That process, which started with Petrarch—for whom, "the pursuit of wisdom must be inseparable from virtue"—continued with humanists like Budé, Ronsard, Erasmus, Vives, and, of course, Pierre Charron, among others (Rice 156). They all tended to privilege a person's active virtue over intellectual knowledge and to recommend an active life over isolated contemplation. Wisdom is conceived as a moral virtue, an ethical concern about how to live well and blessedly in the *civitas christiana*; thus, for instance, for Erasmus wisdom is "virtus cum eruditione liberali coniuncta" (the *Enchiridion* as quoted in Rice 160).

A second element, the rejection of intellectual disciplines—disciplines traditionally forbidden to women—complements the process of moralizing wisdom in humanistic educational treatises. In *Des vertus intellectuelles et morales*, Pierre Ronsard rejects intellectual virtues. He praises Cato the Censor, the archetypal exemplum of *priscus romanus vir*, who "had stigmatized the introduction of so many sciences and so much knowledge as the central cause of Roman decline."[2] In the French poet's view, many of the intellectual virtues are worthless. Mocking as useless all interest in studying the human sciences—vain things such as the motions of stars, meteors, or comets—Ronsard remarks that "que Dieu a mis telles curiositez en l'entendement des hommes pour les tourmenter" (1038–39) [God has put such curiosities in man's mind only to torment him].[3] In doing so, he illustrates a process articulated in Rice's seminal observation: "the transformation of wisdom from contemplation to action, from a body of knowledge to a collection of ethical precepts, from a virtue of the intellect to a perfection of the will is humanism's chief contribution to the development of the idea of wisdom" (149).

The rejection of intellectual virtues as impractical (they are perceived to undermine the active life of virtue), the emphasis on an ethical learning that was aimed at virtuous conduct and the focus on perfection of the will, are probably key ideological underpinnings of Christian humanists' strong and natural interest in the education of women.

Confidence in Education

The rejection of intellectual knowledge coincides with significant changes in the modes of acquisition of wisdom, in the perception of its availability. Medieval wis-

---

[1] Eugene F. Rice Jr., *The Renaissance Idea of Wisdom* (Cambridge, 1958); my exposition on wisdom closely follows Rice's seminal study.

[2] The *Discours prononcé á l'Académie du Palais par Ronsard en présence de Henri III* was given in the late 1570s; cf. Rice, *The Renaissance Idea*, 154–155.

[3] Ronsard, *Oeuvres complètes*, Gustave Cohen, ed. (Paris, 1950), II, 1037–38. English translation from Rice, *The Renaissance Idea*, 154–155.

dom was conceived as a "revealed knowledge of divine things understood in an explicitly Christian sense" (Rice 209). On the contrary, Renaissance secularization of wisdom guaranteed the natural autonomy of its acquisition. Erasmus and Vives—contrary to humanists like Salutati, for whom virtue is a gift from God—"tend to see virtue as a natural human acquisition" (Rice 162). Furthermore, during the Renaissance, human things are included among objects of wisdom, in opposition to the Middle Ages, when "sapiential objects were divine" (Rice 211).

In the minds of Christian humanists, wisdom unites "ethical insights of learning with the practice of virtue. It consists of moral precepts and the actions which obey them" (Rice 161). It needs to be instilled (in both men and women) through appropriate instruction (conceived mainly as a corpus of ethical precepts and *exempla*). Wisdom is perceived as an active virtue, not exclusively God given but also acquired through *eruditio*, learning adequate precepts—mainly from the *Philosophia Christi*—that clearly define virtuous conduct.

The notion that education leads to wisdom, the faith that one can learn active virtue through maxims, sayings, and exempla is, without doubt, another factor that strongly favored the education of women in the mind of humanists like Vives or Erasmus. In fact, confidence in *educatio* as the way to improve all categories of human beings, transforming them into virtuous citizens—from the king to his most humble and mediocre subject, from men to the naturally and theologically inferior women— is paramount in the humanists' idea of morally reforming society. It is not surprising then, that in Vives' concern with improving society through enhancing individual ethics, in his involvement with instructing the pious member of the *civitas christiana*, women could not be left behind.

Wisdom is no longer rustic piety, but *sancta eruditio, docta pietas*, the harmony between religion and a knowledge of the humanities expressed by Petrarch. The study of literature, which "in cogitatione attolit pulcherrimarum rerum, ut a turpitudinum cogitationibus avocet animos" [lifts the mind to the contemplation of beautiful things and rids it of lowly thought] (*De institutione* 38, 39), and the activity of reading, which "mentes hominum occupat totas" [occupies a person's whole attention] (38, 39), thereby protecting against the dangers of idleness, are introduced in Vives' discourse as shields against vices, defenses against a person's strong tendency to evil.[4] Evil

---

[4] I quote *De institutione* from two different sources. For book I (on virgins), my text is C. Fantazzi and C. Matheeussen, eds., C. Fantazzi, trans., *De institutione feminae christianae*, Liber primus (Leiden, 1996). Here I indicate first the Latin page and then the English translation page. Books II and III are quoted from Mayans' Latin edition (Valencia, 1782) of Vives' *Opera omnia* (Basel, 1555), republished by the Gregg Press (London, 1964). In this case, I always indicate the book quoted. All emphases are mine. My translations of the Latin text are indicated. For a modern critical edition of the English translation of *De institutione* and an interesting textual criticism, cf. Betty S. Travitsky, "Reprinting Tudor History: The Case of Catherine of Aragon," *Renaissance Quarterly* 50 (1997): 164–174. Vives' corpus on the instruction of the women is not exclusively limited to his two texts dealing explicitly with the topic: the *De institutione* and *The Office and Duetie of an Husband, made by the excellent philosopher Ludovicus Vives, (De officio mariti liber)* (Bruges, 1528), trans. Thomas Paynell (London, 1550). In at least two other texts, both written in the same period as *De*

Evil is manifested in foolishness and lack of moderation, caused by ignorance and idleness. Eruditio secures the defenses that protect us from "plagam diaboli pugna capitalis" [the implacable hostility of the devil] (26, 27) and the temptations of the flesh. In the opposition between flesh and spirit (transformed into the opposition between *eruditio* and ignorance), Vives contends that the natural weakness and theological inferiority of womankind can be overcome if a woman has a sound knowledge of the *Philosophia Christi*. The Spanish humanist views the practice of reading—activity done in private—as directly reinforcing active obedience and *pudicitia*.

Therefore, the humanistic program united an education in moral virtue as well as in *litteras*: the two dimensions are inextricably linked. Unsurprisingly, *De institutione* contextualizes the education of women in the first words of the *Praefatio* as a moral instruction. Vives observes that even if he admires and praises Catherine of Aragon's Latinism, it is the holiness of her living, her *sancta eruditio*, which impels him to write the text:"Movit me sanctitas morum tuorum et animi tui ardor in sacra studia" [Moved . . . by the holiness . . . of your life and your ardent zeal for sacred studies] (1, 2). Clearly, in Vives' discourse, the aim of education is to show the *"virtutis via."*

Moral probity became a central pedagogical concern for those humanists who believed *"educatio* to be intrinsically morally regenerative and conductive to the formation of a true Christian spirit."[5] Christian humanists believed in an unquestioned equivalence of *litterae* with wisdom and moral integrity, and relied on education to forge virtuous and obedient subjects: in Grafton's and Jardine's words, "good grammarians seem to lead blameless lives"(34). *De institutione*'s main concern is, therefore, to caution women on moral grounds against ignorance: to be ignorant is the best road to vice. The excellencies of studying *litterae* are related closely and conventionally to improving the *mores*, to *recte vivendi*. In Vives' opinion, a woman (as well as a man) who reads will control her passions and be virtuous, but importantly, she will be submissive to patriarchal authority. *Eruditio*—an indispensable dimension of being wise—is envisaged as moral knowledge that includes, in the case of women, awareness of their specific theological inferiority, their natural weakness, and their socially subordinate role.

A Focus on Means, Not Ends

A revealing second remark, introduced also in the *Praefatio* of *De institutione,*

---

institutione (1524) and *De officio* (1528), Vives' aim is, implicitly or explicitly, the education of Catherine of Aragon's daughter, Mary Tudor, future ruler and versed Latinist, who was seven years old at that time and whom Vives will later briefly tutor in Latin. In the first letter of *De ratione studii puerilis* (*Plans of Studies,* 1523), Vives observes in the dedication to Catherine that the letter is intended to guide Mary Tudor's instructor. The following year Vives again dedicated a text to her, *Satellitium animi*, a collection of apophthegms intended to guide the virtuous ruler, in this case, a princess, to govern wisely. The dedication is signed at Bruges on 1 July 1524. It was translated in 1540 by Richard Morison who, like Thomas Paynell, was a student at Oxford when Vives was lecturing there.

[5] Anthony Grafton and Alice Jardine, *From Humanism to the Humanities* (Cambridge, 1986), 125.

illustrates the foundations on which Vives constructs his pedagogical program. He proclaims himself to be the first author to write on the necessary topic of feminine education. Although conceding that he follows the ideas of the Church Fathers, the Spanish humanist indicates that his intentions are more involved with practical instruction. In his goal to guide the feminine will in the quest for wisdom, the Spanish humanist remarks that, in contrast to the Church Fathers, he will not avoid "erudire inferiora"(2). Vives explains that Cyprian, Jerome, Ambrose, and Augustine "vitae genus suadeant quam forment" [advocate a way of life rather than give instruction about it] (2, 3). As the humanist characterizes the Church Fathers:

> Toti sunt in castitatis laudibus celebrandis magnifico vero opere ... sed praecepta formulasque vitae paucissimas perhibuerunt, satius esse rati adhortari ad optima et manum porrigere ad altissima quam erudire inferiora. (2) They spend all the time singing the praises of chastity ... but they gave very few precepts or rules of life, thinking it preferable to exhort their readers to the best conduct and to point the way to the highest examples rather than to give instruction about more lowly matters. (3)

De institutione claims to be more concerned with practicalities of instructing about "lowly matters" and teaching "precepts and rules of life" than with simply "exhortation" or "counselling."

Virtue, active obedience, and a concern for *educatio*—which focuses on the practical level of ordering life, of regulating every facet of daily routine—become inextricably linked. Wisdom is instilled through a carefully designed practice based on "useful precepts" that need to embrace even the minutiae of daily behavior.

As we already observed, human things are included among the objects of wisdom. In fact, wisdom evolved from being knowledge—the "knowledge of the true," to being an activity—the "pursuit of the good" (Rice 212). The result, Rice points out, was a wisdom "rooted in and ruling man's most banal activities, his politics and business, his family and personal relations" (212). The "humanization" of wisdom entails therefore a significant social implication: virtue is anchored in "lowly matters," in a daily practice instilled through knowledge of precepts.

In a prescribed daily routine, then, the activity of reading is deemed essential as a moral action for all human beings. In a remark from *De officio* that applies both to men and women, Vives avers that reading has to teach "multa de componendis affectibus, et sedanda illa animorum tempestate legat" [how to subdue and bring under the affections, and to appease and pacify the tempest and unquietness of the mind] (369, 204). Control of one's own passions is achieved only through knowledge; in the words of Carlos Noreña: "According to Vives, knowledge is not primarily an instrument for the use of the world but a weapon for the conquest of human passions."[6]

Specifically, the humanist education of women, structured from the viewpoint of ethical conduct (that is, moral improvement), is aimed exclusively at reinforcing a daily discipline of active obedience, self-control, and social moderation.

---

[6] Carlos Noreña, *Juan Luis Vives* (The Hague, 1970), 241.

But the link between knowledge and subordination is explicitly articulated in numerous educational humanistic discourses, not only in those related to female instruction. In fact, humanist wisdom is socially constructed as "a code of conduct whose chief rules are *moderation* and *self-control*" (Rice 164; emphasis mine). Ronsard's aforementioned oration is revealing in presenting moral virtue as conceived on social grounds, privileging a "politics of restraint": "Je conclus doncq, puisque les vertues moralles nous font plus charitables, pitoyables, justiciers, attrampez, fors aux perils, plus compaignables et plus obeissans à nos superieurs, qu'elles sont à preferer aux intellectuelles" (1039) [I conclude, therefore, that since the moral virtues make us more charitable, humane, just, *moderate*, firmer in the face of danger, *more sociable and obedient to our superiors*, they are to be preferred to the intellectual] (Rice 155; emphasis mine).

In the case of women, humanist wisdom is oriented to the goal of effectively inculcating practical virtues which reinforce what Joan Kelly-Gadol has denominated the "restoration of classical attitudes of restraint in the Renaissance."[7] For a vast majority of humanistic moralists, the classical attitudes of restraint are exemplified in the *priscorum Romanorum feminae* brought forth to explain women's social submissiveness in *De institutione* (book "On Widows"): "prisci Romani feminas in virorum potestate semper *voluerunt* esse, tum patrum, tum maritorum, tum fratrum, tum propinquorum" (293) [No woman was allowed even to do a private transaction without the presence of a responsible male and [the Romans] wanted her to remain under control of her parents, brothers, or husband] (my translation).[8]

In my view, the moralizing dimensions of humanist *sapientia*, which stress the perfection of will through conduct based on modesty, frugality, restraint, the capacity to govern one's own passions, to be more "charitable" and "humane," and, in Ronsard's words, more "sociable and obedient to our superiors," shape the exclusively restrictive ideological base on which the education of Christian women is established. In sum, while the *virtutis via* is emblazoned on a rejection of ignorance, the necessary role of *educatio* in the (female) quest for wisdom primarily rests on moral grounds and criteria of sociability formulated as a "politics of self-restraint."

Learning and Lasciviousness: Vives' Strategy in His Defense of the Education of Women

The association made between female *eruditio* and lasciviousness is the essential theme with which Vives disagrees in his explicit opposition to hostile attitudes toward feminine instruction. The Spanish humanist is arguing with a conventional point of view, which opposes the humanist education of women on the grounds that

---

[7] Joan Kelly-Gadol, "Did Women Have a Renaissance?" in *Becoming Visible: Women in European History*, ed. Renate Bridenthal and Claudia Koon, 2nd ed. (Boston, 1987), 143.

[8] Cato's words in Livy; cf. *Ab urbe condita*, XXXIV, 2, 11: "quippe sapienter est a vetere opulo Romano institutum, apud quem nulla femina ne privatam quidem rem sinebatur agere sine auctore, in manu esse voluerunt parentum, fratrum, virorum." On two occasions (both in the book on widows), *De institutione* mentions these words.

it will make them "unchaste." In contrast to common associations made between ignorance and virtue, and learning and lasciviousness in women, the Christian humanist
defense of the *docta femina* is articulated on the basis that education does not foster
socially disruptive women or sexual predators but, on the contrary, buttresses the
quintessential patriarchal female virtues of *pudicitia*, temperance, and docility. Bringing
into his argument a strong social component, he presents himself as challenging deep-
rooted assumptions which obstructed women from acquiring knowledge: learned
women behave in a disorderly fashion; literacy leads to a loss of virtue and of *pudicitia*, and encourages socially disruptive behavior and sexual deviancy; and reading inclines the mind to evil designs. Inverting the terms, Vives insists that *eruditio* is the
best way to assure *pudicitia* and its two inseparable companions, *pudor* and *sobrietas*.[9]
Pudicitia is defined not as simple chastity of the body, as exclusive sexual integrity, but
as the virtue that ensures a person's control of his/her passions, and provides a woman
with a modest, sober spirit that engenders appropiate subordinate behavior.[10] Vives'
construction of *pudicitia*—which receives some Stoic connotations—suggests a more
universal, less gendered notion than the one found in writings by the Church Fathers.

Vives' argument in rejecting the exclusion of women from *bonae artes* has a stra-
tegical rhetorical dimension. The humanist's reasoning justifies feminine instruction,
not directly from the spiritual point of view of assuring a woman of her salvation (the
Church Fathers wrote about that), but from the pragmatic point of view of its benefits for the commonwealth. He underlines the advantages of the *docta femina* for men,
on a private as well as a public level. Men will profit substantially from educating
their female companions, since "nihil est aeque molestum ut communionem vitae
habere cum improbo" [nothing is more repulsive than to share our lives with a dis-
honest person] (*De institutione* 65–66).

In sum, Vives structures feminine instruction in terms of a male social obligation,
thereby establishing the equivalence between *eruditio* and *castitas*. His educational
program focuses on inculcating, through reading, reflective habits, and moderate conduct; on the socially constructed need to repress sexuality; and on female subordination, which is "the main guarantee of law and order in the body politic."[11] The
benefits of instructing women are almost exclusively and strategically formulated on
the grounds that it upholds the natural authority of men and undergirds patriarchal
modes of subjection.

---

[9] For Vives, these virtues should be inculcated in all humans beings, male *and* female, through
doctrina: "Sed doctrina quam ego *toti humano generi* velim proponi, sobria est et casta" (*De institutione*, 26) [The learning that I should wish to be available for the whole human race is sober and
chaste] (27).

[10] Anger, jealousy and cruelty are passions traditionally considered feminine. Women, but also
men, need to control their passions in order to achieve "that wisdom which consists in the right
evaluation of everything in virtue of an uncorrupted judgment" (*Introductio ad sapientam* as quoted
in Carlos G. Noreña, *Vives* 238).

[11] Lawrence Stone as quoted in Carole Levin, "Advice on Women's Behaviour in Three
Tudor Homilies," *International Journal of Women's Studies* 6, 2 (1983): 179.

Concluding Remarks

The Spanish educator's defense of learned women presents itself, paradoxically, as both progressive and conservative. It is progressive in that Vives' rhetoric strives to improve the access to education of women by using evolving notions of wisdom—whether related to women or men—to invert existing ideas about the effects of knowledge on women's *pudicitia*. It is reactionary in that this elemental justification appears to be a fortification of the existing structure of patriarchy. But Vives' argument—which represents the most ambitious treatment of the topic and the most influential defense of the necessity to educate women in the sixteenth century—uncovers probably a more fundamental ideological paradox of humanist education: the instruction of women can only be debated within a socially constructed context that stresses the enhancement of patriarchal order, that openly advocates that education leads women to subordination, restraint, and enclosure (and transforms them into controlled subjects), and thus validates men's authority. Borrowing Ian Maclean's words regarding the notion of women, the paradox in Vives' defense of female learning "reflects well the hesitancies and incoherences inherent in Renaissance modes of thought."[12]

Vives' struggle with the idea of wisdom and its implication of fostering instruction for women is a fascinating example of how shocks to social systems occur (here, the changing notions of wisdom and its potentially radical implications) and how systems attempt to reattain their equilibria. In the process, underlying assumptions are revealed as people try to make everything internally consistent again. In this regard, the choices made by Vives and others humanists seem to indicate that the transformation of *sapientia* into a learned virtue was a factor which fostered humanism's interest in the education of women. These same choices reflected humanists' attempts to reconcile female learning with the existing patriarchal order.

Villanova University

---

[12] Ian Maclean, *The Renaissance Notion of Woman: A Study in the Fortunes of Scholasticism and Medical Science in European Intellectual Life* (Cambridge, 1980), 4.

El exilio en la Poesía Latina
de Michele Marullo[1]

MARIA DEL MAR PÉREZ MORILLO

Michele Marullo Tarcaniota nació en Constantinopla en 1453, tan sólo unos meses después de que la ciudad cayera en manos de los turcos[2]. A consecuencia de esta conquista la familia del poeta emprendió el camino del exilio. Su primera escala importante fue Ragusa (la actual Dubrovnik), ciudad libre que fue refugio para muchos exiliados. De allí pasaron a Ancona, ya en la Península Itálica, aunque no está claro si esta ciudad fue sólo lugar de paso o vivieron allí durante algún tiempo. Aparte de Ragusa y Ancona, las ciudades más importantes en la vida literaria de Marullo fueron Nápoles, primero, y Florencia, después. En Nápoles frecuentó la Academia Pontaniana, entablando amistad con personajes tan importantes como Sannazaro, Poliziano y el propio Pontano, a quien Marullo consideró su maestro. En Florencia fue protegido por los hermanos Lorenzo y Giovanni di Pier Francesco y vivió allí varios años, si exceptuamos el paréntesis de su participación en la campaña

---

[1] Este trabajo forma parte del proyecto de investigación PS93-0130 de la DGICYT.

Por otra parte, quiero puntualizar que me he circunscrito aquí al estudio de los *Epigramas* y *Nenias* de Marullo, dejando a un lado sus *Himnos naturales*, que han sido objeto de numerosos trabajos (P. L. Ciceri, "Michele Marullo e i suoi 'Hymni naturales' ", *Giornale storico della letteratura italiana* 44 [1914]: 289–357; M. J. McGann, "Reading Horace in the Quattrocento: The *Hymn to Mars* of Michael Marullus", en S. J. Harrison, ed., *Homage to Horace* [Oxford, 1995], 329–347; C. Harrauer, *Kosmos und Mythos: Die Weltgotthymnen und die mythologischen Hymnen des Michael Marullus* [Wien, 1994]; M. Marulle, *Hymnes Naturels,* ed. J. Chomarat [Genève, 1995]; entre otros).

Quiero hacer constar también aquí mi agradecimiento al profesor De Pinho, de la Universidad de Coimbra, que puso en mi conocimiento la existencia de dos trabajos de Carlos Ascenso André sobre este tema: el primero, sobre Diogo Pires, también un poeta latino del exilio; y el segundo, sobre el mal de ausencia.

[2] Para los datos biográficos de Marullo, véanse B. Croce, "Vita del Marullo", en *Poeti e scrittori del pieno e del tardo Rinascimento* (Bari, 1945), 269–298; y C. Kidwell, *Marullus. Soldier Poet of the Renaissance* (London, 1989).

francesa contra Nápoles. En Florencia, además, contrajo matrimonio con Alessandra Scala, mujer de elevada posición y vastísima cultura.

Éstos son sólo los eslabones más importantes de toda una vida marcada por un constante ir y venir, sin residencia fija, sirviendo a uno u otro señor y en contacto con distintos círculos literarios. Además, en su juventud temprana parece que sirvió en los ejércitos de algún tirano en las costas del Mar Negro.

Marullo, pues, encaja muy bien en el arquetipo de soldado-poeta tan característico de su época, y su vida de exiliado permanente lo incluye en el grupo de los errantes o "stradioti"[3], así llamados a partir de la palabra "strada", en su sentido tardío de "calle". Como él, muchos literatos y eruditos griegos tuvieron que exiliarse a Italia, y aquí formaron círculos literarios, dedicados, entre otras labores intelectuales, a la edición de textos antiguos y a la educación de los hijos de los personajes más influyentes de la época. Entre estos maestros se encontraban Teodoro Gaza, Demetrio Chalcondilas o Juan Lascaris.

En toda la obra de Marullo se deja sentir, unas veces de forma más explícita y otras menos, el dolor por la patria perdida, el amor por su tierra y por sus raíces, y la esperanza, nunca abandonada del todo, de poder volver a ella, si bien, aun en los momentos de más esperanza, embargado por un profundo pesimismo.

El referente ineludible en cuanto al tratamiento literario del tema del exilio lo constituyen las *Tristes* y las *Pónticas* ovidianas. Estas dos obras latinas clásicas están sin duda en la mente de Marullo, pero lo están en lo que se refiere a la idea general del lamento por la patria perdida y en su afán por recuperarla. Por lo demás, sus situaciones respectivas son muy diferentes. Marullo vivió como exiliado toda su vida; más bien se podría decir que fue un hombre sin patria. Y este sentimiento de castración lo marcó para siempre. En el caso de Ovidio, el destierro, que no el exilio, le llegó en su madurez. Y por otra parte, la idea de expiación de una culpa o de castigo por una falta cometida, que se da en el caso de Ovidio, está ausente de la situación de Marullo, que no fue más que un sujeto pasivo de los acontecimientos.

También desde el punto de vista formal Ovidio está presente en la poesía de Marullo. En un estudio de las fuentes ovidianas llevado a cabo sobre algo más de un 37% de los versos de Marullo estudiados en este trabajo (*ep.* I, 22, 1–15; II, 32, 57–80 y 121–126; III, 37; y III, 47), el conjunto de los calcos de *Tristes* y *Pónticas* suponen el grupo más numeroso del total de calcos ovidianos, con un 32,09%. Ahora bien, en el recuento por obras, el número de calcos más abundante procede de las *Metamorfosis*, con un 18,8%; a las que siguen las *Tristes* y las *Heroidas* con un 16,6% cada una; y las *Pónticas*, con un 15,49%. También es digno de mencionar el alto número de calcos procedentes de los *Fastos* (10,7%). La siguiente obra ovidiana de la que aparecen calcos en Marullo, el *Ars amatoria*, está ya más alejada en porcentaje, con un 7,01%.

Dentro de la poesía marulliana, la idea del exilio es unas veces el eje central de sus poemas y otras aparece en composiciones cuyo núcleo temático es otro. Así, en poemas como el extenso II, 32, que constituye una declaración de amor a Neera, la

---

[3] Cf. B. Croce, "Vita del Marullo", 271.

amada tantas veces cantada por él, el poeta, repasando lo que ha sido su dura vida, compara los embates del destino con los golpes del amor:

> Sed furit interea fax intima ad ossa medullis,
>> **qualis in** *Aetnaeo* vix **solet esse** *iugo*:
> **nunc ego** Rhiphaeas **vellem** *calcare* pruinas,
>> nunc gelidum Tanaim pectore habere meo,
> nunc **succos ferrumque** *pati* sensuque minutus
>> stare procelloso littore truncus iners.
> **An gravis** *hic* **etiam Fortunae iniuria** saevit,
>> nequando misero non sit **acerba** *mihi*? (*ep.* II, 32, 57–64)[4]

El verso 58 presenta un calco ovidiano, por una parte, de la epístola 21 de las *Heroidas* ("**qualis in** *Iliaco* Penthesilea *solo*;", 120)[5] y, por otra, de las *Pónticas* ("**qualis in** aeriae tergo **solet esse** columbae", 3, 3, 19). La construcción "solet esse" se repite con bastante frecuencia en Ovidio en la misma posición en la que aparece en Marullo, es decir, seguida sólo por una palabra antes del final del verso, que en los cuatro últimos casos de los seis que voy a citar es una palabra de estructura yámbica al final de un pentámetro, como en el caso de Marullo (*epist.* 16, 351; 17, 41; 20, 124; *Pont.* 1, 2, 116; 4, 10, 24; e *Ib.* 42). El verso siguiente, el 59, también está tomado de tres versos de Ovidio, en este caso de las *Tristes*: "**Nunc ego** Triptolemi *cuperem consistere* curru" (3, 8, 1); "**nunc ego** Medeae **uellem** *frenare* dracones" (3, 8, 3) y "**nunc ego** iactandas *optarem sumere* pennas," (3, 8, 5). La idea del verso 61 está también recogida de forma muy parecida en dos pasajes ovidianos: el primero, pertenece a la epístola 20 de las *Heroidas* ("ut ualeant, aliae **ferrum patiuntur** et ignes; / fert aliis tristem **sucus** amarus opem", vv. 185–186); y el segundo, a los *Remedia amoris* ("Saepe bibi **sucos** quamuis inuitus amaros / [. . .] / Ut corpus redimas, **ferrum patieris** et ignes", vv. 227–229). En cuanto al verso 63, presenta, entre otros, dos calcos, en los que Ovidio se refiere a la injuria y la dureza de la fortuna: "Nempe per *hos* **etiam Fortunae iniuria** mores" (*Epicedion Drusi*, 51) y "**an grauis** inceptum peragit **Fortuna** tenorem / et manet in cursu semper **acerba** *suo*?" (*epist.* 15, 59–60).

Los dos versos siguientes son los que han servido para datar el nacimiento de Marullo. En ellos el poeta nos cuenta cómo, estando su madre embarazada de él, Constantinopla cayó bajo el dominio turco:

> Vix bene adhuc fueram **matris rude semen in alvo,**
>> **cum grave servitium patria victa subit**. (*ep.* II, 32, 65–66)

---

[4] Recojo aquí el texto de Marullo correspondiente a la edición de su poesía completa que hizo Alessandro Perosa en 1951.

[5] Cito los textos latinos de Ovidio de acuerdo con las siguientes ediciones: *Metamorphoses,* ed. W. S. Anderson (Leipzig, 1985 = 1977); *Epistulae siue Heroides,* ed. H. Bornecque (Paris, 1965 = 1928); *Tristes, Epistulae ex Ponto* e *Ibis,* ed. S. G. Owen (Oxford, 1978 = 1915); *Fasti,* ed. J. G. Frazer (Hildesheim-New York, 1973 = 1929); y *Amores, Ars amatoria* y *Remedia amoris,* ed. E. J. Kenney (Oxford, 1977 = 1961).

La expresión "matris . . . alvo" aparece en la misma posición dos veces en Ovidio de forma que la sílaba "-tris" constituye la 4ª arsis del hexámetro y "aluo" ocupa la posición final del verso: "spesque hominum primae **matris** habitauimus **aluo**:" (*met.* 15, 217) y "Qui simul impura **matris** prolapsus *ab* **aluo**" (*Ib.* 219). No obstante, el sintagma "in aluo" aparece con frecuencia en posición final de pentámetro en Ovidio (*am.* 2, 14, 17; *epist.* 6, 61; *met.* 1, 420; 7, 125; y 14, 176), y en dos de estos casos, junto a la palabra "matris" ("uiuaci nutrita solo ceu **matris in aluo**", *met.* 1, 420) o su adjetivo derivado "materna" ("utque hominis speciem *materna* sumit **in aluo**", *met.* 7, 125). También el sintagma "rude semen" lo encontramos en una ocasión en las *Tristes* de Ovidio en el mismo caso y en una posición similar a la que ocupa en Marullo, con la diferencia de que en aquél el verso es un pentámetro: "misit in ignotam qui **rude semen** humum;" (*trist.* 3, 8, 2). Con respecto al verso 66 de Marullo, es evidente su parentesco con un pentámetro de las *Tristes* de Ovidio ("belua, **serui-tium** tempore **uicta subit**.", *trist.* 4, 6, 8) y con otro de las *Heroidas* en el que se recoge la idea de la patria vencida ("**cum**que mea **patria** laus tua **uicta** *iacet*?", *epist.* 3, 124). Pero además el comienzo del verso "cum graue/is . . ." también aparece un par de veces en Ovidio, una de ellas en las *Tristes* (*met.* 7, 355 y *trist.* 3, 4, 12).

En el dístico siguiente Marullo se refiere a su padre, que, desprovisto de las posesiones familiares, ha de buscar su hogar en Italia:

> Ipse **pater**, Dymae **regnis eiectus** avitis,
> cogitur Iliadae quaerere texta Remi: (*ep.* II, 32, 67–68)

La idea del hexámetro está expresada por Ovidio, aunque de forma distinta, en un dístico de la *Heroida* 14: "bella **pater** patruusque gerunt; **regno**que domoque / pellimur; **eiectos** ultimus orbis habet." (*epist.* 14, 111–112).

Los versos 69 y 70 presentan finales repetidos también en Ovidio:

> hic, ubi Pierio quamvis *nutritus* **in antro**,
> mille tuli raram damna **habitura fidem**. (*ep.* II, 32, 69–70)

"In antro" aparece varias veces en Ovidio como final de hexámetro (*rem.* 789; *met.* 11, 251; *Pont.* 2, 2, 113; e *Ib.* 487, caso éste en el que va precedido del participio en nominativo singular masculino "mactatus"); y la expresión "habitura fidem" cierra dos pentámetros en Ovidio, uno de ellos perteneciente a las *Tristes* (*epist.* 16, 60 y *trist.* 1, 5, 50). En otros tres casos encontramos como final de pentámetro la misma expresión, aunque con otras formas del verbo "habeo": "habere fidem" (*fast.* 4, 58 y *trist.* 3, 10, 36) y "habenda fides", en donde también cambia el caso de "fidem" (*trist.* 1, 8, 8).

En los dos dísticos que siguen, Marullo, con una bella imagen que simboliza su paso a la pubertad, se adentra en la etapa de su vida en la que sirvió como mercenario en las orillas del Mar Negro, cerca de donde Ovidio vivió y murió exiliado:

> Iamque nigrescebant **prima lanugine malae**
> iunctaque erat lustris altera bruma tribus,
> cum fato rapiente vagus Scythiamque per altam
> auferor et ge**lidi** per **loca** vas**ta Getae**. (*ep.* II, 32, 71–74)

El grupo final del verso 71 "lanugine malae" se repite en la misma posición en las *Metamorfosis* ovidianas, con la diferencia de que aparece la forma "malas" en vez de "malae" (*met.* 9, 398; 13, 754; y 12, 291). En el último de los casos citados aparece también el adjetivo "prima" concertando con "lanugine": "e quibus ut **prima** tectus **lanugine malas**". El pentámetro 74 tiene reminiscencias de dos pentámetros de Ovidio, uno de ellos perteneciente a las *Tristes* y otro a las *Pónticas*. En ambos la palabra final es "Getae", como en el caso de Marullo. En el primero de ellos las palabras que preceden a "Getae" tienen los mismos finales que las del verso de Marullo: "et rident sto**lidi** verb**a** Latin**a Getae**;" (*trist.* 5, 10, 38). En el segundo caso encontramos la palabra "loca" en la misma posición en que aparece en el verso de Marullo: "quaerere finitimo vix **loca** nota **Getae**" (*Pont.* 1, 2, 76).

En los versos siguientes Marullo interrumpe la relación de los desgraciados avatares de su vida para lamentarse de todo ello con una interrogación retórica:

> Quid referam interea pelagique viaeque labores
> > et *totiens* **strictas in mea fata manus**
> maternosque rogos miserandaque funera fratris,
> > funera non illo tempore agenda mihi?
> Omnia quae tulimus constanti corde, nec inter
> > tot mala mens animis concidit icta suis. (*ep.* II, 32, 75–80)

En el verso 76 encontramos uno de los ecos ovidianos más claros. Ovidio repite prácticamente el mismo verso en dos ocasiones: "non timeo **strictas in mea fata manus**." (*am.* 1, 6, 14) y "ut taceam **strictas in mea fata manus**," (*trist.* 5, 2, 30). No es casual, desde luego, que uno de estos ejemplos corresponda a las *Tristes*. Y menos, teniendo en cuenta que, cambiando el participio y apareciendo la forma "quotiens" en lugar de "totiens" en el verso anterior y posterior, el esquema se vuelve a repetir en las *Pónticas*: "O *quotiens* . . ./ continuit *promptas* **in mea fata manus**! / O *quotiens* . . ." (*Pont.* 1, 9, 21–23).

Algunos versos más adelante el poeta alude a sus ilustres orígenes, enlazándolos con los de la propia Roma. Su ilustre estirpe lo hacen digno de ser correspondido por su amada, y defiende el hecho de haber adquirido su honor por sus propios esfuerzos, lo que considera más meritorio que haber heredado muchos bienes:

> Ipsa **caput rerum quondam pulcherrima** *Roma*
> > —**certa fides**—Graiis condita **gaudet** *avis*.
> Nec te terruerit peregrini nomen inane:
> > crede mihi, nulla est terra aliena viro;
> et quanquam mihi regna et opes Fortuna paternas
> > abstulit, est proprio sanguine partus honos.
> > > (*ep.* II, 32, 121–126)

En el verso 121 se cruzan dos calcos de *Metamorfosis*. Por una parte, recoge el sintagma "caput rerum" en el mismo lugar que el hexámetro ovidiano "iamque **caput rerum** *Romanam* intrauerat urbem:" (*met.* 15, 736), en donde la palabra "Roma" aparece sustituida por el adjetivo "Romanam" y en otra posición. En segundo lugar, el grupo "quondam pulcherrima" aparece en la misma posición que en el verso de

Metamorfosis, en el que dicho grupo va seguido además por un bisílabo final, como en Marullo: "Deianira tuas, **quondam pulcherrima** uirgo" (*met.* 9, 9). En el caso del verso 122 pasa algo parecido. Los grupos "certa fides" y "gaudet avis" corresponden a sendos versos de los *Fastos*, en los que aparecen en la misma posición: "**certa fides** facti: dictus Sceleratus ab illa" (*fast.* 6, 609) y "nec quae Pygmaeo sanguine **gaudet, avem;**" (*fast.* 6, 176). Hay otros calcos que considero de menor importancia, entre otras cosas por encontrarse en posiciones diferentes o con ligeras variantes, y en los que no me puedo detener aquí por cuestión de espacio.

La idea expresada en el verso "crede mihi, nulla est terra aliena viro;" recoge un sentimiento típicamente renacentista: el hombre es ciudadano del mundo y su patria está allí donde está su libertad, idea que defienden, entre otros, Dante y, más tarde, el propio Pontano, maestro y amigo de Marullo. Según Ghiberti[6], "sólo quien todo lo ha aprendido no es en ninguna parte un extraño; aunque se le prive de su fortuna, aunque se encuentre sin amigos, será un ciudadano en cualquier ciudad donde resida y puede aguardar sin miedo las vicisitudes del destino."

No obstante, la esperanza de recuperar su patria se mantiene viva a lo largo de casi toda su vida. El intento de conquistar Nápoles por parte del rey de Francia, Carlos VIII, le hace tomar partido por el bando güelfo en la esperanza de que, tras apoderarse de Italia, Carlos extienda sus conquistas hacia el este y recupere los territorios tomados por los turcos. Así, Marullo, siguiendo también a dos de sus más importantes protectores, Antonello Petrucci y Antonello Sanseverino, príncipe de Salerno, se enrola en el ejército francés en su campaña por arrebatar de las manos aragonesas el dominio sobre Nápoles.

Llevado por una leve esperanza, Marullo dirige a su amigo, paisano y compañero de estudios Manilio Ralo el epigrama III, 47, en el que, a pesar del final, todo el poema está teñido de un amargo pesimismo. La vida para el poeta está llena de incertidumbres; no podemos esperar nada seguro:

> Malli, nec tepidi **grata Favonii**
> spirat temperies, nec vagus Adria
> *secura patitur* **currere** *navitam*
>   pinu perpetua fide.
> Non omnis **tenui gutture** per dies
> integrat volucris carmina Daulias,
> non semper rosa, non lilia vestiunt,
>   **aut** *flos terram* hiacynthinus. (*ep.* III, 47, 1–8)

El comienzo del poema remite de forma evidente a la oda I, 4 de Horacio: "Solvitur acris hiems **grata** vice veris et **Favoni**," (v. 1)[7]. Y también el verso 8 de Marullo se apoya en el 10 de la oda horaciana I, 4: "**aut** *flore terrae* quem ferunt solu-

---

[6] Citado por Burckhardt, *La cultura del Renacimiento en Italia* (Madrid, 1990), 109.

[7] Cito el texto de Horacio por la edición de E. C. Wickham y H. W. Garrod (Oxford, 1984 = 1901).

tae;". No obstante, y a pesar del obstáculo que supone la diferencia del esquema métrico utilizado por uno y otro autor, la influencia de Ovidio en Marullo no deja de apreciarse, si bien de una forma más laxa. Así, por ejemplo, encontramos en Ovidio las expresiones "currere … patiuntur …" (*epist.* 18, 6), "… securus nauita …" (*ars*, 3, 259) o "… tenui gutture …" (*am.* 1, 13, 8).

A pesar de que el pasado de sus respectivas familias les auguraba una vida noble y tranquila en su patria, el exilio ha roto todas las expectativas:

> **Nos**, Malli, *quoque* sat, nos quoque sat diu
> insignes patria viximus et domo.
> Quid mirum, exilio dura per omnia
>   si rerum patimur vices? (*ep.* III, 47, 9–12)

El sintagma "nos quoque" se repite en Ovidio de una forma machacona a principio de verso: cinco veces en las *Tristes* (1, 1, 31; 2, 1, 539; 4, 1, 35; 4, 6, 37; y 5, 8, 19) y otras tantas en las *Pónticas* (1, 2, 143; 2, 1, 15; 2, 8, 55; 3, 1, 56; y 3, 2, 43).

La débil naturaleza humana está en manos del destino. Y el hombre no puede más que resignarse a la voluntad de los dioses. Para ilustrar esta idea el poeta recurre a los ejemplos de Creso y Príamo:

> Sic Croesum miseris fata potentia
> demersere modis, sic Priamus senex
> supplex Iliadum questibus ultimis
>   raptatum petit Hectora. (*ep.* III, 47, 13–16)

Al final, el poeta, sin aparcar del todo su escepticismo, pero poniendo su confianza en el rey Carlos, atisba una leve esperanza de recuperar su patria:

> Qui scis an melior nos manet exitus?
> Vivendus est lare quocumque libet deis.
> Quanvis, auspice ego Caesare, nec larem
>   despero patrium mihi. (*ep.* III, 47, 21–24))

Como he dicho antes, el primer verso de este poema "Malli, nec tepidi grata Favonii" recuerda al primero de la oda I, 4 de Horacio "Soluitur acris hiems grata uice ueris et Fauoni". Y es que, en realidad, muchos de los llamados epigramas por Marullo son más bien odas de clara influencia horaciana. Así, además de éste, compuesto en estrofas asclepiadeas A, tenemos el IV, 17 y el IV, 32, en estrofas alcaicas ambos; el II, 49, en dísticos de trímetro más dímetro yámbico; y sus nenias I, en dísticos de glicónico más asclepiadeo, y II, en estrofas asclepiadeas A, entre otras.

Otro poema en el que Marullo alude indirectamente a su dura condición de exiliado es el I, 22, en dísticos elegíacos, que constituye el lamento por la muerte de su hermano Janus, en el que, dicho sea de paso, se deja ver la admiración que Marullo sentía por Catulo. La inspiración catuliana se refleja además en muchos epigramas de Marullo y en el caso concreto de esta elegía el modelo es el famoso poema 101 del poeta veronés, también dedicado a la muerte de su hermano. El primer dístico ya indica el parentesco del poema de Marullo con el de Catulo:

> *Per Scythiam Bessosque feros, per tela, per hostes*
>> Rhiphaeo *venio tristis* ab usque gelu, (Marull. *ep.* I, 22, 1–2)

> Multas *per gentes* et multa *per aequora* uectus
>> *aduenio* has *miseras*, frater, ad inferias, (Catull. 101, 1–2)[8]

Y más adelante el tercer dístico de Catulo está reelaborado por Marullo en sus versos 9–10 y 13–14:

> quandoquidem *fortuna* **mihi** *tete* **abstulit** ipsum,
>> **heu** *miser* indigne **frater adempte** mihi, (Catull. 101, 5–6)

> *Te* quoque *sors* invisa **mihi**, dulcissime **frater**,
>> **Abstulit**, . . . / (. . .) /
> **Heu**, *miserande puer*, quae *te mihi* **fata tulerunt**,
>> Cui *miseram* linquis, **frater adempte**, domum?
>>> (Marull. *ep.* I, 22, 9–14)

A pesar del predominio de la influencia de Catulo en este poema, como ya he dicho, también aquí se rastrean calcos ovidianos. El primer verso está relacionado de una forma bastante clara con dos versos ovidianos, uno de los *Amores* y otro, cómo no, de las *Tristes*: "*sed* **Scythiam** Cilicas**que feros** uiridesque Britannos," (*am.* 2, 16, 39) y "Sauromatae cingunt, *fera* gens, *Bessique Getaeque*," (*trist.* 3, 10, 5). El final del verso 13 está tomado también de las *Tristes* de Ovidio: "vivat et absentem, quoniam sic **fata tulerunt**." (*trist.* 1, 3, 101). Este verso de Marullo refleja otro calco de *Tristes* más extenso pero también con más diferencias: "inter quos, memini, *dum me mea* **fata** *sinebant*," (*trist.* 5, 3, 5). Además el sintagma "frater adempte" aparece en Ovidio un par de veces en sendos pentámetros en la misma posición que en el verso 14 del constantinopolitano, precediendo a un bisílabo final: "et patria et patriae **frater adempte** tuae," (*epist.* 9, 166) y "atque ait 'invito **frater adempte**, vale!' " (*fast.* 4, 852). Marullo une, a las desgracias que le han acaecido en su vida como consecuencia de su exilio, la muerte de su hermano, a quien tiene que ir a enterrar a tierra extraña:

> Scilicet exequias tibi producturus inanes,
>> Fraternis unus ne careas lacrimis,
> Teque peregrina, frater, **tellure iacentem**
>> Et tua *sparsurus fletibus* **ossa** *meis*,
> Quandoquidem **post** *tot* **casus** *patriaeque domusque*
>> —Tanquam hoc exempto nil nocuisset adhuc—
>>> (*ep.* I, 22, 3–8)

El final del hexámetro 5 reproduce un final de hexámetro ovidiano: "inmanemque ferum multa **tellure iacentem**" (*met.* 8, 422). El pentámetro que sigue (v. 6) tampoco puede negar su parentesco con otro de los *Fastos* de Ovidio: "*spargebant lacrimis* **ossa** perusta *suis*." (*fast.* 5, 454). El verso 7 presenta un final que, en casos distintos,

---

[8] Cito el texto de Catulo por la edición de R. A. B. Mynors (Oxford, 1958).

se repite dos veces en Ovidio: "Graia iuuenca uenit, quae te *patriamque domumque*" (*epist.* 5, 117) y "deseror amissis regno *patriaque domoque*" (*epist.* 12, 161). Pero además este verso evoca también uno de las *Tristes*: "**post**que *meos* **casus** sit tibi pectus iners." (*trist.* 3, 7, 22). El verso 12 ("Iungeret aut **lacrimis** fratris et ipse *suas*.") retoma la idea expresada en dos versos de la *Heroida* 2: "oscula per longas *iungere* pressa moras / cumque *tuis lacrimis* lacrimas confundere *nostras*," (*epist.* 2, 94–95).

Es en los versos 7 (cf. supra) y 15 ("tu mea post patriam turbasti pectora solus,") en los que el poeta relaciona la desgracia de la pérdida de su hermano con la otra gran pérdida y desgracia de su vida: la de su exilio.

Pero, además de estos poemas en los que el exilio aparece como una amarga pincelada, Marullo, como he dicho antes, dedica a este tema composiciones enteras. Este es el caso de la elegía III, 37, la última a la que voy a referirme en este trabajo y que, titulada "De exilio suo", también fue incluida por el autor entre sus *Epigramas*.[9] En esta ocasión, Marullo se lamenta de haber abandonado su patria y no haber afrontado con ella su destino. El poeta comienza justificando la huida de la patria, que llevaron a cabo sus padres: el ilustre linaje de los Marullos no debía someterse a la esclavitud del invasor:

> **Quid iuvat** hostiles totiens *fugisse* catenas
>   **Atque animam** fatis eripuisse suis?
> Non ut cognati restarem sanguinis unus
>   Crudelis patriae qui superesse velim,
> *Nec quia* non animus lucis contemptor **abunde est**
>   Et velit exilium vertere posse nece,
> Sed ne progenies servire antiqua Marulli
>   Cogerer indigno *tractus* **ab hoste** puer. (*ep.* III, 37, 1–8)

El comienzo del primer hexámetro, "quid iuuat", se repite con cierta frecuencia en Ovidio como tal comienzo de hexámetro (*am.* 2, 6, 19; 2, 9a, 13; 2, 14, 1; *epist.* 4, 87; *rem.* 629; y *Pont.* 4, 16, 51). El primero de estos ejemplos, además, coincide con el verso de Marullo en que presenta un infinitivo de perfecto también en penúltima posición: "**quid iuuat**, ut datus es, nostrae *placuisse* puellae?". También el final de ese primer hexámetro es un calco de Ovidio, aunque con una pequeña variación: "scilicet adserui iam me *fugique* **catenas**," (*am.* 3, 11a, 3). El comienzo del pentámetro 2 lo encontramos en un hexámetro de *Metamorfosis*: "**atque animam** ex igni: leuitas sua praebuit alas," (*met.* 13, 606). El verso 5 recuerda a un hexámetro de *Pónticas* con el que comparte el final y cuyo comienzo tiene cierto parecido: "*Sed qui*, quam potuit, dat maxima, gratus **abunde est**," (*Pont.* 4, 8, 37). El sintagma "ab

---

[9] He de puntualizar aquí que, bajo el título de *Epigramas*, Marullo incluye poemas de muy distinto tipo, como odas o elegías, lo que se encuadra dentro del fenómeno de la mezcla de géneros tan frecuente en la literatura latina renacentista. Véase a este respecto el trabajo del profesor J. M. Maestre Maestre, "La mezcla de géneros en la literatura latina renacentista: a propósito de la *Apollinis fabula* del Brocense", en *Actas del Simposio Internacional IV Centenario de la publicación de la "Minerva" del Brocense, 1587–1987* (Cáceres-Brozas, 1987).

hoste" del verso 8 aparece con frecuencia en Ovidio en pentámetros en la misma posición, precedido de participio o adjetivo nominativo masculino singular en -us bisilábico, y seguido de palabra de estructura yámbica: "sustinet et saevo *cinctus* **ab hoste** locus." (*trist.* 5, 2, 32); "et quam sim denso *cinctus* **ab hoste** loqui." (*Pont.* 3, 9, 4); y "nempe tamen vitam *captus* **ab hoste** tulit." (*Pont.* 4, 3, 38), entre otros.[10]

La razón expuesta por el poeta en los versos iniciales para justificar la huida de la patria pierde todo su sentido, ya que luego tuvo que servir a duros tiranos en su juventud, como él mismo nos cuenta. Mejor hubiera sido, dice Marullo, compartir la esclavitud de la tierra que lo vio nacer:

> Si **procul a patria Scythico** *deprensus* **in orbe**,
>> Heu facinus, Bessi iussa superba fero
> Imperiumque ferox patior dominumque potentem,
>> *Nec* **nisi** libertas **nomen inane mea est**,
> **Utilius fuerat** duro servire tyranno
>> **Cumque mea patria** cuncta dolenda pati.
>>>>> (*ep.* III, 37, 9–14)

El final del verso 9 guarda cierto parentesco con un hexámetro de las *Tristes*, en el que el participio empleado es diferente: "quam mala, quae toto patior *iactatus* **in orbe**," (*trist.* 4, 1, 59). Pero su fuente más directa parece ser el siguiente verso de *Metamorfosis*: "quem **procul a patria** *diuerso maximus* **orbe**" (*met.* 2, 323). Además, la expresión "procul a patria" la encontramos, precedida de monosílabo inicial, en un verso de las *Tristes* (5, 3, 11) y otro de *Pónticas* (1, 3, 84). Aún se pueden citar dos versos más de *Tristes* en los que se repite una expresión muy parecida: "qui **procul** *extremo pulsus* **in orbe** latet," (*trist.* 3, 1, 50) y "atque **procul** Latio diversum *missus* **in** *orbem*" (*trist.* 4, 2, 69). Tampoco es de extrañar que el sintagma "Scythico . . . in orbe" esté tomado de *Tristes*: "ei mihi, iamne domus **Scythico** Nasonis **in orbe** est?" (*trist.* 3, 12, 51). Como vemos, es en este verso donde el porcentaje de calcos tomados de las obras ovidianas del exilio es mayor. El pentámetro 12 guarda cierta similitud con uno de *Pónticas*, al menos en lo que al comienzo y al final se refiere: "*Nam* **nisi** iusta tua est, iusta querela **mea est**." (*Pont.* 4, 3, 22). Pero todavía se parece más a otro pentámetro, aunque esta vez de las *Heroidas*: "*nil* **nisi** Leandri **nomen** in ore *meo* **est**." (*epist.* 19, 40). En cuanto al sintagma "nomen inane", aparece en tres pentámetros de Ovidio en la misma disposición y seguido de palabra de estructura yámbica (*epist.* 10, 116; *ars*, 1, 740; y *trist.* 3, 3, 50). También parecen de origen ovidiano por sus comienzos el verso 13: "**utilius fuerat** non *habuisse* nurus." (*fast.* 2, 434); y el 14: "**cumque mea patria** laus tua *uicta* iacet?" (*epist.* 3, 124).

Continúa el poeta, en los versos que siguen, lamentándose por no estar aún en su patria, ya que así, al menos, podría todavía contemplar los restos y las cenizas de los reinos familiares:

---

[10] Véanse también *ars*, 2, 712; *fast.* 3, 424; *fast.* 5, 578; e *Ib.* 330.

> Est aliquid cineres et tot monumenta suorum
>   Cernere et imperiis imperia aucta patrum
> Natalique frui, superest dum spiritus, aura,
>   Nec procul externis ludibrium esse locis:
>
> (*ep.* III, 37, 15–18)

Según Marullo, la nobleza y la honra de la estirpe se pierde cuando se vive como exiliado en tierra extraña:

> Scilicet exuitur generis decus omne domusque,
>   Cum semel ignotam presseris exul humum,
> Nec iam nobilitas nec avum generosa propago
>   Aut iuvat antiquis fulcta domus titulis.
>
> (*ep.* III, 37, 19–22)

En los versos que siguen el poeta lamenta la condición del exiliado, para quien, una vez perdidos todos sus bienes, ya no existe la hospitalidad de antaño, y afirma que hubiera preferido morir con heridas honrosas, defendiendo la libertad, antes que abandonar la patria a manos enemigas:

> At certe, patriae quondam dum regna manebant,
>   Hospitio totus, qua patet orbis, erat.
> Tunc, ah, tunc animam pueri exhalare senesque
>   Debuimus, tantis nec superesse malis;
> Tunc patrii meminisse animi et virtutis avitae
>   Inque necem pulchris vulneribus ruere,
> Nec libertatem patrio nisi Marte tueri:
>   Haec via quaerendae certa salutis erat.
> O pereat numerum primus qui fecit in armis:
>
> (*ep.* III, 37, 23–31)

Desde aquí hasta el final el poeta dirige sus ataques contra la guerra y contra el enemigo que destruyó su patria: el Turco.

He pretendido con este trabajo acercarme a los *Epigramas* de Marullo que tratan el tema del exilio estudiando la presencia en ellos de la obra de Ovidio y en qué porcentaje están presentes las obras del venusino que abordan este mismo tema: las *Tristes* y las *Pónticas*. En este sentido, como ya hemos visto, el peso de estas obras en Marullo es considerable, pero no lo es menos el influjo de otras obras ovidianas como las *Metamorfosis*, las *Heroidas* o los *Fastos*. Por otra parte, he querido centrarme en los *Epigramas*, dejando a un lado sus *Himnos* y *Nenias*, porque a los primeros les han dedicado más atención los estudiosos y las segundas constituyen un bloque de menor entidad dentro de la obra marulliana.

El tema del exilio en la poesía de Marullo nos permite descubrir a un personaje que aúna en su figura algunos de los arquetipos más significativos del renacimiento y que expresa sus sentimientos de una forma intensa y muy personal, sin perder de vista modelos clásicos como Ovidio, Catulo y Horacio.

Universidad de Cádiz

Un'epistola "de amore" di Giovanni Pontano

GIOVANNI PIRRELLI

Nel 1907, in un primo tentativo di ricostruire e pubblicare l'epistolario di Giovanni Pontano, Erasmo Percopo annunciava la scoperta di una sua lettera inedita, indirizzata a Guiniforte Barzizza[1]. L'epistola non tardò ad essere edita da Pirri nel 1912 sulla base dell'unico testimone in nostro possesso, conservato nella Biblioteca Guarneriana di San Daniele del Friuli all'interno di un codice miscellaneo con la segnatura 44, vergato da più mani. Il curatore sottolineò allora l'importanza di questo testo quale documento precoce della cultura di Pontano "imbevuta delle idee morali propalate dal Valla e dal Panormita"[2].

La lettera nasceva come provocatoria risposta ad una missiva, datata al marzo 1439, che Guiniforte Barzizza aveva inviato ad un gentiluomo spagnolo, Francesco Gilabert Centelles, al servizio degli Aragonesi[3]. La questione affrontata da Barzizza, su richiesta del sunnominato condottiero, concerneva l'amore, e Pontano, animato dall'esigenza di ottenere alcuni chiarimenti sul tema, a suo dire liquidato in maniera oscura e sbrigativa dal proprio interlocutore, ne rovesciava ironicamente le affermazioni.

Dalla lontana attribuzione di Percopo l'epistola è concordemente ritenuta opera del celebre Giovanni Gioviano Pontano, tant'è che nel moderno catalogo della Guarneriana questa paternità viene nuovamente ribadita[4]. Paternità, però, che sulla base di nuovi elementi di conoscenza, appare un po' improbabile, considerato che in tempi

---

[1] E. Percopo, *Lettere di Giovanni Pontano a principi ed amici* (Napoli, 1907), 14–15.

[2] L'epistola si legge ai fols. 42r–48v del ms. Guarner. 44 della Biblioteca di San Daniele del Friuli; cf. P. Pirri, "Le notizie e gli scritti di Tommaso Pontano e di Gioviano Pontano giovane," *Bollettino della Regia Deputazione di Storia Patria per l'Umbria* 18 (1912): 420–423, 463–482. Alle pagine di questa edizione, sebbene in alcuni passi scorretta, si rinvierà d'ora in avanti.

[3] La lettera di Barzizza è pubblicata in *Guiniforti Barzizii orationes et epistolae*, ed. J. A. Furiettus (Romae, 1723), 122–131. Per il profilo biografico di Guiniforte Barzizza e le circostanze in cui fu composta l'opera rinvio al contributo di S. Valerio, "Un epistola 'de amore' di Guiniforte Barzizza", nel presente volume.

[4] L. Casarsa, M. D'Angelo, e C. Scalon, *La Libreria di Guarnerio d'Artegna* (Udine, 1991), 244–249.

recenti Salvatore Monti ed in seguito Liliana Monti Sabia hanno stabilito inequivoca-
bilmente nel 1429 l'anno di nascita di Pontano[5]. Sebbene manchino spie crono-
logiche certe che consentano la datazione della lettera, appare verosimile credere che
sia seguita a ridosso di quella di Barzizza. Ad avvalorare questa ipotesi contribuisce
l'allusione all'impresa di Gerba del 1432, avvenuta a detta di Pontano "paucis ante
annis". Ed in generale il tono della lettera suggerisce l'impressione che le critiche
mosse a Barzizza siano seguite quasi a caldo[6]. Alla luce di queste considerazioni
appare poco plausibile che un Pontano, pressoché decenne nel 1439, anno in cui Barzizza scriveva a Centelles, potesse cimentarsi così precocemente in una *querelle* di tale
rilievo. Questi argomenti mettono in discussione quanto affermato da Percopo e da
Pirri, ai quali sembrava plausibile quell'attribuzione, perché credevano Pontano nato
nel 1426.

Se l'attribuzione a Giovanni Gioviano Pontano è poco credibile, chi è l'autore
dell'epistola? L'intestazione parla chiaro: "Iohannes Pontanus spectabili et famoso
artium ac iuriscivilis doctori domino Giniforto Barzizio salutem". In verità un altro
Giovanni Pontano, che i due studiosi d'inizio secolo non conoscevano, è vissuto nella
prima metà del Quattrocento, di cui sappiamo molto poco. Natio di Bergamo, è noto
soltanto come autore di un orazione funebre per la morte del condottiero Erasmo da
Narni detto il Gattamelata[7]. Il suo nome ricorre in un opera del conterraneo Giovanni Michele Alberto Carrara[8], mentre Giordano Orsini, studente dell'ateneo pado-
vano, ne scrisse l'orazione funebre, da cui apprendiamo che fu allievo di Guarino
Veronese; pronunciò a Padova nel 1443 l'orazione in morte del Gattamelata; attese a
studi giuridici e morì giovanissimo nel 1446[9]. Sicuramente non è molto e soprattutto

---

[5] Per un'analitica discussione sugli estremi di nascita e di morte di Giovanni Pontano e relativa
bibliografia si rinvia a M. de Nichilo, *I "Viri illustres" del cod. Vat. Lat. 3920* (Roma, 1997), 147–
184.

[6] Pirri aveva individuato altri due elementi interni alla lettera sulla base dei quali datarla: il
titolo affibbiato ad Alfonso "Aragonum rex", che fa riferimento ad un periodo precedente all'incoronazione dello stesso a re di Napoli, avvenuta nel 1443, ed inoltre l'intestazione che recita
"Iohannes Pontanus" e non ancora "Iovianus Pontanus" ossia il nome accademico: Pirri, "Le notizie e gli scritti di Tommaso Pontano e di Gioviano Pontano giovane," 421, argomenti che appaiono subito inconsistenti.

[7] L'*Oratio Joannis Pontani Bergomatis acta in funere Magistri Gatemelatae in Civitate Patavina* si può
leggere in S. Eroli, *Erasmo Gattamelata da Narni, suoi monumenti e sua famiglia* (Roma, 1876), 354–
365, si veda anche E. Billanovich–M. Billanovich, "Epitafi ed elogi per il Gattamelata," *Italia
Medioevale e Umanistica* 37 (1994): 223–232. Del resto Percopo era stato tratto in inganno dal-
l'omonimia e aveva attribuito l'orazione per il Gattamelata al più famoso Pontano senza rendersi
conto delle incongruenze piuttosto palesi presenti nella sua attribuzione: E. Percopo, *Vita di Giovanni Pontano* (Napoli, 1938), 291–293.

[8] Carrara dedicando il *De fato et fortuna* a Francesco Pontano ne ricorda il fratello Giovanni,
morto prematuramente: "Praefulgidum fuit Johannis ingenium ut candidissima oratio, quam in
Gattomollata imperatoris funere summa cum gloria peroravit, ostendit"; cf. G. M. A. Carrara, "De
fato et fortuna", in *Opere scelte*, G. Giraldi, ed. (Novara, 1967), 2: 79.

[9] *Jordani de Orsinis oratio in funere ornatissimi iuvenis Iohannis Pontani Bergomensis*, fols. 37r–38v
del manoscritto CLIII (141) della Biblioteca Capitolare di Verona.

nessuno lo ricorda come l'autore dell'epistola "de amore" in questione, ma l'ambiente, la sua formazione culturale e l'età corrispondono a quelle di Guiniforte.

Indipendentemente, comunque, dai problemi di paternità, il testo ha un autonomo valore per l'indubbia rilevanza culturale dei temi in esso trattati. Le due lettere di Barzizza e di Pontano tornano a dibattere questioni da secoli oggetto di un continuo riesame nel mondo occidentale. In particolare durante l'autunno del Medioevo, in concomitanza con la grande stagione\della lirica d'amore, gli argomenti in esse affrontati divennero materia di un'attenta e costante meditazione. E difatti da una parte vengono analizzati i criteri che presiedono alla scelta dell'amata e della moglie, due figure che non sempre coincidono, come non coincidono amore e matrimonio, dall'altra ci si interroga sulla natura di Amore. Inoltre, la riscoperta dei classici dotò l'incipiente Umanesimo di un repertorio di *auctores* che ampliarono e alimentarono il dibattito, innescando sovente aspri confronti quale quello che vede per protagonisti i due umanisti settentrionali[10].

Barzizza, sollecitato dall'amico Centelles ad esprimere il suo parere sulla passione d'amore quando a soggiacervi è un giovane di animo gentile, si attesta su una posizione di difesa del matrimonio. A suo vedere, nobiltà ed amore extraconiugale mal si conciliano, anzi sono in patente contraddizione. Quand'anche si seguano criteri confacenti ad uno spirito generoso nella scelta dell'amata, di fatto nessuna donna, quale che sia la sua condizione, può essere l'eletta. Anche una scelta esclusiva, dettata dalla ragione, e che individua virtù e nobiltà nella donna designata, non preserva il magnanimo da una condotta indegna del proprio *status* e di quello dell'amata. La contraddizione appare a Barzizza insanabile, poiché il soddisfacimento della passione implicitamente comporta una negazione della virtù, quindi dell'essenza stessa dell'essere nobile. Solo riconducendo la *libido* in una sfera matrimoniale è possibile conciliare amore e rettitudine: l'invito a rispettare il patto coniugale, che Centelles aveva contratto, è esplicito. Ma dal momento che le richieste dell'amico incalzavano Barzizza a pronunciarsi proprio sull'amore extraconiugale, il letterato sembra voler fare delle concessioni al cavaliere e con l'ausilio di Petrarca mostra gli straordinari benefici che

---

[10] Sulla trattatistica *de amore* e sul matrimonio tra età medievale ed umanistica, sono innumerevoli gli studi; mi limiterò ad indicare soltanto i contributi più recenti: D. de Rougemont, *L'amore e l'Occidente* (Milano, 1977); *Il matrimonio nella società altomedievale*, Atti della XXIV Settimana di Studio del Centro Italiano di Studi sull'Alto Medioevo (Spoleto 22–28 aprile 1976), (Spoleto, 1977); G. Duby, *Matrimonio medievale* (Milano, 1981); M. L. Lenzi, *Donne e Madonne, l'educazione femminile nel primo Rinascimento italiano* (Torino, 1982); D. Herlihy, *La famiglia nel medioevo* (Roma-Bari, 1987); O. Pugliese, "La nouvelle conception de l'amour", in *L'époque de la Renaissance 1400–1600* (Budapest, 1988), 1: 215–225; F. Furlan, "Pour une histoire de la famille et de l'amour à l'époque de l'Humanisme," *Revue des études italiennes* 36 (1990): 89–104; Furlan, "L'idea della donna e dell'amore nella cultura tardomedievale e in L. B. Alberti", *Intersezioni* 10 (1990): 211–238; M. Savini, "Amor sacro e amor profano nella trattatistica quattro-cinquecentesca," *Studi latini e italiani* 4 (1990): 119–137; F. Bruni, "Dal 'De vetula' al 'Corbaccio': l'idea d'amore e i due tempi dell'intellettuale", in *Testi e chierici del Medioevo* (Genova, 1991), 239–288; J. Leclercq, *La figura della donna nel Medioevo* (Milano, 1994); *Storia delle donne in Occidente: Il Medioevo*, ed. Ch. Klapisch-Zuber (Roma-Bari, 1994²); e *Storia del matrimonio*, ed. M. De Giorgio, Ch. Klapisch-Zuber (Roma-Bari, 1996), a cui si rinvia per una bibliografia esaustiva.

quel tipo di amore largisce al nobile assetato di fama e di gloria. Tuttavia la strada che pel tramite di Amore conduce alla virtù è lastricata di ostacoli insormontabili e, come un secondo esempio tratto dai *Trionfi* dimostra, ecco spalancarsi alla vista degli innamorati l'abisso in cui lo spirito è precipitato dall'insana passione[11]. E a Barzizza non resta che opporre un fermo diniego alla richiesta dell'amico, individuando nell'amore per la virtù il mezzo per raggiungere quei benefici che la passione concede a caro prezzo.

È evidente che nel discorso di Barzizza la condanna del modello cortese di amore, extraconiugale ed adulterino per statuto, vero asse portante dell'*ethos* cavalleresco, proceda conformemente ad una implicita contrapposizione tra il Boccaccio del *Filocolo*, in cui confluiva quella tradizione che fa riferimento al *De amore* di Andrea Cappellano, e il Petrarca dei *Trionfi*, dove il *Filocolo*, rappresenta, nel celebre capitolo dedicato alle questioni d'amore[12], la riproposizione di quel modello, i *Trionfi*, invece, la crisi, la messa in discussione più profonda e lacerante dello stesso[13]. La difesa del matrimonio appare come l'unica via di uscita dalla situazione di *impasse*, e quella più umanisticamente allineata al modello proposto da Francesco Barbaro, dove il *coniugium* è elemento regolatore dello Stato, cemento con il quale assicurare la pacifica convivenza, mentre l'adulterio diviene il fomite di contrasti e di disordini ed è quindi la radice del male, dell'anarchia sociale[14].

Veniamo dunque al Pontano. Questi demolisce sistematicamente le tesi esposte dall'avversario, a cominciare dalla prima che vuole l'uomo nobile guidato nella scelta dell'amata dallo *iudicium rationis*. Se il fine a cui perviene l'atto amoroso è naturale, così come afferma Barzizza, l'istinto prevale sulla ragione e Cupido sottrae all'individuo qualsiasi parte nella scelta. Barzizza è reo di voler costruire il rapporto uomo-donna sul modello dell'amicizia, in cui rettitudine e lealtà hanno un ruolo determinante e sono rafforzati dalla ragione. Neanche la nobiltà di nascita è un metro di giudizio valido e non solo sulla scorta degli stoici che ripongono la nobiltà là dove risiede la virtù, ma perché una relazione amorosa con una persona di nobili origini e perciò illustre, diviene immediatamente di pubblico dominio, con il disastroso effetto che ogni azione scandalosa acquista risonanza immediata, mentre quelle conformi alla morale vengono misconosciute.

Il secondo punto su cui Barzizza viene attaccato è quello dell'esclusività dell'amore. Sostiene Pontano che "avara" è l'idea che vuole limitare i sentimenti così come le facoltà intellettuali degli uomini ed indirizzarli verso un unico interesse, perché l'animo può rivolgere gli affetti verso differenti direzioni. Anzi "funesta" e di conseguenza "pericolosa", poiché spesso cagione di disordine, è la pretesa di volere per se soltanto una persona. Ed inoltre l'esclusività in amore è segno di "viltà", perché si ha paura

---

[11] Cf. per un esame delle fonti dei due testi il contributo di D. Canfora, "Amore e matrimonio nel primo Quattrocento latino: Le epistole di Guiniforte Barzizza e di Giovanni Pontano," nel presente volume.

[12] Cf. G. Boccaccio, *Filocolo*, 4.

[13] Cf. F. Petrarca, *Trionfi*, 1, 3, 151–190 e 1, 4, 136–153.

[14] Cf. F. Barbaro, "De re uxoria", in *Prosatori latini del Quattrocento* (Milano-Napoli, 1952), 104–137.

del rivale, che un uomo magnanimo e forte giammai deve temere. Giustificato appare l'adulterio commesso da una moglie a cui è imposto un matrimonio contro i propri voleri, soprattutto se costretta a tollerare un marito odioso o poco solerte. Ne consegue che l'amore per le *nuptae* non sarà illecito ed ogni tentativo di sorvegliare una donna, sposata o nubile che sia, destinato a fallire. Se si dà il caso di una lunga assenza del marito o dell'amante, una donna potrà sfuggire ad ogni controllo e tradire senza difficoltà il proprio uomo lontano. In questo quadro Pontano afferma con sconcertante cinismo che i figli nati da una relazione adulterina sono preferibili ai legittimi. Barzizza a riguardo aveva disapprovato l'incresciosa situazione di chi non può che coprirsi di infamia riconoscendo i figli naturali oppure ignorandoli, per Pontano non solo un figlio illegittimo non compromette il legame con l'amata, ma alleggerisce il genitore di ogni responsabilità nei confronti della sua condotta futura, e della doverosa protezione paterna. Ugualmente leciti sono i rapporti sia con le vergini che con le vedove. Conquistare le prime sarà una prova di ardimento, degna di un cavaliere come Centelles, mentre le seconde, più di qualsiasi altra donna, riserveranno a chi le possiede abbracci voluttuosi e gioie seducenti.

A questo punto, dopo aver ulteriormente argomentato l'insostenibile accortezza di qualsiasi scelta matrimoniale, la lettera di Pontano s'interrompe bruscamente privandoci del piacere leggero delle sue provocazioni. Il suo discorso non tiene volutamente conto dell'intima coerenza del ragionamento di Barzizza, mette in secondo piano la nobiltà d'animo dell'amante che ne è il pre-requisito irrinunciabile e così facendo può procedere facilmente e con assoluta libertà a demolire tutta la logica che presiede all'ordinamento della *res amatoria* ed *uxoria* stabilita dall'antagonista. Più complesso è però individuarne la reale posizione, perché, oltre al fatto che poco si sa di certo sull'identità e sulla fisionomia culturale dell'autore la lettera è senza conclusione, laddove presumibilmente avremmo trovato la proposta e il modello alternativi a quelli del suo antagonista.

Non resta, quindi, che riflettere sui pochi elementi in nostro possesso, così come emergono dal testo ed in particolare dall'esordio, dove l'autore si autodefinisce rispetto alla materia e all'interlocutore. Scrive infatti Pontano:

Sed, etsi nihil ad me hec questio (*scil.* de amore) pertinet, qui quidem, si quod facio, virtute magis quam natura facerem, essem plane alter Hipolitus aut Bellerofon aut denique Israeliticus ille Ioseph, qui Egiptie concubitum fugiens palium in manu mulieris dereliquit: itaque, quamquam nulle sunt mee in hac causa partes, attamen, quoniam es iudex constitutus, petam a te ut nonulla, que me in hac re ancipitem tenent, prudenter, ut assoles, et subtiliter explices. (463–464).

L'affermazione è chiara: ad un comportamento guidato dalla natura, quindi dall'istinto sessuale, è preferita una condotta guidata dalla virtù ovvero dalla castità, interpretazione autorizzata dalla dichiarazione che immediatamente segue, dove Pontano sostiene di conformare il proprio comportamento a tre campioni di castità maschile: Ippolito, Bellerofonte, e Giuseppe l'Ebreo. In questo modo Pontano si tira fuori dall'azione per concedersi unicamente alla riflessione; a differenza di Centelles, quindi, la sua è solo una richiesta di chiarimento intellettuale: Barzizza non deve guidarlo nell'agire amoroso, ma ingaggiare con lui una disputa, dove è subito evidente che Pontano procederà ad un rovesciamento ironico e beffardo delle posizioni assunte dall'avversario, in nome non più dei propri sinceri convincimenti, ma del gusto per la polemica intellettuale e per la finzione retorica. L'esigenza speculativa che domina in queste righe sposta in un ambito tutto retorico la questione, facendo slittare l'impostazione confidenziale e l'intenzione pedagogica insite nella lettera di Barzizza sul piano ben più astratto della *quaestio* accademica. In questo senso appare persino irrilevante sapere se tra le affermazioni di Pontano e le vicende della sua biografia vi siano delle puntuali rispondenze, mentre in primo piano passa la questione di quali siano i modelli culturali riproposti e secondo quale ottica vengano rilanciati. Ecco quindi che la libertà e licenziosità degli argomenti, con cui tutta la materia amorosa è trattata in seguito, diviene una pura ipotesi confinata nello spazio della speculazione astratta senza poggiare sul terreno dell'azione, che di fatto l'intellettuale scarta a priori. L'esperienza personale non interviene od interferisce affatto nella riflessione, tutta affidata a reminiscenze letterarie, classiche e bibliche. Le citazioni hanno un chiaro intento provocatorio: ribaltare le convenzioni su cui per secoli il cristianesimo aveva disciplinato l'etica del matrimonio monogamico, al fine di frenare e confinare la *libido* in una sfera unicamente riproduttiva.

La castità del sapiente immune dalle passioni, il modello che in queste prime righe traspare, non è certo una novità, ma è il frutto dell'elaborazione culturale che soprattutto in ambito monastico aveva considerato il matrimonio un male minore rispetto alla fornicazione, ma che non per questo smetteva di essere un male. A questo punto doveva costituire quasi un passaggio obbligato per Pontano ricollegarsi alla feroce presa di posizione misogamica dell'*Adversus Jovinianum* di Girolamo. Assume quindi un valore programmatico l'apertura dell'epistola con l'esempio biblico di Giuseppe che resiste alle *avances* della moglie del faraone, un episodio con il quale il Santo aveva stigmatizzato il comportamento diabolico della donna e le tentazioni della carne[15]. Ma la scelta di castità di Pontano ha smarrito tutti i significati religiosi che questa tradizione aveva connesso alla prassi ascetica. Non è certo un dono divino, bensì una posizione di comodo dalla quale attaccare gli argomenti filo-matrimoniali dell'avversario, al punto da ribaltarne completamente il ragionamento. Non essere parte in causa nella *res amatoria* consente all'autore di condurre la sua polemica con animo scevro da passioni e quindi di ritagliarsi un margine di giudizio superiore, lucido e disincantato, rispetto a chi invece era invischiato nei legami sentimentali e matrimoniali. Una scelta quindi tutta personale e laica, che non si costituisce come *remedium amoris* al fine di distogliere l'animo degli innamorati dai pericoli del connubio, ma semplicemente di sfatare i luoghi comuni sulla monogamicità del vincolo matrimoniale.

Difatti l'espressione *binarius numerus infelix* che rielabora l'affermazione di Girolamo *non est bonus duplex numerus*, utilizzando gli stessi argomenti biblici portati come prova dal Santo, conferma la ripresa canonica dell'*Adversus Jovinianum* in chiave anti-matri-

---

[15] Girolamo, "Adversus Jovinianum", in *Opera omnia*, *P.L.* [= *Patrologia Latina*], 33, 229: "Unde et noster Joseph, quia tangere eum volebat Aegyptia, fugit ex manibus ejus, et quasi ad morsum rabidissimae canis, ne paulatim virus serperet, pallium quod tetigerat, abjecit."

moniale[16]. E Girolamo, che riporta gli insegnamenti di Teofrasto e Seneca—ma non meno rilevanti sono i precetti di Giovenale ed Ovidio—traspare ancora quando la fedeltà di coppia è messa in discussione sulla base di tesi misogine. L'ingenuo marito è avvertito: la paura da lui suscitata non è un antidoto all'infedeltà della moglie, anzi è un incitamento all'inganno con il quale le donne si prendono gioco dei mariti creduloni. "Meo iudicio sunt et asine mulieres" (p. 464), così Pontano risponde scherzando a Barzizza che aveva distinto l'amore per le donne da quello asinino, intendendo con questo la lussuria e l'istinto bestiale. Un chiaro indizio, poi, della misoginia che attraversa queste pagine emerge quando l'autore accosta il matrimonio all'acquisto di beni commerciali, con la differenza che se questi possono essere alienati, quando ne rileviamo i difetti, le mogli no, riprendendo quasi alla lettera il Seneca tradito da Girolamo[17]. Ogni cautela e lungimiranza nella scelta è destinata a fallire e non mette al riparo da eventuali brutte sorprese. Insomma, conclude Pontano, la donna veramente virtuosa è una *rara avis* (p. 478), ricalcando un *topos* variamente esemplato da Persio, Giovenale, e Seneca[18].

Comunque è evidente che una percezione diversa della donna distanzi enormemente questo testo da quelli che sono i modelli medievali da cui discende. La misoginia di Pontano è un po' come la sua professione di castità iniziale, cioè un abito intellettuale, letterario, tutto proteso a rovesciare le convenzioni di Barzizza. Tant'è

---

[16] Girolamo, "Adversus Jovinianum", 246–247: "Sed et hoc intuendum duntaxat juxta Hebraicam veritatem, quod cum Scriptura in primo, et tertio, et quarto, et quinto, et sexto die expletis operibus singulorum dixerit: *Et vidit Deus quia bonum est*, in secundo die hoc omnino subtraxit; nobis intellegentiam derelinquens non esse bonum duplicem numerum, quia ab unione dividit, et praefigurat foedera nuptiarum. Unde in arca Noe omnia animalia, quaecumque bina ingrediuntur, immunda sunt. Impar numerus est mundus. Quanquam in duplici numero ostendatur et aliud sacramentum, quod ne in bestiis quidem et in immundis avibus digamia comprobata sit. Bina enim ingrediuntur immunda; et septena quae munda sunt, ut haberet Noe, post diluvium, quod de impari numero statim Deo posset offerre." Pontano afferma alle pp. 469–470: "[Binarius numerus infelix] Nec iniuria. Si enim amor iste inter duos tantum concluditur neque ultra progredi potest, duplicem numerum necessario conficit: is autem semper infelix est. Ideoque cum Deus universam machinam et universa quae in ea sunt procrearet, relinquorum quidem dierum opera dicitur bona, in secundo autem die, quoniam binarium efficitur, nusquam additum est *Vidit Deus quod esset bonum*; nec non in archam Noe animalia omnia immunda bina, munda vero septena mitti iubentur. Minime igitur mirum, si infelix numerus infelices abes effectus."

[17] Girolamo, "Adversus Jovinianum", 289: "Adde quod nulla est uxoris electio, sed qualiscumque obvenerit, habenda. Si iracunda, si fatua, si deformis, si superba, si foetida, quodcunque vitii est post nuptiae discimus. Equus, asinus, bos, canis, et vilissima mancipia, vestes quoque, et lebetes, sedile ligneum, calix, et urceolus fictilis probantur prius, et sic emuntur: sola uxor non ostenditur, ne ante displiceat quam ducatur." Cf. anche Seneca, *Contro il matrimonio: ovvero perché all'uomo saggio non convenga prender moglie*, M. Lentano, ed. (Bari, 1997). Così Pontano a p. 478: "In quo sane dura conditio nostra est, cum equos, vasa, vestes, aurum atque argentum, reliqua denique omnia probemus prius et sic emamus, ea demum empta, si displicuerunt, aut alienari aut abici possunt, coniunx et ignota suscipitur et suscepta, seu temulenta seu iracunda seu stulta sive quovis alio vitio laborans, tenenda est cum eaque omnis nostra etas et vita ducenda. Si sunt difficiles, si insane, si prodige, si flagitiose, invitis tamen nobis ferende sunt."

[18] Cf. Seneca, *Contro il matrimonio*, 31, 73.

che i *topoi* misogini desunti da Girolamo sono depurati delle loro implicazioni religiose, hanno poco a che fare con una effettiva condanna della donna come *imago diabolis*, bensì sono riproposti in positivo, laicamente, oggetto più di scherzo e di arguzia, che fonte di insegnamento morale[19]. Del resto poi là dove Barzizza aveva giudicato esecrabili i comportamenti fedifraghi delle adultere, Pontano si lancia in una loro difesa in nome dell'utilità per sé e per l'amante di una condotta che assicuri la felicità di entrambi, piuttosto che in ossequio alle restrizioni di una morale astratta.

L'idolo polemico contro cui Pontano scaglia i suoi strali è rappresentato piuttosto dalla possibilità di discernimento e di guida della ragione. La tradizione, a riguardo, attribuiva questa capacità all'uomo, reale attore della scelta del coniuge, dato che la donna è relegata dall'istintualità della sua natura ad un ruolo di sottomissione. Ma gli esempi maschili storici e leggendari, che hanno abdicato alle proprie facoltà razionali per essere travolti dalla passione, una casistica nutrita e dilatata quasi oltremisura rispetto alle parti strettamente concettuali, costituiscono per Pontano la prova inconfutabile dell'impossibilità di una scelta. Solo Cupido *ioculator amoris* e *cecus et puer deus* presiede alla scelta (p. 466), secondo una iconografia cara anche all'Alberti e di derivazione properziana[20], e se Eros è un fanciullo cieco e burlone, uomini e donne s'incontreranno per un insondabile gioco di coincidenze sospinti unicamente dal desiderio. Non emerge comunque in Pontano una condanna *tout court* dell'amore e della passione, come nella tradizione a cui si è accennato, ma delle restrizioni che una logica monogamica imponeva al libero dispiegarsi della passione, nonostante l'impiego di quei temi quali la castità del sapiente e l'avversione per la donna che la cultura tardo-antica e medievale aveva usato per riprovare l'esperienza amorosa.

A ben vedere non è possibile dare un'interpretazione complessiva di un testo che si interrompe all'incirca a metà, considerando che rimangono fuori dalla serrata critica di Pontano ancora molte delle asserzioni di Barzizza, mentre la porzione superstite testimonia soltanto la *pars destruens* del discorso e non prospetta un modello alternativo alla logica matrimoniale dell'avversario. Sembra in ogni caso fuori discussione una riproposizione del modello cortese, che avrebbe completato il ribaltamento del punto di vista di Barzizza, e non solo per l'assenza di fonti romanze, ma per il fatto che nella galleria di personaggi mossi da Eros, che Pontano esempla, manca completamente qualsiasi anelito al perfezionamento morale ed interiore e tutta quella complessa psicologia delle cause e degli effetti di Amore peculiare al modello cavalleresco.

Università di Bari

---

[19] Il processo che porta gli umanisti ad affrancare la misoginia da ogni valenza ascetica e a trasformare la stessa in un motivo squisitamente letterario è ampiamente documentato da Furlan nel saggio citato, "L'idea della donna e dell'amore nella cultura tardomedievale e in L. B. Alberti", 218–222.

[20] Cf. R. Rinaldi, "Melancholia albertiana: dalla *Deifira* al *Naufragus*," *Lettere italiane* 37 (1985): 1: 48–49.

Andrea Guarna: Simia

FIDEL RÄDLE

Der Dialog *Simia*[1] ist das zweite und zugleich letzte erhaltene literarische Werk des italienischen Humanisten Andrea Guarna. Über den Autor haben wir nur ganz wenige biographische Daten[2]: er entstammt einer alten Salernitaner Familie, die zur Belohnung für politische Dienste unter Francesco Sforza in das Patriziat von Cremona aufgenommen wurde. Andrea studierte in Bologna, das er mehrfach, auch im vorliegenden Dialog, mit spürbarer Sympathie erwähnt, und er hatte Beziehungen zu Rom. Nach seiner Priesterweihe veröffentlichte er im Jahre 1511 in Cremona sein später in ganz Europa bekannt gewordenes und vielfach nachgeahmtes *Bellum Grammaticale.*[3] Diese fiktive Kriegschronik schildert den bewaffneten Kampf zwischen dem *Nomen* und dem *Verbum* um die Vorherrschaft im Reich der Grammatik und darf getrost als das geglückteste Exempel lateinischen Philologenhumors im Humanismus bezeichnet werden. Didaktischer Zweck des *Bellum Grammaticale* ist es, alle *partes orationis* aus Anlaß der Rekrutierung der Truppen für den Kampf und bei der Entscheidung über ihre Zugehörigkeit zu einer der beiden kriegführenden Parteien (des *Nomen* und des *Verbum*) Revue passieren zu lassen und in ihrer grammatischen Funk-

---

[1] Über die sehr raren Exemplare der Mailänder Editio princeps, der die folgenden Zitate, z. T. verbessert und orthographisch zivilisiert, entnommen sind, vgl. Giorgio Nicodemi's "Nota" zu seinem Nachdruck des Exemplars der Biblioteca Trivulziana, Milano (Signatur: H 617) vom Jahre 1943, S. 49. Für den vorliegenden Beitrag wurde außerdem benutzt: Wien, Österreichische Nationalbibliothek 40 Q. 86. Im Jahre 1970 erschien in Rom zu den Celebrazioni Bramantesche die bisher einzige moderne Ausgabe: Andrea Guarna da Salerno, *Scimmia.* Edizione emendata e corretta, a cura di Giuseppina Battisti. Introduzione e traduzione di Eugenio Battisti. Sie hat einen deutlich kunstgeschichtlichem Interessenschwerpunkt und ist philologisch sehr unbefriedigend: viele der über 100 Druckfehler der Erstausgabe sind nicht erkannt und darum nicht emendiert worden, auch die Übersetzung ist (nicht nur aus diesem Grunde) oft verfehlt. Ich bereite eine kommentierte zweisprachige Edition des *Simia* vor.

[2] Sie sind knapp zusammengefaßt von Johannes Bolte in seiner Einleitung zur Edition des *Bellum Grammaticale* (vgl. nächste Anm).

[3] *Andrea Guarnas* Bellum Grammaticale *und seine Nachahmungen,* hrsg. von Johannes Bolte, Monumenta Germaniae Paedagogica 43 (Berlin, 1908), mit wertvoller Einleitung.

tion und Potenz erkennbar zu machen. Eine besondere Behandlung erfahren dabei die Defectiva der lateinischen Sprache, die als Verwundete und Opfer der verlustreichen Entscheidungsschlacht am Fluß Sive übrig geblieben sind.

Ganz im Schatten des populären *Bellum Grammaticale* steht der dramatische Dialog *Simia*, der im Juni 1517 in Mailand in einem geradezu unbegreiflich fehlerhaften Druck herauskam. Nach dem Erscheinungsjahr des *Simia* gibt es keine biographischen Spuren mehr von Guarna. Dem Zeugnis des Widmungsbriefs zufolge ist der Dialog bereits ein Jahr zuvor, also 1516, entstanden, atmosphärisch gehört er, wie zumal die Kunsthistoriker herausgefunden haben[4], sogar in den Sommer 1514, d. h. in das Todesjahr des Renaissance-Architekten Bramante, der wichtigsten zeitgenössischen Person, die in diesem Dialog auftritt. Bramante war ein Jahr nach Papst Julius II., seinem Auftraggeber für den Neubau der Peterskirche, gestorben, und die Erinnerung an Julius ist bei Guarna noch ganz frisch. Julius wird mit Sympathie, zumindest mit Respekt, gezeichnet und befindet sich nach Auskunft des Heiligen Petrus im Himmel. Weit mehr Licht fällt allerdings auf den neuen Papst, Leo X., einen wahren Hoffnungsträger, dessen *clementia*—offenbar im unausgesprochenen Kontrast zu dem harten und kriegerischen Julius—in beschwörendem Ton gerühmt wird. Im übrigen zeichnet sich Leo durch seine humanistische Bildung und seinen Sinn für Gerechtigkeit aus. Die Gerechtigkeit bleibt, jenseits aller Komik, ein erkennbar ernstes Anliegen unseres Autors.

Simia ist ein dramatischer Dialog in Prosa. Außer den impliziten "gesprochenen Regieanweisungen" kennt er zwar keine ausdrückliche szenische Zurüstung, aber er spielt an zwei deutlich markierten Schauplätzen: zuerst und über den Hauptteil der Handlung am Himmelstor, zum Abschluß in Rom. Die im Himmel agierenden Personen sind, zwangsläufig, Verstorbene oder sogar bereits (wie Petrus) Selige (*beati*). Der Jüngste der erst kürzlich Verstorbenen, Angelus (Angelo Massimo), darf am Ende der Unterredung am Himmelstor wieder ins Leben—nach Rom—zurückkehren, um sich bei Papst Leo für die Freilassung eines zu Unrecht in der Engelsburg Eingekerkerten zu verwenden. Diese Szene in Rom ist nur noch mimische und "motorische" Komödie: alles dreht sich hier um den für komische Aktion ergiebigen Schrecken, der bei den Bettlern vor der Kirche Santa Maria della Pace ausbricht, als Angelo, reinkarniert, aus seinem Sarg steigt und einen der Bettler bittet, ihm die bei seiner früheren Bestattung zusammengebundenen Hände zu lösen. Wir können dieses Satyrspiel im folgenden vernachlässigen und uns der weit gewichtigeren, sehr geistreichen und teilweise höchst satirischen[5] zentralen Szene am Himmelstor zuwenden.

Es geht in dieser Situation, wie man sich denken kann, um die Frage, ob die

---

[4] Vgl. darüber zuletzt Christoph Luitpold Frommel in *The Renaissance. From Brunelleschi to Michelangelo. The Representation of Architecture*, ed. Henry A. Millon et al. (Venice, 1994), 612, Nr. 302. Für guten Rat danke ich Bernd Kulawik, Berlin.

[5] In einem originellen Begleitgedicht versieht Marius Bellonus den *Simia*, der übrigens als masculinum behandelt wird, mit zahlreichen (22!) rühmenden Adjektiven, von denen wenigstens die letzten als die treffendsten zitiert seien: *Argutus: lepidus: uafer: seuerus:/ Doctus: candidus: elegans: facetus* (fol. A iir).

Ankommenden würdig sind, in das Himmelreich einzugehen, und es findet zu diesem Zweck ein *ingrediendi iudicium* (fol. A viir) statt. Die Kandidaten werden über ihr vergangenes Leben befragt und zuletzt, nachdem sie ihre Kleidung abgelegt haben, körperlich nach Makeln visitiert. Folgende Personen treten nacheinander Petrus gegenüber: Zunächst Simia, der dem Dialog seinen Namen gegeben hat. Es handelt sich um den Necknamen des Griechen Demetrios Chalkondyles[6], der im Jahre 1449 nach Rom gekommen war und u. a. in Florenz und Mailand Griechisch und griechische Philosophie gelehrt hat. Sein Tod (1511) liegt zum Zeitpunkt der Veröffentlichung des Dialogs schon einige Jahre zurück. Chalkondyles ist mit entschiedener Antipathie, u. a. als verfressen und als Lügner, gezeichnet. Bei seinem Verhör behauptet er zunächst, ein Römer zu sein, doch Petrus erkennt an seiner Sprache und an seinem Gestank, daß er Grieche ist. (Simia verflucht daraufhin insgeheim seine Leichenwäscher, die ihn nicht ordentlich gewaschen haben.) Petrus, grundsätzlich auffallend ausländerfeindlich, ist vor allem auf Griechen, die den Papst nicht anerkennen, schlecht zu sprechen. Schließlich wird Simia ohne Erbarmen in die Hölle geschickt.

Die übrigen Akteure an der Himmelstür sind, bis auf Bramante, Mitglieder der römischen Curie, und Petrus gibt von vornherein zu verstehen, daß er bei Curialen in jedem Fall schwarz sehe: mit Sicherheit würden von denen *nicht alle* in das Himmelreich eingehen: *Si Curiales sunt, non omnes introibunt* (fol. A vr). Glück hat der Venezianer Jurist Franciscus Brevius (gest. 1508), obwohl der, seinem Namen Brevius zum Trotz, als Auditor Rotae seine Prozesse gewöhnlich so lang hingezogen hat, bis viele darüber gestorben sind, ohne für ihre finanziellen Aufwendungen etwas bekommen zu haben. Sein jähzorniges Temperament verdient keine Strafe, da es herkunftsbedingt, "von Venetianer Art", war. Den Ausschlag für die Begnadigung des Brevius gibt seine glaubwürdige Versicherung, daß er keusch gelebt und keine Kinder habe. Gnade finden auch der Generalschatzmeister Julius des II., Erzbischof Enrico Bruni von Tarent (gest. 1509), der die Heiligen unter Sankt Peter ausgraben und auf dem Campo Santo beisetzen ließ, sowie der moralisch vorbildliche Alexander Zambeccari (gest. 1511) aus Guarnas geliebtem Bologna.[7] Er darf sogar neben Petrus Platz nehmen und ihn bei der Vernehmung der folgenden Personen unterstützen.

Gemeinsam mit Simia kommen in die Hölle Petrus Turres aus Novara und Johannes ex Almania. Das Vergehen des ersten ist *avaritia* in einem besonders schweren Fall (erkennbar an dem Gestank, den der nackte Geizhals verbreitet): Turres hat für Julius II. zum Neubau der Peterskirche zwar viel Geld bereitgestellt, aber er hat damit seine Nachkommen um ihr Erbe betrogen. Guarna verrät hier eine deutliche Reserve gegenüber dem aufwendigen Unternehmen, das, wie man bei Ludwig von

---

[6] Über Demetrios Chalkondyles (geb. 1423 in Athen, gest. 1511 in Mailand), der auch mit Reuchlin bekannt war, vgl. Giuseppe Cammelli, *I dotti Bizantini e le origini dell'umanesimo*, III: *Demetrio Calcondila* (Firenze, 1954). Für freundliche Hilfe danke ich Matthias Dall'Asta, z. Zt. Pforzheim.

[7] *O Bona Bononia: Quae huiusmodi viros feras: Dignos marmoreis laudibus . . .* (fol. B iiiir).

Pastor in der '*Geschichte der Päpste*'[8] nachlesen kann, auch sonst sowohl beim Volk wie bei den Kardinälen denkbar unpopulär war. Stiftungen für die Kirche zum Nachteil der Erben werden in einer eigenen Reflexion über diesen Fall ausdrücklich mißbilligt.

Mit dem an Händen und Gesicht tintengeschwärzten Johannes ex Almania ist der langjährige päpstliche Protonotar Johannes Burckard aus Straßburg (gest. 1506)[9] gemeint, der über seine Amtszeit ein als historische Quelle hochgeschätztes *Diarium* verfaßt hat. Dieses Werk trägt auch den Titel *Liber notarum*, und so ist es kein Wunder, daß sich der ganze Leib des Johannes, nachdem er seine Kleider abgelegt hat, als von *notae* übersät erweist. Man hat hier ein schönes Beispiel für den spezifisch philologischen Humor unseres Autors, der sich mit Vorliebe aus der Doppeldeutigkeit der Sprache, oft aus *voces ambiguae*, generiert. Die *notae* des Notars sind insgeheim zu Schandflecken geworden.

Den Höhepunkt des Dialogs bildet zweifellos der Auftritt des eben (1514) verstorbenen Architekten Bramante. Guarna zeichnet ihn als einen gigantomanischen Künstler, der nicht zu zügeln ist und der sich in seinem Ungestüm sogar zu einem Boxkampf am Himmelstor bereitstellt.[10] Dem erfolgverwöhnten Bramante, einem klassischen anmaßenden Renaissancemenschen, sind die traditionellen Maßstäbe christlichen Lebens, die Petrus natürlich einklagt—etwa Askese oder Demut—ganz und gar fremd geworden. Dieses fatale Unverständnis bringt Guarna sehr geschickt dadurch zum Ausdruck, daß er Bramante den Sinn von *voces ambiguae* schwerwiegend verfehlen läßt. Zum Beispiel kennt Bramante offenbar die religiöse Bedeutung von *salus* nicht, er versteht das Wort nur in seiner profanen Bedeutung "Gruß" und ist empört über die Unhöflichkeit des Petrus, der ihm vermeintlich den Gruß nicht erwidert. Dabei hatte Petrus nur gesagt: *Salutem non damus nisi dignis* (fol. B viiir). Ähnlich geht es mit der doppelten Bedeutung von *bene vivere*, das Bramante als Genußmensch nur ganz irdisch versteht. Er nimmt für sich in Anspruch, tatsächlich "gut gelebt" zu haben. Das Spiel mit den *voces ambiguae* wird noch weiter getrieben: Petrus nennt als Regeln für rechtes christliches Leben u. a. *odisse vitia* und *benefacere*—die Sünden verabscheuen und Gutes tun. Bramante kennt den Begriff des *vitium* aber nur noch als "Kunstfehler" und auch *benefacere* versteht er rein technisch; demzufolge kann er versichern, daß er als Architekt immer darauf geachtet habe, keine Fehler zu machen—nämlich, um nicht von der Welt verlacht zu werden —und er nimmt für sich in Anspruch, verglichen mit seinen Konkurrenten gut gearbeitet zu haben: *inter reliquos artifices benefecisse me arbitror posse gloriari* (fol. B viiiv).

Danach kommt Petrus auf einen besonders wunden Punkt zu sprechen. Er fragt Bramante: "Warum hast du meine Kirche in Rom zerstört, die allein auf Grund ihres ehrwürdigen Alters jeden Verbrecher zu Gott hinführte?"—*Cur euertisti templum illud*

---

[8] Ludwig Freiherr von Pastor, *Geschichte der Päpste* III, 2, 5. bis 7. Auflage (Freiburg i.Br., 1924), 921 ff.

[9] Vgl. *Lexikon des Mittelalters* 2: 954 f.

[10] *Edico uobis omnibus siue is Petrus sit siue Paulus: siue Paradisi huius uestri alius quiuis magnus satrapa: ne mihi incipiat manus: neue mihi contumeliam paret facere, alioquin sentiet, quid hisce pugnis Bramantes possit. Faciet spero hoc in scopulo inexspectatum dentifragium . . .* etc. (fol. Ciir).

meum Romae: scelerati cuiusuis animum sola uetustate in Deum prouocans? (fol. Cr)
Tatsächlich hatte man in Rom den Abriß von Alt-Sankt-Peter allgemein als einen
Akt von Vandalismus empfunden. Bramante weist zunächst alle Schuld von sich: die
Arbeiter hätten auf Befehl des Papstes Julius die Kirche kaputtgemacht, doch muß er
zugeben, daß der Papst auf seine, Bramantes, Veranlassung damit begonnen hat und
daß er selber für die Ruinierung der Kirche verantwortlich ist. "Warum hast du das
gewagt?" fragt Petrus, und Bramante antwortet: "Um den Geldbeutel des Papstes, der
so voll war, daß er platzte, zu erleichtern."—*Ut Iulii marsupium nimio tumore crepans
exonerarem* (fol. Cr). Petrus fragt: "Was hat dich gestört an diesem von Gold gefüllten
Geldbeutel?"—*Quid tibi oberat Iulii marsupium auro plenum?* Antwort: "Alle hat es
gestört, und es war auch in der Tat unvernünftig: daß da so viel Gold an einem Ort
und ohne Effekt begraben war. Darum haben die Alten ja gewollt, daß die Münzen
rund sind: damit sie nämlich rollen können."—*Omnibus oberat: et ab re erat tantum auri
uno in loco sepultum otiosum esse. Propterea enim ueteres uoluere nummos esse orbiculatos: ut
possent currere* (fol. Cr). Bramante beklagt, Julius habe nach Beginn der Bauarbeiten
sein Geld zurückgehalten und nur Ablassgelder aufgewendet; außerdem hätten die
kriegerischen Ereignisse die Vollendung des Neubaus verhindert. (Tatsächlich war
Sankt Peter beim Tod Bramantes noch in einem deprimierend unfertigen Zustand.) Im
weiteren Verlauf des Gesprächs geht es wieder um das bedenklich unchristliche Leben
Bramantes, der, wie er selbstbewußt feststellt, zwischen Freiheit und Zügellosigkeit, *libertas* und *licentia*, keinen Unterschied sieht und sich offen zum Epikureismus bekennt.

Schließlich nennt er, Bramante, die Bedingungen, unter denen er überhaupt nur
bereit wäre, in den Himmel einzutreten: er will auf jeden Fall den bisherigen allzu
beschwerlichen Zugang zum Himmel ersetzen durch eine ausladende Wendeltreppe,
auf der auch die Seelen der Alten und Kranken bequem, zu Pferde nämlich, einreiten
könnten. Danach will er das ganze Paradies abreißen und von Grund auf neu gestalten (*funditus evertere* heißt es mit demselben Verb, das vorher für die Ruinierung
von Alt-Sankt-Peter gebraucht wurde): die Seligen sollten jedenfalls angenehmere
und elegantere Wohnungen bekommen:

> *Omnium primum uiam hanc, quae e terris in Caelum ducit: arduam nimis et ascensu
> perdifficilem tollere in animo est: alteramque erigere coclideam*[11] *et spaciosam: per quam
> seniorum: et debilium animae equestres possint scandere. Postmodum Paradisum hunc
> funditus euertere nouumque erigere: qui Beatis iucundiores: ac cultiores habitationes
> praebeat.* (fol. Ciiir)

Petrus sieht hier ein organisatorisches Problem: "Wo sollen sich die bisherigen Bewohner so lange aufhalten, bis das neue Paradies erstanden ist?"—*Ubinam uoles colonos
nostros habitare, quoadusque Paradisus surgat nouus?* (fol. Ciiir) Bramante schlägt vor: *Sub
dio*—"im Freien". Die Seligen seien von ihrem asketischen irdischen Leben her abge-
härtet, außerdem würden sie sich in diesem gesunden Klima gewiß kein Rheuma zu-
ziehen. Als Petrus auf diese Bedingungen nicht eingeht, ist Bramante schwer gekränkt

---

[11] Der Druck hat hier *ioclidem*, gleich darauf auch *seniorem* statt *seniorum*. Als Modell für die
Wendeltreppe ins Paradies, die Bramante vorschwebt, könnte man die von ihm gebaute Treppe
im Belvedere-Hof sehen, die sich schneckenartig zum Museo Gregoriano emporwindet.

und kündigt an, er werde jetzt geradewegs in die Hölle—*ad Plutonem*—gehen; dort warte viel Arbeit auf ihn, die ganze Hölle habe durch die ewigen Flammen Risse bekommen und sei halbverkohlt: "ich werde sie ganz neu machen"—*Infernum nouum faciam omne: euerso hoc fatiscente: et semiconsumpto tam diuturnis flammis* (fol. Ciiir).

Petrus läßt ihn nicht los und erneuert den Vorwurf: "Du hast meine Kirche in Rom kaputtgemacht"—*evertisti tu templum illud meum Romae.* Bramante gibt das zu, aber Leo, sagt er, werde den neuen Bau in kurzer Zeit vollenden: *Factum fateor, verum illud perficiet Leo breui tempore* (fol. Ciiiv). Petrus, der offenbar ahnt, wie lang das in Wirklichkeit noch dauern wird, nimmt ihn beim Wort und verfügt: "Diese 'kurze Zeit' sollst du hier vor den Toren des Paradieses warten, und du wirst nicht früher eingelassen, als bis ich die Nachricht erhalten habe, daß die neue Kirche wirklich ganz fertig ist."—*Interim expectabis hic ante fores paradisi hoc breui tempore: nec admitteris limiti*[12], *priusquam certior efficiar: perfectum esse penitus nouum templum illud* (fol. Ciiiv).

Darauf fragt Bramante kleinlaut: "Und was ist, wenn sie nie fertig wird?"—*Quid si perficiatur nunquam?* Petrus schiebt diese Zweifel, wohl etwas ironisch, beiseite und sagt: "Ach, mein Leo bekommt das fertig!"—*Ha perficiet certe Leo meus* (fol. Ciiiv). Bramante ergibt sich in sein Los und wartet vor dem Paradies auf die Vollendung von Sankt Peter. Er mußte, wie wir Spätgeborenen wissen, immerhin noch gute 70 Jahre warten: die von Michelangelo entworfene Kuppel über dem Zentralbau wurde erst im Jahre 1589 fertiggestellt.

Es fehlt mir der Raum, näher auf die z. T. ausgesprochen virtuose literarische Qualität dieses Dialogs einzugehen, der z. B. viele feine, noch unentdeckte Anspielungen auf die antike Literatur (etwa Plautus) enthält und seine aufgeregte Epoche in einer ungewohnt gelassenen, geistreich-humorigen Weise satirisch kommentiert. Das ist der große Unterschied zu den zeitgenössischen Romsatiren, die in der Regel weit aggressiver und bewußter politisch sind als der *Simia* dieses friedfertigen Sprachspielers. Darin besteht auch der Abstand zu dem thematisch und technisch nahe verwandten Dialog *Iulius exclusus e coelis*, der zur gleichen Zeit entstanden ist und für den Erasmus als Autor in Frage kommt.

Die Idee der literarischen Inszenierung eines Dialogs mit Verstorbenen im Himmel kommt aus der Antike. Als Muster für die Humanisten dienten und wirkten hier vor allem die Dialoge des Lukian, wie etwa in Alberti's *Intercenales* erkennbar ist.[13] Guarna, der Lukian wohl auch den Einfall für sein *Bellum Grammaticale* verdankt, hat aber vermutlich ein anderes, ebenfalls populäres Modell gehabt, nämlich Senecas *Apokolokyntosis.* Er verrät diese Spur durch ein sehr spezifisches Motiv, und damit komme ich zum Schluß. Simia erzählt die Umstände seines Todes, den er übrigens den unfähigen, aber stets nach Geld gierenden Ärzten anlastet—*den mendici medici*: das Entweichen seiner Seele wollte er durch kräftiges Verschließen seines Mundes verhindern, doch suchte sich die Seele einen anderen Ausweg—*magno edito tonitruo* (fol. Biir). Bei Seneca stirbt Claudius, wie man weiß, unter ähnlich unfeinen Umständen.

Universität Göttingen

---

[12] Druck: *limiti.*

[13] Vgl. Leon Battista Alberti, *Dinner Pieces: A Translation of the Intercenales*, trans. David Marsh, Medieval & Renaissance Texts & Studies Vol. 45 (Binghamton, 1987).

El nuevo mundo en los
Commentariorum de sale libri V
del humanista alcañizano Bernardino Gómez Miedes[1]

SANDRA RAMOS MALDONADO

Uno de los tópicos más extendidos en la literatura universal es el de considerar el "libro como un hijo"[2]. Pero en el caso de la primera obra que salió de la pluma de Bernardino Gómez Miedes, los *Commentariorum de sale libri V*[3], el tópico del "libro como hijo" llega aún más lejos[4], pues el proceso de creación literaria de los mismos va a coincidir con el desarrollo vital y existencial del autor en virtud de los más de veinticinco años empleados en la elaboración del texto[5].

En efecto, cuando Gómez Miedes terminó de escribir su diálogo sobre la sal, tenía en torno a los sesenta años[6]. Pero el humanista inició la redacción del texto durante

---

[1] El presente trabajo está incluido en el Proyecto de Investigación PS93–0130 de la DGICYT. Agradezco al Profesor D. José María Maestre Maestre la valiosa ayuda que me ha prestado en la elaboración del mismo.

[2] Véase Ernst R. Curtius, *Literatura europea y Edad Media latina* (Madrid, 1976), I, 196 ss.

[3] Citamos por nuestra edición "Los *Commentariorum de sale libri V*". Introducción, edición crítica, traducción, notas e índices, Tesis Doctoral inédita realizada bajo la dirección del Dr. D. Juan Gil Fernández y el Dr. D. José María Maestre Maestre, Universidad de Cádiz, 1995, especificando, tras la fórmula Mied. *sal.*, el número del libro, del capítulo y del parágrafo correspondiente a nuestra cita.

[4] Su *foetus* o *partus* le llama el autor, cf. Mied. *sal. prooem.* 1,(12).

[5] Esto, unido a un excesivo y obsesivo proceso de *limae labor,* se tradujo *de facto* en dos ediciones realizadas por el propio autor, en un intervalo de siete años, que, además de presentar múltiples correcciones y añadidos, cuenta con una nueva estructuración de la obra, cuyo resultado más evidente es el paso de los cuatro libros de la *editio princeps* de 1572 a los cinco libros de la segunda edición de 1579, ambas publicadas en Valencia.

[6] Se desconoce la fecha exacta de su nacimiento, que suele situarse entre el 1520 y el 1525. Para más datos al respecto cf. José M. Maestre Maestre, *El humanismo alcañizano del siglo XVI. Textos y estudios de latín renacentista* (Cádiz, 1990), 231–313.

su juventud, como él mismo confiesa por diversas partes de la obra, y más concretamente durante sus años de estudiante en París. Este lento proceso de creación, que va a coincidir, como decíamos, con el propio devenir vital del autor, le va a llevar a contemplar su mundo circundante con la distancia y el tiempo suficientes como para realizar, según dice él, juicios más correctos y objetivos inherentes a la "edad senil"[7].

Y como lo que pretende con su obra es reflexionar y transmitir sus ideas al lector con el propósito ideal de transformarlo, qué mejor que hacerlo sobre los acontecimientos de más impacto en la época; de ahí que no falte el de quizá más palpitante actualidad y que despertó un gran interés sobre todo a mediados de siglo: el descubrimiento y la conquista del Nuevo Mundo. Pero hay algo novedoso y original en el texto del prelado alcañizano frente a otros múltiples relatos sobre la gesta española: la sal. Este condimento, del que D. Bernardino realiza un encendido encomio, se convierte en el punto de partida para meditar sobre los más diversos aspectos de su mundo circundante y para sugerir e incitar al lector a reflexionar sobre él. De este modo, al hacerlo sobre algo que nos es común en la vida cotidiana, causa más impacto y al versar sobre cosas en apariencia triviales, establece con más claridad la verdadera dimensión del pensamiento humano. El objetivo, pues, del presente trabajo es presentar aquí todos los pasajes en los que Bernardino Gómez Miedes, a través de la sal, se hace eco de la gesta española con una única intención, que declararemos al final en nuestra conclusión.

1. El primer pasaje se incluye en la *praefatio* a Felipe II que abre la *editio princeps*[8]:

(2) Etenim non solum populos perquam multos Europae atque insularum Oceani Marisque Nostri felicissime gubernas, sed innumerabiles quidem alterius tanquam orbis terrarum prouincias, tam longo a te licet interuallo disiunctas, et aequissime moderaris et in officio contines et, dum sacro religionis sale initiandas curas, ad inmortalitatem conseruas.

(3) Hoc enim a te, parentibus proauisque tuis illuc asportato atque persperso sale, quam multas quamque miserabiles impietatis sectas radicitus euulsistis? Quantam quamque incredibilem animarum multitudinem ab execrabili humani sanguinis effusione immanissimaque antropophagia liberastis? Quot denique regiones (quantas nulli alii ante uos) Christianae in primis religioni atque Hispanico subinde nomini adiunxistis? Nam qui, obsecro, centum illas et uiginti prouincias Assueri, quondam Persarum regis, cum iis quas auro rerumque copia refertissimas in nouo ipso terrarum orbe possides, conferemus? Quorsum illa tam multa Barbarorum regna ab Alexandro Magno debellata, sub quarta fere unius ex caelestibus, ut uocant, zonis parte conclusa, cum praecellentibus inuictissimarum gentium regnis quae in Europa tenes, comparabimus? Neque enim Romanis olim fuit unquam tuo latius imperium, quod illi uix ultra fines bru-

---

[7] Cf. Mied. *sal. prooem.* 1,(33).

[8] Cf. Mied. *sal. praef.* 1,(2–3).

malem inter et solstitialem orbem comprehensos extendere ac nisi a Caucaso monte ad Gades usque, Herculis terminum, proferre potuerunt.

Gómez Miedes en este pasaje utiliza un tópico tan manido como es el del sobrepujamiento (*Überbietung*)[9] para cantar las excelencias del rey Felipe II, al que llama "la sal del mundo", y entre éstas destaca la de ser el monarca que más ha ensanchado de un lado y de otro el Imperio Español y de ser el responsable, con la ayuda de sus antepasados, de haber llevado la religión cristiana a innúmeras regiones salvajes. Ni siquiera el imperio de Asuero fue más grande que el de Felipe II, ni el de Alejandro Magno ni incluso el de los propios romanos, que no fueron capaces de pasar más allá de Cádiz, la meta, como suele decirse, de Hércules. Gómez Miedes alude aquí, pero de forma indirecta, al tema del Descubrimiento con una alusión que se ha convertido en tópica como es la de considerar a Cádiz (o a tierras cercanas a Cádiz) el fin del mundo, donde la mitología ubicó las dos famosas columnas de Hércules y el famoso *NON PLVS VLTRA*. Precisamente, unas líneas después, tras la descripción del Imperio turco y la famosa batalla de Lepanto, el humanista nos expone con más claridad el tópico y un insinuante recordatorio de que, frente al *NON PLVS VLTRA* de la Antigüedad, el nuevo Hércules consiguió ir "más allá" convirtiéndose por tanto en un *Hercules maior*[10]:

(6) Quamobrem neque est cur reliquos, quantumuis licet praepotentes, orbis principes tecum conferamus, quos non modo populorum multitudine ac frequentia, sed etiam terrarum ambitu et latitudine ita excellis, ut imperium Oceano terminasse (quod olim summum fuit) tu merito non magnifacias, qui paternum haereditariumque illud PLVS VLTRA tam longe lateque prouexeris, ut nemo sanus sit qui te reliquis terrarum dominis ultra omnem terminum praecurrisse non uideat.

(7) Nam praeter ea quae in Europa tenes, cum a freto, ut uocant, Magalianico, quod Australi fere subest circulo, per Peruranam et Mexicanam prouincias ad Floridam usque et Bacchalanos, quae iacent Arcto proximae, fines extenderis ac rursum a freto Siculo ad Herculeum indeque a Fortunatis, utroque superato Oceano, ad eas ubi nouus Occidens cum ueteri Oriente committitur regiones perueneris, nonne plus omnibus imperium ultro citroque propagasti?

(8) Quod si, tam magnis denique mundi plagis Hispanorum uirtute partis, illas etiam adnumeremus quae a clarissimis Lusitanorum regibus, maternis atauis tuis, ad utramque Africae oram et ad Orientem exploratae deuictaeque fuerunt, profecto non amplius, ut Maro cecinit[11]:

Cunctus ob Italiam terrarum clauditur orbis.

---

[9] Cf. Curtius, *Literatura europea*, I, 235–236; J. Mª Maestre Maestre, "El tópico del *sobrepujamiento* en la literatura latina renacentista", *Anales de la Universidad de Cádiz* (1990): 167-192.

[10] Cf. Mied. *sal. praef.* 1,(6–9).

[11] Cf. Verg. *Aen.* 1,233.

(9) Quinimmo, te summo Hispaniarum imperatore, canamus:
Cunctus ab Hispania terrarum panditur orbis.

Para ilustrar la grandeza del imperio español traza un mapa con nombres exóticos y novedosos, unos, clásicos y antiguos, otros, del Viejo y el Nuevo Mundo. Y si Virgilio en su momento cantó la gloria del Imperio Romano ahora es el momento de España y así lo rubrica Gómez Miedes con la adaptación de un verso del mantuano.

2. Otra alusión al descubrimiento la encontraremos ahora en el *prooemium* al lector que abre la *editio princeps*. Gómez Miedes cuenta al lector que sus amigos le reprendieron severamente cuando se enteraron de que iba a escribir sobre la sal, un tema novedoso del que poco se podía decir. Y entre otros argumentos, el humanista se justifica comparando su actitud con la de los marineros de su tiempo que se atrevieron a navegar a regiones desconocidas[12]:

(7) Nautae itidem nostri temporis, nonne mathematicis potius caeli dimensionibus quam praegressorum nauigiorum uestigiis confisi, ab Aquilonaribus regionibus soluentes, ad Australes ignotas sibi penitus et prope inauditas peruenerunt? Sed quantum nauigandi arte profecerint quantaque ipsis pro tam constanti nauigatione magnitudo praemii accesserit, incredibilis auri et argenti uis, necnon gemmarum affluentia quae ab eis domum reportata sunt, manifesto indicant.

Como puede observarse, no se hace aquí, como tampoco en los pasajes anteriores, ninguna alusión a Cristóbal Colón. Son *nautae nostri temporis* los que se atrevieron a abrir un camino a través de tantos mares inmensos y no recorridos antes. Por otro lado, aunque los humanistas en general tratan de disimular el verdadero móvil económico del Descubrimiento y disfrazan el mismo con distintos razonamientos entre los que descuella, sin duda, el de la evangelización del Nuevo Orbe, aquí se aducen motivos como la aventura y la recompensa económica.

3. En el siguiente pasaje entramos ya de lleno en la obra, donde la sal se convierte en el pretexto ideal para tratar sobre múltiples aspectos. Como en el libro II, donde el tema de los impuestos y tributos de sal tan esenciales para las arcas de reyes y príncipes de la iglesia le sirve de excusa para introducir la figura de Hernán Cortés[13]:

(7) Quae largitas atque communicatio salis a Ferdinando Cortesio, Hispanorum duce, ad Indica debellanda regna misso procurata eiusque rogatu a Mexicanorum principe Traschallenensibus populis impetrata, nonne extrema fuit illi anchora ad idem Mexicanorum imperium recuperandum totque subinde prouincias expugnandum?
(8) Cuius ego diuini prope uiri atque inuictissimi imperatoris laudes ne in praesenti quidem reticere queo, dum eius magnanimitatem, prudentiam, forti-

---

[12] Cf. Mied. *sal. prooem.* 1,(7).
[13] Cf. Mied. *sal.* II.8,(7–8).

tudinem, religionem et in aduersis superatam, in prosperis contemptam fortunam ab eoque imploratum ubique numen considero, dum ex tam multis hostium millibus cum tam parua Hispanorum manu reportatas ab eo uictorias nullasque amissas perpendo. Vnde quoties ipsius incredibilia facta, non ex historia solummodo, sed ab iis etiam qui sub eo militarunt, maiora quam quae litteris consignata sunt, fuisse intelligo, dubitare soleo profecto num Cortesium in celeberrima illa fortissimorum heroum, quos unice fama colit, enneade reponam an potius eundem nouae illius iam decadis caput sine controuersia constituam. De quo summo uiro plura alio fortasse loco.

Varios son los comentarios que tenemos que realizar aquí.

En primer lugar, es difícil establecer, dada la brevedad del pasaje y la falta de referencia alguna, la fuente o fuentes en las que pudo inspirarse Gómez Miedes. Tlaxcala, llamado por los indígenas Tlaxcallan o Texcallan, es uno de los pueblos que, en efecto, ha desempeñado el papel más importante en la historia de la conquista de México, pues Cortés aprovechó en favor suyo la rivalidad intensa que existía entre ambos pueblos, los tlaxcaltecas y los mejicanos. Pero que fuera la sal, o mejor dicho su escasez, el desencadenante de la conquista, no hemos podido confirmarlo. Hemos consultado varias fuentes:

Ginés de Sepúlveda[14] escribe al respecto: "Ellos no tenían ni sal ni seda, indispensables para comer y vestir, pues ninguno de los dos productos se daban en el territorio de Tlaxcala debido a su clima frío; en cambio la tierra de Moctezuma lo producía en abundancia y desde allí se podía importar a través del comercio. Pese a ello, vivían estoicamente desnudos y sin emplear sal, con tal de no firmar una paz con los reyes de México".

López de Gomara escribe[15]: "Ellos le rogaron por licencia para sacar algodón y sal, pues no la comían a derechas durante aquellos años en que duraron las guerras".

Francisco Hernández a su vez realiza el siguiente relato[16]: "Narraba los grandes trabajos que los tlaxcaltecas prefirieron tolerar a someterse a Moctezuma; como, por ejemplo, la penuria de algodón y de toda clase de vestidos de los cuales aquella región que es sumamente fría carecía; además la falta de la sal, principal condimento de todos los alimentos; en verdad decía, no había nada tan necesario a los hombres y a la que por amor de la libertad, renunciaban de mala gana. [...] Respondioles (Hernán Cortés) plácida y amorosamente, prometiéndoles que cualquier cosa que le pidieran la obtendrían con plenitud".

No puede decirse, pues, que el humanista en sus *Commentarii* falte a la verdad, pero elabora los hechos de la manera que más le interesa, y en este caso concreto, omitiendo numerosos detalles sobre la conquista de México y destacando aquellos que les son útiles a su proyecto[17].

---

[14] Cf. Juan Ginés de Sepúlveda, *Historia del Nuevo Mundo*, Introducción, traducción y notas de A. Ramírez de Verger (Madrid, 1987), 137.

[15] Cf. F. López de Gomara, *La conquista de México*, ed. J. Luis de Rojas (Madrid, 1987), 147.

[16] Cf. F. Hernández, *Antigüedades de la Nueva España,* ed. A. H. de León-Portilla (Madrid, 1986), 212.

[17] En un trabajo nuestro anterior (cf. "Islamismo y mundo árabe en las obras de los huma-

En cuanto a la lista de los nueve héroes más famosos, Caxton en el prefacio a la edición de *La muerte de Arturo* de 1485[18] cuenta que hay nueve grandes héroes, los mejores de todos los tiempos, que merecen ser por siempre recordados. Tres son paganos: Hector de Troya, Alejandro el Grande y Julio César. Tres son judíos: Josué, David y Judas Macabeo. Tres son cristianos: Arturo, Carlomagno y Godofredo de Bouillon. Ese tema de los nueve paladines heroicos era, como Caxton mismo dice, un tópico bien divulgado desde mucho tiempo atrás entre los doctos[19]. La mejor ilustración plástica del mismo lo constituye su representación en el grupo de esculturas de la Fuente Hermosa de Nurembey. Construida entre 1385 y 1392, este espléndido monumento del gótico tardío nos ofrece unas imágenes de los nueve héroes universales, alternando con las figuras de los siete príncipes alemanes y los profetas y los evangelistas, como un testimonio brillante de su gloria y ejemplaridad.

Reynolds mostró en su libro sobre la presencia del conquistador extremeño en la literatura del Siglo de Oro[20] que los escritores de dicha época normalmente identificaban a Cortés no sólo con los grecolatinos, sino también con otros héroes antiguos. Pero lo más significativo era que esos escritores españoles no quisieron traer a la memoria héroes nacionales. Un caso de legítimo patriotismo. Pero ni siquiera se proyecta la grandeza individual de los héroes de la antigüedad sobre Cortés. Al contrario, ellos son representados como los beneficiarios de su grandeza. Los escritores no subordinan a Cortés a ninguno de ellos, ni lo ven como su continuación y algunos como Gómez Miedes dudan incluso si igualarlo con ellos o si más bien ponerlo *sine controuersia* a la cabeza de una nueva lista ahora de diez héroes.

Con respecto a la frase que cierra el pasaje, *De quo summo uiro plura alio fortasse loco*, podemos asegurar que éste es el único lugar donde D. Bernardino hablará de Hernán Cortés, tanto en esta obra como, según los índices consultados, en su restante producción.

4. De nuevo una alusión a la navegación, y aunque los datos, como luego veremos, los hemos confirmado en el diario de a bordo de Colón, otra vez se omite el nombre del navegante italiano[21]:

> (3) [. . .] Nutrit enim Indicum mare salsam herbam, quam uocant salgazum, mobilem in mari summo consistentem adeoque copiosam, ut intuentibus florentissimorum pratorum speciem referat, sicuti primis illis terras ultra mare ad

---

nistas: los *Commentariorum de sale libri V* del alcañizano Bernardino Gómez Miedes", en *Estudios de la UCA ofrecidos a la Memoria del Profesor Braulio Justel Calabozo* (Cádiz, 1998), 179–191, llegamos a las mismas conclusiones.

[18] Cf. T. Malory, *La muerte de Arturo* (Madrid, 1985), I 3-4.

[19] Cf. C. García Gual, *Historia del Rey Arturo y de los nobles y errantes caballeros de la Tabla Redonda* (Madrid, 1984), 14-15.

[20] Cf. W. A. Reynolds, *Hernán Cortés en la literatura del Siglo de Oro* (Madrid, 1978), 117; Alberto Navarro González, "Hernán Cortés en la literatura española", en *Actas de I Congreso Internacional sobre Hernán Cortés* (Salamanca, 1986), 515–538.

[21] Cf. Mied. *sal.* II,47,(3).

partes obeunti soli expositas inquirentibus Hispanis, post diuturnum atque longissimum emensi maris spatium obtigit, quos eiusmodi procul uisa salgazus, planae ac stabilis insulae prospectum prae se ferens uana elusit spe. Nam partim uiridis est, partim crocea, quae pingui humore maris alitur nec nisi ubi salsuginosum est solum enascitur.

Con el nombre de mar de Sargazo se conoce la porción del Océano Atlántico comprendida entre las Antillas, las Bermudas y las Azores. Fue descubierto por Colón, cuya tripulación se asustó ante aquel cúmulo de algas, creyendo que señalaban el límite del mar navegable[22]: "Domingo, 16 de septiembre: [. . .] Aquí comenzaron a ver muchas manadas de hierba muy verde que poco había, según le parecía, que se había desapegado de la tierra, por lo cual todos juzgaban que estaban cerca de alguna isla, pero no de tierra firme, según el Almirante que dice: 'porque la tierra firme yo la hago más adelante'".

La forma *salgazus* empleada por el alcañizano debe ser la etapa intermedia entre "la(s algas)" y "sargazos" tal como se conoce actualmente, aparte del posible interés de nuestro humanista por mantener la forma *sal-* por evidentes razones.

En cuanto al "olvido" de Colón, no es el primero que se produce en las obras de los humanistas. Un ejemplo: otro alcañizano, Juan Sobrarias, en su *Panegyricum carmen de gestis heroicis diui Ferdinandi Catholico* (1511)[23], erige como único protagonista de la gesta del Descubrimiento al rey Católico con total olvido también de la reina Isabel debido, naturalmente, a su condición de aragonés. Y la alusión a Colón quitaría honores a España y por extensión a su rey.

5. En los capítulos que trata sobre las plantas que gustan de la sal, el autor finaliza su catálogo con el lugar en el que todo parece inmenso y singular, donde además nos pone de manifiesto la habilidad de los indígenas para vencer las dificultades agrícolas del terreno:

(5) Ac neque praetereunda est summa illa per salem ubertas, quae apud occidentales Indos comperta est in permagna regione illa Perura in urbe Azua, ulteriori Oceano, qui del Sur dicitur, finitima nonoque gradu ab aequinoctio remota. Quae urbs cum uniuerso circuncirca agro sterilis est ac neque pluuia neque fluuiatili aqua irrigatur et, quia maritima est, puteales duntaxat aquas habet salsuginosas quodammodo neque satis ad bibendum gratas. Vnde cum neque arbores neque stirpes sponte ullas terra ferat neque culturae omnino sit apta, piscatoriam omnes exercent atque icthiophagi sunt ac quoniam copiosissimo suisque modis aptato marino sale abundant, captos certi generis pisciculos saliunt, quos magno sibi usui esse comperiunt ad serendum, tum occandum et colligendum maizium uulgo dictum, quo unico aluntur terrae frumento.

---

[22] Cf. C. Colón, *Diario de a bordo,* ed. Luis Arranz (Madrid, 1985), 78–79.

[23] Cf. José Mª Maestre Maestre, "Sobrarias y el Descubrimiento: notas a los vv. 451–494 del *Panegyricum carmen de gestis heroicis diui Ferdinandi*", en Juan Gil y José Mª Maestre Maestre, eds., *Humanismo Latino y Descubrimiento* (Sevilla-Cádiz, 1992), 151–169.

Pese a los datos tan exactos que nos proporciona Gómez Miedes y haber consultado un buen número de textos y mapas tanto de la época como actuales, no hemos podido localizar Azua. Podría referirse a Azuay, provincia de la República del Ecuador (antaño de la región del Perú) cuya capital es Cuenca y tiene numerosas fuentes de aguas termales[24]. José de Acosta en su *Historia natural y moral de las Indias* describe un vino de maíz que llaman en el Perú "azua" ("chicha" por vocablo de Indias común)[25].

En cuanto al término *maizium*, es un préstamo tomado de las lenguas autóctonas de los pueblos conquistados en el nuevo mundo, probablemente de género neutro. Pero siguiendo la práctica generalizada en estos casos, nuestro humanista presenta el vocablo acompañado de una fórmula introductoria, en este caso *uulgo dictum*[26].

6. D. Bernardino, a pesar de ser conocido como incansable viajero, limitó sus viajes a Europa, por lo que las noticias sobre el Nuevo Mundo las conoció indirectamente, ya sea a través de las crónicas, como también de la cantidad de rumores que debieron circular provenientes de un mundo nuevo de ricas tierras y extrañas gentes, como así lo constata en el texto siguiente[27]:

> (2) Tametsi asserere ausim uel hac nostra aetate inter tot hominum infinita millia dari aliquos qui ad hanc summam sanitatem prope accedant. Quales inueniri crediderim apud occidentales Indos sub Aequinoctio prope Synarum regionem, ubi insulas esse ferunt quarum incolas fama est trecentos fere annos attingere paucissimisque uexari morbis ac neque grauioribus quam esse in extrema aetate taedereque ipsos tam longae uitae.

Estos hombres de casi 300 años, aunque no tan fantásticos y portentosos como los cinocéfalos, las amazonas o los hombres con colas entre otros descritos por J. Gil en su libro *Mitos y utopías del Descubrimiento*[28], son igualmente producto de una antañona tradición de maravillas que los geógrafos clásicos situaban ya entonces en el último cabo de Oriente.

7. Entre los capítulos correspondientes a los lugares más celebres que abundan en sal, en especial la de lago, encontramos un pasaje donde el humanista sitúa a la cabeza de todas, la sal de lago de la ciudad de México, donde no se desaprovecha la oportunidad para celebrar la gesta española, al rey Carlos y a la religión cristiana:

---

[24] Hay un Azua de Compostela, pero está en la República Dominicana.

[25] Cf. José de Acosta, *Historia natural y moral de la Indias*, ed. J. Alcina Franch (Madrid, 1987), 255.

[26] En efecto, para los vocablos no pertenecientes al latín clásico, Gómez Miedes suele presentarlos acompañados de una fórmula introductoria o "excusatoria" del tipo *apud nos . . . nominatum/-atur, sic/ut nostri uocant/nominant/appellant, uulgo dicere/uocare, etc.*, que ya aconsejaban en la época Justo Lipsio, el Brocense, Francesco Florido e incluso Erasmo. Cf. L. Rivero García, *El latín del "De orbe nouo" de Juan Ginés de Sepulveda* (Sevilla, 1993), 86.

[27] Cf. Mied. *sal.* II,59,(2).

[28] Cf. Juan Gil, *Mitos y utopías del Descubrimiento. 1. Colón y su tiempo* (Madrid, 1989), 29–45.

(1) Atque inter hos demum unum omnium de quibus summa ubique fama est, lacum et copiosissimi et imperiosissimi, ut sic dicam, salis feracissimum in medium afferamus, qui nostra tempestate apud occidentales Indos ad solstitialem paulo ultra orbem in Mexicana prouincia repertus est. Quae prouincia, quod auctoribus Hispanis, Carolo Caesari, felicissimo Hispaniarum regi, atque in primis Christianae religioni gloriosissime fuerit subiecta, Noua Hispania uocatur.

(2) In hac igitur uastissimus est lacus ambitu quidem centum milliaria, diametro uero triginta paulo plus continens. Is Themistitanam, urbem maximam, insulae instar mediam cingit [. . .][29].

Mario Hernández en su edición de las *Cartas de relación* de Hernán Cortés escribe[30] que el conquistador extremeño fue el primer español que escribió con caracteres latinos una lengua—la nahuatl o azteca—que nunca se había escrito fonográficamente, es decir, con signos que tuvieran una correspondencia fonética. Por esta razón no estaba muy seguro en la transcripción de nombres de cosas, personas y lugares que tomaba al oído. Insiste en llamar siempre Temixtitán a Tenochtitlán[31].

8. Y para terminar un pasaje que puede servirnos de perfecta conclusión. En él el autor defiende como temas de conversación apropiados a la mesa los relacionados con la comida. Por ejemplo, podría buscarse la explicación filosófica de por qué entre la innúmera cantidad de animales que existen, sólo nos alimentamos de los que son estúpidos, como el cerdo, los salmonetes, la perdiz, mientras que los que destacan por su inteligencia, el gusto humano los aborrece por su carne rugosa y amarillenta como sucede con las águilas, los perros o los delfines. Pues bien, para confirmar su hipótesis he aquí la explicación que de nuevo viene a confirmar que la finalidad de su obra no es otra que la exaltación del pueblo español:

(5) Contra uero quae ingenio atque excellenti aliqua naturae dote praestant, ut aspectu et rapacitate aquilae et accipitres, ut sensu ac docilitate canes et elephanti, ut uersutia atque praesagiis polypi et delphini pisces, haec, inquam, horridas atque luridas carnes habeant ab eisque ut fatuis aut insuauibus humanus gustus omnino abhorreat. Id quod antropophagos in Mexicana prouincia ad Occidentem plagam in esu humanarum carnium peregregie discreuisse compe-

---

[29] Cf. Mied. *sal.* II,75,(1–4). El texto continúa con una detallada descripción de la ciudad y con una nueva alusión a la sal como causante del poderío del imperio de los mejicanos, texto que no transcribimos aquí por falta de espacio, pero que el curioso lector puede consultar en nuestra edición de la obra.

[30] Cf. Hernán Cortés, *Cartas de relación* (Madrid, 1985), 429. Cf. Juan Ginés de Sepúlveda, *De orbe nouo*, VI,41,1: *Temistitanam*; V,23,1: *Temistitlana*.

[31] Para algunas descripciones de la ciudad de México, cf. Cortés, *Cartas de relación*, 132; Ginés de Sepúlveda, *De orbe novo*, 150–151.

rimus, qui Hispanorum, ut ingeniosiorum, carnes aliis suae gentis inuenientes insuauiores, eas deinde intactas reliquerunt[32].

Conclusión

Dos son los hechos que llaman la atención. En primer lugar, la alusión al descubrimiento y a la conquista se resume, en términos de protagonistas, a dos nombres: los españoles, por un lado, como masa anónima y colectiva, por otro lado, Hernán Cortés, héroe de la conquista, nacional e individualizado a falta de uno para la gesta del descubrimiento. En segundo lugar, el humanista, como buen teólogo y tratadista curialista, supo utilizar las fantasías y rumores del Descubrimiento y la conquista que circulaban por su época para hacer un canto propagandístico de los mismos. Vemos, pues, como no siente reparos en omitir nombres y detalles o resaltar otros, en definitiva, en manipular artísticamente la realidad histórica en aras de su proyecto: proclamar la todopoderosa fuerza de la sal, y por extensión de España, su rey, Dios y la religión católica. Una obra, en fin, henchida de un hondo imperialismo y del espíritu de la Contrarreforma.

Universidad de Cádiz

---

[32] Cf. Mied. *sal.* IV,4,(5).

John Donne and Neo-Latin Humanist Works

ANTHONY RASPA

John Donne (1572–1631) is a poet reputed for his secular and religious verse in English and for some haunting passages in his prose works such as his *Devotions* and sermons. But he is also the author of less popular prose works in English, such as *Pseudo-Martyr* (1610) and *Essays in Divinity* (?–1615), that are nevertheless as essential to understanding his intellectual development as his other writings. The humanist scholarship present in these works is remarkable, and the vast majority of it is neo-Latin. In fact, in *Pseudo-Martyr*, which is Donne's first major published work and the longest by far that he ever wrote, the number of neo-Latin writings referred to is so great that it can safely be said that it is a work in English of marked neo-Latin parentage. A bibliography of *Pseudo-Martyr* might read like a Renaissance catalogue of neo-Latin works. To be found there, repeatedly referred to and quoted, are massive historical works such as the German canonist Severinus Binius' *Concilia Generalia* of 1606,[1] theologico-controversial works such as the Italian Jesuit Robert Bellarmine's *De Controversiis Christianae Fidei* of 1590 to 1593,[2] moral theological works such as the Spaniard Juan Azorius' *Institutionum Moralium* of 1610,[3] and bibliographical works such as the Spanish Jesuit Pedro Ribadeneira's *Illustrium Scriptorum* of the members of his Society of 1602.[4] In *Essays in Divinity*, which Donne appears to have written in the five years after the publication of *Pseudo-Martyr*, the prominence of neo-Latin humanist works is equally striking. Many of the same authors appear among its references, such as the French lawyer Barthélemy de Chasseneux or Cassanaeus' *Catalogus Gloriae Mundi* of 1529,[5] but there are new ones such as the Venetian Francis George's *De Harmonia Mundi* of 1525 as well.[6]

How in either broad or specific terms these neo-Latin works influenced one of the

---

[1] Severinus Binius, *Concilia* (Cologne, 1606).

[2] Robert Bellarmine, *De Controversiis Christianae Fidei,* 3 vols. (Ingolstadt, 1590–1593).

[3] Juan Azor, *Institutionum Moralium* (Rome, 1600–1611).

[4] Pedro de Ribadeneira, *Illustrium Scriptorum* (Antwerp, 1602).

[5] Bartholomew Cassanaeus [or Chasseneux], *Catalogus Gloriae Mundi* (Lyons, 1529).

[6] Francis George [or Georgius], *De Harmonia Mundi* (Venice, 1525).

greatest writers of the English Renaissance has never been determined. And yet, Donne appears to have had by far more neo-Latin books in his personal library, if we consult Geoffrey Keynes' bibliography of him, than any other works either classical or contemporary.[7] A number of broad conclusions about this neo-Latin influence can nevertheless immediately be made. The first is that Donne was a humanist, in the sense that Renaissance humanism has come to be accepted as the pursuit of all branches of knowledge, as the Ancients understood them, in order to throw light on the nature of contemporary life. Twentieth-century criticism has tended to ignore Donne's Renaissance humanism by concentrating attention overwhelmingly on the wittiness and modernity of his verse. A second broad conclusion about the neo-Latin influence in Donne is that neo-Latin works were the literary terrain on which he came to solve his own deeply difficult philosophical and religious problems. Donne's study of neo-Latin writings, the majority of them Roman Catholic, led him to make an enormous wrench with the faith of his ancestors (among them Saint Thomas More) and to become a Protestant. His scholarship in both *Pseudo-Martyr* and *Essays* reveals that his conversion, with which he appears never to have been entirely comfortable, was based not only on neo-Latin works that involved London in political controversy with Rome, but also on numerous speculative and exegetical works that had nothing to do with politics or controversy. Yet a third broad conclusion about the influence of neo-Latin works on Donne is that they made him a much more international figure in early seventeenth-century England than the emphasis of modern criticism on the Englishness of his wit and his verse has led us to believe. His international character must have distinguished him among his English contemporaries much more than we in our own century have supposed. We have only to consider the last two never-written chapters of *Pseudo-Martyr* that his friends, he tells us in his preface, convinced him not to write. The chapters were to deal respectively with the legitimate supremacy of French kings in Renaissance France and with Augustine's conversion of Kent to Roman Catholicism in 597.[8]

To assert here that Donne was a humanist is not meant to beg the obvious. But nevertheless there is a problem. In the case of Donne's learning, particularly because of the manner in which twentieth-century criticism has approached it as wit, the obvious has not always been that evident. Donne has to his credit the plaintive declaration in "The First Anniversary" poem of 1611 commemorating the death of Elizabeth Drury that "the new Philosophy calls all in doubt."[9] On the surface of things, the new philosophy, that is, the practice of looking at the natural world inductively on its own terms, forces men to redefine their metaphysics. The declaration, like the poem from which it is drawn, is full of regret over the passing of an Elizabethan world view. The ladder of being has been shaken. The declaration also bewails the

---

7 Geoffrey Keynes, *A Bibliography of Dr. John Donne*, 4th ed. (Oxford, 1973), 263–279.

8 John Donne, *Pseudo-Martyr,* edited with Introduction, Commentary and Textual Apparatus by Anthony Raspa (Montreal, 1993), liii–liv.

9 John Donne, "The First Anniversary," *Poetical Works*, vol. I, ed. H. J. C. Grierson (Oxford, 1968), 237, l. 205.

retreat of the Graeco-Roman ideas about the nature of matter that had propped up the European Judaeo-Christian imaginings about what the created, that is, the material world, was like. But Donne's reader senses throughout the "Anniversary" poem that he had been suspicious of the universe of time and space for some time. Donne is much more concerned in the poem with the transient character of life than with the new philosophy. The new philosophy is only the occasion for him to contemplate that transitoriness. In the "Anniversary" poem he also wishes to put his finger on what, in the transitory concourse of time and space, gives him an intelligible picture of eternity and infinity.

Therefore it can be said that a major characteristic of Donne's humanism is his attempt to employ learning in the task of identifying the unchanging. This characteristic might even be considered the element that distinguishes Donne's humanism. By contrast, let us consider very briefly John Milton's humanism, because Milton's humanism is more classic and common for us than Donne's. In *Areopagitica* in 1642, some thirty years after Donne's comment on the new philosophy, when the Renaissance's doubt about itself was general and when the Renaissance had almost come to an end as an identifiable historical period, Milton writes a prose aphorism about a book, about human reason, and about man as the image of God that sums up the nature of formal humanism in England since Thomas More. "He who destroys a good book," he says, "kills reason itself, kills the image of God, as it were, in the eye."[10] In this aphorism, the angelic part of man is not the adoring medieval soul but promethean Renaissance reason. Reason is the image of God in man, and a good book, being the image of human reason, is also the image of God at two removes. As God thinks, so does the humanist aspire to think.

The difference between Donne's humanism and Milton's is striking. It is much more private and speculative and much less idealistic and public than Milton's. That is to say, it is also much more personal than Renaissance humanism in general. Because of this, and its accompanying anxiety for personal salvation, we are tempted to describe Donne's humanism as medieval. To do so, however, would be an error in light of its quality of speculation. Nevertheless its ultimate concern with interiority reminds us of the constant pressure of the presence of God on the human mind and on its perception of the material universe in the centuries that preceded the Renaissance.

These generalities about the spiritual feelings of the medieval person and about the intellectual aspirations of the Renaissance humanist can both be accounted for in the influence of neo-Latin writings on Donne. For example, in *Essays in Divinity*, Donne deals at length with attempts to define time and to relate it to the beginning of history on earth. In one passage alone he names six such attempts in a row, including two in antiquity. Was the world of 1600 five, six, seven or eight thousand years old, or, according to Chaldaean tradition, was it four hundred and seventy thousand years

---

[10] John Milton, *Areopagitica*, in *The Students' Milton*, ed. Frank Allen Patterson (New York, 1961), 733.

old (*Essays* 33)?[11] That Donne should look for his answer in Augustine of Hippo and Cyprian of Carthage is to be expected in light of his classical learning but, even if he does not mention it, he is also pursuing the sixteenth-century time-fixing habit of Gerhard Mercator's *Chronologia. Hoc Est, Temporum Demonstratio Exactissima, ab Initio Mundi, Usque ad Annum Domini M.D.LXVIII*, a chronology that gives an exact demonstration of the eras of the universe from the beginning of the world up until 1568.[12] Moreover, Donne's speculations were influenced not only by major contemporary writers such as Mercator, to whom it was usual to refer, but also by a wide range of minor and now obscure writers who were, nevertheless, an integral part of his personal intellectual baggage. As important for Donne as Augustine, Cyprian, and Mercator were the German Henry Bunting's *Chronologia Catholica, Omnium Hactenus ab Initio Mundi ad Nostra Usque Tempora* of 1608 (*Essays 19*), and the 1572 edition of Moses Maimonides' *Hebraeorum Breve Chronicon, sive Compendium de Mundi Ordine & Temporibus, ab Orbe Condito ad Annum Christi 1112*.[13] That Donne should conclude in *Essays in Divinity* that it does not matter whether the world is five, six, seven, or eight thousand years old diminishes in no way the importance of the role of neo-Latin works in his reaching his conclusion.

The speculative character of Donne's humanism is therefore tempered for him by the very existence of the neo-Latin works that were at his disposition. Neo-Latin was not only the language of original composition for some of Donne's prominent authorities in *Essays in Divinity*, such as the Italian commentators on cabalism, Archangelus of Burgonovo[14] and Franciscus Patritius,[15] who have receded into the far background of literary history (15–17). It was also the language, either in the works of commentators such as these or in translations, through which writings originally in Greek, Aramaic, Hebrew, and Arabic were communicated to him. As an example of this, Donne's grappling with the meaning of the Hebrew word "Bresit," signifying more or less the beginning of creation, is a kind of speculative word map of neo-Latin influence on him. The same may be said of his attempt to determine a meaning for the other Hebrew word "Elohim." By the early seventeenth century the words "Bresit" and "Elohim" had come to be related to the Jewish Cabala. The Cabala was a system of esoteric theosophy that its adepts since roughly the tenth century used both to uncover and interpret an oral tradition of divine truth insofar as it had been written down. The oral tradition was reputed to go back to the first man at the beginning of creation.[16] If in "The First Anniversary" and *Essays in Divinity*, written not many years apart, Donne's humanism is characterized by a desire to see clearly

---

[11] John Donne, *Essays in Divinity* (London, 1651), 33 (Cambridge University Library shelf mark, Keynes B.4.35).

[12] Gerhard Mercator, *Chronologia* (Cologne, 1569).

[13] Henry Bunting, *Chronologia Catholica* (Magdeburg, 1608); Moses Maimonides, *Hebraeorum Breve Chronicon* (Paris, 1572).

[14] Archangelus of Burgo Novo, *Apologia* (Bologna, 1564).

[15] Francesco Patrizzi, *Magia Philosophica* (Hamburg, 1593), and *Nova de Universis Philosophia* (Venice, 1593).

[16] Archangelus, *Apologia*, 22–23.

how eternity manifests itself in time, his treatment of "Bresit" was made concrete for him by neo-Latin commentators on the Cabala.

Neo-Latin writings, then, not only made available to him the writings of the Ancients but also the half-hidden stream of writings on Judaeo-Christian traditions by esoteric and obscure authors whom other (today obscure) authors in Donne's period led him to. "Bresit" was the title of the first chapter of *Zohar* (*Essays* 21–22),[17] one of the two chief works of the cabalistic tradition (the supposed Patriarch Abraham's *Book of Creation* being the other) (17).[18] In *Heptaplus*, Pico della Mirandola, one of Donne's more famous authorities in *Essays* (21–22), discusses the meaning of "Bresit" as he explains the opening phrase of Genesis, "In the Beginning."[19] However, it is another one of Donne's authorities, now a totally unknown one, the Spanish exegete Alonso Tostato (51–52), whose treatment of the cabalistic meaning of "Bresit" in *Zohar* best describes Donne's inspiration. Tostatus makes a brilliant distinction between the "Beresith" of the original Hebrew text of *Genesis*, meaning the beginning of time, and its translation into the Greek biblical text as "Genesis," signifying the birth of nature and the creation of things.[20] Touching on existence, the beginning of time, and the birth of nature, the passage by Tostatus represents the central problem of Donne's *Essays* (21).

How far neo-Latin writings exercised their influence on Donne's thinking on abstract concepts other than time is evident in his treatment of the term "Elohim." The name of "Elohim" for God appears repeatedly in the Hebrew text of the Old Testament. There is a complete section on it in *Essays* (49) and, if Donne does not adhere to any fixed meaning for the word, the theories about it in neo-Latin works allow him to speculate on the nature of his God. "Elohim" in fact seems to be a name that, for Donne, brings the concept of his God closest to being comprehended in the world of matter even if, as a cabalistic word, it was for him never more than a verbal object of speculation. "Elohim" as a name for God was, according to one of Donne's medieval authorities, Peter Lombard (*Essays*, 50), the plural form of another singular proper noun, "Hel."[21] As such, "Elohim" seemed to include two or more persons joined together under one name. In discussions about the meaning and the biblical implications of this name among Donne's contemporary cabalistic sources, there came to be connected the argument about the nature of the Trinity. Could there be three persons in one God, as there could be several individual persons signified by one name, particularly when the name at stake was an ancient Hebrew word for God? If so, had the ancient Jews believed in the Trinity of the Father, Son, and Holy Ghost

---

[17] *Zohar* [called "The Book of Splendor,"] supposedly compiled by Rabbi Simon ben Iochai (Cremona, 1559).

[18] An apocryphal book of the late centuries before Christ and supposedly written by Abraham, the *Book of Creation* was also called *Liber Abrahae, Liber de Creatione,* and *De Formationibus* (the title Donne uses): Archangelus identified it (*Apologia*, 10) with the Jewish *Sepher litcira Abrahae.*

[19] Pico della Mirandola, *Heptaplus,* in *Opera* (Basel, 1601), 40.

[20] Alonso Tostado, *Commentaria in Genesim,* in *Opera Omnia,* 13 vols. (Cologne, 1613), 1: 64.

[21] Peter Lombard, *Sententiarum,* Book I, 2 "De Mysterio Trinitatis et Unitatis" (Cologne, 1609), 14.

and expressed this belief cabalistically in one of their principal names for God? Donne agrees with Tostatus once more, to the effect, this time, that the word Elohim, like the Trinity, indicated more than one person (*Essays* 51).[22] At the same time, he disagrees with two other neo-Latin authorities, the Italian Dominican cardinal and professor of metaphysics, Tommaso Cajetan,[23] and the Italian jurist and archbishop, Ambrose Catharinus, both of whom held that to ascribe a plural form to the word was tantamount to admitting the existence of many gods equal to one another (*Essays,* 51–52).[24] The argument was as old as the fourth-century heretic Arius' belief that there were not three equal persons in the Trinity,[25] and Donne pursues it through Nicholas de Lyra in the early fourteenth century,[26] picks it up at length in the *De Arcanis Catholicae Veritatis* (1516) of the early sixteenth-century cabalist and Christian convert from Judaism, Peter Galatine,[27] and concludes it in the more contemporary controversialist works of the German theologians Aegidius Hunnius and David Pareus (50–51).[28] What is important to our comprehension of Donne in his use of these numerous medieval and contemporary neo-Latin works is the extent to which they are part of his daily practical learning. They are composite parts of a humanism that defines itself for him in terms of the Judaeo-Christian tradition as part of the learning of the Ancients. As Donne reads in the language of the ancient Romans and as he writes to himself in his reflective *Essays* in English, the popular cabalist arguments are his instrument for bringing the complexities of the past to bear on his comprehension of the concept of God in the present.

Evidence for the influence of neo-Latin works on Donne's personal history, particularly the *Essays in Divinity,* written in the decisive years of his conversion, falls short. It is the neo-Latin authorities and references in his other work, *Pseudo-Martyr,* written late in 1609 and published in January of 1610, a year before the publication of "The First Anniversary," that are pivotal. For his selection of neo-Latin writers here tells us a great deal about the issues that concerned him. The main entries of *Pseudo-Martyr* are often violent controversialist works for and against both Protestantism and Catholicism. Robert Bellarmine is among the principal ones, but we may add other Jesuits such as the Frenchman Nicholas Serarius and the German Johannes Gretser, and the English Protestant William Whitaker, among possibly a hundred

---

[22] Tostatus, *Commentaria, Opera,* 1: 69.

[23] Giacomo Tommaso de Vio Gaetani Cajetani, *In Quinque Libros Mosi* [of 1531] (Paris, 1539), 1.

[24] Ambrosius Catharinus, *Annotationes in Commentaria* (1535), and *Ennarationes* (Rome, 1552), I, cols. 7 and 8.

[25] Arius of Nicomedia was the bishop of Lybia; Donne draws his description of the Arian heresy from Binius' *Concilia,* I, II, on I Nicea in 325, vol. 1: 332, 338.

[26] Nicholas de Lyra (1270–1340), in *Contra Iudaeos* of his *Biblia Sacra* (Lyons, 1545), vol. VII, fol. 275, H.

[27] Peter Colonna of Galatine, *De Arcanis* (1516) (Francfort, 1602), X, 2–7, cols. 533–549.

[28] Aegidius Hunnius, *Calvinus Iudaizans,* I, in *Operum,* 4 vols. (Wittenberg, 1607), vol. 1, col. 639; David Pareus, *Doctrina . . . Calvini Trinitate* (Newstadt, ? 1600), sig. A2r.

others.[29] But there is also in *Pseudo-Martyr* a large selection of more civilized works of moral philosophy and theology in which, on a quieter daily basis than public controversy, the differences between Catholicism and Protestantism were experienced in Donne's day.[30] Among these are works by moral philosophers and theologians like the Spaniard Juan Azor[31] and the Frenchman Claude Carnin,[32] only two of the many who haunt the *marginalia* of Donne's *Pseudo-Martyr*. Donne's approach to them is controversial insofar as *Pseudo-Martyr* is a controversialist work defending James I's right to the throne, but the history of ideas is also at work in his handling of them. Often Donne agrees with Catholic controversialists such as the Spanish Dominicans de Soto and à Victoria, and the French jurist Cassanaeus, even when he is denying the official Catholic position against James (*Pseudo-Martyr* 91).[33] Donne in fact defines his own theological position in *Pseudo-Martyr* by agreeing with both Catholic and Protestant authorities according to the speculative values that characterize his humanism. The speculative character of his humanism feeds at the same time that it lets him rise above the controversy in which he is taking part. The neo-Latin writings, particularly the works of moral theology and philosophy of such writers as Azor, Carnin, the Austrian Adam Tanner, and the Italian Paolo Camitoli,[34] enlightened and sharpened his own ideas about the Catholicism that he was trying to leave and the Protestantism that he was trying to embrace. The speculative character of Donne's humanism may be looked upon as a condition of the religious struggles with which Renaissance humanism as a whole came into being, while the neo-Latin writings enabled Donne to define his personal destiny in the history of his times.

In the philosophical probings of *Essays in Divinity*, this question of personal destiny and the light that it received from the speculative character of his humanism took Donne far into the reaches of our modernity. Inevitably, the inquisitiveness that he deployed on the full gamut of the disciplines of the Ancients to interpret the nature of contemporary life led to his probing into what became the modern sciences. Ironically, if the new philosophy was only the occasion of Donne's search for eternity and infinity in a world of time and space, it was nevertheless helpful to him for scientific demonstration, even if he was again only speculative and sometimes even satiric. He asks in *Essays in Divinity*, in a question relevant to the yet unborn study of anthropology, what are an Englishman and a Chinaman? In passing, Donne delves into contemporary meanings for the word "aboriginal," coming as it does from two Latin words, "ab" meaning "from," and "origin." He does not annotate his sources, but

---

[29] Nicholas Serarius, *Trihaeresium* (Mainz, 1604); Johan Gretser, *Controversiam Roberto Bellarmine* (Ingolstadt, 1607–1609); William Whitaker, *Disputatio de Sacra Scriptura* (Cambridge, 1588).

[30] See "Introduction," *Pseudo-Martyr*, xxxiv–xxxv.

[31] Azor, principally for his *Institutionum Moralium* of 1600–1611.

[32] Claude Carnin, *Tractatus de Vi et Potestate Legum* (Douai, 1608).

[33] Dominic de Soto, *Commentarii* (Salamanca, 1555–1560); Francis à Victoria, *Relectiones Theologicae* (Salamanca, 1532), in (Lyons, 1587), 106; Cassanaeus, *Catalogus,* 5, Con. 28 (Paris, 1559), 235–236; *Pseudo-Martyr*, "Commentary" for 91, ll. 22–33, and 130, ll. 22–31.

[34] Adam Tanner, *Defensio Ecclesiasticae Libertatis* (Ingolstadt, 1602); Paolo Comitoli, *Responsa Moralia* (Lyons, 1609).

contemporary thinkers turned to the Latin translations or original works of the Ancients, Herodotus the Greek historian, Diodorus the Ancient, and also the Englishman William Camden's originally neo-Latin work *Britain, or a Chronological Description of the Most flourishing Kingdomes, England, Scotland, and Ireland . . . Out of Antiquitie,* published in English translation by Philomen Holland in 1610 (*Essays* 33–34).[35]

Though Donne never describes precisely what an Englishman is, he rejects the current of thought that the British are such blessed natives with a satiric remark on those who proudly call themselves aboriginals. Today we think that an aboriginal is a lineal descendant of a people known to have been somewhere before everybody else, but in Donne's time aboriginals were considered original in themselves, and descended from nobody else. The idea was repugnant to Donne. To be a worthy human being, he infers, not only is it not necessary to issue out of an original race, out of what we might imagine as a sort of people all descending from a single independent amoeba, as though this was possible, it is not even necessary to know where we come from to know what we are (33). Similarly, with his reference to the confounding so-called Chinese estimates of the age of the world, based on Western speculations of who and how many the "Chineses" in the plural are, Donne is not really pointing to the estimates of their age that the Chinese have themselves made. Rather, he is alluding to the evident misapprehensions of European writers such as Richard Willis, Richard Eden, and Gerhard Mercator, as to who the Chinese really are.[36] Donne's anthropological probings are genuine, even if all they produce is questions. In the context of his quest to find unchanging truth through human speculation, the importance of these questions and of the neo-Latin writers who provoke them consists in their contribution to revealing what—in the inexorable passage of time—a human being may grasp that is out of time's reach.

The eighty-three surviving copies of *Pseudo-Martyr,* which came out in 1610, displaying Donne's humanist speculations to his English readers, suggest that it had a large edition. But otherwise, the work appears to have had little impact. For its part, *Essays in Divinity* was not published until 1651, twenty years after Donne's death and some thirty-five years after it was written. The reasons for the relative lack of impact of *Pseudo-Martyr* and the delayed publication of *Essays in Divinity* are perhaps understandable in the context of Donne's use of neo-Latin writers. In both works, the reader is left with the impression that, though these are English compositions, Donne is not writing for him but rather, dialoguing with his neo-Latin sources. Donne the incumbent Catholic might be described as being in a state of disputation with the intellectual milieu of his incipient ex-co-religionists. Both works are haunted by the reflective habit of Donne's mind, and in both we find the consciousness of the transi-

---

[35] See Herodotus' *Historiarum Libri IX,* Book I, No. 171 (Francfort, 1608), 71; "The Fifteenth Booke" (l. 12), *Albions England* (London, 1602); Philomen Holland trans., William Camden, *Britain, Or a Chronologicall Description* (London, 1610), 9; Mercator, *Chronologia* (Cologne, 1569), sigs. *1r–*5v.

[36] Richard Willis, *The History of Travayls,* trans. Richard Eden (London, 1577), 237; Mercator, *Atlas,* trans. W. S. Generosus (London, 1635), cols. 864–865.

toriness of time and space that permeates "The First Anniversary." The fleeting character of life is a constituent element in Donne's debate with himself about what true religion and God are. How do true religion and God manifest themselves in that flux in a manner that does not render them its victim? The question is not necessarily un-English, but it makes Donne an international figure because of the neo-Latin terrain in which he sought to argue it out. Both *Pseudo-Martyr* and *Essays* are fundamentally theological and philosophical treatises written in English for more or less specific occasions, but in the context of a neo-Latin milieu. As such, they make of Donne in his own time an international figure, howbeit unattractive to an English public world where it was other figures such as Ben Jonson who shone. Unpopularity was the price Donne paid for conducting his reflections among the neo-Latin publications of an international intellectual set that shone little and thought much.

Université Laval, Québec

Translation and Imitation of Joannes Secundus'
Basia *during the Era of the Civil War
and Protectorate in England: 1640–60*

STELLA P. REVARD

Although Jonson, Campion, and other Elizabethan poets had imitated individual poems and passages from Joannes Secundus' *Basia*, the collection was not translated until 1651, when the royalist poet Thomas Stanley included an almost complete selection of Secundus' "kiss" poems in an expanded collection of original poems and translations. Stanley was not the only royalist to be interested in Secundus. Throughout the *Hesperides*, the collection of lyric pieces that he published in 1648, Robert Herrick imitated lines and sometimes whole poems of Secundus. That Secundus should become a model for the Cavalier poets who followed Jonson in the 1630s is not unexpected. Jonson's imitation of Catullus, "Come my Celia," owes as much to Secundus as to Catullus, and his famous "Drink to me only with thine eyes" borrows nectared kisses from *Basium* 4. But the popularity of Secundus with Stanley and Herrick during the 1640s and 50s cannot simply be accounted for as their legacy from old Ben. Nor can we accept their imitation of the innocent but reckless sensuality of the *Basia* as only an escape from political upheaval or as nostalgia for the courtly courtesies of an earlier era. When poets in the 1640s and 50s imitated the kiss poems, they were making political as well as amatory statements. Surely Englishmen at the height of the Puritan Commonwealth had better things to do than to contemplate a neo-Latin poetic miscellany on the art of osculation. A closer look at Herrick's and Stanley's imitations of Secundus can tell us something about the literary taste of royalists in the Puritan interregnum, as well as about the continuing popularity of Secundus in England.

Although I have coupled Herrick and Stanley as sons of Ben and as lyric poets whose work appears at roughly the same time at the end of the 1640s, as translators and adapters of Secundus they are quite different. Herrick, the country parson from Devon, who published his verses to imaginary mistresses, is quite a different figure from the aristocratic Stanley, who was independently wealthy, surrounded himself with like-minded royalist friends, and remained devoted and active in literary studies during the Cromwellian regime. Also they make quite different statements about the young Dutch poet and his elegies and *Basia*. Herrick inclines to the flippant and slyly sensual aspects of Secundus' poetry, Stanley to its sweetly sorrowful, mournful regretfulness. It is hardly a surprise that Herrick's famous "To the Virgins, to make much of Time" (84) with its timely advice, "Gather ye Rose-buds while ye may!" is a countrified version of Secundus' more erotic counsel (*Elegia* I. 5.13–16).[1]

Throughout the *Hesperides* there are as many versions of kissing as Secundus offers us. Herrick calls the kiss "loves sweetest language" (130), "the sure sweet-Sement, Glue, and Lime of Love" (218).[2] His descriptions of kisses demonstrate that Herrick knew both Catullus and Secundus. Imitating Catullus' lines to Lesbia (Catullus 5), Herrick exhorts his mistress Sappho: "Let us now take time, and play, / Love, and live here while we may" (238). His "Kissing Usurie" is but another version of the Catullan numbers' game; he urges his mistress that he pay her (with interest) for the single kiss he owes:

> If thou will say,
> Ten will not pay
> For that so rich a one;
> Ile cleare the summe,
> If it will come
> Unto a Million. (29)[3]

But, although Herrick imitates both Catullus' lyrics 5 and 7 and Secundus' imitations of them, Basium 6 and 7, Herrick is still more playful than his predecessors—even flippant—in his demand for kisses. It is almost as though it were a game—a country game with this girl or that. Here is no heart-searing courtship. True, Herrick follows the same mythological lore that frames Secundus' sequence. Like Secundus, he asks Venus and Cupid to grant him kisses ("A Hymne to Venus, and Cupid"); he describes his lady's lips as "over-laid / With Loves-sirrop" (138) and the kiss itself as a winged thing that "honie yeelds; but never stings" ("The Kisse. A Dialogue," 130). But he is not a slavish imitator. For Herrick kisses are tokens to be exchanged between lovers. Sometimes he is too shy even to beg a kiss, content "Onely to kisse that Aire, / That lately kissed thee" ("To Electra," 231). Other times he dismisses kisses as mere provocation: "Give me food that satisfies a Guest: / Kisses are but dry banquets to a Feast" (265). What Secundus hints at (in *Basium* 14 and elsewhere) and Stanley suppresses, Herrick directly states. However sweet, however desired, the kiss is not the be-all and end-all of the lover's desire. Herrick's epigram, "Upon Jack and

---

[1] For an account of the influence of Secundus on English poetry, see Dougall Crane, *Johannes Secundus: His Life, Work, and Influence on English Literature* (Leipzig, 1931). For Herrick, see pp. 59–62.

[2] Robert Herrick, *The Poetical Works of Robert Herrick*, ed. L.C. Martin (London, 1956).

[3] Also see "To Dianeme," where the poet coyly pleads for one kiss that he'll "restore / For that one two / Thousand score" (196).

Jill," is a frank statement of this, with the lady rather than the lover demanding more than kisses. It begins with Jill's complaint, "When *Jill* complaines to *Jack* for want of meate; / *Jack* kisses *Jill*, and bids her freely eate." "Of what?" Jill rejoins. "Sayes *Jack*, on that sweet kisse, / Which full of Nectar and Ambrosia is, / The food of Poets." That sweet kiss, of course, is none other than Secundus' fourth *Basium*. For as Secundus says, Neaera does not give kisses; she gives nectar, the sweet-smelling dew of the soul, fragrant with nard, thyme, and cinnamon with honey; a kiss such as would make the poet immortal. But Herrick's Jill is not impressed: "so I thought sayes *Jill*, / That makes them [the poets] looke so lanke, so Ghost-like still." She advises the poets to "feed on aire, or what they will." As for her, she requires a more substantial meal: "Let me feed full, till that I fart, sayes *Jill*" (186).

Herrick is, as it were, replying to Secundus and his ilk who celebrate the kiss and the kiss alone. By bringing it down to the level of a country Jack and Jill, he gives us a realistic view of the kiss. We find a different frankness in "Kisses Loathsome." Neo-Latin poets frequently ask for tongue kisses. Sannazaro demands such kisses in his verses "Ad Ninam," and Secundus celebrates them in Basium 5, describing how Neaera moves her tongue against his lips and how his tongue meets hers as they kiss. English poets such as Stanley, confronted with such erotic foreplay, often simply look the other way, omitting or modifying the offending lines.[4] Herrick, however, is hardly prudish. He objects to such sport on other grounds: "I abhor the slimie kisse, / (Which to me most loathsome is)." He prescribes exactly what he requires from a kiss: "Those lips please me which are plac't / Close, but not too strictly lac't: / Yeilding I wo'd have them; yet / Not a wimbling Tongue admit." So much for the aesthetics of English versus continental kisses. But Herrick is not through. He adds a racy comment, much in the style of his own Jill: "What sho'd poking-sticks make there, / When the ruffe is set elsewhere?" (282).

Thomas Stanley could not be more different in his reaction to Secundus' *Basia*. Both in his original kiss poems, published in 1647, and in his translations from Secundus, published in 1651, he presents an aesthetic distinct from either Herrick's or Secundus'. In so doing, he sometimes translates literally, sometimes modifies Secundus' work. Among the 1647 *Poems*, "The hasty kisse" is a literal version of Secundus' *Basium* 3, with his mistress Chariessa's name taking the place of Neaera's (5). It directly follows his "Imitatio Catulliana," a version of Catullus 7: "Number the sands that do restrain / And fetter the Rebellious main"(5).[5] Stanley may have intended to produce a mini-anthology of kiss poems from several authors when he assembles this sequence. Immediately after these two literal pieces is an original poem, "The cold kisse," that defines more clearly Stanley's views as a poet. The opening lines of "The

____

[4] A later English translator, George Ogle, offers translations of all of Secundus' *Basia*, but modifies considerably Secundus' original text. See *Basia, Joannis Secundi Nicolai Hagensis: or The Kisses of Joannes Secundus Nicolaius of the Hague. In Latin and English Verse* (London, 1731). See Crane, 74–75.

[5] Quotations from the 1647 *Poems*, unless otherwise noted, are from Thomas Stanley, *Poems and Translations* (London, 1647).

cold kisse" could be read as a variation of two lines from *Basium* 9 or as a chaste version of Sannazaro's kiss poem to Nina.

> Such icie kisses Anchorites that live
> Secluded from the world to dead sculls give;
> And those cold Maids on whom Love never spent
> His flame, nor know what by desire is meant,
> To their expiring Fathers such bequeath. . . . (5)

At first glance these lines seem to echo *Basium* 9:

> Dat casta fratri, qualia dat patri
> Experta nullos nata Cupidines.

Stanley's verses to Chariessa, however, are actually closer to the opening verses from Sannazaro's erotic "Ad Ninam." It was Sannazaro who first demanded kisses different from those that daughters give to parents, or sisters to brothers: "Non quas dent bene filiae parenti / Nec quas dent bene fratribus sorores."[6] Even though Stanley urges Chariessa to join her lips with his in an equal flame that will melt her coldness, he never approaches Sannazaro's erotic suggestiveness. He declines to tell his mistress what kind of kisses he prefers. In Stanley there are no erotic nibblings and thrustings, no implication that the kissing is merely prologue to more passionate exercises. Moreover, the poems that follow in Stanley's mini-anthology of kisses—"The killing Kisse" and "Speaking and kissing"—demonstrate that Stanley has an agenda of his own. He is not content merely to translate Catullus or Secundus or even Sannazaro; he wishes to interpret them for his age. The 1651 translations of Secundus further define attitudes already evident in the first kiss sequence of 1647.

When Stanley comes to translate Secundus' *Basia* for the 1651 collection of his *Poems*, he includes only fourteen of the original nineteen *Basia*. He not only omits *Basia* 8, 10, 11, 12, and 14, but also reworks *Basium* 5, omitting lines 6 through 11—Secundus' description of the tongue kiss. The omitted poems contain not only some of the more erotic passages from the *Basia*, but also some of its more humorous and risqué commentary. *Basium* 8 protests that Neaera has bit the very tongue that praised her beauty; *Basium* 10 provides a continental sampler of kissing styles; *Basium* 11 renders Neaera's verdict on kissing; and *Basium* 12 pleads that although Neaera's book lacks a "mentula," Neaera's poet does not. Together with *Basium* 14, which Stanley also omits, these poems add a playfulness and an explicit sexuality to the collection. But, as the translations of Secundus published in 1731 by George Ogle demonstrate, they present no insuperable problem to the English translator, determined to stay within the bounds of so-called English polite taste.

We do not know which edition of Secundus Stanley used for his translations of the *Basia*. Crump suggests it may well have been one of the editions Petrus Scriverius

---

⁶ See Ioannes Nicolai Secundus, *Basia*, ed. Georg Ellinger (Berlin, 1899), 22. Ellinger includes Sannazaro's poem in an anthology of poetry on kisses, both poems that influence Secundus and those he influences (pp. 22–23).

published in 1619 and 1631.[7] The 1619 edition is particularly interesting, for in it the original nineteen kisses become twenty-two. Scriverius has moved Secundus' "Epithalamium" from the *Sylva* to become *Basium* 20. The "Epithalamium" is a passionate celebration of physical consummation that includes a Propertian rhapsody on the blessedness of the lover. As such, it provides the sequence with a "sexual" climax, quite different from its original playful finale—*Basium* 19's disquisition on honey and honey-bees. Following the "Epithalamium," Scriverius adds, moreover, the epigrams in which Secundus defends his *Basia* against charges of obscenity—"De libello suo Basiorum" and "Ad Grammaticos, cur scribat lascivius."[8]

The very existence of these addenda in the Scriverius edition testify to the eroticism that readers and editors connected with the *Basia*. The "Epithalamium" celebrates sexual passion, and the two epigrams are poetic apologies for the frank sexuality of his kissing poems. English translators who approached the *Basia* in a Scriverius edition could have little doubt about the erotic nature of the original Latin poems. One English editor and translator—Ogle—even retains in his 1731 edition of Secundus the "Epithalamium" as *Basium* 20, knowing full well, as his notes explain, that Scriverius had exceeded his authority as an editor in placing it there. Stanley could have done the same. But, in declining to translate the "Epithalamium" and five of the most frankly erotic *Basia*, he chose to offer to the English public of the 1650s a chastened view of Secundus.

It is not that Stanley is irresponsible as a translator. Of the fourteen "Kisses" he includes, most are close and accurate versions of Secundus' originals. But in omitting a fourth of the poems—as well as Secundus' apologies—Stanley has subtly altered the character of the *Basia*. No need now to insist that the book lacks a "mentula," when he has neatly omitted Secundus' defense of that missing organ. Neaera's biting teeth also disappear along with Secundus' outrage that she has attacked the tongue that praised her tangled hair. Stanley has avoided translating the very passage that Milton alludes to in "Lycidas" when he contemplates the tangles of Neaera's hair.

"Soul" is the key word for Stanley both in the original kiss poems of 1647 and in the translations of Secundus that he includes in 1651. The Latin "anima" occurs in Secundus, but not as frequently as the word "soul" appears in Stanley's translations. The kiss for Stanley is the joining of souls, the ecstatic experience—ecstasy is another key word—that brings the lovers to the verge of death and brings them back again. Stanley was already platonically inclined before he completed his translations from Secundus, as several of the kiss poems from 1647 attest. Taking his cue in "The Innocence of Love" from Catullus 61 and *Basium* 2, Stanley makes his lovers imitate the ivy and the vine as they embrace: "See how this Ivy (Dear), doth twine / Her wanton arms about the Vine (21. ll. 1–2).[9] But far from luxuriating in the wanton-

---

[7] Thomas Stanley, *Poems and Translations*, ed. Galbraith Miller Crump (Oxford, 1962), 392.

[8] See *Ioannis Secundi Hagiensis Poetae elegantissimi Opera quae reperiri potuerunt omnia*, ed. Petrus Scriverius (Leiden, 1619), 103–109.

[9] See Catullus 61. 34–35: "Ut tenax hedera huc et huc / arborem implicat errans (the clinging ivy here and there wandring embraces the tree); Secundus, *Basium* 2. ll. 1–3: "Vicina quantum vitis

ness of such embraces, he defends their innocence: "Thus led by those chast guides, we may / Embrace and kisse as free as they" (ll. 11–12). The model he aspires to is spiritual or heavenly: "those blessed souls above, / Whose life is harmony and love" (ll. 13–14). Such love cannot "shame or blushes move / Like Plants to live, like Angels love" (ll. 23–24). Thus, though drawing his metaphor from Catullus or Secundus, his proposition does not recall these poets. Instead it recalls John Donne, who was his master in a score of his love lyrics.[10] Donne's "Aire and Angels," or his "A Valediction, Forbidding Mourning," could have provided Stanley with examples of lovers raised above "dull sublunary love."

"The killing Kisse" also offers a neo-platonic suggestion:

> When on thy lip my soul I breath,
>   Which there meets thine,
> Freed from the fetters by this death
>   They both unite and joyn;
> Thus without bonds of sence they move,
> And like two Cherubins converse and love. (22. ll. 1–6)

Here Stanley has combined suggestions from both Secundus' *Basium* 13 and Donne's "The Ecstasie." In Donne the lovers are lifted to heavenly love, but they are joined in mind and thought by the twisting of their joined eye-beams, not, as in Stanley, with the catalyst of the kiss. In Stanley's "Speaking and kissing," the key Donnian word "ecstasy" appears, but the poem's kiss anticipates the translation of the *Basia*:

> Lost in this pleasing Extasie
>   I joyn my trembling lips to thine
> And back receive that life from thee,
>   Which I so gladly did resigne. (23, ll. 5–8)[11]

In 1651 Stanley not only published his translation of Secundus' *Kisses*, but also *A Platonick Discourse Upon Love*, translated from Giovanni Pico della Mirandola's *Commento sopra una canzona de amore de H. Benivieni* (1487). In it he defines the difference between vulgar and angelic love:

> Vulgar love is onely in Souls immerst in Matter, and overcome by it, or at least hindred by perturbations and passions. Angelick Love is in the Intellect, eternal

---

lascivit in ulmo, / Et tortiles per ilicem / brachia proceram stringunt immensa corymbi" (Just as the vine plays wantonly in the neighboring elm, and the circling ivy presses the immense branches throughout the tall oak). Stanley renders *Basium* 2 in this way: "The flattering Ivy never holds / Her husband Elm in stricter folds."

[10] See, for example, Stanley's "The Bracelet," in *Poems and Translations*, ed. Crump, 39.

[11] In the dialogue, "Exchange of soules," a similar phenomenon occurs, with first the Philocharis and then Chariessa remarking how the kiss has stolen life away and caused an exchange of souls. The Chorus sums up that "Love onely can these wonders show," when "both soules in desire are one" (39–40).

as it. . . . Though Celestial Love liveth eternally in the Intellect of every Soul, yet onely those few make use of it . . . who declin[e] the Care of the Body. To which state a Man sometimes arrives; but continues there but a while, as we see in Extasies. (241, 243)[12]

In his translation of Pico's discourse Stanley makes no mention of the platonic kiss, which Castiglione makes so prominently a part of Bembo's platonic explanation in Book IV of *The Courtier*. But this kiss cannot have been far from his mind when he translated the discourse or when he appropriated the platonic kiss both for his own kiss poems and his translations of Secundus.

It is not in the first, but in the second *Basium* that Stanley's platonizing becomes evident. He begins, just as Secundus does, by suggesting that the lovers emulate the vine and ivy in their embrace:

> So thou about my Neck thy Arms shalt fling,
>> Joyning to mine thy Breast;
> So shall my Arms about thy fair Neck cling,
>> My Lips on thine imprest. (2. ll. 5–8)

In Secundus the kiss inspires the journey to the Elysian fields to see the pairs of famous lovers who will resign their seats to Neaera and her lover. But in Stanley we have something a little different: the expiration of souls: "But we at once will on each others Lip / Our mutual Souls expire" (2. ll. 11–12). Kisses for Stanley confer life and death. In his translation of *Basium* 4, for example, Neaera not only gives nectar in her kisses, but "Nectar 'tis that new Life flows" (4. l. 2).[13] Whereas in *Basium* 5 Secundus' transports are inspired by the little nips that Neaera gives when she captures his tongue with hers, Stanley's transports are inspired by the soul:

> When thou thy pliant Arms dost wreath
> About my Neck, and gently breath
> Into my Breast that soft sweet Air
> With which thy Soul doth mine repair,
> When my faint Life thou draw'st away . . . (5. ll. 1–5)

There is nothing exactly like this in Secundus.

But if we conclude from this that Secundus is sensual where Secundus' translator Stanley is soulful, we err. After the dalliance of "Kisses" 8 through 12, Secundus fully enacts the love-death in *Basium* 13 (number 9 in Stanley) that Stanley had been hinting at earlier in the sequence. Faint from his encounter with Neaera, the poet lies drained of life. Stanley translates it this way:

---

[12] Thomas Stanley, "A Platonick Discourse Upon Love," in *Poems and Translations* (London, 1651).

[13] He follows Secundus exactly in exclaiming, as Propertius also did, that such kisses "soon me Immortal make" (4.8). See Propertius *Elegies* 1.15; also see Secundus I.5 in which the poet suggests that Julia will make him immortal.

. . . . .
> I lay of Life by thee, my Life, bereav'd
> *Styx* now before my Eyes appeard, the dark
> Region, and aged *Carons* swarthy Bark. (9. ll. 5–6)

But then, even as he hovers between life and death, Neaera bestows the life-giving moisture of her mouth on his dry lips, calling him back from the Stygian valley. It is her soul, now joined with his, that sustains the life in his body. Stanley exactly catches Secundus' meaning: "Part of thy Soul within this Body raigns / And friendly my declining Limbs sustains" (9. ll. 13–14). The poem concludes with an impassioned plea that the two would expire together in a final embrace.

> Come then, unite thy melting Lip to mine,
> And let one Spirit both our Breasts combine,
> 'Till in an Extasie of wild desire
> Together both our Breasts one Life expire. (9. ll. 19–22)

Although the word ecstasy is Stanley's and not Secundus', Stanley in no way exaggerates either the passion nor the soulfulness of Secundus' demand. Perhaps Secundus inherits the desire for the love-death from his master Propertius, who wishes to live and die with his Cynthia; perhaps from Catullus, whose demand for endless kisses follows his anticipation of the long night of death. But in the concluding lines of *Basium* 13 Secundus expresses the sense that one life flows in two bodies: "Unica de gemino corpore vita fluet" (*Basium* 13. ll. 22).

This theme is not unique to *Basium* 13, however. In *Basium* 16 (number 11 in Stanley), after he has demanded from Neaera the same number of kisses that Lesbia gave Catullus, Secundus alludes once more to the killing-restorative kiss:

> Rest on my Cheek in Extasie,
> Ready to close thy dying Eye;
> . . . . .
> My warm to thy cold bosome joyn,
>   And call thee back from Death,
>   With a long Kisses Breath
> 'Till me like Fate of Life bereave. (11. 25–26; 30–33)

Although the poem concludes with a rather conventional exhortation to seize the day, at its center is the insistence that the kiss has the power to transcend life itself.

Neither Secundus nor Stanley concludes the sequence of kisses with transcendence. The final kiss—number 19 in Secundus, number 14 in Stanley—is a sportive little trifle on the bees mistaking Neaera's lip for a flower. It is a delightful piece, one that inspired Herrick to write an apian apology in which the bee excuses his mistake ("The captiv'd Bee: or, The little Filcher," 71). But it is not quite what we would expect as a culmination of kisses. No wonder editors such as Scriverius wanted to use the "Epithalamium" to provide the sexual completion the *Basia* seems to demand.

For Stanley's purposes the tale of the bee is, however, just the right conclusion. Throughout his translation he is intent on containing the sensuousness Secundus has been just as intent on exploring. He follows Secundus when he celebrates the ecstasy beyond human life that love inspires, but he is content to let the soft flame of the soul subside and leave the reader with a sweet and not a killing kiss. His reasons, moreover, for this may have been political as well as aesthetic. When Stanley published the *Kisses* in 1651, the Puritan establishment was firmly in control in England. To many Puritans, royal love poetry was simply indecent. Two of the most popular poets of the era preceding the Civil Wars were Thomas Carew and Sir John Suckling, both of whom knew how to turn aside with a suggestive leer. Carew was, moreover, the author of the notorious seduction poem, "The Rapture," that had been modeled on *Basium* 2, but had taken it one step further—frankly to propose sexual intercourse. Secundus had defended himself against charges of indecency, but there was no defending such a poem as "The Rapture." When Stanley undertook his imitations and finally his translations of Secundus, he does not emphasize an unbridled sensuality. In fact, he puts the bridle on. It is a different kind of rapture that he entertains—the ecstasy of the soul. Indeed, he might also have been demonstrating that royalists loyal to Charles I could write innocently of love.

In several of Stanley's manuscript poems written during this period we find exactly this proposition. In a poem addressed to his kinsman and fellow poet Richard Lovelace, Stanley asserts that the chastity of lovers and loyalty to the king went hand-in-hand: "thou thy Love and Loyalty didst sing, / The Glories of thy Mistris, and thy King" (360).[14] To the dramatist Shirley, another friend and intimate of his circle, he also writes praising the propriety of his life and his poetry:

> Smooth as thy verse, thy Conversation flow'd
> Chast as the kisses by the Morn bestow'd
> Upon the Virgin-daughters of the year;
> Thy Lines and life alike unspotted were. (357)

Stanley seems clearly to be telling his fellow royalists that their conduct in poetry and in life in this Cromwellian age must uphold both unblemished moral and political standards. Royalists must woo a chaste Muse. In his translations of Secundus both politics and his own natural predilection govern Stanley. He would have even more strictly than Secundus himself defended the innocence and the chastity of his *Kisses*.

Southern Illinois University

---

[14] See "A Register of Friends," in *Poems and Translations*, ed. Crump.

Modèles séculaires et tradition biblique:
les Septem psalmi *(1538) de Salmon Macrin*

FRANÇOIS ROUGET

La place qu'occupe Salmon Macrin dans la production néo-latine de son temps est désormais bien connue, depuis les travaux de G. Soubeille et de I. McFarlane[1]. L'on sait quel rôle il a joué dans le *sodalitium* lyonnais aux côtés de N. Bourbon et J. Visagier et quelle influence sa lyrique latine a eue sur les précurseurs de la Pléiade. Pourtant, si ses odes et ses hymnes ont retenu l'attention de la critique, ses adaptations des Psaumes semblent avoir été négligées, éclipsées sans doute en partie par le nombre de ses poésies religieuses publiées dès 1537 et qui ne cesseront de s'accroître.

L'adaptation des Psaumes en vers latins (le plus souvent en strophes lyriques) correspond ainsi chez Macrin à une inspiration chrétienne de plus en plus sensible. Mais elle répond aussi à un horizon d'attente de la part du public et à un essor de la *translatio* de la Bible en latin, partout en Europe, vers 1530[2]. En publiant une adaptation métrifiée des sept psaumes pénitentiels, Macrin s'inscrit dans une vogue, un mouvement d'érudits soucieux de véhiculer la morale chrétienne et sensibles aux inflexions lyriques de la parole davidique.

Ce travail d'adaptation en vers latins apparaît également dans un climat religieux particulier: celui de la première Réforme qui favorise cet effort de traduction et qui voit dans le livre des Psaumes un terrain privilégié pour la transmission de son message évangélique. Malgré les ambiguïtés de son christianisme, et malgré la coexistence d'adaptation latine des Psaumes par des Catholiques déclarés, Macrin ne pouvait

---

[1] Voir S. Macrin, *Le Livre des Épithalames (1528–1531) et les Odes de 1530 (I–II)*, éd. crit. de G. Soubeille (Toulouse, 1978); et I. McFarlane, "Jean Salmon Macrin (1490–1557)", *B.H.R.* 21 (1959): 55–84 et 311–349, et 22 (1960): 73–89.

[2] Cf. W. L. Grant, "Neo-Latin Translation of the Bible", *Harvard Theological Review* 52, 3 (1959): 205–211; J. A. Gaertner, "Latin Verse Translation of the Psalms (1560–1620)", *Harvard Theological Review* 49 (1956): 271–305; et plus précisément pour Macrin, voir I. McFarlane, *Buchanan* (London, 1981): 248.

ignorer qu'en entreprenant cette tâche il prenait position dans des débats religieux menaçants. De plus, outre le clivage religieux, existait une autre forme de compétition à laquelle se livraient les traducteurs en latin et en langue vernaculaire. Ami déclaré de Clément Marot qui se mit à traduire les Psaumes en français au même moment, Macrin semble avoir répondu au défi lancé par son ami réformé. Et on peut se demander dans quelle mesure la paraphrase latine de Macrin a pu influencer la version française de Marot.

On le voit, le petit volume publié en 1538 pose plusieurs questions. Il nous invite à nous interroger sur la place des Psaumes dans l'œuvre de Macrin, sur le rôle de celui-ci dans l'adaptation des Psaumes en odes néo-latines métrifiées, et sur ses motivations linguistiques, esthétiques et religieuses.

Pour tenter d'esquisser des éléments de réponse, nous nous proposons de rappeler d'abord la genèse des Psaumes latins chez Macrin, puis de discerner les principales caractéristiques des *Septem psalmi*, et enfin de mieux situer leur place dans l'ensemble de l'adaptation latine des Psaumes en Europe, pour souligner leurs sources et leur impact possibles.

Macrin et la paraphrase des Psaumes: essai de genèse

Essayons d'abord de rappeler succinctement les étapes de l'adaptation des Psaumes en latin par Macrin. Tout semble démarrer, semble-t-il, peu avant 1537 et la publication des *Hymnorum libri sex,* où l'on voit apparaître en ordre dispersé la paraphrase des Psaumes 1, 2, 119, 122, 127, 113, 116, et 99. A cela s'ajoute la paraphrase latine du "Cantique de Siméon" (Luc 2:25–29) qui inspirera peut-être les versions françaises de Calvin (1539)[3] et de Marot (1543)[4]. Comme dans le cas de Marot en français, l'ordre des Psaumes respecté au début donne l'impression que Macrin aurait d'abord eu l'intention de traduire l'ensemble du Psautier et de manière systématique, avant de se résigner à choisir les pièces les plus significatives. Deuxième remarque à propos de ce recueil de 1537: la paraphrase des Psaumes alterne avec des poèmes de registres très variés et avec des pièces d'inspiration chrétienne plus libres[5]. Les Psaumes semblent se fondre dans la masse et illustrer la *varietas* thématique et la virtuosité du poète en matière rythmique.

L'année suivante, Macrin fait paraître à Poitiers chez de Marnef les *Septem psalmi in lyricos numeros . . .* qui présentent la double caractéristique de l'unité (les sept psaumes pénitentiels) et de la totale nouveauté[6]. A une exception près puisque le Psaume 1 en strophes saphiques de 1537 se voit repris mais fait l'objet d'une refonte en vers hendécasyllabiques en 1538 pour ouvrir la seconde partie du recueil, celle des "Péans". Nous reviendrons plus loin sur la constitution de ce recueil pour en définir

---

[3] Cf. *Aulcuns Pseaulmes et cantiques mys en chant,* (Strasbourg, 1539)—recueil qui contient de lui 6 psaumes, les traductions du "Credo" et des "Commandments", et 13 Psaumes de Marot.

[4] Cf. *Trente Pseaulmes de David mis en françoys* (Paris, 1541).

[5] Cf. pp. 59–61: "Ad Christium Genethliacum"; pp. 61–62: "Carmen natalitium . . .", etc.

[6] Nous ne connaissons qu'une édition de ce texte bien que H. Vaganay en indique une autre de 1530 (*Les traductions du psautier en vers latins au XVIe siècle* [Fribourg, 1898]). A moins qu'il ne s'agisse du même texte . . .

la spécificité. On notera que la même année, à Tolède, est édité le recueil des *Septem Elegiae in septem poenitentiae Psalmos* d'Alvarus Gomez et qu'à Bâle paraît une traduction métrifiée des "Proverbes" et de l'"Ecclésiaste" d'Eobanus Hessus à la suite de laquelle on trouve une anthologie de psaumes en latin composés entre autres par Melanchton, Hessus et Macrin!

En 1540, Macrin fait paraître les *Hymnorum libri tres*, version réduite du texte de 1537. On y trouve cependant de nouvelles paraphrases comme celles des Psaumes 146, 112, 22, 23, et 64, mais aussi des refontes de psaumes précédemment adaptés: les Psaumes 127 et 99, publiés en 1537, et les Psaumes 50 et 145, du recueil de 1538. Le travail de réécriture se limite à quelques retouches lexicales comme dans la seconde version du Psaume 127[7] ou bien s'exerce sur la métrique du poème et la paraphrase entière (Ps. 99)[8].

Enfin, on notera qu'en 1556, Macrin inclura 5 paraphrases dans le recueil composé par Henri Estienne intitulé *Davidis psalmi aliquot Latino carmine . . .* et qui réunit des contributions de G. Buchanan, M. A. Flaminio, E. Hessus et Rapicius[9]. On y retrouve les deux premiers psaumes de 1537, les deux versions du Psaume 127 (1537 et 1540), et le Psaume 137, la seule nouveauté, sauf erreur de notre part. La participation de Macrin à ce florilège européen suggère bien l'intérêt constant qu'il avait porté depuis ses débuts en poésie à la paraphrase latine des Psaumes. Elle montre aussi comment le poète les considérait: source d'inspiration pour de nouveaux poèmes, ils constituaient aussi le matériau idéal pour ses recherches métriques. C'est ce que révèle l'anthologie d'Estienne à propos du Psaume 127. En cela, Macrin a fait œuvre de poète néo-latin toujours en quête d'un rythme et d'une langue qui puissent illustrer, voire dépasser, son modèle hébreu, mais également les versions latines de ses contemporains. Car l'exercice de style s'inscrit dans un jeu collectif où chacun rivalise avec les autres[10]. Sur le plan individuel, il sous-entend peut-être le projet resté inachevé de Macrin de traduire en latin l'ensemble du Psautier, ce que réaliseront Buchanan et Bèze en latin, ce dernier complétant par ailleurs le Psautier de Marot en français.

Toujours est-il que l'effort de Macrin, salué en son temps par les traducteurs européens, mérite d'être souligné par l'analyse de son ouvrage le plus significatif dans la paraphrase des Psaumes: les *Septem psalmi*.

La place des *Septem psalmi*: exercice de style ou œuvre de piété?

Justement, à regarder de près ce petit volume, on s'aperçoit de son double intérêt,

---

[7] La version de 1540 supprime en outre les 3 derniers vers de 1537, "credo" d'ailleurs absent du texte hébreu. Voir aussi le Ps. 145.

[8] Les hendécasyllabes suivis de 1537 se voient transformés en quatrains en 1540.

[9] Cf. les commentaires de I. McFarlane, "Macrin", 22 (1960): 78, et *Buchanan,* 250.

[10] Cf. J. A. Gaertner, "Latin verse translation", 274: "What the educated public found in the Latin (and occasionally Greek) metrical translations was something else: a humanistic delight in literary skill and an occasion for a fascinating comparison between original and translation". Gaertner relève en outre une anthologie antérieure à celle d'Estienne (1556) et d'Hessus (1538), un recueil de 1532 réunissant des versions de Melanchton, Hessus, Moltzer . . . (*Psalmi omnium delectissimi adflictis conscientiis . . .* Hagenau).

qui correspond à sa dimension bipartite. D'un côté, la paraphrase des sept psaumes pénitentiels précédés d'une "precatio dominica" en strophes saphiques et conclus par un éloge de la Vierge Marie en distiques élégiaques. De l'autre, quatre livres de péans, c'est-à-dire d'éloges adressés à des contemporains, de prières aux figures du christianisme et aux saints, ou de poèmes évoquant certains épisodes de la Bible et les dates du calendrier catholique ainsi que les articles de la foi[11]. Macrin met un soin tout particulier à faire alterner les pièces de ces divers registres en les associant aux mètres les plus variés. On y trouve aussi quelques paraphrases de Psaumes (liv.I, Ps. 1; liv.III, Ps. 146 . . .)

Malgré la tonalité religieuse dominante du recueil, le poète a su lui conférer une dimension profane au moyen de la phraséologie latine et de la rythmique. L'unité du volume semble préservée grâce au contenu biblique du lyrisme et à des reprises de genre d'une section à l'autre (les Psaumes). L'esthétique de la *varietas* rythmique sert en quelque sorte à amplifier et à illustrer formellement le lyrisme encomiastique qui reste la base du recueil. Exercice de style avec les paraphrases, composition libre avec les péans, l'écriture du volume se veut entièrement tournée vers la "gloria Dei". Et les formes poétiques choisies (les odes, les péans . . .) correspondent au plus près du sujet élu. Les odes sont censées restituer ou s'adapter à la forme des versets bibliques; quant aux péans—traditionnellement chants d'éloge à Apollon[12]—ne sont-ils pas adéquats pour célébrer le culte du Christ et de la Vierge[13]? De par la source choisie (les Psaumes), et les formes rythmiques adoptées, le recueil de Macrin offre l'impression d'un livre liturgique destiné au chant. On retrouve ainsi dans ces textes bibliques aux cadres métriques latins l'essence même du lyrisme. Dans tous les cas, le poète s'apparente à l'orant qui supplie ses protecteurs d'écouter sa prière. Porte-parole de David dans la paraphrase des Psaumes, il véhicule sa propre voix dans la suite du recueil et à la *persona* biblique succède une présence authentique.

Mais revenons au cœur du sujet, la paraphrase des Psaumes, et interrogeons-nous sur le choix des pièces pénitentielles. Au tout début du siècle, Antonius Geraldinus avait fait paraître sa *Metaphrasis psalmorum VII pœnitentialium litaniarumque* à Paris[14], et en 1538, on l'a vu, Alvarus Gomez publiait à Tolède ses *Septem Elegiae in septem pœnitentiae Psalmos*. C'est dire que le goût pour la poésie pénitentielle était dans l'air. Outre le nombre limité et déterminé de ces psaumes qui favorisait une adaptation relativement aisée et rapide, leur unité de ton exemplifiait l'attitude de contrition du pécheur qui correspondait à la sensibilité de Macrin et de son époque. I. McFarlane a bien montré que dans les odes et les hymnes de 1537 surgissait déjà un pessimisme

---

[11] Cf. McFarlane, "Macrin" [1959]: 336–337.

[12] Voir A. Croiset, *Histoire de la littérature grecque* (Paris, 1898), t.II, 270–273, qui définit le péan comme un chant de joie, un hymne à Apollon dont on sollicite guérison et protection. Ce sont là les caractéristiques essentielles du chant davidique.

[13] Cf. A. Croiset, "*Histoire*", 271–272: "[. . .] consacré d'abord, semble-t-il, exclusivement à Apollon, peut-être aussi à sa sœur Artémis, il finit par se chanter en l'honneur de tous les dieux indistinctement, et même de certains hommes, à la façon d'un encomion". Chez Macrin, les péans prennent pour objets Dieu, Jésus, la Vierge, les saints, et certains hommes aussi . . .

[14] Cf. Gaertner, "Latin verse translation", 293.

qui cherchait dans la foi le salut personnel[15]. A leur façon, les psaumes et les péans de 1538 reproduisent cette quête par laquelle le poète substitue aux Muses et aux dieux païens les divinités du christianisme. Les formes métriques latines, héritées de l'Antiquité, vidées de leur contenu profane, servent de cadres ou de réceptacles à la religion chrétienne. Par ailleurs, les incertitudes du temps, la guerre, la peste, la famine, et les débuts de la persécution des Réformés favorisaient également cette poésie de pénitence, riche d'enseignements pour la jeunesse. La fonction didactique perce indéniablement dans les Psaumes et l'on comprend la prédilection des poètes pour ces pièces. Que ce soit Hessus, ou encore Jean de Gagny, M. A. Flaminio, et plus tard Marot, Bèze, Vigenère et Desportes, tous ont bien vu quel parti idéologique ils pouvaient en tirer[16]. En période de troubles politiques et religieux, la figure du psalmiste, porte-parole de David prophétisant la venue du Christ, jouissait ainsi d'une actualité particulière. On comprend pourquoi les Psaumes ont été si souvent choisis aussi bien du côté des Catholiques que de celui des Protestants. Ils permettaient de véhiculer un message tout en restant au plus près de la tradition illustre du lyrisme. On est dès lors peu surpris de voir apparaître en concurrence les adaptations des Psaumes des deux clans unis autour des mêmes thèmes de l'introspection, l'auto-critique, la corruption des corps par la maladie et la mort, la vanité humaine, le vice de philautie et l'inconstance du monde[17].

C'est peut-être pour rivaliser avec les adaptations plus nombreuses des Réformés, ou pour les rejoindre discrètement sur leur terrain, que Macrin a entrepris ce travail de paraphrase. Nous verrons plus loin que cet exercice n'engage pas seulement son talent poétique, mais pose aussi la question de son engagement religieux et la nature de sa foi.

Pour le moment, restons sur le terrain esthétique et observons brièvement les traits saillants de ses paraphrases. Ils peuvent se résumer à trois mots: *fidélité, amplification, transformation*. La fidélité au texte de la Vulgate d'abord semble généralement observée, à supposer que Macrin n'ait pas suivi le texte hébreu original[18]. C'est lorsqu'il recourt à la strophe pour adapter les versets bibliques que Macrin reste proche de la Vulgate. Ainsi le "Miserere" de David du Psaume 51 reproduit-il les 21 versets par 23 strophes de 3 glyconiques et d'un phérécratéen. Seules la strophe 21, libre paraphrase, et la dernière strophe où le poète détaille des sacrifices de nature presque païenne, différent de l'original. De même, le Psaume 102, qui est une prière dans les malheurs, présente 30 strophes de 2 asclépiades, d'un phérécratéen et d'un glyconique

---

[15] Voir "Macrin" [1959]: 324.

[16] Cf. Grant, "Neo-latin translation", 206, et C. Maddison, *M. A. Flaminio, Poet, Humanist and Reformer* (London, 1964), 160.

[17] Cf. Gaertner, "Latin verse translation", 278: "In an explosive century like the 16th the predilection of the reading public and of the humanists for the Psalter, and especially for the Penitential Psalms, may well have reflected the feeling of uncertainty, the special need for the invocation of divine guidance, the heightened religious fervor which the great schism had produced".

[18] Macrin connaissait-il d'ailleurs l'hébreu? Nous l'ignorons. Peut-être en avait-il acquis quelques rudiments sous la conduite de Jacques Lefèvre, son professeur à Paris et traducteur lui aussi de la Bible.

pour restituer les 29 versets bibliques. Enfin, de manière exemplaire, le psaume suivant, Ps. 130, transpose les 8 versets par 8 strophes saphiques.

Pourtant, Macrin prend parfois certaines libertés par rapport au texte d'origine. Il amplifie notamment par l'apport de certains détails de son cru qui visent à accroître l'expressivité. On le voit bien, pour ne prendre qu'un exemple significatif, dans le début du Psaume 6, qui est une prière d'un malade. Alors que deux versets suffisent à exprimer l'acte de contrition dans la Vulgate ("Domine, ne in furore tuo arguas me, / Neque in ira tua corripias me. // Miserere mei, Domine, quoniam infirmus sum; / Sana me, Domine, quoniam conturbata sunt ossa mea"), Macrin éprouve le besoin d'accentuer la violence des châtiments possibles de Dieu sur près de huit vers, et en développant le registre sémantique de la peur:

> Ne me aeterne tuus Rex furor arguat,
> Iustis corripiat neu tua saeviens
> In me suppliciis ira minaciter,
> At parcens potius nec scelerum memor
> Actorum, ueniam dos mihi supplici,
> Nimirum aeger ego, terror et intimus
> Turbas dura premens ossa medullitus,
> Confusamque animam. [. . .]

Au passage, on note que Macrin substitue à la terminologie chrétienne ("misericordia, Domine . . .") un registre neutre ou profane ("Rex . . ."). Il renforce l'expressivité au moyen de détails physiques concrets, plus saisissants que dans l'original, et qui actualisent la dimension visuelle de la prière. Enfin, les hyperboles nombreuses, l'amplification de la douleur subie (en particulier dans les vers 23–26, paraphrase des versets 8–9) mettent en relief l'image d'un poète martyr, assailli de toutes parts:

> Turba consenui septus ab hostica,
> Quae subuertere me uafra cupiuerat.
> A me nunc abeant, qui mihi construunt
> Lethalèsque dolos, et mala fabricant.

De la même manière, le Psaume 38 en 72 vers glyconiques et asclépiades actualise le potentiel élégiaque des 23 versets bibliques. Le dernier mouvement de l'ode amplifie le sort du malheureux calomnié à tort et il met en valeur la morale manichéenne. Alors que la Vulgate disait simplement "Inimici autem mei vivunt, et confirmati sunt super me: / Et multiplicati sunt qui oderunt me inique", Macrin déploie ce verset 20 et le suivant en 8 vers:

> At vivunt vegeti et valent
> Hostes interea, et robore praediti
> Crescunt perniciem in meam,
> Et linguas acuunt iurgia in impia
> Reddentes mala pro bonis. [. . .]

De nombreux passages illustrent cet effort d'expressivité qui modifient la tonalité tout en respectant la leçon originale.

Dans d'autres cas, plus rares, Macrin ne s'en tient pas à la Vulgate mais paraphrase librement et va jusqu'à ajouter du sens aux mots, voire certains vers. C'est le cas du dernier psaume pénitentiel, le Psaume 143, où les quatre derniers vers entonnent le "credo" catholique de la Trinité chrétienne[19]. La prière du juste persécuté que présente ce psaume ajoute ainsi un élément étranger qui oriente la lecture du recueil et se veut comme la profession de foi du poète:

> Patri si almo gloria perpetim,
>   Eiusque proli, ac Spiritu sacro,
>   Quos mente constanter fideli
>   Tres numero et profitemur unum.

Cette touche finale peut être vue comme l'allégeance de Macrin au parti catholique, à la voie droite qu'il ne cesse d'évoquer tout au long du recueil, mais aussi comme l'un des articles de la foi chrétienne qui se verront tour à tour évoqués et célébrés avec faste dans les 4 livres des "Péans".

Au total, Macrin se fait remarquer par une fidélité au texte de la Vulgate malgré des effets de paraphrase (marqués par la multiplication d'épithètes, de redondances, et de détails matériels) et une extrême diversité des rythmes latins. Fidèle à l'esthétique de la *varietas* qu'il prône depuis le *Carminum libellus* (1528)[20], il ne fait jamais se succéder deux rythmes identiques. Cette caractéristique ajoute à la variété d'un recueil uni par une thématique commune et des répétitions lexicales nombreuses, et facilite également la mémorisation de ces psaumes[21]. On comprend mieux à présent pourquoi certains critiques ont vu dans l'adaptation de Macrin un simple exercice de style[22]. Il nous semble plutôt qu'à travers ces adaptations, Macrin ne s'est pas contenté de traduire mot à mot le Psautier ou d'en offrir une paraphrase ornementale, mais qu'il a tenté d'exprimer le sens du texte hébreu, souvent déroutant ou insaisissable, et d'accentuer son expressivité latente.

C'est sans doute sur ce plan qu'on doit rapprocher ses essais littéraires de ceux de ses contemporains, afin de mieux percevoir la nature de son projet esthétique et de sa foi.

L'héritage de Macrin dans la paraphrase des Psaumes en néo-latin

On l'a dit, Macrin a entrepris son adaptation latine au moment où se dessinait en Europe un essor formidable de ces paraphrases de la Bible. C'est donc en émule qu'il faut définir son projet et par rapport à un vaste dessein collectif. Les anthologies que nous avons citées permettent de saisir la dimension collective de la paraphrase des Psaumes. Les contemporains ou les prédécesseurs immédiats sont si nombreux qu'il serait vain de les citer tous[23]. Contentons-nous de rappeler ceux qui étaient en con-

---

[19] Cf. aussi dans les *Hymnorum libri sex* (1537) le psaume 127 qui offre le même cas de figure.

[20] Voir les *Carminum libri quatuor* (1530), et les commentaires de G. Soubeille dans son édition citée (n.l.), 43 et 65.

[21] Sur ce point, voir Grant, "Neo-latin translation", 205–206.

[22] Cf. Gaertner, "Latin verse translation", 274.

[23] Voir Gaertner, "Latin verse translation", 293–303, pour un aperçu chronologique de la

tact direct avec Macrin et qui ont pu influencer son œuvre ou être influencés par elle.

Tout d'abord, à la même époque, le Hollandais Musius, proche de Macrin à Poitiers de 1536 à 1538, fit paraître ses *Odae et Psalmi* chez de Marnef, c'est-à-dire peu avant la parution des *Septem psalmi* de Macrin. Il y a ensuite A. Gomez, le Portugais, déjà évoqué, et surtout Marco-Antonio Flaminio dont les poésies profanes et religieuses étaient largement répandues en France et que Macrin ne pouvait ignorer. Sa paraphrase de 32 psaumes versifiés parut à Venise en janvier 1538, puis fut rééditée à plusieurs reprises[24]. Ses adaptations latines en mètres variés, caractérisées par la grâce et l'ornementation facile, sont des odes à part entière qui circulaient dans les milieux humanistes[25]. Dans une moindre mesure, on peut citer encore le nom de Quintiano Stoa dont les adaptations latines rappellent celles de Macrin[26], de Jean de Gagny (Ganeius) dont la version métrifiée des Psaumes, publiée à Paris en 1547[27], avait été entreprise dès les années 1520, concurremment à celle de Flaminio dont il tente de se démarquer. Enfin, on ne peut sous-estimer l'importance des essais de Buchanan[28], de N. Bourbon, de J. Visagier, ces deux derniers étant membres du *sodalitium* lyonnais avec Macrin, et dont les efforts, soit continus, soit disparates, participaient d'un projet commun de rivaliser dans une même langue pour restituer au moyen de mètres variés les modulations des chants davidiques.

Cette rivalité littéraire n'a d'égale que la communauté d'esprit qui les unissait. N. Bourbon, J. Visagier, puis C. Marot, Th. de Bèze, L. Des Masures plus tard, enfin Flaminio, Hessus, Buchanan étaient connus pour leurs sympathies évangéliques. Macrin, sans doute prudent, et partageant avant tout avec eux un même idéal esthétique et les mêmes protecteurs (les Du Bellay, J. de Morel, F. Olivier . . .), n'ignorait pas que ses fréquentations le rangeaient—peut-être malgré lui—dans le clan des Réformés[29].

Si les *Septem psalmi* présentent toutes les caractéristiques de l'allégeance de Macrin à l'"orthodoxie modérée" (I. McFarlane)[30] du catholicisme, on peut cependant douter de sa profession de foi. I. McFarlane qui a, le premier, examiné cette question, conclut à l'ambiguïté du poète. Bien que celui-ci ne cesse de multiplier les signes de

---

paraphrase des Psaumes en latin, et le chapitre 7 que McFarlane consacre à celle de Buchanan en rappelant le contexte historique de son émergence (*Buchanan*, "The Psalm Paraphrases", 247–286).

[24] Par exemple, en 1545 (Paris, Venise), 1548 (Venise, Lyon), 1549 (Paris), 1552 (Paris, Florence), 1558 (Venise), etc.

[25] Sur les adaptations de Flaminio, voir Maddison, *Flaminio*, 160–161 et *passim*.

[26] Cf. C. Maddison, *Apollo and the Nine, A History of the Ode* (London, 1960), 110–111. Stoa avait fréquenté Macrin à la Cour. Ce dernier avait même corrigé les épreuves de l'*Orpheus* (1514) et des *Ingeniosa Disticha* (1514). Voir G. Soubeille, *Livre des Épithalames*, Introduction, 25 et 83.

[27] J. Ganeius, *Psalmi Davidici Septuaginta quinque, in lyricos versus . . .* (Paris, 1547). Sur ce métricien, voir M. Jeanneret, *Poésie et tradition biblique au XVIe siècle, Recherches stylistiques sur les paraphrases des psaumes de Marot à Malherbe* (Paris, 1969), 211–213; voir aussi Gaertner, "Latin verse translation", 286, et McFarlane, "Macrin" [1959]: 334–335, et *Buchanan*, 281.

[28] Voir McFarlane, *Buchanan*, chap. 7; Gaertner, "Latin verse translation", 290; Grant, "Neolatin translation", 208; et Ph. Ford, *G. Buchanan, Prince of Poets* (Aberdeen, 1982), 6, 44 et 77.

[29] Cf. G. Soubeille, *Livre des Épithalames*, Introduction, 104 et suiv.

[30] Cf. "Macrin" [1959]: 322.

sa "via recta", peut-être même à l'excès (ce qui paraît toujours suspect), en entonnant des prières aux saints et à la Vierge, en proclamant son innocence et l'injustice des menaces pesant sur lui après l'Affaire des Placards (1534)[31], il ne cherche pourtant pas à dissimuler le nom de ces Réformés avec lesquels il entretient des relations privilégiées. Par ailleurs, plusieurs de ses enfants se convertiront au protestantisme[32], ce qui accroît les soupçons pesant sur le père. . . .

Proche des uns et des autres, se mettant sous la protection de partis opposés (les Du Bellay, le Cardinal de Lorraine, Ph. de Cossé à qui il dédie ses *Septem psalmi* [33]), et n'hésitant pas à dissiper dans ses recueils tout soupçon d'activité religieuse clandestine, Macrin offre l'image d'un poète soucieux de l'unité de l'Église mais se refusant de condamner publiquement le courant évangéliste. De là tient son ambiguïté. Il s'apparente ainsi à de nombreux humanistes qui, favorables et sympathisant aux idées de la Réforme, n'y ont jamais totalement adhéré dans leur parole poétique. C'est ce qui sépare Macrin de Marot. Macrin, lui, n'aura jamais franchi le seuil de la provocation et, partant, aura échappé aux persécutions politiques.

Pourtant, leurs projets respectifs se recoupent et leurs destinées se rejoignent par intervalles. Tous deux ont fréquenté la Cour vers 1530, y ont occupé une place officielle, et leurs œuvres témoignent d'un respect mutuel et même d'une admiration[34]. Plus significatif encore, leur projet d'adapter les Psaumes en odes, l'un en latin, l'autre en français. Et c'est sur les interférences entre les deux œuvres que nous aimerions finir cette étude, parce qu'elles illustrent bien les jeux d'opposition littéraires et linguistiques qui les déterminent.

Nous ne revenons pas en détail sur les rapports biographiques et les amitiés communes des deux poètes. Le plus intéressant demeure dans les coïncidences des œuvres: l'adaptation des Psaumes. D'abord, la publication des *Septem psalmi* correspond presque à la parution des premiers psaumes de Marot dans le recueil anonyme strasbourgeois de 1539 qui mêle les pièces de Marot à celles de Calvin[35]. Outre la proximité temporelle, on constate que les deux poètes ont jeté leur dévolu sur les mêmes psaumes: 6 des 7 psaumes pénitentiels de Macrin, ainsi que le Psaume 1 du premier

---

[31] Cf. *Hymnorum libri VII* (1537), 48, 181 et 190, où Macrin fait allusion aux dangers encourus. Victime de délation, il faillit être arrêté. Voir G. Soubeille, *Livre des Épithalames*, Introduction, 107.

[32] Cf. McFarlane, "Macrin" [1959]: 328.

[33] Philippe de Cossé, fils de René de Cossé, issu de la lignée prestigieuse des Cossé-Brissac, fut précepteur des enfants de France et évêque de Coutances. Humaniste cultivé, connaissant l'hébreu (ce qui lui permettait sans doute d'apprécier le travail d'adaptation des psaumes réalisé par son protégé), il était lié également à N. Bourbon.

[34] Sur les relations de Macrin et de Marot, tous deux valets de chambre du Roi, voir I. McFarlane, "Clément Marot and the World of Neo-Latin Poetry", in *Literature and the Arts in the Reign of Francis I. Essays Presented to C. A. Mayer*, éd. P. Smith et I. McFarlane (Lexington, 1985), 107, 109–113, 117, 119 et 122.

[35] *Aulcuns Pseaulmes et cantiques mys en chant*, 1539. Dès 1533, Marguerite de Navarre avait inséré la traduction du Psaume VI par Marot dans une nouvelle édition du *Miroir de l'âme pecheresse*. D'autres adaptations de Marot apparaîtront dans le théâtre de la Reine de Navarre (cf. *L'Inquisiteur*, 1536).

livre des "Péans", se retrouvent chez Marot. Quand on sait, par ailleurs, que Marot fit paraître la paraphrase du Psaume VI (le premier des pénitentiels) à Lyon entre 1527 et 1531, qu'il fait varier dans ses psaumes toutes les combinaisons strophiques possibles, et qu'il fait précéder ses versions françaises de l'*incipit* latin correspondant de la Vulgate, on peut se demander si Marot, à l'exemple de Macrin, n'aurait pas eu pour objectif de traduire les sept psaumes pénitentiels en français pour rivaliser avec la version latine de son émule. D'autres rapprochements viennent compléter les deux œuvres: les Psaumes 1, 2, 127, et le "Cantique de Siméon" inclus dans les *Hymnorum libri sex* de 1537 figurent aussi dans le recueil strasbourgeois de 1539[36]; quant aux Psaumes 50, 112, et 23 publiés dans les *Hymnorum libri III* de Macrin (1540), leur composition remonte avant 1539 et 1541 chez Marot. En somme, les adaptations respectives semblent simultanées. A Macrin revient, semble-t-il, la priorité chronologique mais sans certitude absolue. Car l'on sait que Marot avait songé au Psautier en français dès le début des années 1530.

On ne peut qu'être frappé en tout cas des corrélations implicites. Et on ne saurait négliger l'exemple que les Néo-latins (Flaminio et Macrin) offraient à l'acclimatation du Psautier en vernaculaire[37]. Si l'on constate peu de points communs entre les versions de Macrin et Marot, on est en droit d'avancer sans trop de réserves que tous deux connaissaient le travail de l'autre. Et les échanges par poèmes interposés, par la traduction respective de leur production en latin et en français, suggèrent que les deux hommes étaient unis par une connivence secrète[38]. Séparés par la langue et par leur foi déclarée (Marot le Réformé, Macrin le Catholique), ils se retrouvent sur le même terrain comme pour illustrer l'universalité de la parole davidique. Il est d'ailleurs curieux de noter que c'est Théodore de Bèze, adaptateur du Psautier en latin (1579), qui se chargera à Genève de compléter le projet du Psautier en français (1562) resté inachevé à la mort de Marot (1544).

Dans l'ensemble de la production poétique de Macrin, la paraphrase des Psaumes occupe une place mineure mais l'intérêt que l'auteur y portait ne cessa de grandir à

---

[36] Le "Cantique de Siméon" attribué à Calvin fera l'objet d'une adaptation de Marot (*Vingt Pseaulmes . . .* 1543).

[37] Cf. McFarlane, "Clément Marot . . .", 120–122. On notera que les *Trente Pseaulmes de David* (1541) de Marot semblent répondre au titre de *Paraphrasis in duos et triginta Psalmos* de Flaminio (Venise, 1538).

[38] Cf. la pièce "Ad Clementium Maronem" insérée dans les "Péans" (f° D V v°) où Macrin se plaint de n'avoir pas reçu un exemplaire de son dernier ouvrage sorti des presses de Gourmont (Jérôme?). Nous ignorons le titre de ce livre: s'agirait-il d'une version clandestine et/ou perdue de paraphrase des Psaumes? Une édition des *Saulmes de Clement Marot* remonterait à 1538 ou 1539 mais aurait été publiée chez J. Gérard à Genève. Par ailleurs, Jérôme de Gourmont semble avoir publié une édition de *Cinquante-deux psaumes* ("incerto autore"). Elle se trouve mentionnée parmi les "livres suspectz" saisis chez Jacques Chevalier en février 1549; mais nous ignorons si Marot est l'auteur présumé de ce texte et quelle en est la date de publication (cf. N. Weiss, *La Chambre ardente* [Paris, 1889] et Slatkine [1970], 350). A moins que Macrin ne fasse allusion au *Frotte-Groing du Sagouyn* (Paris, 1537), l'une des nombreuses pièces composées par Marot pour se moquer de son ennemi Sagon. Nous devons cette précision éditoriale à l'extrême obligeance de Madame J. Veyrin-Forrer.

partir de 1537. Cette part du lyrisme latin n'aura pourtant pas reçu toute l'attention que Macrin attendait. Si certains de ses psaumes figurent dans les anthologies collectives de 1538 (E. Hessus) et 1556 (H. Estienne) parmi les humanistes les plus célébrés de son temps, en revanche les commentateurs leur ont réservé un accueil mitigé. Estienne, qui a choisi Macrin dans son recueil comme le représentant de la France, le considérait comme inférieur aux autres adaptateurs, en particulier à Flaminio[39]; plus près de nous, C. Maddison dresse un réquisitoire en règle et considère blasphématoire le traitement horacien qu'il fit des Psaumes[40].

Pourtant, les efforts de Macrin méritent plus d'indulgence car ils nous permettent de voir quel parti un poète néo-latin pouvait tirer de la doctrine chrétienne pour illustrer sa maîtrise de la rythmique antique, et de celle-ci pour restituer la valeur lyrique des textes bibliques. A sa façon, Macrin offre l'exemple d'un lyrisme profane et religieux et montre que leur association pouvait aboutir à un syncrétisme original. En paraphrasant le Psautier en latin, il révèle son intérêt pour les recherches esthétiques et religieuses de son temps, et son goût pour la traduction. Il fait œuvre d'humaniste en ouvrant la voie à la double tendance du lyrisme en langue française, à Marot d'un côté, à Ronsard de l'autre (et avec lui à la Pléiade à partir de 1553)[41], ce qui lui vaudrait sans doute, en plus de son surnom habituel d'"Horace français", celui d'"Horatius christianus"[42].

Queen's University, Canada

---

[39] Cf. sa Préface, 4: "Nam Salmonius noster [. . .] Flaminio non solum sermonis puritate longè est inferior sed versus etiam elegantia ei credit: et ut minus cultum, quam ille, versum facit, ita multo magis humi serpit".

[40] Cf. *Apollo and the Nine*, 200: "[. . .] these odes [. . .] are all hack work whose shallow and frivolous fluency and unabashed pilfering from Horace make the treatment of their religious themes almost blasphemous and the reading of them intolerable".

[41] On songe à la volonté de certains poètes (Du Bellay, N. Denisot . . .) d'abandonner le lyrisme païen pour ne célébrer que les dieux du christianisme.

[42] Cf. la version élégiaque des Psaumes de Hessus qui lui avait valu le titre d'"Ovidius christianus" accordé par Érasme, qui avait en outre conféré au Mantouan, pour ses églogues et son épopée religieuses, le titre de "Vergilius Christianus".

Juan Ginés de Sepúlveda,
Un hispano a la altura del siglo XVI: Lutero y Erasmo

JOAQUÍN J. SÁNCHEZ GÁZQUEZ

Introducción

Lutero y Erasmo, Reforma evangélico-luterana y Humanismo en la primera mitad del siglo XVI, constituyen no sólo el telón de fondo, sino también, por así decirlo, el escenario mismo de los acontecimientos que hicieron tomar la pluma a Juan Ginés de Sepúlveda desde la Italia del joven *Cinquecento* y que dieron razón de ser, de un lado, a sus *De fato et libero arbitrio libri tres* de 1526 y, de otro, a su *Pro Alberto Pio, principe Carpensi, Antapologia in Erasmum Roterodamum* de 1532, obras ambas que son objeto de la presente reflexión.

El marco de la intervención de Juan Ginés de Sepúlveda

La alternancia de las fórmulas "Lutero erasmiano" y "Erasmo luterano", que S. Seidel Menchi constató en la documentación italiana correspondiente a los años que van desde 1520 a 1535 y que apoya la tesis tanto de la *reductio Lutheri ad Erasmum* como de la *reductio Erasmi ad Lutherum*,[1] es la consecuencia, por una parte, de una serie de ideas y actitudes que procedían del lado norte de los Alpes y que se habían dejado sentir ampliamente, o tal vez deberíamos decir, habían encontrado un terreno abonado para su recepción, en la Península Itálica, por otra parte, de la lectura e interpretación que durante un corto período de tiempo el público italiano pudo hacer de las mismas como la manifestación de una realidad única, de un movimiento general de disidencia respecto a Roma. Sin embargo, la fórmula "Lutero erasmiano" estaba destinada a ceder en poco tiempo ante la fórmula "Erasmo luterano".

De un lado, desde que Lutero colocó en Octubre de 1517 sus noventa y cinco tesis contra las indulgencias en la iglesia del castillo de Wittemberg se fueron sucediendo en tierras germánicas acontecimientos que no pasaron desapercibidos a una Italia que no tardó en atribuirle la paternidad histórica y la hegemonía doctrinal de la

---

[1] S. Seidel Menchi, *Erasmo in Italia. 1520–1580* (Torino, 1987), 1–42.

Reforma. Por ello a partir de 1530 la denominada *reductio Lutheri ad Erasmum* no tuvo credibilidad alguna en la Península Itálica y la fórmula "Lutero erasmiano" cayó casi en desuso.

De otro lado, por el contrario, la *reductio Erasmi ad Lutherum*, que daría razón de ser al "Erasmo luterano", estaba sólo al inicio de la que iba a ser una larga trayectoria, estaba adquiriendo cada vez con mayor fuerza carta de entrada y, no azarosamente, sino por una serie de motivos muy determinados y no faltos de coherencia, que S. Seidel Menchi estudió,[2] entre 1520 y 1535 dicha fórmula se consolida definitivamente en la Península Itálica, adquiriendo unos perfiles mucho más precisos y una significación mucho más llena que no había conocido antes—cuando se usaba indistintamente "Lutero erasmiano" y "Erasmo luterano"—mostrándose con una radicalidad como en ningún otro lugar de Europa, hasta el punto de que dicha fórmula puede y debe considerarse una creación genuinamente italiana.

Por tanto, Lutero como adalid del movimiento reformador, Erasmo como la mano derecha de Lutero, por así decirlo, fue el sentir generalizado de la Península Itálica, tanto más cuanto más avanzaba este segundo decenio. Esta fue la razón de ser de toda una literatura que produjo la élite intelectual—y no sólo intelectual—italiana más conservadora, especialmente en contacto con Roma y con la Corte Pontificia, en contra del que en adelante seguiría considerando un único movimiento, primando a menudo las analogías sobre las diferencias entre las diversas variantes doctrinales y confesionales de la Reforma, pero que a partir de ahora vería, salvo cada vez más raras excepciones, en Lutero al responsable principal y en Erasmo a un poderoso promotor. Así pues, si bien a partir de estos años se dan casos de obras concebidas en contra de Lutero en la misma medida que en contra de Erasmo, lo más frecuente es encontrar obras específicamente antiluteranas o específicamente antierasmianas, entre las que se vienen incluyendo sendas obras de Juan Ginés de Sepúlveda.

La intervención de Juan Ginés de Sepúlveda
De fato et libero arbitrio adversus Lutherum libri tres (Romae, 1526)

Desde la postura conservadora, escolástico-aristotélica, que es de esperar en Sepúlveda no tardó éste en componer una elaborada respuesta en sus *De fato et libero arbitrio libri tres*, que salieron publicados en Roma en 1526, contra el virulento *De servo arbitrio Martini Lutheri ad D. Erasmum Roterodamum*, publicado en Wittemberg en Diciembre de 1525, que escribió su autor en respuesta a la *De libero arbitrio* διατριβή *sive collatio* que Erasmo publicó en Basilea en Septiembre de 1524.[3]

"Si la sereine dissertation d'Erasme sur le libre arbitre déchaîna les passions de Luther et de ses partisans, c'est qu'elle touchait l'endroit névralgique".[4] Si la obra de Lutero hace reaccionar tan rápida y tan enérgicamente a Sepúlveda, que no tenía una participación directa en la polémica y que para ello hubo de posponer una tarea de

---

[2] Cf. Seidel Menchi, *Erasmo*, 46–62.

[3] Cf. G. Chantraine, *Erasme et Luther, libre et serf arbitre* (Paris-Namur, 1981), detenido estudio histórico y teológico de ambas aportaciones, previas a la intervención de Sepúlveda.

[4] Chantraine, *Erasme et Luther*, XII.

mayor envergadura, la traducción y exégesis de las obras del Estagirita, comenzada por encargo de Clemente VII, es porque la obra luterana tocaba una cuestión central. En efecto—no parece que haya discrepancias al respecto entre los estudiosos—centro y punto neurálgico de toda la teología luterana constituye esta obra del reformador alemán, una de las pocas obras de las que él mismo se preciaba, como dejó atestiguado en su correspondencia.[5]

En este momento, nos gustaría dejar constancia del significado de la obra de Sepúlveda como documento inserto en toda una producción italiana antiluterana, en tanto que su autor no tardó en ver en el tema de la predestinación y del servil albedrío de Lutero la gravedad y el alcance de la obra y en tanto que supo dar, desde su postura, una respuesta acorde, en consonancia, con la misma, respuesta concebida como una refutación integral del dogma luterano. Este hecho, que en sí puede parecer previsible o, cuando menos, poco significativo, adquiere nueva luz cuando se presta atención a la producción italiana antiluterana[6] y cuando se estudia esta obra de Sepúlveda como parte integrante que fue de dicha producción.

En general, si atendemos a la literatura italiana antiluterana desde 1518, fecha de publicación de la primera obra concebida contra Lutero, el *In praesumptuosas Martini Luther conclusiones de potestate papae dialogus* de Silvester Prierias, hasta finales de siglo, constatamos que la mayor parte de las obras italianas se caracterizó por centrar la atención en las implicaciones más prácticas de la teología evangélico-luterana, soslayando a menudo las que eran cuestiones centrales de la misma, obras, como dijo G. Miccoli,[7] concebidas en una línea tradicional, con argumentos presentados a la manera tradicional, que resultaban insuficientes como respuesta a los interrogantes respecto a la realidad y a la vida cristiana que Lutero había abierto, sin advertir en una amplia mayoría de casos, más allá de unos gestos que debieron tener no pocos visos de excentricidad, el significado profundo de la actitud del monje alemán y el alcance de las cuestiones que, por así decirlo, puso sobre la mesa. Si nos fijamos en las obras antiluteranas de algunos de los más destacados próceres intelectuales italianos de este período, no tanto anteriores a 1525, fecha de aparición del *De servo arbitrio*, cuanto posteriores, como es el caso de un Tommaso Campegio, de un Agostino Steuco, del mismo Alberto Pío, que, si bien polemizó con Erasmo, su primera obra la tituló contra Lutero, etc., constatamos, en efecto, que el tema del libre-servil albedrío, de la gracia y de la predestinación no es objeto preferente de atención.

En particular, no deja de ser significativo, por ejemplo, que de los sesenta y seis autores de obras antiluteranas que F. Lauchert recoge en su conocido libro[8] ni siquiera una veintena haya hecho un tratamiento detenido de dicha cuestión. Si ponemos mientes en la producción de éste último grupo constatamos, en primer lugar,

---

[5] Cf. *D. Martin Luthers Werke. Kritische Gesamtausgabe. Briefwechsel*, vol. 8 (Weimar, 1938), 99, ll. 5–8.

[6] Cf. F. Lauchert, *Die italienischen literarischen Gegner Luthers* (Freiburg im Breisgau, 1912; repr. 1972), libro que es un documento valioso para este respecto.

[7] G. Miccoli, "La scomparsa delle idee 'luterane' in Italia: modi e termini della loro penetrazione iniziale", en *Storia d'Italia*, vol. 2.1 (Torino, 1974), 976.

[8] Lauchert, *Gegner Luthers*.

que sus obras no fueron escritas como reacción al virulento *De servo arbitrio*, algunas de ellas son muy posteriores a la edición de la obra luterana: las primeras, como la *Confutatio articulorum seu quaestionum Lutheri* de Gasparo Contarini o la *Pro religione Christiana adversus Luteranos* de Agostino Steuco, datan de 1530, si bien aquélla quedó inédita hasta la edición póstuma de conjunto de 1571, y las últimas, como la *Ad principes populosque Germaniae exhortatio grauiss.* de Iacobo Sadoleto y los *In D. Pauli epistolas ad Romanos et Galatas commentaria* de Girolamo Seripando, son de 1560 y 1567 respectivamente e incluso hubo casos de autores cuyas obras no fueron editadas hasta finales de siglo a título póstumo, verbigracia los *Commentaria in epistolam ad Romanos* y los *Opuscula omnia* de Gian Antonio Pantusa en 1596.

En segundo lugar, que a menudo no nos encontramos con obras monográficas dedicadas a abordar este asunto de forma individualizada, sino tratados, opúsculos, partes, a veces bastante pequeñas, de obras de conjunto, que incluyen varios tomos dedicados a temas de incidencia más inmediata que éste: así el caso de los tratados *De libero arbitrio* y *De praedestinatione* integrantes de los *Opuscula omnia* de Gian Antonio Pantusa, del tratado *De libero hominis arbitrio deque gratia, praescientia & praedestinatione Dei, & quod neutrum tollatur ab altero* de los *Opuscula* de Vincenzio Giaccari, de los tratados *De libero arbitrio* y *De praedestinatione* de las *Disputationes adversus Lutheranos* de Giammaria Verrati, etc. En tercer lugar, que algunas de ellas no fueron concebidas *ex professo* contra Lutero ni contra su *De servo arbitrio*, que no son éstos el punto inmediato de referencia, hecho por otra parte inteligible dado el sentido lato con que se aplicó el término "luterano": así el primer tratado que hemos citado de Gian Antonio Pantusa, en el que su autor anunciaba que estaba en parte concebido como una lucha contra los autores modernos que negaban la libertad y *de facto* se limitó a ser una presentación de postulados escolásticos sin polemizar contra Lutero ni contra autor coetáneo alguno, los *De praedestinatione dialogi tres* de Bartolomeo Camerario, concebidos a modo de diálogo entre un interlocutor y Calvino, etc. Por soslayar, finalmente, a los autores que no escribieron sobre el tema que nos ocupa por iniciativa propia, sino a petición de otros.

Aunque la producción y la documentación italiana antiluterana no han recibido aún la atención detenida que, por ejemplo, en el caso erasmiano sí ha ocurrido, especialmente por parte de S. Seidel Menchi,[9] creemos que la idea más concluyente al respecto ya la apuntó dicha autora a propósito del período 1520–35, a saber, "Raramente la documentazione italiana di questo periodo e dei decenni successivi rispecchia la teologia riformatrice nella profondità delle sue intuizioni e nella genialità delle sue costruzioni".[10] Y es que, como ella misma recogió en un artículo sobre la recepción de Lutero en Italia,[11] no era el discurso teológico del Reformador en donde reparaba el público italiano, incluso el más culto, sino en un corolario del mismo, teológicamente secundario, pero que suponía un ataque frontal a la iglesia de

---

[9] Seidel Menchi, *Erasmo.*

[10] Seidel Menchi, *Erasmo,* 50.

[11] S. Seidel Menchi, "Le traduzioni italiane di Lutero nella prima metà del Cinquecento", *Rinascimento* 17.2 (1977): 31–108.

Roma y derruía desde sus cimientos una estructura importante de la vida económica, política, moral y religiosa de la Península Itálica: la autoridad del Pontífice y de toda la jerarquía eclesiástica.

Sepúlveda no se detuvo en estos corolarios, sino que atacó directamente aquel discurso teológico, no porque no viese las consecuencias que de éstos se derivaban—las vio, como todos sus contemporáneos, su obra abunda en pruebas de ello—sino porque entendió que no se podían evitar tales consecuencias (es decir, entendió el discurso de Lutero, como pocos parecieron hacerlo) si no se invalidaba en primer lugar, sin dilación y desde sus raíces aquél. Sepúlveda, por encima del tumulto que la causa luterana propició en la Península Itálica y la coyuntura tan poco favorable en la que tuvo que medirse la iglesia de Roma, aspectos ambos que tan de cerca conoció, hizo una refutación del dogma luterano no en las implicaciones o ramificaciones de éste, cuyos efectos eran ya más que perceptibles a la altura de 1526, sino en la cuestión de la justificación por la fe o la gracia sola y del servil albedrío, sin duda de menos incidencia práctica, pero que encerraban un núcleo del mensaje luterano. Sepúlveda dio una respuesta, con independencia ahora de la orientación de su contenido, necesariamente determinado por la postura ortodoxa desde la que escribió—tema que desborda los límites de esta exposición y que es parte de un trabajo en curso—acorde y en consonancia con la naturaleza y con la envergadura de la obra luterana. Una respuesta que en esto distó, por la documentación italiana registrada que hemos recogido, de la que dio gran parte de sus contemporáneos. Pero es que también respecto a la obra detonante de la de Lutero, la *De libero arbitrio* διατριβή *sive collatio* de Erasmo, obra a la que Sepúlveda hace referencia directa al comienzo de la suya, la actitud de éste, la lectura que éste hizo de la obra erasmiana, también distó de la de la mayor parte de sus contemporáneos italianos. Y es que la Península Itálica, excepto el solo caso del benedictino Isidoro Chiari, según S. Seidel Menchi,[12] al que se debe añadir también el del cardenal Contarini,[13] no se hizo eco de esta obra erasmiana o, cuando se lo hizo, no sólo no la interpretó como obra concebida en clave antiluterana, hecho tal vez debido al tono y a los términos tan suaves que Erasmo empleó, sino que además la interpretó en clave proluterana. Sepúlveda leyó a Erasmo en clave antiluterana y, como en su obra dice sin ambages, le pareció insuficiente en argumentación, ya que sólo se apoyó en los testimonios de las Sagradas Escrituras y dejó de lado los argumentos derivados de la razón natural, por lo que él se vio obligado a escribir otra obra más sólidamente argumentada. Ni sus contemporáneos ni la posteridad han hecho justicia a Sepúlveda, ignorando o soslayando a menudo su obra contra Lutero. Nosotros hemos querido exponer tan sólo el punto de partida. Dejemos por ahora la cuestión luterana y veamos resumidamente cuál fue su postura respecto a otra cuestión central de la época, la erasmiana.

Pro Alberto Pio, principe Carpensi, Antapologia in Erasmum Roterodamum (Romae, 1532)
Esta obra fue concebida y escrita en defensa del que fue su protector en Italia,

[12] Seidel Menchi, *Erasmo*, 99.
[13] Cf. Lauchert, *Gegner Luthers*, 375, n. 2.

Alberto Pío, principe de Carpi, quien durante seis años sostuvo una acerva polémica con Erasmo, una polémica que parecía haber quedado inconclusa, ya que la muerte alcanzó al Príncipe siendo éste aún de mediana edad. Sin embargo, era tal el cariz y el tono que para entonces había adquirido la disputa, que Erasmo no dejó de contestar. Éste fue el motivo por el que Sepúlveda se decidió a tomar cartas en el asunto y a salir en defensa del difunto mecenas, en su opinión tan injustamente agraviado.

La *Antapologia*, por las coordenadas de espacio y tiempo en que está inserta, pertenece al *corpus* de literatura antierasmiana que produjeron los círculos intelectuales conservadores y más destacados de la Península Itálica o de ambientes de fuerte influjo italiano entre 1520 y 1535. A figuras como un Girolamo Aleandro, un Battista Casali o el mismo Alberto Pío, por nombrar a algunos, se debe la fortuna tan prolongada que tuvo la fórmula "Erasmo luterano" a lo largo del *Cinquecento*, fórmula que respondió a una serie de motivos, los principales de los cuales ya quedaron señalados.

En este momento, nos gustaría también dejar constancia del lugar que ocupa la *Antapologia* de Sepúlveda en el marco en que fue concebida, en tanto que ésta no fue una obra antierasmiana a la italiana, en tanto que Sepúlveda no fue un antierasmiano a la italiana.

Un estudio general de la obra muestra que, si bien es cierto que Sepúlveda se desenvolvió en ambientes antierasmistas y su protector, el príncipe de Carpi, fue uno de los ejemplos más ilustrativos de antierasmistas italianos, no lo es menos que el pozalbense no llegó a compartir a la manera italiana—esto hubiera sido lo de esperar después de unos veinte años de permanencia en Italia y no pocos de ellos frecuentando los círculos aristocráticos del Príncipe, a quien tan de cerca trató—los presupuestos que conformaron el denominador común de la mayor parte de las obras antierasmianas que se produjeron en Italia en este período, justamente los años en que Sepúlveda desarrolló su labor más productiva en este país. Veámoslo:

Respecto a la teología de lo cotidiano, la impresión general a que parece llevar la lectura de la *Antapologia* es que también Sepúlveda—en tanto que él mismo, no en tanto que portavoz de la opinión de su difunto mecenas a quien defiende—comparte la postura de éste y de otros tantos italianos antierasmistas, a saber, la centralización de la atención y de su discurso en las implicaciones más prácticas y cotidianas de la teología evangélico-luterana, soslayando cuestiones más centrales. Aunque no conociésemos su obra contra Lutero, sobre la que acabamos de tratar y que es la mejor prueba de que no parecía compartir tal supuesto con sus contemporáneos italianos, el hecho de que esta obra, el *De fato et libero arbitrio*, mereciese el elogio del roterodamense en su *Ciceronianus sive de optimo genere dicendi*,[14] habría sido, cuando menos, un indicio fidedigno de que Sepúlveda supo distinguir entre implicaciones concretas y la razón que las motivaba, entre accidentales y esenciales. Creemos que Sepúlveda compartió con su mecenas y con otros muchos teólogos italianos antierasmistas el molde escolástico-aristotélico que dió forma y fondo a su pensamiento y a toda su producción, pero dudamos, a la luz de la obra que seis años antes había escrito contra

---

[14] Cf. *Desiderii Erasmi Roterodami Opera Omnia*, vol. I.2 (Amsterdam, 1971), 691.

Lutero, de que, si no se hubiese tratado de una defensa pormenorizada de hasta las más nimias afirmaciones de Alberto Pío contrastadas con las de Erasmo, hubiese hecho *sua sponte* un tratamiento similar.

Respecto a la denominada "elocuencia de los herejes", la *Antapologia* es una obra de controversia, de naturaleza fundamentalmente doctrinal, no literaria, su fondo, ya lo apuntaba M. Menéndez Pelayo,[15] es más teológico que literario. Por tanto, no se pueden extraer de ella ideas concluyentes acerca de la postura de Sepúlveda en relación a este punto. Sin embargo, de nuevo su obra antiluterana, arroja luz al respecto. En ella leemos que los *studia humanitatis* fueron la causa de la calamidad surgida entre los pueblos germánicos, opinión, empero, que, si no se quiere incurrir en conclusiones rápidas y poco maduradas, será necesario tomar en su contexto, con las debidas precauciones y en relación a la propia práctica del autor. Su epistolario es rico en testimonios que dan muestra, en primer lugar, de que dichos *studia* en sí no son perniciosos, sino sólo si se abusa o se hace mal uso de ellos, como en su opinión les ocurrió a los germanos—es decir, no considera dichos *studia* perniciosos en sí ni los desacredita, como sus teólogos italianos contemporáneos—y, en segundo lugar, de que él mismo desde su juventud se dedicó con ahinco al cultivo de los mismos con el objeto de que en su madurez éstos fueran no un fin en sí, sino un medio privilegiado para acceder a otros estudios y a otra dedicación que consideró superiores, las *graviores disciplinae*, que constituyeron, pese a y en medio de numerosas obligaciones contraídas, su vocación principal.

Respecto a la superioridad cultural de Italia, el autor deja suficientemente claro en la *Antapologia* que nunca compartió semejante idea.[16]

Un estudio más detenido de la obra matiza más su postura y su actitud. Si bien es cierto que el ambiente le influyó hasta el punto de decantarse en algunos pasajes de la obra claramente del lado italiano con el objeto de no granjearse así desfavorables enemistades, no lo es menos que no rehusó seguir el consejo de amigos que le pidieron suavizar algunos pasajes que podrían haber molestado a Erasmo y que él mismo sin reservas esto lo manifestó tal cual al roterodamense en la carta que quiso enviarle junto con un ejemplar romano corregido de la obra.[17] Si bien es cierto que Sepúlveda no sintió por Erasmo la clase de admiración que por él sintieron muchos de sus adeptos, entre ellos sus compatriotas hispanos, no lo es menos que lo apreció y que

---

[15] M. Menéndez Pelayo, "Apuntes sobre el ciceronianismo en España y sobre la influencia de Cicerón en la prosa latina de los humanistas españoles", en *Bibliografía Hispano-Latina Clásica*, vol. 3 (Santander, 1950), 255.

[16] Juan Ginés de Sepúlveda, *Opera*, IV, 549. Por razones de brevedad el texto de la edición matritense de toda la obra sepulvediana, *Ioannnis Genesii Sepulvedae Cordubensis Opera, tum edita, tum inedita*, 4 vols. (Matriti, 1780), se citará en adelante como aquí: *Opera*, número romano de volumen y número arábigo de página/s.

[17] Cf. Allen, 2637, 13–16 *sive Opera*, III, 77 *et* Allen, 2637, 6–13 *sive Opera*, III, 77. Hemos citado el texto de la obra del erudito oxoniense (*Opus epistolarum Des. Erasmi Roterodami*, eds. P. S. Allen, H. M. Allen *et* H. W. Garrod, 12 vols. [Oxford, 1906–1958]) como se suele hacer: Allen, número de carta y número de línea/s.

nunca deseó zaherir su reputación, como sí muchos de los italianos con quienes por ello salió discutiendo en su defensa, como dejó bien claro en la obra.[18]

Y es que la obra misma es la mejor prueba de que supo mantenerse fiel a su designio, a saber, ser la que Sepúlveda entendió como la más legítima defensa de su difunto protector en agradecimiento por todos los servicios prestados y por la admiración que, por encima de cualesquiera diferencias o preferencias, por él sintió. La *Antapologia* fue, en efecto, una defensa de Alberto Pío sin ser un libelo antierasmiano, pese a que su autor fue un teólogo de sólida formación escolástica en una Italia pontificia y pese a que se vio constreñido a tomar parte en la que llegó a ser una agria polémica y a dar respuesta a la obra última y más virulenta que Erasmo publicó en contra de un difunto tan cercano. Defendió a Alberto Pío, expuso a Erasmo las justas razones por las que el Príncipe y la mayoría de los italianos vinculaban su obra a Lutero y le aconsejó que revisara sus escritos, si no quería que esto siguiese ocurriendo, pero la *Antapologia* distó con mucho de ser un libelo antierasmiano que adscribiese a Erasmo a las filas luteranas. No en vano fue Sepúlveda, como hemos dicho, uno de los pocos intelectuales de su época que leyó en clave antiluterana la obra erasmiana sobre el libre albedrío. En las últimas palabras de su *Antapologia*, que en todo momento fue respetuosa pero firme y que, como se puede suponer, no se avino a elogios fáciles para con el humanista holandés, le decía tal que así: "... quoniam, cum studiorum communio non parum aut soleat aut debeat ingenuos animos conciliare, nos eadem via ingressi simus litterarum, nisi quod tu superato monte jam tenes cacumen, ego adhuc in radicibus haereo".[19] Estas palabras, con independencia de su dosis de modestia, son una manifestación poco ambigua de la destacada faceta humanística de Sepúlveda, pero son, a nuestro parecer, algo aún mucho más significativo, esto es, la expresión de un juicio que reconocía a Erasmo su vocación esencialmente humanística, punto en común que dio razón de ser a la correspondencia científica, de crítica textual fundamentalmente, que en adelante y hasta la muerte del roterodamense intercambiaron.[20] Creemos que la *Antapologia* dijo de Sepúlveda más de lo que él mismo se propuso cuando proyectaba la defensa del difunto príncipe de Carpi y tal vez no acabemos de entenderla hasta que no reparemos en el alcance de este hecho.

Conclusión

Casi al final de su *De servo arbitrio* decía Lutero a Erasmo: "Deinde et hoc in te vehementer laudo et praedico, quod solus prae omnibus rem ipsam es aggressus, hoc est summam caussae, nec me fatigaris alienis illis caussis de Papatu, purgatorio, indulgentiis ac similibus nugis potius quam causis, in quibus me hactenus omnes fere venati sunt frustra. Unus tu et solus cardinem rerum vidisti et ipsum iugulum petisti, pro quo ex animo tibi gratias ago".[21]

El 19 de Octubre de 1519, justo al inicio de la prolongada fortuna que tendría la

---

[18] Cf. Sepúlveda, *Opera*, IV, 549.
[19] Cf. Sepúlveda, *Opera*, IV, 591.
[20] Cf. Allen, 2873, 2905, 2938, 2951 *et* 3906 *sive Opera*, III, 81–97.
[21] Cf. *Luthers Werke*, vol. 18 (Weimar, 1908), 786, ll. 26–31.

fórmula "Erasmo luterano", escribía ya el humanista holandés a Alberto de Branden-burgo, cardenal-arzobispo de Maguncia, en los siguientes términos: "Primum enim quid rei bonis studiis cum fidei negotio? deinde quid mihi cum causa ... Luthe-ri?".[22] El 11 de Marzo de 1534, cuando el uso de dicha fórmula se encontraba en su apogeo, decía Lutero a Nicolás de Amsdorf: "Nam, vivit Christus, magnam ei faciunt iniuriam, et defendendus est mihi contra hostes eius, qui eum Lutheranum accusant, cum sit, me nimis certo et fideli teste, nullo modo Lutheranus, sed Erasmus tantum".[23]

Sepúlveda elaboró una refutación directa de la justificación por la fe sola y del servil albedrío de Lutero, una refutación del "cardinem et ... ipsum iugulum" lute-rano, Sepúlveda no hizo a Erasmo luterano y reconoció su vocación humanística, si bien le advirtió seriamente de los riesgos a que esta dedicación exponía y de las ambi-güedades en que hacía incurrir si no se aplicaba una vigilancia continua y un celo atento en una época de ambigüedades, unas a la sazón más comprensibles, otras tal vez más intencionadas, como él mismo tuvo ocasión de experimentar.

Juan Ginés de Sepúlveda con estas dos obras proporcionó a sus contemporáneos y a la posteridad una clave más de interpretación de Lutero y de Erasmo, una interpre-tación que, como las demás, posiblemente necesite de estudio y de revisión, pero una interpretación, no lo olvidemos, que fue, en esencia, la misma que Lutero, por su parte, y Erasmo, por la suya, pidieron de su época.

Universidad de Almería

---

[22] Cf. Allen, 1033, 208–209.
[23] Cf. *Luthers Werke*, vol. 8, 38, ll. 405–408.

Carmina laudatoria: *Humanistische Panegyriken als Textvorlagen für Staatsmotetten der Renaissance*

THOMAS SCHMIDT-BESTE

Das Verhältnis zwischen humanistischer Dichtung und Musik ist erst in den letzten Jahrzehnten etwas mehr in das Blickfeld der Musikwissenschaft gerückt. Traditionell herrschte hier die Ansicht, daß die einzige—die wohl auch vielen Neulateinern geläufige—derartige Verbindung zwischen Text und Musik in der deutschen Humanistenode bestanden habe, in der die Versmetren vor allem des Horaz, aber auch anderer Dichter mit einfachen vierstimmigen Sätzen unterlegt wurden, die genau dem Metrum folgten, um dies in das Gedächtnis der Schüler einzuprägen.[1] Diese Humanistenoden haben jedoch in der Musikgeschichte und Musikforschung eher geringes Interesse hervorgerufen, da sie ausschließlich vom Text ausgehen und die Musik ganz und gar im Hintergrund steht: Die Oden entwickeln keinen eigenständigen Kunstanspruch und stehen noch dazu fast völlig außerhalb der übrigen musikalischen Entwicklung.[2] Im Rahmen eines Kongresses über neulateinische Sprache und Literatur wäre es zudem auch deswegen wenig sinnvoll, über Humanistenoden zu referieren, da es sich bei den Texten fast immer um die der Klassiker selbst (vor allem Horaz) handelt und nicht um Neulatein im Sinne einer kunstvollen Neuschöpfung oder Nachschöpfung lateinischer Texte im Sinne der Antike. Daher soll es hier vielmehr um Texte gehen, die ebenso neu und auch kunstvoll sind wie die Musikstücke, die aus ihren Vertonungen entstanden.

---

[1] Zu den Humanistenoden vgl. R[ochus] von Liliencron, "Die Horazischen Metren in deutschen Kompositionen des 16. Jahrhunderts" *Vierteljahresschrift für Musikwissenschaft* 3 (1887): 26–91; Karl-Günther Hartmann, *Die humanistische Odenkomposition in Deutschland. Vorgeschichte und Voraussetzungen*, Erlanger Studien 15 (Erlangen, 1976); zuletzt Thomas Schmidt-Beste, "Die humanistische Ode", *Die Musik in Geschichte und Gegenwart* 2. Auflage, Sachteil Bd. 7 (Kassel/Stuttgart, 1997), 562–567.

[2] Vgl. u.a. die Round Table-Diskussion "Verse Meter and Melodic Rhythm in the Age of Humanism", in *International Musicological Society, Report of the Eighth Congress, New York 1961*, hrsg. Jan LaRue (Kassel, 1961), 2: 67–71.

Denn die dem Literaturwissenschaftler vielleicht weniger bekannte Tatsache ist die, daß im Herrscherlob der Renaissance sehr oft eine zweite Kunst zu der der humanistischen Panegyrik hinzutrat, die die erste ergänzte und überhöhte: die Musik. Die Praxis, Musikstücke zum Lob des Fürsten zu komponieren und bei festlichen Anlässen aufzuführen, wurde natürlich nicht erst mit dem Humanismus geboren: auch das Personenlob an sich hatte ja in mittellateinischen Texten das gesamte Mittelalter überdauert.[3] Das steigende Bedürfnis der Renaissancefürsten nach Repräsentation und Selbstdarstellung führte jedoch nicht nur zu dem in Philologenkreisen wohlbekannten sprunghaften Anstieg von Panegyriken, die nunmehr ganz unverblümt antike Vorbilder bemühten, sondern auch zu einer entsprechend ansteigenden Anzahl von Musikstücken, die entsprechend ihrer herausgehobenen Funktion bei festlichen Anlässen auch kompositorisch zu den herausragenden Werken der Epoche gehören.[4] Im Sinne dieser repräsentativen Funktion hat sich in der Musikwissenschaft für diese Stücke der Begriff "Staatsmotette" oder "Festmotette" eingebürgert; ihre Texte sind jedenfalls genau solche Panegyriken, wie sie—sonst ohne Musik—zu feierlichen Anlässen dem Herrscher vorgetragen oder überreicht wurden.[5]

Der Einfluß humanistischer Elemente auf diese Motetten, und das heißt zunächst auf ihre Texte, ist so alt wie der Humanismus selbst: Bereits am Anfang des vierzehnten Jahrhunderts stattete der südfranzösische Dichter Philippe de Vitry, ein enger Freund Petrarcas aus dessen Zeit in Avignon, die Texte zu seinen Motetten mit Anspielungen und Zitaten aus dem klassischen Altertum aus: *Colla iugo subdere* schließt in der Oberstimme mit einem Hexameter aus Lukans *Pharsalia*, und auch die Mittelstimme schließt mit vier Hexametern; "Garrit Gallus", beginnt in der Mittelstimme mit dem Eröffnungsvers aus Ovids Metamorphosen, "In nova fert animus mutatas dicere formas".[6] Im Personenlob Vitrys ist zudem die traditionell-mittelalterliche christliche Bildersprache stark mit klassischen Elementen durchmischt: in seinem Gedicht auf Papst Clemens VI., "Petre Clemens", treten neben Petrus, den Propheten und dem Volk Israel auch Pegasus, Thyestes, Atreus und Apollo auf.[7] Die Werke des in der protohumanistischen Tradition stehenden Vitry (Petrarca bezeichnet ihn als "poeta nunc unicus Gallicarum"[8]) stehen allerdings vorerst relativ allein: Im weiteren Verlauf des Jahrhunderts bleibt Humanistendichtung im Motettentext eher die Ausnahme als die Regel, und die Werke Vitrys erfahren so auch als einzige Motetten-

---

[3] Vgl. F. Bittner, *Studien zum Personenlob in der mittellateinischen Dichtung* (Volkach, 1962).

[4] Vgl. hierzu allgemein Thomas Christian Schmidt, " 'Carmina gratulatoria'—Humanismus in der Staatsmotette des 15. Jahrhunderts", *Archiv für Musikwissenschaft* 51 (1994): 83–109.

[5] Der Begriff "Staatsmotette" ist spätestens seit Albert Dunning, *Die Staatsmotette 1480–1555* (Utrecht, 1970), in der Musikwissenschaft fest eingebürgert; er wurde in den letzten Jahren problematisiert durch Laurenz Lütteken, *Guillaume Dufay und die isorhythmische Motette*. Schriften zur Musikwissenschaft aus Münster 4 (Hamburg, 1993), 263–267.

[6] Eine Edition aller erwähnten Vitry-Motetten findet sich in *Polyphonic Music of the Fourteenth Century*, Bd. 1, hrsg. Leo Schrade (Monaco, 1965).

[7] Vgl. Andrew Wathey, "The Motets of Philippe de Vitry and the Fourteenth-Century Renaissance", *Early Music History* 12 (1993): 119–150.

[8] Zit. in Wathey, "Motets of Philippe de Vitry", 120.

texte des vierzehnten Jahrhunderts überhaupt das Privileg einer von der Musik separaten Verbreitung in humanistischen Texthandschriften.[9]

Ab dem Anfang des fünfzehnten Jahrhunderts aber wird die Verwendung neuverfaßter humanistischer Texte für das musikalische Personenlob in Italien zur allgemein verbreiteten Praxis—und zwar zur selben Zeit und an denselben Orten, an denen auch der literarische Humanismus seine erste große Blütezeit erlebte, das heißt in Venedig, Padua, Bologna und Florenz.[10] Der bedeutendste Komponist "humanistischer" Staatsmotetten ist zunächst der aus Cambrai stammende Guillaume Dufay, der zwischen etwa 1420 und 1440 in Bologna, Florenz und am päpstlichen Hof wirkte und dort insgesamt neun Staatsmotetten komponierte, davon fünf auf metrisch wie inhaltlich humanistisch zu nennende Texte; von einigen wird weiter unten noch die Rede sein. Spätestens ab dem letzten Drittel des Jahrhunderts werden dann neu komponierte Staatsmotetten eigentlich nur noch auf solche Dichtungen komponiert, Panegyriken reinsten Wassers vor allem in Hexametern oder Distichen.[11] Der bedeutendste Vertreter der Jahrhundertwende ist dann der Flame Heinrich Isaac, der wiederum an zwei Hauptzentren des Humanismus tätig war: von 1485 bis 1495 am Hofe der Medici in Florenz und danach am habsburgischen Hof Maximilians I. Aber auch alle anderen großen Komponisten der Zeit schrieben entsprechende Werke, so zum Beispiel Jacob Obrecht, Johannes Ockeghem, Josquin Desprez; im sechzehnten Jahrhundert wird die Tradition unter anderem durch Ludwig Senfl, Cipriano de Rore und Orlando di Lasso fortgesetzt.

Die Verwendung metrischer Texte blieb auch nicht ohne Einfluß auf die rhythmische Gestalt der Musik. Da der Rhythmus in der Mensuralpolyphonie des vierzehnten bis sechzehnten Jahrhunderts genau wie die antiken Metren primär nach Längen und Kürzen und nicht nach einer akzentuierenden "Takt"—Rhythmik organisiert war,[12] lag es nahe, die Versquantitäten auch in der Musik wiederzugeben. Die Anpassung der Musik an das Metrum ist dennoch nicht sklavisch wie in der Humanistenode, die nur zwei rhythmische Werte kennt. Die Längen sind vielmehr relativ zu den sie umgebenden Werten und zum allgemeinen Deklamationstempo "länger", ebenso wie in einem modernen akzent— bzw. taktrhythmischen Lied die Betonungen relativ und nicht absolut hervortreten. Die Beziehung zwischen Metrum und musikalischem Rhythmus ist in den Motetten gleichwohl deutlich zu erkennen. Das erste Beispiel hierfür ist Guillaume Dufays Motette "Rite maiorem" auf stichische sapphische Hendekasyllaben, die er im Jahr 1426 in Bologna für den Sekretär des Kardinals Aleman, den Priester Robertus Auclou komponierte:[13]

---

[9] Für eine Übersicht dieser Quellen vgl. Wathey, "Motets of Philippe de Vitry", 123.

[10] Vgl. Schmidt, "Carmina gratulatoria", 91–94.

[11] Dunning, *Die Staatsmotette*, passim; vgl. auch Hans Albrecht, "Humanismus und Musik", in *Die Musik in Geschichte und Gegenwart* (Kassel, 1957), 6: 903–905.

[12] Vgl. Wolf Frobenius, "Tactus", in *Handwörterbuch der musikalischen Terminologie*, hrsg. H. H. Eggebrecht, 3–6.

[13] Vgl. David Fallows, *Dufay* (London, 1980), 29–31, 244; hrsg. in Guillaume Dufay, *Opera Omnia*, ed. Heinrich Besseler, Bd. 1 (Rom, 1966), 38–45; partielle Neuedition mit korrigierter Textunterlegung in Schmidt, "Carmina gratulatoria", 108f.

Rite maiorem Iacobum canamus,
Ordinis summi decus. O fidelis,
Blanda sit semper tibi sors, viator.
Excita laudes hominum patrono.

Rebus est frater paribus Iohannes;
Tam novas Christi facies uterque
Visit, ut Petrus; sequitur magistrum
Sponte, dilectus fieri ‹vocatus›.

Audiit vocem Iacobi sonoram
Corda divinis penitus moventem
Legis accepte Phariseus hostis:
Ora conversus lacrimis rigavit.

Vinctus a turba prius obsequente,
Cum magus sperat Iacobum ligare,
Vertit in penas rabiem furoris,
Respuit tandem magicos abusus.

Arcibus summis miseri reclusi
Tanta qui fidunt Iacobo merentur
Vinculis ruptis peciere terram
Saltibus gressu stupuere planam.

Sopor annose paralisis altus
Accitu sancti posuit rigorem.
Novit ut Christi famulum satelles,
Colla dimisit venerans ligatum.

Tu patri natum laqueis iniquis
Insitum servas. Duce te precamur
Iam mori vi non metuat viator,
At suos sospes repetat penates.

Corporis custos animeque fortis,
Omnibus prosis baculoque sancto
Bella tu nostris moveas ab oris,
Ipse sed tutum tege iam Robertum[14].

Die Deklamation des Textes ist für den Hörer zwar streckenweise leicht verschleiert, da—wie in der Motette der Zeit sehr oft—die erste und die zweite Hälfte des Gedichtes in den beiden Oberstimmen gleichzeitig deklamiert werden. Dennoch ist der Sapphicus vor allem durch die musikalischen Phrasen, die die Versaufteilung

---

[14] Transkription in Leofranc Holford-Strevens, "Dufay the Poet? Problems in the Texts of his Motets", *Early Music History* 16 (1997): 97–165.

widerspiegeln, durch die Zäsur in der Versmitte und den folgenden zwei kurzen Silben, streckenweise recht gut hörbar.[15]

Guillaume Dufay, Rite maiorem Jacobum canamus, m. 19–24 und 26–30 (Motetus)

Noch deutlicheren humanistischen Einfluß in der Befolgung des Metrums zeigen mehr als ein halbes Jahrhundert danach die Werke Heinrich Isaaks. Im zweiten Teil der Motette "Sancti spiritus-Imperii proceres", die der Komponist zur Eröffnung des Konstanzer Reichstages von 1507 durch Kaiser Maximilian I. schrieb, werden die Hexameter streckenweise in geradezu plakativ deutlicher Weise in der Musik wiedergegeben.[16]

Sancti spiritus assit nobis gracia
Illustrator ades summo delapsus olimpo,
ignis amorque deus qui spiritus omnia reples.
Respice concilii cetum, Constancia felix
quem tenet. Imperii rebus pie consule rector:
Ut celo pacem dictas, sic federa terris
auspice te Cesar componat Maximilianus.
Imperii proceres, Romani gloria regni,
vos electores, vos archiepiscopi et omnes
pontifices: totus sit ecclesiasticus ordo.

---

[15] Vgl. Schmidt, "Carmina Gratulatoria", 100–103.

[16] Vgl. Th. Schmidt-Beste, "Heinrich Isaac's Occasional Motets for the Konstanz Reichstag of 1507: Testimonies of Humanism at the Habsburg Imperial Court?", in *Austria 996–1996: Music in a Changing Society*, Kongreßbericht Ottawa 1996, hrsg. Walter Kreyszig [forthcoming].

> Armorumque duces, vos landtgraviique potentes
> marchio quisquis ades, comes nobilis et baro, urbis
> rector seu populi: imperii quem federa iungunt.
> Consulite in medium, rebus succurrite fessis.
> Ecclesiam fulcite sacram; concordia sancto
> vos stringat vinculo, propriis et rebus adeste.
> Auscultate pio pro vobis Maximiliano. ·
> Sollicite accedat favor, optime Iuli,
> qui pater es patrium, populos frenare superbos.
> Da Deus: imperii iustis cadat emulus armis.
> Hinc tibi devote reddamus carmina, grates
> Atque tuas laudes celebret Germanica virtus.[17]

In der Musik sieht dies dann folgendermaßen aus (Vers 8):

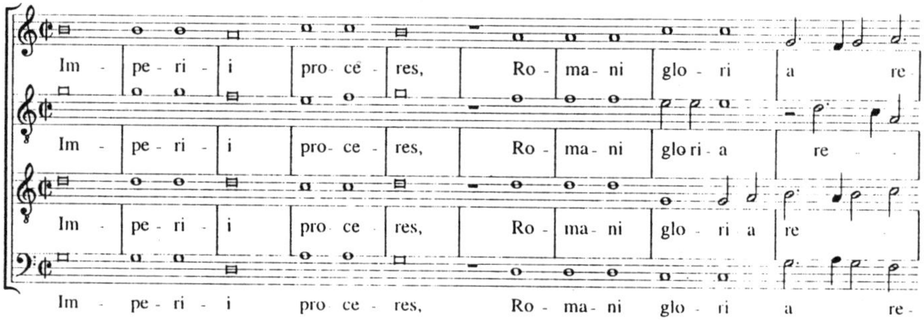

Heinrich Isaac, Sancti Spiritus–Imperii proceres, Anfang des 2. Teils

---

[17] Text nach den Handschriften Basel, Universitätsbibliothek, Musikabteilung Ms. F.IX.55, und Dresden, Landesbibliothek, Mus. Ms. 1/D/505.

Wie verhält es sich aber nun mit den literarischen Qualitäten der Texte? Generell sind zwei Beobachtungen zu machen: Erstens steigt mit dem generellen sprachlichen und metrischen Niveau des Humanistenlateins im Verlauf des 15. und 16. Jahrhunderts auch das der Motettentexte; dies erscheint unmittelbar einleuchtend, da sich die Verfasser der Motettentexte ja prinzipiell im selben höfisch-akademischen Milieu bewegten wie die Verfasser der panegyrischen Texte. Zweitens aber bleibt das Niveau der Motettentexte generell deutlich hinter dem Niveau zumindest der hochwertigeren Produkte aus humanistischer Feder zurück—und zwar im Hinblick auf Sprache, auf Metrik und nicht zuletzt auf Qualität der handschriftlichen Überlieferung. Dies bedarf der Demonstration und der Erklärung. Denn es wird deutlich, daß sich die Komponisten über weite Strecken mit durchaus mittelmäßigen Texten abgaben, obwohl sie doch, wie erwähnt, in den Zentren des Humanismus tätig waren und sicherlich einen der ansässigen Dichter als Textautoren hätten gewinnen können. Guillaume Dufay, der in der ersten Jahrhunderthälfte noch die vergleichsweise anspruchsvollsten Texte vertonte, hätte in Florenz einen Leonardo Bruni und Francesco Filelfo, am päpstlichen Hof einen Poggio und einen Antonio Loschi, in Bologna und Padua ganze Universitäten zur Verfügung gehabt, aber keines der im humanistischen Ton verfaßten Gedichte, die er vertonte, könnte auch nur im Traum von einem dieser Autoren stammen. Man vergleiche hierzu zwei Texte, die Dufay in seinen Florentiner Jahren 1435–1436 vertonte und die beide wie so viele andere Texte das Lob auf die Stadt Florenz singen, mit einem um dieselbe Zeit entstandenen Gedicht desselben Themas von Francesco Filelfo (1434).

Guillaume Dufay (I):

> Salve flos Tusce gentis, Florencia, salve,
>> O salve, Italici gloria magna soli.
> Salve, que doctos felix tot mater alumnos,
>> Tot generas magnos consilio atque fide,
> Que tot prestantes mira integritudine, que tot
>> Prestantes generas religione viros.
> Salve, cui debet quodcumque est artis honeste
>> Ingenii quicquid quicquid et eloquii est.
> Salve, que fama totum diffusa per orbem
>> Et vehere et natos mittis ad astra tuos.
> Nunc cecini et grato voces placuere canore.
>> Premia, mercedes nec periere simul.
> Fessus ego haud cantu, vox est defessa canendo,
>> Sed tu carminibus vive canenda meis.
> Vos nunc Etrusce iubeo salvere puelle.
>> Sic sedet hoc animo nec sine amore moror.
> Stant foribus Nimphis similes, stant Naiades utque
>> Aut ut Amazonides aut proca diva Venus.
> Fervet in amplexus atque oscula dulcia quisque;
>> Si semel has viderit, captus amore cadet.

> Ista, dee mundi, vester per secula cuncta,
>   Guillermus cecini natus et ipse Fay.[18]

Guillaume Dufay (II):

> Mirandas parit hec urbs Florentina puellas
> In quibus est species et summo forma nitore.
> Quale Helenam decus olim nos habuisse putamus,
> Virginibus patriis talis florescit ymago.
> At te precipuam genuit, clarissima virgo;
> Nam reliquas superas et luce et corpore nymphas,
> Ut socias splendore suas dea pulcra Diana
> Vincit et integrior quacumque in parte videtur.[19]

Francesco Filelfo:

> O mihi iam sextum, dulcis Florentia, solem
> per varias habitata vices multoque labore
> inter et invidiae gladios et mentis avarae
> fulmina quae celsos potuissent sternere montes
> tam forti servata manu, iam parce morari.
> Da veniam, sine me tandem capitique reique
> prospexisse meae: livor mihi retia tendit
> improbus; armatur, diris accincta colubris,
> tristis avaritia et virus minitatur et enses.
> Uxor cara mihi, sunt dulcia pignora nati:
> horum si nihili rationem duxero, demens
> censear. Obstrictus magno tibi munere, nunquam
> delabi te mente sinam: tu praemia nobis
> contuleras, alii virtutis nomine quanta
> nulli unquam licuit tanto sperare favore,
> in primisque meum cunctis in rebus honorem
> fovisti, laudem miris successibus augens.[20]

Es handelt sich hierbei sogar um die beiden qualitativ hochwertigsten Gedichte aus Dufays Oeuvre: Anders als in den meisten anderen Gedichten gibt es kaum falsche Quantitäten, und natürlich wimmelt es von inhaltlichen Anspielungen auf die antike Mythologie. Der Satzbau jedoch klammert sich fast sklavisch an die Versgrenzen, und das immer wiederkehrenden "Salve" im ersten der beiden Gedichte wird nach einer Weile doch recht penetrant. Mit der Eleganz des Lobes von Francesco Filelfo anläß-

---

[18] Guillaume Dufay, *Opera Omnia*, 1: 64–69; Text neu transkribiert in Holford-Strevens, "Dufay the Poet".

[19] Guillaume Dufay, *Opera Omnia*, 1: 12–14; Text neu transkribiert in Holford-Strevens, "Dufay the Poet".

[20] Zitiert nach A. Perosa und J. Sparrow, *Renaissance Latin Verse* (London, 1979), 24.

lich seines Abschiedes aus Florenz können die Verse an keiner Stelle konkurrieren.[21]

Erst gegen Ende des Jahrhunderts stieg mit der immer weiteren Verbreitung des Humanistenlateins der sprachliche Standard und offenbar auch der Anspruch so weit, daß die Motettentexte für sich genommen ein gewisses literarisches Niveau beanspruchen können und bisweilen—so weit feststellbar—auch von bedeutenden Autoren stammen. Der bereits erwähnte Isaac vertonte zum Tode von Lorenzo "Il Magnifico" de' Medici zwei solcher Texte, einen aus Versen des *Hercules Oetaeus* von Seneca mit einer Fortsetzung von Angelo Poliziano, "Quis dabit pacem populo timenti", und noch ein weiteres Gedicht, ganz von Poliziano verfaßt, "Quis dabit capiti meo aquam";[22] später in seiner Zeit am habsburgischen Hof folgte noch das Hexameter-Gedicht "Virgo prudentissima", das möglicherweise von dem Schweizer Humanisten Joachim Vadianus stammt.[23] In derselben Zeit wurde es auch üblicher, in der Kunstmusik Originaltexte klassischer Autoren zu vertonen: allein der Monolog der Dido aus Vergils Aeneis, "Dulces exuviae," wurde mindestens achtmal vertont.[24] Andere Motetten zeigen aber nach wie vor ein eher mäßiges sprachliches Niveau. Die oben zitierte Isaac-Motette "Sancti spiritus-Imperii proceres" stolpert selbst nach wohlwollendster Emendierung metrisch recht unbeholfen durch die Hierarchie des habsburgischen Reiches; bis auf wenige Ausnahmen war das sprachliche Niveau nördlich der Alpen um die Jahrhundertwende offenbar noch nicht auf dem Stand der italienischen Lehrmeister.

Der Grund für das allgemeine qualitative Gefälle zwischen den für die Vertonung bestimmten Gedichte und den reinen Texten ist aber wohl darin zu suchen, daß—im Gegensatz zur Humanistenode—der Text im Verhältnis zur Musik zweitrangig war. Der Anspruch der Gedichte erschöpfte sich in ihrer musikalischen Funktion, da sie fast ausnahmslos von vorneherein für Musik bestimmt waren und nicht getrennt von ihr existierten. Ähnlich wie später ein Opernlibretto mußte auch der Motettentext offenbar nicht dieselben literarischen Ansprüche befriedigen wie ein rein zum Lesen oder Rezitieren gedachter Text; wie die angeführten Beispiele belegen, handelt es sich ja auch in aller Regel um Gedichte von nahezu epigrammatischer Kürze. Hinzu kommt, daß noch bis weit ins fünfzehnte Jahrhundert die schon beobachtete Praxis anhielt, zwei Texte gleichzeitig zu deklamieren, was das Textverständnis ebenfalls nicht eben förderte. Es schien offenbar hinreichend, sich einen Text zu verschaffen, der in äußerer Form und Inhalt die modernen Standards humanistischer Dichtung einigermaßen erfüllte—die Feinheiten gingen ohnehin verloren.

Der Vorrang der Musik über das Wort manifestiert sich zudem in der Tatsache, daß der Autor des Textes völlig hinter dem Komponisten zurücktritt. In den Hand-

---

[21] Vgl. zur literarischen Qualität der Dufayschen Texte auch Holford-Strevens, "Dufay the Poet", passim.

[22] Dunning, *Die Staatsmotette*, 20–23; Martin Just, "Studien zu Heinrich Isaacs Motetten" (Diss. Tübingen, 1960), 2: 62f.

[23] Vgl. Louise Cuyler, *The Emperor Maximilian I and Music* (London, 1973), 191; dagegen allerdings Dunning, *Die Staatsmotette*, 40.

[24] Vgl. u.a. *Fünf Vergil-Motetten zu 4–7 Stimmen*, hrsg. Helmuth Osthoff, Das Chorwerk 54 (Wolfenbüttel, 1956).

schriften wird, wenn überhaupt, in Inhaltsverzeichnissen und Überschriften nur der Komponist, nie der Dichter genannt; und, viel wichtiger noch, in den wenigen Fällen, in denen das Gedicht selbst mit der Nennung des Autors als "Verneigung" vor dem Widmungsträger schließt, ist der Genannte immer der Komponist, nie der Dichter; ein Beispiel hierfür ist das zitierte "Salve flos Tuscae gentis" von Dufay (s.o.). Man mag hieraus schließen, daß die Texte zum Teil wohl von den Komponisten selbst stammten, aber auch die bedeutendsten Komponisten des Jahrhunderts wie Dufay, Josquin oder Isaac können eben kaum als Dichter von Rang gelten; sie hatten sich in ihrer Jugend als Chorknaben wohl solide Lateinkenntnisse erworben, und Isaac wird gar als "Magister" genannt; dennoch waren die Musiker als Mitglieder der Kapelle und nicht der Kanzlei eben doch Teil einer anderen Sphäre innerhalb des höfischen Lebens und hatten am akademischen bzw. universitären Leben ohnehin nur in den seltensten Fällen teil. Falls also die Musiker ihre Texte wirklich selber verfaßten, wäre dies sogar eine Erklärung für die schwankende Qualität derselben.

Die wenigen Texte von bekannten Autoren geben schließlich auch Aufschluß über die Probleme der Überlieferung. Einer dieser Texte ist das Italienlob von Petrarca, "Salve cara deo", das am Anfang des fünfzehnten Jahrhunderts von einem "Ludovicus de Arimino" vertont wurde.[25] Ein Vergleich zwischen dem separat überlieferten Originaltext und der Version, die in der einzigen musikalischen Quelle, einer norditalienischen Sammelhandschrift, überliefert ist, zeigt so massive Unterschiede, daß das Original streckenweise kaum noch zu identifizieren ist.[26]

Petrarca:

> Salve, cara Deo tellus sanctissima, salve
> Tellus tuta bonis, tellus metuenda superbis,
> Tellus nobilibus multum generosior oris,
> Fertilior cunctis, terra formosior omni,
> Cincta mari gemino, famoso splendida monte,
> Armorum legumque eadem veneranda sacrarum,
> Pyeridumque domus, auroque opulenta virisque,
> Cuius ad eximios ars et natura favores
> Incubuere simul, mundoque dedere magistram.
> Ad te nunc cupide post tempora longa revertor
> Incola perpetuus. Tu diversoria vitae
> Grata dabis fessae. Tu quantum pallida tandem
> Membra tegant, praestabis humum. Te laetus ab alto
> Italiam video frondentis colle Gebennae.
> Nubila post tergum remanent; ferit ora serenus
> Spiritus, et blandis assurgens motibus aer

---

[25] Vgl. Benvenuto Disertori, "L'Epistola all'Italia del Petrarca musicata nei Codici Tridentini", *Rivista Musicale Italiana* 46 (1942): 65–78.

[26] Vgl hierzu bereits Schmidt, "Carmina gratulatoria", 105–107.

Excipit. Agnosco patriam, gaudensque saluto.
Salve, pulchra parens, terrarum gloria salve![27]

Trient, Museo Provinciale d'Arte, cod. 87, fol. 160v–161:

Salve cara deo tellus sacratissima salve
Tellus tuta bonis tellus metuenda superbis
[Zeile fehlt]
Fertilior cunctis terra formosior ori
cuncto, mari gemino fecunda splendida monte
Pyeridum mater auro opulenta virisque
Armorum legumque veneranda sacrarum.
Huius ad eximios ars et natura favores,
Incubuere simul mundoque dedere magistram.
Ad te nunc cupide post tempora longa revertor,
Incola perpetuus. Tu diversoria vite
Dabis fesse. Tu quartum palida tandem membra
Te gratiam[?] prestabis humani. Te letus ab alto
Ytaliam videam frondentem monte Gebene.
Nubilla post tergum remanent ferit ora serenus
Spiritus, et gratus assurgens montibus aer
Excipit, agnosco gaudens patriamque saluto
Salve sancta parens terrarum gloria salve.

Einige Veränderungen sind möglicherweise inhaltlich gewollt, z.B. "pulchra" zu "sancta" in der letzten Zeile, aber ansonsten handelt es sich in erschreckendem Ausmaß schlicht um Korruption, von zahllosen falschen Quantitäten über vertauschte und fehlende Zeilen bis zu Passagen wie den Versen zwölf und dreizehn, wo das Metrum kaum mehr als solches zu identifizieren ist. Der Schreiber der Musikhandschrift scheint des Lateinischen nur unzureichend mächtig gewesen zu sein, so daß er überhaupt nicht merkte, was er den geplagten Hexametern zufügte. Und damit ist man ist wohl bei dem Hauptproblem in der Überlieferung der Texte überhaupt angelangt, mit denen es die Musikwissenschaftler zu tun haben: Die Schreiber von Musikhandschriften waren eben zunächst Musiker und Notenschreiber, nicht Literaten und Textschreiber. Sie waren Mitglieder der Kapellen und nicht der Kanzleien, hatten als Ausbildung wohl selten mehr als die Chorknabenschule hinter sich; und der Text ist dementsprechend oft in einer sprachlich wie graphisch mehr als fragwürdigen Version überliefert. Die Korruption ist daher—das genannte Petrarca-Gedicht als eines der wenigen nachvollziehbaren Beispiele demonstriert dies sehr deutlich—im Durchschnitt viel schlimmer als in "normalen" Texthandschriften; die Musikwissenschaft ist hier in hohem Maße auf die Hilfe der Neulateiner angewiesen, um die Texte durch Emendierung oder gar Rekonstruktion wieder annähernd in ihren Originalzustand zu versetzen.

---

[27] Perosa und Sparrow, *Renaissance Latin Verse*, 12.

Die Erforschung der humanistischen Panegyriken, die als Grundlage für Staatsmotetten dienten, steht so noch ganz am Anfang. Die Texte sind, wie wir gesehen
haben, sicher nicht der Gipfelpunkt humanistischer Dichtkunst, aber sind in soziologischer Hinsicht als "Gebrauchsdichtung", wenn man so will, doch von gewissem
Interesse. Ein wachsendes Interesse sowohl der Musikwissenschaft als auch der Neolatinistik läßt darauf hoffen, daß das nicht allzu umfangreiche Textkorpus bald soweit
erschlossen ist, daß beide Disziplinen hiervon entsprechend profitieren können.

Universität Heidelberg

Los Errata Petri Alcyonii in interpretatione libri Aristotelis de incessu animalium *de Juan Ginés de Sepúlveda: ¿obra quemada, no impresa o no publicada?*

JULIÁN SOLANA PUJALTE

Dentro de la amplia y polifacética producción del humanista español Juan Ginés de Sepúlveda, ocupan un lugar destacado sus traducciones latinas de diversas obras de Aristóteles y de Alejandro de Afrodisias. A pesar de ello, esta parcela de su obra sigue siendo la que menos ha atraido la atención de los estudiosos. Las únicas excepciones a lo dicho son los artículos de O. H. Green[1], Á. Losada[2], E. Rodríguez Peregrina[3], y sobre todo la tesis doctoral y la serie de trabajos posteriores que ha dedicado al tema A. Coroleu[4]. Aunque lo realizado es enormemente meritorio, queda, sin embargo, por abordar la tarea más importante, la edición y el estudio de estas

---

[1] O. H. Green, "A Note on Spanish Humanism. Sepúlveda and his Translation of Aristotle's Politics", *Hispanic Review* 8 (1940): 339–342.

[2] Ángel Losada, "Juan Ginés de Sepúlveda, traductor y comentarista de Aristóteles", *Revista de Filosofía* 24 (1948): 501–536; 28 (1949): 109–128.

[3] Elena Rodríguez Peregrina, "J. G. de Sepúlveda y sus traducciones comentadas de los filósofos griegos", *Estudios de Filología Latina* 4 (1984): 235–246.

[4] Alejandro Coroleu, "Estudios sobre Juan Ginés de Sepúlveda: sus traducciones latinas de Aristóteles", Tesis doctoral, Barcelona, 1993; "La contribución de Juan Ginés de Sepúlveda a la edición de los textos de Aristóteles y de Alejandro de Afrodisias", *Humanistica Lovaniensia* 43 (1994): 231–245; "Le glosse di Juan Ginés de Sepúlveda alle traduzioni latine di Aristotele", *Giornale Critico della Filosofia Italiana* 73 (75) fasc. 1 (1994): 16–32; "A Philological Analysis of Juan Ginés de Sepulveda's Latin Translations of Aristotle and Alexander of Aphrodisias", *Euphrosyne* 23 (1995): 175–195; "Ioannes Genesius Sepulveda versus Franciscus Vatablus. A propósito de la fortuna de las traducciones latinas de Juan Ginés de Sepúlveda" *Habis* 27 (1996): 277–281; "The *Fortuna* of Juan Ginés de Sepúlveda's Translations of Aristotle and of Alexander of Aphrodisias", *Journal of the Warburg and Courtauld Institutes* 59 (1996): 325–332.

traducciones, que lamentablemente no están contemplados en la edición pozoalbense de sus obras actualmente en curso.

En relación con este campo de las traducciones latinas de Aristóteles de Sepúlveda, aparece citada constantemente otra obra del humanista cordobés de la que hasta hoy apenas sabemos nada y que tanto los estudiosos de Sepúlveda como del *Aristoteles Latinus* consideran unánimemente perdida: los *Errata Petri Alcyonii in interpretatione Aristotelis a Ioanne Genesio Sepulveda Cordubensi collecta.*

1. ¿Qué sabemos sobre esta obra? Resumimos en breves palabras los datos hasta ahora conocidos.

a) En 1521 el humanista veneciano Pietro Alcionio publicó su traducción latina de varios tratados de Aristóteles, entre ellos los *Parva Naturalia*[5]. b) En febrero y marzo de 1522 Cristophe de Longueil en sendas cartas dirigidas a Octaviano Grimaldo le da cuenta de que un español llamado Juan Ginés de Sepúlveda que vive en Bolonia ha reunido los errores cometidos por Alcionio en sus traduciones de Aristóteles y que ya ha editado la obra con el título arriba mencionado[6]. c) Girolamo Nigri en otra carta de septiembre de 1523 dirigida a Marc'Antonio Micheli le da cuenta de lo anterior y le transmite que Alcionio ha comprado todos los ejemplares de la edición, pero que Sepúlveda quiere volver a imprimirlos[7]. d) Paulo Giovio, finalmente, en un caústico *elogium* del humanista veneciano, publicado más de 20 años después, dice que Alcionio no pudo soportar la crítica de Sepúlveda y la aceptación que entre los eruditos tuvieron los *Errata*, y que se vio obligado a comprar todos los ejemplares de la obra para después quemarlos[8]. e) Estos testimonios fueron recogidos por G. M. Mazzucheli en su célebre obra sobre los escritores de Italia, momento a partir del cual todo lo dicho se convierte en una referencia obligada en cuantos estudios se han ocupado de Alcionio o de Sepúlveda[9].

Habitualmente los investigadores (S. D. Wingate[10], M. Rosa[11], C. H. Lohr[12], G. H. Tucker[13]) dan crédito a estos testimonios contemporáneos, consideran que la

---

[5] Pietro Alcionio (Venetia, 1521).

[6] Christophe de Longueil, *Longolii . . . lucubrationes . . . epistolarum libri IV* (Lugduni, 1542), 367, 386–387.

[7] G. Ruscelli, *Lettere di principi. Libro primo nuovamente mandato in luce de G. R.* (Venetia, 1562), fols. 87r y v.

[8] Paulo Giovio, *Elogia veris clarorum virorum imaginibus apposita quae in musaeo Ioviano comi spectantur . . .* (Venetia, 1546), fols. 70v–71.

[9] G. M. Mazzuchelli, *Gli scrittori d'Italia* (Brescia, 1753), I,1, 376–383.

[10] S. D. Wingate, *The Medieval Latin Versions of the Aristotelian Scientific Corpus* (Londres, 1931), 128.

[11] M. Rosa, *Dizionario biografico degli Italiani,* ed. A. M. Ghisalberti et al. (Roma, 1960), II, 77–80.

[12] H. Lohr, *Latin Aristotle Commentaries II. Renaissance Authors* (Firenze, 1988), 419–420.

[13] G. H. Tucker, "Exile Exiled. Petrus Alcyonius (1487–1527?) in a Travelling-Chest", *Journal of the Institute of Romance Studies* 2 (1993): 83–103.

obra se publicó y atribuyen que no se nos haya conservado a que Alcionio quemó cuantos ejemplares cayeron en sus manos.

Discrepa de esta versión L. Minio-Paluello, quien considera que las noticias que nos han llegado son un conjunto de fábulas con escaso fundamento: según él Sepúlveda reunió esos *Errata* pero nunca llegó a publicarlos. Los enemigos de Alcionio, para atacarlo, inventaron la historia de la quema de la obra, basándose en que obviamente no sería posible encontrar ejemplares de un libro que no se había publicado[14]. A confirmar esta hipótesis vendrían las palabras del propio Sepúlveda en el prefacio a la edición del *De incessu animalium* de Bolonia (1522) y París (1532) en el que dice que desistió de imprimir separadamente el opúsculo por la opinión contraria de Alberto Pío, que creyó que bastaba para hacerse un juicio de ambas traducciones simplemente con compararlas[15]. A esta opinión se ha adherido recientemente A. Coroleu[16].

¿Es posible discernir cuál de los dos relatos es el cierto? Veamos en primer lugar qué datos puede aportar a la solución de este pequeño enigma la edición sepulvediana de los *Parva Naturalia* que vio la luz en Bolonia en 1522.

2. Un hecho llama poderosamente la atención al revisar los tan sólo doce ejemplares localizados de la edición boloñesa: la profunda divergencia formal que existe entre ellos. Si fragmentamos todas las partes de que consta esta edición, podemos distiguir las siguientes: 1. Portada de los *Parva Naturalia;* 2. Prefacio a la traducción del tratado *De incessu animalium* dedicado a Alberto Pío; 3. Otro prefacio a la traducción de toda la obra dedicado a Giuliano de Medicis; 4. El texto de la traducción latina de los *Parva;* 5. *Errata librariorum* y colofón.

Pues bien, sólo existen cuatro ejemplares idénticos de los doce que hemos localizado y nos encontramos ocho combinaciones diferentes de estas partes; es decir, hay ocho impresos de hecho diferentes entre sí de la misma edición[17].

¿A qué es atribuible esta curiosa circunstancia? La respuesta se encuentra, en nuestra opinión, en el ejemplar que se conserva en la Biblioteca Marciana de Venecia, que custodia celosamente en su interior dos cuadernillos de seis folios cada uno, que reunen el prefacio dedicado a A. Pío y el texto de los *Errata Petri Alcyonii in interpre-*

---

[14] *Aristoteles latinus XI.1–2. De mundo*, ed. W. L. Lorimer, revisit L. Minio-Paluello (Leiden, 1965), XLIII, n. 1.

[15] "Sed quia tibi (i.e., Alberto Pio) aliter uisum est satisque semota etiam hac notandi diligentia, ex sola comparatione ferri posse iudicium putasti, *destiti ab editione separati opusculi . . . Libellum ergo omni expeditum onere illaque uelut coronide leuatum ad te mitto*" (Ad illustrissimum D. Albertum Pium . . . praefatio in interpretationem libri Aristotelis de incessu animalium).

[16] Coroleu, "Estudios sobre Juan Ginés de Sepúlveda", 43–47.

[17] Los ejemplares que hemos localizado son éstos: Biblioteca de la Universidad de Comillas (Madrid) XVI 2028 (4); Bibliothèque Nationale de France (París) Rés. R 39; Bodleian Library (Oxford) Byw.A.5.14(2); Biblioteca Comunale degli Intronati (Siena); Biblioteca Nazionale Centrale (Roma) 9.18.E.26.2; Biblioteca Apostólica Vaticana R.I.II.733; Biblioteca Vallicelliana (Roma) Borr.I.II.105; Q.VII.56; Biblioteca Comunale Augusta (Perugia) I.E.225; I.E.430; Biblioteca dell'Istituto e Museo di Storia della Scienza (Florencia) coll. 52; Biblioteca Marciana (Venecia) 134.d.36.

tatione libri Aristotelis de incessu animalium, que es el título real del opúsculo.

¿Cuál es la distribución de las partes de que se compone el ejemplar de la Marciana? ¿Eran los *Errata* una obra independiente o formaban un todo con la traducción de los *Parva*? ¿Era la ordenación que presenta el ejemplar de la Biblioteca Marciana la pensada en algún momento por Sepúlveda? La foliación no nos ayuda a averiguarlo, pues únicamente existe en el texto de la traducción propiamente dicho. Los folios precedentes tienen, sin embargo, signaturas que nos pueden servir para ir desvelando una posible interpretación. Por un lado el prefacio a Alberto Pío y los *Errata Petri Alcyonii* forman, como hemos dicho, dos cuadernillos de 6 folios cada uno: AA–BB[6]; por otro, la portada de los *Parva Naturalia* está unida al prefacio dedicado a Giuliano de Medicis en un sólo cuadernillo AA[4]: el texto del prefacio comienza con AA ii, lo que demuestra que su inclusión en el mismo cuadernillo no es debido a un error: la portada sería, naturalmente, el primer folio del cuadernillo, AA.

La duplicidad de la signatura AA, aparentemente en el mismo impreso (en los *Errata* y en el prefacio a Giuliano de Medicis), algo completamente anómalo, es una primera razón para pensar que los *Errata Petri Alcyonii* quizá estaban pensados para ser editados aparte como un opúsculo independiente.

Otro dato corrobora esta hipótesis: el texto del prefacio dedicado a Alberto Pío del ejemplar de la Biblioteca Marciana es bastante diferente al del resto de los ejemplares conservados, pues contiene referencias nominales a Alcionio, que no aparecen en el texto de este prefacio que conserva el resto de los ejemplares, en los que se evita mencionar el nombre del humanista veneciano, aunque se aluda a él. En el ejemplar de la Biblioteca Marciana no se hace referencia alguna, por contra, a que Alberto Pío aconsejase a Sepúlveda no editar los *Errata*. Parece, por tanto, evidente que el prefacio conservado en el ejemplar de la Marciana formaba un todo con los *Errata* y era su prefacio *sensu stricto* y que posteriormente fue retocado.

Un tercer dato a tener en cuenta, y que confirmaría esta hipótesis, es que los dos cuadernillos formados por el prefacio a Alberto Pío y los *Errata* del ejemplar de la Biblioteca Marciana poseen su propio colofón al final de los *Errata*: *Impressum Bononiae per Hieronymum de Benedictis. Anno gratie M.D.XXII. die uero. xxviii. Martii.* En este ejemplar no existe referencia cronológica alguna al final del prefacio dedicado a Alberto Pío, mientras que en su redacción retocada posterior sí está datado *Bononiae. XXIII Martii. M.D.XXII.*

Dos textos parecen confirmar además esta hipótesis: uno es un fragmento de los *Errata*, en el que puede advertirse que Sepúlveda en el momento de su redacción albergaba la idea de la edición del opúsculo precediendo a los *Parva*.

> Sed quia singulorum librorum errata persequi infinitum esset mihi praesertim tam occupato et fortasse nemine perlecturo superuacaneum, satis habui ea dumtaxat, quae in hoc uno libro de incessu animalium notaueram, *operi edendo praemittere* et adiunctis uerbis Aristotelis graecis nostraque interpretatione, ne diuersa uolumina haberes perlegenda, tuo exquisitissimo iudicio aestimanda proponere.

¿Cual es el sentido de este *praemittere*? Parece que enviar por delante, preceder, editar por delante del texto de los *Parva*. Un segundo texto procedente de la segunda versión del prefacio a Alberto Pío, un añadido que no figuraba en la primera versión, es si cabe aun más concluyente: Sepúlveda respeta el consejo de Alberto Pío y renuncia a la edición por separado de los *Errata (opusculum)*, y publica los *Parva (libellus)* sin añadido[18].

Como es patente, Sepúlveda cambió de opinión y esa primera idea, la edición conjunta del Prefacio a Pío y los *Errata Petri Alcyonii* separadamente y precediendo al resto de la obra, tal como se indica en la primera versión del prefacio, fue dejada de lado. En la segunda versión de este prefacio, retocado tras abandonar Sepúlveda la idea de editar los *Errata*, dice el autor que ha tomado la decisión de no publicarlos por consejo de Alberto Pío. Este cambio de planes, probablemente decidido cuando el proceso de impresión ya estaba muy avanzado, es la causa de esa diversidad en la forma de los ejemplares, diversidad que es un reflejo de las diferentes fases por las que pasó el proceso de impresión o de las pruebas que se hicieron en la imprenta hasta que el impreso adquiriese la forma definitiva. Aunque es aventurado poder asegurarlo, nos parece que quizá la forma final del impreso querida por Sepúlveda, tras la decisión de no editar los *Errata*, sea la conservada en el ejemplar de la Bodleian Library: Portada / Prefacio a G. de Medicis / Prefacio a A. Pío / Texto de los *Parva* / *Errata librariorum* – colofón: descartada la edición por separado de los *Errata Petri Alcyonii*, la portada de la traducción de los *Parva Naturalia* ocupa el primer lugar; le sigue la dedicatoria de la traducción completa de la obra a Giuliano de Medicis; la dedicatoria del *De incessu animalium* a Alberto Pío precede la traducción de ese tratado, el primero de la colección; sigue el texto del resto de los tratados que componen la obra y concluye con los *Errata librariorum* y el colofón.

Los *Errata Petri Alcyonii* están datados en su colofón el 28 de marzo de 1522 y el nuevo prefacio retocado dedicado a Alberto Pío el 23 de marzo de 1522. Es decir, el texto de los *Errata* acabó de imprimirse tan sólo cinco días después de concluirse el nuevo texto reformado del prefacio a Alberto Pío. Eso sólo puede significar que cuando se estaban aún imprimiendo los *Errata*, Sepúlveda probablemente ya había decidido no publicarlos, o que la decisión, dicho de otra manera, se tomó cuando ya estaba casi concluida su impresión. El resto de la obra, el texto de la traducción de los *Parva Naturalia* propiamente dicho, se concluyó algo después, como indica su colofón: 15 de mayo de 1522.

A la luz de estos datos, parece bastante improbable la hipótesis hasta ahora mayoritariamente aceptada: Sepúlveda llegó a publicar por separado los *Errata*, Alcionio se hizo con los ejemplares que pudo y los quemó. Si esto hubiese sido cierto, ¿qué sentido habría tenido que Sepúlveda rehiciese el prefacio dedicado a Alberto Pío, que lo integrase en la traducción de los *Parva,* que hubiese renunciado a una nueva impresión de los *Errata*, que hubiese simulado que nunca se habían editado y que responsabilizase de su no edición a Alberto Pío? Esta hipótesis presenta muchos más interrogantes de difícil resolución a los que, en el caso hipotético de que fuera cierta, no estamos en condiciones de responder. Pensamos que los hechos se desarrollaron más bien de esta otra manera:

---

[18] Cf. n. 15.

Con toda seguridad Sepúlveda pensó en un primer momento publicar los *Errata*, precedidos de una dedicatoria a Alberto Pío, como un opúsculo independiente de la traducción de los *Parva*, dedicada a Giuliano de Medicis. Quizá la intención de Sepúlveda fuera encuadernar juntas ambas obras formando un solo volumen, dadas sus características[19].

Cambió de opinión más adelante y decidió, según nos dice, aconsejado por Alberto Pío, no publicar los *Errata*. Como consecuencia de ello, hubo que retocar la redacción del prefacio a Alberto Pío que iba a publicarse de forma separada con los *Errata*, para poder incluirlo en forma de prefacio a la traducción de uno de los tratados de los *Parva*, el *De incessu animalium*.

Esta alteración y posterior reutilización del prefacio dedicado a Alberto Pío nos lleva a suponer que Sepúlveda no publicó finalmente los *Errata*. No tendría sentido, en caso contrario, publicar consecutivamente dos redacciones diferentes del prefacio a Alberto Pío: una en la que se justificase plenamente la razón de ser del opúsculo y otra en la que se explicase por qué acabó por no editarse. Parece, por tanto, una fabulación que Alcionio quemara los ejemplares de los *Errata*. El hecho de que Sepúlveda haya mantenido idéntica en la edición parisina de esta obra en 1532 la segunda redacción del prefacio dedicado a A. Pío, parece confirmarlo.

Todo hace pensar, por tanto, que los *Errata* no se publicaron, pero sabemos que habían sido impresos y que estaban prestos para su difusión: el único ejemplar existente, el conservado en la Biblioteca Marciana así lo demuestra.

Y concluimos ya. Hemos pretendido con esta comunicación dar a conocer el hallazgo de este opúsculo, oculto durante largo tiempo a los estudiosos, hacer una primera aproximación a él y anunciar que estamos trabajando en su edición que esperamos pueda ver la luz en breve.

Universidad de Córdoba

---

[19] Como en el ejemplar de la Biblioteca Marciana, que consta de las siguientes partes: prefacio a Alberto Pío; *Errata Petri Alcyonii*; portada de los *Parva Naturalia*; prefacio a Giuliano de Medicis; texto de los *Parva Naturalia*; *Errata librariorum* y colofón.

Università e Umanesimo

AGOSTINO SOTTILI

Quando si affronta il tema dei rapporti tra Università e Umanesimo, si può dire tutto e il contrario di tutto: che l'Università cioè è stata il luogo che ha propagandato l'Umanesimo e che l'Università è stata il luogo della resistenza all'Umanesimo. Entrambe le cose sono vere: il giurista e il medico del Quattrocento non tenevano lezione nel latino degli Umanisti, ma usavano la lingua che la tradizione secolare offriva loro, una lingua tecnica e precisa, ma lontana dal periodare armonico cui ricorrevano gli Umanisti nella loro reinvenzione della lingua dell'Antichità. Ma l'Università è stata anche il luogo dove il magistero di Leonzio Pilato davanti a Boccaccio ha illustrato Omero[1] e dove Manuele Crisolora ha educato una generazione di Umanisti alla lingua di Bisanzio, ma soprattutto dell'Ellade[2].

Non è possibile dimenticare la polemica che Petrarca ha condotto contro i rappresentanti del mondo accademico; l'avvocato è l'"occupatus" contro cui l'Umanista ha polemizzato nel *De vita solitaria*, i medici sono stati oggetto dei suoi attacchi, contro la scienza filosofica della Facoltà di arti Petrarca ha composto un intero trattato[3]. Ciò nonostante l'Umanista ha intrattenuto, ed era ovvio, tanti amichevoli rapporti con intellettuali di estrazione universitaria e l'Università è stato l'ambiente che più ha favorito l'esportazione all'estero dei suoi scritti[4]; professori universitari hanno commentato sue lettere quando l'Umanesimo ha cominciato a fare la comparsa nelle Università dell'Impero[5].

Ma occorre risalire oltre Petrarca alla generazione che all'Umanesimo ha dato inizio. La riscoperta padovana delle tragedie di Seneca è stato forse l'episodio decisivo

---

[1] A. Pertusi, *Leonzio Pilato fra Petrarca e Boccaccio. Le sue versioni omeriche negli autografi di Venezia e la cultura greca del primo Umanesimo* (Venezia, Roma, 1964).

[2] G. Cammelli, *I dotti bizantini e le origini dell'Umanesimo: Manuele Crisolora* (Firenze, 1941).

[3] *De sui ipsius et multorum ignorantia*.

[4] G. Billanovich, *Petrarca letterato. I. Lo scrittoio del Petrarca* (Roma, 1947), 297–419.

[5] A. Sottili, "In margine al catalogo petrarchesco per la Germania Occidentale", in G. Billanovich, G. Frasso, eds., *Il Petrarca ad Arquà. Atti del Convegno di studi nel VI centenario (1370–1374) (Arquà Petrarca, 6–8 novembre 1970)* (Padova, 1975), 293–311.

per l'avvio dell'Umanesimo letterario e filologico[6]. Abbiamo tutti presente il dialogo di Mussato sulla metrica delle tragedie di Seneca[7]. Il lavoro filologico ed esegetico su Seneca tragico è sfociato nel capolavoro dell'*Ecerinis*, un capolavoro anche metrico che termina con un coro di non facili dimetri anapestici e con una affermazione capitale, quella che la "regula iuris", la norma del diritto è destinata sempre ad avere la meglio. Il dialogo metrico di Mussato si svolge tra l'autore e Lovato, "magna pars" nella scoperta di Seneca e descrittore del trimetro giambico, ma anche sostenitore del professore universitario Pietro da Abano[8]. Il dialogo è poi dedicato a quell'universitario di rango altissimo che fu Marsilio da Padova, dichiaratosi curioso di saperne di più sulla metrica di Seneca.

Vogliamo la prova definitiva sulla connessione tra Università ed Umanesimo nella Padova di inizio Trecento? Essa è data dalla parte avuta dai dottori in arti nella incoronazione poetica di Mussato, storico e tragediografo. È nato l'Umanesimo ed è stato tenuto a battesimo dall'Università. Mussato ha aperto, letto e citato la *Poetica* di Aristotele nella traduzione latina fatta direttamente sul testo greco da Guglielmo di Moerbeke[9], un traduttore che tanti servizi ha reso all'Università con i testi da lui latinizzati. Questa lettura da parte di Mussato è un avvenimento perché della traduzione della *Poetica* in latino fatta da Moerbeke conosciamo quattro lettori, cinque se contiamo il traduttore.

Ma torniamo ancora un momento a Petrarca, "doctor" o, come più propriamente si diceva nella sua Facoltà intesa in senso moderno e nel senso accademico di quei tempi, "magister artium"[10]. Il suo mondo lo ha riconosciuto come accademico perché lo ha chiamato all'insegnamento universitario. Le condizioni erano quelle che si ponevano comunemente ai professori di retorica, leggere cioè il libro che volesse perché il professore di Umanità non era vincolato nell'insegnamento accademico ad un libro canonico, ma insegnava poetica sul testo che preferiva[11]. Attorno a Petrarca c'è un gruppo di universitari e professori, il medico, il giurista, il retore[12], e c'è una ricezione universitaria dell'Umanesimo. Penso che nella fondazione dell'Università di Ferrara abbia avuto un ruolo un fido discepolo di Petrarca, Donato Albanzani. Sarà

---

[6] Guido Billanovich, "Il Seneca tragico di Pomposa e i primi umanisti padovani", in Giuseppe Billanovich, ed., *Pomposia monasterium modo in Italia primum. La biblioteca di Pomposa* (Padova, 1994), 213–232.

[7] A. X. Mega, *Il circolo preumanistico di Padova (Lovato Lovati–Albertino Mussato) e le tragedie di L. A. Seneca* (Tessalonica, 1967), 123–130 (in neogreco).

[8] N. G. Siraisi, *Arts and Sciences at Padua. The Studium of Padua before 1350* (Toronto, 1975), 44.

[9] H. A. Kelly, "Aristotle–Averroes–Alemannus on Tragedy: The Influence of the 'Poetics' on the Latin Middle Ages", *Viator* 10 (1979): 187–193.

[10] Magister è il titolo che gli conferisce il Privilegium laureationis: D. Mertens, "Petrarcas 'Privilegium laureationis'", in M. Bogolte, H. Spilling, eds., *Litterae Medii Aevi. Festschrift für Johanne Autenrieth zu ihrem 65. Geburtstag* (Sigmaringen, 1988), 244.

[11] Lettera della Signoria di Firenze a Petrarca con l'invito a recarsi ad insegnare in quella Università: G. Auzzas, "Studi sulle epistole I: L'invito della Signoria fiorentina al Petrarca", *Studi sul Boccaccio* 4 (1967): 203–240.

[12] Giovanni Dondi dell'Orologio, Giovanni d'Andrea, Pietro da Moglio.

stato lui il primo insegnante di retorica dell'Università di Ferrara o le cure politiche gli impedivano di attendere all'insegnamento?[13] In Umanesimo nel Trecento e ad inizio Quattrocento ci si laureava, a Pavia certamente[14]. Laureato fu Gasparino Barzizza che sapeva veramente scrivere in latino[15]. Laureato fu Pier Paolo Vergerio[16] che aveva per Mentore Francesco Zabarella. Da Giovanni Dondi dell'Orologio a Francesco Zabarella l'Umanesimo ci appare nel suo aspetto interdisciplinare, fornitore prima dello strumento della parola e poi trasformatore delle discipline perché traduttore di Aristotele e introduttore di Platone nell'insegnamento universitario, e insieme, col ricupero dei testi classici, riformatore dell'insegnamento medico.

Nel frattempo dall'Italia si è passati all'Europa. Ho in mente un modestissimo documento d'archivio, il conferimento del suddiaconato a Bernhard Adelmann von Adelsmannsfelden: Pavia, 5 giugno 1479[17]. Non tutte le Università italiane potevano offrire Barzizza, Filelfo, Perotti, Poliziano. Ma le città italiane offrivano tutte il clima della cultura umanistica. L'insegnante ufficiale di retorica a Padova dei tempi di Hartmann Schedel era il modestissimo Antoniolo[18], amico di Schedel e gradito certamente agli studenti che di anno in anno lo rielessero al posto di professore fino alla morte per peste. Le sorti dell'Umanesimo non erano però nelle sue mani, ma in quelle dell'intera cultura cittadina e ad esse partecipava l'Università che si esprimeva in termini umanistici nelle celebrazioni ufficiali.

Leggiamo il diploma di laurea di Johannes Hinderbach: autore fu forse Hinderbach stesso[19]. La prosa fluisce solenne e le dichiarazioni ufficiali che il diploma deve contenere pena la non certificazione dell'atto si esprimono nella prosa della nuova retorica in maniera veramente degna dell'attestazione di un avvenimento cui assistette l'imperatore Federico III. Leggendo Virgilio durante il ricevimento dato da uno studente tedesco in occasione della sua iscrizione all'esame di laurea, un giurista di grido aprì e declamò Virgilio esprimendo il rammarico di non essersi dedicato completamente agli studi di Umanità[20].

All'Università non si insegnava ancora la filologia, ma l'atmosfera era tale da rendere possibile la chiamata del professore di greco. Quando viene istituzionalizzato

---

[13] A. Sottili, "Preumanesimo", in A. Buck, ed., *Die italienische Literatur im Zeitalter Dantes und am Übergang vom Mittelalter zur Renaissance* (Heidelberg, 1989), 264–267.

[14] Il 24 marzo 1388 viene esaminato in grammatica e retorica sotto Pietro da Moglio Guglielmo Guasti che si laurea anche in filosofia: R. Maiocchi, *Codice diplomatico dell'Università di Pavia,* vol. 1 (Bologna, 1971), 145–146.

[15] *Doctor gramatice* è chiamato nel rotolo dell'Università di Pavia per il 1403–1404 edito da R. Maiocchi, *Codice diplomatico.*

[16] A. Gloria, *Monumenti della Università di Padova (1318–1405),* vol. 1 (Padova, 1888), 491.

[17] Archivio di Stato di Pavia, Archivio Notarile di Pavia, 96 fol. 497r.

[18] A. Sottili, *I codici del Petrarca nella Germania Occidentale,* vol. 1 (Padova, 1971), (248); Codex latinus Monacensis 350, fols. 99r–103r.

[19] V. von Hofmann-Wellenhof, "Leben und Schriften des Doctor Johannes Hinderbach, Bischof von Trient (1465–1485)", *Zeitschrift des Ferdinandeums* 3.3 (1893): 259–262.

[20] W. Wattenbach, "Peter Luder der erste humanistische Lehrer in Heidelberg", *Zeitschrift für die Geschichte des Oberrheins* 22 (1869): 107–108.

l'insegnamento del greco, significa che l'Umanesimo ha vinto, che esso è la cultura in cui tutti si riconoscono, è la premessa per il rinnovamento anche delle altre scienze. Se all'Università, a Padova o Pavia, l'insegnamento non è ancora filologico, ma retorico nel senso ampio del termine, nella città circolano i libri dell'Umanesimo, benché non soltanto quelli. Se il professore dalla cattedra insegnava nel latino della tradizione, lo studente Hieronymus Münzer trovava a stampa i classici sul mercato librario pavese e milanese[21].

La tradizione ed il rinnovamento tendono in Italia più a convivere che a polemizzare. Agricola non ha polemizzato coi giuristi pavesi, li ha anzi lodati, ha affermato la superiorità della loro scuola su quella dei colleghi ferraresi, benché a Ferrara avesse trovato le Muse di cui sentiva la mancanza a Pavia[22] perché una precisa scelta di politica culturale aveva fissato a Milano e non all'Università la sede degli studi di Umanità, quello che oggi chiamiamo insegnamento liceale, base però del successivo insegnamento superiore. Non c'era polemica tra Milano, sede delle lettere, e Pavia sede della logica, della filosofia, della medicina, del giure, della teologia, bensì un'integrazione non solo "de facto", ma "de iure", sanzionata in un documento ufficiale, il rotolo, e funzionante nonostante le aspirazioni milanesi a diventare sede universitaria completa. Nel rotolo dell'Università lombarda l'Umanesimo sotto la dizione di *Lettura di retorica* è una voce interdisciplinare; i nomi dei professori sono registrati in coda ai giuristi, ma in coda agli artisti c'è anche la *Lettura di retorica* con rimando per i nomi alla lista giuridica[23]: la disciplina è interdisciplinare, è offerta dalle medesime persone ai giuristi e ai medico-artisti, è strumento di formazione per entrambi. I professori si dividono in due categorie, quelli che leggono a Milano e quelli che leggono a Pavia: i migliori e in alcuni casi anche i meglio pagati, sono i primi, Merula, Calcondila, ma anche il musico Franchino Gaffurio, pagato male, e il matematico Luca Pacioli, pagato meglio[24]. Non due mondi in contrasto, quello delle Umanità e quello delle scienze, ma due mondi che si integrano portando le Università ad accrescere il loro peso. L'aver trovato questo equilibrio ha fatto la fortuna dell'Università italiana. Non ci si poteva attendere che si partisse da Amburgo per venire a Padova a scuola di bel periodare[25].

Lassù avevano però capito che il bel periodare era strumento necessario ormai per

---

²¹ E. P. Goldschmidt, *Hieronymus Münzer und seine Bibliothek* (London, 1938).

²² E. Leibenguth, R. Seidl, "Die Korrespondenz Rudolf Agricolas mit den süddeutschen Humanisten. Einleitung, Text, Übersetzung und Kommentar", in W. Kühlmann, ed., *Rudolf Agricola 1444–1485. Protagonist des süddeutschen Humanismus zum 550. Geburtstag* (Bern, 1994), 209.

²³ A. Sottili, "Die theologische Fakultät der Universität Pavia in der zweiten Hälfte des 15. Jahrhunderts. Die gescheiterte Berufung des Theologen Thomas Penketh und die Einrichtung der "*Lectura Thomae*", in J. Helmrath, H. Müller, eds., *Studien zum 15. Jahrhundert. Festschrift für Erich Meuthen,* vol. 1 (München, 1994), 542.

²⁴ Si veda ad esempio il rotolo per il 1493–94 e per il 1498–99: Pavia, Archivio di Stato, Acta Studii Ticinensis, 22, fols. 201r–v, 222v–223r.

²⁵ È di Amburgo Heinrich Murmester rettore padovano della facoltà di legge per gli anni accademici 1462–63 e 1463–64: G. Pengo, *Acta graduum academicorum Gymnasii Patavini ab anno 1461 ad annum 1470* (Padova, 1992), XIX.

esprimersi in un mondo alla ricerca della dottrina offerta in veste degna. Ho fatto un nome, Bernhard Adelmann. Dicono che la sua fama umanistica sia usurpata[26]. Dall'epistolario di Willibald Pirckheimer appare pio e dotto; il suo latino è quello nuovo e non quello dei "viri obscuri". Il documento che ce lo mostra a Pavia spiega queste qualità: pietà, dottrina, latinità. Non tutti imparavano a scrivere il nuovo latino, ma i più capivano che una novità era in atto. Non scrive un bel latino un altro corrispondente di Willibald Pirckheimer, Lorenz Beheim; l'Italia è tuttavia presente nelle sue lettere, magari in forme che possono far sorridere.

È comunque risaputo che il lessico degli studenti italiani non è dei più casti. Piuttosto bisognerebbe riflettere su di un fenomeno abbastanza particolare che caratterizza la connessione Umanesimo–Università. Si ha l'impressione che si vada ad ondate, che ci siano state concentrazioni di Umanisti o di vita umanistica in certi momenti e in certe Università con successivi affievolamenti. Penso a Siena attorno agli anni trenta, il periodo in cui si è formato un giurista transalpino insigne, Johannes de Lysura, Johann von Leiser[27], ma durante il quale passano nomi come Marrasio, Panormita, Piccolomini, Filelfo. Penso alla Pavia della fine degli anni venti e dei primi anni trenta, l'età di Brivio, Vegio, Panormita, Valla. Penso alla Pavia della fine degli anni sessanta e dei primi anni settanta per gli umanisti stranieri: Liber, Agricola, Bonstetten, Löffelholz, i Plinii. Penso alla Padova dei primi anni sessanta con Luder, Hartmann Schedel, Iohannes Pirckheimer, Ulrich Gossembrot. Può darsi che ci siano ragioni di vario genere, come la chiamata di un professore di grido oppure la peste che spopola una Università per popolarne un'altra; ma può darsi anche che si tratti della dinamica tipica della migrazione accademica: ci si muove ad ondate e ci si concentra ad ondate in un determinato luogo. Al tempo di Agricola compaiono a Ferrara numerosi studenti provenienti dai Paesi Bassi ed altri lasciano Pavia: ci si muove ad ondate e la forza che imprime nuovamente all'onda il movimento questa volta si chiama Agricola. In coincidenza con la sua permanenza a Ferrara si infittiscono le presenze di studenti dei Paesi Bassi del Nord. Agricola è una garanzia che l'Università scelta è giusta sul doppio fronte della formazione professionale e della formazione umana.

Nell'Università si propagano i costumi umanistici, per esempio quello della lettera familiare: l'erudito entra così nel vivo della vita quotidiana e acquisisce conoscenze non di poco conto. Torino è Università umbratile nel Quattrocento; non deve essere stata molto frequentata; ma rotoli di professori ne conosco; spero che le notizie sulle lauree vengano pubblicate presto. In un contesto del genere la lettera di Marquard Brisacher ad Albrecht von Bonstetten diventa una perla[28]. Il latino del Brisacher è quello che è: ricco di notizie, ma non umanistico; non ha la scorrevolezza del latino

---

[26] J. Martínek, "De falsa litterarum gloria Bernhardo Adelmanno adficta", *Listy filologické* 108 (1985): 207–214.

[27] A. Sottili, "Le lettere di Johannes Ruysch da Chieri e Pavia nel contesto dei rapporti tra Umanesimo italiano e Umanesimo tedesco", *Annali della Scuola Normale Superiore di Pisa. Classe di lettere e filosofia* 3.19 (1989): 323–412.

[28] Albrecht von Bonstetten, *Briefe und ausgewählte Schriften*, hrsg. v. A. Büchi (Basel, 1893), 42–43.

delle lettere di un Panormita. Umanistica è la confidenziale familiarità con cui il mittente intrattiene il destinatario sui temi per entrambi interessanti delle vicende universitarie. Gli storici dell'Università di Torino ignorano questa lettera; essa è fondamentale perché dimostra che nell'anno in questione l'Università funzionava con i problemi di tutte le Università di modello bolognese: irrequietezza degli studenti ed i problematici rapporti col governo. La lettera deve essere riedita, commentata, inserita nella storia dell'Università di Torino e degli Stati dei Savoia.

Restiamo a Torino, ma torniamo indietro di qualche decennio. L'Umanesimo è, tra tante cose, un mondo di antologie. Lo studente raccoglie testi per conservarli a ricordo di un periodo vivace che nella sua vita, di solito, non si ripeterà più. Da una di queste antologie[29], più importante tuttavia per Pavia che per altre ragioni, ricavo due testi eccezionali per l'Università di Torino. Il problema di questa Università era il finanziamento. Alla fine del terzo decennio del secolo proprio per questa ragione l'Università deve migrare a Chieri, allora più popolosa di Torino. L'antologia di cui sto parlando ha conservato due testi che ci permettono di entrare nel Duomo di Chieri in occasione dell'intronizzazione del rettore. Quelli di Chieri non furono anni sbiaditi per l'Università di Torino: lo sappiamo da un gruppetto di lettere scritte da uno studente che fece carriera, in Italia prima, in Germania poi[30]. Lo sforzo di fare in esse anche letteratura è evidente ma al primo posto sta la comunicazione degli avvenimenti. Tuttavia la lettera familiare come può essere familiare se non è ricca di avvenimenti e di affetti?

L'Università mostra la sua faccia umanistica perché in essa si produce letteratura. Albrecht von Eyb sul versante latino non è stato un umanista originale, generoso però certamente. Attendiamo in tanti che uno studioso di diritto ci dica che cosa dobbiamo pensare dei pareri di Albrecht von Eyb e che valore dobbiamo attribuire alla sua scienza giuridica. Personalmente vorrei tanto sapere se la carta dell'autografo della *Margarita poetica* è italiana. Il codice porta la data dello stesso anno della laurea pavese di von Eyb[31]. La *Margarita poetica* per me è stata scritta in Italia ed è un prodotto dell'Umanesimo universitario. Un professore come Catone Sacco era tecnico nelle lezioni, ma "orator" in letteratura come dimostra lo sforzo stilistico delle sue orazioni[32].

Ho elencato fatti e svolto qualche considerazione, ma che cosa ci attendiamo dallo studioso dell'Università che non abbia solo interessi di storia istituzionale e attenzione per le dottrine? Un mio sogno è stato studiare gli appunti di Teodorico Plinio alle lezioni di Ubertino da Crescentino sulle *Familiari* di Cicerone[33]. Siamo forse davanti ad un corso completo registrato da persona che sa scrivere almeno qualche parola in greco. Questo sogno non lo realizzerò più perché la scrittura di Teodorico Plinio,

<hr>

[29] Venezia, Biblioteca Marciana, XI 123: P. O. Kristeller, *Iter italicum,* vol. 2 (London–Leiden, 1967), 240. Fols. 14r–17f, Orazione di Mercurino Ranzo per il rettore Stephanus Guigonardus (Chieri, 9.8.1431); fols. 17r–18r, Orazione del rettore Stephanus Guigonardus.

[30] Vedi nota 27.

[31] 1459.

[32] A. Sottili, "Università e cultura a Pavia in età visconteo-sforzesca", in *Storia di Pavia* (Milano, 1990), 392–395.

[33] Stuttgart, Württembergische Landesbibliothek, Inc.2° 5164.

almeno nell'esemplare fotografico dell'incunabulo a mia disposizione, è troppo piccola. O trovo un sistema per ampliarla o devo passare la palla ad un giovane volenteroso che finalmente ci illustri il corso di un professore italiano di retorica come è stato recepito da uno straniero illustre.

L'Università aveva una vita sociale che si esprimeva in feste, specialmente di carnevale. Facciamo edizioni critiche delle commedie e in primo luogo della *Cauteriaria*, universitaria nel contenuto e nella tradizione manoscritta, almeno in parte di essa. Ho collazionato il codice di Fulda, quello di Johannes Zeller[34]; qualcuno collaziona l'Arundel 138 e andremo in tal modo avanti nel chiarire i rapporti tra queste che sono tra le antologie più belle di tedeschi allievi di Università italiane. L'Arundel è stato proprietà di Thomas Pirckheimer e degli altri della sua famiglia che è ozioso ricordare perché tutti li conoscono, ma che è obbligatorio ricordare perché di generazione in generazione hanno passato l'uno all'altro l'amore della giurisprudenza e quello delle lettere.

La lettura degli *Acta graduum* padovani è commovente[35] per chi segue il filo rosso o la strada maestra lungo la quale l'Umanesimo dei giuristi ha rimontato le Alpi per formare una nuova civiltà. Non mi stanco mai di contemplare la placchetta di Orfeo ed Euridice di Peter Vischer il giovane confortato dal commento di Dieter Wuttke[36]. I versi latini sono, come insegna Wuttke, di Teodorico Ulsenio, anche lui accademico e umanista e pellegrino in Italia, pare a Bologna[37]. La presenza tedesca in questa città è la meglio esplorata tra le connessioni dell'Impero con le Università italiane, ma prosopograficamente, non per i risvolti umanistici che certamente ci sono stati: lo testimoniano Eyb, Hans Pirckheimer, Johannes Roth. *Dazwischen*: tra una cultura e l'altra, tra la scienza e l'Umanesimo. Ma per Dieter Wuttke questa parola sta a significare un metodo[38]. Orbene, a questo metodo ci si può ispirare anche quando si progetta il lavoro da compiere sulla connessione umanistica del giurista e del medico.

Dazwischen è la *Cronaca* di Hartmann Schedel da esaminare per la sua mediazione della cultura italiana nel mondo tedesco, il comparire della biografia di Petrarca, di quelle di scienziati e di giuristi, delle tavole delle città. Hartmann Schedel in Italia è un progetto che poco per volta realizzeremo non senza tener conto che il suo *Liber de antiquitatibus*[39] è anche applicazione al mondo tedesco del metodo archeologico creato dagli italiani. Poco alla volta le varie sezioni a partire da Milano e Venezia e soprattutto da Padova verranno filologicamente esaminate. Hartmann non è filologo e fa errori quando copia le epigrafi, anzi fa errori quando copia e basta, ma il suo viaggio nelle antichità germaniche ha almeno il fascino del romanzo scritto sui Fran-

---

[34] "Il Petrarca e l'Umanesimo tedesco", *Quaderni Petrarcheschi* 9–10 (1992–1993): 255–263.

[35] Si veda ad esempio il volume segnalato alla nota 25.

[36] "Die Orpheus-Eurydike-Plaketten Peter Vischers des Jüngeren. Theodoricus Ulsenius als Textquelle", in D. Wuttke, *Dazwischen. Kulturwissenschaft auf Warburgs Spuren*, vol. 1 (Baden-Baden, 1996), 93–103.

[37] C. Santing, *Geneeskunde en humanisme. Een intelectuele biografie van Theodoricus Ulsenius* (Rotterdam, 1992), 28.

[38] Mi riferisco all'opera citata a nota 36.

[39] Codex latinus Monacensis 716.

chi dal suo contemporaneo Tritemio. Vengono offerte al lettore le antichità e le bellezze delle città tedesche, da Augusta e Ratisbona e Norimberga a Francoforte, Magonza e Colonia, alle Fiandre ecc. Il modello va ricercato nelle raccolte conosciute all'Università di Padova. Mi si propone di accettare che Hartmann Schedel abbia conosciuto la famosissima raccolta di epigrafi di Pietro Donato[40], vescovo e cancelliere dell'Università: non so decidermi, spinto da un lato dalla conoscenza dell'amore che in Germania si diffondeva per le antichità locali e dall'altro per l'attaccamento alle radici italiane dell'Umanesimo.

L'Università non è stata solo un luogo di incontro tra tedeschi e civiltà umanistica. A Pavia si recavano i borgognoni. È stato fatto il nome di Agricola, ma non si tratta di un solitario. Si arrivava dai paesi "de par-deça" e dai paesi "de par-dela"; da questi, penso, più, che da quelli. Si veniva per il diritto, ma poi succedeva che un Arnould de Lalaing appena dottorato andasse a Treviri e spedisse a Pavia in francese le sue impressioni sul fatto più memorabile di quel torno di tempo, l'incontro tra l'Imperatore e il Temerario[41]. È un altro dei compiti che attendono uno storico dell'Università di Pavia sensibile ai problemi letterari, un'edizione commentata di questa lettera, scritta da un testimone oculare e completata con vena critica da Agricola. La lettera ha bisogno di un commento storico che la metta a confronto con gli altri testi relativi alla vicenda in essa narrata. Concludo con un ultimo episodio pavese e borgognone. L "incipit" della Vita di Petrarca di Agricola, quell "Antonius Scrofinius avus tuus[42]", non è più un mistero, ma la documentazione è riservata ad altra occasione.

Università di Torino

---

[40] Berlin, Staatsbibliothek, Ham. 254: H. Boese, *Die lateinischen Handschriften der Sammlung Hamilton zu Berlin* (Wiesbaden, 1966), 125–130.

[41] La lettera è edita in *Rodolphi Agricolae Lucubrationes* (Coloniae, 1539), 221–226. Arnould de Lalaing si è laureato a Pavia l'11.8.1473: A. Sottili, *Lauree pavesi nella seconda metà del Quattrocento*, 1 (1450–1475) (Milano, 1995), 264–266.

[42] L. Bertalot, *Studien zum italienischen und deutschen Humanismus*, hrsg. v. P. O. Kristeller, vol. 2 (Roma, 1975), 2.

Martin Luther, the Oreads of Wittenberg, and Sola Gratia

CARL P. E. SPRINGER

While Martin Luther's enormously popular efforts at writing German hymns have been the subject of extensive scholarly study,[1] relatively little attention has been paid to his occasional Latin poetry (some thirty compositions appear in the *Weimar Ausgabe* of his works, ranging from two to twenty lines in length). The German reformer used Latin verse to salute friends like Justus Jonas and Georg Spalatin, to blast enemies of his theology like Erasmus or the pope, and to paraphrase the Psalms or other portions of Scripture, often along classical lines.[2] This paper analyzes one of the more ambitious of Luther's Latin verse compositions, an epigram consisting of ten elegiac distichs, written in 1544 in praise of a spring whose water had been recently routed into the city of Wittenberg. In what follows I suggest that despite Luther's own self-deprecating protestations that he was a mere *rusticus* with only barbarous Latin,[3] a judgment which modern readers of his Latin verse have echoed, in one way or another, we may find in this little poem some glimmerings of the distinctive genius, if not of an outstanding Latin poet, at least of an outstanding man who happened to write Latin poetry.

---

[1] See, for instance, the discussion in L. Schmidt, " 'Und wenn die Welt voll Teufel wär.' Zu Martin Luthers 'Ein feste burg ist unser Gott'," in *Gedichte und Interpretationen, Bd. 1., Renaissance und Barock* (Stuttgart, 1982), 55.

[2] The single most useful volume on Luther's Latin poetry is Udo Frings, *Martinus Lutherus-Poeta Latinus.* Orientierung: Schriftenreihe zur Lehrerfortbildung 10 (Aachen, 1983) [abbreviated hereafter as Frings]. I have also found O. Albrecht's discussion of Luther's Latin verse in *D. Martin Luthers Werke, Kritische Gesamtausgabe,* the so-called *Weimar Ausgabe* of his works [abbreviated hereafter as *WA*], vol. 35:596 ff., particularly helpful. Less critical, but useful, too, is Georg Schleusner, *D. Martin Luthers Dichtungen in gebundener Rede mit den nötigen Anmerkungen* (Wittenberg, 1892). I was unable to see two eighteenth-century discussions of the poems: *Martini Lutheri Poemata dispersa* (Magdeburg, 1729) and M. F. Andreas Hallbauer, *Lutherus Politioris Litteraturae Cultor et Aestimator* (Dissertation, University of Jena, 1717).

[3] Lewis Spitz, "Luther and Humanism," in *Luther and Learning* (Selinsgrove, 1985), 76.

This short epigrammatic poem, probably written to be inscribed on a newly constructed fountain in Wittenberg, owes much to the Latin poetic tradition with which Luther was quite familiar. Throughout his life he quoted often and approvingly from Terence, Horace, Virgil, and Ovid, whose works he had read as a schoolboy. The only two books he took with him into the cloister in Erfurt when he left law school to become a monk, we are told, were the writings of Plautus and Virgil.[4] Even after he had learned to appreciate the Scriptures as the authority of authorities, Luther still felt that some of the classic authors (including the great Greek and Latin epic poets, Homer and Virgil) might serve as a useful propaedeutic to Scripture study (unlike some of the radical reformers, who spurned pagan authors in favor of a narrow biblicism). In his directive to city magistrates to establish Christian schools, Luther hoped that students would read poets "nicht angesehn ob sie Heyden odder Christen weren, Kriechisch odder Lateinisch. Denn aus solchen muss man die Grammatica lernen."[5] His last written observations (on a slip of paper found in the clothes he wore on the day of his death) are well known: "Vergilium in Bucolicis et Georgicis nemo potest intelligere, nisi quinque annis primum fuerit pastor aut agricola. . . . Scripturas sacras sciat se nemo gustasse satis, nisi centum annis cum prophetis ecclesias gubernavit. . . . Hanc tu ne divinum Aeneida tenta, sed vestigia pronus adora. Wir sein pettler. Hoc est verum."[6]

It is true that Luther did criticize Homer and Virgil insofar as their epic poems celebrated war and bloodshed. Like other reformers, he also recommended that poets like Juvenal, Martial, and Catullus, who dealt with erotic subject matter, not be included on school reading lists.[7] We might note, however, that Luther himself used some of the same kind of scurrilous language that characterizes the verse of the three poets just mentioned. A short composition attacking Simon Lemnius, a young humanist at Wittenberg who had attacked the reformer, whom Luther describes colorfully as a *merdipoeta*, stands directly in the tradition of invective familiar to readers of Catullus and Martial.[8]

---

[4] *WA TR* 1. 44. 23 [166]. 1531. As cited in Reinhard Schwarz, "Beobachtungen zu Luthers Bekanntschaft mit antiken Dichtern und Geschichtsschreibern," *Lutherjahrbuch* 54 (1987): 8.

[5] *WA* 15. 52. 5–7.

[6] *WA TR* 5. 317–318. The translation in H. G. Haile, *Luther: An Experiment in Biography* (New York, 1980), 356, follows: "None can comprehend Virgil in his *Bucolics* and *Georgics* who has not first been a herdsman or a farmer for five years. . . . Let none think he has sufficiently tasted Holy Scriptures unless he has governed the churches with the prophets for a hundred years. . . . Lay no hand on this divine *Aeneid*. Rather fall down on your knees and worship at its footsteps. [cf. Statius, *Theb.* 12. 816 f.] We are truly beggars."

[7] Schwarz, "Beobachtungen zu Luthers Bekanntschaft mit antiken Dichtern und Geschichtsschreibern," 12–13.

[8] I use the text from *WA*, Tischreden, vol. 4:89–90. My translation follows: "How well your cause and your poetry are matched, Lemchen! Your cause is manure, your poetry is manure. Lemchen, the man of manure, was worthy of a song of manure, for nothing but manure is fitting for a poet of manure. O unhappy the prince whom you praise with your song of manure, whom you yourself befoul with your manure. You press manure from your bowels and you would like to produce all on your own a large bowel movement, but you produce nothing, O poet of

Quam bene conveniunt tibi res et carmina, Lemchen!
  Merda tibi res est, carmina merda tibi.
Dignus erat Lemchen merdosus carmine merdae,
  Nam vatem merdae nil nisi merda decet.
Infelix princeps, quem laudas carmine merdae!
  Merdosum merda quem facis ipse tua.
Ventre urges merdam vellesque cacare libenter
  Ingentem, facis at, merdipoeta, nihil.
At meritis si digna tuis te poena sequatur,
  Tu miserum corvis merda cadaver eris.

Despite his warnings against Martial, it is obvious that Luther was intimately familiar with the Silver Age poet. His verses on Psalm 128 owe much to Martial 10.47, whose language and meter he closely follows (the first line is virtually identical):

Vitam quae faciunt beatiorem,
O carissime christiane, sunt haec.
Aeternum dominum Deum timere,
Mandatique sui vias amare.
Sit victus manuum labore partus,
Sic vivis bene, sic eris beatus.
Uxor prole tuam domum beabit,
Laetis ut generosa vitis uvis.
·Ad mensam tibi filii sedebunt,
Ut pinguis tenerae novella olivae.
Sic fidus benedicitur maritus
In casto domini timore vivens.
Donet te benedictione semper
Ex Zion dominus Jerusalemque.
Florentem faciat bonis vigere,
Ut natos videas et inde natos.
Et pacem super Israel per aevum!
Hic dicat pius omnis amen. amen.[9]

---

manure. But if a penalty worthy of your deserts follows you, your corpse will be a miserable pile of manure for the crows."

[9] I use the text provided by Frings, 25. My own translation follows: "Those things which make for a happy life, O dear Christian, are these. To fear the eternal Lord God and to love the ways of his command. Let your food be won by the labor of your hands. Thus you live well; thus you will be happy. Your wife will bless your house with children, like an abundant vine with happy grapes. Your sons will sit at your table like the fat shoot of the tender olive. Thus the faithful husband is blessed who lives in the chaste fear of the Lord. From Zion may the Lord alway give you his blessing and from Jerusalem. May he make you thrive as you flower with good things, so that you may see your sons and their sons. And may peace be on Israel for ever! Let every believer say Amen to this: Amen."

Luther's dedication of an epigram to a *fons* can also be seen as fitting squarely within the tradition of classical Latin poetry. Springs and fountains fascinated the ancient Greeks and Romans. Thought to be divine in nature and connected with nymphs who were said to inhabit them, springs such as Callirhoe in Athens, Arethusa in Sicily, or Pirene in Corinth were famous in the ancient world. And springs attracted the attention of poets. The *Greek Anthology* is filled with epigrams devoted to springs and fountains. Many of them, like Luther's, feature the fountain itself speaking to the one who has come to drink.[10] One of the best known of all Latin poems is Horace's praise of *fons Bandusiae* (*Carm.* 3.13) and its crystal clear water. Like this composition of Horace and his poetic precursors, Luther's epigram is a panegyric of sorts. He is praising—although, as we shall see, his praise is not unqualified—the quality of the spring whose pure water will refresh the inhabitants of Wittenberg. In Late Antiquity, Christian poets like Ambrose, Damasus, and Ennodius applied their poetic energies to the description of a different kind of fons, namely, the baptismal font. Their epigrammatic efforts were often inscribed on baptistery walls or on the fonts themselves.[11] Unlike Luther, however, they did not write Christian epigrams for public fountains. It is probably significant that Luther, with his high hopes for the potential influence of the Gospel on every aspect of human endeavor, including those traditionally designated as secular, did. It was not uncommon, either, for Luther's humanist contemporaries to write elegies in praise of springs and fountains. Consider, for example, a poem by Giovanni Giovano Pontano (1426–1503) in praise of the spring Casi, which, unlike Luther's epigram, is replete with learned allusions to the stock figures of classical mythology and contains no reference to Christianity:[12]

> Casis, Hamadryadum furtis iucunde minister
>   et cupidis rupes semper amica deis,
> ad quem saepe, sui linquens secreta Lycaei,
>   Pan egit medios sole calente dies
> Maenalioque tuos implevit carmine montes
>   et septem cecinit fistula blanda modos,
> cum passim iunctaeque manus et bracchia nexae
>   ducebant placidos Naides ante choros
> carpebantque hilares iuxta virgulta capellae
>   haedus et in molli subsiliebat humo;
> quin etiam defessa iugis siquando Diana
>   egit praecipites per cava saxa feras,

---

[10] See, for instance, epigram 315, by Nicias, in the *Greek Anthology*, Book IX.

[11] See my discussion of Ambrose's verses *ad Fontem S. Teclae* in "The Concinnity of Ambrose's *Inluminans Altissimus*," in *Panchaia: Festschrift für Klaus Thraede* (Bonn, 1995), 230.

[12] For a good overview of the tradition of "fountain poetry" and its practice in the early modern period, see Jürgen Blänsdorf, Dieter Janik, Eckart Schäfer, *Bandusia: Quelle und Brunnen in der lateinischen, italienischen, französischen, und deutschen Dichtung der Renaissance*, Beiträge zur Altertumskunde 32 (Stuttgart, 1993).

> hic posuitque latus viridique in margine sedit
>> et vitreo flavas lavit in amne comas;
> te Bacchus, te Phoebus amant, tibi carmina nymphae
>> dulce canunt, tibi se comit amata Dryas,
> Pelignosque suos siquando et rura relinquit,
>> lassa subit fonti Calliopea tuo
> et lenem querula carpit sub fronde quietem,
>> qua cadit arguto murmure lympha fugax.[13]

Luther's epigram on the new city fountain of Wittenberg is certainly classical in form. He uses the familiar elegiac distichs (the same meter used by many of the Greek anthologists as well as Pontano) flawlessly, and the epigram has very few, if any, false quantities. Of the various traditional figures which Luther uses to good advantage, such as anaphora, assonance, alliteration, and metaphor, one of the most conspicuous is prosopopoeia, a device also employed by the Greek anthologists, and one that makes particularly good sense for an inscription of a fountain, if one believes it to be animated with divine presence or inhabited by a nymph. The spring speaks in its own voice throughout the poem. One striking (and possibly humorous) example of irony may be found in the classicizing title of the poem: "De Fonte Oreadum Wittebergensium." While it is not unusual to address the nymphs in such a context as this (Pontano brings up hamadryads, dryads, and naiads in his "Laudes Casis Fontis"), the oreads are usually associated with hills or mountains, and Wittenberg itself, situated rather unpicturesquely on the banks of the Elbe River, is singularly devoid of such topographical features. The name of the town does mean "white mountain," but the name was assigned to the location by Flemish settlers, for whom, E. Schwiebert surmises, "recalling the flat land of their native home, this sandy hill seemed like an actual mountain."[14] While it is true that there are what we might call elevations in the area of Wittenberg, such as the Teucheler Berg, described in the *Wittenberg Urbarium* of 1543 as the source of the town's water, it certainly sounds anachronistic and humorous to the modern reader (and probably to Luther's contemporaries as well) to hear the names of these spritely Mediterranean mountain sylphs mentioned

---

[13] I use the text and translation found in I. D. McFarlane, *Renaissance Latin Poetry* (New York, 1980), 69: "Casi, indulgent accomplice of the secret loves of the hamadryads and crag forever friendly to love-smitten gods, near which often, leaving the hidden regions of his own Lycaeus, Pan spent the heat of the midday sun and filled your hills with song and his charming pipe sounded the seven-note melody, while all around, hands linked and arms entwined, the Naiads led their placid dances before him and the cheerful goats nearby cropped the shrubs and the kid skipped around on the soft ground. Rather, sometimes, Diana, tired of the mountain slopes, drove the wild beasts headlong from grotto to grotto, lay down here and sat on the green edge and washed her yellow hair in the crystal stream. You are loved of Bacchus, of Phoebus, to you the nymphs gently sing their songs, the Dryad loved by you combs her hair for you; and if ever Calliope forsakes her Peligni and her own fields, she comes wearied to your spring and takes a gentle rest beneath the rustling leaves, where the water falls in flight with a lively sound."

[14] E. Schwiebert, *Luther and His Times: The Reformation from a New Perspective* (St. Louis, 1950), 199.

in the same breath as Wittenberg, a town which was regularly disparaged for its lack of amenities and attractions—"a regular beer chamber," one contemporary of Luther observed, "hardly worth 3 farthings"—not only by those who visited it but by its own denizens.[15]

At the same time, it is clear that however much he owed to the classical poetic tradition, Luther was also concerned to write Christian poetry. His invective aimed at humanists who were opposed to his reformation agenda has a more serious, theological, purpose than the raunchy banter of a Catullus. Luther's Latin version of Psalm 128 is not merely an "imitation" of Martial 10.47, but is obviously intended to present a vision of the happy life that is, in the author's view, decidedly superior to the pagan (as the title of Luther's composition suggests: "Psalmus ... oppositus Martialis Epigrammati, Vitam quae faciunt beatiorem ...").

So, too, this fountain epigram cannot be understood or appreciated fully apart from Luther's theological *Weltanschauung*, which permeated every aspect of his life and writing. Other Christian humanists who were contemporary with Luther, like Pontano, found it possible or even desirable to write Latin verse in which nary a trace of their own religious beliefs found expression. Aside from the playful reference to the oreads in the title, this poem is decidedly Christian and even Lutheran in its tone. In fact, one could say that the structure of this poem, which falls so neatly into two distinct and counterpoised halves of ten lines each, follows Luther's own dialectical understanding of Law and Gospel. The preaching of the Law, according to Lutheran theology, fills the heart with despair of one's own goodness and terror of divine judgment, but it is followed in what Luther calls "divine succession"[16] by the comfort of the Gospel, which gives encouragement and hope and life. The effect of this dialectic theology on the Christian's life, as Luther himself put it, is that one feels himself always to be *simul iustus et peccator*. This Wittenberg spring has a very Lutheran understanding of itself. The epigram begins with the spring's fairly realistic self-evaluation. It is not a sea; it is not a river; it is just a *particula* of all of the water which God ever created. Nor does the spring have any grand notion of the place of its origin *(scatebris exilibus)* or the path it must travel to Wittenberg. Luther departs radically from the rhetorical conventions usually associated with the *locus amoenus* topos as he describes how it flows, unpicturesquely, through the prosaic and richly bedunged fields which surround Wittenberg, whose farmers evidently take this work of the great God rather for granted:

> Qui mare, qui fontes, qui flumina cuncta creavit,
> > Me quoque iussit aquae particulam esse suae.
> Corpore sum parvo, scatebris exilibus ortus,
> > Magni me sed opus glorior esse Dei.
> Negligor incultus, dispersis undique venis,

---

[15] For a sample of negative descriptions by contemporaries of Luther's (such as Myconius and Cochlaeus) as well as by Luther, see Gottfried Krueger, "Wie sah die Stadt Wittenberg zu Luthers Lebzeiten aus?" in *Vierteljahrschrift der Luthergesellschaft* 15 (1933).

[16] *Luther's Works*, ed. Jaroslav Pelikan (St. Louis, 1961), vol. 3: 63.

> Et squalere sinor per loca foeda luto.
> Rustica more suo me spernunt turba coloni,
>   Fons, quibus, haud dignus, qui colar, esse putor,
> Forsan, si propior melioribus urbibus essem,
>   Fontibus urbanis cultior ipse forem.[17]

Although this spring cannot claim to compete with the size or reputation of those fountains associated with larger cities (the *peccator* part of the equation outlined above), it is surprisingly unfazed by the lack of respect which it receives from people, because it knows that it is part of the good creation of God (here comes the *iustus* part), a theme often sounded by Luther, as, for example, in his explanation of the first article of the Apostles' Creed in his famous Small Catechism, with its focus on God the creator and giver of all good things. This modest spring, therefore, has the same kind of feisty self-confidence which the controversial professor at the University of Wittenberg himself possessed.

This self-confidence, of course, has nothing to do with one's own merits. Lutherans are justified by grace, through faith, not by works, as the Apostle Paul puts it. This theological principle, of such fundamental importance to the Lutheran reformation, is most clearly articulated in the second half of the epigram, especially in the last four lines, so reminiscent of Luther's reference to "gold and silver" in his explanation of the second article of the Apostles' Creed in the Small Catechism. These lines apply the Reformation principle of *sola gratia* to the fountain's willingness to offer its gift of water gratis to both rich and poor:

> Non movet agrestis tamen haec iniuria vulgi,
>   Dimoveor nullis a bonitate malis.
> Servo meas undas puras, nitidasque ministro,
>   Gratis, ingratis, omnibus, aequus agor,
> Servio namque Deo largo pincerna benignus,
>   Gratuito munus largior inde meum.
> Non moror, argenti nihil aut habeas nihil auri,
>   Hausturus gratis dives inopsque veni.
> Sic Deus ingrato dedit et facit omnia mundo,
>   Cuius ad exemplum me iuvat esse bonum.[18]

---

[17] I use the text found in Frings, 32. My translation follows: "He who created the sea, the springs, and all the rivers, ordered me, too, to be a little part of his water. I am small in size, sprung from little sources, but I rejoice that I am the workmanship of a great God. I am despised because I am uncared for, with my streams running in various directions, and they let me get filthy with mud as I flow through the ugly countryside. The rural folk, the farmers, despise me in their way. They don't think that I am a spring worth cultivating. Perhaps if I were closer to the better cities, I would be better taken care of than the city springs."

[18] My translation follows: "This insult from the country folk, however, does not bother me. I am not swayed from doing good by any evil. I keep my waters pure and I serve them crystal clear, to the grateful and ungrateful alike; I deal fairly with all. For I serve a generous God, as a benevolent butler; without pay I pour out my bounty derived from that source. Without delay,

This theological topos fits particularly well in this context, because drinkers at fountains are not ordinarily charged for the water they consume, unlike those who wish to imbibe other beverages. The reader is reminded of biblical imagery associated with fountains, such as Isaiah's invitation (55.1): "Ho everyone that thirsteth, come ye to the waters, and he that hath no money; come ye, buy and eat," and Revelation 21.6: "I will give unto him that is athirst of the fountain of the water of life freely." Like God's grace, this water can be enjoyed by anyone who is thirsty and comes to drink, no matter how poor or undeserving. The last two lines of the poem echo the same sentiment as the first two, with the accent placed on God's creative activities. There is, however, a new emphasis on the spring's active participation in that good activity (what Lutheran theologians refer to as "sanctification"). Our good works come at the end, not the beginning (according to the Lutheran view) of the salvation process. They are the fruits of justification, not its cause.[19]

There are very few readers of Luther's Latin verse[20] (and certainly not the author of this paper) who would suggest that the corpus of Luther's Latin poetry is particularly distinguished by its quantity or quality. The reformer himself was modest about his own achievements in the area of Latin letters in general: "litteras scribere possum, sed non Ciceronianas et oratorias ut Grickell, sed res habeo, etiamsi verba Latina et elegantia non habeo,"[21] and consistently set other humanists' achievements in this regard above his own. (He compared himself, for instance, to Choerilus, in relationship to Melanchthon, whose poetry Luther over-generously rated on a par with Homer's.)[22] But this paper does suggest that if we read this "Christian humanist's" ventures into Latin verse not simply as frivolous archaizing literary exercises in the "classical" vein, but as lively and often serious expressions of his own distinctive religious faith, we may find that Luther's Latin verse is not only of considerable interest to the serious student of Luther and the Reformation, but also worth at least a passing reference in the history of Latin and Neo-Latin poetry.

Illinois State University

---

whether you have any silver or gold or not, come, if you want to drink for free—both rich and poor. That is how God gave and makes all things for an ungrateful world, whose good example I am pleased to follow."

[19] Frings makes some of these same points in his discussion of the poem, especially in pp. 38–40. We know that at least one of Luther's contemporaries, Johannes Stigel (1515–1562), also read the poem in the light of Lutheran theology, because he quotes it in his poem in praise of the literary achievements of Luther, "In tomos Lutheri" [see Frings, 39]: Fontis ut exigui scatebris exilibus ortus, / allapsa fluvius largius imbre fluit; / ut procul albescens rediturae lucis imago / exorto reddit splendida sole diem: / Sic Evangelii lux est, monstrante Luthero, / exiguis parvae viribus orta facis.

[20] Johannes Schilling, "Latinistische Hilfsmittel zum Lutherstudium," *Lutherjahrbuch* 55 (1988): 87: "Nur am Rande sei erwähnt, dass es auch lateinische Dichtungen von Luther gibt. Sie sind nach Umfang und Bedeutung bescheiden."

[21] *WA TR* 4. 595. 7–9: "I am able to write, but not in Ciceronian style and in orations like Agricola, but I have substance even though I don't have the Latin vocabulary and elegance."

[22] *WA* 35. 596.

Les lettres de Joannes Dantiscus au Roi Sigismond I et la Reine Bona Sforza

JERZY STARNAWSKI

> Sic per bis senos orator regius annos
> Missus in Hispana ter regione fui.
> [Joannes Dantiscus: *Vita Joannis Dantisci*, 51–52]

Parmi les manuscrits de la Bibliothèque Nationale à Paris on trouve un manuscrit (Lat. 11015), contenant les *Joannis Dantisci litterae ad regem et reginam*. C'est une copie de la fin du XVIIIème siècle ou du début du XIXème siècle: les lettres datent de 1526–1528 et de 1538. Dantiscus, un célèbre poète polono-latin, fut longtemps orateur du roi de Pologne en Espagne. La plupart des lettres sont déjà connues, imprimées d'après d'autres sources dans les *Acta Tomiciana*, à l'exception des lettres de 1538. Dantiscus est parti pour la Cour d'Espagne à l'époque ou Maximilien Ier était encore en vie, en octobre 1518. Il n'a posé les pieds sur la Péninsule pyrénéenne qu'en janvier 1519, à l'époque où le roi Maximilien décéda (son décès eut lieu le 12 janvier de la même année). C'est ainsi que Dantiscus accomplit sa mission auprès de Charles Quint.

Le codex manuscrit, appelé *Parisinus* par l'auteur de la conférence à la manière des philologues, comprend 27 lettres connues (1526–1528). L'une de ces lettres, adressée à la reine Bona (qui date du 13 octobre 1526), n'a pas été publiée dans le recueil mentionné ci-dessus; on y a omis de même le postscriptum à la lettre du 21 mai 1527, adressée également à la reine. Comme le recueil de lettres ne s'étend pas jusqu'en 1538, les *Acta Tomiciana* ne contiennent pas de lettres datant de l'an 1538. Les lettres du 1526–1532 ont été écrites de différents endroits en Espagne, la lettre de 1538, de la Résidence des évêques de Warmia (Heilsberg ou Lidzbark). La réponse est médiocre, mais on peut déduire certaines énonciations d'après le texte ainsi transmis. Toutes les remarques concernant ce recueil des lettres sont faites à travers l'optique d'un historien de littérature.

Il convient de commencer par les titres admis et utilisés dans la correspondance de Dantiscus. En s'adressant au roi et à la reine il n'emploie d'une manière conséquente que les formes telles que: "Serenissima Regia Maiestas; Domine, Domine Clementissime; Serenissima Reginalis Maiestas et Domina; Domina mea Clementissima." C'est avec ces en-têtes-ci qu'on commence les lettres. Le contenu des lettres exigeait qu'on y parle des souverains et des dignitaires. L'orateur Dantiscus évoque par conséquent la personne de l'impératrice en utilisant l'expression "Serenissima Domina Imperatrix"; le roi français, en le nommant "Rex Christianissimus" (les rois se servaient du titre Roi Très Chrétien); de temps en temps, on employait aussi les termes "Rex Franciae" ou "Rex Galliae" par analogie avec les appellations "Rex Angliae", "Dux Moscoviae". Il s'adressait à certaines personnes en utilisant leurs prénoms: "Infans Hispanorum Don Philippus, Princeps De Oranges".

Ce sont les affaires italiennes qui sont envisagées, en grande partie, mais non exclusivement, par les lettres adressées à la reine. Quant aux lettres adressées au roi, elles contiennent les explications fournies à sa Majesté sur différents pays par l'ambassadeur. Plusieurs noms de villes espagnoles, souvent éloignées, qui apparaissent successivement dans ces lettres, témoignent d'une conscience géographique approfondie, ce qui n'était pas souvent le cas chez les humanistes polonais de l'époque. La façon d'énumérer des noms de villes est liée à l'emploi de la structure relative aux noms de ville. En latin humaniste, cette structure n'était pas obligatoire sans exception. On écrivait: "in Cracovia", "ex Cracovia", "Cracoviae", "Cracoviam". Chez Dantiscus ces cas sont rares. Au cours de son séjour en Espagne il résida longtemps à Valladolid. S'il note le nom de cette ville en latin, il a recours à deux composants, par exemple, "ex Valle Oleti", et ne va donc pas contre la règle. On trouve chez Dantiscus: "Neapoli", "Granatae", aussi bien que "in Toleto", "ex Granata", "civitate Castiliae in Hispania".

Bien que ce diplomate ait traversé tant de pays, il était très attaché à la Pologne, son pays natal. Il appelait Gdańsk "patria mea" (lettre du 21 mai 1527). Les villes qui l'intéressent sont essentiellement Gdańsk et Elbląg. Il indique les bénéfices dont il aurait pu profiter à son retour en Pologne. Outre le désir d'obtenir les bénéfices, ces lettres manifestent une nostalgie particulièrement émouvante. Dantiscus se sentait mal en Espagne; à plusieurs reprises il évoque son souhait de retourner en Pologne. Dans la lettre adressée à la reine (lettre du 1er septembre 1526) il dit brièvement:

> humillime commendo et rogo [. . .] reditus mei clementer rationem habeat.

Et dans celle du 21 mai 1527, et plus précisement dans le postscriptum découvert récemment, il écrit:

> [. . .] modo mihi ad Vos honeste redire liceat et id reliquum vitae est apud Vos absumere.

Le même jour, dans la lettre adressée au roi, on lit:

> Quid reliquum est, humillime supplico M[aiestati] V[estrae] Serenissimae, cum iam fere negotium Barense transactum est, castellanusque arcis Barensis vi habebitur, in quem prius Reginalis Maiestas consensit, dignetur me tandem post tertium annum in quarto saltem clementer revocare, litterasque mihi de quibus 14 Octobris scripsi, quo tutius redire possem, mittere; reditusque mei ac diuturnae meae servitutis benignam habere rationem.

Ce qui est le plus émouvant dans la lettre à la reine (lettre du 13 octobre 1526), qui n'a pas été publiée dans les *Acta Tomiciana*, c'est que l'auteur s'est servi de la citation d'Ovide, de la lettre poétique *ad Rufinum*, faisant partie du Premier Livre du recueil attendrissant *Epistulae ex Ponto*:

> [. . .] unde me his plerumque exulem non oratorem agere existimo,
> istudque Ovidii verissimum iam experior, quod dicat:
> Nescio qua natale solum dulcedine cunctos
> Attrahit immemores nec sinit esse sui.

Cette citation des *Epistulae ex Ponto* (I 3, 35–36) choisie d'une manière très juste, a été déformée. Au lieu de "Attrahit" on aurait dû mettre "Ducit et" et au lieu de "nec", "non". Ce n'est pas l'unique fois que notre écrivain a recours à Ovide. Dans la lettre du 15 novembre 1527, adressée au roi, où il reconnaît avoir reçu des conseils, il avoue dans une longue phrase que grâce à ceux-ci il se sent rassuré.

> [. . .] sequentes Ovidii iternates: inter utrumque vola, medio tutissimus ibis
> [. . .].

Cette fois-ci il a cité les *Metamorphoseon libri* et il a agencé les idées exprimées dans le passage sur Phaéton (II 140, 137) en effectuant une seule modification: au lieu de "vola" il aurait dû mettre "tene". Les exemples précités n'épuisent pas l'inventaire des références puisées par le diplomate-poète dans le patrimoine antique. Dans la lettre du 6 mai 1527, adressée à la reine, Dantiscus mentionne, dans le contexte adéquat, la massue d'Hercule (*Herculis clava*), renvoyant ainsi à Marc Térence Varron et à son oeuvre *De lingua Latina* (8, 26). Quand, dans la lettre adressée au roi du 17 août 1527 il formule l'idée "Sed timeo, ne in Scillam, vitata Charibdi incidiam", il se souvient de même des images présentées dans l'*Odyssée* d'Homère (livre XII) paraphrasées en-suite par Virgile (*Aeneis* III 430–432).

Comme diplomate Dantiscus rencontra plusieurs personnages illustres et de haut rang. Il a énuméré aussi bien ceux qui étaient le plus hautement placés que celui qui était son serviteur (*amanuensis meus*). Il commandait à toute une suite de gens. Le compte rendu exprimé dans une lettre très longue du 17 août 1527 adressée au roi est digne d'être mentionné:

> Cum nuntio Pontifici Domino Balthasar Castiglione fuit mihi de rebus multis
> longus sermo [. . .].

Un illustre humaniste italien, qui, quelques mois après et plus précisément au mois d'avril 1528, publie l'oeuvre dont la rédaction lui a pris 20 ans, *Il corteggiano*, présentait les affaires politiques à l'envoyé polonais. Cependant, parmi les problèmes considérés comme des "res multae" pouvaient se trouver également les questions culturelles; ce qui est regrettable, c'est que Dantiscus n'a pas fourni de détails. Les informations con-cernant la réception des oeuvres du plus grand savant de cette époque-là dans le mi-lieu catholique, contenues dans la lettre du 17 juin 1527 adressée à la reine sont à cet égard frappantes:

> [. . .] Sunt hic quindecim doctores Theologiae Sanctae qui decernere debent,

> si opera Erasmi Roterd[amensis] hic legi debeant nec ne? Monachi enim ope-
> ribus Erasmi plurimam adversantur. *Enchiridion militis Christiani* per Erasmum
> editum in Hispanam sermonem per episcopos non contradicentes translatum et
> in his typis impressum passim ab omnibus legitur, in quo multa contra caere-
> monias sanctas.

Les textes qui ont fait l'objet de l'analyse ne sont que des lettres. Mais ce sont quand même des lettres adressées au roi et à la reine. Souvent elles sont très longues et ont pour but de fournir des informations sur le monde. Bien qu'elles n'aient pas constitué une oeuvre littéraire dont le but est essentiellement artistique, ces textes, sous la plume d'un écrivain de talent, sont devenues de la bonne prose. Dantiscus se servait d'effets oratoires bien marqués. Il savait profiter de la richesse des conjonctions. Ainsi dans la lettre du 6 décembre 1526, on lit:

> Cum sit et aetate perfecto et prudens et quod tandem post discessum Maiestatis
> Vestrae a Caesare recuperari cogisset [. . .].

Ce n'est pas par hasard qu'il a écrit dans une de ses lettres: "[. . .] de quo gravamen vel gratiam fuisset praevisum vel provisum vel pervisum" (lettre du 21 mai 1527). Ce n'est pas non plus par hasard qu'il met en parallèle: "obsecro et obtestor" (lettre du 13 octobre 1526 qui n'a pas été publiée dans les *Acta Tomiciana*), "labor et dolor" (lettre du 22 avril 1527), "rumor et clamor" (lettre du 21 mai 1527).

Comme cela arrive souvent dans la prose latine du Moyen-Age et celle de la Renaissance, dans les lettres de Dantiscus apparaissent les rimes: "coligerem . . . mitterem" (lettre du 6 mai 1527), "oppressisset . . . interfecisset . . . coepisset" (lettre du 6 mai 1527), "neque quero neque spero" (lettre du 21 mai 1527, le postscriptum qui n'a pas été publié dans les *Acta Tomiciana*). Mais toute la richesse des rimes, nous la rencontrons dans la lettre du 22 avril 1527: "Quod cum fecissem, famuloque nec iniuxissem—ut ab ille cui scripta mea daret, responsum resportaret [. . .]". De même la rime: "[. . .] si verus fuisset, gaudio affecisset plurimos". En plus des rimes apparaissent des allitérations. Par exemple, dans la même lettre "[. . .] durissimo hoc tempore detractis et desideratis". Et dans la lettre du 6 mai 1527:

> [. . .] in iis nihil fuit conclusum quam quod omnes concorditer congrubeant,
> ut nihil Caesari contribuatur quando quod non contra Turcas sed contra Chris-
> tianos subsidia pecuniaria exgerentur.

L'accumulation des mots qui commencent par un "c" ou par un "q" est vraiment riche. Les lettres de Dantiscus, peu analysées jusqu'à présent, constituent donc non seulement un document historique, mais aussi une part essentielle da sa prose latine.

Université de Lodz

L'epistola "de amore" di Guiniforte Barzizza

SEBASTIANO VALERIO

Scrivendo nell'aprile del 1438 ai cugini Giovanni Agostino e Cristoforo, Guiniforte Barzizza[1] annunciava la propria decisione di sposarsi.[2] Giunto all'età di
trentadue anni, egli sentiva ormai la "necessità" del matrimonio per almeno tre ragioni che così definiva: *religio quaedam, respectus aetatis*, e *status mei ratio*. Il matrimonio,
in altri termini, era un esercizio di *pietas*, in quanto in esso, a ben guardare, scriveva
il Barzizza, come in un voto monastico, si ritrovano *castitatem, oboedientiam et pauper-
tatem* (p. 113). Divenuti una sola persona, i due coniugi rispettano la castità al di fuori
del matrimonio e la reciproca obbedienza nel rapporto matrimoniale. Il marito, si intende, ha il dovere di assumere su di sé la responsabilità della moglie, condivide il suo
corpo con lei, che da parte sua si sottomette totalmente ad esso, *ut sese illi gubernan-
dam regendamque committat*. Il matrimonio è poi esercizio di povertà in senso lato, perché *ut monachi se nihil proprium habituros iurant a monasterii substantia separatum* (p. 113),
così anche marito e moglie fanno comunione di beni.

Il *respectus aetatis* invece imponeva ad un uomo dell'età di Guiniforte di non tar-
dare oltre il matrimonio. Come un porto tranquillo richiamava il navigante più di
quel mare aperto e periglioso, che era metafora topica dell'amore, così il matrimonio

---

[1] Su Guiniforte Barzizza cf. innanzitutto la voce in *Dizionario Biografico degli Italiani* (Roma,
1960–), vol. 2; a cura di Martellotti, ripubblicata in G. Martellotti, *Dante e Boccaccio e altri scrittori
dall'Umanesimo al Romanticismo* (Firenze, 1983), 478–482. Notizie interessanti si desumono inoltre
in R. Sabbadini, "Notizie sulla vita e sugli scritti di alcuni dotti umanisti del sec. XV, Guiniforte
Barzizza," *Giornale storico della Letteratura italiana* 6 (1885): 170–176; A. Cappelli, "Guiniforte Barzizza maestro di Galeazzo Maria Sforza," *Archivio Storico Lombardo* s. 3, 21 (1894): 399–442. Sulla
famiglia Barzizza cf. invece R. Cessi, "Cristoforo Barzizza medico del sec. XV," *Bollettino della
Civica Biblioteca di Bergamo* 3.1 (1909): 15 ff.; R. Cessi, "Di alcune relazioni familiari di Gasparino
Barzizza," in *Scritti in onore di R. Reiner* (Torino, 1912), 737–746; G. Billanovich, "Un esercizio
di scrittura umanistica in casa Barzizza," in *Forme e vicende per Giovanni Pozzi* (Padova, 1987), 67–
74.
[2] L'epistolario è pubblicato in G. Barzizii *Orationes et epistolae pars secunda*, ed. J. A. Furiettus
(Roma, 1723). A questa edizione si farà riferimento ogni qualvolta citeremo una lettera del
Barzizza.

richiamava Guiniforte, che ringraziava Dio per avergli fatto incontrare una *virgo* di cui poteva dire: *placet aetas nec forma repudio* (p. 115), di nobili natali, nata a Milano e dunque rispondente ad un altro importante requisito, la nascita in una illustre patria. La lettera elenca i meriti e la nobiltà della famiglia della moglie, nella quale, in ossequio ad un ideale ben consolidato, ritrovava *innocentiam, humilitatem, operosae vitae amorem, sobrietatem, pauciloquium, timorem Dei,* e invece non incontrava *ruditatem incultam, neque exquisitum in exteriori apparatu studium, [. . .] hilaritatem non levem et gravitatem non odiosam* (p. 118).[3] Tutto questo in una sola donna: Caterina dei Malabarba, che in una lettera inviata meno di un mese dopo al di lei cugino Guido Gonzaga poteva già chiamare *coniugem meam* (p. 119).

Guiniforte soggiornava a Milano da ormai qualche tempo, dopo un periodo di frenetici spostamenti. Figlio ed erede spirituale del pedagogo Gasparino, Guiniforte Barzizza era nato nel 1406 e dopo il normale corso di studi, alla morte del padre, avvenuta nel 1431, cercò di succedergli nell'insegnamento. La cattedra del padre, invece, era andata ad Antonio da Rho e Guiniforte, dopo un breve soggiorno a Novara, nel 1432 è in Spagna, alla corte di Alfonso d'Aragona, grazie agli uffici di Ugo di Villafranca.

Il Barzizza non rimase molti anni al servizio dell'Aragonese che però seguì nella sfortunata impresa di Gerba e che quindi accompagnò in Sicilia nel 1432.[4] Nello stesso anno avvertì i primi sintomi di quella malattia che lo costrinse a chiedere nel 1434 ad Alfonso di rimanere in Milano, dove era tornato l'anno precedente in sua vece. Già nel 1433 era stato chiamato all'insegnamento presso l'Università di Milano e nel 1435 finalmente ereditò la cattedra che era stata del padre e che resse fino al 1441. Nonostante tutto i rapporti di Guiniforte con la corte di Alfonso rimasero stretti e furono anzi rafforzati nel breve periodo di prigionia che, a seguito della sconfitta di Ponza del 1435, il futuro re di Napoli trascorse a Milano, periodo nel quale il Barzizza tornò al servizio del re d'Aragona. Così ancora negli anni quaranta Guiniforte rappresentava uno dei referenti più certi e continui degli Aragonesi a Milano e non poco concorse alla formazione della biblioteca alfonsina, con l'invio di numerosi codici, per il tramite di Inico d'Avalos.[5]

Il periodo successivo alla permanenza di Alfonso a Milano, gli ultimi anni Trenta, furono fondamentali per Guiniforte che pose mano alle sue opere più importanti, quali, ad esempio, il Commento all'*Inferno* di Dante, nella stesura del quale era impegnato già nel 1438, l'anno del matrimonio.[6]

---

[3] Simili caratteristiche doveva avere anche la donna per il Barbaro: cf. F. Barbaro, "De re uxoria," in *Prosatori latini del Quattrocento* (Milano-Napoli, 1976), 120–125.

[4] La lettera che descrive quella vicenda bellica è pubblicata dal Furietti a pp. 63–75. Sulla partecipazione di Guiniforte all'impresa di Gerba cf. G. Romano, "Guiniforte Barzizza all'impresa di Gerba del 1432 e un poemetto inedito di Antonio Canobio sullo stesso avvenimento," *Archivio Storico Siciliano* 17 (1892): 1 ff.

[5] Cf. T. De Marinis, *La biblioteca napoletana dei re d'Aragona* (Milano, 1952) vol. 1: 8; vol. 2: 33; e *Molto più preziosi dell'oro. Codici di casa Barzizza alla Biblioteca nazionale di Napoli*, a cura di L. Gualdo Rosa, S. Ingegno, A. Nunziata (Napoli, 1996).

[6] Il commento barzizziano all'*Inferno* dantesco è in *Lo Inferno della Commedia di Dante Alighieri*

Guiniforte non studiò esclusivamente l'opera di Dante, ma di più ampio respiro fu il suo interesse nei confronti della letteratura volgare fiorentina: sotto la spinta dello stesso Filippo Maria Visconti, che già gli aveva commissionato lo studio della *Commedia* dantesca, scrisse un commento all'opera volgare del Petrarca.[7] Egli, come altri intellettuali di area viscontea in questo periodo, ad esempio il Filelfo, si impegnò in una rilettura delle tre corone fiorentine, ma in particolare di Dante e Petrarca, con un chiaro fine "ideologico", quello di fare emergere in essi gli atteggiamenti anticittadini e le inclinazioni universalistiche, in risposta alla propaganda che ne faceva i campioni della *florentina libertas*.[8]

Sempre a quegli anni, con precisione al marzo del 1439, data un'epistola indirizzata da Guiniforte a tale *Franciscus Gilabertus Scintigles*. La lettera, che verteva su una discussione *de re uxoria*, in qualche modo ricalcava nei contenuti quella dell'anno precedente, indirizzata ai cugini in occasione del matrimonio, ma illuminava quella materia da un'angolazione diversa, per comprendere la quale sarebbe necessario ricostruire le circostanze in cui essa fu concepita e la figura del destinatario.

Tratteggiare con precisione questa figura non è indubbiamente semplice, come pure chiarire le circostanze nella quale la lettera fu composta. In primo luogo non tutti i testimoni da cui è conservata concordano sul nome del destinatario:[9] nell'unica edizione a stampa dell'epistola, curata dal Furietti nel 1723, il secondo nome Gilabertus (o Gilbertus) non figura (compare invece nella risposta all'epistola del Barzizza attribuita al Pontano) e il cognome è riportato nella forma *Scitigles*.[10] Già Erasmo Percopo, però, volle riconoscere in costui un personaggio vicino alla corte aragonese e appartenente alla famiglia Centelles, originaria di Valenza.[11] Da molte generazioni

---

col commento di Guiniforto delli Bargigi, G. Zacheroni ed. (Firenze-Marsiglia, 1838). Ma cf. pure E. Lamma, "Del Commento all'Inferno di Guiniforte Barzizza e di un ignoto manoscritto di esso," *Giornale dantesco* 30 (1896): 112–124. Sugli interessi danteschi del Barzizza cf. la voce a cura di P. G. Ricci in *Enciclopedia Dantesca*, 1: 529. Sul commento all'*Inferno* cf. pure G. Finazzi, *Di Guiniforte Barzizza e di un suo commento all'Inferno di Dante recentemente pubblicato* (Bergamo, 1845); K. Hegel, *Ueber den historischen Werth der älteren Dante-Commentare* (Lipsia, 1878). Per una completa e dettagliata analisi di questa opera del Barzizza si veda G. Ferraù, "Il commento all'*Inferno* di Guiniforte Barzizza," in *Dante nel pensiero e nella esegesi dei secoli XIV e XV. Atti del Convegno, Melfi 27 Settembre–2 Ottobre 1970* (Firenze, 1975), 357–373, studio dal quale si ricava appunto il periodo in cui il Barzizza attese a questo lavoro.

[7] Sugli interessi petrarcheschi di Guiniforte e sul suo commento a Petrarca, conservato nel codice Parigino N. A. lat. 1819, assieme ad un commento a Seneca, cf. A. Sottili, "Note biografiche sui petrarchisti Giacomo Publicio e Guiniforte Barzizza," in *Petrarca 1304–1374. Beiträge zu Werk und Wirkung* (Francoforte, 1975), 270–286.

[8] Sull'interesse della cultura milanese di questo periodo per la letteratura volgare fiorentina cf. M. Zaggia, "Appunti sulla cultura letteraria in volgare a Milano nell'età di Filippo Maria Visconti," *Giornale storico della letteratura italiana* 170 (1993): 161–219, 321–382.

[9] I codici che restituiscono l'epistola sono Add. 15336 (cc. 41–45) della British Library e i codd. J 246 inf. (cc. 109–118), L 69 sup. (cc. 162–170), O 159 sup. (cc. 12v–13r) della Biblioteca Ambrosiana di Milano.

[10] L'epistola è edita da Furietti alle pp. 122–131.

[11] Sulla famiglia Centelles e il ramo discendente da Bernardo Centelles, cf. la voce "Bernardo

i Centelles erano al servizio degli Aragonesi: Bernardo Centelles aveva combattuto al loro fianco in Sicilia già alla fine del XIV secolo. Fu figlio di Gelabert de Centelles e il proprio figlio si chiamò allo stesso modo, Francesco Gilabert: potrebbe essere costui il corrispondente del Barzizza. Che il destinatario fosse un personaggio legato agli aragonesi lo si desume dalla stessa epistola, da cui si desume pure che fu un militare, un condottiero. Scrive infatti il Barzizza: *nunc serenissimi regis lateri officiosus assistens, praecipuam eius in te clementiam promereberis* (p. 129). Francesco Gilabert era, dunque, al servizio di un "re", e nell'Italia del 1439 il solo Alfonso d'Aragona poteva fregiarsi di questo titolo. A corroborare questa ipotesi concorre anche la considerazione, avanzata dal Barzizza, sull'impossibilità di godere della propria moglie da parte del proprio interlocutore, *qui longa expeditione a propriis abes laribus* (p. 127). Ora la guerra di conquista del napoletano da parte degli Aragonesi viveva proprio in questi anni la sua fase più importante e decisiva e non mancano le attestazioni di un forte impegno al fianco di Alfonso di Francesco Gilabert Centelles, che si guadagnò fama di valente condottiero. Egli viene ricordato come capitano delle non molte galee aragonesi nel 1440, alla battaglia di Gaeta, incarico che non dovette mantenere a lungo se già nel settembre dello stesso anno figura col titolo di *marescalcus*, e successivamente, forse nel 1448, fu nominato conte d'Oliva e di Montacuto.[12] Non sappiamo, invece, se in questo stesso personaggio o in un suo consanguineo possa identificarsi il Francesco Gilabert Centelles che venne nominato sempre nel 1440, assieme a Battista Platamonte, viceré di Sicilia.[13]

Guiniforte scrive: *Intercipies, non dubito, sermonem meum, amantissime Francisce, tuasque mihi scintillas inicies* (p. 127), giocando sulla traduzione del cognome Centelles, che in spagnolo sta per "scintille" e che appunto egli rendeva nel latino, *scintillas*. Di lui non conosciamo però l'esatta data di nascita, per quanto si possa ipotizzare che sia stato pressoché coetaneo di Guiniforte. Infatti il padre Bernardo nacque intorno al 1380 e Francesco Gilabert fece testamento nel 1467 ed era ancora vivo nel gennaio del 1480. Sappiamo inoltre che sposò, in una data a noi ignota, una nobildonna spagnola, Beatriz de Urrea y Centelles da cui ebbe due figli. Guiniforte potrebbe avere conosciuto il Centelles durante il suo soggiorno presso la corte di Alfonso d'Aragona in Spagna e forse condivise con lui l'esperienza bellica a Gerba.

Più difficile è invece determinare le circostanze nelle quali l'epistola fu concepita

---

Centelles" a cura di E. Putzulu in *Dizionario Biografico degli Italiani* e quindi A. e A. Garcia Carraffa, *Enciclopedia Heráldica Genealógica Hispano-Americana* (Madrid, 1927), vol. 26: 26–31, da cui ricaviamo molte delle notizie che seguono su Francesco Gilabert Centelles.

[12] La notizia, riportata anche dall'*Enciclopedia Heráldica Genealógica*, è in A. Ryder, *The Kingdom of Naples under Alfonso the Magnanimous. The Making of a Modern State* (Oxford, 1976), 298 e 311, che a sua volta la desume da ciò che resta degli archivi aragonesi.

[13] Cf. G. Evangelista, *Storia de' Viceré luogotenenti e presidenti del Regno di Sicilia* (Palermo, 1790), vol. 2: 146. Si può invece sicuramente escludere, per questioni di età, che il nostro possa essere il Francesco Gilabert Centelles che nel 1415 prese in sposa Costanza Ventimiglia, divenendo conte di Galifano. È questa, però, un'ulteriore testimonianza della diffusione della famiglia Centelles nel regno aragonese e del nome di Francesco Gilabert in essa.

e redatta. Sembrerebbe, innanzitutto, il frutto di un dibattito avviato forse da tempo, non sappiamo se sulla base di una discussione verbale o di un altro scritto.

La questione posta dal Centelles è quella dell'amore, ma non in senso generale, bensì, piuttosto, se l'amore "giovanile", quello passionale, sia degno degli "animi generosi". Guiniforte, costituitosi giudice della questione e proclamatosi esperto della materia ma ormai libero da ogni risvolto passionale dell'amore, come un *magister amoris* della tradizione cortese, cerca di dirimerla, procedendo con fare analitico anzitutto alla delimitazione del campo di discussione. La sentenza è presto pronunciata: non è proprio dell'animo generoso amare colei che si ama occasionalmente. L'animo gentile non può disperdersi nell'amore di più di una donna e non deve limitarsi all'esteriorità, ma deve anzitutto badare all'*egregiam indolem, virtutis indicem* (p. 123) e a tutto quel complesso di comportamenti che la denunciano. È un concetto di virtù, quello proposto dal Barzizza, che non si discosta dalla tradizione cortese e anzi in essa pare radicarsi, come suggerisce, oltre che l'esclusività del sentimento amoroso, il nesso tra la nobiltà d'animo della donna e la nobiltà dei natali e di patria. Pur presentando interessanti e significativi scarti da questa tradizione, quali anzitutto la prospettiva strettamente matrimoniale in cui egli delimitava il fenomeno d'amore, le ragioni della forte persistenza di questa tradizione, che potrebbe destare meraviglia in un umanista, trova la propria giustificazione nell'ambiente "cortese" in cui questo dibattito maturò e nella personalità stessa dell'interlocutore, nobile e cavaliere, e quindi probabilmente legato egli stesso ad una educazione di stampo tardo-medievale.

Riprendendo, infatti, una casistica che poteva già ritrovare in Andrea Cappellano, ma che aveva incontrato un'ampia fortuna in ambito umanistico, da Poggio al Piccolomini,[14] Guiniforte discuteva se fosse più consono all'animo generoso l'amore per una donna maritata, vedova o vergine. Con l'apporto di una ricca argomentazione e capovolgendo però gli esiti della tradizione cortese, il Barzizza dimostrava che era risibile l'amore per una donna sposata, perché l'amore non poteva che essere un sentimento esclusivo, che non ammetteva condivisioni e poi chi aveva tradito già una volta poteva tradire ancora. L'impianto stesso della discussione, invece, riprende motivi che non possono che richiamare alla mente il *Filocalo* del Boccaccio, opera nella quale Feramonte poneva alla "reina" Fiammetta la questione se "un giovane … si dee innamorare di queste tre, o di pulcella, o di maritata o di vedova".[15] Oggi sappiamo che accanto a quella di Petrarca e Dante, che Guiniforte studiò in maniera specifica, anche l'opera di Boccaccio faceva parte della biblioteca Barzizza[16] e la circolazione del *Filocalo*, un'opera che fu particolarmente cara alle corti rinascimentali,

---

[14] A. Cappellano, *De amore* (Bologna, 1980), I, XVIII. Cf. Aeneae Sylvii Piccolomini *Opera quae extant omnia* (Basileae, 1551; rist. an. Frankfurt, 1967), 607: *Epist. CVI, Aeneas Sylvius Poeta, Nicolao Vuartenburgensi, Amoris illiciti medula*: "Dixisti te neç virginem, nec nuptam, nec viduam amare, sed mulierem quamvis pulchram meretricem tamen, quibuslibet viris precii causa sese substernentem." Una variazione sul tema è rappresentata dallo scritto *An seni sit uxor ducenda* di Poggio Bracciolini (Poggii Bracciolini Florentini *Dialogus an seni sit uxor ducenda* [Florentiae, 1823]).

[15] G. Boccaccio, *Filocalo* (Milano–Napoli, 1974), IV, 9, 881.

[16] Cf. *Molto più preziosi dell'oro*, 17.

anche in ambito milanese è con sicurezza attestata.[17] Di quanto sostenuto dalla *magistra amoris* Fiammetta nella *Quistione IX* del quarto libro, il nostro *magister amoris* Guiniforte riprendeva anzitutto il tono perentorio nel rifiuto delle maritate, senza attenuante alcuna. A differenza di quanto si leggeva nel *De Amore* del Cappellano, in Guiniforte si negava che l'amore potesse essere extraconiugale, nel momento in cui questo avrebbe costretto l'uomo magnanimo a ricorrere a sotterfugi contraddicendo così la propria indole. Un *amor delicatus et nitidus* (p. 125) poteva invece nutrirsi nei confronti delle vergini, ma ancora una volta non senza il matrimonio, perché le vergini, inesperte dell'amore, non possono essere piegate ai voleri dell'amante se non proprio con il sotterfugio. E anche Boccaccio aveva ricordato che "le zitelle non senza molto affanno si recano abili a' disiderii dell'uomo".[18] Mantenere a lungo quest'amore, senza giungere al matrimonio, poi è assolutamente impossibile con mezzi leciti e senza macchiare l'onore proprio e dell'amante.

Viduam, scio, statim propones, continua Barzizza rivolto al Centelles, ma la nobiltà richiederebbe qualcosa di socialmente più elevato di una vedova, per quanto, ammetta Guiniforte, contro di esse non concorrano *vehementes rationes* (p. 125). Proprio sulle vedove era caduta la preferenza della "reina" Fiammetta nel *Filocolo* in virtù della maggiore esperienza, mentre la discussione lì aveva portato Feramonte ad una diversa risoluzione, cioè a preferire le "pulzelle".

Guiniforte, dunque, non ritiene nessuna di queste donne (maritate, vedove o vergini) adeguate al *vir magnanimus*: non lo è certamente nemmeno l'amore per le monache "incestuose", *quas veluti prostitutas haberi convenit* (p. 126), secondo un accostamento che già era possibile leggere nel *De Amore* del Cappellano, laddove l'amore delle monache era discusso subito prima dell'amore comprato, di quello bestiale e asinino dei contadini e dell'amore per le prostitute.[19] Guiniforte, insomma, nega l'amore per le donne maritate e non permette liberamente l'amore per le vergini e le vedove. Prevenendo possibili obiezioni e fugando il sorgere di ogni dubbio, Guiniforte assicura il Centelles che egli pensa esclusivamente ad un amore confinato *intra naturae leges*[20]: comunque sia una donna, anche se vedova, ma ciò che soprattutto importa è che questa donna risponda ad una precisa serie di requisiti fisici, morali e sociali.

---

[17] Cf. M. Zaggia, *Appunti sulla cultura letteraria*, 173–174. Bisogna notare che lo stupendo codice del *Filocolo* della Landesbibliothek di Kassel, di provenienza milanese, è stato miniato da un personaggio vicino al maestro (detto delle Vite degli Imperatori romani) che miniò il cod. Parigino It. 2017, contenente il commento barzizziano all'*Inferno* dantesco e quel codice Parigino Lat. 8528, che conserva l'epistolario ciceroniano, con postille autografe di Guiniforte Barzizza. Su questi codici cf. P. Toesca, *La pittura e la miniatura nella Lombardia dai più antichi monumenti alla metà del Quattrocento* (Milano, 1912), 528–532; M. Levi D'Ancona, *The Wildenstein Collection of Illuminations. The Lombard School* (Firenze, 1970), 16, 18; E. Pellegrini, *Le Bibliothèque des Visconti e des Sforza ducs de Milan au XV siècle* (Parigi, 1955), 392.

[18] G. Boccaccio, *Filocolo*, IV, 9, 880.

[19] G. Boccaccio, *Filocolo*, I, 20, 200.

[20] Scrive Barzizza (p. 126): "ita vereris, quo mea se intentio referat. Horret animus, cum te cogito fortassis nefanda suspicari, quae tam remota semper a me divino munere fuerunt, quam occasus ab ortu, quam a superis inferi".

La descrizione della donna ideale offerta da Guniforte ricalca una topica ben diffusa nella precettistica del *tor moglie*, con espressioni che devono far pensare alla *Familiare* 22, 1 del Petrarca. Non possiamo, però, fare a meno di notare che Guniforte descriva questa donna ideale riproponendo le medesime parole e i medesimi concetti con cui un anno prima aveva descritto la futura moglie ai cugini, quasi a volere rimarcare la necessità e l'opportunità del matrimonio. Doveva essere di bell'aspetto e di età adeguata, di nobile famiglia e di nobile patria, modesta, benigna, affabile, semplice ma non incolta, una donna che *non se ad puerilem compta modum visendam ambitiose ostendet populo* (p. 126):[21] un angelo del focolare che fosse ubbidiente e che riempisse la casa di canti e dolci suoni. Solo l'amore per una donna di questo genere avrebbe rappresentato una crescita spirituale, solo questo fuoco si conveniva all'uomo nobile e gentile. Altri amori corrompono e corrodono: forse richiamando alla memoria il *Simposio* platonico, Guniforte definisce questo amore *coelestis ignis*, un fuoco che rende due animi e due corpi un corpo e un'anima sola. Questo amore, questo fuoco *et principio rerum caput fuit serendae societatis humanae et conservandae perpetuus custos esse cognoscitur* (p. 127).

L'amore coniugale è l'unico degno di un uomo come il Centelles, e la questione posta, quella dell'amore extraconiugale, non dovrebbe nemmeno essere posta, tanto più che nella vita, sostiene Guniforte sottintendendo che il proprio interlocutore fosse felicemente coniugato, anche Francesco Gilabert ha nei fatti mostrato di pensarla allo stesso modo, ma se proprio di quest'amore "giovanile" si deve discutere, conclude il Barzizza, non si devono comunque perdere di vista anzitutto quei valori etici di cui precedentemente aveva detto.

È un amore, quello che si nutre per le donne ricolme di virtù, che rende attoniti, ma senza il matrimonio non può essere un porto sicuro, non può essere un certo rifugio. L'epistola a Francesco Gilabert Centelles si chiude con quelle citazioni petrarchesche che hanno richiamato l'attenzione della critica. Gli ossimori presenti nei versi tratti dal *Trionfo dell'amore* del Petrarca descrivono l'amore come dissidio, come condizione non già di beatitudine, ma anzi di incertezza. Ciononostante, se nutrito nei confronti di una donna virtuosa, "gentile" avrebbe detto uno stilnovista, questo amore può aprire la via all'incivilimento, rendendo l'amante tanto mansueto, benefico e cortese nelle faccende domestiche, quanto determinato, valoroso e coraggioso nelle imprese belliche. Guniforte, in questo passo, disegna per altro un tipo di educazione che deve richiamare necessariamente l'attenzione di chi in lui, a questo punto, cercherebbe le tracce della pedagogia umanistica. Ebbene, anche in questo caso la rotta seguita sembra divergere da essa o quantomeno presentare interessanti deroghe. Non è vi dubbio, per quanto abbiamo fino a questo momento detto, che l'universo culturale entro cui questa lettera si muove è fortemente caratterizzato dalla tradizione romanza, più che da quella classica e anche in questo frangente questo aspetto emerge.

---

[21] Anche il Cappellano aveva scritto (*De Amore*, 16): "Sed, et si mulierem videris nimia colorum varietate fucatam, eius non eligas formam, nisi alia vice primo ipsam extra festiva diligenter aspicias, quia mulier in solo corporis fuco confidens non multum solet morum muneribus ornari".

L'amore, come risultava al Barzizza da una lunga tradizione, è sprone anzitutto alle imprese belliche, infonde coraggio e audacia, invita ad avere *equi acres domandi*, ad esercitarsi in guerra e nelle giostre con *catapulta, tragula* e *ponderosa silice iacenda* e quindi impone di incedere *exteriori cultu ornatior.*[22] I segni, appena visibili, di un'educazione più squisitamente umanistica si possono rintracciare nella breve e fugace raccomandazione a non aborrire *Musarum studia*, a dare *eloquentiae operam* e ad *historiam noscere*, per quanto, a ben guardare, anche nel *De Amore* la pratica bellica era accostata all'esercizio delle arti liberali.[23]

Si tratta comunque di una strada incerta, scivolosa, piena di pericoli e dolori, che sarebbe meglio non intraprendere perché l'uomo magnanimo non deve essere mosso dall'amore passionale, dalla violenza del *iuvenilis amor*, ma dall'amore per la virtù, che deve ricercare nella donna che, altrimenti, *natura imbecillam fecit.*

È questa la sentenza definitiva che il "giudice" Guiniforte emette, dall'alto della sua esperienza, che all'amore giovanile, al suo furore e al suo cieco dominio era riuscito a sfuggire e che ormai poteva guardare con distacco alle tempeste d'amore da quel tranquillo porto, che, a suo giudizio, era il matrimonio.

Università di Bari

---

[22] Si confrontino queste affermazioni del Barzizza (p. 129) con A. Cappellano, *De Amore*, cit., 12: "Effectus autem amoris hic est, quia verus amator nulla posset avaritia offuscari . . . O, quam mira res est amor, qui tantis facit hominem fulgere virtutibus tantisque docet quemlibet bonis moribus abundare!"

[23] Ivi, 58: "Magna debet antiquorum libenter gesta recolere atque asserere. Animosus debet esse in proelio et contra inimicos arditus, sapiens, cautus et ingeniosus. Plurium non debet simul mulierum esse amator, sed pro una omnium debet feminarum servitor exsistere atque devotus. Corporis cultui moderate debet insistere et sapientem atque tractabilem et suavem se omnibus demonstrare, licet quidam credant, se plurimum mulieri complacere, si stulta quasi vesana proferant verba suisque se valeant gestibus hominibus demonstrare dementes".

El Gonsalus seu de appetenda gloria dialogus, primera obra filosófica de Juan Ginés de Sepúlveda[1]

JUAN JESÚS VALVERDE ABRIL

El relieve intelectual que alcanzó Juan Ginés de Sepúlveda en la Europa del Quinientos lo demuestra su prolífica obra original, que abarca varios géneros, como la historiografía, la epístola, el diálogo, etc., y cuyos postulados a veces lo condujeron a acervas disputas, así como sus traducciones de filósofos griegos. Nuestro objetivo en el presente trabajo será el de presentar y describir una de las que podríamos denominar obras menores de Sepúlveda y que hasta ahora no ha llamado excesivamente la atención de los estudiosos[2], el *Gonsalus seu de appetenda gloria dialogus*.

Las ediciones de las que disponemos de dicha obra son la de Roma, que data del 19 de agosto de 1523, impresa por Marcelo Silber; la de París de 1541, en la imprenta de Simón Colines, cuya novedad con respecto a la anterior radica en la inclusión de correcciones y adiciones del propio autor; la de Colonia de 1602, *in officina Birckmanica sumptibus Arnoldi Milii;* y la de Madrid de 1780, llevada a cabo por la Real Academia de la Historia, que sigue en lo fundamental la edición de Colonia, aunque en ocasiones se aparte de ella[3].

Por lo que respecta a la datación de su composición, el *terminus ante quem* viene evidentemente impuesto por la propia fecha de la primera edición, el 19 de agosto de

---

[1] El siguiente trabajo se incribe dentro del proyecto de investigación financiado por la DGICYT del Ministerio Español de Educación y Cultura PS93-0164: "Juan Ginés de Sepúlveda: obras completas, edición, traducción y estudio".

[2] Tan sólo podemos citar los trabajos de D. Briesemeister, "Die Dialogtraktate Sepúlvedas und Osórios *De gloria*", en A. Buck, ed., *Höfischer Humanismus* (Weinheim, 1989), 183–194; y de Antonio Espigares Pinilla, "La cuestión del honor y la gloria en el humanismo del siglo XVI a través del estudio del 'Gonsalus' de Ginés de Sepúlveda y el 'De honore' de Fox Morcillo", Tesis Doctoral inédita, Madrid, 1992; además de la obra de Ángel Losada, *Juan Ginés de Sepúlveda a través de su 'Epistolario' y nuevos documentos* (Madrid, 1949; repr. 1973).

[3] Cf. Losada, *Juan Ginés de Sepúlveda*, 335–345, 356–357; y nuestro trabajo, "Juan Ginés de Sepúlveda, *Gonsalus seu de appetenda gloria dialogus*. Introducción, edición y traducción", Pozoblanco, en prensa.

1523. Sin embargo, en el establecimiento del *terminus post quem* no nos ayudan ni las referencias que el propio Sepúlveda hace en el Prefacio a la obra sobre las circunstancias en las que se produjo dicha composición, ni los sucesos históricos coetáneos referidos en dicho prefacio, ni siquiera otras alusiones externas, como la inserta en la carta fechada en 1554 dirigida a Francisco de Argote[4]. Por todo ello no nos atrevemos a dar una fecha concreta para el comienzo de la composición de la obra. Podríamos convenir con Á. Losada en el verano del propio año de 1523 como fecha más propicia, aunque no descartamos otra más temprana.

El *Gonsalus* es, como indica su subtítulo, un diálogo, al que nosotros añadiríamos el calificativo de filosófico. Nos hallamos, por tanto, ante uno de los primeros ejemplos hispanos de este género.

No vamos a entrar aquí en la problemática que subyace al cultivo de este género literario, ni a debatir la cuestión de si es posible encontrar en los cultivadores de él una élite intelectual de un marcado talante reformador y humanista[5]. Ni tampoco definiremos la naturaleza del género, pues es éste un debate que excede los límites de nuestro trabajo[6]. Para nuestro interés baste constatar que la tradición clásica ofrecía a los autores renacentistas libre de cualquier preceptiva teórica un amplio espectro de autores y obras a los que imitar: Platón y Sócrates, de un lado; Aristóteles y Cicerón, de otro; Jenofonte y, por último, Luciano de Samósata.

Pues bien, teniendo en cuenta la formación italiana de nuestro humanista (recordemos su estancia en el Colegio Español de San Clemente de Bolonia entre 1515 y 1523), no es de extrañar que Sepúlveda se proponga emular en el *Gonsalus* el modelo ciceroniano o doctrinal, lo que consigue mediante la imitación de una obra determinada, en nuestro caso el *Laelius*. De ahí se desprenden los siguientes rasgos:

---

[4] "Ceterum adulescens ista aetate qua tu nunc es, et isto animi feruore libellum scripsi 'de gloria appetenda' ...": *Ioannis Genesii Sepulvedae Cordubensis Opera cum edita tum inedita*, vol. 3 (Matriti, 1780), 292.

[5] Cfr. J. Gómez, *El diálogo en el Renacimiento español* (Madrid, 1988), 177–199, donde rebate la tesis expuesta por J. Ferreras en *Les dialogues espagnols du XVI° siècle ou l'expression littéraire d'une nouvelle conscience* (Paris, 1985), I–II, 13, 1077–1078.

[6] A modo de bibliografía fundamental remitimos, además de a los estudios citados en la nota anterior, a los siguientes: A. Buck, "Fiktion und Wirklichkeit. Bemerkungen zu den humanistischen Dialogen der italienischen Renaissance", en K. Ley, ed., *Text und Tradition: Gedenkschrift Eberhard Leube* (Frankfurt, 1996), 31–46; E. Garin, "La evolución de la dialéctica desde el siglo XII a principios de la Edad Moderna", en N. Abbagnano, ed., *La evolución de la dialéctica,* trad. F. Moll Camps (Barcelona, 1971), 132–163; F. V. Gómez, "El concepto de 'dialoguismo' en Bajtín: La otra forma del diálogo renacentista", *1616* 5 (1983): 47–54; D. Marsh, *The Quattrocento Dialogue. Classical Tradition and Humanist Innovation* (Cambridge, Mass.–London, 1980); L. Mulas, "La scrittura del dialogo. Teorie del dialogo tra cinque e seicento", en G. Cerina, C. Lavinio, y L. Mulas, eds., *Oralità e scrittura nel sistema letterario* (Roma, 1982), 245–263; M. Roelens, "Le dialogue philosophique? L'opinion des siècles classiques", *Cahiers de l'Association International d'Études Françaises* 24 (1972): 43–58; A. Vian Herrero, "La ficción conversacional en el diálogo renacentista", *Edad de Oro* 7 (1988): 173–186; G. Wyss-Morigi, *Contributo allo studio del dialogo all'epoca del Umanesimo e del Rinascimento* (Monza, 1950).

1. La inclusión de personajes históricos como interlocutores del diálogo es un rasgo que comparten los diálogos clásicos y renacentistas[7]. La razón de ello la da Sepúlveda evocando un pasaje de Cicerón[8]:

> Quare cum genus hoc sermonum, quod Cicero doctissime ut cetera dixit, positum in hominum ueterum auctoritate et eorum illustrium plus nescio quo pacto habeat grauitatis, tres summos et grauissimos uiros . . . quasi loquentes induxi . . . (Praef. 3)[9].

Son tres, por tanto, los personajes que aparecen en el diálogo: Gonzalo Fernández de Córdoba, el Gran Capitán, personaje principal de la obra y que da título a la misma (costumbre esta también tomada del modelo ciceroniano), quien asume la función de maestro, pues expone y defiende las ideas del autor; Diego Fernández de Córdoba, conde de Cabra; y Pedro Fernández de Córdoba, marqués de Priego, quienes hacen las veces de discípulos: ellos son los que plantean el tema a debatir y presentan las objeciones que Gonzalo debe refutar.

2. La clasificación de los diálogos según el modo en el que es presentado el discurso en directos, indirectos y mixtos y la definición de éste último tipo fueron materia de discusión filológica en el siglo XVI, ya se analizase el corpus platónico, ya el ciceroniano. En un principio los dialogos de Cicerón *Cato Maior* y *Laelius* fueron entendidos como mixtos, por la presencia de la voz de un narrador en los primeros compases del mismo, pese a que en el prólogo del *Laelius* Cicerón afirmaba:

> Quasi enim ipsos induxi loquentes, ne "inquam" et "inquit" saepius interponeretur, atque ut tamquam a praesentibus coram haberi sermo uideretur.

En atención a estas palabras con posterioridad tales diálogos fueron reclasificados como dramáticos[10].

Ni que decir tiene que el *Gonsalus* presenta un caso análogo. Si en un principio la voz de un narrador sitúa a los personajes en el acto de conversar, lo cierto es que esa voz no vuelve a aparecer en el resto de la obra y la sucesión de las intervenciones de los personajes están marcadas, primero por las referencias directas que se hacen unos a otros, como vocativos o interrogaciones, y segundo por unas abreviaturas o siglas que encabezan cada intervención[11].

3. Dos características esenciales del diálogo ciceroniano en lo que atañe a la forma interna del discurso son, de un lado, la *disputatio in utramque partem*, que vemos ejem-

---

[7] Cf. R. Hirzel, *Der Dialog. Ein literarhistorischer Versuch*, II (Leipzig, 1895; repr. Hildesheim, 1963), 388.

[8] Cic. *Lael.* 4.

[9] Los números entre paréntesis remiten a los capítulos y parágrafos en los que hemos dividido el texto del *Gonsalus* que ofrecemos en nuestro trabajo citado (Valverde, "Sepúlveda, *Gonsalus*").

[10] Cf. F. Pignati, "Introduzione", en C. Sigonio, *Del dialogo* (Roma, 1993), 58–60.

[11] Tal debió ser el estado observado por los humanistas en los manuscritos que manejaron. Cf. J. Andrieu, *Le dialogue antique. Structure et présentation* (Paris, 1954), 297–303.

plificada en el *De finibus*, y que no es sino el contrapunto formal del eclecticismo y del escepticismo académico que Cicerón profesaba, y, de otro, la *oratio perpetua*, es decir, la práctica desaparición en algunos de sus diálogos, como en el *Laelius* y el *Cato Maior*, del proceso dialogado, consecuencia, en última instancia, de la formación retórica del Arpinate[12].

Ambos rasgos podemos rastrearlos en el *Gonsalus*. Si Sepúlveda parece desconfiar de la *disputatio in utramque partem*, como inferimos de la siguiente afirmación que pone en boca de Pedro:

> ‹philosophi› talia solent ancipiti oratione uersare et in utramque partem dispu-
> tare uerborum tanta subtilitate, ut non liceat, quid uerum sit, dignoscere (9,1),

lo cierto es que veladamente la utiliza, no sólo cuando los discípulos presentan los argumentos en contra de la moralidad del deseo de gloria, sino también cuando en un largo monólogo (llamémoslo así) el maestro recuerda los mismos para rebatirlos, recurriendo en muchas ocasiones a la figura retórica de la *occupatio*. Valga a modo de ejemplo el siguiente pasaje:

> At pium est et euangelicum non resistere malum, fateor atque id optimum esse
> dico et perfectae pietatis; sed haec perfectio in nullo minus desiderari uidetur
> quam in milite. . . . (32,8)

Por lo que atañe al segundo aspecto, la *oratio perpetua*, rasgo este propio del diálogo doctrinal, lo vemos reflejado en el asentimiento de los discípulos hacia las tesis del maestro ya desde el propio planteamiento de la discusión. Dice Pedro:

> A te potius, patrue sapientissime, haec audire cupimus, quem tum naturae
> praestantia, tum multarum rerum usu, quid optimum sit, recte statuisse credi-
> mus. (9,1)

Y más adelante Diego:

> Ego uero, Gonsale, quid in hac quaestione uerum sit, iam nihil ambigo; nam
> tua mihi auctoritas pro summa ratione est. (19,2)

Ello supone la desparición de cualquier proceso contencioso entre los distintos sujetos que forman la trama literaria y la asunción del turno de palabra por parte del maestro. Así, en la obra que analizamos la última intervención de Gonzalo ocupa una extensión de casi la mitad de la misma.

Pero la imitación de los modelos no se restringe a la adquisición de un caparazón formal, sino que supone la absorción de los saberes clásicos por parte de los distintos autores neolatinos. De ahí que la producción filosófica del Renacimiento carezca en

---

12 Cf. G. L. Hendrickson, "Literary Sources in Cicero's *Brutus* and the Technique of Citation in Dialogue", *American Journal of Philology* 27 (1906): 184–199; P. Levine, "Cicero and the Literary Dialogue", *Classical Journal* 53 (1958): 146–151; M. Ruch, *Le préambule dans les oeuvres philosophiques de Cicéron* (Paris, 1958), 39–55; Marsh, *The Quattrocento Dialogue*, 2–3; Gómez, *El diálogo*, 94–101.

muchas ocasiones de originalidad, como han señalado algunos estudiosos[13]. En este sentido la labor del filósofo consiste en amalgamar y adecuar la producción clásica a una nueva matriz ideológica, nacida de unas circunstancias sociales, políticas y económicas totalmente nuevas.

En efecto, vemos que la temática del *Gonsalus*, que podríamos resumir en la justificación de la gloria mundana dentro de una ética cristiana, militarista y ascética a la vez, al servicio de un estado absolutista en expansión, hunde sus raíces en las obras clásicas. Aristóteles planteó el debate y ofreció la solución al respecto en su *Ética Nicomáquea*, cuando afirmó:

ἐπεὶ δὲ τῶν ἐπιθυμιῶν καὶ ‹δὲ› τῶν ἡδονῶν αἱ μέν εἰσι ‹τῶν› τῷ γένει καλῶν καὶ σπουδαίων (τῶν γὰρ ἡδέων ἔνια φύσει αἱρετά), ... οἷον χρήματα καὶ κέρδος καὶ νίκη καὶ τιμή· πρὸς ἅπαντα ... (διὸ ὅσοι μὲν παρὰ τὸν λόγον ἢ κρατοῦνται ἢ διώκουσι τῶν φύσει τι καλῶν καὶ ἀγαθῶν, οἷον οἱ περὶ τιμὴν μᾶλλον ἢ δεῖ σπουδάζοντες ... καὶ γὰρ ταῦτα τῶν ἀγαθῶν, καὶ ἐπαινοῦνται οἱ περὶ ταῦτα σπουδάζοντες[14].

Naturalmente también se deja notar el influjo de autores latinos. Entre ellos el maestro Cicerón ocupa un lugar preeminente. Recordemos que compuso un *De gloria* en dos libros, para nosotros perdido, pero quizá aún manejado por los autores renacentistas, y que en el *De officiis* reflexionaba acerca del tema de la gloria. Pero la lección ciceroniana, como la de Valerio Máximo, autor de los *Dicta et facta memorabilia*, obra ampliamente conocida en el Renacimiento[15], parece reducirse a la asunción de determinados *exempla*, aducidos por el autor como uno de los instrumentos más adecuados en el proceso argumentativo para la confirmación de sus tesis.

Claro que todo este sistema ideológico está tamizado a través de una profundísima y arraigada conciencia cristiana del autor, que busca la sanción del texto bíblico o de escritores tan autorizados en la Cristiandad como el propio Agustín[16].

Sólo nos queda abordar ya el análisis de las unidades temáticas en las que podemos dividir el contenido de la obra, que vienen a coincidir con los elementos estructurales

---

[13] Cf. Paul O. Kristeller, *El pensamiento renacentista y sus fuentes*, trad. F. Patán López (Madrid, 1982; repr. 1993), 336.

[14] Arist. *EN*. 1148a22–32. Transcribimos la traducción de J. Pallí Bonet, *Aristóteles, Ética Nicomáquea. Ética Eudemia* (Madrid, 1985), 299: "Ahora bien, de los apetitos y placeres, unos son genéricamente nobles y buenos (pues algunas cosas agradables son por naturaleza apetecibles), ... por ejemplo la ganancia, la victoria y los honores ... Por eso cuantos, contra la razón, son dominados por ellos o persiguen cosas que naturalmente son buenas y nobles, como aquellos que se afanan por el honor más de lo debido, son alabados (pues estas cosas son buenas y los que se afanan por ellas son alabados)."

[15] Cf. L. Gil Fernández, *Panorama social del Humanismo español (1500–1800)*, 2ª ed. (Madrid, 1997), 499.

[16] "Luceant opera uestra coram hominibus ut uideant bona facta uestra et glorificent Patrem uestrum, qui in caelis est" (Matt. 5:16) puede remitir al parágrafo 24,4; "et ideo melior est uirtus, quae humano testimonio contenta non est, nisi conscientiae suae" (Aug. *ciu*. 5,12,4) lo vemos reflejado en 34,1.

que vertebran a la misma. Para ello recurriremos a la terminología acotada y definida por Carlo Sigonio en su *De dialogo liber* de 1562[17].

El *Gonsalus* se abre con una *praefatio*, redactada en forma de epístola nuncupatoria dirigida a Luis y Elvira de Córdoba. En ella expone el autor las motivaciones que lo llevaron a la composición de la obra, resume el tema de la misma, presenta a los interlocutores del diálogo, además de hacer una aguerrida defensa de la labor del escritor como medio para que la fama de las hazañas perviva hasta el futuro.

Después de ella comienza el diálogo propiamente dicho, en el que dentro de la continuidad que supone todo discurso dialogado podemos establecer los siguientes cortes:

A la *praeparatio* corresponde el encuadre local y temporal del diálogo. En este sentido, Sepúlveda, por guardar el principio de verosimilitud, sitúa la conversación que transcribe, que es una ficción, en la Córdoba de los años 1507-1508, poco después de la vuelta de Gonzalo a su ciudad natal, tras sus victoriosas campañas en Italia, y necesariamente antes del destierro de Pedro en Valencia[18].

Dentro de la *praeparatio* podemos situar también las primeras intervenciones de los interlocutores del diálogo, aquéllas que sirven para introducir al lector en la problemática sobre la que versará la obra. Así, el recuerdo de un tema cotidiano para la época, el de la guerra de Granada y los acontecimientos que la siguieron, como la sublevación en Sierra Bermeja en 1501, sirve para plantear el debate. Dice Diego:

> Itane censes, Gonsale, gloriam excelso magnoque animo uiris ante cetera mortalia bona et uitam esse ponendam? (8,1)

Sigue un proceso de discusión denominado *contentio* (8,2–37,2), en el que los personajes que suelen adoptar el papel de discípulos presentan los argumentos en contra de las tesis del autor, para que posteriormente éste por boca del personaje maestro los refute. A estos dos elementos binarios que conforman la *contentio* se les suele denominar respectivamente *propositio* y *probatio*. En el *Gonsalus* podemos observar tal organización, pero con la salvedad de que tal proceso se halla geminado en dos unidades temáticas, cuya estructura podríamos decir que es paralela.

La primera de ellas (8,2–19,1) recoge y desarrolla la idea del beneficio moral que aporta al individuo la apetencia de gloria, pues ésta lo impulsa a la realización de acciones virtuosas. Diego propone el tema a tratar:

> Rem gratissimam nobis ... effeceris, si gloria sitne et quatenus magnis uiris appetenda, hodierno die nobis explicueris. (8,2)

Y Gonzalo refiere algunos ejemplos de personajes notorios que alcanzaron la gloria gracias a sus acciones. Enumera así las distintas virtudes que cultivaron tales personajes: virtud político-militar, virtud intelectual, y las virtudes éticas, justicia, lealtad,

---

[17] Cf. Sigonio, *Del dialogo*.

[18] Cf. L. Fernández Suárez y M. Fernández Álvarez, *Historia de España, XVII, 2, La España de los Reyes Católicos*, (Madrid, 1969), 691; M. C. Quintanilla Raso, *Nobleza y señoríos en el reino de Córdoba. La Casa de Aguilar. Siglos XIV–XV*, 150–152.

templanza y liberalidad, clasificación esta que nos hace recordar la que ofrece Aristóteles en la *Ética Nicomáquea*.

La segunda unidad temática (19,2–37,2) representa el debate filosófico-religioso que tal tema podía suscitar en los ambientes intelectuales de la época. Comprende dos procesos argumentativos contrapuestos. De un lado los discípulos aducen los argumentos que podían socavar la licitud, entendida en términos morales y religiosos, del apetito de gloria. Y mientras Diego presenta las objeciones que podríamos denominar lógico-filosóficas:

> Aiunt enim gloriam appetere ambitiosi hominis esse, ambitionem autem inter uitia numerari, non esse igitur gloriam appetendam, deinde gloriosum hominem appellare in probris esse, non in laudibus; quid autem esse gloriosum hominem nisi gloriae appetentem; gloriam igitur potius esse contemnendam. (19,4)

Pedro presenta las religiosas:

> Nam qui religionem Christianam sanctius colunt, hanc ipsam religionem in primis opponunt, qua iubemur omnes res humanas contemnere et omnia nostra tum dicta tum facta ad solum deum referre; itaque gloriam istam, quam illi caducam inanemque uocant, appetere hominis esse irreligiosi et diuinorum praeceptorum contemptoris. (20,1)

Evidentemente Gonzalo no comparte tal punto de vista. De forma que comienza una intervención, ya no interrumpida hasta el final de la obra, en la que rebate las anteriores objeciones a la vez que define el concepto de gloria. Acerca de la confusión del apetito de gloria con la ambición refiere:

> Ego enim eam gloriam appeti uolo, quae altis radicibus innitatur, quae per solam uirtutem contingit, immo quae sola, ut doctissimis uiris placere uideo, uirtutis est praemium. (21,5)

Por lo que respecta a la confusión entre gloria y vanagloria dice:

> Qua dementia tantum abest ut quisquam gloriam assequatur, ut, siquid egerit laude non indignum, id totum importuna iactatione perdat. . . . (24,3)

La refutación de estos primeros argumentos la concluye con una *definitio* del concepto de gloria, inspirada en palabras de Cicerón[19]:

> Ad summam ne ambiguitate sermonis erremus; cum gloriae intellectus latissime patere uideatur ad omnemque laudem pertinere, illam gloriam magnis uiris expetendam esse dico, quae uirtutis sequitur et factorum est comes; ea uero est, ut doctissimi uiri definierunt, consentiens laus bonorum, incorrupta uox bene iudicantium de excellente uirtute, res uidelicet solida et expressa, non adum-

---

[19] Cic. *Tusc.* 3,3.

brata, non inanis et quae nec ab stultorum errore pendet nec per temeritatem aut simile aliud uitium exquiritur. (28,1–2)

Con respecto a los argumentos aducidos por Pedro, es decir, los religiosos, responde Gonzalo:

Sic igitur gloriam expetemus oportet, ut prima sit cura religionis. Sed si uera gloria, ut saepe dico, per uirtutes exquiritur et religio Christiana per uirtutes maxime colitur, quid, obsecro, potest obesse, quo minus religionem simul colere et gloriam appetere honeste ualeamus? (31,1)

Añade además Gonzalo como argumento irrefutable el ejemplo de muchos pueblos que utilizaron el apetito de gloria como acicate para el comportamiento virtuoso de sus conciudadanos y la consecución de hazañas ilustres:

Age uero, si licet ex omnium gentium factis institutisque commune hominum iudicium aucupari, qua in re magis omnium mortalium sententiae consensere quam in proponendo honore, qui a nobis ponitur in parte gloriae, pro honestissimo praemio iis, qui magnae cuiuspiam uirtutis aliquod exemplum edidissent? (35,1)

La conclusión que descuella de tal argumentación es evidente y rotunda. Afirma Gonzalo ya al final de su intervención:

Quis dubitare queat, quin gloriae appetitus maxime naturalis sit, pulcher, honestus et cum ipsius uirtutis atque honestatis amore suapte natura coniunctus et colligatus? prorsus ut, si uirtutes amare, amplecti, desiderare, ut est, sic honestum, pium et ex officio esse dicatur, gloriam, quae uirtutum est consectatrix, appetere contra uel religionem uel officium esse dicere irreligiosum et contra officium esse uideatur. (37,1–2)

Y con ella finaliza la obra que estudiamos, no sin olvidar Sepúlveda concluir la misma con una elogiosa alusión a la familia de los Fernández de Córdoba.

Repasados, pues, someramente los distintos niveles desde los que se puede describir una obra latina renacentista de tales características, sólo nos queda ya expresar el deseo de que con nuestra aportación quede cubierto el vacío al que aludíamos, no tanto porque creamos que hemos resuelto todos los problemas que se nos han planteado a lo largo de su estudio, sino porque esperamos que con ella despierte el interés de los estudiosos hacia esta obra.

Universidad de Granada

Ovid's Heroides *in the Netherlands:*
A Dutch Princess in a Heroic Epistle of
Caspar Barlaeus (1629)

OLGA VAN MARION

The heroic epistle was a popular genre in Dutch literature, from about 1600, the time the young Republic was formed, until the establishment of the Kingdom of the Netherlands in 1815. Some hundred poets composed a few hundred epistles, in Neo-Latin and in the vernacular, using a wide range of religious and historical characters derived from classical history, church history, or more recent national and international politics.[1]

The heroic epistle discussed in this paper deals with an episode in the so-called Eighty Years War, the Dutch Revolt against Spanish supremacy.[2] The main characters are key characters in this Revolt, too. The topic of the paper is the relationship between this heroic epistle and Dutch politics, and the influence of this phenomenon on the Dutch poets who felt challenged to translate and answer the letter in Dutch, thus taking a stand in the political discussion and spreading the genre into the vernacular.

The letter was published in 1629 under the title *Epistola Ameliae ad Henricum Fredericum, maritum [. . .]* "A letter from Amalia to Henry Frederick, her husband, too audaciously making war, right under the walls of 's-Hertogenbosch."[3] Countess Amalia van Solms, married to the new stadtholder of the young Dutch Republic, is the leading actor in this rhetorical exercise of *ethopoeia*, the personification in which a poet represents the words of an historical or literary character, imagining how this

---

[1] The heroic epistle genre in European literature is discussed in Heinrich Dörrie, *Der heroische Brief* (Berlin, 1968). A list of heroic epistles in Dutch literature: http://wwwlet.LeidenUniv.nl/www.let.data/Dutch/heroides.html. The research project on Dutch heroic epistles was supported by NWO (the Netherlandic Organisation of Scientific Research).

[2] For literature see Geoffrey Parker, *Spain and the Netherlands 1559–1659* (1974).

[3] "Epistola Ameliae ad Henricum Fredericum, maritum, audacius sub ipsis Sylvae-Ducis moenibus militantem," in *Sylvae-Ducis obsidio* (Leiden, 1629), 49–55.

person would have spoken in a particular situation. The princess is pictured writing to her husband the Prince of Orange, chief-captain of the new Dutch Republic.[4] At that time, the summer of 1629, he was besieging the stronghold of the Spanish in the North, the unconquerable city of 's-Hertogenbosch in Brabant, with its governor Baron Anthony Schetz. A garrison consisting of Spanish, Walloon and German soldiers defended the city and three strong forts. A rescue force sent by the governor of the Netherlands in Brussels, the Spanish Infanta Isabella,[5] arrived late and was successfully distracted; several attacks, however, had to be beaten off.

The ghostwriter of the epistle was the poet Caspar Barlaeus, former professor of philosophy at Leiden University, and from 1632 professor in history and philosophy at the Amsterdam *Athenaeum Illustre*.[6] Barlaeus was one of the great throng of encomiasts of the stadtholder, distinguishing himself as a panegyrist, chiefly through his epic poem *Sylvae Ducis obsidio* 1629, on the siege and conquest of 's-Hertogenbosch, to which he added the letter from Amalia in elegiac distichs.

How could Barlaeus know of the personal details of the royal family at a time when there were no tabloids or glossy magazines? Most of his information came from the secretary of the stadtholder, the poet Constantijn Huygens, whom he knew as a friend. Their extensive correspondence and exchange of poems bears witness to this.[7]

> If you could spare me a moment, without soldiers blowing the harsh trumpet with its barbaric sounds around the tents, and if you do not walk pugnaciously and triumphantly between the trenches, the ditches and the bullets, stained with blood, then read these lines from your worried wife (if I'm permitted to write like this), the sorrowful words of your Amalia.[8]

---

[4] Countess Amalia van Solms (1602-1675), Princess of Orange. For literature see A. Kleinschmidt, *Amalie von Oranien, geborene Gräfin zu Solms-Braunfels* (1905). Frederik Hendrik van Nassau (1584–1647), Prince of Orange and stadtholder of five Northern provinces, captain-general of the Dutch Republic; Eighty Years War (Dutch Revolt) 1567/8–30 Jan. 1648, Peace of Muenster; Siege of 's-Hertogenbosch, 30 April–14 September 1629.

[5] Isabella Clara Eugenia (1598–1633), Spanish Infanta, governor of the Netherlands in Brussels.

[6] Caspar Barlaeus (1584–1648), whose family came from the southern parts of the Netherlands. From 1612 he was a regent of the State College and from 1618 professor of philosophy at the University of Leiden, where he was dismissed in 1619 because of his Arminian leanings. He obtained his doctorate in medicine in 1620, and was a private teacher in Leiden until 1632, when he and G. J. Vossius became the first professors at the *Athenaeum Illustre* in Amsterdam. For literature see Ton Harmsen, "Maurits de Braziliaan en zijn dichters," in *Van Oost tot West* (Leiden, 1995). His complete poetry is at: wwwlet.LeidenUniv.nl/www.let.data/Dutch/Latijn/ BARL01. html.

[7] Constantijn Huygens (1596–1687), secretary of the Prince of Orange. For literature on the correspondence between Barlaeus and Huygens see F. F. Blok, *From the Correspondence of a Melancholic* (1976); K. van der Horst, *Inventaire de la correspondance de Caspar Barlaeus* (1978).

[8] Si vacat, & nullus circum tentoria miles
    Barbaricis inflat classica rauca sonis:
Nec medios inter cuneos, fossasque, globosque
    Efferus, & multa caede cruentus ovas:
Has lege sollicitae, mihi fas ita scribere, voces
    Conjugis, Ameliae tristia verba tuae.
                    (*Epistola Ameliae* [hereafter *EA*], p. 49)

Because 's-Hertogenbosch was surrounded by a swamp, the whole area had to be drained before the city walls could be blown up. Arriving with an army of 28,000 soldiers of fortune—Germans, Scots, Walloons, Frenchmen, and Englishmen—on the last day of April, the prince immediately started to construct a line of defensive works around the city to keep off any rescue force. A second line was built inside, in order to drain the area between the line and the bulwarks of the city with mills, driven by horsepower; two small rivers were diverted. Hundreds of farmers assisted in this Herculean labour.

The princess writes that the trenches are being dug and that the attacks on the walls have started. The explosions and firing must have made a terrible noise. According to the calculations of one of the historians of the siege, Pieter Bor, 116 guns fired 28,517 times. In this cacophony the princess asks for a respite.

> While I'm writing and the letter is running over the paper, young Louise cries near my writing hand. And the young Prince of Orange lies on your side of the bed and calls for his father, when he sees he is not there.[9]

The picture of the princess sadly contemplating at home is not a new topos of Barlaeus. The vernacular poet Joost van den Vondel portrayed her while Henry Frederick besieged Groenlo two years before, in 1627. Barlaeus may also have been inspired by Propertius' elegy from Arethusa to Lycotas and the epistle from Andromache to Hector by his contemporary Daniel Heinsius.[10]

But the original heroic epistles, Ovid's *Epistulae heroidum* or *Heroides*, were of course Barlaeus' main source. His intention was to portray an Ovidian heroine, and he is not at all concerned to represent the courtly style of the real-life princess, who took over the business of her husband during his absence in a professional way, as a redoubtable partner in discussion with envoys and delegates.

Imitating Ovid, Barlaeus modelled the Dutch princess on Laodamia, the Greek heroine who was not aware of the fact that her husband Protesilaus, the first Greek to fall in the Trojan War, was already dead when she wrote to him. In passages of about twenty lines each both Laodamia and Amalia complain that they do not want to live an easy life while their husbands are having a hard time; they both refrain from the same courtly dresses and adornments; they both refuse to go out or run the household or comb their hair. On top of this the poet pays a straightforward literary tribute to Ovid, when the Dutch princess compares herself with no fewer than eleven Ovidian heroines.

Then we arrive at the heart of the epistle. Henry Frederick is far too audacious, risking his life in places full of danger. Amalia argues that her husband should give orders as a commander rather than fight himself:

---

[9] Haec ego dum scribo, tabulis dum littera currit,
    Vagiit ad motam parva Loysa manum.
Auriacusque, tua recubans in parte cubilis,
    Invocat, absentem quem videt esse, patrem. (*EA* p. 49–50)
[10] Daniel Heinsius, "Andromache Hectori" in *Elegiae* (Leiden, 1603), 279–287.

If you enjoy the title of "prince", be in command. Warlords should order rather than fight. Yours is a commander's role, not a soldier's one. The welfare of a country depends on a commander, not on an ordinary soldier.[11]

Historians tell us the prince rode on his horse inspecting all the works, encouraging the soldiers and the farmers, even giving assistance if necessary.[12] Moreover, his helmet was crowned with a clearly visible bunch of white feathers, the martial symbol that made him an easy target. He received warnings from representatives of the States-General and high officers (in Dutch), from friends (in Latin), and from his wife (in French). Through his correspondence with the prince's secretary in the military camp Barlaeus must have been aware of this general fear and these alarming letters. These warnings must have inspired his character's words: the prince should let the British and the French soldiers, the Scots, the Dutch and the Swiss march on the town and attack the walls; he should have them killed in places full of fear. Amalia illustrates her point that a commander should order rather than fight with examples of historical heroes such as Scipio Africanus. She emphasizes the political significance of the continued existence of the House of Orange:

> Please spare yourself. The loss of other dead is easy to accept, but leaders with the name of Orange are rare. Let the many lamentable funerals of members of your kin, and the many Nassau pyres that enlighten the Netherlands, be enough. We brought enough offers to King Philip, in that blood we paid enough for breaking the scepter of the Spanish land.[13]

She ends her letter just like Laodamia and Propertius' Arethusa: "I will follow you wherever you go, even into the realm of the dead."

> One bed we shared, one we were, and I hope the Fates allow us to die in one way.[14]

On July 3 Caspar Barlaeus sent his heroic epistle to his friend Constantijn Huygens: "Quos mitto versiculos, mitto tibi": "I send you these little rhymes; I send them to you, because I know you to be a fair critic of my poetry. What if you should

---

[11] Si titulo gaudes Principis, arma jube.
      Non pugnare Duces, sed sunt dare jussa parati.
   Militis haud partes, imperitantis habes.
      Tota salus patriae Ducis est, non militis illa est. (*EA* p. 52)

[12] E.g., Pieter Bor, *Gelegentheyt van 's Hertogen-Bosch, vierde Hooftstadt van Brabandt* (Den Haag, 1630).

[13] Parce tibi. alterius facilis jactura sepulchri est.
   Rarior Auriaco nomine ductor adest.
   Sufficiant miseranda tuae tot funera gentis,
      Et tot Nassoviis Belgica clara rogis.
   Solvimus inferias Regi sat sanguine in illo
      Hesperii luimus subruta sceptra soli. (*EA* p. 53)

[14] Una thori facies, una est concordia, tandem
      Fata velint uno nos periisse modo. (*EA* p. 55)

answer on behalf of the prince?" Indeed Huygens began an answer from Henry Frederick, as well as a translation into Dutch, but both remained incomplete. As a critic, however, he showed more initiative. Together with a mutual friend he condemned some lines of the Amalia epistle as indecent, advising Barlaeus to remove the expressions that would not amuse the court. With the new chaste version of the epistle Barlaeus and Huygens began searching for a translation into French or Dutch in order to be able to read the epistle aloud to the real-life prince.

Several poets were involved in this Barlaeus project, resulting in a collection of texts of which six poems are complete and have been preserved. Five of them appeared in the form of a pamphlet, written in the very year of the Den Bosch siege or at the beginning of the next.

These texts aim at a wide audience. A former pupil of Barlaeus, Jacobus Westerbaen, composed two responses on behalf of the prince.[15] A devotee of Ovid, who later in his life translated and adapted his works into the vernacular, he versified his answers from the prince both in Latin and in Dutch, publishing them as one pamphlet. The Amalia arguments are refuted carefully, one by one: a commander should lead his army and walk in front. A commander's wife should dress and act according to her status, and continue to do so while her husband carries severe arms. The young Prince of Orange should draw the military camp of his father with his finger in the sand, in order to imitate his father's glorious deeds. At the end of his letter the reader finds political statements. There the prince condemns the Spanish Infanta and, with her, the "old" Roman Catholic church:

> Let the palace of the mighty Spanish gods mourn, and let Clara Isabella sit there neglected on a gloomy spot. Now Iberia notices that the shrines shake to their foundations.[16]

In the same months after the Den Bosch siege a second version of the Amalia epistle, in Dutch, was composed by the historian and poet Petrus Scriverius, one of Barlaeus' friends and an important supporter of vernacular poetry.[17] He was also the first to dedicate the epistle to the most important character involved, the princess herself. The *Send-brief* is an adaptation of the Latin original, explaining difficulties *in margine*, and avoiding classical phraseology. The poet introduced the oppositions between the gods Mars and Pallas, and War and Love, convincing the reader that

---

[15] Jacob Westerbaen, *Fredericus Henricus Ameliae. Antwoordt van mijn Heere den Prince van Orangien; op den Brief van Me-Vrouwe de Princesse* (Den Haag, 1630).

[16] [. . .] Dat Isabel haer kamer houwe,
Dat Spangjens Dochter sitt´ in rouwe.
Nu, nu begint sy al te mercken
Den harden val van hogge Kercken,
Van oude beelden en' Outaren;
Nu wagg'len gronden en' Pilaren, [. . .] (*EA* p. 11)

[17] Petrus Scriverius, *Send-Brief ingestelt op de naem van Me-vrouwe de Princesse Amalia, als schrijvende aen haeren Man Frederick Henrick, prince van Orangien, te dier tijdt als hy hem voor 'sHertogen-Bosch al te seer waeghde,* (Leiden, 1630).

military affairs do not go hand in hand with matters of love. With sentences as "Love does not conceal, Love cannot but take care for a husband" the Dutch Amalia epistle has a more general intent, aiming at a wide audience, and may indeed be addressed to the princess herself, as the dedication poem wants us to believe.

The last text is again an answer to the *Epistola Ameliae*. It is, however, dependent on the Dutch version of the Amalia epistle, not on the Latin original. This "Answer in the name of my lord Frederik Hendrik, Prince of Orange", is a vernacular response on behalf of the prince, written by an otherwise unknown poet, Cornelis Keyser.[18] He depicts the prince defending his military strategy with as many mythological references as possible, using concepts such as honour and the laurel wreath: "No, thou good princess, a hero must not yield, when he wishes to attach more realms to his laurel wreath."[19] Rather than like a woman in mourning, Amalia must behave like an Amazon. How can fear deform her well-formed limbs? Why doesn't she wear her courtly garments any more?

> The wardrobe that thou dost not approach because of fear: will your disgust enlarge my glory?[20]

In other words, the writer of the letter encourages his spouse not to behave like an Ovidian heroine, but as a brave soldier's wife, a true and courageous princess of Orange, living with him in his army camp so that she can give him some advice.

Concluding Remarks

In this paper we have discussed a fine specimen of a Dutch heroic epistle, written in elegiac distichs in the summer of 1629 by the Neo-Latin poet Caspar Barlaeus. His characters are the most important political figures in the Netherlands of his time: the Prince of Orange took the lead in the Dutch Revolt against the Spanish supremacy. Although his characters were still alive and Barlaeus had enough information about their lifestyle, he modelled the princess after the Greek heroine Laodamia, imitating Ovid.

It is not surprising that the epistle provoked reactions in which politics played a role. There were also poets playfully answering the Amalia epistle with letters in the name of her husband. These reactions were all published in the form of a pamphlet within a period of less than one year, 1629–1630. Two of the three answers were written in the vernacular; one of them is even fully dependent on the Dutch translation.

One may have the impression now that after the *Epistola Ameliae* Dutch heroic epistles were always written in the vernacular. That is not true. The fifth adaptation

---

[18] Cornelis Keyser, *Antwoort inghestelt op den Naem van mijn Heer Frederick Henrick Prince van Orange, over den be-anghsten Send-brief van Me-vrouw de Princesse Amelia, soo hy in 't Leger voor den Bosch sijn Victory verwacht* (Rotterdam, 1630).

[19] Neen, ghy brave Vorstin; een Helt en moet niet wijcken,
   Die aen sijn Lauwer-krans, wil hechten noch meer Rijcken. (*EA* p. 9)

[20] De Garde-robbe, die door vrees ghy niet wilt naken,
   Sal 't walgen van de Pracht, mijn Glory grooter maken. (*EA* p. 6)

of the Amalia epistle did not appear until eleven years later, and was again in Latin elegiac distichs.[21] Here the eleven-year-old Prince of Orange is playfully depicted writing to his father, besieging Breda, the next city that had to be reclaimed from the Spanish.

Leiden University

---

[21] Petrus Stratenus, "Guiljelmus Iunior Arausionensium Princeps, Frederico Henrico, Aurausionensium principi, etc. Patri suo, cum Bredam obsideret," in *Venus Zeelanda et alia ejus poëmata*. C. Boyus I.C. collegit et edidit (Den Haag, 1641), 89–91.

Furthermore, the *Epistola Ameliae* was incorporated anonymously and with an abridged title in the collection of elegies by Laurent Le Brun SJ, *Eloquentia poetica* (Paris, 1655), through which it circulated in the international Jesuit milieu.

Jeroni Pau en el umbral de un mundo nuevo:
Quinto centenario de su muerte

MARIÀNGELA VILALLONGA VIVES

La figura y la obra del humanista catalán Jeroni Pau destacan por encima del humanismo de la Península Ibérica por su temprana aparición, por su calidad y por lo que representan de innovación en el panorama literario de la segunda mitad del siglo XV. Consistirá este trabajo en una revisión de su biografía, de su obra y especialmente de su difusión en el humanismo europeo, una puesta al día necesaria a la vista de recientes investigaciones, en la que se darán a conocer unos pocos datos nuevos, aparecidos en senderos no hollados anteriormente que deparan inevitables sorpresas al filólogo, once años después de la publicación de la edición crítica de la obra de Pau, y de obligada referencia en el quinientos aniversario de la muerte de nuestro humanista.

Voy a centrar mi exposición en dos ejes, interrelacionándolos constantemente. Por un lado intentaré ahondar en un aspecto poco estudiado todavía: la difusión y la recepción que tuvo la obra de Jeroni Pau por parte de sus contemporáneos. Por otro lado, y de manera más concreta, intentaré añadir los últimos datos conocidos sobre la vida y la obra del humanista barcelonés. Así, voy a incidir en algunos puntos de su biografía y de su obra, en función solamente de las novedades que sobre ellas pueda aportar. Para un conocimiento más completo del personaje me remito a mis trabajos ya publicados.[1]

Primera cuestión: Fecha de nacimiento de Jeroni Pau

Sigo suponiendo a Jeroni Pau nacido en Barcelona no antes de 1458, fecha que no ha sido posible ni concretar, ni rechazar, once años después de la aparición de su biografía, pero que puede aceptarse por los datos que ya eran conocidos, cuando fue establecida, y por una nueva constatación relacionada con los estudios de nuestro humanista.

---

[1] Me refiero a Mariàngela Vilallonga, *Jeroni Pau. Obres,* 2 vols. (Barcelona, 1986).

Vayamos por partes. Pau estudió en diversas universidades italianas, según sus propias palabras y las afirmaciones de sus biógrafos, pero sin posibilidades de comprobación en el momento en que completé el apartado biográfico referente a sus estudios. Ahora, sin embargo, podemos asegurar su paso al menos por uno de los centros universitarios que se daba por seguro que Pau había visitado. Se trata de su estancia en la universidad de Pisa, que tan sólo había podido ser documentada a través de la correspondencia de Pau con sus amigos.[2] En estos momentos podemos añadir la presencia del nombre de Jeroni Pau en las listas de alumnos de la universidad de Pisa del curso 1475–1476.[3] Pau aparece como *studens iuri canonico* y se le menciona como *egregius legum doctor*.[4] Así pues, parece ser que Pau ya era doctor en leyes en 1475, cuando se trasladó a Pisa para realizar sus estudios de derecho canónico, imprescindibles para acceder a un buen cargo en la corte papal, a las órdenes de Roderic de Borja, su protector.

Si examinamos a los compañeros que tuvo Pau en el curso de derecho canónico impartido aquel año académico, nos daremos pronta cuenta de que hay una serie de características que les igualan. A saber. Muchos de ellos han nacido en fechas próximas a la fecha hipotética establecida para Pau; la mayoría son clérigos; muchos proceden de otros centros universitarios, especialmente de Boloña y de Perugia; casi todos gozan de beneficios eclesiásticos y a lo largo de su vida llegarán a ocupar puestos de relevancia dentro de la jerarquía eclesiástica.

Así por ejemplo, Francesco Soderini había nacido en 1453, había estudiado anteriormente en Boloña, fue nombrado obispo de Volterra en marzo de 1478 y cardenal en 1503. Por otro lado, Giuliano Tornabuoni nació en 1454, era canónigo y llegó también a obispo de Saluzzi. El florentino Bartolomeo Ciai había nacido en 1456 y cuando acabó sus estudios en 1481 pasó a ser profesor del Estudio Pisano. Finalmente Averardo de Medici y Jorge de Almeyda nacieron en 1457, y Almeyda accedió al obispado de Coimbra en 1482. De lo que se deduce que no es en modo alguno descabellada la hipótesis del nacimiento de Pau en 1458, confirmada por una de las biografías de nuestro autor.[5]

Otro condiscípulo de Pau en el curso 1475–76 fue Alberto de Caruccis, de quien

---

[2] Concretamente la carta que Pau dirigió a su amigo el consejero real Bartomeu de Verí, escrita en Pisa en julio de 1476. Cf. Vilallonga, *Jeroni Pau*, I, 32–33.

[3] No había podido consultar las listas en la edición de A. F. Verde, *Lo studio fiorentino (1473–1503). Ricerche e documenti*, especialmente el vol. III *Studenti-"Fanciulli a scuola" nel 1480* (Firenze, 1977). En el tomo I, 388 se puede leer sobre Pau: "studente nel corso 1475–1476", según el texto de la colección "Notarile Antecosimiano dell'Archivio di Stato di Firenze", donde se puede leer "egregius legum doctor dominus Hieronymus Paulus olim Jacobi de Barchinonia modo existens in Studio civitatis Pisarum". En cuanto la conocí, publiqué esta noticia en Mariàngela Vilallonga, "Gli umanisti catalani del XV secolo nei centri universitari della Toscana", *Studi italiani di filologia classica*, 3. ser. 10 (Firenze, 1992): 1131–1143.

[4] Armando Verde califica a Pau de humanista y clérigo en el lugar mencionado.

[5] Conservada en el ms. 425, fol. 155 de la Biblioteca Universitària de Barcelona. En Vilallonga, *Jeroni Pau*, I, 28–30 se analiza la fecha en cuestión. En aquellos momentos mi convencimiento era mínimo.

se conservan los apuntes de las lecciones que le dio su maestro Baldo Bartolini en Perugia durante los años 1471–73 y posteriormente en Pisa. Baldo fue también, recordémoslo, uno de los profesores más respetados por Pau.

Pau compartió el curso con un sobrino de Roderic de Borja, canónigo de Valencia, Juan de Castelar Borja, del círculo romano del cardenal, arzobispo de Trani y de Monreale en Sicilia, muerto en 1505.

Finalmente y habida cuenta del lugar en que nos encontramos, querría destacar un último condiscípulo de Pau en el estudio Pisano, el clérigo de Ávila, Huberto Morian, quien aparece consignado en el mismo documento que Jeroni Pau, en la colección Notarile Antecosimiano del Archivio di Stato di Firenze.[6]

Recordemos, a propósito de la estancia de Pau en Pisa, la relación epistolar que mantuvieron Pere Miquel Carbonell, el archivero barcelonés, y Lorenzo Lippio, el poeta y traductor al latín de las *Halieutica* de Opiano. Fue precisamente Jeroni Pau quien puso en contacto ambos personajes como puede verse en las epístolas que se intercambiaron. Desgraciadamente no se conservan las cartas de Pau a Carbonell con la presentación de Lippio. Sin embargo una vez más hay que dejar constancia de una amistad de Carbonell impulsada por Jeroni Pau. Sobre la relación de Pau con Lippio me preguntaba yo hace años, ¿Hemos de pensar que el año 1476 Pau estudiaba en Pisa, donde tenía como compañero a Lorenzo Lippio? La respuesta es afirmativa a medias. Efectivamente Pau, como hemos podido comprobar, estudiaba en Pisa el curso 1475–76, pero Lorenzo Lippio no era compañero de nuestro humanista sino profesor de Poética y de Retórica en el Estudio Pisano desde 1473 hasta su muerte en 1485. Lippio, seguidor del Poliziano, había sido el encargado de pronunciar el discurso inaugural de apertura de la Universidad de Pisa que tuvo lugar el día de Todos los Santos de 1473. Hasta 1478 no pudo publicar Lippio el *De natura piscium*, según reza el título en latín, tal como tradujo el profesor pisano.[7] Y todo un Lippio, a instancias de Jeroni Pau, dedicó grandes elogios a Pere Miquel Carbonell, precisamente por su buen latín, contra la opinión de algunos estudiosos modernos, y le envió su traducción junto con algunos de sus *Disticha*.[8]

Segunda cuestión: Autógrafo de Pau

No había podido aportar hasta ahora ningún texto manuscrito de Jeroni Pau, ni siquiera breve y en alguno de los manuscritos estudiados. Una revisión más a fondo de algunas páginas, a primera vista poco importantes para obtener datos acerca de nuestro humanista, nos ha sorprendido con unas líneas autógrafas de Jeroni Pau. Se trata del manuscrito 69 del Archivo Capitular de Gerona, tantas veces utilizado y de

---

[6] Cf. Verde, *Lo studio fiorentino*, vol. III, t. 2, 925: "È testimone ad un atto notarile."

[7] Cf. Verde, *Lo studio fiorentino*, vol. IV, t. 1, p. 306: "Tramite uno studente di diritto canonico, m. Girolamo Paolo di Iacopo da Barcellona, l'opera fu richiesta, apprezzata, propagandata dagli ambienti umanistici che facevano capo a Pier Michele Carbonelle segretario del re di Spagna" (vol. III, p. 388).

[8] Todo ello fue publicado por P. Faider y P. van Sint Jan, *Catalogue des manuscrits conservés à Tournai* (Gembloux, 1950), 73–79. Las dos cartas intercambiadas entre Lippio y Carbonell fueron reproducidas en Vilallonga, *Jeroni Pau*, II, 229–231.

tanta importancia para el conocimiento de la obra poética de nuestro autor. Concretamente en el folio 187v aparece un texto autógrafo de Pau. El folio muestra la siguiente disposición. En primer lugar aparece una carta, todavía inédita, de Pere Miquel Carbonell dirigida a Jaume Garcia, y a media página nos encontramos el siguiente encabezamiento: *Beneficia reseruata Barcinonae*.[9] Sigue una lista con algunos canónigos barceloneses. Pero antes de dar a conocer su contenido, debemos fijarnos en las anotaciones marginales, las que nos dan la autoría del texto. En el margen izquierdo y con la inconfundible letra humanística de Carbonell tenemos esta primera anotación: *Haec quae sequuntur scripta sunt per Hieronymo Paulo contribulo et amico meo colentissimo*. En el mismo margen aparece una segunda anotación: *Hieronymus Paulus mense Iulii Anno a Natiuitate Domini MCCCCLXXXI possessionem canonicatus et prebendae Vicensis deo opitulante adeptus est*. Efectivamente, Pau accedió a la canongía de la ciudad de Vic el año 1481, según aparece registrado en el documento de permuta de este beneficio por el mismo cargo en la ciudad de Barcelona, fechado en 1485.[10]

La relevancia del contenido del texto autógrafo de Pau es prácticamente nula. Sin embargo, se da la circunstancia de que no se conocía la letra de nuestro autor. El texto nos aporta datos relacionados con los beneficios de determinadas propiedades religiosas, con nueve canónigos de Barcelona o Girona, y sus relaciones con Roderic de Borja. Sirvan de ejemplo los siguientes:

> Berengarius Vila Canonicus Barcinonensis Rector loci de Perpinya familiaris Reuerendissimi domini Vicecancellarii.
>
> Magister Cosida Canonicus Barcinonensis Rector loci de Montblanc canonicus hierundensis et multa alia beneficia, familiaris Reuerendissimi domini Vicecancellarii.
>
> Dominus Martinus Ioannis Fuxa canonicus Barcinonensis Rector loci de Vlla et multa alia, familiaris Reuerendissimi domini Vicecancellarii.
>
> Dominus Antonius Agullana Canonicus Barcinonensis et multa alia beneficia, familiaris Reuerendissimi domini Vicecancellarii.
>
> Dominus Fexes Canonicus Barcinonensis et hebdomadarius Acolitus bonae memoriae Callisti.
>
> Dominus Sos canonicus et Decanus officialis Papae.
>
> Dominus Lull canonicus et praepositus Barcinonensis et multa alia beneficia, Cubicularius Nicolai.

Podemos suponer que se trata de unos apuntes anotados a vuela pluma por Pau, posiblemente durante alguna de sus contadas estancias en Barcelona, a manera de recordatorio, para su propio uso o para el de Carbonell. Y allí se quedaron, en medio de la miscelánea casi me atrevería a decir caótica que suponen los códices de

---

[9] El texto de Pau pasó desapercibido y no aparece descrito ni en M. A. Adroher Ben, "Estudios sobre el manuscrito Petri Michaelis Carbonelli Adversaria 1492, del Archivo Capitular de Gerona", *Anuario del Instituto de Estudios Gerundenses* 11 (1956–57): 109–162, ni tampoco en el volumen correspondiente a la descripción de los manuscritos gerundenses de P. O. Kristeller.

[10] Podemos ver esta información en Vilallonga, *Jeroni Pau*, I, 47 y 53.

Carbonell. Sólo hay que recordar que en los folios siguientes Carbonell copió las adiciones de Llucià Colomines al tratado gramatical de Villadei. Tema como se ve completamente alejado del que venimos tratando, pero muy en consonancia con el *zibaldone* de Carbonell.

Tercera cuestión: Obras de Pau en un códice de Hartmann Schedel

Han aparecido asimismo nuevos manuscritos que nos legan parte de la obra ya conocida y editada de Pau.[11] Se trata del ms. Clm. 434 de la Bayerische Staatsbibliothek de Munich y del ms. 10565/10567 de la Bibliothèque Royale de Bruselas. Analizaremos con algún detenimiento las aportaciones que dichos manuscritos representan para el conocimiento de la obra del humanista catalán. Hay que señalar que básicamente las copias aparecidas no hacen variar las ediciones críticas de los textos de Pau que se publicaron en su momento.

En el manuscrito conservado en Munich, de 264 folios y copiado por Hartmann Schedel,[12] aparecen reproducidas algunas de las obras de Pau en los folios 13–40. Así, encontramos en primer lugar *De fluminibus et montibus Hispaniarum libellus* (fols 13–27v), a continuación *De priscis Hispaniae episcopatibus et eorum terminis* (fols. 28–32v), para acabar con los *Excepta ex itinerario Antonini Pii et Theodosii de Hispaniis* (fols. 33–38v) y los *Excepta a Prouinciali antiquo Ecclesiae Romanae de Episcopatibus Hispaniae* (fols. 38v–40). Es decir, el manuscrito de Munich reproduce, al completo y con precisión, la edición romana de 1491 realizada por Eucharius Silber, de las mencionadas obras de nuestro autor.[13] El volumen había formado parte *ex Bibliotheca Serenissimorum utriusque Bauariae Ducum 1618*. Pero su anterior propietario y copista nos es señalado en el primer folio: *Liber Doctoris Hartmann Schedel Nurembergensis*.

Hay que poner atención asimismo en los folios primeros y anteriores a los que acabo de reseñar. Los dos primeros folios del volumen, con una numeración en romanas distinta a la del resto del códice, contienen un *Index eorum quae in isto libro ponuntur*. A continuación, en el primero de los folios con la numeración arábiga, aparece un resumen posiblemente de lo más importante del contenido del volumen: *Descriptio Regionum Vrbis Romanae, Libellus de montibus et fluminibus Hispaniarum, pleraque epigrammata et alia per tempora congesta. Et Auicenna de anima.*

Efectivamente, los folios 2–10 están ocupados por una *Romanae Vrbis Regionum breuis descriptio*. Se trata del mismo texto que aparece manuscrito por Pere Miquel Carbonell *De regionibus Vrbis Romae* en su códice gerundense, en los folios 95v–99.

---

[11] Di cuenta de ello en la entrada correspondiente a Jeroni Pau, en mi trabajo *La literatura llatina a Catalunya al segle XV* (Barcelona, 1993), 182–185, sin estudiar las posibles modificaciones respecto de la edición crítica, que reservé para esta ocasión.

[12] El manuscrito muniqués aparece descrito por P.O. Kristeller, *Iter Italicum,* vol. III (Londres-Leiden, 1983), 613, y en el *Catalogus codicum latinorum Bibliothecae Regiae Monacensis,* vol. I, 1 (Munich, 1892), 118–119.

[13] Incluso reproduce, después de todas las obras mencionadas, la entrada del rio *Singilis*, también omitida por el incunable en el lugar conveniente y añadida al final del volumen. Con lo que podemos asegurar que, al igual que el manuscrito 596 de la Biblioteca Nacional de Madrid copiado por Gerónimo Blancas, este códice tambien depende directamente de la edición impresa.

En las páginas anteriores y posteriores del códice gerundense aparecen parte de los poemas de Jeroni Pau y otros humanistas del círculo de Carbonell y Pau, como el mallorquín Bernat Descós o el italiano Antonio Geraldini. Pero en los folios inmediatamente anteriores a la *Descriptio* aparece el diccionario de abreviaturas que Carbonell utilizaba para comprender las inscripciones que Jeroni Pau le enviaba desde Italia. Ninguno de los dos manuscritos, ni el de Munich ni el de Gerona, nos da el nombre del autor del texto, sin embargo, como podemos ver, aparece siempre relacionado de alguna manera con las obras de Pau. Los dos textos presentan la misma estructura, pero con variantes significativas, que merecerían alguna atención, pero no es éste el momento más adecuado para ello.

El resto del manuscrito de Munich contiene ni más ni menos que un conjunto de *uaria ac lepida epigrammata laude digna*, desde el fol. 43 hasta el 68. Entre ellos podemos encontrar epigramas del humanista Conrad Celtis y significativamente su *De situ et moribus Germaniae*, por lo que podemos deducir que el copista o el *comittente* o el destinatario del códice (o ambos) tenía un determinado interés por las descripciones geográficas, una de las novedades del momento, tan útiles para el nuevo mundo que se modelaba a partir de los descubrimientos. No es el único códice de Hartmann dedicado precisamente a texto de consulta. Baste recordar la miscelanea *Liber historiarum*, en la que copió crónicas e historias y también inscripciones, recogidas directamente en los lugares que visitaba en sus viajes,[14] tal como tambien hizo Jeroni Pau. Asimismo debemos destacar la presencia en el manuscrito del discurso *Pro Sauonarolae innocentia*, de Pico della Mirandola (fols. 113–150) al lado de la *Inuectiua in Sauonarolam*, de Samuel Cassinensis (fols. 151–184) para acabar con la *Defensio Sauonarolae*, nuevamente de Pico della Mirandola (fosl. 185 al final). Además de epigramas anónimos o de otros humanistas italianos.

Hay que hacer hincapié también en el hecho de que los textos de Jeroni Pau aparecen en el mismo manuscrito que contiene una selección de poemas del humanista alemán Conrad Celtis,[15] y las defensas de Savonarola de Pico della Mirandola. Con ello podemos situar a nuestro Jeroni Pau entre los más grandes de sus contemporáneos. Con ello podemos pretender además que se reconozca su situación de privilegio dentro del humanismo europeo del siglo XVI. No sólo su manual sobre cancillería vaticana tuvo un éxito considerable y vio edición tras edición, sino que su obra de creación fue valorada hasta el punto de situarle entre los humanistas reconocidos en la Europa finisecular y en pleno Renacimiento.

Cuarta cuestión: Obras de Pau en Bruselas

En el manuscrito conservado en Bruselas,[16] de 57 folios y copiado tambien en el

---

[14] Véase sobre este manuscrito Agostino Sottili, "In margine al catalogo dei codici petrarcheschi per la Germania Occidentale", en *Il Petrarca ad Arquà* (Padova, 1975), 293–314, aqui 307–308.

[15] Hay que recordar que Conrad Celtis había nacido en 1459 y murió en 1508, por tanto era un año más joven que Jeroni Pau, quien había nacido en 1458 y murió en 1497, el 22 de marzo.

[16] El manuscrito belga aparece descrito por P. O. Kristeller, *Iter Italicum*, vol. III, 117–118; en el *Catalogue des manuscrits de la Bibliothèque Royale des Ducs de Bourgogne* (Bruselas, 1842), vol. I,

siglo XVI, aparecen por este orden las siguientes obras de Pau. En primer lugar *Barcino* (fols. 1–24v), a continuación el *Hymnus panegyricus in festo diui Aurelii Augustini episcopi Hipponensis* (fols. 24v–37), y finalmente *De fluminibus et montibus Hispaniarum libellus* (fols. 37v–57v). Así pues, se trata de un manuscrito dedicado por completo a obras de nuestro humanista, una *dedication copy*.

La primera pregunta que se nos plantea es la del porqué de la elección de estas obras de Pau y no otras. La respuesta no es fácil, aunque podemos aventurar una hipótesis verosímil: las tres obras son las más extensas de nuestro autor y probablemente las de mayor solidez, aunque no hayan gozado de la misma difusión. Me explicaré. Las dos obras en prosa, *Barcino* y *De fluminibus et montibus Hispaniarum libellus*, que ya aparecían juntas en el manuscrito de la Biblioteca Vaticana del siglo XV y en las ediciones alemanas del siglo XVII, son, sin lugar a dudas, las mayores aportaciones de Jeroni Pau a la literatura humanística; le sitúan en la línea clara del humanismo italiano, amante de los elogios de las ciudades y de las descripciones geográficas, y son la primera gran descripción de una ciudad, Barcelona, y la primera gran descripción geográfica, de los ríos y de las montañas de la Península Ibérica, en la Hispania cuatrocentista.

La situación de privilegio de Pau dentro del humanismo europeo le viene dada por estas dos obras. Prueba de ello son las numerosas ediciones que se realizaron de ambas obras en los siglos posteriores y el hecho de que sirvieron de modelo a no pocas obras parecidas. Las dos obras pueden considerarse canónicas por la innovación que supusieron y por la difusión que tuvieron. Por el contrario el *Hymnus panegyricus in festo diui Aurelii Augustini episcopi Hipponensis* no gozó de la difusión de las obras anteriores y sin embargo su sola extensión de 387 perfectos hexámetros y su indudable calidad le hacían merecedor de una atención mayor, que alguien le supo prestar.

La reflexión a la que nos conduce el hecho de encontrar por primera vez juntas en un mismo volumen, aunque sea manuscrito, las dos obras en prosa y el más extenso poema de Jeroni Pau debe ser la que nos certifica una vez más la difusión que tuvo su obra en la Europa contemporánea a nuestro personaje o inmediatamente posterior. La reflexión nos añade un aspecto del todo positivo a la recepción y conocimiento de Pau en las cortes europeas, la del interés que sus obras despertaban, y muy especialmente dos de ellas, la descripción de Barcelona y la descripción de los ríos y las montañas de España, que no sólo fueron impresas prontamente, sino que además fueron reservadas a paladares exquisitos que quisieron degustarlas en versión manuscrita para ellos solos.

Hay otro hecho que, a la luz de la aparición de los dos nuevos manuscritos, se nos pone en evidencia. Los dos manuscritos han coincidido significativamente en copiar una sola de las obras de Pau, el *De fluminibus et montibus Hispaniarum libellus*. Con ello la obra se sitúa en primer lugar entre las de Pau, si atendemos a sus distintas reproducciones, y prescindiendo una vez más de la *Practica Cancellariae Apostolicae*. Son

---

212; en R. Calcoen, *Inventaire des manuscrits scientifiques de la Bibliothèque Royale de Belgique* (Bruselas, 1965–1975), vol. III, 36, núm. 301; y finalmente por J. van den Gheyn, *Catalogue des manuscrits de la Bibliothèque Royale des Ducs de Bourgogne* (Bruselas, 1901–1948), vol. X, 36, núm. 6797.

cinco los manuscritos que nos han transmitido el *De fluminibus et montibus Hispaniarum libellus*. Además de los dos que estudiamos ahora, ambos del siglo XVI, se conserva otro en la Biblioteca Vaticana del siglo XV, otro en la Biblioteca Nacional de Madrid del siglo XVI y finalmente otro en la Biblioteca de la Real Academia de la Historia de Madrid del siglo XIX. Tenemos una edición romana de 1491 y dos ediciones del siglo XVII, de Frankfurt y de Colonia. En cambio la obra *Barcino*, se nos ha conservado sólo en tres manuscritos, el de la Biblioteca Vaticana del siglo XV y los de la Bibliothèque Royale de Bruselas y de la Biblioteca del Real Monasterio de El Escorial, ambos del siglo XVI. Tenemos tambien una edición de 1491, pero de Barcelona, las dos ediciones germanas del siglo XVII y dos ediciones de 1914 y 1957.[17]

Quinta cuestión: crítica textual y nuevas variantes para el *Hymnus*

La aparición de los nuevos manuscritos me ha obligado a cotejar nuevamente las distintas versiones de la obra de Pau, añadir las posibles nuevas variantes y buscar la filiación de los manuscritos de Munich y de Bruselas. Aquí trataré solamente del *Hymnus panegyricus*.

El hecho de que, en el manuscrito conservado en Bruselas, se copiase el largo poema de Pau dedicado a San Agustín, significa entre otras cosas que ya no contamos con un manuscrito único para su edición, sino que finalmente hemos podido cotejar nuestro texto, de complicadísima edición en su momento, con una copia, si no contemporánea, muy poco posterior. La revisión del poema nos ha reafirmado en la validez de nuestra edición, puesto que esta copia, mucho más clara y ordenada que nuestro original no aporta grandes ni significativas novedades respecto de lo que ya conocíamos.

Vamos a dar un repaso a las dificultades que presentó la edición crítica del poema hexamétrico. El único texto provenía del Archivo Capitular de Girona y del manuscrito de Pere Miquel Carbonell, donde el archivero barcelonés conservó la mayor parte de la producción poética de Pau. Carbonell copió el texto del poema de manera fragmentaria y con múltiples correcciones. Incluso llegó a añadir páginas sueltas a su códice, con referencias cruzadas sobre el lugar concreto donde debían situarse los versos compuestos con posterioridad por el autor y enviados al copista después de haber copiado éste una primera versión. Se trata efectivamente de un borrador, de las dos primeras versiones de la obra, una primera copiada de manera continuada, corregida encima en un segundo estadio y con muchos añadidos, de manera que el texto no puede leerse seguido, sino con las interrupciones que suponen las constantes llamadas a fragmentos añadidos posteriormente. El propio Carbonell a la vista de lo intrincado del texto que transmitía, tan poco frecuente en él, que destacaba precisamente por la pulcritud de sus manuscritos, se disculpaba en una nota al principio del poema, y aclaraba que nadie debía asombrarse si el Himno resultaba *ita sordidus et male tractatus ac in pluribus locis emendatus, non enim culpa fuit scribentis sed edentis, qui post*

---

[17] El censo completo de las obras de Pau con sus lugares de ubicación se puede consultar en Vilallonga, *La literatura llatina*, 182–186.

illius editionem multum emendauit et resecauit atque addidit. Sin embargo, ahora, a la vista de la copia del texto entero que nos ha llegado, podemos afirmar que Carbonell supo remitir a la perfección los versos que le iba enviando Jeroni Pau.

Evidentemente, debieron de existir más copias del poema, al menos una copia (o quizá una edición?) intermedia entre el borrador que nos legó Carbonell y la versión recientemente conocida e incorporada ahora a la edición crítica del poema. Por lo que, a pesar de la recensión de las nuevas variantes que he realizado, quedará todavía incompleta la edición crítica de la obra. De momento sólo contamos con la copia de Carbonell y la del manuscrito de Bruselas.

Nos fijaremos en algunas de las variantes que he podido recoger y en su significación. Vamos a distribuirlas en diversos grupos. En primer lugar habrá que reseñar los más que probables **errores de copista** detectados en la nueva versión de Bruselas. Entre ellos cabe destacar un *pulisis* por *pulsis* en el v. 22, un *sceua* por *saeua* en el v. 34, un *prestansior* por *praestantior* en el v. 46, un *a tribus* por *artibus* en el v. 49, un *pelagis* por *Pelasgis* en el v. 71, un *sors* por *fors* en el v. 105 (*fors* formaria figura etimológica con un *fortunas* del v. 104), un *possent* por *possint* en el v. 106, un *possis* por *poscis* en el v. 107, un *prefundier* por *perfundier* en el v. 121, un *uidebant* por *iubebant* en el v. 134, un *inuitum* por *inuitus* en el v. 135, un *sacrique* por *sacri quae* en el v. 137, un *immitens* por *immites* en el v. 139, un *aut* por *et* en el v. 145, un *nec* por *non* en el v. 151, un *lacescere* por *lacessere* en el v. 155, un *illi* por *isti* en el v. 160, un *talibus* por *tabulis* en el v. 178, un *ritus uerbis* por *uerbis ritus* en el v. 184, un *nec* por *non* en el v. 191, un *nec* por *haec* en el v. 200, un *ductores* por *ductoris* en el v. 214, un *uidebo* por *iubebo* en el v. 226, un *Olenis* por *Olenes* en el v. 255, un *taceant Tamolsidis* por *taceantque Zemolsidis* en el v. 255, un *allidere* por *alludere* en el v. 265, un *Gynmaneos* por *Cynnameos* en el v. 280, un *sequantur* por *sequuntur* en el v. 290, un *pacatis* por *paccatrix* en el v. 293, un *aeterna* por *aeternae* en el v. 318, un *quodque* por *quidque* en el v. 333 y finalmente un *celebratque* por *celebrataque* en el v. 375.

En segundo lugar hay que reseñar unas pocas **variantes significativas**, que nos han hecho suponer que la copia de Bruselas deriva de una versión distinta de la conocida. Pertenecerían a este grupo un *in* en lugar de un *ne* en el v. 35, un *corpore* por *pectore* en el v. 51, un *censitur* por *censuue* en el v. 133, la omisión de un *est* al final del v. 207, un *necit* por *gessit* en el v. 211, un *dulcia* por *dulci* en el v. 286, un *sacra* por *caeca* en el v. 325, un *cordis* por *mentis* en el v. 329. Algunas de estas variantes podrían ser consideradas como intervenciones directas o correcciones del copista de Bruselas sobre el texto de Pau, o bien variantes procedentes de una versión nueva del texto de Pau, quizá la definitiva, que no conocemos. De todos modos, dadas las características de estas variantes, me inclino más por la primera posibilidad, puesto que no aportan correcciones aceptables.

En cambio hay otro grupo de **variantes significativas** que debemos tener en cuenta, ya que nos ofrecen lecturas que mejoran el texto de Pau. Las veremos una a una. Algunas de ellas tienen relación con las conjeturas que realicé en la edición del Himno. El número de conjeturas no era elevado, puesto que a pesar de las dificultades de recomposición del texto por los motivos ya comentados, Carbonell ponía todo su cuidado en reproducir lo más fielmente posible aquello que nos quería legar, con gran interés por su parte. Así, las conjeturas aducidas en aquellos momentos se refieren más bien a correcciones, que en algunos casos habrán de ser rectificadas a la luz de la nueva versión.

De las ocho conjeturas que había realizado, la mayoría de las cuales no era más que correcciones por falta de rigor sintáctico o métrico, cuatro de ellas pueden ser confirmadas ahora por la copia de Bruselas. Se trata de las siguientes: en el v. 97 aparece un *commitata* en G, que corregí *comitata*, lectura que se ve confirmada por *Bru*. En el v. 228, G daba *miraculo* forma que no podía aceptarse ni métrica ni sintácticamente tal y como expliqué entonces[18] y que corregí por *miracula*, lo mismo que hace *Bru*. Algo parecido ocurre con *fallacis* del v. 252, conjetura que corregía la lectura *fallaciis* del ms. de Gerona y que aparece tambien en el ms. de Bruselas. Por último en el v. 284 se leía *opulentius* en G y corregí por *opulentus*, tambien por las mismas razones anteriores, lectura que aparece en el manuscrito de Bruselas.

Por otro lado en el v. 96 corregí *legis* por *legi*, lectura que daba el manuscrito de Gerona coincidente con la del manuscrito de Bruselas, lo que me ha hecho reconsiderar la conjetura que debo desestimar ahora por razones sintácticas, que producen una ligera variación en el significado del texto, puesto que no se trata de un genitivo, sino de un dativo. Por otro lado me quedé corta al realizar una conjetura en el v. 269, al suponer que la lectura *Phleget* de G debía substituirse por *Phlegethon*, cuando en realidad la conjetura no solucionaba todos los problemas métricos del verso, cosa que sí hace la nueva lectura de *Bru* que aceptaré a partir de ahora *Phlegethontis*.

Sigo pensando que debo mantener las dos conjeturas restantes de los v. 213 *ut* y 221 *tum*, a pesar de que tanto G como *Bru* omiten ambas formas. Y al mismo tiempo creo que debería aceptar las lecturas de *Bru* en los casos siguientes. En el v. 118 la lectura *flexisse* que aparece en Bruselas es mucho más conveniente que la anterior *frexisse* del manuscrito de Girona, que no acerté a corregir. En el v. 219 la lectura del adjectivo *afflictis* de Bruselas calificando a *rebus*, produce una iunctura ciceroniana que me parece mucho más acertada que la lectura de *afflictus* que daba el códice gerundense. Finalmente en el v. 292 la lectura del ms. de Bruselas, más correcta creo, es *iusticia* frente a *iusticiae* que ofrecía el ms. de Gerona.

Para terminar querría aducir un error que se escapó en mi edición, se trata de la forma *quaque* del v. 56, debe leerse *quaeque*, puesto que así aparece tanto en el manuscrito gerundense como en el de Bruselas.

Finalmente debo señalar las coincidencias con alguna versión anterior corregida en el mismo texto que nos legó Carbonell, pero mantenida en la versión de Bruselas, así tenemos en el ms. de Bruselas un *qui prius ut* por *quique prius* procedente de un anterior *quique prius ut* en el v. 45, lo mismo ocurre con un *reddit* por *reddet* en el v. 228, un *fessa* por *fassa* en el v. 230 y un *tinnitibus* por *bombicibus* en el v. 289, lecturas de Bruselas coincidentes con las lecturas de Girona antes de la corrección por una mano distinta de la de Carbonell en los cuatro casos.

En último lugar querría añadir que en la versión de Bruselas faltan los versos 43–

---

[18] Ver al respecto Vilallonga, *Jeroni Pau,* nota 44 del vol. II, 197, en la que comento las razones que me llevaron a realizar la conjetura.

44, y que en el manuscrito de Gerona fueron señalados por Carbonell con una cruz al comienzo de cada uno de ellos como para suprimirlos, igual que en otras ocasiones, pero sin llegar a tacharlos.

Dejo para otra ocasión la revisión del aparato crítico de las obras en prosa de Pau. Su interés es menor, puesto que para fijar el texto conté con muchas más copias e incluso ediciones que para el texto del poema panegírico dedicado a San Agustín, de manuscrito único.

Universitat de Girona

Die spanische Eroberung Mexikos im späten neulateinischen Epos: Giambattista Marienis Cortesius nondum absolutus *von 1729*

HERMANN WIEGAND

Die Erschliessung und Eroberung der neuen Welt durch die Spanier hat in der neulateinischen Literatur und Dichtung breiten Widerhall gefunden. Seit den *De novo orbe decades octo* des Petrus Martyr von Angleria, die gesammelt 1530 publiziert wurden, nahmen humanistische Autoren und neulateinische Poeten immer wieder Bezug auf dieses epochemachende Ereignis an der Wende vom 15. zum 16. Jahrhundert. Christoph Columbus' Entdeckerfahrt wurde ebenso gewürdigt wie die Eroberung Mexikos durch Hernán Cortés.[1] In der neulateinischen Dichtung besteht freilich ein deutliches Ungleichgewicht der Behandlung "amerikanischer" Themen. Während Columbus zwischen 1581 und 1730 nicht weniger als fünfmal Gegenstand z. T. umfangreicher Epen wurde, ist Hernán Cortés aus Medellín, der Eroberer des Aztekenreiches, weit seltener von neulateinischen Poeten als Sujet eines grösseren poetischen Werkes gewählt worden. Hingegen war er in der spanischen Literatur des "Goldenen Zeitalters" bereits mehrfach Held eines volkssprachlichen epischen Gedichtes geworden.[2] Eine Ausnahme von dieser poetischen Nichtbeachtung des Cortés-Stoffes in der neulateinischen Literatur bildet das Jesuitendrama. Allein in der neulateinischen Schuldramenproduktion der Jesuiten in Deutschland wurde Cortés

---

[1] Juan Ginés de Sepúlveda beschreibt etwa in klassischem Latein in den Büchern III bis VII seines Werkes *De orbo novo* ausführlich die Eroberung Mexikos. Vgl. die Edition von de Verger A. Ramírez, *Ioannes Genesius Sepulveda Cordubensis De Orbo Novo* (Stuttgart und Leipzig, 1993).

[2] Zu der Behandlung von Cortés in der spanischen Literatur vgl. Winston A. Reynolds, *Hernán Cortés en la literatura del Siglo de Oro* (Madrid, 1978). Vgl. auch Elisabeth Frenzel, *Stoffe der Weltliteratur. Ein Lexikon dichtungsgeschichtlicher Längsschnitte*, 4 Aufl. (Stuttgart, 1976), 491–498, dort Nennung zahlreicher Bearbeitungen des Cortés-Stoffes.

zwischen 1670 und 1764 nicht weniger als sechzehn Mal auf der Bühne vorgestellt, und zwar nahezu immer unter dem gleichen Aspekt: Herausgestellt wird der spanische *miles et apostolus* vor allem als glühender Marienverehrer.[3] Aber wenige neulateinische Epiker haben sich des Stoffes angenommen, ausser einem kleineren Werk, das auf diesem Kongress vorstellt wird, ist Hernán Cortés meines Wissens nur einmal Titelheld einer grösseren neulateinischen Epos geworden, das—soweit ich sehe—bisher in der wissenschaftlichen Literatur keine Beachtung gefunden hat. Es trägt den Titel JOANNIS BAPTISTAE/ MARIENI/ BRIXIENSIS/ CORTESIUS/ NONDUM ABSOLUTUS und ist in Venedig 1729 publiziert worden.[4] Auf 221 Seiten mit etwa 5400 hexametrischen Versen erzählt der Dichter Episoden aus der Eroberungsgeschichte Mexikos. Von den ursprünglich wohl geplanten zwölf Büchern sind ganz ausgeführt das erste, dritte und sechste bis zehnte, ein Fragment des elften Buches, an dessen Ende ein *Desunt caetera* den schon durch den Titel indizierten fragmentarischen Charakter des Werkes unterstreicht, bricht mitten im Text ab. Dass ein italienischer späthumanistischer Dichter aus Brescia[5] sich einem Stoff zuwendet, der ein national-spanischer ist, mag auf den ersten Blick verwundern, freilich waren amerikanische Stoffe im 18. Jahrhundert in ganz Europa beliebt.

Marienis *Cortesius* ist in seiner poetischen Faktur weit mehr als der Cortés-Stoff-Tradition einem neulateinischen Epos verpflichtet, das vierzehn Jahre vor seinem Werk erstmals in Rom erschienen war und als bedeutendstes der neulateinichen Columbus-Epen gelten kann: der *Columbus. Carmen Epicum* des Soraner Jesuiten Ubertino Carrara.[6] Ohne die Anregung dieses Erneuerers der neulateinischen Dichtung in Italien im 18. Jahrhundert ist das Cortés-Epos Marienis kaum denkbar. Wie der *Columbus* Carraras orientiert sich der *Cortesius* nicht nur an Vergils *Aeneis*—dessen Buchzahl der Brescianer zwar nicht erreicht—aber anstrebt, sondern spiegelt wie Carraras *Columbus* Konfigurationen und Strukturen des vergilischen Epos. Manche Gestalten des *Cortesius* sind wie viele des *Columbus* nach vergilischen Vorbildern modelliert. Marieni folgt Carrara auch darin, dass er die Erzählstruktur des vergilischen Epos über weite Strecken aufbricht: Lange Rückblicke und Exkurse überwuchern streckenweise den Handlungsgang, der wohl in der Eroberung Mexikos gipfeln sollte. Aus der neulateinischen didaktisch-aitiologischen Tradition des gerade im 18. Jahrhundert

---

[3] Vgl. Ruprecht Wimmer, "Hernán Cortés in der Geschichtsschreibung und auf dem Theater der Jesuite", in *Von der Weltharte zum Kuriositätenkabinett. Amerika im deutschen Humanismus und Barock,* hrsg. Karl Kohut, Publikationen des Zentralinstituts für Lateinamerika-Studien der Katholischen Universität Eichstätt, Serie A: Kongress-Akten 14 (Frankfurt am Main, 1995), 231–243.

[4] JOANNIS BAPTISTAE/ MARIENI/ BRIXIENSIS/ CORTESIUS/ NONDUM ABSOLUTUS./ VENETIIS, MDCCXXIX. Typis Dominici Lovisa. *Superiorum Permissu.*

[5] Zu ihm vgl. ganz kurz Vincenzo Peroni, *Biblioteca bresciana*, vol. 2 (Brescia, 1818–1823), 222: Marieni Giambattista di Brescia, poeta latino. Fioriva nel principio del secolo XVIII.

[6] Vgl. jetzt die—leider im lateinischen Text mitunter fehlerhafte—Ausgabe: Ubertino Carrara, *Columbus*. Traduzione poetica e note di Mario Martini. Testo a fronte. Prefazione de Miquel Batllori (Sora, 1992).

in Italien noch lebhaft gepflegten neulateinischen Lehrgedichtes stammt eine lange, von der *Syphilis*-Dichtung Fracastoros inspirierte Erzählung über den *Chocolates* im dritten oder solche über Schwefel und andere für die Pulverherstellung benötigte Substanzen im achten Buch des *Cortesius*. Zahlreiche in das Werk eingelegte Reden reflektieren die antike historiographische Tradition.

Vor allem wird der Einfluss Carraras auf Marieni in der Konzeption seines Helden sichtbar. Wie der Columbus Carraras ist der *Cortesius* Marienis ganz als der glaubensstarke Hidalgo angelegt, dessen Mission es ist, das Aztekenreich dem christlichen Glauben zuzuführen. Historisch getreue Darstellung wird man schwerlich von einem neulateinischen Epos des 18. Jahrhunderts über die Conquista des 16. Jahrhunderts erwarten, ist aber doch erstaunt zu sehen, wie frei Marieni mit der historischen Überlieferung schaltet. Zwar klingen einige Personennamen wie *Aguilarus, Sandovalus, Ordas, Marina* u.a. an Persönlichkeiten an, die aus der Eroberungsgeschichte Mexikos bekannt sind, aber deren Träger im Epos haben meist sehr wenig mit den historischen Personen gemein. So ist etwa der *Ordas* Marienis ein treuer Gefolgsmann des Cortés, während die historische Person ein Anhänger von Cortés Gegenspieler Velasquez war. *Dona Marina,* die aztekische Malintzin, die Cortés als Dolmetscherin und Geliebte diente, wird in Marienis Werk zu einer Amazone, die sogar ihre Heimat verlassen muss, weil sie ihre *virginitas* bewahren will. Ähnlich frei zeichnet Marieni die indianischen Gegner des Cortés. Moctecuzoma-Montezuma kommt überhaupt nicht vor, da Marieni gar nicht von der ersten Expedition des Cortés vor der *noche triste* berichtet, sondern nur einen Feldzug schildert, der zur Belagerung von Mexiko-Tenochtitlan führt. Deshalb tritt als sein Feind gleich zu Beginn *Guatimozinus*-Cuauhtemoc auf, dessen Sohn *Amozinus* in die Gefangenschaft der Spanier gerät und für den Fortgang der Handlung eine nicht unwichtige Rolle spielt. Gleichwohl hat Marieni sicher historische Quellen zur Geschichte des Cortés gekannt. Den Marsch des Conquistadors auf *Mexicus*-Tenochtitlan skizziert er—wenn auch knapp—recht zuverlässig am Ende des 7. Buches: u.a. erwähnt er die sogenannte Schlacht bei Otumba.

Da der *Cortesius* Marienis kaum bekannt sein dürfte—der Text scheint sehr selten zu sein—soll im folgenden zunächst der Gang des Epos nachgezeichnet werden.

(Buch I) Nach der traditionellen Eröffnung durch die Anrufung der Musa bekennt der Autor zunächst, zu erschöpft zu sein, um das Werk noch vollenden zu können. So wie ein Baumeister zunächst nur die Seitenwände aufführe, wolle auch er sein unvollendetes Werk dem Leser darbieten. Mit einer Zeitangabe setzt die eigentliche Erzählung ein. Die Handlung beginnt drei Sommer, nachdem der Spanier Cortés von Gades abgesegelt war. Gleich zu Beginn des Werkes wird seine göttliche Sendung betont: Ein vom Himmel gesandter Engel hatte ihm Gottes Auftrag übermittelt:

> *Ut domitos late populos, & Marte subactos*
> *Relligio sancta instituat, Fideique jubenti*
> *Servit armatum Bellum. . . . (p. 4)*

So ist ihm Gott Urheber seiner heldenhaften Fahrt: *impellit Deus author euntem* (p. 5). Der Bericht wendet sich zunächst der Stadt *Mexicus*-Tenochtitlan zu, deren Charakterisierung nach der Karthagos im ersten Buch der *Aeneis* Vergils gegeben wird:

> *Urbs antiqua, ingens, Princeps, sceptroque superba,*
> *Dives opum . . .* (p. 5)[7]

um dann ihre Lage in einem See näher zu beschreiben.

Zahlreiche *prodigia* beunruhigen den noch jungen *Guatimozinus,* einen kriegsmächtigen Herrscher. Dieser hat einen furchtbaren Traum: Ein Ungeheuer, teils Vogel, teils Fisch, taucht aus dem See um Tenochtitlan auf, dringt in den Palast ein und wird von *Guatimozinus* mit einem Pfeilschuss zwischen die Augen getötet. Der Priester *Orchamus* deutet dieses Ungeheuer als *urbs Mexicus.* Männer von einem anderen Himmelsstrich würden kommen, um das Aztekenvolk auszulöschen. Unterdessen kommen von Cortés Gesandte, die in langer Rede dem Aztekenherrscher, wofern er sich nur Gott unterwerfe, Frieden und Bündnis anbieten. Die Azteken beraten, was zu tun sei, *Carses* stimmt für Frieden, der Spanier werde leicht auf die Religionsbedingung eingehen, da es ihm nur um die *fama* und Beifall gehe, sei so doch die Charakteranlage des spanischen Volkes (*quod ferme gentis Iberae/Ingenium est,* p. 18). Gegen den Frieden äussern sich der vornehme *Tarzarius* und der Priester *Orchamus,* der zur Verteidigung der alten Religion auffordert. Die Meinung der Letzteren setzt sich durch, die spanischen Gesandten werden gegen alles Recht gefangen gesetzt, nach einer Opferprozession getötet und gegessen. Den Spaniern erklären die Azteken den Krieg. Cortés eröffnet seinerseits den Angriff auf die Stadt, die spanischen Kriegshelden passieren in einem Katalog Revue. Unter ihnen befindet sich auch die Indianerin *Marina,* der *Martia virtus* eignet. Sie hatte ihre Heimat verlassen müssen und sich als Krieger verkleidet den Spaniern angeschlossen. Die *virgo* offenbarte sich Cortés und liess sich taufen.

Das dritte Buch, das im spanischen Feldlager spielt, wird zum grössten Teil von einer aitiologischen Erzählung eingenommen, die dem herrlichen Trank *Chocolates* gewidmet ist, den Eingeborene kredenzen. Solche Elemente eines *carmen didascalicum* finden sich in zahlreichen neulateinischen Epen vor allem des 17. und 18. Jahrhunderts, wie überhaupt in den Epen der Spätzeit die Auflösung der strengen epischen Erzählform und Gattungsmischungen gerade mit der Lehrdichtung zu beobachten sind.

Das nicht ausgeführte fünfte Buch sollte nach Ausweis einer Marginalie (p. 68) die Gefangennahme von *Amozinus,* dem Sohn des *Guatimozinus,* durch Cortés schildern. Mit dem sechsten Buch beginnt der bis zum zehnten durchgängig ausgeführte Teil des Epos. Im sechsten erzählt der getreue Gefolgsmann *Ordas* dem gefangenen, auf Befehl des Cortés mit aller Ehrerbietung behandelten Prinzen von der Herkunft und den ritterlichen Taten seines *Ductor.* Obwohl er einen Gegner in einem ritterlichen Turnier bezwungen hatte, neidet ihm eine in diesen verliebte Dame den Erfolg und verlangt einen zweiten Kampf, dem sich Cortés gegen den Rat seiner Freunde erneut siegreich stellt. Dieses Ritterspiel war nur das Vorspiel der *vera certamina,* die Cortés auf Geheiss Gottes nunmehr zu bestehen hat. Cortés landet in Kuba und befiehlt den Bau von fünf Schiffen zu den bereits vorhandenen. Da tritt *Satanas* auf den Plan, der verhindern will, dass Cortés in Mexiko landet und stiftet einen Mann namens *Bartus* an, die Seeleute zur Zerstörung der Flotte aufzuhetzen. Diese Episode hat ihr Vorbild

---

[7] Vgl. Vergil, *Aeneis* 1, 12–14.

in der Zerstörung der troischen Schiffe im fünften Buch der *Aeneis* Vergils (V. 605–699). Zugleich bildet wohl eine Episode in mehreren Columbus-Epen das Vorbild dieser Szene. Auch in der poetischen Cortés-Tradition taucht das Motiv der Schiffeverbrennung auf, allerdings ist es dort zumeist Hernán Cortés selbst, der die Schiffe nach der Landung in Yucatan selbst in Brand steckt, um seinen Gefolgsleuten die Möglichkeit zur Rückkehr nach Kuba zu nehmen.[8] Marienis Gestaltung des Themas ist der vergilischen ganz analog: So wie die Troerinnen das Verbleiben in Sizilien erzwingen wollen, will der Satan Cortés an der Erfüllung seiner göttlichen Mission hindern. Der *Cortesius* Marienis wird in seiner Reaktion ganz als erhabener Held gezeichnet, der den Gegnern schon durch seine Erscheinung Furcht einflösst (p. 85).

Durch Cortés Eingreifen wird der Brand gelöscht, der unedle *Bartus* in Ketten gelegt und die Schiffe zu Wasser gelassen. Mit dem goldenen Kreuz als Zeichen des Cortés (*Crux aurea, signum Cortesii*, p. 91) setzt die Flotte ihre Fahrt fort (Buch VII). Trotz weiterer Ränke Satans landet die Flotte schliesslich in *Cozumel*, wo es *Ordas* gelingt, *Aguilarus* vor eingeborenen Verfolgern zu retten. Dieser *Aguilarus*, eine historische Persönlichkeit,[9] erzählt seinem Lebensretter von seinem Schicksal: Als Schiffbrüchiger heiratet er eine Eingeborene, mit der er mehrere Kinder zeugt. Alle bekennen sich zum Christentum. Als sie sich weigern, dem Gott *Cozumel* Opfer darzubringen, ja *Aguilarus* sogar versucht, die Eingeborenen zu bekehren, soll er mit seiner ganzen Familie nach dem Urteil des Oberpriesters getötet werden. Diese Opferszene wird von Marieni in düsteren Farben gemalt, die die brutale Grausamkeit der heidnischen Priester und die Blutgier der Zuschauer illustrieren und die Heilstat der Spanier in ein helles Licht rücken soll: Die Kinder des *Aguilarus* sterben als christliche Märtyrer und ihr Vater ist stolz, sie gezeugt zu haben:

> *Non alius pater, aut genitrix foelicior ulla*
> *Esse potest nobis, qui nostri quotquot amoris*
> *Pignora sunt suscepta, Deo, Fideique dicamus.* (p. 120)

Mit der Beschreibung des Weges von Yucatan nach Mexiko endet die Erzählung des *Ordas.*

Das achte Buch knüpft an das nicht ausgeführte fünfte an: Die Spanier leiden unter Pulvermangel und beratschlagen, was zu tun sei. In breit ausgeführten Reden erörtern *Floresius*, der zum zeitweiligen Rückzug rät, *Bravo Ruiz*, der das Aushungern der Stadt empfiehlt, und *Sotelius Sisaponensis*, der einen den Spaniern allein angemessenen heldischen Angriff empfiehlt, die Lage. Man entschliesst sich, den Kastilier *Sandovalus* und den *Cantaber Ordas* loszuschicken, um Nitrat zu suchen. Inzwischen haben aber die Bewohner Mexikos gemerkt, dass die Spanier kaum mehr über Pulver

---

[8] Vgl. Frenzel, *Stoffe*, 494f.

[9] Gerónimo de Aguilar war 1511 an der Küste von Yukatan gestrandet, hatte bei den Mayas als Sklave gedient und fungierte nun für Cortés als Dolmetscher. Zu ihm vgl. Hugh Thomas, *Die Eroberung Mexikos. Cortés und Montezuma* (Frankfurt/Main, 1998), 93 und öfter. Thomas' Werk ist die derzeit ausführlichste Darstellung der historischen Vorgänge und auch für die übrigen Personen heranzuziehen.

verfügen. Der Magier *Chasaphus*, der verbrecherische Bastard einer Priesterin, erbietet sich, Zwietracht unter den Spaniern zu säen, indem er durch eine nekromantische Beschwörung einen zweiten *Ordas* auftreten lässt, der *Sandovalus* angreift und damit den echten *Ordas* dem Verdacht aussetzt, aus Herrschgier Verrat an der Sache der Spanier verübt zu haben. Diese ausführlich wiedergegebene nekromantische Szene ist offensichtlich von der Nekromantieszene der Hexe Erictho aus dem sechsten Buch der *Pharsalia* Lucans beeinflusst, deren Physiognomie ebenso für die des *Chasaphus* Pate gestanden hat wie manche Einzelheit der Darstellung des wiederbelebten Leichnams.[10] Unterdessen sucht der nichtsahnende und Cortés treu ergebene *Ordas* überall nach Pulver, bis er endlich auf einem rauchenden Vulkan fündig wird—es ist wohl der Popocatepetl. Gegen den Willen seiner Gefährten ist *Ordas* bereit, für Cortés sein Leben zu opfern und den Berg zu erkunden. Als er zurückkehrt, sind sie doch willens ihm zu folgen und den Schwefel zu holen, dessen verschiedene Arten wieder wie in einem *carmen didascalicum* am Ende des achten Buches beschrieben werden. Zu Beginn den neunten Buches, das wie die folgenden den Kampfbüchern der *Aeneis* korrespondiert, kehren die Gefährten des *Sandovalus* in das spanische Lager zurück und berichten von dem Überfall des vermeintlichen *Ordas* auf ihre Gruppe. *Ordas* wird vor Cortés, der in Zweifel gestürzt wird, des Verrats beschuldigt. Während im spanischen Lager Unfrieden herrscht, als *Sandovalus* schwer verletzt zurückkehrt, entschliesst sich *Guatimozinus* zum Angriff. Marieni erzählt als Einschub wohl unter dem Einfluss Torquato Tassos die Liebesgeschichte von dessen Tochter *Myrteis*, die von den Rivalen *Arastes*, den sie liebt, und *Tarzarus* umworben wird.

Im Kampf selbst sticht *Guatimozinus* durch Tapferkeit hervor, gegen ihn kämpft der Spanier *Barbas*, den der Mexikaner im erbitterten Reitergefecht tötet. Von den übrigen Kämpfern wird besonders das indianische Brüderpaar *Marsus* und *Lycas* gerühmt, in ihrer unzertrennlichen brüderlichen Treue ein Gegenpaar zu *Nisus* und *Euryalus* im neunten Buch der *Aeneis*. Ihre verwitwete Mutter will sie vom Krieg abhalten, aber die Jungen stürmen in den Kampf. Ihre Siege rufen die *bellatrix Virgo Marina* auf den Plan, deren Gestalt nach der Amazone Camilla im elften Buch der *Aeneis* modelliert ist.[11] Die beiden Brüder, die füreinander zu sterben bereit sind— ein *fraterni exemplar amoris* (p. 173)—werden von *Marina* getötet. Es gelingt ihr aber als *maior [. . .] gloria dextrae Arastes*, der auf der Suche nach *Amozinus* über das Schlachtfeld reitet, gefangen zu nehmen. Ausführlich schildert Marieni die sich anschliessende Reiterschlacht—er trägt offensichtlich keine Bedenken, auch die Azteken ohne weiteres zu Pferd kämpfen zu lassen—im vergilischen Farben. Die beiden Protagonisten des Kampfes, *Guatimozinus* und Cortés, beherrschen die Szene: *Guatimozinus* tötet den engen Gefährten des Cortés *Barbas*, dem zu Beginn des zehnten Buches ein feierliches Leichenbegängnis zuteil wird—eine Spiegelung der *Pallas*-Episode in der *Aeneis*.[12] *Cortés* erweist sich in seinem Einsatz als unüberwindlicher

---

[10] Beispielsweise hat sie ein Gesicht *foeda situ macies*, Lucan, *Pharsalia* 6, 616, und Chasaphus *Stat macie absumptus senior* (*Cortesius*, p. 143), auch tötet sie für ihre magischen Praktiken wie Chasaphus Kinder.

[11] Vgl. Vergil, *Aeneis* 11, 532ff.

[12] Vgl. besonders Vergil, *Aeneis* 10, 445–489; 11, 139–181.

Heros, der mit mehreren Feinden gleichzeitig kämpfen kann. Seine durch den Tod des *Barbas* gesteigerte Kampfeswut gipfelt in der Aristie bei der Begegnung mit *Guatimozinus*. Beide kämpfen mit höchster Anstrengung, Cortés nicht zuletzt angestachelt durch *Fidei contemptus honos, & Numinis alti Relligio* (p. 178). Cortés' Gefolgsmann *Portillus* ist jedoch nicht damit zufrieden, bei dem Kampf nur Zuschauer zu sein, sondern fordert seine Landsleute als tapfere Spanier auf (*Cur fecit natura viros? cur fecit Iberos?*, p. 179), für den Feldherrn zu den Waffen zu greifen. Das Kriegsglück neigt sich schliesslich ze den Azteken. Als *Chasaphus*, darüber erfreut, auf neue Listen sinnt, trifft ihn die rächende Hand Gottes.

Das elfte Buch wird von drei Themenkreisen bestimmt: Zunächst wird—wie schon erwähnt—*Barbas* in einem feierlichen Leichenbegängnis bestattet. Dann wird der Faden der *Myrteis*-Erzählung aus dem achten Buch wiederaufgenommen. Da ein Zweikampf ihrer beiden Liebhaber unentschieden ausgeht, entschliesst sich *Myrteis*, nachts aus Mexiko zu fliehen und sich mit *Arastes* zu verheiraten. Diese Episode wird auf der Folie der *Pyramus* und *Thisbe*-Erzählung Ovids, aber auch des vierten Buches des *Aeneis* mit wörtlichen Anklängen gestaltet. *Arastes* weigert sich aus Ehrgefühl, auf dieses Ansinnen einzugehen. Das Baumgleichnis aus dem Dido-Buch der *Aeneis* wird auf ihn als einen *alter Aeneas* übertragen (p. 200 im Vergleich mit Aeneis 4, 441–449). Verzweifelt begeht *Myrteis* also *altera Dido* Selbstmord; *Arastes* tötet sich darauf mit dem Schwert und Cortés lässt beide ehrenvoll bestatten.

Im folgenden wird die *Ordas*-Episode aus dem achten Buch wiederaufgenommen. *Ordas* kehrt nichtsahnend ins spanische Lager zurück und die erzürnten Spanier wollen ihn töten. Cortés mahnt zur Besonnenheit und veranlasst ein Gericht über den vermeintlichen Verräter. Da greift Gott ein und lässt einen gefangenen Azteken die list des *Chasaphus* aufdecken. *Ordas'* Unschuld wird offenbar. Dem Fragment des elften Buches kommt für die Zielsetzung des ganzen Epos grosse Bedeutung zu: In ihm werden die Mächte der Hölle unter Führung Satans direkt den himmlischen Heerscharen unter Führung des Erzengels Michael konfrontiert. Das weitere Geschehen, also wohl der siegreiche Angriff der Spanier auf die Stadt *Mexicus*, wird damit auf die Ebene einer Auseinandersetzung der transzendenten Mächte der gefallenen und noch bei Gott seienden Engel projiziert. Die Höllenmächte, deren gefallene Engel in einem etwas merkwürdigen Katalog aufgeführt werden, sind durch *furentes . . . irae* (p. 218) gekennzeichnet—Affekte, von denen auch die indianischen Führern ergriffen sind und die schon in der neulateinischen christlichen Epik des sechzehnten Jahrhunderts die Mächte der Hölle charackterisieren, so etwa in der *Syrias* des Petrus Angelius Bargaeus. Einer der Teufel übernimmt die Rolle des vergilischen *Aeolus* im ersten Buch der *Aeneis*, um die neugewonnenen Pulvervorräte der Spanier durch Blitzschlag zu vernichten. Diese Aktionen der Hölle bemerkt der *coeli Dominator & Orbis* (p. 219) und schickt den Erzengel *Michael* mit seinen Heerscharen in den Kampf. *Michael* lenkt mit Hilfe seines glänzenden Schildes den Blitz des Teufelsheeres in einen Turm ab gegen seine Urheber. So kann am Ende des Fragments Marieni den spanischen Feldherrn in einer Apostrophe ansprechen:

> *O foelix Fernande! o praestantissime Ductor,*
> *Et nimius dilecte Deo! Tibi militat aether,*

Atque Erebus, pariuntque novos tibi damna triumphos. . . . (p. 220f.)

Versucht man, den literaturgeschichtlichen Standort des *Cortesius nondum absolutus* zu bestimmen, lässt sich die durchgehende Orientierung am vergilischen Modell konstatieren. In Faktur und Modellierung der Gestalten ist Marieni wie sein Vorbild Ubertino Carrara auf Vergil orientiert, übernimmt aber auch Motive und etwa das *furor*-Konzept für Azteken und Satan oder die Zeichnung des Magiers *Chasaphus* aus Lucans *Pharsalia*. Marienis Konzept seines Haupthelden ist wie bei Carrara das des christlichen Hidalgos, der direkt durch Gottes Weisung geleitet wird. Die transzendenten Mächte, die den antiken Götterapparat ersetzen, bilden der christliche Gott, der nicht selten selbst in die Handlung eingreift, und sein Widersacher, der Satan. Das hängt entscheidend mit Marienis Auffassung der Entdeckung und Eroberung Mexikos zusammen: Für ihn bedeutet die Entdeckung keine zivilisatorische, sondern eine rein religiöse Aufgabe: Cortés ist wie in den Jesuitendramen der Apostel Mexikos. Hier wird der Einfluss von Torquato Tasso's *Gerusalemme liberata* sichtbar. Daraus erwächst für Marienis Vergilisieren ein Problem. Wenn er etwa *Marina* ganz im Gegensatz zur historiographischen Tradition zur alleinkämpfenden Amazone vor der Folie der *Camilla* Vergils macht, so kann er sie zwar im neunten Buch als *altera Camilla* auftreten lassen, dieses Motiv steht aber in deutlichem Widerspruch zum christlich getönten *Virginitas*-Ideal *Marinas* im ersten Buch. Das so gezeichnete *Marina*-Bild spiegelt zugleich die Cortés-Auffassung, der als orthodoxer christlicher Held natürlich keine Geliebte haben darf. Analog zu diesem *Marina*-Bild ist das des *Aguilarus* und seiner Familie angelegt. Es dient nicht nur dazu, die Grausamkeit der heidnischen Bewohner Mexikos zu illustrieren, sondern auch die Sendung der Spanier in der Neuen Welt zu unterstreichen: Nicht die Spanier sind wie in der *leyenda negra* grausam und unmenschlich, sondern ausschliesslich die Repräsentanten des alten Mexiko: Der Grausamkeit des Magiers *Chasaphus* und des *Cozumel*-Priesters—er lässt die Kinder vor den Augen der Eltern töten—enspricht die der Bewohner *Cozumels*, die *laeto [. . .] clamore* (p. 119) die grausame Tötung begleiten.

Im Gegensatz zum Bild der Bewohner Mexikos ist das der Spanier in Marienis Epos durchweg positiv gezeichnet: So erweisen sie sich etwa gegenüber dem gefangenen *Amozinus* als ritterlich. Ihrem Selbstbild nach sind sie besonders tapfer und auf ehrenhaften Ruhm aus. Hernán Cortés schliesslich verkörpert in allem die besten Tugenden der Spanier. Als ritterlicher Kämpfer zeigt er sich schon in seiner Jugend im Turnier, sein Handeln steht immer im Einklang mit dem Willen Gottes, und er erweist sich als fromm, wenn auch diese Frömmigkeit im Unterschied zur jesuitischen Tradition nur marginal Marienfrömmigkeit ist: so errichtet er in Tabasco eine Marienkirche.

Marienis Epos steht damit im Einklang mit der voraufklärerischen, spanienfreundlichen epischen "Entdeckertradition" der italienischen Neulateiner in der Nachfolge von Torquato Tassos *Gerusalemme liberata*. Er will weder von "edlen Wilden" noch von den kritischen Stimmen schon der Zeitgenossen der Conquista in der *leyenda negra* etwas wissen.

Mannheim

Index

Achilles Tatius, 320
Adam, 201, 428
Adelmann von Adelmannsfelden, Bernhard, 605–607
Aelianus, Claudius, 133, 320
Aeneid, 221, 222, 245, 304, 311, 377, 378, 535, 593, 612, 621, 660, 661–662, 663, 664, 665; *see also* Virgil
Africa, 34, 84, 389–396
Agricola
    Rudolf, 606, 607, 610
    Rudolf Junior, 293–299
Agrippa von Nettesheim, Cornelius, 53
Agrippina, 233, 235, 485
Aguilarus, Geronimo de, 663, 666
Albanzani, Donato, 604
Alanus ab Insulis (Alain de Lille), 398
Alcaeus, 271
alchemy, 180
Alciati, Andrea, 95–96, 404
    Emblemata, 19, 96
Alexander VI, Pope, 467, 468, 470
Alexander of Aphrodisias, 597
Alfonso of Aragon, 624, 626
Alighieri, Dante, 223, 361, 624–625, 627
Allegretti, Allegretto, 30
Altieri, Marcantonio, *Li Nuptiali*, 461
Amatus, Johannes Silvius, 295
Amazons, 434, 644, 661
Ambrose, Saint, 260, 337, 503, 614
Amerbach, Johannes, 399
Ammianus Marcellinus, 337, 477
Amozinus, 662, 666
Amphion, 217–226
Angera, Pietro Martire d' (Peter Martyr of Antwerp), 29–39, 659
Angeriano, Girolamo, 11–12
    Carmina, 12

Annius of Viterbo, 87, 215, 363
anthologies, 13–15
anti-colonialism, 237–246
anti-scholasticism, 439–447
Apollinaris, Sidonius, 136
Apuleius, 213
Arabic, study of, 353, 356, 546
Aragón, 227, 247
Arastes, 664, 665
Aréchaga y Casas, Juan de
    Commentaria juris civilis, 156, 157
    Extemporaneae commentationes, 156–157
Argyropoulos, Giovanni, 460, 462
Arias Montano, Benito, 24–25, 20, 106, 107, 109, 110, 193–204, 337
    Commentaria in Isaiae Prophetae Sermones, 201–202
    De Varia Republica, 199–200
    Escorial, Latin distichs at, 20
    Humanae Salutis Monumenta, 25
    Hymni et Secula, 200–201
    Liber Generationis et Regenerationis Adam, 201
    Naturae Historia, 202–204
Ariosto, 320, 372
Aristotle, 61, 71, 153, 154, 218, 219, 223, 337, 489, 597–602, 603–605, 632
    De incessu animalium, 597–602
    Parva Naturalia, 598
    theory of seeds, 285, 286, 289
ars poetica (genre), 217–226
art, theories of, 473–480
Artemidorus, 323
Ascensius, Jodocus Badius, 397–402
Asso, Ignacio Jordán de, 108
astrology, 206
atheism, 284, 288

Atlantis, 32, 73, 74, 80, 86, 87, 89, 90
atomic physics, theories of, 284
Auclou, Robertus, 587
Augustine, of Hippo, Saint, 43, 64, 71,
        184, 211–216, 337, 384, 419, 503,
        546, 635, 653–654
    De Civitate Dei, 211–216
Aulus Gellius, 148, 184, 337, 477
Ausonius, 14
automata, hypothesis of (theory of soul),
        284
Avanzo, Girolamo, 364
Ávila, 409
"azua", 540

Bacon, Francis, 319, 320, 322
Bad Hunneff, 482, 484
Baetica, 83
Balboa, Vasco Nuñez, 38
Baldhove, Georg Martin von, 177–178,
        181
Balearic Islands, 186
Barbaro
    Ermolao, 147
    Francesco, 299
Barbas, 664, 665
Bargaeus, Petrus Angelius, 12, 665
Barlaeus, Caspar, 122
Baronius, Cardinal, 474
Bartholin
    Jacob, 132
    Thomas, 129–138
        correspondence with Ole Wurm,
        130
Bartus, 662–663
Barzizza
    Gasparino, 605
    Guiniforte, 147, 154, 519–526, 623–
        630
Battista, Fregosi, 33
Bayle, Pierre, 283
Beccadelli, Antonio (Antonio Panormita),
        17, 397, 519, 607, 608
Becelli, Guido Cesare, 367
Beheim, Lorenz, 607
Bellarmine, Robert, Cardinal, 543, 548
Bellum Grammaticale, 527
Bembo, Pietro, 12, 14, 17, 490, 494,
        496, 497, 559
Benavides y de la Cueva, Diego de,

Marqués de Solera, viceroy of Peru,
        333–344
    Hispania nautica elogium, 340–344
    Horae Successivae, 335–344
Beroaldo, Filippo, 362
Berossus, 215, 363
Bèze, Théodore de, 565, 567, 572
Bible, 26, 59–60, 87, 148, 152, 179, 184,
        207, 219, 240, 255, 259, 297, 298,
        320, 372, 382–383, 386, 428, 437,
        451, 467, 468, 480, 523–525, 563–
        573, 611, 614
    Complutensian Polyglot, 107
    Estienne printings, 374
    Hebrew, 546–548, 567; *see also*
        Reuchlin
    Neo-Latin, 563
    Septuagint, 215
    Vulgate, 567, 568, 569
Bindoni, Francesco, 371–378
Binet, Etienne, 477
Blancas, Jerónimo de, 247–252
    Aragonensium rerum commentarii, 247
Boccaccio, Giovanni, 43, 147, 184, 219–
        220, 224, 372, 522, 603, 627–628
    De claris mulieribus, 179
    De genealogia gentilium deorum, 42 n. 5,
        148, 219–220, 224
Boethius, 337, 402 n. 38, 459–460
Bogard, Jean, 366
Boiardo, Matteo Maria, 426
Bologna, 403–404, 529
Bonini, Bonino de, 362
Bonn, 481, 483, 484
Bonstetten, Albrecht von, 607
book, history of the, 371–378
Bor, Pieter, 641
Boulenger
    Jules-César, 473–480
    Pierre, 474
Bracciolini, Poggio, 147
Bramante, Donato, 528, 529, 530–532
Brant, Sebastian, 399, 400
Brazil, 238–246
Brendan, St., voyage of (narrative), 81
Brevius, Franciscus, 529
Brisacher, Marquard, 607
Brivio, Giuseppe, 607
Brocense (F. Sánchez de las Brozas), 95–
        103

Browne, Thomas (Sir), 55–72; *see also names of translators*
  The Gardens of Cyrus, 70
  Hydriotaphia (Urn Burial), 70
  Religio Medici, 55–72
Brune
  Jan de (l'Ancien), 321
    Emblemata of Sinne-werck, 381–388
  Jan de (le Jeune), 319–324
    Wetsteen der vernuften, 319–324
Bruni, Enrico, from Tarentum, 529
Bruni, Leonardo, 184, 295, 413–414, 417–418, 421, 424, 591
  Laudatio Florentinae urbis, 424
  Oration of Heliogabalus to the Prostitutes, 413–421
Buchanan, George, 237–246, 565, 570
Budé, Guillaume, 500
Burckard, Johannes, 529, 530
Burton, Robert, 387
Buschius, Hermann, 439, 442, 443, 444, 447

cabalism, 546–548
Caballero y Rodríguez de la Barrera, José Agustín, 158
Caesar, Julius, 170, 184, 185, 189, 336, 428, 490
Calderini, Domizio, 362, 363
Calderón de la Barca, Pedro, *El gran duque de Gandía*, 27
Callimachus, Filippo Buonaccorsi, 294
Calvin, John, 56, 67, 571
Camilla, 664, 666
Campo Santo, 529
Canter, William, 365
Cappellanus, Andreas, 522, 627–628
Carbone, Lucovico, 426, 429
Carew, Thomas, 561
carmen didascalicum, 664
Carrara, Giovanni Michele Alberto, 520
Carrara, Ubertino, 660, 666
Carvajal, Bernardinius, 32
Caspar, Barlaeus, 639–645
Cassiodorus, 337
Castañeda, Juan de, 108, 111
Castellesi, Adriano, 298
Castiglione, Baldassare, 15, 125, 208, 461, 492, 559, 621
Castilian, 410

Castro, Alvar Gómez de, *see* Gómez de Castro
Catalonia, 183–191, 647–657
Cato, 254, 255, 260, 261, 490, 493, 500
Catullus, 17, 51, 241, 242, 337, 356, 361, 365, 367, 373, 397, 513–514, 517, 553–558, 560, 612, 616
Celtis, Conrad, 295, 652
censorship, 374–375
Centelles, Francesco Gilabert, 147, 153, 519, 520, 521, 523, 625–629
Cervantes, Miguel de, 82
Chalkondyles, Demetrios, 508, 529, 606
Charlemagne, 428
Charles V, emperor, 29, 33, 87, 259, 403, 540–541, 619
Charles the Bold, 610
Chasaphus, 664, 665, 666
Chaucer, Geoffrey, 55, 179
chocolate, epic poetry on, 661, 662
Christ, imitation of, 254–255, 258–261
Christian, Prince of Denmark, 133
chronicles, false, see *Bellum Grammaticale*, *Crónica de San Pedro de Taberna*
Chrysoloras, Manuel, 413, 603
Cicero, 61, 68, 98, 148, 150, 151, 184, 225, 258 n. 8, 337, 346, 356, 418, 419, 420, 424, 428, 489–497, 608, 632–635, 637
Cid, El, 336
Cisneros, Francisco Ximenes de, 345, 389–396
cities, praise of, 423–430
Clariti, Constantius, 295
Claudian, 337, 373
Claudius, 532
Clement VI, Pope, 586
Clement VIII, Pope, 72
Clénard, Nicolas,
  Institutiones Arabicae, 356
  Institutiones Grammaticae Latinae, 353–360
  Institutiones in linguam graecam, 353–360
Cleophilus, Octavius, 296
Clusius, Carolus, 105–111
Coccio, Marcus Antonio (de Sabellico), 31
Cockaigne, 433–434
Codro, Urceo, 299
Coimbra, 237, 357

Collège de Guyenne, 237
Colomb, Fernand, 353
colonialism, 237–246
Columbus, Christopher, 30, 34, 35, 158, 301–306, 343, 433, 438, 536, 538, 539, 659, 660
commonplace books, 371–378
Conde y Oquendo, Francisco Javier, 158
Conde de Santisteban (Diego de Benavides), 333–344
Constantinople, 478, 507, 509
Conti, Federico de', 361
conversos, 261–262
copia (literary), 179, 312
Cornazzano, Antonio, 428
Cortés, Hernán, 37, 536–538, 541, 542, 659–666
Cortesi, Paolo, 32
Cossé, Philippe de, 571
Cox, Leonard, 293–299
Cozumel, 663, 666
Cracow, 293–299, 403–407
Cremona, 527
Criep (Cripius), Wilhelmus, 44
criticism, poetic, 42, 43
Crónica de San Pedro de Taberna, 247–252
Cuba, 155–161
Cudworth, Ralph, 285
Cuneo, Michele da, 31
Cyllenius, Dominicus, 482

Damasus, Pope, 614
Dantiscus, Johannes, 619–622
Dati
    Augustino, 295
    Augusto, 400
    Carlo, 473, 477
    David, 428, 566; *see also* Psalms, penitential
De Ferrarica, Antonio (de Galateo), 32
De pacificatione, 253–263
Decembrio
    Angelo, 425
        Politia literaria, 425
    Pier Candido, 151, 424
        De laudibus Mediolanensium urbis panegyricus, 424
    Umberto, 151
democracy, 275–281
Demosthenes, 337

Descartes, René, 284
Desprez, Josquin, 587, 594
dialogue, literary form/genre, 419, 532, 632–635
Diodorus Siculus, 184, 190, 218, 550
Diogenes Laertius, 180, 181
Dionysius Periegetes, 91, 184
Doña Marina (Cortés's translator), 661, 662, 666
Donato, Pietro, 610
Dondi dell'Orologio, Giovanni, 605
Donne, John, 543–551, 558
    Essays in Divinity, 543, 544, 545–548, 549–550, 551
    "The First Anniversary", 544–545, 546, 551
    Pseudo-Martyr, 543, 544, 548–549, 550, 551
Dorp, Maarten van, 115, 116
Dousa, Janus, 326, 365, 366
Du Bellay, Joachim, 265, 266–267, 272–273
    Epigrammata, 265–273
    Tombeau de (de la Taille), 82
Dufay, Guillaume, 587, 591–592, 594
Dutch language, 120–121
Dutch Revolt, 644
dystopia, 431–438

Earle, John (Latin translation of *Of the Laws of Ecclesiastical Polity* [Hooker]), 55, 56–60, 63–67, 72
Eck, Valentin, 293–299
editions, philological, 129
education, 376–378, 397, 449–458; *see also* Greek, Hebrew, Virgil
Egypt, 34, 36, 39
encomium, paradoxical, 413–421
Ennodius, 337, 614
Epictetus, 100
Epicurus, 284, 288
Epidorpides, 381–388; *see also* Scaliger, Julius Caesar
epigrams, 19, 21–28, 205–210, 265–273, 611–618; *see also individual authors*
    Christian, 336–337; *see also* Arias Montano, Benito; More, Thomas
Epistolae clarorum virorum, 440, 443
Epistolae obscurorum virorum, 439, 443–446, 447

epistolography, 129–138, 295–296
epitaph, 165–168, 208–209, 437
epithalamium, 331
Erasmus (of Rotterdam), 44, 139–140, 258 n. 8, 309–318, 326, 364, 416, 443, 489, 491, 494–495, 496–497, 499–506, 532, 575–583, 611, 622
    De ratione studii, 169
Eschenbrender, Pantaleon, 485
Espinosa, José Julián Parreño, 157
Estaço, Achilles, 365, 366
Este
    Borso d', 423–430
    Ercole d', 426, 427
    Leonello d', 424, 425, 426
    Niccolò (di Leonello) d', 427
    Polissena d', 429
    Sigismondo d', 426
Estienne family, printers, 365; *see also next*
Estienne
    Henri, 565, 573
    Robert (Robertus Stephanus), 373, 374–375, 376, 377
Euclid, 384
Eusebius of Caesarea, 215, 468, 480
exercises, stylistic, 266, 272–273
exile, in poetry, 507–517
Eyb, Albrecht von, 299, 608, 609

Ferrara, 423–430
"Festmotette", 586
Ficino, Marsilio, 217–226, 323, 460
fictionalization, 43
Filareto, Apollonio, 377–378
Filelfo, Francesco, 295, 591–592, 605–607
Flaminio, Marco Antonio, 23, 565, 567, 572, 573
Fleming, Paul, 54
Folger Library MS V.b. 34, 57–58
fountains and springs, poems about, 611, 612, 614–618
Fracastoro, Girolamo, 661
Francis I, 259, 374
Frederick III, emperor, 423, 424, 425, 605
Frederick, Henry, 639, 641, 643
frontiers of the world, concept, 73–91

Gabbema, Simon, 366

Gaffurio, Franchino, 606
Gallo, Antonio, 33
Gamrat, Piotr (Bishop), 403, 406
Garcilaso, 12, 14, 15, 28
Gardiner, Stephen (Bishop), 328
Gassendi, Pierre, 284
Gauricus, Pomponius, 474, 475, 478, 479
Gaza, Theodore, 459, 508
geography, ancient and Renaissance, 73–91, 133
George of Trebizond, *see* Trebizond, George of
Geraldini, Alessandro, 32–33
Giselin, Victor, 365
Giustiniani, Agostinius, 32
Goethe, Johann Wolfgang von, 54, 368
Golden Age, 271, 315–316, 428–430
Gomarus, Franciscus, 321
Gómez de Castro, Alvarus (Alvaro), 16, 17, 565, 566, 570
    De rebus gestis a Francisco Ximenio Cisnerio libri octo, 389–396
Gómez Miedes, Bernardino, *Commentariorum de sale libri V*, 533–542
Gossembrot, Ulrich, 607
Gouda, 309, 310
Gouveia, André de, 237
Graevius, Johannes Georgius, 366, 473
Gram, Hans, 129–131, 135–136
grammar, 353–360, 527, 612
Granada, 301–307
Gratius, Ortwin, 440, 441, 443, 444–446, 447
Greek, study of, 353, 355, 356, 374, 413, 449, 450; *see also* Argyropoulos, Chalcondyles, Chrysoloras
Greek Anthology, 614, 615
Gregory XII, Pope, 413
Gronovius, Johannes Fredericus, 473
Groot, Peter de, 321
Grotius, Hugo, 123, 385
growth (in science), 284
Gruter, Jan (Ianus), 13
Gruterus, Isaac, 321
Guarna, Andrea, 527–532
Guarino, Battista, 376, 420
Guatimozinus (Cuauhtemoc), 662, 664, 665
Guicciardini, Francesco, 30
Guldensterrius, Nicolaus, 332

Guzmán, Gaspar de (Conde-Duque de Olivares), 101, 102

Haarlem, 325
Haccius, Johann Berthold, 165
Háfiz (Persian poet), 367
Hall, Joseph, 431, 432, 436, 437–438
Hammius, 289
Hannibal, 428
harpies, 245
Hartsoeker, Nicolas, 285
Harvey, William, 134
Hebrew, study of, 353, 356, 449, 450; *see also* Reuchlin
Hegius, Alexander, 364
Heinrich, Maximilian, 482
Heliodorus, *Aethiopika*, 82
Heliogabalus (Elagabalus), emperor, 413–414
Henry II (of France), 269, 271–272, 374
Hermetica, 220–221
Herodotus, 36, 150, 180, 184, 550
Herrick, Robert, *Hesperides*, 553–555, 560
Hesiod, 74, 219, 480
Hessus, Eobanus, 565, 570, 573
Heyen, Berta de, 309–318
hidalgo, 661
Hinderbach, Johannes, 605
historiography, theory of, 345–352
Hobbes, Thomas, 275, 279, 284
Hoffmann, Karl, 367
Holland (Netherlands), 486, 639–645; *see also* Orange
Homer, 42, 70, 74, 243, 320, 327, 337, 428, 480, 603, 612, 618, 621
Hoogstraten, Jacob, 439, 440, 441, 443
Hooker, Richard, *Of the Laws of Ecclesiastical Polity*, 55–72
Horace, 52, 62, 148, 218, 222–223, 240, 309, 337, 356, 364, 365, 373, 398, 512–513, 517, 573, 585, 612, 614
    Ars Poetica, 218, 223
Horozco, Sebastián de, *Cancionero*, 17
humanism, 213–214, 253–263, 499–506, 544, 603–610; *see also* Humanists
    English, 543–551; *see also* Donne, More
    German, 439–447
    Italian, 217–226

Portuguese, 237
    Spanish, 449–458, 499–506
humanist poetry, 218–219, 585–596
Humanists, 293–299, 403–407; *see also* humanism
humor, learned, 527
Hurtado de Mendoza, Diego, 14–15, 18
Hutten, Ulrich von, 439, 442, 444, 445, 447
Huygens, Constantijn, 119–127, 640, 642–643
hymns, 297, 611

Iberia, 79
imitatio, 293
Inghirami, Tommaso (de Fedra), 32
Inquisition, 213 n. 2, 237, 261–263, 375
invective, 612–613
irony, 413–421
Isaac, Heinrich, 587, 589, 594
Isidore of Seville, 184, 219
Islam, 302, 356, 394

James I (of England), 434, 549
Jerome, Saint, 180, 181, 184, 187, 337, 468, 503, 524–526
Jesuits, drama of, 659–660, 666
John the Baptist, Saint, 297
John III Sobieski, King of Poland, 283
Josephus, Flavius, 184
Julius II, Pope, 528, 529, 531
Junius
    Franciscus, 321, 473, 477, 480
    Hadrianus, 325–332
Justin (Roman historian), 148, 150, 184
Justinian, 323, 337
Juvenal, 148, 149, 373, 398, 415, 418, 525, 612

Kaempfer, Engelbert (Dr.), 163–165
    children of, 164, 166–168
Karben, Victor von, 439–447
Keck, Thomas, 60
Kelley, Edward, 177
Kepler, Johannes, 285
Kircher, Athanasius, 285
Köln, 482, 484, 485
Konstanz, Reichstag of 1507, 589
Kromer, Marcin, 405

Lactantius, 43, 152, 184, 320
Laeto, Pomponio, 33, 295
Lalaing, Arnould de, 610
Landa, Diego de, 39
Landino, Cristofero, 217, 220–223
Landsberg, Martin, 363
Laskaris, Ioannes (Janus), 508
Lasso, Orlando di, 587
Latin translations of vernacular English works, 55–72
Le Parmesan, 479
LeBeau, Charles, 283
Leeuwenhoek, Antoni van, 286–290
Leiden University, 326, 640
Lemnius, Simon, 612–613
Leo X, Pope, 528, 532
Leo Africanus, 84
Leonzio, Pilato, 603
Léry, Jean de, 240, 246
Leto, Pomponio, 33, 461
letters of reply, 131, 134
"leyenda negra", 666
Liber, Antonius (Anton Vrije), 607
Lipsius, Justus, 97, 99–100, 102, 380, 381, 384, 475
literary criticism, 43, 120–124
Lithuania, 407
Livy, 184, 212, 347–348, 356, 415, 490, 504
Locke, John, 275–276, 367
Löffelholz, Johannes, 607
Longchamps, Pierre de, 368
Lope de Vega, Félix, 10, 12, 20–28
    Circe, con otras Rimas y Prosas, 23
    El poder en el discreto, 27
    epigrams, 21–28
    La Filomena, 22
    Rimas, 23
Lotichius, Petrus, 41–54; see also Secundus
Louis XIV, 283, 284
Lovati, Lovato, 604
love, 147–154, 519–526, 623–630
    erotic, 553–561
    Neo-Platonic, 557–559
Lucan, 180, 184, 190, 255, 336, 337, 356, 373, 586, 664, 666
Lucian, 36, 80, 372, 413, 416, 418–419, 420, 436, 439, 532, 586, 632
Lucilius, 418

Lucretius, 51, 283–285, 288, 368, 373
Luder, Peter, 607
Luther, Martin, 575–583, 611–618
Lycas, 664
Lysura, Johannes de, 607

Maciejowski, Samuel (Bishop), 403, 406
Macrin, Salmon, 563–573
Macrobius, 184
Maffei, Raffaele, 32
Maimonides, Moses, 546
Mal Lara, Juan de, 19–20
Malintzin, 661
Malipiero, Domenico, 30
Mancinelli, Antonio, 295
Manrique, Alfonso, Archbishop of Seville, 261–263
Mantuanus, Baptista, 10, 24, 295, 297, 397–402
manuscripts:
    Brussels B.R. 10565/10567, 651
    London B.L. Harl. 3475, 462
    Madrid B.N.M. 5554, 184–185
    Madrid B.N.M. 5785, 465–471
    Munich B.S.B. Clm. 434, 651
    Paris B.N. lat. 11015, 619–622
Manuzio (Manutius)
    Aldo, 364, 373
    Paolo, 364, 365
Margarit, Joan, Paralipomena, 183–191
Marguerite of Valois, 267
Marieni, Giambattista, Cortesius nondum absolutus, 659–666
Marillier, Clément, 368
Marineo, Lucio, 31
Marolles, Michel de, 366
Marot, Clément, 564, 567, 571, 572, 573
Marrasio, Giovanni, 607
marriage, 205–209, 298–299
Marsilio of Padua, 604
Marso, Pietro, 362–363
Marsus, 664
Martial, 14, 17, 184, 320, 356, 373, 612, 613, 616
Marullo, Michele (Michael Marullus), 12, 15, 43, 45, 51–52, 397, 507–517
    Hymni naturales, 43–44, 51
Mary, Virgin, 50, 312–316, 317, 336–337, 566, 660
Mary of England, Queen, 325–332

Mary Magdalen, Saint (*Diuae Magdalenae Libri IV* [Petreyo]), 10
Mary Stuart, Queen of Scots, 26
Mason, Peter, 88
Massimo, Angelo, 528
Maureus, Royzius (Pedro Ruiz de Moroz), 403–407
Maximilian I (Emperor), 587, 589, 619
Mayr, Franz Xavier, 367
McFarlane, Ian, 14, 563, 566, 567, 570
medallion bindings, 378
Medea, 49
Medici, Lorenzo de', 593
Meier, Christoff, 165
Melanchthon, Philip, 323, 565, 618
Mendoza, Manuel Sarmiento de, 97
Meneses, Francisco, 358
mensural polyphony, 587
Mercator, Gerhard, 546, 550
Merryweather, John (Latin translation of *Religio Medici* [Browne]), 55, 58, 59–60, 67–72
Merula, Giorgio, 606
meter, 310, 312, 507–517, 565–573, 585–596, 604, 615; *see also individual poets*
Mexico, Spanish conquest of, 536–538, 659–666
Mexico City (Tenochtitlán), 661, 662
Michael, archangel, 665
Michelangelo, 479, 532
microscope, 283, 286–288
Milton, John, 438, 545
    Areopagitica, 545
Minturno, Antonio, 223–226
Modrzewski, Andrzej Frycz, 405
Montaigne, Michel de, 319, 320, 322, 383
Montezuma, 37, 661
More, Thomas (Sir), Saint, 83, 113–118, 205–210, 431, 436, 438, 494–495, 544, 545
    children of, 209–210; *see also* Roper, Margaret
    Epigrammata, 205–210
    Utopia, 113–118, 431, 436, 438
Morell, Claude, 365
Moretus, Iohannes, 193–204
Moroz, Pedro Ruiz de (Royzius Maureus), 403–407; *see also* Maureus

Moses, 217–226, 428
Mundus Alter et Idem, *see* Hall, Joseph
Münzer, Hieronymus, 606
Muret, Marc-Antoine, 364, 365, 366
Murmell, Johann, 364
Murmester, Heinrich, 606
Murrho, Sebastianus, 397–402
music, and humanist poetry, 585–596; *see also individual composers*
Musius, 570
Mussato, Albertino, 604
Mutius, M., 317
Myrteis, 664, 665
mythology, ancient, 32, 37, 41–54, 207, 329–330, 342–343, 523
    Christian reception and use of, 41, 46, 148, 180, 217–226, 240, 243, 330–331, 586
    function of, 43, 44

Nebrija, Antonio de, 100, 189–190, 351–352, 357, 449
Neo-Latin, 1–5, 155–161, 543–551
Neo-Platonism, 43, 460, 461; *see also* love
Neo-Stoicism, 99–101
New World, 242, 246, 301–307, 533–542
Niccoli, Niccolò, 417–418
Niger, Franciscus, 295
Nine Worthies, 538
Noah, 428

Obrecht, Jacob, 587
Ocean, 74, 75, 76, 80, 81, 84, 85
Ockeghem, Johannes, 587
Oldenbarnevelt, Johan van, 385
Olivares, Conde-Duque de, *see* Guzmán
Oppian, 649
Orange, Princes of, 119, 125, 644
Oration of Heliogabalus to the Prostitutes (Bruni), 413–421
Ordas, 662, 663–664, 665
Orosius, 184
Orpheus, 217–226
Orphic Hymns, 45, 220
Orry, Marc, 365
Ortelius, Abraham, 85, 86, 90, 433, 435
Orzechowski, Stanisław, 405
Otumba, battle of, 661

Ovid, 42, 49, 51, 148, 149, 152, 154,
177, 184, 190, 242, 244, 330, 337,
356, 363, 373, 415, 485, 487, 508–
517, 525, 586, 612, 621, 641, 643,
644, 665
  Epistulae ex Ponto, 508–517, 621
  Heroides, 49, 179, 259, 508–510, 639–
  645
  Metamorphoses, 42, 180, 242–243, 330,
  508, 586, 621
  Remedia Amoris, 509
  Tristia, 508–517
Oviedo, Gonzal Fernandez de, 87
"ovulists" (scientific theoreticians), 286

Pacheco, Doña María, 16
Pacific Ocean, discovery of, 38
Pacioli, Luca, 606
Pafraet brothers, printing firm, 363
Palazzolo, Antoniolo, 605
Palmireno, Juan Lorenzo, *Lexicon nauti-
  cum et aquatile*, 169–175
panegyrics, 586
Panormita, Antonio, 17, 519, 607, 608;
  see also Beccadelli
Paris, 371–378
Parthenica (Weston, q.v.), 178–182
Pascual y Villegas, Tomás, 158
Pasini, Maffeo, 371–378
Passerat, Jean, 365
Pau, Jeroni, 647–657
  Barcino, 653
  *De fluminibus et montibus Hispaniarum
  libellus*, 653
  *Hymnus panegyricus in festo diui Aurelii
  Augustini episcopi Hipponensis*, 653–
  654
Paul, Saint, 384, 617
Paul II, Pope, 459, 460
Paul III, Pope, 449, 451
Paul IV, Pope, 243–244, 374
Pausanias, 218
peace, 253–263, 395
Peerlkamp, Petrus Hofman, 327
Perotti, Niccolò, 605
Persius, 373, 398, 525
Peter, Saint, 528, 529, 530–532
Petit, Jean, 357
Petrarch (Petrarca), Francesco, 153, 184,
219, 337, 490, 500, 501, 521, 522,

586, 594, 603, 609, 625, 627, 629
Pfefferkorn, Johannes, 440, 441, 446
Philip II of Spain, 19, 20, 139, 227, 325–
  332, 457, 534, 535
Philo, 337
Photius, 80–81
Piccolomini, Enea Silvio (Pope Pius II),
  294, 425, 607, 627
  Descriptio urbis Viennensis, 425
Pico della Mirandola
  Gianfrancesco, 44
  Giovanni, 460, 547, 558–559, 652
Pietro da Abano, 604
Pimentel y Sotomayor, Antonio, 157
Pindar, 76, 179, 270
Pirckheimer
  Hans, 609
  Johannes, 607
  Willibald, 607
Plantin, Christophe, 364, 365
Plantino, Cristóbal, 197–204
Platina (Bartolomeo Sacchi), 459–463
  De amore, 461–462
  De falso et vero bono, 459–460
  De flosculis quibusdam linguae latinae,
  460, 461
  De principe, 462
  Lives of the Popes, 460
  "Parentalia", 462
Plato, 32, 151, 154, 213, 337, 384, 415–
  416, 420–421, 453, 605, 632
  Timaeus, 80
Plautus, 27, 356, 371–378, 490, 532, 612
Plinius
  Johannes (Johannes von Plieningen),
  607
  Theodoricus (Dietrich von Plienin-
  gen), 607, 608
Pliny the Elder, 34, 36, 77, 190, 337,
  462, 479, 490
Pliny the Younger, 136, 356
Plutarch, 151, 184, 337, 384, 424, 461
Poelman, Theodor, 365
poeta theologus, 217–226
poetry
  humanist, 585–596
  Latin, 165, 166, 168, 205–210, 265–
  273, 462, 611–618
  Neo-Latin, 9–28
  occasional, 596, 611

and origin myths, 217–226
Poggio Bracciolini, 148, 299, 413, 419, 420, 591, 627
Poland, 283, 293–299, 403–407, 619–622
Polenton, Sicco, *Catinia*, 419–420
Polignac, Melchior de, 283–290
Poliziano, Angelo, 10, 11, 17, 18, 24, 507, 592, 605, 649
    Hermaphroditus (attr.), 17
Polybius, 184, 337
polyphony, 587
Pompeii, 428
Pompilio, Paolo, *De vero et probabili amore*, 461
Pontano
    Giovanni, 17, 296–297
    Giovanni da Bergamo, 147–154, 520–526
    Giovanni Gioviano, 147, 153, 519–526, 614–615
pope, female, legend of (Pope Joan), 178, 180–181
Popocatepetl, 664
Porphyry, 213
Portillus, 665
Portugal, 237–246
Prado, Lorenzo Ramírez de, 101
preformation theory, in science, 289–290
Presocratics, 224–225
prisci poetae, 217–226
Priscian, 134, 184
Proba, 180
Propertius, Sextus, 14, 361–370, 373, 559–560
prose, English (sixteenth and seventeenth centuries), 61–72; *see also* Donne
Protestantism, *see* Reformation
prototypes (in science), 286
Prudentius, 309–318
Prunius, Cornelius, 365
Psalms, penitential, 563–573
Ptolemy, *Geographia*, 84, 184, 190
publishing, 371–378
pudicitia, 499–506
Puritanism, English, 56–57, 553, 561
Pyramus and Thisbe, 665
Pyrrhonists, 284

quantities (poetic), 122, 123
Quintilian, 346, 356, 489, 490, 492

Raleigh, Walter (Sir), 434
Ramée, Pierre de la, *Ciceronianus*, 489–497
Raphael, 479
Raphelingen, Franciscus, 365
Ravisius Textor, 23–24
    Catalogue of Learned Women, 177–182
    Officina, 23, 178–182
reading process, 376–377
Recino y Hormachea, Tomás, 157
Reformation, doctrines of, 56–57, 67, 181, 218, 244, 246, 374–375, 384–386, 435, 548–549, 562–564, 567, 570–572, 575–579, 611–618, 643; *see also* Calvin, Luther
Rej, Mikołaj, 405
Reuchlin, Johannes, 439, 440, 441, 443, 446–447
rhetoric, 169–175, 203, 253–263, 345–352
rhythm (musical), 587
Riviera, Guido, 367
Rochette, Louis de, 385
Roman history, as model, 214, 415, 500; *see also* Cato, Livy, Tacitus, Virgil
Romano, Egidio, 424
Rome, 212, 243–244, 413–421, 527, 528, 531, 532
Romei, Giovanni, 429
Romulus, 428
Ronsard, Pierre de, 265–273, 320, 383, 500, 504
Roper, Margaret, 316
Rore, Cipriano de, 587
Rossi, Tebaldo de, 30
Rostgaard, Frederik, 129
Roth, Johannes, 609
Rothelin, Charles d'Orléans de, 283
Rousseau, Jean Jacques, 368
Rubeanus, Crotus, 439, 442, 443, 447
    Contra sentimentum Parrhisiense, 442, 446
Rudolf II, emperor, 177, 181
rulers, praise of, 336, 586
Rybisch, Heinrich, 299

Sacchi, Bartolomeo (Platina), 459–463
Sacco, Catone, 608
Sahagún, Bernardino, 39
saints, *see individual names*
Salazar, Francisco Cervantes de, 140–142

Comentarios, 143–146
Sallust, 184, 337, 356, 487, 490
Salutati, Coluccio, 347, 413, 418, 501
San Juan Bautista, Manuel de, 157
Sandovalus, 663–664
Sannazaro, Iacopo, 10, 11, 23, 555, 556
Santa Maria della Pace, Rome (church), 528
Sanudo, Marino, 364
Sappho, 179
Sargasso Sea, 539
Satan, 665, 666
satire, 206–208, 413–421, 431–438, 439–447
Savonarola, Michele, 423
Scaliger
    Joseph Justus, 323, 365, 366, 381, 382, 382, 384
    Julius Cæsar, 44
        Epidorpides, 381–388
        Pro Cicerone, 493–494
Schedel, Hartmann, 605, 609, 651–652
Schefferus, Johan, 133–134
Schiller, Friedrich, 50
Schipano, Mario, 133
Scillacio, Nicolò, 33–35
Scipio Africanus, 148, 428
Scriptores Historiae Augustae, 413–414
Scriverius, Petrus, 556, 557, 643
Scrovegni, Antonio, 610
Secundus
    Janus, 12, 326
    Joannes, 553–561
        Basia, 553–561
        Epigrammata, 23
    Petrus Lotichius, 41–54; *see also* Lotichius
Seneca, 68, 153, 180, 320, 337, 373, 424, 490, 525, 532, 592
Seneca the Younger, 603, 604
Senfl, Ludwig, 587
Sententiae et proverbia ex poetis Latinis, 371–378
Septem psalmi, see Psalms, penitential
Sepúlveda, Juan Ginés de, 392, 465–471, 575–583, 597–602, 631–638
    Apologia, 465–471
    De fato et libero arbitrio adversus Lutherum libri tres, 575, 576–579
    Errata Petri Alcyonii, 597–602
    Gonsalus seu de appetenda gloria dialogus, 631–638

Pro Alberto Pio, principe Carpensi, Antapologia in Erasmum Roterodamum, 575, 579–582
Severinus, Marcus Aurelius, 133, 134
Seville, 186
Sforza, Bona, queen of Poland, 619–622
    Francesco, 527
Sidney, Philip, 63
Sigea, Luisa, 449–451, 456–458
    Duarum virginum Colloquium de vita aulica et privata, 452–457
Sigeo, Diego, 449, 450, 451, 452
Sigismund I, king of Poland, 619–622
Sigüenza, Fray José de, 20
Silber, Eucario, 362, 363
Silius Italicus, 373
Sixtus IV, Pope, 460, 462
social contract theory, 275–281
Socrates, 424, 478, 632
Solera, Marqués de, *see* Benavides, Diego de
Solórzano, Juan de, 96, 97
Spain, 403–407
Spanish literature, 9–28
"spermatists" (scientific theoreticians), 286
Spinoza, Benedict (Baruch) de, *Tractatus Theologico-Politicus*, 276–281
"Staatsmotetten", 585–596
Stanley, Thomas, 553, 554, 555, 561
Statius, 180, 317, 373, 612 n. 6
Stella, Julio César, *Columbeida*, 302
Steyn, 312, 318
Strabo, 78–79, 83, 85, 184, 185, 190
Strozzi, Ercole, 23
    Tito Vespasiano, *Borsias*, 427
Suetonius, 337, 415 n. 10
Swammerdam, Jan, 285–286

"Tacitismo", 95–103, 227–235
Tacitus, Cornelius, 68, 95–103, 227–235, 337, 415, 490
Taille, Jacques de la, 82
Tartarus, 664
Tartessos, 85, 90
Tasso, Torquato, 320, 664, 666
Terence, 148, 149, 356, 371–378, 490, 612
Teresa of Ávila, Saint, 409–411
Tertullian, 43
Textor, Ravisius (Jean Tixier, Seigneur de Ravisi), 178–182

Theophrastus, 476, 525
Thucydides, 337
Thule, 73–91
Tibullus, Albius, 14, 48, 62, 177, 361,
    363, 365, 373
Tifernate, *Carmina*, 317
Tongern, Arnold, 441, 443
Tonson, Jacob, 367
toponymy, 183–191
Tostatus (Alonso Tostato), 547, 548
Tovar, Simón de, 107
Trebizond, George of, 345–352
Trips, Franciscus Xaverius, 481–488
Trithemius, Johannes, 610
Triumphus Doctoris Reuchlini, 442–443,
    446
Trzecieski, Andrzej, 405
Turks, 483, 506, 509, 535
Turres, Petrus, 529

Ubertino da Crescentino, 608
Ulsenius, Theodoricus (Dirk van Ulsen),
    609
Ulysses, 150, 243
universities, and humanism, 603–610
Urban VIII, Pope, 25–26

Vachiantus, Joachim, 51
Vadianus, Joachim, 593
Valerius Flaccus, 373
Valerius Maximus, 148, 150, 635
Valla, Lorenzo, 347, 402, 417, 420–421,
    460, 519, 607
    De voluptate, 417, 420–421, 460
Valois, Marguerite de, 267
van der Venne, Adriaen, 383
Varela y Morales, Félix, 158–159
Varro, 184, 212, 214, 219, 490, 621
Vasæus, Jean, 353, 354, 357, 358, 359
vates, 218, 219, 222, 225
Vegio, Maffeo, 296, 607
Velásquez, 661
Velleius Paterculus, 337
Venice, 371–378
Vergerio, Pier Paolo, 414, 605
Verona, 483
Veronese, Guarino, 425, 426
Verzosa, Juan de, 15
Vigenère, Blaise de, 475, 476, 477, 478,
    567
Vintimiglia, Aprosio, 132

Virgil, 51, 62, 79, 83, 148, 150, 184,
    190, 245, 309, 311–315, 330, 356,
    364, 373, 376–377, 398, 405, 446,
    462, 535, 593, 605, 612, 621, 661,
    663, 664, 666; *see also Aeneid*
virginity, ideal of, 666
viri obscuri, 439–447
Vischer, Peter, the younger, 609
Vives, Juan Luis, 101, 139–146, 169,
    211–216, 253–263
    *Commentaria ad Diui Aurelii Augustini
    De Civitate Dei*, 211–216
    De disciplinis, 495–496
    De institutione foeminae Christianae,
    450–452, 453, 454–455, 499–506
    Prooemia, 211–216
Volsco, Antonio, 362, 363
Voltaire, 368
von Knebel, Karl Ludwig, 367
von Moltke, Levin Nicolas, 58, 60–61,
    71
Vondel, Joost van den, 322
Vossius
    Franciscus, 321
    Gerard, 321, 323, 324
    Matthaeus, 322
Vrije, Anton (Antonius Liber), 607

Walpole, Robert (Sir), 367
Walton, Isaac, 72
war, 392, 395
Weston, Elizabeth Jane (Westonia), 177–
    182
William of Moerbeke, 604
Wimpfeling, Jakob, 399
wisdom, 499–502
Wittenberg, 611, 612, 615–616, 617
women
    attitudes toward, 205–210, 414–417,
    420–421, 434–435, 449–458, 461–
    462, 499–506
    education of, 210, 449–458, 499–506
    writers, 177–182, 449–458
Wurm (Worm), Ole, 129–131, 132, 135
    correspondence with Thomas Bartho-
    lin, 130
Wuttke, Dieter, 609

Xenophon, 337, 632

Yucatan, 663

Zabarella, Francesco, 605
Zambeccari, Alexander, 529
Zamorano, Rodrigo, 108
Zeller, Johannes, 609
Zurita y Castro, Jerónimo de, *Indices rerum ab Aragoniae Regibus gestarum*, 227–235

MRTS

MEDIEVAL AND RENAISSANCE TEXTS AND STUDIES
is the major publishing program of the
Arizona Center for Medieval and Renaissance Studies
at Arizona State University, Tempe, Arizona.

MRTS emphasizes books that are needed —
texts, translations, and major research tools.

MRTS aims to publish the highest quality scholarship
in attractive and durable format at modest cost.